# Frommer's®
# France

## 22nd Edition

by Jane Anson, Mary Anne Evans,
Lily Heise, Tristan Rutherford,
Caroline Sieg, Louise Simpson,
and Amelia Smith

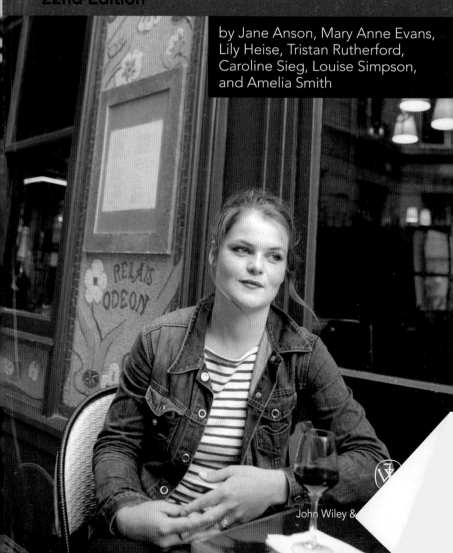

John Wiley &

Published by:
**JOHN WILEY & SONS, INC.**
111 River St.
Hoboken, NJ 07030-5774

ISBN 978-1-118-28860-3 (paper); ISBN 978-1-118-33496-6 (ebk); ISBN 978-1-118-33165-1 (ebk); ISBN 978-1-118-33385-3 (ebk).

Editor: Jamie Ehrlich
Production Editor: Eric T. Schroeder
Cartographer: Andrew Murphy
Photo Editors: Cherie Cincilla, Richard Fox
Design and Layout by Vertigo Design

Production by Wiley Indianapolis Composition Services

Front cover photo: Carcassonne © Chris Warren / SuperStock / Alamy Images
Back cover photos: LEFT: Gorges du Fier © Kirsten Scully. MIDDLE: Lavender field in Buis les Baronnies, Provence © Kirsten Scully. RIGHT: Detail at Lascaux Caves © Kirsten Scully.

For information on our other products and services or to obtain technical support, please contact our Customer Care Department within the U.S. at 877/762-2974, outside the U.S. at 317/572-3993 or fax 317/572-4002.

Wiley also publishes its books in a variety of electronic formats. Some content that appears in print may not be available in electronic formats.

Manufactured in China

5  4  3  2  1

# CONTENTS

# 6 THE LOIRE VALLEY 244

# 7 NORMANDY & MONT-ST-MICHEL 295

# 8 BRITTANY 329

# FRANCE
# LIST OF MAPS

# ABOUT THE AUTHORS

 **Jane Anson** spent many family holidays in France, but headed to Japan and Hong Kong after graduating, spending five years in Asia. On moving back to Europe, the pull of France won out, and she has lived in Bordeaux since 2003 with her husband and two daughters. She has authored or co-authored over 10 books on southwest France and its wines. Getting fully into Bordeaux's favorite pastime, she teaches wine tasting at the Bordeaux Ecole du Vin, as well as working as Bordeaux correspondent for *Decanter* magazine in London.

 **Mary Anne Evans** has a house in the remote Auvergne region of France and writes for about.com, producing articles and blogs that take her through the whole country. Her writing career includes books on Japanese prints and guitars, guide books to Belgium and Stockholm, and articles on Finland. She has written for Gault/Millau and gayot.com about hotels and restaurants in London and has written and updated *Frommer's London.*

 **Lily Heise** has been living in Paris for over 10 years, having refused to go back to Canada after studying art first in Italy and then in France. She has extensive experience in the travel and culture sectors and, in addition to contributing to *Frommer's Paris* and *Frommer's France*, she reports on Paris cultural news for local and international online and print publications. She lives in Montmartre and spends her free time exploring off-beat Paris and traveling around Europe.

 **Tristan Rutherford** moved to Nice and began a career in freelance travel journalism in 2002. He writes travel features for *The Guardian* and London's *Sunday Times Travel Magazine* among others and lectures in travel journalism at Central Saint Martins in London. His hottest picks along the Cote d'Azur remain the 1€ no.100 bus from Nice to Monaco, the sandy beaches of Juan-les-Pins, and Nice's locals-only street market of Libération.

 **Caroline Sieg** is half-Swiss, half-American, and her relationship with France began with childhood trips to Strasbourg to visit her Alsatian family. Later, she studied French, resided in Paris and worked several seasons in a ski resort bordering France and Switzerland. These days, Caroline heads to France as often as possible—to ski, sniff out the best wine, cheese, and bread, or simply meander along quiet side streets.

 **Louise Simpson** fell in love with all things French as a teenager on holidays to her family home in the Dordogne and as a French and Spanish student at Cambridge University. Since moving to Southern France in 2003, she has authored 10 print and online travel guides to Southern and Central France and written for *Financial Times Weekend, Independent on Sunday,* and *Timesonline,* among others.

 **Amelia Smith** skipped the "tu" form of conjugation after her high school French teacher said the chances of her ever knowing an actual French person were close to none. Thirteen years after moving to France, she continues to address French family and friends like royalty. Her work has appeared in the *New York Times, Huffington Post,* and *Daily Beast,* among others.

## HOW TO CONTACT US

In researching this book, we discovered many wonderful places—hotels, restaurants, shops, and more. We're sure you'll find others. Please tell us about them, so we can share the information with your fellow travelers in upcoming editions. If you were disappointed with a recommendation, we'd love to know that, too. Please write to:

*Frommer's France*, 22nd Edition
John Wiley & Sons, Inc. • 111 River St. • Hoboken, NJ 07030-5774
frommersfeedback@wiley.com

## ADVISORY & DISCLAIMER

Travel information can change quickly and unexpectedly, and we strongly advise you to confirm important details locally before traveling, including information on visas, health and safety, traffic and transport, accommodations, shopping, and eating out. We also encourage you to stay alert while traveling and to remain aware of your surroundings. Avoid civil disturbances, and keep a close eye on cameras, purses, wallets, and other valuables.

While we have endeavored to ensure that the information contained within this guide is accurate and up-to-date at the time of publication, we make no representations or warranties with respect to the accuracy or completeness of the contents of this work and specifically disclaim all warranties, including without limitation warranties of fitness for a particular purpose. We accept no responsibility or liability for any inaccuracy or errors or omissions, or for any inconvenience, loss, damage, costs, or expenses of any nature whatsoever incurred or suffered by anyone as a result of any advice or information contained in this guide.

The inclusion of a company, organization, or website in this guide as a service provider and/or potential source of further information does not mean that we endorse them or the information they provide. Be aware that information provided through some websites may be unreliable and can change without notice. Neither the publisher nor author shall be liable for any damages arising herefrom.

# FROMMER'S STAR RATINGS, ICONS & ABBREVIATIONS

Every hotel, restaurant, and attraction listing in this guide has been ranked for quality, value, service, amenities, and special features using a **star-rating system.** In country, state, and regional guides, we also rate towns and regions to help you narrow down your choices and budget your time accordingly. Hotels and restaurants are rated on a scale of zero (recommended) to three stars (exceptional). Attractions, shopping, nightlife, towns, and regions are rated according to the following scale: zero stars (recommended), one star (highly recommended), two stars (very highly recommended), and three stars (must-see).

In addition to the star-rating system, we also use **eight feature icons** that point you to the great deals, in-the-know advice, and unique experiences that separate travelers from tourists. Throughout the book, look for:

Special finds—those places only insiders know about

Fun facts—details that make travelers more informed and their trips more fun

Best bets for kids and advice for the whole family

Special moments—those experiences that memories are made of

Places or experiences not worth your time or money

Insider tips—great ways to save time and money

Great values—where to get the best deals

Warning—traveler's advisories are usually in effect

The following **abbreviations** are used for credit cards:

| | | | | | |
|---|---|---|---|---|---|
| **AE** | American Express | **DISC** | Discover | **V** | Visa |
| **DC** | Diners Club | **MC** | MasterCard | | |

## TRAVEL RESOURCES AT FROMMERS.COM

Frommer's travel resources don't end with this guide. Frommer's website, **www. frommers.com**, has travel information on more than 4,000 destinations. We update features regularly, giving you access to the most current trip-planning information and the best airfare, lodging, and car-rental bargains. You can also listen to podcasts, connect with other Frommers.com members through our active-reader forums, share your travel photos, read blogs from guidebook editors and fellow travelers, and much more.

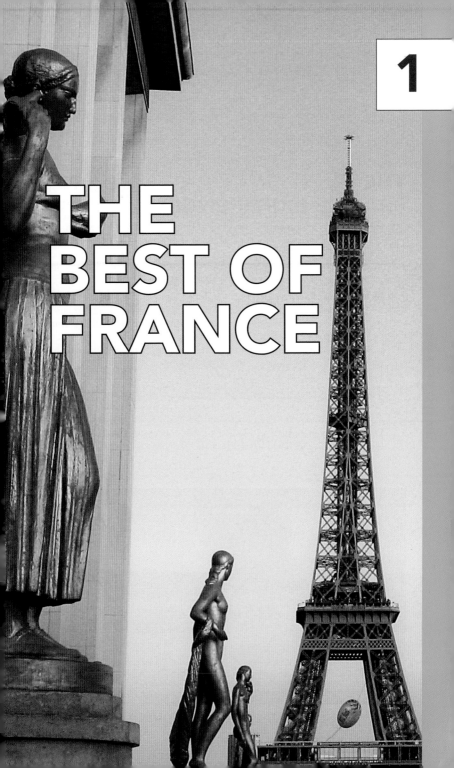

THE
BEST OF
FRANCE

1

France presents visitors with an embarrassment of riches—you may find yourself bewildered by all the choices. We've tried to make the task easier by compiling a list of our favorite experiences and discoveries. In the following pages, you'll find the kind of candid advice we'd give our closest friends.

# THE most unforgettable
# FRANCE EXPERIENCES

- **Hunting for Antiques:** The 18th- and 19th-century French aesthetic was gloriously different from that of England and North America, and many objects bear designs with mythological references to the French experience. France has some 13,000-plus antiques shops throughout the country. Stop where you see the sign ANTIQUAIRE or BROCANTE.

- **Biking in the Countryside:** The country that invented La Tour de France offers thousands of options for bike trips. For a modest charge, trains in France will carry your bicycle to any point. **Euro-Bike & Walking Tours** (www.eurobike.com; ✆ 800/575-1540) offers some of the best excursions, including walking and cycling tours of areas such as Provence, Burgundy, and the Loire Valley. See chapter 20 for other options.

- **Shopping in Parisian Boutiques:** The French guard their image as Europe's most stylish people. The citadels of Right Bank chic lie on rue du Faubourg St-Honoré and its extension, rue St-Honoré. The most glamorous shops are along these streets, stretching between the Palais Royal to the east and the Palais de l'Elysée to the west. Follow in the footsteps of Coco Chanel, Yves Saint Laurent, and Karl Lagerfeld on the shopper's tour of a lifetime. See chapter 4.

Biking in the French countryside. PREVIOUS PAGE: **A view of the Eiffel Tower.**

- **Exploring the Loire Valley:** An excursion to the châteaux dotting the valley's rich fields and forests will familiarize you with the French Renaissance's architectural aesthetics and with the intrigues of the kings and their courts. Nothing conjures up the aristocratic *ancien régime* better than a tour of these landmarks. See chapter 6.

- **Paying Tribute to Fallen Heroes on Normandy's D-Day Beaches:** On June 6, 1944, the largest armada ever assembled departed on rough seas and in dense fog from England. For about a week, the future of the civilized world hung in a bloody and brutal balance between the Nazi and Allied armies. Today you'll find only the

Window shopping at Chanel in Paris.

sticky sands and wind-torn, gray-green seas of a rather chilly beach. But even if you haven't seen *Saving Private Ryan* or *The Longest Day*, you can picture the struggles of determined soldiers who paid a terrible price to establish a bulkhead on the Continent. See "The D-Day Beaches" in chapter 7.

- **Climbing to the Heights of Mont-St-Michel:** Straddling the tidal flats between Normandy and Brittany, this Gothic marvel is the most spectacular fortress in northern Europe. Said to be protected by the archangel Michael, most of it stands as it did during the 1200s. See "Mont-St-Michel" in chapter 7.

- **Touring Burgundy During the Grape Gathering:** Medieval lore and legend permeate the harvests in Burgundy, where thousands of workers (armed with vintner's shears and baskets) head over the rolling hills to gather the grapes that have made the region's wines so famous. You can sample the local wines in the area restaurants, which always stock impressive collections. See chapter 11.

- **Schussing down the Alps:** France offers world-class skiing and luxurious resorts. Our favorites are Chamonix, Courchevel, and Megève. Here you'll find cliffs only experts should brave, as well as

Mont-St-Michel.

runs for intermediates and beginners. The après-ski scene roars into the wee hours. See chapter 13.

o **Marveling at the Riviera's Modern-Art Museums:** Since the 1890s, when Signac and Bonnard discovered St-Tropez, artists and their patrons have been drawn to the French Riviera. Experience an unforgettable drive across southern Provence, interspersing museum visits with wonderful meals, sunbathing, and stops at the area's architectural and artistic marvels. Highlights are Aix-en-Provence (Cézanne's studio), Biot (the Léger Museum), Cagnes-sur-Mer (the Renoir Museum), Cap d'Antibes (the Grimaldi Château's Picasso Museum), La Napoule (the Henry Clews Museum), and Nice (the famed Matisse Museum and Chagall Museum). In addition, Monaco, St-Paul-de-Vence, and St-Tropez all have world-class modern art collections. See chapters 14 and 15.

# THE best ROMANTIC MOMENTS

o **Soaking up the Glamour of Deauville** (Normandy): Using the resort of Deauville to propel herself to stardom, Coco Chanel added greatly to its sense of glamour and romance. Try your hand at the casinos, ride horses, stroll along the elegant boardwalk, or simply revel in the resort's sense of style and nostalgia. See "Deauville" in chapter 7.

o **Escaping the World in Belle-Ile-en-Mer** (Brittany): If crashing waves and windswept coastline put you in the mood for a cuddle, consider an escape with your significant other to this island on Brittany's Côte Sauvage ("Wild Coast"). Partake of quaint hotels and copious seafood platters in the Port de Goulphar. Pricey (but worth it): the Castel Clara Hotel and Spa. Priceless: a bundled up stroll along the cliffs above the sea. See p. 352.

o **Living Like a Fairytale at the Château d'Azay-le-Rideau** (Loire Valley): Visitors are enthralled by this château's beauty. Poised above the waters of

Belle-Ile-en-Mer.

St-Tropez coastline.

the Indre River, it boasts decorative remnants of medieval fortifications and an atmosphere that prefigures the Renaissance embellishments of later Loire Valley châteaux. See p. 280.

o **Relaxing in the Alps in Talloires** (the French Alps): The bracing climate, the history that goes back to the Middle Ages, and the Gallic flair of the innkeepers make for a memorable stay. The accommodations include a converted medieval monastery, and the village's cuisine is superb. See "Talloires" in chapter 13.

o **Hiding out in Les Baux** (Provence): The isolated, cinematic setting of the ancient fortress of Les Baux had troubadours singing in its streets during the Middle Ages. Today it is no less romantic, with an abundance of hideaways within minutes of the village itself. See "Les Baux" in chapter 14.

o **Exploring a Monument to Love at Monastère Royal de Brou** (Rhône Valley): One of the great artistic treasures of France, this Flamboyant Gothic monastery is a testament to eternal love built for Margaret of Austria, the ill-fated daughter of Emperor Maximilian. Over the ornate Renaissance doorway, the tympanum depicts Margaret and her "handsome duke," Philibert, who died prematurely at the age of 24 after catching a cold on a hunting expedition. Inside cherubs watch over their tombs. See chapter 12, p. 460.

o **Hitting the Beach in Sexy St-Tropez** (French Riviera): Any blonde feels like Brigitte Bardot in sunny St-Tropez, and the number of scantily clad satyrs and nymphs in town during summer could perk up the most sluggish libido. The real miracle here is that the charm of the place manages to survive its hype and the hordes of visitors. See "St-Tropez" in chapter 15.

# THE most unforgettable
# FOOD & DRINK EXPERIENCES

o **Having a Picnic in Paris:** When the weather is nice, the banks of the Seine River and the Canal St-Martin in Paris and the city's many parks become lined with Parisians enjoying a picnic in the open air. Bring a baguette, some cheese, and a bottle of wine (don't forget the bottle opener!), and join the locals for some of the cheapest fun to be had in Paris.

o **Slurping Fresh Oysters in Cancale** (Brittany): The Breton port of Cancale has been famous for its oysters since Louis XIV began requesting them for his table at Versailles. Strong tides and currents help make the *huîtres creuses* cultivated here one of the most sought-after mollusks in France, appreciated for their pure, ocean-like flavor. Enjoy a dozen at any of the restaurants along the port, or, even better, on a takeaway plate sitting on the pier. See p. 336.

Enjoying a picnic near the Eiffel Tower.

A tasty crêpe from Brittany.

o **Enjoying Crepes in Brittany:** Crepes may make you think of France, but they make the French think of Brittany. Once the bread staple of that region, thin buckwheat galettes are still found everywhere, finished with savory fillings and served as a light (and economical) meal. Start with the classic ham and cheese version and work your way up to more exotic varieties such as Roquefort with walnuts or scallops with leeks. Fillings for dessert crepes, made with white flour, can be as simple as lemon juice and powdered sugar or as gourmande as ice cream and gooey caramel.

o **Sampling Norman Cider** (Normandy): Normandy's cider (*cidre* in French) is a delicate, fermented version of apple juice that produces a refreshing alcoholic beverage. Some are sparkling but others are still, and you can find both sweet versus dry versions. Normandy is also famous for its delicate pear ciders, which are less common worldwide so this is a great place to try them. Look out for ciders on regional menus too, where they use cider instead of wine for sauces.

o **Filling a Box of Chocolates:** It's impossible to walk into a chocolaterie and not be tempted to take home a box. Choose the size of the box, and then begin the fun task of pointing out whatever *pralinés* and *ganaches* you'd like to try. Our favorite *chocolatiers* are **Christian Constant** in Paris (see p. 170), **Max Vauché** in Blois (see p. 256), and **Cadiot-Badie** in Bordeaux (see p. 711).

o **Savoring Roast Bresse Chicken** (Rhône Valley): Roast chicken in France is delectable and can be enjoyed throughout the country. **Bourg-en-Bresse** is a small town that's famous for its poultry. You can enjoy the local birds at low prices, and food critics travel here from all over France for the hearty roast chicken.

○ **Consuming Gooey Melted Cheese in the Alps:** The French Alps are home to three mmmm-worthy cheese dishes. **Tartiflette** is a decadent mix of diced potatoes, cream, lardons, and reblochon (a pungent, creamy soft cheese), baked until it bubbles into a creamy, hearty dream. Or indulge in **raclette,** sizzling-hot cheese poured over baby potatoes. Then there's **fondue Savoyard,** a regional version of this classic mixing Beaufort, Emmenthal, and Comte cheeses into the pot. Dip in your cube of bread and you're officially in Alpine land.

○ **Sipping Pastis in Provence:** Pastis is synonymous with Provence. This anise-flavored liquor is sipped at sundown on every town square, from Arles to the Italian border. Beware: the Provençal are seriously brand conscious. Order a "51" if you want to look like a local, or a "Janot" for the region's latest organic offering. Impress the barman by ordering a tomate (pastis with a dash of grenadine) or a perroquet (literally a parrot, which is pastis with a splash of green mint syrup).

○ **Going au naturel in Languedoc-Roussillon:** Natural wines, which are made from organic grapes and use few preservatives or stabilizing agents, are all the rage in France right now. Languedoc-Roussillon is one of the leaders in producing organic wines. Try **Domaine Malavieille** in Merifons, west of Montpellier in the Herault (www.domainemalavieille.com). The **Cave cooperative of Cabrières** (www.cabrieres.com/english/present.html), south of Clermont l'Herault, offers a good selection.

○ **Surrendering Control:** Tasting menus that offer no choices are becoming increasingly popular. If you're ready to put yourself in the hands of a talented chef, try **Le Chateaubriand** (p. 144) or **Spring** (p. 134) in Paris, **Restaurant Bistro Saveurs** in Castres (see p. 656), or **Chateau Prieuré** near Saumur (see p. 290).

# THE best SCENIC DRIVES

○ **La Route des Crêtes** (Alsace-Lorraine): The Vosges, one of the oldest mountain ranges in France, once formed a boundary with Germany. Richly forested with hardwood trees and firs, they skirt the western edge of the Rhine and resemble the Black Forest. La Route des Crêtes (the Crest Road), originally chiseled out of the mountains as a supply line, begins west of Colmar, at the Col du Bonhomme. High points are Münster (home of the cheese), Col de la Schlucht (a resort with panoramas as far as the Jura and the Black Forest), and Markstein. At many points along the way, you can stop and strike out on a well-marked hiking trail. See "La Route des Crêtes" in chapter 10.

La Côte d'Or.

- **The Routes Touristiques du Champagne** (Champagne Country): Wind your way through the back roads and villages of Champagne along this 70-kilometer (45-mile) drive. In addition to hillside vineyards, woods and views of the Marne River, you'll pass dozens of independent Champagne houses, some open for drop-in tasting. See p. 368.

- **La Côte d'Or** (Burgundy): Stretching only 60km (37 miles) from Santenay to Dijon, this route is for wine lovers. Rows of terraced vines rise in tiers above the D122/N74/D1138 highways (La Route des Grands Crus), passing through the towns of Chassagne-Montrachet, Meursault, Beaune, Nuits-St-Georges, Vosne-Romanée, Gevrey-Chambertin, and Marsannay-la-Côte. Travel at your leisure, stopping to sample the noble vintages (look for the signs sprouting from the sides of the highway). See chapter 11.

- **The Gorges of the Ardèche** (the Rhône Valley): The river that carved these canyons (the Ardèche, a tributary of the Rhône) is the most temperamental French waterway. Riddled with alluvial deposits, grottoes, caves, and canyons more than 285m (935 ft.) deep, the valley is one of France's most unusual geological spectacles. A panoramic road (D290) runs along one rim of the canyons, providing views over a striking, arid landscape. Plan to park and walk a little on some of the well-marked paths. The drive, which you can do in a day even if you make frequent stops, stretches between Vallon-Pont-d'Arc and Pont St-Esprit. See "The Ardèche" in chapter 12.

- **La Route des Grandes Alpes** (the French Alps): One of the most panoramic drives in western Europe stretches south from the lakefront town of Evian to coastal Nice. You'll see Alpine uplands, larch forests, glaciers, and the foothills of Mont Blanc. Plan on driving 2 to 6 days, stopping in such towns as Morzine, Avoriaz, Chamonix, and Megève. The route covers 740km (459 miles) and crosses many of France's dramatic mountain passes. Some sections are passable only in midsummer. See chapter 13.

# THE best VINEYARD & WINERY VISITS

- **Couly-Dutheil** (Chinon): Many of its medieval cellars are carved into the rock undulating through the area's forests. Most production here involves Chinon wines (mostly reds), though its Bourgueil and St-Nicolas de Bourgueil wines are growing in popularity in North America. See "Chinon" in chapter 6.

- **Moët et Chandon Champagne Cellars** (Champagne Country): Go straight to the source to learn the secrets of one of the world's most prestigious champagne houses. The informative tour includes an explanation of the *methode champenoise* as well as anecdotes about illustrious clients

Tasting wine at Couly-Dutheil.

including Napoleon Bonaparte. In Epernay, 90-minutes away from Paris by train, this also makes for great rainy day Plan B.

**Taittinger** (Reims): Taittinger is a grand *marque* of French champagne, one of the few still controlled by members of the family that founded it, in 1930. It's one of the most visitor-friendly houses. See p. 364.

**Domaines Schlumberger** (Guebwiller, near Colmar): Established in 1810, these cellars blend early-19th-century brickwork and modern stainless steel; a visit will enhance your understanding of the subtle differences among wines produced by the seven varieties of grape cultivated in Alsace. See "Colmar" in chapter 10.

**Domaine Maurice Protheau** (Mercurey): The 50 hectares (124 acres) of grapevines straddle at least two *appellations contrôlées* (a regulation system that ensures a wine has been produced where the bottle says), so you'll have a chance to contrast reds (both pinot noirs and burgundies), whites, and rosés produced under the auspices of both Rully and Mercurey. Headquarters is in a château built in the late 1700s and early 1800s.

**Château de Meursault**: Meursault is famed for its buttery white chardonnay wines and there's no better place to taste them than Château de Meursault. This 60-hectare domain covers vineyards stretching from Aloxe Corton to Pommard, and of course Meursault. You can turn up without prior reservation for a visit to the cellars of this fabulous 19th-century castle followed by a tasting of pinot noir reds and chardonnay white wines in the old castle kitchens for 15€. See chapter 11, p. 431.

**Château de Chassagne-Montrachet** (Chassagne-Montrachet): The Côte de Nuits produces the most sought-after pinot noir red wines in the world. A good place to taste them where you can turn up without an appointment is Château de Chassagne-Montrachet. Owner Michel Picard runs one of the largest and most successful domains in the area selling wine, spirits, and *Crémant de Bourgogne* sparkling wines. Visits to the 12th-century cellars, including a wine-tasting, are available from March to November. See chapter 3, "A Wine Lover's Tour of Burgundy," p. 72.

**The Winegrowing Region around Bordeaux:** This area is among the most glamorous in France, with a strong British influence, thanks to centuries of trade with London- and Bristol-based dealers. Increasingly the big-name chateaux, such as Chateau Pichon Longueville, Pauillac (*©* **05-56-73-17-17**), and Chateau Soutard, Saint Emilion (*©* **05-57-24-71-41**), welcome visitors for tours. Visits to the striking cellars and vineyards are followed by a *dégustation des vins*. See p. 715.

# THE best HISTORIC EXPERIENCES

**Remembering Marie Antoinette at the Conciergerie** (Paris): The seat of royal power for 400 years, from the 10th to the 14th centuries, this is the oldest royal palace in the capital. After Charles V abandoned the palace for a new residence in the current Marais, it was converted into a prison, and during the French Revolution, Marie Antoinette was held there before being guillotined. It's a great example of the architecture of the Middle Ages; don't miss the Gens d'Armes room, the Guard room, and the kitchens. On the northeastern corner you can still see the city's first public clock, installed in 1370. See p. 102.

o **Drinking with the Literary Greats at Café de Flore** (Paris): The Café de Flore has been at the center of the city's intellectual life since it opened its doors in 1887. The writer Charles Maurras wrote his book *Au signe de Flore* there. The cafe has been associated with poets Guillaume Apollinaire, Louis Aragon, and Jacques Prévert; philosopher Jean-Paul Sartre; and expat American writers Arthur Koestler, Ernest Hemingway, and Truman Capote. Today, you can still order a glass of *vin,* and toast to all the drinks, arguments, and ideas that have passed through this exceptional place. See p. 154.

o **Being a King for a Day at the Château de Versailles** (Ile de France): Versailles is the most spectacular palace in the world. Its construction was fraught with ironies and tragedies, and its costs were a factor in the bloodbath of the French Revolution. Ringed with world-class gardens and a network of canals whose excavation required an army of laborers, the site also contains the Grand and Petit Trianons, as well as miles of ornate corridors lined with the spoils of a vanished era. See p. 203.

o **Trekking through the Château and Forest of Fontainebleau** (Ile de France): Since the days of the earliest Frankish kings, the forest has served as a royal hunting ground. Various dwellings had been erected for medieval kings, but in 1528, François I commissioned the core of the building that subsequent monarchs would enlarge and embellish. Napoleon declared it his favorite château, delivering an emotional farewell to his troops from its exterior staircase after his 1814 abdication. See p. 219.

o **Touring the Towers and Turrets of the Loire** (Loire Valley): The Loire Valley is dotted with hundreds of castles. You won't have time to see them all, but from the medieval fortresses of **Chinon** and **Loches** to fairytale châteaux of **Chenonceau** and **Ussé,** you can trace France's transition from the feudal age to birth of the Renaissance and be charmed with the area's beauty along the way.

o **Exploring "The Corsaire City" of St-Malo** (Brittany): With the king's blessing, sea pirates used this walled fortress in the English Channel as a base for their conquests (the bounty going to France, of course). Later it was a major

Palais de Fontainebleau.

The Loire Valley's Château d'Azay-le-Rideau.

trading port for gold, coffee and spices brought back from exotic lands. Watch the waves crash against the centuries-old ramparts, stroll the cobblestone streets, or visit the *Musée d'Histoire* or *Fort National* to take in the town's unique nautical history. See p. 330.

o **Viewing the Iconic Cathédrale Notre-Dame in Rouen** (Normandy): Consecrated in 1063 and rebuilt after a fire in 1200, parts of it are masterpieces of the Flamboyant Gothic style; others are plainer, though equally dignified. This cathedral was immortalized in the 19th century, when Monet painted a series of impressions of the facade. See p. 298.

o **Learning about Film's Early Days in Lyon** (Rhône Valley): Film buffs from all over the globe flock to see the historic home of the Lumière family, pioneers of the motion picture. As well as founding a factory producing photographic plates, paper, and chemicals, they invented the Cinématographe, an early motion picture camera. In 1895, they produced the film *La Sortie de L'Usine,* considered the world's first movie. **L'Institut & Musée Lumière** is a living museum of cinema displaying early films, posters, and the earliest cinematographic equipment. See p. 445.

o **Wandering through Europe's Greatest Fortress City** (Languedoc-Roussillon): **Carcassonne** was built for war with its fortifications, imposing château, and double ring of defensive walls. But even the 14 towers around the outer ring and 24 around the inner ring didn't keep it safe from conquest and reconquest during the endless feuds of medieval power politics. Its inevitable decline was reversed in the 19th century with a massive restoration overseen by Viollet-le-Duc, fresh from working on Notre-Dame in Paris, and today Carcassone is one of the great sites of Europe. See p. 650.

o **Breaking the Bank at Monte-Carlo:** The **Casino de Monte-Carlo** has been the most opulent place to have a flutter for exactly 150 years. Its creation by architect Charles Garnier (of Paris Opera house fame) in 1863 turned the tables for Monaco, turning a weary port into a world-class tourist destination. Expect frescoed ceilings and a wealthy, well-dressed clientele from as far afield at China, Russia, and the U.S. See chapter 15, p. 621.

o **Seeing the Pomp of the Pope's Medieval Party Pad:** Those medieval popes knew a thing or two about interior design. Avignon's **Palais des Papes,** or Pope's Palace, is a moneyed medley of banqueting halls, fine art, and suites fit for a Hollywood celebrity. The Châteauneuf-du-Pape papal vineyards just north of Avignon still produce some of the most noted wine in France. See chapter 14, p. 500.

o **Visiting a Prehistoric Art Gallery:** The "Sistine Chapel of Prehistory" will impress all but the toughest audiences. Try to decipher the mystery of the prehistoric cave paintings on the walls of Lascaux, painted by Cro-Magnon man over 15,000 years ago. See p. 726.

# THE best WAYS TO SEE FRANCE LIKE A LOCAL

o **Buying Your Daily Bread:** That cute little boulangerie just down the street? Depending on where you are, there's likely to be another—or several—a short walk away. The daily baguette run is a ritual for many French people; in the early evenings, bakeries have lines out their doors. Get your coins ready (one euro, give or take 10 centimes) and join the queue. To really fit in, ask for your baguette chewy *(pas trop cuite)*, or crusty *(bien cuite)*.

o **Hitting the Sales:** Twice a year Paris shops sacrifice their current collections, with up to 75% reductions, to make way for new stock. Summer sales start in the last week of June, and winter sales start in early January. Parisians stock up on everything from clothes to home goods to electronics at these city-wide sales. See p. 156.

o **Donning Your Chapeau and Heading to the Races:** From April through to late October, the greater Parisian Region and Deauville (Normandy) host a number of world famous races. Great venues for people-watching, you can rub shoulders with the French elite and get caught up in the excitement. Hemmingway spent a good deal of his earnings out at the Longchamp track in the Bois de Boulogne; we suggest attending the Prix Diane held in June at the track of the lovely **Château de Chantilly** (p. 234).

o **Strolling Along the Harbor in Honfleur** (Normandy): Gawk at the colorful yachts and ponder the skinny houses—this harbor was made for wandering. Join the locals and meander without a care while scoping out where to perch with a plate of crustaceans and a dollop of brisk sea air. See p. 305.

o **Shopping on a Market Day:** Market days are one of the best ways to explore French towns like a local. Burgundy's liveliest market is held in **Beaune** (see p. 428). Locals arrive early to avoid the tourist crowds, before settling down at a street-side cafe to gossip over a drink. We also recommend the open-air market in **Arles,** Provence's most authentic destination. A colorful line of vendors sell olives, fresh bread, cheese, and local ham underneath the city ramparts, a few blocks from the town's Roman amphitheater. See p. 515.

o **Partying in Perpignan:** The second city of Catalonia takes its clue from its Spanish neighbor and parties late into the night. Make your way to the quays of the Basse River or stay around place de la Loge in old Perpignan for bars, cafes, and restaurants serving tapas, beer, and sangria when the rest of the city has gone to sleep. See chapter 16, p. 649.

o **Sunbathing like a Local** (French Riviera): The beaches along France's Cote d'Azur are the nation's sandiest and most chic. However, bathing on the Riviera may be a little different from home. Firstly, most beaches feature private clubs with mattresses, parasols, and chilled champagne on demand. Secondly, topless bathing is popular on most stretches of sand, with naturism a common feature in St-Tropez. We can advise on where (or where not!) to lay your towel. See chapter 15.

**Shopping for cherries on a market day in Nice.**

# THE best FAMILY EXPERIENCES

o **Stunning the Kids at Les Catacombs** (Paris): Les Catacombes, a creepy underground ossuary, will have the kids transfixed. Wander through almost 2km (1⅓ miles) of labyrinthine corridors lined with six million bones, transferred here from Parisian cemeteries over 200 years ago. In the past, it served as a quarry, where stone was extracted for building, and during World War II, the French Resistance used the tunnel system to outsmart the German soldiers. See p. 132.

o **Experiencing the "Animals" of Nantes' Les Machines de l'Ile** (Brittany): Fantastical? Fantastic? *Both.* The attractions at this mechanized art installation, based on the stories of Jules Verne, include a 12-meter (147-foot) elephant ride and a tri-level carousel with articulated sea creatures including a manta ray, squid, and flying fish. While awaiting your turn, watch the artisan mechanics tinkering and blow-torching the newest additions into being. See p. 355.

o **Meeting Mademoiselle Minnie and Monsieur Mickey:** The riches and beauty of France make it its own magic kingdom, however, **Disneyland Paris** still rules when it comes to family entertainment. With two parks encompassed in a vast entertainment complex, the European Disney is a fun-filled destination for families seeking to take in the culture of the capital city in addition to some R&R. See p. 225.

o **Watching Figures Spin on the Astronomical Clock in Strasbourg** (Alsace-Lorraine): The astronomical clock in Strasbourg's Cathedrale Notre Dame is one of the world's largest and most entertaining to watch. Its animated allegorical figures launch into action at 12:30 daily—be sure to get there on time when the angel makes the bell ding. This starts the procession of allegorical wooden figures: Apollo drives his sun horses; a skeleton spins by, representing death; and the twelve apostles spin by at the top, taking a bow in front of Christ while a rooster crows and spreads its wings. See p. 383.

o **Playing all Day in Lyon's Parc de la Tête d'Or** (Rhône Valley): France's largest city-based public garden, Parc de la Tête d'Or is the perfect day out for the whole family. Created in 1856 by the landscape architect Denis Bühler, the park has a magnificent lakeside setting with broad tree-lined avenues, fountains, and rose gardens. Kids will love the pony rides, carousels, swings, pedal cars, and pedalos around the lake, as well as the 20-minute train ride around the park. After visiting the Zoological Park with 1,000 animals including rose-pink flamingos and Senegalese dwarf goats, a trip to the Botanical Garden will keep you busy as you explain the

Lyon's Parc de la Tête d'Or.

Les Baux's ruins.

concept of carnivorous plants to your kids in the Dutch greenhouse. See chapter 12, p. 446.

- **Getting Medieval in the Hilltop Town of Les Baux** (Provence): The age-old hilltown of **Les Baux** commands views over hundreds of miles of Provençal countryside. Its film-set location, including the hilltop ruins of its "ghost village," plus a volley of great restaurants have made it a retreat for France's rich and famous. Kids will love its car-free medieval streets and awesome views, plus the daily display of a siege engine catapult. See chapter 14, p. 521.

- **Getting a Taste of Modern Art in Antibes** (French Riviera): The **Musée de Picasso,** or Picasso Museum in Antibes, highlights some of the most accessible art in France. The Spanish painter set up shop in the atmospheric old quarter of Antibes's Château Grimaldi some 70 years ago. In such relaxed surroundings, children can appreciate the color, vibrancy, and playfulness that made Picasso one of the 20th century's greats. The far-out sculptures and sunny views of the surrounding coastline will please non-art fans, too. See chapter 15, p. 579.

- **Joining the Cowboys in the Camargue** (Languedoc-Roussillon): Riding a sturdy Camarguais horse and with a local cowboy to guide you, make your way through the marshes of these beautiful, remote wetlands. You'll spot pink flamingos, wildlife you've only seen on a TV nature program, and the *Gardians* with their large felt hats rounding up the black bulls bred for the bull rings of the south. If the children don't ride, there are the great alternatives of a slow boat or a jeep. See chapter 16, p. 636.

- **Get on board in Biarritz** (Basque Country): The beaches of Biarritz might offer the perfect family experience in southwest France. Here you'll find waves and surfboards on one side, and shops, museums, and restaurants on the other. See p. 679.

# FRANCE
# IN DEPTH

by Tristan Rutherford

LE PENSEVR
DE RODIN OFFERT
PAR SOVSCRIPTION
PVBLIOVE AV PEVPLE
DE PARIS MCMVI

The civilization and history of France and the French way of life makes the country easily the most visited in the world. The savoir-faire of its people lures travelers from across the globe to this country that covers an area smaller than Texas. Yet despite the size, you can get lost in France, lost in the sense that each region is so intriguing and varied that you may immerse yourself in one province for so long that you'll never have time to go on to see what's on the other side. France, often referred to as "the garden of Europe," is—perhaps more than any country in the world—a land to be savored. It's better to get to know intimately one, two, or three regions than try to explore them all. This is not a destination to rush through on one of those quick bus tours ("If it's Tuesday, it must be Nice"). It is ideally explored by car or on the country's magnificent rail network, allowing you to stop whenever and wherever you wish.

---

No European country, not even England, can beat France in its pageantry of personalities, from Madame de Pompadour to Charles de Gaulle, from Jean-Luc Godard to Françoise Hardy, from Catherine de Médicis to Joan of Arc, from Napoleon to its current president, François Hollande. You'll be introduced to some of these figures in the pages ahead. Seeing where they lived, worked, loved, and became legends is part of the experience of going to France.

This guide is meant to help you decide where to go in France, but ultimately the most gratifying experience will be your own serendipitous discovery of France—sunflowers, a picnic in a poppy field, an hour spent chatting with a small winemaker—whatever it is that stays in your memory for years to come.

# FRANCE TODAY

France remains one of the world's most hyped and written-about destinations. It can inspire a masterpiece—and has on countless occasions. Even the cantankerous James McNeill Whistler would allow his masterpiece, a portrait of his mother, to hang in no other city save Paris.

Although not large by North American standards (about the size of the state of Texas, or of Britain and Germany combined), France is densely packed with attractions, both cultural and recreational. Even better, it's permeated with style and known for its *joie de vivre*.

The French claim credit, among other things, for developing the Gothic style of architecture and the cathedrals that stand as legacies of soaring stone for future generations. Creators of everything from palaces to subway stations have drawn at least some inspiration from designs inaugurated in France. However,

PREVIOUS PAGE: *The Thinker* **at Musée Rodin.**

## Impressions

*I tried to think it out. Why did Paris still draw us to its fascination, why did it draw those who felt themselves creative—talent or no talent? Why had it been, since Franklin, that all of us felt that we were freer there than elsewhere? Why did art, literature, and sex, and the feeding and drinking seem more genuine there? Generations of Americans had run a whole gamut of desires, hopes in Paris—all so opposite to those they had found at home, on the farm, in the city.*

*—Stephen Longstreet,*
*We All Went to Paris (1972)*

despite the thrilling architectural monuments peppering the country's land-scapes, it would be wrong to assume that the culture's main contribution to the world is derived from stone, mortar, stained glass, and gilt. Its contributions to painting, literature, cuisine, fashion, and savoir-faire are staggering.

When other parts of Europe were slumbering through the Dark Ages, Provence was alive with creativity as Provençal poetry evolved into a truly lyrical, evocative, and (in some cases) erotic verse form. Despite the frequent absences of its monarchs, who sequestered themselves with their entourages in remote Loire Valley châteaux, Renaissance Paris developed into one of Europe's most cosmopolitan cities, embellishing itself with majestic buildings and sculpture.

As for style, it has always been foolhardy to try to compete with the French on their terms. The theatrical backdrops of the sometimes-silly Gallic monarchs have been interpreted by latter-day aesthetes as history's crowning achievement when it comes to conspicuous displays of wealth and prestige.

In politics and ideology, France has always been a leader and remains so today. Fueled by Enlightenment writings, whose most articulate voices were French, the 1789 Revolution toppled Europe's most deeply entrenched regime and cracked the foundations of dozens of other governments. After a period of murky maneuverings by diverse coalitions of strange bedfellows, post-revolution-ary Paris became a magnet for the greatest talents of the 19th and early 20th centuries in many fields of endeavor.

Newcomers have commented (often adversely) on the cultural arrogance of the French. But despite its linguistic and cultural rigidity, France has received more immigrants and political exiles than any other European country. Part of this derives from France's status as one of Europe's least densely populated nations per square mile, and part of it from the tendency of the French to let others be until their actions become dangerous or obnoxious, not necessarily in that order.

This guidebook represents our effort to introduce first-time visitors to France's subtle pleasures and—if possible—to open new doors to those who might have already spent time here. We've set for ourselves the formidable task of seeking out France at its finest and condensing that information so you can access it easily. But the best need not always be the most expensive or the most chic or the most widely publicized.

If you're a first-timer, everything in Paris, of course, is new. But if you've been away for a long time, expect changes. Taxi drivers may no longer correct your fractured French, but address you in English—and that's tantamount to a revolution. More Parisians have a rudimentary knowledge of English, and the country, at least at first glance, seems far less hysterically xenophobic than in decades gone by. Part of this derives from Parisians' interest in music, culture,

# France

UNITED KINGDOM

Southampton
Brighton
Portsmouth
Exeter
Plymouth
Penzance

*English Channel*

Channel Is.
(U.K.)
Guernsey
Jersey

Cherbourg
*Baie de la Seine*
Le Havre
Bayeux
Saint-Lô
Caen

Dunkerque
Calais

NORD-PAS
DE CALAIS

Abbeville
Dieppe
Amiens
Beauvais
Rouen

HAUTE-
NORMANDIE

*Normandy*

PARIS
Versailles
ILE-DE-
FRANCE

Chartres

*I. de Batz*
Ile
d'Ouessant
Brest
*Iroise*
Quimper
*Iles des Glénan*
Lorient
Vannes

*I. de Bréhat*
Mont-St-
Michel
St-Brieux
*Brittany*
BRETAGNE
Rennes

BASSE-NORMANDIE

Mayenne
Laval
PAYS DE
LA LOIRE
Châteaubriant
Angers

Le Mans

*Loire Valley*
Orléans
Blois
CENTRE
Tours
Bourges

Belle-Ile-
en-Mer
St-Nazaire
Nantes
*Loire*
Saumur

*Ile de Noirmoutier*
*Ile d'Yeu*
La Roche-sur-Yon

Châtellerault
Poitiers

Châteauroux
Montluçon

ATLANTIC
OCEAN

Niort
*Ile de Ré*
La Rochelle
Rochefort
*Ile d'Oléron*
Saintes
Cognac

POITOU-
CHARENTES
Angoulême

Limoges
LIMOUSIN
Ussel

Brive-la-Gaillarde

Bordeaux
Gujan-Mestras
*Bassin d'Arcachon*

Bergerac
*Dordogne*
Aurillac

*The Dordogne
& The Lot*

*Bay of
Biscay*

AQUITAINE
*Bordeaux &
The Atlantic Coast*

*Lot*
Agen
Rodez

Mont-de-Marsan
Montauban
Albi

Santander

Dax
Orthez
Bayonne
Biarritz
*Basque
Country*
Pau
San
Sebastian
Bilbao
Lourdes
Pamplona

MIDI-PYRENEES
Toulouse
Castres

*Garonne*
Carcassone

*Pyrenees
National Park*
Andorra
la Vella
ANDORRA

P y r e n e e s

SPAIN

★ National Capital
◉ Regional Capital

18

and films from foreign countries, and part from France's growing awareness of its role within a united Europe.

Yet France has never been more concerned about the loss of its unique identity within a landscape that has attracted an increasing number of immigrants from its former colonies. Many have expressed the legitimate concern that France will continue to lose the battle to keep its language strong, distinct, and unadulterated by foreign slang or catchwords. But as the country moves deeper into the millennium, foreign tourists spending much-needed cash are no longer perceived as foes or antagonists. *Au contraire:* The rancor of France's collective xenophobia has been increasingly redirected toward the many immigrants seeking better lives in Paris, where the infrastructure has nearly been stretched to its limits.

# THE MAKING OF FRANCE

**EARLY GAUL** When the ancient Romans considered France part of their empire, their boundaries extended deep into the forests of the Paris basin and up to the edges of the Rhine. Part of Julius Caesar's early reputation came from his defeat of King Vercingetorix at Alésia in 52 B.C., a victory he was quick to publicize in one of the ancient world's literary masterpieces, *The Gallic Wars.* In that year, the Roman colony of Lutetia (Paris) was established on an island in the Seine (Ile de la Cité).

As the Roman Empire declined, its armies retreated to the flourishing colonies that had been established along a strip of the Mediterranean coast—among others, these included Orange, Montpellier, Nîmes, Narbonne, and Marseille, which retain some of the best Roman monuments in Europe.

As one of their legacies, the Roman armies left behind the Catholic church, which, for all its abuses, was the only real guardian of civilization during the anarchy following the Roman decline. A form of low Latin was the common language, and it slowly evolved into the archaic French that both delights and confuses today's medieval scholars.

The form of Christianity adopted by many of the chieftains was viewed as heretical by Rome. Consequently, when Clovis (king of northeastern Gaul's Franks and founder of the Merovingian dynasty) astutely converted to Catholicism, he won the approval of the pope, the political support of the powerful archbishop of Reims, and the loyalty of the many Gallic tribes who'd grown disenchanted with anarchy. (Clovis's baptism is viewed as the beginning of a collusion between the Catholic church and the French monarchy that flourished until the 1789 Revolution.) At the Battle of Soissons in 486, Clovis defeated the last vestiges of Roman power in Gaul. Other conquests that followed included expansions westward to the Seine, then to the Loire. After a battle in Dijon in 500, he became the nominal overlord of the king of Burgundy. Seven years later, his armies drove the Visigoths into Spain, giving most of Aquitaine, in western France, to his newly founded Merovingian dynasty. Trying to make the best of an earlier humiliation, Anastasius, the Byzantium-based emperor of the Eastern Roman Empire, finally gave the kingdom of the Franks his legal sanction.

After Clovis's death in 511, his kingdom was split among his squabbling heirs. The Merovingian dynasty, however, managed to survive in fragmented form for another 250 years. During this period, the power of the bishops and the great lords grew, firmly entrenching the complex hierarchies and preoccupations of what we today know as feudalism. Although apologists for the Merovingians are quick to point out their achievements, the feudalistic quasi-anarchy of their tenuous reign has been (not altogether unfairly) identified by many historians as the Dark Ages.

**THE CAROLINGIANS** From the wreckage of the intrigue-ridden Merovingian court emerged a new dynasty: the Carolingians. One of their leaders, Charles Martel, halted a Muslim invasion of northern Europe at Tours in 743 and left a much-expanded kingdom to his son, Pepin. The Carolingian empire eventually stretched from the Pyrénées to a point deep in the German forests, encompassing much of modern France, Germany, and northern Italy. The heir to this vast land was Charlemagne. Crowned emperor in Rome on Christmas Day in 800, he returned to his capital at Aix-la-Chapelle (Aachen) and created the Holy Roman Empire. Charlemagne's rule saw a revived interest in scholarship, art, and classical texts, defined by scholars as the Carolingian Renaissance.

Despite Charlemagne's magnetism, cultural rifts formed in his sprawling empire, most of which was eventually divided between two of his three squabbling heirs. Charles of Aquitaine annexed the western region; Louis of Bavaria took the east. Historians credit this division with the development of modern France and Germany as separate nations. Shortly after Charlemagne's death, his fragmented empire was invaded by Vikings from the north, Muslim Saracens from the south, and Hungarians from the east.

**THE MIDDLE AGES** When the Carolingian dynasty died out in 987, Hugh Capet, comte de Paris and duc de France, officially began the Middle Ages with the establishment of the Capetian dynasty. In 1154, the annulment of Eleanor of Aquitaine's marriage to Louis VII of France and subsequent marriage to Henry II of England placed the western half of France under English control, and vestiges of their power remained for centuries. Meanwhile, vast forests and swamps were cleared for harvesting (often by the Middle Ages' hardest-working ascetics, Cistercian monks), the population grew, great Gothic cathedrals were begun, and monastic life contributed to every level of a rapidly developing social order. Politically driven marriages among the ruling families more than doubled the size of the territory controlled from Paris, a city that was increasingly recognized as the country's capital. Philippe II (reigned 1179–1223) infiltrated more prominent families with his genes than anyone else in France, successfully marrying members of his family into the Valois, Artois, and Vermandois. He also managed to win Normandy and Anjou back from the English.

Louis IX (St. Louis) emerged as the 13th century's most memorable king, though he ceded most of the hard-earned military conquests of his predecessors back to the English. Somewhat of a religious fanatic, he died of illness (along with most of his army) in 1270 in a boat anchored off Tunis. The vainglorious and not-very-wise pretext for his trip was the Eighth Crusade. At the time of his death, Notre-Dame and the Sainte-Chapelle in Paris had been completed, and the arts of tapestry making and stonecutting were flourishing.

During the 1300s, the struggle of French sovereignty against the claims of a rapacious Roman pope tempted Philip the Fair to encourage support for a pope based in Avignon. (The Roman pope, Boniface VIII, whom Philip publicly insulted and then assaulted in his home, is said to have died of the shock.) During one of medieval history's most bizarre episodes, two popes ruled simultaneously, one from Rome and one from Avignon. They competed fiercely for the spiritual and fiscal control of Christendom, until years of political intrigue turned the tables in favor of Rome and Avignon relinquished its claim in 1378.

The 14th century saw an increase in the wealth and power of the French kings, an increase in the general prosperity, and a decrease in the power of the feudal lords. The death of Louis X without an heir in 1316 prompted more than a decade of scheming and plotting before the eventual emergence of the Valois dynasty.

The Black Death began in the summer of 1348, killing an estimated 33% of Europe's population, decimating the population of Paris, and setting the stage for the exodus of the French monarchs to safer climes in such places as the Loire Valley. A financial crisis, coupled with a series of ruinous harvests, almost bankrupted the nation.

During the Hundred Years' War, the English made sweeping inroads into France in an attempt to grab the throne. At their most powerful, they controlled almost all the north (Picardy and Normandy), Champagne, parts of the Loire Valley, and the huge western region called Guyenne. The peasant-born charismatic visionary Joan of Arc rallied the dispirited French troops as well as the timid dauphin (crown prince), whom she managed to have crowned as Charles VII in the cathedral at Reims. As threatening to the Catholic Church as she was to the English, she was declared a heretic and burned at the stake in Rouen in 1431. Led by the newly crowned king, a barely cohesive France initiated reforms that strengthened its finances and vigor. After compromises among the quarreling factions, the French army drove the discontented English out, leaving them only the Norman port of Calais.

In the late 1400s, Charles VIII married Brittany's last duchess, Anne, for a unification of France with its Celtic-speaking western outpost. In the early 1500s, the endlessly fascinating François I, through war and diplomacy, strengthened the monarchy, rid it of its dependence on Italian bankers, coped with the intricate policies of the Renaissance, and husbanded the arts into a form of patronage that French monarchs continued to endorse for centuries.

Meanwhile, the growth of Protestantism and the unwillingness of the Catholic Church to tolerate it led to civil strife. In 1572, Catherine de Médicis reversed her policy of religious tolerance and ordered the St. Bartholomew's Day Massacre of hundreds of Protestants. Henri IV, tired of the bloodshed and fearful that a fanatically Catholic Spain would meddle in the religious conflicts, converted to Catholicism as a compromise in 1593. Just before being fatally stabbed by a half-crazed monk, he issued the Edict of Nantes in 1598, granting freedom of religion to Protestants in France.

**THE PASSING OF FEUDALISM**  By now France was a modern state, rid of all but a few of the vestiges of feudalism. In 1624, Louis XIII appointed a Catholic cardinal, the duc de Richelieu, his chief minister. Amassing enormous power, Richelieu virtually ruled the country until his death in 1642. His sole objective was investing the monarchy with total power—he committed a series of truly horrible acts trying to attain this goal and paved the way for the eventual absolutism of Louis XIV.

Although he ascended the throne when he was only 9, with the help of his Sicilian-born chief minister, Cardinal Mazarin, Louis XIV was the most powerful monarch Europe had seen since the Roman emperors. Through first a brilliant military campaign against Spain and then a judicious marriage to one of its royal daughters, he expanded France to include the southern provinces of Artois and Roussillon. Later, a series of diplomatic and military victories along the Flemish border expanded the country toward the north and east. The estimated population of France at this time was 20 million, as opposed to 8 million in England and 6 million in Spain. French colonies in Canada, the West Indies, and America (Louisiana) were stronger than ever. The mercantilism that Louis's brilliant finance minister, Colbert, implemented was one of the era's most important fiscal policies, hugely increasing France's power and wealth. The arts flourished, as did a sense of aristocratic style that's remembered with a bittersweet nostalgia today. Louis's palace of Versailles is the perfect monument to the most flamboyantly consumptive era in French history.

Louis's territorial ambitions so deeply threatened the other nations of Europe that, led by William of Orange, they united to hold him in check. France entered a series of expensive and demoralizing wars that, coupled with high taxes and bad harvests, stirred up much civil discontent. England was viewed as a threat both within Europe and in the global rush for lucrative colonies. The great Atlantic ports, especially Bordeaux, grew and prospered because of France's success in the West Indian slave and sugar trades. Despite the country's power, the total number of French colonies diminished thanks to the naval power of the English. The rise of Prussia as a militaristic neighbor posed an additional problem.

**THE REVOLUTION & THE RISE OF NAPOLEON**   Meanwhile, the Enlightenment was training a new generation of thinkers for the struggle against absolutism, religious fanaticism, and superstition. Europe was never the same after the Revolution of 1789, though the ideas that engendered it had been brewing for more than 50 years. On August 10, 1792, troops from Marseille, aided by a Parisian mob, threw the dimwitted Louis XVI and his tactless Austrian-born queen, Marie Antoinette, into prison. After months of bloodshed and bickering among violently competing factions, the two thoroughly humiliated monarchs were executed.

France's problems got worse before they got better. In the ensuing bloodbaths, both moderates and radicals were guillotined in full view of a bloodthirsty crowd that included voyeurs like Dickens's Mme. Defarge, who brought her knitting every day to place de la Révolution (later renamed place de la Concorde) to watch the beheadings. The drama surrounding the collapse of the *ancien régime* and the beheadings of Robespierre's Reign of Terror provides the most heroic and horrible anecdotes in the history of France. From all this emerged the Declaration of the Rights of Man, an enlightened document published in 1789; its influence has been cited as a model of democratic ideals ever since. The implications of the collapse of the French aristocracy shook the foundations of every monarchy in Europe.

Only the militaristic fervor of Napoleon Bonaparte could reunite France and bring an end to the revolutionary chaos. A political and military genius who appeared on the landscape at a time when the French were thoroughly sickened by the anarchy following their revolution, he restored a national pride that had been severely tarnished. He also established a bureaucracy and a code of law that has been emulated in other legal systems around the world. In 1799, at the age of 30, he entered Paris and was crowned first consul and master of France. Soon after, a decisive victory in his northern Italian campaign solidified his power at home. A brilliant politician, he made peace through a compromise with the Vatican, quelling the atheistic spirit of the earliest days of the Revolution.

Napoleon's victories made him the envy of Europe. Beethoven dedicated his *Eroica* symphony to Napoleon—but later retracted the dedication when Napoleon committed what Beethoven considered atrocities. Just as he was poised on the verge of conquering all Europe, Napoleon's famous retreat from Moscow during the winter of 1812 reduced his formerly invincible army to tatters. As a plaque in the Lithuanian town of Vilnius once told the tale: "Napoleon Bonaparte passed this way in 1812 with 400,000 men" – on the other side are the words "Napoleon Bonaparte passed this way in 1812 with 9,000 men." Napoleon was then finally defeated at Waterloo by the combined armies of the English, Dutch, and Prussians. Exiled to the British-held island of St. Helena in the South Atlantic, he died in 1821, probably the victim of an unknown poisoner.

**THE BOURBONS & THE SECOND EMPIRE**   In 1814, following the destruction of Napoleon and his dream of empire, the Congress of Vienna redefined the map of Europe. The new geography was an approximation of the boundaries that had existed in 1792. The Bourbon monarchy was reestablished, with reduced powers for Louis XVIII, an archconservative, and a changing array of leaders who included the prince de Polignac and, later, Charles X. New oppressions, however, didn't sit well in a France that had already spilled so much blood in favor of egalitarian causes.

In 1830, after censoring the press and dissolving Parliament, Louis XVIII was removed from power after yet more violent uprisings. Louis-Philippe, duc d'Orléans, was elected king under a liberalized constitution. His reign lasted for 18 years of calm prosperity during which England and France more or less collaborated on matters of foreign policy. The establishment of an independent Belgium and the French conquest of Algeria (1840–47) were to have resounding effects on French politics a century later. It was a time of wealth, grace, and expansion of the arts for most French people, though the industrialization of the north and east produced some of the 19th century's most horrific poverty.

A revolution in 1848, fueled by a financial crash and disgruntled workers in Paris, forced Louis-Philippe out of office. That year, Napoleon I's nephew, Napoleon III, was elected president. Appealing to the property-protecting instinct of a nation that hadn't forgotten the violent upheavals of less than a century before, he initiated a repressive right-wing government in which he was awarded the totalitarian status of emperor in 1851. Rebounding from the punishment they'd received during the revolution and the minor role they'd played during the First Empire, the Second Empire's clergy enjoyed great power. Steel production was begun, and a railway system and Indochinese colonies were established. New technologies fostered new kinds of industry, and the bourgeoisie flourished. And the baron Georges-Eugène Haussmann radically altered Paris by laying out the grand boulevards the world knows today.

By 1866, an industrialized France began to see the Second Empire as more of a hindrance than an encouragement to its expansion. The dismal failure of colonizing Mexico and the increasing power of Austria and Prussia were setbacks to the empire's prestige. In 1870, the Prussians defeated Napoleon III at Sedan and held him prisoner with 100,000 of his soldiers. Paris was besieged by an enemy who only just failed to march its vastly superior armies through the capital.

After the Prussians withdrew, a violent revolt ushered in the Third Republic and its elected president, Marshal MacMahon, in 1873. Peace and prosperity slowly returned, France regained its glamour, a mania of building occurred, the Impressionists made their visual statements, and writers like Flaubert redefined the French novel into what today is regarded as the most evocative in the world. As if as a symbol of this period, the Eiffel Tower was built as part of the 1889 Universal Exposition.

Émile Zola.

By 1890, a new corps of satirists (including Zola) had exposed the country's wretched living conditions, the cruelty of the country's vested interests, and the underlying hypocrisy of late-19th-century French society. The 1894 Dreyfus Affair exposed the corruption of French army officers who had destroyed the career and reputation of a Jewish colleague (Albert Dreyfus), falsely and deliberately punished—as a scapegoat—for treason. The ethnic tensions identified by Zola led to further divisiveness in the rest of the 20th century.

**THE WORLD WARS** International rivalries, thwarted colonial ambitions, and conflicting alliances led to World War I, which, after decisive German victories for 2 years, degenerated into the mud-slogged horror of trench warfare. Mourning between four and five million casualties, Europe was inflicted with psychological scars that never healed. In 1917, the United States broke the European deadlock by entering the war.

After the Allied victory, grave economic problems, plus the demoralization stemming from years of fighting, encouraged the growth of socialism and communism. The French government, led by a vindictive Georges Clemenceau, demanded every centime of reparations it could wring from a crushed Germany. The humiliation associated with this has often been cited as the origin of the German nation's almost obsessive determination to rise from the ashes of 1918 to a place in the sun.

The worldwide Great Depression had devastating repercussions in France. Poverty and widespread bankruptcies weakened the Third Republic to the point where successive coalition governments rose and fell with alarming regularity. The crises reached a crescendo on June 14, 1940, when Hitler's armies arrogantly marched down the Champs-Elysées, and newsreel cameras recorded French people openly weeping. Under the terms of the armistice, the north of France was occupied by the Nazis, and a

> ## Impressions
>
> *Paris is a sphinx. I will drag her secret from her.*
>
> —Mirabeau

puppet French government was established at Vichy under the authority of Marshal Pétain. The immediate collapse of the French army is viewed as one of the most significant humiliations in modern French history.

Pétain and his regime cooperated with the Nazis in unbearably shameful ways. Not the least of their errors included the deportation of more than 75,000 French Jews to German work camps. Pockets of resistance fighters (*le maquis*) waged small-scale guerrilla attacks against the Nazis throughout the course of the war, and free-French forces continued to fight along with the Allies on battlegrounds like North Africa. Charles de Gaulle, the irascible giant whose personality is forever associated with the politics of his era, established himself as the head of the French government-in-exile, operating first from London and then from Algiers.

The scenario was radically altered on June 6, 1944, when the largest armada in history successfully established a bulkhead on the beaches of Normandy. Paris rose in rebellion even before the Allied armies arrived, and on August 26, 1944, Charles de Gaulle entered the capital as head of the government. The Fourth Republic was declared even as pockets of Nazi snipers continued to shoot from scattered rooftops throughout the city.

**THE POSTWAR YEARS**  Plagued by the bitter residue of colonial policies that France had established during the 18th and 19th centuries, the Fourth Republic witnessed the rise and fall of 22 governments and 17 premiers. Many French soldiers died on foreign battlefields as once-profitable colonies in North Africa and Indochina rebelled. It took 80,000 French lives, for example, to put down a revolt in Madagascar. After suffering a bitter defeat in 1954, France ended the war in Indochina and freed its former colony. It also granted internal self-rule to Tunisia and (under slightly different circumstances) Morocco.

Algeria was to remain a greater problem. The advent of the 1958 Algerian revolution signaled the end of the much-maligned Fourth Republic. De Gaulle was called back from retirement to initiate a new constitution, the Fifth Republic, with a stronger set of executive controls. To nearly everyone's dissatisfaction, de Gaulle ended the Algerian war in 1962 by granting the country full independence. Screams of protest resounded long and loud, but the sun had set on most of France's far-flung empire. Internal disruption followed as vast numbers of *pieds-noirs* (French-born residents of Algeria recently stripped of their lands) flooded back into metropolitan France, often into makeshift refugee camps in Provence and Languedoc.

In 1968, major social unrest and a violent coalition hastily formed between the nation's students and blue-collar workers eventually led to the collapse of the government. De Gaulle resigned when his attempts to placate some of the marchers were defeated. The reins of power passed to his second-in-command, Georges Pompidou, and his successor, Valéry Giscard d'Estaing, both of whom continued de Gaulle's policies emphasizing economic development and protection of France as a cultural resource to the world.

**THE 1980S & 1990S**  In 1981, François Mitterrand was elected the first Socialist president of France since World War II (with a close vote of 51%). In almost immediate response, many wealthy French decided to transfer their assets out of the country, much to the delight of banks in Geneva, Monaco, the Cayman Islands, and Vienna. Though reviled by the rich and ridiculed for personal mannerisms that often seemed inspired by Louis XIV, Mitterrand was reelected in 1988. During his two terms, he spent billions of francs on his *grands projets* (like the Louvre pyramid, Opéra Bastille, Cité de la Musique, and Grande Arche de La Défense), some of which are now beginning to fall apart or reveal serious weaknesses.

In 1992, France played a leading role in the development of the European Union (E.U.), 15 countries that will ultimately abolish all trade barriers among themselves and share a single currency, the euro. More recent developments include France's interest in developing a central European bank for the regulation of a shared intra-European currency, a ruling that some politicians have interpreted as another block in the foundation of a European superstate.

In April 1993, voters dumped the Socialists and installed a new conservative government. Polls cited corruption scandals, rising unemployment, and urban insecurity as reasons for this. The Conservative premier Edouard Balladur had to "cohabit" the government with Mitterrand, whom he blamed for the country's growing economic problems. Diagnosed with terminal prostate cancer near the end of his second term, Mitterrand continued to represent France with dignity, despite his deterioration. The battle over who would succeed him was waged against Balladur with epic rancor by Jacques Chirac, tenacious survivor of many terms as mayor of Paris. Their public discord was among the most venomous since the days of Pétain.

On his third try, on May 7, 1995, Chirac won the presidency with 52% of the vote and immediately declared war on unemployment. Mitterrand turned over the reins of government on May 17 and died shortly thereafter. But Chirac's popularity soon faded in the wake of unrest caused by an 11.5% unemployment rate, a barrage of terrorist attacks by Algerian Muslims, and a stressed economy struggling to meet European Union entry requirements.

A wave of terrorist attacks from July to September 1995 brought an unfamiliar wariness to Paris. Six bombs were planted, killing 7 people and injuring 115. In light of this, Parisians proved cautious, if not fearful. Algerian Islamic militants, the suspected culprits, may have brought military guards to the Eiffel Tower, but they failed to throw France into panic.

Throughout 1995 and early 1996, France infuriated everyone from the members of Greenpeace to the governments of Australia and New Zealand by resuming its long-dormant policy of exploding nuclear bombs on isolated Pacific atolls for testing purposes. This policy continued until public outcry, both in France and outside its borders, exerted massive pressure to end the tests.

In May 1996, thousands of Parisian workers took to the streets, disrupting passenger train service to demand a workweek shorter than the usual 39 hours. They felt that this move would help France's staggering unemployment figures. Employer organizations resisted this idea, claiming that even if the workweek were cut to 35 hours, businesses wouldn't be able to take on many new employees.

The drama of 1996 climaxed with the heat of the summer, when the police took axes to the doors of the Paris church of St-Bernard de la Chapelle. Nearly 300 African immigrants were removed by force from this place of refuge and deported. Strikes and protests continued to plague the country, and Chirac's political horizon became dimmer still—with a 12% unemployment rate and crime on an alarming increase. Terrorist scares continued to flood the borders of France throughout 1997, forcing a highly visible armed police force, as part of a nationwide program known as Vigipirate, to take to the streets of major cities. One of the unusual offshoots of the Vigipirate program involved the closing of the crypts of many of France's medieval churches to visitors, partly in fear of a terrorist bomb attack on national historic treasures.

In the latest power struggle between the Conservatives and the Socialists, in the spring of 1998, Conservatives were ousted in a majority of France's regional provinces, amounting to a powerful endorsement for Prime Minister Lionel Jospin's Socialist-led government.

In 1999, France joined with other European countries in adopting the euro as its standard of currency. The new currency accelerated the creation of a single economy comprising nearly 330 million Europeans, although the ability for several fiscally wayward states to borrow at preferential rates has led to a sovereign debt crisis today. Nonetheless, the European Union now boasts a combined gross national product approaching 18€ trillion, larger than that of the United States.

France moved into the millennium by testing the practicality of new and progressive social legislation. On October 13, 1999, the French Parliament passed a new law giving legal status to unmarried couples, including homosexual unions. The law allows couples of same sex or not to enter into a union and be entitled to the same rights as married couples in such areas as housing, inheritance, income tax, and social welfare.

**CONTEMPORARY POLITICS (2000–PRESENT)** In February 2005, President George W. Bush flew to Europe to mend fences with some of his worst critics, notably French President Chirac. The two political foes found common ground on such issues as Syria and Lebanon, but Iraq remained a thorny problem. Chirac, a self-styled expert on cows after serving as a former agriculture minister, was not invited to Bush's Texas ranch. When asked why not, Bush enigmatically said, "I'm looking for a good cowboy."

Late in 2005, decades of pent-up resentment felt by the children of African immigrants exploded into an orgy of violence and vandalism. Riots began in the suburbs of Paris and spread around the country. Throughout France, gangs of youths battled the French police; torched schools, cars, and businesses; and even attacked commuter trains. Rioting followed in such cities as Dijon, Marseille, and Rouen. Most of the rioters were the sons of Arab and black African immigrants, Muslims living in a mostly Catholic country. The reason for the protests? Leaders of the riots claimed they live "like second-class citizens," even though they are French citizens. Unemployment is 30% higher in the ethnic ghettos of France.

Against a backdrop of discontent regarding issues of unemployment, immigration, and healthcare, the charismatic Nicolas Sarkozy swept into the presidential office in May 2007. Sarkozy, the combative son of a Hungarian immigrant, promised to reinvigorate ties with France's traditional ally, the United States, and he made a summer vacation trip to New England directly after his election.

In the ensuing years, Sarkozy found time to divorce a wife and take a beautiful new bride. A glamorous model-turned-singer, Carla Bruni became first lady of France in 2008. The tabloids had a field day with the Bruni, whose former lovers include Mick Jagger, Eric Clapton, Donald Trump, and even Laurent Fabius (a former French prime minister). "The Carla effect," as it's called in Paris, initially decreased Sarkozy's popularity—although the birth of the presidential child born in office, Giulia Sarkozy, in October 2011 coincided with a poll boost.

Many French citizens became uncertain of their future as a European Union member in 2010. The financial instability in Greece and the continuing woes of debt-ridden Ireland, Italy, Spain, and Portugal contributed to the drop in the euro's value. Along with Germany, France found a new voice within the group as it pressed for greater fiscal and monetary union. But politically, Sarkozy remained a divisive figure. His attempt to reform the pension system by raising the age of retirement from 60 to 62 caused a wave of strikes and protests across France in the autumn of 2010. Despite widespread opposition to the legislation, the French parliament approved the reforms in October 2010. Outside of politics, the French looked at Sarkozy's personal life with ridicule. His holidays with the rich and famous earned him the title of the "bling bling president."

The French Presidential elections of April 2012 were held against a backdrop of growing debt, moribund economies, and squabbles with EU partners. Added to the mix was the odd touch of nasty nationalism from far right candidate Marine Le Pen. The voter choice was stark: either France continues with the state-heavy status quo, or reworks the economy under Sarkozy with measures of austerity, and further modernization. The big surprise in the first round of voting was Communist Party boss Jean-Luc Mélenchon, a man who proposed a 100% rate of income tax on earnings over 360,000€, who gained a massive 13% of the vote. But this figure wasn't enough to keep either him or Le Pen into the Presidential race, so a final runoff between Sarkozy and Social Party candidate François Hollande was held the following May.

Hollande won the runoff with a vote of 51.63%, against Sarkozy's 48.37%. This statistic served to confirm the divided nature of modern French politics. France's first socialist president in 17 years got off to a rocky start, unsurprisingly perhaps for a man who has never held government office before. In short, the French gave globalization only a half-hearted *non* in 2012, and it remains to be seen how the world's fifth largest economy will beat a path in today's connected world.

# ART & ARCHITECTURE

## Art

France's art treasures range from medieval stained glass and Ingres portraits to Monet's Impressionist *Water Lilies;* its architecture encompasses Roman ruins and Gothic cathedrals, as well as Renaissance châteaux and postmodern buildings like the Centre Pompidou. This brief overview will help you make sense of it all.

## PREHISTORIC, CELTIC & CLASSICAL (25,000 B.C.–A.D. 500)

After England's Stonehenge, Europe's most famous prehistoric remains are France's **Paleolithic cave paintings.** Created 15,000 to 20,000 years ago, they depict mostly hunting scenes and abstract shapes.

The **caves at Lascaux,** the Sistine Chapel of prehistoric art, have been closed since 1963, but experts have created a replica, Lascaux II. To see the real stuff, visit **Les Eyzies-de-Tayac,** which boasts four caves (Font de Gaume is the best). In the neighboring Lot Valley, outside Cahors, is the **Grotte du Pech-Merle,** with France's oldest cave art (about 20,000 years old). Little remains of the art of **Celtic** (ca. 1000 B.C.–A.D. 125) and **Roman** (A.D. 125–500) Gaul. Surviving items—small votive bronzes, statues, jewelry, and engraved weapons and tools—are spread across France's **archaeology museums.** Burgundy preserves the most of Celtic Gaul, including sites at **Dijon, Châtillon-sur-Seine, Alise-Ste-Reine,** and **Auxerre.** To see artifacts of Roman Gaul, visit the southern towns of **Nîmes, Arles, Orange, St-Rémy-de-Provence,** and **Vienne.**

## ROMANESQUE (900–1100)

Artistic expression in medieval France was largely church related. Because Mass was in Latin, images were used to communicate the Bible's lessons to the mostly illiterate people. **Bas-reliefs** (sculptures that project slightly from a flat surface) were used to illustrate key tales that inspired faith in God and fear of sin (the *Last Judgment* was a favorite). These reliefs were wrapped around column capitals and fitted into the **tympanums,** or arched spaces above doorways (the complete door, tympanum, arch, and supporting pillars assemblage is the **portal**).

The best examples of Romanesque art include a *Last Judgment* tympanum by Gislebertus at **St-Lazare** in Autun; 76 Romanesque cloister capitals and one of France's best-carved 11th-century portals at **St-Pierre Abbey** in Moissac near Montauban; and the tympanum over the inner main portal of huge **Ste-Madeleine** in Vézelay. The **Bayeux Tapestry** (1066–77) is the most notable example of Romanesque artistry, 69m (226 ft.) of embroidered linen telling the story of William the Conqueror's defeat of the English.

## GOTHIC (1100–1400)

Paris retains almost no art from the classical or Romanesque eras, but much remains from the medieval Gothic era, when artists created sculpture and stained glass for churches.

Outstanding examples include the **Cathédrale de Chartres** (1194–1220), a day trip from Paris, boasting magnificent sculpture and some of the best stained glass in Europe; the **Cathédrale de Notre-Dame** (1163–1250), with sculpture on the facade, an interior choir screen lined with deep-relief carvings, and three rose windows filled with stained glass; and **Sainte-Chapelle** (1240–50), a tiny chapel adorned with the finest stained glass in the world.

## THE RENAISSANCE & BAROQUE (1450–1800)

Humanist thinkers rediscovered the wisdom of ancient Greece and Rome, while artists strove for naturalism, using newly developed techniques like linear perspective. The French had little to do with this movement, which started in Italy and was picked up only in Germany and the Low Countries. However, many Renaissance treasures are in French museums, thanks to collectors such as **François I.**

Not until the 17th-century **baroque** did a few French masters emerge. This period is hard to pin down. In some ways a result of the Catholic

Counter-Reformation, it reaffirmed spirituality in a simplified, monumental, and religious version of Renaissance ideals. In other ways, it delved even deeper into classical modes and a kind of super-realism based on using peasants as models and the *chiaroscuro* (contrast of light and dark) of the Italian painter Caravaggio.

Paris's **Louvre** abounds with Renaissance works by Italian, Flemish, and German masters, including **Michelangelo** (1475–1564) and **Leonardo da Vinci** (1452–1519). Leonardo's *Mona Lisa* (1503–05), perhaps the world's most famous painting, hangs there. Great baroque and rococo artists include **Antoine Watteau** (1684–1721), a rococo painter of colorful, theatrical works; and **Jean-Honoré Fragonard** (1732–1806), a master of rococo pastel scenes, including the famous *The Bathers*.

## NEOCLASSICAL & ROMANTIC (1770–1890)

As the baroque got excessive, the rococo got cute, and the somber Counter-Reformation got serious about the limits on religious art, several artists looked to the ancients for relief. This gave rise to a **neoclassical** artistic style that emphasized symmetry, austerity, clean lines, and classical themes.

The **romantics,** on the other hand, felt that both the ancients and the Renaissance had gotten it wrong and that the Middle Ages was the place to be. They idealized romantic tales of chivalry and the nobility of peasantry.

Some great artists and movements of the era, all with examples in the **Louvre,** include **Jean Ingres** (1780–1867), who became a defender of the neoclassicists and the Royal French Academy and opposed the romantics; **Theodore Géricault** (1791–1824), one of the great early romantics, who painted *The Raft of the Medusa* (1819), which served as a model for the movement; and **Eugène Delacroix** (1798–1863), whose *Liberty Leading the People* (1830) was painted in the romantic style.

## IMPRESSIONISM (1870–1920)

Seeking to capture the *impression* light made as it reflected off objects, the Impressionists adopted a free, open style; deceptively loose compositions; swift, visible brushwork; and often light colors. For subject matter, they turned to landscapes and scenes of modern life. You'll find some of the best examples of their works in the **Musée d'Orsay.**

Impressionist greats include **Edouard Manet** (1832–1883), whose groundbreaking *Picnic on the Grass* (1863) and *Olympia* (1863) helped inspire the movement with their harsh realism, visible brush strokes, and thick outlines; **Claude Monet** (1840–1926), who launched the movement officially in an 1874 exhibition in which he exhibited his Turner-inspired *Impression, Sunrise* (1874), now in the **Musée Marmottan; Pierre-Auguste Renoir** (1841–1919), known for his figures' ivory skin and chubby pink cheeks; **Edgar Degas** (1834–1917), an accomplished painter, sculptor, and draftsman—his pastels of dancers and bathers are particularly memorable; and **Auguste Rodin** (1840–1917), the greatest Impressionist-era sculptor, who crafted remarkably expressive bronzes. The **Musée Rodin,** his former Paris studio, contains, among other works, his *Burghers of Calais* (1886), *The Kiss* (1886–98), and *The Thinker* (1880).

## POST-IMPRESSIONISM (1880–1930)

The smaller movements or styles of Impressionism are usually lumped together as "post-Impressionism." Again, you'll find the best examples of these works at the

**Musée d'Orsay,** though you'll find pieces by Matisse, Chagall, and the cubists, including Picasso, in the **Centre Pompidou.** Important post-Impressionists include **Paul Cézanne** (1839–1906), who adopted the short brush strokes, love of landscape, and light color palette of his Impressionist friends; **Paul Gauguin** (1848–1903), who developed **synthetism** (black outlines around solid colors); **Henri de Toulouse-Lautrec** (1864–1901), who created paintings and posters of wispy, fluid lines anticipating Art Nouveau and often depicting the bohemian life of Paris's dance halls and cafes; **Vincent van Gogh** (1853–90), who combined divisionism, synthetism, and a touch of Japanese influence, and painted with thick, short strokes; **Henri Matisse** (1869–1954), who created **fauvism** (a critic described those who used the style as *fauves,* meaning "wild beasts"); and **Pablo Picasso** (1881–1973), a Málaga-born artist who painted objects from all points of view at once, rather than using such optical tricks as perspective to fool viewers into seeing three dimensions. The fractured result was **cubism.** You can see art from all of his periods at museums across France, including the Picasso museums in Antibes and Paris, the latter set to reopen in summer 2013.

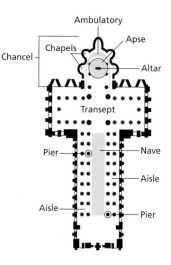

Church Floor Plan

## Architecture

It's worth pointing out that very few buildings (especially churches) were built in one particular architectural style. These massive, expensive structures often took centuries to complete, during which time tastes would change and plans would be altered.

### ANCIENT ROMAN (125 B.C.– A.D. 450)

**Provence** was Rome's first transalpine conquest, and the legions of Julius Caesar quickly subdued the Celtic tribes across France, converting it into Roman Gaul.

Pont du Gard, Nîmes.

**Nîmes** preserves from the 1st century B.C. a 20,000-seat **amphitheater,** a **Corinthian temple** called the "Square House," a fine **archaeology museum,** and the astounding **pont du Gard,** a 47m-long (154-ft.), three-story aqueduct made of cut stones fitted together without mortar. The Roman ruins of **Arles** are similarly spectacular.

## ROMANESQUE (800–1100)

The Romanesque style took its inspiration from ancient Rome (hence the name). Early Christians in Italy had adapted the basilica (ancient Roman law-court buildings) to become churches.

The **Cathédrale St-Bénigne** in Dijon was the first French Romanesque church, but of that era, only the crypt remains. The **Cathédrale St-Pierre** in Angoulême has a single large nave, a rounded apse with small radiating chapels, and a pair of transept mini-apses.

## GOTHIC (1100–1500)

By the 12th century, engineering developments freed church architecture from the heavy, thick walls of Romanesque structures and allowed ceilings to soar, walls to thin, and windows to proliferate. Gothic interiors enticed churchgoers' gazes upward to high ceilings filled with light. Graceful buttresses and spires soared above town centers.

The best examples in and around Paris of the Gothic are **Basilique St-Denis** (1140–44), the world's first Gothic cathedral, in a Paris suburb; **Cathédrale de Chartres** (1194–1220), a Gothic masterpiece with some 150 glorious stained-glass windows; and, of course, **Cathédrale de Notre-Dame** (1163–1250), which possesses

Cathédrale Notre-Dame de Chartres.

pinnacled flying buttresses, a trio of France's best rose windows, good portal carvings, a choir screen of deeply carved reliefs, and spiffy gargoyles.

## RENAISSANCE (1500–1630)

In architecture, as in painting, the Renaissance came from Italy and was only slowly Frenchified. And as in painting, its rules stressed proportion, order, classical inspiration, and precision to create unified, balanced structures.

The Loire Valley and Burgundy are home to many Renaissance **châteaux.** Foremost is the Loire's **Château de Chambord,** started in 1519, probably according to plans by Leonardo da Vinci (who may have designed its double helix staircase). In contrast, the **Château de Chenonceau,** home to many a French king's wife or mistress, is a fanciful fairy tale built in the middle of a river. The best example in Burgundy is the **Château de Tanlay,** east of Chablis.

Château de Chambord.

## CLASSICISM & ROCOCO (1630–1800)

While Italy and Germany embraced the opulent baroque, France took the fundamentals of Renaissance **classicism** even further, becoming more imitative of ancient models. During the reign of Louis XIV, art and architecture were subservient to political ends. Buildings were grandiose and severely ordered on the Versailles model. Opulence was saved for interior decoration, which increasingly (especially in 1715–50, after the death of Louis XIV) became a detailed and self-indulgent **rococo** (*rocaille* in French). Externally, rococo is noticeable only in a greater elegance and delicacy.

François Mansart built town houses, châteaux, and churches (**Val-de-Grâce** in Paris, the **Palais du Tau** in Reims) and laid out Dijon's **place de la Libération.** But the Parisian architect is chiefly remembered for his steeply sloping namesake, "**mansard" roofs.**

**Louis Le Vau** (1612–70) was the chief architect of the Louvre from 1650 to 1670 and of the **Château de Vaux-le-Vicomte** (1656–61) outside Paris, a gig that put him and his collaborators—including Mansart, interior decorator **Charles Le Brun** (1619–90), and the unparalleled landscape gardener **André Le Nôtre** (1613–1700)—on Louis XIV's radar and landed them the commission to rebuild **Versailles** (1669–85). Versailles is France's—indeed, Europe's—grandest palace.

Cornice
Modillion — Entablature
Frieze
Architrave
Capital
Shaft
Base
Corinthian Order      Ionic Order      Doric Order

**Classical Orders**

## THE 19TH CENTURY

Architectural styles in 19th-century Paris were eclectic, beginning in a severe classical mode and ending with an identity crisis torn between Industrial Age technology and Art Nouveau organic.

Identifiable styles include the neoclassical **First Empire,** with its strong lines often accented with a simple curve—the rage during Napoleon's reign; and **Second Empire,** which occurred during Napoleon III's reign, a reinterpretation of classicism in an ornate mood. During this period, Paris became a city of wide boulevards courtesy of **Baron Georges-Eugène Haussmann** (1809–91), commissioned by Napoleon III in 1852 to redesign the city. Haussmann lined the boulevards with simple six-story apartment blocks, such as elongated 18th-century town houses with continuous balconies wrapping around the third and sixth floors and mansard roofs with dormer windows.

The **Third Republic** expositions in 1878, 1889, and 1900 used the engineering prowess of the Industrial Revolution to produce such Parisian monuments as the Tour Eiffel and Sacré-Coeur.

**Art Nouveau** architects and decorators rebelled against the Third Republic era of mass production by creating asymmetrical, curvaceous designs based on organic inspiration (plants and flowers) in such media as wrought iron, stained glass, and tile.

The best examples are the **Arc de Triomphe** (1836), Napoleon's oversize imitation of a Roman triumphal arch, the ultimate paean to the classic era; **Tour Eiffel** (1889), which **Gustave Eiffel** (1832–1923) slapped together to form the world's tallest structure, at 324m (1,063 ft.); and **Métro station entrances.**

## THE 20TH CENTURY

France commissioned some ambitious architectural projects in the last century, most of them the *grand projets* of the late François Mitterrand. The majority were considered controversial or even offensive when completed.

At **Centre Pompidou** (1977), British designer Richard Rogers (b. 1933) and Italian Renzo Piano (b. 1937) turned architecture inside out—literally—to craft Paris's eye-popping modern-art museum, with exposed pipes, steel supports, and plastic-tube escalators wrapping around the exterior; the **Louvre's**

Centre Pompidou.

**glass pyramids** (1989) were created by Chinese-American architect I. M. Pei (b. 1917); and **Opéra Bastille** (1989) is a curvaceous, dark glass mound of space designed by Canadian Carlos Ott (b. 1947).

The 21st century looks set for more of the same. British architect Baron Foster (b. 1935) completed the skyline topping **Millau Viaduct** in 2004, and plans to top out Paris' **Hermitage Plaza** in 2016. At 323m high (1,062 ft) the Hermitage will be a symbolic meter shorter than the Eiffel Tower, France's tallest building. Two jaw-dropping branches of the capital's major museums offer architecture aficionados a novel treat. Japanese architects are behind both the **Metz Centre Pompidou** (2010) and the **Lens Louvre** (2012)—Shigeru Ban (b.1957) for the former, and the combined team of Kazuyo Sejima (b.1956) and Ryue Nishizawa (b.1966) for the latter.

# FRANCE IN POPULAR CULTURE
## Books

There are numerous books on all aspects of French history and society—ranging from the very general, such as the section on France in the *Encyclopedia Americana,* International Edition (Grolier Incorporated, 2004), which presents an excellent, illustrated overview of the French people and their way of life; to the very specific, such as Judi Culbertson and Tom Randall's *Permanent Parisians: An Illustrated Guide to the Cemeteries of Paris* (Chelsea Green, 1986), which depicts the lives of famous French and expatriates who are buried in Paris.

**HISTORY**   In addition to the encyclopedia reference above, a broad overview of French history can be found in other encyclopedias and general history books. One very good one is *History of France,* by Guillaume de Bertier de Savigny and David H. Pinkney, a comprehensive history with illustrations and plenty of obscure but interesting facts.

Two books that present French life and society in the 17th century are Warren Lewis's *The Splendid Century* and Madame de Sévigné's *Selected Letters,* edited by Leonard W. Tancock, which contains imaginative and witty letters written to her daughter during the reign of Louis XIV. Simon Schama's *Citizens* is a long but enjoyable new history of the French Revolution.

Moving into the 20th century, *Pleasure of the Belle Epoque: Entertainment and Festivity in Turn-of-the-Century France,* by Charles Rearick, depicts public diversions in the changing and troubled times of the Third Republic. *Paris Was Yesterday, 1925–1939* is a fascinating collection of excerpts from Janet Flanner's "Letters from Paris" column of the *New Yorker,* while *On Paris* comprises a newly bound series of essays by Ernest Hemingway, written for the *Toronto Star* between 1920 and 1924. Larry Collins and Dominique Lapierre have written a popular history of the liberation of Paris in 1944 called *Is Paris Burning?*

Finally, two unusual approaches to French history are Rudolph Chleminski's *The French at Table,* a funny and honest history of why the French know how to eat better than anyone and how they go about it; and *Parisians: An Adventure History of Paris* by Graham Robb, entertaining historical snippets that range from the French Revolution through the 1968 riots and up to coverage of Nicolas Sarkozy's politics.

**TRAVEL** Since 1323, some 10,000 books have been devoted to exploring Paris. One of the best is *Paris: Capital of the World,* by Patrice Higonnet. This book takes a fresh social, cultural, and political look at the City of Light, exploring Paris as "the capital of sex" and, in contrast, the "capital of art."

Showing a greater fondness for gossip is Alistair Horne in his *Seven Ages of Paris.* Horne is certainly not a timid writer: he calls the Palais de Chaillot fascistic and hideous, the Pompidou Center a horror. We even learn that a woman once jumped off the Eiffel Tower, bounced off the roof of a parked car, and survived.

In *The Flâneur: A Stroll Through the Paradoxes of Paris,* Edmund White wants the reader to experience Paris as Parisians do. Hard to translate exactly, a *flâneur* is someone who wanders, loafs, or idles. And for the frequent visitor, Jean-Christophe Napais's *Quiet Corners of Paris: Unexpected Hideaways, Secret Courtyards, Hidden Gardens* is sure to turn up plenty of undiscovered gems. For a lighter read, David Sedaris's *Me Talk Pretty One Day* describes the funny frustrations of an American expat in Normandy as he tries to get to grips with French culture.

**BIOGRAPHY** You can get a more intimate look at history through biographies of historical figures. The best book yet on the architect who changed the face of Paris is *Haussmann: His Life and Times and the Making of Modern Paris,* by Patrick Camiller. Leonie Frieda brings to life the 16th-century French queen *Catherine de Medici,* mother of three kings of France, a queen of Spain, and a queen of Navarre.

Representing a very different era are *A Moveable Feast,* Ernest Hemingway's recollections of Paris during the 1920s, and Morley Callaghan's *That Summer in Paris: Memories of Tangled Friendships with Hemingway, Fitzgerald and Some Others,* an anecdotal account of the same period. Another great read is *The Autobiography of Alice B. Toklas,* by Gertrude Stein. It's not only the account of 30 years in Paris, but also the autobiography of Gertrude Stein.

*Simone de Beauvoir,* by Deirdre Bair, was described by one critic as ". . . a biography 'à l'Americaine'—that is to say, long, with all the warts of its subject unsparingly described." The story of the great feminist intellectual was based in part on tape-recorded conversations and unpublished letters.

*Colette: A Life,* by Herbert R. Lottman, is a painstakingly researched biography of the celebrated French writer and her fascinating life—which included not only writing novels and appearing in cabarets, but also dabbling in lesbianism and perhaps even collaborating with the enemy during the Nazi occupation.

**THE ARTS** Much of France's beauty can be found in its art. Three books that approach France from this perspective are *The History of Impressionism,* by John Rewald, which is a collection of writings about and quotations from the artists, illuminating this period in art; *The French Through Their Films,* by Robin Buss, an exploration of more than 100 widely circulated films; and *The Studios of Paris: The Capital of Art in the Late Nineteenth Century,* by John Milner. In the last, Milner presents the dynamic forces that made Paris one of the most complex centers of the art world in the early modern era.

*Nightlife of Paris: The Art of Toulouse-Lautrec,* by Patrick O'Connor, is an enchanting 80-page book with anecdotes about the hedonistic luminaries of Belle Epoque Paris, with paintings, sketches, and lithographs by the artist.

*Olympia: Paris in the Age of Manet,* by Otto Friedrich, takes its inspiration from the celebrated artwork in the Musée d'Orsay in Paris. From here the book takes off on an anecdote-rich gossipy chain of historical associations, tracing the rise of the Impressionist school of modern painting, but incorporating social commentary, too, such as the pattern of prostitution and venereal disease in 19th-century France.

Gustave Flaubert.

**FICTION** The *Chanson de Roland,* edited by F. Whitehead, written between the 11th and 14th centuries, is the earliest and most celebrated of the "songs of heroic exploits." *The Misanthrope* and *Tartuffe* are two masterful satires on the frivolity of the 17th century by the great comic dramatist Molière. François-Marie Arouet Voltaire's *Candide* is a classic satire attacking the philosophy of optimism and the abuses of the ancient regime.

A few of the masterpieces of the 19th century are *Madame Bovary,* by Gustave Flaubert, in which the carefully wrought characters, setting, and plot attest to Flaubert's genius in presenting the tragedy of Emma Bovary; Victor Hugo's *Les Misérables,* a classic tale of social oppression and human courage set in the era of Napoleon I; and *Selected Stories,* by the master of short stories, Guy de Maupassant.

More recently, one of France's leading 20th-century thinkers, Jean-Paul Sartre, shows individuals struggling against their freedom in *No Exit and Three Other Plays,* while Henry Miller's *Tropic of Cancer* is the semiautobiographical story of the author's years in Paris.

Michel Houellebecq is currently one of France's most controversial authors, renowned for nihilist masterpieces such as *Atomised* and *Platform.*

## Films

Although Americans understood—and very quickly, too—the commercial wealth to be made from films, the French are credited with the scientific and technical inventions that made them possible. French physicists had laid the groundwork for a movie camera as early as the mid-1880s, and the world's first movie was shown in Paris on December 28, 1895. Its makers were the Lumière brothers, who considered filmmaking a scientific oddity and stubbornly confined its use to the production of international newsreels. Later, a vaudevillian actor and illusionist, Georges Méliès, used film to convey plot and drama.

Charles Pathé and Léon Gaumont were the first to exploit filmmaking on a grand scale. Beginning in 1896, they produced and distributed their own films, building their company into a giant before World War I. When Gaumont made his first film, he enlisted his secretary, Alice Guy-Blanché, to create the plot, design the scenery, and direct it. She proved so successful that she was eventually promoted to the head of Paris's largest studio and became the world's first female director.

Before World War I the many talented actors arriving *en scène* included Max Linder, a popular French comic, whose style influenced Charlie Chaplin and helped him develop his keen sense of timing. After World War I, a flood of film imports from the United States and an economic depression slowed down the growth of French filmmaking.

By the 1920s, the French began to view filmmaking as an art form and infused it with surreal and dada themes. These were eventually named avant-garde and included experiments viewed (sometimes skeptically, sometimes encouragingly) in Hollywood and around the world. Examples include Man Ray's *Le retour à la raison* (1923), Fernand Léger's *Le ballet mécanique* (1924), and Jean Cocteau's *Le sang d'un poète* (1930).

The golden age of the French silent screen on both sides of the Atlantic was 1927 to 1929. Actors were directed with more sophistication, and technical abilities reached an all-time high. One of our favorite films—despite its mind-numbing length—is Abel Gance's sweepingly evocative masterpiece *Napoleon* (1927); its grisly battle scenes are easily as chilling as any war film made today. Other highlights from this era include René Clair's *Un chapeau de paille d'Italie* (*An Italian Straw Hat,* 1927), Carl Dreyer's *La passion de Jeanne d'Arc* (1928), and an adaptation of Emile Zola's *Thérèse Raquin* (1928) by Jacques Feyder.

Experiments with the early productions of "talkies" were less successful. Popular film director, Marcel Pagnol, declared outright that the role of films was to publicize to the masses the benefits of the theatrical stage. During this period, many of the counterculture's most gifted directors either left France altogether (as did René Clair, who emigrated to England in 1934) or died (Jean Vigo, *Zéro de Conduite*).

In 1936, the Cinémathèque Française was established to find and preserve old (usually silent) French films. By that time, French cinematographers had divorced themselves completely from the value system of the stage and had found a style of their own. An average of 130 films a year was made in France, by (among others) Jean Renoir, Charles Spaak, and Marcel Carne. This era also brought such French luminaries as Claudette Colbert and Maurice Chevalier to Hollywood.

During World War II, the best-known (to Americans) of the French directors fled to Hollywood. The Vichy government heavily censored the ones who chose to remain. Despite that, more than 350 French films, many relating to long-past (and, therefore, uncontroversial) events were produced. Exceptions were Carne's *Les enfants du paradis* (*Children of Paradise,* 1945).

In 1946, France slapped a heavy quota system onto the importation of foreign (especially American) films. A semigovernmental film authority (le Centre national du Cinéma Français) financed independent French film companies and encouraged liaisons between the French and Italian film industries. Many directors who had supported the Vichy government's Nazi collaboration were soon accepted back into the cinematic community.

Two strong traditions—film noir and a return to literary traditions—began to flourish. Film noir included such existentially inspired nihilistic themes as André Cayatte's *Nous sommes tous des assassins* (*We Are All Assassins*, 1952) and Yves Allegret's *Dedée d'Anvers* (1948). Examples of the literary tradition include Bresson's *Journal d'un curé de campagne* (*Diary of a Country Priest*, 1951) and a film rendition of Stendhal's *Le rouge et le noir* (*The Red and the Black*, 1954), by Autant-Lara. By the 1950s, comedy adopted a new kind of genre with Jacques Tati's *Les vacances du Monsieur Hulot* (*Mr. Hulot's Holiday*). By the mid-1950s, French filmmaking ushered in the era of enormous budgets, a la Hollywood, and the creation of such frothy potboilers as *And God Created Woman*, which helped make Brigitte Bardot a celebrity around the world, contributing greatly to the image in America of France as a kingdom of sexual liberation.

By the late 1950s, François Truffaut, widely publicizing his auteur theories, rebelled with a series of short films (the most famous of which was *The 400 Blows*, 1959) that were partly financed by government funds, partly by wealthy benefactors. With Jean-Luc Godard (*À bout de souffle*, or *Breathless*, 1960) and Claude Chabrol (*Le beau Serge*, 1959), they pioneered one of the most publicized movements in 20th-century French art, *la nouvelle vague*. In the early 1960s, dozens of new directors joined the movement, furiously making films, some of which are considered classics, others of which have been thrown into the dustbin of forgotten artistic endeavors. Enthusiastically endorsed by the countercul-

A scene from *A bout de souffle*.

ture on both sides of the Atlantic, these directors included Alain Resnais (*Muriel*), Roger Vadim, Agnès Varda (*Le Bonheur*), Jacques Demy (*Les parapluies de Cherbourg*, or The Umbrellas of Cherbourg), Louis Malle, Chris Marker, and Marguerite Duras (*Detruire, dit-elle*).

After a switch to political themes (Costa Gavras's *Z*) during the 1968 rebellions (and a politically motivated abandonment of the film festival at Cannes by at least a dozen prominent French directors), French cinema turned to comedy in the early 1970s. Examples include Luis Buñuel's *Le charme discret de la bourgeoisie* (Discrete Charm of the Bourgeoisie, 1972) and Jean Yanne's *Tout le monde il est beau, tout le monde il est gentil* (1972).

Many American films—still shown rather frequently on TV—were filmed in Paris (or else used sets to simulate Paris). Notable ones have included the classic *An American in Paris*, starring Gene Kelly, and *Moulin Rouge*, starring José Ferrer as Toulouse-Lautrec. *Last Tango in Paris*, with Marlon Brando, was one of the most controversial films set in Paris. Woody Allen's acclaimed *Midnight in Paris* is the most recent film to celebrate the City of Light. The film features beautiful shots of the city and includes cameos of iconic figures who lived in Paris in the 1920s.

Truffaut's *The Last Metro* and Clément's *Is Paris Burning?* gained worldwide audiences. *Betty Blue*, the stylish Jean-Jacques Beineix film about a torrid summertime love affair, was released in English in 1992. It was first shown in France in 1986 when it was that country's nominee for the Oscar as best foreign film.

One French film that continues to enchant is Jean-Pierre Jeunet's *Amélie*, with its beautiful scenes shot in Montmartre. *La Vie en Rose* won Marion Cotillard an Oscar in 2008 for her performance as "The Little Sparrow," Edith Piaf.

## Music

Music and France have gone together since the monks in the 12th century sang Gregorian chants in Notre-Dame. Troubadours with their ballads traveled all over France in the Middle Ages. In the Renaissance era, **Josquin des Prez** (c. 1440–1521) was the first master of the High Renaissance style of polyphonic vocal music. He became the greatest composer of his age, a magnificent virtuoso. **Jean-Baptise Lully** (1632–87) entertained the decadent court of Versailles with his operas. During the reign of Robespierre, **Claude-Joseph Rouget de Lisle** (1760–1836) immortalized himself in 1792 when he wrote *La Marseillaise*, the French national anthem. Regrettably, he died in poverty.

The rise of the middle class in the 1800s gave birth to both grand opera and *opéra comique*. Both styles merged into a kind of lyric opera, mixing soaring arias and tragedy in such widely popular hits as Bizet's *Carmen* in 1875 and St-Saën's *Samson et Dalila* in 1877.

During the romantic period of the 19th century, foreign composers moving to Paris often dominated the musical scene. **Frédéric Chopin** (1810–49) was half French, half Polish. He became the most influential composer for piano and even invented new musical forms such as the *ballade*. **Félix Mendelssohn** (1809–47) had to fight against anti-Semitism to establish himself with his symphonies, concerti, and chamber music.

At the dawn of the 20th century, music became more impressionistic, as evoked by **Claude Débussy** (1862–1918). In many ways, he helped launch modernist music. His *Prélude à L'Après-midi d'un Faune* in 1894 and *La Mer* in 1905 were performed all over Europe. From Russia came **Igor Stravinsky**

Frédéric Chopin.

(1882–1971), who made *Time* magazine's list of the 100 most influential people of the 20th century. He achieved fame as a pianist, conductor, and composer. His *Le sacre du printemps (The Rite of Spring)* provoked a riot in Paris when it was first performed in 1913, with its pagan rituals.

A revolutionary artist, **Yves Klein** (1928–62) was called a "neo-Dada." His 1960 "The Monotone Symphony" with three naked models became a notorious performance. For 20 minutes, he conducted an orchestra on one note. Dying of a heart attack at the age of 34, Klein is considered today an enigmatic postmodernist. **Pierre Boulez** (b. 1925) developed a technique known as integral serialism using a 12-tone system pioneered in the 1920s. As director of the IRCAM institute at the Centre Pompidou from 1970-92, he influenced young musicians around the world.

France took to American jazz like no other country. Louis Armstrong practically became a national hero to Parisians in the 1930s, and in 1949 Paris welcomed the arrival of Miles Davis. **Stéphane Grappelli** (1908–97), a French jazz violinist, founded the Quintette du Hot Club de France, the most famous of all-string jazz bands. **Django Reinhardt** (1910–53) became one of the most prominent jazz musicians of Europe, known for such works as "Belleville" and "My Sweet."

Some French singers went on to achieve world renown, notably **Edith Piaf** (1915–63), "The Little Sparrow" and France's greatest pop singer. Wherever you go in France, you will hear her "La Vie en Rose," which she first recorded in 1946. Born in 1924, **Charles Aznavour** remains an eternal favorite. He's known for his unique tenor voice with its gravelly and soulful low notes. **Jacques Brel** (1929–78), a singer-songwriter, has seen his songs interpreted by everybody from Frank Sinatra to David Bowie. A popular *chanson* singer, **Juliette Gréco** (b. 1927) became known as "the High Priestess of Existentialism" on Paris's Left Bank and was beloved by Jean-Paul Sartre. She dressed all in black and let her long, black hair hang free before coming to Hollywood and becoming the mistress of mogul Darryl Zanuck.

Among rock stars, the French consider **Johnny Halladay** (b. 1943) their equivalent of Elvis Presley. He has scored 18 platinum albums, selling more than 100 million records. Another pop icon is **Serge Gainsbourg** (1928–91). He was a master of everything from sexy rock to jazz and reggae. Upon his death, President François Mitterrand called him "our Baudelaire, our Apollinaire." In the late 1990s, dreamy French house secured international notoriety with bands such as **Air** and **Daft Punk.**

Artists with immigrant backgrounds often are the major names in the vibrant French music scene of today, with influences from French Africa, the French Caribbean, and the Middle East. Along with rap and hip-hop, these sounds rule the nights in the *boîtes* of France's biggest cities. **Khaled** (b. 1960), from Algeria, has become known as the "King of Raï." The most influential French rapper today is **MC Solaar** (b. 1969); born in Senegal, he explores racism and ethnic identity in his wordplays.

# EATING & DRINKING IN FRANCE

As any French person will tell you, French food is the best in the world. That's as true today as it was during the 19th-century heyday of the master chef Escoffier. A demanding patriarch who codified the rules of French cooking, he ruled the kitchens of the Ritz in Paris, standardizing the complicated preparation and presentation of haute cuisine. Thanks to Escoffier, with his legendary flare-ups and those of his French-born colleagues, whose kitchen tantrums have been the bane of many a socialite's life, the French chef for years has been considered a temperamental egomaniac, bearing single-handedly the burden of diffusing French civilization into the kitchens of the Anglo-Saxon world.

The demands of these chefs, however, aren't as far-fetched as they might seem, considering the intense scrutiny that has surrounded every aspect of France's culinary arts since the start of the Industrial Revolution.

Until the early 1800s, most French citizens didn't eat well. Many diets consisted of turnips, millet, fruits, berries, unpasteurized dairy products, and whatever fish or game could be had. Cooking techniques and equipment were unsanitary and crude, and starvation was a constant threat. Fear of famine was one of the rallying cries of the Revolution; everyone knows Marie Antoinette's "Let them eat cake" response to cries that the poor couldn't afford bread. (However, to be fair to Marie, this comment has been taken out of context. At the time, bread flour was much more expensive than cake flour, so her words weren't quite as callous as they might seem.)

At the foundation of virtually every culinary theory ever developed in France is a deep-seated respect for the *cuisine des provinces* (also known as *cuisine campagnarde*). Ingredients usually included only what was produced locally, and the rich and hearty result was gradually developed over several generations of *mères cuisinières*. Springing from an agrarian society with a vivid sense of nature's cycles, the cuisine provided appropriate nourishment for bodies that had toiled through a day in the open air. Specific dishes and cooking methods were as varied as the climates, terrains, and crops of France's many regions.

The revolution against Escoffier has been raging for so long that many of the early rebels are now returning to the old style of cookery, as exemplified by the boeuf bourguignon, the *blanquette de veau,* and the *pot-au-feu*.

*Cuisine moderne* is here to stay, and some restaurants feature both traditional and contemporary. The new cooking is often based on the classic principles of French cookery, but with a big difference. Rich sauces, for example, are eliminated. Cooking times that can destroy the best of fresh ingredients are considerably shortened. The aim is to release the natural flavor of food without covering it with heavy layers of butter and cream. New flavor combinations in this widely expanding repertoire are often inspired.

The most promising trend for those who don't want to sell the family homestead is to patronize one of the *neo-bistros* springing up across France. Some of the top chefs of Paris, even Guy Martin of Grand Véfour, have opened these more simplified bistros simply serving good-tasting and often regionally inspired dishes. Chefs have fun creating these more affordable menus, perhaps borrowing dishes that their *grande-mère* taught them.

Volumes have been written about French gastronomy—our comments are meant to be a brief introduction only. More than ever, young *chefs du cuisine* are making creative statements in the kitchen, and never in the history of the country has there been such an emphasis on superfresh ingredients. One chef we know in Paris has been known to shut down his restaurant for the day if he doesn't find exactly what he wants in the marketplace that morning.

There is a vast array of expensive restaurants in France that exist almost exclusively for the tourist trade. Luckily, there are others—hundreds of others. Paris, which is said to have more restaurants than any other city on Earth, has many good, reasonably priced ones. And they aren't hard to find. Once you arrive in the countryside, except for the French Riviera and certain citadels of haute cuisine, food prices become more reasonable.

**CUISINE BOURGEOISE & HAUTE CUISINE**  Cuisine bourgeoise and its pretentious cousin, haute cuisine, were refinements of country cooking that developed from the increased prosperity brought on by 19th-century industrialization. As France grew more affluent, food and the rituals involved in its preparation and presentation became one of the hallmarks of culture. And as refrigerated trucks and railway cars carried meats, fish, and produce from one region to another, associations were formed and entire industries spawned, revolving around specific ingredients produced in specific districts. The country's wines (demarcated with "Appellation d'Origine Contrôlée"); lamb from the salt marshes of Pauillac; poultry from Bresse in Burgundy; and melons, strawberries, apples, and truffles from specific districts command premiums over roughly equivalent ingredients produced in less legendary areas.

France often names a method of preparation (or a particular dish) after its region of origin. Dishes described as *à la normande* are likely to be prepared with milk, cream, or cheese or with Calvados, in honor of the dairy products and apple brandy produced in abundance within Norman borders. **Cassoulet** (a stewed combination of white beans, duck, pork, onions, and carrots) will forever be associated with Toulouse, where the dish originated. And something cooked *à la bordelaise* has probably been flavored with ample doses of red bordeaux (along with bone marrow, shallots, tarragon, and meat juices).

Other than caviar (which the French consume in abundance but don't produce), the world's most elegant garnish is **truffles,** an underground fungus with a woodsy, oaky smell. Thousands of these are unearthed yearly from the Dordogne and Périgord forests, so if your menu proclaims a dish is *à la périgourdine,* you'll almost certainly pay a premium for the truffles and foie gras.

And what's all the fuss about **foie gras?** It comes from either a goose or a duck (the rose-hued gooseliver is the greater delicacy). The much-abused goose, however, has a rough life, being force-fed about a kilogram (2¼ lb.) of corn every day in a process the French call *gavage.* In about 22 days, the animal's liver is swollen to about 25 ounces (in many cases, far

Cassoulet.

more than that). When prepared by a Périgourdine housewife (some of whom sell the livers directly from their farmhouses to passing motorists), it's truly delicious. Foie gras is most often served with truffles; otherwise, it's called au naturel.

## Regional Cuisines

What exactly is "French food"? That's a hard question to answer. Even cities have their own specialties.

Gastronomy alone would be good enough reason for going to the Loire Valley. From Nantes to Orléans, the specialties are many, including, for example, shad cooked with sorrel, Loire salmon, chitterling sausage, lark pâté, goat's milk cheese, partridge, rillettes (shredded and potted pork), herb-flavored black pudding, plus good Loire wines, including rosés.

The Normans are known not only as good soldiers, but as hearty eaters. Their gastronomic table enjoys world renown. Many Parisians drive up for *le weekend* just to sample the cuisine. Harvested along the seacoast are sole, brill, mackerel, and turbot. Shellfish are also common, especially fat black mussels, the prawns of Cherbourg, the demoiselles of Dieppe. Try also Madame Poulard's featherweight omelet, sole *normande* (stewed in rich cream), tripe *à la mode de Caen,* chicken from the Auge Valley, and duckling from Rouen. Normandy apples, especially those from the Auge Valley, produce a most potent cider. Matured in oaken casks, the apples also are turned into Calvados, a sort of apple-jack, a distillation of cider flavored with hazelnuts. A true Norman drinks this cider spirit at breakfast. Benedictine, the liqueur made at Fécamp, also enjoys acclaim. The rich Norman Camembert is imitated but never equaled. Pont l'Evêque cheese has been known here since the 13th century. The Livarot is delicious for diners who can get past the smell.

The province of Brittany offers sublime seafood, the mainstay of its diet, including Aulne salmon, pike (best with *beurre blanc*), scallops, trout, winkles, cockles, spiny lobsters, and Lorient sardines. The pré-sale (salt-meadow lamb) is the best meat course, traditionally served with white beans. The finest artichokes come from Roscoff, the most succulent strawberries from Plougastel. Nearly every village has its own crêperie, specializing in those paper-thin pancakes with an infinite variety of fillings. Savory crepes are most often made with buckwheat. Oysters are ubiquitous and fantastic, with the best coming from Cancale (p. 336)—splurge and try the flat, green-tinged *plates.* Breton food is washed down with cider (perhaps inferior to the Norman variety, but quite good nevertheless). Unlike much of France, the province lacks wine, except for Muscadet, a light white wine produced from the vineyards around the old Breton capital of Nantes in the lower Loire Valley.

The cuisine of Alsace-Lorraine has been influenced by Germany, as reflected by its sauerkraut garni, its most popular dish. It is also the home of foie gras, an expensively delicious treat. The Savoy, in the French Alps, also has many specialties, many using rich cream and milk, which makes the cuisine heavy but tasty. Game such as woodcock is common.

Some of the best food and best wines are found in Burgundy. You'll also see written "*à la Bourgogne*" after a dish, which means bourguignon—cooked in a red-wine sauce and often garnished with buttonhole mushrooms and pearl onions. Lyon is regarded as the gastronomic capital of France. For example, tripe Lyonnaise is known around the world. Lyonnaise sausage is also well known, and the city's many famous dishes include *quenelles* (fish dumplings, often made with pike).

The Périgord and Dordogne regions are known for their foie gras and truffles. Many farmers sell foie gras—from goose or duck—directly from their kitchen doors. Even if you don't like foie gras, you'll surely want to try the fish from the rivers of the Dordogne, along with morels, strawberries, and porcini mushrooms—called *cèpes*—from the field.

Gourmets, not just beach lovers, go to the Riviera. The food, especially fish, can be exceptionally good. It also tends to be expensive. Bouillabaisse, an exquisite fish soup said to have been invented by Venus, is the area's best-known dish. *Rascasse* (rockfish), a fish found only in the Mediterranean, is very popular as are *rouget* (red mullet) and *loup de mer* (sea bass) cooked with fennel. *Aïoli*, mayonnaise with a garlic-and-olive-oil base, is usually served with a large plate of steamed vegetables, white fish, and a hard-boiled egg. Other specialties include *daube* (slow-cooked beef stew), *soupe au pistou* (vegetable soup with basil), *salade Niçoise* (likely to include other items, but traditionally made with tomatoes, olives, radishes, scallions, peppers, and tuna or anchovies), and *pain bagnat* (bread doused in olive oil and stuffed with *salade Niçoise*).

**MEALS & DINING CUSTOMS**    In many of the less expensive places described in this guide, the menu will be handwritten, in French only. Don't let that intimidate you. Nor should you be timid about ordering dishes without knowing precisely what they are. You'll get some delightful surprises. We know a woman who wouldn't have dreamed of asking for escargots if she'd realized they were snails cooked in garlic sauce. As it was, she ate this appetizer in a spirit of thrift rather than adventure—and has been addicted to it ever since. As for vegetables, the French regard them as a separate course and eat them apart from the meat or poultry dishes. But we wouldn't advise you to order them especially unless you're an exceptionally hearty eater. Most main courses come with a small helping, or *garni*, of vegetables anyway.

As a rule, it's better to order an aperitif—often the house will have a specialty—rather than a heavy drink such as a martini before a classic French dinner. Vodka or scotch can assault your palate, destroying your taste buds for the festive repast to come. Allow plenty of time for a gourmet dinner. Orders are often prepared individually, and it takes time to absorb the wine and the flavors.

Most meals consist of several small courses. You can begin, for example, with hors d'oeuvres or a light *potage* (soup). The classic restaurant used to serve a small order of fish after the appetizer, then the meat or poultry course, but nowadays it's likely to be either fish or meat. A salad may follow the main course, then a selection of cheese (there are now more than 1,000 registered French cheeses) and dessert (often a fruit concoction or a sorbet). In this book, prices are given for fixed-price or a la carte main courses.

If you find the food "too rich, with too many sauces," that may be because you've been overdoing it. Elaborately prepared gourmet banquets should not be consumed for both lunch and dinner, or even every day. Sometimes an omelet or a roast chicken can make a delightful light meal, and you can "save up" for your big dining experience.

**WINE**  French cookery achieves palate perfection only when lubricated by wine, which is not considered a luxury or even an addition, but rather an integral part of every meal. Certain rules about wine drinking have been long established in France, but no one except traditionalists seems to follow them anymore. "Rules" would dictate that if you're having a roast, steak, or game, a good burgundy should be your choice. If it's chicken, lamb, or veal, you would choose a red from the Bordeaux country, certainly a full-bodied red with cheese such as Camembert, and a blanc-de-blanc with oysters. A light rosé can go with almost anything, especially if enjoyed on a summer terrace overlooking the Mediterranean or the Seine.

Let your own good taste—and, sometimes almost as important, your wallet—determine your choice of wine. Most wine stewards, called sommeliers, are there to help you in your choice, and only in the most dishonest of restaurants will they push you toward the most expensive selections. Of course, if you prefer only bottled water, or perhaps a beer, then be firm and order either without embarrassment. In fact, bottled water might be a good idea at lunch if you're planning to drive later. Some restaurants include a beverage in their menu rates *(boisson compris),* either as part of a set tasting menu in ritzy restaurants or as part of a fixed price formula in cheaper establishments. Some of the most satisfying wines we've drunk in France came from unlabeled house bottles or carafes, called a *vin de la maison.* In general, unless you're a real connoisseur, don't worry about labels and vintages.

When in doubt, you can rarely go wrong with a good burgundy or bordeaux, but you may want to be more adventurous than that. That's when the sommelier can help you, particularly if you tell him or her your taste in

**Bottles of Bordeaux.**

wine (semidry or very dry, for example). State frankly how much you're willing to pay and what you plan to order for your meal. If you're dining with others, you may want to order two or three bottles with an entire dinner, selecting a wine to suit each course. However, French at informal meals—and especially if there are only two persons dining—select only one wine to go with all their platters, from hors d'oeuvres to cheese. As a rule of thumb, expect to spend about one-third of the restaurant tab for wine.

**WINE LABELS**   Since the latter part of the 19th century, French wines sold in France (and sometimes elsewhere) have been labeled. The general label is known as *appellations contrôlées*. These controls, for the most part, are by regions such as Bordeaux and the Loire. These are the simple, honest wines of the district. They can be blended from grapes grown at any place in the region. Some are composed of the vintages of different years.

In most cases, the more specific the label, the better the wine. For example, instead of a Bordeaux, the wine might be labeled medoc (pronounced *may*-doc), which is the name of a triangle of land extending some 81km (50 miles) north from Bordeaux. Wine labels can be narrowed down to a particular vine-growing property, such as a Château Haut-Brion, one of the most famous and greatest of red wines of Bordeaux (this château produces only about 10,000 cases a year).

On some burgundies, you are likely to see the word *clos* (pronounced "cloe"). Originally, that meant a walled or otherwise enclosed vineyard, as in Clos-de-Bèze, which is a celebrated Burgundian vineyard producing a superb red wine. *Cru* (pronounced "croo," and meaning "growth") suggests a wine of superior quality when it appears on a label as a *vin-de-cru*. Wines and vineyards are often divided into crus. A grand cru or premier cru should, by implication, be an even more superior wine.

Labels are only part of the story. It's the vintage that counts. Essentially, vintage is the annual grape harvest and the wine made from those grapes. Therefore, any wine can be a vintage wine unless it is a blend. But there are good vintages and bad vintages. The variation between wine produced in a "good year" and wine produced in a "bad year" can be great, and even noted by the neophyte.

Finally, champagne is the only wine that can be correctly served through all courses of a meal—but only to those who can afford its astronomical cost.

# WHEN TO GO

The best time to visit France is in the spring (Apr–June) or fall (Sept–Nov), when things are easier to come by—from Métro seats to good-tempered waiters. The weather is temperate year-round. July and August are the worst for crowds. Parisians desert their city, leaving it to the tourists.

Hotels used to charge off-season rates during the cold, rainy period from November to February; now they're often packed with business travelers, trade fairs, and winter tour groups, and hoteliers have less incentive to offer discounts. Airfares are still cheaper during these months, and more promotions are available. They rise in the spring and fall, peaking in the summer, when tickets cost the most.

In even-numbered years, don't come to Paris during the first 2 weeks of October without a confirmed hotel room. The weather's fine, but the city is jammed for the auto show.

# Weather

France's weather varies from region to region and even from town to town. Despite its latitude, Paris never gets very cold. Snow used to be rare, although recent winters have seen blizzards and city closures. The hands-down winner for wetness is Brittany. Brest (known for the mold—probably caused by the constant damp—that adds flavor to its blue cheeses) receives a staggering amount of rain between October and December. May is the driest month.

The Mediterranean coast in the south has the most arid climate. When it does rain, storms tend to be concentrated in spring and autumn. Summers are comfortably dry—beneficial to humans, but deadly to vegetation, which (unless it's irrigated) often dries and burns up in the parched months.

Provence dreads le mistral (an unrelenting wind), which most often blows in the winter for bouts of a few days at a time, but can also last up to 2 weeks.

## Paris's Average Daytime Temperature & Rainfall

|  | JAN | FEB | MAR | APR | MAY | JUNE | JULY | AUG | SEPT | OCT | NOV | DEC |
|---|---|---|---|---|---|---|---|---|---|---|---|---|
| TEMP. °F | 38 | 39 | 46 | 51 | 58 | 64 | 66 | 66 | 61 | 53 | 45 | 40 |
| TEMP. °C | 3 | 4 | 8 | 11 | 14 | 18 | 19 | 19 | 16 | 12 | 7 | 4 |
| RAINFALL (IN.) | 3.2 | 2.9 | 2.4 | 2.7 | 3.2 | 3.5 | 3.3 | 3.7 | 3.3 | 3.0 | 3.5 | 3.1 |

# France Calendar of Events

For an exhaustive list of events beyond those listed here, check http://events.frommers.com, where you'll find a searchable, up-to-the-minute roster of what's happening in cities all over the world.

## JANUARY

**Monte Carlo Motor Rally (Le Rallye de Monte Carlo).** The world's most venerable car race. For information, call the Monaco Automobile Club (www.acm.mc; ✆ 377/93-15-26-00). Usually mid-January.

## FEBRUARY

**Carnival of Nice.** Parades, music, fireworks and *Les Batailles des Fleurs* (Battles of the Flowers) are all part of this celebration. The climax is the 131-year tradition of burning the Carnival king effigy. For details, contact the Nice Convention and Visitors Bureau (www.nicecarnaval.com; ✆ 08-92-70-74-07; fax 04-92-14-46-49). Late February to early March.

## MARCH

**International Ready-to-Wear Fashion Shows (Le Salon International de Prêt-à-Porter),** Jardin des Tuileries, Esplanade des Feuillants, 1er, Paris. See what you'll be wearing next season. Visit www.whosnext.com or call ✆ 01-40-13-74-74. Early March; also held late January.

## APRIL

**Foire du Trône,** on the Reuilly Lawn of the Bois de Vincennes, 12e, Paris. This mammoth amusement park operates daily from noon to midnight. Visit www.foiredutrone.com. Early April to early June.

**Cinéscénie de Puy du Fou,** *son-et-lumière*, Château du Puy du Fou, Les Epesses (La Vendée), Brittany. A cast of 2,500 actors, dozens of horses, and laser shows recreate the achievements of the Middle Ages. Visit www.puydufou.com or call ✆ 08-20-09-10-10. Early April to late September.

**International Marathon of Paris.** Runners from around the world compete along the Champs-Elysées. Visit www.parismarathon.com or call ✆ 01-41-33-15-68. Mid-April.

## MAY

**Cannes Film Festival (Festival International du Film).** Movie madness transforms this Mediterranean town into a media circus. Admission to the films in competition is by invitation only. Other films play 24 hours a day. Contact the Festival International du Film, 3 rue Amélie, 75007 Paris (www.festival-cannes.com; ☏ **01-53-59-61-00**). Two weeks before the festival, its administration moves to the Palais des Festivals, La Croisette, Cannes 06400. Mid-May.

**Monaco Formula 1 Grand Prix.** Hundreds of cars race through Monaco's narrow streets and winding roads in a fusion of high-tech machinery and medieval architecture. Visit www.formula1monaco.com or call ☏ **377/93-15-26-00.** Mid-May.

**Festival de St-Denis.** A celebration of music in the burial place of the French kings, a grim early Gothic monument in Paris's northern suburb of St-Denis. Visit www.festival-saint-denis.com or call ☏ **01-48-13-06-07.** Late May to late June.

**French Open Tennis Championship,** Stade Roland-Garros, 16e, Paris (Métro: Porte d'Auteuil). The open features 10 days of men's, women's, and doubles tennis on the hot, red, dusty courts. For information, call ☏ **01-47-43-48-00,** or visit http:rolandgarros.fft-tickets.com. Late May to early June.

## JUNE

**Prix du Jockey Club** and **Prix Diane-Hermès,** Hippodrome de Chantilly. Thoroughbreds from as far away as Kentucky and Brunei compete in this race. On race days, dozens of trains depart from Paris's Gare du Nord for Chantilly, where racegoers take free shuttle buses to the track. Visit www.france-galop.com or call ☏ **01-49-10-20-30,** or for information on these and other Chantilly events. Early to mid-June.

**Fête Chopin,** Paris. Everything you've ever wanted to hear by the Polish exile, who lived most of his life in Paris. Piano recitals take place in the Orangerie du Parc de Bagatelle, 16e. Visit www.frederic-chopin.com or call ☏ **01-45-00-22-19.**. Mid-June to mid-July.

**Paris Air Show.** France's military-industrial complex shows off its high-tech hardware. Fans, competitors, and industrial spies mob Le Bourget Airport. Visit www.paris-air-show.com or call ☏ **01-53-23-33-33.** Mid-June in alternate years; next is mid-June 2013.

**Les 24 Heures du Mans Voitures,** for stock cars, is in the same circuit as the September motorcycle rally, but on a 13km (8-mile) radius. For information, visit www.lemans.org or call l'Automobile Club de l'Ouest (☏ **02-43-40-24-24**). Mid-June.

**Gay Pride Parade,** place du 18 Juin 1940 to place de la Bastille, Paris. A week of expositions and parties climaxes in a parade patterned after those in New York and San Francisco. For more information about gay pride and any other aspect of gay, lesbian, and transgendered life in and around Paris, contact Inter-LGBT, 3 rue Perrée, Box 8, Paris 75003 (www.inter-lgbt.org; ☏/fax **01-72-70-39-22**). Late June.

## JULY

**Colmar International Festival,** Colmar. Classical concerts are held in public buildings of one of the most folkloric towns in Alsace. Visit www.festival-colmar.com or call ☏ **03-89-20-68-97.** First 2 weeks of July.

**Les Chorégies d'Orange,** Orange. One of southern France's most important lyric festivals presents oratorios, operas, and choral works in France's best-preserved Roman amphitheater. Visit www.choregies.asso.fr or call ☏ **04-90-34-24-24,** or Early July to early August.

**Les Nocturnes du Mont-St-Michel.** This sound-and-light tour meanders through the stairways and corridors of one of Europe's most impressive medieval monuments. Check out www.monuments-nationaux.fr or call ☏ **02-33-60-14-30**

## Getting Tickets

**Keith Prowse Tickets** can order tickets to many of the musical and theatrical events at the Avignon festival, as well as other cultural happenings throughout France. You'll pay a fee (from a couple of dollars up to 20%) for the convenience. Visit www.keithprowse.com.

for more information. Performances are Monday through Saturday evenings from early July to late August.

**Tour de France.** Europe's most hotly contested bicycle race sends crews of wind tunnel–tested athletes along an itinerary that detours deep into the Massif Central and ranges across the Alps. The finish line is on the Champs-Elysées. Visit www.letour.fr. First 3 weeks of July.

**Festival d'Avignon.** This world-class festival has a reputation for exposing new talent to critical scrutiny and acclaim. The focus is usually on avant-garde works in theater, dance, and music. Many of the performances take place in the 14th-century courtyard of the Palais des Pâpes. For information, visit www.festival-avignon.com or call ✆ **04-90-27-66-50.** Last 3 weeks of July.

**Bastille Day.** Celebrating the birth of modern-day France, the nation's festivities reach their peak throughout the country with street fairs, pageants, fireworks, and feasts. In Paris, the day begins with a parade down the Champs-Elysées and ends with fireworks at Montmartre. July 14.

**Paris Quartier d'Eté.** For 4 weeks, music rules sounds around the city. Two-dozen French and international performances take place at a variety of locales, including Montmartre's Arènes, the Cour d'Honneur des Invalides and the Parc de Belleville. Visit www.quartierdete.com or call ✆ **01-44-94-98-00.** Mid-July to mid-August.

**Nice Jazz Festival.** The most prestigious jazz festival in Europe. Concerts begin in the afternoon and go on until late at night (sometimes all night) in place Masséna

and the Jardin Albert 1er, overlooking Nice's promenade des Anglais. Contact the Nice Tourist Office (www.nicejazzfestival.fr; ✆ **08-92-70-74-07**). Mid-July.

**Festival d'Aix-en-Provence.** A musical event par excellence, with everything from Gregorian chant to operas and melodies composed on synthesizers. Recitals are in the medieval cloister of the Cathédrale St-Sauveur. Expect heat, crowds, and traffic. Visit www.festival-aix.com or call ✆ **08-20-92-29-23.** Throughout July.

### AUGUST

**Festival Interceltique de Lorient,** Brittany. Celtic verse and lore are celebrated in the Celtic heart of France. The 150 concerts include classical and folkloric musicians, dancers, singers, and painters. Traditional Breton *pardons* (religious processions) take place in the once-independent maritime duchy. Visit www.festival-interceltique.com or call ✆ **02-97-21-24-29.** Early August.

### SEPTEMBER

**La Villette Jazz Festival.** Some 50 concerts are held in churches, auditoriums, and concert halls in the Paris suburb of La Villette. Past festivals have included Herbie Hancock, Shirley Horn, and other international artists. Visit www.villette.com or call ✆ **01-40-03-75-75.** Early to mid-September.

**Les 24 Heures du Mans Moto.** This motorcycle race is on a grueling 4km (2½-mile) circuit 4.5km (2¾ miles) south of Le Mans. For information, visit www.lemans.org or call l'Automobile Club de l'Ouest ((✆ **02-43-40-24-24**). Mid-September.

**Festival d'Automne,** Paris. One of France's most famous festivals is one of its most eclectic, focusing mainly on modern music, ballet, theater, and art. Contact the Festival d'Automne (www.festival-automne.com or ✆ **01-53-45-17-00**). Mid-September to late December.

**Paris Auto Show,** Parc des Expositions, Porte de Versailles, 15e, Paris. This showcase for European car design comes complete with glistening metal, glitzy attendees, lots of hype, and the latest models. Visit www.mondial-automobile.com or call ✆ **01-56-88-22-40.** Usually first 2 weeks of October (dates vary).

**Perpignan Jazz Festival.** Musicians from everywhere jam in what many consider Languedoc's most appealing season. Visit www.jazzebre.com or call ✆ **04-68-35-37-46.** Month of October.

**Prix de l'Arc de Triomphe,** Hippodrome de Longchamp, 16e, Paris. France's answer to England's Ascot is the country's most prestigious horse race, culminating the equine season in Europe. Visit www.france-galop.com or call ✆ **01-49-10-20-30.** Early October.

**Armistice Day,** nationwide. In Paris, the signing of the document that ended World War I is celebrated with a military parade from the Arc de Triomphe to the Hôtel des Invalides. November 11.

**Les Trois Glorieuses,** Clos-de-Vougeot, Beaune, and Meursault. Three Burgundian towns stage the country's most important wine festival. Though you may

not gain access to many of the gatherings, tastings and other amusements will keep you occupied. Reserve early, or visit as day trips from nearby villages. Contact the Office de Tourisme de Beaune (www.ot-beaune.fr; ✆ **03-80-26-21-30**). Third week in November.

**Christmas Fairs,** Alsace (especially Strasbourg). More than 60 villages celebrate a traditional Christmas. The events in Strasbourg have continued for some 430 years. Other towns with celebrations are Münster, Sélestat, Riquewihr, Kaysersberg, Wissembourg, and Thann. Visit www.tourism-alsace.com or call ✆ **03-89-24-73-50.** Late November to December 24.

**The Boat Fair (Le Salon Nautique de Paris).** Europe's major exposition of what's afloat, at Salon Nautique de Paris, 52–54 quai de Dion-Bouton, 15e, Paris (www.salonnautiqueparis.com; Métro: Porte de Versailles). Ten days in early December.

**Fête des Lumières,** Lyon. In honor of the Virgin Mary, lights are placed in windows through the city. Visit www.fetedeslumieres.lyon.fr or call ✆ **04-72-10-30-30.** Early December.

**Fête de St-Sylvestre (New Year's Eve),** nationwide. In Paris, this holiday is most boisterously celebrated in the Quartier Latin. At midnight, the city explodes. Strangers kiss and boulevard St-Michel and the Champs-Elysées become virtual pedestrian malls. December 31.

# RESPONSIBLE TRAVEL

From pioneering eco-friendly *autopartage* (car-sharing) programs to an unabashed enthusiasm for *biodynamique* wines, the French have embraced sustainability. In an age when environmental, ethical, and social concerns are becoming ever more important, France's focus on green principles—whether through traditional markets, carbon-neutral public transport, or all-natural outdoor adventure—offers visitors and residents alike plenty in the way of sustainable tourism.

Paris was recently ranked one of the top 10 cities committed to ecological issues by the European Green City Index. It has an excellent public transportation system, which is cheap and user-friendly, and most Parisians get around the city by public transport. In 2007, **Bertrand Delanoë,** Paris's mayor since 2001, introduced the **Vélib'** scheme (www.velib.paris.fr), a public bicycle "sharing" program; with thousands of bicycles and bike rental stations spread throughout the city, it is a fast and inexpensive way to get around the city, and you will see both Parisians and visitors taking advantage of this program. Similar schemes are in place in many other major French cities, including Bordeaux, Toulouse, Lyon, Nice, Avignon, Aix-en-Provence, and Marseille.

Also under Delanoë's guidance, a similar car-sharing program called the **Autolib'** (www.autolib.fr) was launched in Paris in December 2011. More than 5,000 eco-friendly and exhaust-free public cars now slip silently around the Parisian streets; passes for their use can be purchased by the hour, day, month, or year. Nice and Lyon also boast smaller Autolib' programs.

In order to criss-cross France's vast countryside, many French ditch their cars and opt instead for travel on a **TGV** (www.tgv-europe.com). This network of high-speed trains is powered by SNCF, France's government-owned rail company, which is dedicated to becoming completely carbon-neutral. TGVs run from Paris's hub to cities throughout the country, including Lille, Brest, Rennes, Bordeaux, Strasbourg, Lyon, and Marseille, among others.

Many hotels in France have undertaken measures to preserve the environment, and those that have are awarded with a green label. Look for hotels with the title of **La Clef Verte** (Green Key; www.laclefverte.org) or the European Eco-Label. Both labels reward hotels that take a more environmental approach to water, energy and waste, and raise the awareness of their guests. Although there are currently only a few hotels that boast such labels, sustainable tourism is becoming increasingly important in the hotel industry. Even if you don't stay at a green hotel, you can still do your bit: turn off the air-conditioning when you leave the room, request that your sheets aren't changed every day, and use your towels more than once. Laundry makes up around 40% of an average hotel's energy use.

When planning your travels, it's equally important to consider the impact your visit will have on the environment. France's rippling vineyards, **Grande Randonée (GR)** hiking trails, and pristine coastline all make for enchanting (and eco-friendly) escapes. Alternatively, you could consider participating in **WWOOF** (www.wwoof.fr), or World Wide Opportunities on Organic Farms, where you'll swap volunteer work for food and lodging on French organic farms.

Responsible tourism also means leaving a place in the same condition as you found it. You can do this by not dropping litter and respecting the color-coded garbage bin system: Yellow or brown bins are for recyclable materials, including glass, paper, plastic, and aluminum cans, while gray bins are for garbage. Support the local economy and culture by shopping in small neighborhood stores and at open-air markets that showcase the seasonal harvest of local, often organic (*bio*) producers. Look out for organic and *biodynamique* (biodynamic) wines, frequently sold at wine shops and farmers' markets too. And given the myriad of tiny, family-run restaurants scattered throughout France's cities, towns, and countryside, it's easier to dig into a home-cooked meal, rather than the mass-produced fare purveyed at big chain stores and restaurants.

**3**

# SUGGESTED ITINERARIES IN FRANCE

**W**hen we first launched this guidebook, founding father Arthur Frommer gave us a warning: "You can get lost in France." And we did—and still do on occasion.

If you have unlimited time, one of the world's great pleasures is getting "lost" in France, wandering about at random, making new discoveries every day off the beaten path. But few of us have this luxury, and so below we present both 1- and 2-week itineraries to help you make the most of your time.

France is so vast and so treasure filled that you can't even skim the surface in 1 or 2 weeks, so relax and don't even try. Instead, we recommend that you enjoy the nuggets—Paris, Versailles, and Mont-St-Michel—among other allures, saving the rest for another day. You may also review chapter 1, "The Best of France," to find out what experiences or sights have special appeal to us and then adjust the itineraries to suit your particular travel plans.

France ranks with Germany in offering Europe's fastest and best-maintained superhighways, and it also has one of the fastest and most efficient public transportation systems in the world, especially in its national train system. For example, the highlights of Normandy and the Loire Valley (the château country) are just 1 or 2 hours away from Paris by train. You can travel from Paris to Nice on the Riviera in 5½ hours—or fly much more quickly, of course.

The itineraries that follow take you to some major attractions and some charming towns. The pace may be a bit breathless for some visitors, so skip a town or sight occasionally to have some chill-out time—after all, you're on vacation. Of course, you can use any of these itineraries as a jumping-off point to develop your own custom-made trip.

# THE REGIONS IN BRIEF

Though France's 547,030 sq. km (211,209 sq. miles) make it slightly smaller than the American state of Texas, no other country has such a diversity of sights and scenery in such a compact area. A visitor can travel through the north's flat, fertile lands; the Loire Valley's green hills; the east's Alpine ranges; the Pyrénées; the Massif Central's plateaus and rock outcroppings; and the southeast's Mediterranean coast. Even more noteworthy are the cultural and historical differences that define each region.

Destinations in France are within easy reach from Paris and each other. **French National Railroads (SNCF)** offers fast service to and from Paris—though trains tend to crawl on routes that do not serve the capital. The train trip from Paris is 4 hours to Alsace, 5 to the Alps, 7 to the Pyrénées, and 8 to the Côte d'Azur—and the newer TGVs (high-speed trains) cut that travel time dramatically.

PREVIOUS PAGE: **A street in the town of Sarlat-la-Canéda, Dordogne.**

Giverny.

You'll find nearly 71,000km (about 44,020 miles) of roads, mostly in good condition. Try not to travel the Route Nationale network all the time. Nearly all of France's scenic splendors are along secondary roads.

A "grand tour" of France is nearly impossible for the visitor who doesn't have a lifetime to explore. If you want to get to know a province, try to devote at least a week to a specific region; you may have a more rewarding trip if you concentrate on getting to know two or three areas at a leisurely pace rather than racing around trying to see everything. To help you decide where to spend your time, we've summarized the highlights of each region for you.

**ILE DE FRANCE**   The Ile de France is an island only in the sense that rivers—with odd-sounding names such as Essonne, Epte, Aisne, Eure, and Ourcq—and a handful of canals delineate its boundaries (about an 81km/50-mile radius from the center of Paris). France was born in this temperate basin, where the attractions include **Paris, Versailles, Fontainebleau, Notre-Dame de Chartres,** and **Giverny.** Despite industrialization (and Disneyland Paris), pockets of charm remain, including the forests of Rambouillet and Fontainebleau, and the artists' hamlet of Barbizon. For more information, see chapter 5.

**THE LOIRE VALLEY**   This area includes two ancient provinces, Touraine (centered on Tours) and Anjou (centered on Angers). It was beloved by royalty and nobility until Henry IV moved his court to Paris. Head here to see the most magnificent castles in France. Irrigated by the Loire River and its many tributaries, the valley produces many superb wines. For more information, see chapter 6.

**NORMANDY**   This region will forever be linked to the 1944 D-day invasion. Some readers consider a visit to the D-day beaches the most emotionally worthwhile part of their trip. Normandy boasts 599km (371 miles) of coastline and a maritime tradition. It's a popular weekend getaway from Paris, and many hotels and restaurants thrive here, especially around the casino town of **Deauville.** Normandy's great attractions include the **Rouen** cathedral, the abbey of **Jumièges,** and medieval **Bayeux.** For more information, see chapter 7.

**BRITTANY** Jutting into the Atlantic, the westernmost region (and one of the poorest regions) of France is known for its rocky coastlines, Celtic roots, frequent rain, and ancient dialect, akin to the Gaelic tongues of Wales and Ireland. Many French vacationers love the seacoast (rivaled only by the Côte d'Azur) for its sandy beaches, cliffs, and relatively modest—by French standards—prices. **Carnac** is home to ancient Celtic dolmens and burial mounds, and the region's most sophisticated resort, **La Baule,** is near some of Brittany's best beaches. For more information, see chapter 8.

**CHAMPAGNE** Every French monarch since A.D. 496 was crowned at **Reims,** and much of French history is linked with this holy site. In the path of any invader wishing to occupy Paris, Reims and the Champagne district have seen much bloodshed, including the World War I battles of the Somme and the Marne. Industrial sites sit among patches of forest, and vineyards sheath the steep sides of valleys. The 126km (78-mile) road from Reims to Vertus, one of the **Routes du Champagne,** takes in a trio of winegrowing regions that produce 80% of the world's bubbly. For more information, see chapter 9.

**THE ARDENNES & NORTHERN BEACHES** This northern region is often ignored by North Americans. In summer, French families arrive by the thousands to visit Channel beach resorts such as **Le Touquet-Paris-Plage.** This district is quite industrialized and has always suffered in wars. Its best-known port, Calais, was a bitterly contested English stronghold for centuries. Calais is now the port of disembarkation for ferries, hydrofoils, and Channel Tunnel arrivals from Britain. **Notre-Dame Cathedral** in **Amiens,** the medieval capital of Picardy, is a treasure, with a 42m-high (138-ft.) nave—the highest in France.

**ALSACE & LORRAINE** Between Germany and the forests of the Vosges is the most Teutonic of France's provinces: Alsace, with cosmopolitan Strasbourg as its capital. Celebrated for its cuisine, particularly its foie gras and choucroute, this area is home to villages with half-timbered designs that make you think of the Black Forest. If you travel the Route de Vin (Wine Road), you can visit towns such as **Colmar, Riquewihr,** and **Illhaeusern,** famous for great food and wine. Lorraine, birthplace of Joan of Arc, witnessed many battles during the world wars. Its capital, **Nancy,** is the guardian of a grand 18th-century plaza, place Stanislas. The much-eroded peaks of the Vosges forest, the closest thing to a wilderness in France, offer lovely hiking. For more information, see chapter 10.

**BURGUNDY** Few trips will prove as rewarding as several leisurely days spent exploring Burgundy, with its splendid old cities such as **Dijon.** Besides its famous cuisine (*boeuf* and *escargots à la bourguignonne*), the district contains, along its Côte d'Or, hamlets whose names (Mercurey, Beaune, Puligny-Montrachet, Vougeot, and Nuits-St-Georges) are synonymous with great wine. For more information, see chapter 11.

**THE RHÔNE VALLEY** A fertile area of Alpine foothills and sloping valleys in eastern and southeastern France, the upper Rhône Valley ranges from the

Vineyards in Burgundy.

French suburbs of the Swiss city of Geneva to the northern borders of Provence. The district is thoroughly French, unflinchingly bourgeois, and dedicated to preserving the gastronomic and cultural traditions that have produced some of the most celebrated chefs in French history.

Only 2 hours by train from Paris, the region's cultural centerpiece, **Lyon,** is France's "second city." North of here, you can travel the Beaujolais trail or head for Bresse's ancient capital, **Bourg-en-Bresse,** which produces the world's finest poultry. You can explore the Rhône Valley en route to Provence. Try to visit the medieval villages of **Pérouges** and **Vienne,** 27km (17 miles) south of Lyon; the latter is known for its Roman ruins. For more information, see chapter 12.

**THE FRENCH ALPS**   This area's resorts rival those of neighboring Switzerland and contain incredible scenery: snowcapped peaks, glaciers, and Alpine lakes. **Chamonix** is a famous ski resort facing **Mont Blanc,** western Europe's highest mountain. **Courchevel** and **Megève** are more chic. During the summer, you can enjoy such spa resorts as **Evian** and the restful 19th-century resorts ringing **Lake Geneva.** For more information, see chapter 13.

**PROVENCE**   One of France's most popular destinations stretches from the southern Rhône River to the Italian border. Long frequented by starving artists, *la bourgeoisie,* and the downright rich and famous, its premier cities are **Aix-en-Provence,** associated with Cézanne; **Arles,** famous for bullfighting and Van Gogh; **Avignon,** the 14th-century capital of Christendom; and **Marseille,** a port city established by the Phoenicians that today is the melting pot of France. Quieter and more romantic are villages such as **St-Rémy-de-Provence, Les Baux,** and **Gordes.** The strip of glittering beach towns along Provence's southern edge is known as the **Côte d'Azur,** or the French Riviera (see the following section). For more information, see chapter 14.

**THE FRENCH RIVIERA (CÔTE D'AZUR)**   The resorts of the fabled Côte d'Azur (Azure Coast, or Blue Coast) still evoke glamour: **Cannes, St-Tropez, Cap d'Antibes,** and **St-Jean-Cap-Ferrat.** July and August are the most buzzing months, while spring and fall are still sunny but way more laid-back. **Nice** is the biggest city and most convenient for exploring the area. The principality of **Monaco** occupies only about 2 sq. km (¾ sq. mile) but has enough sights, restaurants, and glamour to go around. Along the coast are some sandy beaches, but many are pebbly. Topless bathing is common, especially in St-Tropez, and some of the restaurants are citadels of conspicuous consumption. Dozens of artists and their patrons have littered the landscape with world-class galleries and art museums. For more information, see chapter 15.

**LANGUEDOC-ROUSSILLON**   Languedoc may not be as chic as Provence, but it's less frenetic and more affordable. **Roussillon** is the rock-strewn French answer to Catalonia, just across the Spanish border. The **Camargue** is the marshy delta formed by two arms of the Rhône River. Rich in bird life, it's famous for its grassy flats and such fortified medieval sites as **Aigues-Mortes.** Also appealing are **Auch,** the capital of Gascony; **Toulouse,** the bustling pink capital of Languedoc; and the "red city" of **Albi,** birthplace of Toulouse-Lautrec. **Carcassonne,** a marvelous walled city with fortifications begun around A.D. 500, is the region's highlight. For more information, see chapter 16.

**THE BASQUE COUNTRY**   Since prehistoric times, the rugged Pyrénées have formed a natural boundary between France and Spain. The Basques, one of Europe's most unusual cultures, flourished in the valleys here. In the 19th century, resorts such as **Biarritz** and **St-Jean-de-Luz** attracted the French aristocracy; the empress Eugénie's palace at Biarritz is now a hotel. Four million Catholics make annual pilgrimages to the city of Lourdes. In the villages

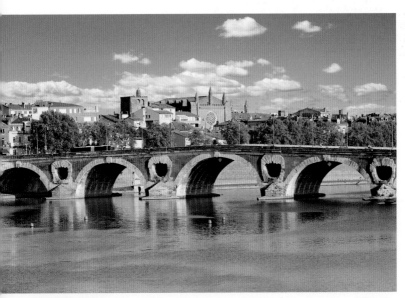

Pont Neuf, Toulouse.

and towns of the Pyrénées, the old folkloric traditions, permeated with Spanish influences, continue to thrive. For more information, see chapter 17.

**BORDEAUX & THE ATLANTIC COAST** Flat, fertile, and frequently ignored by North Americans, this region includes towns pivotal in French history (**Poitiers, Angoulême,** and **La Rochelle**), as well as wine- and liquor-producing villages (**Cognac, St-Emilion,** and **Sauternes**) whose names are celebrated around the world. **Bordeaux,** the district's largest city, has an economy based on wine merchandising and showcases grand 18th-century architecture. For more information, see chapter 18.

**THE DORDOGNE & THE LOT** The splendid Dordogne River valley has been a favorite vacation spot since Cro-Magnon peoples were painting bison on cave walls in **Lascaux.** Today visitors flock to the valley to marvel at prehistoric sites near **Les Eyzies-de-Tayac** and to ramble through exquisite villages like **Sarlat-le-Canéda** and **Beynac-et-Cazenac.** The land of truffles and foie gras, Périgord has long been famed as a gastronomic Mecca, while nearby **Cahors** is celebrated for its rich red wine. For more information, see chapter 19.

**THE MASSIF CENTRAL** The rugged heartland of south-central France, this underpopulated district contains ancient cities, unspoiled scenery, and an abundance of black lava, from which many buildings were created. The largest cities are **Clermont-Ferrand** and **Limoges**—the medieval capitals of the provinces of the Auvergne and the Limousin. **Bourges,** a gateway to the region and once capital of Aquitaine, has a beautiful Gothic cathedral. For more information, see chapter 19.

# FRANCE IN 1 WEEK

The title of this tour is a misnomer. There is no way you can see France in 1 week. But you can have a memorable vacation in Paris and see other highlights of France in a week if you budget your time carefully. One week provides enough time—barely—to visit the major attractions of Paris, such as the **Musée du Louvre** (world's greatest art gallery), the **Eiffel Tower,** and **Notre-Dame.** After 2 days in Paris, head for the former royal stamping grounds of **Versailles,** followed by Normandy (an easy commute from Paris), visiting such highlights as **D-day beaches,** the cathedral city of **Rouen** (where Joan of Arc was burned alive), the tapestry of **Bayeux,** and the incredible monastery of **Mont-St-Michel.**

## DAYS 1 & 2: Arrive in Paris ★★★

Take a flight that arrives in Paris as early as possible on **DAY 1.** Check into your hotel and hit the nearest cafe for a pick-me-up café au lait and a croissant before sightseeing. Take the Métro to the Palais Royal–Musée du Louvre for a visit to the **Musée du Louvre** (p. 93). Spend at least 2 hours here viewing world-class masterpieces such as Leonardo da Vinci's *Mona Lisa.* After leaving the Louvre, walk south toward the **quays of the Seine,** spending an hour taking in the tree-shaded banks and panoramic vistas of Paris. Head for that island in the Seine, **Ile de la Cité,** to explore its attractions, including **Ste-Chapelle** (p. 104) and the monumental

**1** Arrive in Paris
**2** Paris
**3** Day Trip to Versailles
**4** Rouen: Normandy's Capital
**5** Bayeux & Caen
**6** The D-Day Beaches
**7** Mont-St-Michel

**Notre-Dame** (p. 97) and its gargoyles. As the evening fades, head for the **Eiffel Tower** for the greatest cityscape view in Europe.

On **DAY 2,** arrive at the **place de la Concorde** and its Egyptian obelisk, and take a stroll up the 1.8km (1-mile) avenue of French grandeur, the **Champs-Élysées,** until you reach the **Arc de Triomphe** (p. 105), which you can scale for another panoramic view of Paris. Afterward, head for the **Ile St-Louis** (p. 82), which, after Cité, is the second island in the Seine. Lacking monumental attractions, this little isle is a sight in itself, with quays to stroll and small side streets where you can discover hidden wonders such as antiques shops and little bistros.

After lunch in one of those bistros, visit **Musée d'Orsay** (p. 128) and the world's greatest collection of Impressionist paintings. As the afternoon fades, head for **Basilique du Sacré-Coeur** (p. 113) for a crowning view of Paris as the sun sets. Have a final dinner in a Montmartre cafe.

## DAY 3: A Day Trip to Versailles ★★★

Having survived 2 days in the capital of France, bid an adieu and take the RER Line C to the **Versailles/Rive Gauche station.** You can spend a full day at Versailles—and then some—or else you can see the highlights in 3 hours, including the Grands and Petits appartements, the glittering Hall of

Basilique du Sacré-Coeur.

Eglise St-Maclou.

Mirrors, Gabriel's Opera House, the Royal Chapel, and the Gardens of Versailles, which contain the Grand and Petit Trianons.

### DAY 4: Normandy's Capital of Rouen ★★★

Take an early train to Rouen and check into a hotel. Spend at least 2 hours exploring the city's ancient core, especially its **Cathédrale Notre-Dame** (p. 298), immortalized in paintings by Monet. Stand at the **place du Vieux-Marché** (p. 301), where Joan of Arc was executed for heresy in 1431, and then visit the **Eglise St-Maclou** (p. 299), a 1432 church in the Flamboyant Gothic style. After lunch, rent a car for the rest of your trip and drive to **Giverny** (p. 230)—it's only 60km (37 miles) southeast of Rouen. At Giverny, visit the **Claude Monet Foundation** (p. 230), returning to your hotel in Rouen for the night.

### DAY 5: Bayeux ★★ & Caen ★★★

Strike out toward Bayeux, stopping en route to visit **Abbaye de Jumièges,** one of the most evocative ruins in France. Even with a stopover, you can easily be in the city of Caen in time for lunch before visiting **Abbaye aux Hommes** (p. 315), founded by William the Conqueror. After Caen, continue west to the city of **Bayeux,** where you can arrive in time to view the celebrated **Musée de la Tapisserie de Bayeux** (p. 319). Stay overnight in Bayeux.

### DAY 6: The D-Day Beaches ★★

Reserve this day for exploring the D-day beaches, where Allied forces launched "the Longest Day," the mammoth invasion of Normandy in June 1944 that signaled the beginning of the end of Hitler's Third Reich.

From Bayeux, head east to explore the coastline. Your voyage of discovery can begin at the seaside resort of Arromanches-les-Bains, where you can visit the **Musée du Débarquement** (p. 322), **Omaha Beach** (p. 322), and the **Normandy American Cemetery** (p. 322). You can have lunch in the town of Grandcamp-Maisy (p. 324), later checking out **Utah Beach.**

That evening, drive to **Mont-St-Michel** (less than 2 hr. away) and overnight in the pedestrian village on "the Rock," giving you plenty of time for an early-morning visit to this popular attraction. If it's summer, you can also take an illuminated night tour.

### DAY 7: Mont-St-Michel ★★★

You can explore one of the great attractions of Europe, **Mont-St-Michel** (p. 325), in a minimum of 3 hours. This great Benedictine monastery, founded in 966, is best enjoyed by taking an English-language tour that covers the highlights. After viewing the abbey, drop in at **La Mère Poulard** (p. 328) for a legendary omelet. After lunch, return your car to Rouen, where you'll find frequent train service back to Paris and your flight home the following day.

# FRANCE IN 2 WEEKS

If you have 2 weeks to explore France, you'll have time to visit several regions—not only Paris, but also the best of the Loire Valley châteaux, the most history-rich town of Provence (Avignon), and several resorts on the Riviera, taking in the beaches, modern art galleries, and even the principality of Monaco.

For **days 1 through 7,** follow the "France in 1 Week" itinerary, above.

### DAY 8: Orléans–Gateway to the Loire Valley ★

Leave Paris on an early train to **Orléans** (trip time: 1 hr., 15 min.). Heavily bombed in World War II, Orléans is a fairly dull town. Rent a car here and drive west to the **Château de Chambord** (p. 253), the largest château in the Loire Valley, representing the apogee of the French Renaissance architectural style. Allow 2 hours for a visit. Back on the road again, continue southwest to the **Château de Blois** (p. 256), called "the Versailles of the Renaissance" and a virtual illustrated storybook of French architecture. Stay overnight in Blois.

### DAY 9: Amboise ★★ & Chenonceau ★★★

In the morning, continue southeast from Blois to **Amboise,** where you can check into a hotel for the night. Visit the 15th-century **Château d'Amboise** (p. 264), in the Italian Renaissance style, and also **Clos-Lucé** (p. 264), last residence of Leonardo da Vinci. In the afternoon, drive southeast to the **Château de Chenonceau** (p. 267), famous for the French dames who have occupied its precincts, including Diane de Poitiers (mistress of the king) and Catherine de Médicis (the jealous queen). You can spend 2 hours at the château before driving back to Amboise for the night.

### DAY 10: Avignon, Gateway to Provence ★★★

From Amboise, get an early start and drive east to Orléans to return your rental car. You now face a choice: take an early train from Orléans to Paris's Gare d'Austerlitz, then the Métro or a taxi to the Gare de Lyon, and hop on to a TGV bound for Avignon (2½ hr.); or, perhaps more simply, take a train from Orléans to Lyon and then change trains for Avignon.

Check into a hotel in **Avignon,** one of Europe's most beautiful medieval cities. Before the day fades, you should have time to wander through

**Looking upward in the Château d'Amboise.**

the old city to get your bearings, shop for Provençal souvenirs, and see one of the smaller sights, such as the **Pont St-Bénézet** (also known as the Bridge of Avignon). See p. 499.

### DAY 11: Avignon to St-Tropez ★★

In the morning, spend 2 hours touring the **Palais des Papes** (p. 500), the capital of Christendom during the 14th century. After lunch in one of Avignon's cozy bistros or cobblestoned outdoor cafes, rent a car and drive to **St-Tropez** (p. 547). If it's summer, get in some beach time and spend a good part of the early evening in one of the cafes along the harbor, indulging in that favorite French pastime of people-watching.

**Palais des Papes.**

France in 2 Weeks

1  Arrive in Paris
2  Paris
3  Day Trip to Versailles
4  Rouen: Normandy's Capital
5  Bayeux & Caen
6  The D-Day Beaches
7  Mont-St-Michel
8  Orléans
9  Amboise & Chenonceau
10  Avignon
11  Avignon to St-Tropez
12  Cannes
13  Nice
14  Nice to Monaco

## DAY 12: Cannes, Capital of the Riviera Chic ★★★

Before leaving St-Tropez in the morning, check out the Impressionist paintings at **Musée de l'Annonciade** (p. 550). Drive 50km (31 miles) east along the coast until you reach Cannes.

Assuming it's summer, get in some time at the beach, notably at **Plage de la Croisette** (p. 556), and feel free to wear your most revealing swimwear. In the afternoon, take the ferry to **Ile Ste-Marguerite** (p. 560), where the "Man in the Iron Mask" was imprisoned. You can visit his cell. That evening, you may want to flirt with Lady Luck at one of the plush **casinos** (p. 563).

## DAY 13: Nice, Capital of the Riviera ★★★

It's only a 32km (20-mile) drive east from Cannes to **Nice,** the Riviera's largest city. After checking into a hotel (the most affordable along the Riviera), stroll through **Vieille Ville** (p. 594), the old town, beginning at the foot of "the Rock." Enjoy a snack of *socca,* a round crepe made with chickpea flour that's sold steaming hot by street vendors. Then head for the **promenade des Anglais** (p. 594), the wide boulevard along the waterfront. Stop in at one of the grand cafes along the water for a light lunch. In the afternoon, head for the best of the hill towns above Nice, **St-Paul-de-Vence,** only 31km (19 miles) to the north. Here you can wander its ramparts in about 30 minutes before descending on the greatest modern art museum in the Riviera, the **Foundation Maeght** (p. 586).

Continue over to Vence (p. 588) for a visit to **Chapelle du Rosaire** (p. 589), where the great Henri Matisse created his artistic masterpiece for some Dominican nuns. From there, it's just 24km (15 miles) southeast to Nice.

Have dinner at a typical bistro, serving a traditional Niçoise cuisine with its inevitable Italian influences.

## DAY 14: Nice to Monaco ★★★

While still overnighting in Nice, head east for the most hair-raising but thrilling drive in all of France, a trip along the **Grande Corniche** highway that stretches 31km (19 miles) east from Nice to the little resort of **Menton** near the Italian border. Allow 3 hours for this trip. Highlights along this road include **Roquebrune-Cap Martin** and **La Turbie.** The greatest view along the Riviera is at the **Èze Belvedere,** at 1,200m (3,936 ft.).

# FRANCE FOR FAMILIES

France offers many attractions for kids. Perhaps your main concern with having children along is pacing yourself with museum time. Our suggestion is to limit **Paris** to 2 days and then spend a day wandering the spectacular grounds and glittering interiors of **Versailles,** 2 days in **Disneyland Paris,** and 2 days on the **Riviera.**

## DAYS 1 & 2: Paris ★★★

Take the kids for a morning visit to **Notre-Dame** (p. 97). The highlight is climbing the 387 narrow and winding steps to the top of one of the towers for a fabulously Quasimodo view of the gargoyles and Paris. After a visit, head for the **Eiffel Tower** (p. 113). In addition to scaling this fantastic monument, you can order lunch—allow at least 2 hours for your visit, one just to access the elevators on levels one and two. Food is available at the Altitude 95 restaurant on the first floor, but it's a bit pricey for most families. A first-floor snack bar and a second-floor cafeteria offer the best values for the family on a budget.

After touring the tower, take the kids for a donkey ride in the nearby **Champ de Mars,** which also stages the best puppet shows.

In the afternoon, take the children for a stroll through the **Jardin des Tuileries** (p. 89), where there are more donkey rides, ice-cream stands, and a marionette show. At the circular pond, you can rent a toy boat.

On **DAY 2,** visit the **Musée du Louvre** (p. 93). Even if your child is not a museum buff and bores easily, he or she will surely be intrigued by the many displays. Over the years, we've observed that, even more than the paintings, kids are fascinated by the Egyptian art and antiquities displayed in the Sully and Denon wings, a total of 7,000 items, the largest exhibition of such artifacts outside of Cairo.

After the Louvre, take the Métro to Porte de la Villette, where you can spend 2 or 3 hours at **Cité des Sciences et de l'Industrie** (p. 116). The mammoth structure is home to a planetarium, a 3-D cinema, video workshops, and interactive exhibits.

### France for Families

**1 & 2** Paris
**3** Versailles
**4 & 5** Disneyland Paris
**6** Nice
**7** Monaco

Space is too tight in this book to document all activities in Paris of interest to children, but you'll want to spend a good 2 hours in the **Jardin d'Acclimatation,** in the northern part of the Bois de Boulogne. The visit starts with a ride on a narrow-gauge train through a stretch of wooded park, and attractions include a zoo, a house of mirrors, a puppet theater, a playground, and kiosks selling waffles.

As the afternoon fades, head for **Butte Montmartre,** with its fiesta atmosphere. Take the Métro to Anvers and walk to the funicular, the cable car that carries you to the **Basilique du Sacré-Coeur** (p. 113). Once you arrive at "the top of Paris," follow the crowds to the **place du Tertre,** where a Sergeant Pepper–style band often blasts off-key, and you can have a local artist create a sketch of your kids. Finally, reward your brood with ice cream sold on the square.

### DAY 3: Versailles ★★★

Tear yourself away from the glories of Paris for a day spent at the **Château de Versailles** (p. 203). Take the RER line C to the Versailles/Rive Gauche station. Kids delight in the Hall of Mirrors and in the grand apartments. Take the children for a walk through the garden, where they can visit the hamlet where the ill-fated Marie Antoinette strolled with her lambs. You can buy the makings of a picnic lunch in Paris and enjoy it on the grounds, or

Jardin d'Acclimatation.

Place du Tertre, Montmartre.

else you can purchase fast food at one of the stalls placed in discreet corners of the garden.

Return to Paris in time to visit **Parc Zoologique de Paris,** in the Bois de Vincennes on the southeastern outskirts of Paris. Quickly reachable by Métro, this is one of France's greatest zoos, complete with playful animals in natural habitats, as well as lions roaming a veldt. There's even a cement mountain similar to Disneyland's Matterhorn.

### DAYS 4 & 5: Disneyland Paris ★★

Disneyland Paris is the top family vacation destination in France. Allow a full day to see the highlights of the park, plus another day to absorb its secondary adventures. Our recommendation is to visit **Main Street, U.S.A., Frontierland,** and **Adventureland** on the first day, saving **Fantasyland, Discoveryland,** the entertainment center at **Village Disney,** and **Sleeping Beauty Castle** for the second day. You can stay in the Disney hotels on-site, coming in various price ranges from very expensive to budget. The RER commuter express train A takes you from Etoile in Paris to Marne-la-Vallée/Chessy in 45 minutes.

### DAY 6: Nice ★★★

Return to Paris and fly to Nice, capital of the French Riviera. If you flew Air France transatlantic, Nice can often be attached as a low-cost extension of your round-trip fare.

In Nice, you can check into your hotel for 2 nights, as the city has the most affordable hotels on the Riviera. Set out to explore this old city. The people-watching on the Riviera alone is likely to leave your kids wide-eyed. Beware that they'll see plenty of skin, as topless bathing is rampant. There's always a lot of free entertainment in summer along the boardwalk in Nice, called the **promenade des Anglais** (p. 594).

In the afternoon, journey to the hill town of **St-Paul-de-Vence** (p. 584). This is the most evocative of the hill towns of Nice, and children delight in touring the ramparts and strolling along the pedestrian-only rue

Grande. You can have a late lunch in the cafeteria of the **Foundation Mae-ght** (p. 586), the Riviera's greatest modern-art museum.

Return to Nice for the evening and take your kids for a stroll through the Old Town, dining in a typical Niçoise bistro.

### DAY 7: Monaco ★★★

While still based in Nice, head for the tiny principality of Monaco, which lies only 18km (11 miles) east of Nice.

Children will enjoy the changing-of-the-guard ceremony at **Les Grands Appartements du Palais** (p. 618), where Prince Rainier took his young bride, film star Grace Kelly, years ago. But the best part of Monaco for kids is the **Musée Océanographique de Monaco** (p. 618), one of Europe's biggest aquariums, with sharks and other exotic sea creatures. Monaco also has the **Collection des Voitures Anciennes de S.A.S. le Prince de Monaco** (p. 618) and the **Musée National de Monaco** (p. 619), with a mammoth antique doll collection.

Return to Nice that night and prepare for your flight home in the morning.

# A WINE LOVER'S TOUR OF BURGUNDY

For lovers of French wine and landscapes alike, a tour of the world-famous Burgundy wine region is one of the highlights of France. Taste chardonnays and pinot noirs that have been sought after since time immemorial by everyone from Roman emperors to Cistercian monks. This wine tour curves along the River Saône past the key wine-growing areas of Burgundy from **Mâconnais** in the South, through the **Côte Chalonnaise** towards the Côte d'Or vineyards of **Côte de Beaune** and **Côte de Nuits.**

### DAY 1: MÂCONNAIS: Chardonnay to Tournus ★★

A good place to start your tour of Burgundy is in **Chardonnay**, the village that gave its name to the region's most celebrated white grape variety. This village is at the northern end of **Mâconnais,** a wine region known for its good-value, white chardonnay wines. You'll find Chardonnay bordered by vineyards and green pastures dotted with cream-colored Charolais cattle on the D56, route de Plottes driving southwest from Tournus, 98km (61 miles) north of Lyon along A6.

From there, head south on the D56, then west on D82 to Bissy-la-Mâconnaise before heading north on D161 to **Cruzille,** home to some of the oldest organic vineyards in Burgundy. Here you can visit **Domaine Guillot-Broux** (www.guillot-broux.com; ✆ 03-85-33-29-74), whose reasonably priced wines from 9€ to 27€ per bottle show a surprising complexity and fruitiness. In 1991, proprietors Jean-Gérard and Jacqueline moved to organic viticulture so discreetly that some of their older clients were not even aware of the change. Free wine tasting (groups of 10 or more pay a small fee) can be organized from Monday to Friday between 9:30am and 4:30pm and weekends by prior appointment. The domaine also runs a gîte (chalet) for weekend and weekly rentals from 190€ to 340€.

You can stop off for lunch in picturesque Ozenay (driving north along D161, then east on D14) at the **Relais d'Ozenay** (www.le-relais-dozenay.com;

## A Wine Lover's Tour of Burgundy

1 Chardonnay to Tournus
2 Chalon-sur-Saône to Givry
3 Mercurey
4 Côtes de Beaune
5 Beaune
6 Côte de Nuits
7 Dijon

**℡ 03-85-32-17-93**) a village restaurant with a Michelin Bib Gourmand and a well-stocked Mâcon wine list. Afterwards, drive west along D14 to Cormatin for an afternoon visit to one of Burgundy's finest moated châteaux, **Château de Cormatin** (www.chateaudecormatin.com; **℡ 03-85-50-16-55**) with its sumptuous Renaissance garden. Stay the night in Tournus at the 17th-century **La Tour du Tresorier,** 9 place de l'Abbaye (www.tour-du-tresorier.com; **℡ 03-85-27-00-47**), where you can organize a tasting of Burgundy wines with owner Thierry Lindbergh.

## DAY 2: LA CÔTE CHALONNAISE: Chalon-sur-Saône to Givry ★★

Begin your day with a different perspective on Burgundy's winelands from the air. You'll grasp the nature of *terroir* as you stare at the intricate pattern of vineyards: each one with its own combination of exposure, slope, and soil. Drive north on the A6 past the bustling market town of Chalon-sur-Saône to the aerodrome in Champforgeuil, **Procoptère** (www.procoptere-aviation.com; **℡ 03-85-46-93-93**), which organizes tourist helicopter flights for two to five passengers from 89€ per person over the Côte Chalonnaise (15 min.), Hautes Côtes de Beaune (25 min.), or Côte de Beaune and Côte de Nuits (40 min.).

Head south on the A6, then west on D69 to **Givry,** whose pinot noir red wines with hints of cherry and raspberry were said to be the favorite wines of French king Henri IV. Givry is in the heart of the **Côte Chalonnaise.** Known for its well-priced pinot noir red wines, this limestone-rich sub-region of Burgundy extends in a thin strip for 25km (16 miles) between Tournus and Chagny.

In Givry, start your wine tasting at **Clos Salomon,** 16 rue du Clos Salomon (www.du-gardin.com/clossalomon; **℡ 03-85-44-32-24**), a Premier Cru vineyard dating back to the 14th-century when Hugues Salomon sold wines to the Pope in Avignon. Wine tastings can be organized from Monday to Saturday by appointment only. Minutes away (west off the D170 in the neighboring hamlet Poncey), you'll find **Domaine Ragot,** 4 rue de l'Ecole (www.domaine-ragot.com; **℡ 03-85-44-35-67**), with its award-winning Givry Premier Cru red and white wines. Energetic owner Nicolas Ragot took over this family-run domain in 2008 and is happy to offer tastings Monday to Friday 9am to noon and 2 to 5pm by appointment.

If you'd like to overnight at the former summer residence of the Bishops of Autun, head to **Côté Park,** 18 rue Georges Clémenceau, Givry (www.cotepark.com; **℡ 03-85-94-88-91**).

## DAY 3: LA CÔTE CHALONNAISE: Mercurey ★★

Mercurey is your first stop today. From Givry, drive north along D981, then northwest along the D978 to Mercurey. This pretty Gallo-Roman village, lined with winegrowers' houses, is the most coveted appellation in the Côte Chalonnaise. Mercurey is known for its spicy-cherry, red pinot noir wines and produces over 3 million bottles of red wine per year. There are 32 Premier Cru appellations within Mercurey AOC, but no Grand Cru appellations in this part of Burgundy. Along Grande Rue, you'll find **Domaine de Suremain** (at no.71; www.domaine-de-suremain.com; **℡ 03-85-98-04-92**) where you can call in advance to organize a tasting of predominantly Premier Cru pinot noir reds and **Domaine Michel Juillot** (at no. 59;

www.domaine-michel-juillot.fr; ℭ **03-85-98-99-89**) whose 30-hectare (74-acre) domaine produces both Mercurey Premier Cru red and white wines, as well as Côte de Beaune wines, *Crémant de Bourgogne* (sparkling wines), and *Marc de Bourgogne* (cognac-like liqueur). You can drop by for wine tastings at Domaine Michel Juillot from Monday to Saturday 9am to 6pm and Sunday 9:30am to 12:30pm. Up-and-coming wine producer **Bruno Lorenzon** welcomes wine lovers by prior appointment to his domaine nearby at 14 rue du Réu (www.domainelorenzon.com; ℭ **03-85-45-13-51**). Bruno's favorite saying is *"Un grand raisin, c'est 90% du travail."* (Great grapes are 90% of the work).

After a morning of wine tasting, backtrack along the D978 and then go north on the D981. Summertime visitors can take a break at the magnificent medieval **Château de Rully** (www.chateau-rully-bourgogne.com; ℭ **03-85-87-20-89**). Visits are available in July and August Wednesday to Sunday at 3, 4, and 5pm.

Continue up the D981. Just south of Chagny in Bouzeron, an AOC known for its Aligoté white grape variety, lies **Domaine de Villaine,** 2 rue de la Fontaine (www.de-villaine.com; ℭ **03-85-91-20-50**) where you can taste their organic wines from Bouzeron, Rully, and Mercurey.

Foodies may like to overnight at **Maison Lameloise,** 36 place d'Armes (see p. 432) in Chagny, whose three Michelin-starred cuisine draws visitors from all around the globe. Reservations are required. It's closed all day Tuesday and Wednesday.

## DAY 4: Route des Grands Crus: Côtes de Beaune ★★★

Now begins the mythical Route des Grands Crus that stretches from Santenay in the south to Dijon in the north. The route sweeps through some of Burgundy's prettiest villages with geranium-strewn cobbled streets and stone houses. You'll pass through miles of sunny, limestone slopes where vines have been tended since before 500 B.C. 32 of the 33 Grand Cru appellations in Burgundy are along this route.

From Chagny, drive west on D62 to Santenay. With its brightly colored tiled roof, **Château de Santenay,** 1 rue du Château (www.chateau-de-santenay.com; ℭ **03-80-20-61-87**), was a fabulous stately residence from the 9th to the 16th centuries. Commonly called *Château Philippe-Le-Hardi,* the castle was home to Philip the Bold, the first Duke of Burgundy, whose 1395 edict imposed pinot noir as the only red wine grape variety of Burgundy and reinforced the concept of single-variety wines. The wine estate now produces 600,000 bottles of white and red wines. Their tasting cellar is open from April to October daily 10am to 6pm.

From Santenay, take the D113 north to **Château de Chassagne-Montrachet,** 5 rue du Château (www.michelpicard.com; ℭ **03-80-21-98-57**). With 135 hectares (334 acres), owner Michel Picard runs one of the largest and most successful domaines in the village selling wine, spirits, and *Crémant de Bourgogne* sparkling wines. You can turn up without an appointment for a visit of the 12th-century cellars and a wine tasting from April to November daily 10am to 5pm. Alternatively, you can have a lazy wine-tasting lunch with six to 12 wines accompanying a *table d'hôtes* menu. For those who'd like to unwind with a longer stay, the château has five luxurious suites.

Curve through more of the Côte de Beaune's finest wine-producing villages on D113 and then the D973 on your way to Beaune: Puligny-Montrachet, Meursault (see p. 431 for information on **Château de Meursault**), Volnay, and Pommard (see p. 431 for information on **Château de Pommard**). Although red wines are produced in these villages (in particular Pommard), these appellations are most famous for their white chardonnay wines. Spend the night in Beaune.

## DAY 5: Beaune ★★

Beaune is the home to many of Burgundy's *négotiants* (wine merchants who process and bottle the produce of smaller winemakers and then sell under their own name) where you'll often be able to taste a wider variety of appellations than at an individual vineyard. Take your pick from well-known *négotiants* such as **Patriarche** (www.patriarche.com; ✆ **03-80-24-53-78**), offering 1-hour visits to its fabulous 13th-century vaulted tasting cellars and **Bouchard Père et Fils,** 15 rue du Château (www.bouchard-pereetfils. com; ✆ **03-80-24-80-45**), with cellars in the 15th-century Castle of Beaune, a former royal fortress. Housed in a former Cordeliers church, wine merchant **Marché aux Vins** (✆ **03-80-25-08-20**) has over 100 hectares (247 acres) of vineyards and offers a wide range of appellations to taste. Its nearby sister property, **Caves du Couvent des Cordeliers,** 6 rue de l'Hôtel-Dieu, offers tastings and visits around its 13th-century convent cellars. For more information on opening hours and prices, see p. 430.

Just opposite is **Musée de l'Hôtel-Dieu,** rue de l'Hôtel-Dieu (see p. 429). With its multicolored patterned roof, this 15th-century hospital is one of the town's most visible antique buildings. An exciting time to visit is November when the world's most celebrated charity wine auction is held here.

## DAY 6: Route des Grands Crus: Côte de Nuits ★★★

As you head north from Beaune on the D974, the first village is **Aloxe-Corton,** where Charlemagne once owned vineyards. The emperor is honored with "a white wine of great character," Corton-Charlemagne, which is still produced here.

Further north along the D974, the Côte de Nuits is famed for its fruity Pinot Noir red wines and the closed-door policy of most of its eminent wine domains. Make a stop at Nuits-Saint-Georges, made famous by Jules Verne's hero in "From the Earth to the Moon" who opened bottles of Nuits-St-Georges wine when he first saw the moon. A curious diversion is **Le Cassissium,** 8 passage Montgolfier (www. cassissium.fr; ✆ **03-80-62-49-70**), a museum dedicated to the cassis liqueur added to white wine to make Kir (see p. 414). The visit lasts 1½ hours. It's open April to

Harvesting grapes in Aloxe-Corton.

mid-November daily 10am to 1pm and 2 to 7pm; mid-November to March Tuesday to Saturday 10:30am to 1pm and 2 to 5:30pm. The village is a good place for an early lunch stop at the diminutive **La Cabotte,** 24 Grande Rue (www.restaurantlacabotte.fr; © **03-80-61-20-77**).

On your way to Vougeot along the D974, you'll pass by **Vosne-Romanée,** where the mythical Domaine de la Romanée-Conti keeps its gates firmly closed to passersby. In Vougeot, you can visit Château du Clos-de-Vougeot (www.closdevougeot.fr; © **03-80-62-86-09**). This Renaissance-style château started life as a wine farm built in the 12th century by the Abbey de Cîteaux monks who played a pivotal role in molding Burgundy's *terroir* and developing the single variety method of viticulture. Sadly the château no longer produces wine, but is still open for visits year-round (Apr–Sept daily 9am–6:30pm, Sat until 5pm only; Oct–Mar 9–11:30am and 2–5.30pm, Sat until 5pm only). Admission is 4.10€ for adults and 3.10€ for children 8 to 16 years; free for kids 7 years and under; 2.90€ for students.

The D974 continues north to Dijon, but you can branch off onto D122 past Chambolle-Musigny and Gevrey-Chambertin, where nine of the region's 33 Grands Crus are produced. On the outskirts of Dijon in the village of Marsannay-la-Côte lies **Château de Marsannay** (www.chateau-marsannay.com; © **03-80-51-71-11**). This château was bought in 1990 by the Boisseaux family, founders of Beaune-based wine merchants Patriarche and owners of Château de Meursault. Marsannay is the only village in the Côte de Nuits to produce three colors of wine: red, white, and rosé. The chateau is open for wine-tasting visits March to November daily 10am to noon and 2 to 6pm and in winter by appointment only.

Continue into **Dijon** (p. 410), where you can spend the night. If you arrive early enough in the day, you can visit some of the town's attractions.

## DAY 7: Dijon: En Route to Paris ★★★

Surrounded by some of the world's most splendid vineyards, Dijon was the former seat of the powerful dukes of Burgundy. A university town and regional center today, it has had a long and rich history. Its monumental attraction is the **Musée des Beaux-Arts** (see p. 412), housed in an old palace and showcasing a stunning collection of European art from the 14th to the 19th centuries. Next, pick up a map at the **Office de Tourisme** (see p. 411) and walk through the historic core of this ancient city.

Dijon is one of the major transportation hubs in this part of France, and you can easily return to Paris from here. If you're driving, the distance is 312km (193 miles), which you can do in a morning, reaching Paris to the northwest in time for lunch.

View over Dijon.

3

# PARIS

F rom the Louvre to the Eiffel Tower, Paris is home to some of the world's most famous museums and monuments. While all of these sights are well worth visiting, the city itself is much more than a mere collection of buildings. Visiting Paris is as much about soaking up the atmosphere as sightseeing. With all the layers of history, it's easy to forget that Paris is a 21st-century capital, but some of the more recent additions to the city, such as the Vélib' biking scheme, have injected Paris with a new sense of dynamism.

Each of Paris's 20 *arrondissements* possesses a unique style and character. Our guide to the different neighborhoods of Paris will give you an insight into the city and help you decide where you want to stay and what you want to see. Once you arrive in Paris, try to explore as many neighborhoods as you can in order to appreciate the diversity of the city. If you have only a few days, you'll probably spend most of your time in the center of Paris, seeing the major sites. In a week, you'll be able to wander off the beaten track and explore some of Paris's neighborhoods in a bit more depth. And if you can stay for several weeks, you'll soon be an expert on *la vie parisienne*.

# ORIENTATION
## Arriving
### BY PLANE

Paris has two international airports: **Aéroport d'Orly,** 13km (8 miles) south of the city, and **Aéroport Roissy–Charles de Gaulle,** 22km (14 miles) northeast. A shuttle (19€) makes the 50- to 75-minute journey between the two airports about every 30 minutes.

**CHARLES DE GAULLE AIRPORT (ROISSY)**   At Charles de Gaulle (© **01-48-62-12-12,** or 39-50 in France), foreign carriers use Aérogare 1, while Air France uses Aérogare 2. From Aérogare 1, you take a moving walkway to the passport checkpoint and the Customs area. A *navette* (shuttle bus) links the two terminals.

Fast RER (Réseau Express Régional) trains depart the airport and **Roissy rail station** every 10 minutes between 5am and midnight for Métro stations including Gare du Nord, Châtelet, Luxembourg, Port-Royal, and Denfert-Rochereau. A typical fare from Roissy to any point in central Paris is 8.20€ per person (5.60€ children 4–10). Travel time from the airport to central Paris is around 35 to 40 minutes.

You can also take an **Air France shuttle bus** (© **08-92-35-08-20** or 01-48-64-14-24; www.cars-airfrance.com) to central Paris for 15€ one-way. It stops at the Palais des Congrès (Port Maillot) and continues to place Charles-de-Gaulle–Etoile, where subway lines can carry you to any point in Paris.

## The Paris Airport Shuttle

The **Paris Airport Shuttle** (www.parisshuttle.com; ℂ **01-53-39-18-18;** fax 01-53-39-13-13) is the best option. It charges 25€ for one person or 19€ per person for two or more going to and from Charles de Gaulle or Orly. Service is daily 6am to 11pm. Both shuttles accept American Express, Visa, and MasterCard, with 1-day advance reservations required.

That ride, depending on traffic, takes 45 to 55 minutes. The shuttle departs about every 20 minutes between 5:40am and 11pm.

The **Roissybus** (ℂ **01-58-76-16-16**), operated by the RATP, departs from the airport daily 6am to 11:45pm and costs 8.60€ for the 45- to 50-minute ride. Departures are about every 15 minutes, and the bus leaves you near the corner of rue Scribe and place de l'Opéra in the heart of Paris.

A **taxi** from Roissy into the city will cost about 47€ to 60€; from 8pm to 7am, the fare is 40% higher. Long orderly lines for taxis form outside each of the airport's terminals.

**ORLY AIRPORT**    Orly (ℂ **01-49-75-52-52,** or 39-50 in France) has two terminals—Orly Sud (south) for international flights and Orly Ouest (west) for domestic flights. A free shuttle bus connects them in 3 minutes.

**Air France buses** leave from Exit E of Orly Sud and from Exit F of Orly Ouest every 12 minutes between 6am and 11:30pm for Gare des Invalides; the fare is 9€ one-way, 14€ round-trip. Returning to the airport (about 30 min.), buses leave both the Montparnasse and the Invalides terminal for Orly Sud or Orly Ouest every 15 minutes.

Another way to get to central Paris is to take the RER from points throughout central Paris to the station at Pont-de-Rungis/Aéroport d'Orly for a per-person one-way fare of 6€, and from here, take the free shuttle bus that departs every 15 minutes from Pont-de-Rungis to both of Orly's terminals. Combined travel time is about 45 to 55 minutes.

A **taxi** from Orly to central Paris costs about 30€ to 50€, more at night. Don't take a meterless taxi from Orly; it's much safer (and usually cheaper) to hire one of the metered cabs, which are under the scrutiny of a police officer.

## BY TRAIN

Paris has six major stations: **Gare d'Austerlitz,** 55 quai d'Austerlitz, 13e (serving the southwest, with trains to and from the Loire Valley, Bordeaux, the Pyrénées, and Spain); **Gare de l'Est,** place du 11-Novembre-1918, 10e (serving the east, with trains to and from Strasbourg, Reims, and beyond, to Zurich and Austria); **Gare de Lyon,** 20 bd. Diderot, 12e (serving the southeast, with trains to and from the Côte d'Azur [Nice, Cannes, St-Tropez], Provence, and beyond, to Geneva and Italy); **Gare Montparnasse,** 17 bd. Vaugirard, 15e (serving the west, with trains to and from Brittany); **Gare du Nord,** 18 rue de Dunkerque, 15e (serving the north, with trains to and from London, Holland, Denmark, and northern Germany); and **Gare St-Lazare,** 13 rue d'Amsterdam, 8e (serving the northwest, with trains to and from Normandy). Buses operate between the stations, and each station has a Métro stop. For train information and to make reservations, call ℂ **08-92-35-35-35,** or **36-35** in France, between 8am and 8pm daily. From Paris, one-way rail passage to Tours costs 30€ to 51€; one-way to Strasbourg costs 55€ or 80€, depending on the routing.

***Warning:*** The stations and surrounding areas are usually seedy and frequented by pickpockets, hustlers, hookers, and addicts. Be alert, especially at night.

### BY BUS

Most buses arrive at the **Eurolines France** station, 28 av. du Général-de-Gaulle, Bagnolet (www.eurolines.fr; 🕻 **08-92-89-90-91;** Métro: Gallieni).

### BY CAR

Driving in Paris is *not* recommended. Parking is difficult and traffic dense. If you drive, remember that Paris is encircled by a ring road, the *périphérique.* Always obtain detailed directions to your destination, including the name of the exit on the *périphérique* (exits aren't numbered). Avoid rush hours.

The major highways into Paris are A1 from the north; A13 from Rouen, Normandy, and other points northwest; A10 from Spain and the southwest; A6 and A7 from the French Alps, the Riviera, and Italy; and A4 from eastern France.

## Visitor Information

The **Paris Convention and Visitors Bureau** (🕻 **08-92-68-30-00;** .35€ per minute; www.paris-info.com) has offices throughout the city, with the main headquarters at 25–27 rue des Pyramides, 1er (Métro: Pyramides). It's open Monday through Saturday 10am to 7pm (June–Oct from 9am), Sunday and holidays from 11am to 7pm. Less comprehensive branch offices include Clémenceau Welcome Center, corner of avenue Champs-Élysées and avenue Marigny (8e; Métro: Champs-Élysées), open April 6 to October 20 daily 9am to 7pm. **Espace Tourisme Ile-de-France,** in the Carrousel du Louvre, 99 rue de Rivoli, 1er (Métro: Palais-Royal–Louvre), open daily 10am to 6pm; in the **Gare de Lyon,** 20 bd. Diderot, Paris 12e (Métro: Gare de Lyon), open Monday through Saturday 8am to 6pm; in the **Gare du Nord,** 18 rue de Dunkerque, 10e (Métro: Gare du Nord), open daily 8am to 6pm; and in **Montmartre,** 21 place du Tertre, 18e (Métro: Abbesses or Lamarck-Caulaincourt), open daily 10am to 7pm. You can walk in at any branch to make a hotel reservation; the service charge is free. The offices are extremely busy year-round, especially in midsummer, so be prepared to wait in line.

## City Layout

Compared to many capitals, Paris is surprisingly compact. The river Seine divides the city into the *Rive Droite* **(Right Bank)** to the north and the *Rive Gauche* **(Left Bank)** to the south. The larger Right Bank is where you find the city's business sector, stately monuments, and high-fashion industry. The smaller Left Bank has the publishing houses, universities, and a reputation as bohemian because students, philosophers, and creative types have been congregating here for centuries.

Paris is divided into 20 numbered municipal districts called **arrondissements.** The layout of these districts follows a distinct pattern. The first (abbreviated 1er for *premier*) arrondissement is the dead center of Paris, comprising an area around Notre-Dame and the Louvre. From there, the rest of the districts spiral outward, clockwise, in ascending order, like a snail shell. The lower the *arrondissement* number, the more central the location. If you want to be within walking distance of all the major sites and monuments, be sure to stay in one of the first eight arrondissements. There are only six arrondissements—the 5e, 6e, 7e, 13e, 14e, and 15e—on the Left Bank. The Right Bank is much larger, and it comprises the remaining 14 arrondissements.

Most city maps are divided by arrondissement, and addresses include the arrondissement number (in Roman or Arabic numerals and followed by *ème* or *e,* as in *10ème*). Arrondissement numbers are key to locating an address in Paris, and this book lists addresses the way they appear in Paris, with the arrondissement number following the specific street address (for instance, 29 rue de Rivoli, 4e, is in the fourth arrondissement). Paris also has its own version of a zip code. The mailing address for a hotel is written as, for example, "Paris 75014." The last two digits, 14, indicate that the address is in the 14th arrondissement—in this case, Montparnasse. Arrondissements are indicated on the blue enamel street signs, above the street name.

Finding an address can be a complicated process in Paris, but once you know the arrondissement in which an address is located, finding that spot is much easier. Numbers on buildings running parallel to the Seine usually follow the course of the river east to west. On north–south streets, numbering begins at the river. To enter a building, you'll usually need a code for the outside door. Once inside, you'll need a letter indicating which staircase to take, the floor number, and the position of the apartment (right, left, last door etc). *Bis* and *ter* after a building number are the equivalent of *b* or *c* and indicate a separate address.

A good way to orientate yourself is the Métro. As you're rarely more than 10 minutes' walk away from a Métro station, it's easy to work out which part of Paris you're in by finding your nearest station.

There is a pull-out map showing Paris's neighborhoods at the back of this book. For a more detailed map of Paris, we recommend *Paris Pratique par arrondissement,* available at newsstands and bookshops for around 7€. This guide provides you with a Métro map and maps of each arrondissement, with all streets listed and keyed. Free maps of the Paris Métro, bus, and RER networks are available at all Métro stations.

## Neighborhoods in Brief
### THE RIGHT BANK

**LES HALLES, LOUVRE & PALAIS ROYAL (1ER & 2E)**  Home to some of Paris's most important historical sites, the area around the **Louvre** and **Palais-Royal** is one of the most visited (but least residential) parts of the city. Whether you're strolling through the **Jardin des Tuileries** or admiring the classic beauty of the **place Vendôme,** this is one of the most elegant neighborhoods in the city. It's also one of the most luxurious, with designer boutiques filling the arcades of the Palais-Royal and *haute couture* lining the sidewalks of the **rue St-Honoré. Rue de Rivoli,** the main artery running through the 1st arrondissement, is one of the busiest streets in Paris, full of shops, cafes, and restaurants. For a little peace and quiet, head south for a walk along the banks of the Seine or take refuge in the gardens of the Palais-Royal.

**RIGHT BANK**

**1** Les Halles, Louvre, & Palais Royal (1er & 2e)

**2** Le Marais, Île St-Louis & Île de la Cité (3e & 4e)

**3** Champs Elysées & Western Paris (8e, 16e, & 17e)

**4** Opéra & Canal St-Martin (9e & 10e)

**5** Pigalle & Montmartre (18e)

**6** République, Bastille & Eastern Paris (11e & 12e)

**7** Belleville & Northeast Paris (19e & 20e)

**LEFT BANK**

**8** Latin Quarter (5e)

**9** St-Germain-des-Prés & Luxembourg (6e)

**10** Eiffel Tower & Nearby (7e)

**11** Montparnasse & Southern Paris (13e, 14e, 15e)

# Paris Neighborhoods

North of the Palais-Royal is the **Bourse** (stock exchange). You'll find fewer tourists, but it still remains close to the center of the action. Like most financial districts, this area is lively during the week but much quieter at weekends. To the east is **Sentier,** the traditional center of the wholesale clothing trade, and the picturesque, cobbled market street, **rue Montorgueil.** Over the past few decades, the area around **Etienne Marcel** has gained a reputation as a trendy fashion district. For a more classic shopping environment, explore the various *passages* (covered arcades) that the 2nd arrondissement is famous for, the loveliest of which is Galerie Vivienne.

**Les Halles** was the name of Paris's great food market, which was located here from the Middle Ages to the 1960s, when the market was moved to Rungis, outside Paris. The 19th-century iron and glass pavilions were torn down and replaced by an ugly Seventies-style shopping complex, Forum des Halles. Seen as one of central Paris's biggest eyesores, both the Forum and the surrounding gardens are currently being redeveloped. However, it'll be years before all the work is finished, and at the moment most of this area is a building site. The huge underground shopping center and Métro/RER station means that Les Halles is always hectic and heaving with people. It's not the safest area, and it's worth avoiding at night. The same is true of the seedy rue St-Denis, just east of Les Halles, as this is one of Paris's red light districts.

**LE MARAIS, ILE ST-LOUIS & ILE DE LA CITÉ (3E & 4E)**    There's no better place to begin your exploration of Paris than at the Seine and the two islands in its center as it was here that Paris's history began all those thousands of years ago. There are magnificent views of the river from the Ile de la Cité and the Ile St-Louis, but apart from that the two islands could not be more different from each other. Although the **Ile de la Cité** does have some quieter spots, such as the square du Vert-Galant, as it is where you'll find the majestic Gothic cathedral **Notre-Dame** and the beautiful **Sainte-Chapelle,** it is visited by thousands of tourists every day. The **Ile St-Louis,** with its aristocratic town houses, is much calmer and more picturesque. Far removed from the hustle and bustle of Paris, the *quais* of the Ile St-Louis are perfect for a romantic stroll.

Having avoided Haussmann's 19th-century transformation of Paris, **Le Marais** has a more intimate atmosphere than other parts of Paris. It's home to the beautiful **place des Vosges** and is full of *hôtels particuliers* (private mansions that were built by the aristocracy). Stretching across the 3rd and 4th arrondissements, the southern part of Le Marais is a lively area, full of elegant boutiques and small, contemporary art galleries. It's a great area for wining and dining, and very popular on Sundays as, unlike many other parts of Paris, most of the shops here are open. The area around **rue des Rosiers** has long been home to the city's Jewish community, while the **rues St-Croix-de-la-Bretonnerie, des Archives,** and **Vieille-du-Temple** are the center of Paris's gay and lesbian life.

The upper part of the Le Marais, north of the rue des Francs-Bourgeois is more up and coming but considerably quieter than the 4th. The heart of the 3rd is the **rue de Bretagne.** There's a great antiques market along this street on Sunday mornings, and it's here you'll find the **Marché des Enfants Rouge,** a food market full of delicious goodies. Nearby, the beautiful iron market hall designed by Gustave Eiffel, the Carreau du Temple, is undergoing restoration. The plan is for it to become a cultural center. The streets around this hall, such as **rue de Picardie,** are home to some cool bars, and you'll also find a lot of small contemporary art galleries in this neighborhood.

**CHAMPS-ÉLYSÉES & WESTERN PARIS (8E, 16E & 17E)** One of the most famous avenues in the world, the tree-lined avenue **des Champs-Élysées** is the embodiment of Parisian grandeur. While strolling along the Champs-Élysées may be something of a disappointment thanks to the fast-food restaurants, overpriced cafés, and chain stores, leading off to the south are **avenue George V** and **avenue Montaigne,** home to *haute couture* boutiques and several of Paris's most luxurious hotels. The Champs-Élysées continues to be a rallying point for parades and festivities, and there's a popular Christmas market here in winter.

You'll find similar levels of wealth and grandeur in the 16th arrondissement, which is full of embassies, diplomats, and exclusive residences. Fans of Art Nouveau will enjoy walking around the 16th as it was here that Hector Guimard built nearly all of his buildings, the most famous of which is Castel Béranger. There are several interesting museums, including Paris's **Musée d'Art Moderne,** and the hip **Palais du Tokyo,** but this remains one of Paris's most bourgeois districts and can feel quite soulless and far from the action.

Heading north from the Champs-Élysées, you'll come to the picturesque **Parc Monceau** and the area known as **Batignolles.** This sophisticated neighborhood became fashionable during the 19th century and is full of elegant Haussmannian-style buildings. Today, it's a wealthy, predominantly residential area. The area around **place de Clichy** is more lively but a lot less elegant. On the nearby **rue des Dames** there are a number of hip bars and good restaurants.

**OPÉRA & GRANDS BOULEVARDS (9E)** Sandwiched between the 2nd and 18th arrondissements, the 9th is a good base for exploring Paris's Right Bank. The area around the glitzy **Opéra Garnier** is one of the busiest, most commercial areas of Paris. It's a great place for shopping, and it's where you'll find the landmark 19th-century department stores **Galeries Lafayette** and **Printemps.** Heading east from Opéra you come to the area known as **Grands Boulevards.** This is the collective name for the streets that run from Madeline to République and they follow the lines of the ramparts built by Charles V in the 14th century. This was one of the most fashionable neighborhoods of Paris in the 18th and 19th centuries as it was the epicenter of cafe and theater life. It was also, in the days before department stores, a popular shopping district thanks to the numerous covered *passages* (arcades). **Passage Jouffroy** is well worth a visit. But although there is still lively nightlife here—bars, cinemas and theaters—the grandeur of Grands Boulevards has faded and the area can seem rather shabby and inauthentic

North of rue de Châteaudun, the 9th arrondissement becomes much quieter and more residential. **Rue Cadet** is a pretty market street and several of the streets leading up to Pigalle, such as **rue des Martyrs** and **rue de Rochechouart** are full of interesting boutiques, delicious food shops and cozy cafés. The area around St-Georges is a quarter known as La Nouvelle Athènes (the New Athens). It got this name when a wave of Romantic artists and writers came to live here in the 19th century. Take some time to admire the mansions on the rue de la Tour des Dames.

**PIGALLE & MONTMARTRE (18E)**   Located on a hill in the north of Paris, Montmartre's winding, narrow streets are a far cry from the wide avenues and boulevards of central Paris. Despite its distance from the center, **Montmartre**—or *la butte* (the hill), as it is affectionately referred to by locals—is one of the city's most popular neighborhoods for visitors and residents alike. At the end of the 19th century, Montmartre was full of avant-garde writers and artists, including Picasso, van Gogh, and Toulouse-Lautrec, who were attracted by the cheap rents and cheap booze. Despite the busloads of tourists who climb the hill to visit **Sacré Coeur,** this area has retained its bohemian atmosphere and if you avoid the tourist traps—such as place du Tertre—you'll find plenty of charm and romance. There's a great selection of bars and restaurants around **rue des Abbesses** and **rue Lepic,** and one of the advantages of being a little farther away from the center is that the prices are lower.

Place Pigalle was named after a French sculptor, Jean-Baptiste Pigalle, who is buried in a tiny cemetery at the top of *la butte*. Unfortunately for him, it's not usually art that springs to mind when you hear the name "Pigalle." This neighborhood has long been one of Paris's red-light districts and between place Pigalle and place Blanche, you'll discover the seedier side of this neighborhood with flashing neon signs advertising sex shops and adult-only cinemas. There are lots of good music venues in **Pigalle,** such as Le Trianon and La Cigale, and although there are less dance halls and absinthe dens these days, the neighborhood is still a popular area for drinking and clubbing.

To the east of the 18th, around rue de la Goutte d'Or and Barbès Rochechouart, there is a large North African community. There's a lively atmosphere here but it's quite hectic, particularly on Saturdays when there is a popular fruit and vegetable market. If you do get off the Métro here, be wary of pickpockets. Located on the northernmost edge of the 18th is the city's most famous flea market, the **Marché aux Puces de Clignancourt.**

**RÉPUBLIQUE, BASTILLE & EASTERN PARIS (11E & 12E)**   The districts of eastern Paris—the 11th and 12th arrondissements—were traditionally home to Paris's working classes but over the last several decades they have become predominantly middle-class, residential neighborhoods. In spite of this, both place de la Bastille and **place de la République,** with its statue of the great symbol of the Revolution, *Marianne,* remain symbolic places for the French Left and are often the scenes of large public demonstrations.

To the east of République, is the leafy **boulevard Richard Lenoir,** which covers the southern section of Canal Saint Martin as it makes its way to the Seine. The gardens along this boulevard, originally designed by Second Empire architect Gabrial Davioud and updated by David Mangin in 1993, make this a pleasant way to walk from République to Bastille. The area between Goncourt, Menilmontant, Parmentier, and Oberkampf is young and hip, and boasts some of the best nightlife in the city.

**Place de la Bastille** is dominated by the modern **Opéra Bastille,** which was met with mixed reactions when it opened in 1989. Nearby, in the streets around **rue de Lappe** and **rue de Roquette,** you'll find numerous bars and clubs, but compared to other areas in Paris the nightlife in Bastille can seem overpriced and inauthentic. To the east of the place is the **rue du Faubourg St-Antoine,** which has been the center of the furniture-makers district for centuries. It's now a pleasant shopping street, but if you go up some of the side streets you can still find some artisans at work. Head down the rue d'Aligre and you'll find the delightful food market the **Marché d'Aligre.** One of the most peaceful parts of the 12th arrondissement is the **Promenade Plantée,** a leafy walkway built along an old railway viaduct. It starts just south of the opera house and continues to Jardin de Reuilly before going on to the **Bois de Vincennes** just outside Paris. The 12th is also home to **Bercy Village.** Up until the 1980s, wine was unloaded from boats and stored in warehouses here, but the warehouses were recently renovated and are now home to shops, bars and a multiplex cinema.

**BELLEVILLE, CANAL ST-MARTIN & NORTHEAST PARIS (10E, 19E & 20E)** The 10th arrondissement is one of Paris's most multiethnic neighborhoods, and the streets around **rue du Faubourg Saint-Denis** are home to large numbers of Indians, Pakistanis, Bangladeshis, West Indians, Africans, and Turks. It's a vibrant, thriving area and the **passage Brady** is one of the best places in Paris to eat Indian and Pakistani food. However, the streets around Strasbourg St-Denis, Gare du Nord, and Gare de l'Est are not the safest parts of the city and should be avoided late at night.

The main attraction of the 10th is the increasingly popular **Canal Saint Martin.** With its picturesque footbridges and cobbled, tree-lined *quais,* this is the ideal place for a summer picnic or Sunday stroll. There's a very *bobo* (short for *bourgeois bohemian*) atmosphere around here, thanks to the stylish boutiques and trendy bars and cafes.

Heading east from the Canal, you'll come to the traditionally working-class district of **Belleville,** which is home to large numbers of immigrants. North African Muslims and Jews, many of Tunisian origin, live alongside Chinese and Vietnamese immigrants, and Belleville is Paris's second Chinatown. Cheap rents have attracted a number of artists to this area and you'll come across a lot of artists' studios and street art. Paris property prices mean that this area, like many others before it, is slowly being gentrified. There's a lively atmosphere in the streets of Belleville, and it's a great place to come for cheap bars and restaurants.

The 19th is not the most attractive of Paris's arrondissements, but there are some places that are worth visiting. At the top of the Canal St-Martin is the **Bassin de la Villette,** where two MK2 cinemas (MK2 is one of Paris's biggest movie theater chains) face each other across the canal. There's a pleasant atmosphere here during the summer, when people gather outside the local bars, picnicking, or playing *pétanque.* If you continue along the Canal de l'Ourcq you'll reach the **Parc de la Villette,** which hosts an outdoor cinema festival in the summer and a jazz festival in September. A little farther south is one of Paris's loveliest green spaces, the **Parc des Buttes Chaumont.** If you continue south, the 19th becomes the 20th, a sprawling, predominantly residential district, some parts of which are not easily accessible on the Métro. The main attraction in the 20th is definitely the **Père Lachaise Cemetery,** where the likes of Jim Morrison, Edith Piaf, and Chopin are buried. However, it's not just the dead who are drawing people to the 20th these days. There are several good bars and music venues both north of the cemetery, around **Menilmontant,** and south, around **place St-Blaise.**

## THE LEFT BANK

**LATIN QUARTER (5E & 13E)**    From a historical perspective, the Latin Quarter is not to be missed. From the Roman settlement of Lutetia to the heady days of May 1968, layers of Parisian history are visible in the 5th arrondissement. Home to the **Sorbonne**—the administrative center of the University of Paris—the Latin Quarter has been associated with education and learning since the Middle Ages. A number of academic institutions are still based in the 5th and parts of the neighborhood, particularly around rue Mouffetard and place de la Contrescarpe, are filled with students. There are lots of art house cinemas here that give the neighborhood an offbeat, indie vibe, and a trip to the charming English-language bookshop, **Shakespeare & Co.** (see p. 163), on rue de la Bûcherie is a must for literature lovers.

Many visitors are disappointed by how tacky and commercial parts of the 5th have become. The area around place St-Michel and rue de la Huchette, although very central, is one of most touristy parts of the city. To do the Latin Quarter justice, it's best not to spend much time in these streets. Instead, admire Ile de la Cité from the terrace of the **Institut du Monde Arabe,** visit the hammam in the **Mosquée de Paris,** or take a leisurely stroll through the **Jardin des Plantes.** As you head further south you can see the quieter, more residential side of the 5th.

You'll see quite a different side of Paris in the 13th arrondissement. It's one of the few districts in the city where there are modern, high-rise tower blocks. It's also home to Paris's principal **Chinatown:** The area around place d'Italie, Tolbiac, and Olympiades is a great place to come for authentic Chinese and Vietnamese food. Just south of place d'Italie is the pretty, village-like neighborhood of **Butte-aux-Cailles.** The main streets of this area are the cobbled rue de la Butte aux Cailles and rue des Cinq Diamants, and walking around you'll come across quaint old houses and charming bars and restaurants.

**ST-GERMAIN-DES-PRÈS & LUXEMBOURG (6E)**    Today one of the city's most exclusive neighborhoods, St-Germain oozes *Rive Gauche* glamour. For most of the 20th century, the area around the Eglise-St-Germain-des-Prés was the intellectual heartland of Paris, and everywhere you turn, you'll encounter historic and literary associations. Here you'll find three of Paris's most famous cafes, all within a few meters of one another. Known as **The Golden Triangle, the Brasserie Lipp, Les Deux Magots,** and **Café de Flore** were frequented by the likes of Hemingway and Picasso in the 1920s, and Jean-Paul Sartre and Simone de Beauvoir in the 1950s. However, the neighborhood has lost a lot of its intellectual appeal in the last few decades and nowadays, you'll find more *haute couture* (Christian Dior, Louis Vuitton, and more) than highbrow culture.

Despite being one of the smaller arrondissements (in terms of both surface area and population) you can find a little of everything in St-Germain. It's home to two of the city's most famous churches, **Eglise-St-Germain-des-Près** and **St-Sulpice,** as well as the **Institut de France** and former mint, the **Hôtel des Monnaies.** There's art, thanks to the **Ecole des Beaux Arts** on rue Bonaparte, and you'll find an abundance of art dealers and small, private galleries on the nearby streets. If you want to go shopping you can choose from the designer names mentioned above, the smart, upmarket boutiques around St-Sulpice, or the more reasonably priced high street stores on rue de Rennes. Despite being a little on the pricey side, this neighborhood boasts some great bars and restaurants and there's a lively atmosphere in the evenings in the narrow streets around St-Germain and **Odéon.** Not forgetting one of Paris's largest and loveliest green spaces, the charming **Jardin du Luxembourg.** This 24-hectare (59-acre) park, the design of which is based in the Boboli Gardens in Florence, is full of 19th-century park furniture and allegorical statues. Popular with everyone, from toddlers to joggers to lovers, this park is well worth strolling around.

**EIFFEL TOWER & NEARBY (7E)**   The 7th arrondissement is a calm, elegant but rather formal neighborhood. The main attraction is, of course, the **Eiffel Tower.** Despite the fact that many people hated it when it was showcased at the 1889 Great Exhibition, the Eiffel Tower has become the symbol of Paris itself. The panoramic views from the top and the sheer magnificence of the structure attract thousands of visitors everyday. But where there are tourists, there are pickpockets and you should be very vigilant when strolling around beneath the tower. Similarly, the Champ de Mars attracts some dodgy characters and it's not the safest place to hang out after dark.

The 7th arrondissement is also home to the world famous and recently renovated **Musée d'Orsay,** where you'll find many of the Impressionist masterpieces, as well as the **Musée Rodin.** In the center of the 7th, you'll also find the **Hôtel des Invalides,** where Napoleon's body was interred, the **Assemblée Nationale** (National Assembly), and a number of key government ministries. Although there are a lot of civil servants running—or being chauffeured—around during the week, this makes it one of the quieter neighborhoods at the weekends. There's a bit more of life on either side of Invalides. **Rue St-Dominique** and **rue de Grenelle** are popular shopping streets and **rue Cler** is a busy, well-heeled market-street full of gourmet food shops, and classy cafés. On the other side of the 7th, you'll find the chic **rue du Bac,** which winds its way down to the lively shopping district around Sèvres Babylone. It is impossible to come here without paying a visit to the beautiful 19th-century department store, **Le Bon Marché,** on the rue des Sèvres.

**MONTPARNASSE & SOUTHERN PARIS (14E & 15E)**   After WW1, the artistic center of Paris shifted from Montmartre to Montparnasse, and this lively, cosmopolitan neighborhood witnessed the birth of Modernism. Picasso, Matisse, Modigliani, and Chagall, along with expats Ernest Hemingway, Henry Miller, and Gertrude Stein, were all well-known figures in Montparnasse. Today, it's difficult to imagine this area as a literary and artistic heartland. Montparnasse is a busy, commercial neighborhood dominated by the rather ugly **Montparnasse Tower,** which was built in the 1970s. It's still reasonably close to central Paris and is very well connected in terms of public transport but it has lost much of its former soul. Along boulevard Montparnasse you can find, however, several famous Art Deco brasseries—La Coupole, Le Select, and Le Dôme—which were patronized by the all the movers and shakers of the interwar period, including Hemingway, Picasso, and Trotsky.

You'll find some peace and quiet in the **Cimetière du Montparnasse,** the resting place of a number of artists, writers and intellectuals including Serge Gainsbourg, Samuel Beckett, and both Jean-Paul Sartre and Simone de Beauvoir. As you head south, the 14th becomes increasingly residential and there's very little to see or do down here. The same is true for the 15th arrondissement, which does not have any significant buildings or landmarks. There are a couple of nice parks including Parc André-Citroën and Parc Georges-Brassens, which hosts a book market on Saturdays and Sundays. You'll find a busy shopping district around **Métro La Motte Picquet Grenelle** and **rue du Commerce.**

# EXPLORING PARIS

The city of Paris has a long history: There has been civilization here for more than 2 millennia, ever since Julius Caesar's troops invaded the city in 52 B.C., snatching power from the Gaulish tribe the *Parisii.* Two thousand years of art, architecture, war, religion, and politics—not to mention power, passion, and intrigue—have left its mark on the city. Paris counts hundreds of museums and monuments. It's a city that can transport you back centuries, where you can lose yourself in the labyrinth of Royal power and opulence or get captivated by the violence of the French Revolution. Or, the city can bring you up-to-date, with the most avant-garde art, design, and architecture that the world has to offer today. But the special thing about Paris is that just walking the streets feels like visiting the world's most magical museum.

Area by area, the following pages will highlight the best that Paris can offer, from iconic sights known the world over to quirky museums and hidden gardens, from 1,000-year-old castles to galleries celebrating the most challenging contemporary art.

---

### The New Les Halles

For eight centuries, **Les Halles** was the city's primary wholesale fruit, meat, and vegetable market. In the 19th century, Zola famously called it "the belly of Paris." The smock-clad vendors, beef carcasses, and baskets of vegetables all belong to the past, for the original market was torn down in the early '70s and relocated to a massive steel-and-glass edifice at Rungis, a suburb near Orly. Today, Les Halles includes the city's chief transportation hub and a major shopping complex, the **Forum des Halles** (1–7 rue Pierre-Lescot, 1er). This large mall, much of it underground, contains shops, restaurants, and movie theaters. In 2010, the city embarked on a massive 810-million euro renovation program that will overhaul the underground shopping and transportation zones as well as the garden above. Renovations are slated to be completed in 2016, but the complex should remain open and operational during the renovations. For more information, visit www.parisleshalles.fr.

# The Right Bank

## LES HALLES, LOUVRE & PALAIS ROYAL (1E & 2E)

Crowned by the Louvre, this central area that flanks the Seine packs in a high density of important museums, centered on the magnificent former royal palace and its expansive Jardin des Tuileries. Though the Louvre is on top of most visitors' to do lists, don't forget that there are also some wonderful smaller museums close by, and great shopping, too.

**Jardin des Tuileries** ★★ ☺ GARDEN   The spectacular statue-studded Jardin des Tuileries, bordering place de la Concorde, is as much a part of Paris as the Seine. Le Nôtre, Louis XIV's gardener and planner of the Versailles grounds, designed the gardens. Some of the gardens' most distinctive statues are the 18 enormous bronzes by Maillol, installed within the Jardin du Carrousel, a subdivision of the Jardin des Tuileries, between 1964 and 1965, under the direction of Culture Minister André Malraux.

About 400 years before that, Catherine de Médicis ordered a palace built here, the **Palais des Tuileries;** other occupants have included Louis XVI (after he left Versailles) and Napoleon. Twice attacked by Parisians, it was burned to the ground in 1871 and never rebuilt. The gardens, however, remain. In orderly French manner, the trees are arranged according to designs, and even the paths are arrow-straight. Bubbling fountains break the sense of order and formality.

Each summer, over the months of July and August, the parks hosts a traditional **funfair** (www.feteforaine-jardindestuileries.com) alongside the rue de Rivoli—be sure to take a Ferris wheel ride for excellent views.

Near place de la Concorde, 1er. 📞 **01-40-20-90-43.** Free admission. Daily Apr–May 7am–9pm; June–Aug 7am–11pm; Sept 7am–9pm; Oct–Mar 7:30am–7:30pm. Métro: Tuileries or Concorde.

Jardin des Tuileries.

# Paris's Top Attractions

1 Arc de Triomphe
2 Palais du Tokyo
3 Musée du Quai Branly
4 Eiffel Tower
5 Hôtel des Invalides/
   Napoleon's Tomb
6 Sacré-Coeur
7 Opéra Garnier
8 Jardin des Tuileries
9 Musée d'Orsay
10 Musée du Louvre
11 Église St-Germain-
   des-Pres
12 Jardin du Luxembourg
13 Sainte-Chapelle
14 Cathédrale de Notre-Dame
15 Centre Pompidou
16 Cimetière du Père-Lachaise

1/4 mi
0.25 km

**Jeu de Paume** ★★ MUSEUM   After knowing many roles, this museum, in the northeast corner of the Tuileries gardens, has become a national center for photography and video, exploring "the world of images, their uses, and the issues they raise" from the 19th to the 21st centuries. It is one of the finest museums of its type in the world, and presents ever-changing exhibitions, many of them daringly avant-garde.

Originally, in this part of the gardens, Napoleon III built a ball court on which *jeu de paume,* an antecedent of tennis, was played—hence the museum's name. The most infamous period in the gallery's history came during the Nazi occupation, when it served as an "evaluation center" for works of modern art. Paintings from all over France were shipped to the Jeu de Paume; art condemned by the Nazis as "degenerate" was burned.

1 place de la Concorde, 8e. www.jeudepaume.org. ℰ **01-47-03-12-50.** Admission 8.50€ adults, 5.50€ students and children. Tues noon–9pm; Wed–Fri noon–7pm; Sat–Sun 10am–7pm. Métro: Concorde.

**Musée de l'Orangerie** ★★ MUSEUM   In the Tuileries stands another gem among museums. It has an outstanding collection of art and one celebrated work on display: Claude Monet's exquisite *Nymphéas* (1915–27). The two galleries were purpose-built by the French state to house eight massive murals by Monet, in which water lilies float amorphously on the canvas. The paintings are displayed as the artist intended them to be: lit by sunlight in large oval galleries that evoke the shape of the garden ponds at his former Giverny estate.

Creating his effects with hundreds and hundreds of minute strokes of his brush (one irate 19th-c. critic called them "tongue lickings"), Monet achieved unity and harmony, as he did in his Rouen Cathedral series and his haystacks. Artists with lesser talent might have stirred up "soup." But Monet, of course, was

Monet's *Nympheas* at Musée de l'Orangerie.

# Les Halles, the Louvre & Palais Royal (1er & 2e)

**ATTRACTIONS**

Cour Napoléon & I.M. Pei Pyramid **11**
Jardin des Tuileries **6**
Jeu de Paume **1**
Musée de l'Orangerie **2**
Musée des Arts Décoratifs **7**
Musée du Louvre **12**
Palais Royale **10**

**HOTELS**

Hôtel de Vendôme **4**
Hôtel du Cygne **21**
Hôtel Meurice **5**
Hôtel Thérèse **8**
Park Hyatt Vendôme **3**

**RESTAURANTS**

Frenchie **20**
Higuma **9**
La Régolade-St.Honoré **16**
Le Fumoir **19**
Le Garde Robe **18**
Restaurant Chez Denise - La Tour de Monthéry **14**
Passage 53 **13**
Spring **17**
Yam'Tcha **15**

a genius. See his lilies and evoke for yourself the mood and melancholy as he experienced them so many years ago. Monet continued to paint his water landscapes right up until his death in 1926, although he was greatly hampered by failing eyesight.

The renovated building also houses the art collections of two men, John Walter and Paul Guillaume, who are not connected to each other, except that they were both married at different times to the same woman. Their collection includes more than 24 Renoirs, including *Young Girl at a Piano*. Cézanne is represented by 14 works, notably *The Red Rock,* and Matisse by 11 paintings. The highlight of Rousseau's nine works displayed here is *The Wedding,* and the dozen paintings by Picasso reach the pinnacle of their brilliance in *The Female Bathers.* Other outstanding paintings are by Utrillo (10 works in all), Soutine (22), and Derain (28).

It is possible to buy a joint ticket to both the Musée d'Orsay (p. 128) and the Musée de l'Orangerie, which is valid for 4 days and costs 14€.

Jardin des Tuileries, 1er. www.musee-orangerie.fr. ✆ **01-44-77-80-07.** Admission 7.50€ adults, 5€ students 25 and younger. Free 1st Sun of every month. Wed–Mon 9am–6pm. Métro: Concorde.

**Musée des Arts Décoratifs ★★** MUSEUM   In the northwest wing of the Louvre's Pavillon de Marsan, this imposing museum is home to a treasury of furnishings, fabrics, wallpaper, objets d'art, and items displaying living styles from the Middle Ages to the present. Notable are the 1920s Art Deco boudoir, bath, and bedroom done for couturier Jeanne Lanvin by the designer Rateau, plus a collection of the works donated by Jean Dubuffet. Decorative art from the Middle Ages to the Renaissance is on the second floor; collections from the 17th, 18th, and 19th centuries occupy the third and fourth floors. The fifth floor has specialized centers, such as wallpaper and drawings, and exhibits detailing fashion, textiles, toys, crafts, and glass trends. The space also includes a lovely ground-floor shop, **107Rivoli** (p. 162), selling all sorts of craft pieces, and a restaurant, Le Saut du Loup, which boasts an outdoor eating area in the Tuileries Gardens.

Palais du Louvre, 107 rue de Rivoli, 1er. www.lesartsdecoratifs.fr. ✆ **01-44-55-57-50.** Admission 9.50€ adults, 8€ ages 18–25, free for children 17 and younger. Tues–Wed, Fri 11am–6pm; Thurs 11am–6pm; Sat–Sun 10am–6pm. Métro: Palais-Royal or Tuileries.

**Musée du Louvre ★★★** MUSEUM   The Louvre is the world's largest palace and museum, and it houses one of the greatest art collections ever. To enter, pass through I. M. Pei's controversial 21m (69-ft.) **glass pyramid ★**—a startling

### Leaping Over the Louvre Line

If you don't want to wait in line for tickets to the Louvre, you can order tickets in advance by visiting **http://louvre. fnacspectacles.com** or calling ✆ **08-92-68-46-94;** tickets can be mailed to you, or you can pick them up at any Paris branch of the FNAC electronics chain. You can also order advance tickets and take a virtual tour at **www.louvre.fr**. Note that the Louvre is open until 10pm on Wednesday and Fridays—usually a quiet time to visit.

**THE PYRAMID**

**The Louvre**

to Richelieu

audiovisual rooms

restaurants cafes

to Carrousel, Hall Charles V, parking, Métro

auditorium

*Hall Napoléon*

(i)

to Sully

bookshop boutique

guided visits workshops "Accueil des groupes"

to Denon

**THE WINGS**

rue de Rivoli

**Marly Horses** (ground floor)

**Richelieu**

**The Pyramid**

*cour Napoléon*

**Sully**

*cour Carrée*

**Denon**

*Venus de Milo* (ground floor)

*Mona Lisa* (first floor)

*Winged Victory* (first floor)

though effective contrast of the ultramodern against the palace's classical lines. Commissioned by the late president François Mitterrand and completed in 1989, it allows sunlight to shine on an underground reception area with a complex of shops and restaurants.

People on one of those "Paris-in-a-day" tours try to break track records to get a glimpse of the Louvre's two most famous ladies: the beguiling ***Mona Lisa*** and the armless ***Venus de Milo*** ★★★. The herd then dashes on a 5-minute stampede in pursuit of ***Winged Victory*** ★★★, the headless statue discovered at Samothrace and dating from about 200 B.C. In defiance of the assembly line theory of art, we head instead for David's ***Coronation of Napoleon,*** showing Napoleon poised with the crown aloft as Joséphine kneels before him, just across from his ***Portrait of Madame Récamier*** ★, depicting Napoleon's opponent at age 23; she reclines on her sofa agelessly in the style of classical antiquity.

Then a big question looms: Which of the rest of the 30,000 works on display would you like to see?

Between the Seine and rue de Rivoli, the Palais du Louvre suffers from an embarrassment of riches, stretching for almost 1km (½ mile). In the days of Charles V, it was a fortress, but François I, a patron of Leonardo da Vinci, had it torn down and rebuilt as a royal residence. Less than a month after Marie Antoinette's head and body parted company, the Revolutionary Committee decided

**Musée du Louvre.**

the king's collection of paintings and sculpture should be opened to the public. At the lowest point in its history, in the 18th century, the Louvre was home for anybody who wanted to set up housekeeping. Laundry hung in the windows, corners were pigpens, and families built fires to cook their meals in winter. Napoleon ended all that, chasing out the squatters and restoring the palace. In fact, he chose the Louvre as the site of his wedding to Marie-Louise.

So where did all these paintings come from? The kings of France, notably François I and Louis XIV, acquired many of them, and others were willed to or purchased by the state. Many contributed by Napoleon were taken from reluctant donors: The church was one especially heavy and unwilling giver. Much of Napoleon's plunder had to be returned, though France hasn't yet seen its way clear to giving back all the booty.

The collections are divided into seven departments: Egyptian Antiquities; Oriental Antiquities; Greek, Etruscan, and Roman Antiquities; Sculpture; Painting; Decorative Arts; and Graphic Arts. If you don't have to do Paris in a day, you might want to visit several times, concentrating on different collections or schools of painting. Those with little time should take a guided tour.

Acquired by François I to hang above his bathtub, Leonardo's **La Gioconda (Mona Lisa)** ★★★ has been the source of legend for centuries. Note the guard and bulletproof glass: The world's most famous painting was stolen in 1911 then found in Florence in 1913. At first, both the poet Guillaume Apollinaire and Picasso were suspected, but it was discovered in the possession of a former Louvre employee, who'd apparently carried it out under his overcoat. Two centuries after its arrival at the Louvre, the *Mona Lisa* in 2003 was assigned a new gallery of her own. Less well known (but to us even more enchanting) are Leonardo's **Virgin and Child with St. Anne** ★ and the **Virgin of the Rocks.**

After paying your respects to the "smiling one," allow time to see some French works stretching from the Richelieu wing through the entire **Sully wing** and even overflowing into the **Denon wing.** It's all here: Watteau's *Gilles* with the mysterious boy in a clown suit staring at you; Fragonard's and Boucher's rococo renderings of the aristocracy; and the greatest masterpieces of David, including his stellar 1785 *The Oath of the Horatii* and the vast and vivid *Coronation of Napoleon.* Only Florence's Uffizi rivals the Denon wing for its Italian Renaissance collection—everything from Raphael's *Portrait of Balthazar Castiglione* to Titian's *Man with a Glove.* Veronese's gigantic *Wedding Feast at Cana* ★, a romp of Venetian high society in the 1500s, occupies an entire wall (that's Paolo himself playing the cello).

Of the Greek and Roman antiquities, the most notable collections, aside from the *Venus de Milo* and *Winged Victory,* are fragments of a **Parthenon frieze** (in the Denon wing). In Renaissance sculpture, you'll see Michelangelo's *Esclaves (Slaves),* originally intended for the tomb of Julius II but sold into other bondage. The Denon wing houses masterpieces such as Ingres's *The Turkish Bath,* the **Botticelli frescoes** from the Villa Lemmi, Raphael's *La Belle Jardinière,* and Titian's *Open Air Concert.* The Sully wing is also filled with old masters, such as Boucher's *Diana Resting After Her Bath* and Fragonard's *Bathers.*

The **Richelieu wing ★★★** houses northern European and French paintings, along with decorative arts, sculpture, Oriental antiquities (including a rich collection of both Islamic and Far Eastern Art), and the Napoleon III salons. One of its galleries displays 21 works that Rubens painted in a space of only 2 years for Marie de Médicis's Palais de Luxembourg. The masterpieces here include Dürer's *Self-Portrait,* van Dyck's *Portrait of Charles I of England,* and Holbein the Younger's *Portrait of Erasmus of Rotterdam.*

When you tire of strolling the galleries, you may like a pick-me-up at the Richelieu Wing's **Café Richelieu** (℃ **01-47-03-99-68**) or, under the arcades and overlooking Pei's pyramid, at **Café Marly,** 93 rue de Rivoli, 1er (℃ **01-49-26-06-60**). Boasting Napoleon III opulence, the Marly is a perfect oasis. Try a cafe crème, a club sandwich, a pastry, or something from the bistro menu.

34–36 quai du Louvre, 1er. Main entrance in the glass pyramid, Cour Napoléon. www.louvre.fr. ℃ **01-40-20-53-17,** 01-40-20-50-50 for operator, or 08-92-68-46-94 for advance credit card sales. Admission 10€, children 17 and younger free, free to all 1st Sun of every month. Sat–Mon and

---

## Contemporary Art & the Louvre

With all those centuries-old masterpieces grabbing the spotlight, the museum's contemporary works can get overlooked—but they're worth seeking out. In 2010, the museum unveiled a painted ceiling in the Salle des Bronzes by American artist Cy Twombly, the third contemporary artist who was commissioned to install a permanent work at the Louvre.

(He was preceded by contemporary artists Anselm Kiefer and François Morellet.) Twombly's painting appears on the ceiling of one of the Louvre's largest galleries, and it covers more than 350 sq. m (3,770 sq. ft.). The ceiling depicts an immense blue sky that is dotted with spheres and white insets inscribed with the names of famous Greek sculptors.

Thurs 9am–6pm; Wed and Fri 9am–10pm. 1½-hr. English-language tours (Mon and Wed–Sun) 9€, 6€ children 12 and younger with museum ticket. Métro: Palais-Royal–Musée du Louvre.

**Palais Royal ★★** HISTORIC SITE/GARDEN    The Palais Royal was origi-nally known as the Palais Cardinal, for it was the residence of Cardinal Riche-lieu, Louis XIII's prime minister. Richelieu had it built, and after his death it was inherited by the king, who died soon after. Louis XIV spent part of his childhood here with his mother, Anne of Austria, but later resided at the Louvre and Ver-sailles. The palace was later owned by the duc de Chartres et Orléans, who encouraged the opening of cafes, gambling dens, and other public entertain-ment. Today the building is occupied by the French Culture Ministry.

The lovely **Jardin du Palais Royal** is at the center of the arcaded former palace, and features a fountain and gardens. Don't miss the main courtyard, close to the rue St Honoré, with the controversial 1986 Buren sculpture—280 prison-striped columns, oddly placed. The arcades of the Palais Royal have become a high fashion destination over the last few years, with high-end boutiques such as Marc Jacobs and Stella McCartney.

Rue St-Honoré, 1er. No phone. Free admission. Gardens daily 7:30am–dusk. Métro: Palais Royal–Musée du Louvre.

# LE MARAIS, ILE ST-LOUIS & ILE DE LA CITÉ (3E & 4E)

This historic neighborhood, home to royalty and aristocracy in the 17th and 18th centuries, preserves exceptional architecture—some of it dating back to the Renaissance. Its narrow, winding streets are from another age. While it features some blockbuster attractions, including the **Hôtel de Ville** and the **Centre Pompidou,** the Marais is notable for its density of charming smaller museums, where you hopefully won't be fighting through crowds. The two islands in the Seine, Ile St-Louis and Ile de la Cité, set the stage for some impressive medieval monuments, the **Cathédrale de Notre-Dame,** the **Conciergerie,** and the glo-rious **Sainte-Chapelle.**

**Cathédrale de Notre-Dame ★★** CATHEDRAL    Notre-Dame is the heart of Paris and even of the country itself: Distances from the city to all parts of France are calculated from a spot at the far end of place du Parvis, in front of the cathedral, where a circular bronze plaque marks **Kilomètre Zéro.**

The cathedral's setting on the banks of the Seine has always been memo-rable. Founded in the 12th century by Maurice de Sully, bishop of Paris, Notre-Dame has grown over the years, changing as Paris has changed; often fall-ing victim to whims of taste. Its flying buttresses (the external side supports, giving the massive interior a sense of weightlessness) were rebuilt in 1330. Though many disagree, we feel Notre-Dame is more interesting outside than in, and you'll want to walk all around it to fully appreciate this "vast symphony of stone." Better yet, cross over the Pont au Double to the Left Bank and view it from the quai.

The histories of Paris and Notre-Dame are inseparable. Many prayed here before going off to fight in the Crusades. The revolutionaries who destroyed the Galerie des Rois and converted the building into a secular temple didn't spare "Our Lady of Paris." Later, Napoleon crowned himself emperor here, yanking the crown out of Pius VII's hands and placing it on his own head before crowning his Joséphine empress (see David's *Coronation of Napoléon* in the Louvre). But

# Marais, Ile St-Louis & Ile de la Cité (3e & 4e)

Pedestrians only
Ⓜ Métro station
ℝℰℝ RER station
✉ Post office

98

Cathédrale de Notre-Dame.

carelessness, vandalism, embellishments, and wars of religion had already demolished much of the previously existing structure.

The cathedral was once scheduled for demolition, but because of the popularity of Victor Hugo's *Hunchback of Notre-Dame* and the revival of interest in the Gothic period, a movement mushroomed to restore the cathedral to its original glory. The task was completed under Viollet-le-Duc, an architectural genius. The houses of old Paris used to crowd in on Notre-Dame, but during his redesign of the city, Baron Haussmann ordered them torn down to show the cathedral to its best advantage from the parvis. This is the best vantage for seeing the three sculpted 13th-century portals (the Virgin, the Last Judgment, and St. Anne).

On the left, the **Portal of the Virgin** depicts the signs of the zodiac and the coronation of the Virgin, an association found in dozens of medieval churches. The restored central **Portal of the Last Judgment** depicts three levels: the first shows Vices and Virtues; the second, Christ and his Apostles; and above that, Christ in triumph after the Resurrection. The portal is a close illustration of the Gospel according to Matthew. Over it is the remarkable **west rose window ★★**, 9.5m (31 ft.) wide, forming a showcase for a statue of the Virgin and Child. On the far right is the **Portal of St. Anne,** depicting scenes such as the Virgin enthroned with Child; it's Notre-Dame's best-preserved and most perfect piece of sculpture. Equally interesting (though often missed) is the **Portal**

## Pont Neuf

Don't miss the ironically named **Pont Neuf (New Bridge)** at the tip of the Ile de la Cité, opposite from Notre-Dame. The span isn't new—it's Paris's oldest bridge, begun in 1578 and finished in 1604. In its day, it had two unique features: It was paved, and it wasn't flanked with houses and shops. Actually, with 12 arches, it's not one bridge but two (they don't quite line up)—one from the Right Bank to the island and the other from the Left Bank to the island. At the **Musée Carnavalet** (p. 103), a painting called *The Spectacle of Buffoons* shows what the bridge was like between 1665 and 1669. Duels were fought on it, the nobility's great coaches crossed it, peddlers sold their wares, and entertainers such as Tabarin went there to seek a few coins from the gawkers. As public facilities were lacking, the bridge also served as a *de facto* outhouse.

# Notre-Dame de Paris

- Statue of Louis XIV
- Statue of Louis XIII
- Ambulatory
- Pietà
- High Altar
- Choir
- To Treasury
- Virgin & Child (13th cent.)
- Statue of St. Denis
- Virgin & Child (14th cent.)
- Portal of the Cloisters
- North Transept
- Crossing
- South Transept
- Portal of St. Stephen
- North Rose Window
- South Rose Window
- North Aisle
- Nave
- South Aisle
- Entrance to the Towers
- West Rose Window
- Portal of the Virgin
- Portal of the Last Judgment
- Portal of St. Anne

of the Cloisters (around on the left), with its dour-faced 13th-century Virgin, a survivor among the figures that originally adorned the facade. (Alas, the Child she's holding has been decapitated.) Finally, on the Seine side of Notre-Dame, the **Portal of St. Stephen** traces that saint's martyrdom.

If possible, see Notre-Dame at sunset. Inside of the three giant medallions warming the austere cathedral, the **north rose window** ★★ in the transept, from the mid–13th century, is best. The main body of the church is typically Gothic, with slender, graceful columns. In the **choir,** a stone-carved screen from the early–14th century depicts such biblical scenes as the Last Supper. Near the altar stands the 14th-century ***Virgin and Child*** ★, highly venerated among Paris's faithful. In the **treasury** are displayed vestments and gold objects, including crowns. Exhibited is a cross presented to Haile Selassie, former emperor of Ethiopia, and a reliquary given by Napoleon. Notre-Dame is especially proud of its relics of the True Cross and the Crown of Thorns.

To visit the **gargoyles** ★★ immortalized by Hugo, you have to scale steps leading to the twin **towers,** rising to a height of 68m (223 ft.). When there, you can inspect devils, hobgoblins, and birds of prey. Look carefully, and you may see hunchback Quasimodo with Esmeralda.

Approached through a garden behind Notre-Dame is the **Mémorial des Martyrs Français de la Déportation de 1945 (Deportation Memorial),** out on the tip of Ile de la Cité. Here, birds chirp and the Seine flows gently by, but the memories are far from pleasant. The memorial commemorates the French citizens who were deported to concentration camps during World War II. Carved into stone are these blood-red words (in French): "Forgive, but don't forget." The memorial is open Monday to Friday 8:30am to 9:45pm, and Saturday to Sunday 9am to 9:45pm. Admission is free.

6 place du Parvis Notre-Dame, 4e. www.notredamedeparis.fr. ℭ **01-53-10-07-02.** Admission free to cathedral. Towers 8.50€ adults, 5€ seniors and ages 13–25, free for children 12 and younger. Treasury 3€ adults, 2.20€ seniors, 1.60€ ages 13–25, free for children 12 and younger. Cathedral year-round daily 8am–6:45pm (Sat–Sun 7:15pm). Towers and crypt daily 10am–6pm

(until 11pm Sat–Sun June–Aug). Museum Wed and Sat–Sun 2–5pm. Treasury Mon–Fri 9:30am–6pm; Sat 9:30am–6:30pm; Sun 1:30–6:30pm. Métro: Cité or St-Michel. RER: St-Michel.

**Centre Pompidou ★★★ ☺** MUSEUM   When it first opened in the 1970s, the Centre Pompidou was hailed as "the most avant-garde building in the world," and today it still continues to pack in the art-loving crowds—about six million people visit it each year.

Conceived by former French president Georges Pompidou and designed by architects Renzo Piano and Richard Rogers, this building originally opened in 1977, and it underwent a major renovation in 2000, which expanded and improved the space. The building's exterior is very bold: brightly painted pipes and ducts crisscross its transparent facade (green for water, red for heat, blue for air, and yellow for electricity), and an outdoor escalator flanks the building, freeing up interior space for exhibitions.

Inside, the big attraction is the impressive **Musée National d'Art Moderne (National Museum of Modern Art) ★★**, which is home to some 40,000 works from the 20th and 21st centuries—though only about 850 works can be displayed at one time. If you want to view some real charmers, seek out Calder's 1926 *Josephine Baker,* one of his earlier versions of the mobile, an art form he invented. You'll also find two examples of Duchamps's series of Dada-style sculptures he invented in 1936: *Boîte en Valise* (1941) and *Boîte en Valise* (1968). And every time we visit, we have to see Dalí's *Hallucination partielle: Six images de Lénine sur un piano* (1931), with Lenin dancing on a piano. A new gallery, the Espace 315, is dedicated to exhibitions by a younger generation of international artists. A dedicated area for children **La Galerie des Enfants** on the mezzanine hosts great interactive artist-conceived projects for kids.

Other attractions inside the Centre Pompidou include: the **Bibliothéque Publique d'Information (Public Information Library),** a vast public library with a huge collection of French and foreign books, periodicals, films, music records, slides, and more; the **Institut de Recherche et de Coordination Acoustique-Musique (Institute for Research and Coordination of Acoustics/Music),** which brings together musicians and composers; and the **Atelier Brancusi ★**, a minimuseum that re-creates the Jazz Age studio of Romanian sculptor Brancusi. There are also a movie theater, performance halls that often host concerts and events, shops, and restaurants. The Centre Pompidou holds regularly changing public exhibitions and events, so check their website for information.

Outside, there is a large open **forecourt,** which is a free "entertainment center" often featuring mimes, fire-eaters, circus performers, and sometimes musicians. Here you can admire a monumental sculpture by Alexander Calder. Dating from 1974 and made in France, the piece *Horizontal* is one of Calder's last *stabiles-mobiles.* And don't miss the nearby **Stravinsky fountain,** containing mobile sculptures by Tinguely and Niki de Saint Phalle.

Place Georges-Pompidou, 4e. www.centrepompidou.fr. ℰ **01-44-78-12-33.** Admission 11€–13€ adults, students 9€–10€ students, free for children 17 and younger; admission varies depending on exhibits. Wed–Mon 11am–10pm. Métro: Rambuteau, Hôtel de Ville, or Châtelet–Les Halles.

**Conciergerie** ★★ HISTORIC SITE   London has its Bloody Tower, and Paris has its Conciergerie. Even though the Conciergerie had a long regal history before the French Revolution, it was forever stained by the Reign of Terror and lives as an infamous symbol of the time when carts pulled up constantly to haul off fresh supplies of victims of Dr. Guillotin's wonderful little invention.

Much of the Conciergerie was built in the 14th century as an extension of the Capetian royal Palais de la Cité. You approach through its landmark twin towers, the **Tour d'Argent** (where the crown jewels were stored at one time) and **Tour de César,** but the **Salle des Gardes (Guard Room)** is the actual entrance. Even more interesting is the dark and foreboding Gothic **Salle des Gens d'Armes (Room of People at Arms),** utterly changed from the days when the king used it as a banquet hall. However, architecture plays a secondary role to the list of prisoners who spent their last days here. Few in its history endured tortures as severe as those imposed on Ravaillac, who assassinated Henri IV in 1610. In the Tour de César, he received pincers in the flesh and had hot lead and boiling oil poured on him like bath water before being executed. During the revolution, the Conciergerie became a symbol of terror to the nobility and enemies of the State. A short walk away, the Revolutionary Tribunal dispensed a skewed, hurried justice—if it's any consolation, the jurists didn't believe in torturing their victims, only in decapitating them.

After being seized by a crowd of peasants who stormed Versailles, Louis XVI and Marie Antoinette were brought here to await their trials. In failing health and shocked beyond grief, *l'Autrichienne* ("the Austrian," as she was called with malice) had only a small screen (sometimes not even that) to protect her modesty

Conciergerie.

from the gaze of guards stationed in her cell. By accounts of the day, she was shy and stupid, though the evidence is that on her death, she displayed the nobility of a true queen. (What's more, the famous "Let them eat cake," which she supposedly uttered when told the peasants had no bread, is probably apocryphal—besides, at the time, cake flour was less expensive than bread flour, so even if she said this, it wasn't meant coldheartedly.) It was shortly before noon on the morning of October 16, 1793, when the executioners arrived, grabbing her and cutting her hair, as was the custom for victims marked for the guillotine.

Later, the Conciergerie housed other prisoners, including Mme Elisabeth; Mme du Barry, mistress of Louis XV; Mme Roland ("O Liberty! Liberty! What crimes are committed in thy name!"); and Charlotte Corday, who killed Marat while he was taking a sulfur bath. In time, the revolution consumed its own leaders, such as Danton and Robespierre. Finally, one of Paris's most hated men, public prosecutor Fouquier-Tinville, faced the guillotine to which he'd sent so many others. Among the few interned here who lived to tell the tale was American Thomas Paine, who reminisced about his chats in English with Danton.

1 quai de l'Horloge, 4e. www.monum.fr. (**01-53-40-60-80.** Admission 8.50€ adults, 5.50€ ages 18–25, free for children 17 and younger. Mar–Oct daily 9:30–6pm; Nov–Feb daily 9am–5pm. Métro: Cité, Châtelet, or St-Michel. RER: St-Michel.

**Musée Carnavalet-Histoire de Paris** ★★ ☺ MUSEUM   If you enjoy history, but history tomes bore you, spend some time here for insight into Paris's past, which comes alive in such details as the chessmen Louis XVI used to distract himself while waiting to go to the guillotine. The comprehensive and lifelike exhibits are great for kids. The building, a Renaissance palace, was built in 1544 and later acquired by Mme de Carnavalet. François Mansart transformed it between 1655 and 1661.

The palace is best known for one of history's most famous letter writers, Mme de Sévigné, who moved here in 1677. Fanatically devoted to her daughter (she moved in with her because she couldn't bear to be apart), she poured out nearly every detail of her life in her letters, virtually ignoring her son. A native of the Marais district, she died at her daughter's château in 1696. In 1866, the city of Paris acquired the mansion and turned it into a museum. Several salons cover the Revolution, with a bust of Marat, a portrait of Danton, and a model of the Bastille (one painting shows its demolition). Another salon tells the story of the captivity of the royal family at the Conciergerie, displaying the bed in which Mme Elisabeth (the sister of Louis XVI) slept and the Dauphin's exercise book.

Exhibits continue at the **Hôtel le Peletier de St-Fargeau,** across the courtyard. On display is furniture from the Louis XIV period to the early 20th century, including a replica of Marcel Proust's cork-lined bedroom with his actual furniture, including his brass bed. This section also exhibits artifacts from the museum's archaeological collection, including some Neolithic pirogues, shallow oak boats used for fishing and transport from about 4400 to 2200 B.C.

23 rue de Sévigné, 3e. www.carnavalet.paris.fr. (**01-44-59-58-58.** Free admission. Special exhibits from 5€ adults, 4.20€ students and children. Tues–Sun 10am–6pm. Métro: St-Paul or Chemin Vert.

**Place des Vosges** ★★ ☺ SQUARE   The exquisite place des Vosges was built by Henri IV and inaugurated in 1612 to celebrate the wedding of Louis XIII

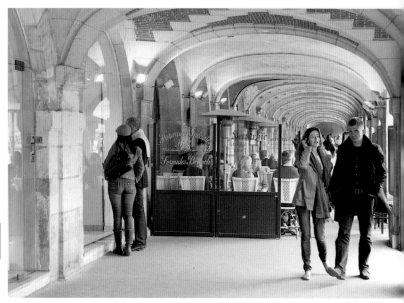

**Place des Vosges.**

to Anne of Austria. It is Paris's oldest planned square and is in the heart of the Marais, actually marking the division between the 3rd and 4th arrondissements. Lined with large buildings of red brick and blue-tiled roofs, the square was previously named "place Royale" under the reign of Henri IV, then "place des Fédérés," "place de la Fabrication-des-Armes," and "place de l'Indivisibilité" during the French Revolution. It was only in 1800 that it was given the name it has today, in honor of the French department the Vosges. Adorned with linden trees, water fountains, and an equestrian statue of Louis XIII, it makes a charming spot for a picnic *en famille.* There's free Wi-Fi here too.

4e. Métro: St-Paul.

**Sainte-Chapelle ★★★ CHURCH**   Countless writers have called this tiny chapel a jewel box, yet that hardly suffices. Go when the sun is shining, and you'll need no one else's words to describe the remarkable effects of natural light on Sainte-Chapelle. You approach the church through the cour de la Sainte-Chapelle of the Palais de Justice.

Begun in 1246, the bi-level chapel was built to house relics of the True Cross, including the Crown of Thorns acquired by St. Louis (the Crusader King, Louis IX) from the emperor of Constantinople. (In those days, cathedrals throughout Europe were busy acquiring relics for their treasuries, regardless of their authenticity. It was a seller's, perhaps a sucker's, market.) Louis IX is said to have paid heavily for his relics, raising the money through unscrupulous means. He died of the plague on a crusade and was canonized in 1297.

You enter through the ***chapelle basse* (lower chapel),** used by the palace servants; it's supported by flying buttresses and ornamented with fleur-de-lis designs. The king and his courtiers used the ***chapelle haute* (upper chapel),** one of the greatest achievements of Gothic art; you reach it by ascending a narrow spiral staircase. On a bright day, the 15 stained-glass windows seem to glow with Chartres blue and wine-colored reds. The walls consist almost entirely of the glass, 612 sq. m (6,588 sq. ft.) of it, which had to be removed for safekeeping during the revolution and again during both world wars. In the windows' Old and New Testament designs are embodied the hopes and dreams (and the pretensions) of the kings who ordered their construction. The 1,134 scenes depict the Christian story from the Garden of Eden through the Apocalypse; you read them from bottom to top and from left to right. The great rose window depicts the Apocalypse.

Sainte-Chapelle stages **concerts** from March to November, daily at 7 and 8:30pm; tickets cost 19€ to 25€. Call ✆ **01-44-07-12-38** from 11am to 6pm daily for details.

Palais de Justice, 4 bd. du Palais, 4e. www.monum.fr. ✆ **01-53-40-60-80.** 8.50€ adults, 5.50€ ages 18–25, free 17 and younger. Mar–Oct daily 9:30am–6pm; Nov–Feb daily 9am–5pm. Métro: Cité, St-Michel, or Châtelet–Les Halles. RER: St-Michel.

## CHAMPS-ÉLYSÉES & WESTERN PARIS (8E, 16E & 17E)

Money and power dominate this neighborhood and its emblematic avenue, the Champs-Élysées. There is also a wealth of exceptional museums here from **Musée d'art Moderne,** a testament to Paris's Modernist glory days, to the **Palais de Tokyo,** a pioneering contemporary art space.

**Arc de Triomphe ★★** MONUMENT  At the western end of the Champs-Élysées, the Arc de Triomphe suggests an ancient Roman arch, only it's larger. Actually, it's the biggest triumphal arch in the world, about 49m (161 ft.) high and 44m (144 ft.) wide. To reach it, *don't try to cross the square,* Paris's busiest traffic hub. With a dozen streets radiating from the "Star," the roundabout has been called by one writer "vehicular roulette with more balls than numbers," death is certain! Take the underground passage, and live a little longer.

Commissioned by Napoleon in 1806 to commemorate the victories of his Grand Armée, the arch wasn't ready for the entrance of his empress, Marie-Louise, in 1810 (he divorced Joséphine because she couldn't provide him an heir). It wasn't completed until 1836, under the reign of Louis-Philippe. Four years later, Napoleon's remains, brought from St. Helena, passed under the arch on their journey to his tomb at the Hôtel des Invalides. Since then, it has become the focal point for state funerals. It's also the site of the tomb of the Unknown Soldier, in whose honor an eternal flame burns.

**Arc de Triomphe.**

# The Champs-Élysées &
# Western Paris (8e, 16e & 17e)

bd. Maurice Barrès

Les Sablons **M**

Palais des
Congrès
de Paris

**4** **17e**

*Jardin
d'Acclimatation*

bd. Maillot

Porte Maillot

place de la
Porte Maillot

pl. Saint-
Ferdinand

des

Ternes

**1**

route de la Porte des Sablons à la Porte Maillot

**M**

av.

**Musée National
des Arts et
Traditions
Populaires**

Longchamp

Porte
Maillot

**M**

Grande Armée

av.

**M**

Argentine

Charles de

**5**

**6**

bd. Périphérique

bd. de l'Amiral Bruix

de

Malakoff

Piccini

le Sueur

**RER** Gaulle-
Étoile

de

*allée*

**Arc de
Triomphe** **7**

Foch

place Charles
de Gaulle

BOIS DE
BOULOGNE

**2**

Porte Dauphine

*place du
Mal. de Lattre
de Tassigny*

**M** Porte Dauphine

Paul

av. Victor Hugo

Kléber

de Presbourg

route de Suresnes

**RER**
Avenue Foch

av. Bugeaud

**M** Victor Hugo

Copernic

pl. des
États
Unis

Lannes

Avenue Foch
**RER**

place Jean
Monnet

Raymond
Poincaré

Boissière

**M** Boissière

**16e**

**3** St-Didier

Kléber

Longchamp

pl. d'Iéna

**14**

**M**

**15**

Porte de la Muette

*place de
Colombie*

square
Lamartine

Henri Martin

Georges Mandel

pl. de
Trocadéro
et du 11 Novembre

**M** Trocadéro

**Palais de Chaillot**

av. Albert de Mun

To Stade Roland Garros

*Jardin
du
Ranelagh*

chausée de la
Muette

La Muette

**M** **RER**

Boulainvilliers

**M**

Cimetière
de Passy

av. Paul Doumer

*Jardins du
Trocadéro*

place de
Varsovie

**13**

**Tour
Eiffel**

quai Branly

La Muette

place
d'Andorre

place
Chopin

place de
Costa Rica

sq.
Alboni

**M**
Passy

Champ de Mars-
Tour Eiffel
**RER**

av. de Suffren

Ranelagh

**M**

parc de
Passy

pont de Bir
Hakeim

Bir-Hakeim

**M**

r. Jean Rey

**15e**

l'Assomption

av. de Lamballe

quai de Grenelle

bd. de Grenelle

Jasmin

Av. du Prest. Kennedy
Maison de Radio-France

**RER**

square
Bela Bartok

place
Dupleix

| 0 | | 1/4 mi |
|---|---|---|
| 0 | 0.25 km | |

The greatest state funeral was Victor Hugo's in 1885; his coffin was placed under the arch, and much of Paris came to pay tribute. Another notable funeral was in 1929 for Ferdinand Foch, commander of the Allied forces in World War I. The arch has been the centerpiece of some of France's proudest moments and some of its most humiliating defeats, notably in 1871 and 1940. The memory of German troops marching under the arch is still painful to the French. Who can forget the 1940 newsreel of the Frenchman standing on the Champs-Élysées weeping as the Nazi storm troopers goose-stepped through Paris? The arch's happiest moment occurred in 1944, when the liberation-of-Paris parade passed beneath it. That same year, Eisenhower paid a visit to the tomb of the Unknown Soldier, a new tradition among leaders of state and important figures. After Charles de Gaulle's death, the French government (despite protests from anti-Gaullists) voted to change the name of this site from place de l'Etoile to place Charles de Gaulle. Today it's often known as place Charles de Gaulle–Etoile.

Of the sculptures on the monument, the best known is Rude's *Marseillaise,* or *The Departure of the Volunteers.* J. P. Cortot's *Triumph of Napoléon in 1810* and Etex's *Resistance of 1814* and *Peace of 1815* also adorn the facade. The monument is engraved with the names of hundreds of generals (those underlined died in battle) who commanded French troops in Napoleonic victories.

You can take an elevator or climb the stairway to the top, where there's an exhibition hall with lithographs and photos depicting the arch throughout its history, as well as an observation deck with an exceptional view.

Place Charles de Gaulle–Etoile, 8e. www.monum.fr. ℂ **01-55-37-73-77.** Admission 9.50€ adults, 6€ for those 18–24. Apr–Sept daily 10am–11pm; Oct–Mar daily 10am–10:30pm. Métro: Charles-de-Gaulle–Etoile. Bus: 22, 30, 31, 52, 73, or 92.

**Bois de Boulogne ★★ ☺ PARK**   One of the most spectacular parks in Europe is the **Bois de Boulogne,** often called the "main lung" of Paris. Horse-drawn carriages traverse it, but you can also drive through. You can discover its hidden pathways, however, only by walking. You could spend days in the Bois de Boulogne and still not see everything.

Porte Dauphine is the main entrance, though you can take the Métro to Porte Maillot as well. West of Paris, the park was once a forest kept for royal hunts. It was in vogue in the late 19th century: Along avenue Foch, carriages with elegantly attired and coiffured Parisian damsels would rumble along with their foppish escorts. Nowadays, it's more likely to attract run-of-the-mill picnickers. (Be careful at night, when hookers and muggers proliferate.)

When Napoleon III gave the grounds to the city in 1852, they were developed by Baron Haussmann. Separating Lac Inférieur from Lac Supérieur is the **Carrefour des Cascades ★** (you can stroll under its waterfall). The Lower Lake contains two islands connected by a footbridge. From the east bank, you can take a boat to these idyllically situated grounds, perhaps stopping off at the cafe/restaurant on one of them.

Restaurants in the *bois* are numerous, elegant, and expensive. The **Pré Catelan ★** contains a deluxe restaurant of the same name (www.precatelan paris.com; ℂ **01-44-14-41-00**), occupying a gem of a Napoleon III–style château, and also a Shakespearean theater in a garden planted with trees mentioned in the bard's plays. Nearby is **La Grande Cascade** (ℂ **01-45-27-33-51**), once a hunting lodge for Napoleon III.

Jardin d'Acclimatation (www.jardindacclimatation.fr; *℃* **01-40-67-90-82**), at the northern edge of the park, is for children, with a zoo, an amusement park, and a narrow-gauge railway (see listing below for more information).

Two racetracks, the **Hippodrome de Longchamp ★★★** and the **Hippodrome d'Auteuil,** are in the park. The Grand Prix is run in June at Longchamp (the site of a medieval abbey). Fashionable Parisians always turn out for this, the women in their finest haute couture. To the north of Longchamp is the **Grand Cascade,** an artificial waterfall.

In the western section of the *bois,* the 24-hectare (59-acre) **Parc de Bagatelle ★** (*℃* **01-43-28-47-63**) owes its existence to a bet between the comte d'Artois (later Charles X) and Marie Antoinette, his sister-in-law. The comte wagered he could erect a small palace in less than 3 months, so he hired nearly 1,000 craftsmen (cabinetmakers, painters, Scottish landscape architect Thomas Blaikie, and others) and irritated the locals by requisitioning all shipments of stone and plaster arriving through Paris's west gates. He won his bet. If you're here in late April, it's worth visiting the Bagatelle just for the tulips. In late May, one of the finest rose collections in Europe is in full bloom.

16e. Métro: Porte d'Auteuil, Les Sablons, Porte Maillot, or Porte Dauphine.

**Grand Palais ★★** HISTORIC SITE    Built for the 1900 Universal Exhibition, this giant exhibition hall spans a total area of 72,000 sq. m (775,000 sq. ft.), with the biggest glass roof in Europe—an elegant lighting solution, since the building was constructed prior to electricity. After years of renovations, the Grand Palais reopened in 2007, and today it hosts a changing array of sporting and cultural events, including FIAC (Paris's annual contemporary art fair), "Monumenta" (an annual event which commissions and displays an original monumental work by a contemporary artist in the Grand Palais' nave), the Hermès horse jumping competition, and fashion shows; check their website for events. The Grand Palais faces the Petit Palais.

1 avenue Géneral Eisenhower, 8e. www. grandpalais.fr. *℃* **01-44-13-17-17.** Opening hours and admission prices vary according to the exhibitions and events. Métro: Champs-Élysées Clémenceau.

**Jardin d'Acclimatation ★ ☺**
AMUSEMENT PARK/GARDEN
This 20-hectare (49-acre) children's park in the northern part of the Bois de Boulogne is the kind of place that amuses tykes and adults but not teenagers. The visit starts with a ride on a narrow-gauge train from Porte Maillot to the Jardin entrance, through a stretch of wooded park. The train operates at 10-minute intervals daily from 10:30am until the park closes; round-trip fare costs 2.70€. En route you'll find a **house of mirrors,** an **archery range,** a

Jardin d'Acclimatation, in the Bois de Boulogne.

miniature-golf course, zoo animals, a **puppet theater** (performances Wed, Sat–Sun, and holidays), a **playground**, a **hurdle-racing course, junior-scale rides, shooting galleries**, and **waffle stalls.** You can trot the kids off on a **pony** (Sat–Sun only) or join them in a **boat** on a mill-stirred lagoon. **La Prévention Routière** is a miniature roadway operated by the Paris police: Youngsters drive through in small cars equipped to start and stop, and are required by two genuine gendarmes to obey street signs and light changes. Inside the gate is an easy-to-follow map.

In the Bois de Boulogne, 16e. www.jardindacclimatation.fr. ℭ **01-40-67-90-82.** Admission 2.90€, free for children 3 and younger. Apr–Sept daily 10am–7pm; Oct–Mar daily 10am–6pm. Métro: Sablons.

**Musée d'Art Moderne de la Ville de Paris** ★★ MUSEUM    Paris's Modern Art Museum borders the Seine and is in fact housed in the Eastern Wing of the monumental Palais de Tokyo (below), a building designed for the 1937 World Fair. The museum opened in 1961, and it is home to works of modern art, including Henri Matisse's *The Dance,* Pierre Bonnard's *Nude in the Bath* and *The Garden,* and Fernand Léger's *Discs.* There are also works by Chagall, Rothko, Braque, Dufy, Picasso, Utrillo, and Modigliani. Seek out Pierre Tal Coat's *Portrait of Gertrude Stein,* and keep Picasso's version of this difficult subject in mind. The museum also presents excellent ever-changing exhibits on individual artists from all over the world or on contemporary international trends.

11 av. du Président-Wilson, 16e. www.mam.paris.fr. ℭ **01-53-67-40-00.** Free admission to general collections, temporary exhibition admission 5€–11€. Tues–Sun 10am–6pm. Métro: Iéna or Alma-Marceau.

**Palais de Tokyo** ★★★ ☺ MUSEUM    This art center, which opened in 2002, is one of the most original and avant-garde in Europe. Dedicated to "emerging" art and artists, the Palais de Tokyo emphasizes edgy, contemporary art and ideas. Its monumental raw concrete architecture immediately sets it apart from a classic museum, and its opening hours (noon to midnight) are radical too. The installations and vast open spaces invariably appeal to kids. The exhibits change frequently, so check to see what's showing—perhaps a video or sculpture exhibition, fashion events, or performance art. The space also includes a bookshop, a cafeteria, and a first-rate restaurant and bar called Tokyo Eat. In 2012 the Palais de Tokyo underwent a major expansion—its surface area expanded from 8,000 square meters (86,111 sq. ft.) to 22,000 square

Palais de Tokyo.

## Opéra & Grands Boulevards (9e)

**ATTRACTIONS**
Opera Garnier 5

**RESTAURANTS**
Chartier 8
Restaurant de
l'Opéra 6
Wally Le
Saharien 3

**HOTELS**
Hotel Amour 1
Hôtel Arvor St Georges 2
Hôtel Chopin 7
Hôtel de la Tour
d'Auvergne 4

meters (236,806 sq. ft.)—and it is now one of the largest sites devoted to contemporary creativity in Europe.

13 av. du Président-Wilson, 16e. www.palaisdetokyo.com. ℂ **01-47-23-54-01.** Admission 6€ adults, 4.50€ students, free for ages 18 and younger. Tues–Sun noon–midnight. Métro: Iéna.

## OPÉRA (9E)

The impressive **Opéra Garnier** dominates its dynamic neighborhood, which delivers perhaps more opportunities for outstanding retail experiences than for cultural ones.

**Opéra Garnier ★★** OPERA HOUSE   This neobaroque masterpiece was built in 1875, under Napoleon III, by architect Charles Garnier, and was known as the Palais Garnier. The stunning grand foyer, restored in 2004, is lined with mirrors and adorned with crystal chandeliers; it resembles the famous Galerie des Glaces at Versailles. It has a magnificent painted ceiling by Paul Baudry portraying themes from the history of music. The gilded auditorium has 1,900 seats and is lit by an immense crystal chandelier that hangs below a once-controversial ceiling painted by Marc Chagall in the 1960s. Today, the venue is home to the fine Paris Opera Ballet. The site also famously hosts beehives on its roof, and the exclusive honey from those hives can be purchased from the Opéra's souvenir store.

8 rue Scribe, 9e. www.operadeparis.fr. (📞) **01-40-01-17-89.** Admission 9€ adults, 6€ students, children under 10 enter for free. Daily 10am–5pm. Métro: Opéra.

## PIGALLE & MONTMARTRE (18E)

Perched on the city's highest point, the **Sacré-Coeur** basilica may be the area's only significant monument, but Montmartre's cobblestone streets and unique, villagelike architecture are an attraction in themselves. The harmless red-light district of neighboring Pigalle can't be reduced to a single attraction either, but it is an exciting area to explore.

**Basilique du Sacré-Coeur ★★ ☺ CHURCH**   Sacré-Coeur is one of Paris's most characteristic landmarks and has been the subject of much controversy. One Parisian called it "a lunatic's confectionery dream." An offended Zola declared it "the basilica of the ridiculous." Sacré-Coeur has had warm supporters as well, including poet Max Jacob and artist Maurice Utrillo. Utrillo never tired of drawing and painting it, and he and Jacob came here regularly to pray. Atop the *butte* (hill) in Montmartre, its multiple gleaming white domes and campanile (bell tower) loom over Paris like a 12th-century Byzantine church. But it's not that old. After France's 1870 defeat by the Prussians, the basilica was planned as a votive offering to cure France's misfortunes. Rich and poor alike contributed money to build it. Construction began in 1876, and though the church wasn't consecrated until 1919, perpetual prayers of adoration have been made here day and night since 1885. The interior is brilliantly decorated with mosaics: Look for the striking Christ on the ceiling and the mural of his Passion at the back of the altar. The stained-glass windows were shattered during the struggle for Paris in

Detail on a Montmartre building.

## Pigalle & Montmartre (18e)

**ATTRACTIONS**

Basilique du Sacré-Coeur **8**

Cimetiére de Montmartre **1**

**HOTELS**

Hôtel des Arts **3**

Hôtel Particulier **2**

Le Chat Noir Design Hotel **6**

**RESTAURANTS**

Le Bal Cafe **7**

Café des Deux Moulins **4**

Chéri Bibi **9**

Nansouty **5**

| | |
|---|---|
| ‖‖‖‖ | Steps |
| ⊦⊦⊦⊦⊦ | Funicular |
| Ⓜ | Métro station |

0        200 yds

0        200 m

---

1944 but have been well replaced. The crypt contains what some of the devout believe is Christ's sacred heart—hence, the name of the church. Kids will delight in taking a turn on the merry-go-round, then taking the funicular up the hill to the church.

    ***Insider's tip:*** Although the view from the Arc de Triomphe is the greatest panorama of Paris, we also want to endorse the view from the gallery around the inner dome of Sacré-Coeur. On a clear day, your eyes take in a sweep of Paris extending for 48km (30 miles) into the Ile de France. You can also walk around the inner dome, an attraction even better than the interior of Sacré-Coeur itself.

Place St-Pierre, 18e. www.sacre-coeur-montmartre.com. ℰ **01-53-41-89-00.** Free admission to basilica, joint ticket to dome and crypt 8€/ 5€. Basilica daily 6am–11pm; dome and crypt daily 9am–6pm. Métro: Abbesses; take elevator to surface and follow signs to funicular.

**Cimetière de Montmartre** ★ CEMETERY    This cemetery, established in 1795, lies west of Montmartre and north of boulevard de Clichy. Russian dancer **Vaslav Nijinsky,** novelist **Alexandre Dumas** *fils,* Impressionist **Edgar Degas,** and composers **Hector Berlioz** and **Jacques Offenbach** are interred here, along with **Stendhal** and lesser literary lights such as **Edmond** and **Jules de Goncourt** and **Heinrich Heine.** A more recent tombstone honors **François Truffaut,** film director of the *nouvelle vague* (new wave). We like to pay our respects at the tomb of **Alphonsine Plessis,** heroine of *La Dame aux Camélias,*

113

**Basilique du Sacré-Coeur.**

and **Mme Récamier,** who taught the world how to lounge. **Émile Zola** was buried here, but his corpse was exhumed and promoted to the Panthéon in 1908. In 1871, the cemetery was used for mass burials of victims of the Siege and the Commune.

20 av. Rachel (west of the Butte Montmartre and north of bd. de Clichy), 18e. ℭ **01-53-42-36-30.** Mon–Fri 8am–6pm; Sat 8:30am–6pm; Sun 9am–6pm. Métro: La Fourche.

## BELLEVILLE, CANAL ST-MARTIN & NORTHEAST PARIS (10E, 19E & 20E)

Perhaps the greatest attraction in this area is the picturesque **Canal St-Martin** itself. Beyond that is **La Villette,** which encompasses Paris's biggest park, Parc de la Villette. It is also an exceptional 21st-century cultural compound including museums, concert halls, circus tents, and exhibition spaces that host a great year-round program. The lure of this former industrial zone is its outdoor attractions: In addition to La Villette, the renowned **Père-Lachaise cemetery** and the wonderful **Buttes Chaumont park** are also located in this area. Note that the area around the Belleville Métro station is also home to one of the city's bustling Chinatowns.

**Cimetière du Père-Lachaise ★★★ ☺ CEMETERY**   When it comes to name-dropping, this cemetery knows no peer; it has been called the "grandest address in Paris." Everybody from Sarah Bernhardt to Oscar Wilde to Richard Wright is resting here, along with Honoré de Balzac, Jacques-Louis David, Eugène Delacroix, Maria Callas, Max Ernst, and Georges Bizet. Colette was taken here in 1954; her black granite slab always sports flowers, and legend has it that cats replenish the roses. In time, the "little sparrow," Edith Piaf, followed. The lover of George Sand, poet Alfred de Musset, was buried under a weeping willow. Napoleon's marshals, Ney and Masséna, lie here, as do Frédéric Chopin and Molière. Marcel Proust's black tombstone rarely lacks a tiny bunch of violets (he wanted to be buried beside his friend/lover, composer Maurice Ravel, but their families wouldn't allow it).

Some tombs are sentimental favorites: Love-torn graffiti radiates 1km (½ mile) from the grave of Doors singer **Jim Morrison,** and could appeal to jaded teens. The great dancer **Isadora Duncan** came to rest in the Columbarium, where bodies have been cremated and "filed" away. If you search hard enough, you can find the tombs of that star-crossed pair **Abélard** and **Héloïse,** the ill-fated lovers of the 12th century—at Père-Lachaise, they've found peace at last.

Other famous lovers also rest here: A stone is marked **"Alice B. Toklas"** on one side and **"Gertrude Stein"** on the other; and eventually, France's First Couple of film were reunited when **Yves Montand** joined his wife, **Simone Signoret.**

Covering more than 44 hectares (109 acres), Père-Lachaise was acquired by the city in 1804. Nineteenth-century sculpture abounds, as each family tried to outdo the others in ostentation. Monuments also honor Frenchmen who died in the Resistance or in Nazi concentration camps. Some French Socialists still pay tribute at the **Mur des Fédérés,** the anonymous gravesite of the Communards who were executed in the cemetery on May 28, 1871. When these last-ditch fighters of the Commune, the world's first anarchist republic, made their final desperate stand against the troops of the French government, they were overwhelmed, lined up against the wall, and shot in groups. A few survived and lived hidden in the cemetery for years, venturing into Paris at night to forage for food.

Chopin's grave at the Cimetière du Père-Lachaise.

A free map of Père-Lachaise is available at the newsstand across from the main entrance.

16 rue de Repos, 20e. www.pere-lachaise.com. ℗ **01-55-25-82-10.** Mon–Fri 8am–6pm; Sat–Sun 8:30am–6pm (closes at 5pm Nov to early Mar). Métro: Père-Lachaise or Philippe Auguste.

## The Canal St-Martin

The Canal St-Martin is a picturesque waterway that connects the river Seine, near Bastille, to the Canal de l'Ourcq, near the Villette in the 19th arrondissement. When Parisians talk about *le canal,* they are usually referring to the popular stretch of the quais Jemmapes and Valmy, which begins just above République and runs up by the Gare de l'Est. The canal was inaugurated in 1825 with the aim of bringing fresh drinking water to the heart of the city. During the 19th and early 20th centuries, this water highway attracted much commerce and industry to the surrounding areas. Painter Alfred Sisley was inspired by this canal—you can admire his painting "Vue du canal Saint-Martin à Paris" (1870) at the Musée d'Orsay (p. 128). After almost being destroyed in the 1970s to make way for more roads, the canal was classified as a historic monument in 1993, and today, visitors can explore the canal at their leisure. If you'd like to take a scenic boat tour of the canal, contact **Paris Canal** (www.pariscanal.com; ℗ **01-42-40-96-97**) or **Canauxrama** (www.canauxrama.com; ℗ **01-42-39-15-00**).

4

**Cité des Sciences et de l'Industrie ★★ ☺ MUSEUM**
A city of science and industry has risen here from unlikely ashes. When a slaughterhouse was built on the site in the 1960s, it was touted as the most modern of its kind. It was abandoned in 1974, and the location on the city's northern edge presented the government with a problem. What could be built in such an unlikely place? In 1986, the converted premises opened as the world's most expensive ($642-million) science complex, designed to "modernize mentalities" in the service of modernizing society. It is located within the Parc de La Villette compound (see below).

The place is so vast, with so many exhibits, that a single visit gives only an idea of the scope of the Cité. Busts of Plato, Hippocrates, and a double-faced Janus gaze silently at a tube-filled riot of high-tech girders, glass, and lights. The sheer dimensions pose a challenge to the curators of its constantly changing exhibits. Some exhibits are couched in Gallic humor—imagine using the comic-strip adventures of a jungle explorer to explain seismographic activity. **Explora,** a permanent exhibit, occupies the three upper levels of the building and examines four themes: the universe, life, matter, and communication. The Cité also has a **multimedia library,** a **planetarium,** and an **"inventorium"** for kids. The silver-skinned geodesic dome called **La Géode**—a 34m-high (112-ft.) sphere with a 370-seat theater—is the city's IMAX theater, regularly screening 3-D films on a giant 400 sq. m (4,305 sq. ft.) screen.

**Belleville, Canal St-Martin & Northeast Paris (10e, 19e & 20e)**

**ATTRACTIONS**
Cimetière du Père-Lachaise **10**
Cité des Sciences et de l'Industrie **1**
Parc de la Vilette **2**

**HOTELS**
Le Citizen **6**
Libertel Canal St-Martin **4**
Mama Shelter **11**
St Christopher's Paris Hostel **3**

**RESTAURANTS**
Brasserie Flo **9**
La Verre Volé **8**
Pink Flamingo **7**
Rosa Bonheur **5**

Cité des Sciences et de l'Industrie.

In the Parc de La Villette, 30 av. Corentine-Cariou, La Villette, 19e. www.cite-sciences.fr. ℰ **01-40-05-70-00.** Varied ticket options 11€–21€ adults, 8€–16€ ages 7–24, free 6 and younger. Tues–Sat 10am–6pm; Sun 10am–7pm. Métro: Porte de La Villette.

**Parc de la Villette** ★★★ ☺ PARK   This modern 21st-century park, designed by architect Bernard Tschumi, cleverly combines nature and architecture. Twice the size of the Jardin des Tuileries, it is Paris's largest park. The Canal de l'Ourcq runs through the park, feeding into various waterfalls, fountains, and ponds. Two walkways crisscross the park: the first runs from the Porte de Pantin to the Porte de la Villette, and the second is elevated and runs along the southern bank of the canal. The park is famous for its 26 red "follies," a contemporary version of the 18th-century gazebo, which are both ornamental and functional. In the center of the park are large grassy areas known as the circle and the triangle, where people can relax; during the summer, the triangle hosts a popular outdoor cinema program.

211 avenue Jean Jaurès, 19e. www.villette.com. ℰ **01-40-03-75-75.** Daily 6am–1am. Métro: Porte de Pantin or Porte de la Villette.

## The Left Bank
### LATIN QUARTER (5E & 13E)
This leafy neighborhood is defined by the medieval university at its heart: the Sorbonne. In fact, it gets its name from the Latin the students spoke in their classes there up until 1793. The Roman occupation, from 52 B.C. until A.D. 486, remains visible too; the rue Saint-Jacques and boulevard Saint-Michel mark the former Roman cardo, and you can explore Roman ruins at the Cluny Museum. French architect Dominique Perrault is behind the massive new national library out in the 13th arrondissement, signaling the resurrection of this former industrial heartland.

# The Latin Quarter &
# Southern Paris (5e & 13e)

**Musée National du Moyen Age/Thermes de Cluny (Musée de Cluny)** ★★ MUSEUM   Along with the Hôtel de Sens in the Marais, the Hôtel de Cluny is all that remains of domestic medieval architecture in Paris. Enter through the cobblestoned **Cour d'Honneur (Court of Honor),** where you can admire the flamboyant Gothic building with its vines, turreted walls, gargoyles, and dormers with seashell motifs. First, the Cluny was the mansion of a rich 15th-century abbot, built on top of/next to the ruins of a Roman bath. By 1515, it was the residence of Mary Tudor, widow of Louis XII and daughter of Henry VII and Elizabeth of York. Seized during the Revolution, the Cluny was rented in 1833 to Alexandre du Sommerard, who adorned it with medieval artworks. After his death in 1842, the government bought the building and the collection.

This collection of medieval arts and crafts is superb. Most people come to see *The Lady and the Unicorn* tapestries ★★★, the most acclaimed tapestries of their kind. All the romance of the age of chivalry—a beautiful princess and her handmaiden, beasts of prey, and house pets—lives on in these remarkable yet mysterious tapestries discovered only a century ago in Limousin's Château de Boussac. Five seem to deal with the senses (one, for example, depicts a unicorn looking into a mirror held by a dour-faced maiden). The sixth shows a woman under an elaborate tent with jewels, her pet dog resting on an embroidered cushion beside her, with the lovable unicorn and his friendly companion, a lion, holding back the flaps. The background forms a rich carpet of spring flowers, fruit-laden trees, birds, rabbits, donkeys, dogs, goats, lambs, and monkeys.

The other exhibits range widely: Flemish retables; a 14th-century Sienese John the Baptist and other sculptures; statues from Sainte-Chapelle (1243–48); 12th- and 13th-century crosses, chalices, manuscripts, carvings, vestments, leatherwork, jewelry, and coins; a 13th-century Adam; and recently discovered heads and fragments of statues from Notre-Dame de Paris. In the fan-vaulted medieval chapel hang tapestries depicting scenes from the life of St. Stephen.

*The Lady and the Unicorn* tapestries at the Musée National du Moyen Age.

**Inside the Panthéon.**

Downstairs are the ruins of the **Roman baths,** from around A.D. 200. The best-preserved section is seen in room X, the frigidarium (where one bathed in cold water). Once it measured 21×11m (69×36 ft.), rising to a height of 15m (49 ft.), with stone walls nearly 1.5m (5 ft.) thick. The ribbed vaulting here rests on consoles evoking ships' prows. Credit for this unusual motif goes to the builders of the baths, Paris's boatmen. During Tiberius's reign, a column to Jupiter was found beneath Notre-Dame's chancel and is now on view in the court; called the "Column of the Boatmen," it's believed to be the oldest sculpture created in Paris.

6 place Paul Painlevé, 5e. www.musee-moyenage.fr. (C) **01-53-73-78-00.** Admission 7.50€ adults, 5.50€ youths 18–25. Add 2€ for access to the temporary exhibitions. Wed–Mon 9:15am–5:45pm. Métro: Miromesnil or St-Philippe-du-Roule.

**Panthéon ★★** CHURCH    Some of the most famous men in French history (Victor Hugo, for one) are buried here on the crest of the mount of St. Geneviève. In 1744, Louis XV vowed that if he recovered from a mysterious illness, he'd build a church to replace the Abbaye de St. Geneviève. He recovered but took his time fulfilling his promise. It wasn't until 1764 that Mme de Pompadour's brother hired Soufflot to design a church in the form of a Greek cross with a dome reminiscent of St. Paul's in London. When Soufflot died, his pupil Rondelet carried out the work, completing the structure 9 years after his master's death.

After the revolution, the church was converted to a "Temple of Fame" and became a pantheon for the great men of France. Mirabeau was buried here, though his remains were later removed. Likewise, Marat was only a temporary tenant. Voltaire's body was exhumed and placed here—and allowed to remain. In the 19th century, the building changed roles so many times—a church, a pantheon, a church again—that it was hard to keep its function straight. After Hugo was buried here, it became a pantheon once again. Other notable men entombed within are Rousseau, Soufflot, Zola, and Braille. Only one woman has so far been deemed worthy of placement here: Marie Curie, who joined her husband, Pierre. Most recently, in 1996, the ashes of André Malraux were transferred to the Panthéon because, according to former French president Jacques Chirac, he "lived [his] dreams and made them live in us." As Charles de Gaulle's culture minister, Malraux decreed the arts should be part of the lives of all French people, not just Paris's elite.

Before entering the crypt, note the striking frescoes: On the right wall are scenes from Geneviève's life, and on the left is the saint with a white-draped head looking out over medieval Paris, the city whose patron she became, as well as Geneviève relieving victims of famine with supplies.

Place du Panthéon, 5e. www.monum.fr. ✆ **01-44-32-18-00.** Admission 8.50€ adults, 5.50€ ages 18–25, free for children 17 and younger. Apr–Sept daily 10am–6:30pm; Oct–Mar daily 10am–6pm (last entrance 45 min. before closing). Métro: Cardinal Lemoine or Maubert-Mutualité.

## ST-GERMAIN-DES-PRÉS & LUXEMBOURG (6E)

This neighborhood in the 6th arrondissement was the postwar home of existentialism, associated with great writers and philosophers Jean-Paul Sartre, Simone de Beauvoir, Albert Camus, and an intellectual bohemian crowd that gathered at **Cafe de Flore** (p. 154) or **Les Deux Magots.** St-Germain-des-Prés still retains an intellectually stimulating bohemian street life, full of many interesting bookshops, art galleries, *caveau* (basement) clubs, bistros, and coffeehouses. But the stars of the area are two churches, **St-Germain-des-Prés** and **St-Sulpice,** and **Musée National Eugène Delacroix.**

**Jardin du Luxembourg** ★★ ☺ GARDEN   Hemingway once told a friend that the Jardin du Luxembourg "kept us from starvation." He related that in his poverty-stricken days in Paris, he wheeled a baby carriage (the vehicle was considered luxurious) through the garden because it was known "for the classiness of its pigeons." When the gendarme went across the street for a glass of wine, the writer would eye his victim, preferably a plump one; lure him with corn; "snatch him, wring his neck"; and hide him under the blanket. "We got a little tired of pigeons that year," he confessed, "but they filled many a void."

The Luxembourg has always been associated with artists, though children, students, and tourists predominate nowadays. Watteau came this way, as did Verlaine. In 1905, Gertrude Stein would cross them to catch the Batignolles/Clichy/Odéon omnibus, pulled by three gray mares, to meet Picasso in his studio at Montmartre, where he painted her portrait.

Marie de Médicis, the wife of Henri IV, ordered the **Palais du Luxembourg** built on this site in 1612, shortly after she was widowed. A Florentine by birth, the regent wanted to create another Pitti Palace, where she could live with her "witch" friend, Leonora Galigal. Architect Salomon de Brossee wasn't entirely successful, though the overall effect is Italianate. Alas, the queen didn't get to enjoy the palace, as her son, Louis XIII, forced her into exile when he discovered she was plotting to overthrow him. She died in poverty in Cologne. For her palace, she'd commissioned 21 paintings from Rubens, which glorified her life, but they're now in the Louvre. It is extremely difficult to visit the palace, because it is the chamber of French senators. A few visits are organized throughout the year but there is no schedule. You can call ✆ **01-44-54-19-49** and take a

# St-Germain-des-Prés, Luxembourg & Montparnasse (6e & 14e)

**ATTRACTIONS**

Cimetière du
Montparnasse **22**
Jardin du Luxembourg **17**
Les Catacombes **23**
St-Germain-des-Prés **3**
St-Sulpice **12**
Tour Montparnasse **18**

**HOTELS**

Hôtel d'Aubusson **5**
Hôtel Mayet **16**
Hôtel Récamier **13**
Le Placide **15**
Relais Christine **8**

**RESTAURANTS**

Café de Flore **2**
La Cerisaie **19**
Crêperie Josselin **20**
La Crémerie Restaurant
Polidor **14**
La Palette **4**
La Régalade **24**
La Rotonde **21**
L'Avant Comptoir **10**
Le Comptoir du Relais **11**
Le Procope **9**
Le Relais de l'Entrecôte **1**
Le Relais Louis XIII **7**
Ze Kitchen Galerie **6**

Jardin du Luxembourg.

chance. Even so, when tours are offered only 30 tickets are available. The cost is 8€ per person.

You don't really come to the Luxembourg to visit the palace; the gardens are the attraction. For the most part, they're in the classic French tradition: well groomed and formally laid out, the trees planted in patterns. Urns and statuary on pedestals—one honoring Paris's patroness, St. Geneviève, with pigtails reaching to her thighs—encircle a central water basin. Kids can sail a toy boat, ride a pony, or attend an occasional Grand Guignol puppet show. And you can join a game of *boules* (lawn bowling) with a group of men who wear black berets and have Gauloises dangling from their mouths.

Place Edmond Rostand, place André Honnorat, rue Guynemer, rue de Vaugirard, 6e. 8am–dusk. Métro: Odéon; RER: Luxembourg.

**St-Germain-des-Prés** ★★ CHURCH   It's one of Paris's oldest churches, from the 6th century, when a Benedictine abbey was founded here by Childebert, son of Clovis. Alas, the marble columns in the triforium are all that remain from that period. The Normans nearly destroyed the abbey at least four times. The present building has a Romanesque nave and a Gothic choir with fine capitals. At one time, the abbey was a pantheon for Merovingian kings. Restoration of the site of their tombs, **Chapelle de St-Symphorien,** took place in 1981, when unknown Romanesque paintings were discovered on the triumphal arch. Among the others interred here are Descartes (his heart, at least) and Jean-Casimir, the king of Poland who abdicated his throne. The Romanesque tower, topped by a 19th-century spire, is the most enduring landmark in St-Germain-des-Prés. Its church bells, however, are hardly noticed by the patrons of Les Deux Magots across the way.

3 place St-Germain-des-Prés, 6e. www.eglise-sgp.org. ℂ **01-55-42-81-33.** Free admission. Mon–Sat 8am–7:45pm; Sun 9am–8pm. Métro: St-Germain-des-Prés.

**St-Sulpice ★★** CHURCH   Pause first outside St-Sulpice. The 1844 fountain by Visconti displays the sculpted likenesses of four bishops of the Louis XIV era: Fenelon, Massillon, Bossuet, and Flechier. Work on the church, at one time Paris's largest, began in 1646. Though laborers built the body by 1745, work on the bell towers continued until 1780, when one was finished and the other left incomplete. One of the priceless treasures inside is Servandoni's rococo **Chapelle de la Madone (Chapel of the Madonna),** with a Pigalle statue of the Virgin. The church has one of the world's largest organs, comprising 6,700 pipes; it has been played by musicians such as Marcel Dupré and Charles-Marie Widor.

The real reason to come here is to see the Delacroix frescoes in the **Chapelle des Anges (Chapel of the Angels),** the first on your right as you enter. Look for his muscular Jacob wrestling (or dancing?) with an effete angel. On the ceiling, St. Michael is having some troubles with the Devil, and yet another mural depicts Heliodorus being driven from the temple. Painted in Delacroix's final years, the frescoes were a high point in his baffling career. If these impress you, pay the painter tribute by visiting the Musée Delacroix.

> **Gregorians Unplugged**
>
> St-Germain-des-Prés stages wonderful concerts on the Left Bank; it boasts fantastic acoustics and a marvelous medieval atmosphere. The church was built to accommodate an age without microphones, and the sound effects will thrill you. For more information, call ℂ **01-55-42-81-33** or visit www. eglise-sgp.org. Arrive about 45 minutes before the performance if you'd like a front-row seat. Tickets are 15€ to 50€.

Rue St-Sulpice, 6e. ℂ **01-42-34-59-98.** Free admission. Daily 8:30am–8pm. Métro: St-Sulpice.

## EIFFEL TOWER & NEARBY (7E)

The **Eiffel Tower** has become a symbol for Paris itself. After admiring and climbing the elegant structure, stroll west along the river to two other important attractions: **Musée du quai Branly** and **Musée d'Orsay.**

**Hôtel des Invalides/Napoleon's Tomb ★★** HISTORIC BUILDING   In 1670, the Sun King decided to build this "hotel" to house soldiers with disabilities. It wasn't an entirely benevolent gesture, considering that the men had been injured, crippled, or blinded while fighting his battles. When the building was finally completed (Louis XIV had long been dead), a gilded dome by Jules Hardouin-Mansart crowned it, and its corridors stretched for miles. The best way to approach the Invalides is by crossing over the Right Bank via the early-1900s Pont Alexander-III and entering the cobblestone forecourt, where a display of massive cannons makes a formidable welcome.

Before rushing on to Napoleon's Tomb, you may want to visit the world's greatest military museum, the **Musée de l'Armée.** In 1794, a French inspector started collecting weapons, uniforms, and equipment, and with the accumulation of war material over time, the museum has become a documentary of man's self-destruction. Viking swords, Burgundian battle axes, 14th-century blunderbusses, Balkan *khandjars,* American Browning machine guns, war pitchforks, salamander-engraved Renaissance serpentines, a 1528 Griffon, musketoons, grenadiers—if it can kill, it's enshrined here. As a sardonic touch, there's even the wooden leg of General Daumesnil, the governor of Vincennes, who lost his leg in the battle of Wagram. Oblivious to the irony of committing a crime against a place that documents man's evil nature, the Nazis looted the museum in 1940.

Among the outstanding acquisitions are suits of armor worn by the kings and dignitaries of France, including Louis XIV. The best are in the new Arsenal. The most famous one, the "armor suit of the lion," was made for François I. Henri II ordered his suit engraved with the monogram of his mistress, Diane de Poitiers, and (perhaps reluctantly) that of his wife, Catherine de Médicis. Particularly fine are the showcases of swords and the World War I mementos, including those of American and Canadian soldiers—seek out the Armistice Bugle, which sounded the cease-fire on November 7, 1918, before the general cease-fire on November 11. The west wing's Salle Orientale has arms of the Eastern world, including Asia and the Mideast Muslim countries, from the 16th century to the 19th century. Turkish armor (look for Bajazet's helmet) and weaponry, and Chinese and Japanese armor and swords are on display.

Then there's that little Corsican who became France's greatest soldier. Here you can see the death mask Antommarchi made of him, as well as an oil by Delaroche painted at the time of Napoleon's first banishment (Apr 1814) and depicting him as he probably looked, paunch and all. The First Empire exhibit displays Napoleon's field bed with his tent; in the room devoted to the Restoration, the 100 Days, and Waterloo, you can see his bedroom as it was at the time of his death on St. Helena. The Turenne Salon contains other souvenirs, such as the hat Napoleon wore at Eylau; the sword from his Austerlitz victory; and his "Flag of Farewell," which he kissed before departing for Elba.

**Napoleon's Tomb.**

# Near the Eiffel Tower (7e & 15e)

Pedestrians only
Ⓜ Métro station
RER RER station
⊠ Post office

0   0.25 km
0   1/4 mi

**ATTRACTIONS**

Hôtel des Invalides/
Napoleon's Tomb **8**
Les Egouts
(Sewers of Paris) **3**
Musée d'Orsay **13**
Musée du quai Branly **2**
Musée Rodin **9**
Tour Eiffel **1**

**HOTELS**

Hôtel Le Bellechasse **12**
Hôtel Thoumieux **5**

**RESTAURANTS**

Chez l'Ami Jean **4**
Eric Kayser **14**

Jadis **7**
Jean-François Piège **5**
L'Arpège **10**
L'Atelier Saint-Germain
de Joël Robuchon **15**
Le Casse Noix **6**
Restaurant Auguste **11**

126

You can gain access to the **Musée des Plans-Reliefs** through the west wing. This collection shows French towns and monuments done in scale models (the model of Strasbourg fills an entire room), as well as models of military fortifications since the days of the great Vauban.

A walk across the Cour d'Honneur (Court of Honor) delivers you to the **Eglise du Dôme,** designed by Hardouin-Mansart for Louis XIV. The architect began work on the church in 1677, though he died before its completion. The dome is the second-tallest monument in Paris (the Tour Eiffel is the tallest, of course). The hearse used at the emperor's funeral on May 9, 1821, is in the Napoleon Chapel.

To accommodate **Napoleon's Tomb ★★★**, the architect Visconti had to redesign the church's high altar in 1842. First buried on St. Helena, Napoleon's remains were exhumed and brought to Paris in 1840 on the orders of Louis-Philippe, who demanded that the English return the emperor to French soil. The remains were locked inside six coffins in this tomb made of red Finnish porphyry, with a green granite base. Surrounding it are a dozen Amazon-like figures representing Napoleon's victories. Almost lampooning the smallness of the man, everything is done on a gargantuan scale. In his coronation robes, the statue of Napoleon stands 2.5m (8¼ ft.) high. The grave of the "King of Rome," his son by second wife, Marie-Louise, lies at his feet. Surrounding Napoleon's Tomb are those of his brother, Joseph Bonaparte; the great Vauban, who built many of France's fortifications; World War I Allied commander Foch; and the vicomte de Turenne, the republic's first grenadier (actually, only his heart is entombed here).

Place des Invalides, 7e. www.invalides.org. ℭ **01-44-42-37-72.** Admission to Musée de l'Armée, Napoleon's Tomb, and Musée des Plans-Reliefs 9€ adults, 7€ students, free for children 17 and younger. Oct 1–Mar 31 Mon–Sat 10am–5pm, Sun 10am–5:30pm; Apr 1–Sept 30 Mon, Wed–Sat 10am–6pm, Sun 10am–6:30pm, Tues 10am–9pm; June–Aug daily 10am–7pm. Closed Jan 1, May 1, Nov 1, and Dec 25. Métro: Latour-Maubourg, Varenne, Invalides, or St-Francois-Xavier.

**Musée des Egouts de Paris ★ ☺** HISTORIC SITE   Some sociologists assert that the sophistication of a society can be judged by the way it disposes of waste. If so, Paris receives good marks for its mostly invisible sewer network. Victor Hugo is credited with making them famous in Les Misérables: Jean Valjean takes flight through them, "all dripping with slime, his soul filled with a strange light." Hugo also wrote, "Paris has beneath it another Paris, a Paris of sewers, which has its own streets, squares, lanes, arteries, and circulation."

In the early Middle Ages, drinking water was taken directly from the Seine, and wastewater poured onto fields or thrown onto the unpaved streets transformed the urban landscape into a sea of smelly mud. Around 1200, the streets were paved with cobblestones, and open sewers ran down the center of each. These open sewers helped spread the Black Death, which devastated the city. In 1370, a vaulted sewer was built on rue Montmartre, draining effluents into a Seine tributary. During Louis XIV's reign, improvements were made, but the state of waste disposal in Paris remained deplorable.

During Napoleon's reign, 31km (19 miles) of sewer were constructed beneath Paris. By 1850, as the Industrial Revolution made the manufacture of iron pipe and steam-digging equipment more practical, Baron Haussmann developed a system that used separate channels for drinking water and sewage. By 1878, it was 580km (360 miles) long. Beginning in 1894, the network was enlarged, and laws required that discharge of all waste and storm-water runoff be funneled into the sewers. Between 1914 and 1977, an additional 966km (600 miles) were added. Today, the network of sewers is 2,093km (1,300 miles) long.

The city's sewers are constructed around four principal tunnels, one 5.5m (18 ft.) wide and 4.5m (15 ft.) high. It's like an underground city, with the street names clearly labeled. Sewer tours begin at Pont de l'Alma on the Left Bank, where a stairway leads into the city's bowels. Visiting times might change during bad weather, as a storm can make the sewers dangerous. The tour consists of a film, a small museum visit, and then a short trip through the maze. **Warning:** The smell is pretty bad, especially in summer, but kids should love the gross-out factor.

Pont de l'Alma, 7e. ℭ **01-53-68-27-81.** Admission 4.30€ adults; 3.50€ seniors, students, and children 5–16; free for children 4 and younger. May–Sept Sat–Wed 11am–5pm; Oct–Apr Sat–Wed 11am–4pm. Métro: Alma-Marceau. RER: Pont de l'Alma.

**Musée d'Orsay ★★★** MUSEUM   Architects created one of the world's great museums from an old rail station, the neoclassical Gare d'Orsay, across the Seine from the Louvre and the Tuileries. Don't skip the Louvre, of course, but come here even if you have to miss all the other art museums in town. The Orsay boasts an astounding collection devoted to the watershed years 1848 to 1914, with a treasure-trove by the big names plus all the lesser-known groups (the symbolists, pointillists, nabis, realists, and late romantics). The 80 galleries also include Belle Époque furniture, photographs, objets d'art, and architectural models.

A monument to the Industrial Revolution, the Orsay is covered by an arching glass roof allowing in floods of light. It displays works ranging from the creations of academic and historic painters such as Ingres to romanticists such as Delacroix, to neorealists including Courbet and Daumier.

The museum's Impressionist and post-Impressionist galleries, as well as the four floors of the "Pavillon Amont," underwent a major renovation in 2011 which enlarged exhibition spaces and improved displays. The Impressionists still draw the crowds to this museum. Led by Manet, Renoir, and Monet, the Impressionists shunned ecclesiastical and mythological set pieces for a light-bathed Seine, faint figures strolling in the Tuileries, pale-faced women in hazy bars, and even vulgar rail stations such as the Gare St-Lazare. And the Impressionists were the first to paint that most characteristic feature of Parisian life: the sidewalk cafe, especially in the artists' quarter of Montmartre.

The most famous painting from this era is Manet's 1863 **Déjeuner sur l'herbe (Picnic on the Grass),** whose forest setting with a nude woman and two fully clothed men sent shock waves through respectable society when it was first exhibited. Two years later, Manet's **Olympia** created another scandal by depicting a woman lounging on her bed and wearing nothing but a flower in her hair and high-heeled shoes; she's attended by an African maid in the background. Zola called Manet "a man among eunuchs."

One of Renoir's most joyous paintings is here: the **Moulin de la Galette** (1876). Degas is represented by his paintings of racehorses and dancers; his 1876 cafe scene, **Absinthe,** remains one of his most reproduced works. Paris-born Monet was fascinated by the effect of changing light on Rouen Cathédrale and brought its stone bubbles to life in a series of five paintings; our favorite is

*Rouen Cathédrale: Full Sunlight.* Another celebrated work is by an American, Whistler's **Arrangement in Grey and Black: Portrait of the Painter's Mother,** better known as **Whistler's Mother.** It's said that this painting heralded modern art, though many critics denounced it at the time because of its funereal overtones. Whistler was content to claim he'd made "Mummy just as nice as possible."

You'll also see works by Matisse, the cubists, and the expressionists in a setting once used by Orson Welles to film a nightmarish scene in *The Trial,* based on Kafka's unfinished novel. You'll find Millet's sunny wheat fields, Barbizon landscapes, Corot's mists, and Tahitian Gauguins.

1 rue de Bellechasse or 62 rue de Lille, 7e. www.musee-orsay.fr. ✆ **01-40-49-48-14.** Admission 9€ adults, 6.50€ ages 18–24, free ages 17 and younger. Joint ticket to this museum and the Musée de l'Orangerie (p. 91) 13€. Tues–Wed and Fri–Sun 9:30am–6pm; Thurs 9:30am–9:45pm. Closed Jan 1 and Dec 25. Métro: Solférino. RER: Musée d'Orsay.

**Musée du quai Branly ★★★ ☺ MUSEUM**   The architect Jean Nouvel said he wanted to create something "unique, poetic, and disturbing." And so he did with this $265-million museum, which opened in 2006. Set in a lush, rambling garden on the Left Bank in the shadow of the Eiffel Tower, this museum houses nearly 300,000 tribal artifacts from Africa, Asia, Oceania, and the Americas. Galleries stand on sculpted pillars that evoke totem poles.

Housed in four spectacular buildings with a garden walled off from the quai Branly are the art, sculpture, and cultural materials of a vast range of non-Western civilizations, separated into different sections that represent the traditional cultures of Africa, East and Southeast Asia, Oceania, Australia, the Americas, and New Zealand. The pieces here come from the now-defunct Musée des Arts Africains et Oceaniens, from the Louvre, and from the Musée de l'Homme. Temporary exhibits are shown off in boxes all along the 183m-long (600-ft.) exhibition hall.

Incredible masterpieces are on display made by some very advanced traditional civilizations; some of the most impressive exhibits present tribal masks of different cultures, some of which are so lifelike and emotional in their creation that you can feel the fear and elation involved in their use, which is well documented by descriptions in English. The exhibitions are very engaging for children. Allow 2 hours for a full visit; also take a stroll in the carefully manicured garden, or have a café au lait in the small cafeteria across from the main building. There are numerous entrances to the museum grounds from the area near the Eiffel Tower; the main entrance is on quai Branly.

27–37 quai Branly and 206–208 rue de Université, 7e. www.quaibranly.fr. ✆ **01-56-61-70-00.** Admission to permanent exhibitions 8.50€ adults, 6€ seniors and students 18–26, free for children 17 and younger; admission to temporary exhibitions 7€ adults, 5€ seniors and students 18–26 Tues–Wed and Sun 11am–7pm; Thurs–Sat 11am–9pm. Métro: Alma-Marceau. RER: Pont d'Alma.

**Musée Rodin ★★ ☺ MUSEUM**   Today Rodin is acclaimed as the father of modern sculpture, but in a different era, his work was labeled obscene. The world's artistic taste changed, and in due course, in 1911, the French government purchased Rodin's studio in this gray-stone, 18th-century mansion in the Faubourg St-Germain. The government restored the rose gardens to their 18th-century splendor, making them a perfect setting for Rodin's most memorable works.

In the courtyard are three world-famous creations. Rodin's first major public commission, **The Burghers of Calais,** commemorated the heroism of six citizens of Calais who in 1347 offered themselves as a ransom to Edward III in return for ending his siege of their port. Perhaps the single best-known work, **The Thinker,** in Rodin's own words, "thinks with every muscle of his arms, back, and legs, with his clenched fist and gripping toes." Not completed when Rodin died, **The Gate of Hell,** as he put it, is "where I lived for a whole year in Dante's *Inferno*."

Inside, the recently renovated museum presents sculptures, plaster casts, reproductions, originals, and sketches that reveal the freshness and vitality of a remarkable artist. You can almost see his works emerging from marble into life. Everybody is attracted to **Le Baiser (The Kiss),** of which one critic wrote, "The passion is timeless." Upstairs are two versions of the celebrated and condemned **Nude of Balzac,** his bulky torso rising from a tree trunk (Albert E. Elsen commented on the "glorious bulging" stomach). Included are many versions of his **Monument to Balzac** (a large one stands in the garden), Rodin's last major work. Other significant sculptures are the soaring **Prodigal Son; The Crouching Woman** (the "embodiment of despair"); and **The Age of Bronze,** an 1876 study of a nude man modeled after a Belgian soldier. (Rodin was falsely accused of making a cast from a living model.) Generally overlooked is a room devoted to Rodin's mistress, Camille Claudel, a towering artist in her own right. She was his pupil, model, and lover, and created such works as **Maturity, Clotho,** and the recently donated **The Waltz** and **The Gossips.** The little alley behind the Musée Rodin winds its way down to a pond with fountains, flower beds, and even sand pits for children. It's one of the most idyllic hidden spots in Paris.

In the Hôtel Biron, 79 rue de Varenne, 7e. www.musee-rodin.fr. ℭ **01-44-18-61-10.** Admission 7€ adults, 5€ ages 18–25, free for children 17 and younger. Apr–Sept Tues–Sun 9:30am–5:45pm; Oct–Mar Tues–Sun 10am–5:45pm. Métro: Varenne, Invalides, or St-Francois-Xavier.

**Tour Eiffel ★★★ ☺ MONUMENT**    This is without doubt one of the most recognizable structures in the world. Weighing 7,000 tons, but exerting about the same pressure on the ground as an average-size person sitting in a chair, the wrought-iron tower wasn't meant to be permanent. Gustave-Alexandre Eiffel, the French engineer whose fame rested mainly on his iron bridges, built it for the 1889 Universal Exhibition. (Eiffel also designed the framework for the Statue of Liberty.) Praised by some and denounced by others (some called it a "giraffe," the "world's greatest lamppost," or the "iron monster"), the tower created as much controversy in the 1880s as I. M. Pei's glass pyramid at the Louvre did in the 1980s. What saved it from demolition was the advent of radio—as the tallest structure in Europe, it made a perfect spot to place a radio antenna.

The tower, including its antenna, is 317m (1,040 ft.) high. On a clear day you can see it from

## Tour Eiffel Bargain

The least expensive way to see the Tour Eiffel (www.tour-eiffel.fr) is to walk up the first two floors at a cost of 4.50€ adults, or 3.50€ ages 25 and younger. That way, you also avoid the long lines waiting for the elevator—although the views are less spectacular from this platform. If you dine at the tower's own **58 Tour Eiffel** (ℭ **01-45-55-20-04**), an Eiffel restaurant on the first floor, management allows patrons to cut to the head of the line.

65km (40 miles) away. An open-framework construction, the tower unlocked the almost unlimited possibilities of steel construction, paving the way for skyscrapers. Skeptics said it couldn't be built, and Eiffel actually wanted to make it soar higher. For years it remained the tallest man-made structure on earth, until skyscrapers like the Empire State Building surpassed it.

We could fill an entire page with tower statistics. (Its plans spanned 5,400 sq. m/58,000 sq. ft. of paper, and it contains 2.5 million rivets.) But forget the numbers. Just stand beneath the tower, and look straight up. It's like a rocket of steel lacework shooting into the sky.

After undergoing major renovations, the Eiffel Tower's first floor reopened in 2013 with entirely redeveloped public spaces including a new pavilion for visitor services, restaurants, and shops; a new entertaining and educational museum circuit; and two new attractions: a glass floor giving you a view plunging 57m (188 ft.) down to the ground, and an immersive, emotionally powerful film.

**Tour Eiffel.**

From December to February, it is possible to ice-skate inside the Eiffel Tower. Skating takes place on an observation deck 57m (188 ft.) above ground. The rectangular rink is a bit larger than an average tennis court, holding 80 skaters at once. Rink admission and skate rental are free, after you pay the initial entry fee below.

To get to **Le Jules Verne** (www.lejulesverne-paris.com; ✆ **01-45-55-61-44**), the Ducasse–owned fine dining restaurant on the second platform, take the private south foundation elevator. You can enjoy an aperitif in the piano bar and then take a seat at one of the dining room's tables, all of which provide an inspiring view. The menu changes seasonally, offering fish and meat dishes that range from filet of turbot with seaweed and buttered sea urchins to veal chops with truffled vegetables. Reservations are recommended.

Champ de Mars, 7e. www.tour-eiffel.fr. ✆ **01-44-11-23-23.** Admission to 2nd landing 8.20€ adults, 6.60€ ages 12–24, 4.10€ ages 4–11; admission to 3rd landing 13€ adults, 12€ ages 12–24, 9.30€ ages 4–11; admission for stairs to 2nd floor 4.70€ adults, 3.70€ ages 12–24, 3.20€ ages 4–11. Free admission for children 3 and under. Sept–May daily 9:30am–11:45pm; June–Aug daily 9am–12:45am. Sept–June stairs open only to 6:30pm. Métro: Trocadéro, Ecole Militaire, or Bir Hakeim. RER: Champ de Mars–Tour Eiffel.

**TIME OUT AT** the tower

To see the Eiffel Tower best, don't sprint—approach it gradually. We suggest taking the Métro to the Trocadéro stop and walking from the Palais de Chaillot to the Seine to get the full effect of the tower and its surroundings; then cross the Pont d'Iéna and head for the base, where you'll find elevators in two of the pillars—expect long lines. (When the tower is open, you can see the 1889 lift machinery in the east and west pillars.) You visit the tower in three stages: The first landing provides a view over the rooftops, as well as a cinema museum showing films, restaurants, and a bar. The second landing offers a panoramic look at the city. The third landing gives the most spectacular view; Eiffel's office has been re-created on this level, with wax figures depicting the engineer receiving Thomas Edison.

## MONTPARNASSE & SOUTHERN PARIS (14E & 15E)

For the "Lost Generation," life centered on the cafes of Montparnasse, at the border of the 6th and 14th arrondissements. Picasso, Amedeo Modigliani, Man Ray, and Hemingway frequented this neighborhood, as did Fitzgerald when he was poor (when he was rich, you'd find him at the Ritz). Today Montparnasse plays second fiddle to St-Germain-des-Prés.

**Cimetière du Montparnasse ★** CEMETERY   In the shadow of the Tour Montparnasse, this debris-littered cemetery is a burial ground of yesterday's celebrities. A map to the left of the main gateway will direct you to the gravesite of its most famous couple, **Simone de Beauvoir** and **Jean-Paul Sartre.** Others resting here include **Samuel Beckett; Guy de Maupassant; Pierre Larousse** (famous for his dictionary); **Capt. Alfred Dreyfus;** auto tycoon **André Citroën;** sculptors **Ossip Zadkine** and **Constantin Brancusi;** actress **Jean Seberg;** composer **Camille Saint-Saëns;** photographer **Man Ray;** poet **Charles Baudelaire,** who wrote about "plunging into the abyss, Heaven or Hell"; and American intellectual and activist **Susan Sontag,** who was interred here in 2005.

3 bd. Edgar-Quinet, 14e. ℰ **01-44-10-86-50.** Mon–Fri 8am–6pm; Sat 8:30am–6pm; Sun 9am–6pm (closes at 5:30pm Nov–Mar). Métro: Edgar-Quinet.

**Les Catacombes ★** HISTORIC SITE   Every year, about 50,000 visitors explore some 910m (2,986 ft.) of tunnel in these dank catacombs to look at six million ghoulishly arranged, skull-and-crossbones skeletons. First opened to the public in 1810, this "empire of the dead" is now illuminated with electric lights over its entire length. In the Middle Ages, the catacombs were quarries, but by the end of the 18th century, overcrowded cemeteries were becoming a menace to public health. City officials decided to use the catacombs as a burial ground, and the bones of several million persons were transferred here. In 1830, the prefect of Paris closed the catacombs, considering them obscene and indecent. During World War II, the catacombs were the headquarters of the French Resistance.

1 place du Colonel Henri Rol-Tanguy, 14e. www.catacombes-de-paris.fr. ℰ **01-43-22-47-63.** Admission 8€ adults, 6€ seniors, 4€ ages 14–25, free for children 13 and younger. Tues–Sun 10am–5pm. Métro: Denfert-Rochereau.

Les Catacombes.

**Tour Montparnasse** ☺ ARCHITECTURE   Completed in 1973 and rising 206m (676 ft.) above the skyline, the Tour Montparnasse was denounced by some as "bringing Manhattan to Paris." The city soon passed an ordinance outlawing any further structures of this size in the heart of Paris. Today, the modern tower houses an underground shopping mall, as well as much of the infrastructure for the Gare de Montparnasse rail station. You can ride an elevator up to the 56th floor (where you'll find a bar and restaurant) and then climb three flights to the roof terrace. The terrific view encompasses virtually every important Paris monument, including Sacré-Coeur, Notre-Dame, and La Défense.

33 avenue de Maine, 15e. www.tourmontparnasse56.com. ✆ **01-45-38-52-56.** Admission 7€ adults, 4€ students, 3€ children 7–15, Free for children 6 and younger. Apr–Sept daily 9:30am–11:30pm, Oct–Mar daily 9:30am–10:30pm. Métro: Montparnasse-Bienvenüe.

# WHERE TO EAT

Paris has always been a haven for high-rolling gastronomes who collect luxury restaurants like playing cards. That's still the case today. Whether you're looking for an opulent culinary experience or edgy, provocative cooking, Paris's range of quality restaurants—from three-star restaurants to casual bistros—remains unmatched by any other city in the world.

Although Paris has long been home to high-end gourmet restaurants, a growing number of affordable, high-end bistros serving gourmet food have entered Paris's culinary scene. For more than a decade now, chefs who have trained under three-star chefs have been leaving these "palace" restaurants to open more reasonably priced neo-bistrots, where you can get a three-course meal for about 30€ to 40€. Combining classic technique with an emphasis on fresh, seasonal ingredients, this new generation of chefs is revitalizing the culinary scene.

One important challenge remains, even at the informal bistro level: getting in. Paris restaurants tend to be small in size, and they rarely offer multiple seatings during a lunch or dinner service. The result is a smaller number of available seats, and these are often reserved in advance. Reservations are a very good idea at most of the restaurants we recommend, but you needn't worry about booking weeks in advance. The majority will have space if you call the same day or a few days in advance. Ask your hotel concierge to help if you can't manage the telephone, but don't shy away from this step if food is an important part of your Paris visit. The quality of what you can "stumble in" and find, versus what you can experience when you reserve, is radically different.

# The Right Bank

## LES HALLES, LOUVRE, & PALAIS ROYAL (1ER & 2E)

Les Halles takes its name from the soaring food pavilions that once stood on this spot as part of the city's largest outdoor market. That market, which writer Émile Zola famously nicknamed "the belly of Paris," has since moved to the suburbs, but Les Halles still has plenty of gourmet offerings today. Three of the city's most heralded newcomers—**Yam'Tcha, Spring,** and **La Régalade–St. Honoré**— have opened here in recent years. Just to the northwest, the 2nd arrondissement is another hotbed of restaurant activity. Sandwiched between the Louvre and Grand Boulevards you'll find the city's Japanese quarter along rue St-Anne. Here, foodies come from across the city to taste the freshly made gyoza and noodle soups—often even lining up in the street to get a table. You'll also find a sprinkling of excellent eateries, like **Passage 53,** inside the city's olde-worlde covered passages.

### Expensive

**Passage 53** ★★ MODERN FRENCH   After a stint at L'Astrance (p. 140), chef Shinichi Sato joined forces with famous butcher Hugo Desnoyer to open this petite restaurant inside the city's oldest covered passage. His cuisine has been so successful that it earned the restaurant two Michelin stars in 2011. Start with a splash of Champagne Jacquesson before diving into a tasting menu that might begin with pink cubes of raw veal topped with a bracing and briny raw oyster. Up next, you might be served some pristine fish or a *civet* (a type of stew) of wild hare served with chocolate sauce. Flavors are bold and clear, and the technical skill on display is impressive. End the meal with a delicious tart with the thinnest-possible pastry crust.

53 passage des Panoramas, 2e. www.passage53.com. ✆ **01-42-33-04-35.** Reservations recommended. Fixed-price lunch 60€; fixed-price dinner 110€. MC, V. Tues–Sat noon–2:30pm and 7–10pm. Métro: Grands Boulevards.

**Spring** ★★ MODERN FRENCH   This media-hyped restaurant was created by young American chef Daniel Rose. Spring initially opened in a remote Pigalle location, but after garnering rave reviews from French critics, Rose moved the restaurant to this space near the Louvre. Today, Spring has a 16th-century wine cave, an underground wine bar with vaulted ceilings, an open kitchen, and a sleek modern dining room. The fixed-price tasting menu is improvisational—it changes nearly every day—but it might begin with a little beignet of fried sole, followed by roasted pigeon or sweetbreads with wild mushrooms. Desserts might include a crustless lemon tart or berries floating in a tea made from the pit of a peach. The wine list is well chosen but it only offers a few moderately priced bottles. Spring also offers wine-tasting lessons on most Thursday afternoons (60€).

6 rue Bailleul, 1er. www.springparis.fr. (C) **01-45-96-05-72.** Reservations required. Fixed-price dinner 58€–76€; fixed-price lunch 44€. MC, V. Wed–Fri noon–2pm and 7–10pm; Tues-Sat 7–10pm. Closed mid-Feb-early March. Métro: Louvre-Rivoli.

**Yam'Tcha ★★★** MODERN FRENCH/CHINESE   A seat at this modern restaurant, on an ancient side street in Les Halles, is one of the city's most difficult to reserve. That has something to do with the small number of tables, but it is mostly due to the fact that Chef Adeline Grattard has received almost universal acclaim for her Franco-Chinese cooking. After spending time at the Michelin three-starred restaurant L'Astrance, Grattard set out on her own in 2009 and has been solidly booked ever since. The dishes on her prix-fixe menus reflect the seasons and change regularly; a recent menu included a flash-seared lobster with corn coulis, and a bouillon of beef with foie gras that one French critic called "the best dish of the year." Both wine and tea pairings (Yam'Tcha means "drink tea") are available. Reserve a month in advance for lunch and more than three months in advance for dinner.

4 rue Sauval, 1er. (C) **01-40-26-08-07.** Reservations required far in advance. Fixed-price lunch 50€; fixed-price dinner 85€. AE, MC, V. Métro: Louvre-Rivoli.

## Moderate
**Frenchie ★★ 🍴** MODERN FRENCH   Greg Marchand acquired the nickname Frenchie when he left his native France to work for Jamie Oliver in England and later at New York's Gramercy Tavern. In 2009, Marchand returned to Paris and opened up this tiny bistro in an unfashionable part of the Sentier. Word spread quickly about the delicious and wonderfully priced cuisine, and Frenchie began to win various "Best Bistro" awards and features in magazines. As a result, this simple place requires booking (at least) several months in advance. Marchand's cooking remains astonishingly good. Starters like house-smoked fish with pickled vegetables are bright and clean, and main dishes—like duck with blood orange and dandelion—manage to be both comforting and provocative. Desserts, like a cheesecake composed of Brillat Savarin (a delicious triple cream cheese), are never too sweet.

5 rue du Nil, 2e. www.frenchie-restaurant.com. (C) **01-40-39-96-19.** Reservations required far in advance. Fixed-price dinner 34€–45€. MC, V. Mon–Fri 7–10:30pm. Métro: Sentier.

**La Régalade–St. Honoré ★★** TRADITIONAL FRENCH/BISTRO   It used to be that fans of the bistro La Régalade had to travel to the southern edge of the 14th arrondissement in order to enjoy the cooking of Bruno Doucet. Not anymore. In 2010, Doucet opened a second restaurant under the Régalade banner right on the rue Saint-Honoré. Now you can enjoy famously comforting dishes like sautéed morel mushrooms in cream with parsley and crispy croutons or farm-raised pork belly with a creamy interior and crispy skin. Just as at the restaurant down south, the same "help-yourself" crock of homemade pork terrine arrives with *cornichons* (gherkin pickles) and butter as you sit down to the table. Desserts, as you can imagine, are sometimes hard to face after all that pork fat, but they're included in the three-course prix fixe for a remarkable 32€—although note that some dishes come with supplementary charges.

123 rue Saint-Honoré, 1er. (C) **01-42-21-92-40.** Reservations required. Fixed-price dinner 32€. MC, V. Mon–Wed noon–2:30pm and 7–10:30pm; Thurs–Fri noon–2:30pm and 7–11:30pm. Métro: Louvre-Rivoli.

**Le Fumoir** ★★ CONTEMPORARY FRENCH    With views onto the Louvre's eastern edge, this chic colonial-style restaurant, with a zinc bar and leather chesterfield armchairs is a plum spot for escaping the tourists. Cocktails and coffee are served throughout the day, and at mealtimes inventive, affordable dishes are served to swarms of those in the know. The menu might include a starter of beef marinated in port wine, turnips, and salmon roe (an unsual combination, but it works); followed by pan-roasted cod with citrus and rosemary crust; and for dessert, blood-orange rice-pudding. The 22€ Sunday brunch menu is popular too: Fruit juice, hot drinks, pancakes, poached eggs, and smoked ham or a juicy French steak with fries are on offer—and of course, there are those chesterfields for slumping into.

6 rue de l'Amiral Coligny, 1e. http://lefumoir.com. ✆ **01-42-92-00-24.** Reservations recommended. Main courses 20€–25€; 3-course fixed-price menu 35€. AE, DC, MC, V. Daily 11am–2am. Métro: Louvre-Rivoli.

**Restaurant Chez Denise - La Tour de Montlhéry** ★★ TRADITIONAL FRENCH/BISTRO    Diners looking for the classic Paris bistro experience come to this raucous old dining room near Les Halles. Chez Denise (as the locals call it) stays open until the early hours of the morning and serves sturdy platters of *côte de boeuf* (a giant rib steak), grilled marrow bones, and brochettes of grilled meat so long they look like swords. The long-aproned waiters are used to encountering English speakers, but Chez Denise hasn't yet lost its bawdy, authentic local vibe. This might not be, however, the place to bring your vegetarian friend.

5 rue des Prouvaires, 1er. ✆ **01-42-36-21-82.** Reservations recommended. Main courses 22€–30€; fixed-price dinner 50€. MC, V. Mon–Fri noon–3pm and 7:30pm–4am. Closed July 15–Aug 15. Métro: Les Halles.

### Inexpensive

**Higuma** ★ JAPANESE    This no-frills Japanese canteen in the Japanese quarter is always full, so get there early if you don't want to queue in the street at meal times. The reason behind its popularity is its quirky open kitchen, which fills the air with delicious-smelling steam, and the low prices—around 11€–13€ for a starter of gyoza (grilled dumplings filled with pork meat)—and its giant bowls of soup, rice, or noodles piled high with meat, seafood, of stir-fried vegetables. For some theater with your meal, arrive early and request a table at the bar surrounding the open kitchen. From your perch you can watch your food being cooked, and even dodge the steam and flames.

32 bis rue St-Anne, 2e. ✆ **01-47-03-38-59.** Main courses 9€–14€. MC, V. Daily 11:30am–10pm. Métro: Pyramides.

**Le Garde Robe** FRENCH/WINE BAR    In a quaint side street off rue de Rivoli in Châtelet, Le Garde Robe is a tiny wine bar with exposed stone walls and wine bottles lining the walls. Fans of French wine come for the large selection of organic and biodynamic wines, which you can buy to take away; or if you decide to stay (which you will) corkage is 7€ extra. A laidback, suited crowd usually rolls up to the bar afterwork for a glass of red or white, accompanied by a *petit chèvre au pesto* (creamy goat cheese with pesto) or the excellent *croque robe* (a house take on traditional French *croque monsieur*, with cheese, ham, and salad). For extra comfort (the bar stools can be awkward), reserve one of the tables in the back, then relax and enjoy the buzzy atmosphere.

41 rue de l'Arbre Sec, 1er. ✆ **01-49-26-90-60.** Reservations recommended. Main courses 10€–16€; MC, V. Mon–Sat 7:30–11pm; Métro: Louvre Rivoli or Châtelet.

## LE MARAIS, ILE ST LOUIS & ILE DE LA CITÉ (3E & 4E)

The Marais is packed with contemporary art galleries and cutting-edge fashion boutiques, but our favorite restaurants in this neighborhood are utterly traditional, whether they're serving the city's best roast chicken (**L'Ami Louis**) or classic dishes from the Basque region (**Au Bascou**), Brittany (**the Breizh Café**), or Provence (**Chez Janou**). Any stroll through the historic Jewish quarter around the rue des Rosiers requires a stop at **L'As du Fallafel** for the beloved (and messy) falafel sandwich.

### Expensive

**Benoit** TRADITIONAL FRENCH   There's something weighty about this historical monument, lined with mirrors, zinc, and tiles; every mayor of Paris has dined here since the restaurant was founded in 1912. Today Benoit is owned by the Alain Ducasse group, which adds extra pizazz to the traditional bistro fare. Crowd-pleasers include cassoulet (home-made sausage, duck, and white bean hot-pot), filet of sole, and *tête de veau* (head cheese) with a *ravigote* sauce. The three-course lunch menu is particularly good value. It might include pork with pumpkin gratin, black pudding (sausage), or apple chocolate tart. There are over 350 types of wine to go with your meal, so ask the sommelier for a helping hand.

20 rue St-Martin, 4e. www.benoit-paris.com. ✆ **01-42-72-25-76.** Reservations required. Main courses 24€–44€; fixed-price lunch 36€. AE, DC, MC, V. Daily noon–2pm and 7:30–10pm. Métro: Hôtel-de-Ville.

### Moderate

**Au Bascou** BASQUE   The succulent cuisine of France's "deep southwest" is the specialty here, where art objects, paintings, and tones of ocher celebrate the beauty of the region, and hanging clusters of pimentos add spice to the air. Try *pipérade basquaise* (a spicy omelet loaded with peppers and onions), pimentos stuffed with purée of codfish, and *axoa* (a stew of veal shoulder, peppers and onions). Also noteworthy are the *soupions* (baby squid) sautéed with chorizo and duck breast with pan-fried foie-gras.

38 rue Réaumur, 3e. www.au-bascou.fr. ✆ **01-42-72-69-25.** Reservations recommended. Main courses 17€; fixed-price lunch menu 18€. AE, DC, MC, V. Mon–Fri noon–2pm and 7:30–10:30pm. Métro: Arts-et-Métiers.

**Jaja** MODERN FRENCH/BISTRO   Tucked into a charming courtyard in the southern Marais, this bistro is coveted by the foodies and style hounds of the neighborhood. It's a place to be seen, sure, but also a place to eat well for not much money, especially at lunch. Jaja's take on the hot dog (an artisanal sausage topped with pungent cheese) and the croque-monsieur (ham and cheese grilled sandwich) are playful and delicious. Stick to the basics here, and wash them down with wine from Jaja's very well-curated wine list.

3 rue Sainte-Croix-de-la-Bretonnerie, 4e. www.jaja-resto.com. ✆ **01-42-74-71-52.** Reservations recommended. Main courses 15€–23€; fixed-price lunch 16€. Mon–Sun noon–2:30pm and 8–11pm. Métro: Hotel de Ville.

### Inexpensive

**Breizh Café** ★ ✦ CRÊPERIE/CAFÉ   This popular spot in the Marais serves crepes like you've never had them before. Run by a Breton-Japanese couple, this warm and modern wood-paneled space that is decorated with funky Japanese art has friendly service and quality food. Start with oysters or go straight to a savory buckwheat galette, which is crisp and nutty and filled with high-quality organic ingredients, such as farm fresh eggs, Bordier butter, and seasonal produce. Sip on one of the artisanal ciders, and save room for a sweet crepe, drizzled with chocolate or salted butter caramel. Reservations highly recommended.

109 rue Vieille du Temple, 3e. www.breizhcafe.com. ✆ **01-42-72-13-77.** Reservations recommended. Main courses 5.50€–11€. MC, V. Wed–Sat noon–11pm; Sun noon–10pm. Métro: Filles du Calvaire.

**L'As du Fallafel ★** FALAFEL/LIGHT FARE    You can distinguish the "king of falafel" from other pretenders on the street by the presence of a long line snaking away from the dark green shop front. Join the line (it moves fast) for a sandwich to go, or push through into one of two dining rooms and ask for a table. There are many options on the menu, including chicken shawarma and lamb kabobs, but you want the falafel sandwich. Stuffed with light and crispy balls of falafel (fried chickpeas) and topped with grilled eggplant and fresh salad, this really is one of the most delicious cheap bites in town. With a plate of fries to share and an Israeli beer, you can escape for less than 10€ per person. Note that L'As is closed Friday night and all day Saturday to honor the Jewish Sabbath.

34 rue des Rosiers, 4e. ✆ **01-48-87-63-60.** Reservations not accepted. Main courses 5€–16€. Sun–Thurs 11am–11:30pm; Fri 11am–5pm. Métro: St. Paul.

**Le Potager du Marais ★** VEGETARIAN    Arguably the best vegetarian restaurant in Paris, vegetarians flock to this place for its range of delicious organic offerings. Dishes are so tasty, even meat eaters won't complain. Many items are gluten-free. Your veggie meal might start with mushroom paté, followed by tofu and pumpkin parmentier (pumpkin baked with mashed potato) seasoned with herbs and lentils, and finished with homemade apple compote. Just be prepared to get friendly with your neighbors: the restaurant is so narrow that the tables are packed in like sardines along just one wall.

22 rue Rambuteau, 3e. www.lepotagerdumarais.com. ✆ **01-42-74-24-66.** Entrees 9€–16€. MC, V. Daily noon–2pm and 7–10:30pm. Métro: Rambuteau.

## CHAMPS-ÉLYSÉES & WESTERN PARIS (8E, 16E & 17E)

The posh avenues that radiate from the Champs-Élysées are home to some of the most expensive and elegant dining in the city. If you're looking to splurge on a lavish gastronomic experience, this is the right neighborhood. Dress sharp and be ready to drop at least 100€ per head, unless you uncover one of the rare moderate tables in these parts.

### Very Expensive
**Antoine ★★** SEAFOOD    Seafood fans go wild for chef Mickaël Féval's perfect-every-time, innovative fish and shellfish dishes, which earned this restaurant its first Michelin star in 2011. The bouillabaisse is as good as any in Marseille, and the oysters come with tangy shallot vinegar and creamy salted butter for your bread. It's a handy address to have up your sleeve when you're exploring the Chaillot quarters, Champs-Élysées, and the Eiffel Tower. Come at night and you can just make out the Eiffel Tower sparkling through the trees on the other side of the river.

10 ave. de New York, 16e. www.antoine-paris.fr. ✆ **01-40-70-19-28.** Main courses 50€–70€; fixed-price lunch 35€. MC, V. Daily noon–2pm and 7–10:30pm. Métro: Alma Marceau.

**Le Cinq** ★★ MODERN FRENCH   Since it was established in 1928 in honor of the king of England, there has always been a world-class dining venue associated with the Hotel George V. Today, the grand decor of this high-ceilinged room evokes the Grand Trianon at Versailles. Critics have been lavishing Chef Eric Briffard with praise, saying that he's a shoe-in to regain the restaurant's third Michelin star. Briffard trained under both Joël Robuchon and Alain Ducasse and cooks with precision and expertise. The menu changes frequently, but you may start with something like abalone and razor clams with algae butter and fried watercress, and move on to a main dish of venison with smoky bacon and a chocolaty peppercorn sauce.

In the Four Seasons Hotel George V, 31 av. George V, 8e. www.fourseasons.com. © **01-49-52-71-54.** Reservations recommended 4 weeks in advance for dinner, 1 week in advance for lunch. Main courses 80€–135€; fixed-price lunch 78€–160€; fixed-price dinner 160€–230€. AE, DC, MC, V. Daily 12:30–2:30pm and 7–10:30pm. Métro: George V.

**Pierre Gagnaire** ★★★ MODERN FRENCH   Of all the three-star chefs working in Paris today, Gagnaire is by far the most playful and experimental. He spent years collaborating with molecular gastronomy pioneer Hervé This to create boundary-pushing dishes with unusual textures and forms. The menu changes regularly, but recent meals have featured lobster hidden under brightly colored blankets of vegetable gel, and raw clams on a bed of sweet and sour pumpkin. One tip if you plan to order a la carte: each *plat* is actually made up of four to five small dishes, so ordering both a starter and a main dish may yield more food than you could possibly eat. Perhaps it's not a bad thing that the desserts here are not as strong as you'll find at other three-star restaurants.

6 rue Balzac, 8e. www.pierre-gagnaire.com. © **01-58-36-12-50.** Fax 01-58-36-12-51. Reservations required. Main courses 65€–165€; fixed-price lunch 105€; fixed-price dinner 265€. AE, DC, MC, V. Mon–Fri noon–1:30pm; Sun–Fri 7:30–10pm. Métro: George V.

**Restaurant Plaza Athénée (Alain Ducasse)** ★★ TRADITIONAL FRENCH   This three-star restaurant bears the name of internationally renowned chef Alain Ducasse and serves as the flagship of his restaurant empire. The globe-trotting chef is rarely here himself, but he has left his kitchen in the capable hands of Christophe Saintagne. A special emphasis is placed on "rare and precious ingredients"; the chef whips up flavorful and very expensive combinations of caviar, lobster, crayfish, and truffles (both black and white). Dishes may include sea scallops with salsify and black truffles, duck liver "pot au feu," or sole meunière with Belgian endives. The wine list is superb, with selections deriving from the best vintages of France, Germany, Switzerland, Spain, California, and Italy. The dining room, designed by Patrick Jouin and featuring a jaw-dropping "deconstructed" chandelier, is among the most beautiful in Paris.

In the Hôtel Plaza Athénée, 25 av. Montaigne, 8e. www.alain-ducasse.com. © **01-53-67-65-00.** Fax 01-53-67-65-12. Reservations required 4–6 weeks in advance. Main courses 90€–180€; fixed-price menu 260€–360€. AE, DC, MC, V. Thurs–Fri 12:45–2:15pm; Mon–Fri 7:45–10:15pm. Closed mid-July to Aug 25 and 10 days in late Dec. Métro: Alma-Marceau.

**Shang Palace** ★★★ CHINESE   The palatial Hôtel Shangri-La (the former Palace of Roland Bonaparte, Napoleon's great nephew) is a veritable foodie heaven with no less than three fabulous, high-end eating opportunities. Our favorite is **Shang Palace,** the city's first-ever gourmet Cantonese restaurant serving the best dim sum and Peking duck in town in a beautiful dining room reminiscent of a 1930s Hong Kong gentleman's club. The 58€ lunch menu offers a wide selection of gourmet dim sum and noodle dishes. The hotel's other restaurants—**L'Abeille,** which serves up French gastronomy in a magazine-perfect gray and yellow setting, and **La Bauhinia Brasserie,** which serves lip-smacking Chinese and French dishes—are both worth a visit if you have time (and money).

10 ave. Iéna, 16e. www.shangri-la.com. ✆ **01-53-67-19-98.** Reservations recommended. Main courses 22€–125€; fixed-price lunch from 58€; fixed-price dinner from 98€. AE, DC, MC, V. Daily 11:30am–2:30pm and 6:30–10:30pm. Métro: Iéna.

## Expensive

**L'Astrance ★★★** MODERN FRENCH   This small and charming spot is owned by two former employees (some say "disciples") of megachef Alain Passard, scion of L'Arpège; Christophe Rohat supervises the dining room, while Pascal Barbot is a true culinary force in the kitchen. The menu changes seasonally, but might include an unusual form of "ravioli," wherein thin slices of avocado encase a filling of seasoned crabmeat, all of it accompanied by salted almonds and a splash of almond oil. Other delights to the palate include turbot flavored with lemon and ginger, or sautéed pigeon with potatoes au gratin. The signature dish is a galette of thinly sliced raw mushrooms and verjus-marinated foie gras with hazelnut oil and lemon confit.

4 rue Beethoven, 16e. ✆ **01-40-50-84-40.** Reservations required at least one month in advance. Main courses 24€–80€; fixed-price lunch 70€–120€; fixed-price dinner 125€–290€. AE, DC, MC, V. Tues–Fri 12:15–1:30pm and 8:15–9pm. Closed Aug. Métro: Passy.

## Moderate

**Le Hide ★**  TRADITIONAL FRENCH   This bistro near the Eiffel Tower takes its name from chef Hide Kobayashi, who describes his food as French bistro cooking. The cuisine is certainly French, but a few of the recipes hint at his Japanese origins. Kobayashi perfected his craft in the kitchens of some of the world's greatest chefs, including Joël Robuchon. The menu changes regularly, and main courses, like fricassee of rabbit flavored with mustard or sweetbreads in cream with truffles, all carry the same price tag. In a neighborhood full of expensive and unmemorable restaurants, Le Hide is one of the best options for well-executed French bistro cuisine at an affordable price.

10 rue du General Lanrezac, 17e. www.lehide.fr. ✆ **01-45-74-15-81.** Reservations required. Main courses 16€; fixed-price menu 23€–30€. MC, V. Mon–Fri noon–3pm and Mon–Sat 7–10:30pm. Métro: Charles-de-Gaulle-Etoile.

---

### Personalized Food Tours

Canadian Rosa Jackson is a self-declared foodie and an acclaimed food critic who shares her time between Paris and Nice. Through her company, **Edible Paris** (www.edible-paris.com), she concocts personalized food itineraries around the city. Whether you're into chocolate, cheese, bread, luxury restaurants, or all of these things, she provides you with routes to follow for a half-day, a whole day, or over 2 days. She can also set you up with your very own food gurus—English-speaking restaurant critics, food writers, and professional cooks in Paris who spend their spare time sniffing out the very best food shops and restaurants to share with you during your break. These experiences cost 100€ to 350€.

### Inexpensive
**Monte Carlo** 🍴 FRENCH   Local business types flock to this excellent self-service canteen at lunchtime for the quality 3-course menus—possibly the cheapest around the Champs-Élysées, starting at 11€. Being served over the counter probably isn't your dream dining experience for Paris, but the food is tasty, the staff friendly, and at these prices you simply can't complain. The dishes of the day (think *boeuf bourguignon* and *coq au vin*) are served with a choice of side dish—usually French fries, rice, or boiled vegetables. Desserts range from healthy yogurts to cream cakes. This is a top spot when you're on the run.

9 ave. de Wagram, 17e. www.monte-carlo.fr. ✆ **01-43-80-02-20.** Reservations not accepted. Main courses 9€. MC, V. Daily 11am–11pm. Métro/RER: Charles-de-Gaulle Etoile.

## OPÉRA & CANAL ST-MARTIN (9E & 10E)
This area, which stretches from the Opéra Garnier eastwards along the grand boulevards—Haussmann, Montmartre, and Bonne Nouvelle—is filled with good-value bistros and wine bars, often hidden down side streets. Recently, the Opéra Garnier saw the opening of its first-ever restaurant, the **Restaurant de l'Opéra,** a boldly modern affair nestled inside the former entrance for horse-drawn carriages.

### Expensive
**Restaurant de l'Opéra** MODERN FRENCH   It took five years for director Pierre François Blanc to open the opera house's first ever restaurant—the building is so historically important that planning permission was almost impossible to obtain. However, it was worth the wait. Today's dining room is both edgy and beautiful. The bold, curvaceous red and white structure, designed by Odile Decq, fills the space without touching the Garnier's protected walls. Expect well-cooked, if not a little over-priced, dishes with prime ingredients like lobster, whiting, and sole as well as guinea fowl and pata negra pork. End the night with a cocktail from the Martini bar: Phantom (in reference to Leroux's 1910 Phantom of the Opera novel inspired by the Opéra Garnier) is the house special. You can also work your meal around a night at the ballet or opera in the adjoining opera house.

Palais Garnier, place Jacques-Rouché, 9e. www.opera-restaurant.fr. ✆ **01-42-68-86-80.** Reservations recommended. Main courses 26€–45€; fixed-price lunch 36€. MC, V. Daily noon–10pm. Métro: Opéra; RER Auber.

### Moderate
**Le Pantruche** ★ 🍴 TRADITIONAL FRENCH/BISTRO   From the moment it opened in early 2011, this modern bistro not far from Pigalle impressed critics with its friendly atmosphere, affordable prices, and better-than-average bistro fare. Dishes include a rich celery root soup, tender glazed beef cheeks, oyster tartare, and a classic Grand Marnier soufflé. Although it's dressed like a humble neighborhood joint, Franck Baranger's cooking puts Le Pantruche in another league altogether.

3 rue Victor Massé, 9e. http://lepantruche.com. ✆ **01-48-78-55-60.** Reservations recommended. Fixed-price dinner 32€; fixed-price lunch 17€. Mon–Fri noon–2:30pm and 7:15–10:30pm. Métro: Pigalle.

**Wally Le Saharien** MIDDLE EASTERN   Head to this dining room—lined with desert photos and tribal artifacts crafted from ceramics, wood, and weavings—for an insight into the spicy, slow-cooked cuisine that fueled the colonial expansion of France into North Africa. The prix-fixe dinner menu might begin with a trio of starters: spicy soup, stuffed and grilled sardines, and a savory pastilla of pigeon in puff pastry. Next comes any of several kinds of couscous or a *méchouia* (slow-cooked tart). Merguez, the cumin-laden spicy sausage of the North African world, factors importantly into any meal, as do homemade pastries.

36 rue Rodier, 9e. *© 01-42-85-51-90.* Reservations recommended. Main courses 20€–25€; fixed-price lunch 30€; fixed-price dinner 45€. MC, V. Tue–Sat noon–2pm and 7–10:30pm. Closed July. Métro: St-Georges or Anvers.

### Inexpensive

**Chartier** TRADITIONAL FRENCH/BRASSERIE   Opened in 1896, this unpretentious *fin-de-siècle* restaurant is now an official historic monument featuring a whimsical mural with trees, a flowering staircase, and an early depiction of an airplane (it was painted in 1929 by an artist who traded his work for food). The menu follows brasserie-style traditions, including items you might not dare to eat—beef tartare, chitterling sausages, tongue of beef with spicy sauce—as well as some classic temptations, like duck confit. The waiter will steer you through such dishes as *choucroute* (sauerkraut), *pavé* (a thick slice of rump steak), and at least five kinds of fish. High gastronomy this isn't, but you can't beat Chartier for a cheerful night on the cheap. Arrive early to avoid the queues.

7 rue du Faubourg Montmartre, 9e. www.restaurant-chartier.com. *© 01-47-70-86-29.* Main courses 9€–12€. AE, DC, MC, V. Daily 11:30am–10pm. Métro: Grands-Boulevards.

## PIGALLE & MONTMARTRE (18E)

Montmartre today is home to a good number of reputable restaurants, including great finds like **Le Bal Café.** However, if you're looking for a good meal, avoid place du Tertre, where hopeful portrait artists sit waiting for tourists with their easels. Instead head to the northern side of the Butte around Lamarck-Caulincourt, where you'll find lovely low-key bistros like **Nansouty.**

### Moderate

**Chéri Bibi** 🍴 TRADITIONAL FRENCH   Decorated with flea-market finds and featuring an affordable menu of classic French fare, Cheri Bibi has become the unofficial canteen for the young and artsy Montmartre crowd. The chalk-board menu includes rustic dishes like *boudin noir* (blood sausage), *andouillette*, head cheese, and steak frites. This might not be the place to bring a vegetarian friend. A crowd often gathers around the restaurant's zinc bar just to sip wine, sometimes spilling out onto the sidewalk that lies just below the eastern slope of the Sacré-Coeur.

15 rue André del Sarte, 18e. *© 01-42-54-88-96.* Reservations recommended. Main courses 16€–35€; fixed-price dinner 22€–26€. MC, V. Mon–Sat 8pm–midnight (until 2am for the bar). Métro: Barbes-Rochechouart.

**Nansouty** ★ 🎒 MODERN FRENCH   Just north of the Butte de Montmartre, Nansouty is an epicurean find, serving traditional French cuisine with a modern twist. Groups of friends tend to cluster at the large *table d'hôte* at the entrance, while couples make a beeline for the smaller tables nearest the semi-open kitchen at the back, where you can catch delicious odors wafting out of bubbling pots and sizzling frying pans. The menu changes with the seasons but a typical meal here might include pan-fried foie gras with vegetable stew, *côte de boeuf,* or a humongous rum baba (cake doused in rum and sugar) covered in cream. Nansouty is also about the wine, so tell the waiter your price range and he'll make suggestions to match your food.

35 rue Ramey, 18e. ☏ **01-42-52-58-87.** Reservations recommended. Main courses 16€–35€; fixed-price dinner 35€. MC, V. Mon–Sat noon–3pm and 7:30–11:30pm. Métro: Lamarck-Caulincourt or Château Rouge.

### Inexpensive
**Le Bal Café ★** ENGLISH    Brunch-loving Parisians have flipped for the traditional English breakfast that's served on the weekends here. Tucked inside a cultural center and photography museum near the place de Clichy, Le Bal Café is more than just eggs and bacon (and scones, kippers, and pancakes). The chef, who used to work at London's renowned Saint John restaurant, prepares an impressive array of modern British cuisine, with dishes like guinea hen with endives, lamb shoulder with carrots, and head cheese with prunes. The sturdy fare is complemented by a well-chosen and affordable wine list. Kill time waiting for your reservation by browsing the adjoining bookstore or taking in some of the wonderful photography exhibits at the center.

6 impasse de la Défense, 18e. www.le-bal.fr. ☏ **01-44-70-75-51.** Reservations not required. Main courses 5.50€–20€; brunch 12€. MC, V. Wed, Fri noon–8pm; Sat 11am–8pm; Sun 11am–7pm; Thu 11am–10pm. Métro: Place de Clichy.

## RÉPUBLIQUE, BASTILLE & EASTERN PARIS (11E & 12E)

With a mix of working-class families, hipsters, and *bobos,* the area between République and Nation is diverse, young, and fun. It's also one of the best food neighborhoods in the city, thanks to stand-out restaurants like **Le Chateaubriand, Le Bistrot Paul Bert,** and **La Gazzetta.** The atmosphere in these places is casual and buzzing, the waiters tend to be handsome and unshaved, and the wine is mostly natural. Don't let the informality trick you into believing that you don't need to book in advance or that prices will be low.

### Expensive
**La Gazzetta ★★** MODERN FRENCH    Within one of the prettiest bistro settings in all of Paris, and just down the street from the bustling outdoor food market at Aligre, Chef Petter Nilsson is serving some of the city's most avantgarde cuisine. The beautiful Art Deco–inspired dining room, with its soft lighting, leafy palm trees, and dark polished wood, suggests a place serving classic bistro fare. But Nilsson's dishes are anything but traditional. A recent meal featured a soft poached egg floating in a broth of anise-scented cardoon that was spiked with briny mullet roe. That was followed by scallops roasted with beetroot and almonds, and seaweed scones served with Roquefort cheese and lemon caramel. For fans of experimental cooking, the seven-course tasting menu at 56€ is one the city's best values.

29 rue de Cotte, 12e. www.lagazzetta.fr. ☏ **01-43-47-47-05.** Reservations recommended. Fixed-price dinner 42€ and 56€; fixed-price lunch 17€. Tues–Sat noon–2pm and 8–11pm. Métro: Ledru-Rollin.

**Le Chateaubriand ★★★** MODERN FRENCH   Chef Inaki Aizpitarte is the unofficial leader of France's neo-bistrot movement, and his restaurant, Le Chateaubriand, still receives superlative praise. Aizpitarte's regularly changing 55€ prix-fixe menu offers no choices, but open-minded diners are rewarded with some of the most innovative flavor pairings in Paris. You may try rare tuna slices in pink beet foam flavored with pomegranate seeds or eel flavored with orange juice and olive oil. Not every single plate is a winner, but usually at least three of four dishes tend to be brilliant. If you don't have a reservation, you can try to score a seat at the second seating, which begins around 10pm.

129 av. Parmentier, 11e. ℰ **01-43-57-45-95.** Reservations required. Fixed-price dinner 55€. AE, DC, MC, V. Tues–Sat 8–11:30pm. Métro: Goncourt.

## Moderate

**Le Bistrot Paul Bert ★★** BISTRO/TRADITIONAL FRENCH   Ask any local food writer to name his or her favorite classic bistros and there's a very good chance that you'll be directed here. The chalkboard menu is long and changes with the seasons, but a typical meal might begin with a plate of sunny-side up eggs with truffle cream and shaved black truffle, followed by one of the city's best steak frites (it's crowned with a glistening morsel of marrow), and ending with a generous slice of *tarte tatin* (apple tart) and its accompanying pitcher of thick crème fraîche. The decor is a jumble of wooden tables, cracked tile floors, flea market finds, and a polished zinc bar—exactly how you imagine a neighborhood bistro should be. The crowd is predominantly local, although the staff is used to dealing with the occasional food-minded traveler. The wine list features many unusual and affordable bottles from small wine producers.

18 rue Paul Bert, 11e. ℰ **01-43-72-24-01.** Reservations required. Mains 17€–25€; fixed-price dinner 34€. MC, V. Tues–Sat noon–2pm and 7:30–11pm. Métro: Faidherbe-Chaligny.

**Mansouria** MOROCCAN   One of Paris's most charming Moroccan restaurants occupies a restored building midway between place de la Bastille and place de la Nation. The minimalist decor combines futuristic architecture with bare sand-colored walls, accented only with sets of antique doors and portals from the sub-Sahara. Look for eight different varieties of couscous and six different *tagines,* including versions with chicken, beef, lamb, and vegetables.

11 rue Faidherbe, 11e. www.mansouria.fr. ℰ **01-43-71-00-16.** Reservations recommended. Main courses 17€–26€; fixed-price dinner 28€–36€. AE, MC, V. Mon 7:30–11pm; Tues–Sat noon–2pm and 7:30–11pm. Métro: Faidherbe-Chaligny.

**Septime** CONTEMPORARY FRENCH   This neo-bistrot is one of Paris's most exciting new restaurants. Here, Chef Bertrand Grébaut (who gave up a career in graphic design to become a cook) lets his imagination and culinary expertise run loose. Amid chic but understated décor, with light walls and old tiled flooring, the ever-changing menu might include a creamy tarragon and watercress risotto, veal tartare, roasted black pig with fennel, and a *p'tit suisse* (creamy fresh cheese tart). The 26€ lunch menu is a fine introduction to Grébaut's cuisine and includes a glass of wine. If you're curious, come in the evening for the 55€ tasting menu.

**HOTELS**

Cosmos Hotel **5**
Gabriel Paris Marais **3**
Le Général Hotel **2**

**RESTAURANTS**

Jeanne A **4**
La Gazzetta **9**
Le Bistrot
    Paul Bert **7**
Le Chateaubriand **1**
Mansouria **8**
Septime **6**

---

80 rue de Charonne, 11e. www.septime-charonne.fr. (℃) **01-43-67-38-29.** Reservations recommended. Main courses 18€–26€; fixed-price lunch 26€; fixed-price dinner 55€. MC, V. Mon 8–10:30pm;
Tues–Fri 12:30–2pm, 8–10:30pm. Métro: Ledru Rollin or Charonne.

### Inexpensive

**Jeanne A ★ 🔖** TRADITIONAL FRENCH/WINE BAR   This restaurant/
wine bar/takeout shop represents a new trend in Paris, providing an informal
place to eat and drink well for not a lot of money. Run by the renowned Astier
restaurant next door, Jeanne A turns out spit-roasted meats (Challans duck or
crispy-skinned chicken) served with salad and heaping portions of *potato gratin
dauphinois*. These mains are bookended by delicious charcuterie and an impressive selection of artisanal cheeses, and complemented by high-quality wines that
are well-priced. Order by the glass or the magnum (that's two bottles' worth), and
take home what you're not able to drink.

42 rue Jean-Pierre Timbaud, 11e. (℃) **01-43-55-09-49.** Reservations recommended. Main courses
12€–17€; fixed-price lunch 15€. MC, V. Thurs–Mon 10:30am–10:30pm. Métro: Parmentier.

## BELLEVILLE, CANAL ST-MARTIN & NORTHEAST PARIS (10E, 19E AND 20E)

Between the two parks of Belleville and Buttes Chaumont and along the Canal St-Martin lie some of the city's most quirky, delightful, and wine-centered restaurants.

### Moderate

**Brasserie Flo ★★** TRADITIONAL FRENCH/BRASSERIE This well-known restaurant is tough to find, located down a discreet cobblestoned passage, but you'll be glad you tracked it down when you try the onion soup, sole meunière, or guinea hen with lentils. The 19th-century decor, reminiscent of a German beer tavern, is stunning, with rich wooden paneling and frescoes depicting little people making beer. As you tuck in, don't forget to watch the black-and-white–clad waiters at work; it's a veritable choreography of sevice as they wind in between tables carrying giant silver platters and hot pots.

7 cour des Petites-Ecuries, 10e. www.floparis.com. (✆ **01-47-70-13-59.** Reservations recommended. Main courses 16€–30€; price-fixed lunch 24€–40€, price-fixed dinner from 35€. AE, DC, MC, V. Métro: Château d'Eau or Strasbourg-St-Denis.

**Le Verre Volé ★★** WINE BAR/MODERN FRENCH This wine bar, along the charming Canal Saint-Martin, has been open for more than 10 years, but it recently added a second dining room annex and brought in some real culinary talent in the form of Chef Delphine Zampetti. The sharable plates of charcuterie and cheese are still on the menu, but more inventive fare like octopus carpaccio, smoked swordfish, and pâté en croûte with pigeon and foie gras are also offered. Select a bottle of wine from the shelves that line the walls, and enjoy it (for a nominal corkage fee) in this informal and fun setting. It may be a casual place, but the popularity of the Verre Volé requires that you reserve in advance.

67 rue de Lancry, 10e. www.leverrevole.fr. (✆ **01-48-03-17-34.** Reservations recommended. Main courses 25€–30€; plate of the day 16€. MC, V. Daily 12:30–2pm and 7:30–10:30pm. Métro: Jacques Bonsergent.

**Rosa Bonheur ★ 🎁😊** TAPAS This restaurant inside the Parc des Buttes Chaumont boasts a sprawling terrace and one of the best panoramic views in town. A huge crowd gathers to drink and nibble tapas outside, but the menu also features main dishes such as stuffed and grilled shrimp, lamb and carrot stew, and monkfish with sage sauce. The real reason to visit is for the relaxed and friendly ambience, though—and the possibility of strolling through the city's largest and wildest park before or after your meal. That park, plus an indoor play area and kids' menu, makes Rosa Bonheur a great family option, too.

2 ave. de la Cascade, 19e. www.rosabonheur.fr. (✆ **01-42-00-00-45.** Reservations not accepted. Tapas 5€–8€; fixed-price menus at 29€ and 35€; children's menu 14€. MC, V. Wed–Sun noon–midnight. Métro: Botzaris.

### INEXPENSIVE

**Pink Flamingo** PIZZA Not only are the Pink's pizzas quirky (try the Poulidor: goat cheese and sliced duck breast), they're also put together with the best, freshest ingredients, and the crusts are made with organic flour. If you picnic by the canal, take a pink helium balloon, find your spot, and wait for the pizza delivery boy to cycle to you. There are other locations at 105 rue Vieille du Temple in the 3rd, 23 rue d'Aligre in the 12th, and 30 rue Muller in the 18th.

67 rue Bichat, 10th. www.pinkflamingopizza.com. ℰ **01-42-02-31-70.** Pizzas 11€–16€. MC, V. Sun noon–11:30pm; Mon 7–11:30pm; Tues–Sat noon–3pm and 7–11:30pm. Métro: Jacques Bonsergent.

# The Left Bank

## LATIN QUARTER (5E & 13E)

This neighborhood, stretching south from the river near Notre-Dame, past the market street of Mouffetard (one of the oldest and best preserved street markets in the city), leads to the area around place d'Italie and Paris's main Chinese quarter. The chefs who have set up shop here most recently are not content to merely perpetuate tradition. Some restaurants, such as **Le Pré Verre,** are using foreign flavors and techniques to update traditional French recipes, while others, like **Dans Les Landes,** are trying to relax the rules and make restaurant dining a less formal experience.

### Moderate

**Bouillon Racine** ★ BISTRO/BRASSERIE    This jewel-box dining room is the best example of baroque Art Nouveau in Paris—a magnificent affair of swirling iron and woodwork, with twinkling stained glass, mirrors, and tiles. The excellent brasserie fare might include carpaccio of beef with basil, lemon, and Parmesan; scallop risotto; or chicken blanquette. If you've got a sweet tooth, the crème brûlée flavored with maple syrup is delicious. The two-course lunch menu offered Monday to Friday is a steal at just 15€.

3 rue Racine, 6e. www.bouillon-racine.com. ℰ **01-44-32-15-60.** Mains 15€–23€; fixed-price dinner 30€ and 41€; fixed-price lunch 15€. MC, V. Daily noon–11pm. Métro: Odéon.

**Dans Les Landes** ★ 🥢 SOUTHWESTERN FRENCH    Julien Duboué's modern eatery is named after the southwestern French region that inspired the chef's long list of tapas and small plates. Go for grilled quail breasts or the unmissable fried *chipirions* (small squid that are crisp, golden, and dusted with smoky pepper). Duboué's southwestern take on the spring roll—rice paper stuffed with foie gras, duck breast, and salad—is also compelling. Finish with an unusual dessert of warm anise-scented liquor with toasted crème anglaise.

119 bis rue Monge, 5e. ℰ **01-45-87-06-00.** Reservations recommended. Tapas 6€–15€; plat du jour 16€. MC, V. Mon–Sat noon–11pm. Métro: Censier-Daubenton.

**Le Pré Verre** ★ 🥢 MODERN FRENCH/ASIAN FUSION    Around the corner from the Sorbonne in the heart of the Latin Quarter sits a refreshing restaurant where you can get seriously good food at an affordable price. The Delacourcelle brothers are firmly based in the French tradition but many of their chosen flavorings are inspired by Asia (they've got a second Pré Verre in Tokyo). In a welcoming, relaxed, and convivial atmosphere, tables are placed so close together that you're literally dining and rubbing elbows with your neighbors. For starters, dig into a well-flavored terrine—like the one made with layers of foie gras and mashed potatoes—or oysters marinated with ginger and poppy seeds or

**Bouillon Racine.**

scallops with cinnamon. Main courses might include suckling pig with aromatic spices and crisp-cooked cabbage, or roasted codfish.

8 rue Thenard, 5e. www.lepreverre.com. ✆ **01-43-54-59-47.** Reservations required. Main courses 18€; fixed-price lunch 13€–29€; fixed-price dinner 39€. MC, V. Tues–Sat noon–2pm and 7:30–10:30pm. Closed Aug. Métro: Maubert-Mutualité.

### Inexpensive

**Breakfast in America** ☺ AMERICAN  Connecticut-born Hollywood screenwriter Craig Carlson opened this replica of a down-home U.S.-based diner in 2003, building it with funds from members of the California film community who donated memorabilia from their films. Its self-proclaimed mission involves dispensing proper, rib-sticking American breakfasts and diner food to Parisians. The setting replicates a 1950s-era railway car, replete with scarlet-and-black Naugahyde banquettes, faux windows with mirrored insets, and an unabashedly Americanized staff. Breakfast (heaping portions of the egg-and-waffle-and-bacon combinations, as well as omelets) is served throughout the day and evening. Also available are half a dozen variations of burgers, tacos, club sandwiches, and BLTs.

17 rue des Ecoles, 5e. ✆ **01-43-54-50-28.** Reservations not accepted. Breakfast platters 7€–11€; lunch and dinner platters and "blue-plate specials" 8€–12€; fixed-price Sun brunch 16€. MC, V. Daily 8:30am–10:30pm. Métro: Cardinal Lemoine or Jussieu.

**Chez Gladines** ✦ BASQUE  Penny pinchers climb the cobblestone hill of the Butte aux Cailles to dine on the large portions at this dive. The setting is laid back (actually a bit grimy), but the food is hearty and authentic. This may not be the place to go to impress a date, but you can gorge on Gladines' giant "salads" (which consist of meat, cheese, garlic potatoes, and a few leaves of lettuce) and main dishes such as *pipérade* (Basque-style scrambled eggs with vegetables), cassoulet, potatoes with ham and cantal cheese, and our favorite, ham in a creamy sauce with layers of gratin-style potatoes that have been fried in duck fat. It's a bit leaden, but devotees love it.

30 rue des Cinq Diamants, 13e. ℂ **01-45-80-70-10.** Reservations not accepted. Main courses 8€–15€; fixed-price lunch 10€. No credit cards. Daily noon–3pm and 7pm–midnight; Sun noon–4pm. Closed 3 weeks in July. Métro: Corvisart or Place d'Italie.

## ST-GERMAIN-DES-PRÉS & LUXEMBOURG (6E)

Our favorite restaurants in Saint-Germain are classic bistros, serving traditional French fare with a few modern accents. **Le Comptoir du Relais, Le Relais Louis XIII**, and **Ze Kitchen Galerie** are run by notable chefs and require advance reservations, but the rest of our restaurant recommendations here are more casual and accept walk-ins and same-day bookings.

### Very Expensive

**Le Relais Louis XIII** ★ FRENCH    Chef Manuel Martinez upholds French traditions in this atmospheric, two-Michelin starred dining room, an old world space with dark wooden beams that wouldn't look amiss in an Alexandre Dumas novel. The key to Martinez's success is his mastery of traditional French cuisine, which he revisits with modern flair. For a treat, order the *canard au sang* (literally "bloody duck"), made with cognac and madeira wines and prepared at your table with much pomp and circumstance (upon advance request). The impeccable wine list offers bottles from the Champagne, Bordeaux, Rhône Valley, and Burgundy regions.

8 rue des Grands-Augustins, 6e. www.relaislouis13.fr. ℂ **01-43-26-75-96.** Reservations recommended. Main courses 58€–60€; fixed-price lunch 50€; fixed price dinner 80€-130€. AE, DC, MC, V. Tues–Sat noon–2:30pm, 7.30–10.30pm.

### Expensive

**Le Comptoir du Relais** ★★ TRADITIONAL FRENCH/BISTRO    Le Comptoir is the domain of Yves Camdeborde, the pioneering chef who kicked off the bistronomy movement, serving high-caliber food in a casual bistro setting, when he left a three-star kitchen to open his own bistro at the edge of the city. He sold La Régalade (which remains good) years ago to open this "counter," serving guests of the attached hotel and foodies who book dinner months and months in advance. Lunch is an easier table to score because reservations are not accepted—just line up before the doors open at noon and you're likely to get a table. All this fuss can be attributed to Camdeborde's well-executed bistro cuisine that reflects his southwestern roots and is made from high-quality ingredients. The menu changes regularly—it's comfort food with a touch of luxury, and it will spoil you for all subsequent bistros.

9 carrefour de l'Odéon, 6e. www.hotel-paris-relais-saint-germain.com. ℂ **01-44-27-07-97.** Reservations required several weeks in advance;. Main courses weekends 27€–35€; fixed-price dinner weeknights 50€. MC, V. Daily noon–2am. Métro: Odéon.

**Ze Kitchen Galerie** ★ INTERNATIONAL/MODERN FRENCH    At this colorful loft space in an antique building with an open showcase kitchen, most of the paintings on display are for sale (the place doubles as an art gallery). The innovative cuisine fuses Asian influences with French dishes. The menu changes about every 5 weeks. For starters, you might try the octopus with lemongrass and kalamenji. A pasta dish might feature homemade linguine with Bouchot mussels and dried fish eggs. Other mains might include grilled mackerel with miso or Challans duck with mostarda and plums. Dessert could be the restaurant's "cappuccino of the month," a frothy dessert concoction with ingredients that change with the seasons.

4 rue des Grands-Augustins, 6e. www.zekitchengalerie.fr. ☎ **01-44-32-00-32**. Reservations recommended. Main courses 24€–42€; fixed-price lunch with water and coffee 27€–70€; fixed-price dinner 82€. AE, DC, MC, V. Mon–Fri noon–2:30pm; Mon–Sat 7–11pm. Métro: St-Michel or Pont-Neuf.

## Moderate

### Le Relais de l'Entrecôte ☺ TRADITIONAL FRENCH/STEAK    For those
who are tired of making decisions, Le Relais de l'Entrecôte has only one question for you: "La cuisson?" Tell them how you like your steak done (*"bien cuit"* for medium-well, *"à point"* medium rare, or *"saignant"* for rare) and then sit back and let the show begin. You'll start with a fresh green salad and then proceed to the main event: a giant silver platter of steak, doused in an addictive "secret sauce," and served with crispy golden fries. That platter is refillable, by the way— you can expect to see your server return with a second helping once you've finished. Desserts, if you can find the strength, are classic and delicious, including profiteroles and crème brûlée. The crowd that gathers inside the pretty-postcard dining room includes tourists, locals, and chefs; it also includes plenty of families with kids.

20 rue St. Benoît, 6e. www.relaisentrecote.fr. ☎ **01-45-49-16-00.** Reservations not required. Daily noon–3pm and 7–11pm. Fixed-price lunch and dinner 25€. MC, V. Métro: St. Germain des Prés.

## Inexpensive

### La Crémerie Restaurant Polidor ☺ TRADITIONAL FRENCH/BISTRO
Crémerie Polidor is the most traditional (and heavily touristed) bistro in the Odéon area, serving *cuisine familiale.* Its name dates from the early 1900s, when it specialized in frosted cream desserts, but the restaurant can trace its history from 1845. The Crémerie was André Gide's favorite, and Joyce, Hemingway, Valéry, Artaud, and Kerouac also dined here. Peer beyond the lace curtains and brass hat racks to see drawers where, in olden days, regular customers used to lock up their cloth napkins. Try the day's soup followed by kidneys in Madeira sauce, *boeuf bourguignon* (beef braised in red wine), *confit de canard* (leg of duck), or *blanquette de veau* (veal ragout in cream sauce). For dessert, order a chocolate, raspberry, or lemon tart.

39 rue Monsieur-le-Prince, 6e. www.polidor.com. ☎ **01-43-26-95-34.** Main courses 12€–20€; fixed-price menu 22€–32€. No credit cards. Daily noon–2:30pm; Mon–Sat 7pm–12:30am; Sun 7–11pm. Métro: Odéon.

### L'Avant Comptoir ★ WINE BAR/SOUTHWESTERN FRENCH    This
shoebox-size wine bar is just steps from the Odéon and run by bistro maestro Yves Camdeborde. Next door to his seminal restaurant Le Comptoir, this place sells crepes and sandwiches during the day and hors d'oeuvres to a raucous crowd at night. Basque and Béarnais-inspired nibbles include fried croquettes stuffed with Iberian ham, a filling cod *brandade,* oxtail canapés with horseradish cream, and chicken hearts grilled with garlic and parsley. Plates of charcuterie

are meant to be eaten (and shared) with the crocks of Bordier butter and gherkins that line the counter. No more than a dozen people can crowd into this place at a time and there are no chairs.

3 carrefour de l'Odéon, 6e. No phone and no reservations accepted. Main courses 3.50€–8€. MC, V. Daily 9am–1am. Métro: Odéon.

## EIFFEL TOWER & NEARBY (7E)

The chic 7th arrondissement is home to some of the city's most respected and innovative chefs, including Alain Passard (**L'Arpège**), **Jean-François Piège,** and **Joël Robuchon.** A table at one of their celebrated tables doesn't come cheap, but you'll never forget the experience. There are several *bistronomique* restaurants here too, including **Chez l'Ami Jean,** where gastronomes can go for a memorable meal at more modest prices.

### Very Expensive

**Jean-François Piège** ★ MODERN FRENCH    This new restaurant, above the bustling brasserie Thoumieux, is the newest stage for star chef Jean-François Piège. After leaving the palatial kitchens of Les Ambassadeurs, Piège partnered with Thierry Costes to open a hotel and restaurant complex near Invalides. His namesake restaurant is an intimate 20-seat showcase, which has been enthusiastically welcomed by the critics, receiving two Michelin stars in 2011, just a year after opening. Dishes are creative and whimsical; you might try a mussel with a heap of fried frizzled potatoes—his version of *moules frites.* For dessert, the *tarte tatin* (apple tart)—a puff of sweet pizza dough topped with sliced apples and cream—is excellent. Piège's cooking has been called witty and precise, and the funky decor—featuring brightly colored sofas with black and white accents—has garnered almost as much attention as the food.

79 rue St. Dominique, 7e. www.jfpiege.com. ✆ **01-47-05-49-75.** Reservations recommended. Main courses 37€–75€; fixed-price menus 70€–165€.MC, V, Daily noon–midnight. Métro: La Tour Maubourg.

**L'Arpège** ★★★ MODERN FRENCH    Chef Alain Passard made waves years ago when he decided to put vegetables, not meat, in the spotlight at his three-star restaurant L'Arpège. Although meat is still featured on the menu, his dedication to carrots and turnips was something previously unseen. This pristine produce, which he raises on a farm near Le Mans, is often picked in the morning and served the same day in Paris. Uneaten food from his restaurant makes the return journey to become compost. Food politics aside, the flavors that Passard coaxes from these vegetables (often with the welcome addition of butter and cream) are truly remarkable. Service is discreet, as one expects at a restaurant frequented by diplomats and executives, and the dining room, with etched glass, burnished steel, and pearwood paneling, is beautiful, if a bit dated. Don't miss the cheese course, served on a giant polished plank of wood, or the *tarte aux pommes bouquet de roses* (a tart composed of apple ribbons rolled into tiny rosettes).

84 rue de Varenne, 7e. www.alain-passard.com. ✆ **01-47-05-09-06.** Fax 01-44-18-98-39. Reservations required 2 weeks in advance. Main courses 48€–180€; fixed-price lunch 125€; fixed-price dinner 420€. AE, DC, MC, V. Mon–Fri 12:30–2:30pm and 8–10:30pm. Métro: Varenne.

### Expensive

**L'Atelier Saint-Germain de Joël Robuchon** ★★ MODERN FRENCH
World-renowned Chef Joël Robuchon came out of a short-lived retirement in

2003 in order to open this ground-breaking culinary workshop on the left bank. He recently added the words "Saint-Germain" when he opened a second Atelier near the Arc de Triomphe. This original location remains packed with gastronomes who want to eat well without the fuss implied by a three-star restaurant. Sitting informally upon high stools at a U-shaped bar, you can order the tasting menu or a series of sharable small plates including sea bream carpaccio, caviar with smoked eel and horseradish, grilled marrow bones, and the famous Robuchon mashed potatoes. Reservations are accepted for the extremely early and late seatings only (at 11:30am and 2pm for lunch, and 6:30pm for dinner); these spots are booked well in advance. Otherwise, it's first come, first served.

5 rue Montalembert, 7e. www.joel-robuchon.net. ℂ **01-42-22-56-56.** Reservations required. Main courses 28€–75€; dinner tasting menu 150€. AE, MC, V. Daily 11:30am–3:30pm, 6:30pm–midnight. Métro: Rue du Bac.

**Restaurant Auguste** ★★ TRADITIONAL FRENCH/SEAFOOD  Right by the Assemblée Nationale (the seat of French *governement* along with the Senat), chef Gael Orieux's red and white contemporary eatery is coveted by politians—a handy clientele for this young chef, whose love of the sea has led him to represent "Mr. Goodfish," a European association dedicated to protecting the oceans. Serving some of the best seafood in town, Orieux's meals might include red mullet with Thai condiments; scallops with creamy risotto; and oysters in horseradish mousse. But there are also meat dishes, with fabulous preparations like celtic duck with caramelized citrus fruits, and *ris de veau* (veal sweetbreads) with oyster mushrooms and apricots. For dessert, delicacies like pistachio soufflé, finish everything off perfectly.

54 rue de Bourgogne, 7e. www.restaurantauguste.fr. ℂ **01-45-51-61-09.** Reservations required. Main courses 30€–48€; fixed-price lunch 35€; fixed-price dinner 80€. MC, V. Daily noon–2:30pm and 7–10:30pm. Métro: Assemblée Nationale.

## Moderate

**Chez l'Ami Jean** ★ BASQUE/SOUTHWESTERN FRENCH  This restaurant was originally opened by a Basque nationalist in 1931, but it was Chef Stéphane Jego who really put the bistro on the map. Jego maintained the original decor (if one can call wood panels and sports memorabilia a decor) but turned L'Ami Jean into a destination for *cuisine bistronomique*—high-caliber cooking served in a homey neighborhood setting. Reserve in advance and arrive hungry because the Basque dishes served here are anything but light—even the fish dishes here are accented by foie gras and chorizo. However much you may have already eaten, say yes to the cheese plate with Basque brebis (sheep's milk cheese) and black cherry preserves, and finish with a heaping bowl of *riz au lait* (rice pudding).

27 rue Malar, 7e. www.amijean.eu. ℂ **01-47-05-86-89.** Reservations required. Main courses 20€–40€; fixed-price dinner at 35€, 42€, and 60€. MC, V. Tues–Sat noon–2pm and 7pm–midnight. Closed Aug. Métro: Invalides.

## Inexpensive

**Eric Kayser** ★★ BAKERY/LIGHT FARE  If you're in the 7th arrondissement for breakfast or lunch, a good refueling stop is this bakery, bar, and café. Kayser's forte is bread making—he is known for the long fermentation of his dough. He's always coming up with new ideas for his breads, including one made with apricots and pistachios and another with chorizo. This Alsatian baker offers many luxe breads and pastries, and breakfast is a delight here. At lunch you have a choice of 20 different combinations of *tartines* (open-faced sandwiches), and teatime features gourmet snacks such as a sweet tartine with meringue and chestnuts.

18 rue du Bac, 7e. © **01-42-61-27-63.** Sandwiches and savory tartes 4€–8.50€. MC, V. Tues–Sun 7am–8pm. Métro: Bac or Musée d'Orsay.

## MONTPARNASSE & SOUTHERN PARIS (13E, 14E & 15E)

The largely residential 15th arrondissement has exploded with restaurants in recent years. Although this area may seem remote, those who venture here are rewarded with a large selection of fabulous and affordable bistros.

### Expensive

**La Régalade ★★** TRADITIONAL FRENCH/BISTRO   The *bistronomique* movement started here, under Chef Yves Camdeborde (who now works at Le Comptoir du Relais, p. 149), when people flocked to this sweet little bistro, with its cracked tile floors, polished wood, and burgundy banquettes, to taste excellent food in a low-key setting. In 2006, Camdeborde sold La Régalade to Bruno Doucet, who has maintained the tradition and become a respected chef in his own right. Meals here begin with a help-yourself crock of homemade terrine, served with bread and gherkins, and continue with starters such as foie gras in asparagus bouillon or marinated sea scallops with basil and Parmesan. Mains are comforting, such as caramelized pork belly with mashed potatoes or sea bream with caramelized fennel and black olives. Dessert could be a stinky Reblochon cheese, a molten Guanaja chocolate cake, or rice pudding.

14 av. Jean-Moulin, 14e. © **01-45-45-68-58.** Reservations recommended. Fixed-price menus 34€–50€. MC, V. Tues–Fri noon–2:30pm; Mon–Fri 7–11:30pm. Closed Aug. Métro: Alésia.

### Moderate

**Jadis ★** TRADITIONAL FRENCH/BISTRO   In the up-and-coming 15th arrondissement, Chef Guillaume Délage uses fresh seasonal ingredients to resuscitate "forgotten" bistro dishes from the past; start with an egg poached in red wine sauce and move on to beef stroganoff or stuffed breast of veal. Délage's nose-to-tail approach to cooking makes use of the whole animal, so don't be surprised to see cock's comb or kidney on the menu. The cheese course (if you've got room) is generally so ripe that it still smells like the farm, and desserts, like the bittersweet chocolate soufflé and coffee-flavored *pot de crème*, are pure comfort.

208 rue de la Croix Nivert, 15e. www.bistrot-jadis.com. © **01-45-57-73-20.** Reservations required. Main courses 21€; fixed-price lunch 29€; fixed-price dinner 36€. AE, MC, V. Mon–Fri 12:15–2:30pm and 7:15–10:30pm. Métro: Convention.

**La Cerisaie ★ ▥** SOUTHWESTERN FRENCH/BISTRO   This shoebox-size dining room near the Tour Montparnasse serves the soul-warming cuisine of southwestern France. Depending on the season, you might start with chestnut soup or an egg baked in porcini cream sauce, and foie gras is always on the menu. In autumn and winter, Chef Cyrill Lalanne does amazing things with wild game and his menu features every animal in the forest from hare to partridge to boar. Finish with the southwestern take on the classic *baba*, made with the region's Armagnac instead of rum. The atmosphere at La Cerisaie is informal and unpretentious, but the restaurant's popularity means that you need to reserve a few days in advance.

70 boulevard Edgar-Quinet, 14e. www.restaurantlacerisaie.com. ☎ **01-43-20-98-98.** Reservation recommended. Main courses 15€–35€. MC, V. Mon–Fri noon–2pm and 7–9pm. Métro: Montparnasse-Bienvenüe or Edgar Quinet.

**Le Casse Noix ★** 🏠 TRADITIONAL FRENCH/BISTRO    After cooking for six years at La Régalade (p. 153), Chef Pierre-Olivier Lenormand opened his own *bistro*—a place that serves high-caliber food in a casual setting—in 2010. The decor is nostalgic and the traditional French cooking is sincere and generous. Dishes like smoked chestnut soup, Iberian pork belly with choucroute of turnips, and the classic *petit salé aux lentilles* (lentils with smoky ham) are followed by crowd-pleasing desserts such as *île flottante* ("floating island," a meringue floating on custard). The wine list includes a good selection by the glass as well as many moderately priced bottles. This is a good option if you're looking for an affordable, traditional bistro that's not yet overrun with tourists.

56 rue de la Fédération, 15e. www.le-cassenoix.fr. ☎ **01-45-66-09-01.** Reservations recommended. Fixed-price dinner 32€; fixed-price lunch 25€. Mon–Fri noon–2:30pm and 7:30–10:30pm. Métro: Dupleix.

### Inexpensive
**Crêperie Josselin ★** 🥄 ☺ CRÊPERIE    Josselin is just one of maybe 20 crêperies that are concentrated around the "gateway to Brittany" Montparnasse train station, but it stands above all others as the city's best. The Breton working the griddle knows exactly how to achieve the lacy, golden edges of a perfect galette, and he's not shy with the butter. Our idea of a perfect lunch (especially after too much wine the night before) is Josselin's *complete*—a buckwheat galette stuffed with egg, cheese, and ham—paired with a ceramic bowl of hard cider and followed by a salted butter caramel crepe. The easy prices, continuous service, and wide range of flavor combinations make this a great option for children as well.

67 rue du Montparnasse, 14e. ☎ **01-43-20-93-50.** Reservations not required. Crepes 6€–15€; fixed-price menu 11€. MC, V. Tue–Sun noon–11pm. Métro: Montparnasse-Bienvenüe.

# THE TOP CAFES

As surely everyone knows, the cafe is a Parisian institution. Parisians use cafés as combination club/tavern/snack bars, almost as extensions of their living rooms. They're spots where you can sit alone and read your newspaper, do your homework or write your memoirs; meet a friend or lover; nibble on a hard-boiled egg; or drink yourself into oblivion. At cafes, you meet your dates, and then go on to a show or stay and talk. Above all, cafes are for people-watching.

Now, just a few words on cafe etiquette: Your bill will probably arrive with your order, but you're not expected to pay until you leave. *Service compris* means the tip is included in your bill, so it isn't necessary to tip extra. Still, tips are appreciated, but keep them small—a tip of small change (1€) is more than enough if you're only having a few drinks.

**Café de Flore**    This is perhaps the most famous cafe in the world, still fighting to maintain a Left Bank aura despite hordes of visitors from around the world. Jean-Paul Sartre—the granddaddy of existentialism, a key figure in the Resistance, and a renowned café-sitter—often came here during World War II. Wearing a leather jacket and beret, he sat and wrote his trilogy *Les Chemins de la Liberté (The Roads to Freedom)*. Camus, Picasso, and Apollinaire also frequented the Flore. The café is still going strong, although the existentialists have been replaced by tourists and sometimes fashionistas.

172 bd. St-Germain, 6e. www.cafedeflore.fr. ☏ **01-45-48-55-26.** Café espresso 4.10€; glass of beer 9€; snacks from 9€; full meal 25€–50€. AE, DC, MC, V. Daily 7:30am–1:30am. Métro: St-Germain-des-Prés.

**Café des Deux Moulins**  *Amélie* was a quirky low-budget film that was nominated for five Oscars and was seen by more than 25 million people around the world following its release in 2001. The film was set in Montmartre, and the cafe featured in the film has developed into a mandatory stopping-off place for the constantly arriving "cult of Amélie." In the film, Amélie worked as a waitress at the Café des Deux Moulins. The musty atmosphere, with its 1950s decor, mustard-colored ceiling, and lace curtains, has been preserved—even the wall lamps and unisex toilet. The menu has retained classic, hearty dishes such as calf's liver, green frisée salad with bacon bits and warm goat cheese, and pigs' brains with lentils. They also serve hamburgers, with or without a fried egg on top.

### Did You Know?

You'll pay substantially less in a cafe if you stand at the counter rather than sit at a table, partly because there's no service charge, and partly because clients tend to linger at tables.

15 rue Lepic, 18e. ☏ **01-42-54-90-50.** Main courses 11€–18€. MC, V. Daily 7am–2am. Métro: Blanche.

**La Belle Hortense**  This is the most literary cafe in the Marais, loaded with literary antecedents and references. It contains an erudite and accessible staff; an inventory of French literary classics as well as modern tomes about art, psychoanalysis, history, and culture; and two high-ceilinged, 19th-century rooms, little changed since the days of Baudelaire and Balzac. Near the entrance is a zinc-covered bar that sells glasses of wine. If you're fluent in French, you might be interested in attending a reading, a book signing, or a lecture (check the website for information).

31 rue Vieille du Temple, 4e. http://cafeine. com. ☏ **01-48-04-71-60.** Glass of wine 4€–10€; coffee 2.10€; *plats du jour* 12€–24€. MC, V. Daily 5pm–2am. Métro: Hôtel-de-Ville or St-Paul.

**La Palette ★**  The interior of this desperately romantic cafe, inhabited

**La Belle Hortense.**

by amiably crotchety waiters and formerly frequented by Picasso and Braque, consists of tiled murals installed around 1935 advertising the virtues of a brand of liqueur that's no longer manufactured. If you happen to drop in during mealtime, you'll have a limited selection of salads and croque-monsieur (toasted ham and cheese), plus one *plat du jour,* always priced at 15€, which may include roast beef, lamb stew, fish, or lamb. The real reason to come, though, is the terrace, a beautiful outdoor space not far from the river where you can get a real sense of the village life in Saint-Germain.

43 rue de Seine, 6e. www.cafelapaletteparis.com. ☎ **01-43-26-68-15.** Sandwiches, omelets, and *plats du jour* 6€–15€. MC, V. Café and bar daily 8am–2am. Restaurant daily noon–3pm. Métro: Mabillon or St-Germain-des-Prés.

**La Rotonde**   Once patronized by Hemingway, the original Rotonde faded into history but is immortalized in the pages of *The Sun Also Rises,* in which Papa wrote, "No matter what cafe in Montparnasse you ask a taxi driver to bring you to from the right bank of the river, they always take you to the Rotonde." Having since been lavishly upgraded, its reincarnation has a paneled Art Deco elegance and shares the site with a cinema. The menu includes such hearty fare as pepper steak with French fries, shellfish in season, a superb and succulent version of *sole meunière,* and sea bass filets with herb-flavored lemon sauce.

105 bd. du Montparnasse, 6e. www.rotondemontparnasse.com. ☎ **01-43-26-48-26.** Glass of wine 4€–11€; main courses 10€–38€; fixed-price lunch 18€–35€; fixed-price dinner 39€. AE, MC, V. Café daily 7:15am–2am; food service daily noon–1am. Métro: Vavin.

**Le Procope**   To fans of French history, this is the holy grail of Parisian cafes. Opened in 1686, it occupies a three-story town house categorized as a historic monument. Inside, nine salons and dining rooms, each of whose 300-year-old walls have been carefully preserved and painted a deep red, are available for languorous afternoon coffee breaks or old-fashioned meals. Menu items include platters of shellfish, onion soup *au gratin, coq au vin* (chicken stewed in wine), duck breast in honey sauce, and grilled versions of various meats and fish. Every day between 3 and 6pm, the place makes itself available to sightseers who come to look but not necessarily eat and drink at the site that welcomed such movers and shakers as Diderot, Voltaire, George Sand, Victor Hugo, and Oscar Wilde. Especially charming is the ground-floor room outfitted like an antique library.

13 rue de l'Ancienne-Comédie, 6e. www.procope.com. ☎ **01-40-46-79-00.** Reservations recommended. Coffee 3€; glass of beer 5€–7€; main courses 20€–29€. AE, DC, MC, V. Daily 11:30am–1am. Métro: Odéon.

# SHOPPING IN PARIS

Paris is, of course, a world-famous shopping destination—and for good reason. The city marries art and commerce, elevating an afternoon of window shopping into a high-culture experience. Parisian department stores sell everything you could ever want under one elegant roof, while specialty shops hold countless small treasures, from jeweled safety pins to handcrafted candles. But true shoppers come to Paris for the fashion—Chanel, Dior, Hermès, and Louis Vuitton call Paris home. The city is also home to iconic cosmetic and perfume houses, as well as endless gourmet food shops. But you don't have to buy anything to appreciate shopping in Paris: Peer in the *vitrines* (window displays), keep an eye out for new trends, and return home with a whole new interepretation of style.

# Business Hours

**Usual shop hours** are Monday to Saturday from 10am to 7pm, but hours vary, and Monday mornings don't run at full throttle. Small shops sometimes close for a 2-hour lunch break, and some do not open at all until after lunch on Monday. Thursday is the best day for late-night shopping, with stores open to 9 or 10pm.

**Sunday shopping** is limited to tourist areas and flea markets, though there's growing demand for full-scale Sunday hours. The department stores are now open on the 5 Sundays before Christmas. The **Carrousel du Louvre** (© **01-43-16-47-10**), a mall adjacent to the Louvre, is open daily 10am to 8pm. The tourist shops lining rue de Rivoli across from the Louvre are open on Sunday, as are the antiques villages, flea markets, and specialty events. Several food markets enliven the streets on Sunday. For our favorites, see the box "Food Markets" (p. 160). Most of the shops along the Champs-Élysées stay open on Sunday.

*Note:* Many independent stores close for about a month at the height of summer, from late July to late August.

# Great shopping areas

**LES HALLES, LOUVRE & PALAIS ROYAL (1E & 2E)**  Subterranean shopping mall **Les Halles** is a short stroll from major shopping strip **rue de Rivoli.** Both these destinations are a who's who of the major international fashion chains, including H&M, Zara, Sephora, Etam, and Gap. At another end of the 1st is the **Palais Royal,** just north of the Louvre and one of the city's best shopping secrets. The 18th-century arcade of boutiques flanks the garden of a former palace and includes some of the hottest names in fashion and accessories. It signals the beginning of the busy part of rue St-Honoré to the south, and to the north, behind the Palais Royal, is another sophisticated shopping destination, **place des Victoires,** which joins up with to the east with the **Etienne-Marcel** shopping neighborhood, known for its jeans and streetwear. In the 19th century, this area became known for its *passages,* glass-enclosed shopping streets—in fact, the world's first shopping malls. They were also the city's first buildings to be illuminated by gaslight. Many have been torn down, but a dozen or so have survived. The **passage de Grand Cerf,** between 145 rue St-Denis and 10 rue Dussoubs (Métro: Etienne-Marcel), is filled with everything from ethnic-chic to jewelry and accessory shops. **Place Vendôme** is the city's fine jewelry quarter, set like a crown around the mythical Ritz hotel.

**LE MARAIS, ILE ST-LOUIS & ILE DE LA CITÉ (3E & 4E)**  The Marais provides two dramatically different shopping experiences. The Lower Marais is concentrated around **rue des Francs-Bourgeois,** where you'll find a succession of charming fashion, accessories, and beauty stores. But don't be afraid to strike off into the neighborhood's medieval warren of twisting streets chockablock with up-to-the-minute fashions and trends. The Northern Marais, concentrated around **rue de Bretagne,** is a hotbed of independent French designers. Some in-the-know shoppers are skipping St-Germain and St-Honoré and heading here instead, for guaranteed cutting-edge fashion and design.

**CHAMPS-ÉLYSÉES & WESTERN PARIS (8E, 16E & 17E)**  The heart of the international designer parade is here on the Right Bank. **Rue du Faubourg St-Honoré** was the traditional miracle mile until recent years, when many of

Place Vendôme.

the exclusive shops shunned it for the even more deluxe **avenue Montaigne** at the other end of the arrondissement. (It's a long but pleasant walk from one fashion strip to the other.) Paris's most glamorous shopping street is lined with almost unspeakably fancy shops, and in a few hours, you can see Dior, Chanel, and everything in between. The neighboring **Champs-Élysées** shouts "teen scene," with mass-market flagships. The zone around the **Madeleine** hosts many fine speciality food shops.

**OPÉRA & CANAL ST-MARTIN (9E & 10E)** These two neighborhoods offer wildly different shopping experiences. Opera has at its beating heart the "other" two department stores: Le Printemps and Les Galeries Lafayette, built in a row along **boulevard Haussmann.** Their commercial energy draws many other big names and chains. The sleepy Canal St-Martin offers boho local charm along little streets rue de Marseille, Beaurepaire, the quais de Valmy, and Jemmapes.

**PIGALLE & MONTMARTRE (18E)** Villagey Montmartre's charming winding streets, fanning out around Abbesses, are filled with small speciality shops in design, fashion, jewelery, and food. Wander along rue des Abbesses, down rue Houdon, and up rue des Martyrs for a sweet afternoon of discovery.

**RÉPUBLIQUE, BASTILLE & EASTERN PARIS (11E & 12E)** Shopping in Bastille is concentrated on and around **rue du Faubourg St-Antoine,** which heads east from place de la Bastille and counts big names and chains; and winding streets nearby, like **rue de Charonne.** The **Viaduc des Arts,** running parallel to avenue Daumesnil, is a collection of about 30 specialist craft stores occupying a series of narrow vaulted niches under what used to be railroad tracks.

**BELLEVILLE & NORTHEAST PARIS (19E & 20E)** Not a shopping zone, tourists come here to soak up the cosmopolitan atmospheres and explore speciality shops from the city's various immigrant communities.

**LATIN QUARTER (5E)** More of a residential neighborhood, the Latin Quarter is better known for its major sights—the Luxembourg Gardens and the Sorbonne University—than for its shopping strips. However a host of specialist bookshops, which feed the local student population, remain a real draw.

**ST-GERMAIN-DES-PRÉS & LUXEMBOURG (6E)** This area is the soul of the Left Bank and is one of the most famous shopping districts in Paris. In this traditionally more literary neighborhood, high-fashion addresses are gradually taking over the bookshops, and the Left Bank now rivals classic Right Bank shopping zones like St-Honoré and avenue Montaigne. Wander avenue St-Germain, rue St-Sulpice, rue du Cherche Midi, rue du Vieux Colombier, rue Bonapart, and rue Jacob down to the Seine, or gourmet paradise rue de Buci, for some elevated shopping experiences.

**EIFFEL TOWER & NEARBY (7E)** The city's most glamorous department store, Le Bon Marché, sets the scene for another high-voltage shopping experience. If much of this neighborhood is more dedicated to culture and architecture than fashion, along its eastern edge, some of the glamour of adjacent St-Germain rubs off, and around **rue du Bac** and **rue du Grenelle,** you'll find all that wealth can buy.

**MONTPARNASSE & SOUTHERN PARIS (13E, 14E & 15E)** Located behind St-Germain, this neighborhood is dominated by both Paris's only skyscraper and France's tallest building, the Montparnasse tower, and a major railway station. Montparnasse might be worth a trip for the major shopping center located under the tower and the shopping along adjacent **rue de Rennes.**

# Malls & Markets

**Carrousel du Louvre ★★** If you want to combine an accessible location, a fun food court, boutiques, and plenty of museum gift shops with a touch of culture, don't miss the Carrousel. Always mobbed, this is one of the few venues allowed to open on Sunday. There's an Apple Store, Starbucks, Virgin Megastore, a branch of L'Occitane, and several other emporiums for conspicuous consumption. Check out Fragonard or Pylones for original souvenir ideas. Open daily, 10am to 8pm. 99 rue de Rivoli, 1er. www.carrouseldulouvre.com. ✆ **01-43-16-47-10.** Métro: Palais-Royal or Musée du Louvre.

**Le Forum des Halles** This major transport and shopping hub draws suburban Parisians to its subterranean labyrinth of chain stores, including H&M, FRAC, Zara, or Muji, as well as a heated swimming pool, and the UGC cinema multiplex. The complex is undergoing major renovations until 2016, but the shopping mall remains open throughout. Open Monday to Saturday 10am to 8pm. 101 Porte Berger, 1er. www.forumdeshalles.com. Métro: Châtelet-Les Halles.

**Marché aux Fleurs et aux Oiseaux ★** Artists and photographers love to capture the Flower Market on canvas and film. Most of the time, the stalls are ablaze with color, and each is a showcase of flowers, most of which escaped the

Marché aux Fleurs.

perfume factories of Grasse on the French Riviera. The Flower Market is along the Seine, behind the Tribunal de Commerce. But on Sunday, it becomes the poetic Bird Market. Open daily 8:30am to 4pm. Place Louis-Lépine, Ile de la Cité, 4e. No phone. Métro: Cité.

**Marché aux Puces de la Porte de Vanves** ★★ 🎁 This weekend event sprawls along two streets and is the best flea market in Paris—dealers swear by it. There's little in terms of formal antiques and furniture. It's better for old linens, vintage Hermès scarves, toys, ephemera, costume jewelry, perfume bottles, and bad art. Asking prices tend to be high, as dealers prefer to sell to nontourists. On Sunday, there's a food market one street over. Open Tuesday to Sunday 7am to 5pm. Av. Georges-Lafenestre, 14e. No phone. Métro: Porte de Vanves.

**Marché aux Puces St-Ouen de Clignancourt** ★ Paris's most famous flea market is a grouping of more than a dozen flea markets—a complex of 2,500 to 3,000 open stalls and shops on the northern fringe of the city, selling everything from antiques to junk, from new to vintage clothing. The market begins with stalls of cheap clothing along avenue de la Porte de Clignancourt. As you proceed, various streets will tempt you. Hold on until you get to rue des Rosiers; then turn left. Vendors start bringing out their offerings around 9am Saturday to Monday and take them in around 6pm. Hours are a tad flexible, depending on weather and crowds. Monday is traditionally the best day for bargain seekers—attendance is smaller and merchants demonstrate a greater desire to sell.

First-timers always want to know two things: "Will I get any real bargains?" and "Will I get fleeced?" It's all relative. Obviously, dealers (who often have a prearrangement to have items held for them) have already skimmed the best

---

### Food Markets

Outdoor markets are plentiful in Paris. Some of the better known are the **Marché Buci;** the **rue Mouffetard market,** open Tuesday to Sunday from 9:30am to 1pm and Tuesday to Saturday from 4 to 7pm (6e; Métro: Monge or Censier-Daubenton); and the **rue Montorgueil market,** behind the St-Eustache church, open Monday to Saturday from 9am to 7pm (1er; Métro:

Les Halles). The covered Marché d'Aligre in the 12e dates back to the 18th century and boasts a lovely family atmosphere (p. 85). The trendiest market is **Marché Biologique,** along boulevard Raspail, a tree-lined stretch lying between rue de Rennes and rue du Cherche-Midi, 6e. It's open Sunday from 8:30am to 6:30pm (Métro: Montparnasse).

buys. And it's true that the same merchandise displayed here will sell for less in the provinces. But for the visitor who has only a few days to spend in Paris—and only half a day for shopping—the flea market is worth the experience.

Dress casually and show your knowledge if you're a collector. Most dealers are serious and get into the spirit of things only if you speak French or make it clear you know what you're doing. The longer you stay, the more you chat and show your respect for the goods, the more room you'll have for negotiating. Most of the markets have restroom facilities; some have central offices to arrange shipping. Cafes, pizza joints, and even a few restaurants are scattered around. *Note:* Beware of pickpockets and teenage troublemakers while shopping the market. Open Saturday to Monday 9am to 7pm. Av. de la Porte de Clignancourt, 18e. No phone. www.marchesauxpuces.fr. Métro: Porte de Clignancourt (turn left, cross bd. Ney, and then walk north on av. de la Porte Montmartre). Métro: Porte de Clignancourt.

**Marché des Enfants Rouges ★** This charming covered fresh food market is the oldest in Paris and dates from 1777. In the heart of the rapidly gentrifying Northern Marais neighborhood, it's a lively place for stocking up on picnic supplies (organic if you like), including wine and flowers, or for sitting down for a bite at any of the food stands. We recommend traditional French dishes at L'Estaminet in the western corner, or the excellent Japanese canteen Taeko on the eastern edge. Open Monday to Saturday, 8:30am to 7:30pm, Sunday 8:30am to 2pm. 39 rue de Bretagne, 3e. ℰ **01-42-72-28-12.** Métro: Filles du Calvaire.

# Shopping A to Z
## ANTIQUES, COLLECTIBLES & VINTAGE

### Le Louvre des Antiquaires ★★

Across from the Louvre, this store offers three levels of fancy knick-knacks and 250 vendors. It's just the place if you're looking for 30 matching Baccarat-crystal champagne flutes from the 1930s, a Sèvres tea service from 1773, or a signed Jean Fouquet gold-and-diamond pin. Too stuffy? No problem. There's always the 1940 Rolex with the eggplant crocodile strap. Prices can be high, but a few reasonable items are hidden here. What's more, the Sunday scene is fabulous, and there's a cafe with a variety of lunch menus. Pick up a free map and brochure of the premises from the information desk. Open Tuesday to Sunday 9am to 7pm. Closed Sunday. 2 place du Palais Royal, 1er. www.louvre-antiquaires.com. ℰ **01-42-97-27-27.** Métro: Palais-Royal.

### L'Objet qui Parle ★★ This
almost ridiculously charming shop sells a perfectly curated jumble of

Le Louvre des Antiquaires.

vintage finds, including Art Deco sunburst mirrors, teapots, kitchen canisters and crockery, hunting trophies, religious paraphernalia, and old lace. Great for souvenir shopping! Open Monday to Saturday 1pm to 7:30pm. 86 rue des Martyrs, 18e. ☎ **06-09-67-05-30.** Métro: Abbesses.

## ART & CRAFTS

**Artcurial ★**   Set within minimalist showrooms in one of the most spectacular 19th-century mansions in Paris, this is one of the best outlets in Europe for contemporary art. Since it was established in 1975, it has represented megastars such as Man Ray and the "enfant terrible" of France's postwar intelligentsia, Jean Cocteau. Today, the names of showcased artists read like a who's who of contemporary art: Arman, Sonia Delaunay, and Niki de Saint Phalle for painting and sculpture; Claude Lalanne for jewelry design; and Matta for contemporary carpets. Technically, it's an auction house, similar in some ways to Sotheby's and Christie's, albeit with a specialization in modern and contemporary art, vintage photographs by "important" photographers, antique books and posters, and sculpture. Despite an address that might be among the most expensive in the world (the intersection of av. Montaigne and Champs-Élysées), the place is more welcoming than its location implies. A great arts bookshop, and a recently renovated daytime cafe provide respite from the shops. Open Monday to Friday 10am to 7pm; Saturday 11am to 7pm. 7 rond-point des Champs-Élysées, 8e. www.artcurial. com. ☎ **01-42-99-20-20.** Métro: Franklin-D-Roosevelt.

**107Rivoli ★★**   Inside the city's Decorative Arts Museum, itself located within a wing of the Louvre, this ground floor store presents a wonderful selection of contemporary ceramic, textile, glass and design pieces, plus a great collection of books dedicated to the arts, architecture, fashion, and design, as well as take-home pieces inspired by the current exhibitions. Great for inspired souvenir shopping. Open Monday to Sunday 10am to 7pm. 107 rue de Rivoli, 1er. www. lesartsdecoratifs.fr. ☎ **01-42-60-64-94.** Métro: Palais-Royal.

## BEAUTY, COSMETICS & PERFUME

**Annick Goutal ★**   Although there are other branches, and you can test Goutal bathroom amenities at many upscale hotels, the sidewalk mosaic tile and the gold accented boudoir vibe of this central flagship make it worth stopping by. Try their bestseller Eau d'Hadrien for a unisex splash of citrus and summer. Store hours are Monday to Saturday from 10am to 7pm. 14 rue Castiglione, 1er. www. annickgoutal.com. ☎ **01-42-60-52-82.** Métro: Concorde.

**Diptyque ★★**   This contemporary Parisian perfumery and candle maker has a truly unique range of aromatic plant–based scents, including bestsellers Philosykos, a woody blend of fig tree leaves and white cedar, or Tubéreuse, an intoxicating blend based on the heady tuberose flower. Open Monday to Saturday 10am to 7pm. 34 bd St Germain, 5e. www.diptyqueparis.com. ☎ **01-43-26-77-44.** Métro: Maubert-Mutualité.

**The Different Company ★ 🎁**   Many fashionistas are deserting the fabled houses of scent and heading for this corner of counterculture chic in the Marais. The perfume shop is run by the father-daughter team of Jean-Claude and Céline Ellena. Dad is perfumer for Hermès and continues here a commitment to exceptional quality. Scents, which include Osmanthus, Sel de Vétiver, and Rose Poivrée, have been called "fragrances for the 21st century." Open Tuesday to

Saturday noon to 7:30 or 8pm. 10 rue Ferdinand Duval, 4e. www.thedifferentcompany. com. ✆ **01-47-83-65-88.** Métro: Saint-Paul.

## BOOKS

If you like rare and unusual books, there's not only the choice of the city's exceptional bookshops; you also have the choice to patronize one of the *bouquinistes,* the owners of those army-green stalls that line the Seine (on the Left Bank between the quai de la Tournelle and quai Malaquais, and on the Right Bank between Pont Marie and the quai du Louvre). This is where tourists in the 1920s and 1930s went to buy "dirty" French postcards. You might get lucky and come across a treasured first edition that was banned for decades in the United States.

**Cassegrain ★**   Nothing says elegance more than thick French stationery and notecards. Cassegrain, originally an engraver in 1919, offers beautifully engraved stationery, most often in traditional patterns, and business cards engraved to order. Several other items for the desk, many suitable for gifts, are for sale as well; there are even affordable pencils and pens, leather wallets, and small desktop accessories. Open Monday to Saturday 10am to 7pm. 422 rue St-Honoré, 8e. www. cassegrain.fr. ✆ **01-42-60-20-08.** Métro: Concorde.

**7L ★**   Monsieur Karl Lagerfeld is not only the creative director of Chanel, the city's emblematic fashion label, but also a prolific photographer and publisher. Here is where he sells his coffee table tomes on art, architecture, photography and design, in an elegant space designed by Japanese architect Tadao

Ando. Open Tuesday to Saturday 10:30am to 6:45pm. Closed Sunday and Monday. 7 rue de Lille, 7e. www.steidlville.com/bookshops/ ✆ **01-42-92-03-58.** Métro: St Germain des Près.

**Shakespeare and Company ★**
The most famous bookstore on the Left Bank is Shakespeare and Company, on rue de l'Odéon, home to Sylvia Beach, "mother confessor to the Lost Generation." Hemingway, Fitzgerald, and Stein were frequent patrons, as was Anaïs Nin, the diarist noted for her description of struggling American artists in 1930s Paris. Nin helped her companion Henry Miller publish *Tropic of Cancer,* a book so notorious in its day that returning Americans who tried to slip copies through Customs often had them confiscated as pornography. (When times were hard, Nin herself wrote pornography for a dollar a page.) Long ago, the shop moved to rue de la Bûcherie, a rickety old

Shakespeare and Company.

place where expatriates still swap books and literary gossip and foreign students work in exchange for modest lodgings. Monday nights host free readings; check the program on their site. Open daily 10am to midnight. 37 rue de la Bûcherie, 5e. www.shakespeareandcompany.com. ✆ **01-43-25-40-93**. Métro: St-Michel.

**Village Voice Bookshop** This favorite of expatriate Yankees is on a side street in the heart of the best Left Bank shopping district, near some of the gathering places described in Gertrude Stein's *The Autobiography of Alice B. Toklas*. Opened in 1981, the shop is a hangout for literati. Its name has nothing to do with the New York weekly. Regular author events are publicized on their website. Open Monday 2 to 8pm; Tuesday to Saturday 10am to 8pm; Sunday 2 to 7pm. 6 rue Princesse, 6e. www.villagevoicebookshop.com. ✆ **01-46-33-36-47**. Métro: Mabillon.

## CLOTHING & ACCESSORIES

### Women's

**agnès b ★** Agnès b's take on relaxed but elegant urban fashion has been winning over Parisians, and the rest of the planet, since the '70s. She produces collections for the whole family; note that you will find her menswear collections on sale around the corner at agnès b. Homme (1 rue Dieu, 10e). There are numerous other addresses scattered around the city. Open Monday 1 to 7pm, Tuesday to Saturday 11am to 7pm. Closed Sunday. 13 rue de Marseille, 10e. www.agnesb.com. ✆ **01-42-06-66-58**. Métro: Jacques Bonsergent.

**Bensimon ★** This popular French label designs wearable fashion and sportswear for the whole family. They also produce an important range of accessories, including a model of canvas sneaker that has become a cult summer classic. Just down the street at no. 8 rue des Francs Bourgeois you'll find Home Autour du Monde, stocking their ethnic-chic interiors range. Open Monday to Saturday 11am to 7pm, Sunday 1:30 to 7pm. 12 rue des Francs Bourgeois, 3e. www.bensimon. com. ✆ **01-42-77-06-08**. Métro: St-Paul.

**Chanel ★** If you can't have the sun, the moon, and the stars, at least buy something with Coco Chanel's initials on it—either a serious fashion statement or something fun and playful. Karl Lagerfeld's designs come in all flavors and have added a subtle twist to Chanel's classicism. This mythical flagship store is located just behind the Ritz, where Mlle Chanel once lived. Check out the beautiful staircase of the *maison* before you shop the two-floor boutique—where a series of rooms display Chanel fashion, accessories, beauty, and perfumes, including store exclusives. It's well worth a peek. Open Monday to Saturday 10am to 7pm. 31 rue Cambon, 1er. www.chanel.fr. ✆ **01-42-86-28-00**. Métro: Tuileries or Madeleine.

**Hermès ★★** France's single most important status item is a scarf or tie from Hermès. Patterns on these illustrious scarves, retailing from about 220€, have recently included the galaxies, Africa, the sea, the sun, and horse racing and breeding. But the choices don't stop there—this large flagship store sells everything from beach towels and accessories, dinner plates, *prêt-à-porter* for men and women, the complete collection of Hermès fragrances (including their "24 Faubourg," named after this mythic address), to saddles; a package of postcards could be the least expensive item sold. Outside, note the horseman on the roof with his scarf-flag flying. The illustrious brand opened a magnificent new flagship on the Left Bank in late 2010, which concentrates more on homeware than on the fashion lines, and features a bookshop, florist, and pricey cafe (17 rue de Sèvres, 6e; ✆ **01-42-22-80-83**; Mon–Sat 10:30am–7pm). Open Monday to

Saturday 10:30am to 7pm. 24 rue du Faubourg St-Honoré, 8e. www.hermes.com. ℰ **01-40-17-46-00.** Métro: Concorde.

**Isabel Marant** ★★ With her elegant but wearable urban fashion, Isabel Marant has defined this generation of Parisian chic, and now exports to all the fashion capitals. This is her original store, opened in 1996 when the Bastille neighborhood was where it was at. Here you'll find her signature range of trendy looks, sporting ethnic and vintage details, for women and children. Open Monday to Saturday 10:30am to 7:30pm. Closed Sunday. Also at 47 rue Saintonge, 3e, and 1 rue Jacob, 6e. 16 rue Charonne, 11e. www.isabelmarant.tm.fr. ℰ **01-49 29-71-55.** Métro: Bastille or Ledru-Rollin.

**L'Eclaireur** ★ You might feel as if you're stepping into an art gallery when you enter this, the latest address in this prestige string of multibrand emporiums created by the pioneering Madame and Monsieur Hadida. Their beautifully curated selection of high-end fashion is available in five exceptional stores around Paris. This Marais address was designed by Belgian artist Arne Quinze, and conceived of as a multimedia experience, or a sculpture, rather than a simple store. You'll discover women's wear from designers like Rick Owens, Maison Martin Margiela, Lanvin, Dries Van Noten, and Balenciaga. Open Monday to Saturday 11am to 7pm. 40 rue Sévigné, 3e. www.leclaireur.com. ℰ **01-48-87-10-22.** Métro: St-Paul.

**Sonia Rykiel** ★★ The emblematic Left Bank fashion designer has been dressing the independent and audacious women of St-Germain-des-Prés since 1968. Her modern wardrobe of elegant, comfortable clothes is instantly recognizable by its bestselling signature range of stripey knits. So you'll find a piece of the city's fashion history in this glamorous two-floor flagship. Open Monday to Saturday 10:30am to 7pm. 175 boulevard St Germain, 6e. www.soniarykiel.fr. ℰ **01-45-49-13-10.** Métro: St-Germain-des-Prés.

**Zadig & Voltaire** This trendy young French brand is doing well at capturing a contemporary European rock 'n' roll spirit. This spacious first-floor store, overlooking the place St-Sulpice in the heart of the Left Bank, displays their popular collections of up-to-date luxury: perfectly worn jeans, comfortable cashmeres, biker boots, and more, for men, women, and children. Open Monday to Saturday 10:30am to 7:30pm. 1 rue du Vieux Colombier, 6e. www.zadig-et-voltaire.com. ℰ **01-43-54-72-56.** Métro: St-Sulpice.

## Men's

**Citadium** A whole department store over four floors dedicated to streetwear and "lifestyle" for men. You'll find all the usual, international, suspects like North Face, Adidas, and Diesel, but also quality local brands including Petit Bateau, Veja, or The Kooples. The Beaubourg branch is smaller, but more central. Monday to Saturday 10am to 8pm (9pm Thurs). 50/56 rue Caumartin, 9e. www.citadium.fr. ℰ **01-55-31-74-00.** Métro: Havre-Caumartin. Other location at 33 rue Quincampoix, 4e. ℰ **01-70-06-99-89.** Métro: Rambuteau.

**Sandro Homme** If you're wanting to resemble the nonchalantly elegant gentlemen you see lounging around Parisian cafes, this Paris label is for you, with flannel pants in tones of charcoal or chocolate, merino turtlenecks, leather biker jackets, woolen suits, silk scarfs, and more. There's no compromising on style, but prices remain reasonable. The brand has a string of stores dedicated to its equally appealing women's wear. Open Monday to Saturday 10:30am to 7pm. 11 rue des Francs Bourgeois, 4e. www.sandro-paris.com. ℰ **01-44-59-84-51.** Métro: St-Paul.

## Children's

**Bonpoint** ★★ 🎁 This stylish brand helps parents transform their darlings into models of well-tailored conspicuous consumption. Though you'll find some garments for real life, the primary allure of the place lies in its tailored, fairly traditional—and expensive—garments. This breathtaking flagship is located inside a mansion set around an interior courtyard, and includes a secret cafe with chairs outside under the trees. Open Monday to Saturday 10am to 7pm. 6 rue de Tournon, 6e. www.bonpoint.com. ✆ **01-41-51-98-20.** Métro: Odéon.

**Bonton** ★ This fun three-floor emporium includes a candy counter, a hairdresser, a retro photo booth, toys, books, a basement knickknack and interiors department, plus the French label's signature collections of trendy clothing for boys and girls, from birth to age 16. It's hard to walk out empty-handed. Open Monday to Saturday 10am to 7pm. 5 boulevard des Filles du Calvaire, 3e. www.bonton. fr. ✆ **01-42-72-34-69.** Métro: Filles du Calvaire.

## Shoes & Accessories

**Goyard** ★ Like its rival Louis Vuitton, this luxury trunk maker was established in France in the mid-19th century. But while Louis Vuitton went on to international stardom and a listing on the stock market, Goyard has remained a relatively modest family business. However, the brand's range of totes and trunks have been quietly picking up a cult following. Goyard also has a store dedicated to luxury pet accessories, or *"le chic de chien,"* across the street at number 352. Open Monday to Saturday 10:30am to 7pm. 233 rue Saint-Honoré, 1er. www.goyard. fr. ✆ **01-42-60-57-04.** Métro: Tuileries.

**Louis Vuitton** ★★ Its luggage is among the most famous and prestigious in the world, a standard accessory aboard the first-class cabins of aircraft flying transatlantic and transpacific. Not content to cover the world's luggage with his initials, Vuitton also creates breathtaking ready-to-wear lines for men and women, as well as bags and other leather accessories, writing instruments, travel products, and more. The Champs-Élysées flagship rivals the Eiffel Tower as a destination for jet loads of flushed Japanese tourists, and note that the building includes a quality exhibition space (free entry) on its top floor (entry via rue Bassano). Open Monday to Saturday 10am to 8pm, Sunday, 11am to 7pm. 101 avenue Champs-Élysées, 8e. www.louisvuitton.com. ✆ **01-53-57-52-00.** Métro: George V. Other location 6 place St-Germain-des-Prés, 6e. ✆ **01-45-49-62-32.** Métro: St-Germain-des-Prés.

**Maison Fabre** ★ Three generations of the Fabre family have taken this family-owned glove factory in rural France to the pages of the world's finest fashion magazines. The brand sells an exquisite range of gloves, for day and night, summer or winter, that will wow your friends back home. Open Monday to Saturday 10am to 7pm. 128–129 Galerie de Valois, 1er. www.maisonfabre.com. ✆ **01-42-60-75-88.** Métro: Palais-Royal. Other location: 60 rue des Saints Pères, 7e. ✆ **01-42-22-44-86.**

**Pierre Hardy** ★ Another of the city's iconic cobblers. Pierre Hardy presents his cutting-edge, urban footwear collections from within sleek, black-lacquered spaces. You'll find shoes for men and women, as well as a range of leather accessories. Hardy was one of the first to propose luxury trainers. Open Monday to Saturday 11am to 7pm. 156 galerie de Valois, 1er. www.pierrehardy.com. ✆ **01-42-60-59-75.** Métro: Palais-Royal. Other location: 9 place du Palais Bourbon, 7e. ✆ **01-45-55-00-67.** Métro: Assemblée Nationale.

## Vintage Clothing

**Didier Ludot ★**   Fashion historians salivate when they're confronted with an inventory of vintage haute couture. In this frenetically stylish shop, albeit at prices that rival what you'd expect to pay for a serious antique, you'll find a selection of gowns and dresses created between 1900 and 1980 for designing women who looked *faaabulous* at Maxim's, at chic cocktail parties on the avenue Foch, in Deauville, or wherever. Open Monday to Saturday 11am to 7pm. 24 galerie de Montpensier, in the arcades surrounding the courtyard of the Palais Royal, 1er. www.didier ludot.fr. ✆ **01-42-96-06-56.** Métro: Palais-Royal.

**Kiliwatch ★**   The city's biggest central vintage emporium will not disappoint. It has everything from second-hand jeans and military wear to Hermès scarves and couture pieces. Plus there's a great arts book corner. Open Tuesday to Sunday 11am to 7pm, Monday 2 to 7pm. 64 rue Tiquetonne, 1er. http://espacekiliwatch.fr. ✆ **01-42-21-17-37.** Métro: Etienne-Marcel.

## Discount Stores

**L'Habilleur ★**   This northern Marais institution discounts last season's collections of quality brands including the Italian knit brand Roberto Collina or French fashion for men and women by Paul and Joe and Antik Batik. The garments are impeccably maintained and most aesthetically organized by their color, creating a rainbow of fashion opportunities. Open Tuesday to Saturday 11am to 7pm. 44 Rue du Poitou, 3e. ✆ **01-48-87-77-12.** Métro: St-Sébastien Froissart.

**Réciproque ★**   Forget about serious bargains, but celebrate what could be your only opportunity to own designer clothing of this caliber. Within a series of six storefronts side by side along the same avenue, you'll find used clothing from every major name in fashion, along with shoes, accessories, menswear, and wedding gifts. Everything has been worn, but some items were worn only on fashion runways or during photo shoots. Open Tuesday to Saturday 11am to 7pm. 89–101 rue de la Pompe, 16e. www.reciproque.fr. ✆ **01-47-04-30-28.** Métro: Pompe.

## Lingerie

**Chantal Thomass ★★**   This lingerie brand sells luxury French underwear for the contemporary pin-up with a penchant for suspenders and corsets. The boutique is a delicious burlesque boudoir lined in pink satin. Open Monday to Saturday 10am to 7pm. 211 rue St-Honoré, 1er. www.chantalthomass.fr. ✆ **01-42-60-40-56.** Métro: Tuileries.

**Erès ★★**   Minimal collections of luxury French lingerie and swimwear flaunt a subtle palette and high prices. Open Monday to Saturday 10am to 7pm. 4 bis, rue du Cherche Midi, 6e. www.eresparis.com. ✆ **01-45-44-95-54.** Métro: St-Sulpice.

## Jewelry

**Bijoux Blues ★** 🎁   This Marais boutique offers unique jewelry handmade in Paris with a variety of different materials, including Austrian and bohemian crystals, natural and semiprecious stones, pearls, coral, and mother-of-pearl. Custom requests are welcomed for individually-designed pieces. The store offers jewelry at what the staff calls "atelier prices." Open Tuesday to Saturday noon to 7pm, Sunday 2 to 6pm. 30 rue St-Paul, 4e. www.bijouxblues.com. ✆ **01-48-04-00-64.** Métro: St. Paul.

**Dior Joaillerie ★★**   The talented Parisian aristocrat with the dreamy name Victoire de Castellane launched Dior's fine jewelry department in 1998. Colored stones, bright enamels, flower and insect motifs, are some of the signature elements. Discover her astounding, dreamy collections displayed within a jewel box of a store installed on the magnificent place Vendôme. Open Monday to Saturday 11am to 7pm. 8 place Vendôme, 1er. www.diorjoaillerie.com. ☎ **01-42-96-30-84.** Métro: Tuileries.

**White Bird** ★ This new multi-brand shop offers a fine selection of jewelry, including limited edition pieces by a unique selection of international craftsmen. Store owner Stephanie Roger carefully curates the collection by selecting independent-minded international jewelry designers with a unique aesthetic. The boutique manages to exude neither the coolness of a contemporary art gallery nor the hushed and stifling atmosphere of the classic jewelry store. It's a stone's throw from the place Vendôme, but a world away from the trade jewelry scene. Open Monday to Saturday 11:30am to 7pm. 38 rue du Mont Thabor, 1er. www.white birdjewellery.com. ☎ **01-58-62-25-86.** Métro: Concorde.

## CONCEPT STORES

**Colette** ★★ Colette is a swank citadel for a la mode fashion. It buzzes with excitement, stocking fashion by some of the city's most promising young talent, from Comme des Garçons to Carven. This is for the sophisticated international shopper who'd never be caught dead shopping at Galeries Lafayette and the like. A pioneering concept store, it also curates home furnishings by designers such as Tom Dixon, books, music, DVDs, and even zany Japanese accessories. If you're not in the mood for shopping, head straight for the basement "water bar," with its fresh quiches, salads, and cakes, plus three dozen brands of bottled water. Open Monday to Saturday 11am to 7pm. 213 rue St-Honoré, 1er. www.colette.fr. ☎ **01-55-35-33-90.** Métro: Tuileries or Pyramides.

**Le 66** ★★ This appealing labyrinthine space in an arcade off the Champs-Élysées provides some welcome relief from the hysteria on the avenue. Explore

the considered selection of edgy fashion and accessories for men and women at your leisure. Discover the latest pieces from an impressive list of local and international brands such as Le Mont St Michel, Thomsen, JC de Castelbajac, and Vivienne Westwood. Plus there's a satellite Kiliwatch vintage bazaar on site. Open Monday to Saturday 11am to 8pm, Sunday 2 to 8pm. 66 ave des Champs-Élysées, 8e. www. le66.fr. ☎ **01-53-53-33-80.** Métro: George V or Franklin-D-Roosevelt.

**Merci** ★★ This airy, three-floor superstore brings together a carefully selected selection of furniture, home goods, fashion, and beauty. There's a delicious and healthy basement canteen overlooking a courtyard herb garden, and a literary cafe on the ground level for further refreshments. This imposing address in the northern

**Shopping at Merci.**

Marais exemplifies the neighborhood's panache and creativeness, and you don't know who you might run into. Open Monday to Saturday 10am to 7pm. 11 boulevard Beaumarchais,3e. www.merci-merci.com. ☏ **01-42-77-00-33.** Métro: Saint Sébastien-Froissart.

**Spree ★ 🎁** Possibly the best store in Montmartre, Spree has been doing its bohemian thing since 2000, and slowly drawing other quality retail to the vicinity. This relaxed concept store presents an inspiring fusion of fashion and accessories, art and design, with pieces from talents including Isabel Marant, Tsumori Chisato, Vanessa Bruno, Jerome Dreyfuss, Acne, and APC. The staff is warm and helpful. Open Monday to Saturday 11am to 7:30pm, Sunday 3 to 7pm. 16 rue Vieuville, 18e. www.spree.fr. ☏ **01-42-23-41-40.** Métro: Abbesses.

## DEPARTMENT STORES

**Le Bon Marché ★★** This Left Bank landmark has worked hard positioning itself as the most exclusive of the city's departments stores. Its modest size makes it manageable to wander the exclusive selection of fashion for men, women, and children; cosmetics and perfumes; furniture; upscale gifts; and housewares. It also boasts one of the largest food halls in Paris, which should not be missed. The magnificent displays of the finest fresh and preserved produce from France and around the world is a feast for the senses. Open Monday to Wednesday and Saturday 10am to 8pm; Thursday and Friday 10am to 9pm. 22–24 rue de Sèvres, 7e. www.lebonmarche.fr. ☏ **01-44-39-80-00.** Métro: Sèvres-Babylone.

Printemps.

**Les Galeries Lafayette ★** Opened in 1896, with a lobby capped by an early-1900s stained-glass cupola classified as a historic monument, the family-owned Galeries Lafayette remains Paris's most popular department store. This store could provision a small city with its thousands of racks of clothing for men, women, and children, and a staggering array of cosmetics, and perfumes. Also in the complex is **Lafayette Gourmet,** one of the fanciest grocery stores in Paris, selling culinary exotica at prices usually lower than those at Fauchon (see "Food and Drink: Specialty," later in this chapter); **Lafayette Sports; Galeries Lafayette Mariage** (for wedding accessories); and two other general-merchandise stores, both known simply as **"GL."** The floor above street level has a concentration of high-end, corners, including Cartier, Vuitton, and Prada. The **Galerie des Galeries** is located within this Luxury department and presents regular quality contemporary art exhibitions (free entry). At the street-level Welcome Desk, a multilingual staff will tell you where to find various items in the store, where to get a taxi back to your hotel, and so on. Across the street at 35 boulevard Haussmann you'll find the 3-story **Lafayette Maison,** dedicated to everything you might need for the home. Open Monday to Wednesday and Friday to Saturday 9:30am to 8pm; Thursday 9:30am to 9pm. 40 bd. Haussmann, 9e. www.galerieslafayette.com. ✆ **01-42-82-34-56.** Métro: Chaussée d'Antin. RER: Auber.

**Printemps ★**   Take a look at the elaborate facade of this store for a reminder of the Gilded Age. Inside, the merchandise is divided into housewares (**Printemps Maison**), women's fashion (**Printemps de la Mode**), and men's clothes (**Le Printemps de l'Homme**). Since a change in ownership in 2006, the Printemps has been chasing a serious luxury market, and now displays a cavalcade of high-end brands across its selection. Inside is a magnificent stained-glass dome, through which turquoise light cascades into the sixth-floor **La Brasserie Printemps;** you can have a coffee or a full meal here. Interpreters at the Welcome Service in Printemps de la Mode will help you find what you're looking for, claim your VAT refund, and so on. Printemps also has a tourist discount card, offering a flat 10% discount. Open Monday to Wednesday and Friday to Saturday 9:35am to 7pm; Thursday 9:35am to 9pm. 64 bd. Haussmann, 9e. www.printemps.com. ✆ **01-42-82-50-00.** Métro: Havre-Caumartin. RER: Auber or Haussmann–St-Lazare.

## FOOD & DRINK
### Bread & Cakes

**Ladurée ★★**   Japanese tourists have been known to faint when reaching the celadon and gilt entry to this mythical French patisserie. Sofia Coppola even called on the *maison* to prepare their famous macaroons for her 2006 film "Marie Antoinette." Although the branch on the Champs-Élysées is the most spacious, the one on rue Royale is the original store, which opened back in 1862 and where the modern day macaroon is credited with actually being invented. But you can expect queues at all three Parisian outposts. As well as their exquisite macaroons available in classic flavors like chocolate, raspberry and rose petal, Ladurée makes all the traditional French cakes, and includes an onsite tea room cum restaurant where you can enjoy the desserts. Open Monday to Friday from 7:30am to 11pm, Saturday from 7:30am to midnight, Sunday 7:30am to 10pm. 75 avenue des Champs-Élysées, 8e. www.laduree.fr. ✆ **01-40-75-08-75.** Métro: George V. Other locations at 16–18 rue Royale, 8e. ✆ **01-42-60-21-79.** Métro: Madeleine; 21 rue Bonaparte, 6e. ✆ **01-44-07-64-87.** Métro: St-Germain-des-Prés.

**Pierre Hermé ★★**   The cult of the macaroon, a delicate sweet biscuit, has swept the city over the last few years, and Monsieur Hermé is one of its pioneers. From this elegant Left Bank flagship you will find Pierre Hermé's full range, with original flavor combinations like passion fruit and chocolate, or wasabi and strawberry. There is also an incomparable selection of cakes, to eat in, take out or simply admire. Open daily 10am to 7pm. 72 rue Bonaparte, 6e. www.pierreherme.com. ✆ **01-43-54-47-77.** Métro: St-Sulpice.

**Poilâne ★★**   One of Paris's best-loved bakeries, Poilâne hasn't changed much since it opened in 1932. Come here to taste and admire the beautiful loaves of bread decorated with simple designs of leaves and flowers that'll make you yearn for an all-but-vanished Paris. Specialties include apple tarts, butter cookies, and a chewy sourdough loaf cooked in a wood-fired oven. Breads can be specially wrapped to stay fresh during your journey home. Cherche-Midi location open Monday to Saturday 7:15am to 8:15pm; Grenelle location Tuesday to Sunday 7:15am to 8:15pm. 8 rue du Cherche-Midi, 6e. www.poilane.fr. ℂ **01-45-48-42-59.** Métro: St-Sulpice. Also: 49 bd. de Grenelle, 15e. ℂ **01-45-79-11-49.** Métro: Dupleix.

Chocolates at Christian Constant.

## Chocolate

### Christian Constant ★★

Opened in 1970, Christian Constant sells some of Paris's most delectable chocolates by the kilo. Each is a blend of ingredients from Ecuador, Colombia, or Venezuela, usually mingled with scents of spices and flowers such as orange blossoms, jasmine, the Asian blossom ylang-ylang, and vetiver and *verveine* (herbs more usually used to brew tea). Open daily 9am to 8pm. 37 rue d'Assas, 6e. www.christianconstant.fr. ℂ **01-53-63-15-15.** Métro: St-Placide.

**Jean-Paul Hévin ★★** One of the great chocolatiers of Paris, its owner has mastered the fusion of *chocolat* with *fromage* (cheese, of course). Sweet luscious chocolates with tart cheeses such as Camembert or Roquefort are infused to satisfy both the cheese fan and the chocolate lover's sweet tooth. Savory chocolates are also served without cheese. New offerings—unique in Paris—have caused this place to become one of the most acclaimed in Europe for chocolate devotees. Open Monday to Saturday 10am to 7:30pm. 231 rue St-Honoré, 1er. www.jphevin.com. ℂ **01-55-35-35-96.** Métro: Tuileries or Concorde.

## Cheese

**Barthélémy ★** This historic cheese monger has been supplying the country's presidents since 1973 with an incredible range of specialty produce from the four corners of France. Their specialty? The Mont d'Or, a creamy cow's milk cheese from the Alps available between September and May. Open Tuesday to Saturday 7.30am to 7:30pm. 51 rue de Grenelle, 7e. ℂ **01-42-22-82-24.** Métro: Rue du Bac.

## Specialty

**Fauchon ★★★** At place de la Madeleine stands one of the city's most popular sights—not the church, but Fauchon, a hyper-upscale mega-delicatessen that thrives within a city famous for its finicky eaters. In the original store (26 place de la Madeleine) you'll find a *pâtissier* and *boulangerie,* for breads and pastries, and a *traiteur,* for fresh produce including cheeses, terrines, pâtés, caviar, and fruits. Prices are steep, but the inventories—at least to serious foodies—are without equal. The selection of cakes is mouth-watering; try one of their famous *éclairs,* with new flavor combinations each season. Or a *Paris-Brest,* a ring in the shape of a bicycle wheel that's loaded with pastry cream, almond praline, butter cream, and hazelnut paste capped with almonds. At the second, neighboring address (30 place de la Madeleine), you'll discover an *épicerie* (for jams, crackers, pastas, and exotic canned goods), a *confiserie* selling chocolates and confectionary, a wine cellar, plus two dining areas (a casual basement lunch space La Cantine and upstairs more formal dining at Le Café). At some of the counters, you'll indicate to attendants what you want from behind glass display cases and get an electronic ticket, which you'll carry to a *caisse* (cash register). Surrender your tickets, pay the bill, and then return to the counter to pick up your groceries. In other cases, you simply load up a shopping basket with whatever you want and pay for your purchases at a cash register, just as you would at any grocery store. Open Monday to Saturday 9:30am to 7pm. 26 and 30 place de la Madeleine, 8e. www. fauchon.com. ✆ **01-70-39-38-00.** Métro: Madeleine.

**Hédiard ★★**    Another fine Parisian delicatessen, this 1850 temple of *haute gastronomie* has a more traditional style than its neighbor Fauchon. The old-fashioned decor is a series of red and black salons filled with towering displays of exotic and specialty foodstuffs, giving the store the look of an early-1900s spice emporium. Hédiard is rich in coffees, teas, jams, and spices. They have a quality wine cellar, and the fresh produce department displays exotic fruit and vegetables from the four corners of the planet, in all seasons. Open Monday to Friday 8am to 10pm, Saturday noon to 10:30pm. 21 place de la Madeleine, 8e. www.hediard.fr. ✆ **01-43-12-88-99.** Métro: Madeleine.

### Wines

**Lavinia ★**    This is the largest wine-and-spirits store in Europe, opened in 2002 to great acclaim in Paris. Spread over three floors near place de la Madeleine, it stocks more than 3,000 brands of French wine and spirits, along with more than 2,000 brands from other parts of the world. A simple lunch-only restaurant is onsite, as well as a tasting bar. Wine sales here are big business and reflective of France's marketing ideas that regard wine as a part of life. This is the only place in Paris where you can buy a good bottle of South Dakota wine. But who would want to? Open Monday to Saturday 10am to 8pm. 3–5 bd. de la Madeleine, 1er. www. lavinia.fr. ✆ **01-42-97-20-20.** Métro: Madeleine.

## HOUSEWARE

### Ceramics, China & Porcelain

**Astier de Villatte ★★**    This impossibly charming two-story shop sells a range of white, uncompromisingly handmade earthenware in a range of designs inspired by 18th-century styles. There's regular special collections in collaboration with other Paris creatives, and a corner devoted to all sorts of other objects that appeal to the owners, from postcards to scented candles. Astier de Villatte also produce a cult range of annual diaries and notebooks. Everything they do radiates good taste. Open Monday to Saturday 11am to 7:30pm. 173 rue Saint-Honoré, 1er. www.astierdevillatte.com. ✆ **01-42-60-74-13.** Métro: Palais Royal.

### Crystal

**Baccarat ★★**    Opened in 1764, Baccarat is one of Europe's leading purveyors of full-lead crystal. They sell luxury jewelry pieces based on colored crystal and precious gems, tableware, glassware, and contemporary chandeliers and other crystal light fittings. The most prestigious outlet is on place de la Madeleine, but the exquisite, Philippe Starck–designed **Maison Baccarat** at 11 place des Etats-Unis, 16e, is larger and includes the **Musée Baccarat**. Branches are open

Tuesday to Friday 10am to 7pm; Monday and Saturday 10am to 7:30pm. 11 place de la Madeleine, 8e. www.baccarat.fr. ℰ **01-42-65-36-26.** Métro: Madeleine. Also: 11 place des Etats-Unis, 16e. ℰ **01-40-22-11-22.** Métro: Boissière.

### Kitchenware

**Dehillerin ★**   Established in 1820, Dehillerin is Paris's most famous cookware shop, in the "kitchen corridor" around Les Halles, where all the city's chefs once came to stock up on provisions at the central fresh food market. The shop has a professional, though dusty, feel to it, but don't be intimidated. Equipped with the right tools from Dehillerin, you, too, can learn to cook like a master chef. Open Monday 9am to 12:30pm and 2 to 6pm; Tuesday to Saturday 9am to 6pm. 18–20 rue Coquillière, 1er. www.e-dehillerin.fr. ℰ **01-42-36-53-13.** Métro: Les Halles.

**Les Fleurs ★**   Tucked down a little alleyway in Bastille, this is a charming clutter of curated accessories for the home or for you. Unique products by young designers are piled together; expect to find everything from leather bags to coffee mugs, but always with a twist. Great for gifts. Open Monday to Saturday Noon to 7:30pm; Closed Sunday. 6 passage Josset, 11e. http://lesfleurs.canalblog.com. ℰ **06-64.35.75.54.** Métro: Ledru-Rollin

## MUSIC

**FNAC ★**   This is a large chain of music, books, and electronics stores known for their wide selection and discounted prices. Great for the traveler, it offers everything you need for your computer, iPod, or digital camera. Most branches include digital photo development services. Stock up on French music in the CD department, or browse the bookshelves. Seven branches are in Paris, with the largest being at 136 rue de Rennes, Montparnasse. Other locations include rue St-Lazare, avenue des Champs-Élysées, Forum des Halles, avenue des Ternes, and avenue d'Italie. All are open Monday to Saturday 10am to 7:30pm except Champs-Élysées, which is open daily noon to midnight. 136 rue de Rennes, 6e. www.fnac.com. ℰ **08-25-02-00-20.** Métro: St-Placide.

## TOYS & GAMES

**Au Nain Bleu ★**   This is the largest, oldest, and most centrally-located toy store in Paris. More important, it's probably the fanciest toy store in the world. But don't panic—in addition to the expensive stuff, you'll find rows of cheaper items on the first floor. Open Monday 2 to 7pm; Tuesday to Saturday 10am to 7pm. 5 bd. Malesherbes, 8e. www.aunainbleu.com. ℰ **01-42-65-20-00.** Métro: Concorde or Madeleine.

# ENTERTAINMENT & NIGHTLIFE

It seems that every resident of this luminous city has a higher education in pleasure. Whatever your diversional whim, Paris can answer it. As its nickname indicates, Parisian streets and monuments remain illuminated all night. Restaurants won't expect you before 8pm, and by midnight, the party is just getting started at hundreds of bars or dance clubs throughout the city.

## The Performing Arts

Home to a broad range of performing arts, Paris showcases everything from world-renowned opera and contemporary dance to classical music, slap-stick comedy and edgy and modern theater. The **Opéra Garnier** and **Opéra Bastille** are the stalwart venues of world-class opera and ballet, kicking out classics by the likes of Puccini and Mozart (often with cutting-edge mise-en-scènes), or hosting performances from foreign ballet powerhouses as well as their own Opera de Paris corps. Theater in Paris is generally in French, but check the programs for the occasional play in English.

**LISTINGS**    Announcements of shows, concerts, and operas are plastered on kiosks all over town and in the Métro. You'll find listings in the weekly *Pariscope,* an entertainment guide with an English-language section, or in *L'Officiel des Spectacles,* available at newsstands. Also check out **http://en.parisinfo.com**, the city's official English-language tourism website. The "What's On" section has detailed listings for every concert and show in town. *Note:* Performances tend to start later in Paris than in London or New York—from 8 to 9pm—and Parisians tend to dine after the theater.

**GETTING TICKETS**    Your best bet for cheap tickets is to try the theater's box office at the last minute. Or head for a discount agencies such as the **Kiosque-Théâtre,** 15 place de la Madeleine, 8e (✆ **01-42-65-35-64;** www.kiosquetheatre.com; Métro: Madeleine), offering leftover tickets for up to 50% off on the day of performance. Tickets for evening shows sell Tuesday to Saturday from 12:30 to 8pm, for matinees, Sunday 12:30 to 4pm. Other branches are in front of Gare Montparnasse and at the exit of Ternes Métro station.

Another option is **FNAC**. There are several branches across the city, but two handy ones are at 136 rue de Rennes, 6e (✆ **08-25-02-00-02;** Métro: St. Placide); and 1–7 rue Pierre-Lescot, in the Forum des Halles, 1er (✆ **08-25-02-00-20;** Métro: Châtelet–Les Halles). The chain sells music, movies, electronics, and books, as well as tickets for festivals, concerts, and the theater. You can pick up your tickets at the *billitterie* (ticket booth) of any of these locations, or online at www.fnacspectacles.com. Two other great websites for reduced-price tickets are www.ticketnet.fr and **www.billetreduc.fr**.

*Tip:* Students with ID can get great last-minute deals by applying for the lottery at box offices an hour before curtain time.

The easiest (and most expensive) way to get tickets is to ask your concierge to arrange for them. A service fee is added, but it's a lot easier if you don't want to waste precious hours in Paris trying to secure often hard-to-get tickets.

Cité de la Musique.

## THEATER

**Comédie-Française** ★★ Those with an understanding of French can delight in a sparkling production of Molière at this national theater, established to keep the classics alive and to promote important contemporary authors. Nowhere else will you see the works of Molière and Racine so beautifully staged. In 1993 a Left Bank annex was launched, the **Comédie Française-Théâtre du Vieux-Colombier,** 21 rue du Vieux-Colombier, 4e (② **01-44-39-87-00**). Though its repertoire varies, it's known for presenting serious French dramas and the occasional foreign adaptation. The troupe's contemporary plays are usually shown in the **Studio Théâtre** (just opposite in the Carousel du Louvre, 99 rue de Rivoli, 1e). 2 rue de Richelieu, 1er. www.comedie-francaise.fr. ② **08-25-10-16-80.** Tickets range from 12€–40€. Métro: Palais-Royal or Musée du Louvre.

**Théâtre de Châtelet** ★★ The Châtelet's Belle Époque interior makes a stunning setting for some the best musical theater in Paris. Troupes from the West End and Broadway, as well as the best French companies, frequently perform classic musicals like Sweeney Todd, West Side Story, and The Sound of Music, in English, with full orchestras. Check the website for up-to-the-minute details. 1 place du Châtelet, 1er. www.chatelet-theatre.com. ② **01-40-28-28-40.** Tickets range from 12€–130€. Métro: Palais-Royal or Musée du Louvre.

## OPERA, DANCE & CLASSICAL CONCERTS

**Cité de la Musique** ★★★ This testimony to the power of music has been the most widely applauded of the late François Mitterrand's *grands projets*. At the city's northeastern edge in what used to be a run-down neighborhood, this $120-million stone-and-glass structure incorporates a network of concert halls, a library and research center for the study of all kinds of music, and a museum. The complex hosts a rich variety of concerts, ranging from Renaissance music through 19th- and 20th-century works, including jazz and traditional music from nations around the world. There's a great café on site if you'd like to sip some wine on the sunny terrace before your concert. 221 av. Jean-Jaurès, 19e. www.cite-musique.fr. ② **01-44-84-44-84.** Tickets 8€–39€. Métro: Porte de Pantin.

Opéra Garnier.

**Opéra Bastille ★★**  This controversial building—it has been called a "beached whale"—was designed by Canadian architect Carlos Ott, with curtains by Japanese designer Issey Miyake. Since the house's grand opening in July 1989, the Opéra National de Paris has presented works such as Mozart's *Marriage of Figaro* and Tchaikovsky's *Queen of Spades*. The main hall is the largest of any French opera house, with 2,700 seats, but the building also contains two smaller concert halls, including an intimate 250-seat room that usually hosts chamber music. Both traditional opera performances and symphony concerts are presented here, as well as classical and modern dance. 2 place de la Bastille, 4e. www. operadeparis.fr. ℭ **08-92-89-90-90.** Tickets 5€–180€ opera, 8€–100€ dance. Métro: Bastille.

**Opéra Garnier ★★★**  With its grand décor, underground lake and cellars, and haunted history—a falling chandelier killed a man here in 1896—this place served as the inspiration for Gaston Leroux's 1910 novel (and later a musical hit), *The Phantom of the Opera*. Today, this is once again the premier venue for dance and opera. Charles Garnier designed this 1875 rococo wonder during the heyday of the French Empire under Napoleon III; the facade is adorned with marble and sculpture, including *The Dance* by Carpeaux. You can see the original gilded busts and statues, the rainbow-hued marble pillars, the mosaics, and inside, the ceiling painted by Chagall. The Opéra Garnier combines ballet and opera, and provides one of the most elegant evenings you can spend in the City of Light. The box office is open Monday to Saturday from 10:30am to 6:30pm. You can also visit the building outside performance times. Place de l'Opéra, 9e. www.opera deparis.fr. ℭ **08-92-89-90-90** or 01-40-01-18-50. Tickets 5€–180€ opera, 8€–89€ dance. Métro: Opéra.

**Salle Pleyel** ★★★  New York has Carnegie Hall, but for years Paris lacked a permanent home for its orchestra. That is, until several years ago when the restored Salle Pleyel opened once again. Built in 1927 by the piano-making firm of the same name, Pleyel was the world's first concert hall designed exclusively for a symphony orchestra. Ravel, Debussy, and Stravinsky performed their masterpieces here, only to see the hall devastated by fire less than 9 months after its opening. In 1998, real estate developer Hubert Martigny purchased the concert hall and pumped $38 million into it, restoring the Art Deco spirit of the original and also refining the acoustics it once knew. Nearly 500 seats were removed to make those that remained more comfortable. The Orchestre Philarmonique de Radio France and the Orchestre de Paris now have a home worthy of their reputations, and the London Symphony Orchestra makes Pleyel its venue in Paris. The box office is open Monday to Friday 10am to 6pm. You'll also find jazz and high-brow pop on the agenda. 252 rue du Faubourg-St-Honoré, 8e. www.sallepleyel.fr. ℭ **01-42-56-13-13.** Tickets 10€–160€. Métro: Miromesnil.

## CABARET

Decidedly expensive and wholly kitsch cabarets give you your money's worth by providing lavishly spectacular floor shows with bare-breasted ladies in feathers and sequins, and fun acts by ice-skaters and ventriloquists. The dancing is beautiful—the music less so—but Paris just wouldn't be Paris without its cabarets.

**The Crazy Horse**  Since 1951, this sophisticated strip joint has thrived, thanks to good choreography and an avant-gardist, coquettish celebration of the female form. The Crazy Horse has been getting more attention in recent years ever since the famous burlesque performer Dita Von Teese decided to make it her home away from home in Paris. Shows last less than 2 hours. You'll find a

Moulin Rouge.

small number of women among the audience of mainly businessmen. Shows Sunday to Friday 8:15 and 10:45pm; Saturday at 7, 9:30, and 11:45pm. The Crazy doesn't have a restaurant but you can buy a combined show-dining ticket and eat at affiliated restaurants like La Fermette Marbeuf. 12 av. George V, 8e. www. lecrazyhorseparis.com. © **01-47-23-32-32.** Reservations recommended. Entry from 100€ for the show and champagne; show plus dinner packages 180€–240€. Métro: George V or Alma Marceau.

**Moulin Rouge** This place is a camp classic. The establishment that Toulouse-Lautrec immortalized is still here, but the artist would probably have a hard time recognizing it today, surrounded as it is by so many tour buses. Colette once created a scandal here by offering an on-stage kiss to Mme de Morny, but shows today have a harder time shocking audiences. Try to get a table—the view is much better on the main floor than from the bar. What's the theme? Synchronized dancing by handsome men and girls, girls, girls, virtually all topless. Dance finales usually include two dozen of the belles doing a topless cancan. Revues begin nightly at 9 and 11pm. 82 bd. Clichy, place Blanche, 18e. www.moulinrouge.fr. © **01-53-09-82-82.** Tickets for the show alone range from 105€–105€, and packages including dinner range from 175€–200€. Métro: Blanche.

# The Bar Scene
## BARS & PUBS

You will find Parisians enjoying their drinks at any of the ubiquitous cafes and bars throughout town (many of which often double as an extension of personal living rooms). What follows are among the best places to enjoy a beer or cocktail, in part because of the interesting crowds they draw. Paris is also home to quite a few luxurious, world-class bars, including those at the **Plaza Athénée** and the **Ritz**—imbibing at these bars is a uniquely Parisian experience. Just dress up for the occasion. As a general rule, bars and pubs are open daily from 11am to 2am.

**Andy Whaloo ★** This bar has a 1970s Moroccan vibe, with colorful rugs and other North African collectables. The cocktails are expensive, but people-watching among the youthful and *branché* (hip) Parisians perched on the stools makes up for the prices, and DJs play into the wee hours most nights. Open Tuesday to Saturday 6pm to 2am. 69 rue des Gravilliers, 3e. © **01-42-71-20-38.** Métro: Arts et Métiers.

**Experimental Cocktail Club** This cosmopolitan lounge has the feel of a retro speakeasy. The cocktails here are spot-on and the crowd is fashionable—starchitect Philippe Starck and actor Adrian Grenier have been spotted sipping drinks here late into the evening. Drinks start at 12.50€. Open daily from 6pm to 2am, until 5am Friday and Saturday. 37 rue St-Sauveur, 2e. www.experimental cocktailclub.com. © **01-45-08-88-09.** Métro: Sentier.

**Le Bar (Hôtel Plaza Athénée)** This classy, historic joint is all glamour and fabulousness with a shockingly 21st-century decor. It will cost you a small fortune to drink a glass of champagne (24€), but for some it's definitely worth it. The specialty Love Mojito (a mix of vodka, litchis, pink champagne, and rose petals) is as delicious as it is decadent (28€). Dress to the nines if you're going—but if you're planning on making the trip, you already knew that. Drinks start at 20€. Open daily from 6pm to 2am. Hotel Plaza-Athénée, 25 av. Montaigne, 8e. www.plaza-athenee-paris.fr. © **01-53-67-66-65.** Métro: Alma-Marceau.

**Le China** This site has been home to various clubs stretching back decades. In the 1930s, it was an opium den and jazz club. Today, in its latest incarnation, it is all dark colors, candles, soft lights, and intimacy. The onsite restaurant evokes 1930s Shanghai with red-painted walls and asian cuisine. There is a long zinc bar (the longest in Paris) on the ground floor, and the basement bar hosts regular jazz concerts. Cocktails cost from 10€. The Chinatown (gin, fresh mint, lemon, and soda) was invented here in the 1990s. Open Monday to Friday noon to 2am and Saturday and Sunday from 5pm to 2am. 50 rue de Charenton, 12e. www.lechina.eu. ℂ **01-43-46-08-09.** Métro: Ledru Rollin.

**Le Forum** The polished oak paneling, ornate stucco, and selection of single-malt whiskeys on offer here recall a posh English gentleman's club. The Forum, however, is all about cocktails. You can sample from among 180 of them, including many that haven't been popular since the Jazz Age. Champagne by the glass is common, as is that social lubricant, the martini. Open Monday to Thursday noon to 1am, Friday noon to 2am, Saturday 5:30pm to 2am. 4 bd. Malesherbes, 8e. www.bar-le-forum.com. ℂ **01-42-65-37-86.** Métro: Madeleine.

## WINE BARS

The wine bar, or *bar à vin*, is a welcome departure from sitting down at a typical café or restaurant. They are often calm and warmly decorated, and many have regional themes. All offer diverse and interesting selections of wines and serve simple small dishes and platters—perfect for those in the mood for a delectable snack with their drinks.

**5e Cru ★** 🎁 This shabby-chic spot, with only three pine tables as well as a few barrels converted to dining stations, is a favorite of foodies. Jean de Toalier boasts that he's got "every *terroir* of France covered" in his kitchen, offering more than 150 different French wines. He may well be right. You can get a simple menu, or daily small plate special, for 15€; a glass of wine for 4€ to 8€, with bottles priced as low as 8€ and rarely more than 60€. Open Tuesday to Friday 10:30am to midnight, Saturday 3pm to 1am. 7 rue du Cardinal Lemoine, 5e. www.5ecru.com. ℂ **01-40-46-86-34.** Métro: Jussieu.

Le Baron Rouge.

**Le Baron Rouge ★★** This immensely popular Bacchanalian temple only has four tables, so get here before the pre-dinner crowds sweep in if you want to sit. If not, be prepared to slurp any one of its 50 or so labels standing, or resting on a giant wine barrel outside. Snacks of cheese, charcuterie, and (when in season) oysters add to the attraction. Being in the middle of the Marché Aligre, it's also a coveted bar with the Sunday market crowds. It's open Tues–Thurs 10am–3pm and 5–10pm; Fri–Sat 10am–10pm; Sun 10am–3pm. 1 rue Théophile Roussel, 75012. ✆ **01-43-43-14-32.** Metro: Ledru-Rollin.

**Les Caves Populaires**   The name says it all: This is a hugely popular wine bar with friendly waiters, rustic decor, cheap platters of cheese and meat, and even cheaper wine, starting at just 2.50€ a glass. It's a real local's joint in the heart of the Batignolle's district and a place to mix with 30-something artsy types and students. It's open Mon–Sat 8am–2am, and Sun 11am–2am. 22 rue des Dames, 75017. ✆ **01-53-04-08-32.** Metro: Place de Clichy.

# The Club & Music Scene

The live music and club scene in Paris is legendary. The City of Light is home to everything from the swankiest of chic nightclubs—with thousand-euro bottle service and models—to the smallest and sweatiest dive bars and glitzy cabarets. There is also a world-class jazz scene here, as well as a varied live music scene; clubs and concert halls host everything from cutting-edge electronica music to hip-hop to the soft glamour of indie rock, and just about everything else in between. Paris is a moveable dance floor.

## LIVE MUSIC
### Jazz Clubs
The great jazz revival that long ago swept America is still going strong here, with Dixieland, Chicago, bop, and free-jazz rhythms being pounded out in dozens of cellars, mostly called *caveaux*, where music lovers of all ages gather to listen to jazz.

**Caveau des Oubliettes ★**   It's hard to say which is more intriguing—the entertainment and drinking or the setting. An oubliette is a dungeon with a trap door at the top as its only opening, and the name is accurate. Located in the Latin Quarter, just across the river from Notre-Dame, this night spot is housed in a genuine 12th-century prison, complete with dungeons and spine-tingling passages, where prisoners were tortured and sometimes pushed through port-holes to drown in the Seine. The *caveau* is beneath the subterranean vaults that many centuries ago linked it with the fortress prison of Petit Châtelet. Today patrons laugh, drink, talk, and flirt in the narrow *caveau* or else retreat to the jazz lounge. There's a free jam session every night, which might be funk, jazz, or rock. At some point on Friday and Saturday nights concerts are staged, sometimes with a cover charge. Open daily 5pm to 4am. 52 rue Galande, 5e. www.caveaudesoubliettes. fr. ✆ **01-46-34-23-09.** Métro: St-Michel.

**Le Sunset/Le Sunside ★**   This is a dual temple of jazz, one of the hottest addresses on the after-dark scene in Paris, lying between the Forum des Halles and the Centre George Pompidou. Le Sunset Jazz, created in 1983, is dedicated to electric jazz and international music, whereas le Sunside, launched in 2001, is devoted to acoustic jazz for the most part. Some of the most innovative names in European jazz appear here regularly, along with jazz legends, many from abroad. Both clubs form a single complex with two concerts every night. Open Monday to Saturday 9:30pm to 1am. 60 rue des Lombards, 1er. www.sunset-sunside.com. ✆ **01-40-26-46-60.** Tickets 20€–30€. Métro: Châtelet.

**New Morning** ★   Jazz maniacs come to drink, talk, and dance at this enduring club. It's sometimes a scene, attracting such guests as Spike Lee and Prince. Recent bookings have included Robin McKelle, The Klezmatics, Patricia Barber, and folk rock acts such as Steve Earle. It opens nightly at 8pm, with concerts beginning at 9pm. 7 rue des Petites-Ecuries, 10e. www.newmorning.com. ⓒ **01-45-23-51-41.** Cover 18€–26€. Métro: Château-d'Eau.

## Modern Concert Halls

**La Boule Noire**   The Black Ball is one of those intimate, divey Parisian haunts that attract biggies such as the Dandy Warhols, Metallica, Cat Power, Franz Ferdinand, and Jamie Cullum. Despite the star-studded line up, prices tend to hover around the 20€ mark, making this one of the cheapest venues around. 120 bd. Rochechouart, 75018. www.laboule-noire.fr. ⓒ **01-49-25-81-75.** Métro: Anvers or Pigalle.

**La Cigale** ★   This 19th-century music hall, next door to the Boule Noire, draws some of the biggest artists working in music today—everything from indie rock to hip-hop and jazz. Recent bookings include Band of Horses, Cee Lo Green, and the Eric Truffaz Quartet. Balcony seating is available for those who arrive early, and there's plenty of open floor space for those who want to dance. 120 boulevard de Rochechouart, 18e. www.lacigale.fr. ⓒ **01-49-25-81-75.** Tickets 8€–55€. Métro: Pigalle or Anvers.

**La Flèche d'Or**   Set inside a converted train station and boasting beautiful windows that look out over the tracks below, this concert hall books both unknown and major label bands. Recent performances have included England's Razorlight, Band of Horses, and the Walkmen. Tickets tend to be cheap here, but beers are expensive. 102 bis rue de Bagnolet, 20e. www.flechedor.fr. ⓒ **01-44-64-01-02.** Tickets 8€–20€. Métro: Alexandre Dumas or Gambetta.

**La Maroquinerie** ★   This little club atop the Ménilmontant hill is the place to catch local and international music artists before they blow up big and start playing

New Morning Jazz Club.

La Cigale. The roster leans heavily toward the indie rock genre but there are electro and folk acts in the mix, too. An attached restaurant and bar with a pretty outdoor courtyard are good places to hang before and after the show. 23 rue Boyer, 20e. www. lamaroquinerie.fr. ☏ **01-40-33-64-85.** Tickets 10€–20€. Métro: Ménilmontant.

## Live Music Bars

**L'Alimentation Générale**  This ode to all things kitsch has oodles of unusual beers (Flag, Sagres and Orval) for 3€ to 5€, and inventive cocktails from 8€. But that's not the only reason to visit: DJs or live bands (often world music) play here practically every night, and only the biggest names tend to have a cover charge (10€ including one free drink). Open Wednesday and Sunday 7pm to 2am and Thursday to Saturday 7pm to 4am. 64 rue Jean-Pierre Timbaud, 75011. www. alimentation-generale.net. ☏ **01-43-55-42-50.** Métro: Parmentier.

**L'International**  The already cool 11th arrondissement got a little cooler when this joint opened—a breath of fresh air for music lovers with its free entry and a string of on-the-up bands playing to hip indie crowds. Beer is a steal at 3€, and once a month there's an after-show party until 4am. 5/7 rue Moret, 75011. www. linternational.fr. ☏ **01-49-29-76-45.** Métro: Ménilmontant.

**OPA**  Industrial-chic OPA is like a live MySpace music joint: it's free, and Paris's up-and-coming bands play from 9pm until late, before DJs take over and play into the wee hours. Tuesday is rock or folk, Wednesday pop or French *chanson*, Thursday varies, and Friday and Saturday nights are electro rock and pop. 9 rue Biscornet, 75012. www.opa-paris.com. ☏ **01-46-28-12-90.** Métro: Bastille.

# NIGHTCLUBS

From the dance halls of the cancan and raucous and energetic jazz clubs of the 1920s, Parisians have historically made it a point to get out at night and go dancing. Stepping into a Parisian club today (known as *les boîtes de nuit*, or just *une boîte*) with the locals is one of the best ways to experience a night on the town in the City of Lights. Like in any big city, Parisian clubs are divided into different scenes: some places more "see and be seen," while others tend to focus less on what you're wearing and more on the music being played—not to suggest that the glitz and glam spots don't have great music. Certain locations stay popular for years, but most will wax and wane in their level of "coolness." Also, the French love their fashion, so dressing to impress is obligatory—sneakers will rarely get you past the line outside. Check *Time Out: Paris* (www.timeout.fr/paris/en) or *Pariscope* to get a sense of current trends. Most of these clubs don't really get going until at least 11pm, if not later.

**Batofar** ★  While most clubs would never last more than a few years before the crowds moved on, somehow Batofar remains fresh and consistently full. The fact that it sits on a converted barge floating on the Seine must have something to do with it. It has also opened a restaurant so hungry clubbers can fill up without leaving the boat. On good nights you'll see hundreds of gyrating dancers moving in rhythm to house, garage, techno, and live jazz music. Beer costs about 10€ a bottle, while cover runs from free to 15€, depending on the band or DJ. Open Tuesday to Saturday from 6pm to 4am (restaurant open Tues–Sat noon–2pm and 7:30–11pm). Facing 11 quai François Mauriac, 13e. www.batofar.org. Métro: Quai de la Gare.

**Cab** ★★  Although it's not as glamorous as it once was, the former cabaret still sees crowds of rich international types, young bourgeois Parisians, and impossibly skinny fashion models. Located in an underground restaurant/lounge right next to the Louvre, after 11pm the space converts into a dimly lit, classy affair. Cozy up in a nook behind the red velvet ropes or hit the expertly–lit dance floor. You'll hear the latest dance and electro-lounge hits, as well as trendy American sounds, even the occasional hip-hop. Open Wednesday to Saturday 11:30pm to 6am. 2 place du Palais Royal, 1er. www.cabaret.fr. ( **01-58-62-56-25.** Cover 20€–30€, including 1 drink. Métro: Palais Royal-Musée du Louvre.

**Le Baron ★**  Once the most expensive brothel in Paris, much of Le Baron's original decor remains, including the 1920s-era tile of frolicking nude ladies, sexy red walls, and tasseled lamps. It's long been regarded as the playground of the rich and bored, or sometimes just fabulous and occasionally androgynous. The dance floor is regularly packed with some of the world's most beautiful people. Drinks are costly but so is being trendy. It's open daily 11pm to 6am, although hours can vary. 6 av. Marceau, 8e. www.clublebaron.com. ( **01-47-20-04-01.** Cover free to 15€ depending on the event and the night of the week. Métro: Champs-Élysées.

**Nouveau Casino**  Rue Oberkampf is still hyper-hip and in this former movie theater adjacent to the Café Charbon (a drafty space centered on a dance floor and an enormous bar crafted to resemble an iceberg) you can listen to live concerts most nights of the week. On Friday and Saturday, the party continues from 1am till dawn, with a DJ who spins some of the most avant-garde dance music in Paris. Celebrity spotters have picked out Prince Albert of Monaco, British pop star Jarvis Cocker and such French-language film stars as Vincent Cassel and Mathieu Kassovitz. 109 rue Oberkampf, 9e. www.nouveaucasino.net. ( **01-43-57-57-40.** Cover free to 30€. Métro: St-Maur, Parmentier, or Ménilmontant.

**Showcase**  Set almost unbelievably beneath the Pont Alexandre III, with incredible views of the Seine, this may be the only club you'll ever enter that's literally under a bridge. Unique location aside, they have DJs and live bands and gorgeous lighting along the endlessly long bar. Expect a BCBG crowd dressed in Gucci blazers and impossibly high heels. While the live bands are all over the map, the DJs play mostly electro, house, and disco beats. Open Friday

## FRANCE'S PALACE hotels

After adding a 5th star to their official hotel rating system back in 2009, putting France more in line with international standards, in 2011 the French tourism authorities launched a new hotel label called "Distinction Palace." Criteria for this new label include the hotel's location, historical significance, room comfort, personalized service, multilingual staff, and health and spa facilities. France counts a total of 127 five-star hotels, but at launch of the new category, only eight hotels earned the distinction immediately, and this restricted selection is as notable for who it included as for who it left out. The four hotels in Paris to go straight to the top are the Bristol, the Meurice (p. 184), Park Hyatt Paris-Vendôme (p. 185) and the Plaza Athénée (p. 189). Certainly in response to the snub, the majestic George V is undertaking a major renovation program until the end of 2013 (though it remains open to the public throughout), and the place Vendôme's legendary Ritz Hotel closed for at least two years of renovations in mid-2012.

and Saturday nights from 11pm until 7am. Port des Champs-Élysées under the Pont Alexandre III. www.showcase.fr. ☎ **01-45-61-25-43.** Entry ranges from free to 20€. Métro: Invalides.

# The Gay & Lesbian Scene

Paris has a vibrant gay nightlife scene, centered on **le Marais, les Halles,** and to some extent, **Bastille.** The area with the greatest concentration of gay and lesbian clubs, restaurants, bars, and shops is the area surrounding the Hôtel de Ville and Rambuteau Métro stops. Gay dance clubs come and go so fast that even the magazines devoted to them, such as *2x*—distributed free in the gay bars and bookstores—have a hard time keeping up. For lesbians, there is *Lesbia Magazine.* Also look for *Têtu* magazine, sold at most newsstands—it has special nightlife inserts for gay bars and clubs. Also see Le Gibus.

## GAY & LESBIAN BARS & CLUBS

**Le Cox**    This place gets so busy early in the evening that the muscled, tank-top-wearing crowd overflows out onto the sidewalk. This is where you'll find a dependably mixed gay crowd in Paris—from hunky American tourists to sexy Parisians. 15 rue des Archives, 4e. www.cox.fr. ☎ **01-42-72-08-00.** Métro: Hôtel de Ville.

**Le Duplex**    This welcoming bar is a good choice if loud club music isn't your cup of tea. Usually piping in jazz and some hip rock, actual conversation can take place and the clientele is mostly local and quite friendly. Open daily 8pm–2am (until 4am Friday and Saturday). 25 rue Michel Le Comte, 3e. www.duplex-bar.com. ☎ **01-42-72-80-86.** Métro: Rambuteau.

**Le Raidd ★**    The bartenders here may be hunks and so are most of the patrons. Be prepared for attitude galore. A special feature is a plexiglass shower box where nude shower boys flaunt their assets throughout the night. It's shoulder-to-shoulder action here with pickup possibilities at every turn. Only the best dressed can expect to get invited in at the door. Open daily 5pm to 5am. 23 rue du Temple, 4e. www.raiddbar.com. ☎ **01-92-77-09-88.** Métro: Hôtel-de-Ville or Rambuteau.

**Le 3w Kafé**    The 3w means "Woman with Woman." This is the best-known lesbian bar in the Marais, where an unattached woman usually will have little trouble finding a drinking buddy. On weekends there's dancing downstairs with a DJ in control of the sounds. Straight men are welcome too, if accompanied by a woman. Gay men are admitted without problem. Open Wednesday to Sunday 5pm to 2am, Friday and Saturday 5pm to 4am. 8 rue des Ecouffes, 4e. ☎ **01-48-87-39-26.** Métro: St. Paul.

**Open Café**    Although this bar is side-by-side with Le Cox, each place has an independent feel, even if their clientele is not. Both places define themselves as bars rather than dance clubs, but on particularly busy nights, someone will inevitably begin to dance. Simple café-style food is served from noon to around 5pm. Patrons include just about every type of man that roams the streets of gay Europe today. Open daily from 11am to 2 am, Friday and Saturday to 3am. 17 rue des Archives, 4e. ☎ **01-42-72-26-18.** Métro: Hôtel-de-Ville.

# WHERE TO STAY

Naturally, the most-visited city in the world boasts an overwhelming number of hotels, which range from mythical palaces including the Ritz and the Crillon to dives so repellent that even George Orwell, author of *Down and Out in Paris and*

*London,* wouldn't have considered checking in. (Of course, you won't find those in this guide!) We include deluxe places for those who can afford to live like the Sultan of Brunei, as well as a wide range of moderate and budget choices for the rest of us.

# The Right Bank

## LES HALLES, LOUVRE & PALAIS ROYAL (1ER & 2E)

Located on the right bank, this area is the *très chic* center of Paris. This part of Paris—by the Seine river and clustered around the Louvre—boasts exquisite monuments, boulevards, gardens, and shopping.

### Very Expensive

**Hôtel de Vendôme ★★** This luxury boutique hotel sits on one of Paris's most prestigious addresses, the place Vendôme, surrounded by the city's finest jewelers. The soundproof rooms are opulent and designed in classic Second Empire style, with prestige beds and well-upholstered, hand-carved furnishings. Suites have generous space and such extras as blackout draperies and quadruple-glazed windows. The security is fantastic, with TV intercoms, and the service is warm and professional. This hotel is a short walk from the Louvre and Tuileries gardens.

1 place Vendôme, 75001 Paris. www.hoteldevendome.com. ℂ **01-55-04-55-00.** Fax 01-49-27-97-89. 29 units. 535€–865€ double; 835€–1,525€ suite. AE, DC, MC, V. Parking 27€. Métro: Concorde or Opéra. **Amenities:** Restaurant; piano bar; babysitting; concierge; room service. *In room:* A/C, TV, hair dryer, minibar, MP3 docking station, Wi-Fi (free).

**Hôtel Meurice ★★★** This landmark hotel, which lies between the place de la Concorde and the Grand Louvre, facing the Tuileries Gardens, is media-hip and style-conscious. Since the 1800s, it has welcomed the royal, the rich, and even the radical. The mad genius Salvador Dalí made the Meurice his headquarters, and in 2008 that other mad genius, Philippe Starck, overhauled the hotel's public areas, bringing an exquisite contemporary touch of the surreal to the lobby and downstairs bar and restaurant. Each room is individually decorated with period pieces, fine carpets, Italian and French fabrics, marble bathrooms, and modern features. Our favorites and the least expensive are the sixth-floor rooms. Some have painted ceilings of puffy clouds and blue skies, along with canopy beds. Suites are among the most lavish in France.

228 rue de Rivoli, 75001 Paris. www.meuricehotel.com. ℂ **01-44-58-10-10.** Fax 01-44-58-10-15. 160 units. 790€–1,070€ double; 1,300€–1,900€ junior suite; from 2,100€ suite. AE, DC, MC, V. Parking 45€. Métro: Tuileries or Concorde. **Amenities:** 2 restaurants; bar; babysitting; concierge; health club and spa; room service. *In room:* A/C, TV, TV/DVD player, fax, hair dryer, minibar, Wi-Fi (24€ per day).

**Park Hyatt Vendôme ★★★** American interior designer Ed Tuttle took five separate Haussmann-era buildings and wove them into a seamless entity to create this citadel of 21st-century luxury living. High ceilings, colonnades, and interior courtyards speak of the buildings' former lives, but other than the facades, all is completely modern and luxurious inside. The third Hyatt in Paris, this palace enjoys the greatest and most prestigious location in "Ritz Hotel country." Graced with modern art, it is filled with elegant fabrics, huge mirrors, walk-in closets, mahogany doors, and Jim Thompson silk. Bedrooms and bathrooms are spacious and state-of-the-art, with elegant furnishings and glamorous bathrooms with "rain showers," plus separate tubs.

5 rue de la Paix, 75002 Paris. www.paris.vendome.hyatt.com. ✆ **800/492-8804** in the U.S. and Canada, or 01-58-71-12-34. Fax 01-58-71-12-35. 168 units. 800€–910€ double; from 1,010€ suite. AE, DC, DISC, MC, V. Métro: Tuileries or Opéra. Free parking. **Amenities:** 2 restaurants; bar; babysitting; concierge; health club and spa; room service. *In room:* A/C, TV, DVD, CD player, hair dryer, minibar, Wi-Fi (19€ per day).

## Moderate

**Hôtel Thérèse ★★**   Close to the Louvre, place Vendôme, and the Tuileries Gardens, this hotel combines French charm with English classicism. For example, the library and bar evoke a London club with wood-paneled walls and plush armchairs, but the lounge is adorned with Parisian art. Owner Sylvia de Lattre, who likes shades of pistachio and royal blue, trolled the flea markets for paintings and prints to personalize each bedroom. The rooms are unpretentious but filled with quality furnishings, from the soft, efficient lighting by Philippe Starck to the natural wool quilts. The hotel's public areas were redecorated in late 2011.

5–7 rue Thérèse, Paris 75001. www.hoteltherese.com. ✆ **01-42-96-10-01.** Fax 01-42-96-15-22. 43 units. 165€–295€ double. AE, MC, V. Métro: Musée du Louvre. **Amenities:** Library/bar; room service; smoke-free rooms. *In room:* A/C, TV, hair dryer, Wi-Fi (free).

## INEXPENSIVE

**Hôtel du Cygne**   This centrally located hotel is within walking distance of the charming gourmand–friendly rue Montorgueil, the place des Victoires, the Marais, and the Louvre. In a restored 17th-century building, the hotel combines the old with touches of the new; much of the eclectic decor has been handpicked by the hotel's friendly owner, Isabelle. The staff is helpful, but there is no elevator, so be prepared to carry your luggage up the narrow, winding stairs. Avoid the rooms overlooking the street, as they can be noisy. Room 35 is the largest.

3–5 rue du Cygne, 75001 Paris. www.cygne-hotel-paris.com. ✆ **01-42-60-14-16.** Fax 01-42-21-37-02. 18 units. 122€–132€ double; 147€ suite. MC, V. Métro: Etienne Marcel. **Amenities:** Breakfast room. *In room:* TV, hair dryer, Wi-Fi (free).

## LE MARAIS, ILE ST-LOUIS & ILE DE LA CITÉ (3E & 4E)

This busy neighborhood includes the city's gay and Jewish quarters. Most of the important contemporary galleries are here, too. You'll find a concentration of great stores from independent local labels in the northern Marais, around rue de Bretagne. But it's the architecture that really sets this area apart, as it conserves buildings dating back to the Renaissance.

## Expensive

**Hôtel du Jeu de Paume ★**   This small-scale hotel encompasses a pair of 17th-century town houses accessible through a timbered passageway from the street outside. The hotel is located on the incredibly quaint and charming Ile St-Louis in the Seine, and is just a 5-minute walk from Notre-Dame. Originally, the hotel was a clubhouse used by members of the court of Louis XIII, who amused themselves with *les jeux de paume* (an early form of tennis) nearby. Public areas are outfitted in a simple version of Art Deco. Renovated in 2010, guest rooms have a sleek contemporary style, with elegant materials such as oak floors and fine craftsmanship. Some have wooden-beamed ceilings. The rooms are a bit larger than those of some nearby competitors. The most luxurious units are the five duplexes and two junior suites, each individually decorated and opening onto an indoor courtyard.

54 rue St-Louis-en-l'Ile, 75004 Paris. www.jeudepaumehotel.com. © **01-43-26-14-18.** Fax 01-40-46-02-76. 30 units. 285€–360€ double; 360€–560€ suite. AE, DC, MC, V. Métro: Pont Marie. **Amenities:** Bar; babysitting; concierge; exercise room; room service. *In room:* A/C, TV, hair dryer, minibar, Wi-Fi (free).

**Hôtel Duo ★ 📷** Fashionistas flock to this restored hotel in the Marais, which is one of the cutting-edge places to stay in Paris. The location is convenient to the Centre Pompidou, Notre-Dame, and the Louvre. The building has been in the family of Veronique Turmel since 1918. In 2002, she decided to completely convert the interior while retaining the facade. She hired Jean-Philippe Nuel, who kept many of the original architectural features, including exposed beams, old stones, and hardwood floors. He created a modern and stylish look graced with Wenge-wood furnishings, white walls, and bronzed sconces—old-world charm in a tasteful and refined setting. The midsize bedrooms are completely up-to-date, with beautiful and comfortable furnishings. The so-called breakfast "cave" is a charming room with slipcovered chairs and sea-grass matting.

11 rue du Temple, 75004 Paris. www.duo-paris.com. © **01-42-72-72-22.** Fax 01-42-72-03-53. 58 units. 200€–380€ double; 400€–550€ suite. AE, DC, MC, V. Métro: Hôtel-de-Ville. **Amenities:** Exercise room; room service. *In room:* A/C, TV, hair dryer, Wi-Fi (free).

**Pavillon de la Reine ★★ 📷** This is a hidden gem that opens onto the most romantic square in Paris: the place des Vosges. You enter through an arcade that opens onto a small formal garden. In days of yore the 1612 mansion was a gathering place for the likes of Racine, La Fontaine, Molière, and Madame de Sévigné. Today, the Louis XIII decor evokes the heyday of the square itself, and iron-banded Spanish antiques create a rustic aura. Each guest room is individually furnished in a historic or modern style—take your pick. Some units are duplexes with sleeping lofts above cozy salons.

28 place des Vosges, 75003 Paris. www.pavillon-de-la-reine.com. © **01-40-29-19-19.** Fax 01-40-29-19-20. 56 units. 330€–450€ double; 600€–800€ suite. AE, MC, V. Métro: Bastille. **Amenities:** Bar; concierge; room service. *In room:* A/C, TV, minibar, Wi-Fi (free).

## Moderate
**Hôtel Caron de Beaumarchais ★ 🍴** Built in the 18th century, this good-value choice features floors of artfully worn gray stone, antique reproductions, and elaborate fabrics based on antique patterns. Hotelier Alain Bigeard intends his primrose-colored guest rooms to evoke the taste of the French gentry in the 18th century, when the Marais was the scene of high-society dances and even duels. Most rooms retain their original ceiling beams. The smallest units overlook the courtyard, and the top-floor rooms are tiny, but have panoramic balcony views across the Right Bank.

12 rue Vieille du Temple, 75004 Paris. www.carondebeaumarchais.com. © **01-42-72-34-12.** Fax 01-42-72-34-63. 19 units. 145€–195€ double. AE, MC, V. Métro: St-Paul or Hôtel-de-Ville. **Amenities:** Breakfast room; babysitting. *In room:* A/C, TV, hair dryer, minibar, Wi-Fi (free).

**Hôtel du Bourg Tibourg ★** What you get here is a sophisticated and supercharged color palette, a sense of high-profile design, and a deliberately cluttered venue that looks like an Edwardian town house decorated by an individual on psychedelic drugs. It is set behind an uncomplicated, cream-colored facade in the Marais and marked only with a discreet brass plaque and a pair of carriage lamps. Bedrooms are genuinely tiny, but rich with romantic, neo-Gothic, and in some cases neo-Venetian swirls and curlicues. Decorated by Jacques Garcia, each room is quirky, idiosyncratic, richly upholstered, and supercharged with tassels, faux leopard skin, contrasting stripes, fringes, and lavish window treatments. Rooms facing the front get more sunlight; rooms facing the courtyard tend to be quieter.

19 rue du Bourg-Tibourg, 75004 Paris. www.hotelbourgtibourg.com. ✆ **01-42-78-47-39.** Fax 01-40-29-07-00. 30 units. 250€–270€ double; 370€ suite. AE, DC, MC, V. Métro: Hôtel-de-Ville. **Amenities:** Room service. *In room:* A/C, TV, hair dryer, minibar, Wi-Fi (free).

**Hôtel Jules & Jim ★★**   Proudly gay friendly, this new boutique hotel opened in late 2011. Spread across three buildings, it's a little urban oasis arranged around two beautiful, paved courtyards. The rooms either look out at the rooftops of Paris or into the lush vertical garden in the courtyard. Guest rooms are sleek, and designed with durable materials, like glass, wood, stone, and concrete; they are soundproofed and equipped with sophisticated amenities, like luxury linens and an iPod docking station. The bar is a great place to wind down your day, with a working outdoor fireplace (in winter) and live music (in summer).

11 rue des Gravilliers, 75003 Paris. www.hoteljulesetjim.com. ✆ **01-44-54-13-13.** Fax 01-42-78-10-01. 23 units. 180€–310€ double; 390€–550€ suite. AE, MC, V. Métro: Arts-et-Métiers. **Amenities:** Bar; concierge; room service. *In room:* AC, TV, hair dryer, iPod Dock, Wi-Fi (free).

### Inexpensive
**Castex Hotel 🎣**   Long known to thrifty travelers, the Castex lies on the fringe of both the Bastille sector and the Marais. Bedrooms are small and somewhat simple, decorated in a 17th-century style with Louis XIII furnishings and wrought iron features. There's a complimentary bottle of wine in every room. Several of the units open onto a courtyard patio that bursts into full bloom in the spring.

5 rue Castex, 75004 Paris. www.castexhotelparis.com. ✆ **01-42-72-31-52.** 30 units. 155€ double; 220€ triple. AE, MC, V. Métro: Bastille. **Amenities:** Breakfast room. *In room:* A/C, TV, hair dryer, Wi-Fi (free).

## CHAMPS-ÉLYSÉES & WESTERN PARIS (8E, 16E & 17E)

This is where most of the city's money and power is concentrated. The "Golden Triangle" (av. Montaigne, George V, and the Champs-Élysées) is bling-bling heaven, with all the major fashion labels jostling for position. It's also a business neighborhood, so get ready to navigate the suits.

### Very Expensive
**Fouquet's Barrière ★★★**   This deluxe boutique hotel on the corner of the Champs-Élysées may lack the historic cachet of the neighboring George V or Plaza Athénée, but it's a more contemporary brand of glitz and glamour. Standing alongside its namesake, the legendary restaurant, Fouquet's, it offers some of the most luxurious and spacious bedrooms in Paris, its decor dominated by ceiling-high padded headboards in shiny gold. The hotel contains such novel features as waterproof floating TV remotes in the bathtub, and a bedside button that, when pressed, will summon your butler. There's one butler to every eight guests, and the service is the best in Paris. That butler even arrives to unpack your luggage and serve you champagne.

46 av. George V, 75008 Paris. www.fouquets-barriere.com. ✆ **01-40-69-60-00.** Fax 01-40-69-60-05. 107 units. 750€–1,300€ double; 1,100€–1,700€ junior suite; 1,700€–3,600€ suite. AE, MC, V.

Métro: George V. Parking 45€. **Amenities:** 2 restaurants; 2 bars; concierge; health club and spa; pool (indoor); room service. *In room:* A/C, TV, TV/DVD, hair dryer, minibar, Wi-Fi (free).

**Le Royal Monceau - Raffles Paris ★★★** This five-star Raffles hotel opened in late 2010 and immediately wowed Paris with its luxurious chic interiors designed by Philippe Starck. The decor is contemporary, but is still in tune with the Art Deco heritage of the building. The spacious rooms offer all the comfort and amenities that you would expect from a hotel of this caliber, but maintain a relaxed vibe. There's even an electric guitar in each room, if you feel like expressing your inner rock star. The hotel has a unique commitment to contemporary art: it regularly hosts art exhibitions, has a fully-stocked art bookstore, and it publishes a sophisticated website (www.artforbreakfast.com), which gives an insider's perspective on the Paris art scene. The hotel offers cutting-edge fashion in its satellite L'Éclaireur store. The icing on the cake? Star *pâtissier* Pierre Hermé is responsible for the desserts.

37 av. Hoche, 75008 Paris. www.leroyalmonceau.com. ☏ **01-42-99-88-00.** Fax 01-42-99-89-00. 160 units. 780€–930€ double; from 1,200€–10,000€ suite. AE, DC, MC, V. Métro: Ternes. **Amenities:** 2 restaurants; bar; children's programs; cigar lounge; concierge; health club; movie theater; pool (indoor); room service; spa. *In room:* A/C, TV/DVD, hair dryer, iPod dock, minibar, Wi-Fi (free).

**Plaza Athénée ★★★** The Plaza Athénée, an 1889 Art Nouveau marvel, is a landmark of discretion and style and one of the city's most emblematic hotels. About half the celebrities visiting Paris have been pampered here; in the old days, Mata Hari used to frequent the place. The **Salon Gobelins** (with tapestries against rich paneling) and the **Salon Marie Antoinette,** a richly paneled and grand room, are two public rooms that add to the ambience of this lavish hotel.

There's also a calm, quiet interior courtyard draped with vines and dotted with geraniums. The quietest guest rooms overlook a courtyard with awnings and parasol-shaded tables. Some rooms overlooking avenue Montaigne have views of the Eiffel Tower. The hotel is also home to **Alain Ducasse au Plaza Athénée,** where Alain Ducasse presents a gourmet French menu. The spa is by Dior. During Paris Fashion Week, the bar becomes the event's nonofficial HQ.

25 av. Montaigne, 75008 Paris. www.plaza-athenee-paris.com. ☏ **866/732-1106** in the U.S. and Canada, or 01-53-67-66-65. Fax 01-53-67-66-66. 191 units. 865€–965€ double; 1,160€–1,800€ junior suite; 1,900€–22,000€ suite. AE, MC, V. Parking 28€. Métro: Franklin-D.-Roosevelt or Alma-Marceau. **Amenities:** 5 restaurants; bar; babysitting; concierge; state-of-the-art health club; room service; smoke-free rooms; spa. *In room:* A/C, TV, TV/DVD, CD player, hair dryer, minibar, Wi-Fi (24€ per day).

**Le Royal Monceau.**

## Expensive

### Best Western Premier Regent's Garden ★★

Near the convention center (Palais des Congrès) and the Arc de Triomphe, the Regent's Garden boasts a proud heritage: Napoleon III built this château for his physician. The hotel prides itself on its sustainability; it was awarded a prestigious European Eco-Label for its efforts in preserving the environment by reducing the consumption of water, gas, electricity, and waste. The smart guest rooms feature tall sound-proof windows, traditional French furniture, and modern textiles—the environmental approach extends to the guest rooms, as the duvets in each room are made from fair trade cotton. Even breakfast is composed of organic ingredients. Guests have access to a neighboring fitness center and spa, Eclipse & Vous. A garden with ivy-covered walls and umbrella-shaded tables makes for a perfect place to meet other guests. The hotel is smoke free throughout.

6 rue Pierre-Demours, 75017 Paris. www.hotel-regents-paris.com. © **800/528-1234** in the U.S., or 01-45-74-07-30. Fax 01-40-55-01-42. 40 units. 290€–440€ double; from 490€ suite. AE, DC, MC, V. Parking 20€. Métro: Ternes or Charles-de-Gaulle–Etoile. **Amenities:** Babysitting; spa. *In room:* A/C, TV, hair dryer, minibar, Wi-Fi (free).

### Le Pavillon des Lettres ★

If you're a literature fan, this hotel—Paris's first literary-themed hotel—might just be the place for you. Located in the 8th arrondissement, this charming boutique hotel opened in 2010, and is owned by the same owners of the Pavillon de la Reine. It features 26 rooms—one for each letter of the alphabet. Each room is dedicated to the life and work of great writers, from Andersen to Proust to Zola, and you'll find excerpted texts from these writers printed on the bedroom walls. There's also an iPad in each room loaded with a rich digital library. The comfortable rooms are designed to encourage relaxation and are decorated in metallic tones. Lounge in the hotel's library over a well-thumbed classic, and when you're tired of reading, just step outside to reach the many nearby shops and restaurants in the thick of Right Bank.

12 rue des Saussaies, 75008 Paris. www.pavillondeslettres.com. © **01-49-24-26-26.** Fax 01-49-24-26-27. 26 units. From 300€–340€ double; 460€ suite. AE, DC, MC, V. Métro: Madeleine. **Amenities:** Restaurant; bar; library; room service. *In room:* A/C, TV, iPad, iPod docking stations, minibar, Wi-Fi (free).

## Moderate

### Radisson Blu Le Dokhan's Hotel ★★

If not for the porters walking through its public areas carrying luggage, you might suspect that this well-accessorized hotel was a private home. It's in a stately 19th-century Haussmann-styled building vaguely inspired by Palladio, and it contains accessories such as antique paneling, Regency-era armchairs, and chandeliers. Each guest room has a different decorative style, with antiques or good reproductions, lots of personalized touches and triple-glazed windows. Beds are often antique reproductions with maximum comfort. Suites have a larger living space and spacious bathrooms with such extras as makeup mirrors and luxe toiletries.

117 rue Lauriston, 75116 Paris. www.radissonblu.com/dokhanhotel-paristrocadero. © **01-53-65-66-99.** Fax 01-53-65-66-88. 45 units. 250€–350€ double; from 470€ suite. AE, DC, MC, V. Parking 30€. Métro: Trocadéro. **Amenities:** Babysitting; champagne bar; concierge; room service. *In room:* A/C, TV, fax, hair dryer, minibar, Wi-Fi (free).

### Inexpensive

**Hôtel Galileo ★ 🎁**   This is one of the 8th's most charming hotels. Proprietors Roland and Elisabeth Buffat have won friends from all over with their Hôtel des Deux-Iles and Hôtel de Lutèce on St-Louis-en-l'Ile. A short walk from the Champs-Élysées, this town house is the epitome of French elegance and charm. The medium-size rooms are a study in understated taste. Within this hotel, rooms with numbers ending in 3 (specifically 103, 203, 303, 403, and 503) are more spacious than the others. Rooms 501 and 502 have private glassed-in verandas that you can use even in winter.

54 rue Galilée, 75008 Paris. www.galileo-paris-hotel.com. ℰ **01-47-20-66-06.** Fax 01-47-20-67-17. 27 units. 105€–335€ double. AE, DC, MC, V. Métro: Charles-de-Gaulle–Etoile or George V. *In room:* A/C, TV, hair dryer, minibar, Wi-Fi (free).

## OPÉRA & GRANDS BOULEVARDS (9E)

Two of Paris's major department stores are located just above Opéra, and they set the tone for this dynamic shopping district which extends west along the tree-lined boulevard Haussmann and east up to the "Grands Boulevards" Metro station.

### Moderate

**Hotel Amour ★★ 🎁**   This hotel oozes streetwise chic and attitude. One critic claimed that thanks to the hotel bar being frequented by young European fashionistas, each flaunting his or her respective allure and neurosis, "waiting in a queue for the toilets has never been so entertaining." Each bedroom is decorated by a celebrity friend of the owner (like Sophie Calle, Marc Newson), so the trendy decor varies widely, from minimalist white-on-white with touches of faux baroque to disco balls to graffiti written directly on the walls. The relaxed downstairs bar and restaurant are a great destination at any time for seeing and being seen. And the ivy-covered courtyard is perfect for sipping champagne on warm days or nights.

8 rue Navarin, 75009 Paris. www.hotelamourparis.fr. ℰ **01-48-78-31-80.** 20 units. 155€–215€ double; 285€ duplex. AE, MC, V. Métro: St-Georges. **Amenities:** Restaurant; bar; room service. *In room:* A/C, minibar, no phone, Wi-Fi (free).

**Hôtel Arvor St Georges ★★ 🎁**   This fresh, contemporary hotel is located in the charming "New Athens" neighborhood, off the tourist beat and nestled below Montmartre. In the 19th century, this neighborhood was frequented by Romantic artists such as Victor Hugo, George Sand, and Frédéric Chopin, but today the neighborhood is a gourmand's paradise, with the restaurant-lined rue des Martyrs nearby. The hotel is relaxed and comfortable, and you'll feel like a guest in a chic Parisian's private home as you flip through some of the art and photography titles over a cup of coffee in the airy downstairs lobby. The tasty breakfast (14€) is served here or outside in the flower-filled patio when the weather is nice. The rooms have a clean, designer style, and the six suites boast views over Paris to the Eiffel Tower. Service is friendly and professional.

8 rue Laferrière, 75009 Paris. www.arvor-hotel-paris.com. ℰ **01-48-78-60-92.** Fax 01-48-78-16-52. 30 units. 125€–190€ double. AE, DC, MC, V. Métro: St-Georges. **Amenities:** Bar; room service. *In room:* TV, hair dryer, Wi-Fi (free).

**Hôtel Particulier.**

### Inexpensive

**Hôtel Chopin** ♦ Enter this intimate, offbeat hotel through a passageway that includes a toy store, a bookstore, the exit from the Musée Grevin, and the architectural trappings of its original construction in 1846. Just off the Grands Boulevards, this old-fashioned hotel evokes the charm of yesteryear. In honor of its namesake, the Chopin has a piano in its reception area. The inviting lobby welcomes you behind its 1850s facade of elegant woodwork and Victorian-era glass. In the style of the Paris of long ago, the comfortably furnished bedrooms open onto a glass-topped arcade instead of the hysterically busy street, so they are rather tranquil. We prefer the bedrooms on the top floor, as they are larger and quieter, with views over the rooftops of Paris. The least expensive bedrooms lie behind the elevator bank and get less light.

10 bd. Montmartre or 46 passage Jouffroy, 75009 Paris. www.hotel-chopin.com. ⓒ **01-47-70-58-10.** Fax 01-42-47-00-70. 36 units. 98€–114€ double; 136€ triple. AE, MC, V. Métro: Grands-Boulevards. **Amenities:** Wi-Fi (free). *In room:* TV, hair dryer.

**Hôtel de la Tour d'Auvergne** ★ Here's a good bet for those who want to be near the Opéra or the Gare du Nord. This building was erected before Baron Haussmann reconfigured Paris's avenues around 1870. Later, Modigliani rented a room here for 6 months, and Victor Hugo and Auguste Rodin lived on this street. The interior has been recently redecorated in a chic international style. The guest rooms are meticulously coordinated, yet the small decorative canopies over the headboards can make them feel cluttered. Though the views over the back courtyard are uninspired, some guests prefer the quiet of the rear rooms.

10 rue de la Tour d'Auvergne, 75009 Paris. www.hoteltourdauvergne.com. © **01-48-78-61-60.**
Fax 01-49-95-99-00. 24 units. 115€–135€ double. AE, DC, MC, V. Métro: Cadet. **Amenities:** Bar;
room service. *In room:* A/C, TV, hair dryer, minibar, Wi-Fi (free).

## PIGALLE & MONTMARTRE (18E)

The wedding-cake Sacré-Coeur basilica crowns the city's highest point, on the
summit of Montmartre. A neighborhood apart in Paris, with a rich artistic history
and all the charm of a village, Montmartre runs into Pigalle below, a harmless red
light district with a high concentration of concert and club venues.

### Expensive

**Hôtel Particulier ★★**　No hotel in Paris seems quite as special as this one,
lying between avenue Junot and rue Lepic and nestled in a "secret" passageway
called le passage du Rocher de la Sorcière, or the Witch's Rock Passage. Modern
Paris meets Old Montmartre in this Directoire mansion from the 18th century, and
the marriage is harmonious. Louis Bénech, one of the landscape architects who
renovated the Tuileries, created the intimate gardens of the hotel. Each of the five
suites has a different personality, the work of various artists that range in decor from
an erotic window by Philippe Mayaux to poems and hats by Olivier Saillard. The
most unusual is the suite "Curtain of Hair," a loft created in the attic with images
of the long hair of photographer Natacha Lesueur. The downstairs bar has exceptional cocktails. Service may not be on a par with hotels in a similar price range.

23 av. Junot, 75018 Paris. www.hotel-particulier-montmartre.com. © **01-53-41-81-40.** Fax 01-42-
58-00-87. 5 units. 390€–590€ suite. MC, V. Métro: Blanche. **Amenities:** Bar; garden. *In room:* A/C,
TV, hair dryer, Wi-Fi (free).

### Moderate

**Le Chat Noir Design Hotel ★**　Located two steps from the Moulin Rouge
cabaret in the heart of Paris's red light district, this stylish hotel takes its name
from another 19th-century cabaret just next door; Le Chat Noir was one of the
favorite haunts of painter Henri de Toulouse-Lautrec. Making reference to the
cabaret's glory days, the hotel is decorated in red and black throughout, with
black motifs making reference to the shadow plays once so popular at the cabaret. Guest rooms are contemporary and spotlessly clean, and some rooms on the
8th floor boast Eiffel Tower views. The generous buffet breakfast (15€) is served
on the ground floor (beware: rooms 101 and 102 are just outside the breakfast
room so they can be noisy). The staff is very friendly and helpful.

68 boulevard de Clichy, Paris 75018. www.hotel-chatnoir-paris.com. © **01-42-64-15-26.** Fax
01-46-06-35-03. 38 units. 210€ double. AE, DC MC, V. Métro: Blanche. *In room:* A/C, TV, DVD
player, hair dryer, Wi-Fi (free).

### Inexpensive

**Hôtel des Arts ★**　In the center of Montmartre between place du Tertre and
the Moulin Rouge, this hotel lies in a delightful quarter of Paris once made famous
by poets and painters. It has a warm, welcoming atmosphere and in a former life it
was a dormitory for the dancers of the Moulin Rouge. As you might expect, the
rooms are small yet comfortable, with country-style curtains and bedspreads. Opt
for one of the four bedrooms on the sixth floor for a panoramic view of Paris. Keeping up with the zeitgeist, the hotel now offers iPads on loan to hotel guests.

5 rue Tholozé, Paris 75018. www.arts-hotel-paris.com. ℰ **01-46-06-30-52.** Fax 01-46-06-10-83. 50 units. 85€–160€ double. AE, MC, V. Métro: Blanche. **Amenities:** Breakfast room. *In room:* TV, Wi-Fi (free).

# RÉPUBLIQUE, BASTILLE & EASTERN PARIS (11E & 12E)

Paris's former industrial heart has been converted into a string of cosmopolitan neighborhoods with a bohemian vibe.

## Moderate

**Gabriel Paris Marais ★ 🏠** This chic boutique hotel calls itself Paris's first "detox hotel." The hotel takes an active approach to purifying the bodies of its guests, with an emphasis on restful sleep and healthy food. One example of this is that some accommodations are outfitted with "NightCove," a system that uses sound and light to encourage natural sleeping patterns; the rooms are also sound-proofed to ensure a restful night. You can continue to detox with an organic breakfast and spa treatments in their Bioo Detox Room. Located close to place de la République and the Canal St-Martin, this hotel offers comfortably furnished rooms with modern amenities and stylish lighting that range from small to midsize. In the surrealist but harmoniously decorated "detox bar," guests can order a large choice of antioxidant drinks and teas.

25 rue du Grand-Prieure, 75011 Paris. www.gabrielparismarais.com. ℰ **01-47-00-13-38.** 41 units. 155€–280€ double. AE, DC, MC, V. Métro: République. **Amenities:** Cafeteria; room service; small spa. *In room:* A/C, TV/DVD, hair dryer, minibar, MP3 docking station, Wi-Fi (free).

**Le Général Hotel ★** As the neighborhood around place de la République, Canal St-Martin and rue Oberkampf becomes increasingly tuned to Paris's sense of counterculture chic, this is a good example of that neighborhood's improving fortunes. Opened within the premises of a run-down hotel that was radically renovated and decorated by noted designer Jean-Philippe Nuel, the hotel's upbeat interior revolves around prominent rectilinear lines, spartan-looking decors, and an intelligent distribution of spaces. The result is a seven-story hotel with floors linked by two separate elevator banks and pale, monochromatic beige-and-off-white color schemes, and with furniture that is either dark (specifically, rosewood-toned) or pale (specifically, birch- or maple-toned). Bathrooms include L'Occitane products.

5–7 rue Rampon, 75011 Paris. www.legeneralhotel.com. ℰ **01-47-00-41-57.** Fax 01-47-00-21-56. 46 units. 167€–260€ double; 290€–320€ suite. AE, MC, V. Métro: République. **Amenities:** Bar; exercise room; room service; sauna. *In room:* A/C, TV, hair dryer, iPod dock, Wi-Fi (free).

## Inexpensive

**Cosmos Hotel 🏠** This no-frills option in the heart of the animated Oberkampf neighborhood has got to be one of the best deals in town. The simply furnished rooms are clean and have fresh towels provided on a daily basis. The staff is help-ful, and the hotel is also home to a little furry feline mascot. The only downside is that the hotel can be noisy on the weekends as people spill out of the busy local bars and restaurants.

35 rue Jean-Pierre Timbaud, 75011 Paris. www.cosmos-hotel-paris.com. ℰ **01-43-57-25-88.** Fax 01-43-57-25-88. 36 units. 62€–70€ double; 78€ triple. AE, MC, V. Métro: Parmentier. *In room:* TV, hair dryer, Wi-Fi (free).

Mama Shelter.

## BELLEVILLE, CANAL ST-MARTIN & NORTHEAST PARIS (10E, 19E & 20E)

Not as many tourists venture to these cosmopolitan areas, located in the city's old industrial heartland. But up-and-coming Belleville includes one of the city's Chinatowns, a new wave of contemporary art galleries, and the must-see Buttes Chaumont park, while on the charming and leafy Canal St-Martin, you can linger over coffee with bohemian locals.

### Moderate

**Le Citizen** ★★  This chic 12-room boutique hotel on the Canal St-Martin opened in 2011. The hotel has a low-key, contemporary vibe, with a minimalist Swedish look featuring natural wood accents throughout. The soundproofed rooms include top-of-the-line bedding, flatscreen TVs with a variety of international channels, free Wi-Fi access, an iPad, and a complimentary minibar. The hotel is eco-friendly, and strives to conserve water, paper, and energy; it's also entirely smoke free.

96 quai de Jemmapes, 75010 Paris. www.lecitizenhotel.com. ✆ **01-83-62-55-50.** Fax 01-83-62-55-71. 69 units. 175€–235€ double, 275€–450€ suite. Rates include breakfast. AE, MC, V. Métro: Jaques Bonsergent. **Amenities:** Room service; smoke-free rooms. *In room:* A/C, TV, hair dryer, iPad, minibar (free), Wi-Fi (free).

**Mama Shelter** ★★ *✦*  Even though it's located off the beaten track, this Philippe Starck–designed hotel nevertheless attracts the in-crowd with its buzzing downstairs restaurant-bar space, sleek design, and high-tech features. The stylish yet simple rooms are equipped with iMac computers, offering on-demand movies, Internet access, and television programs. Plus, the low rates make the rooms a great value. This is a place for the young and hip, and the in-house bar and restaurant are local hot spots.

109 rue de Bagnolet, 75020 Paris. www.mamashelter.com. ✆ **01-43-48-48-48.** Fax 01-43-48-48-49. 170 units. 89€–209€ double. Rates include breakfast. MC, V. Free parking. Métro: Gambetta. **Amenities:** Restaurant; bar; babysitting; bicycle rental; concierge. *In room*: A/C, iMac, microwave, minibar, Wi-Fi (free).

### Inexpensive
**Libertel Canal St-Martin ★**   This hotel consists of three small typical Parisian buildings that are connected by a charming courtyard and a small garden. Though small, guest rooms are clean and contemporary, with flatscreen TVs and Wi-Fi access. Located in the Canal St-Martin neighborhood, the hotel is near some charming shops and restaurants, as well as the beautiful Buttes-Chaumont Park; it is also very close to the Jaurès Métro stop. The hotel is entirely nonsmoking.

5 avenue Secrétan, 75019 Paris. www.hotel-canal-st-martin.com. ✆ **01-42-06-62-00.** Fax 01-42-40-64-51. 69 units. 105€–145€ double. Rates include breakfast. MC, V. Métro: Jaurès. **Amenities:** Smoke-free rooms. *In room*: A/C (in most rooms), TV, Wi-Fi (free).

**St Christopher's Paris Hostel ★ ⚡**   Located on the picturesque Bassin de la Villette, which connects the Canal St-Martin to the Seine, this massive purpose-built hostel, opened in 2008, is close to some great bars, cinemas, restaurants, and clubs, and is particularly lovely in summer, when the banks of the canal come to life. The hostel is home to an animated bar called Belushi's.

159 rue Crimée, 75019 Paris. www.st-christophers.co.uk/paris-hostels. ✆ **01-40-34-34-40.** Fax 01-40-34-31-38. 70 units. 75€–100€ double. Rates include breakfast. MC, V. Métro: Crimée or Laumière. **Amenities:** Restaurant; bar; bicycle rental. *In room:* Wi-Fi (free).

# The Left Bank

## LATIN QUARTER (5E & 13E)

The Sorbonne University is at the heart of this Left Bank neighborhood, which gets its name from the Latin the students and professors spoke there until the end of the 18th century. To feed those minds, the 5th arrondissement boasts some of the city's best specialty bookshops. This neighborhood dates from the time when the Romans ruled—Paris was conquered by the Romans in 52 B.C.— and the area still conserves Roman ruins, which you can explore at the Cluny Museum. Nearby, the 13th arrondissement is a former industrial zone in the process of gentrification; it's home to the capital's newest national library.

### Moderate
**The Five Hotel ★★ 🎁**   A charmer among Left Bank boutique hotels, the Five is named for the 5th arrondissement and lies in a restored 1800s town house on a U-shaped street off boulevard de Port-Royal. The funky interior design is not to everyone's taste, including a red leather paneled hall or a red-painted gas fireplace. The rooms are individually designed in various colors (blood red or Halloween orange, for example), and tiny white lights evoke a planetarium. Of course, if you want a room the color of a prune, that too is available. A Chinese lacquer artist, Isabelle Emmerique, has certainly been busy here. Some rooms are small, but all the beds are exceedingly comfortable.

3 rue Flatters, Paris 75005. www.thefivehotel.com. ℂ **01-43-31-74-21.** Fax 01-43-31-61-96. 24 units. 245€–315€ double. AE, MC, V. Métro: Bastilel or Gobelins. **Amenities:** Bar; room service. *In room:* A/C, TV, hair dryer, Wi-Fi (free).

### Hôtel Design de la Sorbonne ★★

Located near the Sorbonne University and a short walk from the Luxembourg Gardens, this boutique hotel is stylish and comfortable. Though small, guest rooms are sleek and trendy, and are decorated in bold colors and patterns; rooms feature new bathrooms and modern amenities such as Apple iMac computers. The owners, who manage several other quality hotels in Paris, demonstrate inventiveness through the hotel design—look down at the floor to read excerpts from French literary classics woven into the hotel's carpets. The hotel is smoke free.

6 rue Victor Cousin, 75005 Paris. www.hotelsorbonne.com. ℂ **01-43-54-58-08.** Fax 01-40-51-05-18. 38 units. 250€–340€ double. AE, DC, MC, V. Métro: Cluny–La Sorbonne. RER: Luxembourg. **Amenities:** Smoke-free rooms. *In room:* A/C, TV, Apple iMac, hair dryer, minibar, Wi-Fi (free).

### Hôtel St-Jacques ★ ♘

Try for a room with a balcony view of Notre-Dame and the Panthéon. The Belle Epoque atmosphere of the hotel was made famous in the movie *Charade* (1963), which starred Cary Grant and Audrey Hepburn. Jean-Paul and Martine Rousseau, the owners, welcome you to this old-fashioned Latin Quarter gem, filled with Second Empire overtones, including frescoes in the breakfast room and lounge, 18th-century ceiling murals in some of the bedrooms, wedding cake plasterwork, and corridors painted with *trompe l'oeil* marble. Bedrooms are generally spacious and have been attractively and comfortably restored. Street-side rooms can be a bit noisy.

35 rue des Ecoles, 75005 Paris. www.paris-hotel-stjacques.com. ℂ **01-44-07-45-45.** Fax 01-43-25-65-50. 26 units. 168€–290€ double; 278€ triple. AE, DC, MC, V. Métro: Maubert-Mutualité. **Amenities:** Babysitting. *In room:* A/C TV, hair dryer, Wi-Fi (free).

## Inexpensive

### Hôtel des Grandes Ecoles ★★ ✒

Few hotels in the neighborhood offer so much low-key charm at such reasonable prices. It's composed of a trio of high-ceilinged buildings, interconnected via a sheltered courtyard, where in warm weather, singing birds provide a worthy substitute for the TVs deliberately missing from the rooms. Accommodations, as reflected by the price, range from snug, cozy doubles to more spacious chambers. Each room is comfortable, but with a lot of luggage, the very smallest would be cramped. The decor is old-fashioned, with feminine touches such as flowered upholsteries and ruffles. Many have views of a garden where trellises and flower beds evoke the countryside.

75 rue de Cardinal-Lemoine, 75005 Paris. www.hotel-grandes-ecoles.com. ℂ **01-43-26-79-23.** Fax 01-47-47-65-48. 51 units. 118€–145€ double. Extra bed 20€. MC, V. Parking 30€. Métro: Cardinal Lemoine, Jussieu, or Place Monge. RER: Port-Royal, Luxembourg. **Amenities:** Babysitting; room service. *In room:* Hair dryer, Wi-Fi (free).

### Hôtel Le Vert Galant ★

Verdant climbing plants and shrubs make this family-run hotel feel like an *auberge* (inn) deep in the French countryside. The smallish guest rooms have tiled or carpeted floors, unfussy furniture, and (in most cases) views of the private garden or the public park across the street. One of the hotel's best aspects is the Basque restaurant next door, the Auberge Etchegorry, sharing the same management; hotel guests receive a discount.

41 rue Croulebarbe, 75013 Paris. www.vertgalant.com. ✆ **01-44-08-83-50.** Fax 01-44-08-83-69. 15 units. 90€–130€ double. AE, MC, V. Parking 15€. Métro: Corvisart or Gobelins. RER: Gare d'Austerlitz. **Amenities:** Restaurant; room service; smoke-free rooms. *In room:* TV, hair dryer, minibar, Wi-Fi (free).

## ST-GERMAIN-DES-PRÉS & LUXEMBOURG (6E)

This glamorous neighborhood is home to great shops and cafes. Intellectuals like Simone de Beauvoir and Jean-Paul Sartre put St-Germain on the map post-war, when they and their friends had high-minded conversations at cafes like Les Deux Magots or Cafe de Flore. The area still draws many of the city's artists and thinkers, and most of the modern art galleries are here, too.

### Expensive

**Hôtel d'Aubusson ★★**   This mansion in the heart of St-Germain-des-Prés was the site of the city's first literary salon. Fully restored, it is today one of the best luxe boutique hotels in Paris. Lying 2 blocks south of Pont Neuf and the Seine, the hotel has taken over a former private residence from the 1600s, to which is attached a 1950s building. You enter a grand hall under a beamed ceiling with a baronial fireplace, original Aubusson tapestries, and furnishings in the style of Louis XV. There are also a number of smaller, more intimate lounges. The bedrooms are midsize to large, each attractively and comfortably furnished, often in a Directoire style and sometimes with exposed ceiling beams. Antiques are often placed in front of the original stone walls. For the most traditional flair, ask for one of the rooms on the top two floors. Bathrooms are stocked with Hermès toiletries.

33 rue Dauphine, Paris 75006. www.hoteldaubusson.com. ✆ **01-43-29-43-43.** Fax 01-43-29-12-62. 49 units. 315€–480€ double; 625€ suite. AE, DC, MC, V. Parking 25€. Métro: Odéon. **Amenities:** Bar; cafe; babysitting; room service. *In room:* A/C, TV, hair dryer, minibar, Wi-Fi (free).

**Relais Christine ★★**   This hotel welcomes you into a former 16th-century Augustinian cloister. From a cobblestone street, you enter a symmetrical courtyard and find an elegant reception area with sculpture and Renaissance antiques. Each room is uniquely decorated with wooden beams and Louis XIII–style furnishings; the rooms come in a range of styles and shapes. Some are among the Left Bank's largest, with extras such as mirrored closets, plush carpets, and some balconies facing the courtyard. The least attractive rooms are in the interior. Bed configurations vary, but all mattresses are on the soft side, offering comfort with quality linens.

3 rue Christine, 75006 Paris. www.relais-christine.com. ✆ **01-40-51-60-80.** Fax 01-40-51-60-81. 51 units. 300€–510€ double; 450€–930€ duplex or suite. AE, DC, MC, V. Free parking. Métro: Odéon or St-Michel. **Amenities:** Bar; babysitting; concierge; exercise room; room service; spa. *In room:* A/C, TV, TV/DVD, hair dryer, minibar, Wi-Fi (free).

### Moderate

**Hôtel Récamier ★★**   Sitting on the picturesque place-Sulpice, this intimate little hotel resembles a charming private home. Its 24 individually decorated rooms offer elegant calm and comfort, with quality textiles and linens spiced up with original art works and unexpected details. The deluxe rooms have views over the square and its 17th-century church. The quality of the service is excellent, there's a complimentary tea time in the salon every day between 4 and 6pm, and room service is available until 11pm (the home-made soups are especially popular). If you do make it out, all St-Germain lies at your feet.

3 bis place-Sulpice, Paris 75006. www.hotelrecamier.com. ⓒ **01-43-26-04-89.** Fax 01-43-26-35-76. 24 units. 260€–450€ double. AE, DC, MC, V. Métro: Saint Sulpice. **Amenities:** Bar; room service. *In room*: A/C, TV, hair dryer, minibar, Wi-Fi (free).

**Le Placide** ★★ 🏠 Converted from a former family home in the 19th century, Le Placide has the aura of a private club. This small boutique hotel—there are only two rooms per floor—lies just steps from the chic Bon Marché Department Store. It was designed by a member of Philippe Starck's firm, who brought a 21st-century style of luxury and comfort to the interior, featuring white Moroccan leather, lots of glass, a bit of chrome, and a crystal pedestal table. Fresh flowers adorn each room, and rose petals are placed on your bed at night. The spacious bathrooms provide natural light.

6 rue St-Placide, 75006 Paris. www.leplacidehotel.com. ⓒ **01-42-84-34-60.** 11 units. 153€–530€ double. AE, MC, V. Métro: St-Placide. **Amenities:** Bar. *In room*: A/C, TV, TV/DVD, CD player, hair dryer, minibar, MP3 docking station, Wi-Fi (free).

### Inexpensive
**Hotel Mayet** ★ 🏠 This affordable hotel has a great location close to shopping heaven Le Bon Marché and St-Germain. The compact rooms are clean, comfortable, and contemporary, designed in a bordeaux and gray color scheme. The low-key lobby sets the scene: deep, comfortable sofas are set against a brightly painted wall with some original graffiti by Parisian artist André. There's an iMac computer in the lobby with Internet access. Service goes the extra mile.

3 rue Mayet, 75006 Paris. www.mayet.com. ⓒ **01-47-83-21-35.** Fax 01-40-65-95-78. 23 units. 140€–175€ double. Rates include breakfast. AE, DC, MC, V. Métro: Duroc. **Amenities:** Bar; breakfast room. *In room*: A/C, minibar, TV, Wi-Fi (free).

## EIFFEL TOWER & NEARBY (7E)
Running along the Seine on the Left Bank, from Musée d'Orsay to the Eiffel Tower and opposite the Louvre, this elegant residential neighborhood counts M. Karl Lagerfeld as one of its well-heeled inhabitants.

### Expensive
**Hôtel Thoumieux** ★★ 🌶 This hotel-cum-dining destination is a collaboration between Chef Jean-François Piège and Paris dining baron Thierry Costes. Parisians and visitors flock here to eat in either the buzzing brasserie downstairs or the fine dining restaurant, with two Michelin stars, upstairs. The restaurants are so successful that in 2011, the owners opened up this boutique hotel in the rest of the building. Decorated by celebrated interior designer India Mahdavi, the rooms evoke the 1950s, and are colorful yet elegant, adorned with loud prints on the wallpaper, carpet, and upholstery. Though the hotel lacks an elevator, each room is an oasis, with an iPad, an iHome system, a coffee machine, and a complimentary (alcohol free) minibar. This place oozes contemporary Parisian extravagance.

79 rue St-Dominique, 75007 Paris. www.thoumieux.fr. ⓒ **01-47-05-79-00.** Fax 01-47-05-36-96. 15 units. 200€–400€ double. AE, DC, MC, V. Métro: Rue du Bac. **Amenities:** 2 restaurants; bar; room service. *In room*: A/C, TV, hair dryer, iHome, iPad, minibar, Wi-Fi (free).

## Moderate

**Hôtel Le Bellechasse ★★ 🎁**   This gem of a hotel, seconds on foot from the Musée d'Orsay, is still one of the city's most fanciful designer hotels. It's the creation of couturier Christian Lacroix, who let his imagination go wild. A stay here is like wandering into a psychedelic garden. Each guest room is different in a pastiche of colors with baroque overtones. One French critic called Lacroix's designs "magpie sensibility," perhaps a reference to one room where top-hatted, frock-coated Paris dandies with butterfly wings wrap around both walls and ceilings. The helpful staff is part of the fun—that and taking a bath in a fiberglass tub.

8 rue de Bellechasse, 75007 Paris. www.lebellechasse.com. ✆ **01-45-50-22-31.** Fax 01-45-51-52-36. 34 units. 160€–245€ double. MC, V. Métro: Solferino. RER: Musée d'Orsay. **Amenities:** Dining room (breakfast). *In room:* A/C, TV, TV/DVD, CD player, hair dryer, minibar, MP3 docking station, Wi-Fi (free).

## MONTPARNASSE & SOUTHERN PARIS (14E & 15E)

Back in the early days of the 20th century, Montparnasse was a hotbed of creativity. Between World War I and World War II, artists, expats, and extravagant figures like Kiki de Montparnasse and Gertrude Stein reinvented the world in the bars and cafes of the area.

## Moderate

**Hôtel La Manufacture ★ 🎁**   With good rooms and decent prices, this place is a real find. Lying on a small street near place d'Italie in the 13th arrondissement, it is only 10 minutes by Métro from the stations at Montparnasse and Gare de Lyon. Small to midsize bedrooms are decorated in printed fabrics and soothing pastels. The most desirable room is no. 74 because of its distant views of the Eiffel Tower. This restored 19th-century building has a wrought-iron door and is graced with iron lamps, wicker chairs, oak floors, and bright paintings. It contains a number of old-fashioned armoires called *chapeau de gendarme* (police hat).

8 rue Philippe de Champagne (av. des Gobelins), 75013 Paris. www.hotel-la-manufacture.com. ✆ **01-45-35-45-25.** Fax 01-45-35-45-40. 56 units. 145€–195€ double; 310€ triple. AE, DC, MC, V. Métro: Place d'Italie. **Amenities:** Bar; room service. *In room:* A/C, TV, hair dryer, Wi-Fi (10€ per 3 hr.).

# Near the Airports

## ORLY

**Hilton Paris Orly Airport ★**   Boxy and bland, the Hilton at Orly is a well-maintained and convenient business hotel. Noise from incoming planes can't penetrate the guest rooms' sound barriers, giving you a decent shot at a night's sleep. (Unlike the 24-hr. Charles de Gaulle Airport, Orly is closed to arriving flights from midnight–6am.) The midsize rooms are standard for a chain hotel; each has been renovated.

Aéroport Orly, 267 Orly Sud, 94544 Orly Aérogare Cedex. www.hilton.com. ✆ **800/445-8667** in the U.S. and Canada, or 01-45-12-45-12. Fax 01-45-12-45-00. 351 units. 90€–250€ double; 300€ suite. AE, DC, MC, V. Parking 14€. Transit to and from airport by complimentary shuttle bus. **Amenities:** Restaurant; bar; babysitting; concierge; exercise room; room service. *In room:* A/C, TV, TV/DVD player, hair dryer, Wi-Fi (13€ per day).

## CHARLES DE GAULLE

**Hyatt Regency Paris–Charles de Gaulle ★** This property is adjacent to the Charles de Gaulle Airport. Lying only a 25-minute drive from Disneyland Paris and a half-hour from the attractions of central Paris, the Roissy property was designed by the renowned architect Helmut Jahn. He created a stunning five-story structure of sleek design and tech-smart features. Jet-lagged passengers find comfort in the elegantly furnished and soundproof guest rooms, which meld modern convenience with European style.

351 av. du Bois de la Pie, 95912 Roissy. www.paris.charlesdegaulle.hyatt.fr. ☎ **01-48-17-12-34.** Fax 01-48-17-17-17. 388 units. 155€–255€ double; 265€–400€ suite. AE, DC, MC, V. RER-B train to its final destination (Aéroport Charles de Gaulle-Terminal Two). From there, take the hotel's shuttle bus (departures every 20 min.) directly to the hotel. Parking 29€. Free shuttle to and from airport. **Amenities:** Restaurant; bar; babysitting; concierge; exercise room; pool (indoor); room service; 2 tennis courts. *In room:* A/C, TV, TV/DVD, hair dryer, minibar, Wi-Fi (12€ per day).

**ibis Paris CDG Terminal Roissy ★** Conveniently located near CDG's Terminal 3, this two-star hotel is the cheapest option near the airport. Recently renovated, the hotel rooms are clean and comfortable, though they are decorated in that bland aesthetic common to airports.

Roissy Aéroport, 95701 Roissy en France. www.ibishotel.com. ☎ **01-49-19-19-19.** Fax 01-49-19-19-21. 556 units. 79€–139€ double. AE, DC, MC, V. Parking 16€ per day. Transit to and from airport by complimentary shuttle bus. **Amenities:** 2 restaurants; bar; room service. *In room:* A/C, TV, hair dryer, minibar, Wi-Fi (free).

**5**

# SIDE TRIPS FROM PARIS

by Lily Heise

**W**hether you are escaping busy Paris for the day or embarking on an adventure to another region of France, there are a myriad of wonderful destinations a mere hour's journey from the capital. Bask in the glory of the French royals and nobles at the magnificent Château de Versailles or the more discrete Vaux-le-Vicomte. Step into the paintings of Monet and van Gogh at the picturesque villages of Giverny and Auvers-sur-Oise. Travel back to medieval France while wandering the narrow laneways of Senlis or marveling at the amazing stained glass of the Cathedral of Chartres. Fans of the great outdoors can trek through the forests of Fontainebleau or Rambouillet, and kids of all ages can get their thrills at Disneyland Paris.

# VERSAILLES ★★★

21km (13 miles) SW of Paris; 71km (44 miles) NE of Chartres

Back in the *grand siècle,* all you needed was a sword, a hat, and a bribe for the guard at the gate. Provided you didn't look as if you had smallpox, you'd be admitted to the Château de Versailles, where you could stroll through salon after glittering salon and watch the Sun King gossiping, dancing, plotting, and flirting. Louis XIV was accorded about as much privacy as an institution.

Today Louis XIV would be shocked to find 5.4 million commoners parading through the chateau each year and happy families regularly picnicking along the Grand Canal. What was once the terrain of the elite is now open to the masses, who are invited to enjoy the 7,000 paintings, 2,900 sculptures, and 2,500 *objets d'art* that decorate the castle and its vast grounds. With over 2,000 rooms and 787 hectares (1,944 acres) of grounds, Versailles' upkeep is a Herculean feat, and parts of the domain are still not open to the public. But thanks to a massive, multi-decade restoration project, visitors will have even more to visit in years to come.

## Essentials

**GETTING THERE**   To get to Versailles, catch the **RER** line C1 to Versailles–Rive Gauche at the Gare d'Austerlitz, St-Michel, Musée d'Orsay, Invalides, Ponte de l'Alma, Champ de Mars, or Javel stop, and take it to the Versailles/Rive Gauche station. The trip takes 35 to 40 minutes. Make sure you take the train marked "Versailles/Rive Gauche" and not "Versailles Chantier," which takes a round-about route and will leave you on the other end of town, a long walk from the château. The round-trip fare is 6.50€. A section of the RER C line within Paris (a stretch of key stations from Gare d'Austerlitz to Invalides) may be closed from mid-July to mid-August for renovation works which are scheduled to continue every summer until 2017. See information in an RER metro station or ask any metro ticket agent for re-routing assistance. **SNCF trains** make frequent runs from Gare St-Lazare and Gare Montparnasse in Paris to Versailles. Trains departing from Gare St-Lazare arrive at the Versailles/Rive Droite railway station; trains departing from Gare Montparnasse arrive at Versailles/Chantiers station, a long walk, as mentioned.

Both Versailles/Rive Gauche and Versailles/Rive Droite stations are within a 10-minute walk of the château, and we recommend the walk as a means of orienting yourself to the town, its geography, its scale, and its architecture. Directions to the château are clearly signposted from each railway station.

If you're **driving,** take the *périphérique* (the ring road around Paris) to the autoroute A13 (direction Versailles/Rouen); take exit 5 to Versailles Centre and park on place d'Armes in front of the château.

**TICKETS**  The **Château Passeport** offers access to the entire domain (palace, gardens, Trianons, Domaine de Marie Antoinette, and temporary expositions) and costs 25€ from April to October and 18€ from November to March. If you are feeling less ambitious, the **Palace Ticket** (Billet Château) will let you in to just the palace and the temporary exhibits; it costs 15€ and includes an audioguide in English. Buying tickets in advance will save you headaches and extra lines at the entrance; tickets can be purchased online on the château's website (www.chateauversailles.fr) or through the FNAC bookstores (www.fnac.com; ✆ **08-92-68-36-22**). You can also buy tickets in person at any Fnac store (branches all over Paris—visit the website for locations).

If you hold the **Paris Museum Pass**, admission is free to most of the sight (but does not include the gardens on Tuesdays and the weekend in high season or evening spectacles). The pass also lets you use the priority entrance so you don't have to wait in line to get in. Due to the ongoing renovations at the château, this privilege may occassionally be revoked, and you'll be obliged to stand in line with everyone else.

**VISITOR INFORMATION**  The **Office de Tourisme** is at 2 bis av. de Paris (www.versailles-tourisme.com; ✆ **01-39-24-88-88;** fax 01-39-24-88-89).

**EVENING SPECTACLES**  Every summer, usually on Saturday nights between June and August, the palace grounds are the setting for "Les Grandes Eaux Nocturnes" a program of fireworks and illuminated fountains. Starting around 9pm, ticket holders get to stroll around and visit colorfully lit bosquets, fountains, and statues and gaze at fireworks set to music. Tickets are 17€ to 21€. Before the fountains start, for an extra 13€ to 18€ you can enjoy 50 minutes of "La Serenade," period dancing and music in the Hall of Mirrors. Tickets for these events can be purchased on the same day at the entrance to the gardens from 10am to 7:30pm.

In late summer or early fall there are open-air spectacles or concerts in the gardens ranging from choreographed fireworks display featuring prerecorded classical music and hundreds of live players and exclusive concerts by international dance companies or performing artists. Ticket prices are 35€ to 55€.

# Paris & the Ile de France

Beauvais
Compiègne
*FORÊT DE COMPIÈGNE*
Clermont — N31 — A1
Noailles
OISE
N14
A16
N16
Senlis
Chantilly
Villers-Cotterêts
*FORÊT D'HALATTE*
N2
Chambly
Vernon
Giverny
Vigny
VAL-D'OISE
Auvers-sur-Oise
A1
N330
Marne
A4
**Pontoise**
Roissy-en-France
*Charles de Gaulle*
N15
A15
SEINE-ST-DENIS
Pacy-sur-Eure
A13
A14
St-Denis
N3
Meaux
EURE
St-Germain-en-Laye
**Bobigny**
Ivry-la-Bataille
**Nanterre**
★**PARIS**
Disneyland Paris
Château de Versailles
**Versailles**
**Créteil**
Coulommiers
N12
HAUTS-DE-SEINE
VAL-DE-MARNE
A4
Dreux
YVELINES
*FORÊT DE RAMBOUILLET*
Orsay
*Orly*
N4
SEINE-ET-MARNE
N19
N36
Nogent-le-Roi
Rambouillet
Évry
N104
Vaux-le-Vicomte
A10
N10
Maintenon
N154
N20
ESSONNE
Melun
A11
**Chartres**
Notre-Dame de Chartres Cathedral
N191
Milly-la-Forêt
Fontainebleau
A5
Seine
Etampes
N20
N837
*FORÊT DE FONTAINEBLEAU*
Montereau-Fault-Yonne
A10
A6
Malesherbes
Nemours
LOIRET

0    10 mi
0    10 km

Since it reopened after an extensive restoration, big names in classical music, theater, and dance are filling the stage at the magnificent Opéra Royal; reserve well in advance and expect royal ticket prices (45€–100€). Tickets can be purchased online at www.chateauversailles-spectacles.fr, by phone at ☏ **01-30-83-78-89,** or through FNAC (see above).

**DAYTIME SPECTACLES**   Saturdays and Sundays from April through October, between 11am and noon and 3:30 and 5pm, Versailles broadcasts classical music throughout the park and opens the valves on as many fountains as are currently in operation as part of a program known as "Les Grandes Eaux Musicales de Versailles." The spectacles showcase the landscaping vision of the palace's designers and encourage participants to walk, promenade, or meander the vast park, enjoying the juxtaposition of supremely grand architecture with lavish waterworks. Admission is included in the Passport or separate garden tickets can be purchased to onsite 8€ for adults and 6€ for ages 6 to 18. A similar event, "Les Jardins Musicaux," takes place on Tuesdays from May through September from 9am to 5:30pm: Music is broadcast in the gardens; however, the fountains are not running (adults 7€, ages 6–18 6€). Tickets can be purchased at the garden; entrance from 9am to 5pm. For information, visit www.chateauversailles-spectacles.fr or call ☏ **01-30-83-78-89.**

## Contemporary Versailles

Even though it is one of France's most visited sights, Versailles still attempts to bring in regular visitors through by a program of controversial temporary exhibits by international contemporary artists such as Jeff Koons and Takashi Murakami. They shows might have the Sun King rolling in his grave; however, they have drawn in huge crowds of new admirers to the château.

# Exploring the Château & Gardens

**Château de Versailles** ★★★ PALACE/MUSEUM/GARDEN   In 1661, Louis XIV set out to build a palace that would be the envy of Europe and created a symbol of opulence copied, yet never duplicated, the world over. Less than 40 years and more than 40,000 workmen later, the Château de Versailles was transformed from Louis XIII's humble hunting lodge into an extravagant palace and century-long base of the French court.

Wishing (with good reason) to keep an eye on the nobles of France, Louis XIV summoned them to live at his court. Here he amused them with constant entertainment and lavish banquets. To some he awarded such tasks as holding the hem of his robe. While the aristocrats played at often-silly intrigues and games, the peasants on the estates sowed the seeds of the Revolution.

When Louis XIV died in 1715, his great-grandson Louis XV succeeded him and continued the outrageous pomp, though he is said to have predicted the outcome: *"Après moi le déluge"* (After me, the deluge). His wife, Marie Leszczynska, was shocked by the blatant immorality at Versailles.

The next monarch, Louis XVI, found his grandfather's behavior scandalous—in fact, on gaining the throne, he ordered that the "stairway of indiscretion" (secret stairs leading to the king's bedchamber) be removed. The well-intentioned but weak king and his queen, Marie Antoinette, were well liked at first, but the queen's frivolity and spending led to her downfall. Louis and Marie Antoinette were at Versailles on October 6, 1789, when they were notified that mobs were marching on the palace. As predicted, *le déluge* had arrived.

Napoleon stayed at Versailles but never seemed fond of it. Louis-Philippe (who reigned 1830–48) prevented the destruction of the palace by converting it into a museum dedicated to the glory of France. To do that, he had to surrender some of his own riches. Decades later, John

Château de Versailles.

D. Rockefeller contributed toward the restoration of Versailles, and work continues today.

Upon entering the palace before going up to the second floor where the main highlights are located, have a quick glance at the **Chapel.** Designed by Hardouin-Mansart, it was the fifth chapel to be built at Versailles. This was where the Sun King attended Mass every morning and where Louis XVI married Marie Antoinette in 1770, while he was the Dauphin.

Upstairs, step into the magnificent **Grands Appartements ★★★**, in the Louis XIV style; each bears the name of the allegorical painting on the ceiling. The best known and largest is the **Hercules Salon ★★**, with a ceiling painted by François Lemoine, depicting the Apotheosis of Hercules. In the **Mercury**

**Salon** (with a ceiling by Jean-Baptiste Champaigne), the body of Louis XIV was put on display in 1715; his 72-year reign was one of the longest in history.

The most famous room at Versailles is the 73m-long (239-ft.) **Hall of Mirrors ★★★**. Begun by Mansart in 1678 in the Louis XIV style, it was decorated by Le Brun with 17 arched windows faced by beveled mirrors in simulated arcades. On June 28, 1919, the treaty ending World War I was signed in this corridor. The German Empire was proclaimed here in 1871. In 2007, a $16-million makeover was completed, returning the Hall of Mirrors to much as it was during the reign of the Sun King. The restoration marked the first time in more than 3 centuries that the hall was restored from top to bottom. Even so, hawk-eyes will notice nips and tucks. But Frédéric Didier, the chief architect of France's monuments, claimed, "All the wrinkles in her face tell a story."

The royal apartments were for show, but Louis XV and Louis XVI retired to the **Petits Appartements ★★** to escape the demands of court etiquette. Louis XV died in his bedchamber in 1774, a victim of smallpox. In a second-floor apartment, which you can visit only with a guide, he stashed away first Mme. de Pompadour, and then Mme. du Barry. The **Grand Appartement de la Reine** was the private suite of several queens though Marie Antoinette had many aspects of the rooms redecorated to her liking. Her **bathroom** is one of the latest rooms to be restored and was unveiled in late 2011.

Louis XVI had a sumptuous **Library,** designed by Jacques-Ange Gabriel, the designer of place de la Concorde in Paris. Its panels are delicately carved, and the room has been restored and refurnished. The **Clock Room** contains Passement's astronomical clock, encased in gilded bronze. Twenty years in the making, it was completed in 1753. The clock is supposed to keep time until the year 9999. At age 7, Mozart played for the court in this room.

Gabriel also designed the **Opéra ★★** for Louis XV in 1748, though it wasn't completed until 1770. In its heyday, it took 3,000 candles to light the place. After two years of renovations, the Opéra reopened to the public and performances in 2009.

In 2005, previously off-limits sections of the vast palace were opened to the public for the first time, including the mammoth **Battle Gallery,** which, at 119m (390 ft.), is the longest hall at Versailles. The gallery displays monumental paintings depicting all of France's great battles, ranging from the founding of the monarchy by Clovis, who reigned in the 5th and 6th centuries, through the Napoleonic wars in the early 19th century.

## ○ Versailles' *Jardins Secrets*

Tucked away in the wooded areas of the gardens are various *bosquets* (groves). These hidden gardens each have a specific theme, and several have significant links to certain royals. The **Apollo Baths,** surrounded by a mix of English and Chinese gardens, were constructed on the request of Louis XIV's mistress Mme. de Montespan. The **Queen's Grove** was the setting of the infamous 1785 Affair of the Diamond Necklace (when Marie Antoinette was wrongly accused of arranging the purchase of an exorbitantly priced diamond necklace), which forever tarnished Marie Antoinette's image—despite her innocence. Today they offer visitors a quiet escape from the masses marching along the Grand Canal.

Spread across 100 hectares (247 acres), the **Gardens of Versailles ★★★** were laid out by landscape artist André Le Nôtre. At the peak of their glory, 1,400 fountains spewed forth. One of the most famous, located at the base of the Grand Canal, is the Apollo Fountain, by Jean-Baptiste Tuby, which features the god rising out of the water in his chariot pulled by four horses. Le Nôtre created a Garden of Eden using ornamental lakes and canals, geometrically designed flower beds, and avenues bordered with statuary. On the mile-long Grand Canal, Louis XV used to take gondola rides with his favorite of the moment.

A long walk across the park (or a shorter ride on the little train) takes you to the pink-and-white-marble **Grand Trianon ★★**, designed by Hardouin-Mansart in 1687. Traditionally, it has been lodging for VIPs, though de Gaulle wanted to turn it into a weekend retreat. Nixon slept here in the room where Mme. de Pompadour died. The original furnishings are gone, replaced today by mostly Empire pieces.

In 2006, the 34-hectare (84-acre) **Domaine de Marie-Antoinette** opened, offering a glimpse into the private life of the ill-fated queen. Encompassing the Petit Trianon, its gardens, and the queen's private "hamlet," complete with cows and a dairy, the estate can be visited separately or as part of the "Chateau Passport" package. Gabriel designed the **Petit Trianon ★★** in 1768 for Louis XV who used it for his trysts with Mme. du Barry. In time, Marie Antoinette adopted it as her favorite residence, a place to escape the rigid life at the main palace. Many of the current furnishings, including a few in her rather modest bedchamber, belonged to the ill-fated queen. After redecorating, she commissioned an English garden, complete with a pavilion where she often dined and a marble-columned structure known as the Temple of Love, as well as Belvédère Hall, where small recitals were held.

The Gardens of Versailles.

Riders and horse lovers shouldn't miss **Les Grandes Ecuries** (the Stables) situated immediately opposite the château's main front facade, where horses and carriages of the kings were housed. Today the Académie de Spectacle Equestre is housed here, directed by Bartabas, whose equestrian theater company, Zingaro, has garnered world fame. Visitors can watch a team of up to a dozen students, with their mounts, strut their stuff during hour-long riding demonstrations. Hour-long demonstrations are conducted Saturdays and Sunday and certain Thursdays at 11:15am (6.50€–12€). On some weekend afternoons, a more elaborate "equestrian ballet" is on offer; tickets to those shows are 25€. After the shows visitors are able to tour the stables. For more information and ticketing, visit the Académie's website, www.bartabas.fr/Academie-du-spectacle-equestre.

www.chateauversailles.fr. © **01-30-83-78-00.** Passport 18€–25€ adults, Palace Ticket 15€ adults, Domaine de Marie Antoinette (includes both Trianons) 10€ adults; free for ages 18 and under. Palace: Apr–Oct Tues–Sun 9am–6pm; Nov–Mar Tues–Sun 9am–5pm. Domaine de Marie Antoinette: Tues–Sun noon–6pm. Grounds daily dawn to dusk.

# Shopping

Founded by the Sun King himself, Louis XIV, **Marché Notre-Dame,** place du Marché Notre-Dame, is the major public market in Versailles, housed in a series of red-brick buildings. The present look dates from the 19th century. Indoor shops selling local cheeses, meats, and fresh fruits are open daily from 7am to 7pm, but the outdoor stalls in the center of the square flourish only on Tuesday, Friday, and Sunday, from about 9am to 2pm.

Close to the mammoth market, **passage de la Geôle** (www.antiques-versailles.com; © **01-30-21-15-13**) is open Friday to Sunday 10am to 7pm, housing antiques shops selling furniture and *objets d'art* at "all prices." More antique gems can be found in **Les Carrés Saint-Louis** on the streets around rue d'Anjou and rue Royale. Built by Louis XV in 1755, these square blocks of low slate-roofed houses make up one of the first ever shopping malls.

# Where to Eat

## VERY EXPENSIVE

**Gordon Ramsay au Trianon ★★★** FRENCH/INTERNATIONAL   One of the kings of cuisine reigns over this Art Deco restaurant in the swanky **Trianon Palace Hotel** (see above)—and he's not French. Scottish-born and Michelin laureate Gordon Ramsay, the *enfant terrible* of chefs, designs a seasonal French menu with modern flair. Treat yourself to the exceptional tasting menu or choose à la carte from bubbly wild roasted sea bass with mussels, baby squid and champagne, or the rich pressed foie gras and Scottish venison with Périgord truffle, figs and raspberries. Finish with the delicate roasted apple with spices and iced almond mousse. The food is of the highest order—and so are the prices. For more relaxed dining, opt for its little sister **La Veranda,** located in the terrace of the hotel, perfect for summer dining.

In the Hotel Trianon Palace, 1 bd. de la Reine. www.gordonramsay.com. © **01-30-84-55-55.** Reservations required. Main courses 55€–72€; fixed-price menu 160€. AE, DC, MC, V. Fri–Sat noon–2pm; Tues–Sat 7–10:30pm. Closed first 2 weeks of Jan, 1 week in Mar.

## MODERATE

**Le Potager du Roy** ★ MODERN FRENCH   It's not often you can eat as a king—or at least from his vegetable garden. Philippe Letourneur spent years perfecting a distinctive cuisine that now adds novelty to the dining scene in Versailles. Letourneur rotates his skillfully prepared menu with the seasons. Examples are gazpacho with anchovy toasts, pork cheeks on a bed of lentils, pink salmon with warm asparagus, and filet of lamb with a tian of vegetables. The wine list might not date back as far as the château, but it's equally impressive.

1 rue du Maréchal-Joffre. www.lepotagerduroy.com. © **01-39-50-35-34.** Reservations required. Main courses 28€; fixed-price menu 34€–44€. AE, MC, V. Tues–Sat noon–2pm and 7:30–10pm.

## INEXPENSIVE

**La Flottille** FRENCH   One of the few restaurants inside the château's grounds (at the head of the Grand Canal), it has a sweeping view over some of Europe's most famous landscaping. Both restaurant and snack-bar service are available. In warm weather, the traditional French cuisine is also served at outside tables. Reservations are recommended.

Parc du Château. www.laflotille.fr. © **01-39-51-41-58.** Fax 01-39-50-51-87. Main courses 18€–22€; fixed-price menu 28€. AE, MC, V. Daily noon to château closing.

**Le Resto du Roi** ★ 🍴 MODERN FRENCH   In an 18th-century building overlooking the western facade of Versailles, this bistro recently got a new owner and a chic makeover in tones of cream and chocolate. The new chef, Olivier Pariaud, has updated the menu as well, which features high-quality bistro classics made with fresh seasonal ingredients. Old-fashioned steak with *gratin dauphinoise* shares the stage with poached tuna steak draped in coco and lime sauce. There are also large *salades* including the vegetarian *estivale* with hot goat cheese toasts and melon. For dessert, try the divine profiterole *royale* with grilled almonds. Warm-weather meals can be taken on the ample terrace overlooking the château.

1 av. de St-Cloud. www.restaurant-versailles.com. © **01-39-50-42-26.** Reservations recommended. Main courses 15€–16€; fixed-price menus 20€–38€. AE, MC, V. Daily 11:45am–2:30pm and 7–10:30pm.

# Versailles Nightlife

**O'Paris Pub,** 15 rue Colbert, off place d'Armes (www.puboparis.com; © **01-39-50-36-12**), is an Irish pub where you can order the best brews in town. A bit more upmarket, **Bar à Vins-Restaurant Le Ducis,** 13 rue Ducis (© **01-30-21-93-76**), provides a mellow atmosphere on a summer evening, with tables spilling onto a side street. A bottle of wine and a good companion should get you through an evening, enhanced perhaps by a plate of food selected from the chalkboard menu.

# Where to Stay

## VERY EXPENSIVE

**Trianon Palace** ★★★   This luxe hotel is the grandest in the Ile de France, and after a recent renovation, it has a more modern feel, with redesigned public and private rooms. A Westin property, it was built in 1910 on a 2-hectare (5-acre) garden bordering the gardens of the Petit Trianon. Since being the headquarters of the peace conference marking the Treaty of Versailles in 1919, the hotel has hosted illustrious guests including Woodrow Wilson, John D. Rockefeller, Queen Elizabeth II, and Marlene Dietrich, who made headlines by wearing pants in the dining room. The hotel is in a classically designed palace and connected to a late-20th-century annex (Le Pavillon) by an underground tunnel. Accommodations in both buildings are decorated in traditional style with reference to château living, using rich fabrics and a mixture of antiques and reproductions. The hotel has also joined with Guerlain to create an outstanding spa.

1 bd. de la Reine, Versailles 78000. www.trianonpalace.com. ✆ **800/937-8461** in the U.S. and Canada, or 01-30-84-50-00. Fax 01-30-84-50-01. 199 units. 239€–369€ double; from 609€ suite. AE, DC, MC, V. Parking 20€. **Amenities:** 2 restaurants; cafe; bar; babysitting; health club; indoor pool; room service; sauna; spa; tennis courts. *In room:* A/C, TV, hair dryer, Internet (7€ per hour), minibar.

## MODERATE

**Novotel Château de Versailles**　A 15-minute walk north of one of the side wings of the château, this chain hotel, built in 1988, has a modern facade with columns and large windows. It's not too expensive and is a convenient choice for visitors to Versailles. All bedrooms have been recently renovated and sport a contemporary style.

4 bd. St-Antoine, Le Chesnay 78150. www.novotel.com. ✆ **01-39-54-96-96.** Fax 01-39-54-94-40. 105 units. 99€–159€ double; 165€–185€ suite. Children 16 and under stay free in parent's room. AE, DC, MC, V. Parking 11€. **Amenities:** Restaurant; bar; room service. *In room:* A/C, TV, hair dryer, minibar, free Wi-Fi

# THE FOREST & CHÂTEAU OF RAMBOUILLET

55km (34 miles) SW of Paris; 42km (26 miles) NE of Chartres

Once known as La Forêt d'Yveline, the **Forest of Rambouillet ★** is one of the loveliest forests in France. More than 20,000 hectares (49,421 acres) of greenery stretch from the valley of the Eure to the high valley of Chevreuse, the latter rich in medieval and royal abbeys. Hills and dales, rocky outcroppings, and lakes and waterfalls are but some of the natural attractions of this "green lung," which is also home to a wide variety of wildlife. Most people, however, come to Rambouillet to visit its beautiful château, which has welcomed generations of French kings, presidents, and visiting foreign heads of state. Today the château and its gardens are open to the public, which take about 2 hours visit, or allot more time if you would like to explore the forest (see Moments box).

## Essentials

**GETTING THERE**　**Trains** depart frequently from Paris's Gare Montparnasse (35-min. trip). Tickets cost 15€ round-trip, for information and train schedules visit www.transilien.com or call ✆ **3658**). By **car,** take N10 southwest from Paris, passing Versailles along the way.

**VISITOR INFORMATION**　The **tourist office** is at the Hôtel de Ville, place de la Libération (www.rambouillet-tourism.com; ✆ **01-34-83-21-21**).

## Seeing the Château

**Château de Rambouillet ★** CASTLE    Stately and elegant, the château is surrounded by formal French gardens and a 100-hectare (247-acre) park, and is located in one of the largest forests in northern France. While its origins lie deep in the Middle Ages, most of château's facades were reconstructed in the 19th century. Much of the interior dates from the 18th and 19th centuries, including superb woodwork, tapestries from the famous Gobelins Manufactory, and fine Dutch ceramics. The magnificent 16th century **Marble Room** features the oldest decor in the château. François I, the Chevalier king, died of a fever here in 1547 at age 52. When the château was later occupied by the comte de Toulouse, the youngest legitimated son of Louis XIV and his mistress, Madame de Montespan, Rambouillet was often visited by Louis XV, who enjoyed a (very) close friendship with the comte's charming wife. Particularly taken with the hunting opportunities that Rambouillet provided, Louis XVI eventually acquired the château in 1783, but Marie Antoinette found it to be far beneath her standards and deplored spending time there. In an effort to persuade her otherwise, Louis offered the queen her own dairy farm and tasting room on the château grounds, built in the form of a neo-Greek temple and furnished with Carrara marble sculptures and Sèvres porcelain tasting bowls.

After the Revolution, Napoleon Bonaparte inhabited and heavily restored the château. The emperor's apartments still feature an ornate **bathroom**, inspired by the Pompeii style, as well as a **dining room** and **bedchamber**, where he insisted on spending his final night before his final exile to the remote island of St. Helena.

In 1830, the elderly Charles X, Louis XVI's brother, abdicated the throne at Rambouillet as a mob marched on the château and his troops began to desert

Château de Rambouillet.

Rambouillet and its forests can provide a verdant interlude. If you've exhausted the idea of a ramble through the gardens that surround the château (or if they're closed because of visiting dignitaries), consider discovering the **Rochers d'Angennes,** rocky hillocks that remain as leftovers from the Ice Age. To reach them, park your car on the D107, where you'll see a sign pointing to the **Rochers**

**et Etang d'Angennes,** about 4km (2½ miles) north of the hamlet of Epernon. Walk along a clearly marked trail through a pine forest before you eventually reach a rocky plateau overlooking the hills and a pond (*l'Etang d'Angennes*) nestled into the surrounding countryside. Round-trip, from the site of your parked car to the plateau and back, your promenade should take between 30 and 45 minutes.

him. From Rambouillet, he embarked for a safe but controversial haven in England. Afterward, Rambouillet fell into private hands until 1852 when Napoleon III returned it to the Crown. In 1896, it was designated an official residence for the president of France. In 1944, Charles de Gaulle lived here briefly before giving the order for the remaining French army to join the Americans in liberating Paris. In more recent years, the château has welcomed the G6 summit meeting, Kosovo peace agreement discussions, and state visits by Boris Yeltsin and Nelson Mandela.

Two must-sees in the park include the aforementioned **Queen's Dairy** and the **Shell Cottage,** a "humble" thatched cottage built for the Princesse de Lamballe featuring an interior decorated with an astonishing array of seashells, marble, and mother-of-pearl.

Parc du Château. www.monuments-nationaux.fr. ✆ **01-34-83-00-25.** Admission 8.50€ adults, 5.50€ students 18–25, free for children 17 and under. Apr–Sept Wed–Mon 10am–noon and 2–6pm; Oct–Mar Wed–Mon 10am–noon and 2–5pm.

## Where to Eat

**La Poste** TRADITIONAL FRENCH   On a street corner in the town's historic center, this restaurant dates from the mid–19th century, when it provided meals and shelter for the region's mail carriers. The two dining rooms have rustic beams and old-fashioned accents that complement the flavorful old-fashioned food. Tasty menu items include a fricassee of chicken and crayfish, and noisettes of lamb "prepared in the style of a roebuck," with a *grand Veneur* sauce. Also popular are civets of both *une biche* (female venison) and rabbit during hunting season.

101 rue du Général-de-Gaulle. ✆ **01-34-83-03-01.** Reservations recommended Sat–Sun. Main courses 18€–20€; fixed-price menus 24€–36€. AE, MC, V. Tues–Sun noon–2pm; Fri–Sat and Tues–Wed 7:30–9:30pm. Closed 1st week of Jan and Sept.

# THE GLORIOUS CATHEDRAL OF CHARTRES ★★★

98km (61 miles) SW of Paris; 76km (47 miles) NW of Orléans

An hour south of Paris, amid a sea of wheat fields, rises the city of Chartres. Crowned with one of the world's most breathtaking cathedrals along with its quaint

## Notre-Dame de Chartres

Chapelle St-Piat

Chapelle St-Sacrement

Ambulatory

Notre-Dame du Pilier

Choir Screen

Sacristy

Choir

Choir Screen

Crypt Entrance

Notre Dame de la Belle Verrière

North Portal

North Transept

**North Rose Window**

Crossing

South Transept

**South Rose Window**

South Portal

Nave

North Aisle

South Aisle

**Chapelle Vendôme**

**Labyrinth**

**New Bell Tower**

**West Rose Window**

**Old Bell Tower**

Royal Portal

historic center, it gives visitors the perfect glimpse of a quintessential French town. In a half-day excursion you'll be captivated by the splendid Notre-Dame; spend a full day to explore the local farmers market, enjoy a lunch of *pâté de Chartres,* wander along its medieval laneways, or visit its lovely Fine Arts Museum.

## Essentials

**GETTING THERE**   From Paris's Gare Montparnasse, **trains** run directly to Chartres, taking around an hour. Tickets cost 29€ round-trip and can be bought at the station; for more information see www.voyages-sncf.com or call ☏ **36-35**. If **driving,** take A10/A11 southwest from the *périphérique* and follow signs to Le Mans and Chartres. (The Chartres exit is clearly marked.)

Inside the Cathédrale Notre-Dame de Chartres.

**VISITOR INFORMATION**    The **Office de Tourisme** is on place de la Cathédrale (www.chartres-tourisme.com; ✆ **02-37-18-26-26;** fax 02-37-21-51-91).

## Seeing the Cathedral

**Cathédrale Notre-Dame de Chartres ★★★** CATHEDRAL    It's not hard to understand why visitors flock to see the awe-inspiring Cathédrale de Chartres, a UNESCO World Heritage Site since 1979. With its mixed-and-matched bell towers; its weather-worn, revolution-damaged exterior; and above all, its shimmering stained-glass windows, the phenomenal church seduces the eyes and the spirit. Rodin reputedly once sat for hours on the sidewalk, admiring the cathedral's Romanesque sculpture. His opinion: Chartres is the French Acropolis. When it began to rain, a kind soul offered him an umbrella—which he declined, so transfixed was he.

The cathedral's origins are uncertain; some suggest it grew up over a Druid site that later became a Roman temple. As early as the 4th century, a Christian basilica was here. An 1194 fire destroyed most of what had then become a Romanesque cathedral, sparing the western facade and crypt. The cathedral today dates principally from the 13th century, when it was rebuilt with the efforts of kings, princes, churchmen, and pilgrims from all over Europe. One of the world's greatest High Gothic cathedrals, it was one of the first to use flying buttresses to support the soaring dimensions within. As you approach the building, stop to admire the beautiful 12th-century sculptures on the **Royal Portal ★★★**. A landmark in Romanesque art, the sculptured bodies are elongated, often formalized beyond reality, in long, flowing robes. But the faces are amazingly (for the time) lifelike, occasionally betraying Mona Lisa smiles. In the central tympanum, Christ is shown at the Second Coming, with his descent depicted on the right, his ascent on the left. Before you enter, admire the Royal Portal and walk around to both the **North Portal** and the **South Portal**; both date from the 13th century. Look carefully and you can read some of the biblical scenes such as the expulsion of Adam and Eve from the Garden of Eden.

Upon entering the cathedral visitors are immediately overcome by the amazing light from the **stained glass ★★★**. Covering an expanse of more than 2,500 sq. m. (26,910 sq. ft.), the glass is unlike anything else in the world. Most of it dates from the 12th and 13th centuries and was spared in both world wars by being painstakingly removed, piece by piece, and stored away. See the windows in the morning, at noon, in the afternoon, at sunset—as often as you can. Like the petals of a kaleidoscope, they constantly change. It's difficult to single out one panel or window above the others, but an exceptional one is the 12th-century *Vierge de la Belle Verrière* (**Our Lady of the Beautiful Window**) on the south side. Of course, there are three fiery rose windows, but you couldn't miss those if you tried.

Though you might be too transfixed by the heavenly light, don't neglect to take in the celebrated **choir screen;** work on it began in the 16th century and lasted until 1714. The niches, 40 in all, contain statues illustrating scenes from the life of the Madonna and Christ—everything from the *Massacre of the Innocents* to the *Coronation of the Virgin*. Before exiting, have a look at the floor of the **nave,** which still contains its ancient floor labyrinth, a 262m-long (858 ft.) pilgrimage path that used to be walked by pilgrims in prayer or often traveled on one's knees as an act of repentance. The wooden *Notre-Dame du Piller* (**Virgin of the Pillar),** to the left of the choir, dates from the 14th century. The crypt was built over 2 centuries, beginning in the 9th century. Enshrined within is *Our Lady of the Crypt,* a 1976 Madonna that replaced one destroyed during the revolution. If you're fit enough, don't miss the opportunity, especially in summer, to climb to the top of the tower.

 **Music of the Spheres**

If you visit Chartres on a Sunday afternoon in July or August, the church features free organ concerts at 4:45pm, when the filtered light brings the cathedral's western windows vibrantly to life.

Try to take a tour conducted by Malcolm Miller (millerchartres@aol.com; *C* **02-37-28-15-58;** fax 02-37-28-33-03), an Englishman who has spent 3 decades studying the cathedral and giving tours in English. His rare blend of scholarship, enthusiasm, and humor will help you understand and appreciate the cathedral. He usually conducts 75-minute tours at noon and 2:45pm Monday to Saturday for 10€ per person or 5€ per student. Tours are canceled during pilgrimages, religious celebrations, and large funerals.

16 cloître Notre-Dame. www.monuments-nationaux.fr. *C* **02-37-21-22-07.** Free admission to cathedral. Admission to the treasury and towers 7€ adults; 4.50€ adults 18–25; free for children 17 and under. Cathedral open daily 8:30am–7:30pm.

# Exploring the Town

Next to the cathedral is the **Musée des Beaux-Arts de Chartres** ★, 29 cloître Notre-Dame (✆ **02-37-90-45-80**), open May 2 through October 3 Wednesday to Monday 10am to noon and 2 to 6pm (closed Sun morning); the rest of the year, it's open only until 5pm. Admission is 3.20€ for adults, 1.60€ for students, free for children 18 and under. In a former Episcopal palace, the building at times competes with its exhibitions. The collection covers the 16th to the 20th centuries and includes works by Zurbarán, Chardin, and Soutine.

At the foot of the cathedral, the lanes contain gabled houses. Humped bridges span the Eure River. From the Bouju Bridge, you can see the lofty spires in the background. Our favorite stroll is along **rue du Pont-St-Hilaire** ★, where you get the best views of the old rooftops that lie beneath the towering cathedral. The street of St-Hilaire is east of the Gothic **church of St-Pierre,** on rue St-Pierre, a 10-minute stroll south of the cathedral. Two evocative streets of old Chartres, each a 3-minute walk south of the cathedral, are **rue du Cygne** and **rue des Ecuyers.** To the east, the most charming old *quartier* is **St. André,** once home to cobblers and tanners. Most of the buildings are restored but date from the 1700s and are known for their embossed doorways crowned by bull's-eye glass.

# Shopping

Your best shopping bet in Chartres is **place des Epars**. This pedestrian area is home to most of the apparel shops and even some haute couture boutiques. Many shops selling regional items line the narrow streets that fan southeast from the cathedral. Along rue Noël-Balay is a small mall with about 15 interesting shops, which can also provide a dry respite if it's raining. A colorful array of local produce and delicacies can be found in the Saturday morning market held in **place Billard**.

At **Galerie du Vitrail,** 17 cloître Notre-Dame (www.galerie-du-vitrail.com; ✆ **02-37-36-10-03**), you'll find a huge selection of stained glass. **Lassaussois Antiquités,** 17 rue des Changes (✆ **02-37-21-37-74**), specializes in antique objets d'art and contemporary furnishings.

# Where to Eat

**La Vieille Maison** ★★ MODERN FRENCH    Even if the food here wasn't superb, the 14th-century building could be visited for its historical value. The dining room, outfitted in the Louis XIII style, is centered on a narrow ceiling vault, less than 2m (6½ ft.) across, crafted of chiseled white stone blocks during the 800s. Bruno Letartre, the only *maître cuisinier de France* (master French chef) in Chartres, supervises the cuisine. The menu changes four or five times a year, reflecting the seasonality of the Ile de France and its produce. Some good examples include cream of green and white asparagus soup topped with shellfish and beef in a bordeaux wine sauce. Dessert raves go to the profiteroles with *Grand Cru* chocolate.

5 rue au Lait. www.lavieillemaison.fr. ✆ **02-37-34-10-67.** Reservations recommended. Main courses 28€–32€; fixed-price menu 30€–58€. MC, V. Tues–Sun noon–2:15pm; Tues–Sat 7–9:30pm.

**Le Georges** ★★ FRENCH    The most upscale and delicious dining experience in Chartres is in the Grand Monarque, a hotel with roots that date from the 15th century, when the site served food and drink to weary travelers and postal workers. Today's diners feast in a formal, high-ceilinged dining room outfitted in soft reds and grays. Menu items change with the seasons but might include savory portions of *pâté de Chartres*, made with a combination of minced meats that includes wild duck baked in a giant puff pastry, farm-raised duckling, or superb roasted veal "Grand Monarque," served with a casserole of mushrooms and cheese. Desserts are sumptuous, and the chef is known locally for his Grand-Marnier soufflé.

In the Grand Monarque Best Western, 22 place des Epars. www.bw-grand-monarque.com. 02-37-18-15-15. Reservations recommended. Main courses 18€–36€; fixed-price menus 51€–90€. AE, DC, MC, V. Tues–Sun noon–2pm; Tues–Sat 7–10pm.

## Chartres Nightlife

For an evening of theater or modern dance from September to June, try the **Théâtre de Chartres,** place de Ravennes (www.theatredechartres.fr; 02-37-23-42-79). For dancing, go to **Le Privilège,** 1 place St-Pierre (02-37-35-52-02), where you'll find a range of dance music from zouk to disco.

## Where to Stay

**Grand Monarque Best Western**    Located in the town center, this is certainly the most appealing and desirable hotel in Chartres. Functioning as an inn since its original construction in the 15th century and expanded and improved many times since then, it's a grand hotel that remains under the direction of the Jallerat family. It attracts guests who enjoy its old-world charm—such as Art Nouveau stained glass and Louis XV chairs in the dining room. The guest rooms are decorated with reproductions of antiques; most have sitting areas.

22 place des Epars, Chartres 28005. www.bw-grand-monarque.com. 800/528-1234 in the U.S., or 02-37-18-15-15. Fax 02-37-36-34-18. 60 units. 130€–180€ double; 250€ suite. AE, DC, MC, V. Parking 8€. **Amenities:** 2 restaurants; bar; room service, spa. *In room:* A/C (in some), TV, hair dryer, minibar, free Wi-Fi.

**Hôtel Châtelet**    This modern hotel has many traditional touches. The rustic guest rooms are inviting, with reproductions of Louis XV and Louis XVI furniture. The larger, more expensive units face a garden and avoid street noise. But many windows along the front (street) side of the hotel open onto a view of the cathedral. Each room comes with a tidy, tiled bathroom with shower and tub. In chilly weather, there's usually a fire burning in one of the salons. Breakfast is the only meal served, but numerous restaurants are close by.

6–8 av. Jehan-de-Beauce, Chartres 28000. www.hotelchatelet.com. 02-37-21-78-00. Fax 02-37-36-23-01. 48 units. 112€–139€ double. Extra person 25€. AE, MC, V. Parking 8€. **Amenities:** Bar; room service. *In room:* TV, hair dryer, minibar, free Wi-Fi.

# FONTAINEBLEAU: REFUGE OF KINGS ★★★

60km (37 miles) S of Paris; 74km (46 miles) NE of Orléans

From the elegant Renaissance castle of François I to 19th century Napoleonic stronghold, the hallways and vast forest of Fontainebleau have played host to some of the most important figures and events in French history. Far from the overwhelming glitz and pomp of Versailles, Fontainebleau, which Napoleon referred to as "the house of the centuries," offers visitors a more intimate look at the real lives of French monarchs, and its immense forest provides a great get-away for travelers craving some fresh air and nature. Allow 2½ hours to see the château and gardens, or a full day to explore the forest.

## Essentials

**GETTING THERE** **Trains** to Fontainebleau depart from the Gare de Lyon in Paris. The trip takes 40 minutes each way and costs 8.50€ one-way. Fontainebleau's railway station lies 3km (1¾ miles) north of the château, in the suburb of Avon. A local bus (marked CHATEAU and part of line A) makes the trip to the château at 15-minute intervals Monday through Saturday and at 30-minute intervals on Sunday; the fare is 1.80€ each way. If you're **driving,** take A6 south from Paris, exit onto N191, and follow signs.

**VISITOR INFORMATION** The **Office de Tourisme** is at 4 rue Royale, Fontainebleau (www.fontainebleau-tourisme.com; ✆ **01-60-74-99-99**), opposite the main entrance to the château.

## Seeing the Château & Gardens

**Musée National du Château de Fontainebleau ★★★** CASTLE/MUSEUM/GARDEN   Napoleon's affection for this palace is understandable. He followed the pattern of a succession of French kings who used Fontainebleau as a resort and hunted in its forests. François I converted the hunting lodge into a royal palace in the Italian Renaissance style, bringing artists, including Benvenuto Cellini, there to work for him. Under François I's patronage, the School of Fontainebleau (led by the painters Rosso, Fiorentino, and Primaticcio) increased in prestige. These artists adorned one of the most outstanding rooms at Fontainebleau: the 63m-long (207-ft.) **Gallery of François I ★★★**. Surrounded by pomp, François I walked the length of his gallery while artisans tempted him with their wares, job seekers asked favors, and courtesans attempted to lure him from the duchesse d'Etampes. The stucco-framed panels depict such scenes as Jupiter carrying off Europa, the Nymph of Fontainebleau (with a lecherous dog peering through the reeds), and the king holding a pomegranate, a symbol of unity. Everywhere is the salamander, symbol of the Chevalier King.

If it's true that François I built Fontainebleau for his mistress, then Henri II, his successor, left a memorial to the woman he loved, Diane de Poitiers.

### Hiking Along Trails Left by French Kings

The 20,000-hectare (49,400-acre) Forest of Fontainebleau is riddled with *sentiers* (hiking trails) made by French kings and their entourages who went hunting in the forest. A trail guidebook is available at the tourist information center (see above). Bike paths also cut through the forest. You can rent bikes at **A La Petite** **Reine** (4 rue de la Paroisse; www.alapetitereine.com; ✆ **01-60-74-57-57**), located in the center of town, a few blocks from the chateau. The cost of a regular bike is 5€ per hour or 15€ per full day. The shop is open Tuesday through Saturday 9am to 7:30pm, and Sunday from 9am to 6pm.

**Musée National du Château de Fontainebleau**

Sometimes called the Gallery of Henri II, the **Ballroom (La Salle de Bal)** ★★★ is the château's second splendid interior. The monograms H & D are interlaced in the decoration. At one end of the room is a monumental fireplace supported by two bronze satyrs, reproduced in 1966 (the originals were melted down during the Revolution). A series of 16th-century frescoes depict mythological subjects.

An architectural curiosity is the **Louis XV Staircase** ★★. To make room for the monumental stairway, the floor was removed from the upper level bedroom of the duchesse d'Etampes, but luckily the beautiful sculpture and paintings by artist Primaticcio, which decorated the duchess's suite, were incorporated into the final staircase design. One fresco depicts the Queen of the Amazons climbing into Alexander the Great's bed.

Fontainebleau found renewed glory under Napoleon, who used it as one of his bases. Imperial influences include the **throne room**, where he abdicated (the abdication document displayed is a copy), his **offices**, his **bedroom** (look for his symbol, a bee), and his **bathroom**. Some of the smaller rooms, especially those containing his personal mementos and artifacts, are accessible by guided tour only. Second Empire decor can be observed in the **Papal Apartment,** where Pope Pius VII lodged for Napoleon's coronation in 1804 and was later held as the emperor's hostage in 1812–14. The ceilings date from the 16th century when the suite was the Queen Mother's Apartment.

You will leave the château via the very horseshoe-shaped stairway where Napoleon stood to bid farewell to his shattered army before departing for Elba. Save time to visit the **gardens** and especially the carp pond; the gardens, however, are only a prelude to the forest of Fontainebleau and not nearly as spectacular as those surrounding Versailles.

Place du Général-de-Gaulle. www.musee-chateau-fontainebleau.fr. ℂ **01-60-71-50-70.** Combination ticket including *grandes appartements*, Pope's rooms, Renaissance rooms, chapel, Napoleon museum and *Gallerie de Diane*, and audioguide 10€ adults, 8€ students 18–25, free for children 17 and under. Ticket to *petits appartements* 6.50€ adults, 5€ students 18–25, free for children 17 and under, Adults can also purchase a combined ticket for the *grands* and *petits appartements* for 15€. Apr–Sept Wed–Mon 9:30am–6pm; Oct–Mar Wed–Mon 9:30am–5pm.

## Where to Eat

**Auberge de la Croix d'Augas ★ 🎁** SAVOYARD    Located in the forest of Fontainebleau, just 2km (1¼ miles) from the town center, this country inn features specialties from Savoy, an Alpine region known for its fondues, raclettes, and tartiflettes. Potatoes, cheese, and ham feature heavily in these stick-to-your-ribs dishes, but don't worry—there are salads and pasta plates for the faint of heart, as well as your classic steak-frites fare. The setting is truly rustic, including checked tablecloths and hanging copper pots; weather permitting, tables are set up outside on the terrace or under the veranda.

Exit Fontainebleau on bd. de Maréchal Foch (rte. D606) to rte. D116, about 1km (½ mile) into the forest. www.restaurant-fontainebleau.fr. ℂ **01-64-23-49-25.** Main courses 9.70€–20€; fixed-price menu 19€; children's menu 9€. MC, V. Daily noon–2pm and 7–10pm.

**Chez Bernard ★** TRADITIONAL FRENCH    The premier dining choice in Fontainebleau has a covered terrace overlooking the château and the cour des Adieux. Chef Bernard Crogiez's cuisine is meticulous highlighting product provenance with such dishes as oysters from the Bay of Quiberon or Aubrac regional steak with Roquefort sauce and home fries. Cheese lovers should save room for some local Brie de Meaux.

3 rue Royale. www.chez-bernard.fr. ℂ **01-64-22-24-68.** Reservations required. Main courses 14€–29€; fixed-price lunch Mon–Fri only 15€; fixed-price dinner 20€-25€. AE, MC, V. Tues–Sun noon–2pm; Mon–Sat 7:30–9:30pm. Closed 2 weeks in Aug and 1 week in Dec.

## Where to Stay

**Hôtel Aigle-Noir ★**    This mansion, once the home of Cardinal de Retz, sits opposite the château. The formal courtyard entrance has a high iron/board grille and pillars crowned by black eagles. It became a hotel in the 1760s and is the finest lodging in Fontainebleau. The rooms are decorated with Louis XVI, Empire, or Regency-era antiques or reproductions, with plush beds and elegant bathroom amenities. Enjoy a drink in the Napoleon III–style bar.

27 place Napoleon-Bonaparte, Fontainebleau 77300. www.hotelaiglenoir.com. ℂ **01-60-74-60-00.** Fax 01-60-74-60-01. 53 units. 170€–240€ double; 320€–380€ suite. AE, DC, MC, V. Parking 10€. **Amenities:** Bar; exercise room; room service. *In room:* A/C, hair dryer, minibar, free Wi-Fi.

# VAUX-LE-VICOMTE: A PRELUDE TO VERSAILLES ★★

47km (29 miles) SE of Paris; 19km (12 miles) NE of Fontainebleau

Ambition, jealousy, and treachery underlie the troubled history of the château de Vaux-le-Vicomte, the most influential baroque castle in all of Europe. For the first time, a château's architectural plan, its interior, and grounds were designed in unison by the era's top artistic minds, creating a perfectly harmonious effect. However, the lavish château would become the theater of the tragic downfall of its owner, Nicolas Fouquet, and the birth of an even more extravagant palace: the Château de Versailles.

## Essentials

**GETTING THERE**    Though it's close to Paris, Vaux-le-Vicomte is hard to reach by mass transit. By **car,** take the N6 to the A5 autoroute and get off at Saint

Germain-Laxis, 1km (½ miles) from the château (around 50 min.). Take a **regional train** from Gare de Lyon to Melun or **RER line D** from Châte-let–Les Halles or Gare de Lyon to Melun, (30 minutes, 16€ round-trip) and then a taxi from the station 6.5km (4 miles) to Vaux-le-Vicomte (16€ each way). On weekends and holidays between April and October, there is a shuttle bus ("Chateaubus") from the Melun train station (3.5€ per person). Once there, allow 2 hours to see the château.

The nearest **tourist office** is in Melun, at 18 rue Paul Doumer (www. ville-melun.fr; *©* **01-64-52-64-52**); it's open Monday 1:30 to 6pm, Tues-day to Saturday 10am to 12:30pm and 1:30 to 6pm.

## Seeing the Château

**Château de Vaux-le-Vicomte ★★** CASTLE/GARDEN   "On August 17, at 6 in the evening, Nicolas Fouquet was the King of France; at two in the morning, he was nobody." So Voltaire summed up the grim events of the fateful day in 1661 when Louis XIV's finance minister held a sumptuous party for the king, his court, and the crème de la crème of French society to inaugurate his spectacular resi-dence. Thinking he was honoring his king, Fouquet went all out—after showing off his splendid castle and gardens, he served a fabulous meal (served on solid silver and gold tableware), presented a new comedy by Molière, and set off fireworks to wow his guests. The king, who had enough of being upstaged by his flamboyant minister, had other ideas. Within 2 weeks, Fouquet was arrested on trumped-up charges of embezzlement and imprisoned for life. The king seized the castle, con-fiscated its contents, and hired its artists and architects to work on Versailles.

Vaux-le-Vicomte was eventually released to Fouquet's widow, and the castle has remained in private hands ever since. The ancestors of the current owners, Patrice and Cristina de Vogüé, bought the palace in 1875, when they started a

The garden at Château de Vaux-le-Vicomte.

much-needed restoration program to restore Vaux to its original splendor.

Today the view of the château from the main gate reveals the splendor of 17th-century France. The entrance hall leads to 12 staterooms, including the Italian-inspired oval rotunda, left in its unfinished state, as it was the night of Fouquet's arrest. Many rooms feature allegorical Le Brun wall and ceiling paintings; some of the finest are in **King's Apartments** and **Fouquet's bedroom.** If you have enough energy, climb to the top of the dome for the best views of the impressive gardens.

The true highlight of Vaux is the famed **Le Nôtre gardens.** Here, Le Nôtre fused various new landscaping principles developed in the first half of the 17th century, creating what would become the model *jardin à la française.* Le Nôtre designed the perspective so that the composition is balanced from every point of view, creating an optical illusion with widening canals, water basins, and patterned parterres (mirror motifs that Le Brun also used indoors), which extend nearly 3km (1½ miles) along the central axis.

Musée des Equipages.

Included in either ticket is entrance to the château's carriage museum, **Musée des Equipages,** in the stables. Some 25 restored 18th- and 19th-century carriages are on display, each accessorized with mannequin horses and people.

Candlelight evenings, **Soirées aux Chandelles,** take place every Saturday from May to mid-October between 6pm and midnight. During the events, the electric lights go out and thousands of candles illuminate both the château and its gardens. The effect is mystical, a memorable re-creation of the way of life that prevailed during the building's heyday. Admission for the "simple visit" during candlelight evenings is 17€ for adults, 15€ for students and children 6 to 15, free for children 5 and under; add another 2€ for the Pass.

77950 Maincy. www.vaux-le-vicomte.com. © **01-64-14-41-90.** Admission "simple visit" 14€ adults, 11€ students and children 6–16, free for children 5 and under. Vaut-le-Vicomte Pass 16€ adults, 13€ students and children 6–16, free for children 5 and under. April–June Thurs–Tues 10am–6pm; July–Aug daily 10am–6pm. Closed Nov–Mar, except for certain days during the Christmas holidays, generally the last 2 weeks of Dec.

## Where to Eat

The **Ecureuil** restaurant located in a wing of the château's outbuildings also offers casual dining.

**Les Charmilles** MODERN FRENCH    Located on the Diane parterre, facing the south facade of the château and the gardens, Les Charmilles' seasonal menu features light salads to more elaborate *plats du jour*. Take a break from the summer heat with the cool langoustine and salmon tartare before savoring the flambée tagliatelles with white truffle sauce or grilled suckling pig with Mojette beans. Finish off with pineapple soup with vanilla essence and mango sorbet. It is also open on the candlelight evenings, making it ideal for a romantic *dîner-à-deux* or glass of champagne under the stars before the fireworks begin.

Located in the Vaux Gardens 🕿 **01-60-66-95-66.** Reservations recommended for candlelight evenings; ask about their special packages for these evenings. Main courses 10€–18€; fixed-price menu 35€. MC, V. Daily 11:30am–6pm and 11pm on candlelight evenings. Closed Nov–Mar.

**La Table de Saint Just** TRADITIONAL FRENCH   You're bound to be charmed while dining at this elegant 17th-century farmhouse, whose oak beams and exposed stone walls were once associated with the nearby **Château de Vaux-le-Pénil.** Menu items change with the seasons but may include foie gras with figs served with spice bread, lobster with green apples, scallops roasted with truffles, and roasted rack of lamb with moussaka of fresh vegetables.

11 rue de Libération, Ferme Saint Just, Vaux-le-Pénil. www.restaurant-latablesaintjust.com. 🕿 **01-64-52-09-09.** Reservations recommended. Main courses 33€–48€; fixed-price menu 46€ and 90€. AE, MC, V. Tues–Sat noon–1:30pm and 7:30–9pm. Closed 3 weeks in Aug, 2 weeks at Christmas, and 1 week at Easter. From Vaux-le-Vicomte, drive 5.5km (3½ miles) west, following signs to Melun, then to Maincy, and then to Vaux-le-Pénil.

# DISNEYLAND PARIS ★

32km (20 miles) E of Paris

It might be an ocean away from the other Disney parks, but Disneyland Paris looks, tastes, and feels like the ones in California and Florida—except this fairytale castle belongs to *Belle au Bois Dormant* instead of Cinderella, and Mickey might greet you with a friendly *bonjour!* The controversy over the opening of Disneyland Paris in 1992 has long been forgotten, and the resort has surpassed the Eiffel Tower and the Louvre to become France's number-one tourist attraction—drawing a whopping 50 million visitors annually. Take a day to get your fill of thrills at the main park or two to enjoy the full Disney atmosphere and movie action at the **Walt Disney Studios.**

## Essentials

**GETTING THERE**   The RER A commuter **train** stops within walking distance of the park. Board the RER A in Paris at Charles-de-Gaulle–Etoile, Auber, Châtelet–Les Halles, Gare de Lyon, or Nation. Make sure you are taking the branch that terminates at Marne-la-Vallée/Chessy (as opposed to Boissy-St-Leger) and get off at the last stop. The trip takes about 40 minutes from central Paris. The round-trip fare is 14€. Trains run daily every 10 to 20 minutes from 5:30am to midnight.

    **Shuttle buses** connect Orly and Charles de Gaulle airports with each hotel in the resort. Buses depart the airports every 30 to 45 minutes. One-way transport to the park from either airport is 17€ for adults, 13€ for children 3 to 11.

    If you're **driving,** take A4 (direction "Metz/Nancy") east from Paris and get off at exit 14, DISNEYLAND PARIS. Parking begins at 15€ per day but is free if you stay at one of the park hotels. A series of moving sidewalks speeds up pedestrian transit from parking areas to the park entrance.

**VISITOR INFORMATION**    All the hotels we recommend offer general information on the theme park. For details and reservations at any of its hotels, contact the **Disneyland Paris Guest Relations Office,** located in City Hall on Main Street, U.S.A. (www.disneylandparis.com; ✆ **01-60-30-60-53** in English, or 08-25-30-60-30 in French). For information on Disneyland Paris and specific details on the many other attractions and monuments in the Ile de France and the rest of the country, contact the **Maison du Tourisme,** just next to the TGV train station and Disney Village (✆ **01-60-43-33-33**).

**ADMISSION**    Admission varies depending on the season. In peak season, a 1-day, one-park ticket costs 57€ for adults, 51€ for children 3 to 12, free for children 2 and under; a 2-day park-hopper ticket is 122€ for adults, 109€ for kids; and a 3-day park-hopper ticket is 151€ for adults, 130€ for kids. There are lots of advance special offers and package deals including park entry and hotel stay available online (www.disneylandparis.com). Peak season is from mid-June to mid-September, as well as Christmas and Easter weeks. Entrance to Disney Village is free, though there's usually a cover charge at the dance clubs.

**HOURS**    Hours vary throughout the year but most frequently are 10am to 7pm. Be warned that autumn and winter hours vary the most; it depends on the weather. It's good to phone ahead if you're contemplating a visit at this time.

# Seeing Disneyland

Situated on a 2,000-hectare (4,942-acre) site (about one-fifth the size of Paris) in the suburb of Marne-la-Vallée, the resort was designed as a total vacation destination: In one enormous unit, the park includes five "lands" of entertainment, a dozen hotels, a campground, an entertainment center, a 27-hole golf course, and dozens of restaurants, shows, and shops. **Disney Village** contains dance clubs, shops, restaurants (one of which stages a dinner spectacle based on the original *Buffalo Bill's Wild West Show*), bars for adults trying to escape their children, a French Government Tourist Office, and a post office.

Visitors stroll amid flower beds, trees, reflecting ponds, fountains, and a large artificial lake flanked with hotels. An army of smiling employees and Disney characters—many of whom are multilingual, including Buffalo Bill, Mickey and Minnie Mouse, and, of course, the French-born Caribbean pirate Jean Laffite— are on hand to greet the thousands of *enfants*. You'll see characters from *Aladdin, The Lion King, Pocahontas,* and *Toy Story.* As Disney continues to churn out animated blockbusters, look for the newest stars to appear in the theme park.

**Main Street, U.S.A.,** abounds with horse-drawn carriages and barbershop quartets. Steam-powered railway cars embark from the Main Street Station for a trip through a Grand

 **FASTPASS Those Long Lines**

Disneyland Paris has instituted a program that's done well at the other parks. With the **FASTPASS** system, visitors to the various rides reserve a 1-hour time block. Within that block, the waiting is usually no more than 8 minutes.

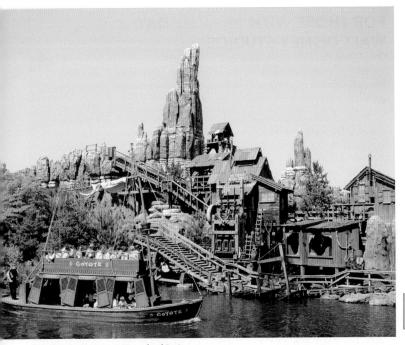

Catastrophe Canyon at Disneyland Paris.

Canyon diorama to **Frontierland,** with its paddle-wheel steamers reminiscent of Mark Twain's Mississippi River. Other attractions are the **Big Thunder Mountain** roller coaster and the ghosts and ghouls of **Phantom Manor.**

The park's steam trains chug past **Adventureland**—with its swashbuckling **Pirates of the Caribbean,** stomach-churning **Indiana Jones and the Temple of Doom,** and the kinder, gentler **Aladdin's Magic Carpet**—to **Fantasyland.** Here you'll find the **Sleeping Beauty's Castle,** whose pinnacles and turrets are an idealized (and spectacular) interpretation of French châteaux. In its shadow are Europeanized versions of *Blanche Neige et les Sept Nains* (Snow White and the Seven Dwarfs), Peter Pan, Dumbo, Alice (from Wonderland), the Mad Hatter's Teacups, and Sir Lancelot's Magic Carousel. Fairy tale dreams come true for young visitors at the recently opened **Princess Pavilion**, featuring Cinderella, Aurora, Jasmine, and your other favorite Disney princesses.

Visions of the future are in **Discoveryland,** where tributes to invention and imagination draw from the works of Jules Verne, H. G. Wells, and the *Star Wars* series. Favorites here include hyperfast **Space Mountain** and **Buzz Lightyear's Lazer Blast.**

## Where to Eat

Disneyland Paris offers a gamut of cuisine in more than 45 restaurants and snack bars. You can live on burgers and fries, or you can experiment at the following upscale restaurants.

# FOR THOSE WITH another DAY: WALT DISNEY STUDIOS

You don't need to go all the way to Hollywood to experience movie magic—**Walt Disney Studios** takes guests on a behind-the-scenes interactive discovery of film, animation, and television through four thematic Studio Lots.

The main entrance to the studios, called the **Front Lot,** consists of Disney Studio 1, an elaborate sound stage complete with film props, shops, and restaurants. The **Toon Studio** reveals the trade secrets of Disney animators; here families can have gigantic fun in the oversized **Toy Story Playland,** speed around on the **RC Racer** or soar through the skies on the **Toy Soldiers Parachute Drop.** The **Production Courtyard** lets guests take a look behind the scenes of film and TV production; bigger and braver kids enter the spooky **Hollywood Tower Hotel** at their own risk. The abandoned hotel's rickety elevator sends you flying 13 floors to the depths of the **Twilight Zone Tower of Terror.** Finally, the **Back Lot** is home to special effects and stunt workshops. A live stunt show features cars, motorbikes, and jet skis.

This ode to Hollywood and the films it produced since the end of its "golden age" has a roller coaster, the **Rock 'n' Roller Coaster,** featuring the music of Aerosmith, which combines rock memorabilia with high-speed scary twists and turns.

**California Grill** ★★ ☺ CALIFORNIAN/FRENCH   The resort's showcase restaurant serves cuisine that's the equivalent of the fare at a one-Michelin-star restaurant. East meets west in their appetizers such as the crispy *mille-feuille* of crab and fresh herbs or pan-fried skate wing with lemon flavored butter and capers. Another winning selection is the roasted pigeon with cinnamon juice, served with baby squash, tomatoes and glazed potatoes. Many items are specifically for children. If you want a quiet, mostly adult venue, go here as late as your hunger pangs will allow; the restaurant is open only for dinner.

In the Disneyland Hotel. ✆ **01-60-45-65-76.** Reservations required. Fixed-price menu 57€–79€; children's menu 21€. AE, DC, MC, V. Daily 6:30pm–10:30pm.

**Inventions** ✦ INTERNATIONAL   This may be the only buffet restaurant in Europe where animated characters from the Disney films go table-hopping. With views over a park, the restaurant contains four enormous buffet tables. Don't expect *grande cuisine*—that's the domain of the more upscale California Grill (see above), in the same hotel; however, the quality is much better than your average buffet, with a mix of French and international delicacies such as chilled asparagus, Italian prosciutto, or even escargot and bouillabaisse, plus lots of kid-friendly dishes from spaghetti with meatballs to Buzz Lightyear éclairs.

In the Disneyland Hotel. ✆ **01-60-45-65-83.** Buffet 52€ adults, 26€ children 7–11, 20€ children 3–6. Fixed-price lunch menu 36€ adults, 18€ children 6–11, 16€ children 3–6. Brunch (Sun only) 58€ adults, 27€ children. AE, DC, MC, V. Daily 12:30–3pm and 6–10:30pm.

## Disneyland Nightlife

The premier theatrical venue is **Le Legende de Buffalo Bill,** in Disney Village (✆ **01-60-45-71-00**). The twice-per-night stampede of entertainment recalls the show that once traveled the West with Buffalo Bill and Annie Oakley. You'll dine at tables arranged amphitheater style around a rink where sharpshooters, runaway stagecoaches, and dozens of horses and Indians ride fast and perform alarmingly realistic acrobatics. A Texas-style barbecue, served in an assembly line by waiters in 10-gallon hats, is part of the experience. Shows start at 6:30 and 9:30pm; the cost (dinner included) is 59€ to 71€ for adults and 45€ to 57€ for children 3 to 11.

# Where to Stay

You can easily make Disney a day trip from Paris—the transportation links are excellent—or you can spend a night . . . or two. Most overnight guests take a package that includes park entry, breakfast, and a couple of nights in a hotel. The per-night hotel prices listed below can range wildly, depending on the package you book, the number of days you stay, the time of year, and so on. Your best bet is to study the website or call the reservations service shared by the resort's seven theme hotels. In North America, call ✆ **407/W-DISNEY** (934-7639). In France, contact the **Central Reservations Office,** Euro Disney Resort, S.C.A., B.P. 105, F-77777 Marne-la-Vallée Cedex 4 (www.disneylandparis.com; ✆ **08-25-30-60-30**).

## VERY EXPENSIVE

**Disneyland Hotel** ★★   At the park entrance, this flagship four-story hotel has a Victorian facade, with red-tile turrets and jutting balconies. The spacious guest rooms are plushly furnished but evoke the image of Disney, with cartoon depictions and candy-stripe decor. The beds are king-size, double, or twin; in some rooms, armchairs convert to beds. Accommodations in the rear overlook Sleeping Beauty's Castle and Big Thunder Mountain. Some less desirable units open onto a parking lot. The exclusive Castle Club on the third floor pampers guests with a separate elevator, free newspapers, all-day beverages, and access to a well-equipped private lounge.

Disneyland Paris, B.P. 111, F-77777 Marne-la-Vallée Cedex 4. www.disneylandparis.com. ✆ **01-60-45-65-89.** Fax 01-60-45-65-33. 495 units. 530€–860€ double; from 775€ suite. AE, DC, MC, V. **Amenities:** 2 restaurants; bar; cafe; babysitting; health club w/indoor pool; room service; sauna; spa. *In room:* A/C, TV, hair dryer, Internet (5€ per 15 min.), minibar.

## EXPENSIVE

**Newport Bay Club** ★★   The Disney lake might not be the Atlantic, but with its central cupola, balconies, awnings, and pergolas, The Newport Bay mirrors a harborfront New England hotel (ca. 1900). The yacht club atmosphere carries over to the nautically decorated blue and cream rooms, arranged in various shapes and sizes. Try to book a corner unit, which is the most spacious, in one of these you'll hardly realize you are staying in the biggest hotel in France.

Disneyland Paris, B.P. 105, F-77777 Marne-la-Vallée Cedex 4. www.disneylandparis.com. ✆ **01-60-45-55-00.** Fax 01-60-45-55-33. 1,093 units. 245€–460€ double; from 370€ suite. AE, DC, MC, V. **Amenities:** 2 restaurants; bar; health club; indoor and outdoor pools; room service; sauna. *In room:* A/C, TV, minibar, Wi-Fi (15€ per day).

## MODERATE

**Hotel Cheyenne/Hotel Santa Fe** ☺   Head to the far West for the best hotel bargains at the resort. These two Old West–style lodgings stand side-by-side near a re-creation of Texas's Rio Grande. The Cheyenne consists of 14 two-story buildings along Desperado Street; the desert-themed Santa Fe encompasses four "nature trails" winding among 42 adobe-style pueblos. The Cheyenne is a favorite among families, offering a double bed and bunk beds. Children have an array of activities, including a play area in a log cabin with a lookout tower and a section where you can explore the "ruins" of an ancient Anasazi village. The only disadvantage, according to some parents, is the absence of a pool.

More recently constructed, but charging the same prices, is the nearby **Kyriad Hotel,** a chain hotel designed for families that evokes the aesthetics and layout of a French country inn. Whenever the Cheyenne and the Santa Fe are full, Disney usually directs the overflow to the Kyriad.

Disneyland Paris, B.P. 115, F-77777 Marne-la-Vallée Cedex 4. www.disneylandparis.com. ✆ **01-60-45-63-12** (Cheyenne) or 01-60-45-79-22 (Santa Fe). Fax 01-60-45-62-33 (Cheyenne) or 01-60-45-78-33 (Santa Fe). 2,000 units. Hotel Cheyenne 140€–310€ double; Hotel Santa Fe 120€–274€ double. AE, DC, MC, V. **Amenities:** Restaurant; bar; Internet (15€ per 100 min.). *In room:* A/C, TV.

# GIVERNY: IN THE FOOTSTEPS OF MONET

81km (50 miles) NW of Paris

When artist Claude Monet moved to Giverny in 1883, looking for some peace and quiet, little did he know he would forever change the fate of this sleepy Norman village. Soon after his arrival, the town was invaded by eager young artists who'd come from all over the world in search of the Impressionist master. Today, artists and art lovers alike still trek out to Giverny to tour his restored home and gardens, and to be inspired themselves. Budget 2 hours to explore the museum and gardens at Giverny or a full day to take your time, have a nice lunch then wander the village.

## Essentials

**GETTING THERE**  Take the **train** from Paris's Gare St-Lazare to the Vernon station (45-min. ride; 13€ each way). From Vernon, you can take either the **shuttle bus** (15-min. ride, timed to leave about 5 or 10 min. after the train arrives; 2€ each way), the **local bus** no. 240 (timed to leave about 15 min. after the train arrives; 2€ each way), or a **taxi** for the remaining 7km (4¼ miles) to Giverny. If you are feeling plucky, you can **walk** or **bicycle** to Giverny along a pretty bike path (bike rental at the Vernon train station). If you're **driving,** take the A14 autoroute, merging into the A13 toward Rouen. Take exit 14 at Vernon/Bonnières, and then follow the signs to Bonnières and cross the Seine to Bennecourt. From here, a

### Giverny's Other Sites

After you've explored the Claude Monet Foundation, take a stroll along the main street up the cemetery to visit the Monet family tomb. The **Musée des Impressionismes** (99 rue Claude Monet; www.musee desimpressionnismesgiverny.com; ✆ **02-32-51-94-65**), the former American museum, also has notable temporary exhibits that occasionally feature some Monet works.

direct road with signs leads to Giverny. Expect it to take about an hour; try to avoid weekends.

## Show Me the Monet

**Claude Monet Foundation** ★★★ HISTORIC HOME/GARDEN    Monet is certainly one of France's most renowned artists. One of the founders of Impressionism, it was his painting titled *Impression, Sunrise* (at the **Musée Marmottan**) that gave the movement its name. A brilliant innovator, he excelled at presenting the effects of light at different times of the day. His paintings of the Rouen cathedral and of water lilies are just a few of his masterpieces.

After settling in Giverny, Monet barely left, preferring to paint in his peaceful gardens. However, many of his friends came to visit him here at *Le Pressoir,* including Clemenceau, Cézanne, Rodin, Renoir, Degas, and Sisley. When Monet died in 1926, his son, Michel, inherited the house but left it abandoned. The gardens became almost a jungle, inhabited by river rats. In 1966, Michel died and left house and gardens to the Académie des Beaux-Arts. It wasn't until 1977 that Gerald van der Kemp, who restored Versailles, decided to work on Giverny.

Unfortunately, you won't find any original Monet paintings here; however, his house and famous gardens are open to the public. The house contains Monet's collection of 18th- and 19th-century Japanese prints, as well as antique (though not original) furnishings. You can stroll the garden and view the thousands of flowers, including the *nymphéas.* The Japanese bridge, hung with wisteria, leads to a setting of weeping willows and rhododendrons. Monet's studio barge was installed on the pond.

84 rue Claude-Monet, Giverny 27620. www.fondation-monet.com. ✆ **02-32-51-28-21.** Admission 9€ adults, 5€ students and children 7–12, free for children 6 and under. Daily 9:30am–6pm. Closed Nov–Mar.

**Claude Monet Foundation.**

## Where to Eat

**Baudy** FRENCH    While the hotel Baudy might be overrun with tourists, it's still well worth dining at this legendary *auberge* (inn), especially for true art fans. In Monet's time, it was an *epicerie-buvette* (casual hangout) run by the painter's friends Angelina and Gaston Baudy. During the town's 19th-century heyday, the American painters used the pink villa as their lodging. Classic French standards are offered, such as chicken liver terrine with Armagnac liquor, the Baudy omelet with *confit de canard* and sautéed potatoes, or deluxe "wine merchant" *faux filet*.

81 rue Claude-Monet. www.restaurantbaudy.com. ✆ **02-32-21-10-03.** Reservations recommended. Main courses 14€–25€; fixed-price menu 24€. MC, V. Daily 10am–9:30pm. Closed Nov–Mar.

**L'Esquisse Gourmande** FRENCH    Located at the far end of town near the church, this is a refreshing alternative to the tourist traps near le Fondation Monet. This combined tea salon and restaurant is perfect for a relaxing summer lunch. The seasonal menu is inspired by regional specialties and the apple reigns. Start with a kir-normand, local cider with crème de cassis, followed by the Camembert crumble, one of their creative salads, or daily specials such as lamb brochettes or supreme of quail with caramelized baby vegetables and apples.

73 bis rue Claude-Monet. www.lesquissegourmande.fr. ✆ **02-32-51-86-95.** Main courses 8€–20€. AE, MC, V. Wed–Sun noon–2pm; Tues–Sat 7:30–10pm.

# 5

# AUVERS-SUR-OISE: AN AUDE TO VAN GOGH

30km (18 miles) N of Paris

"Here we are far from Paris, far enough for it to be the real country . . . Auvers is truly beautiful," was how post-Impressionist master Vincent van Gogh described scenic Auvers-sur-Oise. While the town itself has not changed much since the artist's brief stay in 1890, his 70-day sojourn here and his tragic death immortalized this country nook both on canvas and in history. Auvers can be combined with Giverny if traveling by car.

## Essentials

**GETTING THERE**    There is a direct train to Auvers-sur-Oise every Saturday, Sunday, and public holidays April to October departing from Gare du Nord around 10am and a direct return train to Paris at 6pm (approx. 35 min. each way). Alternatively, take a suburban train at Saint-Lazare or Gare du Nord toward Pontoise. Change at St-Ouen L'Aumone (be careful, it's the second St-Ouen stop, not the first), to the Persan Beaumont Creil line for the train to Auvers-sur-Oise (approx. 1 hr. 15 min.) 11€ round-trip. **BY CAR** take the A15 highway direction Cergy-Pontoise. After 5km (3 miles) take the A115, in the direction of Amiens-Beauvais. Exit at Méry-Auvers-sur-Oise, follow signs to "Maison de Van Gogh" (30 min.).

**VISITOR INFORMATION**    **THE Office du Tourisme** is located in the Manoir des Colombières, rue de la Sansonne, across from the entrance to the Maison de Van Gogh (www.lavalleedeloise.com; ✆ **01-30-36-10-06**).

Auberge Ravoux (Maison de Van Gogh).

## Exploring Auvers

**Auberge Ravoux** MUSEUM/HISTORIC BUILDING   An inn and restaurant since 1876, l'Auberge Ravoux is often referred to as the Maison de van Gogh, as this the artist lodged here in a tiny 7 sq. m (75 sq. ft.) room for 3.5 francs a day. Vincent had been encouraged to come to Auvers by fellow painter **Paul Cezanne** to be treated of his friend **Dr. Gachet**. From the moment he arrive at the end of May 1890, Dr. Gachet pushed van Gogh to paint to help overcome his psychological problems. And paint he did, with frenetic energy, creating virtually a painting a day. The room at the Auberge also acted as his studio, and after a day of painting in the village he would stack his works in his room or outside on the landing.

On July 27, 1890, the artist headed out to the fields armed with his brushes, easel, and apparently a pistol. At the end of the day, he came crawling back to the Auberge with a fatal gunshot wound to the chest. He lay dying for almost 2 days in his bed, with Theo by his side. The Auberge still functions as a restaurant, which distinguishes itself with its unique, historically accurate approach to cuisine.

52 rue du Général de Gaulle. www.maisondevangogh.fr. ✆ **01-30-36-60-63.** Admission 6€ adults, 4€ ages 12–17 and under, free for children 11 and under. Mar to Oct Wed–Sun 10am–6pm. Closed Nov to Feb.

After visiting the Auberge, amble along the *Chemin des Peintres* to visit the various intriguing sights around Auvers (all well indicated with signposts). Hike up the gentle hill to visit the **Notre-Dame church,** which features in one of van Gogh's tableaux (now at the Musée d'Orsay). A little further up the hill is the **Auvers Cemetery,** the final resting place of both Vincent and Theo, who died 6 months after Vincent. You'll find their ivy-covered graves side-by-side against the far left cemetery wall.

If you stay the whole day there are various other museums in town including two in honor of painter Charles Daubigny; the **Manoir des Colombières,** rue de la Sansonne (www.musee-daubigny.com; ✆ **01-30-36-80-20**), and his home and studio the **Atelier de Daubigny**, 61 rue Daubigny (www.atelier-daubigny.com; ✆ **01-30-36-60-60**). Serious van Gogh should visit **La Maison du Docteur Gachet** (Dr. Gachet's home), 78 rue du Docteur Gachet (✆ **01-30-36-81-27**) and those looking for a little fun to end their time in Auvers can stop in at the **Absinthe Museum,** 44 rue Alphonse Callé (www.musee-absinthe.com; ✆ **01-30-36-83-26**), where you'll learn about the strong liquor enjoyed by the Impressionist artists. The museums of Auvers are only open from spring to late autumn.

## Where to Eat

In addition to the suggestion below, the restaurant of the Auberge Ravoux is an excellent choice.

**Chemin des Peintres** FRENCH    Various restaurants in Auvers are returning to authentic gastronomic philosophies and recipes, and the Chemin des Peintres is among the best. Set in a restored 19th-century barn, it serves tasty traditional dishes with a dash of creativity using local organic and farm products. The atmosphere is friendly and relaxed, fitting its country locale. Try the warm Chauvy goat-cheese salads, local Commency rabbit seasoned with cumin and ginger, and free-range chicken with a red wine reduction.

3 bis rue de Paris. ✆ **01-30-36-14-15.** Main courses 12€–24€; fixed-price menu 18€–24€. MC, V. Mon–Fri 11am–4pm; Sat 11am–11pm; Sun 11am–7pm.

# CHANTILLY: A DAY AT THE RACES ★★★

42km (26 miles) N of Paris; 50km (31 miles) SE of Beauvais

This is a resort town for Parisians who want a quick weekend getaway. Known for its frothy whipped cream and its black lace, it is also home to one of the loveliest chateaux near Paris and a world-class racetrack.

Two of the great French horse races, **Le Prix du Jockey Club** and the **Prix Diane,** take place at the Hippodrome on the first and second Sundays of June, respectively. Thoroughbreds from as far away as Kentucky and Brunei, as well as entrants sponsored by old and new European money, compete in a very civil format that's broadcast throughout France.

## Essentials

**GETTING THERE**    **Trains** depart frequently for Chantilly from Gare du Nord in Paris. The ride takes about 30 minutes; the round-trip cost is 15.60€. On race days, free shuttle buses take fans from the Chantilly station to the

Château de Chantilly.

track. Alternatively, RER line D will get you from Métro stop Châtelet–Les Halles to Chantilly in about 45 minutes.

**VISITOR INFORMATION** The **Office Tourisme** is at 60 av. du Maréchal-Joffre (www.chantilly-tourisme.com; ☎ **03-44-67-37-37**).

## Seeing the Château & Museums

**Château de Chantilly/Musée Condé ★★★** CASTLE/MUSEUM/GARDEN Once the seat of the grand Condé, head of the Bourbon-Condé dynasty, this château and the museum within it are on an artificial lake and surrounded by meticulous French gardens. Approach on the same forested drive that Louis XIV rode for a banquet prepared by his chef, Vatel. (One day when the fish didn't arrive on time, Vatel committed suicide.)

The château, commissioned by the once powerful Montmorency family, was built by Jean Bullet around 1560. It is an excellent example of French Renaissance architecture, with gables and towers. Inherited by the Condé family in 1632, they tasked Le Nôtre with designing its Versailles-esque gardens. A forest once filled with stag and boar skirts it.

In 1875, the château's owner, the duc d'Aumale, embarked on a campaign to rebuild parts of the château. Upon his death, he bequeathed the park and palace to the Institut de France, along with his art collection and library. The château houses one of the best art collections in France outside the Louvre with works by Botticelli, Poussin, Watteau, Rubens, Memling, Van Dyck, Ingres, Delacroix, Corot, and Vernet. Highlights include Raphael's *Madonna of Lorette, Virgin of the House d'Orléans,* and *Three Graces* (sometimes called the *Three Ages of Woman*). A series of about 40 miniatures represents the foremost French painter of the

235

15th century, Jean Fouquet. A copy of the rose diamond that received worldwide attention when it was stolen in 1926 is occasionally on display in the jewel collection. Don't miss the **library**, lined with 30,000 books including one of the most celebrated Condé acquisitions, the Limbourg brothers' *Les Très Riches Heures du Duc de Berry,* a 15th-century illuminated manuscript (not always on view). A stroll through the **Grands** and **Petits Appartements**, with sumptuous period furnishings, provides a peak into the private lives of the duke and duchess. The **stables** (see below), a hallmark of French 18th-century architecture, were constructed to house 240 horses, with adjacent kennels for 500 hounds. If you have time, take a walk in the **gardens**. A hamlet of rustic cottages, similar to the one built by Marie Antoinette at Versailles and the Maison de Sylvie, a graceful building constructed in 1604 and rebuilt by Maria-Felice Orsini, is in the park.

You can also ride a motorized "train" (touristy and loaded with children) through the park (5€ for adults, 3€ for children), or take a boat ride on the château's ornamental lake (12€ per hour for up to four people).

Chantilly. www.chateaudechantilly.com. ✆ **03-44-62-62-62.** Admission to the château, museum, and gardens 13€ adults, free for children 17 and under accompanied by an adult, gardens only 6€ adults, free for children 17 and under. Nov–Mar Wed–Mon 10:30am–5pm (park until 6pm); Apr–Oct Wed–Mon 10am–6pm (park until 8pm).

**Les Grandes Ecuries/Musée Vivant du Cheval** ★★ MUSEUM/RACE-COURSE ☺ This museum occupies the restored Grandes Ecuries, the stables built between 1719 and 1735 for Louis-Henri, prince de Bourbon and prince de Condé, who occupied the château. Besides being fond of horses, he believed in reincarnation and expected to come back as a horse in his next life, so he built stables fit for a king.

The stables and an adjoining kennel fell into ruin, but they've been restored as a museum of the living horse, with thoroughbreds housed alongside old breeds of draft horses, Arabs and Hispano-Arabs, and farm horses. Exhibits trace the horse's association with humans and include a blacksmith shop and displays of saddles, equipment for the care of horses, and horse-race memorabilia.

At press time, the museum was undergoing more restorations and is scheduled to reopen in 2014. Meanwhile, parts of the stables are open and continue to present equestrian demonstrations daily and more elaborate thematic shows several times a week and during the holiday season; see the website for exact hours and prices.

Chantilly. www.museevivantducheval.fr ✆ **03-44-27-31-80.** Equestrian demonstrations Wed–Mon 11am and/or 2pm. Admission 11€–21€ Special shows throughout the year Admission 18€–32€, special ticket packages château/gardens/Grandes Ecuries available.

# Where to Eat

In addition to the below, the restaurant at the castle is a fine lunch option and the **Château de la Tour** (see next page) is open to the public for lunch and dinner.

**Carmontelle** ★★ MODERN FRENCH 🍴 A short drive from the château is the area's most refined restaurant. Its bright and spacious dining room overlooks Chantilly's coveted golf course. Chef Alain Montigny has earned a Michelin star with his delicious and inventive culinary creations. His seasonal menu can feature goose foie gras with black truffle and meringue or French sweetbreads with limoncello juice and "Isigny" cream. Desserts are divine with creative names such as the "Carmelized of the Sun" with apples, chestnuts, dried fruit, and cinnamon foam.

In the Hotel Dolce Chantilly, route d'Apremont, Vineuil-Saint-Firmin. www.dolce-chantilly-hotel. com. $\textcircled{C}$ **03-44-58-47-57.** Reservations required. Lunch menu 50€, dinner menus including wine 62€–120€. AE, DC, MC, V. Daily noon–2pm and 7–9:30pm.

**La Ferme de Condé** TRADITIONAL FRENCH   Some of the best traditional food in Chantilly is served in this 100-year-old stone-sided former Anglican church. It's on the periphery of town, about 1.6km (1 mile) north of the château. Antique farm implements, racks of wine bottles, and barrels give the space a cozy feel. The cuisine is old-fashioned, with variations based on seasonal ingredients and the chef's inspiration. Look for fresh oysters from Brittany or homemade foie gras, followed by duck *magret* with honey and spices, or succulent sweetbreads with morels.

42 av. du Maréchal-Joffre. www.lafermedeconde.fr. $\textcircled{C}$ **03-44-57-32-31**. Reservations recommended. Main courses 15€–44€; fixed-price menus 25€–28€. AE, DC, MC, V. Daily noon–2pm and 7–10:30pm.

## Where to Stay

**Château de la Tour ★★**   A wealthy Parisian banking family built this elegant turn-of-the-20th-century château with a 4.8-hectare (12-acre) park as a weekend getaway. During World War II, it was the home of the German l'Etat Major, and in 1946, it became a luxury hotel. The likes of Edith Piaf, Tino Rossi, and Jean Gabin met and mingled in the restaurant. In 1990, it gained a new wing; guests can choose rooms with a modern flavor or a more traditional ambience. All units are large and feature hardwood floors, high ceilings, and first-class furnishings, and three-quarters of the units are air-conditioned.

Chemin de la Chaussée, Gouvieux 60270. www.lechateaudelatour.fr. $\textcircled{C}$ **03-44-62-38-38.** Fax 03-44-57-31-97. 41 units. 160€–190€ double; 190€–265€ suite. AE, DC, MC, V. Free parking. **Amenities:** Restaurant; bar; babysitting; free bikes; outdoor pool; room service; tennis court. *In room:* A/C (in 31 rooms), TV, hair dryer, minibar, free Wi-Fi.

# SENLIS ★★

52km (32 miles) S of Paris; 100km (62 miles) S of Amiens

Sleepy Senlis, which some Parisians treat as a suburb, is a quiet township surrounded by forests. Its memories are many and regal. Hugh Capet, founder of the Capetian dynasty that fathered all the Louises, was elected king here in 987. The town belonged to his royal descendants through the centuries until the monarchy finally ended in 1848. You can tie a visit to this town with a trek to nearby Chantilly (see p. 234). Today the core of Vieux Senlis is a medieval bonanza that attracts visitors from all over the world. Budget 2 hours to see Senlis.

## Essentials

**GETTING THERE**   From Paris's Gare du Nord, you can take a **train** to Chantilly (see above), and from the station take the SNCF **bus** (marked SENLIS), which has a schedule that coincides with the arrival of trains from Paris. You can also take the TER regional **train** from Gare du Nord to Creil and transfer to the SNCF bus to Senlis. The round-trip bus and train fare is 20€ to 25€, depending on the route. If you visit Chantilly in the morning, you can take the bus to Senlis directly from a stop near the château. Total travel time from downtown Paris to Senlis should be around an hour but can be longer, depending on connections; visit the SNCF website (www.voyages-sncf.com) for schedules. If you're **driving,** take the Paris–Lille motorway (A1) for 52km (32 miles).

**VISITOR INFORMATION** The **Office de Tourisme** is on place parvis Notre-Dame (www.senlis-tourisme.fr; ✆ **03-44-53-06-40).**

Rue du Chat-Harét, Senlis.

# Seeing the Sights

Take a stroll around town to admire the medieval streets loaded with antique masonry and evocative doorways. Leaving the cathedral or the museum complex, take rue de Villevert to rue du Chat-Harét, one of the most picturesque streets, granting a view over the ruined château and the Gallo-Roman foundations. Stay on it as it changes names and winds its way left around to the main shopping street, **rue de l'Apport à Pain,** bustling with nice shops and a few *salons de thé,* such as **Le Comptoir** (2, impasse de la Chaufferette; www.lecomptoir-senlis.fr; ✆ **03-44-60-62-02**). Amble off the main street to find charming streets such as on the **rue des Cordeliers,** the site of a (since demolished) medieval convent, and nos. 14 and 10 on that street are particularly beautiful and old, but neither is open to the public.

**Cathédrale Notre-Dame de Senlis** ★★ CATHEDRAL   This cathedral has a 13th-century spire that rises 78m (256 ft.) and dominates the countryside. The severe western facade contrasts with the Flamboyant Gothic southern portal. A fire swept the structure in 1504, and much rebuilding followed. Damaged during the Revolution, the church, whose origins date from 1153, was restored in the 19th century. Before you enter, walk around to the western porch to see the sculptures. Depicted in stone is a calendar of the seasons, along with scenes showing the ascension of the Virgin. The builders of the main portal imitated the work at Chartres. In the forecourt are memorials to Joan of Arc and Marshal Foch.

3 place Notre-Dame. ✆ **03-44-53-01-59.** Free admission. Daily 8:30am–7pm.

**Musée d'Art et d'Archéologie** MUSEUM   At press time, this museum was getting a thorough overhaul and was scheduled to reopen in at an undetermined date in 2012. Housed in a former Episcopal palace, the museum contains a fine collection of Gallo-Roman artifacts from the region, as well as rare sculptures and church art from the Middle Ages. The collection also features paintings, some by local artists working in an untrained style that art historians refer to as "naive," executed between the 17th and 20th century.

Place du Parvis. www.musees-senlis.fr. (𝄢 **03-44-32-00-83.** Admission 2€ adults, 1€ students and children 16–18, free for children 15 and under. Mon and Thurs–Fri 10am–noon and 2–6pm; Wed 2–6pm; Sat–Sun 11am–1pm and 2–6pm.

**Parc du Château Royal and Musées de la Vénerie (Hunting Museum) et des Spahis** ★ HISTORIC SITE/MUSEUM Across from the cathedral stands this curious archaeological ruin. Its stones have more royal associations than virtually anywhere else in France. The most impressive aspect remaining today is a massive Gallo-Roman wall, in some places more than 6m (20 ft.) tall. It encircles an area of about 6 hectares (15 acres), some of them occupied by parts of medieval Senlis. Of the wall's 28 original watchtowers, 16 remain. Within the circumference, the best-preserved fortification of its kind in France, are the ruins of a château that was occupied, or at least visited, by virtually every monarch of France from Hughes Capet (in the 10th c.) to Henri IV (late Renaissance). Abandoned by the monarchs around 1600, the château was demolished after the French Revolution. Today you can wander freely among the ruins, imagining the grandeur of life as it used to be.

The complex's highlight, in the verdant park that surrounds the ruin, is the **Prieuré St-Mauritius,** a monastery that not only honors a saint, but also was founded by one, Louis IX. It houses the **Musée de la Vénerie (Hunting Museum),** where you'll see hunting-related works of art from the 15th century to the present. Exhibits include arms, horns, trophies, drawings, engravings, and old hunting suits and costumes, all of which evoke the passion and pageantry that used to surround royal hunting expeditions. You can visit the museum only as part of a 1-hour tour (in French); tours begin every hour on the hour.

In another building lies the **Musée des Spahis,** a small museum dedicated to the North African cavalry troops of the French army. The Spahi troops were first recruited from Algeria, Tunisia, and Morocco in 1831, when those countries were still French colonies, and served in both World Wars. A unit was posted in Senlis for 30 years in this former house, which now displays trumpets, banners, and the striking uniforms of this unique cavalry division.

Senlis. www.musees-senlis.fr. (𝄢 **03-44-32-00-81.** Free admission to the park. Admission to the Hunting and Spahi Museums, including guided tour, 2€ adults, 1€ adults over 60 and students under 25, free under 16. Mon and Thurs–Fri 10am–noon and 2–6pm; Wed 2–6pm; Sat–Sun 11am–1pm and 2–6pm.

# Where to Eat & Stay

**Hostellerie de la Porte Bellon** In a town of lackluster inns, this is a good oasis for the night. The stately but relatively inexpensive hotel was built as a convent 300 years ago and later functioned as a coaching inn. A short walk east of Senlis's historic core, it has three floors of big-windowed guest rooms and a facade dotted with old-fashioned shutters and window boxes filled with pansies and geraniums. The recently renovated rooms are each decorated differently with hints of traditional French style and colorful modern touches. The hotel boasts a noteworthy **gastronomic restaurant** and an impressive wine cellar fit for Senlis's royal roots.

51 rue Bellon, Senlis 60300. www.portebellon.fr. ☏ **03-44-53-03-05.** Fax 03-44-53-29-94. 17 units. 80€–93€ double; 245€ 3-bedroom suite. AE, MC, V. Closed 1st 2 weeks of Jan. **Amenities:** Restaurant; bar. *In room:* TV, free Wi-Fi.

**Le Scaramouche** FRENCH    The best restaurant in Senlis is facing its best monument—the cathedral. A family affair, Mr. and Mrs. Noiret and their son work their magic in the kitchen. The dining room is homey and the service exceptional though discrete. Dishes are sophisticated and the seasonally inspired menu has items such as baked goat cheese cocotte served with rocket sorbet, parmentier of duck confit, duo of monkfish and gambas with risotto, and saddle of hare which might have come from the town's surrounding forests. In summer, you can dine on the lovely terrace while admiring the soaring cathedral.

4 place Notre Dame. www.le-scaramouche.fr. ☏ **03-44-53-01-26.** Reservations recommended Fri–Sat. Main courses 22€–42€; fixed-price menu 32€ and 42€. AE, MC, V. Thurs–Mon 12:15–2pm; 7–10:30pm. Closed last 2 weeks in Aug.

# COMPIEGNE ★★★

81km (50 miles) N of Paris

A visit to this Oise River valley town can be combined with an excursion to Senlis (see above), some 32km (20 miles) away. Like Senlis, this town north of Paris has a rich though mixed history. Most come to celebrate the town's royal heritage. Graced with two royal castles in its environs, there are several centuries' worth of history to visit, not to mention the 14,160-hectare (34,975-acre) forest of Compiègne and the **Wagon de l'Armistice**, a must for war history buffs.

## Essentials

**GETTING THERE    Trains** run frequently from the Gare du Nord in Paris. The ride takes 40 to 60 minutes. The station is across the river from the town center. A round-trip ticket costs 28€. However, to see some of the best sites you need a car. **Driving,** take the Paris–Lille motorway (A1 or the less convenient E15) for 81km (50 miles).

**VISITOR INFORMATION    The Office de Tourisme** is located on the place de l'Hôtel-de-Ville (www.compiegne-tourisme.fr; ☏ **03-44-40-01-00**).

## Seeing the Sights

An imposing statue of **Joan of Arc,** who was taken prisoner at Compiègne by the Burgundians on May 23, 1430, stands in the town square.

**Château de Pierrefonds ★★ ☺** CASTLE    One of the Compiègne forest's most evocative medieval buildings lies 12km (7½ miles) north of the town. (To reach it from the center, follow signs to Soissons.) Originally built in the 1100s as a château-fortress, it was partially destroyed in the 17th century and was in ruins when it was bought by Napoleon for a pittance. In 1857, his nephew, Napoleon III, asked Viollet-Le-Duc, monument restorer par excellence, to not only fix it up, but rebuild it. The result is not entirely authentic, but impressive. Surrounded by a moat, it looks feudal, with rounded towers capped by funnel-shaped pointed roofs. Artifacts from the Middle Ages are displayed inside. Save time for a stroll through the tiny village of Pierrefonds at the base of the château. Here, half-timbered houses recall the château's medieval heyday.

**Château de Compiegne.**

Rue Viollet-Le-Duc in the Forêt de Compiègne. www.pierrefonds.monuments-nationaux.fr.
*C* **03-44-42-72-72.** Admission 7€ adults, 4.50€ students 18–25, free for ages 17 and under.
May–Aug daily 9:30am–6pm; Sept–Apr Tues–Sun 10am–1pm and 2–5:30pm.

### Musée de la Figurine Historique (Museum of Historical Figurines) ★

MUSEUM   Housed in one of Compiègne's finest monuments, the Flamboyant
Gothic Hôtel de Ville, built from 1499 to 1503, this museum showcases a collection of about 100,000 tin soldiers, from a Louis XIV trumpeter to a World War II
soldier. The Battle of Waterloo, staged in miniature on a landscape with thousands of figurines, is depicted in all its gore.

28 place de l'Hôtel-de-Ville. www.musee-figurine.fr. *C* **03-44-40-72-55.** Admission 3€ adults,
1.50€ students and children 7–18, free for ages 5 and under. Tues–Sat 9am–noon; Tues–Sun
2–6pm (until 5pm Nov–Feb).

### Musée National du Château de Compiègne ★★★ CASTLE/MUSEUM

In its heyday, Compiègne attracted royalty and two Bonaparte emperors. But
this wasn't always a place of pageantry. Louis XIV once said: "In Versailles, I live
in the style befitting a monarch. In Fontainebleau, more like a prince. At Compiègne, like a peasant." But the Sun King returned again and again. His successor, Louis XV, started rebuilding the château, based on plans by Gabriel. The
king died before work was completed, and Louis XVI and Marie Antoinette
expanded it.

Napoleon's second wife, Marie-Louise, arrived at Compiègne to marry him;
in a dining room, which you can visit only on the guided tour, she had her first

meal with the emperor. Accounts maintain that she was paralyzed with fear of the older man (Napoleon was in his 40s; she was 19). After dinner, he seduced her and is said to have only increased her anxiety.

During the Second Empire, Compiègne reached its pinnacle. Under Napoleon III and Eugénie, the hunting season was the occasion for balls and parties. Women in elegant hoop skirts danced to Strauss waltzes; Offenbach's operas echoed through the chambers and salons; and Eugénie, who fancied herself an actress, performed in the palace theater for her guests.

On the tour, you'll see the gold-and-scarlet Empire Room, where Napoleon spent many a troubled night, and his library, known for its secret door. In the Queen's Chamber, Marie-Louise used the "horn of plenty" bed.

In addition to the Imperial apartments, there are two museums stashed in the wings of the castle, both of which can be visited only on a guided tour (in French). The **Musée National de la Voiture (National Automobile Museum)** exhibits about 150 vehicles, from Ben-Hur chariots to a Citroën "chain-track" vehicle. The **Musée du Second Empire** is devoted to sculpture, paintings, and furniture from Napoleon III's glory days (1852–1870), including works by Meissonier, Giraud, and Carpeaux.

Place du Général de Gaulle. www.musee-chateau-compiegne.fr. ℭ **03-44-38-47-02.** Admission (including access to museums) 6.50€ adults, free for adults and children 25 and under. Wed–Mon 10am–6pm.

**Wagon de l'Armistice (Wagon du Maréchal-Foch)** ★★ HISTORIC SITE   In 1940, in one of the most perverse twists of fate in European history, Hitler forced the vanquished French to capitulate in the same rail coach where German officials signed the Armistice on November 11, 1918. The triumphant Nazis transported the coach to Berlin and then to Ordüff in the Thuringian Forest, where an Allied bomb destroyed it in April 1945. Seven kilometers (4¼ miles) into the forest of Compiègne lies the **Clarière de l'Armistice,** a clearing where the original coach came to a stop, and where today you can visit a replica that recounts the events of 1918 and 1940 in graphic detail, assisted by newspapers, photos, maps, and slide shows.

Rte. de Soissons, Compiègne. http://armistice.chez-alice.fr ℭ **03-44-85-14-18.** Admission 4€ adults, 2€ children 7–13, free for children 6 and under. Apr to mid-Oct Wed–Mon 10am–noon and 2pm–6; mid-Oct to Mar Wed–Mon 10am–noon and 2–5pm.

# Where to Eat

The restaurant at the **Hostellerie du Royal-Lieu** (see next page) is also open to the public.

**La Part des Anges** ★ 🍴 FRENCH   Our favorite restaurant in Compiègne occupies two warmly decorated dining rooms within a tile-roofed building from the early 1990s in the commercial center of town. The decor creates an old-fashioned warmth, with tapestry fabrics, indirect lighting, and a floor covered with antique beige-and-brown ceramic tiles. Items likely to appear on the menu include lobster spring rolls, John Dory fish with asparagus *mille-feuille,* and homemade foie gras with figs.

18 rue de Bouvines. ☎ **03-44-86-00-00.** Reservations recommended. Main courses 20€–27€; set-price menus 35€–60€. AE, MC, V. Tues–Fri and Sun noon–1:30pm; Tues–Sat 7:30–9pm. Closed 3 weeks in Aug, 1 week btw. Christmas and New Year's Day.

# Where to Stay

**Hostellerie du Royal-Lieu** ★   This half-timbered inn is the best choice for food and lodging close to the town, about 2km (1¼ miles) away. Guest rooms are medium in size, sleekly designed, and the bathrooms are tidily organized. The rooms and the restaurant's terrace overlook a garden. Gastronomic meals in the elegantly rustic dining room may include foie gras with red fruit chutney and raspberry vinegar or sautéed veal sweetbreads with capers. Menus from 35€ to 75€.

9 rue de Senlis, Compiègne 60200. www.host-royallieu.com. ☎ **03-44-20-10-24.** Fax 03-44-86-82-27. 15 units. 140€ double; 170€ suite. AE, MC, V. Follow signs southwest toward Senlis until you reach rue de Senlis, a 5-min. drive east of the town center. Free parking. **Amenities:** Restaurant; bar; room service. *In room:* TV, hair dryer, free Wi-Fi.

# THE LOIRE VALLEY

by Lily Heise

The Loire Valley, 2 hours south of Paris, enchants visitors with stunning castles, vineyards, and landscapes straight out of a fairy tale. The heart of France during the Renaissance period, François I made Amboise his capital, and he and his court left a spectacular legacy of castles and monuments, designed and decorated by the era's most famous Italian artists, including Leonardo da Vinci. This immense cultural heritage has earned the entire valley a place on the World Heritage Site list. Spend a few days châteaux-hopping or take your time to soak up the regional character while biking along the various rivers, exploring sleepy hamlets, or sampling the regional wines.

**Sightseeing**    Start your tour of the châteaux at the grandest of them all; the monumental **Château de Chambord** featuring a forest of chimneys and pepperpot turrets, as well as a massive double staircase. Drive further into château country to **Azay-le-Rideau,** a dreamy Renaissance castle that seems to float in a pond dotted with lily pads. Then move on to **Château d'Ussé,** said to be the model for the castle in Perault's *Sleeping Beauty.* The graceful gardens of **Villandry** dazzle with acres of intricate ornamental flowerbeds, a stark contrast to the foreboding medieval keep of the **Loches.**

**Eating & Drinking**    The Loire Valley is home to some of the world's most prestigious wine appellations, from Vouvray to Saumur-Champigny and dozens of others around **Saumur, Angers,** and **Tours.** The dining is world class as well, from smart Michelin-starred restaurants to rustic *auberges,* where you can sample scrumptious regional specialties like freshly caught pikeperch in wine and butter sauce, or local products like Sainte-Maure goat cheese and rillettes, a buttery pork pâté.

**History**    The Loire abounds in history. A parade of famous figures marched across the valley at one time or another, from Julius Caesar to Richard the Lion-Hearted. At the hauntingly beautiful **Abbaye Royale de Fontevraud,** the largest medieval abbey in France, you can see the tombs of four members of the royal house of Plantagenet. Trail Joan of Arc to **Chinon,** where the martyr begged the Dauphin to fight the English during the Hundred Years' War or stop in at **Blois,** with its thick intrigue during the Wars of Religion. **Angers's** striped slate and tufa château houses the Apocalypse tapestry, a 14th-century masterwork that is over 90m (300 ft.) long.

**Active Pursuits**    The Loire Valley is relatively flat and crisscrossed with cycling paths, including the 800km-long (496-mile) Loire à Vélo trail, so you can easily bike from one château to another and stay at bike-friendly hotels associated with the trail. You'll pass through jewel-like villages, enjoy the natural riches of the Loire ecosystem, and be tempted by the offerings of wineries you'll pass along the way.

PREVIOUS PAGE: **Château de Chenonceau.**

Trains serve some towns, but the best way to see this region is by car. There are **two regional tourist offices** that can help you plan your stay: Comité Régional de Tourisme Val de Loire, 37 av. de Paris, Orléans 45000 (www.visa loire.com; ☏ **02-38-79-95-28**), and SEM Régionale des Pays de la Loire, 1 place de la Galarne, BP 80221, Nantes 44202 Cedex 2 (www.westernloire.com; ☏ **02-40-48-24-20**).

 # BIKING YOUR WAY through THE LOIRE

After more than 10 years and several million euros, 800km (496 miles) of bike paths are now available for your cycling pleasure along the banks of the Loire. Thanks to a vast program called **"La Loire à Vélo"** (The Loire on a Bike), you can now safely pedal from Sancerre to the sea on a dedicated bike path past châteaux, villages, and natural areas. Relatively flat, the path was designed primarily for low-key cycling with family and friends, and is linked to cycling-friendly hotels and bike rental outfits along the way (look for the ACCUEIL VÉLO signs). More paths are added every year, the project will hook up to an even more massive project called EuroVelo 6, a cycling path that leads all the way to the Black Sea.

La Loire à Vélo has partnered with various tourist offices and travel agencies to offer a range of bike-trip packages that include hotel, meals, bike rental, and baggage transport (very important if you don't want to haul extra weight). For more information, visit their site (in English), www.cycling-loire.com, or one of the two regional tourist offices (listed above). The website also has detailed information on dozens of bike-rental outfits along the route, as well as brochures and links to guidebooks on various sections of the path.

One of the better-known outfitters is **Detours de Loire,** 35, rue Charles Gille, Tours (www.locationdevelos.com; ☏ **02-47-61-22-23**), which has three other shops in Blois, Saumur, and Nantes, as well as 20 or so associated outlets up and down the Loire à Vélo circuit. This means that you can pick up your bike in one town and leave it in any partner outlet along the way, without having to worry about returning the bike to the place where you rented. If you are arriving in the Loire Valley by train, the four main shops are all located close to the town station. Prices for all-purpose bikes are from 14€ to 21€ per day, with discounts for multiple-day rentals. A 300€ deposit (usually a credit card imprint) is required. Detours de Loire can also organize hotel-bike packages, deliver your bike to your accommodations, and store your baggage while you are out pedaling. **Note:** Most outlets are open only from April to October.

**BikeToursDirect,** 1638 Berkley Circle, Chattanooga, TN (http://biketours direct.com; ☏ **877/462-2423**), has six Loire Valley tours, including a three-stage program that, when linked together, takes cyclists from Orléans to the Atlantic. BikeToursDirect represents overseas bike tour operators whose low overhead and frequent departures allow them to offer prices as much as 70% below those of United States bike-tour companies. Self-guided tours start at 665€ per person, based on double occupancy, and include hotels, breakfasts, rental bikes, luggage transfers, and detailed route information.

# ORLÉANS ★

119km (74 miles) SW of Paris; 72km (45 miles) SE of Chartres

Ever since **Joan of Arc** relieved the besieged city from the Burgundians and the English in 1429, the city has honored the "Maid of Orléans." This deliverance is celebrated every year on May 8, the anniversary of her victory, but even if you aren't in town for the celebration, it's impossible to overlook the city's affection for the warrior, her name adorning everything from streets and cafes to chocolates and candies. Though suffering damage in World War II, Orléans' downtown still remains quaint; however, it has gradually been losing its regional prominence to the more prosperous Tours.

# Essentials

**GETTING THERE**   About two **trains** per hour arrive from Paris's Gare d'Austerlitz (1 hr., 10 min; 19€ one-way); there are also a dozen connections from Tours (50–70 min.). The one-way fare from Tours to Orléans is about 18€. Orléans lies on the road between Paris and Tours. If you're **driving** from Paris, take A10 south; from Tours, take A10 north.

**VISITOR INFORMATION**   The **Office de Tourisme** is at 2 place de L'Etape (www.tourisme-orleans.com; ✆ **02-38-24-05-05**).

# Exploring the Town

Orléans, pop. 116,000, is the chief town of Loiret, on the Loire, and beneficiary of many associations with the French aristocracy. It gave its name to the dukes and duchesses of Orléans. Wander the narrow lanes of the city center to get the feel of what the city might have been like during Joan of Arc's time. An equestrian statue of Jeanne d'Arc is on place du Martroi. From the square, you can drive past the elegant arched galleries on rue Royal (rebuilt in 18th-c. style) across pont George-V (erected in 1760). A simple cross marks the site of the Fort des Tourelles, which Joan of Arc and her men captured.

**Cathédrale Ste-Croix ★** CATHEDRAL   Begun in 1287, after an earlier Romanesque church here collapsed from old age, the cathedral was burned by the Huguenots in 1568. Henri IV laid the first stone of the present building in 1601, and work continued until 1829. The cathedral boasts a 17th-century organ and woodwork from the early 18th century in its chancel, the masterpiece of Jules Hardouin-Mansart and other artists associated with Louis XIV.

Place Ste-Croix. ✆ **02-38-77-87-50.** Free admission. May–Sept daily 9:15am–6pm; Oct–Apr daily 9:15am–noon and 2–6pm.

**Eglise St-Aignan** CHURCH   One of the most frequently altered churches in the Loire Valley, St-Aignan was consecrated in 1509 in the form you see today. It possesses one of France's earliest vaulted hall crypts, complete with polychromed capitals. Scholars of pre-Romanesque art view are interested in its rare 10th- and 11th-century aesthetics. Above ground, the church's Renaissance-era choir and transept remain, but the Protestants burned the nave during the Wars of Religion. In a wood-carved shrine are the remains of the church's patron saint.

Place St-Aignan. No phone. Crypt can be visited only on a guided tour; sign up at the tourist office.

**Hôtel Groslot** HISTORIC HOME   This brick Renaissance mansion was begun in 1550 and embellished in the

Hôtel Groslot.

19th century. François II (the first husband of Mary, Queen of Scots) lived here during the fall of 1560 and died on December 5. It was here that his brother and successor Charles IX met his lovely Marie Touchet. Between the Revolution and the mid-1970s, it functioned as the town hall. Marriage ceremonies, performed by the town's magistrates, are still held here. The statue of Joan of Arc praying was the work of Louis Philippe's daughter, Princesse Marie d'Orléans. In the garden, you can see the remains of the 15th-century Chapelle St-Jacques.

Place de l'Etape (northwest of the cathedral). ☎ **02-38-79-22-30.** Free admission. July–Sept Mon–Fri and Sun 9am–6pm, Sat 5–8pm; Oct–June Mon–Fri and Sun 10am–noon and 2–6pm, Sat 5pm–7pm.

**Musée des Beaux-Arts ★★** MUSEUM  A museum of mostly French, but also Italian, Dutch, and Flemish works dating from the 15th to 20th centuries. The collection includes some impressive paintings by Tintoretto, Correggio, and Van Dyck, as well as a fine array of portraits, including one of Mme. de Pompadour by Drouais. The museum also has one of the largest collections of pastels in French, includes works by Quentin de la Tour and Chardin.

Place Saint-Croix. www.coeur-de-france.com/orleans-beauxarts.html. ☎ **02-38-79-21-55.** Admission 3€ adults, 1.50€ students, free for children 18 and under and for all visitors on the 1st Sun of the month; Tues–Sun 10am–6pm.

# Shopping

Near rue Royale is **place du Châtelet,** with many boutiques, including a Galeries Lafayette. Look for fashionable clothing, jewelry, books, and leather goods. For antiques, walk along **rue de Bourgogne,** where a host of dealers sell everything from objets d'art to furniture.

Vinegar making was one of the city's main industries from the Middle Ages well into the 20th century. You can buy some of the famous Orléans vinegar north of town at **Martin Pouret,** 236 Faubourg Bannier, Fleury-les-Aubrais (www. martin-pouret.com; ✆ **02-38-88-78-49**). The family-owned business dates from 1797. The current M. Pouret is the only person in the region carrying on the slow, traditional vinegar-making method. You can do a wine tasting at one of the region's most comprehensive wine merchants, **Cave de Marc & Sebastien,** 7 place du Châtelet (www.cavedemarcetsebastien.fr; ✆ **02-38-62-94-11**), in the heart of the commercial center, just north of the Loire and west of rue Royale; see the website for a calendar of tastings.

## Where to Eat

**Chez Jules ★ ▮** TRADITIONAL FRENCH   This small bistro may not look like much, but it serves some of the best regional cuisine in the city. Tables are limited, so it's important to reserve in advance. Given the quality of the cuisine, prices are very reasonable. The menu is seasonally adjusted; some examples are eggplant caviar with ratatouille for an opener and marinated mussels and beets or a goat cheese pastry to start. There is usually a changing array of seafood dishes as well as hardier dishes such as parmentier of pigeon with foie gras.

136 rue de Bourgogne. ✆ **02-38-54-30-80.** Reservations required. Main courses 18€–22€; fixed-price lunch 19€, dinner 25€–33€. AE, MC, V. Tues–Sat noon–2pm and 7–9:30pm. Closed 2 weeks in July.

**La Vieille Auberge ★** MODERN FRENCH   You can dine inside in a stylish room or, if the weather's right, order your food in a lovely garden. The restaurant is housed in a building from the 17th century, and all the food is prepared fresh daily by skilled chefs. The menu changes with the season to take advantage of the freshest available ingredients, which may include lobster, oysters, game (in autumn), shellfish, and lamb.

2 rue du Faubourg St-Vincent. ✆ **02-38-53-55-81.** Reservations recommended. Main courses 18€–35€; fixed-price lunch 25€, dinner 35€–49€. AE, MC, V. Mon–Thurs noon–2pm and 7–9:30pm; Fri–Sat noon–2pm and 7–10pm; Sun noon–2pm.

## Orleans Nightlife

You'll find most of the action in the bars along **rue de Bourgogne** and a handful of places on **rue Bannier.** A trendy young crowd drinks the night away at **Le Moog,** 245 rue de Bourgogne (✆ **02-38-54-93-23**), in a modern setting of stainless steel and bordello red lighting, with pop music playing in the background. There's also a terrace for fair weather. A few streets over is one of the better jazz clubs, **Paxton's Head,** 264 rue de Bourgogne (✆ **02-38-81-23-29**), with a down-home English pub feel. **Havana Café,** 28 place du Châtelet (✆ **02-38-52-16-00**), crawls with young and beautiful 20- to 30-year-olds. This joint serves strong, party-colored drinks and loud music.

## Where to Stay

**Best Western Hôtel d'Arc**   This four-story hotel, built in the 1920s, has an Art Deco facade and old-fashioned elevator. It sits in the middle of the town and is close to the railway station and the pedestrian-only shopping streets. The guest rooms feature ceiling moldings and paneling. Most are of average size; the largest units have numbers that end in 2. Most rooms are peaceful, but avoid those that face rue de la République, which tends to be noisy. Although the hotel has no restaurant, it serves breakfast in an ornate room with a carved marble fireplace.

37 ter rue de la République, Orléans 45000. www.hoteldarc.fr. ℂ **02-38-53-10-94.** Fax 02-38-81-77-47. 35 units. 107€–176€ double. AE, DC, MC, V. **Amenities:** Room service. *In room:* TV, hair dryer, minibar, free Wi-Fi.

**Hôtel de l'Abeille** ★   A touch of the 19th century lingers in these cozy lodgings—bedrooms are decorated with period prints and antique armoires, and even the facade of the building has a certain *fin-de-siècle* flourish. The hotel has been in the family for four generations; the feeling here is of a grand old house that is open to visitors. Not high luxury, but clean and comfortable. There's a pretty roof garden with a view of the cathedral for lazing about on sunny days. You'll notice a Joan of Arc theme on the walls; the hotel owners collect artworks that celebrate Orléans' favorite liberator.

64 rue Alsace-Lorraine, Orléans 45000. www.hoteldelabeille.com. ℂ **02-38-53-54-87.** Fax 02-38-62-65-84. 27 units. 69€–98€ double; 98€–130€ family suite. AE, DC, MC, V. Parking 7€. **Amenities:** Bar; room service. *In room:* TV, hair dryer, free Wi-Fi.

# BEAUGENCY ★

150km (93 miles) SW of Paris; 85km (53 miles) NE of Tours

On the right bank of the Loire, the town of Beaugency boasts a long 12th-century bridge with 23 arches, said to have been built by the Devil himself. A major medieval event took place here: the 1152 annulment of the marriage of Eleanor of Aquitaine and her cousin, Louis VII. She then married Henry II of England, bringing southwestern France as her dowry, an act that set off the Hundred Years' War. This remarkable woman was the mother of Richard the Lion-Hearted. (The film *The Lion in Winter* dramatizes these events.) Allow 2 hours to see Beaugency.

The 15th-century **Château Dunois** is currently closed for renovations and may not reopen again into 2013 or beyond, so you'll have to see it from its exterior. The château is brooding and impressive, its historical links stretching back to almost-mystical medieval antecedents. The current castle was built by Jean d'Orléans, who fought alongside Joan of Arc in the siege of Orléans, on the foundations of an earlier 10th-century fortress that belonged to the lords of Beaugency, whose feudal power extended throughout the region. Astride the street (la rue du Pont) that leads to one of the château's secondary entrances, the Voûte St-Georges (St. George's Vault) is an arched gateway from the earlier château.

More medieval moodiness is on hand at **La Tour César,** a 36m-tall (118-ft.) castle keep that is all that remains of an 11th-century citadel. A fine example of Romanesque military architecture, the interior of this five-story structure is in ruins.

Beaugency.

**Eglise Notre-Dame,** place Saint-Fermin, a 12th-century abbey, was rebuilt after it was burned during the Wars of Religion (1562–1598). You can still see traces of its original Romanesque architecture in the chancel and transept. Nearby, the 16th-century **Tour St-Fermin,** a bell tower with a panoramic view of the valley, is famous for its bells, which ring out a traditional tune three times a day.

The 10th-century **Eglise St-Etienne,** place du Martroi, is one of the oldest churches in France. Now deconsecrated, it is owned by the municipality and is open only for temporary exhibitions of painting and sculpture.

## Essentials

**GETTING THERE**   If you're **driving** from Blois to Beaugency, take N152 northeast. About 20 **trains** per day run between Beaugency and either Blois or Orléans; each trip takes about 20 minutes, and the one-way fare ranges from 5.70€ to 6.30€. For railway information, visit www.voyages-sncf.com or dial (✆ **36-35.** From Orléans, there are about four to eight **buses** a day that go to Beaugency. For bus schedules and information, visit www.ulys-loiret.com or contact the tourist office (see below).

**VISITOR INFORMATION**   The **Office de Tourisme** is at 3 place du Dr.-Hyvernaud ((✆ **02-38-44-54-42**).

## Where to Eat & Stay

**Abbaye de Beaugency ★**   This three-star hotel offers the most historic accommodations in Beaugency. Built in 1640 as a monastery, it retains the stone window and door frames of its original construction and an elegant brick facade that may remind you of a château. A hotel since 1935, it sits beside the Loire, and all rooms have either partial or full views of the river. Guest rooms are large and bright; the decor includes lots of exposed beams and nice period touches.

2 quai de l'Abbaye, Beaugency 45190. www.hotel-abbaye-beaugency.com. ☎ **02-38-45-10-10.**
Fax 02-38-44-98-14. 19 units. 89€–159€ double; 159€-199€ suite. MC, V. **Amenities:** Bar; room
service. *In room:* TV, minibar, free Wi-Fi.

**La Tonnellerie ★ 🏨**   About 1.5km (1 mile) south of the center of Beaugency,
this well-managed hotel is intimate and charming. It was originally built as a
manor house in the 19th century, and it retains its original L-shaped design,
walled garden, and sense of the era of Balzac and Flaubert. Rooms are comfortable and traditional, furnished with reproduction antiques and period prints. The
restaurant serves regional classics; main courses run 19€.

12 rue des Eaux-Bleues, Tavers, Beaugency 45190. www.tonelri.com. ☎ **02-38-44-68-15.** Fax
02-38-44-10-01. 20 units. 105€–180€ double; 174€–210€ suite. AE, MC, V. Closed Dec 13–Jan 31.
Take A10, exit at Beaugency, and then take N152 to Beaugency/Tavers. **Amenities:** Restaurant;
bar; outdoor pool; bike rental. *In room:* TV, hair dryer, free Wi-Fi.

# CHAMBORD

191km (118 miles) SW of Paris; 18km (11 miles) E of Blois

The **Château de Chambord ★★★** (www.chambord.org; ☎ **02-54-50-40-
00**) is the culmination of François I's two biggest obsessions: hunting and architecture. Built as a "hunting lodge," this colossal edifice is a masterpiece of
architectural derring-do. Some say Leonardo da Vinci had something to do with
it, and when you climb the amazing double spiral staircase, that's not too hard to
believe. The staircase is superimposed upon itself so that one person may
descend and a second ascend without ever meeting. While da Vinci died a few

**Bedroom of Ludwig XIV at Château de Chambord.**

months before construction started in 1519, what emerged after 20 years was the pinnacle of the French Renaissance, the largest château in the Loire Valley. The castle's proportions are of an exquisite geometric harmony, and its fantastic arrangement of turrets and chimneys makes it one of France's most recognizable châteaux.

Construction continued for decades; François I actually stayed at the château for only a few weeks during hunting season, though he insured Chambord would forever carry his legacy by imprinting his "F" emblem and symbol, the salamander, wherever he could. After he died, his successors, none too sure what to do with the vast, unfurnished, and unfinished castle, basically abandoned it. Finally, Louis XIII gave it to his brother, who saved it from ruin; Louis XIV stayed there on several occasions and saw to restorations, but not a single monarch ever really moved in. The state acquired Chambord in 1932, and restoration work has been going on ever since.

Four monumental towers dominate Chambord's facade. The three-story keep has a spectacular terrace from which the ladies of the court used to watch the return of their men from the hunt. While many of the vast rooms are empty, several have been restored and filled with an impressive collection of period furniture and objects, giving an idea of what the castle looked like during the periods when parts of it were occupied. The château is in a park of more than 5,260 hectares (12,992 acres), featuring miles of hiking trails and bike paths, as well as picnic tables and bird-watching observation posts.

The château is open daily April to September 9am to 6pm, and October to March 9am to 5pm (until 7pm mid-July to mid-August). Admission is 9.50€ for adults and free for ages 17 and under accompanied by an adult. Allow 1½ hours to visit the château.

## Essentials

**GETTING THERE**   It's best to **drive** to Chambord. Take D951 northeast from Blois to Saint Dyé, turning onto the rural road to Chambord. You can also rent a **bicycle** in Blois and ride the 18km (11 miles) to Chambord, or take a **tour** to Chambord from Blois in summer. From May to September, **Transports du Loir et Cher** (www.tlcinfo.net; ℂ **02-54-58-55-44**) operates bus service to Chambord.

**VISITOR INFORMATION**   The **Maison de Tourisme,** on place Saint Louis (ℂ **02-54-33-39-16**), is open April to October.

## Where to Eat & Stay

**Hôtel du Grand-St-Michel**   Across from the château, and originally built as a kennel for the royal hounds, this inn is the only one of any substance in the tiny village. Try for a front room overlooking the château, which is dramatically floodlit at night. Accommodations are plain but comfortable, with provincial decor. Most visitors arrive for lunch, which in summer is served on a terrace. High points from the menu include pheasant with chestnuts (in late autumn and winter), filet mignon with black chanterelle mushrooms and artichokes, and several local pâtés and terrines, including coarsely textured, flavorful rillettes of regional pork.

103 place St-Louis, Chambord 41250, near Bracieux. www.saintmichel-chambord.com. ℂ **02-54-20-31-31.** Fax 02-54-20-36-40. 40 units. 61€–102€ double; 85€–114€ triple. MC, V. Free

parking. Restaurant: Main courses and fixed menus 19€–26€. Closed 2 weeks in Jan. **Amenities:** Restaurant; Internet; tennis court. *In room:* TV.

# BLOIS

180km (112 miles) SW of Paris; 60km (37 miles) NE of Tours

The star attraction in this town of 52,000 is the **Château de Blois ★★★**, but if time remains after a visit to the château, you may want to walk around the town. It's a piece of living history, with cobblestone streets and restored white houses with slate roofs and red-brick chimneys. Blois (pronounce it "Blwah") hugs a hillside overlooking the Loire. Some of its "streets" are mere alleyways originally laid out in the Middle Ages, or lanes linked by a series of stairs. Allow 1½ hours to see Blois.

## Essentials

**GETTING THERE**   A dozen or so **trains** run from Paris's Gare de Austerlitz every day (1 hr., 45 min.; 27€ one-way), and several others depart from the Gare Montparnasse, which involves a change in Tours (around 1 hr., 50min.; 26.60€–62€). From Tours, trains run almost every hour (trip time: 40 min.), at a cost of 10€ one-way. For information and schedules, visit www.voyages-sncf.com or dial ☏ **36-35.** From June to September, you can take a **bus** (www.tlcinfo.net; ☏ **02-54-58-55-44**) from the Blois train station to tour châteaux in the area, including Chambord, Chaumont, Chenonceau, and Amboise. If you're **driving** from Tours, take RN152 east to Blois, which runs along the Loire; if you want to get there fast, take the A10 autoroute. If you'd like to explore the area by **bike,** check out **Traineurs de Loire,** 1 rue Chemonton (www.traineursdeloire.com; ☏ **02-54-79-36-71**). Rentals start at 6€ per hour, 13€ per day.

**VISITOR INFORMATION**   The **Office de Tourisme** is at 23 place du Château (www.bloispaysdechambord.com; ☏ **02-54-90-41-41**).

## Exploring the Town & the Château

If you have time for **shopping,** head for the area around **rue St-Martin** and **rue du Commerce** for high-end items such as clothing, perfume, shoes, and jewelry. Find a one-of-a-kind piece of jewelry; have something created by the master jeweler **Philippe Denies,** 3 rue St-Martin (www.atelierdeniesphilippe.com; ☏ **02-54-74-78-24**). If you prefer antique jewelry, stop by **Antebellum,** 12 rue

---

### ◉ Lights, Sound, Action!

Many of the Loire châteaux present *son-et-lumière* (sound and light) shows on summer nights providing visitors with original evening entertainment. The Château de Blois hosts one of the best. Catch it from May to September, beginning at 10-10:30pm; on Wednesday nights, the show is in English. As a taped lecture plays, colored lights and readings evoke the age in which the château was built. The show costs 7.50€ for adults, 6€ students, 4€ for children 6 to 17, and is free for children 5 and under (see château website for full details).

**Blois.**

St-Lubin (☎ **02-54-78-38-78**), and browse its selection of precious and semi-precious stones set in gold and silver. If you want to acquire a copy of tapestries like the ones at the nearby châteaux, you'll find a wide range at **Tapisserie Langlois,** Voûte du Château (☎ **02-54-78-04-43**). Chocoholics flock to award-winning **Max Vauché,** 50 rue du Commerce (www.maxvauche-chocolatier.com; ☎ **02-54-78-23-55**). On Saturday all day, a **food market** is on place Louis XII and place de la République, lining several blocks in the center of town at the foot of the château.

**Château de Blois ★★★** CASTLE   A wound in battle earned him the name Balafré (Scarface), but he was quite a ladies' man. In fact, on the misty morning of December 23, 1588, Henri I, the duc de Guise, had just left a warm bed and the arms of one of Catherine de Médicis's ladies-in-waiting. His archrival, King Henri III, had summoned him, but when the duke arrived, only the king's minions were about. The guards approached with daggers. Wounded, the duke made for the door, where more guards awaited him. Staggering, he fell to the floor in a pool of his own blood. Only then did Henri emerge from behind the curtains. "Mon Dieu," he reputedly exclaimed, "he's taller dead than alive!" The body couldn't be shown: The duke was too popular. Quartered, it was burned in a fireplace.

   The murder of the duc de Guise is only one of the events associated with the Château de Blois, begun in the 13th century by the comte de Blois. Blois reached the apex of its power in 1515, when François I moved to the château. For that reason, Blois is often called the "Versailles of the Renaissance," the second capital of France, and the "City of Kings." Blois soon became a palace of exile. Louis XIII banished his mother, Marie de Médicis, to the château, but she escaped by sliding into the moat down a mound of dirt left by the builders.

A mix of different styles, if you stand in the courtyard, you'll find that the château is like an illustrated storybook of French architecture. The Hall of the Estates-General is a beautiful 13th-century work; Louis XII built the Charles d'Orléans gallery and the Louis XII wing from 1498 to 1501. Mansart constructed the Gaston d'Orléans wing between 1635 and 1637. Most remarkable is the François I wing, a French Renaissance masterpiece, containing a spiral staircase with ornamented balustrades and the king's symbol, the salamander.

Blois 41000. www.chateaudeblois.fr. ② **02-54-90-33-33.** Admission 8€ (Oct–May) and 9.50€ (June–Sept) adults, 6.50€ (Oct–May) and 7€ (June–Sept) students, 4€ children 6–17, free for children 5 and under. July–Aug daily 9am–7pm; Apr–June and Sept daily 9am–6:30pm; Oct daily 9am–6pm; Nov–Mar daily 9am–12:30pm and 1:30–5:30pm.

# Where to Eat

**Au Rendez-vous des Pêcheurs** ★★ TOURAINE/SEAFOOD   This restaurant occupies a 16th-century house and former grocery a short walk from the château. Chef Christophe Cosme enjoys a reputation for quality, generous portions, and creativity. He prepares two or three meat dishes, including roasted Racan pigeon with caramelized cabbage, and seared Charolais steak with potatoes Maxime. These appear alongside a longer roster of seafood dishes, such as poached filet of local *sandre* (a freshwater fish; "zander" in English) served with citrus flavored fennel confit, and freshwater pike stuffed with mussels.

27 rue du Foix. www.rendezvousdespecheurs.com. ② **02-54-74-67-48.** Reservations required. Main courses 31€–37€; fixed-price menu 30€–69€. AE, MC, V. Tues–Sat noon–2:30pm; Mon–Sat 7–10pm. Closed 1 week in Jan and the 1st 2 weeks of Aug.

**Le Médicis** ★ TRADITIONAL FRENCH   Members of the Garanger family maintain one of the most sophisticated inns in Blois, just 1km (½ mile) from the château. It's ideal for a gourmet meal or an overnight stop. Fresh fish is the chef's specialty. Typical dishes are lobster with tonka bean mousse, crispy tandoori-flavored cod, potatoes with green olives and shellfish coulis, and veal sweetbreads with morels. Chocolate in many manifestations is the dessert specialty. The Garangers rent 10 elegant rooms with air-conditioning, TV, minibar, and hair dryer. Double rates are 87€ to 150€.

2 allée François 1er, Blois 41000. www.le-medicis.com. ② **02-54-43-94-04.** Fax 02-54-42-04-05. Reservations required. Main courses 18€–36€; fixed-price menu 23€–72€. AE, MC, V. Daily noon–1:15pm and 7–9pm. Closed Jan and Sun night and Mon Nov–Mar. Bus: 2.

**L'Orangerie du Château** ★★★ ☺ TOURAINE   Next to the château, one of the castle's former outbuildings holds the grandest and best restaurant in the area, with a floral-themed dining room. Faithful customers and the most discerning foodies visiting Blois delight in the filet mignon with truffles. You can also sample a freshly caught monkfish flavored with fresh thyme or autumny venison with sweet potatoes purée and roasted figs. Everything tastes better with a Sauvignon de Touraine. Junior gastronomes can satisfy their palates with the special children menu.

1 av. Jean-Laigret. www.orangerie-du-chateau-fr. ② **02-54-78-05-36.** Reservations required. Main courses 23€–37€; fixed-price menu 35€–79€; children's menu 14€. AE, MC, V. Thurs–Tues noon–1:30pm; Thurs–Sat and Mon–Tues 7:15–9:15pm. Closed mid-Feb to mid-Mar.

# Blois Nightlife

There's not much in the way of nightlife in Blois, but you could saunter down to the fun and friendly **L'Hendrix Café,** 1 rue du Puits-Châtel (📞 **02-54-58-82-73**), for a drink. Another possibility is **Le Velvet Jazz Lounge,** 15 bis rue Haute (www.velvet-jazz-lounge.com; 📞 **02-54-78-36-32**), off rue Denis Papin. This is part of a 13th-century abbey but is now a venue for weekly jazz concerts. Otherwise, this is a classy joint for a drink.

# Where to Stay

Some of the best rooms in town are at **Le Médicis** (see "Where to Eat," on previous page).

**Côté Loire–Auberge Ligérienne**   About a 5-minute walk from Blois Castle, these B&B-like lodgings include impeccably maintained rooms decorated with an interesting mix of antique headboards, country throw rugs, and 1930s shipping posters. There is a low-key maritime theme here, which makes sense for a hotel that sits on the edge of a river that served as a major transportation link up until the 19th century. Parts of this small inn were constructed in the 12th, 15th, and 16th centuries, which explains the narrow stairways and exposed beams. One of the owners does double duty as chef: There is a tiny restaurant on the ground floor that features fresh, local ingredients.

2 place de la Grève, Blois 41000. www.coteloire.com. 📞 **02-54-78-07-86.** Fax 02-54-56-87-33. 8 units. 57€–89€ double. MC, V. **Amenities:** Bar; restaurant. *In room:* TV, hair dryer, free Wi-Fi. Closed Jan.

**Mercure Centre**   This is one of the best-located hotels in Blois—three stories of reinforced concrete and big windows beside the quays of the Loire, a 5-minute walk from the château. Though rooms never rise above the chain format, they attempt a modern look and are roomy and soundproof.

28 quai St-Jean, Blois 41000. www.mercure.com. 📞 **02-54-56-66-66.** Fax 02-54-56-67-00. 96 units. 90€–245€ double. AE, DC, MC, V. Parking 7€. Bus: Quayside marked PISCINE. **Amenities:** Restaurant; bar; babysitting; Jacuzzi; indoor pool; room service; sauna. *In room:* A/C, TV, hair dryer, minibar, free Wi-Fi.

# CHEVERNY

192km (119 miles) SW of Paris; 19km (12 miles) SE of Blois

The upper crust heads to the Sologne area for the hunt as if the 17th century had never ended. However, 21st-century realities—like formidable taxes—can't be entirely avoided, so the **Château de Cheverny ★★★** (www.chateau-cheverny.fr; 📞 **02-54-79-96-29**) opens its rooms to visitors.

Unlike most of the Loire châteaux, Cheverny is the residence of the original owner's descendants. The family of the vicomte de Sigalas can trace its lineage from Henri Hurault, the son of the chancellor of Henri III and Henri IV, who built the château in 1634. Designed in classic Louis XIII style, it is resolutely symmetrical, with square pavilions flanking the central pile. Its elegant lines and sumptuous furnishings provoked the Grande Mademoiselle, otherwise known as the Duchess of Montpensier, to proclaim it an "enchanted castle."

You, too, will be impressed by the antique furnishings, tapestries, and objets d'art. A 17th-century French artist, Jean Mosnier, decorated the fireplace with motifs from the legend of Adonis. The Guards' Room contains a collection of medieval armor; also on display is a Gobelin tapestry depicting the abduction of Helen of Troy. In the king's bedchamber, another Gobelin traces the trials of Ulysses. Most impressive is the stone stairway of carved fruit and flowers. To complete the regal experience, your arrival or departure from the château might be heralded by red-coated trumpeters accompanied by an enthusiastic pack of hunting hounds.

The château is open daily November to March 9:45am to 5pm, April to June and September 9:15am to 6:15pm, July and August 9:15am to 6:45pm, and October 9:45am to 5:30pm. Admission is 7.70€ for adults, 5€ for students under 25, and children 7 to 18, and free for children 6 and under. Allow 2 hours for your visit.

Fireplace in the Guards' Room at the Château de Cheverny.

## Essentials

**GETTING THERE**   Cheverny is 19km (12 miles) south of Blois, along D765. It's best reached by **car** or on a **bus tour** (April–Aug only) from Blois with **TLC Transports du Loir et Cher** (www.tlcinfo.net; *©* **02-54-58-55-44**). Bus no. 4 leaves from the railway station at Blois once or twice per day; see the TLC website for the schedule. You can also take a **taxi** (*©* **02-54-78-07-65**) from the railway station at Blois.

**VISITOR INFORMATION**   The **Maison de Tourisme** is at 12 rue Chêne des Dames (www.bloispaysdechambord.com; *©* **02-54-79-95-63**).

## Where to Eat & Stay

**Les Trois Marchands** TRADITIONAL FRENCH   This coaching inn, more comfortable than St-Hubert (see below), has been handed down for many generations. Jean-Jacques Bricault owns the three-story building, which has a mansard roof, a glassed-in courtyard, and sidewalk tables under umbrellas. In the tavern-style main dining room, the menu may include foie gras, lobster salad, frogs' legs, fresh asparagus in mousseline sauce, game dishes, or fish cooked in a salt crust. The inn rents 24 well-furnished, comfortable rooms with TVs for 42€ to 55€ for a double.

60 place de l'Eglise, Cour-Cheverny 41700. *©* **02-54-79-96-44.** Fax 02-54-79-25-60. Dining room main courses 18€–47€; fixed-price menu 22€–45€. AE, DC, MC, V. Tues–Sun 7am–11pm. Closed Sun night Dec–Mar.

**St-Hubert** TRADITIONAL FRENCH   About 500m (1,640 ft.) from the château, this inn was built in the 1950s in the provincial style. The least expensive menu (served only at lunchtime Mon–Fri) may include terrine of wild boar with pistachios, poached ray with mustard sauce, and *tarte tatin* with vanilla bourbon ice cream. The most expensive menu may list sautéed scallops with red onion fondue, filet of Rossini beef with truffles, and profiteroles with ginger and chocolate sauce. The St-Hubert offers 20 conservatively decorated rooms with TVs for 57€ to 65€ for a double. Each room comes with free Wi-Fi.

122 rte. Nationale, Cour-Cheverny 41700. www.hotel-sthubert.com. ✆ **02-54-79-96-60.** Fax 02-54-79-21-17. Main courses 18€–22€; fixed-price menu 19€–39€; children's menu 12€. AE, MC, V. Daily noon–2pm and 7–9pm. Closed Sun night off season.

# VALENÇAY

233km (144 miles) SW of Paris; 56km (35 miles) S of Blois

**Château de Valençay** ★★ ☺ (www.chateau-valencay.fr; ✆ **02-54-00-10-66**) is one of the Loire's most handsome Renaissance châteaux. Talleyrand acquired it in 1803 on the orders of Napoleon, who wanted his minister of foreign affairs to receive dignitaries in style. The d'Estampes family built Valençay in 1520. The dungeon and west tower are of this period, as is the main body of the building, but other wings were added in the 17th and 18th centuries. The effect is grandiose, with domes and turrets.

The apartments are sumptuously furnished, mostly in the Empire style, but with Louis XV and Louis XVI trappings as well. A star-footed table in the main drawing room is said to have been the one on which the final agreement of the Congress of Vienna was signed in June 1815 (Talleyrand represented France).

A 45-minute audioguide visit gives detailed explanations of the castle's history and decor. After your visit to the château, you can walk through the garden and deer park. There are plenty of activities here for kids, including a giant labyrinth, a miniature farm, a playground, a golf cart circuit through the forest and, in high season, historic reenactments (at 3, 4, and 5pm). A few nights per summer the château and its grounds return to the Renaissance decked out with thousands of candles, costumed performers and musical entertainment (see website for details). Admission to the castle, car museum, and park is 11.50€ for adults, 8€ for students, 2.50€ for children 4 to 6, and free for ages 5 and under. The château is open daily mid-March to April 10:30am to 6pm, May 10am to 6pm, June 9:30am to 6:30pm, July and August 9:30am to 7pm, September 10am to 6pm, October to November 9 10:30am to 5:30pm. Allow 1½ hours to see the castle.

Within 200m (656 ft.) of the château, the **Musée de l'Automobile de Valençay,** route du Blois, 12 av. de la Résistance (http://museedevalencay.voila.net; ✆ **02-54-00-07-74**), features a collection of more than 60 antique automobiles. Of special interest is a Bédélia (ca. 1914). The tandem-style automobile (the driver rode behind the passenger) with a pulley-operated two-speed gearshift is the rarest in the collection. The Bédélia, like 80% of the cars in the collection, was made in France. The museum is open from March to November.

## Essentials

**GETTING THERE** If you're **driving** from Tours, take A85 east, turning south on D956 (exit 13 to Selles-sur-Cher) to Valençay. From Blois, follow D956 south.

**VISITOR INFORMATION** The **Office de Tourisme** is at 2 av. de Résistance (✆ **02-54-00-04-42**).

## Where to Eat & Stay

**Hôtel Le Relais du Moulin** The town's best overnight choice is a 5-minute walk from the entrance to the château. It's also immediately adjacent to a stream and the now-disabled water wheel of an 18th-century textile mill that, during the age of Talleyrand and Napoleon, produced fabrics for curtains, clothing, and upholsteries. The hotel is in a modern building with a cream-colored façade; rooms are simple but functional, in tones of pale yellow and soft red, with views that overlook the château, the river, vineyards, and/or the verdant grounds. Fixed-price menus in the dining room cost from 14€ to 32€ and focus on traditional and well-prepared French food.

94 rue Nationale, Valençay 36600. www.hotel-lerelaisdumoulin.com. ✆ **02-54-00-38-00.** Fax 02-54-00-38-79. 54 units. 67€–70€ double. AE, MC, V. Closed Nov–Mar. **Amenities:** Restaurant; bar; exercise room; indoor pool; sauna. *In room:* TV, minibar (in some).

# CHAUMONT-SUR-LOIRE

200km (124 miles) SW of Paris; 40km (25 miles) E of Tours

On the morning when Diane de Poitiers first crossed the drawbridge, the **Château de Chaumont** ★★ (www.domaine-chaumont.fr; ✆ **02-54-51-26-26**) looked grim. Henri II, her lover, had recently died. The king had given her Chenonceau, but his angry widow, Catherine de Médicis, forced her to trade her favorite château for Chaumont, a comparatively virtual dungeon for Diane, with its medieval battlements and pepper-pot turrets and position perched high above the Loire.

The château belonged to the Amboise family for 5 centuries. In 1465, when one of them, a certain Pierre, rebelled against the rule of Louis XI, the king had the castle burned to the ground as a punishment. Pierre and his descendants rebuilt for the next few decades. The castle's architecture spans the period between the Middle Ages and the Renaissance, and the vast rooms still evoke the 16th and 17th centuries. In the bedroom occupied by Catherine de Médicis, you can see a portrait of the Italian-born queen. The superstitious Catherine housed her astrologer, Cosimo Ruggieri, in one of the tower rooms (a portrait of him remains). He reportedly foretold the disasters awaiting her sons.

The château passed through the hands of various owners and was eventually acquired and restored by the eccentric Marie Say and Amédée de Broglie in the late 18th century, who also added elaborate stables, a farm, and gardens. Since 1992, the latter has hosted the **International Garden Festival,** a world-renowned gathering

Medallions at the Château de Chaumont.

of cutting-edge landscape designers that lasts from mid-April to mid-October that is open to the public. Each year, a dozen different gardens are created, using thousands of different plants and innovative garden designs. Since 2008, the château has also been a site for contemporary art and photography exhibits; check the website for this year's program. Entrance to the festival is 10€ for adults, 7.50€ for children 12 to 18, 4.50€ for children 6 to 11, and free for 5 and under.

The château is open daily November through March 10am to 5pm, April through June 10am to 6:30pm, July through August 10am to 7pm, September 10am to 6:30pm, and October 10am to 6pm. Admission is 9.50€ for adults, 6€ for children 12 to 18, 3.50€ for children 6 to 11, and free for ages 5 and under. Allow 2 hours to see Chaumont castle and its park, more if you are visiting the festival.

## Essentials

**GETTING THERE** Several **trains** per day travel to Chaumont from Blois (trip time: 10–15 min.) and Tours (about 40 min.). The one-way fare is 3.40€ from Blois, 7.90€ from Tours. The railway station serving Chaumont is in Onzain, a nice 1½-mile walk north of the château. For train schedules and ticketing information, visit www.voyages-sncf.com or call ℭ **36-35**.

**VISITOR INFORMATION** The **Office de Tourisme** is on rue du 24 Maréchal-Leclerc (www.chaumont-sur-loire.eu; ℭ **02-54-20-91-73**).

## Where to Eat & Stay

**Hostellerie du Château** 🦋 Visitors to the château who want to stay close to the castle can stay at this completely renovated half-timbered inn located directly in front of the gateway to the château. Accommodations open onto the riverbank of the Loire; ask for a room with a view. The rooms are modestly yet comfortably furnished. In the summer, you can enjoy regional specialties in the restaurant and swim in the terrace-flanked pool.

2 rue Maréchal de-Lattre-de-Tassigny, Chaumont-sur-Loire 41150. www.hostellerie-du-chateau. com. ℭ **02-54-20-98-04.** Fax 02-54-20-97-98. 15 units. 66€–83€ double. MC, V. **Amenities:** Restaurant; bar; outdoor pool; room service. *In room:* TV, hair dryer, free Wi-Fi. Closed mid-Nov to mid-Mar.

**Le Domaine des Hauts de Loire** ★★ Less than 3km (1¾ miles) from the Château de Chaumont, this property sits on the opposite side of the Loire. The manor house was built by the owner of a Paris-based newspaper in 1840 and called, rather coyly, a "hunting lodge." It's the most appealing stopover in the neighborhood, with rooms decorated in Louis Philippe or Empire style. More than half of the rooms are in the slightly less desirable half-timbered annex that was originally the stables.

The stately dining room's creative menu includes a salad of sautéed eel with shallot vinaigrette, local *sandre* fish with frog leg tempura and watercress mousseline, organic guinea hen with chestnut ravioli, and filet of venison with parsnips and quince. Main courses range from 36€ to 68€, with fixed-price menus ranging from 55€ to 150€.

Rte. d'Herbault, Onzain 41150. www.domainehautsloire.com. ℭ **02-54-20-72-57.** Fax 02-54-20-77-32. 36 units. 130€–290€ double; 320€–550€ suite. AE, DC, MC, V. Closed Dec–Feb. **Amenities:** Restaurant; bar; outdoor pool; room service. *In room:* TV, hair dryer, minibar, Wi-Fi (10€ per hour).

# AMBOISE ★★

219km (136 miles) SW of Paris; 35km (22 miles) E of Tours

Amboise is on the banks of the Loire in the center of vineyards known as Touraine-Amboise. The good news: This is a real Renaissance town. The bad news: Because it is so beautiful, tour buses overrun it, especially in summer. Other than the myriad of notable royal residences, the town has also played host to Leonardo da Vinci, who spent his last years here and more recently, royal rocker Mick Jagger, lord of a nearby château.

## Essentials

**GETTING THERE**　About a dozen **trains** per day leave from both Tours and Blois. The trip from Tours takes 20 minutes and costs 5.10€ one-way; from Blois, it takes 20 minutes and costs 6.50€ one-way. Several conventional trains a day leave from Paris's Gare d'Austerlitz (trip time: about 2 hr., 15 min.), and several TGVs depart from the Gare Montparnasse, with a change to a regular train at St-Pierre-des-Corps, next to Tours (trip time: 1 hr., 30 min.). Fares from Paris to Amboise start at 23€. For information, visit www.voyages-sncf.com or call ✆ **36-35.**

If you prefer to travel by bus, **Fil Vert Buses** (www.tourainefilvert.com), which operates out of Gare Routière in Tours, just across from the railway station, runs about six to eight **buses** every day between Tours and Amboise. The one-way trip takes about 45 minutes and costs 1.70€.

If you're **driving** from Tours, take the D751, following signs to Amboise.

**VISITOR INFORMATION**　The **Office de Tourisme** is on quai du Général-de-Gaulle (www.amboise-valdeloire.com; ✆ **02-47-57-09-28**).

Amboise.

# Exploring the Town

**Château d'Amboise** ★★ CASTLE   On a rocky spur above the town, the medieval château was rebuilt in 1492 by Charles VIII, the first in France to reflect the Italian Renaissance.

You enter on a ramp that opens onto a panoramic terrace fronting the river. At one time, buildings surrounded this terrace, and fetes took place in the enclosed courtyard. The castle fell into decline during the Revolution, and today only about a quarter of the once-sprawling edifice remains. You first come to the Flamboyant Gothic **Chapelle de St-Hubert,** distinguished by its lacelike tracery and where you can visit the **tomb of Leonardo da Vinci,** who died in Amboise. Tapestries cover the walls of what's left of the château's grandly furnished rooms, which include **Logis du Roi (King's Apartment).** The vast **Salle du Conseil,** bookended by a Gothic and a Renaissance fireplace, was once the venue of the lavish fetes designed by da Vinci. Exit via the **Tour des Minimes** (also known as the Tour des Cavaliers), noteworthy for its ramp up which horsemen could ride. The other notable tower is the Heurtault, which is broader than the Minimes, with thicker walls.

www.chateau-amboise.com 🕿 **02-47-57-00-98.** Admission 10€ adults, 8.50€ students, 6.50€ ages 7–14, free for children 7 and under. Daily as follows: Jan 9am–12:30pm and 2–4:45pm; Feb 9am–12:30pm and 1:30–5pm; Mar 9am–5:30pm; Apr–June 9am–6:30pm; July–Aug 9am–7pm; Sept–Oct 9am–6pm; Nov 2–15 9am–5:30pm; Nov 16–Dec 31 9am–12:30pm and 2–4:45pm.

**Château du Clos-Lucé** ★ HISTORIC HOME/MUSEUM   Within 3km (1¾ miles) of the base of Amboise's château, this brick-and-stone building was constructed in the 1470s. Bought by Charles VII in 1490, it became the summer residence of the royals and also served as a retreat for Anne de Bretagne, who, according to legend, spent a lot of time praying and meditating. Later, François I installed "the great master in all forms of art and science," Leonardo himself. Da Vinci lived here for 3 years, until his death in 1519. (The paintings of Leonardo dying in François's arms are probably symbolic; the king was supposedly out of town at the time.) Today the site functions as a small museum, offering insights into Leonardo's life and a sense of the decorative arts of the era. The manor contains furniture from his era; examples of his sketches; models for his flying machines, bridges, and cannon; and even a primitive example of a machine gun.

2 rue de Clos-Lucé. www.vinci-closluce.com. 🕿 **02-47-57-00-73.** Mar–Nov 15 admission 13€ adults, 8€ students and children 6–18, 35€ family ticket (2 adults, 2 children), free for children 5 and under; Nov 16–Feb admission 10€ adults, 7€ students, 6.50€ children 6–18, 28€ family ticket (2 adults, 2 children), free for children 5 and under. Jan daily 10am–6pm; Feb–June daily 9am–7pm; July–Aug daily 9am–8pm; Sept–Oct daily 9am–7pm; Nov–Dec daily 9am–6pm.

# Nearby Attractions

The region around Amboise has attractions that resemble a mix of Disney's Magic Kingdom and the court of the Renaissance kings. The most frequently visited attraction, the **Aquarium du Val de Loire,** Parc des Mini-Châteaux 😊 (www.aquariumduvaldeloire.com; 🕿 **02-47-23-44-44**), lies 9.5km (6 miles) west of Amboise. It has more than 10,000 freshwater and saltwater fish, including about a half-dozen sharks. Admission is 14€ for adults and 9.50€ for children 4 to 14; it's open daily 10:30am to 6pm January through March and September through December, 10:30am to 7pm April through May, 10am to 7pm June through July, and 10am to 8pm late July through mid August. The aquarium is usually closed two weeks in November and January.

At the same address (same phone) is the **Parc des Mini-Châteaux,** which holds replicas of France's most famous castles, built at ⅓₀ the size of the originals. Chambord, for example, is less than 3.5m (11 ft.) tall. It's all very patriotic—a sort of learning game that teaches French schoolchildren the glories of their *patrimoine* (heritage) and collects some of the most celebrated architecture in Europe. Admission is 13.50€ for adults, 9.50€ for students and children 4 to 14, and free for children 3 and under (discounted joint ticket with Aquarium available). The Parc des Mini-Châteaux is open daily 10:30am to 7pm April through May, 10am to 7pm June through August (8pm), 10:30am to 6pm September through November 14. The park is closed from mid-November through early April.

To get here from Amboise, follow signs to Tours and take RD751 along the southern bank of the Loire. The aquarium is 1km (½ mile) beyond the village of Lussault-sur-Loire (it's clearly marked).

## Where to Eat

For fine dining, the restaurants at **Le Choiseul, Le Fleuray,** and the **Château de Pray** are excellent (see "Where to Stay," below).

**Brasserie de l'Hotel de Ville** ☺ FRENCH   In the town's historic core, a short walk from the château, this bustling Paris-style brasserie has a solid local reputation. Expect a noisy environment focused on rows of banquettes, hassled waiters, and steaming platters that emerge relatively quickly from the overworked kitchen. Menu items include a full range of old-fashioned cuisine that locals may remember from their childhoods, like local sausage splashed with Vouvray sparkling wine, standard grilled beefsteak with french fries, duck with honey and rosemary, as well as lighter salads and omelets.

1 and 3 rue François 1er. ☏ **02-47-57-26-30.** Reservations recommended. Main courses 7€–18€; fixed-price menu 15€–26€; children's menu 6.90€. AE, MC, V. Daily noon–2pm and 7–9:30pm.

## Where to Stay

**Le Château-de-Pray** ★★   This château 1.6km (1 mile) west of the town is flanked by imposing towers that date from the 13th century. Rich in noble history, it was one of the first château-restaurants in the Loire and has been managed by the Cariou family for several decades. You'll find an elegant yet cozy atmosphere with a fireplace in the drawing room and a fine collection of antique furniture and oil paintings throughout. The manicured gardens and pool compliment your château experience. Rooms in the main building are conservative and comfortable; many of the beds sport canopies. The more spacious guest rooms are near the ground floor. The rooms in the 1990s annex do not have as much character, though each has its own private terrace. The Michelin-starred restaurant, open to nonguests, offers fixed-price menus (52€–65€) with excellent Loire cuisine; reservations are required.

Rue de Chargé 37400. www.chateaupray.com ☏ **02-47-57-23-67.** Fax 02-47-57-32-50. 19 units. 145€–195€ double; 225€–305€ suite. AE, DC, MC, V. Free parking. Closed 2nd half of Nov and 3 weeks in Jan. **Amenities:** Restaurant; babysitting; massage; bike rental. *In room:* TV, hair dryer, free Wi-Fi.

**Le Choiseul** ★★★   This 18th-century mansion, nestled on the banks of the Loire River, harbors the best hotel in Amboise and serves its best cuisine. Guest rooms are luxurious; though modernized, they retain their old-world charm. The small bathrooms contain combination tub/showers. The formal dining room has a view of the Loire and welcomes nonguests who phone ahead. The restaurant is superb; the menu features classic and regional French, utilizing the freshest ingredients. Lunch ranges from 27€ to 60€, with dinner going for 46€ to 80€.

36 quai Charles-Guinot, Amboise 37400. www.le-choiseul.com. © **02-47-30-45-45.** Fax 02-47-30-46-10. 32 units. 108€–305€ double; 292€-365€ suite. AE, DC, MC, V. **Amenities:** Restaurant; bar; bicycles; outdoor pool; room service. *In room:* A/C, TV, hair dryer, minibar, free Wi-Fi.

**Le Fleuray ★★ 🏠**    One of the most appealing hotels in the region is this well-maintained ivy-covered manor house, a short drive from Amboise. A 19th-century farm, it was purchased in 1991 by the Newingtons, a family of English expatriates, whose hard work restoring the site was honored with a French medal of tourism in 2011. Guest rooms have been recently renovated and evoke an elegant but not terribly formal English country house, several have private terraces. The peaceful surroundings make it an excellent base for château touring and unwinding as there's also plenty to do on the extensive grounds: Aside from a swimming pool and Jacuzzi, there is a tennis court, 9-hole golf course, and children's play area.

Don't miss the restaurant—it's one of the best in the area and is manned by a hot young chef. Items on the fixed-price menus (27€–51€) include carpaccio of monkfish drizzled with dried fruit and lemon vinaigrette, farmer's citrus chicken with young leeks and polenta, braised lamb shank with buttered berry lentils, or vegetarian-friendly wild mushroom risotto.

Route D74, Cangey 37530, near Amboise. www.lefleurayhotel.com. © **02-47-56-09-25.** Fax 02-47-56-93-97. 23 units. 78€–148€ double. MC, V. Free parking. From Amboise, take the D952 on the north side of the river, following signs to Blois; 12km (7½ miles) from Amboise, turn onto D74, in the direction of Cangey. **Amenities:** Restaurant; bar; free bikes; golf course; Jacuzzi; massage; outdoor pool; room service; tennis court. *In room:* TV, hair dryer.

**Le Manoir Les Minimes ★★**    This restored 18th-century mansion is a welcoming, cozy hotel built on the foundation of an ancient convent. On the river's edge, in the shadow of the château, it is surrounded by acres of gardens. Inside, furnishings are elegant in both the public and private rooms, with much use made of antiques. The most desirable rooms are in the main building; a comfortable, well-furnished trio of units is in an annex, although these lack character. No. 10 is a particularly beautiful corner suite with panoramic views. Many of the second-floor bedrooms open onto views of the Loire. The best-value rooms are smaller and on the third floor. Each room has unique decor and comes with an elegant bathroom with tub.

34 quai Charles Guinot, Amboise 37400. www.manoirlesminimes.com. © **02-47-30-40-40.** Fax 02-47-30-40-77. 15 units. 131€–200€ double; 290€–489€ suite. MC, V. **Amenities:** Breakfast room. *In room:* A/C, TV, minibar, free Wi-Fi.

# CHENONCEAUX

224km (139 miles) SW of Paris; 26km (16 miles) E of Tours

Chenonceau is one of the most remarkable castles in France because it spans an entire river. Its impressive setting along with its intriguing history and renowned residents make it many visitors' favorite château in the whole country.

A Renaissance masterpiece, the **Château de Chenonceau ★★★** (www.chenonceau.com; ✆ 02-47-23-90-07) is best known for the dames de Chenonceau, who once occupied it. (The village, whose year-round population is less than 300, is spelled with a final *x,* but the château isn't.) Built first for Katherine Briçonnet, the château was bought in 1547 by Henri II for his mistress, Diane de Poitiers. For a time, this remarkable woman was virtually queen of France, infuriating Henri's dour wife, Catherine de Médicis. Diane's critics accused her of using magic to preserve her celebrated beauty and to keep Henri's attentions from waning. Apparently, Henri's love for Diane continued unabated, and she was in her 60s when he died in a jousting tournament in 1559.

When Henri died, Catherine became regent (her eldest son was still a child) and one of the first things she did was force Diane to return the jewelry Henri had given her and to abandon her beloved home. Catherine added her own touches, building a two-story gallery across the bridge—obviously inspired by her native Flor-

**Garden at the Château de Chenonceau.**

ence. The gallery, which was used for her opulent fetes, doubled as a military hospital in WWI. It also played a crucial role in WWII serving as the demarcation line between Nazi occupied France and the "free" zone.

Gobelin tapestries, including one depicting a woman pouring water over the back of an angry dragon, and several important paintings by Poussin, Rubens and Tintoretto adorn the château's walls. The chapel contains a marble *Virgin and Child* by Murillo, as well as portraits of Catherine de Médicis in black and white. There's even a portrait of the stern Catherine in the former bedroom of her rival, Diane de Poitiers. In François I's Renaissance bedchamber, the most interesting portrait is that of Diane as the huntress Diana.

The women of Chenonceau are the subject of the **Musée de Cire (Wax Museum),** located in a Renaissance-era annex a few steps from the château.

The château is open daily 9am to 8pm July and August; 9am to 7pm for the last two weeks of March; 9am to 7:30pm in June and September, October 9am to 6pm; 9am to 5pm the rest of the year. Admission is 11€ for adults and 8.50€ for students and children 7 to 17. You can purchase a combination ticket including entrance to the château and the museum for 13€ for adults, 11€ ages 7 to 17, free for 6 and under. Allow 2 hours to see this château.

# Essentials

**GETTING THERE**   About a dozen daily **trains** run from Tours to Chenonceaux (trip time: 30 min.), costing 6.30€ one-way. The train deposits you at the base of the château; from there, it's an easy walk. For information, visit www.voyages-sncf.com or call ☏ **36-35**. If you're **driving,** from the center of Tours, follow the signs to the D40 east, which will take you to the signposted turnoff for Chenonceaux.

**VISITOR INFORMATION**   The **Syndicat d'Initiative** (tourist office), 1 rue du Dr. Bretonneau (☏ **02-47-23-94-45**), is open year-round.

# Where to Eat

**La Roseraie** and the **Auberge du Bon-Laboureur** (see below) have very good restaurants.

**Au Gâteau Breton** TRADITIONAL FRENCH   This pretty 18th-century inn was once a grocery store run by an "immigrant" from the distant land of Brittany. Just a short walk from the château, today this restaurant makes a refreshing stop for a casual lunch or tea. Gravel paths run among beds of pink geraniums and lilacs, and bright umbrellas adorn the red tables. In cool months, meals are served in the rustic dining rooms. Worthwhile dishes include homey favorites like *boudin* (blood sausage) with apples, *poulet Tourangelle* (sautéed chicken with mushroom and cream sauce), and steak with *beurre maitre d'hôtel* (butter mixed with parsley, garlic, and lemon).

16 rue du Dr. Bretonneau. www.restaurant-gateau-breton.com. ☏ **02-47-23-90-14.** Reservations required July–Aug. Main courses 14€–18€; fixed-price menus 15€–27€. MC, V. Apr–Sept daily noon–2:30pm, daily 7–10pm; Nov–Mar daily noon–2:30pm.

# Where to Stay

**Auberge du Bon-Laboureur** ★★   This inn, within walking distance of the château, is your best bet for a comfortable night's sleep and exceptional Loire Valley cuisine. Founded in 1786, the hotel maintains the flavor of that era, thanks to thick walls, solid masonry, and a scattering of antiques. Most guest rooms open out onto the garden, which features formally planted roses. Menu choices in the restaurant include crispy lobster with beet vinaigrette, and roasted pigeon with red cabbage celery root compote; the kitchen uses fresh produce direct from the hotel's garden. The prix-fixe menu at lunch is 30€; dinner menus run from 48€ to 85€.

6 rue du Dr. Bretonneau, Chenonceaux 37150. www.amboise.com/laboureur. ☏ **02-47-23-90-02.** Fax 02-47-23-82-01. 25 units. 125€–170€ double; 230€–280€ suite. AE, MC, V. Closed mid-Nov to mid-Dec and Jan 7–Feb 14. **Amenities:** Restaurant; bar; outdoor pool; room service. *In room:* A/C, TV, hair dryer, free Wi-Fi.

**La Roseraie** ★ 🍴   If charm is what you are after, you will be very happy at this friendly inn, where cheerful rooms are individually decorated with lots of period prints and old-fashioned furniture. History has left its mark: Just after World War II, Churchill, Truman, and Eleanor Roosevelt all came through; a framed letter from Mrs. Roosevelt hangs in the cozy salon. The exceptionally helpful and enthusiastic owners also welcome guests at the restaurant, which features homemade foie gras, haddock with dill and pork medallions with mustard sauce.

7 rue du Dr. Bretonneau, Chenonceaux 37150. www.hotel-chenonceau.com. ✆ **02-47-23-90-09.** Fax 02-47-23-91-59. 18 units. 69€–135€ double. AE, DC, MC, V. Closed mid-Nov to mid-Feb. Free parking. **Amenities:** Restaurant; bar; outdoor pool; Wi-Fi in lobby and bar. *In room:* A/C, TV.

**Le Relais Chenonceaux** ✒ Like the two other hotels listed above, this one is the center of the village and just a short walk to the château. The building has a dormer roof and an inviting courtyard filled with flowers in summer. Inside, exposed beams and an old fireplace decorate the restaurant, which serves traditional Loire Valley cuisine. There is also an on-site crêperie for light meals. The rustic bedrooms are personalized and comfortable, nothing fancy but tidily maintained.

10 rue du Docteur Brettoneau, Chenonceaux 37150. www.chenonceaux.com. ✆ **02-47-23-98-11.** Fax 02-47-23-84-07. 24 units. 52€–72€ double. MC, V. Closed mid-Nov to Jan. **Amenities:** Restaurant; bar. *In room:* TV, free Wi-Fi.

# TOURS ★

232km (144 miles) SW of Paris; 113km (70 miles) SW of Orléans

Though it doesn't have a major château, Tours (pop. 137,000), at the junction of the Loire and Cher rivers, is known for its food and wine. Many of its buildings were bombed in World War II, and 20th-century apartment towers have taken the place of châteaux. However, the downtown core is quite charming and as Tours is at the doorstep of some of the most magnificent châteaux in France, it makes a

Outdoor dining in Tours.

good base or starting point from which to explore. Pilgrims en route to Santiago de Compostela in northwest Spain once stopped here to pay homage at the tomb of St-Martin, the "Apostle of Gaul," who was bishop of Tours in the 4th century. One of the most significant conflicts in European history, the 732 Battle of Tours, checked the Arab advance into Gaul. In the 15th century, French kings started setting up shop here, and Tours became the capital of France for over 100 years.

Most Loire Valley towns are rather sleepy, but Tours is where the action is, with busy streets and cafes. A quarter of the residents are students, who add a vibrant touch to a soulless commercial enclave. Allow a morning or an afternoon to see Tours.

## Essentials

**GETTING THERE**   There are as many as 14 high-speed TGV **trains** per day departing from Paris's Gare Montparnasse and arriving at St-Pierre des Corps station, 6km (3¾ miles) east of the center of Tours, in an hour. Free *navettes,* or shuttle buses, await on your arrival to take you to the center of town (the Tours Centre train station). There are also a limited number of conventional trains that depart from Gare d'Austerlitz and arrive in the center of Tours, but they take twice as long (about 2¼ hr.). One-way fares range from 18.30€ to 56€. For information, visit www.voyages-sncf.com or call ✆ **36-35.** If you're **driving,** take highway A10 to Tours.

**GETTING AROUND**   It's easy to walk from one end of central Tours to the other, and many of the good hotels are near the train station. For taxi service, call **Taxi Radio** (✆ **02-47-20-30-40**). You can rent a car at **Avis** (www.avis.fr; ✆ **02-47-20-53-27**), located in the Tours Centre train station, or **Europcar,** at the St-Pierre des Corps station (www.europcar.fr; ✆ **02-47-63-28-67**). You can rent a bike at **Detours de Loire,** 35 rue Charles Gilles (www.locationdevelos.com; ✆ **02-47-61-22-23**), at a cost of 14€ per day. A deposit is required.

**VISITOR INFORMATION**   The **Office de Tourisme** is at 78–82 rue Bernard-Palissy (www.ligeris.com; ✆ **02-47-70-37-37**).

## Exploring the City

The heart of town is **place Jean-Jaurès.** The principal street is **rue Nationale,** running north to the Loire River. Head west along rue du Commerce and rue du Grand-Marché to Vieux Tours/Vieille Ville (old town).

**Cathédrale St-Gatien** CATHEDRAL   This cathedral honors a 3rd-century evangelist and has a Flamboyant Gothic facade flanked by towers with bases from the 12th century. The lanterns date from the Renaissance. The choir is from the 13th century, with new additions built in each century through the 16th. Sheltered inside is the handsome 16th-century tomb of Charles VIII and Anne de Bretagne's two children. Some of the glorious stained-glass windows are from the 13th century.

5 place de la Cathédrale. ✆ **02-47-70-21-00.** Free admission. Daily 9am–7pm.

**Musée des Beaux-Arts** ART MUSEUM   This fine provincial museum in the Palais des Archevêques is worth a visit just to see its lovely rooms and gardens. There are old masters here as well, including works by Rubens, Delacroix,

Rembrandt, and Boucher. The sculpture collection includes works by Houdon and Bourdelle.

18 place François Sicard. www.tours.fr/culture/musees/bxarts. ℂ **02-47-05-68-73.** Admission 4€ adults, 2€ seniors and students, free for children 12 and under. Wed–Mon 9am–6pm. Bus: 3.

## Shopping: To Market We Go

In the pedestrian area of rue de Bordeaux, from the train station to rue Nationale, you'll find dozens of mall-type shops and department stores selling clothes, shoes, jewelry, leather goods, and the like. Up rue Nationale toward the river are more shops and upscale boutiques, and a small mall with chain stores. If you turn left on rue du Commerce toward the old town center, you can explore the streets and courtyards for regional specialties, books, toys, and crafts. A hotbed for antiques is east of rue Nationale (toward the cathedral), along rue de la Scellerie.

Of the more than 30 markets here, the most animated are the **gourmet market (Marché Gourmand),** the first Friday of each month, 4 to 10pm, place de la Résistance; the **antiques market,** the first and third Friday of the month in the pedestrian zone on rue de Bordeaux, and on the fourth Sunday of the month, a larger version of the event with more *brocante* than genuine antiques; the **flower market,** Wednesday and Saturday 8am to 6pm, boulevard Béranger;

and the **craft market (Marché Artisanal),** Saturday 9am to 1pm, place des Halles. The covered market, **Les Halles et Grand Marché,** with a huge selection of fresh local meat, cheese, and produce, is at place Gaston-Pailhou Tuesday through Saturday 6am to 1pm and 3pm to 7pm, and Sunday 6am to 1pm.

# Where to Eat

Restaurants can be pricey, but you can keep costs low at **La Souris Gourmande,** 100 rue Colbert (http://lasourisgourmande.com; ☎ 02-47-47-04-80), where the chef is respected for the diversity of his cheese selection. Try it in half a dozen fondues. You may be asked to join a communal table. Main courses cost 13€ to 15€. At the raffish but cheerful bistro **Le Lapin qui Fume,** 90 rue Colbert (☎ 02-47-66-95-49), a fixed-price menu costs 11€ to 14€ at lunch and 17€ to 24€ at dinner.

## EXPENSIVE

**La Roche le Roy ★★** MODERN FRENCH   Alain Couturier, one of the hottest chefs in town, blends new and old techniques in a gabled 18th-century manor south of the town center. Couturier's repertoire includes lobster risotto, foie gras with caramelized apples, bass with champagne cream sauce, and *matelote* (stew) of eel with Vouvray wine. His masterpiece is supreme of pigeon with "roughly textured" sauce. For dessert, try a warm orange soufflé flavored with Grand Marnier.

55 rte. St-Avertin. www.rocheleroy.com. ☎ **02-47-27-22-00.** Reservations recommended. Main courses 25€–38€, lunch menu 34€, dinner menu 78€. AE, MC, V. Wed–Sat noon–1:30pm and 7:30–9:30pm. Closed 2 weeks in Feb and 3 weeks in Aug. From the center of town, take av. Grammont south (follow signs to St-Avertin–Vierzon).

## MODERATE

**Rive Gauche ★** TRADITIONAL FRENCH   Having recently changed chefs, this gourmet restaurant now touts "responsible gastronomy," which takes into consideration both taste and environmental impact. The talented young chef, Gaëtan Evrard, uses his lively imagination and high-quality local and/or artisanal products to create surprising dishes like steamed Loire mullet with crushed apples, gambas with Rioja chorizo, foie gras stuffed Orléans partridge with Japanese dashi bouillon and sancho pepper. Dessert includes an award-winning *nougat de Tours,* a light almond cake, served warm and topped with apricot sherbet. You can savor these delicacies in either of the two cozy dining rooms or, in warm weather, outdoors on the terrace.

23 rue du Commerce. www.tours-rivegauche.com. ☎ **02-47-05-71-21.** Reservations required. Main courses 15€–32€; fixed-price menu 26€–69€. AE MC, V. Daily 12:30pm–2pm and 7:30–10pm.

## INEXPENSIVE

**Le Petit Patrimoine** TRADITIONAL FRENCH   This pocket-size, long-established restaurant exudes a powerful, albeit quirky and idiosyncratic, appeal. Outfitted in a rustic and old-fashioned style that might have been inspired by someone's early-20th-century grandmother, it has exposed ceiling beams, old masonry walls, and a sense of respect for old-fashioned French aesthetics and values. Your hosts, each a distinct personality known by clients as either independent-minded or curmudgeonly, depending on their mood of the moment, will propose dishes that include a savory *matelote* of veal with baby vegetables, a salad of *rillons* (a meat byproduct made from bacon), and grilled beefsteaks with goat cheese.

58 rue Colbert. (©) **02-47-66-05-81.** Reservations recommended. Main courses 14€; fixed-price menu 12€—14€ lunch, 18€–25€ dinner. MC, V. Tues–Sat noon–2pm and 7–10pm.

## Tours Nightlife

Long a student town, Tours has a lively young population. Even during summer, when most students have left, a youthful crowd rules the hot spots. **Place Plumereau** (often shortened to "place Plume"), a square of medieval buildings, houses a concentration of restaurants and bars. In the warmer months, the square explodes with tables, which fill with people who like to people-watch (and be watched themselves). In addition to the bars and clubs around the place Plumereau, an even trendier street, **rue Colbert,** has emerged as a hip and fashionable strip. Rue Colbert lies in the heart of Tours, midway between the place Plumereau and the cathedral.

The hottest place in town is **L'Excalibur,** 35 rue Briçonnet ((©) **02-47-64-76-78**), with an electro beat and video system. A clientele of all ages, many from the surrounding countryside, heads to **Le Pyms,** 170 av. de Grammont (www.lepyms.com; (©) **02-47-66-22-22**), where there are two spaces, one playing '80s nostalgia and the other contemporary electro.

And if you're gay, relatively energetic, and like to dance, check out the town's most popular gay bar and disco, **Le G.I.,** 13 rue Lavoisier (www.giclub.fr; (©) **02-47-66-29-96**). Positioned on a dark street in a safe but somewhat rundown neighborhood, it attracts a local, mostly male crowd that packs the place on weekends.

## Where to Stay

**Best Western Le Central** Off the main boulevard, this old-fashioned hotel is within walking distance of the train station, the river, and the cathedral. Despite its central location, there is plenty of greenery here: The back of the hotel looks out on a leafy garden, and the front is set off by a lawn. The decor is classic and conservative, and blends well with the 19th-century building. Half of the guest rooms have tub/showers, the others only showers.

21 rue Berthelot, Tours 37000. www.bestwesterncentralhoteltours.com. (©) **800/528-1234** in the U.S. and Canada, or 02-47-05-46-44. Fax 02-47-66-10-26. 37 units. 95€–155€ double; 195€–250€ suite. AE, DC, MC, V. Parking 10€. **Amenities:** Bar; babysitting; room service. *In room:* A/C, TV, hair dryer, minibar, free Wi-Fi.

**Hôtel du Manoir** On a quiet street near the train station, this 19th-century residence is a comfortable and affordable place to stay. The cheerful reception area reflects the quality of the rooms. Though small to average in size, all units have windows that let in lots of light and afford views of the neighborhood or the hotel courtyard. Most have simple furnishings.

2 rue Traversière, Tours 37000. http://hotel.manoir.tours.voila.net. (©) **02-47-05-37-37.** Fax 02-47-05-16-00. 20 units. 65€–75€ double. AE, MC, V. Parking 7€. *In room:* TV, hair dryer, free Wi-Fi.

**Château-Hopping Made Easy**

Several tour companies in Tours arrange full- and half-day visits to nearby castles, and three of them offer mini bus tours that leave daily from the tourist office. **Acco-Dispo** (www.accodispo-tours.com; ☎ **06-82-00-64-51**), **Saint-Eloi Excursions** (http://saint-eloiexcursions.com; ☎ **06-70-82-78-75**), and **Quart de Tours** (www.quartdetours.com; ☎ **06-30-65-52-01**) all offer mini bus tours that depart around 9am; you can reserve on the tourist office website (see above) or contact them directly. Costs range from 20€ to 52€ per person, depending on the company and how many castles you want to see. The price does not include meals or admission to the châteaux, but participation in the tour qualifies you for reduced group rates. Keep in mind that less is sometimes more when it comes to castle viewing; after two or three, you may not be able to remember which was which.

# Where to Eat & Stay Nearby

**Château d'Artigny ★★★** This is perhaps the grandest address in the Loire Valley. About 1.5km (1 mile) west of the hamlet of Montbazon and 15km (9¼ miles) south of Tours, the château was built between 1912 and 1920 for perfume and cosmetics king François Coty, who lived and entertained lavishly. Set in a forest, overlooking formal gardens, the château combines Jazz Age ostentation and 18th-century French aesthetics. The drawing room and corridors are furnished with fine antiques, Louis XV–style chairs, and bronze statuary. The grounds contain acres of parks and a large garden with a reflecting pool. Guest rooms are outfitted in period style, with many antiques, comfortable mattresses, and all the perks of upscale country living. Only 31 units are in the main building; the others are in four annexes—a former chapel, gatehouse, mill, and staff dormitory.

Rte. des Monts (D17), Montbazon 37250. www.artigny.com. ☎ **02-47-34-30-30.** Fax 02-47-34-30-39. 65 units. 136€–380€ double; 390€–490€ junior suite. AE, DC, MC, V. From Tours, take N10 south for 11km (6¾ miles) to Montbazon, and then take D17 1.5km (1 mile) southeast. **Amenities:** Restaurant; bar; babysitting; exercise room; outdoor pool; room service; sauna; spa; 2 tennis courts. *In room:* TV, hair dryer, minibar, free Wi-Fi (in some).

**Château de Beaulieu ★★** At this 18th-century estate, about 5km (3 miles) south of Tours, you can experience the lifestyle of another era. Beyond the entrance, a double-curving stairway leads to the reception hall. Guest rooms have mahogany and chestnut furniture, decorative fireplaces, and chic modern bathrooms. Nine are in the château (we recommend these); the others, a bit more sterile, are in a turn-of-the-20th-century pavilion a stone's throw away. All have elegant beds outfitted with comfortable mattresses.

67 rue de Beaulieu, Joué-les-Tours 37300. www.chateaudebeaulieu37.com. ☎ **02-47-53-20-26.** Fax 02-47-53-84-20. 19 units. 97€–275€ double. AE, MC, V. From Tours, take av. de Grammont south, and turn right on bd. Winston Churchill and then left on av. de Pont Cher and right on rue de Beaulieu. **Amenities:** Restaurant; bar; bike rental. *In room:* A/C, TV, hair dryer, minibar, free Wi-Fi.

# LOCHES ★★

258km (160 miles) SW of Paris; 40km (25 miles) SE of Tours

Forever linked to legendary beauty Agnès Sorel, Loches is an exquisite village, situated on the banks of the Indre. Sitting high on a bluff overlooking the valley, the château and its satellite buildings form a complex called the **Cité Royale ★**. The House of Anjou, from which the Plantagenets descended, owned the castle from 886 to 1205. Its royal legacy continued with its occupation by the kings of France from the mid–13th century until Charles IX became king in 1560.

**Château de Loches ★★**, 5 place Charles-VII (www.chateau-loches.fr; ✆ 02-47-59-01-32), is one of the region's best examples of medieval architecture and is remembered for the *belle des belles* (beauty of beauties) Agnès Sorel, who lived there in the 15th century. Maid of honor to Isabelle de Lorraine, Charles VII became so enamored by Agnès that he bestowed his new mistress with the château. She bore the king three daughters and wielded great influence over him until her mysterious death. She was immortalized on canvas posthumous by Fouquet as a practically topless Virgin Mary–with a disgruntled Charles VII looking on. (The original is in Antwerp; the château has a copy.) The château also contains the oratory of Anne de Bretagne, decorated with ermine tails. One of its outstanding treasures is a triptych of *The Passion* (1485) from the Fouquet school.

The massive 36 meter-high (118 feet) keep, or *donjon,* of the comtes d'Anjou was built in the 11th century and turned into a prison by Louis XI. The Round Tower contains rooms used for torture; a favorite method involved suspending the victim in an iron cage. In the 15th century, the duke of Milan,

Dungeon at Loches.

Ludovico Sforza, was imprisoned in the Martelet and painted frescoes on the walls to pass the time; he died here in 1508.

You can visit the château, the keep, and medieval garden without a guide daily. It's open April to September from 9am to 7pm, and October to March 9:30am to 5pm, in August there is usually a medieval festival held at the castle.

Tickets to the château and the dungeon cost 7€ for adults, 4.50€ for students, and 4.50€ for children 12 to 18. Children 11 and under enter free.

The tomb of Agnès Sorel rests nearby at the Romanesque **Collégiale St-Ours (Collegiate Church of St-Ours),** 1 rue Thomas-Pactius (✆ 02-47-59-02-36), which was erected in the 11th and 12th centuries. Sculpted figures of saints and animals decorate the portal. Stone pyramids (*dubes*) surmount the nave; the carving on the west door is exceptional. The church is open daily from 9am to 7pm, except during mass; admission is free.

Finally, you may want to walk the ramparts and enjoy the view of the town, including a 15th-century gate and Renaissance inns.

Allow 3 hours to see Loches.

## Essentials

**GETTING THERE**   Six to 10 **buses** run daily from Tours, run by the SNCF railway; the 50-minute trip costs 8.60€ one-way. For schedules, visit www.voyages-sncf.com or call ✆ 02-47-05-30-49. If you're **driving** from Tours, take N143 southeast to Loches.

**VISITOR INFORMATION**   The **Office de Tourisme** is near the bus station on place de la Marne (www.loches-tourainecotesud.com; ✆ 02-47-91-82-82).

## Where to Eat & Stay

Loches is short on inns and good restaurants. If you're here for lunch, we recommend the 19th-century **Hôtel George-Sand,** 39 rue Quintefol (www.hotel restaurant-georgesand.com; ✆ 02-47-59-39-74), for its Touraine cuisine, including filet of pikeperch from the Loire. It also rents 19 rooms; doubles go for 65€ to 130€.

**Hotel de France ★**   This charming hotel was a postal relay station until the mid–19th century. In 1932, it gained three floors and became an inn. Before the turn of the 21st century, management upgraded and redecorated the guest rooms, added new beds, and restored the small bathrooms. The most tranquil rooms overlook the courtyard. You can dine in the wood-paneled dining room or under the parasols in the courtyard.

6 rue Picois, Loches 37600. http://h.france.loches.free.fr. ✆ **02-47-59-00-32.** Fax 02-47-59-28-66. 17 units. 62€–90€ double. AE, DC, MC, V. Parking 5€. Closed Jan 5 to early Feb and mid-Nov to mid-Dec. **Amenities:** Restaurant; bar; free Internet; room service. *In room:* TV.

**Le Château de Reignac ★★ 🎁**   The former château of the Marquis de la Fayette has been entirely renovated and is today one of the most luxurious châteaux in the Loire. You can explore the landscaped grounds with their ancient trees, have a drink in a plush 18th-century living room, or relax in the book-lined library as you listen to your favorite opera. The antiques-filled bedrooms, each sumptuously furnished, were named for famous people in French history, each a guest who had stayed here with the marquis. Gourmet-level food is served in the evening along with wine from the Touraine. A stay here is like wandering back to a more elegant age.

19 rue Louis de Barberin, Reignac-sur-Indre 37310. www.lechateaudereignac.com. ✆ **02-47-94-14-10.** Fax 02-47-94-12-67. 13 units. 172€–202€ double; 252€ junior suite; 354€ family suite for 4. AE, MC, V. 15km (9¼ miles) north of Loches. **Amenities:** Restaurant for guests; room service; tennis court, babysitting, Wi-Fi in common areas. *In room:* Hair dryer.

# VILLANDRY

253km (157 miles) SW of Paris; 32km (20 miles) NE of Chinon; 18km (11 miles) W of Tours; 8km (5 miles) E of Azay-le-Rideau

The 16th-century-style gardens of the Renaissance **Château de Villandry** ★★★ (www.chateauvillandry.com; ✆ **02-47-50-02-09**) are celebrated throughout Touraine and amaze visitors from around the world with their beauty and faithful historic preservation.

Every square of the gardens is like a geometric mosaic. Designed on a trio of superimposed cloisters with a water garden on the highest level, they were restored by the Spanish doctor and scientist Joachim Carvallo, great-grandfather of the present owner. The grounds contain 17km (11 miles) of boxwood sculpture, which the gardeners cut to style in only 2 weeks each September. The borders symbolize the faces of love: tender, tragic (represented by daggers), and crazy (with a labyrinth that doesn't get you anywhere). Pink tulips and dahlias suggest sweet love; red, tragic; and yellow, unfaithful. All colors signify crazy love. The vine arbors, citrus hedges, and walks keep six men busy full-time. They are also reverting the French vegetable garden to being completely organic.

Château de Villandry.

277

A feudal castle once stood at Villandry. In 1536, Jean le Breton, François I's Finance Minister and former Ambassador to Italy, acquired the property and built the present château with strong influences of the Italian Renaissance. The buildings form a U and are surrounded by a moat. Near the gardens is a terrace from which you can see the small village and its 12th-century church. A tearoom on-site, **La Doulce Terrasse** (www.chateauvillandry.com; ℭ **02-47-50-02-10**; closed mid-Nov to mid-Feb), serves regional cuisine, including hot dishes, with vegetables for the garden, freshly baked bread, and homemade ice cream.

Admission to the gardens, including a guided tour of the château, costs 9.50€ for adults, 5.50€ for children 8 to 18, and is free for children 7 and under. Visiting the gardens separately, without a guide, costs 6.50€ for adults and 4€ for children 8 to 18. The gardens are open daily 9am to between 5 and 7:30pm, depending on the hour of sunset; the château is open daily from 9am to between 4:30 and 6:30pm, depending on a complicated seasonal schedule. Tours are conducted in French; leaflets are available in English. Allow 1½ hours to see Villandry.

## Essentials

**GETTING THERE**   There are three daily **buses** from Tours that operate from July to October only; the trip takes about 30 minutes and costs 1.70€. For bus information, visit www.touraine-filvert.com or call ℭ **02-47-05-30-49**. Villandry has no train service. The nearest connection from Tours is at the town of Savonnières; the trip takes around 15 minutes and costs 3.20€ one-way. For information, visit www.voyages-sncf.com or call ℭ **36-35**. From Savonnières, you can walk along the Loire for 4km (2½ miles) to reach Villandry, rent a **bike** at the station, or take a **taxi.** You can also **drive,** following D7 from Tours.

**VISITOR INFORMATION**   The **Office de Tourisme** is located in a kiosk in front of the hotel Le Cheval Rouge (see below), in the center of town (www.villandry-tourisme.com; ℭ **02-47-50-12-66**).

## Where to Eat & Stay

**Le Cheval Rouge** MODERN FRENCH   The well-known dining stopover near the château extends a congenial welcome. The conservatively decorated dining room lies about 91m (298 ft.) from the banks of the Cher. Specialties include bream flavored with vanilla, scallops flambéed with whiskey, roast lamb with thyme, and veal with *pleurotes,* a type of wild mushroom. The inn also rents 41 rooms, all with free in-room Wi-Fi. A double is 47€ to 62€.

9 rue Principale, Villandry 37510. www.lecheval-rouge.com. ℭ **02-47-50-02-07.** Fax 02-47-50-08-77. Reservations recommended. Main courses 15€–18€; fixed-price menu 20€–35€. AE, DC, MC, V. Daily noon–2:30pm and 7–9pm.

# LANGEAIS

259km (161 miles) SW of Paris; 26km (16 miles) W of Tours

On December 6, 1491, 15-year-old Anne de Bretagne was wed to Charles VIII at Langeais, permanently attaching Brittany to France. It was the castle's golden hour.

## Château de Langeais ★★ CASTLE ☺

Dominating the town on a steep slope, this medieval fortress is one of the few châteaux actually on the Loire. The facade is forbidding, but once you cross the drawbridge, you'll find the apartments so richly decorated that they soften the effect. The original castle was built in the 10th century when Fulk III (972–1040), count of Anjou, sometimes called The Black Falcon, seized Langeais from the Count of Blois. He erected the first keep, the ruins of which can still be seen. The present structure was built in 1465 in the late medieval style. The interior is well preserved and furnished, thanks to Jacques Siegfried, who not only restored it over 20 years, but also bequeathed it to the Institut de France in 1904.

The rooms re-create the ambience of a regal residence of the late Middle Ages, rich with ornamental fireplaces and tapestries. A remark-

**View from the Château de Langeais.**

able 15th-century "millefleurs" tapestry decorates the Chambre de la Dame, and seven superb tapestries known as the Valiant Knights cover the walls of the Salle des Preux.

The Banquet Hall features a mantelpiece carved to resemble a fortress, complete with crenellated towers. The Wedding Hall includes a recreation of the marriage of Anne de Bretagne and Charles VIII with lavishly costumed wax figures. In the Luini Room is a large 1522 fresco by that artist, removed from a chapel on Lake Maggiore, Italy. It depicts Saint Francis of Assisi and Saint Elizabeth of Hungary with Mary and Joseph. Kids can learn medieval castle construction with interactive displays and with reconstructed scaffolding, they can also have some fun exploring the tree house and the two playgrounds. Allow 1½ hours to go through the château.

Langeais 37130. www.chateau-de-langeais.com. ✆ **02-47-96-72-60.** Admission 8.50€ adults, 7.20€ students and ages 18–25, 5€ for children 10–17, free for 9 and under. Daily Apr–June and Sept to mid-Nov 9:30am–6:30pm; mid-Nov to Jan 10am–5pm; Feb–Mar 9:30am–5:30pm; July–Aug 9am–7pm.

## Essentials

**GETTING THERE** Several **trains** per day stop here en route from Tours or Saumur. The one-way fare from Saumur is 7.50€, the one-way fare from Tours 5.10€. Transit time from both cities is around 20 minutes. For schedules and information, visit www.voyages-sncf.com or call ✆ **36-35.** If you're **driving** from Tours, take D952 southwest to Langeais.

**VISITOR INFORMATION** The **Office de Tourisme** is at place du 14-Juillet (www.tourisme-langeais.com or ☏ **02-47-96-58-22**).

## Where to Eat & Stay

**Hotel Errard Hosten ★** This ivy-draped country inn in the center of town was built in 1853. In 2002, it added a neighboring house, creating a hotel–restaurant complex. The restaurant, which has received many honors, is elegant and formal, while the hotel that houses it is a bit more relaxed. Guest rooms are rustic and comfortable, and some (particularly the suites in the annex) are surprisingly large. Most of the well-maintained tiled bathrooms have tub/showers. Guests dine indoors or at tables in the open courtyard under umbrellas and flowering trees. The *menu de prestige* accompanied by regional wines includes Anjou escargots with thyme, and filet of guinea fowl with tarragon. For a standout dessert, try Creole spring rolls filled with exotic fruit and sprinkled with aged rum.

2 rue Gambetta, Langeais 37130. www.errard.com. ☏ **02-47-96-82-12.** Fax 02-47-96-56-72. Restaurant: main course menus 28€–59€. 10 units. 72€–82€ double; 98€–115€ apt. AE, MC, V. Parking 5€. Closed mid-Dec–Jan. **Amenities:** Restaurant; bar. *In room:* TV, hair dryer, free Internet.

# AZAY-LE-RIDEAU

261km (162 miles) SW of Paris; 21km (13 miles) SW of Tours

With its idyllic location and fairy tale turrets the Renaissance **Château d'Azay-le-Rideau ★★**, rue Pineau, Azay-le-Rideau 37190 (http://azay-le-rideau.monuments-nationaux.fr; ☏ **02-47-45-42-04**) instantly enchants visitors and was even deemed by neighboring writer Honoré de Balzac as "a facetted diamond set in the Indre." Its machicolated towers and blue-slate roof pierced with dormers give it a medieval air; however, its defensive-fortress–like appearance is all for show. The château was actually commissioned in the early 1500s for Gilles Berthelot, François I's finance minister, and his wife, Philippa, who supervised its construction. They didn't have long to enjoy their elegant creation: In 1527, Berthelot was accused of misappropriation of funds and forced to flee, and the château reverted to the king. He didn't live here, but granted it to Antoine Raffin, one of his high-ranking soldiers. It became the property of the state in 1905.

Château d'Azay-le-Rideau.

Before you enter, circle the château and note the perfect proportions of the crowning achievement of the Renaissance in the Touraine. Check out its most fancifully ornate feature, the bay enclosing a grand stairway with a straight flight of steps.

From the second-floor Royal Chamber, look out at the gardens. This lavish bedroom

## For Literary Fans: An Ode to Balzac

Seven kilometers (4¼ miles) east of Azay-le-Rideau (take D17), you can visit **Saché,** the hometown of Honoré de Balzac. Here he wrote several of his novels, including *The Lily of the Valley* and *Père Goriot.* He declared that his affection for the Touraine was like "the love of the artist for his art." Of interest to fans is the **Musée Balzac,** in the 19th-century Château de Saché, Saché 37190 (www.musee-balzac.fr; ℂ **02-47-26-86-50**). The small château contains the writer's bedrooms, preserved as they were when he lived here. A collection of Balzac's notes, first editions, etchings, letters, and cartoons are on display, as is a copy of Rodin's sculpture of the writer. The castle and museum are open daily April to June (and Sept) 10am to 6pm, July and August 10am to 7pm; closed Tuesdays October to March, when its opening hours are 10am to 12:30pm and 2 to 5pm. Admission is 5€ for adults, 4€ for seniors and students, and free for children 11 and under.

housed Louis XIII when he came through in 1619. The private apartments are lined with rich tapestries dating from the 16th and 17th centuries and feature examples of rare period furniture, like the Spanish *bargueno,* a carved wooden chest that held writing materials.

The château is open daily in July and August 9:30am to 7pm, April to June and September 9:30am to 6pm, and October to March 10am to 12:30pm and 2 to 5:30pm. Admission is 8.50€ for adults, 5.50€ for ages 18 to 25, and free for children 17 and under. Allow 2 hours for a visit.

In July and August, there is a guided outdoor tour/performance that features actors in period dress, animals, recorded music, and lights beaming on the exterior of the château. The tour, which lasts about 1hours, begins at 9:15 and 10:20pm. Tickets are 10€ for adults, 6€ for ages 12 to 25, and free for children 11 and under.

## Essentials

**GETTING THERE**   To reach Azay-le-Rideau, take the **train** from Tours or Chinon. From either starting point, the trip time is about 30 minutes; the one-way fare is 4.70€ from Chinon, 5.30€ from Tours. For the same fare, the SNCF railway also operates a bus between Tours and Azay; the trip takes 50 minutes. For schedules and information, visit www.voyages-sncf.com or call ℂ **36-35**. If you're **driving** from Tours, take D751 southwest to Azay-le-Rideau.

**VISITOR INFORMATION**   The **Office de Tourisme** is on place de L'Europe (www.ot-paysazaylerideau.com; ℂ **02-47-45-44-40**).

## Where to Eat & Stay

**L'Aigle d'Or ★** TRADITIONAL FRENCH   This excellent restaurant is set in a century-old house. Located in the village center, the service is professional, the welcome charming, and the food the best in Azay. In a dining room accented with ceiling beams, a fireplace, and pastel colors, you can savor dishes including foie gras with pears and *blanquette* (stew) of Loire Valley whitefish prepared with local white wine. Desserts include baked apple with rice pudding mousse, and chocolate cake with sour cherry coulis. In summer, dining extends onto an outdoor terrace.

10 av. Adélaïde-Riché. ℰ **02-47-45-24-58.** Reservations recommended. Main courses 12€–24€; fixed-price menus 27€–54€. V. Mon–Tues and Thurs–Sat noon–1:30pm and 7:30–9pm.

**Le Grand Monarque**    The ivy that covers the exterior of this hotel—less than 150m (492 ft.) from the château—seems to protect it from the modern world. The large guest rooms are outfitted with antiques; ancient exposed beams adorn the lobby ceiling. Units in the annex aren't as well decorated but are more tranquil; those looking out on the wide courtyard are particularly quiet.

The restaurant features dishes like a brochette of crayfish with sesame sauce, suprême of *sandre* in shallot-flavored broth, and rack of Touraine pork with oyster mushrooms and tarragon. Fixed-price menus range from 29€ to 35€. During warmer months, you can dine out on the courtyard terrace.

3 place de la République, Azay-le-Rideau 37190. www.legrandmonarque.com. ℰ **02-47-45-40-08.** Fax 02-47-45-46-25. 24 units. 75€–148€ double. AE, MC, V. Parking 10€. Closed Dec to mid-Jan. **Amenities:** Restaurant; bar; babysitting; room service. *In room:* TV, hair dryer, free Wi-Fi.

# CHINON ★★

283km (175 miles) SW of Paris; 48km (30 miles) SW of Tours; 31km (19 miles) SW of Langeais

In the film *Joan of Arc,* Ingrid Bergman identified the dauphin as he tried to conceal himself among his courtiers. This took place in real life at the Château de Chinon, one of the oldest fortress-châteaux in France. Charles VII centered his government at Chinon from 1429 to 1450. In 1429, with the English besieging Orléans, the Maid of Orléans prevailed upon the dauphin to give her an army. The rest is history. The seat of French power stayed at Chinon until the end of the Hundred Years' War.

Today Chinon remains a tranquil town known mainly for its delightful red wines. After you visit the attractions, we recommend taking a walk along the Vienne River; definitely stop to taste the wine at one of Chinon's terraced cafes. Allow 3 hours to see Chinon.

## Essentials

**GETTING THERE**    The SNCF runs about seven **trains** and four **buses** every day to Chinon from Tours (trip time: 45 min. by train; 1 hr., 15 min. by bus), the one-way fare is 8.90€. For schedules and information, visit www.voyages-sncf.com or call ℰ **36-35**. Both buses and trains arrive at the train station, which lies at the edge of the very small town. If you're **driving** from Tours, take D751 southwest through Azay-le-Rideau to Chinon.

**VISITOR INFORMATION**    The **Office de Tourisme** is at place Hofheim (www.chinon-valdeloire.com; ℰ **02-47-93-17-85**).

## Exploring the Town & the Château

On the banks of the Vienne, the winding streets of Chinon are lined with many medieval turreted houses, built in the heyday of the court. The most typical street is rue Voltaire, lined with 15th- and 16th-century town houses. At no. 44, Richard the Lion-Hearted died on April 6, 1199, from a wound suffered during the siege of Chalus in Limousin. The Grand Carroi, in the heart of Chinon, served as the crossroads of the Middle Ages. For the best view, drive across the river and turn right onto quai Danton. From this vantage point, you'll be able to see the castle in relation to the town and the river.

**Château de Chinon** ★★ CASTLE   The château, which was more or less in ruins, has undergone a massive excavation and restoration effort that started in 2003 and so far has resulted in beautifully restored ramparts, castle keep, and royal apartments, which now look more or less as they did in the good old days. After being roofless for 200 years, the apartments now sport pitched and gabled slate roofs and wood floors, and the keep is once again fortified. The restoration, while not exact (due to the state of the original building), gives the overall impression of what the castle looked like around the time of Joan of Arc's visit. The buildings are separated by a series of moats, adding to its medieval look. A new building has been construction on the foundations of the Fort of St-George, which serves as an entrance hall and museum, featuring new archeological finds discovered during the restoration, as well as objects and interactive displays that recount the story of Joan of Arc, Charles VII, and the history of the castle.

Btw. rue St-Maurice and av. Francois Mitterrand. www.forteressechinon.fr. ℰ **02-47-93-13-45.** Admission 7€ adults, 4.50€ students, free for children 12 and under. Open daily May-Aug 9:30am–7pm; Mar, Apr and Sept 9am–6pm; Oct–Feb 9:30am–5pm.

Château de Chinon.

# IN PURSUIT OF THE grape

Chinon is famous for its wines, which crop up on prestigious lists around the world. Supermarkets and wine shops throughout the region sell them; families that have been in the business longer than anyone can remember maintain the two most interesting stores. At **Caves Plouzeau,** 94 rue Haute-St-Maurice (www.plouzeau.com; ✆ **02-47-93-32-11**), the 12th-century cellars were dug to provide building blocks for the foundations of the château. The present management dates from 1929; bottles of red or white wine cost from 6€ to 12€. You're welcome to climb down to the cellars. They are open for wine sales and visits April to September Tuesday to Saturday 11am to 1pm and 3 to 7pm.

The cellars at **Couly-Dutheil,** 12 rue Diderot (www.coulydutheil-chinon.com; ✆ **02-47-97-20-20**), are suitably medieval; many were carved from rock. This company produces largely Chinon wines (mostly reds), and it's proud of the Bourgueil and St-Nicolas de Bourgueil, whose popularity in North America has grown in recent years. Tours of the caves and a *dégustation des vins* (wine tasting) require an advance call and cost 4€ to 6€ per person. Visits are conducted year round 8am to noon and 1:45 to 5:45pm.

**Musée Rabelais–La Devinière** MUSEUM   The most famous son of Chinon, François Rabelais, the earthy and often bawdy Renaissance writer, lived in town on rue de la Lamproie. (A plaque marks the spot where his father practiced law and maintained a home and office.) This site, just outside of the hamlet of Seuilly, 5.5km (3½ miles) west of Chinon, was an isolated cottage at the time of his birth. It was maintained, because of local superstition and custom, for the sole purpose of delivering the children of the Rabelais clan into the world.

The museum has three floors of exhibition space, each focusing on an aspect of Rabelais, his times, and his role in Chinon. In two neighboring buildings, you'll find exhibits on aspects of life during the Middle Ages, including an unusual display on medicinal plants.

La Devinière, just outside of Seuilly off the N751. www.monuments-touraine.fr ✆ **02-47-95-91-18**. Admission 4.50€ adults, 3€ students, free for children 11 and under. Open daily Apr–June 10am–12:30pm and 2–6pm; July–Aug 10am–7pm; Sept 10am–12:30pm and 2–6pm; Oct–Mar Wed–Mon 10am–12:30pm and 2–5pm. From Chinon, follow the road signs pointing to Saumur and the D117.

## Where to Eat

**Les Années 30** FRENCH   On the oldest street in Chinon, you'll find the town's most innovative restaurant. If the charming 16th-century building doesn't entice you, the excellent value menu certainly will. In summer, savor lobster duo with avocado and papaya salsa on the shady terrace and in winter, feast on pheasant with roasted figs or venison marinated with spiced gin with a vegetable and chestnut tart beside the cozy fireplace.

78 rue Haute St-Maurice www.lesannees30.com. ✆ **02-47-93-37-18**. Reservations recommended. Main courses 18€–32€; fixed-price lunch menu 16€, dinner menus 27€–43€. MC, V. Thurs–Mon 12:15–2:00pm; Tues–Sat 7:30–10pm.

# Chinon Nightlife

A charming bar and nighttime hangout is **Le Café Français,** 37 place du Général-de-Gaulle (www.cafefrancais.fr; ℂ **02-47-93-32-78**). Behind the Hotel de Ville (town hall), it attracts the local young crowd. There's a modest admission charge for occasional concerts.

# Where to Stay

**Hostellerie Gargantua** ★   This 15th-century building was once a courthouse where the father of François Rabelais worked as a lawyer in the 15th century. Art historians admire the building's early Renaissance staircase and its chiseled-stone details. The hotel has some quirks as one would expect due to its age, but its large guest rooms have a lot of charm featuring high ceilings and canopy beds, and a few have stone fireplaces and/or views of the castle. Try to stop here for a meal, served in a medieval hall. You can sample Loire *sandre* prepared with Chinon wine or duckling with dried pears and smoked lard, followed by a medley of seasonal red fruits in puff pastry.

73 rue Haute St. Maurice, Chinon 37500. www.hotel-gargantua.com. ℂ **02-47-93-04-71.** Fax 02-47-93-08-02. 7 units. 55€–81€ double. AE, MC, V. Closed Dec **Amenities:** Restaurant; bar. *In room:* TV, free Wi-Fi.

**Hôtel Diderot** ★ 👜   Within a 5-minute walk of the town's historic core, this is a comfortable hotel with strands of ivy climbing romantically up its stone front. Although the foundations date from the 14th century, the building was radically altered in the 1700s; today you'll see remnants of thick wall and ceiling beams throughout the public rooms and in some of the guest rooms. Rooms are midsize to spacious, outfitted in Henry II or Napoleon III style, usually with big windows letting in maximum sunlight. One of the architectural highlights is a magnificent 15th-century fireplace in the breakfast room, where you'll enjoy as many as 52 kinds of jams and jellies as part of your morning ritual. The congenial hosts' enthusiasm for the charms of their home town is contagious.

4 rue du Buffon, Chinon 37500. www.hoteldiderot.com. ℂ **02-47-93-18-87.** Fax 02-47-93-37-10. 27 units. 55€–82€ double. AE, DC, MC, V. Parking 7€. **Amenities:** Bar. *In room:* TV, hair dryer, free Wi-Fi. Closed 1st 2 weeks of Dec and last week of Jan through 1st week of Feb.

# Where to Eat & Stay Nearby

**Château de Marçay** ★★★   This property began in the 1100s as a fortress and took its present form during the Renaissance. The centerpiece of the wine-producing hamlet of Marçay, it's sumptuously decorated. The main building houses the more opulent lodgings; a handful of less expensive, less dramatic rooms are in an annex a short walk away. Menu specialties change with the season at the restaurant, and the chef works hard to maintain high standards. The garden terrace and elegantly rustic dining room afford a panoramic view.

Marçay, Chinon 37500. www.chateaudemarcay.com. ℂ **02-47-93-03-47.** Fax 02-47-93-45-33. 33 units. 105€–225€ double; 240€–290€ suite. AE, DC, MC, V. Closed mid-Jan to mid-Mar. Take D116 for 7km (4¼ miles) southwest of Chinon. **Amenities:** Restaurant; bar; outdoor pool; room service; tennis court. *In room:* TV, hair dryer, minibar, Wi-Fi.

**Manoir de la Giraudière**   Built during the mid-1600s, this elegant manor house resembles a small château because of its use of *tuffeau* (the beige stone used in residences of many of the French monarchs). In a 2.4-hectare (6-acre) park surrounded by hundreds of acres of fields and forests, this midrange establishment offers classic decor and modern comforts. Each good-size room comes with a fine bed and quality linen. Air-conditioning isn't necessary because the thick walls act as natural insulation against heat and cold. A small on-site restaurant serves light meals.

15 rue de la Giraudiere, Beaumont-en-Veron 37420. www.giraudiere.com. ☏ **02-47-58-40-36.** Fax 02-47-58-46-06. 24 units. 71€–135€ double; 100€–130€ apartment. AE, DC, MC, V. Head 5km (3 miles) west of Chinon along D749 toward Bourgueil. **Amenities:** Restaurant; bar. *In room:* TV, hair dryer, free Wi-Fi.

# USSÉ

295km (183 miles) SW of Paris; 14km (8¾ miles) NE of Chinon

At the edge of the dark forest of Chinon in Rigny-Ussé, **Château d'Ussé ★** (www.chateaudusse.fr; ☏ **02-47-95-54-05**) was the inspiration for Perrault's legend of *The Sleeping Beauty (La Belle au bois dormant)*. Conceived as a fortress in 1424, the complex of steeples, turrets, towers, and dormers was erected at the dawn of the Renaissance on a hill overlooking the Indre River. The terraces, laden with orange and lemon trees, were laid out by royal gardener Le Nôtre. When the need for a fortified château passed, the north wing was demolished to open up a greater view.

The château was later owned by the duc de Duras and then by Mme. de la Rochejaquelein; its present owner, the marquis de Blacas, has opened many rooms to the public, most recently the private dining room and the dungeon. The visit begins in the Renaissance chapel, with its sculptured portal and handsome stalls. You then proceed to the royal apartments, furnished with tapestries and antiques. One gallery displays an extensive collection of swords and rifles. A spiral stairway leads to a tower with a panoramic view of the river and a waxwork Sleeping Beauty waiting for her prince to come.

The château is open daily from mid-February to March 10am to 6pm, April to August 10am to 7pm, and September to November 10am to 6pm; closed the rest of the year. Entrance costs 14€ for adults, 4€ for students and children 8 to 16, and is free for children 7 and under. Allow 1½ hours to visit the castle and its grounds. The château is best visited by car or on an organized bus tour from Tours. If you're driving from Tours or Villandry, follow D7 to Ussé.

## Where to Stay

**Le Clos d'Ussé ★ 🏠** Although most visitors make Ussé a day trip, this little hotel across the street from the castle makes a good overnight stop. The Duchemin family offers well-maintained rooms that are midsize and comfortably furnished. The least expensive rooms are small and without in-suite bathrooms; the others have full facilities with either shower or bathtub. The friendly owners are experts on the lore of the castle. Its restaurant serves up fine local specialties, menus from 17€ to 19€.

7 rue Principale, on D7, Rigny-Ussé 37130. www.leclosdusse.fr. ☏ **02-47-95-55-47.** Fax 02-47-95-55-47. 7 units. 35€–55€ double. DC, MC, V. Closed Nov–Feb. **Amenities:** Restaurant; free Wi-Fi. *In room:* TV, hair dryer, no phone.

# FONTEVRAUD-L'ABBAYE ★★

304km (188 miles) SW of Paris; 16km (10 miles) SE of Saumur

You'll find the Plantagenet dynasty buried in the **Abbaye Royale de Fonte-vraud** (www.abbayedefontevraud.com; ℭ **02-41-51-73-52**). The kings, whose male line ended in 1485, were also the comtes d'Anjou, and they wanted to be buried in their native soil, and this regal patronage led to the building of one of Europe's largest medieval monastery complex.

In the 12th-century Romanesque church—with four Byzantine domes—are the remains of two English kings or princes, including Henry II of England, the first Plantagenet king, and his wife, Eleanor of Aquitaine, the most famous woman of the Middle Ages. Her crusading son, Richard the Lion-Hearted, was also entombed here. The Plantagenet line ended with the death of Richard III at the 1485 Battle of Bosworth. The tombs fared badly during the Revolution, when mobs desecrated the sarcophagi and scattered their contents on the floor.

More intriguing than the tombs is the octagonal **Tour d'Evraud,** the last remaining Romanesque kitchen in France. Dating from the 12th century, it contains five of its original eight *apsides* (half-rounded indentations originally conceived as chapels), each crowned with a conically roofed turret. A pyramid tops the conglomeration, capped by an open-air lantern tower pierced with lancets.

Robert d'Arbrissel, who spent much of his life as a recluse, founded the abbey in 1101. Aristocratic ladies occupied one part; many, including discarded mistresses of kings, had been banished from court. The four youngest daughters of Louis XV were educated here. Since 1975, the abbey has also functioned as a cultural center, offering expositions, concerts, and seminars.

Admission is 9€ adults, 6€ students, free for ages 8 and under. Hours are April to June and September to October daily 9:30am to 6pm, July and August daily 9:30am to 7pm, November to December daily 10am to 5:30pm, and February to March Tuesday through Sunday 10am to 5:30pm. The abbey is closed in January. Allow ½ hour for the abbey.

**Abbaye Royale de Fontevraud.**

## Essentials

**GETTING THERE** If you're **driving,** take D147 about 4km (2½ miles) from the village of Montsoreau. In season, you can take a **bus** (Line 1) from Saumur; schedules vary according to school holidays—visit the bus company's website, www.agglobus.fr, to download the schedule or call (ℭ **02-41-51-11-87**). The one-way fare for the 30-minute trip is 1.35€.

**VISITOR INFORMATION**  The **Office de Tourisme,** allée Ste-Catherine (© **02-41-51-79-45**), within the compound of the medieval abbey, is open only from Easter to September 30.

## Where to Eat

The **Hôtel Abbaye Royale de Fontevraud** (see below) has a good restaurant.

**La Licorne ★** MODERN FRENCH  For the perfect combination of medieval history and culinary sensuality, visit the abbey and then dine at this 35-seat restaurant on a linden-lined walkway between the abbey and a nearby parish church. Its symmetrical proportions and neoclassical pilasters, built in the 1700s just before the French Revolution, evoke the *ancien régime* at its most graceful and opulent. In summer, guests sit in the garden or the elegantly rustic dining room. Service can be a tad slow but the excellent-value menu is well-worth the wait. It includes refined dishes such as royal Maine d'Anjou Pigeon topped with Chinon truffles, farm-raised veal with foie gras sauce, and luscious desserts such as local **Alienor** pastries with strawberries and roses.

Allée Ste-Catherine. © **02-41-51-72-49.** Reservations required. Main courses 18€–36€; fixed-price menu 25€–55€. AE, MC, V. Nov–Apr Tues–Sun noon–2pm; Tues and Thurs–Sat 7–9pm; May–Oct daily noon–2pm and 7–9pm. Closed 1 week in Dec.

## Where to Stay

**Hôtel Abbaye Royale de Fontevraud ★ 🎁**  This unusual hotel is set on 11th-century foundations within the perimeter of the Abbaye Royale in one-time monks' quarters. It became a hotel in 1990. The guest rooms are well maintained and monastically simple, though with colorful drapery, modern furniture, and exposed sections of cream-colored *tuffeau,* the easy-to-carve rock used to build the abbey during the early Middle Ages.

Le Prieuré St-Lazare, rue St-Jean de l'Habit, Fontevraud-l'Abbaye 49590. www.hotels-francepatrimoine.fr/hotel/abbaye-royale-de-fontevraud. © **02-41-51-73-16.** Fax 02-41-51-75-50. 52 units. 67€–147€ double; 190€ suite. AE, MC, V. Closed Nov 16–Mar 15. **Amenities:** Restaurant; bar; babysitting; free Wi-Fi. *In room:* TV, hair dryer.

# SAUMUR

299km (185 miles) SW of Paris; 53km (33 miles) SE of Angers

Saumur is in a region of vineyards, where the Loire separates to encircle an island, and makes one of the best bases for exploring the western Loire Valley. A small but thriving town, it doesn't entirely live off its past: Saumur produces some 100,000 tons per year of the mushrooms the French adore. Balzac left us this advice: "Taste a mushroom and delight in the essential strangeness of the place." The cool tunnels for the *champignons* also provide the ideal resting place for the celebrated sparkling wines of the region. Enjoy both of these local favorites at a neighborhood cafe.

## Essentials

**GETTING THERE**  **Trains** run frequently between Tours Centre and Saumur. Some 20 trains per day arrive from Tours (trip time: 30–40 min.); the one-way fare is 11.10€. Over a dozen trains per day pull in from Angers (trip time: 20–30 min.), costing 8.20€ one-way. From the station, take bus A into town. For schedules and information, visit www.voyages-sncf.com or call ✆ **36-35**. If you're **driving** from Tours, follow D952 or the A85 autoroute southwest to Saumur.

**VISITOR INFORMATION**    The **Office de Tourisme** is on place de la Bilange (www.ot-saumur.fr; ✆ **02-41-40-20-60**).

## Exploring the Area

Of all the Loire cities, Saumur remains the most bourgeois; perhaps that's why Balzac used it for his classic characterization of a smug little town in *Eugénie Grandet.* Saumur is also famous as the birthplace of the *couturière* Coco Chanel.

The men of Saumur are among the best equestrians in the world. Founded in 1768, the city's riding school, **Cadre Noir de Saumur ★**, avenue de l'Ecole Nationale d'Equitation (www.cadrenoir.fr; ✆ **02-41-53-50-50**), is one of the grandest in Europe, rivaling Vienna's, enough so to be deemed a UNESCO world heritage site in 2011. The stables house some 350 horses. Mid-February to October, tours (7€ adults, 5€ children) begin at 9:30 to 11am and 2 to 4pm from Monday afternoon to Saturday afternoon. Tours depart about every 20 minutes. Tours last about 1 hour. Some 48km (30 miles) of specialty tracks wind around the town—to see a rider carry out a curvet is a thrill. The performances peak during the **Carrousel de Saumur ★★** on the last 2 Saturdays and Sundays in July.

Regrettably, **Château de Saumur,** the main reason for visiting the town, is closed for extensive renovations, with no announced opening date. The 12th-century château was the royal residence of Philippe II in the early 13th century, it hasn't changed much since being immortalized in the September scene of the famous illuminated manuscript *Les Très Riches Heures* in 1410. Until the renovations are finished, you can view the exterior and enjoy the panorama from the terrace. A selection of equestrian statues is on display, as well as panels recounting

Riding at Cadre Noir de Saumur.

the history of the chateau, Admission is 3€ adult, 2.50€ children 7–16, free under 7, Tuesday to Sunday April to June and September to October 10am to 5:30pm, July and August 10am to 6pm.

The area surrounding the town has become famous for its delicate sparkling wines. In the center of Saumur, you can wander the many aisles of **La Maison du Vin,** quai Lucien Gauthier (www.vinsvaldeloire.fr; ℂ **02-41-38-45-83**), and choose from a large stock direct from the many surrounding vineyards.

An alternative is to travel east of Saumur to the village of St-Hilaire, where you'll find a host of vineyards. One of the better ones is **Veuve Amiot,** 21 rue Jean-Ackerman (www.veuveamiot.fr; ℂ **02-41-83-14-14**), where you can tour the wine cellars, taste different vintages, and buy bottles and gift boxes right in the showroom.

Mushrooms enthusiasts can learn about the cultivation of the local fungi first hand at **the Musée du Champignon** (www.musee-du-champignon.com; ℂ **02-41-50-31-55**), don't miss the annual mushroom festival in October, entrance costs 8€ adult, 6€ under 18, open daily February to mid-November 10am to 7pm.

## Where to Eat

**Le Prieuré** (see below) serves excellent cuisine.

**Le Gambetta ★★** MODERN FRENCH   This is certainly not the cheapest restaurant in Saumur, but if you want to savor cutting-edge cuisine made with top-quality ingredients, it's the place to go. Since Mickaël Pihours took over the kitchen in 2006, the restaurant has received a coveted Michelin star. The cuisine is creative and absolutely delicious—the menu includes dishes like free-range lamb Gremolata served with bulgur pilaf and olive caponata, duck foie gras served with orange and ground, roasted cacao beans, and the adventurous smoked cod and eel with squid ink Coco de Paimpol beans (a nod to Pihours' native Brittany).

12 rue Gambetta. www.restaurantlegambetta.com. ℂ **02-41-67-66-66.** Reservations recommended. Main courses 19€–30€; lunch menu 23€, dinner menu 29€–94€. Tues and Thurs–Sun noon–2pm; Tues and Thurs–Sat 7–9pm. Closed 2 weeks in Jan, 3 weeks in Aug.

## Where to Stay

**Hôtel St-Pierre ★**   Nestled among tiny winding streets and built against the Eglise St-Pierre, this hotel overflows with character. Appointments include finely upholstered antiques, half-timbered walls, beamed ceilings, stone fireplaces, and spiral staircases. Guest rooms are individually decorated in the same rich style; even the bathroom walls showcase custom tile designs. Overall, the hotel is an appealing middle-bracket choice in a historic location. The intimate breakfast room opens onto a small garden terrace.

Rue Haute-Saint-Pierre, Saumur 49400. www.saintpierresaumur.com. ℂ **02-41-50-33-00.** Fax 02-41-50-38-68. 14 units. 100€–180€ double. AE, DC, MC, V. **Amenities:** Babysitting; room service. *In room:* A/C, TV, hair dryer, minibar, free Wi-Fi.

**Le Prieuré ★★★**   This is one of the grandest addresses in the region, a bastion of comfort, charm, and grace. The 12th-century priory is in a 24-hectare (59-acre) park 8km (5 miles) from town. The hotel has a steep roof, dormer windows, and a large peaked tower. It provides gracious, comfortable rooms; two of the most beautiful are in a 10th-century chapel. The least expensive (and less desirable) rooms are in an outlying pavilion. The Grand Salon features an ornately carved stone fireplace, crystal chandeliers, oak furniture, and a bar with a fleur-de-lis motif.

From the dining room, you'll enjoy a magnificent view of the Loire—it's truly beautiful at sunset. The chef's oeuvre includes Mouliherne escargots with parsnip purée, *sandre* with ginger and heritage vegetables, and filet of pigeon with artichoke mousseline. Even if you're not a guest, consider dining here. Fixed-price menus cost 34€ to 72€ at dinner, and 25€ to 32€ at lunch.

Chênehutte-les-Tuffeaux 49350. www.grandesetapes.fr. ℭ **02-41-67-90-14.** Fax 02-41-67-92-24. 36 units. 135€–280€ double; 350€ suite. AE, DC, MC, V. **Amenities:** Restaurant; bar; babysitting; outdoor pool; room service; tennis court. *In room:* TV, hair dryer, minibar, free Wi-Fi.

# ANGERS ★★★

288km (179 miles) SW of Paris; 89km (55 miles) E of Nantes

Once the capital of Anjou, Angers straddles the Maine River at the western end of the Loire Valley. Though it suffered extensive damage in World War II, it has been restored, blending provincial charm with a suggestion of sophistication. The bustling regional center is often used as a base for exploring the château district to the west. Young people, including some 30,000 college students, keep this vital city of 155,700 jumping until late at night. Allow 3 hours to see the attractions at Angers.

## Essentials

**GETTING THERE** High-speed **trains** make the 1½ hour trip every hour from Paris's Gare Montparnasse; the cost is 28€ to 61€ one-way. From Tours, about 10 trains per day make the 1-hour trip; a one-way ticket is 17€. The Angers train station is a convenient walk from the château. For schedules and information, visit www.voyages-sncf.com or call ℭ **36-35**. From Saumur, there are direct **bus** connections (1½ hr.); visit www.anjoubus.fr or call ℭ **08-20-16-00-49** (.12€ per minute) for schedules. If you're **driving** from Tours, take the A85 autoroute west and exit at Angers Centre.

**VISITOR INFORMATION** The **Office de Tourisme,** 7 place Kennedy (www.angers-tourisme.com; ℭ **02-41-23-50-00**), is opposite the entrance to the château.

Château d'Angers.

# Exploring the Town

If you have time for shopping, wander to the pedestrian zone in the center of town. Its boutiques and small shops sell everything from clothes and shoes to jewelry and books. For regional specialties, head to **Maison du Vin de l'Anjou,** 5 bis place Kennedy (www.vinsdeloire.fr; © **02-41-88-81-13**), where you can learn about the area's vineyards and buy a bottle or two for gifts or a picnic.

**Cathédrale St-Maurice ★★** CATHEDRAL   The cathedral dates mostly from the 12th and 13th centuries; the main tower is from the 16th century. The statues on the portal represent everybody from the Queen of Sheba to David at the harp. The tympanum depicts Christ enthroned. The stained-glass windows from the 12th through the 16th centuries have made the cathedral famous. The oldest one illustrates the martyrdom of St. Vincent; the most unusual is of St. Christopher with the head of a dog. The 12th-century nave, a landmark in cathedral architecture, is a work of harmonious beauty. If you're interested in a guided tour, call the church's presbytery at the number below. Tours are conducted erratically, often by an associate of the church, and usually with much charm and humor. The tours are available in French, English (offered July–Aug), and Italian.

Place Freppel. © **02-41-87-58-45.** Free admission; donations appreciated. Daily 9am–7pm.

**Château d'Angers ★★★** CASTLE   The château, dating from the 9th century, was the home of the comtes d'Anjou. The notorious Black Falcon lived here, and in time, the Plantagenets took up residence. From 1230 to 1238, the outer walls and 17 enormous towers were built, creating a fortress. King René favored the château, and during his reign, a brilliant court life flourished until he was forced to surrender to Louis XI. Louis XIV turned the château into a prison. In World War II, the Nazis used it as a munitions depot, and the Allies bombed it in 1944.

Visit the castle to see the **Apocalypse Tapestries ★★★**. They weren't always so highly regarded—they once served as a canopy to protect orange trees and were also used to cover the damaged walls of a church. Woven in Paris by Nicolas Bataille from cartoons by Jean de Bruges around 1375 for Louis I of Anjou, they were purchased for a nominal sum in the 19th century. The series of 77 sections, illustrating the Book of St. John, stretches 100m (328 ft.).

In 2009, the roof of the Logis Royal burned in an electrical fire and the château suffered damage (fortunately, the tapestries are housed in a separate building and were untouched). The Logis, which includes the royal apartments, is currently closed for repairs, but you can still tour the fortress, including the courtyard, ramparts, windmill tower, and 15th-century chapel, and see the tapestries. Once you've paid the entrance fee, you can take an hour-long guided tour focusing on the architecture and history of the château, or a tour devoted to the Apocolypse Tapestries. Both are available only in French; a self-guided tour with audioguides is available in English.

2 promenade du Bout-du-Monde. http://angers.monuments-nationaux.fr. © **02-41-86-48-77.** Admission 8€ adults, 5€ seniors and students 18–25, free for children 17 and under. Sept–Apr daily 10am–5:30pm; May–Aug daily 9:30am–6:30pm.

**Musée Jean Lurçat ★★** MUSEUM   The town's most intriguing museum is in the Ancien Hôpital St-Jean, founded in 1174 to care for the sick. The museum

> ## A Toast with the Home-Brew—Cointreau
>
> Another libation unique to Angers is Cointreau. Two confectioner brothers set out to create a drink of "crystal-clear purity." The result was Cointreau, a twice-distilled alcohol from the peels of two types of oranges, bitter and sweet. The factory has turned out the drink since 1849. Cointreau flavors such drinks as the cosmopolitan and the sidecar. Recent marketing campaigns, including one featuring seductress Dita Von Teese, have help modernize the brand and today some 13 million bottles of Cointreau are consumed annually.
>
> **La Carée Cointreau,** 2 bd. des Bretonnières (www.cointreau.fr; ✆ **02-41-31-50-50**), is in the suburb of St-Barthèlemy, a 10-minute drive east of the town center. If you call ahead to reserve, you can take a 1½-hour guided tour of the distillery and then visit the showroom, where you can sample and stock up on the fruity liqueur. Hours are variable; tours run on Saturdays only from October to April, and Tuesday through Saturday the rest of the year (9.80€ adult, 3.60€ children 12–17, free 12 and under).

is known for its famous tapestry, *Le Chant du Monde* (*The Song of the World*), designed by Jean Lurçat and executed in 10 panels between 1957 and 1966. It depicts an abstract conglomeration of beneficent suns, popping champagne bottles, and life cycles. You can visit a 17th-century dispensary, with earthenware jars and trivets still on its wooden shelves, and see everything from a Romanesque cloister with a secret garden to a pewter vessel from 1720 that once contained an antidote for snakebites.

4 bd. Arago. www.musees.angers.fr ✆ **02-41-24-18-45.** Admission 4€ adults, free for 25 and under. June–Sept daily 10am–6:30pm; Oct–May Tues–Sun 10am–noon and 2–6pm.

## Where to Eat

**La Salamandre** ★ CLASSIC FRENCH    The salamander was the symbol of Renaissance king François I. In this formal, elegant restaurant, you'll see portraits of and references to that cunning strategist everywhere. Beneath massive sculpted ceiling beams, beside a large wooden fireplace, you'll enjoy the most impeccable service and best food in town. Shining examples include scallops with chanterelle mushrooms, lobster stew, roasted Challans region duck, and sautéed filet of beef and fresh foie gras with a reduction of red Anjou wine.

In the Hotel d'Anjou, 1 bd. du Maréchal Foch. www.restaurant-lasalamandre.fr. ✆ **02-41-88-99-55.** Reservations recommended. Main courses 21€–38€; fixed-price menu 28€–48€. AE, DC, MC, V. Daily noon–2pm and Mon–Sat 7:30–9:30pm.

**Provence Caffè** PROVENÇAL    If you have had your fill of Loire specialties, dine here to experience a taste of Provence. The chic decor includes bundles of herbs and souvenirs of the Mediterranean. The chef delights diners with such dishes as risotto served with rabbit and basil, and roasted filet of hake fish with garlic confit and baby spinach.

9 place du Ralliement. www.provence-caffe.com. ✆ **02-41-87-44-15.** Reservations recommended. Main courses 15€; fixed-price menu 16€–32€. MC, V. Tues–Sat noon–2pm and 7–10pm.

## Angers Nightlife

Head to **place du Ralliement** or **rue St-Laud,** with its many bars and cafes. For a great night of beer drinking with friends, go to **Le Kent,** 7 place Ste-Croix (✆ **02-41-87-88-55**). If a night of dancing seems the perfect antidote to a day of château gazing, consider **Le Boléro,** 38 rue St-Laud (✆ **02-41-88-61-19**), to rub shoulders with the young crowd or join slightly older revelers at **Studio 49,** 8 place Vigan (www.lestudio49.com; ✆ **02-41-48-15-28**); the entrance fee is 10€, including a beverage.

## Where to Stay

**Best Western Hôtel d'Anjou**    Beside a park, this hotel built in 1846 is the best choice for overnighting in the area. It has upscale appointments and amenities, along with a good restaurant, La Salamandre (see "Where to Eat," above). The lower rooms have higher ceilings and are more spacious.

1 bd. de Maréchal Foch, Angers 49100. www.hoteldanjou.fr. ✆ **800/528-1234** in the U.S. and Canada, or 02-41-21-12-11. Fax 02-41-87-22-21. 53 units. 89€–193€ double. AE, DC, MC, V. Parking 8.50€. **Amenities:** Restaurant; bar. *In room:* TV, minibar, free Wi-Fi.

**L'Hôtel de France**    For a good night's sleep near the railway station, this comfortable 19th-century hotel is your best bet. Run by the Bouyer family since 1893, the rooms are decorated in light shades of cream and beige, nicely furnished and well maintained. Room rates go up 15€ to 25€ per night when trade shows are in town.

8 place de la Gare, Angers 49100. www.hoteldefrance-angers.com. ✆ **02-41-88-49-42.** Fax 02-41-87-19-50. 55 units. 80€–140€ double. AE, DC, MC, V. Parking 7€. **Amenities:** Restaurant; bar; room service. *In room:* A/C, TV, hair dryer, minibar, free Wi-Fi.

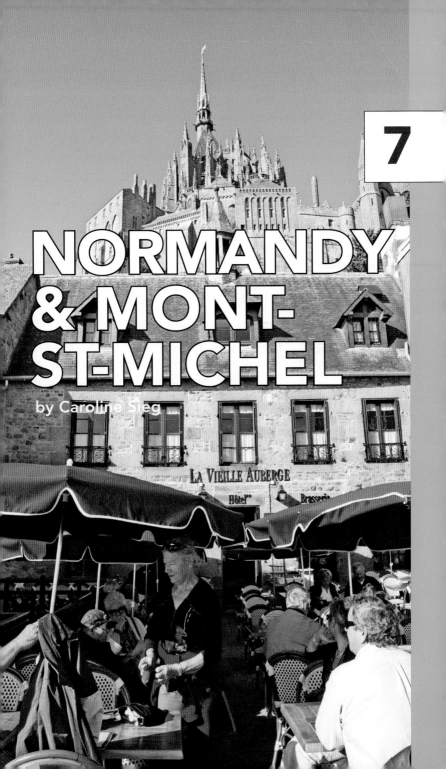

# NORMANDY & MONT-ST-MICHEL

by Caroline Sieg

# T

en centuries have passed since the Vikings invaded Normandy. The early Scandinavians came to seize the land, but they stayed to cultivate it. The Normans produced great soldiers, none more famous than William the Conqueror, who defeated King Harold at the Battle of Hastings in 1066. The English and the French continued to battle for centuries.

The invasion of June 6, 1944, ravaged much of Normandy. The largest armada ever assembled was responsible for regaining control of Europe from the Nazis. Today many visitors come to Normandy to see the D-day beachheads.

Some of this province may remind you of a Millet landscape, with cattle grazing in fields and wood-framed houses alongside modern buildings. Not far from the Seine is the hamlet where Monet painted his waterlilies. Here and there are stained-glass windows and Gothic architecture that survived the bombardments; however, many great buildings were leveled. Normandy's wide beaches attract families, and in August, the Deauville sands draw the chicest of the chic from Europe and North America. The resort towns of Deauville and Trouville are part of the region known as La Côte Fleurie (the Flower Coast), so called because of the profusion of flowers that grow there in the summer.

### A 4-Day Normandy Itinerary

On your first day, head to Rouen and explore its old town and cathedral. On your second day, go for Caen, William the Conqueror's seat of government. Stay in Caen or in Bayeux and take a look at the local cathedral and the Bayeux tapestry. On your third day (from Caen or Bayeux), explore the D-day beaches. On your fourth day, continue west toward the ancient island-abbey of Mont-St-Michel.

# ROUEN ★★★

135km (84 miles) NW of Paris; 89km (55 miles) E of Le Havre

The capital of Normandy and the fifth-largest port in France, Rouen is a hub of commerce. It's a bustling, vibrant place, bursting with activity generated by the industries connected to the port and the students at nearby universities and art schools. Former occupants include the writers Pierre Corneille and Gustave Flaubert, Claude Monet (who endlessly painted Rouen's Cathédrale de Notre-Dame), and Joan of Arc ("Oh, Rouen, art thou then my final resting place?"). Today it's a city of half a million people.

Victor Hugo called Rouen "the city of a hundred spires." Half of it was destroyed during World War II, mostly by Allied bombers, and many Rouennais were killed. During the reconstruction of the old quarters, some of the almost-forgotten crafts of the Middle Ages were revived. The city on the Seine is rich in historical associations: William the Conqueror died here in 1087, and Joan of Arc was burned at the stake on place du Vieux-Marché in 1431.

PREVIOUS PAGE: **Mont-St-Michel.**

As in Paris, the Seine splits Rouen into a **Rive Gauche (Left Bank)** and **Rive Droite (Right Bank).** The old city is on the right bank.

## Essentials

**GETTING THERE**   From Paris's Gare St-Lazare, **trains** leave for Rouen about once an hour (trip time: 1½ hr.). The one-way fare is 20€. The station is at the corner of rue Jeanne d'Arc and rue Verte. For information, visit www. voyages-sncf.com or call ℗ **36-35** or 08-92-35-35-35. To **drive** from Paris, take A13 northwest to Rouen (trip time: 1½ hr.).

Rouen.

**GETTING AROUND**   The **Métro** is part of the city's MétroBus system (℡ **02-35-52-52-52**). It has one north–south line. The most central stations in Old Rouen are Palais de Justice and Gare Rue Verte. Tickets cost 1.40€ per ride and are good for bus transfers within 1 hour of entering the Métro. Buy tickets from kiosks or automated machines.

**VISITOR INFORMATION**   The **Office de Tourisme** is at 25 place de la Cathédrale (www.rouentourisme.com; ℡ **02-32-08-32-40**).

## Seeing the Sights

**Cathédrale Notre-Dame de Rouen ★★★**   CATHEDRAL Monet immortalized Rouen's cathedral (particularly the facade, with its galaxy of statues) in his paintings. The main door, **Porte Central,** is embellished with sculptures (some decapitated) depicting the Tree of Jesus. The 12th-century Porte St-Jean and Porte St-Etienne flank it. Consecrated in 1063, the cathedral, a symphony of lacy stonework, was reconstructed after suffering damage in World War II. Two towers distinguish it: **Tour de Beurre** was financed by the faithful who were willing to pay for the privilege of eating butter during Lent. Containing a carillon of 56 bells, the **Tour**

Cathédrale Notre-Dame de Rouen.

**Rouen**

Map legend:

Cathédrale Notre-Dame de Rouen **6**

Eglise St-Maclou **7**

Eglise St-Ouen **8**

Musée de la Céramique **1**

Musée des Beaux-Arts **2**

Musée Flaubert et d'Histoire de la Médecine **4**

Musée Jeanne-d'Arc **5**

Musée Le Secq des Tournelles (Wrought Ironworks Museum) **3**

Information ⓘ

Post Office ✉

| 0 | | 1/4 mi |
|---|---|---|
| 0 | 0.25 km | |

**Lanterne (Lantern Tower)**—built in 1877 and using 740 tons of iron and bronze—rises to almost 150m (492 ft.).

The cathedral's interior is fairly uniform. The choir is a masterpiece, with 14 soaring pillars. The Booksellers' Stairway, in the north wing of the transept, is adorned with a stained-glass rose window that dates, in part, from the 1500s. The 13th-century chancel is beautiful, with simple lines. Especially interesting is the **Chapelle de la Vierge,** adorned with Renaissance tombs of the cardinals d'Amboise. Also entombed is the heart of Richard the Lion-Hearted, a token of his affection for the people of Rouen.

Behind the cathedral is the **Palais de l'Archevêché (Archbishop's Palace),** which was bombed in the war. Now it stands naked against the sky. The broken arches and rosette windows witnessed the trial of Joan of Arc in 1431, and her rehabilitation was proclaimed here in 1456.

Place de la Cathédrale. www.cathedrale-rouen.net. ⓒ **02-35-71-71-60.** Free admission. Mon 2–6pm; Tues–Sat 7:30am–noon and 2–6pm; Sun 8am–6pm. Closed during Mass and on bank holidays.

**Eglise St-Maclou ★★** CHURCH   St-Maclou was built in the Flamboyant Gothic style, with a step-gabled porch and cloisters, and is known for the 16th-century panels on its doors. Our favorite (to the left) is the Portail des Fontaines

(Portal of the Fonts). The church was built in 1200, rebuilt in 1432, and consecrated in 1521; its lantern tower is from the 19th century. It sits on a square full of old Norman crooked-timbered buildings. Inside, pictures dating from June 4, 1944, document St-Maclou's destruction and its subsequent restoration.

3 place Barthélémy, behind the cathedral. ✆ **02-35-71-28-09.** Free admission. Apr–Oct daily 10am–noon and 2–6pm; Nov–Mar daily 10am–noon and 2–5:30pm.

**Eglise St-Ouen** ★★ CHURCH   This church is the outgrowth of a 7th-century Benedictine abbey. Flanked by four turrets, its 115m (377-ft.) octagonal lantern tower is called "the ducal crown of Normandy." The church represents the work of 5 centuries. Its nave is from the 15th century, its choir from the 14th (with 18th-c. railings), and its stained glass from the 14th to the 16th. On May 23, 1431, Joan of Arc was taken to the cemetery here, and officials sentenced her to be burned at the stake unless she recanted. She signed an abjuration, condemning herself to life imprisonment, but that sentence was later revoked.

Place du Général-de-Gaulle. ✆ **02-32-08-31-01.** Free admission. Mar–Oct Tues–Sun 10am–noon and 2–6pm; Nov–Feb Tues–Sun 10am–noon and 2–5:30pm.

**Musée de la Céramique** ★★ MUSEUM   One of the great treasures here is the collection of 17th- and 18th-century Rouen faïence (opaquely glazed earthenware), which has a distinctive red hue because of the color of the local clay. The exhibits provide a showcase for Masseot Abaquesne, the premier French artist in faïence. An exceptional display is devoted to chinoiserie from 1699 to 1745.

94 rue Jeanne d'Arc. www.rouen-musees.com. ✆ **02-35-07-31-74.** Admission 3€ adults, 2€ students, free for children 17 and under. Wed–Mon 2–6pm.

**Musée des Beaux-Arts** ★★ MUSEUM   This is one of France's most important provincial museums, with more than 65 rooms of art that ranges from medieval primitives to contemporary paintings. You'll find portraits by David and works by Delacroix and Ingres (seek out his *La Belle Zélie*). A Gérard David retable (altarpiece), *La Vierge et les Saints (The Virgin and the Saints),* is a masterpiece. One salon is devoted to Géricault, including his portrait of Delacroix. Other works here are by Veronese, Velázquez, Caravaggio, Rubens, Poussin, Fragonard, and Corot, and by Impressionists such as Monet, including several paintings of the Rouen cathedral.

Esplanade de Marcel Duchamp. www.rouen-musees.com. ✆ **02-35-71-28-40.** Admission 5€ adults, 3€ students, free for children 17 and under. Wed–Mon 10am–6pm.

**Musée Flaubert et d'Histoire de la Médécine** MUSEUM   Gustave Flaubert, author of *Madame Bovary,* was born in the director's quarters of Rouen's public hospital (his father was the director) in 1821. The room in which he was born is intact. You'll see the glass door that separated the Flauberts from the ward and its patients. Family furniture and medical paraphernalia are also displayed.

51 rue de Lecat. ✆ **02-35-15-59-95.** Admission 3€ adults, 1.50€ for students and ages 18–25, free for children 17 and under. Tues 10am–6pm; Wed–Sat 10am–noon and 2–6pm.

**Musée Jeanne-d'Arc** MUSEUM   The life and the martyrdom of Joan of Arc, France's national heroine, are the focus here. In a vaulted cellar, dioramas, waxworks, and commentary in four languages tell the story of her life—from Domrémy, where she was born, to Rouen, where she was burned at the stake. The museum also contains a research library that concentrates on her life and

## A Ride on "the Little Train"

The rubber-wheeled **Petit Train** ((*C* **02-32-18-40-23**) is the most fun way to see this ancient city. The 40-minute tours leave from the front of the tourist office, 25 place de la Cathédrale ((*C* **02-32-08-32-40**). Departures are daily and hourly at 10 to noon and 2 until 5pm. Tickets cost 6.50€ for adults and 4.50€ for children 12 and under. The train operates from April 1 to mid-October, with limited service over the Christmas holidays.

the politics of her era. Visitors can hear, without charge, recorded narration on hand-held devices.

33 place du Vieux-Marché. www.jeanne-darc.com. (*C* **02-35-88-02-70.** Admission 5€ adults, 3€ students and children 17 and under. Mid Apr–mid Sept daily 9:30am–7pm; mid Sept–Mid Apr daily 10am–noon and 2–6:30pm.

**Musée Le Secq des Tournelles (Wrought Ironworks Museum) ★** MUSEUM Housed in the 15th-century Eglise St-Laurent, this museum showcases ironwork, a Norman art form. Its collection ranges from what a critic once called "forthright masculine forging to lacy feminine filigree, from Roman keys to the needlepoint balustrade that graced Mme. de Pompadour's country mansion." The collection displays some 14,000 pieces.

2 rue Jacques-Villon. www.rouen-musees.com. (*C* **02-35-88-42-92.** Admission 3€ adults, 2€ students, free for children 17 and under. Wed–Mon and 2–6pm.

**Place du Vieux-Marché ★** SQUARE Joan of Arc was executed for heresy at the Old Marketplace. Tied to a stake, she was burned on May 30, 1431. Her ashes were gathered and tossed into the Seine. A modern church with stained-glass windows from St-Vincent sits in the center of a monumental complex in the square; beside it, a bronze cross marks the position of St. Joan's stake.

**Rue du Gros-Horloge ★★** WALKING TRAIL The "Street of the Great Clock" runs between the cathedral and place du Vieux-Marché. Now a pedestrian mall, it's named for an ornate gilt Renaissance clock mounted on an arch, Rouen's most popular monument. The arch bridges the street and connects to a Louis XV fountain with a bevy of cherubs and a bell tower. At night the bells still toll a curfew.

## Shopping

Rouen was once one of France's major producers of the fine decorative ceramic ware known as *faïence de Rouen.* Examples of both antique and contemporary faïence abound, and it's worth picking up one or two pieces. For contemporary faïence, your best bet is **Faïencerie Carpentier Augy,** 26 rue St-Romain ((*C* **02-35-88-77-47**). The well-known studio sells reproductions of historical styles in an array of colors.

Another Rouen specialty is *les coffret de Rouen.* The little hand-painted wooden boxes were all the rage during the 18th and 19th centuries. The original versions continue to be popular, but watch out for modern forgeries.

Rouen is also an antiques capital, with more than 80 vendors in the Old Town. The best hunting ground is in Vieux Rouen (the Old Town), along **rue Eau-de-Robec, place Barthélémy, rue Damiette,** and **rue St-Romain.** The city has two **flea markets,** on Saturday and Sunday at place St-Mare, and on Thursday at place des Emmurés. Medium- and large-scale auctions take place year-round at **Les Salles des Ventes** and 20 rue de la Croix-de-Fer (✆ **02-35-71-54-48**).

Other antiques shops worth visiting are **Michel Bertran,** 108 rue Molière (✆ **02-35-98-24-06**), with a good selection of 18th- and 19th-century paintings, especially by School of Rouen Impressionists; **Etienne Bertran,** 110 rue Molière (✆ **02-35-70-79-96**), with its collection of antique books dating to the 16th century; and **Patrick Chasset,** 12 rue de la Croix-de-Fer (✆ **02-35-70-59-97**), for toys and cards from the 1700s and 1800s, as well as bottles and glassware. You'll find watercolors by local artists, as well as antique Norman and English engravings.

Lovers of chocolate will discover a veritable paradise at **La Chocolatière,** 18 rue Guillaume-le-Conquérant (✆ **02-35-71-00-79**). The specialty that has attracted local gourmets for as long as anyone can remember is a praline-layered *paillardises,* rich in velvety chocolate that many readers describe as sinful.

# Where to Eat

**Gill ★★★** MODERN FRENCH    The best restaurant in town sits beside the traffic of the Seine's quays. The minimalist decor, with high-tech lighting and accessories, is an appropriate backdrop for the sophisticated cuisine. Who can resist ravioli stuffed with foie gras and served in a bouillon sprinkled with fresh truffles? The best items on the menu are pan-fried foie gras of duckling served with caramelized turnips and a turnip-green salad; a salad of crayfish tails with tomato-and-black-pepper chutney; and the most famous and popular specialty, Rouen-style pigeon with vegetables floating in densely concentrated consommé.

9 quai de la Bourse. www.gill.fr. ✆ **02-35-71-16-14.** Reservations required far in advance. Main courses 30€–57€; business lunch 38€; fixed-price dinner 95€. AE, DC, MC, V. Tues–Sat noon–1:45pm and 7:30–9:30pm. Closed Aug and 2 weeks in Apr.

**Les Nymphéas ★★★** MODERN FRENCH    One of the most appealing restaurants in Rouen bears the name of a painting by Monet *(Water Lilies).* The setting is a 16th-century half-timbered house that fits gracefully into the centrally located neighborhood (place du Vieux-Marché). The restaurant features sophisticated, savory cuisine. It's celebrated for its warm foie gras with cider sauce; wild duckling Rouennais style, served with wild mushrooms and caramelized onions; and *civet* (stew) of lobster with sauternes. An award-winning dessert that evokes the Norman countryside is a warm soufflé flavored with apples and Calvados.

7 rue de la Pie. www.lesnympheas-rouen.com. ✆ **02-35-89-26-69.** Reservations required. Main courses 24€–55€; fixed-price menu 40€–75€. AE, MC, V. Tues–Sat 12:15–2pm and 7:30–9:45pm. Closed late Aug to mid-Sept.

**Pascaline** 🍴 TRADITIONAL FRENCH    This informal bistro is often filled with regulars and has been a favorite since its opening in 1880. The decor hasn't changed much since. The cheapest fixed-price menus are among the best bargains in town. Menu items include seafood dishes such as pavé of monkfish with roughly textured mustard sauce, breast of duck cooked in beer, and savory *pot-au-feu maison* (house stew). Don't come for refined cuisine—you should expect hearty, time-tested favorites.

5 rue de la Poterne. www.pascaline.fr. ✆ **02-35-89-67-44.** Reservations recommended. Main courses 10€–22€; fixed-price menu 16€–29€. AE, MC, V. Daily noon–2:30pm and 7–11pm.

# Rouen Nightlife

For highbrow entertainment, **Théâtre des Arts,** 7 rue du Dr.-Rambert (© 02-35-71-41-36), presents ballet, opera, and classical music. **Théâtre des Deux Rives,** 48 rue Louis-Ricard (© 02-35-89-63-41), presents plays in French. **Théâtre des Arts/Opéra Léonard de Vinci,** 7 rue du Dr.-Rambert (© 02-35-71-41-36), has a busy schedule of classical and contemporary opera. A variety of concerts takes place at **Eglise St-Ouen,** place du Général-de-Gaulle. For information about who's playing, contact the tourist office.

Much of the nightlife, especially pubs, centers on place du Vieux-Marché. **La Bohème,** 18 rue St-Amand (www.laboheme-discotheque.com; © 02-35-71-53-99), is a small discothèque with a cozy, publike ambience. Many students meet at the **Underground Pub,** 26 rue des Champs-Maillets (© 02-35-98-44-84), which has a street-level bar and an underground bar fitted with wood and British bric-a-brac.

**WINE BAR** Le P'tit Zinc, 20 place du Vieux-Marché (© 02-35-89-39-69), is a bistro-style wine bar with early-1900s decor and one of the best wine selections in town. Tired of wine? They've also got an excellent selection of Norman cider.

# Where to Stay

## MODERATE

**Hôtel de Dieppe** The Gueret family has run this Best Western property, across from the train station, since 1880. Although it has been modernized, it's still a traditional French inn and barely a skip away from all the action. It's a bit noisy (though double-glazed windows help), but it quiets down after the last train from Paris arrives around 10:30pm. Rooms are a tad bland but comfortable and spotlessly clean. **Le Quatre Saisons,** the adjoining rotisserie, is famous for its duckling *à la presse* (pressed duck).

Place Bernard-Tissot, Rouen 76000. www.hotel-dieppe.fr. © **800/528-1234** in the U.S. and Canada, or 02-35-71-96-00. Fax 02-35-89-65-21. 41 units. 100€–140€ double. AE, DC, MC, V. Parking 5€. **Amenities:** Restaurant; bar; room service. *In room:* TV, hair dryer, free Wi-Fi.

## INEXPENSIVE

**Alive Hôtel De Québec**  In the historic core, this budget hotel stands close to the cathedral and its surrounding antiques shops. It is a very typical Norman city hotel, without any grand design, but offering affordable, solid rooms. Bedrooms don't offer a lot of wiggle room, but many open onto a view of a garden. Some units have both a double bed and a single—ideal for families.

## Finding Old Normandy in Calvados Country

For a taste of old Normandy, motorists heading from Rouen to Deauville should stop in Pont-Audemer, 50km (31 miles) west of Rouen. On the banks of the River Risle, Pont-Audemer is in the heart of Calvados country. In spite of war damage, Pont-Audemer retains much of its old look, especially if you wander its historic streets, rue de la Licorne (unicorn) and rue de la République. Along rue de la République, look for Eglise St-Ouen, dating from the 11th century.

18–24 rue Québec, Rouen 76000. www.hotel-rouen.com. ℰ **02-35-70-09-38.** Fax 02-35-15-80-15. 38 units. 55€–60€ double; 55€–99€ triple. AE, MC, V. **Amenities:** Breakfast room. *In room:* TV, hair dryer, free Wi-Fi.

**Hôtel Cardinal** ✦   Not only is this hotel ideally located, it's also affordable. It's across from the cathedral (imagine waking up to a view of the majestic structure and the surrounding half-timbered buildings), in the middle of a neighborhood known for antiques, art galleries, and fine dining. With so much to do in the area, you won't mind the hotel's simplicity. Rooms are business-class plain with built-in furnishings and a small bathroom with tub or shower.

1 place de la Cathédrale, Rouen 76000. www.cardinal-hotel.fr. ℰ **02-35-70-24-42.** Fax 02-35-89-75-14. 18 units. 66€–99€ double; 86€–116€ triple or family room. MC, V. Parking 6€ nearby. Closed mid-Dec to mid-Jan. **Amenities:** Room service. *In room:* TV, hair dryer, free Wi-Fi.

**Hôtel de la Cathédrale**   Built around a timbered and cobble-covered courtyard, this hotel evokes serious charm. The location is ideal: a pedestrian street midway between the cathedral and the Eglise St-Maclou, opposite the Archbishop's Palace where Joan of Arc was tried. The remodeled rooms are well maintained and tastefully furnished, accessible by both stairs and an elevator. Breakfast is the only meal served.

12 rue St-Romain, Rouen 76000. www.hotel-de-la-cathedrale.fr. ℰ **02-35-71-57-95.** Fax 02-35-70-15-54. 26 units. 70€–110€ double. AE, MC, V. Parking 10€ nearby. **Amenities:** Tea lounge; babysitting; room service. *In room:* TV, hair dryer, free Wi-Fi.

**Hôtel du Vieux Carré ★ 🎁**   In a restored half-timbered 18th-century house, this is one of the most charming and tranquil lodgings in Rouen. After inspecting too many impersonally furnished hotels, this one stands out for its personal touch. The enthusiastic and much-traveled owner has tastefully decorated the midsize guest rooms in comfortable rustic fashion. Unusual for central Rouen, its restaurant opens onto a flower-filled courtyard.

34 rue Ganterie, Rouen 76000. www.hotel-vieux-carre.com. ℰ **02-35-71-67-70.** Fax 02-35-71-19-17. 13 units. 60€–68€ double. AE, MC, V. **Amenities:** Restaurant (lunch only); tearoom/cafe. *In room:* TV, free Wi-Fi.

# HONFLEUR ★★

201km (125 miles) NW of Paris; 63km (39 miles) NE of Caen

At the mouth of the Seine opposite Le Havre, Honfleur is one of Normandy's most charming fishing ports. Having escaped major damage in World War II, the working port looks like an antique. Thanks to the pont de Normande, the bridge that links Honfleur to Le Havre, visitors flock here. Honfleur is 500 years older than Le Havre, dating from the 11th century. Artists, including Daubigny, Corot, and Monet, have long favored this township.

## Essentials

**GETTING THERE**   If you're **driving** from Pont l'Evêque or other points south (including Paris), D579 leads to the major boulevard, rue de la République. Follow it to the town center. Driving time from Paris is 2 to 2½ hours.

There's no direct **train** service into Honfleur. From Paris, take one of the dozen or so daily trains from Gare St-Lazare to Deauville for 30€

Honfleur.

one-way. From there, bus no. 20 makes the 25-minute ride to Honfleur; the one-way fare is about 2.15€. From Rouen, take the train to Le Havre and transfer to bus no. 50, which costs 4.20€ each way, for the 30-minute ride to Honfleur. Several **buses** run daily between Caen and Honfleur (trip time: 2 hr.); the one-way fare is 7.20€. For information, call **Bus Verts du Calvados** (✆ **08-10-21-42-14**).

**VISITOR INFORMATION**    The **Office de Tourisme** is on quai Lepaulmier (www.ot-honfleur.fr; ✆ **02-31-89-23-30**).

## Seeing the Town

Begin your tour, which should take about an hour, at place de la Porte-de-Rouen. Stroll along the **Vieux Bassin,** the old harbor, taking in the fishing boats and narrow, slate-roofed houses. On the north side of the basin, the former governor's house, **Lieutenance,** dates from the 16th century. Nearby is the **Eglise Ste-Catherine,** place Ste-Catherine (✆ **02-31-89-11-83**), constructed of timber by 15th-century shipbuilders. The church's wooden belfry is on the other side of the street. The church is open July and August daily from 8am to 8pm, September through June daily 8:30am to noon and 2 to 6pm.

**Maisons Satie** MUSEUM    Opened in 1998, this high-tech museum honors Honfleur's native son Erik Satie in the house where he was born in 1866. Satie was a "complete artist": He became most famous for his music, but he was also a painter and acted as a muse and inspiration to Picasso, Braque, Cocteau, Debussy, Ravel, and Stravinsky. This is not a traditional museum. The walk-through exhibitions incorporate sound, light, and recordings of Satie's compositions. Visitors wear high-tech helmets that transmit sound, which allows for a degree of play and experimentation in some of the exhibits.

67 bd. Charles V. ✆ **02-31-89-11-11.** Admission 5.10€ adults, 3.60€ ages 10–17, free for children 9 and under. May–Sept Wed–Mon 10am–7pm; Oct–Apr Wed–Mon 11am–6pm. Closed Jan–early Feb.

**Musée d'Ethnographie et d'art populaire** MUSEUM   This place celebrates the unique cultural and aesthetic contributions of Normandy to the rest of Europe. You'll find old furniture, lace headdresses, embroidery, candle-making equipment, and farm implements, as well as several rooms outfitted with period art and antiques.

Quai St-Etienne. ✆ **02-31-89-14-12.** Admission 3.50€ adults, 2.10€ students and children 10–18, free for children 9 and under. July–Aug daily 10am–noon and 2–6:30pm; Apr–June and Sept Tues–Fri 10am–noon and 2–6pm; Oct to mid-Nov and mid-Feb to Mar Tues–Fri 2–5:30pm, Sat–Sun 10am–noon and 2:30–5:30pm.

**Musée Eugène-Boudin** MUSEUM   This museum showcases a good collection of works by the painters who flocked to this port when Impressionism was new. The largest collections comprise the pastels and paintings of Boudin.

Place Erik-Satie. ✆ **02-31-89-54-00.** Admission 5.30€ adults, 3.80€ students and children 10 and over. Mar 15–Sept Wed–Mon 10am–noon and 2–6pm; Oct–Mar 14 Wed–Mon 2:30–5:30pm, Sat–Sun 10am–noon and 2:30–5:30pm. Closed Jan to mid-Feb, July 14, and Christmas.

**NaturoSpace** MUSEUM   Inaugurated in 1999 on the western outskirts of town, adjacent to the seacoast, Honfleur's modern attraction displays the flora and butterfly life of some of the most exotic climates on Earth. Designed like an enormous greenhouse bursting with tropical plants and butterflies, it contains a labyrinth of walkways that cut through Normandy's approximation of a tropical rainforest. Most visitors spend about an hour in this environment, which is in distinct contrast to the old Norman ethnicity that's otherwise associated with Honfleur.

Bd. Charles V. www.naturospace.com. ✆ **02-31-81-77-00.** Admission 8.20€ adults, .406€ students and children 13 and under, family package 32€. Apr–June and Sept daily 9:30am–1pm and 2–6:30pm; Feb–Nov 9:30am–1pm and 2–5:30pm; July–Aug daily 9:30am–6:30pm.

# Where to Eat

**La Terrasse et l'Assiette** ★★ TRADITIONAL FRENCH   Outfitted "in the Norman style" with heavy beams and lots of exposed brick, the gourmet citadel of Honfleur attracts an upscale international clientele. Dishes include crayfish with sautéed vermicelli and truffles, an omelet studded with chunks of lobster, unctuous fried foie gras served with lentils, and braised scallops with a purée of Brussels sprouts and smoked-ham sauce. Leave room for *petit gateau moelleux au chocolat* (very moist chocolate-fudge cake). In summer, if the weather is agreeable, ask for a table on the terrace, overlooking the historic Eglise Ste-Catherine.

8 place Ste-Catherine. ✆ **02-31-89-31-33.** www.laterrasseetlassiette.com. Reservations recommended. Main courses 26€–42€; fixed-price menu 22€–39€. AE, MC, V. Wed–Sun noon–2pm and 7:30–9pm. Closed Jan.

**Restaurant/Hôtel L'Absinthe** ★★ TRADITIONAL FRENCH   This tavern, named for the drink preferred by many 19th-century writers, is known for its beautiful decor, extravagant portions, and well-prepared cuisine. Rooms in the 16th-century building have beamed ceilings, parquet floors, and furniture that matches the architectural grandeur. The restaurant consists of two dining rooms (one from the 15th c. with exposed beams and exposed stone, and one from the 17th c. with a stately fireplace). The menu changes frequently. The best menu items include foie gras with caramelized ginger and apples, and sea bass roasted with laurel leaves and red wine.

The restaurant is part of the Hotel Absinthe—an equally atmospheric choice with doubles running 120€ to 185€, and the suite goes for 245€. Parking costs 12€.

10 quai de la Quarantaine. www.absinthe.fr. ✆ **02-31-89-39-00.** Fax 02-31-89-53-60. Reservations required. Main courses 26€–48€; fixed-price menu 31€–59€. AE, DC, MC, V. Daily 12:15–3pm and 7:15–10pm. Closed Nov 15–Dec 17.

# Where to Stay

**Restaurant/Hôtel L'Absinthe** (see "Where to Eat," above) also rents rooms.

**Castel Albertine ★ 🏨**   Management takes great care to maintain the character of this home of Albert Sorel, a 19th-century historian and scholar. The impressive house, of red brick and rose-hued stone, is a 3-minute walk from the port. It is a handsome, welcoming hotel. All of the individually decorated rooms have floor-to-ceiling windows that open onto views of gardens and trees. Bathrooms are small but tidily kept, with either a tub or a shower.

19 cours Albert-Manuel, Honfleur 14600. www.honfleurhotels.com. ✆ **02-31-98-85-56.** Fax 02-31-98-83-18. 27 units. 80€–160€ double. MC, V. Parking 10€. Closed Jan. **Amenities:** Bar; babysitting; room service; sauna. In room: TV, hair dryer, free Wi-Fi.

**Hotel des Loges ★★★**   Take four former fisherman's cabins, deck them out with designer-worthy pieces, soothing muted colors, and contemporary oak furnishings, and you get an escape you won't want to leave. The modern feel is gentle under the hotel's traditional wood beams. The location, right in the center of the town near a cluster of restaurants close to the harbor, makes this one of our favorite hotels. Standard rooms are spread across three of the houses. The fourth is a separate 3-story, 2-bedrooms cottage (less modern, more traditional with a hodgepodge of shabby-chic antiques) and sleeps up to 5. The hotel rents bikes too—perfect for tooling around the town.

18 rue Brûlée, 14600 Honfleur. www.hoteldesloges.com. ✆ **02-31-89-38-26.** Fax 02-31-89-42-79. 14 units. 115€–150€ double; from 140€ cottage. AE, V. **Amenities:** Babysitting; room service. In room: TV, minibar, free Wi-Fi.

**La Ferme St-Siméon ★★★**   Take a 17th-century half-timbered slate hotel set on an old farmhouse and ta-da! This is one of Normandy's most elegant and prestigious inns. Looming up in the hills above Honfleur, about 1.5km (1 mile) from the old port, the shimmering water of the English Channel draws artists to the hilltop inn, said to be where Impressionism was born in the 19th century. We love the terra-cotta floors, carved wood, and copper and faïence touches. Rooms are cozy and elegant with fabric-covered walls; some feature exposed half-timbering or ceiling beams and others contain canopy-covered beds. Regardless, you can be certain to find antique or heirloom furnishings.

20 rue Adolphe-Marais, Honfleur 14600. www.fermesaintsimeon.fr. ✆ **02-31-81-78-00.** Fax 02-31-89-48-48. 34 units. 220€–470€ double; 550€–850€ suite. AE, MC, V. **Amenities:** Restaurant; bar; babysitting; indoor pool; room service; sauna; spa. In room: TV, hair dryer, minibar, free Wi-Fi.

**Les Maisons de Léa Hotel & Spa ★★**   In 1900, the hotel owners converted a 16th-century fish market into this romantic and tranquil retreat: think Laura Ashley goes Zen and moves to Normandy. The hotel has soothing colors, polished antiques, a touch of wicker here and there, and sofas that beg you to take a nap. The on-site spa all includes a heavenly *hammam*—inquire about special spa and hotel packages. Oh, and do not leave without tucking in with a spot of tea in their inviting library.

Place Ste-Catherine, Honfleur 14600. www.lesmaisonsdelea.com. © **02-31-14-49-49.** Fax 02-31-89-28-61. 30 units. 145€–220€ double; 210€–340€ suite. AE, MC, V. Bus: 20 or 50. **Amenities:** Snack bar; babysitting; room service (breakfast only). *In room:* TV, hair dryer, free Wi-Fi.

# DEAUVILLE ★★★

206km (128 miles) NW of Paris; 47km (29 miles) NE of Caen

Deauville has been associated with the rich and famous since the duc de Morny, Napoleon III's half-brother, founded it as an upscale resort in 1859. In 1913, it entered sartorial history when Coco Chanel launched her career here, opening a boutique selling tiny hats that challenged the fashion of huge-brimmed hats loaded with flowers and fruit. (Coco's point of view: "How can the mind breathe under those things?")

## Essentials

**GETTING THERE**  There are 6 to 10 daily **rail** connections from Paris's Gare St-Lazare (trip time: 2 hr., 15 min.); prices start at 30€ one-way. The rail depot lies between Trouville and Deauville, south of town. Take a taxi from the station. **Bus Verts du Calvados** (www.busverts.fr; © 08-10-21-42-14) serves the Normandy coast from Caen to Le Havre. To **drive** from Paris (trip time: 2½ hr.), take A13 west to Pont L'Evêque, and then follow N177 east to Deauville.

**VISITOR INFORMATION**  The **Office de Tourisme** is on place de la Mairie (www.deauville.org; © 02-31-14-40-00).

**SPECIAL EVENTS**  For a week in September, the **Deauville Festival of American Film** (www.festival-deauville.com; © 02-31-14-40-00) honors movies made in the United States. Actors, producers, directors, and writers flock here and briefly eclipse the high rollers at the casinos and the horse-racing and polo crowd.

## Exploring the Resort

Coco Chanel cultivated a tradition of elegance that survives in Deauville and in its smaller and less prestigious neighbor Trouville, on the opposite bank of the Toques (see the next section). Don't expect flash; in its way, restrained and ever-so-polite Deauville is the most British seaside resort in France.

However, in its heart, Deauville is less English than French. It has even been dubbed "Paris's 21st arrondissement." The crowds here tend to be urban and hip. Deauville is stylish and not (by anyone's definition) inexpensive.

With its golf courses, casinos, deluxe hotels, La Touques and Clairefontaine racetracks, regattas, a yachting harbor, polo grounds, and tennis courts, Deauville is a formidable contender for the business of the upper class. Looking for a charming place to stroll? Head for boutique-lined **rue Eugène-Colas, place Morny** (named for the resort's founder), and **place du Casino.**

**BEACHES**  Expect to spend time on Deauville's boardwalk, **Les Planches,** a promenade running parallel to the beach. Beaux Arts and half-timbered

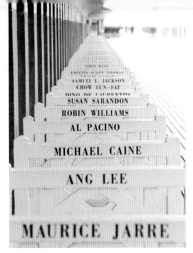
Les Planches, Deauville.

Norman-inspired buildings line its edges. In summer, especially August, parasols dot the beach and oiled bodies cover seemingly every inch of sand. The resort's only beach is **Plage de Deauville,** a strip that's part of La Côte Fleurie.

If you're looking for a gay and nude beach, you can go to **Merville-France-Ville,** 39km (24 miles) from Deauville toward Caen. But considering how permissive most Deauville fans are, many gay travelers feel perfectly comfortable here.

Access to every beach in Normandy is free; in Deauville, you'll pay from 2€ per hour for parking in any of the many public lots beside the sea.

The **Piscine Municipale,** boulevard de la Mer (✆ 02-31-14-02-17), is a large indoor seawater pool. Depending on the season, bathers pay 4€ to 5€ per person. Hours are July and August daily 9:30am to 7:30pm, June and September daily 10am to 7pm, and October to December and February to May daily 10:30am to 7pm.

**HORSE RACES/POLO** You can watch horses every day from late June to early October. There's either a race at 2pm or a polo match at 3pm. The venues are the **Hippodrome de Deauville La Touques,** boulevard Mauger (✆ 02-31-14-20-00), in the heart of town near the Mairie de Deauville (town hall); and the **Hippodrome de Deauville Clairefontaine,** route de Clairefontaine (✆ 02-31-14-69-00), within the city limits, 2km (1¼ miles) west of the center.

## Shopping

This seaside town has a pedestrian shopping area between the polo field and the port; the main drags are **rue Mirabeau, rue Albert-Fracasse,** and the west end of **avenue de la République.** The leading shops, selling some of the world's most elegant merchandise (with prices to match), cluster on **rue Eugène-Colas, place Morny,** and **place du Casino.** At **La Cave de Deauville,** 48 rue Mirabeau (www.cave-de-deauville.com; ✆ 02-31-87-35-36), you'll find a wide selection of apple ciders, Calvados, and the apple aperitif known as *pommeau.*

For an overview of the bounty of the fertile Norman soil, head for the **Marché Publique** (open-air market) in the place du Marché, adjacent to place Morny. From July to mid-September, it's open daily 8am to 1pm. The rest of the year, market days are Tuesday, Friday, Saturday, and occasionally Sunday. In addition to fruits, vegetables, poultry, cider, wine, and cheese, you'll find cookware, porcelain tableware, and cutlery.

## Where to Eat

**Chez Miocque** TRADITIONAL FRENCH   This hip cafe near the casino and the boutiques does a bustling business at its sidewalk tables. The place serves hearty brasserie-style food, including succulent lamb stew with spring vegetables, filet of skate with cream-based caper sauce, and steaks. Portions are filling, and the atmosphere can be lively. The dish of the day is always from the sea.

81 rue Eugène-Colas. ⓒ **02-31-88-09-52.** Reservations recommended. Main courses 19€–43€. AE, MC, V. July–Sept daily 9am–midnight; mid-Feb to June and Oct–Dec Fri–Mon noon–4pm and 7–11:30pm.

**Le Ciro's Barrière ★★★** FRENCH/SEAFOOD   Hot on the resort's social scene, Le Ciro's serves Deauville's best seafood. It's expensive but worth it. If you want a bit of everything, ask for the *plateau de fruits de mer,* brimming with lobster and shellfish. For an elaborate appetizer, we recommend lobster salad with truffles. Marmite of scallops with sweet sauterne wine and saffron makes a superb main course. The collection of bordeaux wine is exceptional. The ambience is airy, stylish, and evocative of the Belle Epoque heyday of Deauville.

Promenade des Planches. ⓒ **02-31-14-31-31.** Fax 02-31-88-32-02. Reservations required. Main courses 23€–54€; fixed-price menu 29€. AE, DC, MC, V. Thurs–Mon 12:30–2:45pm and 7:30–9:30pm. Closed 2 weeks in Jan.

**Le Spinnaker ★** NORMAN   Owner-chef Pascal Angenard's charming yellow-and-blue restaurant features regional cuisine. The satisfying specialties include terrine of foie gras with four spices, roast lobster with cider vinegar and cream-enriched potatoes, slow-cooked veal flank, and hot apple tart. Pascal recommends roast turbot flavored with shallots *en confit.* A fine array of wines can accompany your meal. On some nights, a dish here or there might not be sublime, but most are excellent.

52 rue Mirabeau. www.spinnakerdeauville.com. ⓒ **02-31-88-24-40.** Reservations required. Main courses 20€–50€; fixed-price menu 38€–52€. AE, DC, MC, V. Wed–Sun noon–1:30pm and 7:30–10pm. Closed June 21–28, Nov 15–30, and Jan 2–31.

# Deauville Nightlife

Opened in 1912, the **Casino de Deauville,** rue Edmond-Blanc (www.lucien barriere.com; ⓒ **02-31-14-31-14**), is one of France's premier casinos. Its original Belle Epoque core has been expanded with a theater, a nightclub, three restaurants, and an extensive collection of slot machines (*machines à sous*). The casino distinguishes areas for slot machines from more formal locales containing such games as roulette, baccarat, blackjack, and poker. The slots are open daily from 11am to 2am (to 3am Fri and 4am Sat) and have no dress code; access to this area is free. The areas containing *les jeux traditionnels* (traditional games) are open daily at 4pm and close between 3 and 4am, depending on business and the day of the week. Entrance is free, and you must present a passport or identity card to gain admission. The most interesting nights are Friday and Saturday, when the cabaret theater and all the restaurants are open. The theater presents glittering, moderately titillating shows at 10:30pm on Friday and Saturday. Admission is 25€ Friday, rising to 29€ on Saturday. Dinner and the show costs 55€ to 59€.

If it's a dance club you're looking for, head to the high-energy **Y Club,** 14 bis rue Désiré-le-Hoc (ⓒ **02-31-88-30-91**), which charges a cover of 15€. For salsa, merengue, and reggae, visit **Brok Café,** 14 av. du Général-de-Gaulle (ⓒ **02-31-81-30-81**). If you want to re-create the restrained but decadent ambience of the 1970s, consider **Le Régine's,** inside Deauville's casino, rue Edmond-Blanc (ⓒ **02-31-14-31-96**).

**Dancing Les Planches,** Le Bois Lauret, Blonville (*✆* **02-31-87-58-09**), 4km (2½ miles) from Deauville, is a club where you'll find up-to-date music, a dance floor, and even an indoor swimming pool near an indoor/outdoor bar. It's open from 11pm until dawn every Friday and Saturday night.

# Where to Stay

## EXPENSIVE

### Hôtel du Golf Barrière ★★★ ☺

Golfers gravitate to this half-timbered hotel created by the Lucien Barrière chain in the late 1980s. The location, in the hills above Deauville, about 3km (1¾ miles) from the center of town, creates an aura of country-club tranquillity. Outfitted in English country house style, it's one of the few hotels in Normandy with its own golf course. If the links aren't your thing, you might consider the Normandy or Royal hotels (reviewed below, and all three Lucien Barrière properties). The children's center and activities program are the best in Deauville. Rooms come in a wide range of sizes; those in back open onto the links, those in front have better views of the Channel. The best rooms, called "prestige luxe," feature antique-style furnishings, French windows, and spacious bathrooms and balconies.

At New-Golf Club, Mont Canisy, St-Arnoult Deauville 14800. www.lucienbarriere.com. *✆* **02-31-14-24-00.** Fax 02-31-14-24-01. 178 units. 245€–620€ double; 500€–655€ junior suite. AE, MC, V. Closed mid-Nov to mid-Mar. From Deauville, take D278 south for 2.5km (1½ miles). **Amenities:** 2 restaurants; bar; babysitting; children's center; exercise room; 27-hole golf course; massage; heated outdoor pool; room service; rooms for those w/limited mobility; sauna; smoke-free rooms; 3 tennis courts. *In room:* TV, hair dryer, minibar, Wi-Fi.

### Normandy Barrière ★★★ ☺

This is the most famous hotel in Deauville, a legendary place that dates back to the Edwardian age. The Anglo-Norman design includes half-timbering, dovecotes, turrets, and gables; the 1912 building resembles a cozy but stately English country house. A renovation updated all the rooms, public areas, and security systems. Because of its extensive facilities for children, including a nursery and babysitting, it attracts upscale families with children—although that doesn't interfere with the hotel's image as a chic nest for French celebrities. During the Deauville Festival of American Film, it attracts French stars, the press, and jury members. Originally built to house well-heeled gamblers from the nearby casino, it continues to draw the gambling crowd today.

38 rue Jean-Mermoz, Deauville 14800. www.lucienbarriere.com. *✆* **02-31-98-66-22.** Fax 02-31-98-66-23. 298 units. 319€–719€ double; 700€–1,020€ suite. AE, DC, MC, V. Parking 30€ in garage. **Amenities:** Restaurant; children's dining room; bar; babysitting; exercise room; heated outdoor pool; room service; steam room; 2 tennis courts. *In room:* TV, hair dryer, minibar, Wi-Fi (8€ per hour).

### Royal-Barrière ★★★

The Royal adjoins the casino and fronts a park near the Channel. It rises like a palace, with columns and exposed timbers. Although it doesn't have the insider cachet of the Normandy Barrière (see above), it is a grander and more opulent hotel. It's a member of Leading Hotels of the World, and its architecture evokes an Edwardian-era grand palace hotel. The hotel was built in 1913 on architectural principles conceived by Gustav Eiffel (an iron skeleton supports walls and ceilings). Post-millennium, the hotel concluded a 5-year renovation program that included virtually every aspect of the establishment, including elegant bathrooms with tubs and showers. The decor of the guest rooms, conceived

Deauville

by megadesigner Jacques Garcia, is a reinterpretation of Directoire and Napoleon III styles. During the Deauville Festival of American Film, the U.S. stars stay here.

Bd. Eugène-Cornuché, Deauville 14800. www.lucienbarriere.com. ✆ 02-31-98-66-33. Fax 02-31-98-66-34. 290 units. 330€–750€ double; 685€–1,065€ suite. AE, DC, MC, V. Closed Nov to early Mar. **Amenities:** 2 restaurants; bar; health club; heated outdoor pool; room service; sauna. *In room:* TV, hair dryer, minibar, Wi-Fi (8€ per hour).

### INEXPENSIVE

**Hôtel Ibis** ✦   Built in the 1980s as part of the nationwide chain, the Ibis is on the periphery of Deauville about 1km (½ mile) from the casino. The modern building, overlooking the harbor, is one of the best bargains in town. Rooms are comfortable and tidy, but decorated in dull chain style. The small tiled bathrooms contain showers and the restaurant offers a traditional French menu.

9–10 quai de la Marine, Deauville 14800. www.hotelibis.com. ✆ 02-31-14-50-00. Fax 02-31-14-50-05. 95 units. 76€–175€ double; 120€–185€ duplex suite for 2–6 people. AE, DC, MC, V. Parking 10€. **Amenities:** Restaurant; bar; babysitting. *In room:* A/C, TV, free Wi-Fi.

**L'Augeval** ★   Across from the racetrack and just blocks from the beach and casino, this hotel mixes city flair and country charm. The former private villa was built in the early 1900s and sits amid well-kept lawns and gardens. The cozy rooms range from medium to spacious, and each has at least one high-quality antique. Some units have Jacuzzis.

15 av. Hocquart-de-Turtot, Deauville 14800. www.augeval.com. ✆ 02-31-81-13-18. Fax 02-31-81-00-40. 52 units. 95€–110€ double; 222€–333€ suite. AE, DC, MC, V. Parking 8€. **Amenities:** Bar; babysitting; exercise room; small heated outdoor pool; room service. *In room:* TV, hair dryer, minibar, free Wi-Fi.

# TROUVILLE ★★

206km (128 miles) NW of Paris; 43km (27 miles) NE of Caen

Across the Touques River from the fashionable (and expensive) Deauville, Trouville feels more like a fishing port. The town is similar to Honfleur, but with fewer boutiques and art galleries. Don't expect the grand atmosphere of Deauville; Trouville is more low-key. It's also less dependent on resort euros; when the bathers leave its splendid sands, Trouville continues to thrive—its resident population of fishermen sees to that.

## Essentials

**GETTING THERE**   There are **rail** connections from Gare St-Lazare in Paris to Trouville (see the "Deauville" section, earlier in this chapter). **Bus Verts du Calvados** (www.busverts.fr) links Trouville, Deauville, and the surrounding region with the rest of Normandy. For bus information, call the **Gare Routière** (✆ 08-10-21-42-14). If you're traveling by **car** from Deauville, drive west along D180.

**VISITOR INFORMATION**   The **Office de Tourisme** is at 32 quai Fernand-Moureaux (www.trouvillesurmer.org; ✆ 02-31-14-60-70).

## Exploring the Town

In the heyday of Napoleon III, during the 1860s, *boulevardiers* (men about town) used to bring their wives and families to Trouville and stash their mistresses in

Seafood on offer in Trouville.

Deauville. Deauville was just coming into existence; it's a planned city, with straight avenues and a sense of industrial-age orderliness. By contrast, the narrow, labyrinthine alleyways of Trouville hint at its origins as a medieval fishing port.

Our recommendation? Explore Trouville, enjoying its low-key charm, and when you tire of it, join the caravan of traffic that heads across the river to the bright lights and glamour of Deauville.

**Les Planches** is a stretch of seafront boardwalk dotted with concessions on one side and overlooking the sea on the other. In midsummer, expect lots of flesh sprawled on the sands in various states of undress. There's only one beach, **Plage de Trouville** (though when you've tired of it, you only have to cross the river to reach the Plage de Deauville). On Trouville's seafront is the **Piscine de Trouville,** promenade des Planches (✆ 02-31-14-48-10), an indoor fresh-water pool that gets very crowded in summer. Depending on the season, bathers pay 6€ to 7€ per person. Hours are July and August daily 9:30am to 7:30pm, June and September daily 10am to 7pm, and October to May daily 10:30am to 7pm.

## Where to Eat

**La Petite Auberge** NORMAN    For a quality meal, head to this Norman bistro a block from the casino. Try cream of cauliflower soup with scallops or a *pot-au-feu Dieppoise* featuring filet of sole, scallops, monkfish, and salmon beautifully simmered together. You can also order grilled beef and chicken thighs braised in cider. Because the bistro seats only 30, reservations are vital in summer.

7 rue Carnot. ✆ **02-31-88-11-07.** Reservations required. Main courses 22€–33€; fixed-price menu 33€–55€. MC, V. Thurs–Mon noon–2:30pm and 7:15–9:30pm.

**Les Vapeurs** ★★ FRENCH/SEAFOOD    This Art Deco brasserie, one of the most popular on the Norman coast, is frequented by stylish Parisians on *le week-end*. Established in 1926, it has been called the Brasserie Lipp of Normandy. The windows face the port, and in warm weather you can dine at sidewalk tables.

Seafood—a wide range of shrimp, mussels laced with cream, crinkle-shelled oysters, and fish—is the specialty. Sauerkraut is also popular.

162 bd. Fernand-Moureaux. www.lesvapeurs.fr. ☏ **02-31-88-15-24.** Reservations recommended. Main courses 14€–33€. AE, MC, V. Mon–Fri noon–10:30pm; Sat–Sun noon–12:30am.

## Trouville Nightlife

If the casino in Deauville is too stuffy for you, you'll feel more comfortable in its smaller, less architecturally distinctive sibling in Trouville, **Casino Barrière de Trouville,** place du Maréchal-Foch (www.lucienbarriere.com; ☏ **02-31-87-75-00;**). It has more of a New Orleans–style environment, with a blues and jazz bar that schedules live music Friday and Saturday night, and a small-scale replica of Bourbon Street. Entrance to the slot machines is free. Entrance to the more formal area—with roulette, blackjack, and craps—costs 14€ per person. You must present a passport or identity card to gain admission. The formal area is open Sunday through Thursday 8pm to 2am, Friday 8pm to 3am, and Saturday 8pm to 4am. The rest of the casino is open daily from 10am. Men aren't required to wear jackets and ties, but sneakers are not allowed.

## Where to Stay

**Best Western Hostellerie du Vallon ★**   The best place to stay in town is this modern hotel constructed in a traditional Norman style. Lying a short walk from the beach, the hotel is far more affordable than so many of the properties at neighboring Deauville. Well run and spacious, it boasts a modern interior with such facilities as an indoor swimming pool, which makes it a good year-round choice. Many of the attractively and comfortably furnished bedrooms open onto private balconies with a view.

12 rue Sylvestre Lassere, 14360 Trouville. www.hostellerie-du-vallon.com. ☏ **02-31-98-35-00.** 62 units. 120€–180€ double; 200€–260€ junior suite. AE, DC, MC, V. **Amenities:** Bar; exercise room; Jacuzzi; indoor pool; sauna; steam room. *In room:* TV, hair dryer, minibar.

**Le Beach Hotel**   Although a poor relation to the palaces of Deauville, Le Beach Hotel provides comfort at more affordable prices. The seven-story hotel emerges from a lackluster lot only 45m (148 ft.) from the beach. Its average-size rooms have modern furniture and comfortable beds, plus views of Trouville harbor; most bathrooms have showers only.

1 quai Albert-1er, Trouville 14360. ☏ **02-31-98-12-00.** Fax 02-31-87-30-29. 110 units. 105€–220€ double. AE, DC, MC, V. Parking 9€. Amenities: Restaurant; bar; babysitting; indoor pool; room service. In room: TV, minibar, free Wi-Fi.

# CAEN ★

238km (148 miles) NW of Paris; 119km (74 miles) SE of Cherbourg

Situated on the banks of the Orne, the port of Caen suffered great damage in the 1944 invasion of Normandy. Nearly three-quarters of its buildings, 10,000 in all, were destroyed, though the twin abbeys founded by William the Conqueror and his wife, Mathilda, were spared. The city today is essentially modern and has many broad avenues and new apartment buildings. Completely different from Deauville and Trouville, the capital of Lower Normandy is bustling, congested, and commercial; it's a major rail and ferry junction. The student population of 30,000 and the hordes of travelers have made Caen more cosmopolitan than ever.

## Essentials

**GETTING THERE**   From Paris's Gare St-Lazare, 12 **trains** per day arrive in Caen (trip time: 1 hr., 50 min.–2½ hr.). One-way fares start at 32€ to 47€. One-way fares from Rouen (trip time: 1 hr., 45 min.) start at 23€. To **drive** from Paris, travel west along A13 to Caen (driving time: 2½–3 hr.).

**VISITOR INFORMATION**   The **Office de Tourisme** is on place St-Pierre in the 16th-century Hôtel d'Escoville (www.tourisme.caen.fr; ✆ **02-31-27-14-14**).

## Exploring the City

**Abbaye aux Dames** RELIGIOUS SITE   Founded by Mathilda, wife of William the Conqueror, this abbey embraces Eglise de la Trinité, which is flanked by Romanesque towers. Its spires were destroyed in the Hundred Years' War. The 12th-century choir houses the tomb of Queen Mathilda; note the ribbed vaulting.

Place de la Reine-Mathilde. ✆ **02-31-06-98-98.** Free admission. Daily 2–5:30pm. Free guided 1-hr. tour of choir, transept, and crypt (in French) daily 2:30 and 4pm.

**Abbaye aux Hommes** ★★ RELIGIOUS SITE   Founded by William and Mathilda, this abbey is adjacent to the Eglise St-Etienne, which you enter on place Monseigneur-des-Hameaux. During the height of the Allied invasion, residents of Caen flocked to St-Etienne for protection. Twin Romanesque towers 84m (276 ft.) tall dominate the church; they helped earn Caen the appellation "city of spires." A marble slab inside the high altar marks the site of William's tomb. The Huguenots destroyed the tomb in 1562—only a hipbone was recovered. During the French Revolution, the last of William's dust was scattered to the wind. The hand-carved wooden doors and elaborate wrought-iron staircase are exceptional. From the cloisters, you get a good view of the two towers of St-Etienne.

Esplanade Jean-Marie-Louvel. ✆ **02-31-30-42-81.** Obligatory tours (in French, accompanied by broken-English translation) 2.40€ adults, 1.20€ students, free for children 17 and under. Daily 8:30am–12:30pm and 1:30–7:30pm (2:30–7:30pm Sun). Tours daily 9:30 and 11am, and 2:30 and 4pm. Ticket office for tours daily 8am–4pm.

Abbaye aux Hommes.

**Le Château de Caen** CASTLE This complex was built on the ruins of a fortress erected by William the Conqueror in 1060. Enter the grounds at esplanade de la Paix. The gardens are ideal for strolling and, from the ramparts, a panoramic view of Caen unfolds. Within the compound are two museums. The **Musée de Normandie** (www.musee-de-normandie.caen.fr; ✆ 02-31-30-47-60) displays artifacts from Normandy, including archaeological finds, along with a collection of regional sculpture, paintings, and ceramics. Admission is free, and it's open Wednesday to Monday 9:30am to 6pm. Also within the walls is the **Musée des Beaux-Arts** (www.ville-caen.fr/mba; ✆ 02-31-30-47-70), with a collection of works—though not their finest—by old masters including Veronese and Rubens. Admission is free except for temporary exhibits costing 3€ to 5€. It's open Wednesday through Monday from 9:30am to 6pm.

**Le Mémorial de Caen (Caen Memorial)** MONUMENT/MEMORIAL
The memorial is a 15-minute drive away from the Pegasus Bridge and 15 minutes from the landing beaches. The museum presents a journey through history from 1918 to the present. It's an ideal place to relax. You can walk through International Park, have a meal or drink at the restaurant, or browse through the boutique. Expect to spend at least 2½ hours at this site—anyone intrigued by 20th-century European history will be fascinated. One wing is dedicated to a depiction of the American and global role after World War II. Its photo documentaries and exhibits illustrate the Cold War, the construction and collapse of the Berlin Wall, and the assault of military weapons (especially nuclear testing) on the environment.

Esplanade Général Dwight-Eisenhower. www.memorial-caen.fr. ✆ 02-31-06-06-45. Admission Apr–Sept 18€ adults, 15€ students and children 10–18; Oct–Mar 17€ adults, 14€ students and children 10–18; free to World War II veterans, those with war disabilities, war widows, and children 9 and under. Daily 9am–7pm (until 8pm mid-July to mid-Aug). Closed Jan 4–26.

## Shopping

Caen has some good boutique-lined shopping streets, including **boulevard du Maréchal-Leclerc, rue St-Pierre,** and **rue de Strasbourg. Antiques** hunters

 **AN** excursion **TO THE FORBES CHÂTEAU**

Built by François Mansart between 1626 and 1636, the **Château de Balleroy** ★, between Bayeux and Caen, has been owned by the Forbes family for more than 3 decades. The late Malcolm Forbes was an internationally known balloonist, and his dream of opening the world's first balloon museum has been fulfilled at the château. Today it is the venue for the biannual international ballooning festival.

The museum, in a converted stable, is filled with artifacts related to the history of ballooning. The château also contains many period rooms that abound with elegant art and antiques. Admission to the museum and castle is 8€ for adults or 6€ for students and children 7 to 18, and free for those 6 and under; entrance to just the grounds costs 3€ for everyone. Visiting times are from mid-March to mid-October Wednesday to Monday 10am to noon and 2 to 6pm (July–Aug hours are 10am–6pm).

The museum (www.chateau-balleroy.com; ✆ 02-31-21-60-61) lies at Balleroy F-14490 outside the village of Balleroy. To reach it from Caen (40km/25 miles), head west along N13, cutting south at the junction with D572, and follow the road to Balleroy, where the château is signposted.

should check out the shops along rue Ecuyère and rue Commerçantes, and the antiques show at the **Parc des Expositions,** rue Joseph-Philippon (*©* **02-31-29-99-99**), in early May. The **markets** at place St-Sauveur on Friday morning and place Courtonne on Sunday morning also sell secondhand articles.

For custom-built reproduction antique furniture, visit **La Reine Matilde,** 47 rue St-Jean (*©* **02-31-85-45-52**); it also sells decorative items, including a selection of bed linens and curtains. **Le Chocolaterie Hotot,** 13 rue St-Pierre (*©* **02-31-86-31-90**), has a cornucopia of chocolate products, as well as local jams and jellies. At **Le Comptoir Normand,** 7 rue de Geôle (*©* **02-31-86-34-13**), you'll find many regional items, including Calvados and various charcuterie products, such as tripe in the style of Caen.

## Where to Eat

**Le Carlotta** FRENCH/SEAFOOD   This is a well-established brasserie, one of the best known in town, with a high-volume turnover and a penchant for seafood. With an Art Deco decor, it's a bustling venue. Tried-and-true menu items include platters of shellfish, especially oysters; strips of duck breast with parsley sauce; braised oxtail with truffles and mashed potatoes; and roasted shoulder of lamb *en confit,* served with Middle Eastern spices and mashed potatoes. Desserts usually include a homemade version of tiramisu and a gratin of seasonal berries.

16 quai Vendeuvre. www.lecarlotta.fr. *©* **02-31-86-68-99.** Reservations recommended. Main courses 18€–28€; set menus 23€–36€. AE, MC, V. Mon–Sat noon–2pm and 6–10:30pm.

**Le P'tit B** ♠ FRENCH/NORMAN   A growing number of local diners are enthusiastic about this place, which is set in a 17th-century house in the center of town. Its fixed-price menu, with loads of good choices, is a great deal. You might begin with *terrine maison* or a slice of Norman-style Camembert tart, followed by a seafood brochette.

15 rue de Vaugueux. *©* **02-31-93-50-76.** Reservations recommended. Main courses 14€–18€; fixed-price lunch 16€; fixed-price dinner 32€. AE, MC, V. Daily noon–3pm and 7pm–midnight.

## Caen Nightlife

Take a walk down rue de Bras, rue St-Pierre, and the north end of rue Vaugueux to size up the action. If you want to connect with the hip 18-to-35 crowd, go to **Le Chic,** rue des Prairies St-Gilles (*©* **02-31-94-48-72**), where disco music begins at 10:30pm. **Le Carré,** 32 quai Vendeuvre (*©* **02-31-38-90-90**), is a disco that caters to patrons over 27 with rock 'n' roll, cutting-edge techno, and an assortment of music from the '70s and '80s. Upstairs, there's the hip and often charming Bar de Nuit.

## Where to Stay

**Hôtel des Quatrans** ✦  This agreeable, unpretentious hotel was rebuilt after World War II, and thanks to continual renovations, it's one of Caen's best bargains. Don't expect luxury: The hotel has four floors of old-fashioned rooms that offer basic amenities, including small, shower-only bathrooms. A buffet breakfast, available in the breakfast room or delivered to your room, is the only meal served.

17 rue Gémare, Caen 14300. www.hotel-des-quatrans.com. ✆ **02-31-86-25-57.** Fax 02-31-85-27-80. 47 units. 65€ double; 75€ triple. MC, V. Parking free. **Amenities:** Restaurant; bar. *In room:* TV, hair dryer, free Wi-Fi.

**Hôtel Kyriad**  This hotel is a reliable bargain. The original was destroyed during a World War II bombing raid. Rebuilt several years later, it's surrounded by a commercial area of shops and restaurants, as well as more tranquil pedestrian streets. The hotel provides bedrooms in attractive color schemes such as soft yellows and reds. There's no restaurant, but an independent grill-style restaurant across the street offers inexpensive breakfast plans for hotel guests.

1 place de la République, Caen 14000. ✆ **02-31-86-55-33.** Fax 02-31-79-89-44. 47 units. 57€–90€ double. AE, MC, V. Parking 7€. **Amenities:** Bar. *In room:* A/C, TV, hair dryer, free Wi-Fi.

# BAYEUX ★★

267km (166 miles) NW of Paris; 25km (16 miles) NW of Caen

The *ducs de Normandie* sent their sons to this Viking settlement to learn the Norse language in the ninth century. Bayeux has changed a lot since then but was spared from bombardment in 1944. This was the first French town liberated, and the citizens gave de Gaulle an enthusiastic welcome when he arrived on June 14. The town is filled with timbered houses, stone mansions, and cobblestone streets.

   Visitors wanting to explore sites associated with "the Longest Day" flood the town, because many memorials (not to mention the beaches) are only 9.5 to 19km (6–12 miles) away. Shops line the cozy little streets. Many sell World War II memorabilia, and more postcards and T-shirts than you'll ever need.

## Essentials

**GETTING THERE**  Twelve **trains** depart daily from Paris's Gare St-Lazare. The 2½-hour trip to Bayeux costs 35€. Most trains stop in Caen. Travel time between Caen and Bayeux is about 20 minutes and costs 5.80€. To **drive** to Bayeux from Paris (trip time: 3 hr.), take A13 to Caen and E46 west to Bayeux.

**VISITOR INFORMATION**  The **Office de Tourisme** is at pont St-Jean (www.bayeux-bessin-tourism.com; ✆ 02-31-51-28-28).

**SPECIAL EVENTS**  The town goes wild on the first weekend in July during **Fêtes Médiévales;** the streets fill with wine and song during 2 days of medieval revelry. For information, call ✆ **02-31-92-03-30.**

A pretty evening in Bayeux.

## Seeing the Sights

**Musée de la Tapisserie de Bayeux** MUSEUM ★★★   The most famous tapestry in the world is actually an embroidery on linen, 69m (226 ft.) long and .5m (20 in.) wide, depicting 58 scenes in eight colors. Contrary to legend, it wasn't made by Queen Mathilda, the wife of William the Conqueror, but was probably commissioned in Kent and created by unknown embroiderers between 1066 and 1077. The first mention of the embroidery was in 1476, when it decorated the nave of the Cathédrale Notre-Dame de Bayeux.

Housed in a Plexiglas case, the embroidery tells the story of the conquest of England by William the Conqueror, including such scenes as the coronation of Harold as the Saxon king of England, Harold returning from his journey to Normandy, the surrender of Dinan, Harold being told of the apparition of a comet (a portent of misfortune), William dressed for war, and the death of Harold. The decorative borders include scenes from *Aesop's Fables.*

Admission to the museum includes access to an annex whose collections are not as spectacular. The **Collections Baron Gérard** is housed in **Le Musée de l'Hôtel du Doyen,** 6 rue Lambert le Forestier (*©* 02-31-92-14-21). Exhibitions feature examples of regional lacework, porcelain, and religious and secular paintings, many of them created within this region.

Centre Guillaume-le-Conquérant, 13 rue de Nesmond. www.tapisserie-bayeux.fr. *©* **02-31-51-25-50.** Admission 7.80€ adults, 3.80€ students, free for children 9 and under. Mar 15–Nov 15 daily 9am–6:30pm; off season daily 9:30am–12:30pm and 2–6pm.

**Musée Memorial de la Bataille de Normandie** MUSEUM   This museum deals with the military and human history of the Battle of

A section of the Bayeux Tapestry.

Normandy (June 6–Aug 22, 1944). In a low-slung building designed like a bunker are 132m (433 ft.) of window and film displays, plus a diorama. Wax soldiers in uniform, along with the tanks and guns used to win the battle, are on exhibit. Across from the museum, the **Commonwealth Cemetery** (✆ **03-21-21-77-00**) lies on the northwestern perimeter of Bayeux, containing 4,144 graves of soldiers from throughout the British Commonwealth, all of them killed during the Battle of Normandy.

Bd. Fabian Ware. ✆ **02-31-51-46-90.** Admission 6.50€ adults, 3.80€ students and children, free for children 9 and under. May–Sept 15 daily 9:30am–6:30pm; Sept 16–Apr daily 10am–12:30pm and 2–6pm.

**Notre-Dame de Bayeux** ★★ CATHEDRAL    This cathedral was consecrated in 1077 and partially destroyed in 1105. Romanesque towers from the original church rise on the western side. The central tower is from the 15th century. The nave is a fine example of Norman Romanesque style. The 13th-century choir, a perfect example of Norman Gothic style, is rich in sculpture and has Renaissance stalls. The crypt was built in the 11th century and then sealed, its existence unknown until 1412.

Rue du Bienvenu. ✆ **02-31-92-14-21.** Admission 4€, free ages 14 and under. Daily 8:30am–6pm (to 7pm July–Aug).

# Where to Eat

**Le Pommier** ★ 🍴 NORMAN    One of the most appealing restaurants in Bayeux's historic zone occupies an 18th-century building. Ceiling beams and exposed masonry enhance the trio of dining rooms. The establishment is devotedly Norman, with cuisine that reflects the region's long tradition of baking with apples (the name translates as "The Apple Tree") and cream (though its use is limited, to make the food a bit healthier). The health-conscious staff is proud that the dishes "aren't drowned in gravies and sauces." Menu items evolve with the seasons. You can usually expect dishes such as rabbit stew braised in cider and a platter that contains two kinds of fish, served with chitterling sausage and a sauce of cream and chitterling drippings.

38 rue des Cuisiniers. www.restaurantlepommier.com. ✆ **02-31-21-52-10.** Fax 02-31-21-06-01. Reservations recommended. Main courses 17€–25€; fixed-price menus 25€–42€. AE, MC, V. Apr–Sept daily noon–2:30pm and 7–9:30pm; Oct–Mar Mon–Sat noon–2pm and 7–9:30pm. Closed mid-Dec to mid-Jan.

# Where to Stay

**Churchill** ★ 🍴    Open from March to November, this hotel lies in the heart of the medieval town, close to the famous tapestry and the cathedral. Excursions for the D-day beaches leave from the square behind the hotel, and a shuttle to Mont-St-Michel can also be arranged. The staff is among the most accommodating in town. Their midsize bedrooms are personalized, each comfortably furnished on an individual basis. Of course, their deluxe rooms are the way to go, unless you're economizing, in which case you'll find their standard units most adequate.

14 rue St-Jean, 14400 Bayeux. www.hotel-churchill.fr. ✆ **02-31-21-31-80.** 32 units. 100€–170€ double. MC, V. **Amenities:** Free Internet. *In room:* TV.

**Le Lion d'Or** ★★  This old-world hotel is the oldest and most nostalgic in town, dating from 1928. The property, built in 1734, has an open courtyard with lush flower boxes decorating the facade. As befits an old inn, rooms come in various shapes and sizes. The midsize bathrooms are well equipped; each has a shower, and more than half have tubs. Guests are required to take at least one meal here, but that shouldn't be a problem—the traditional cuisine is delicious. The restaurant serves lots of reasonably priced wines.

71 rue St-Jean, Bayeux 14400. www.liondor-bayeux.fr. *C* **02-31-92-06-90.** Fax 02-31-22-15-64. 28 units. 115€–200€ double. AE, MC, V. Parking 9€. **Amenities:** Restaurant; bar; babysitting; exercise room. *In room:* TV, minibar, free Wi-Fi.

# THE D-DAY BEACHES ★★

Arromanches-les-Bains: 272km (169 miles) NW of Paris, 11km (6¾ miles) NW of Bayeux; Grandcamp-Maisy (near Omaha Beach): 299km (185 miles) NW of Paris, 56km (35 miles) NW of Caen

During a rainy week in June 1944, the greatest armada ever—soldiers and sailors, warships, landing craft, tugboats, jeeps—assembled along the southern coast of England. At 9:15pm on June 5, the BBC announced to the French Resistance that the invasion was imminent, signaling the underground to start dynamiting the railways. Before midnight, Allied planes began bombing the Norman coast. By 1:30am on June 6 ("the Longest Day"), members of the 101st Airborne were parachuting to the ground on German-occupied French soil. At 6:30am, the Americans began landing on the beaches, code-named Utah and Omaha. An hour later, British and Canadian forces made beachheads at Juno, Gold, and Sword.

The Nazis had mocked Churchill's promise in 1943 to liberate France "before the fall of the autumn leaves." When the invasion did come, it was swift, sudden, and a surprise to the formidable "Atlantic wall." Today veterans walk with their children and grandchildren across the beaches where "Czech hedgehogs," "Belgian grills," pillboxes, and "Rommel asparagus" (all military barriers or structures) once stood.

## Essentials

**GETTING THERE**  The best way to get to the D-day beaches is to **drive.** Public transportation is unreliable. The trip takes about 3 hours from Paris. Take A13 west to Caen, and continue west along A13 to Bayeux. From Bayeux, travel north along D6 until you reach the coast at Port-en-Bessin. From here, D514 runs along the coastline; most D-day sites are west of Port-en-Bessin. Parking is not a problem, and most of the designated areas along the roadway are free. It's best to visit on a weekday, because weekends (especially in summer) can be crowded with tourists and sunbathers.

**Bus** service from Bayeux is uneven and usually involves long delays. **Bus Verts** (www.busverts.fr; *C* **08-10-21-42-14**) runs to Port-en-Bessin and points west, and bus no. 75 offers service year-round to Arromanches and other points in the east. Bus no. 70 travels west (June–Sept only) from Bayeux toward Omaha Beach and the American cemetery.

If you don't have a car, the best way to see the D-day beaches is on a **tour. Normandy Tours,** Hotel de la Gare, Bayeux (www.normandy-landing-tours. com; *C* **02-31-92-10-70**), runs a 4- to 5-hour tour (in English) to

Arromanches, Omaha Beach, the American Military Cemetery, and Pointe du Hoc for 48€ adults and 40€ students and seniors. **D-Day Tours,** 52 rte. de Porte en Bessin, Bayeux (www.normandywebguide.com; ✆ **02-31-51-70-52**), conducts tours with a bit more pizzazz and guides who speak better English. A half-day trip costs 45€ for adults and 40€ for students; a full-day trip is 75€ for adults and 65€ for students. The company picks you up at your hotel in Bayeux. A final option, **Battlebus** (www.battlebus.fr; ✆ **02-31-22-28-82**), leads a full-day tour encompassing all sites and beaches that were pivotal during the D-day landing and Battle of Normandy; cost is 85€ per person. Most participants have found this latter option the best tour of all—simultaneously riveting, exhausting, and stimulating.

**VISITOR INFORMATION**   The **Office de Tourisme,** 4 rue du Maréchal-Joffre, Arromanches-les-Bains (✆ **02-31-21-47-56**), is open year-round.

## Reliving the Longest Day

Start your exploration at the seaside resort of **Arromanches-les-Bains.** In June 1944, this was a fishing port until the 50th British Division took it. A mammoth prefabricated port known as Winston was towed across the Channel and installed to supply the Allied forces. "Victory could not have been achieved without it," Eisenhower said. The wreckage of that artificial harbor is just off the beach, **Plage du Débarquement. Musée du Débarquement,** place du 6-Juin (www.normandy1944.com; ✆ **02-31-22-34-31**), in Arromanches, features maps, models, a cinema, photographs, and a diorama of the landing, all with English commentary. Admission is 6.50€ for adults and 4.50€ for students and children. From June to August, hours are daily 9am to 7pm; September Monday to Saturday 9am to 6pm, Sunday 10am to 6pm; October and March daily 9:30am to 12:30pm and 1:30 to 5:30pm; November to December and February daily 10am

Sand yachts at Omaha Beach.

**Normandy American Cemetery.**

to 12:30pm and 1:30 to 5pm; April Monday to Saturday 9am to 12:30pm and 1:30 to 6pm, Sunday 10am to 12:30pm and 1:30 to 6pm; and May Monday to Saturday 9am to 7pm, Sunday 10am to 7pm. It's closed December 24 to 26, December 31, and the month of January.

Moving along the coast, you'll arrive at **Omaha Beach,** where you can still see the war wreckage. "Hanging on by their toenails," the men of the 1st and 29th American Divisions occupied the beach that June day. The code name Omaha became famous; until then, the beaches had been called St-Laurent, Vierville-sur-Mer, and Colleville. A monument commemorates the heroism of the invaders. Covering some 70 hectares (173 acres) at Omaha Beach, the **Normandy American Cemetery** (www.abmc.gov; *©* **02-31-51-62-00**) is filled with crosses and Stars of David in Lasa marble. The remains of 9,387 American military were buried here on territory now owned by the United States, a gift from the French nation. Admission is free. The cemetery is open daily 9am to 5pm, the visitor center until 6pm (both are closed Christmas and New Year's Day).

## Americans Return to Normandy

The **Normandy American Visitor Center,** opened at Colleville-sur-Mer 14710 (www.abmc.gov; *©* **02-31-51-62-00**), dedicated to those heroes of World War II who liberated mainland France from the Nazis, tells the story of the 9,387 Americans buried on French soil. The center relates that dramatic story through narrative text, photos, films, interactive displays, and artifacts. Admission is free. The center is open April 15 through September 15 daily 9am to 6pm, and off season daily 9am to 5pm.

# reliving THE ALLIED INVASION OF NORMANDY

One of the most evocative ways to re-create the sensations that the combat troops felt just prior to their invasion of Normandy involves signing up for a waterborne tour. Maintained by **Les Vedettes de Normandie,** and entitled "Balades sur les plages du Débarquement," the tour offers prerecorded English-language commentary on a cassette player, live commentary from a French-language guide, and boats with a capacity of 200 sightseers at a time. Commentary focuses on the physicality of the Norman coastline; the region's construction, shipping, and fishing industries; and the historic events associated with the invasion of Normandy by Allied troops in 1944.

Between mid-April and mid-October, boats depart between one and three times a day, with a schedule that varies with the tides, the season, the day of the week, and French national holidays. All tours depart from the harborfront quays of the hamlet of Port-en-Bessin. Tours lasting 90 minutes each, and which cost 15€ per participant, focus on either Arromanches or Omaha beaches. Lasting 3 hours, tours (at 23€) focus on Omaha Beach and the Pointe du Hoc. There's no discount for children. For information about departure times and reservations, contact *Les Vedettes de Normandie,* Ste. H.C., bd. De Général de Gaulle Point de Cabourg, 14160 Dives-sur-Mer (🕽 **02-31-43-86-12**).

Farther along the coast, you'll see the jagged lime cliffs of the **Pointe du Hoc.** A cross honors a group of American Rangers, led by Lt. Col. James Rudder, who scaled the cliffs using hooks to get at the pillboxes (gun emplacements). The scars of war are more visible here than at any other point along the beach. Farther along the Cotentin Peninsula is **Utah Beach,** where the 4th U.S. Infantry Division landed at 6:30am. The landing force was nearly 3km (1¾ miles) south of its intended destination, but Nazi defenses were weak. By midday the infantry had completely cleared the beach. A U.S. monument commemorates their heroism.

Nearby, you can visit the hamlet of **Ste-Mère-Eglise,** which was virtually unknown outside of France before paratroopers dropped from the sky. In Ste-Mère-Eglise is Kilometer 0 on the Liberty Highway, marking the first of the milestones the American armies reached on their way to Metz and Bastogne.

## Where to Eat & Stay at Grandcamp-Maisy

**Hôtel Duguesclin** TRADITIONAL FRENCH    We recommend this Norman inn for lunch or even an overnight stay. The fish soup, grilled scallops, Norman sole (when it's available), and grilled turbot with white butter are excellent. Everything tastes better with the dining room's country bread and Norman butter.

The hotel rents 23 simple, comfortable rooms, all with bathroom, phone, and TV. Accommodations have a shower or tub (sometimes both). A double costs 45€ to 66€.

4 quai Crampon. 🕽 **02-31-22-64-22.** Fax 02-31-22-34-79. Reservations recommended. Main courses 12€–33€; fixed-price menu 15€–35€. AE, MC, V. Daily noon–2pm and 7–9pm.

**La Marée** NORMAN   Set beside the port, this small, nautically decorated restaurant serves mostly fish and only fish caught in the English Channel or within a reasonable distance out in the Atlantic, guaranteeing a local culinary experience. During nice weather, the dining room expands onto a terrace.

5 quai Henri Chéron. ℭ **02-31-21-41-00.** Reservations required. Main courses 18€–22€; fixed-price menus 14€–25€. AE, MC, V. Daily 12:30–2:30pm and 7–9:30pm. Closed Jan 1–Feb 7.

## Where to Stay at Arromanches

**Hôtel de la Marine**   A hotel has stood on this spot since 1837, although the one you see today wins over any of its earlier incarnations when it comes to comfort and style. The hotel directly faces the beach that played a keynote role during the U.S. invasion of Normandy and offers many of the charming details of a Norman private country estate. Bedrooms are rustically outfitted with colorful fabrics and solid, traditional furnishings. The restaurant appeals even to nonguests. It's open daily noon to 2pm and 7 to 9:30pm, and serves set-price, thoroughly French meals priced at 22€ to 35€ each.

1 quai du Canada, Arromanches les Bains 14117. www.hotel-de-la-marine.fr. ℭ **02-31-22-34-19.** Fax 02-31-22-98-80. 33 units. 78€–185€ double. Rates include breakfast and dinner. AE, MC, V. Free parking. **Amenities:** Restaurant; bar. *In room:* A/C, TV, hair dryer, free Wi-Fi.

# MONT-ST-MICHEL ★★★

324km (201 miles) W of Paris; 129km (80 miles) SW of Caen; 76km (47 miles) E of Dinan; 48km (30 miles) E of St-Malo

Massive walls measuring more than half a mile in circumference surround one of Europe's great attractions, the island of Mont-St-Michel. Connected to the shore by a causeway, it crowns a rocky islet at the border between Normandy and Brittany. The rock is 78m (256 ft.) high.

Grand Rue.

## Essentials

**GETTING THERE**   The most efficient way to reach Mont-St-Michel is to **drive.** From Caen, follow A84 southwest to Pontorson, continuing a few more kilometers to Avranches; from there, merge onto D43, following signs to its end at Mont-St-Michel. Total driving time from Paris is about 4½ hours.

There are no direct trains between Paris and Mont-St-Michel. We suggest taking the high-speed **TGV train** from Paris's Gare Montparnasse to Rennes, where you can transfer to the **bus** run by the **SNCF** (www.voyages-sncf.com; ℭ **36-35** or 08-92-35-35-35) for the 75-minute trip to Mont-St-Michel. Depending on the season, two to five buses a day run to Rennes for 12€ per

Mont-St-Michel.

person. Another company, **Les Courriers Bretons** (www.lescourriers bretons.fr; ✆ **02-99-19-70-70**), also operates buses that make the 75-minute ride to Mont-St-Michel from St-Malo two to five times a day for 13€ per person.

**VISITOR INFORMATION** The **Office de Tourisme** is in the Corps de Garde des Bourgeois (the Old Guard Room of the Bourgeois), at the left of the town gates (www.ot-montsaintmichel.com; ✆ **02-33-60-14-30**). The tourist office is open daily year-round except Christmas and New Year's Day.

## Exploring Mont-St-Michel

You'll have a steep climb up Grande Rue, lined with 15th- and 16th-century houses, to reach the **abbey** (www.monuments-nationaux.fr; ✆ **02-33-89-80-00**). Those who make it to the top can begin their exploration of the Marvel of the West. In the 8th century, St. Aubert, the bishop of Avranches, founded an oratory on this spot. A Benedictine monastery, founded in 966 by Richard I, replaced it. That burned in 1203. Philip Augustus financed the building of an abbey in the 13th century.

Ramparts encircle the church and a three-tiered ensemble of 13th-century buildings called **La Merveille** that rise to the pointed spire of the abbey church. This terraced complex is one of Europe's most important Gothic monuments, a citadel in which the concept of an independent France was nurtured during the darkest years of the English occupation of Aquitaine.

On the second terrace of La Merveille is one of Mont-St-Michel's largest and most beautiful rooms, a 13th-century hall known as the **Salle des Chevaliers.**

Crowning the mountain's summit is the **Eglise Abbatiale** (not to be confused with the parish church, Eglise St-Pierre, lower on the mountain). Begun in the 11th century, the abbey church consists of a Romanesque nave and transept, plus a choir in Flamboyant Gothic style. The rectangular refectory dates from 1212, and the cloisters with their columns of pink granite are from 1225.

**Mont-St-Michel**

The abbey is open daily May through September 9am to 7pm, and October to April 9:30am to 5:30pm. From June to September, it's also open Monday to Saturday 9pm to 1am (last entrance at midnight). Mass begins at 12:15pm Tuesday to Sunday. Entrance during daytime or nighttime tours includes a group tour, but you can also wander on your own. Year-round, day or night visits, with or without the tour, cost 9€ for adults, 5.50€ for students and ages 18 to 25, and free for children 17 and under.

Guided tours in French depart at intervals of 30 to 45 minutes, depending on the season. There are usually two to four English-language tours per day. Everything is closed New Year's Day, May 1, and Christmas.

**Archeoscope,** chemin de la Ronde (*©* **02-33-89-01-85**), is a small theater that presents *L'Eau et La Lumière (Water and Light),* celebrating the legend and lore of Mont-St-Michel and its role as a preserver of French medieval nationalism. The 30-minute shows begin every 30 to 60 minutes between 9:30am and 5:30pm. An unusual diversion is the adjacent **Musée de la Mer,** Grande Rue (*©* **02-33-89-02-02**). It showcases marine crafts throughout history, the ecology of the local tidal flats, and illustrations of the French government's ongoing project intended to reactivate the tidal cleansing of the nearby marshes. **Musée Grevin (Musée Historique de Mont-St-Michel),** chemin de la Ronde (*©* **02-33-89-02-02**), traces the history of the abbey.

A museum that's worth a visit is the **Logis Tiphaine,** Grande Rue (✆ **02-33-89-02-02**), a 15th-century home originally under the control of the Dugesclin family, noted defenders of the fortress from English intrigue. In the building, next to the Église St-Pierre, you'll find furniture and accessories from that era, and a sense of pride at the fortress's durability as a bastion of all things French.

A combined ticket for all four of these attractions costs 18€ for adults and 14€ for students, 10€ ages 10 to 18. Free 9 and under. Other than the Archeoscope, whose hours are noted above, the museums are open daily from 9am to 5pm.

## Where to Eat & Stay

**Hôtel du Mouton-Blanc**   Occupying a pair of buildings, parts of which date from the 14th century, this inn stands between the sea and the basilica and has hosted guests since the 1700s. Rooms are small but cozy. Eight are in a comfortable annex, where all units have small bathrooms with showers. The seven better-equipped units in the main building have bathrooms with both tubs and showers. A rustic Norman-style dining room sits on a terrace overlooking the sea. Popular dishes include omelets with seafood, and two marvelous versions of lamb.

Grande Rue, Mont-St-Michel 50116. ✆ **02-33-60-14-08.** Fax 02-33-60-05-62. 15 units. 93€ double; 124€ suite. AE, MC, V. **Amenities:** Restaurant; bar. *In room:* TV.

**La Mère Poulard** NORMAN   This country inn is a shrine to those who revere the omelet that Annette Poulard created in 1888, when the hotel was founded. It's under the same ownership as the more rustic Les Terrasses Poulard. Annette Poulard's secret has been passed on to the inn's operators. Other specialties are *agneau du pré salé* (lamb raised on the saltwater marshes near the foundations of the abbey) and an array of fish.

Grande Rue, Mont-St-Michel 50116. www.mere-poulard.fr. ✆ **02-33-89-68-68.** Fax 02-33-89-68-69. Reservations recommended. Main courses 36€–45€; fixed-price lunch 55€–84€; fixed-price dinner 39€–87€. AE, DC, MC, V. Daily noon–10pm.

# BRITTANY

by Amelia Smith

"ittle Britain," as it was called by the 4th- and 5th-century Celts who came to settle this northwestern peninsula, always seems a bit apart from the rest of France. While this was once politically true (the region resisted conquest and incorporation into Charlemagne's Frankish empire, remaining an independent duchy until 1532), even today's Bretons hold fast to their traditions, and their independent spirit is undeniable. The original Breton language, with its roots in Welsh and Cornish, is still widely spoken. The *Gwenn-ha-du*—the black-and-white Breton flag—still flies proudly in every town.

Promontories, coves, and beaches stud the rocky coastline, some 1,207km (748 miles) long. The interior is a land of hamlets, stone farmhouses, and medieval fortresses.

The British, just a channel-hop away, think of Brittany as a resort region. The French, who typically go south to chase their sun, appreciate it for its untamed beauty, serious sailing, and unique culture and cuisine. We suggest first-time visitors stick to the coast, where you can experience the best of all these in the shortest time.

If you're coming from Mont-St-Michel, use St-Malo, Dinan, or Dinard as a base to explore the north. Visitors from the eastern Loire Valley can reach the coastline of southern Brittany in under 3 hours.

# ST-MALO ★★★

414km (257 miles) W of Paris; 69km (43 miles) N of Rennes; 13km (8 miles) E of Dinard

Despite past lives as a fortress and the site of a monastery, St-Malo is best known for the *corsaires* who used it as a base during the 17th and 18th centuries. During wartime, a decree from the French king sanctioned the seafaring mercenaries to intercept British ships and requisition their cargo. During peacetime, they acted as intrepid merchant marines, returning from Asia and the Americas with gold, coffee, and spices. Indeed, the sea is in the hearts of all *Malouins*, as natives of St-Malo are called–especially during the city's famous transatlantic sailing race, the *Route du Rhum*, which is held every 4 years and finishes in Guadeloupe.

Walking the ramparts and cobblestone streets, it's hard to imagine that 80% of St-Malo was destroyed in World War II. What you see today is thanks to a meticulous, decades-long restoration.

St-Malo encompasses the communities of St.-Servan and Paramé, but most tourists head for the walled city, or *Intra-muros*. In summer, the Grande Plage du Sillon towards Paramé is dotted with hopeful sun-seekers; year-round it's sought after for its deluxe seawater spa. St-Servan's large marina is adjacent to a large terminal where ferries depart for and arrive from the Channel Islands and England.

PREVIOUS PAGE: **Scallops from the region.**

Brittany

## Essentials

**GETTING THERE**    From Paris's Gare Montparnasse, about 14 TGV **trains** per day make the journey; a one-way ticket costs approximately 89€. Three of these trains are nonstop, making the journey in 2¾ hours; transferring at Rennes takes 4 hours. For information, visit www.voyages-sncf.com or call ☎ **08-92-35-35-35**. If you're **driving** from Paris, take A13 west to Caen and continue southwest along N175 to the town of Miniac Morvan. From there, travel north on N137 directly to St-Malo. Driving time is 4 hours from Paris.

**VISITOR INFORMATION**    The **Office de Tourisme** is on esplanade St-Vincent (www.saint-malo-tourisme.com; ☎ **08-25-13-52-00**).

**SPECIAL EVENTS**   The **Festival de la Musique Sacrée,** from mid-July to mid-August, stages evening concerts twice a week in the cathedral. The next **Route du Rhum** departs from St-Malo in November 2014; contact the tourist office for information.

## Exploring the City

The 15th-century **Porte St-Vincent**, with a Belle Epoque carousel just in front of it, is the main entrance to St-Malo *Intra-muros*. Walk to your right past the restaurant terraces on place Chateaubriand—a portal leads to steps up to the **ramparts ★★★**. Built and rebuilt over several centuries, some parts of these walls date from the 14th. Weather cooperating, they're an ideal place to start a walking tour and take in sweeping views of the English Channel and the **Fort National** (see below).

About halfway round, you'll see an islet called the **Ile du Grand-Bé ★★**—during low tide you can walk to it and visit French Romantic novelist **Chateaubriand's tomb**. His last wish was to be buried here, where he'd "hear only the sounds of the wind and the ocean." Also within sight is the **Piscine de Bon-Secours**, a 1930's outdoor public swimming pool whose three walls catch the receding seawater. On warm days you'll see brave divers leaping from its cement platform.

If it's too windy, get off the ramparts here by descending the ramp that joins the rue de la Crosse. Turn left onto the rue de la Pie Qui Boit and follow it until you reach the rue Broussais. Alternatively, continue along the ramparts (where the view just keeps getting better) until you reach the **Porte de Dinan**. The street below it, rue de Dinan, becomes rue Broussais. Both routes lead to the

St-Malo's ramparts.

**place de Pilori** back in the center. Head back toward the Porte St-Vincent for the greatest concentration of shopping and dining options.

**Cathédrale St-Vincent ★★★** CATHEDRAL    Transformation of a monastic church into this cathedral began in 1146. Over the centuries, various architects added Romanesque, Gothic, and neoclassic elements—only to have the steeple knocked off and the transept destroyed during fierce fighting in 1944. It took nearly 30 years to restore the structure and its magnificent stained glass. A floor mosaic commemorates the 1535 blessing of St-Malo native Jacques Cartier before he set off to discover Canada. Cartier's tomb is here, along with that of René Duguay-Trouin, a legendary privateer so successful he was made a commander in the French navy.

12 rue St-Benoît. *©* **02-99-40-82-31.**

**Musée d'Histoire de St-Malo ★★** MUSEUM    Situated in the great keep and gatehouse of the Château de St-Malo, this museum abounds with insights into the history and commercial importance of St-Malo. Souvenirs of the city's most famous citizens—Chateaubriand, Jacques Cartier, and the privateers Duguay-Trouin and Surcouf—are displayed along with ship models, exhibits on fishing, and photos of the extensive damage the city incurred during World War II.

Porte St-Vincent. *©* **02-99-40-71-57.** Admission: 6€ for adults, 3€ for ages 8–18, free for children 7 and under. Apr–Oct daily 10am–12:30pm and 2–6pm (closed May 1); Oct–Mar Tues–Sun 10am–noon and 2–6pm.

**Fort National ★** HISTORIC SITE    Construction of this fortress began in 1689, based on plans drawn by famed military architect Sébastien de Vauban. You can access it by walking 300m (984 ft.) over sand at low tide (heed the tidal information, or you may find yourself wading back). Thirty-five minute guided tours take you into the dungeon and explain the fort's history; it's equally rewarding to wander on your own and enjoy the views of the Bay of St-Malo.

Grande Plage de Sillon. www.fortnational.com. *©* **06-72-46-66-26.** Tours: 5€ adults, 2.50€ ages 6-16, free for children 5 and under. Open Jun through Sept. Hours, which depend on the tide, vary. Call in advance or look to the fort itself (when the French flag is flying, it's open to visitors).

## Beaches

Along the coast, stretches of sand intersperse with rugged outcroppings that suggest fortresses protecting Brittany from Atlantic storms. Both the **Grande Plage du Sillon** and the **Plage de Bon Secours,** west of the city walls, are very popular. Situated between the two, the **Plage de l'Eventail** is small and especially rocky.

## Shopping

If you're in St-Malo on Tuesday or Friday between 8am and 1pm and want to experience a great Breton market, head for the Halle au Blé, in the heart of the old city. You can't miss the bustle and the hawking of seafood, fresh produce, local dairy products, and baked goods.

Check out **Marin-Marine,** 5 Grand Rue (*©* **02-99-40-90-32**), for men's and women's fashions including mariner's shirts and Breton wool sweaters.

Gauthier Marines, 2, rue Porcon de la Barbinais (📞 02-99-40-91-81), is a walk-in treasure chest of model ships, wooden sculpture, and marine-themed gift items.

Brittany's most revered chef and modern-day spice hunter, Olivier **Roellinger**, has an eponymous shop at 12 rue Saint-Vincent (📞 06-18-80-44-10). His beautifully presented blends, made from spices found all over the world, are worth collecting. And just try leaving **Maison Larnicol**, 6 rue St-Vincent (📞 02-99-40-57-62), empty handed. It specializes in Breton sweets including baked goods, chocolates and a variety of flavored caramels.

# Where to Eat

**Hôtel France et Chateaubriand** (see next page) has one of the finest dining rooms in town.

**La Brasserie du Sillon** ★ SEAFOOD/FRENCH    Choosing a restaurant inside the old city can feel like a crapshoot. Walk in front of this beachside brasserie, and you'll know you're in for something good. Several prix-fixe menus offer excellent values. And that "shellfish tower," as Chef Anthony Bourdain likes to call them, over at the next table? That's a *plateau de fruit de mer*, and this is a great place to try one. There are 13 different varieties on the menu, including a deluxe version for two, with all manner of creatures, for 120€. Meat dishes are on level with the seafood.

3 chaussée du Sillon. www.brasseriedusillon.com. 📞 **02-99-56-10-74.** Reservations recommended. Main courses 15€–35€; fixed-price menus 26€–39€. AE, MC, V. Daily noon–2pm; Sun–Thurs 7–10pm; Fri–Sat 7–10:30pm).

**Le Chalut** ★★ SEAFOOD/FRENCH    The interior might be a bit kitschy, but this restaurant is the place to go for fresh fish. The flavorful cuisine, based on fresh ingredients, includes a tart with layers of salmon and scallops, sprinkled with lime juice; John Dory with wild mushrooms, essence of lobster, and fresh coriander; and succulent line-caught sea bass with sherry sauce and braised endive. For dessert, try gateau of bitter chocolate with almond paste, or homemade ice cream flavored with malt whiskey.

8 rue de la Corne-de-Cerf. 📞 **02-99-56-71-58.** Reservations required. Main courses 23€–29€; fixed-price lunch and dinner menus 26€–70€. AE, MC, V. Wed–Sun noon–1:30pm and 7–9:30pm.

# St-Malo Nightlife

For an evening of gambling, head to **Le Casino Barrière,** 2 chaussée du Sillon (📞 02-99-40-64-00). You can also order dinner, sometimes accompanied by live music. A passport must be presented.

For dancing, consider **L'Escalier,** La Buzardière (www.escalier.fr; 📞 02-99-81-65-56), open Thursday to Saturday midnight to 5am. The cover doesn't exceed 13€. You'll need wheels, as the club is in the countryside 5km (3 miles) east of town. It does have a free shuttle, however; for information and reservations call **06-85-31-27-64**. **Le 109,** 3 rue des Cordiers (www.le-109.com; 📞 02-99-56-81-09), is a futuristic bar and dance club in a 300-plus-year-old vaulted cellar. It isn't as fashionable as L'Escalier, but is accessible without a car. It's open Tuesday to Sunday 8pm to 3am; the price of your first drink (10-12€) is considered the cover charge.

Popular pubs include **L'Aviso,** 12 rue du Point du Jour (✆ **02-99-40-99-08**), offering 300 types of beer and Breton beer on tap, and **Pub Saint Patrick,** 24 rue Sainte-Barbe (✆ **02-99-56-66-90**), serving 50 different Irish whiskeys, along with Breton beer. Concerts are regularly scheduled at the latter.

## Where to Stay

While some hotels inside the city walls are up to snuff, others are a bit run down. An alternative is to stay along the Plage du Sillon and walk the 10 minutes into the historic center.

**Hotel Alba ★ ☺**    For those who want to stay outside the walls near the beach, this boutique hotel is a winning choice, with rooms opening onto panoramic views of the English Channel. Guest rooms are small but attractively decorated in earthy tones, with contemporary furnishings; some are large enough for families. In fair weather, guests gather on the sunny terrace or else enjoy a drink at night from the scenic bar. The best rooms have an ocean view and private balcony.

17 rue des Dunes, St-Malo 35400. www.hotelalba.com. ✆ **02-99-40-37-18.** 22 units. 99€–171€ double; 200€ family room. DC, MC, V. Free parking. **Amenities:** Bar; room service. *In room:* TV, hair dryer, free Wi-Fi.

**Hôtel Beaufort**    A neighbor to the Hotel Alba (see above), recent renovations and new ownership have given this hotel modern amenities while retaining a seaside home feel. Rooms have spectacular beach and sunset views, and some rooms have a bed for a third person. Breakfast for 13€ is served in a dining room looking out over the waves.

25 chausée du Sillon, St-Malo 35400. www.hotel-beaufort.com. ✆ **02-99-40-99-99.** Fax 02-99-40-99-62. 22 units. 177€–247€ double. AE, DC, MC, V. Parking 15€. **Amenities:** Bar; babysitting. *In room:* TV, hair dryer, free Wi-Fi.

**Hôtel France et Chateaubriand ★**    The birthplace of Chateaubriand, inside the walls of old St-Malo, is one of the old town's most highly regarded hotels. Recent renovations create a Jekyll-and-Hyde feeling between up-to-date rooms and more dated ones—but they're priced accordingly (if possible, ask to see a couple so you'll be happy with what you pay for). Twenty rooms have panoramic ocean views; those overlooking the square provide some eye candy too. In the chic bar with gold-trimmed Corinthian columns, you can chat over drinks and occasionally hear the pianist play the baby grand.

12 place Chateaubriand, St-Malo 35412. www.hotel-fr-chateaubriand.com. ✆ **02-99-56-66-52.** Fax 02-99-40-10-04. 80 units. 71€–196€ double. AE, DC, MC, V. Parking 15€. **Amenities:** Restaurant; cafe; bar; babysitting; room service. *In room:* TV, hair dryer, free Wi-Fi.

**Quic en Grogne**    An excellent budget option within the *Intra-muros*. Rooms are small but clean with basic nautical decoration. Breakfast is served in a glassed-in sun porch, and private parking means you can avoid the huge lots outside the ramparts. The welcoming and attentive owners merit this hotel an additional star to its current two.

8 rue d'Estrées, St-Malo 35400. www.quic-en-groigne.com. ✆ **02-99-20-22-20.** Fax 02-99-20-22-30. 15 units. 67€–102€ double. MC, V. Parking 11€. *In room:* TV, hair dryer, free Wi-Fi.

**8**

**BRITTANY**

St-Malo

# LUNCH ON THE half-shell

If you're driving east from St-Malo to Mont-St.-Michel, consider a stop in **Cancale ★★★**—a harbor town famous for its oysters since the 17th century, when Louis XIV had them delivered regularly to Versailles.

Head to the northernmost end of the Port de la Houle, just beyond the jetty, where you'll see a handful of blue and white covered stalls selling shellfish out of crates. Come armed with a baguette and half-bottle of Muscadet (easily found on the port's main street) and order a dozen oysters to go. The sellers will shuck them immediately and hand them to you on a plastic plate. Find a spot on a bench or the rocks, slurp down your molluscs and toss the shells onto the sun-bleached pile below.

For a second course, pop in to the **Crêperie du port**, 1 place du Calvaire, 7 quai Thomas (✆ **02-99 89-60-66**) for inventive savory buckwheat galettes and dessert crêpes.

# DINARD ★★

417km (259 miles) W of Paris; 23km (14 miles) N of Dinan

Dinard (not to be confused with its inland neighbor, Dinan) sits on a rocky promontory at the top of the Rance River, opposite St-Malo. Once a small fishing community, by the late 19th century it was a favorite of the European jet set, thanks largely to wealthy British families who built grand Victorian villas along the coast.

Though its golden age has tarnished somewhat, Dinard is still one of France's best-loved resorts. It's also a destination for cinephiles, who flock to the film festival here every October.

## Essentials

**GETTING THERE**  If you're **driving**, take D186 west from St-Malo to Dinard. SNCF **trains** go only as far as St-Malo; from there, take bus no. 16A, which departs from the St-Malo rail station daily for the 30-minute ride to Dinard. The one-way fare is 1.80€. **Buses** arrive from many towns and cities in Brittany, including Rennes. Schedule and fare information is available via **Illenoo** (www.illenoo-services.fr; ✆ **08-25-13-81-30**). Between April and October, **Compagnie Corsaire,** Gare Maritime de la Bourse, St-Malo (www.compagniecorsaire.com; ✆ **02-23-18-15-15**), operates ferryboats from St-Malo to Dinard. The trip takes 10 minutes and costs 4.20€ one-way. A **taxi** to Dinard from St-Malo is another option; it costs 22€ during the day, with a 50% surcharge after 7pm and on Sundays and holidays. For information, call ✆ **06-84-92-55-73.**

**VISITOR INFORMATION**  The **Office de Tourisme** is at 2 bd. Féart (www.ot-dinard.com; ✆ **02-99-46-94-12**).

## Enjoying the Resort

A 10-minute walk from the town's historic core to the Pointe du Moulinet encircles most of the old town and encompasses views as far away as St-Malo.

Dinard's coast.

**BEACHES & SWIMMING**  Dinard's main beach is the **Plage de l'Ecluse (La Grande Plage)**, the strip of sand between the peninsulas that defines the edges of the old town. Favored by families and vacationers, it's crowded on hot days. Smaller and more isolated is the **Plage de St-Enogat** (you pass through the village of St-Enogat on the 20-min. hike east from Dinard). The **Plage du Prieuré,** a 10-minute walk from the center, has a few trees that shade the sand. Because there's such a difference between high and low tides, the municipality has built swimming pool–style basins along the Plage de L'Ecluse and the Plage du Prieuré to catch the seawater.

The **Piscine Olympique,** boulevard du Président-Wilson, next to the casino (© **02-99-46-22-77**), is a covered, heated seawater pool open year-round. Entrance is 4.70€ for adults, 3.60€ for ages 5 to 17, and free for children 4 and under. From July to mid-September, it's open Monday to Friday 10am to 12:30pm and 3 to 7:30pm, weekends 10am to 12:30pm and 3 to 6:30pm. Hours vary the rest of the year according to the needs of school groups and swim teams (inquire at the tourist office).

**SHOPPING**  For shops and boutiques, concentrate on rue du Maréchal-Leclerc, rue Levavasseur, and boulevard Féart. In the 15th-century house containing **Galerie d'Art du Prince Noir,** 70 av. George-V (© **02-99-46-29-99**), you'll find paintings and sculptures by some of the most talented artists in France. The gallery is closed from October to April. Another worthwhile destination is **L'Ancien Temple,** 29 rue Jacques-Cartier (© **02-99-46-82-88**), in a former Protestant church. The high-ceilinged showrooms feature upscale porcelain, stoneware, kitchen utensils, gift items, and fresh flowers.

# Where to Eat

The **Grand Hôtel Barrière de Dinard** (see below) offers fine dining.

**Didier Méril** ★★ FRENCH/BRETON   The finest dining room in town offers tables with a panoramic view of the Bay of Prieuré. Filled with designer furniture, it offers traditional gourmet fare in spite of its contemporary look. Chef Didier Méril takes full advantage of the local seafood and vegetables from neighboring farmland. He also offers the finest and most varied wine list in the area. In good weather, tables are placed on a sea-bordering terrace. Try such tasty specialties as sweetbread with lemon, foie gras with caramelized apples, roast pigeon with cabbage, and lobster flavored with cognac. John Dory, sea bass, and turbot are regularly featured, depending on the catch of the day.

The restaurant also rents six stylish bedrooms, some with bay views; the simplest rents for 85€, the best for 160€.

1 place du Gen. de Gaulle. ℂ **02-99-46-95-74.** www.restaurant-didier-meril.com. Reservations required. Main courses 20€–60€; fixed-price menu 29€–65€. AE, DC, MC, V. Daily noon–2:30pm and 7–9:30pm.

**La Passerelle** ★ SEAFOOD   Situated at one end of the Promenade du Claire de Lune, this restaurant offers great views and the freshest seafood around. Main dishes, many with Asian flavors, include grilled prawns with satay sauce, seared tuna with coriander seeds, and John Dory served with wheatberry risotto and morels. It's a good value, especially considering its privileged location.

3 avenue George-V. ℂ **02-99-16-96-37.** Reservations recommended. Main courses 20€–60€; fixed-price menu 25€–35€. AE, DC, MC, V. Daily noon–2:30pm and 7–9:30pm.

# Dinard Nightlife

Like many French beach resorts, Dinard has a casino. **Le Casino Barrière,** 4 bd. du Président-Wilson (ℂ **02-99-16-30-30**), is liveliest from Easter to late October with games including roulette, blackjack, and slot machines. Hours are Sunday through Thursday from 11am to 3am, Friday and Saturday from 11am to 4am. Admission is free. An alternative is **La Suite,** Zone Artisanale La Mare (ℂ **02-99-46-46-46**), a nightclub and dance club on the outskirts with a loyal following thanks to a good wine selection and amiable ambience. It's open Thursdays through Saturdays, with varying cover charges and free shuttlebus service to Dinard and St-Malo. According to its club rules, "Homosexuality is not a problem—but homophobia is."

In the evenings from June to September, tourists stroll the **Promenade du Clair de Lune** to admire specially illuminated buildings and gardens and hear all kinds of music performed outside.

# Where to Stay

**Didier Méril** (see "Where to Eat," above) also rents rooms.

**Grand Hôtel Barrière de Dinard** ★   A member of the Lucien Barrière luxury chain, Dinard's largest, swankiest hotel dates from 1858. Its location, a 2-minute walk from the town center, commands an excellent view of the harbor. It rises in two impressive wings, separated by a heated indoor pool. Most rooms have balconies and are equipped with traditional furnishings and fabrics, though their wow factor isn't equal to the exterior. The inviting bar is a popular spot before and after dinner.

46 av. George V, Dinard 35801. www.lucienbarriere.com. ℂ **02-99-88-26-26.** Fax 02-99-88-26-27. 90 units. 165€–480€ double. AE, DC, MC, V. Closed late Nov to early Mar. **Amenities:** Restaurant; bar; babysitting; kids' club; indoor pool; fitness center; sauna; spa; room service; rooms for those w/limited mobility. *In room:* TV, hair dryer, minibar, Wi-Fi (10€ per day). Closed Jan to mid-Mar.

**Hôtel Printania ★**   Your impression of this family-owned hotel will depend on how you feel about nostalgia. Originally built in 1920, it refers to itself as a *musée-hôtel*, in that the public spaces and individually-decorated rooms are meant to retain the spirit of that earlier era (including all its tchotchkes). On the other hand, in-room facilities are right up-to-date, with flat screen TVs and Wi-Fi access. Some of the bedrooms contain *lits clos*—Breton-style beds enclosed in wooden paneling, somewhat like ships' bunks. Terraces and a glassed-in veranda overlook the water; beaches are a 5-minute walk away.

5 av. George-V, Dinard 35801. www.printaniahotel.com. ℂ **02-99-46-13-07.** Fax 02-99-46-26-32. 56 units. 83€–154€ double; 220€–290€ suite. DC, MC, V. Closed mid-Nov to mid-Mar. **Amenities:** 3 restaurants; bar. *In room:* TV, hair dryer, free Wi-Fi.

**Villa Reine-Hortense ★★**   This beachside hotel was built in 1860 as a retreat for one of the Russian-born courtiers of Queen Hortense de Beauharnais, daughter of Joséphine de Beauharnais (who married Napoleon). It offers glamorously outfitted public salons and guest rooms decorated in either Louis XV or Napoleon III style. Most units have private balconies. One high-ceilinged room (no. 4) has Hortense's silver-plated bathtub, dating from the early 1800s. Breakfast (16€) is the only meal served.

19 rue de la Malouine, Dinard 35800. www.villa-reine-hortense.com. ℂ **02-99-46-54-31.** Fax 02-99-88-15-88. 8 units. 150€–245€ double; 305€–385€ suite. AE, DC, MC, V. Closed Oct to mid-Apr. **Amenities:** Bar. *In room:* TV, hair dryer, free Wi-Fi.

# DINAN ★★★

396km (246 miles) W of Paris; 52km (32 miles) NW of Rennes

Once a fortified stronghold of the Dukes of Brittany, Dinan is one of the prettiest and best-preserved towns in the region. It's noted for its *maisons à piliers,* medieval-half-timbered houses built on stilts over the sidewalks. For centuries the town has served as a hub of cultural and commercial activity, from the original merchants and traders to today's artists and craftspeople. There's tourist bustle on a busy day, but it's hard not to be moved by a walk atop the ramparts or a visit to the basilica.

## Essentials

**GETTING THERE**   Dinan has an SNCF station, but service is infrequent. The trip from Rennes, with one stop, takes about one hour and costs 14€. From St-Malo it takes about as long and costs 9.30€. Most rail passengers just transfer to one of the **buses** that line up in front of the train stations. The trip time is almost the same, but tickets are 2€. For information on bus schedules visit www.tibus.fr or call **08-10-22-22-22.** If you're **driving** from Dinard, take highway D166 south to Dinan.

**VISITOR INFORMATION**   The **Office de Tourisme** is at 9 rue du Château (www.dinan-tourisme.com; ℂ **02-96-87-69-76;** fax 02-96-87-69-77).

**SPECIAL EVENTS** One of the biggest medieval festivals in the world, the **Fêtes des Remparts** is held the third weekend of July in even-numbered years. Mingle amongst the knights and maidens and enjoy authentic street entertainment, food, and crafts. Take in an archery competition or even a jousting match.

## Exploring the Town

Dinan's ramparts, which include 14 watchtowers and four gates, extend for almost 3.5km (2 miles) around the town. The tourist office can provide you with a printed walking guide.

An authentic and appealing street is the sloping rue du Jerzual, flanked with 15th-century dwellings and shops with craftspeople selling their wares. In the middle is the **Porte du Jerzual,** a 13th- and 14th-century gate—you can still see traces of its drawbridge in the stone. In the direction of the river the street becomes **rue du Petit-Fort** and leads to the town's small port and its Gothic style bridge.

**Basilique St-Sauveur ★★** CHURCH Built between the 12th and 16th centuries, this church has Romanesque, Gothic, baroque, and classical elements. A monument holds the heart of Bertrand du Guesclin, the beloved Breton knight who defended Dinard during the Hundred Years' War. Just behind the basilica the terraced **Jardin Anglais (English Garden)** provides a panoramic view of the Rance Valley and direct access to the ramparts.

Place St-Sauveur. ℭ **02-96-39-06-67.**

**Château Musée de Dinan ★** MUSEUM The dungeon of Dinan's massive 14th-century fortress has served in the past as a residence for the Duke of Brittany and also a jail. For the last hundred years, along with one of the towers, it has housed the municipal museum. The exhibits focus on history, including prehistory, while a chapel contains holy objects, furniture, and silver. It's worth a visit, if only to see the interior of the castle.

Rue du Château. ℭ **02-96-39-45-20.** Admission: 4.55€ for adults, 1.85€ ages 12–18, free for children 11 and under. June–Sept daily 10am–6:30pm, Oct–May daily 1:30–5:30pm. Closed Jan.

**Tour de l'Horloge** HISTORIC SITE This structure boasts a clock made in 1498 and a bell donated by Anne de Bretagne in 1507. After 158 steps you'll be rewarded with a view of Dinan from the 23m (75-ft.) belfry—one of only two intact belfries in all of Brittany. Its main bell is named after Anne—three smaller ones are engraved with the names Jacqueline, Françoise, and Noguette.

Rue de l'Horloge. ℭ **02-96-87-58-72.** Admission is 2.95€ for adults, 1.90€ for ages 12–18, and free for children 11 and under. Apr–May 2–6pm; June–Sept 10am–6:30pm.

## Where to Eat

**L'Auberge du Pélican ★** FRENCH/BRETON This traditional restaurant's decor is contemporary, but the food is often based on time-honored recipes (even the bread is homemade). An excellent dish is the casserole of fresh fish served daily with *beurre blanc,* a sauce made with vinegar, white wine, shallots, and butter. Succulent scallops from the bay are also a satisfying choice for seafood lovers. The chef prepares meat and poultry dishes equally well, particularly the *magret de canard* (duck breast) with figs and a tender filet of beef with mushrooms. For

# AN idyll ON AN ILE

The **Ile de Bréhat** is home to some 350 hearty folk who live most of the year in isolation—until the summer crowds arrive. The tiny island (actually two islands, Ile Nord and Ile Sud, linked by a bridge, Le Pont Vauban) is in the Gulf of St-Malo, north of Paimpol. A visit to Bréhat is an adventure, even to the French. The only settlement on the islands is Le Bourg, in the south. The only bona fide beach is a strip of sand at Guerzido.

Walking is the primary activity, and it's possible to stroll the footpaths around the island in a day. Cars, other than police and fire vehicles, aren't allowed. Tractor-driven carts carry visitors on an 8km (5-mile) circuit of Bréhat's two islands, charging 14€ for the 45-minute jaunt (it's 11€ for children 4 to 11 and free for 3 and under). A number of places rent bikes, but they aren't necessary.

The rich flora here astonishes many visitors, who arrive expecting a wind-swept island only to discover a more Mediterranean clime. Flowers abound in summer, though both the gardens and houses appear tiny because of the scarcity of land. At the highest point, Chapelle St-Michel, you'll be rewarded with a panoramic view.

The tourist office, place du Bourg, Le Bourg (✆ **02-96-20-83-16**), is open Monday to Saturday mid-June to mid-September.

To reach Paimpol, **drive** west on D768 from Dinard to Lamballe, then take E50 west to Plérin and D786 north to Paimpol. To reach the island, take D789 4km (2½ miles) north of Paimpol, where the peninsula ends at the Pointe de l'Arcouest. From Paimpol, 6 to 10 **Tibus** (www.tibus.fr; ✆ **08-10-22-22-22**) buses make the 10-minute run to the point for a one-way fare of 2€. Then catch one of the **ferries** operated by **Les Vedettes de Bréhat** (www.vedettesdebrehat.com; ✆ **02-96-55-79-50**). Ferries depart about every 30 minutes in summer, around 7 times per day in the off season; the round-trip costs 9€ for adults, 4.50 for ages 4 to 11€, and is free for children 3 and under. Visitors in April, May, June, and September will find the island much less crowded than in July and August. Cars are not allowed on the ferry.

a lighter meal, the busy, solid Creperie Ahna is just around the corner on rue de la Poissonniere.

3 rue Haute Voie. ✆ **02-96-39-47-05.** Reservations recommended. Main courses 14€–28€; fixed-price menus 20€–60€. MC, V. July–Aug daily noon–2pm and 7–10pm; Sept–June Tues–Sun noon–2pm, Tues–Wed and Fri–Sun 7–9:30pm. Closed Jan.

## Dinan Nightlife

Cafes and bars line the cobbled **rue de la Cordonnerie,** nicknamed *la rue de la soif* ("the street of the thirsty") by long-ago sailors.

## Where to Stay

**Hôtel d'Avaugour** ★★ ☺ Just inside the ramparts, and across from the site of Dinan's Thursday morning food market, this is one of best hotels in town. The simple but charming guest rooms have modern, midsize bathrooms with tub/shower combinations. Nine of the units face the large and lovely backyard garden, where you can take tea in the afternoon. A copious breakfast buffet, for 14€, is the only meal served.

1 place du Champs, Dinan 22100. www.avaugourhotel.com. ☏ **02-96-39-07-49.** Fax 02-96-85-43-04. 24 units. 125€–260€ double; 230€–350€ suite. MC, V. Closed Nov–Mar 1. *In room:* TV, hair dryer, free Wi-Fi.

**Hôtel Arvor** ✦ ☺   This comfortable, relatively inexpensive hotel is housed in a Renaissance building constructed on the site of a 14th-century Jacobin convent. The carved stone entrance is in contrast to the guest rooms, which are well decorated but without historic ambience. Bathrooms are small but the rooms themselves are spacious—there's even a duplex suite that sleeps six. Overall, a cozy haven in one of Dinan's oldest neighborhoods. Only breakfast (8€) is served, but many restaurants lie within a short walk.

5 rue Pavie, Dinan 22100. www.hotelarvordinan.com. ☏ **02-96-39-21-22.** Fax 02-96-39-83-09. 23 units. 80€–105€ double. Parking 4€. MC, V. Closed Jan. *In room:* TV, hair dryer, free Wi-Fi.

# QUIMPER ★★

570km (353 miles) W of Paris; 205km (127 miles) NW of Rennes

Quimper, the town that pottery built, is the historic capital of Brittany's most traditional region, La Cornouaille. It takes its name from the Breton word *kemper*, the meeting of two rivers—in this case the Odet and the Steir. There's no better place to get a feel for southern Breton culture, whether during its annual festival or just trolling the *vieux centre* for Quimperware, the hand-painted faience that's symbolized Brittany for centuries. Modern-day Quimper is somewhat bourgeois, home to some 67,000 *Quimperois* who walk narrow streets spared from World War II damage.

## Essentials

**GETTING THERE**   Speedy **TGV trains** take only 4½ hours from the Montparnasse station in Paris. The one-way fare is 77€. For information, visit www.voyages-sncf.com or call ☏ **08-92-35-35-35**. If you're **driving,** the best route is from Rennes: Take E50/N12 west to just outside the town of Montauban, continue west along N164 to Châteaulin, and head south along N165 to Quimper.

**VISITOR INFORMATION**   The **Office de Tourisme** is on place de la Résistance (www.quimper-tourisme.com; ☏ **02-98-53-04-05**).

**SPECIAL EVENTS**   For 6 days around the third week of every July, the **Festival de Cornouaille** celebrates Breton culture. The festivities include parades in traditional costume and Celtic and Breton concerts throughout the city. For information, contact the tourist office.

## Exploring the Town

In some quarters, Quimper maintains its old-world atmosphere, with narrow medieval streets and footbridges spanning the rivers.

**Cathédrale St-Corentin** ★★ CATHEDRAL   Characterized by two towers that climb 75m (246 ft.), this cathedral was built between the 13th and 15th centuries. The twin steeples were added in the 19th. Inside, note the

Quimper.

15th-century stained glass—windows on the north side were funded by religious donors, those on the south by secular ones. The year 2008 marked the end of a 20-year restoration that revitalized the architectural details and finishings.

Place St-Corentin. ℭ **02-98-95-06-19.** Admission free. Sept–Jun daily 9:45am–noon and 1:30–6:30pm; July–Aug daily 9:45am–6:30pm, except during Sun morning services.

**Musée des Beaux-Arts ★★** MUSEUM This museum has been open since 1872; it was renovated and extended in the early 1990s. The collection includes work by Rubens, Boucher, Fragonard, and Corot, plus an exceptional exhibit of the Pont-Aven school (Bernard, Gaugin, Sérusier, Lacombe, Maufra, Denis). Tribute is also paid to Surrealist poet and painter Max Jacob, who was born in Quimper.

40 place St-Corentin. ℭ **02-98-95-45-20.** Admission 5€ for adults, 2.50€ for ages 12–26, free for 11 and under. July and Aug daily from 10am–7pm; Apr–Jun and Sept-Oct Wed–Mon 9:30am–noon and 2–6pm; and Nov–Mar Wed–Mon 9:30am–noon and 2–5:30pm, Sun 2–5:30pm.

**Musée Departemental Breton ★★★** MUSEUM In the medieval Palais des Eveques de Cornouaille (Palace of the Bishops of Cornwall), adjacent to the cathedral, this museum showcases the archaeological and decorative history of the region. And not in a dusty, clear-out-the-attic kind of way: the architecturally pleasing interior is divided into areas for stained glass, sculpture, furniture, painting, and faience (see below), with four rooms dedicated to everyday and ceremonial Breton costumes.

1–3 rue Roi Gradlon. www.museedepartementalbreton.fr. ℭ **02-98-95-21-60.** Admission: 4€ for adults, 2.50€ for ages 18–25, and free for children 17 and under. Free on weekends from Jan–May and Oct–Dec. Tues–Sat 9am–noon and 2–5pm.

# Shopping

Quimper's proximity to the rivers gave it plenty of access to clay; it's been known as a pottery town since the late 1600s. Faience, the French term for glazed earthenware (as opposed to porcelain, manufactured to be more delicate) is your go-to souvenir here. Quimperware is recognized for its bright, hand-painted motifs, often Breton figures, fruits, and flowers. One of the most popular designs is a male *Breton* or female *Bretonne,* both in profile and in traditional costume. Today this 19th-century motif is copyrighted and fiercely protected.

The best shopping streets are **rue Kéréon** and **rue du Parc,** where you'll find Breton products including pottery, dolls and puppets, clothing made from regional cloth and wool, jewelry, lace, and beautiful Breton costumes.

One of three sites that produce stoneware is open for tours. From April to September, Monday to Friday 9am to 4:30pm, five to seven tours per day depart from the visitor information center of **HB-Henriot Faïenceries de Quimper,** rue Haute, Quartier Locmaria (www.hb-henriot.com; ✆ **02-98-90-09-36**). Tours in English, French, or both last 40 to 45 minutes and cost 5€ for adults, 2.50€ for children 8 to 14, and are free for children 7 and under. On-site, a store sells the most complete inventory of Quimper porcelain in the world. You can invest in first-run (nearly perfect) pieces or slightly discounted "seconds," with almost imperceptible flaws. Everything can be shipped.

For more Breton pottery, as well as fine tablecloths, linens, and other household items, visit **François le Villec,** 4 rue Roi-Gradlon (www.levillec.com; ✆ **02-98-95-31-54**).

# Where to Eat

**Les Acacias** ★ ☺ BRETON/SEAFOOD   This is Quimper's leading restaurant, focusing on seafood and very fresh fish, with a few meat dishes, including game. Your meal may include roasted crayfish with sweet spices, delectable smoked John Dory perfumed with algae, or roast pigeon with baby vegetables. Customers rave about the dessert specialty of local strawberries marinated in spiced wine. The wine list features 150 to 200 mostly French vintages.

88 bd. Creac'h Gwen. ✆ **02-98-52-15-20.** Reservations recommended. Main courses 27€–60€; fixed-price menu 20€–45€; children's menu 12€. MC, V. Sun–Fri 12:30–2:30pm; Mon–Fri 8–9:30pm. Closed Aug, 1 week in May. From Quimper, drive 2km (1¼ miles), following signs to Benodet.

**Ambroisie** ★ ☺ BRETON/FRENCH   Although it's surpassed by Les Acacias, this restaurant remains one of the most respected in Quimper. A 5-minute walk north of the cathedral, the airy, ocher-and-gold dining room has contemporary furniture and large paintings in a style inspired by the English neosurrealist Francis Bacon. Menu items incorporate Breton traditions, with an occasional contemporary twist. The finest examples include a crusty buckwheat galette stuffed with spiced crabmeat, braised scallops with asparagus and citrus sauce, and filet of John Dory on a colorful bed of vegetable ragout.

49 rue Elie Fréron. ✆ **02-98-95-00-02.** www.ambroisie-quimper.com. Reservations recommended. Fixed-price menu 36€–58€; children's menu 15€. MC, V. Tues–Sun noon–1:30pm; Tues–Sat 7:30–9:15pm.

# Quimper Nightlife

You'll likely hear the **Céili Pub** before you find it at 4 rue Aristide-Briand (✆ **02-98-95-17-61**). It has lots of polished wood, Celtic/Breton music, and jolly regulars. Two animated pubs with modern recorded music and a lot of innate Breton/Celtic pride are **O Patchwork,** place Pierre de Ronsard (✆ **02-98-95-05-72**), and **An Poitin Still,** 2 av. Libération, (✆ **02-98-90-02-77**), the latter featuring Irish music Fridays at 10pm.

The young and stylish flock to **Les Naïades Discothèque,** boulevard Creac'h Gwen (✆ **02-98-53-32-30**), where you can dance to the latest tunes. It sometimes charges a cover.

## Where to Stay

**Hôtel Gradlon** 🔔 Consistent lodgings can be found in this 19th-century landmark a 5-minute walk from the town center. It has a modern annex a few steps away. Some of the guest rooms are a bit grandmotherly, with floral wallpaper and whitewashed furniture, but they are clean and comfortable, and the English speaking staff are very attentive. There's a courtyard as well as a fireplace near the bar. Breakfast, for 9€, is the only meal served.

30 rue de Brest, Quimper 29000. www.hotel-gradlon.com. ✆ **02-98-95-04-39.** Fax 02-98-95-61-25. 20 units. 89€–135€ double; 130€–175€ suite. AE, DC, MC, V. Parking 10€. Closed mid-Dec to mid-Jan. Pets 9€. **Amenities:** Bar. *In room:* TV, hair dryer, free Wi-Fi.

**Hôtel Kregenn** The best hotel in town boasts spacious, stylish rooms that are a real value. This family-run establishment under the Best Western umbrella might not be terribly Breton, but it's not so modern that it lacks a soul. Breakfast, for 13€, is the only meal served, though light items can be requested at any time.

11–15 rue des Réguaires, Quimper 29000. www.hotel-kregenn.fr. ✆ **02-98-95-08-70.** Fax 02-98-53-85-12. 32 units. 105€–180€ double, 185€–220€ suite. AE, DC, MC, V. Parking 7€. Pets 15€. **Amenities:** Bar; limited room service. *In room:* TV, hair dryer, Internet.

## Where to Eat & Stay Nearby

**Manoir du Stang ★★** In an orchard district 13km (8 miles) from Quimper, the sleepy village of La Forêt-Fouesnant is home to one of Brittany's finest 16th-century manors. At the end of a tree-lined lane and through a stone gateway, the impressive Manoir du Stang is surrounded by formal flower-filled gardens and 10 hectares (25 acres) of natural woodland. Guests stay in the main building or in the even older but less desirable annex, which has a circular stone staircase. Rooms are furnished sparingly with antiques; each midsize bathroom comes with a combination tub/shower. Best of all, breakfast is brought to your bed.

La Forêt-Fouesnant 29940. www.manoirdustang.com. ✆ **02-98-56-96-38.** Fax 02-22-44-21-49. 22 units. 60€–190€ double. AE, MC, V. Free parking. Closed end-Sept to mid-May. Drive 1.5km (1 mile) north of the village center and follow signs from N783; access is by private road. **Amenities:** Bar. *In room:* Hair dryer, free Wi-Fi.

# CONCARNEAU ★★

539km (334 miles) W of Paris; 93km (58 miles) SE of Brest

This port is a favorite of painters, who never tire of capturing the subtleties of the fishing fleet. It's also unique among the larger coastal communities because fishing, not tourism, is its main industry (Concarneau's canneries produce most of the tuna in France). Walk along the quays, especially in the evening, and watch the Breton fishers unload their catch; later, join them for a pint of cider in the taverns.

## Essentials

**GETTING THERE**   There's no **rail** service to Concarneau. If you're **driving,** the town is 21km (13 miles) southeast of Quimper along D783. A **bus** runs from Quimper to Concarneau (trip time: 30 min.); the one-way fare is 2€. The bus from Rosporden, site of another SNCF railway station, runs about eight times per day (trip time: 20 min.) for a fare of 2€. For information call (✆ **08-10-81-00-29**).

**VISITOR INFORMATION**   The **Office de Tourisme** is on quai d'Aiguillon (www.tourismeconcarneau.fr; ✆ **02-98-97-01-44**).

## Exploring the Area

The town is built on three sides of a natural harbor whose innermost sheltered section is the **Nouveau Port.** In the center of this is the heavily fortified **Ville Close ★★,** an ancient hamlet surrounded by ramparts, some from the 14th century. From the quay, cross the bridge and descend into the town. Souvenir shops have taken over, but don't let that spoil it. You can spend an hour wandering the alleys, gazing up at the towers, peering at the stone houses, and stopping in secluded squares.

For a splendid view of the port, walk the **ramparts ★.** They're open to pedestrians daily 10am to 7:30pm, with seasonal variations.

Also in the old town is a fishing museum, **Musée de la Pêche ★,** 3 rue Vauban (www.musee-peche.fr; ✆ **02-98-97-10-20**). The 17th-century building has ship models and exhibits tracing the development of the fishing industry; you can also view the ship *Hemerica,* currently under restoration. Admission is 6.50€ for adults, 4€ for ages 5 to 15, and free for children 4 and under. It's open daily February, March, and October from 10am to noon and 2pm to 6pm, from April to June and September 10am to 6pm, and July and August 9:30am to 8pm.

**BEACHES**   Concarneau's largest, most beautiful beach, popular with families, is the **Plage des Sables Blancs,** near the historic core. Within a 10-minute walk are the **Plage de Cornouaille** and two small beaches, the **Plage des Dames** and **Plage de Rodel,** where you'll find fewer families with children. The wide-open **Plage du Cabellou,** 5km (3 miles) west of town, is less crowded than the others.

**SEA EXCURSIONS**   Boat rides are usually fine between June and September but can be treacherous the rest of the year. The spectacular Glenans archipelago, ten miles off the coast, is a must if you have the time and sea legs. For excursions, contact **Vedettes Glenn** (www.vedettes-glenn.fr; ✆ **02-98-97-10-31**) or **Vedettes de l'Odet** (www.vedettes-odet.com; ✆ **02-98-57-00-58**). During midsummer, you can arrange deep-sea fishing with the captain of the **Santa Maria** (www.santamariapeche.com; ✆ **06-62-88-00-87**).

## Where to Eat

**La Coquille ★** SEAFOOD/TRADITIONAL FRENCH   This 4 decade-old restaurant occupies one end of a stone-sided harbor-side building; guests dine in a trio of rooms with stone walls, ceiling beams, and century-old oil paintings from the School of Pont-Aven. Seafood is the focus at La Coquille, and much of what is on the menu is offered simply because the fish is so fresh and succulent. Try the abalone salad or sautéed scallops with caramelized endives. The service is bistro style, with a cheerful, old-fashioned panache enhanced by the harbor view.

1 quai du Moros, at Nouveau Port. ✆ **02-98-97-08-52.** www.lacoquille-concarneau.com. Reservations required Sat–Sun and in summer. Main courses 14€–39€; fixed-price menu 29€–45€. AE, DC, MC, V. Tues–Sun noon–1:30pm; Tues–Sat 7:30–9:30pm.

**Le Vauban** ✔ FRENCH/SEAFOOD It's always best not to mess with a good thing, especially fish. This restaurant's owner is a former fisherman, which gives him a bead on where to get the good stuff, and his wife, the chef, makes the best of what they get. Tasty oysters are served with a tangy sourdough bread and churned butter. Try ground cuttlefish rolled around algae and salmon, sprinkled with paprika—a mouthful of smoky sea. There's a pleasant bar and more sophisticated dining room hidden in the back.

10 rue Vauban. ✆ **02-98-97-34-93.** Reservations recommended. Main courses 10€–24€; set-price menus 16€–19€. MC, V. Wed–Sun noon–2pm and 7–9:30pm. Closed mid-Jan to mid-Feb.

## Where to Stay

**Hôtel des Halles** 👬 The tourist board gives only two stars to this cement-sided 1960s-era hotel, which is short on historical charm. Yet it's affordable, warm, and ecofriendly, with rooms that are cozier than you might expect. It's also conveniently located, a short distance from the fortifications encircling the town's historic core. Uncomplicated, marine-themed guest quarters have paneling and shower-only bathrooms. Breakfast, including many homemade items and organic products, is the only meal served.

Rue Charles Linement, Concarneau 29900. www.hoteldeshalles.com. ✆ **02-98-97-11-41.** Fax 02-98-50-58-54. 25 units. 64€–84€ double. AE, MC, V. Parking 6€. Small pets accepted free. *In room:* TV, hair dryer, free Internet.

**Les Sables Blancs** ★★ This modern boutique hotel—a clever renovation of a '60s era building—is on Concarneau's prettiest beach. All rooms face the sea and have small terraces, giving them a boatlike feel. The beds and curtains are white, and except for a modern lamp or chair here and there, nothing else in the rooms distracts from the unbeatable view. La Coquille, the hotel's restaurant, offers upscale surf and turf in a very stylish atmosphere (you can eat on the deck), but you'll find much more authentic, and less expensive, food in town, a short drive or twenty-minute walk away.

Plage des Sables Blancs, Concarneau 29900. www.hotel-les-sables-blancs.com. ✆ **02-98-50-10-12.** Fax 02-98-97-20-92. 16 units. 110€–195€ double. 230€–370€ suite. AE, MC, V. Closed mid-Nov to mid-Dec. *In room:* TV, hair dryer, free Wi-Fi.

# PONT-AVEN ★★

522km (324 miles) W of Paris; 32km (20 miles) SE of Quimper; 16km (10 miles) S of Concarneau

Paul Gauguin loved this inland village, with its white houses flanking the River Aven on its gentle course to the Atlantic. It's also known for 15 *moulins,* or water mills, that once operated along the waterways. Only one of them is still functional, but the rest have been restored for historical and aesthetic purposes. With such picturesque surroundings, one might suspect Pont-Aven of being a tourist trap, but its modest, pleasant atmosphere endures.

## Essentials

**GETTING THERE** If you're **driving** from Quimper, go southeast on N165 and follow signs into Pont-Aven. From Quimperlé, head west along D783 until N165 and follow signs. SNCF **trains** stop at Quimper, where you can transfer to between four and six daily **buses** to Pont Aven (trip time: 30 min.; one-way fare 2€). For bus information, call the Pont-Aven tourist office (see below). For train information visit www.voyages-sncf. com or ✆ **08-92-35-35-35**.

**VISITOR INFORMATION** The **Office de Tourisme** is at 5 place de l'Hôtel-de-Ville (www.pontaven. com; ✆ **02-98-06-04-70**).

## Exploring the Area

In the village there are themed walking tours possible, such as the artists' trail or the *promenade des moulins*—the tourist office can provide maps. You can also visit one of the shops that pro-duce the famous *galette de Pont-Aven*, a

Pont-Aven.

round, butter-rich cookie that Bretons like to dunk in their coffee. **Traou Mad**, rue du Port (✆ **02-98-06-18-18**), has a second shop on the bridge. **Délices de Pont-Aven**, 1, quai Théodore Botrel (✆ **02-98-06-02-75**), offers tours of their nearby production facilities in July and August (Tuesdays and Thursdays at 10am; admission 2€).

The 16th-century **Chapelle de Trémalo,** lieu-dit Trémalo (✆ **02-98-06-01-68**), is 1.2km (¾ mile) north of the town center. Here is the wooden crucifix that inspired two of Gauguin's best-known paintings, *The Yellow Christ* (displayed today in a museum in Buffalo, New York) and his *Self-Portrait with the Yellow Christ* (displayed at the Musée d'Orsay in Paris). On private lands that still belong to descendants of the family who originally built and consecrated it in 1532, the chapel is unlocked every morning at 10am and closed at 5pm (6pm July–Aug). It's still a place of worship, so Masses are conducted from time to time. Plunk a coin or two into a machine to briefly illuminate the interior—oth-erwise, midday sunlight from the windows is sufficient.

## Where to Eat & Stay

**Le Moulin de Rosmadec** ★★★ 🎁 TRADITIONAL FRENCH Atmo-sphere-wise, nothing compares to this hotel/dining complex converted from one of the town's 15th-century stone mills. Owner/Michelin-starred chef Frédéric Sébilleau's artfully prepared specialties include ragout of freshwater crayfish, *croustillant de pigeon* (crisply baked pigeon in puff pastry), and grilled lobster with two butters. Sébillau's brother Franck has a second, less formal restaurant, **Sur Le Pont,** 11 place Paul Gauguin, (✆ **02-98-60-16-16**), which is open on Thursdays when the Moulin is closed. The cuisine here has a modern touch that goes with the decor.

The Moulin rents 4 comfortable double rooms for 90€ to 120€. Each has a TV and a tidy bathroom with tub and shower. Because of the location at the end of a cul-de-sac, the accommodations are quiet and calm.

Pont-Aven 29123. ✆ **02-98-06-00-22.** www.moulinderosmadec.com. Reservations recommended. Main courses 30€–50€; fixed-price menu 38€–76€; *menu tradition* (with oysters and lobster) 78€. MC, V. Tues–Sun 12:30–2pm and Tues–Sat 7:30–9pm. Closed Jan and Feb.

# Where to Stay & Eat Nearby

**Château de Locguénolé** ★★★ Tucked into an inlet near the once-fortified town of **Hennebont,** 56km (35 miles) southeast of Concarneau, this is the most delightful hotel in southern Brittany It sits on a 120-hectare park run through with footpaths and gardens that go all the way down to the sea. The stately main house is filled with antiques, tapestries, and paintings—from a sea-view room you can watch dinghies glide lazily by. Rooms in the annex, a modernized 1720 Breton cottage, lack spectacular views but are quite comfortable. Some have Jacuzzis. The gourmet restaurant, in an elegant drawing room, excels in delicate preparations of local seafood and shellfish.

Rte. de Port-Louis en Kervignac, Hennebont 56700. www.chateau-de-locguenole.com. ✆ **02-97-76-76-76.** Fax 02-97-76-82-35. 22 units. 155€–240€ double; 250€–410€ suite. AE, DC, MC, V. Closed Jan 2 to mid-Feb. From Hennebont, follow hotel signs, 4km (2½ miles) south. **Amenities:** Restaurant; babysitting; outdoor pool; room service; 2 saunas. *In room:* TV, hair dryer, minibar, free Wi-Fi.

---

## In the Footsteps of Gauguin

In the summer of 1886, Paul Gauguin arrived in the Breton village of Pont-Aven. Lesser-known artists, including Maurice Denis, Paul Sérusier, and Emile Bernard, soon followed. Breaking from mainstream Impressionism, the Pont-Aven School—as the style of Gaugin and his 20 or so followers came to be known—emphasized pure colors, shunned perspective and shadowing, and simplified human figures. Both *The Yellow Christ* and *The Green Christ*, two of Gauguin's most memorable works, exemplify this method, also known as Synthetism.

The **Musée des Beaux-Arts de Pont-Aven,** place de l'Hôtel de Ville (✆ **02-98-06-14-43**), provides a comprehensive exhibit of these 19th-century painters. Expect muted greens and blues and lots of Breton patriotism as interpreted through the most famous artistic movement to emerge from Brittany. Admission is 4.50€ for adults, 2.50€ for students under 26, and free for ages 17 and under. Prices go up 1.50€ when larger exhibits are on display from June to October. The museum is open in July and August daily 10am to 7pm, September through March daily 10am to 12:30pm and 2 to 6pm, and April through October daily 10am to 12:30pm and 2 to 6:30pm.

# CARNAC ★★

Aside from being a popular beach resort, Carnac is home to the largest mega-lithic site in the world. Spread out over 4km (2½ miles), **Les Alignements,** as three fields of huge, upright stones are known, date back more than 6,000 years to Neolithic times. Scholars have debated their purpose for centuries, though most suggest they had astronomical or religious significance. One theory is that the stones marked burial sites. Another legend claims they are Roman soldiers turned to stone by the wizard Merlin. In all, the town contains 2,732 *menhirs* some rising to heights of 20m (66 ft.).

Carnac's five beaches stretch over nearly 3km (1¾ miles). Protected by the Quiberon Peninsula, they back up onto sand dunes and shady forests. **Carnac-Plage** is a family resort and camping hotspot beside the ocean and along the waterfront boulevard de la Plage. Expect the area to be packed in July and August.

## Essentials

**GETTING THERE**   **Driving** is the most convenient way to get to Carnac. From Pont-Aven, travel southeast along N165, passing through Hennebont. At the intersection with D768, continue south along the signposted road to Carnac. From Nantes, take N165 northwest to Auray and then D768.

Links to Carnac by public transport are inconvenient, as there's no railway station. **Train** travelers leave the SNCF network at either Quiberon or Aurayand take a bus into town (see below). An additional

Field of megaliths.

option, available between June and August only, is to get off the train in Plouharnel-Carnac station, 3km (1¾ miles) from Carnac. For more information about bus transit from any of these hamlets, call ✆ **08-10-10-10-56.**

**VISITOR INFORMATION**   The **Office de Tourisme** is at 74 av. des Druides (www.ot-carnac.fr; ✆ **02-97-52-13-52**).

# Exploring the Area

Out of fear of vandalism, the local tourist authorities have fenced in the megaliths and now allow visitors to wander freely among the menhirs only between October and March, when the park is open daily from 10am to 5pm, and when entrance is free. From April to September, the park can be visited only as part of a rigidly controlled 1-hour guided tour, priced at 4.50€ per person (4€ for students or anyone between 18 and 24; under 18 are free). Tours are usually in French but, depending on the perceived need, may include some additional commentary in English; the only way to be sure is to call the visitor center, La Maison des Mégalithes, at ✆ **02-97-52-29-81,** for a rundown on the tours arranged for the day of your intended visit. For more information, visit www.carnac.monuments-nationaux.fr.

At Carnac Ville, **Musée de Préhistoire,** 10 place de la Chapelle (✆ **02-97-52-22-04**), displays collections from 450,000 B.C. to the 8th century. Admission is 5€ for adults, 2.50€ for ages 6 to 18, and free for children 5 and under. Hours are as follows: July and August daily 10am to 6pm; October to March Wednesday to Monday 10am to 12:30pm and 2 to 5pm; April, May, June, and September Wednesday to Monday 10am to 12:30pm and 2 to 6pm.

# Shopping

Carnac has two shopping areas: one along the beachfront called Carnac-Plage, and the other about 2.5km (1½ miles) inland in Carnac proper. Along the beach, you'll find souvenir shops. Venture down avenue des Druids and avenue de l'Atlantique for more specialized galleries and antiques stores. Other good areas are rue St-Cornély and place de l'Eglise, with a host of clothing and shoe stores, antiques dealers, and jewelers.

# Where to Eat & Stay

**Auberge le Ratelier** ★ 🏠 BRETON   A short walk from the center of Carnac Ville, this vine-covered, time-mellowed inn is a charming alternative to the beachfront tourist traps. It highlights local seafood, often using recipes handed down from generation to generation. Other dishes have been modernized: gazpacho with fresh prawns, seasoned with basil from the garden; and sea bream, flavored with lemongrass and served with potatoes. The owners are proud of their dessert specialty, a candied fruit ice cream with strawberries and honey.

The inn offers eight small, simple guest rooms with showers, comfortably furnished and quite affordable. Doubles cost 52€ to 62€.

4 chemin du Douët. www.le-ratelier.com. ✆ **02-97-52-05-04.** Reservations required. Main courses 19€–34€; fixed-price menu 24€–46€. AE, MC, V. Sept–June Thurs–Mon noon–2:30pm and 7:30–9:30pm; July–Aug daily (same hours). Closed mid-Nov to mid-Dec and Jan.

## THE WILD, WILD coast

Follow the D768 south from Carnac over the isthmus connecting the mainland to **Quiberon,** with its crescent of white-sand. You'll probably see weathered Breton fishers hauling in their sardine catch.

The entire **Côte Sauvage,** or Wild Coast, is rugged and dramatic, with waves breaking ferociously against the reefs. Winds, especially in winter, lash the dunes, shaving the short pines that grow here. On the landward side, the beach is calm and relatively protected.

A 45-minute ferry ride from Quiberon is **Belle-Ile-en-Mer,** an 83 sq. km (32 sq. mi.) outpost of sand, rock, and vegetation. It feels blissfully isolated, despite a scattering of hotels and seasonal restaurants. Depending on the season, 5 to 15 ferries depart daily from Port Maria in Quiberon (✆ **08-20-05-61-56**). a round-trip ticket costs 31.10€ for adults, 19.35€ for ages 4 to 17, and is free for children 3 and under. In summer, you must reserve space for your car, as well as for passengers. The ferry docks at **Le Palais,** a fortified 16th-century port that is the island's window to mainland France. The Office de Tourisme is here, on quai Bonnelle Le Palais (✆ **02-97-31-81-93**).

Excellent accommodation and dining can be found in **Port de Goulphar,** an inlet on the southern shore framed by cliffs. The standout is the 63-unit Relais & Châteaux property **Castel Clara,** (www.castel-clara.com; ✆ **02-97-31-84-21;** fax 02-97-31-51-69) with restful rooms, two heated swimming pools (one seawater) and extensive spa services. Ideal service and first-class cuisine add to the sense of peace. Depending on the season, rates range from 188€ to 395€ in a double, 263€ to 665€ in a suite. The hotel is closed from mid-December to mid-February.

A fitting souvenir is sardines from La Belle-Iloise boutique on the place de la République (✆ **02-97-31-29-14).** Even if you' don't like sardines, the attractive tins make unusual *objets.* The last cannery in Belle-Ile-en-Mer closed in 1975, but production continues in Quiberon, where there are two other Belle-Iloise boutiques.

## Carnac Nightlife

Carnac doesn't stay up very late, but a few places are worth checking out. **Whisky Club,** 8 av. des Druides (✆ 02-97-52-10-52), operates in an old stone house with two floors devoted to entertainment. The first offers an atmosphere conducive to conversation over drinks; the second offers dancing and music. **Les Chandelles,** avenue de l'Atlantique (✆ **02-97-52-90-98**), pulls in a young, flashy crowd. Playing whatever's current and popular, it has hosted some of France's most well-known DJs. Cover is usually around 11€. As at most dance clubs in France, no jeans or sneakers are allowed.

# NANTES ★★★

385km (239 miles) W of Paris; 325km (202 miles) N of Bordeaux

Technically, Nantes (pop. 283,000) is outside of Brittany. In 1941 the Vichy Government transferred it from the region into a newly-created one, the Pays de la Loire. This administrative action did nothing to change Nantes' deeply Breton soul, however, and no guide to Brittany would be complete without its inclusion.

**Nantes**

| | |
| --- | --- |
| 0 | 1/4 mi |
| 0 | 0.25 km |

Information ⓘ

Post Office ✉

Cathédrale St-Pierre **2**
Château des Ducs de Bretagne **4**
Les Machines de l'Ile **5**
Musée des Beaux-Arts de Nantes **3**
Musée Jules Verne de Nantes **1**

The capital of Brittany is Rennes (pop. 207,000), but comparing the two cities, many agree that Nantes is more vibrant. It's best known for its busy port, which suffered great damage in World War II, and for the 1598 Edict of Nantes, which guaranteed religious freedom to Protestants (this was later revoked). During the Middle Ages, Nantes expanded from an island in the Loire to the northern edge of the river, where its center lies today. Many famous people, from Molière to Stendhal, have lived here.

Despite a lackluster reputation, Nantes has taken on a kind of Atlantic Coast chic. Impressive revitalization is changing the city, as once-dreary industrial suburbs are being transformed into places you'd actually like to visit.

## Essentials

**GETTING THERE** The **TGV train** from Paris's Gare Montparnasse takes about 2 to 2½ hours to get to Nantes and costs about 70€. For information visit www.voyages-sncf.com or call ☎ **08-92-35-35-35**. Nantes's **Gare SNCF,** 27 bd. de Stalingrad, is a 5-minute walk from the town center. If you're **driving,** take A11 for 385km (239 miles) west of Paris. The trip takes about 4 hours. **Aéroport Nantes-Atlantique** (☎ **02-40-84-80-00**) is 12km (7½ miles) southeast of town. **Air France** (www.airfrance.fr; ☎36-54 within France only) offers daily flights from Paris. A shuttle bus between the airport and the Nantes train station takes 25 minutes and costs 7.20€. A taxi from the airport costs 25–35€ and takes about 20 minutes.

**VISITOR INFORMATION** The **Office de Tourisme** is at 9 rue des Etats (www. nantes-tourisme.com; ☎ **08-92-46-40-44**).

# Exploring the City

The **Pass Nantes,** available at the airport, tourist office, and certain hotels, allows you to enter museums and ride any of the city's public conveyances, including buses, trams, and some of the boats that cruise through town along the river Erdre. The pass costs 18€ for 1 day, 28€ for 2 days, and 36€ for 3 days; passes for families of 4 are a good value.

**Cathédrale St-Pierre et St-Paul ★★** CATHEDRAL   Begun in 1434, this cathedral wasn't finished until the late 19th century. Still, it managed to remain architecturally harmonious—a rare feat. Two square towers dominate the facade; more impressive is the 100m-long (328-ft.) interior. Its *pièce de résistance* is the Renaissance tomb of François II, duc de Bretagne, and his second wife, Marguerite de Foix. The couple were the parents of Anne de Bretagne, who commissioned sculptor Michel Colombe to create their final resting place. White walls and pillars contrast with the rich colors of the stained-glass windows; helpful signs explain the significance of most objects.

Place St-Pierre. ☎ **02-40-47-84-64.** Free admission. Daily 8:30am–6:15pm. Crypt: Sat–Sun 3–6pm.

**Château des Ducs de Bretagne ★★** CASTLE/MUSEUM   This enormous complex, seat of the Dukes of Brittany, was constructed in the 9th or 10th century, enlarged in the 13th century, destroyed, then rebuilt into its present shape by François II in 1466. The comtesse du Barry, royal courtesan, was imprisoned here, as was Gilles de Retz (aka "Bluebeard"), one of France's most notorious mass murderers. The castle's rich inventory has been presented as a museum since the 17th century. About 30 rooms are devoted to a depiction of the history of the port, displaying evocative objects such as scale models of the city during different eras. The museum charges admission, but you can visit the courtyard and stroll along the ramparts for free.

4 place Marc-Elder. ☎ **08-11-46-46-44.** www.chateau-nantes.fr. Ramparts free daily 10am–7pm (July–Aug until 8pm, Sat 11pm). Museum 5€ adults, 3€ students 25 and under, free for children 17 and under. Sept–June Tues–Sun 10am–6pm; July–Aug daily 10am–7pm. Closed Jan 1, May 1, Nov 1, and Dec 25.

**Les Machines de l'Ile ★★★** THEME PARK ☺   On the island splitting the Loire river in the center of Nantes is a fantastical workshop that does Jules Verne proud. Based on the author's imagined creatures and the mechanical drawings of Leonardo da Vinci, a team of artist/mechanics build articulated moving sculptures that really must be seen—or ridden—to be believed. A 12m (147-ft.) elephant, made from 45 tons of wood and steel, takes 50 passengers at a time for a stroll around the premises. The Carrousel des Mondes Marins (Marine Worlds Carousel) is a work in progress, featuring a manta ray, squid, crab, and flying fish. Seating about 75 for now, the carousel will eventually accommodate 300 "voyagers" on three levels representing the ocean, sea bed, and abyss. One ticket gives access to the rides, another admits you to the Galerie, where you can see future creations taking shape. As the site is a functioning workshop its opening hours change weekly; check the English pages of their website for details.

3 rue de l'Hermitage. www.lesmachines-nantes.fr. ✆ **02-40-69-72-52.** Admission (to rides or the Galerie; together they require 2 tickets): 7€ adults, 5.50€ ages 18 and under. Wed–Sun, call or consult website for daily schedule.

**Musée des Beaux-Arts de Nantes** ★ MUSEUM  In one of western France's most interesting provincial galleries, you'll find an unusually fine collection of sculptures and paintings from the 12th to the late 19th centuries. The street level is devoted to mostly French modern or contemporary art created since 1900, with special emphasis on painters from the 1950s and 1960s.

10 rue Georges Clemenceau. ✆ **02-51-17-45-00.** Admission 2€ adults, 1€ students 19–26, free for children 18 and under. Wed–Mon 10am–6pm (Thurs until 8pm).

**Musée Jules Verne de Nantes** MUSEUM  The novelist Jules Verne (*Journey to the Center of the Earth, Around the World in Eighty Days*) was born in Nantes in 1828. This museum is filled with memorabilia and objects inspired by his writings, from ink spots to a "magic" lantern with glass slides. Fans also seek out Verne's house at 4 rue de Clisson in the Ile-Feydeau, which is privately owned and not open to the public. In a historic, mostly 18th-century neighborhood in the heart of the town, the house was named after an island (l'Ile Feydeau) that became part of "mainland" Nantes after the river was diverted into a series of canals during the 18th century.

3 rue de l'Hermitage. ✆ **02-40-69-72-52.** Admission 3€ adults, 1.50€ for students, free for ages 18 and under. Wed–Sat and Mon 10am–noon and 2–6pm; Sun 2–6pm.

## Shopping

Nantes overflows with shops and boutiques. The principal shopping streets are rue du Calvaire, rue Crébillon, rue Boileau, rue d'Orléans, rue de la Marne, and rue de Verdun. Most of these encompass the shopping districts around place

Shopping at passage Pommeraye.

Graslin, place Royale, the château, and the cathedral. The passage Pommeraye, a historic gallery that dates back to 1843, houses a small, upscale shopping center. One of the prime areas for antiques is around place Aristide-Briand and rue Mercoeur.

Interesting antiques dealers include **Ecritoire Antiquités Poidras,** 12 rue Jean-Jaurès (*C* **02-40-47-78-18**), offering 18th- and 19th-century furniture and decorative pieces such as historic mantels.

For unusual gifts, check out the stores of two master artisans. **Devineau,** 4 rue de la Belle Image (*C* **02-40-47-19-59**), brings the art of waxworking to a new level, offering a huge array of candles in different sizes, colors and shapes including fruits, flowers, and vegetables. **Gautier Debotte,** 9 rue de la Fosse (*C* **02-40-48-23-19**), a historic *chocolatier* established in 1823, is the maker of "Le Muscadet Nantais"—a chocolate-covered white grape mascerated in Muscadet wine (Muscadet being a Loire varietal and Brittany's most popular wine). Other Debotte boutiques are at 2 rue des Hauts Pavé, 3 rue de Budapest, and 15 rue Crébillon.

# Where to Eat

**L'Atlantide** ★★★ MODERN FRENCH   On the fourth floor of the complex that houses the city's chamber of commerce, this panoramic restaurant, with views over the semi-industrial landscape and the river, serves the finest cuisine in the area. World-renowned designer Jean-Pierre Wilmotte created the minimalist, ocean-liner look of the dining area, but Jean-Yves Guého's innovative cooking is what draws patrons. Menu items, steeped in the traditions of both the Loire Valley and the Breton coast, may include lobster salad with a sauce made from *vin jaune* from the Jura, potato-and-herb tart capped with foie gras, Breton turbot with Cantonese spices, and braised sweetbreads with Anjou wine. An excellent dessert is bananas braised in local beer. The cellar is known for some of the finest vintages of Loire Valley wine anywhere, with an emphasis on Anjous and Muscadets.

Centre des Salorges, 16 quai Ernest Renaud. www.restaurant-atlantide.net. *C* **02-40-73-23-23.** Reservations required. Main courses 23€–58€; fixed-price lunch 32€, dinner 60€–95€. AE, MC, V. Mon–Fri noon–2pm; Mon–Sat 8–9:45pm. Closed Aug and Dec 23–Jan 3.

**La Cigale** FRENCH/SEAFOOD   Nantes's most historic and charasmatic brasserie, decorated in jaw-dropping Belle Epoque style, has changed little since it opened in 1895 across from the landmark Théâtre Graslin. Know that you're paying for the atmosphere as much as the food, but the latter is better than average. On the menu are classics such as *confit des cuisses de canard* (duck confit) and *boeuf tartare*, as well as shellfish platters. The sprawling restaurant is usually quite loud, and the staff members tend to be overworked. The terrace is an excellent spot for people-watching.

4 place Graslin. www.lacigale.com. *C* **02-51-84-94-94.** Reservations recommended. Main courses 16€–23€; fixed-price menu 14€–28€. MC, V. Daily 7:30am–12:30am. Bus: 11 or 34.

**Le Lieu Unique** FRENCH/BRETON   The chief attraction of this restored biscuit factory is its restaurant and bar, which have become a major nighttime rendezvous spot for the young people of Nantes. In an atmospheric setting, diners can order from a market-fresh menu. Begin perhaps with a homemade terrine or a "duet" of smoked salmon and rillettes. At least three fish dishes are featured nightly; other options are likely to be honey-basted duck breast or roast lamb flavored with thyme. For dessert, you might order roast pineapple with vanilla ice cream or a crème brûlée.

2 rue de la Biscuterie. www.lelieuunique.com. ✆ **02-51-72-05-55.** Reservations recommended. Main courses 10€–17€; fixed-price lunch 12€, dinner 15€–27€. MC, V. Mon–Sat noon–2pm; Tues–Thurs 7–11pm; Fri–Sat 7pm–midnight.

## Nantes Nightlife

When the sun goes down, the town turns into one big party. On **place du Bouffay, place du Pilori,** and **rue Kervégan,** you'll find lots of cafes and pubs, many with live music and fun people. A younger crowd rules **rue Scribe.**

The hippest location in Nantes, and the town's leading cultural center, is **Le Lieu Unique,** 2 rue de la Biscuiterie (✆ 02-51-82-15-00). Converted from a 19th-century biscuit factory, the venue offers presentations ranging from plays (in French) to art exhibitions. Admission is free to the dimly lit, concrete-floored bar at ground level, which is frequented by students and artists who pack the dance floor. The bar is open Monday 11am to 8pm, Tuesday and Wednesday 11am to 1am, Thursday 11am to 2am, Friday and Saturday 11am to 3am, and Sunday 3 to 8pm.

Catch live blues, jazz, or rock at **L'Univers Café,** 16 rue Jean-Jacques-Rousseau (✆ 02-40-73-49-55), or techno and disco at **L.C. Club,** 21 quai des Antilles (www.lcclub.fr; ✆ 02-40-47-68-45), open all night. A great piano bar with a dance floor and occasional jazz concerts is **Le Tie Break,** 1 rue des Petites-Ecuries (✆ 02-40-47-77-00).

The pump-it-up dance scene has a huge following of everyone from students to seniors. The over-30 crowd heads to the vintage 1970s gay-friendly disco **L'Evasion,** 3 rue de l'Emery (✆ 02-40-47-99-84). Other discos include **Le Royal Club Privé,** 7 rue des Salorges (www.leroyal.fr; ✆ 02-40-69-11-10). Don't wear jeans to any of these places, and be prepared to pay 15€ to 20€ to get in.

A favorite with gays and lesbians is **Le Petit Marais,** 15 rue Kervégan (www.lepetitmarais.fr; ✆ 02-40-20-15-25), where people meet and talk in a friendly atmosphere that welcomes everything from leather to lace. **Le Temps d'Aimer,** 14 rue Alexandre-Fourny (www.letandem.com; ✆ 02-40-89-48-60), is mixed and gay-friendly. This disco with its small dance floor attracts a sophisticated crowd. Cover is around 15€.

## Where to Stay

**Hôtel Pommeraye** ★ Steps from the passage Pommeraye, this hip, forward-thinking hotel is close to shopping, restaurants, and many sights. The rooms are compact, with simple but sleek decoration and a whimsical piece here and there. Breakfast is based on organic and low-carbon-footprint items—if the breakfast room feels too small, you can request a tray brought to your room for no extra charge. As the hotel is right in the center of the action, it can be noisy on weekend nights; be sure to request a quiet room. Public parking is located 150m (492 ft.) away.

2 rue Boileau, Nantes 44000. www.hotel-pommeraye.com. ✆ **02-40-48-78-79.** Fax 02-40-69-75-75. 74 units. 69€–164€ double; 118€–228€ suite. AE, DC, MC, V. Small pets 5€. **Amenities:** Restaurant; bar; room service. *In room:* TV, hair dryer, free Wi-Fi.

**L'Hôtel**   Within sight of the château and the cathedral, this hotel is, for the price, a perfect base in Nantes. Built in the 1980s, it's sleek and contemporary but maintains an inviting atmosphere. With firm beds, modern furnishings, and a brown-grey-beige color scheme, the guest rooms are small but well organized. Some have private patios overlooking the château, while others open onto a garden and terrace. Bathrooms have tubs or showers. The softly lit breakfast room has terrace views.

6 rue Henri IV, Nantes 44000. www.nanteshotel.com. ✆ **02-40-29-30-31.** Fax 02-40-29-00-95. 31 units. 99€–160€ double. AE, MC, V. Parking 9€. **Amenities:** Room service. *In room:* A/C, TV, hair dryer, free Wi-Fi.

# THE CHAMPAGNE COUNTRY

## by Amelia Smith

**9**

G eographical luck—both good and bad—has played a large part in the history of Champagne. Warm enough to grow grapes in, but cold enough for snow in winter, the climate frustrated early winemakers by causing an uneven fermentation that resulted in bubbles—a "fault" that led to one of France's most famous luxury products. On the less-good side, the region's position between the Western Front and Paris meant that the 20th century saw many of its buildings destroyed, especially during the First World War.

Champagne's major tourist towns are easily reached by train from Paris in under 90 minutes. Travelers with their own wheels, however, will get the most out of the winding roads, vineyard-draped hills, deciduous forests, and farmland that lend themselves to this area's natural beauty.

# REIMS ★★

143km (89 miles) E of Paris; 45km (28 miles) NW of Châlons-en-Champagne

The undisputed capital of Champagne, Reims (pronounced "rahns"), was an important city under the Roman Empire. A few hundred years later, its majestic cathedral acted as a kind of French Westminster Abbey: it hosted many royal coronations, including that of Charles VII, who was led to the ceremony by Joan of Arc.

Today Reims is a bustling university town of nearly 200,000 inhabitants—if you count its suburbs, it's the twelfth largest city in France. Since it became a stop on the TGV network in 2007, expansion and improvements have been nonstop, such as a new tramway that links the outer neighborhoods with town center (tickets are 1.30€, sold at distributors around town and onboard).

## Essentials

**GETTING THERE** If you're **driving** from Paris, take A4 east. **TGV trains** direct to the Reims station depart from Paris's Gare de l'Est every 1½ hours (trip time: 45 min.; 32€–56€ one-way). Less expensive, but longer, non-TGV itineraries are possible. Ten trains per day arrive from Strasbourg into the Champagne Ardennes TGV station 8km (5 miles) outside of town, with connections to the center (trip time: approximately 2 hr.; 52€–72€ one-way). For information, visit www.voyages-sncf.com or call ℭ **08-36-35-35-35.** For information on bus service linking Reims to other towns in Champagne, visit www.vitici.fr (choose the English option).

**VISITOR INFORMATION** The **Office de Tourisme** is at 2 rue Guillaume-de-Machault (www.reims-tourisme.com; ℭ **08-92-70-13-51;** fax 03-26-77-45-19).

# Exploring the City

**Cathédrale Notre-Dame de Reims ★★★** CATHEDRAL   Not only is this cathedral where all the kings of France from 815 to 1825 were crowned, it stands upon the site where the first one was baptized. In a baptistery situated here in 496, Rémi, bishop of Reims, anointed the newly-converted Clovis I, Frankish king.

The structure and its religious treasures were almost completely destroyed in World War I. Restoration began as early as 1919, funded largely by contributions from John D. Rockefeller.

Laden with statuettes, the cathedral has three spectacular western facade portals. A rose window above the central one is dedicated to the Virgin. The right portal portrays the Apocalypse and the Last Judgment; the left, martyrs and saints. Particularly impressive are a trio of stained glass windows in the apse created by Marc Chagall in 1974.

Place du Cardinal Luçon. ⓒ **03-26-35-36-00.** Free admission. Daily 7:30am–7:30pm.

**Palais de Tau ★** MUSEUM   Opposite the southern side of the cathedral, this is the former Archbishop's Palace. Today it's a museum dedicated to the royal coronations that took place next door. Lavish banquets were held in the

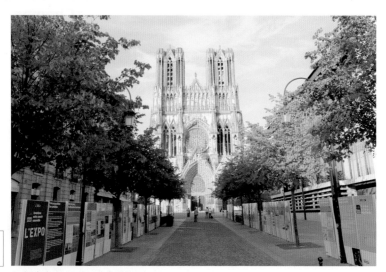

Cathédrale Notre-Dame de Reims.

Salle de Tau, lined with huge tapestries and containing an enormous 15th-century fireplace. Among the objects to be seen are Saint Rémi's 12th-century coronation chalice and the Sainte-Ampoule, a holy flask that held the oil used to anoint new kings.

Place du Cardinal Luçon. ✆ **03-26-47-81-79.** Admission 6.50€ adults, free for children under 18. Free 1st Sun of every month from Oct 1–Mar. Tues–Sun 9:30am–6:30pm May 6 to Sept 8; 9:30am–12:30pm and 2–5:30pm Sept 9–5 May 5. Closed Jan 1, May 1, July 14, Nov 1 and 11, and Dec 25.

**Basilique St-Rémi** ★★ CHURCH This church dates from 1007, making it the oldest in Reims. Though an example of classic medieval French masonry, it's often unfavorably compared to the more spectacular cathedral. Within the complex is the former royal abbey of the aforementioned, canonized Rémi; it now houses an extensive collection covering the history of Reims, regional archaeology, and military history. The church contains St. Rémi's tomb and a collection of 12th-century stained glass windows.

Place Chanoine Ladame. ✆ **03-26-85-31-20.** Free admission. Daily 8am–7pm (or nightfall in winter). Musée: 53 rue Simon. ✆ **03-26-35-36-90.** Admission 3€ adults, free for children 16 and under. Mon–Fri 2–6:30pm; Sat–Sun 2–7pm.

**Salle de Reddition** HISTORIC SITE At 2:41am on May 7, 1945, the Germans surrendered to General Eisenhower and the Allies in this room in what was a technical school near the railroad tracks. Battle maps line the walls exactly as they did on the day of surrender. The exhibit includes military uniforms and a short film in French, German, and English.

12 rue Franklin-D-Roosevelt. ✆ **03-26-47-84-19.** Admission 3€ adults, free for children under 16. Wed–Mon 10am–noon and 2–6pm. Closed Jan 1, May 1, July 14, Nov 1 and 11, and Dec 25.

**Reims**

To Laon

Cimetière du Nord

Porte Mars

Gare de Reims

Gallo-Roman Cryptoporticus

Musée Hôtel Le Vergeur

place A. Briand

place Royale

Palais du Tau

Centre des Congrès

← To Epernay

ERLON

LA BARBATRE

← To Soissons

HINCMAR

LES COUTURES

→ To Paris

Ancien Collège des Jésuites

place du Général-Gouraud

place St-Nicaise

FLECHAMBAULT

place des Droits-de-l'Homme

To Verdun

Paris · Reims · FRANCE

To Rethel →

0 — 1/4 mi
0 — 0.25 km

Information ⓘ
Post Office ✉

Basilique St-Rémi **8**

Cathédrale Notre-Dame
de Reims **4**

Musée des Beaux-Arts **3**

Palais du Tau **5**

Salle de Reddition **1**

Maison de Pommery **7**

Mumm **2**

Taittinger **6**

**Musée des Beaux-Arts** MUSEUM   Housed in the 18th-century buildings belonging to the old Abbaye St-Denis, this gallery contains more than a dozen portraits of German princes by Renaissance painters Lucas Cranach "the Elder" and "Younger". The museum has owned them since it opened in 1795. You can see *toiles peintes* (light painting on rough linen) that date from the 15th and 16th centuries and paintings and furniture from the 17th and 18th. There's an excellent series of 27 of Corot's tree-shaded walks.

8 rue Chanzy. ☎ **03-26-35-36-00.** Admission 3€ adults, free for students and children 16 and under; free to all 1st Sun of every month. Wed–Mon 10am–noon and 2–6pm. Closed Jan 1, May 1, July 14, Nov 1 and 11, and Dec 25.

## Exploring the Champagne Cellars ★★

There are over 250km (155 miles) of champagne cellars beneath Reims, holding some 200 million bottles. During the German siege of 1914 and throughout the war, people lived and even published a daily paper in them. If you go to visit them, take a sweater—temperatures are rarely above 50°F.

**Mumm** WINERY Founded in 1827, Mumm welcomes visitors with a video that explains how champagne is made. An in-house museum exhibits casks and illustrates the ancient role of the vintner. The 1-hour tour covers a labyrinth of tunnels and storage cellars in the chalky bedrock; they contain a vast inventory—almost 25 million bottles—of slowly aging champagne. The more expensive tours tack on oenological insights and tastings.

34 rue du Champ-de-Mars. www.mumm.com. ✆ **03-26-49-59-70.** Reservations required. Tours (in English) 10€–20€ adults, free for children 16 and under. Mar–Oct daily 9–11am and 2–5pm; out of season, phone ahead for tours.

**Pommery** WINERY Among the most-visited cellars are those under the 17-acre hilltop park housing Les Crayères (see "Where to Eat" and "Where to Stay" below). The *real* crayeres—chambers dug into the chalk for storing champagne—are reached here via a magnificent 116-step stairway. The complex comprises 18km (11 miles) of tunnels about 30m (98 ft.) below ground, set within Gallo-Roman quarries. Art exhibits are occasionally held on the premises.

Place du Général-Gouraud. www.pommery.com. ✆ **03-26-61-62-56.** Reservations recommended. Admission 12€, free for children 9 and under. Daily 9:30am–7pm Apr to mid-Nov, 10am–6pm mid-Nov to Mar. Closed Jan 1 and Dec 25.

**Taittinger** WINERY Taittinger is a *grande marque* of French champagne, one of the few still controlled by members of the family that founded it in 1930. The cellars were dug from the site of Gallo-Roman chalk mines in use from the 4th to the 13th centuries and contain vestiges of a Benedictine abbey. Tours—including a film, guided cellar visit, anecdotes about Reims, and Taittinger family lore—last about an hour and include everything from how a corking machine works to the art of sediment removal.

9 place St-Nicaise. www.taittinger.com. ✆ **03-26-85-45-35.** Admission 12€ adults, free for children 11 and under. May 1 to mid-Nov daily 9:30am–noon and 2–5pm; Nov 15-30 and Mar 15 to Apr 30 Mon–Sat 9:30am–noon and 2–4:30pm. Dec 1 to Mar 14 Mon–Fri 9:30am–noon and 2–4:30pm.

**Mumm champagne cellar.**

## Shopping

The city's main shopping district is northwest of the cathedral. The

# TINY bubbles

department store **Galleries Lafayette** and several fashion chains flank the **rue de Vesle**, which is closed to cars.

For take-home gifts, your best bet is either the **place Drouet d'Erlon** or the **cours Langlet,** where plenty of shops sell edibles and gift items. A local specialty is *biscuits roses de Reims,* crunchy-chewy pink cookies that originated in the 17th century. **La Maison Fossier/Biscuits Fossier,** with a shop at 25 cours Langlet (✆ 03-26-47-59-84) has been making them for 250 years and is the only commercial bakery left to do so. For miniature liqueur-filled chocolate champagne bottles and corks in pretty packages, try **La Petite Friande,** 15 cours Langlet (✆ 03-26-47-50-44).

If you don't have time for a tasting and want to bring home some bubbly, stop by the **Grande Boutique du Vin,** 3 place Léon-Bourgeois (✆ 03-26-40-12-12). It stocks one of the most comprehensive inventories of champagne in Reims, with 150 types from more than 100 houses, many of which are not available in North America. Excellent lesser-known brands include Deutz, Billecart Salmon, Henriot, and Gimonnet. Very good *cuvées* can be had for 20€ to 38€. English is spoken.

## Where to Eat

**L'Assiette Champenoise** (see "Where to Stay" on p. 367) has an excellent restaurant.

**Les Crayères** ★★★ MODERN FRENCH   Local foodie gossip usually includes talk of **Le Parc,** Les Crayères' gastronomic restaurant. Whether the current chef is up to snuff, whether it deserves its current number of Michelin stars or got robbed—the Reimois are extremely proud of this hallowed institution, with good reason. For most people a meal here is a once-in-a-lifetime experience. Located in the same chateau as the hotel (see below) it offers an ever-changing, seasonal menu with exclusive items such as foie gras, lobster, and black truffles nearly always making an appearance. **Le Jardin** ★★, Les Crayères' less formal restaurant, is a conservatory-like building with lots of iron and glass and a couple of fireplaces to keep it cozy. With a young, stylish crowd, the atmosphere here is more urban chic. The food is upscale bistro and, as at Le Parc, the wine list is as heavy as a phone book.

64 bd. Henri-Vasnier. ☎ **03-26-82-80-80.** Fax 03-26-82-65-52. Reservations required a few days in advance for weekday dinners, at least a month in advance for weekend dinners. Main courses 50€–140€; fixed-price menus (including red bordeaux and champagne) 185€–305€; fixed-price lunch 70€. AE, DC, MC, V. Wed–Sun noon–1:30pm and 7–9:30pm.

**Le Millénaire** ★★★ MODERN FRENCH Competing for supremacy in a town where the culinary competition is severe, Le Millénaire emerges near the very top. Set near the place Royale and the cathedral, its contemporary setting features frequently changing art exhibitions. The cuisine is sublime, with market-fresh ingredients transformed by Chef Laurent Laplaige and his talented staff into singular dishes such as "cappuccino" of Champagne lentil cream, black truffle and Bellota ham; roast venison with celery root fries; or turbot in a champagne sauce with leeks. Desserts are just as inventive—the problem is saving room for them.

4-6 rue Bertin. www.lemillenaire.com. ☎ **02-26-08-26-62.** Reservations required. Main courses 34€–50€; fixed-price menus 32€–50€. AE, DC, MC, V. Mon–Fri noon–2pm and Mon–Sat 7–10pm.

**Le Jamin** FRENCH Airy, well respected, outfitted in a pleasantly contemporary, noncontroversial style, and a fixture in Reims for more than a decade, this restaurant describes itself as "*semi-gastronomique*" and, as such, offers reasonable prices for some remarkably stylish food. The best examples include a salad composed of scallops, crayfish, and sweetbreads; St-Marcellin cheese, fried and served with pine nuts as a salad; and a *declinaison* of duckling whereby four different preparations (*rilletes, magret* both smoked and unsmoked, and terrine of duck liver) are assembled onto a single flavorful platter. Delectable main courses include roasted turbot in champagne sauce, stingray with garlic butter, and English-style calves' liver.

18 bd. Jamin. www.lejamin.com. ☎ **03-26-07-37-30.** Reservations recommended. Main courses 13€–22€; set menus 21€–32€. AE, MC, V. Tues–Sun noon–2:30pm; Tues–Sat 7:30–9:30pm. Closed last 2 weeks in Aug and last 2 weeks in Jan.

# Reims Nightlife

Reims has the most vibrant nightlife in the region. The best place to start is **place Drouet-d'Erlon,** home to the city's premier clubs. Locals call it simply "place d'Erlon."

For a break from champagne, consider an Irish pub. The **James Joyce,** 80 place Drouet-d'Erlon (☎ **03-26-40-33-06**) offers more than 120 types of beer. **The Sherlock,** 81 place Drouet-d'Erlon (☎ **03-26-40-19-46**), is just next door, and **The Kilberry,** 182 rue de Vesle (☎ **03-26-88-46-47**), has themed nights, including for rugby.

The best dance floors are at **Le Vogue,** 93 bd. Général-Leclerc (☎ **03-26-03-38-03**), which attracts the 18–25 set; the see-and-be-seen **Z Club**, 41 bd. Général Leclerc (☎ **03-26-86-83-32**) for 25 to 40-somethings; and **Bar Lilas,** 75 rue des Courcelles (☎ **03-26-47-02-81**), welcoming an older gay and lesbian crowd.

# Where to Stay

## EXPENSIVE

**Les Crayères ★★★**   There's no finer place to stay in eastern France than this palatial neoclassic chateau. In 2008, *Travel and Leisure* readers voted it the best hotel in France; it continues to rank among the top 5. Located in a 7-hectare (17-acre) park, the chateau's public areas have 5.5-meter (18-foot) ceilings, ornate paneling and opulent details. The guest rooms, with terraces and all the latest amenities, are luxuriously decorated in country manor style and are usually available when a champagne mogul isn't in residence. Bathrooms have deluxe toiletries and tub/showers. The restaurant, Le Parc, is the most renowned in the region (p. 365).

64 bd. Henri-Vasnier, Reims 51685. www.lescrayeres.com. ℂ **03-26-24-90-00.** Fax 26-24-90-01. 20 units. 345€–700€. AE, DC, MC, V. Closed Jan. **Amenities:** Restaurant; bar; babysitting; room service; tennis court. *In room:* A/C, hair dryer, minibar, free Wi-Fi.

## MODERATE

**L'Assiette Champenoise ★★▮▮**   About 3km (1¾ miles) southwest of Reims in the suburb of Tinqueux, this is the second-best hotel and restaurant in the area. Built in the 1970s among century-old trees, it occupies part of a former Norman estate, standing in a 1.6-hectare (4-acre) park. Inside the atmosphere is sleek and even club-like in the dining areas. Rooms are attractively furnished in French traditional style; newer suites are elegantly modern. The cuisine covers a medley of classics with simple but innovative twists. Try John Dory with ragout of vegetables, suckling veal with seven vegetables, or langoustines with wasabi. Homemade foie gras is always a reliable starter. You don't need to be a guest to enjoy the restaurant—it has a faithful local clientele.

40 av. Paul-Vaillant-Couturier, Tinqueux 51430. www.assiettechampenoise.com. ℂ **03-26-84-64-64.** Fax 03-26-04-15-69. 39 units. 165€–255€ double; 395€-59(€ suite. AE, DC, MC, V. Free parking. From Reims, take A4 west toward Paris and exit at sortie 22–tinqueux; av. Paul-Vaillant-Couturier will lead you directly to Tinqueux. **Amenities:** Restaurant; bar; indoor pool; sauna. *In room:* TV, hair dryer, minibar, free Wi-Fi.

**Best Western Hôtel de la Paix ★**   Conveniently located between the train station and the cathedral, this is the only modern hotel in France with a medieval chapel (built for Benedictine nuns in the 1200s) overlooking its garden and pool. The rooms are contemporary and well maintained, and many are air-conditioned. Furnishings are what one expects from this chain, with comfortable beds and tub/shower combinations in most bathrooms. Considering the lack of moderately-priced hotels in Reims with any character, it's a smart choice. There's a decent champagne bar, too.

9 rue Buirette, Reims 51100. www.hotel-lapaix.fr. ℂ **800/528-1234** in the U.S. and Canada, or 03-26-40-04-08. Fax 03-26-47-75-04. 170 units. 155€–210€ double; 350€ suite. AE, DC, MC, V. Parking 11€. **Amenities:** Restaurant; bar; exercise room; indoor pool; room service; sauna. *In room:* A/C, TV, hair dryer, minibar, free Wi-Fi.

## INEXPENSIVE

**Mercure Reims Cathédrale ₰**   This chain hotel from the 1970s sits on the banks of the Aisne-Marne Canal, a 10-minute walk from the town center and the

The **Routes Touristiques du Champagne** are five itineraries developed by tourist offices to show motorists the best their region has to offer. From 70km up to 220km (45–136 miles), they wind their way through vineyards, villages, and sites of interest, clearly marked by black and white road signs. One of the shortest, and prettiest, is the route dedicated to the Montagne de Reims, which is not really a mountain at all but a forested plateau between Reims and Epernay.

Along this route, as with the others, you'll pass dozens of small champagne producers, sometimes as small as in a residence or garage. Tourist offices can give you a list of those open to tastings or where English is spoken; sometimes you'll happen along one with a drop-in policy. Champagne being the livelihood of most of these producers, it's polite to buy at least one bottle in exchange for their time, but you'll likely pay less than you would for two flutes in a restaurant.

For more information, visit any tourist office or see (in French, but with maps) www.tourisme-en-champagne.com.

cathedral. It's near the entrance to the A4 autoroute and easy to find. The good-size rooms have all the modern conveniences and bathrooms with tubs and showers; some have views of the waterway. Furnishings are standard motel style.

31 bd. Paul-Doumer, Reims 51100. www.mercure.com. ⊘ **03-26-84-49-49.** Fax 03-26-84-49-84. 126 units. 82€–164€ double. AE, DC, MC, V. Parking. **Amenities:** Restaurant; bar; room service; swimming pool. *In room:* A/C, TV, hair dryer, Wi-Fi.

# EPERNAY ★

140km (87 miles) E of Paris; 26km (16 miles) S of Reims

Although it has one-sixth the population of Reims, Epernay produces nearly as much champagne, with an estimated 322km (200 miles) or more of cellars and tunnels. Day-trippers also find it more doable, as the town center and major champagne houses are within walking distance of the train station. Unlike urban Reims, it has a more quiet, yet monied, atmosphere.

Invading armies have destroyed or burned Epernay nearly two dozen times—this explains a somewhat disappointing lack of architectural character. The stately avenue de Champagne helps make up for it though, with neoclassical villas housing the headquarters of Moët et Chandon, Perrier-Jouet, and Pol Roger, among others.

## Essentials

**GETTING THERE** If you're **driving** to Epernay from Reims, head south on E51. From Paris, take the A4. Ten **trains** per day arrive from Paris's Gare de l'Est (trip time: 1 hr., 15 min.; 22€ one-way). From Reims, there are 28 trains per day (trip time: 25 min.; 6.40€ one-way). For information, visit www.voyages-sncf.com or call ⊘ **08-36-35-35-35.** For information on bus service linking Epernay to other towns in Champagne, visit www.vitici.fr (choose the English option).

The **Office de Tourisme** is at 7 av. de Champagne (www.ot-epernay.fr; ℂ **03-26-53-33-00;** fax 03-26-51-95-22).

# Exploring the Town

The center of town and shopping district radiate out from the **place Hugues Plomb** and its fountain. Gourmet foodstuffs can be found in and around the iron-and-glass **Halle Saint-Thibault** near the place d'Europe (a very seductive food market is held inside on Wednesday and Saturday mornings).

For champagne, you can go to the individual houses along the avenue de Champagne or one of the shops representing a variety. Both **La Cave Salvatori,** 11 rue Flodoard (ℂ **03-26-55-32-32**), and **Le Domaine des Crus,** 2 rue Henri Dunant (ℂ **03-26-54-18-60**), stock a wide array of labels and vintages.

Boutiques are dedicated mostly to locals' daily needs (clothing, etc.) but there are a few gift and housewares shops. For wine-themed items such as champagne buckets and flutes, try **Home,** 12 rue du Professeur Langevin (ℂ **03-26-51-83-83**).

**Champagne de Castellane** WINERY    De Castellane gives you a more comprehensive view of how champagne is actually produced than the two houses recommended below. You see workers doing it all—corking, labeling, even removing sediment. The on-site museum may be a bit dull, but the climb to the tower (237 steps) for a panoramic view of the area is not. The tower is from 1904 and has become an Epernay landmark.

57 rue de Verdun. www.castellane.com. ℂ **03-26-51-19-11.** Admission 8.50€; free for ages 12 and under. Daily mid-Mar to Dec 10am–noon and 2–6pm. Tasting only Jan to mid-Mar. Closed Dec 24–8 Jan.

**Mercier** WINERY    Mercier is near Moët et Chandon, and you can visit them both on the same day. Mercier conducts tours in English of its 18km (11 miles) of tunnels from laser-guided trains—reached by an elevator that descends past rudimentary champagne-themed dioramas. The caves contain one of the world's largest wooden barrels, with a capacity of more than 200,000 bottles. No reservation is necessary if there are fewer than 10 in your group, though you may want to call ahead for the schedule of English tours. Ticket includes tasting.

70 av. de Champagne. www.champagnemercier.fr. ℂ **03-26-51-22-22.** Admission 10€, 18 and under 5€. 9:30–11:30am and 2–4:30pm daily Mar 24–Nov 14; Thurs–Mon. Feb 10–Mar 23 and Nov 15–Dec 18. Closed mid-Dec to 1st week in Feb.

**Moët et Chandon Champagne Cellars** WINERY    One of the most prestigious champagne houses runs an informative tour, describing the champagne-making process and filling you in on champagne lore: Napoleon, a friend of Jean-Rémy Moët, used to stop by for thousands of bottles on his way to battle. The only time he didn't take a supply was at Waterloo—and look what happened there. The basic tour includes a glass of champagne; more expensive tickets entitle you to more glasses.

20 av. de Champagne. www.moet.com. ℂ **03-26-51-20-20.** Admission 16.50€–29€, 17 and under 9€, 9 and under free. Feb to Mar 23 and Nov 12 to Dec 28: Mon-Fri 9:30–11:30am and 2–4:30pm; Mar 24 to Nov 10: Mon–Sun 9:30–11:30am and 2–4:30pm. Closed Jan.

**Moët et Chandon Champagne Cellars.**

## Where to Eat

The **Royal Champagne** houses a gourmet restaurant. The cuisine at **L'Hostellerie La Briqueterie** is excellent.

**Les Berceaux ★★★** CHAMPENOISE    Here chef-owner Patrick Michelon serves generous portions of the first-class regional cuisine that has earned him a Michelin star. Particularly scrumptious are such dishes as spit-roasted suckling lamb, snails in champagne sauce, and roast filet of John Dory. If you find the slight stuffiness of the dining room intimidating, opt for the less formal Bistro le 7, just next door, for more simple fare and a large selection of wines by the glass.

Available upstairs are 29 comfortable guest rooms, each with TV. A double with a tub/shower rents for 95€, or 140€ for a junior suite.

13 rue des Berceaux, Epernay 51200. ℂ **03-26-55-28-84.** Fax 03-26-55-10-36. www.lesberceaux. com. Reservations recommended. Main courses 34€–72€; fixed-price menu 59€–69€. AE, DC, MC, V. Wed–Sun noon–2pm and 7–9pm. Closed early Feb to early Mar.

**La Table Kobus ★★** CHAMPENOISE    Just behind the church of Notre Dame, this gourmet brasserie scores well in all categories. It's quaint enough for a dinner *en couple*, yet laid back enough to be child friendly (glass panels between tables help with this).

The menu offers a seasonal selection of creatively prepared meat, fish, and poultry, such as cider-caramelized pigeon with sautéed apples and pumpkin gnocchi or lamb stuffed with prunes. In any case, you can't go wrong with seafood, as the owners also run a well-respected fish shop in town. The wine list features several dozen local champagnes.

3 rue Docteur Rousseau, Epernay 51200. ℂ **03-26-51-53-53.** www.la-table-kobus.com. Reservations recommended. Main courses 20€–34€; fixed-price menu 29€–49€. MC, V. Tues–Sun noon–2pm and 7:30–9:30pm. Closed Thurs evening, 2 weeks in Apr, 1st 3 weeks of Aug, Dec 28–Jan 8.

**La Grillade Gourmande ★** GRILL   The cuisine here is uncomplicated and delicious, based mostly on meat and fish grilled over a wood fire—a nice change if you've indulged in one too many French sauces. The atmosphere is far from that of a steakhouse, though—well-dressed businesspeople are often among the clientele. Inside there's a fireplace and outside, a shaded terrace.

16 rue de Reims, Epernay 51200. www.lagrilladegourmande.com. (C) **03-26-55-44-22.** Reservations recommended. Main courses 14€–26€; fixed-price menu 19€–55€. MC, V. Tues–Sat noon–2pm and 7–9pm. Closed 2 weeks in Aug and Feb.

# Epernay Nightlife

Start out at the chic cafe and bar **Le Progrès**, 5 place de la République ((C) **03-26-55-22-72**). The tasting bar **C Comme**, 8 rue Gambetta ((C) **03-26-32-09-55**) stays open till 1:30am on Fridays and Saturdays. Plan a *soirée* around discovering excellent but little known champagnes by the glass (a six-glass sampler costs around 30€; you can order cheese plates and other finger food).

   **The Vintage Café**, 34 rue du Docteur Verron ((C) **03-26-55-18-79**), transforms at night from champagne bar to a dance club featuring mostly electronic music. From Thursday to Saturday, **Le Coeur Kriss**, 160 avenue Foch ((C) **03-26-55-37-91**) starts bar service at 6 p.m. with dancing from 9 p.m. onwards. Free chauffeur service is offered within 10 kilometers (6 miles) from 9pm until 3am. English is spoken.

# Where to Stay

Les Berceaux (see "Where to Eat," previous page) also rents rooms.

## EXPENSIVE

**Royal Champagne ★★★**   This heart of this hotel is an 18th-century postal relay station. Perched on a hillside overlooking acres of vineyards and the Marne River, it affords one of the prettiest views in all of Champagne. The establishment's historic core contains the reception area, bar, and dining facilities; guest rooms are in town house–style accommodations just below. Decoration ranges from sumptuous in the larger rooms to elegant contemporary in the standard ones (these can feel a bit cramped). Private terraces provide a lovely breakfast spot in warm weather.

Champillon Bellevue 51160. www.royalchampagne.com. (C) **03-26-52-87-11.** Fax 03-26-52-89-69. 28 units. 280€–440€ double; 500€–660€ suite. AE, DC, MC, V. Closed early Nov–1 Mar. Drive 8km (5 miles) north from Epernay toward Reims on the rte. du Vignoble (N2051) to Champillon.
**Amenities:** Restaurant; bar; babysitting; room service. *In room:* A/C, TV, hair dryer, minibar, free Wi-Fi.

**Hostellerie La Briqueterie ★★★**   Surrounded by vineyards four kilometers (6.5 miles) from the center of Epernay, from the outside this hotel looks like it could have been transplanted from the California wine country. Make no mistake, however: the service, decor, and outstanding restaurant are thoroughly French. The low-ceilinged, colorful rooms are well decorated and cozy—request one away from the main road, which can be noisy during commute hours. La Briqueterie is the only hotel in the area offering spa services.

4 route de Sézanne, Vinay 51530. www.labriqueterie.fr. (C) **03-26-59-99-99.** Fax 03-26-59-92-10. 40 units. 190€–330€ double; 390€–460€ suite. AE, MC, V. From Epernay, follow signs for Sezanne

---

### Battles of the Marne

World War I history buffs automatically think of Verdun and its trenches but the Marne Valley saw more than its share of bloody conflict. The German offensive got no further west than **Château-Thierry** (87km/54 miles NE of Paris, 51km/32 miles SW of Reims via A4) thanks to a ferocious standoff with U.S. forces in early June 1918. Today an imposing hilltop monument commemorates the battle. Two days later, fighting began at the Bois de Belleau (**Belleau Wood**). Control of the area switched sides six times before the

Americans triumphed, having suffered more than 9,000 casualties. The American cemetery, also known as **Le Cimetière de Belleau** (✆ **03-23-70-70-90**), contains 2,288 graves and a chapel damaged in World War II. In a peaceful park in **Dormans,** the **Mémorial des Batailles de la Marne,** Parc du Château (✆ **03-26-53-35-86**) honors all soldiers killed in the summers of 1914 and 1918. The site houses a chapel and ossuary containing the bones of a thousand soldiers from the U.S. and Europe.

---

on D40, then take D951 4km (6.5 miles) to Vinay. **Amenities:** Restaurant; bar; babysitting; spa. *In room:* A/C, TV, hair dryer, minibar, free Wi-Fi.

## MODERATE

**La Villa Eugene ★★** This boutique hotel, just up the street from the grand villas of the avenue de Champagne, has gained steadily in popularity since it opened its doors a just a few years ago. A 19th-century mansion, it once belonged to the Mercier family. Comfortable rooms and suites are elegantly decorated in a variety of styles, from colonial to Louis XVI. Breakfast is served in a glass veranda overlooking the heated outdoor swimming pool.

82-84 avenue de Champagne, Epernay 51200. www.villa-eugene.com. ✆ **03-26-32-44-76.** Fax 03-26-32-44-98. 15 units. 129€–294€ double, 329€–344€. AE, MC, V. **Amenities:** Swimming pool. *In room:* A/C, TV, minibar.

**Le Clos Raymi ★** Guests of this boutique hotel, set inside a charming 19th-century residence once occupied by Monsieur Chandon (as in Moët et...), are treated to sumptuous beds and antique furnishings, and made to feel at home. It's a short (10-min.) but pleasant walk from the center of town.

30 rue Joseph de Venoge, Epernay 51200. www.closraymi-hotel.com. ✆ **03-26-51-00-58.** 7 units. 110€–170€ double. AE, MC, V. Free parking. *In room:* TV, free Wi-Fi.

# TROYES ★★

143km (89 miles) SE of Paris; 108km (67 miles) S of Reims

In the southwestern part of Champagne bordering Burgundy, the old center of Troyes is an architectural delight. The underwhelming approach past outlet malls and apartment-filled suburbs might tempt you to turn around and leave–but don't. In store is a walk-through history lesson, thanks to one of the largest remaining medieval residential quarters in France.

Troyes was known in Roman times as Augustobona and served as a meeting point between major roads. What's left of the Agrippa Way, linking Milan and Boulogne-sur-Mer on the northern coast, is buried 3m (10 ft.) under the current rue de la Cité. Stone from the ancient ramparts, long since destroyed, serves as foundations for some of the city's buildings, including the former Bishop's palace, now the Museum of Modern Art.

Gorgeously-restored, half-timbered 16th-century houses are the real show-stopper here. A project to bring them back to life, using antique engravings as a guide, began fifty years ago; today the jewel-colored dwellings are well on their way to earning UNESCO World Heritage status.

## Essentials

**GETTING THERE**  Troyes is a 2-hour **drive** southeast from Paris on the A104, then A105 and A5/E54 autoroutes. It's most easily reached by **train**, with departures out of Paris's Gare de l'Est nearly ever hour (trip time: 1½ hr.; 25€ one-way). Unfortunately, from Reims and Epernay you must go back through Paris. For information, visit www.voyages-sncf.com or call ✆ **08-36-35-35-35.** For information on bus service linking Troyes to other towns in Champagne, visit www.vitici.fr (choose the English option).

**VISITOR INFORMATION**  There are two **Offices de Tourisme.** One is next to the train station, 16 boulevard Carnot (✆ **03-25.82-62-70;** fax 03-25-73-06-81); the other is in the pedestrian district on rue Mignard across from the Eglise St. Jean (✆ **03-25-73-36-88**). Or visit www.tourisme-troyes.com.

## Exploring the Town

Keep your head up and camera ready: Wandering the ancient streets you'll find surprises around every corner, such as the **ruelle des Chats** (Cat's Alley)

**Ruelle des Chats.**

between 30 and 32 rue Champeaux. The buildings on either side lean so close that a cat can easily jump from one roof to the other. Sit on one of the benches in front of the **Carousel de Temps Moderne** (Carousel of the Modern Age), place de Hôtel de Ville, to admire its remarkable animals, chariots, and hand-painted depictions of 20th-century inventions and innovators.

**Cathédrale St-Pierre et St-Paul ★★★** CATHEDRAL  The spectacular stained glass windows in this cathedral—180 of them—helped Troyes earn its nickname, the "Holy City of Stained Glass." It can be rather dark inside, but on a sunny day you'll feel like you're in a jewel box.

Place St. Pierre. Free admission.

**Maison de l'Outil et de la Pensée Ouvrière (Museum of the Tool and Workers' Thought) ★★** MUSEUM  If you're short on time or antique tools are not your cup of tea, at least pop in to the courtyard of this museum, housed in the

Renaissance-style Hôtel de Mauroy, built in 1556. Embellished with exquisitely carved wooden gargoyles and crenellated pillars, it's a testament to the master craftsmanship of a much earlier time. Inside are 10,000 hand tools—each with a specific function, demonstrated in some cases with a video. The bookshop is extensive and worth browsing.

7 rue de la Trinité. www.maison-de-l-outil.com. ✆ **03-25-73-28-26.** Admission 6.50€; 3€ ages 12–18; free 11 and under. Daily 10am–6pm Apr–Sept, Wed–Mon 10am–6pm Oct–Mar. Closed 1st week in Jan, May 28, and Dec 25.

**Musée d'Art Moderne ★★** MUSEUM    Amazing what a tiny embroidered crocodile can lead to. The magnificent collection of Lacoste founders Pierre and Denise Lévy is displayed here, inside the 16th- to 19th-century Bishop's Palace. Among the works amassed by the couple are paintings by Picasso, Modiligiani, Matisse, Courbet, and Cezanne, making it one of the most varied exhibitions outside Paris.

Place St. Pierre. ✆ **03-25-76-26-80.** Free admission. May–Sept Tues-Fri 10am–1pm and 2–7pm, weekends 11am–7pm; Oct–Apr Tues–Fri 10am–noon and 2–5pm, weekends 11am–6pm. Closed Jan 1, Nov 11, and Dec 25.

**Musée de la Bonneterie (Hosiery and Knitwear Museum)** MUSEUM    Located in the ornate Hôtel de Vauluisant, this museum celebrates Troyes' long history as knitwear capital of France. The collection features knitting machines and wooden looms dating back to the 18th century, plus examples of intricate handiwork in the form of bonnets and stockings.

4 rue de Vauluisant. ✆ **03-25-43-43-20.** Free admission. May–Sept Wed 2–7pm, Thurs–Fri 10am–1pm and 2–7pm, weekends 11am–1pm and 2–7pm; Oct–Apr Wed–Thurs 2–5pm, Fri–Sun 10am–noon and 2–5pm. Closed Jan 1, Nov 11, and Dec 25.

# Shopping

Speaking of surprises, Troyes is home to one of the most renowned *pâtissier-chocolatiers* in the world. **Pascal Caffet** has taken first place in a half dozen international pastry and chocolate competitions—he's even been decorated by the French government for his cultural contribution. Caffet's sleek, eponymous shop, 2 rue de la Monnaie (✆ **03-25-73-35-73**), captivates eyes and sweet tooths in equal measure. Edible works of art include chocolates, fantastical cakes, and the most beautiful éclairs you'll ever see.

Opposite the cathedral, **Le Cellier St. Pierre,** 1 place St. Pierre (✆ **03-25-80-59-25**), has been open since 1840 and is the oldest continuously running shop in Troyes. It's also a distillery, where *Prunelle de Troyes,* a prune-based liqueur, is still made and for sale along with dozens of wines in every price category.

For whimsical souvenirs, especially for kids, head to **Enfantillages,** 27 rue Champeaux (✆ **03-25-73-71-99**), a tiny shop offering hand puppets and dozens of figurines including Le Petit Prince and Tintin (who is actually Belgian).

# Where to Eat

**La Mignardise ★★** CLASSIC FRENCH    This restaurant tucked away on the ruelle des Chats oozes character, and the food doesn't disappoint. Among the specialties offered by Chef Didier Defontaine are crispy duck breast with morel mushroom cream sauce and classic Tournedos Rossini with Burgundy truffles. If you're intrepid enough to try the local "delicacy" *andouillette de Troyes*—pork stomach sausage encased in intestine—this is surely the best place to do it (don't worry, most French people can't stand the idea either).

1 ruelle des Chats, Troyes 10000. www.lamignardise.net. *©* **03-25-73-15-30.** Reservations recommended. Main courses 27€–43€; fixed-price menu 34€–85€. AE, MC, V. Tues–Sun noon–2pm and 7:30–9pm. Closed early Feb to early Mar.

**Le Jardin Gourmand** ★ FRENCH   Here's another chance to try *andouillette*. Nearly a dozen different preparations feature on the menu, alongside unusual dishes such as chicken with dark chocolate and coffee. The interior is a bit fusty, so try to eat in *le jardin*, a tranquil courtyard seating 20.

31 rue Paillot de Montabert, Troyes 10000. *©* **03-25-73-36-13.** Reservations recommended. Main courses 21€–50€; fixed-price menu 17€–30€. MC, V. Mon–Sat noon–2pm and 7:30–10:30pm. Closed 2 weeks in Mar and Sept.

**La Clef de Voute** SWISS/FRENCH   Families will especially enjoy this cheerful corner spot, whose decoration may remind you of an Alpine chalet. The menu items are rather Alpine too: fondue and many other plates involving cheese. Even the salads are filling and enough for a meal. Heartier fare is served in winter, with a lighter menu offered during the warmer months, when tables spill out onto the cobbled street.

35 rue du Général Saussier, Troyes 10000. *©* **03-25-73-72-07.** Main courses 10€–25€; fixed-price menu 11€–30€. MC, V. Tues–Sat noon–2pm and 7:30–10pm.

# Where to Stay

**La Champ des Oiseaux** ★★   Comprising three 15th and 16th century buildings grouped around a pretty courtyard, this hotel contains 14 charming rooms, each rustically chic with lots of wood, cloud-like white beds, and antique furnishings. The public spaces are equally inviting, from the large fireplace in the lobby to the intimate library. Breakfast in the courtyard is a treat. Not a luxury property, but one with great style and personal service.

20 rue Linard Gonthier, Troyes 10000. www.champdesoiseaux.com. *©* **03-25-80-58-50.** Fax 03-25-80-98-34. 12 units. 149€–189€ double; 239€ suite. Parking 7€–10€. AE, DC, MC, V. **Amenities:** Babysitting. *In room:* TV, hair dryer, free Wi-Fi.

**Hôtel Clarion le Relais Saint Jean** ★   This hotel's half-timbered exterior belies the fact that there are 26 very contemporary rooms inside. They're a bit small, but the ideal location and attentive, mostly English-speaking staff make up for it. An unusual feature is a Jacuzzi installed in the 16th-century cellar, free to guests who reserve. The underground parking is somewhat hard to navigate but welcome in the mostly pedestrian neighborhood. There's no restaurant, but several choices lie within a 5-minute walk.

51 rue Paillot de Montaberte 51160. www.hotel-relais-saint-jean.com. *©* **03-25-73-89-90.** Fax 03-26-73-88-60. 24 units. 130€–150€ double; 160€–210€ suite. AE, DC, MC, V. **Amenities:** Bar; Jacuzzi. *In room:* A/C, TV, hair dryer, minibar, free Wi-Fi.

**Hôtel Best Western De La Poste**   Best Westerns in France tend to have more character than those in the United States. The Hôtel de la Poste is no exception. Standard rooms are decorated in basic business style, but suites under the roof manage to work in exposed beams and skylights (reaching them means climbing a short staircase, as the elevator stops one floor below). Private parking is available 5 minutes away (drop your bags at the hotel first).

35 rue Emile Zola, Troyes 10000. www.hotel-de-la-poste.com. 📞 **03-25-73-05-05.** Fax 03-25-73-80-76. 32 units. 118€–138€ double; 177€ suite. Parking 10€. AE, DC, MC, V. **Amenities:** Bar. *In room:* A/C, TV, hair dryer, minibar, free Wi-Fi.

---

## A Side Trip to Amiens

Is it worth it to drive from Reims Cathedral to see yet another one? If that cathedral is in Amiens, the answer is absolutely. **Amiens,** the capital of Picardy, has been a textile center since medieval days. Its old town is a warren of jumbled streets and canals, branching off from the south bank of the Somme River. It's main draw is the boldly Gothic **Cathédrale Notre-Dame d'Amiens** (Place Notre-Dame; 📞 **03-22-71-60-50**), France's largest cathedral. The dazzling, UNESCO-protected cathedral was started in 1220 to house the head of St. John the Baptist (still visible today), brought back from the Crusades in 1206. One of the biggest Gothic cathedrals ever constructed, it's 145m (475 ft.) tall with a girth of 200,000 cubic meters (more than 7 million cubic feet).

From the cathedral, head to the city's **Quartier St-Leu.** Just below the cathedral, across the water, the quarter used to be a thriving medieval craft center, bustling with water mills. Today its narrow streets contain art galleries, bookshops, and antiques boutiques, making the area a wonderful place to wander. During the Saturday morning *marché sur l'eau* (water market, which takes place throughout June), farmers from the nearby Hortillonnages marshlands hawk their fares from small boats floating on the waters.

While in Amiens, be sure to also visit the **Museé de Picardie** (48 rue de la République; 📞 **03-22-97-14-00**), with a fine collection of Egyptian and Greek antiquities, pieces from around the Picardie region, and an amazing assembly of paintings from the 17th to the 20th centuries. Another big attraction is the **Maison de Jules Verne** (2 rue Charles Dubois; 📞 **03-22-45-45-75**), a stately townhouse where the author plunged himself into his imaginary worlds. Period rooms convey how the house would have looked in Verne's day, and a collection of more than 700 objects reveals the author's inspiration.

To get to Amiens from Reims, take the A26 north 45 km (28 miles) to Laon, and then head west on N44 to N32, which becomes D394 to Amiens. Amiens is also on the main autoroute (A1) from Paris, about a 90 minute drive. There are also 3 trains a day from Reims, which requires a transfer in Laon or Tergnier, and 4 or 5 trains a day direct from Paris.

# ALSACE & LORRAINE

by Caroline Sieg

10

**A**lsace and Lorraine, with ancient capitals at Strasbourg and Nancy, have been the object of many disputes between Germany and France. In fact, they were annexed by Germany from 1870 until after WWI and from 1940 to 1944. Though they've remained part of France since the end of WWII, they feel a bit different from the rest of France. In fact, Alsace has been called "the least French of French provinces," more reminiscent of the Black Forest across the Rhine. Lorraine, with its rolling landscape, appears and feels more French in character.

In the Vosges Mountains, you can follow **La Route des Crêtes (Crest Road)** or skirt the foothills, visiting the wine towns of Alsace. In its cities and cathedrals, the castle-dotted landscape evokes a past filled with military glory or defeat. Lorraine is Joan of Arc country, and many of its towns still suggest their medieval heritage.

# STRASBOURG ★★★

488km (303 miles) SE of Paris; 217km (135 miles) SW of Frankfurt

Situated about 483km (300 miles) southeast of Paris and tucked in the elbow of northwest France, Strasbourg ping-ponged between Germany and France for centuries. Today this capital of wine-growing Alsace blends Teutonic might with a cosmopolitan flair. All canals and cobblestones, half-timbered houses and Gothic spires, this UNESCO World Heritage Site on the River Ill weaves fairy-tale charm with the European Parliament's political clout.

**Things to Do**   Whatever you do, be sure to visit the **Gothic Cathédrale Notre-Dame de Strasbourg**. The big event here occurs at 12:30pm, when carved wooden figures whirl and change in its astronomical clock. After, admire the cathedral's stunning 12th- to 14th-century stained-glass windows. **La Petite France** is worth a slow stroll; the area is home to an enchanting scene of half-timbered houses, canals, and medieval bridges. The sumptuous, rococo **Palais de Rohan** shelters the Musée des Beaux-Arts, with work by Rubens and Rembrandt. All of the above sit on Grand Ile, a designated UNESCO Heritage Site and an island ensconced within the city.

**Shopping**   Delicate **ceramics and pottery** and high-quality **textiles** abound throughout Strasbourg's historic center; your best bets are around the Cathédrale and place des Halles; head to **Nappes d'Alsace** for Alsatian napkins, tea towels, and the like, or **Bastian** for 18th- and 19th-century ceramic tureens. In late November and December, the place de Cathédrale erupts with the magical **Marché de Noël** (Christmas Market), where you can purchase handmade ornaments and gifts and warm up with hot vin chaud (mulled wine).

**Nightlife & Entertainment**   Each summer, the illuminated **place de la Cathédrale** and other outdoor venues in town come alive after dark with

PREVIOUS PAGE: **Alsatian buildings in Strasbourg.**

**Alsace & Lorraine**

world-class drama, dance, and classical concerts. For innovative ballet and opera, make your way to **Opéra du Rhin,** while the **Orchestre Philharmonique de Strasbourg** performs at the Palais de la Musique et des Congrès, north of the center. Dance the night away at one of the biggest discos in the region, **Le Chalet,** a few miles north of the city.

**Restaurants & Dining**   Strasbourg cuisine mixes hearty local staples with French finesse. But it's most famous dish is **flammekueche,** a thin, crispy tart often topped with cheese, ham, and/or mushrooms. It's best sampled at one of the traditional restaurants on and around place de la Cathédrale. Also, kick back and sip **Alsatian wine** such as pinot blanc or local sparkling wine **Crémant d'Alsace** on a riverside terrace in **La Petite France.**

# Essentials

**GETTING THERE**   The **Strasbourg-Entzheim Airport** (Aéroport International Strasbourg; www.strasbourg.aeroport.fr; ✆ **03-88-64-67-67**), 15km (9¼ miles) southwest of the city center, receives daily flights from many European cities, including Paris, London, Rome, Vienna, and Moscow. The **shuttle train** (look for the signs to pedestrian footbridge connecting the airport to the station platform) whisks you to Strasbourg main station in 9 minutes. They run every 15 minutes from 5am until 10pm Monday through Friday, twice an hour on Saturday between 6am and 9pm and once to twice per hour on Sundays between 8am and 9pm. The one-way cost is 3.60€ and includes connection to the municipal tram system. For information, call ✆ **03-88-77-70-70.**

The superfast TGV train makes round-trips from Paris to Strasbourg, cutting travel time nearly in half to 2 hours, 20 minutes. At least 15 **trains** a day arrive from Paris's Gare de l'Est (trip time: 4 hr.); the one-way fare is 65€ to 95€. For information and schedules, call ✆ **36-35** or 08-92-35-35-35.

By **car,** the giant A35 crosses the plain of Alsace, with occasional references to its original name, the N83. It links Strasbourg with Colmar and Mulhouse.

**VISITOR INFORMATION**  The **Office de Tourisme** is on 17 place de la Cathédrale (www.otstrasbourg.fr; ✆ **03-88-52-28-28;** fax 03-88-52-28-29); There is a second branch inside the main train station (same telephone number as above).

**SPECIAL EVENTS**  The **Classical Music Festival** runs for 2 weeks in June, and the **Festival de Jazz** runs in early July (both www.festival-strasbourg.com; ✆ **03-88-15-29-29**). They feature international artists and draw large crowds. Ticket prices range from 24€ to 75€ and go on sale in mid-April. **Wolf Music,** 24 rue de la Mésange (✆ **03-88-32-43-10;** http://wolf-musique.musicunivers.com), arranges ticket sales for these festivals. The Association Musica (www.festival-musica.org; ✆ **03-88-23-46-46**) organizes the **Festival International des Musiques d'Aujourd'hui.** It takes place from the end of September to the first week of October and combines contemporary music concerts with movies and modern opera performances. Tickets are 8€ to 25€ and go on sale at the end of June.

# Exploring Strasbourg

Despite WWI and WWII damage, much remains of Old Strasbourg, including covered bridges and towers from its former fortifications, plus many 15th- and 17th-century dwellings with painted wooden fronts and carved beams.

La Petite France.

# Strasbourg

Parc du Contades

**ATTRACTIONS**
Cathédrale Notre-Dame de Strasbourg **16**
Église St-Thomas **8**
Hôtel du Commerce **7**
Musée Alsacien **10**
Musée de l'Oeuvre Notre Dame **12**
Musée d'Art Moderne et Contemporain Strasbourg **1**
Palais de Rohan **17**

**HOTELS**
Hilton International Strasbourg **21**
Hôtel Beaucour **9**
Hôtel Cardinal de Rohan **13**
Hôtel de l'Ill **18**
Hôtel Gutenberg **14**
Le Régent Contades **19**
Le Régent Petite France **3**

**RESTAURANTS**
Au Crocodile **4**
Brasserie de l'Ancienne Douane **11**
Chez Yvonne **5**
Le Buerehiesel **22**
Maison des Tanneurs **2**
Maison Kammerzell **15**
Winstub Le Clou **6**

381

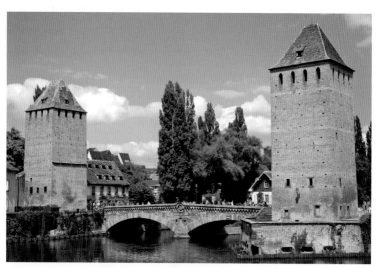

Ponts Couverts, one of Strasbourg's medieval bridges.

The city's traffic hub is **place Kléber ★**, dating from the 15th century. Sit here with a tankard of Alsatian beer and get to know Strasbourg. The bronze statue in the center is of J. B. Kléber, born in Strasbourg in 1753; he became one of Napoleon's most noted generals and was buried under the monument. Apparently, his presence offended the Nazis, who removed the statue in 1940. This Alsatian bronze was restored to its proper place in 1945.

From here, take rue des Grandes-Arcades southeast to **place Gutenberg,** one of the city's oldest squares. The central statue (1840), by David d'Angers, is of Gutenberg, who perfected his printing press in Strasbourg in the winter of 1436 and 1437. The former town hall, now the **Hôtel du Commerce,** was built in 1582 and is one of the most significant Renaissance buildings in Alsace. The neighborhoods within a few blocks of the city's **cathedral** are loaded with medieval references and historical charm.

**La Petite France ★★** is the most interesting quarter of Strasbourg. A virtual island, it's surrounded by scenic canals on four sides, and its 16th-century houses reflect in the waters of the Ill River. In "Little France," old roofs with gray

---

 **Strasbourg by Boat**

Floating through Strasbourg on a boat excursion on the Ill River from the Palais de Rohan is one of the best ways to see the city. The 75-minute cruises cost 9.20€ for adults and 4.80€ for children. They include recorded commentary in six languages. From March to early November, rides depart at 30-minute intervals daily between 9:30am and 9pm, with hours extended to 10pm May to September. In November, departures are at 10:30am, and 1, 2:30, and 4pm; in December-February, rides depart every half-hour from 9:30am to 5pm. For information, call Batorama, 9 rue de Nantes (www. batorama.fr; © **03-88-84-13-13**).

Cathédrale Notre-Dame de Strasbourg.

tiles have sheltered families for ages, and the cross-beamed facades with roughly carved rafters are in typical Alsatian style. For a good view, walk along rue des Moulins, branching off from rue du Bain-aux-Plantes.

**Cathédrale Notre-Dame de Strasbourg ★★★** CATHEDRAL   The city's crowning glory is an outstanding example of Gothic architecture, representing a transition from the Romanesque. Construction began in 1176. The pyramidal tower in rose-colored stone was completed in 1439; at 141m (462 ft.), it's the tallest one from medieval times. This cathedral is still in use. Religious ceremonies, particularly on feast days, meld perfectly with the architectural majesty. Individual tourists can visit the tower only in the summer (you may have to wait to climb it). The Office de Tourisme (see above) organizes tours for groups; call for the schedule.

Four large counterforts divide the **main facade ★★★** into three vertical parts and two horizontal galleries. Note the **rose window,** which looks like stone lace. The facade is rich in decoration: On the portal of the south transept, the *Coronation and Death of the Virgin* in one of the two tympanums is the finest such medieval work. In the north transept, see also the facade of the **Chapelle St-Laurence,** a stunning achievement of the late Gothic German style.

A Romanesque **crypt** lies under the chancel, which is covered with square stonework. The stained-glass window is the work of Max Ingrand. The **nave** is majestic, with windows depicting emperors and kings on the north Strasbourg aisle. Five chapels cluster around the transept, including one built in 1500 in the Flamboyant Gothic style. In the south transept stands the **Angel Pillar ★★,** illustrating the Last Judgment, with angels lowering their trumpets.

The **astronomical clock ★** was built between 1547 and 1574. It stopped during the Revolution, and from 1838 to 1842, the mechanism was replaced. Each day at 12:30pm, crowds gather to see its show of allegorical figures. On Sunday, Apollo drives his sun horses; on Thursday, you see Jupiter and his eagle.

The body of the clock has a planetarium based on the theories of Copernicus. Close-up views of the clock are available Monday to Saturday noon to 12:30pm; tickets (2€ adults, 1.50€ ages 5–18 and students) go on sale in the south portal at 11:45am.

Place de la Cathédrale. ℂ **03-88-32-75-78** for times of services. Cathedral: Daily 7am–7pm. Tower: ℂ **03-88-43-60-40.** Apr–Sept daily 9am–7:15pm; Oct–Mar daily 10am–5:15pm. Tower admission 4.70€ adults, 2.30€ children 17 and under and students.

**Eglise St-Thomas** CHURCH   Built between 1230 and 1330, this Protestant church houses five naves. It contains the **mausoleum ★★** of Maréchal de Saxe, a masterpiece of French art by Pigalle (1777).

Rue Martin-Luther (along rue St-Thomas, near pont St-Thomas). ℂ **03-88-32-14-46.** Free admission. Apr–Oct daily 10am–6pm; Nov–Dec & Mar daily 10am–5pm; Feb daily 2–5pm. Closed Jan.

**Musée Alsacien ★** MUSEUM   This museum occupies three mansions from the 16th and 17th centuries. It's like a living textbook of the folklore and customs of Alsace, containing arts, crafts, and tools of the old province.

23 quai St-Nicolas. www.musees.strasbourg. ℂ **03-88-52-50-01.** Admission 6€ adults, 3€ students, free for children 17 and under. Wed–Fri and Mon noon–6pm; Sat–Sun 10am–6pm.

**Musée d'Art Moderne et Contemporain Strasbourg (MAMCS)** MUSEUM   In the heart of La Petite France, this is Strasbourg's showcase of modern European art. Don't take the word *modern* too literally—the collection dates from 1870 to the present. The layout of the museum starts with a historical section tracing the emergence of modern art and going forward to the 21st century. Other facilities include a graphic art and photography room, an art library, a museum shop, and a cafe-restaurant on the terrace.

1 place Jean-Hans Arp. www.musees.strasbourg.eu. ℂ **03-88-23-31-31.** Admission 7€ adults, 3.50€ students 24 and under and seniors, free for children 17 and under. Tues–Wed and Fri noon–7pm; Thurs noon–9pm; Sat–Sun 10am–6pm.

**Musée de l'Oeuvre Notre-Dame ★★★** MUSEUM   This museum illustrates the art of the Middle Ages and Renaissance in Strasbourg and Alsace. Some pieces were displayed in the cathedral, where copies have been substituted. The most celebrated is a stained-glass head of Christ from about the 11th century. There's also a window depicting an emperor from around 1200. The sculpture is of great interest, as are the works of Strasbourg goldsmiths from the 16th and 17th centuries. The winding staircase and interior are in the Renaissance style. The 13th-century hall contains sculptures from the cathedral, including the wise and foolish virgins from 1280.

3 place du Château. www.musees.strasbourg.eu. ℂ **03-88-52-50-00.** Admission 6€ adults, 3€ students, free for children 17 and under. Tues–Fri noon–6pm; Sat–Sun 10am–6pm.

**Palais de Rohan ★★** PALACE   This palace south of the cathedral was built from 1732 to 1742. It's an example of supreme elegance and proportion. Noted for its facades and rococo interior, it's one of the crowning design achievements in eastern France. On the first floor is a fine-arts museum (Musée des Beaux-Arts) with works by Rubens, Rembrandt, Van Dyck, El Greco, Goya, Watteau, Renoir, and Monet. On the street level is a decorative-arts museum that exhibits ceramics and the original machinery of the cathedral's first astronomical clock. Also on the premises are collections of artifacts excavated from nearby digs,

ALSACE & LORRAINE

focusing especially on art and utilitarian objects from the Roman and early medieval (Merovingian) eras.

2 place du Château. (✆ **03-88-52-50-00.** Admission 6€ adults, 3€ students, free for children 17 and under; combo ticket 8€ adults, 4€ students, free for children 17 and under. Wed–Mon noon–6pm.

## Shopping

Strasbourg overflows with antiques shops, artisans, craftspeople, and beer makers. Every well-accessorized home in Alsace owns some of the napkins, aprons, tablecloths, and tea and bath towels of the Beauvillé textile mills. **Nappes d'Alsace,** 6 rue Mercière, near the cathedral ((✆ **03-88-22-69-29**), has one of the widest selections of textiles in town.

**Bastian,** 22–24 place de la Cathédrale ((✆ **03-88-32-45-93**), specializes in 18th- and 19th-century ceramic tureens that Alsace produced in abundance. Look for ragout pots in the forms of a cabbage, a trout, a boar's head, or a turkey, painted in bright colors. There's also a selection of Louis XV and Louis XVI furniture, crafted in the region during the 18th and 19th centuries following Parisian models from the same era.

Bastian's main competitor is **Ville et Campagne,** 23 quai des Bateliers ((✆ **03-88-36-96-84**), housed in a Renaissance-style 17th-century building across from the Palais de Rohan. Standout items are polychromed Alsatian antiques (especially 18th- and 19th-c. armoires and chests), Louis- and Directoire-style furnishings, statues, and antique paintings.

One of the most appealing shops in Strasbourg is **Arts et Collections d'Alsace,** 4 place du Marché aux Poissons ((✆ **03-88-14-03-77**), which sells copies of art objects and utilitarian ware from museums and private collections through Alsace. You'll see upscale gift items for the home and kitchen, made from pottery, stone, wrought iron, glass, copper, and carved wood. The shop also sells fabric by the yard.

A name in pottery that you're likely to encounter is **Soufflenheim,** a provincial rococo pattern—usually in blues and reds—named after the Alsatian village north of Strasbourg where the style originated. To get there, take N63 north of the center of Strasbourg for 24km (15 miles). In the village, ceramics and pottery have been made since the Bronze Age. Soufflenheim is home to at least a dozen outlets selling cake molds, tureens, saucers and cups, dinnerware, and more, usually in rustic patterns. One of the most prominent retailers is **Gérard Wehrling,** 64 rue de Haguenau ((✆ **03-88-86-65-25**), known for pottery that can withstand the rigors of modern ovens, microwaves, and refrigerators.

If you're driving, you may want to check out the villages of Obernai, Illhaeusern, Ribeauvillé, and Schiltigheim. The last is beer-drinking territory; the others offer country wares and antiques.

## Where to Eat

### VERY EXPENSIVE

**Au Crocodile ★★★** ALSATIAN   A beautiful sky-lit restaurant, Au Crocodile serves the most inventive food in Strasbourg—they manage to offer both regional specialties alongside exotic flavors. Some of the best dishes include sautéed scallops with purée of celery and Indian-style spiced butter sauce; delicate local freshwater whitefish (*sandre*) served in sauerkraut; and duck liver cooked in a salt crust and pigeon served with an amer sauce (Amer is a local specialty which mixes beer and an orange-flavored bitter). Note that their wine list is on the pricey side, but well worth the splurge.

10 rue de l'Outre. www.au-crocodile.com. (✆ **03-88-32-13-02.** Reservations required. Main courses 49€–74€; fixed-price menu 138€–175€. AE, DC, MC, V. Tues–Sat noon–1:30pm and 7:30–9:30pm. Closed last 3 weeks of July and Dec 24–29.

**Le Buerehiesel** ★★★ MODERN FRENCH   Also known as Le Restaurant Westermann, Buerehiesel is famous for its *cuisine moderne* and for its prime location in l'Orangerie, a park at the end of the allée de la Robertsau planned by the landscape artist Le Nôtre, who gave the park to Joséphine during her marriage to Napoleon. The decor includes richly grained wooden ceilings and a conservatively modern design. The kitchen recycles heirloom recipes in innovative and exciting ways. Of special merit are foie gras of goose with truffles; frogs' legs fried with local herbs; ravioli stuffed with confit of onions; and steamed sea bass with a marinade of crisp, al dente vegetables and aromatic herbs. Appealingly old-fashioned, and prepared for only two diners at a time, is one of the Alsace's most classic recipes, *poularde baeckoffe:* Consisting of a top-quality Bresse hen that's slow-cooked in a covered ceramic dish, it comes in versions appropriate to both summer (with potatoes, artichoke hearts, and a confit of lemons) and winter (with leeks, potatoes, and truffles).

4 parc de l'Orangerie. www.buerehiesel.fr. (✆ **03-88-45-56-65.** Reservations required. Main courses 21€–53€; fixed-price menu 35€–90€. AE, DC, MC, V. Tues–Sat noon–2pm and 7–10pm. Closed 1st 3 weeks of Jan and 1st 3 weeks of Aug.

## MODERATE

**Chez Yvonne** ★ FRENCH/ALSATIAN   Journalists and other political dignitaries frequent this traditional Alsatian *winstub,* which has operated here since 1873. It's located near the cathedral in the middle of the historic core. The backdrop is in the traditional bistro style, with lots of wood and red-checked curtains. Steaming platters of well-prepared food emerge from the kitchen, including such appetizers as snails Alsatian or foie gras of the house. For a main course, opt for such temptations as hen cooked in Riesling and served with spaëtzle, or choucroute (sauerkraut) with pork products. Suckling pig is another one of the specialties.

10 rue du Sanglier. www.chez-yvonne.net. (✆ **03-88-32-84-15.** Reservations required. Main courses 13€–25€. AE, DC, MC, V. Daily noon–2:15pm and 6pm–midnight.

**Maison des Tanneurs** ★ ALSATIAN   This longtime favorite, housed in a building from 1572, opened in 1949. The antique-filled restaurant features a warm atmosphere, and has a terrace that opens onto the canal. The restaurant has been called "La Maison de la Choucroute" because its sauerkraut-and-pork platter is the finest in the area. But the chef prepares many other tasty dishes, including snails cooked Alsatian style with local white wine, a traditional version of Strasbourg foie gras, and guinea fowl stuffed with green peppers. We recommend crayfish tails in court bouillon and *coq au Riesling* (chicken cooked in white wine, with noodles).

42 rue du Bain-aux-Plantes. (✆ **03-88-32-79-70.** Reservations required. Main courses 20€–25€; fixed-price lunch 20€–26€. AE, DC, MC, V. Tues–Sat noon–1:45pm and 7–10pm (also Sun noon–2pm in Dec). Closed first 2 weeks in Jan.

**Maison Kammerzell** ★ ☺ ALSATIAN   The gingerbread Maison Kammerzell is an attraction as well as a fantastic restaurant. The carved-wood framework was constructed during the Renaissance, the overhanging stories in 1589. We suggest *la choucroute formidable,* the Alsatian specialty prepared with goose fat, Riesling wine, and Strasbourg sausages. The owner, Guy-Pierre Baumann, also prepares homemade foie gras, guinea hen with mushrooms, medallion of young wild boar, and other regional dishes. A concession to modern cuisine is the chef's version of sauerkraut with fish.

16 place de la Cathédrale. www.maison-kammerzell.com. ℂ **03-88-32-42-14.** Reservations required. Main courses 17€–26€; fixed-price menu 32€–48€. AE, DC, MC, V. Daily noon–2:30pm and 7–11pm.

## INEXPENSIVE

**Brasserie de l'Ancienne Douane** ★ ALSATIAN   This is the largest and most colorful dining spot in Strasbourg. The high-ceilinged rooms are somewhat formal, with Teutonic chairs and heavily timbered ceilings. Among the Alsatian specialties are the well-known "sauerkraut of the Customs officers" and the foie gras of Strasbourg. Onion pie and ham knuckle with potato salad and horseradish are also popular.

6 rue de la Douane. www.anciennedouane.fr. ℂ **03-88-15-78-78.** Reservations recommended. Main courses 16€–24€; fixed-price menu 25€–32€. AE, DC, MC, V. Daily 11:30am–2:30pm and 6:30–11pm.

**Winstub Le Clou** ★★ 🍴 ALSATIAN   With its long communal tables, this restaurant has a typical *winstub* vibe (a *winstub*—which literally means "wine room"—is a traditional Alsatian restaurant oozing coziness and warmth). They specialize in typical Alsatian fare, like *baeckoffe* (a hearty meat stew) or *jambon en cruote* (ham wrapped with a crispy crust). One of their specialties is *choucroute en wädele*—Alsatian sauerkraut with think hunks of ham. It's gut-filling comfort food in a convivial atmosphere.

3 rue de Chaudron. www.le-clou.com. ℂ **03-88-32-11-67.** Main courses 16€–24€; fixed-price menu 17€–26€. AE, MC, V. Mon–Tues and Thurs–Sat 11:30am–2:15pm; Mon–Sat 5:30–midnight.

# Strasbourg Nightlife

A bastion of outdoor entertainment is **place de la Cathédrale,** where you can find an assortment of performers and artists. Dancers perform spontaneously against the illumination of the cathedral. From mid-July to early August, additional folk dances take place in La Petite France on Monday night in place des Tripiers, Tuesday in place Benjamin Zix, and Wednesday in place du Marché aux Cochons de Lait. Performance dates vary; check with the Office de Tourisme (www.otstrasbourg.fr; ℂ 03-88-52-28-29) for a schedule.

**THE PERFORMING ARTS**   For opera and ballet, seek out the **Opéra du Rhin,** 19 place Broglie (www.operanationaldurhin.fr; ℂ **03-88-75-48-23**); tickets cost 12€ to 80€. The **Orchestre Philharmonique de Strasbourg** performs at the Palais de la Musique et des Congrès, place de Bordeaux (www.philharmonique-strasbourg.com; ℂ **03-69-06-37-00**). Tickets cost 20€ to 55€. The **Théâtre National de Strasbourg** plays a busy schedule at 1 av. de la Marseillaise (www.tns.fr; ℂ **03-88-24-88-00**). Tickets cost 5.50€ to 25€.

**CLUBS**  Head to the streets surrounding place de la Cathédrale: rue des Frères, rue des Soeurs, and rue de la Croix. **Jeannette et les Cycleux,** 3 rue des Tonneliers (www.lenetdejeannette.com; ℂ **03-88-23-02-71**), is a wine bar with a jukebox playing rock 'n' roll and other hits from America in the 1950s. Entrance is free.

Le Seven, 25 rue des Tonneliers (ℂ **03-88-32-77-77**; http://leseven strasbourg.com), has a below-street-level dance floor that features all types of music except disco. The place packs in a stylish crowd ages 20 to 35.

One of the biggest and most visible discos in the region, **Le Chalet,** 376 rte. de Wantzenau (ℂ **03-88-31-18-31**), lies 8km (5 miles) north of Strasbourg. The cover buys the first drink and access to two huge and distinctly different sections. One is designed for techno fans, another for less harsh dance music, with a good mix of disco classics. It's open 10pm to 4am Friday and Saturday and cover charges vary: Free entry 10 to 11pm Friday; 5€ Friday 11 to midnight or Sat 10 to 11pm; 8€ Saturday 11pm to midnight; 10€ Friday and Saturday after midnight. To get here, follow signs to Wantzenau.

# Where to Stay
## EXPENSIVE
### Hilton International Strasbourg ★  The luxurious, seven-story steel-and-glass Hilton stands over a university complex opposite the Palais de la Musique et des Congrès. The decor incorporates five kinds of Iberian marble, much of it chosen to resemble the ruddy sandstone of the famous cathedral, which is visible from the hotel. Midsize guest rooms are standard business chain style—comfortable and solid. But they do contain spacious marble-trimmed bathrooms.

Av. Herrenschmidt, Strasbourg 67000. www.hilton-strasbourg.com. ℂ **800/445-8667** in the U.S. and Canada, or 03-88-37-10-10. Fax 03-88-25-55-03. 243 units. 180€–390€ double; from 470€ suite. AE, DC, MC, V. Parking 19€. Take the Strasbourg-Centre exit from the autoroute and follow signs to the Wacken, Palais des Congrès, and Palais de l'Europe. **Amenities:** 2 restaurants; 1 bar; babysitting; exercise room; room service; sauna. *In room:* A/C, TV, hair dryer, minibar, free Wi-Fi.

### Le Régent Petite France ★★  This well-run hotel gives serious competition for best in town. Many guests choose it for its more comfortable rooms, atmosphere, and prime location in the picturesque Petite France. This site was once an ice factory, and many of the old steam machines remain. The marble lobby sets the tone, with ice-cream colors and potted palms. Guest rooms come in various sizes, the best of which are spacious and open onto river views. The beds are top luxury; the bathrooms are marble-clad and fit for a royal.

5 rue des Moulins, Strasbourg 67000. www.regent-petite-france.com. ℂ **800/223-5652** in the U.S. and Canada, or 03-88-76-43-43. Fax 03-88-76-43-76. 72 units. 160€–510€ double; 245€–740€ suite. AE, DC, MC, V. Parking 22€. **Amenities:** Restaurant; bar; babysitting; exercise room; room service; sauna. *In room:* A/C, TV, hair dryer, Jacuzzi (in suites), minibar, free Wi-Fi.

## MODERATE
### Hôtel Beaucour ★★  This hotel is geared toward business travelers, but anyone will find it ideal—it's the city's most tranquil lodging. At the end of a private street a few blocks east of the cathedral, within what used to be an umbrella factory, it occupies a 17th-century building with timbered ceilings. Every double

and suite contains a whirlpool tub. Furnishings are of standard international style, but comfortable. The staff is exceptionally friendly and are happy to give you insider tips based on your needs.

5 rue des Bouchers, Strasbourg 67000. www.hotel-beaucour.com. © **03-88-76-72-00.** Fax 03-88-76-72-60. 49 units. 116€–165€ double; 115€–220€ suite. AE, DC, MC, V. Parking 8.50€. **Amenities:** Babysitting. *In room:* TV, hair dryer, minibar, free Wi-Fi.

### Hôtel Cardinal de Rohan ★ 

In the pedestrian zone steps from the cathedral, this five-story hotel is one of the city's best values and within walking distance of the Palais de Rohan. The 17th-century building was rebuilt shortly after World War II. It offers a choice of elegantly furnished rooms, the cheapest of which are small and have a French bed called a *matrimonial* (a standard double bed). Guest-room decor ranges from Louis XV to a regional Alsatian look with lots of wood paneling.

17–19 rue du Maroquin, Strasbourg 67060. www.hotel-rohan.com. © **03-88-32-85-11.** Fax 03-88-75-65-37. 36 units. 65€–185€ double. AE, DC, MC, V. Parking 17€. **Amenities:** Babysitting. *In room:* A/C, TV, hair dryer, minibar, free Wi-Fi.

### Le Régent Contades ★★ 

Our favorite moderately priced choice is this glorified B&B, in a five-story structure with dormers, close to the cathedral. Diplomats may consider it a secret, but word is out. The stylish hostelry has an intelligent, helpful staff. The guest rooms are furnished in a romantic style with a variety of monochromatic colors that include pink, blue, or soft browns or reds. Breakfast is the only meal served.

8 av. de la Liberté, Strasbourg 67000. www.regent-contades.com. © **03-88-15-05-05.** Fax 03-88-15-05-15. 47 units. 105€–325€ double; 170€–560€ suite. AE, DC, MC, V. Parking 20€. **Amenities:** Bar; room service. *In room:* A/C, TV, hair dryer, minibar, free Wi-Fi.

## INEXPENSIVE

### Hôtel de l'Ill 

A 5-minute walk from the cathedral, this is a solid budget choice. Originally a restaurant, it added rooms in the 1920s and later, in the 1990s, the property became a hotel only and gained a modern wing. An inviting and unpretentious place, it houses quiet, comfortably furnished rooms decorated in either modern or Alsatian traditional style. Two rooms at the rear have a private terrace or balcony opening onto a view of neighboring gardens. Each room comes with a tidily kept shower-only bathroom, but no amenities other than a phone (some have a TV).

8 quai des Bateliers, Strasbourg 67000. www.hotel-ill.com. 27 units. © **03-88-36-20-01.** Fax 03-88-35-30-03. 70€–110€ double. AE, MC, V. Parking 9€. **Amenities:** Free Wi-Fi. *In room:* A/C (in some), TV.

### Hôtel Gutenberg ★ 

Just off place Gutenberg, this many-windowed hotel is both a bargain and a discovery. The mansion exudes old-fashioned charm with the sculptured walls dating to 1745. Many of the guest rooms, with flowery draperies and antiques, have wooden beams. The most romantic accommodations, evoking old France, are on the fifth floor under timbers. All rooms have superb modern bathrooms and flat screen TVs.

31 rue des Serruriers, Strasbourg 67000. www.hotel-gutenberg.com. © **03-88-32-17-15.** Fax 03-88-75-76-67. 42 units. 85€–165€ double. AE, MC, V. **Amenities:** Free Internet. *In room:* A/C (in some), TV.

## Where to Eat & Stay Nearby

Many visitors head north 12km (7½ miles) to La Wantzenau, which has very good restaurants. From Strasbourg, take D468 along the west bank of the Rhine.

**Relais de la Poste ★★★** FRENCH/ALSATIAN   The leading restaurant in this citadel of fine dining is a cozy half-timbered 18th-century house in the heart of the little Alsatian village. The chefs depend on the changing seasons for their inspiration. They prepare traditional dishes with a modern twist, lighter versions of old favorites. Their succulent concoctions include boned and stuffed quail with a sauce of morels, and fried turbot osso buco with Szechuan peppercorn sauce. Two superb appetizers are fresh goose liver and game terrine.

The inn also rents 18 comfortably furnished guest rooms, each in a rustic style, for a double rate of 85€ to 160€.

21 rue du Général-de-Gaulle, La Wantzenau 67610. www.relais-poste.com. *℃* **03-88-59-24-80.** Fax 03-88-59-24-89. Main courses 28€–49€; fixed-price menu 50€–130€. AE, DC, MC, V. Tues–Fri and Sun noon–2pm; Tues–Sat 7–10pm. Closed 1st 2 weeks of Jan.

# LA ROUTE DU VIN (WINE ROAD) ★★★

The fastest route between Strasbourg and Colmar, 68km (42 miles) south, is N83. But if you have time, the famous Route du Vin makes a rewarding experience. It rolls through 60 charming villages—don't miss one of the jewels of the route, Wangen (30km/19 miles from Strasbourg) which features a city gate crowned by a tower and twisting, narrow streets—one of the most typical of the wine towns. Along the way are inns where you can sample wine, take a leisurely meal, or spend the night.

The Wine Road runs along the Vosges foothills, with medieval towers and feudal ruins evoking faded pageantry. The vine-covered slopes sometimes reach a height of 435m (1,427 ft.), and an estimated 20,000 hectares (49,400 acres) of vineyards line the road. Some 30,000 families earn their living tending the grapes. The best time to go is for the harvest in September and October. The well-marked route starts at Marlenheim.

## Marlenheim

This agreeable town, noted for its Vorlauf red wine, is 21km (13 miles) west of Strasbourg on N4. Even if you can't drive the full length of the Wine Road, you may want to visit for the excellent inn.

### WHERE TO EAT & STAY

**Le Cerf ★★★**   In the heart of this medieval village, occupying a half-timbered building at least 300 years old, this hotel offers pleasantly furnished rooms adjoining an excellent restaurant. The elegant, esoteric, and upscale menu items include, depending on the mood of the chef, such dishes as a fricassee of crayfish and wild mushrooms, a gratin of mushrooms with Riesling, an exotic version of sauerkraut that supplements the normal roster of pork and sausage with smoked foie gras, and a roulade of lobster with spinach and a broth that's brewed from the lobster shells. Fixed-price menus range from 39€ to 129€. The restaurant (but not the hotel) is closed on Tuesday and Wednesday year-round.

30 rue du Général-de-Gaulle, Marlenheim 67520. www.lecerf.com. ℰ **03-88-87-73-73.** Fax 03-88-87-68-08. 14 units. 187€–287€ double; 347€–447€ suite. AE, DC, MC, V. Parking 14€. **Amenities:** Restaurant; free Wi-Fi. *In room:* A/C, TV, hair dryer.

## Mittelbergheim

Mittelbergheim, 43km (27 miles) from Strasbourg, is a special village. Houses in the Renaissance style border its **place de l'Hôtel-de-Ville.**

### WHERE TO EAT & STAY

**Winstub Gilg** ★   This is an excellent inn. Though parts of the building date from 1614, its showpiece is a two-story stone staircase, classified as a historic monument. Medieval stonemasons who worked on the cathedral at Strasbourg carved it. Each attractively furnished guest room has a tub/shower. Chef Vincent Reuschlé attracts a loyal following with regional specialties such as onion tart, sauerkraut, and foie gras in brioche. Main courses include stewed kidneys and sweetbreads, duck with oranges, and, in season, roast pheasant with grapes. The hotel and restaurant close in January and from late June to early July. The rest of the year, the restaurant closes on Tuesday and Wednesday.

1 rte. du Vin, Mittelbergheim, Barr 67140. www.hotel-gilg.com. ℰ **03-88-08-91-37.** Fax 03-88-08-45-17. 15 units. 60€–90€ double. AE, DC, MC, V. **Amenities:** Restaurant; Wi-Fi in lobby. *In room:* TV.

## Andlau

This gardenlike resort, 42km (26 miles) from Strasbourg, was the site of an abbey founded in 887 by the disgraced wife of Emperor Charles the Fat. It has now faded into history, but a church remains that dates from the 12th century. In the tympanum are noteworthy Romanesque carvings. The **Office de Tourisme,** 5 rue du Général-de-Gaulle (www.pays-de-barr.com; ℰ **03-88-08-22-57**), is open Monday through Friday 9am to noon.

### WHERE TO EAT

**Au Boeuf Rouge** TRADITIONAL FRENCH   This bustling, unpretentious bistro has a busy bar and a comfortably battered dining room. Its menu of time-tested specialties includes homemade terrines, gamecock, fresh fish, and a tempting dessert cart. Noted chef Pierre Kieffer prepares a fabulous quenelle of brochet, a local whitefish, according to his grandmother's recipe. Although the fare is reliable and consistent, it isn't the most innovative cookery on the wine trail, excepting his seasonal version of wild boar with cassis sauce and spaetzle. For dessert, try a slice of Baettelman, an Alsatian cake baked with apples and cherries. There's also a *winstub* (tavern) on-site to the right as you enter. From March to October, you can sit on the terrace in front.

6 rue du Dr.-Stoltz. ℂ **03-88-08-96-26.** Reservations recommended. Main courses 17€–37€; fixed-price menu 15€–25€. AE, DC, MC, V. Oct–July 12 Fri–Wed 11:30am–2:30pm, Fri–Tues 6–9:30pm; July 15–Sept daily 11:30am–2:30pm and 6–9:30pm. Closed 10 days in Feb and 3 weeks June–July.

# Dambach

In the midst of its vineyards, Dambach (48km/30 miles from Strasbourg) is one of the delights of the Wine Road. The town, formally Dambach-la-Ville, has ramparts and three fortified gates. Its timbered houses are gabled with galleries, and many contain oriels. Wrought-iron signs still tell you if a place is a bakery or a butcher shop. A short drive from the town is the **Chapelle St-Sebastian,** with a 15th-century ossuary. The **Office de Tourisme** (www.dambach-la-ville.fr; ℂ **03-88-92-61-00;** fax 03-88-92-47-11) is in La Mairie (town hall), place du Marché.

# Ribeauvillé ★

At the foot of vine-clad hills, Ribeauvillé (87km/54 miles from Strasbourg) is picturesque, with old shop signs, pierced balconies, turrets, and flower-decorated houses. The town is noted for its Riesling and Gewürztraminer wines. See its Renaissance fountain and **Hôtel de Ville,** place de la Mairie, which has a collection of silver-gilt medieval and Renaissance tankards known as *hanaps.* For information, go to the tourist office at 1 Grand'Rue (www.ribeauville-riquewihr. com; ℂ **03-89-73-23-23**).

Guided tours showcase the *hanaps,* the building's architecture, and the history of the town. The free 90-minute tours run from May to September, on Sunday and Tuesday through Friday at 10am, 11am, and 2pm. On tour days at 3pm, the same guide leads a 90-minute walking tour of the town. Tours are in French, German, or halting English.

Also of interest in Ribeauvillé is the **Tour des Bouchers** (Butcher's Tower), built in stages from the 13th to the 16th century.

Every year on the first Sunday in September, visitors fill the town for its **Jour des Menetriers (Day of the Minstrels).** Beginning at 3pm and lasting almost 2½ hours, it features a parade of flute players from Alsace, the rest of France, Switzerland, and Germany, and as many as 600 parade participants. You can stand anywhere to watch the spectacle, but seats on the medieval stone benches line either side of the parade route.

## WHERE TO EAT & STAY

**Clos St-Vincent ★★★**   This is one of the most elegant choices along Route du Vin. Most of the individually decorated guest rooms have a balcony or terrace, but you get much more than a view of the Haut-Rhin vineyards and summer roses. The rooms, ranging from medium to large, are furnished with grand comfort; each has a bed covered in fine linen and a bathroom with state-of-the-art plumbing and tub/shower. Some have air-conditioning. The Chapotin family's cuisine is exceptional: hot duck liver with nuts, turbot with sorrel, roebuck (in season) in hot sauce, and veal kidneys in pinot noir. The wines are smooth, especially the popular Riesling and Gewürztraminer.

Rte. de Bergheim, Ribeauvillé 68150. www.leclossaintvincent.com. $\textcircled{C}$ **03-89-73-67-65.** Fax 03-89-73-32-20. 24 units. 165€–225€ double; 255€ suite. AE, MC, V. Closed mid-Dec to mid-Mar. **Amenities:** Restaurant (dinner only Wed–Mon); bar; babysitting; Jacuzzi; indoor pool; room service; sauna. *In room:* TV, hair dryer, minibar, free Wi-Fi.

# Kaysersberg ★★

Once a free city of the empire, Kaysersberg (93km/58 miles from Strasbourg) lies at the mouth of the Weiss Valley, between two vine-covered slopes; it's crowned by a castle ruined in the Thirty Years' War. From one of the many ornately carved bridges, you can see the city's medieval fortifications along the top of one of the nearby hills. Many of the houses are Gothic and Renaissance, and most have half-timbering, wrought-iron accents, leaded windows, and multiple designs carved into reddish sandstone.

In the cafes, you'll hear a combination of French and Alsatian. The age of the speaker usually determines the language—the older ones remain faithful to the dialect of their grandparents.

Dr. Albert Schweitzer was born here in 1875; his house is near the bridge over the Weiss. You can visit the **Musée du Albert Schweitzer,** 126 rue du Général de Gaulle ($\textcircled{C}$ **03-89-47-36-55**), from April to November daily from 9am to noon and 2 to 6pm. Admission is 2€ adults and 1€ for students and children 11 and under.

The **Office de Tourisme** is at 39 rue du Général-de-Gaulle (www.kaysersberg. com; $\textcircled{C}$ **03-89-78-22-78;** fax 03-89-71-34-11).

## WHERE TO EAT & STAY

**Au Lion d'Or** FRENCH/ALSATIAN   This 1521 building boasts an exceptionally beautiful decor. A carved lion's head adorns the oak door leading into the restaurant, which has a beamed ceiling, stone detailing, brass chandeliers, and a massive fireplace. If you eat at an outdoor table, you'll have a view of one of Alsace's prettiest streets. The classic Alsatian dishes include wild game, foie gras (which Alsatians claim to have invented), and yummy pork dishes, often with hams and sausage. Sauerkraut, served in its traditional meat-and-potato form or with fish, is an enduring specialty and a favorite with the loyal clientele.

66 rue du Général-de-Gaulle. www.auliondor.fr. $\textcircled{C}$ **03-89-47-11-16.** Reservations required. Main courses 15€–24€; fixed-price menu 25€–40€. AE, MC, V. Thurs–Mon noon–2:30pm and 6:30–9:30pm.

**Le Chambard** ★★★ FRENCH/ALSATIAN   The regional cuisine here is so good, it's worth planning a stop. You'll recognize the restaurant by the gilded wrought-iron sign above the cobblestones. Exposed stone and polished wood accent the rustic interior. Regional specialties with Mediterranean influences attest to the mastery of the kitchen. The imaginative chef presents impeccably flavored and sophisticated cuisine. The restaurant is known for sauerkraut served with a host of (mostly smoked) pork specialties, as well as foie gras and pungent Münster cheese. Other choices include a "cake" of eggplant with goose foie gras, an upscale version of traditional Alsatian stew made with foie gras, and

La Route Du Vin (Wine Road)

traditional Alsatian cake (*kugelhof*) with cinnamon-flavored ice cream. The cellar stocks the best local vintages.

A 20-room hotel annex (with an elegant spa) was built to match the other structures on the street. A double goes for 157€ to 246€, a suite from 269€.

9–13 rue du Général-de-Gaulle, Kaysersberg 68240. www.lechambard.com. ℰ **03-89-47-10-17.** Fax 03-89-47-35-03. Reservations required. Main courses 32€–59€; fixed-price menu 82€–122€. AE, MC, V. Thurs–Sun noon–2pm; Tues–Sun 7–9pm.

# Ammerschwihr

Ammerschwihr, 9km (5½ miles) north of Colmar (79km/49 miles from Strasbourg), is a good stop to cap off your Wine Road tour. Once a free city of the empire, the town was almost destroyed in 1944 and has been reconstructed in the traditional style. More and more travelers visit to sample the wine, especially Käferkopf. Check out the town's gate towers, 16th-century parish church, and remains of early fortifications.

## WHERE TO EAT & STAY

**Aux Armes de France ★★★** FRENCH/ALSATIAN    This is the best restaurant along the Wine Road. Although you can rent one of 10 rooms here (doubles go for 72€–92€), the real reason to come is the cuisine. In a flower-filled setting, Philippe Gaertner and his staff attract many French and German gourmets. A specialty is fresh foie gras served in its own golden aspic. Main courses include classics with imaginative variations, such as roebuck (in season) in hot sauce, and lobster fricassee with cream and truffles. Terrine of lobster and calf's head in aspic (*presskopf*), which we've never seen in any other restaurant in France, is a particular enticement for adventurous gastronomes.

1 Grand'Rue, Ammerschwihr 68770. www.aux-armes-de-france.com. ℰ **03-89-47-10-12.** Fax 03-89-47-38-12. Reservations required. Main courses 22€–50€; fixed-price menu 29€–53€. AE, DC, MC, V. Fri–Tues noon–2pm and 7:30–9pm.

Clos St-Landelin.

## Rouffach

Rouffach is south of Colmar. One of the highest of the Vosges Mountains, Grand-Ballon shelters the town from the winds that bring rain, which makes for a dry climate and a special grape. Make a beeline for the excellent vineyard **Clos St-Landelin** (www.mure.com; ✆ **03-89-78-58-00**), on the Route du Vin, at the intersection of RN83 and route de Soultzmatt. A clerical estate from the 6th century until the Revolution, it has been celebrated over the centuries for the quality of its wine. Clos St-Landelin covers 21 hectares (52 acres) at the southern end of the Vorbourg Grand Cru area. Its steep slopes call for terrace cultivation.

The soil that produces these wines is anything but fertile. Loaded with pebbles, sand, and limestone, the high-alkaline earth produces low-yield, scraggly vines whose fruit goes into superb Rieslings, Gewürztraminers, and pinot noirs. Members of the Muré family have owned these vineyards since 1648. In their cellar is a 13th-century wine press, the oldest in Alsace, and one of only three like it in France. (The other two are in Burgundy.) The family welcomes visitors who want to tour the cellars and ask about the wine, which is for sale. It's open Monday to Friday 8am to 6:30pm, and Saturday 10am to 1pm and 2 to 6pm.

# COLMAR ★★★

440km (273 miles) SE of Paris; 140km (87 miles) SE of Nancy; 71km (44 miles) SW of Strasbourg

One of the most attractive towns in Alsace, Colmar abounds with medieval and early Renaissance buildings, half-timbered structures, gables, and gracious loggias. Tiny gardens and wash houses surround many of the homes. Its old quarter looks more German than French, filled with streets of unexpected twists and turns. As a gateway to the Rhine country, Colmar is a major destination for travelers heading south from Strasbourg. Near the vine-covered slopes of the southern Vosges, it's the third-largest town in Alsace.

Colmar has been so well restored that it's Alsace's most beautiful city—you'd never guess Colmar was hard hit in two world wars.

Pretty home in Colmar.

## Essentials

**GETTING THERE** If you're **driving,** take N83 from Strasbourg; trip time is 1 hour. Because of the narrow streets, we suggest that you park and walk. Leave the car in the Champ-de-Mars, or in the underground place Rapp for a fee of around 1.20€ per hour, northeast of the railway station, and then walk a few blocks east to the old city; or park in the lot designated PARKING VIEILLE

VILLE, accessible from rue de l'Est at the edge of the Petite Venise neighborhood, and walk a few blocks southeast to reach the old city. **Trains** link Colmar to Nancy, Strasbourg, and Mulhouse, as well as to Germany via Strasbourg, across the Rhine. Twenty to twenty-two trains per day arrive from Paris's Gare de l'Est (trip time: 4–6 hr.); the one-way fare is 68€-75€. For information, call ℂ **36-35,** or 08-92-35-35-35 from outside France.

**VISITOR INFORMATION** The **Office de Tourisme** is at 4 rue Unterlinden (www.ot-colmar.fr; ℂ **03-89-20-68-92;** fax 03-89-41-34-13).

For information on wines, vintages, and winery visits, contact the **CIVA** (Alsace Wine Committee), Maison du Vin d'Alsace, 12 av. de la Foire-aux-Vins (www.vinsalsace.com; ℂ **03-89-20-16-20**). It's usually open Monday to Friday 8am to noon and 2 to 5pm. Make arrangements far in advance.

**SPECIAL EVENTS** Alsatian **folk dances** on place de l'Ancienne-Douane begin around 8pm on Tuesday from mid-May to mid-September. If you want to listen to classical music, visit during the first 2 weeks in July for the **Festival International de Musique de Colmar** (www.festival-colmar.com; ℂ **03-89-20-68-97**), which schedules 24 concerts in venues around the city, such as churches and public monuments. **Les Mardis de la Collégiale,** at place de la Cathédrale (ℂ **06-71-06-50-18**), stages concerts every Tuesday at 8:45pm from the end of July to mid-September. Tickets for these events cost 10€ to 15€. You can get complete information on any of the events in town at the Office de Tourisme.

# Exploring Colmar

Colmar is rich with historic houses, many half-timbered and, in summer, accented with geranium-draped window boxes. One of the most beautiful is **Maison Pfister,** 11 rue des Marchands, at the corner of rue Mercière, a 1537 building with wooden balconies. On the ground floor is a wine boutique owned by a major Alsace winegrower, **Muré,** proprietor of the vineyard Clos St-Landelin (ℂ **03-89-41-33-61**).

If you take pont St-Pierre over the Lauch River, you'll have an excellent view of Old Colmar and can explore **Petite Venise,** which is filled with canals.

**SHOPPING** Head for the old town of Colmar, particularly rue de Clefs, Grand'Rue, rue des Têtes, and rue des Marchands.

Antiques abound, and you'll find a large grouping of stores in the old town, especially along rue des Marchands. Shops that deserve particular attention include **Geismar Dany,** 32 rue des Marchands (ℂ/fax **03-89-23-30-41**), specializing in antique painted furniture, and **Antiquités Guy Caffard,** 56 rue des Marchands (www.caffard-antiquites.com; ℂ **03-89-41-31-78**), with its mishmash of furniture, postcards, books, toys, bibelots, and the like. Also worth noting are **Lire & Chiner,** 36 rue des Marchands (www.lire-et-chiner.fr; ℂ **03-89-24-16-78**), and **Antiquité Arcana,** 13 place l'Ancienne Douane (ℂ **03-89-41-59-81**).

One of the most appealing stores is **Arts et Collections d'Alsace,** 1 rue des Tanneurs (ℂ **03-89-24-09-78**), which stocks copies of art objects and utilitarian wares of yesteryear. There are items for the home and kitchen, made from wrought iron, pottery, glass, copper, carved wood, and fabric.

**WINERIES** Because Colmar is one of the gateways to the wine-producing Rhine country, local wine is one of the best purchases you can make. If you don't have time to visit the vineyards along the Wine Road, stop in at **Cave du Musée,** 11 rue Kléber (www.lacavedumusee.com; ✆ **03-89-23-85-29**), for one of the largest selections of wines and liqueurs from the region and the rest of France.

You can drive to one of the most historic vineyards in Alsace-Lorraine. **Domaines Schlumberger** (www.domaines-schlumberger.com; ✆ **03-89-74-27-00**) lies 26km (16 miles) southwest of Colmar in Guebwiller. The cellars, established by the Schlumberger family in 1810, are an unusual combination of early-19th-century brickwork and modern stainless steel. These grapes become such famous wines as Rieslings, Gewürztraminers, muscats, sylvaners, and pinots (blanc, gris, and noir). Views of the vineyards and tasting rooms are available without an appointment, but group tours of the cellars are conducted only when a staff member is available. Call before you go to find out when that might be. The vineyard is only open to tastings Monday to Thursday 8am to 6pm and to 5pm on Fridays. They are also closed 2 weeks in August and December 21 or 22 to January 2 (varies each year—call for details).

**Eglise des Dominicains** CHURCH    This church contains one of Colmar's most famous treasures: Martin Schongauer's painting *Virgin of the Rosebush,* or *Vierge au buisson de rose* (1473), all gold, red, and white, with fluttering birds. Look for it in the choir.

Place des Dominicains. ✆ **03-89-24-46-57.** Admission 1.50€ adults, 1€ students, .50€ ages 12–16, free for children 11 and under. Apr–Dec daily 10am–1pm and 3–6pm.

**Eglise St-Martin** ★ CHURCH    In the heart of Old Colmar is a collegiate church begun in 1230 on the site of a Romanesque church. It has a choir erected by William of Marburg in 1350 and a steeple that rises to 70m (230 ft.).

Place de la Cathédrale. ✆ **03-89-41-27-20.** Free admission. Daily 8am–7pm. Closed to casual visitors during Mass.

**Musée Bartholdi** MUSEUM    Statue of Liberty sculptor Frédéric-Auguste Bartholdi was born in Colmar in 1834. This small memento-filled museum is in the house where he was born. It has Statue of Liberty rooms containing plans and scale models, and documents related to its construction and other works regarding U.S. history. Bartholdi's Paris apartment, with furniture and memorabilia, has been reconstructed here. The museum supplements its exhibits with paintings of Egyptian scenes that Bartholdi collected during his travels in 1856.

30 rue des Marchands. www.musee-bartholdi.com. ✆ **03-89-41-90-60.** Admission 5€ adults, 2.50€ students and children 12–18, free for children 11 and under. Wed–Mon 10am–noon and 2–6pm. Closed Jan–Feb, May 1, Nov 1, and Christmas.

**Musée d'Unterlinden (Under the Linden Trees)** ★★ MUSEUM    This former Dominican convent (1232), the chief seat of Rhenish mysticism in the 14th and 15th centuries, became a museum around 1850, and it's been a treasure house of the art and history of Alsace ever since.

The jewel of its collection is the **Issenheim Altarpiece (Le Retable d'Issenheim)** ★★★, created by Würzburg-born Matthias Grünewald, "the most furious of realists," around 1515. His colors glow, and his fantasy will overwhelm you. One of the most exciting works in German art, it's an immense altar screen with two-sided folding wing pieces—designed to show the Crucifixion, then the Incarnation, framed by the Annunciation and the Resurrection. The carved altar screen depicts St. Anthony visiting the hermit St. Paul; it also shows the Temptation of St. Anthony, the most beguiling part of a work that contains some ghastly birds, weird monsters, and loathsome animals. The demon of the plague is depicted with a swollen belly and purple skin, his body blotched with boils; a diabolical grin appears on his horrible face.

Other attractions include the magnificent altarpiece (dating from 1470) of Jean d'Orlier by Martin Schongauer, a large collection of religious woodcarvings and stained glass from the 14th to the 18th centuries, and Gallo-Roman lapidary collections, including funeral slabs. The armory collection contains ancient arms from the Romanesque to the Renaissance, featuring halberds and crossbows.

1 rue d'Unterlinden. www.musee-unterlinden.com. ✆ **03-89-20-15-58.** Admission 7€ adults, 5€ students and children 12–17, free for children 11 and under. May–Oct daily 9am–6pm; Nov–Apr Wed–Mon 9am–noon and 2–5pm. Closed national holidays.

# Where to Eat

**Chez Hansi** ✦ ALSATIAN   Set within two rooms of a half-timbered house dating from 1532, this is the most historic and most folklorically charming restaurant in a town that's loaded with worthy competitors. Even its name is a reference to the pen name (Hansi) of Jean-Jacques Waltz, a 19th-century illustrator who, in his artwork, elevated Alsatian kitsch to an art form rivaled in America by Norman Rockwell. You'll find this hypertraditional place in the Vieille Ville, beneath massively beamed ceilings and a staff whose women are clad in dirndls. Come here for steaming and heaping platters of choucroute (sauerkraut garnished with pork products), foie gras, onion tarte, *pot-au-feu* that's redolent with gravy and chunks of beef, and, for the ultra-adventurous, calf's head (*tete de veau*) garnished with an apple in its mouth.

23 rue des Marchands. ✆ **03-89-41-37-84.** Reservations recommended. Main courses 17€–28€; prix-fixe menus 18€–50€. MC, V. Fri–Tues 11:45am–1:45pm and 6:45–9:30pm. Closed Jan.

**La Maison des Têtes** TRADITIONAL FRENCH   This Colmar monument is the town's leading hotel and one of its top restaurants. It opens off a covered cobblestone drive and courtyard. The 17th-century house lies in the center of town, near the Unterlinden Museum. The dining rooms are decorated with aged-wood beams and paneling, Art Nouveau lighting fixtures, and stained-glass and leaded windows. Dishes include foie gras with truffles, choucroute, seasonal roebuck with morels and dried fruits, and fresh trout or Rhine salmon braised in Riesling. The Alsatian wines are sublime. There are also 21 nicely furnished rooms with minibars, safes, air-conditioning, and TVs; some have Jacuzzis. Rates are 91€ to 235€ for a double, 205€ to 270€ for a suite.

In the Hôtel des Têtes, 19 rue des Têtes. www.la-maison-des-tetes.com. ✆ **03-89-24-43-43.** Fax 03-89-24-58-34. Reservations required. Main courses 10€–29€; fixed-price menu 29€–75€; menu dégustation 65€. AE, DC, MC, V. Wed–Sun noon–2pm; Tues–Sat 7–9:30pm. Closed Feb.

**Winstub Le Cygne** ★★★ ALSATIAN   Wander down this unassuming side street for simple but flavorful Alsatian fare in a wood-paneled room. Its quietly buzzing with locals most nights, who come for fare that tends to be a bit lighter than the average Winstub grub. They serve flammekueche in both savory and sweet variations (we love the simple ham and cheese version, and sweet tooths can't go wrong with the sugar and lemon version).

17 rue Edouard Richard. ℂ **03-89-23-76-26.** Main courses 12€–25€. AE, MC, V. Wed–Fri noon–2pm; Tues–Sat 7pm–midnight.

# Colmar Nightlife

Head for the seductive **La Fiesta/Le Cotton Club,** place de la Gare (www.fiestaclub.fr; ℂ **03-89-23-43-04**). Popular and busy, this nightclub consists of two strikingly different venues: On street level, La Fiesta is a bar with lots of suds, margaritas, and a busy after-work scene. Upstairs there's a cocktail lounge with a dance floor and a calmer, more urban (think Paris or Berlin) ambience. For a mellow atmosphere, try the piano bar **Louisiana Club,** 3A rue Berthe-Molly (ℂ **03-89-24-94-18**), where you can groove to authentic blues and jazz.

# Where to Stay

Rooms are also available in **La Maison des Têtes** (see "Where to Eat," on previous page).

**Grand Hôtel Bristol**   This 1926 red sandstone "grand hotel" right at the train station provides modern, renovated rooms—even if they are not quite as grand as the name of the hotel suggests, you're certain to have all the standard amenities of a business class hotel. Frankly, this is excellent value if you don't mind giving up local character for comfort and convenience. The hotel is part of the Best Western chain.

7 place de la Gare, Colmar 68000. www.grand-hotel-bristol.com. ℂ **03-89-23-59-59.** Fax 03-89-23-92-26. 91 units. 118€–148€ double. AE, DC, MC, V. **Amenities:** 2 restaurants; bar; babysitting; room service; rooms for those w/limited mobility; smoke-free rooms. *In room:* A/C (in some), TV, hair dryer, minibar, free Wi-Fi.

**Hostellerie Le Maréchal ★★**   Three 16th-century houses make up this hotel, the most tranquil in town. You climb a wide staircase to reach the guest rooms, most of which are air-conditioned. In the east wing is a small, partially timbered room with a sloping ceiling. Accommodations are small but neatly organized, each with a tiled bathrooms; the more expensive doubles and both suits feature Jacuzzi tubs. The restaurant has a fireplace in winter; in summer, seating moves to the terrace, where you can enjoy a water view and east on stuffed quail, good beef and veal dishes, and lamb Provençal accompanied by Alsatian wines.

4–6 place des Six-Montagnes-Noires, Colmar 68000. www.hotel-le-marechal.com. ℂ **03-89-41-60-32.** Fax 03-89-24-59-40. 30 units. 105€–225€ double; 255€ suite. AE, DC, MC, V. Parking 15€. **Amenities:** Restaurant; room service; smoke-free rooms. *In room:* TV, hair dryer, minibar, free Wi-Fi.

**Le Colombier ★**   Originally built as a half-timbered house in the 14th century, this building is among the town's finest hotels. Very old beams and masonry contrast pleasantly with contemporary lighting and furniture. The staff is engaging and helpful. If the government-rated three-star hotel had a restaurant (breakfast is the only meal served), it would surely earn four-star status. With the exception of the cozy unit beneath the steeply pitched pinnacle of the roof, all of the guest rooms have high ceilings; they vary in size and shape. Each contains comfortable appointments and fine linen, plus a small but tidy shower-only bathroom. Some rooms overlook the canals of Petite Venise; others open onto a half-timbered courtyard.

7 rue Turenne, Colmar 68000. www.hotel-le-colombier.fr. ✆ **03-89-23-96-00.** Fax 03-89-23-97-27. 28 units. 95€–190€ double; 205€–255€ suite. AE, DC, MC, V. Parking 10€. **Amenities:** Bar; room service. *In room:* A/C, TV, hair dryer, minibar, Wi-Fi (3.50€ per day).

## Where to Eat & Stay Nearby

Gourmets flock to **Illhaeusern,** 18km (11 miles) from Colmar, east of the N83 highway, to dine at the Auberge de l'Ill, one of France's great restaurants. The signs for the restaurant, beside the main highway, are difficult to miss.

**Auberge de l'Ill ★★★** MODERN FRENCH    This is the greatest restaurant in eastern France. Run by the Haeberlin family in their 19th-century farmhouse, Auberge de l'Ill combines the finest Alsatian specialties with *cuisine moderne* and classic offerings. You can enjoy your aperitif or coffee under the weeping willows in a beautiful garden with a river view. Chef Marc Haeberlin takes dishes of Alsatian origin and makes them into *grande cuisine*—freshwater eel stewed in Riesling, *matelotes* (small glazed onions) in Riesling, and an inventive foie gras. Two unsurpassed choices are braised slices of pheasant and partridge served with winey game sauce, chestnuts, wild mushrooms, and Breton cornmeal; and salmon soufflé. Some dishes require 24 hours' notice, so inquire when you make reservations.

You can spend the night in one of 13 rooms at the **Hôtel des Berges,** in a delightfully furnished, air-conditioned room overlooking the Ill River. The rates are 265€ to 300€ for a double, 350€ to 520€ for a suite, and 465€ for a decade-old cottage on the grounds.

Rue de Collonges, Illhaeusern 68970. www.auberge-de-l-ill.com. ✆ **03-89-71-89-00.** Fax 03-89-71-82-83. Reservations required (1 week in advance for summer weekends). Main courses 46€–145€; fixed-price menu 121€–160€. AE, DC, MC, V. Wed–Sun noon–2pm and 7–9pm. Closed 1st week of Jan and mid-Feb to mid-Mar.

# LA ROUTE DES CRETES ★★★

From Basel, Switzerland, to Mainz, Germany, a distance of some 242km (150 miles), the Vosges Mountains stretch along the west side of the Rhine Valley, bearing a similarity to the Black Forest of Germany. Many German and French families spend their summer vacation exploring the Vosges. Travelers with less time may want to settle for a quick look at the ancient mountains that once formed the boundary between France and Germany. They are filled with tall hardwood and fir trees, and a network of twisting roads with hairpin curves traverses them. The depths of the mountain forests are the closest France comes to wilderness.

**Along La Route des Cretes.**

## Exploring the Area

You can explore the mountains by heading west from Strasbourg, but there's a more interesting route from Colmar. La Route des Crêtes (Crest Road) begins at **Col du Bonhomme,** west of Colmar. The French High Command created it during World War I to carry supplies over the mountains. From Col du Bonhomme, you can strike out on this magnificent road, once the object of bitter fighting but today a series of panoramic vistas, including one of the Black Forest.

By **Col de la Schlucht,** 62km (38 miles) west of Colmar, you'll have climbed 1,472m (4,828 ft.). Schlucht is a summer and winter resort, one of the most beautiful spots in the Vosges, with a panoramic view of the Valley of Münster and the slopes of Hohneck. As you skirt the edge of this glacier-carved valley, you'll be in the midst of a land of pine groves with a necklace of lakes. You may want to turn off the main road and go exploring in several directions; the scenery is that tempting. But if you're still on the Crest Road, you can circle **Hohneck,** one of the highest peaks, at 1,590m (5,215 ft.), dominating the Wildenstein Dam of the Bresse winter-sports station.

At **Markstein,** you'll come to another resort. From here, take N430 and then D10 to **Münster,** where the savory cheese is made. You'll go via the Petit-Ballon, a landscape of forest and mountain meadows with grazing cows. Finally, **Grand-Ballon,** at 1,400m (4,592 ft.), is the highest point you can reach by car in the Vosges. Get out of your car and go for a walk; if it's a clear day, you'll be able to see the Jura, with the French Alps beyond.

# NANCY ★★★

370km (229 miles) E of Paris; 148km (92 miles) W of Strasbourg

Nancy, in France's northeast corner, was the capital of old Lorraine. The city was built around a fortified castle on a rock in the swampland near the Meurthe River. A canal a few blocks east of the historic center connects the Marne to the Rhine.

The city is serenely beautiful, with a history, cuisine, and architecture all its own. It once rivaled Paris as the center for the design and production of Art Nouveau. Nancy has three faces: the medieval alleys and towers around the old Palais Ducal where Charles II received Joan of Arc, the rococo golden gates and fountains, and the dull modern sections.

With a population of more than 100,000, Nancy remains the hub of commerce and politics in Lorraine. Home to a large university, it's a center of mining, engineering, metallurgy, and finance. Its 30,000 students, who have a passion for *le cool jazz,* keep Nancy jumping at night.

## Essentials

**GETTING THERE**  The fast **TGV train** from Paris's Gare de l'Est arrives in Nancy after just 90 minutes, making the city a virtual commute from Paris. Many Parisians now visit for *le weekend.* The one-way fare ranges between 50€ and 65€. Trains from Strasbourg arrive in Nancy every hour, a one-way fare costing 20€ to 32€. For information and schedules, call ✆ **36-35,** or 08-92-35-35-35 from outside France. If you're **driving** to Nancy from Paris, follow N4 east (trip time: 4 hr.).

**VISITOR INFORMATION**  The **Office de Tourisme** is at place Stanislas (www.ot-nancy.fr; ✆ **03-83-35-22-41;** fax 03-83-35-90-10).

**SPECIAL EVENTS** Serious jazz lovers come to town for 2 weeks in October to attend **Jazz Pulsations** (www.nancyjazzpulsations.com; ✆ 03-83-35-40-86). Some kind of performance takes place every night around sundown in a tent in the Parc de la Pépinière, a very short walk from the place Stanislas. Tickets cost 102€ to 35€.

# Exploring Nancy

A **Passe-Musée** is a combination ticket that allows entrance to three of the town's most visited attractions, all for a net price of 10€ per person (another 14€ pass gives access to six museums in town), with no discounts for students or children. Included in the pass is access to the Musée de l'Ecole de Nancy, the Musée des Beaux-Arts, and the Musée Historique Lorraine (which is also known as the Musée des Arts et Traditions Populaires). Ask about the ticket at the tourist office.

Place Stanislas.

The most monumental square in eastern France, and the heart of Nancy, is **place Stanislas ★★★**, named for Stanislas Leszczynski, the last of the ducs de Lorraine, ex-king of Poland, and father-in-law of Louis XV. His 18th-century building programs transformed Nancy into one of Europe's most palatial cities. The square stands between Nancy's two most notable neighborhoods: the **Ville Vieille** (old town), in the medieval core in the northwest, centered on the cathedral, Grande Rue, and the labyrinth of narrow, meandering streets that funnel into it; and the **Ville Neuve,** in the southwest. Built in the 16th and 17th centuries, when streets were laid out in straight lines, Ville Neuve centers on rue St-Jean.

Place Stanislas was laid out from 1752 to 1760 according to the designs of Emmanuel Héré. Its ironwork gates are magnificent. The square is fabled for the brilliant and fanciful railings, the work of Jean Lamour. His gilded railings with flowery decorations and crests evoke Versailles. The entire plaza is an all-pedestrian zone.

The **Arc de Triomphe,** constructed by Stanislas from 1754 to 1756 to honor Louis XV, adjoins the place de la Carrière, a tree-lined promenade leading to the 1760 **Palais du Gouvernement.** This governmental palace adjoins the **Palais Ducal,** built in 1502 in the Gothic style with Flamboyant Gothic balconies.

**Musée de l'Ecole de Nancy ★** MUSEUM   In a turn-of-the-20th-century building is a museum displaying the works of Emile Gallé, the greatest artist of the Nancy style. See Gallé's celebrated "Dawn and Dusk" bed and, our favorite, the "Mushroom Lamp." Works by Eugène Vallin, another outstanding artist, are also on display.

36–38 rue Sergent-Blandan. www.ecole-de-nancy.com. ✆ **03-83-40-14-86.** Admission 6€ adults, 4€ students, free for children 17 and under. Free for students on Wed. Wed–Sun 10am–6pm.

**Musée des Beaux-Arts** ★★ MUSEUM   At press time, this museum was closed for renovations and due to reopen in June 2012. See the website for the most up to date information—this place is worth a visit. Built in the 1700s, this is an outstanding regional museum, encompassing the Collection Galilée, works displayed in Paris between 1919 and 1930. It houses a rare Manet portrait of the wife of Napoleon III's dentist—remarkable because of its brilliance and intensity. There are also works by Delacroix, Utrillo, Modigliani, Boucher, and Rubens. Italians such as Perugino, Caravaggio, Ribera, and Tintoretto are represented as well.

3 place Stanislas. http://mban.nancy.fr. ⓒ **03-83-85-30-72.**

**Musée Historique Lorrain** ★★★ MUSEUM   This is one of France's great museums, covering the art and history of the Lorraine region from ancient times. The first floor devotes an entire room to Jacques Callot, an engraver born in Nancy in 1592. Galerie des Cerfs displays tapestries. You'll see a collection of 17th-century masterpieces by Jacques Bellange, Jacques Callot, Georges de la Tour, and Claude Deruet, dating from when the duchy was known as a cultural center.

Until the Revolution, this was a Franciscan convent. Franciscans were known as Cordeliers—hence the name of the church that adjoins the museum. The Flamboyant Gothic **Eglise des Cordeliers** ★ is the burial site of the dukes of Lorraine. The most notable of the burial monuments are those of René II (1509; attributed to the sculptor Mansuy Gauvain) and a reclining statue of his second wife, Philippa of Gueldres, by Ligier Richier. The limestone rendering of Philippa is one of Nancy's most stunning examples of Renaissance portraiture. The octagonal Chapel of the Dukes (1607) holds the baroque sarcophagi.

In the Palais Ducal, 64 Grande Rue. ✆ **03-83-32-18-74.** Admission 6€ adults, 4€ students and children 12–18, free for children 11 and under (combo ticket for Palais Ducal and Eglise des Cordeliers). Free for students 1st Sun of each month. Tues–Sun 10am–12:30pm and 2–6pm.

## Shopping

Many of Nancy's antiques shops specialize in Art Nouveau. Visit **Denis Rugat,** 13 rue Stanislas (✆ **03-83-35-20-79**), for the best pieces. Another good outlet is **Galerie d'Art International,** 17 rue Amerval (www.galerie-art-international. com; ✆ **03-83-35-06-83**). Both stock inventories of Lalique crystal, brightly colored vases, and enameled boxes made with a technique known locally as *les émaux de Longwy,* plus an assortment of glass-shaded lamps. You'll find more glass and crystal by Daum, at more reasonable prices, than virtually anywhere else in France. The company's premier outlet is **Boutique Daum,** 14 place Stanislas (www. daum.fr; ✆ **03-83-32-21-65**), where the most perfect specimens from the Daum factory are sold at prices that are usually about 30% less than what you'd pay in other glass galleries in France. Each piece, a work of art in its own right, is signed "Daum." In contrast, and for prices that are about 30% to 40% less than what's sold in the above-mentioned boutique, you can head to Daum's factory outlet, **Magasin d'Usine Daum,** 17 rue Cristallerie (✆ **03-83-30-80-24**), a 5-minute walk from the place Stanislas. Their "slightly flawed" factory seconds are gift-wrapped and sold, each signed with the more enigmatic (and less prestigious) "Nancy."

## Where to Eat

While exploring the city, you can stop for food and wine at the minuscule **Le V'Four,** 10 rue St-Michel (✆ **03-83-32-49-48**), where set menus are priced from 26€ to 40€. A special fixed-price lunch is 18€. The best version of the celebrated quiche Lorraine (the egg, ham, and cheese tart) is sold at **Nathalie Lalonde,** 3 rue Stanislas (✆ **03-83-51-67-08**), a tradition since 1901.

The macaroon, that almond cookie so beloved by foodies, was said to have been invented in Nancy by Benedictine nuns. Their original recipe is followed at **Soeurs Macarons,** 21 rue Gambetta (✆ **03-83-32-24-25**). You might end your sightseeing day by calling at the century-old brasserie, **L'Excelsior,** 50 rue Henri Poincare (✆ **03-83-35-24-57**), a period piece from 1911 with stained-glass windows and polished brass chandeliers. Just a block from the rail station, it serves Lorraine specialties with fresh oysters, a delight in season.

**Le Capucin Gourmand ★★** TRADITIONAL FRENCH    This is the leading grand restaurant of Nancy, within a 5-minute walk of place Stanislas, and has a warm, cozy decor with tones of gray and wood paneling. On our last visit, we savored such creations as minced scallops and truffles pressed into patties and served with a walnut-oil vinaigrette, a "marble" of foie gras with exotic mushrooms, and a turbot steak that was "clothed" in baby vegetables. A signature dish is a civet of rabbit *à la royale*—in a sauce of its own blood mixed with red wine and just a hint of bitter chocolate. For dessert, a "passion of chocolate" came with baked fresh figs marinated in honey and served with a yogurt-flavored ice cream.

31 rue Gambetta. www.lecapu.com. ✆ **03-83-35-26-98.** Reservations required. Main courses 28€–38€; fixed-price menu 30€–78€. AE, MC, V. Tues–Fri and Sun noon–2pm; Tues–Sat 7:30–10pm.

**Les Pissenlits (The Dandelions)** 🍴 TRADITIONAL FRENCH    At this cost-conscious brasserie, the food is simple but flavorful and artfully prepared. Chef Jean-Luc Mengin's specialties are likely to include *matelote* of freshwater zander with shallots, dandelion salad with bacon and creamy vinaigrette, and aiguillettes of duckling with spice-flavored honey sauce. The chef's wife, Danièle, is one of the few accredited female wine stewards in France. Art Nouveau antiques, many of them crafted in Nancy, fill the dining room.

27 bis rue des Ponts. www.les-pissenlits.com. ℂ **03-83-37-43-97.** Reservations recommended. Main courses 14€–17€; fixed-price menu 18€–40€. MC, V. Tues–Sat 11:45am–2:30pm and 7:15–10:30pm.

# Nancy Nightlife

As night approaches, most of the student population heads to the Old Town. **Blue Note Why Not,** 3 rue des Michottes (ℂ 03-83-30-31-18), has a room for rock performances, a piano bar, a lounge with a fireplace and comfy armchairs, and a rowdy beer hall. It's open Wednesday through Sunday. Entrance is free except on Friday and Saturday night, when there's a 12€ cover. Women enter free on those nights before 12:30am.

Nancy's most popular dance club is **Les Caves du Roy,** 9 place Stanislas (ℂ 03-83-35-24-14), where a techno crowd flails around in a chrome-and-metallic space. It's open Tuesday to Thursday 11pm to 4am, Friday 11pm to 5am, Saturday midnight to 6:15am.

The hottest nightclub in the region is a converted warehouse in the suburb of Vandoeuvre, 4km (2½ miles) south of the center of town. **Le Circus,** 42 rue Jean-Mermoz (www.circusmedia.fr; ℂ 03-83-57-53-85; for many events, you can print out a "pass" from their website that gives free or discounted access), sits near the town's wholesale food market (le Marché en Gros). It features fire-eaters, jugglers, and techno music. Expect up to 2,000 revelers on a Friday or Saturday night, when the cover is 11€ and includes the first drink; it's open from 11pm to 5am.

# Where to Stay

**All Seasons Nancy Centre Gare**    Near the back of the railway station, this hotel was built after World War II and has an annex just around the corner. Guests select this efficiently operated, government-rated two-star hotel for its reasonable prices and central location. It provides comfortable but not particularly plush guest rooms, outfitted in contemporary style with a monochromatic color scheme. The hotel has a pleasant garden. Breakfast is the only meal served.

3 rue de l'Armée-Patton, Nancy 54000. www.all-seasons-hotels.com. ℂ **03-83-40-31-24.** Fax 03-83-28-47-78. 85 units. 74€–100€ double. AE, MC, V. Parking 6.50€. **Amenities:** Bar. *In room:* A/C, TV, hair dryer, free Wi-Fi.

**Grand Hôtel de la Reine** ★★★    This is the grandest hotel in Nancy. The 18th-century mansion was built simultaneously with the monumental square that contains it. The Louis XV–style guest rooms are appointed with draped testers over comfortable beds, Venetian-style chandeliers, and gilt-framed mirrors. All accommodations contain roomy bathrooms with tub/showers. Units overlooking place Stanislas are expensive. If you can live without a view, some suites (those overlooking the hotel's back and sides) are cheaper than the most expensive double. The elegant and very grand Stanislas restaurant serves classic and modern dishes.

**Pompidou Metz.**

2 place Stanislas, Nancy 54000. www.hoteldelareine.com. ☎ **800/777-4182** in the U.S. and Canada, or 03-83-35-03-01. Fax 03-83-32-86-04. 43 units. 140€–280€ double; 300€ suite. AE, DC, MC, V. Parking 16€. **Amenities:** Restaurant; bar; babysitting; room service. *In room:* A/C, TV, hair dryer, minibar, free Wi-Fi.

**Hotel D'Haussonville ★★**   This grand town house originally dating from the 1500s has been magnificently restored and is today the finest B&B in Nancy. Standing in the town's medieval heart, the hotel is an elegant, tranquil choice and its antique charm is ideal if you're seeking an old Lorraine ambience, yet each room has a special theme evident in its art, ranging from "Ming" to "Nairobi." Bedrooms are elegant, with parquet flooring, and fireplaces and bathrooms are thoroughly modernized and clad in marble.

9 rue Mgr. Trouillet, Nancy 54000. www.hotel-haussonville.fr. ☎ **03-83-35-85-84.** Fax 03-83-32-78-96. 7 units. 140€–230€ double. AE, DC, MC, V. Closed most of Aug and 1st 2 weeks of Jan. **Amenities:** Breakfast room. *In room:* TV.

---

## The Other Centre Pompidou

Amidst much fanfare, Paris's Centre Pompidou unveiled a futuristic, brand-spanking new outpost in Metz, the capital city of Alsace's neighboring region, Lorraine. In addition to a theater and performance auditorium, the prime draw is its contemporary museum, where you'll encounter modern art from the 20th and 21st centuries. This newbie, a satellite of the Centre Pompidou in Paris (see p. 101), features rotating exhibits from the National Modern Art Museum (housed inside the Paris original). The easiest way to get to Metz is by taking a train from Nancy. Trains run every 20 minutes and take 35-55 minutes (9.80€ one-way). The museum is located at 1 parvis des Droits de l'Homme (www.centrepompidou-metz.fr ; ☎ **03-87-15-39-39;** admission 7€ adults, free for seniors and children 26 and under).

# DOMREMY-LA-PUCELLE

443km (275 miles) SE of Paris; 10km (6¼ miles) NW of Neufchâteau

Most often visited on a day trip, Domrémy is a plain village that would have slumbered in obscurity, but for the fact that Joan of Arc was born here in 1412. Today it's a pilgrimage center attracting tourists from all over the world.

Her family's house is known as **Maison Natale de Jeanne d'Arc,** 2 rue de la Basilique (✆ **03-29-06-95-86**). Here you can see the chamber where she was born. A museum beside the house shows a film depicting St. Joan's life. The house is open April to September Wednesday to Monday 10am to 6pm, and October to March Wednesday to Monday 10am to noon and 2 to 5pm. Admission is 3€ for adults, free for children 9 and under. The house is closed in January.

Maison Natale de Jeanne d'Arc.

Adjacent to the museum, on rue Principale, is **Eglise St-Rémi;** repairs and partial reconstructions have masked its 12th-century origins. All that remains from the age of Joan of Arc are a baptismal font and some stonework. On a slope of the Bois-Chenu 1.5km (1 mile) uphill from the village is a monument steeped in French nationalism, the **Basilique du Bois-Chenu.** It was begun in 1881 and consecrated in 1926. To reach it, follow signs from the center and along rue de la Basilique.

## Essentials

**GETTING THERE**   If you're **driving,** take N4 southeast of Paris to Toul, and then A31 south toward Neufchâteau/Charmes. Then take N74 southwest (signposted in the direction of Neufchâteau). At Neufchâteau, follow D164 northwest to Coussey. From there, take D53 into Domrémy.

There is no railway station in Domrémy—you must take one of four **trains** daily going to either Nancy or Toul, where you can make bus and rail connections to Neufchâteau, 9.5km (6 miles) away. You can also take a **taxi,** MBM Assistance 88 (✆ **03-29-06-12-13**), for about 100€ each way.

# VERDUN ★★

261km (162 miles) E of Paris; 66km (41 miles) W of Metz

Built on both banks of the Meuse and intersected by a series of canals, Verdun has an old section, the Ville Haute, on the east bank, which includes the cathedral and Episcopal palace. Today stone houses on narrow cobblestone streets give Verdun a medieval appearance. However, most visitors come to see the famous World War I battlefields, 3km (1¾ miles) east of the town, off N3 toward Metz.

## Essentials

**GETTING THERE**   Two **trains** arrive daily from Paris's Gare de l'Est; you'll have to change at Châlons-en-Champagne. Several daily trains also arrive from Metz, after a change at Conflans. The one-way fare from Paris is 33€ to 40€;

from Metz, it's 13€. For train information and schedules, call ✆ **36-35** or 08-92-35-35-35. Driving is easy; Verdun is several miles north of the Paris-Strasbourg autoroute (A4).

**VISITOR INFORMATION** The **Office de Tourisme** is on place de la Nation (www.verdun-tourisme.com; ✆ **03-29-84-18-85**). It's closed on bank holidays.

# Touring the Battlefields

At this garrison town in eastern France, Maréchal Pétain said, "They shall not pass!" And they didn't. Verdun is where the Allies held out against a massive assault by the German army in World War I. Near the end of the war, 600,000 to 800,000 French and German soldiers died battling over a few miles along the muddy Meuse between Paris and the Rhine. Two monuments commemorate these tragic events: Rodin's *Defense* and Boucher's *To Victory and the Dead.*

The local tourist office provides maps for two tours of the brutal and bloody battlefields that helped define World War I. They include the "Circuit Champs de Bataille Rive Droite," which encompasses the better-known battlegrounds on the River Meuse's right bank. They also have maps for two self-guided tours. The first, whose estimated length is about 4 hours, includes, on the Meuse's right bank, a 32km (20-mile) run, taking in **Fort Vaux,** where Raynal staged a heroic defense after sending his last message by carrier pigeon. After passing a **French cemetery** of 16,000 graves—an endless field of crosses—you arrive at the **Ossuaire de Douaumont,** where the bones of those blown to bits were embedded. Nearby, at the **Fort de Douaumont,** the "hell of Verdun" was unleashed. From the roof, you can look out at a vast field of corroded tops of "pillboxes." Then you proceed to the *Tranchée des Baïonettes (Trench of Bayonets).* Bayonets of French soldiers entombed by a shell burst from this unique memorial.

Within a few paces of the Tranchée des Baïonettes, you'll see the premises of the **Mémorial de Verdun** (built around 1967), Fleury Devant Douaumont (www.memorial-de-verdun.fr; ✆ **03-29-84-35-34**), a museum that commemorates the weapons, uniforms, photographs, and geography of one of the bloodiest battles of World War I. From February to mid-December, it's open daily 9am to noon and 2 to 6pm. Entrance is 7€ for adults and students, 3.50€ for children 8 to 16, free for children 7 and under.

The second self-guided tour, known as **"Circuit Champs de Bataille Rive Gauche"** (or "Circuit de l'Argonne"), also requires about 4 hours, and during its 97km (60 miles), it focuses on mostly outdoor sites. It takes in the **Butte de Montfaucon,** a hill on which Americans erected a memorial tower, and the **Cimetière Américain at Romagne,** with some 15,000 graves.

Because public transportation is inadequate, only visitors with cars should attempt to make these circuits.

# BURGUNDY

by Louise Simpson

B ordered by the River Saône to the east and the River Loire to the west, Burgundy is an agricultural region famed for its wines. Cistercian monasteries rising from vineyards and medieval churches mark the landscape: The delineation of this region's prestigious vineyards by their *terroir* goes back to the medieval monks. Once an independent province, its Valois dukes weathered many struggles defending their independence during the 14th and 15th centuries before being annexed by Louis XI in 1477. The ducs de Bourgogne are but a memory, but they left a legacy of vintage red and white wines to please and excite the palate. The major winegrowing regions of Burgundy are Chablis, Côte de Nuits, Côte de Beaune, Côte Chalonnaise, Mâconnais, and Nivernais.

---

**THE CÔTE D'OR** evokes mythical Premier cru appellations such as Richebourg and Vosne-Romanée, while the region's grassy agricultural plains are home to mouth-watering produce such as Charolais beef, garlic-infused snails, and pungent Epoisses cheese. Sleepy historic towns and villages have been awoken by the appeal of Michelin-starred restaurants: L'Espérance in Vézelay, Le Relais Bernard Loiseau in Saulieu, Maison Lameloise in Chagny, and Georges Blanc in Vonnas. Today, Burgundy is awakening to the importance of wine tourism and of adapting with the times.

# DIJON ★★★

312km (193 miles) SE of Paris; 320km (198 miles) NE of Lyon

Located to the north of the Côte d'Or, Dijon is the capital of Burgundy. This ancient city is being given a 400 million–euro facelift, including a new tramway and restored landmark squares such as place Darcy and place de la République.

On the doorstep of the illustrious Côte d'Or wine region, this city combines world-class wines with good food. As well as being famed for its mustard, Dijon is also the home of *Kir* (a mix of white wine and black currant liqueur, named after a former Dijon major Canon Félix Kir). After admiring the city's impressive Gothic churches and the sumptuous Palais des Ducs et des Etats de Bourgogne, make time to get lost in Dijon's medieval heart: Here you'll happen upon extravagant stone-façaded *hôtels particuliers* (private mansions) and glimpse at ornately paneled interiors through half-timbered shop-front windows.

## Essentials

**GETTING THERE**  The best way to reach Dijon is by **driving.** From Paris, follow A6 southeast to Pouilly-en-Auxois, and then go east along A38 and finally onto the D905 (around Plombières-lès-Dijon) into central Dijon. Dijon also

PREVIOUS PAGE: **Harvesting wine in Burgundy.**

# Burgundy

has excellent rail and bus connections to the rest of Europe. A dozen or so TGV **trains** arrive from Paris's Gare de Lyon each day (trip time: under 1 hr., 45 min.); the one-way fare is 49€ to 62€. Trains arrive from Lyon every hour (trip time: 1 hr., 35 min. to 2 hr.; 28.70€–34€ one-way). For information, visit www.voyages-sncf.com or call ℭ **08-92-33-53-35.**

**VISITOR INFORMATION**   The **Office de Tourisme** is at 11 rue des Forges (www.visitdijon.com; ℭ **08-92-70-05-58;** ).

**SPECIAL EVENTS**   Every June, the streets of Dijon experience a lively renaissance when **Estivade** comes to town. This week-long festival uses the city's parks as a stage for dance shows and musical concerts. It's always a big hit. You can get a schedule of events from the city tourist office (see above) or

---

## Insider Tip

An easy way to get around central Dijon is by Velodi (www.velodi.net; ℭ **0800-20-03-05**) bike along numerous cycle paths. This eco-friendly bike rental offers self-service pick-up and drop-off points all around town such as rue Chabot-Charny, place Grangier, and place Notre-Dame.

La Mairie (the town hall; ✆ **03-80-74-51-51**). New since 2009, the 4-14 Festival (www.4-14-festival.org) combines American and Burgundian cuisine and music for an eclectic, weekend-long celebration in mid-July.

## Seeing the Sights

One of the most historic buildings in this ancient province is the **Palais des Ducs et des Etats de Bourgogne,** which symbolizes the independent (or semi-independent, depending on the era) status of this fertile region. Capped with an elaborate tile roof, the complex is arranged around a trio of courtyards. The oldest section, only part of which you can visit, is the **Ancien Palais des Ducs de Bourgogne,** erected in the 12th century and rebuilt in the 14th. The newer section is the **Palais des Etats de Bourgogne,** constructed in the 17th and 18th centuries for the Burgundian parliament. Today the palace is *la mairie* (the town hall); all of its newer section and much of its older section are reserved for the municipal government and not open to the public. However, there's a fine museum, the **Musée des Beaux-Arts** (see below).

The **Musée Archéologique,** 5 rue du Dr-Maret (www.musees-bourgogne. org; ✆ **03-80-48-83-70**), contains findings unearthed from Dijon's archaeological digs. Admission is free, and it's open Wednesday to Sunday 9am to 12:30pm and 1:30 to 6pm; from mid-May to September the museum is also open on Mondays.

A medieval nunnery, **L'Ancien Couvent des Bernardines,** 17 rue Ste-Anne (✆ **03-80-48-80-90**), is home to two museums. The chapel holds the Musée d'Arts Sacrés, devoted to art from regional churches, and the cloister contains the **Musée de la Vie Bourguignonne** (also known as the Musée Perrin de Puycousin), which exhibits folkloric costumes, farm implements, and some 19th- and early-20th-century storefronts from Dijon's center. Admission is free to both museums (Oct–Apr Wed–Mon 9am–noon and 2–6pm, and May–Sept 9am–12:30pm and 1:30–6pm).

**Musée des Beaux-Arts** ★★ MUSEUM    A 14.3 million–euro renovation is set to transform one of France's oldest and richest museums with renovated facades and a new glass-and-wood roof extension due to be completed by 2013. Although part of the building is currently under tarpaulin, you can still visit most of the exhibits via a temporary entrance on rue Rameau. The museum showcases exceptional sculpture, ducal kitchens from the mid-1400s (with great chimney pieces), a collection of European paintings from the 14th to the 19th centuries, and modern French paintings and sculptures. Take special note of the Salle des Gardes, the banquet hall of the old palace built by Philip the Good (Philippe le Hardi). The tomb of Philip the Bold was created between 1385 and 1411 and is one of the best in France: a reclining figure rests on a slab of black marble, surrounded by 41 mourners.

Musée des Beaux-Arts.

In the Palais des Ducs et des Etats de Bourgogne, cour de Bar. ℰ **03-80-74-52-09.** Free admission. Temporary expositions cost around 2€ each (free Sun). May–Oct Wed–Mon 9:30am–6pm; Nov–Apr Wed–Mon 10am–5pm.

**Musée Magnin** MUSEUM   This museum was built in the 19th century as the home of an arts-conscious member of the *grande bourgeoisie*. The city of Dijon inherited the building and its contents following the death of the family's last descendant. Retaining the look of a lived-in home, it contains an eclectic display of 19th-century antiques and art objects, as well as a collection of paintings accumulated or painted by the former owners.

4 rue des Bons-Enfants. www.musee-magnin.fr. ℰ **03-80-67-11-10.** Admission 3.50€ adults, 2.50€, free for ages 26 and under. Tues–Sun 10am–noon and 2:30–6pm.

**Chartreuse de Champmol** MONASTERY   On N5, 1.5km (1 mile) west from the center of town, stands this Carthusian monastery built by Philip the Bold as a burial place; it's now a psychiatric hospital. Much of it was destroyed during the Revolution. Following a 1.2 million–euro renovation project, the much-admired Well of Moses in the garden is open again to the public. This classified historic monument was designed by Claus Sluter at the end of the 14th century.

1 bd. Chanoine-Kir. (✆ **08-92-70-05-58** Admission 3.50€, free for children under 18. Daily 9:30am–12:30pm and 2–5pm (Apr–Oct until 5:30pm).

## Shopping

Your shopping list may include robust regional wines, Dijon mustard, antiques, and the black currant liqueur, cassis (try a splash with white wine for a kir, or use champagne for a kir royale). The best shopping streets are rue de la Liberté, rue du Bourg, rue Bossuet, place Grangier for designer shops, and rue Verrerie for antiques and interiors. The market at **Les Halles Centrales,** rue Odebert, sells fruits, vegetables, and foodstuffs on Tuesday, Thursday, and Friday from 8am to noon, and Saturday from 8am to around 5pm. At the same time along the market's periphery, a separate endeavor specializes in used clothing, kitchen utensils, housewares, and flea-market castoffs.

Mustard from the region.

For the ideal picnic lunch, begin on rue Musette with **Le Chalet Comtois** at no. 28 (✆ **03-80-30-48-61**) for quiches and artisanal cheese; then **La Vie Saine** (✆ **03-80-30-15-10**) just opposite for organic foods including salads, fruits, and yogurts; and **Paul** at no. 25 for filled baguettes and patisseries. Further along the street at no. 15, you'll find **A La Bonne Choucroute**: this butcher has been tempting customers with its famed choucroute, pâtés, and sliced meats since 1912. Follow with a visit to the **Crémerie Porcheret,** 18 rue Bannelier (✆ **03-80-30-21-05**), to pick up several regional cheeses, including *citeaux*, made by the brothers at a nearby monastery. The new kid on the block, **Le 2 bis Epicerie Gourmande** (✆ **03-80-67-84-22**), on rue Jeannin, is a delicatessen run by charming Breton Hélène Le Cler where you can stock up on fresh hams, pâtés, biscuits, wines, and regional beers as well as huge bottles of popcorn until 8pm on Tuesday to Saturday and until 1pm on Sunday. At **La Boutique Maille,** 32 rue de la Liberté (✆ **03-80-30-41-02**), you can purchase many varieties of the world-famous mustard. Finish your journey at one of the three locations of **Mulot et Petitjean,** 1 place Notre-Dame, 16 rue de la Liberté, or the ornately paneled flagship at 13 place Bossuet (✆ **03-80-30-07-10**), where you can pick up a pastry (especially gingerbread) for dessert.

For antiques and interiors, head to the half-timbered streets around rue Verrerie: **Dubard,** at no. 25 bis rue Verrerie (✆ **03-80-30-50-81**) has an interesting collection of equine-inspired antiques. Around the corner, **Antiquaires Golmard,** 3 rue Auguste Comté (✆ **03-80-67-14-15**), specializes in objects originating on private estates in the region. This store is flexible about trading antiques with individuals and other dealers, making it something of a clearinghouse for unusual antiques from throughout Europe. **Le Consortium,** 37 rue de Longvic (www.leconsortium.com; ☏ **03-80-68-45-55**), is one of Dijon's most interesting modern-art galleries.

For the last 30 years, **Le Baldaquin**, 13 rue Verrerie ☏ **03-80-30-59-69**), has been a children's treasure trove of wooden toys and mobiles. Personalised bags and pictures can be ordered and prepared in 48 hours. For a sweet-smelling gift, **Les Ateliers du Parfumeur**, 11 rue Mably (www.lesateliersduparfumeur. com; ☏ **03-80-30-97-04**) hits the spot with its perfumes and toiletries by sought-after Parisian brands including Artisan Parfumeur and Diptyque, as well as pretty silver jewelry.

# Where to Eat

Hotels offer some of the city's best and most reliable cuisine: in particular, the Michelin-starred **Hostellerie du Chapeau-Rouge** under the helm of the acclaimed chef William Frachot and the garden-facing **La Cloche** at **Hôtel de la Cloche** (see "Where to Stay," p. 417) both have impressive restaurants.

**La Maison des Cariatides** ★★ ⊞ BURGUNDIAN/FRENCH    This new gastronomic restaurant is the one to watch for a Michelin star in Dijon. The venue is one of Dijon's most famous monuments—a listed 17th-century house whose facade comes complete with ornately sculpted caryatids. The chef, Thomas Collomb, believes in fresh ingredients over fuss, and his pitch-perfect cuisine keeps well-heeled diners flocking back. The wild seabass with olive oil–infused mashed potatoes and pan-fried mushrooms with sun-dried tomatoes is a revelation. The thoughtfully selected wine list features independent winegrowers from all corners of Burgundy. A stylishly sober decor is highlighted by a pristine open-plan kitchen lined with gleaming pans.

28 rue Chaudronnerie. www.lamaisondescariatides.fr. ☏ **03-80-45-59-25.** Reservations requi-red. Main courses 19€–25€; fixed-price lunch 21€; fixed-price dinner 29€ –49€. MC, V. Tues–Fri noon–1:45pm; Tues–Sat 7:30–9:30pm.

**Le Pré aux Clercs** ★★★ BURGUNDIAN/FRENCH    In an 18th-century house across from the Palais des Ducs, this is one of Dijon's finest Michelin-starred restaurants, with a reputation that dates to 1833. Chef-owner Jean-Pierre Billoux, assisted by his son, Alexis, prepare meals that consistently win acclaim. Menu items, served beneath an intricately beamed ceiling, may include pâté of pigeon cooked in garlic and red wine or roasted pear with gingerbread ice-cream. The array of wines will delight any connoisseur. In summertime, make sure you book a table outside on the pedestrianized crescent with its privileged view over the magnificent Palais des Duc (dining inside on a recent winter visit, the view was largely obscured by badly placed pot plants, except for those lucky enough to secure the one table in the middle of the window). A new addition is five gor-geously appointed guest rooms from 180€ to 400€. Jean-Pierre also runs the neighboring B9: a contemporary brasserie where you'll find a simpler menu.

13 place de la Libération. www.jeanpierrebilloux.com. ☏ **03-80-38-05-05.** Reservations requi-red. Main courses 25€–45€; fixed-price lunch 35€, dinner 52€ and 95€. AE, MC, V. Tues–Sun noon–1:45pm; Tues–Sat 7:30–9:30pm. Closed 10 days in Aug.

**Les Pieds Bleus** ★ 🍃 VEGETARIAN    A modest purple facade hides this excellent vegetarian restaurant in one of Dijon's pretty pedestrianized squares. Once inside, you'll find a shabby chic decor: wall friezes of exotic locations, wooden communal dining tables, and a long buffet table stacked with mouth-watering salads, hot dishes, and soup. The self-service formula is simple: 12€ for as much food as you can eat. Desserts at 2.50€ are extra. Tables fill up quickly, so it's best to arrive early to grab a place.

13 place Emile Zola. © **03-80-50-06-66.** Fixed-price lunch 12€. AE, MC, V. Mon–Fri 11:45am–2pm.

**Stéphane Derbord** ★★ FRENCH    Given the prices and acclaim of this Michelin-starred restaurant, customers have a right to expect perfection—and they get it. Stéphane Derbord is the most sought-after restaurant in Dijon. Stéphane's charming wife presides over the cozy dining room. Saône River *sandre* (a local whitefish) is roasted and served with tarragon cream, and caramelized duckling with black currant. Chef Derbord recommends the *filet de boeuf*, "the emblem of our region," with a pinot noir reduction and organic potatoes.

10 place Wilson. www.restaurantstephanederbord.fr. © **03-80-67-74-64.** Reservations required. Main courses 36€–44€; fixed-price lunch menu 25€; dinner menus 66€–95€. AE, DC, MC, V. Tues–Sat noon–1:45pm; Mon–Sat 7:30–9.15pm. Closed 1 week in Jan and 2 weeks in Aug.

## Where to Eat Nearby

**Restaurant des Gourmets** ★★ FRENCH    Gourmets have been coming to this aptly named village restaurant for over 50 years. Romain Detot's imaginative cuisine is reason enough to journey to a charming medieval village 6km (3¾ miles) south of Dijon. In a modern room overlooking a garden, you can enjoy a seasonal menu that may include main-course delights such as red-legged partridge with licorice. The cellar contains more than 600 wines; many are burgundies from lesser-known, small-scale wineries.

8 rue du Puits de Têt, Marsannay-la-Côte 21160. www.restaurant-lesgourmets.com . © **03-80-52-16-32.** Reservations recommended. Main courses 24€–34€; fixed-price lunch menu 17€; dinner menus 25€–89€. AE, DC, MC, V. Wed–Sun noon–1:30pm and 7–9:30pm. Closed 2 weeks in Aug. Drive 9.5km (6 miles) south of Dijon on D122, following the signs for Beaune and then Marsannay-la-Côte.

## Dijon Nightlife

A new nightclub, **Bal'tazar,** 20 avenue Garibaldi (www.bal-tazar.fr; © **06-25-82-76-71**) is the latest place to rock Dijon. With its tree-trunk benches and naturalistic friezes, this stylishly modern and eco-friendly venue is open every Thursday to Saturday from 10pm. Bordello chic reigns at another popular venue, **Le Cercle Jamaïque,** 14 place de la République (www.lecerclejamaique.com; © **03-80-73-52-19**). It's a bar (open Tues–Sat from 2pm) and nightclub (open Thurs–Sat from 10.30pm) rolled into one, with jazz, rock, and Latin tunes until 4am.

The long-awaited arrival of **L*Hôtel Particulier** (www.lhotelparticulier-dijon.com) transformed an 18th-century mansion on rue Musette into Dijon's funkiest venue. Life-size Playmobil figures, black-and-white canvases of pop legends, and high vaulted ceilings set the scene. Open Tuesday to Saturday until 2am, it's the place to go for pre-dinner aperitifs and post-dinner cocktails before heading onto one of Dijon's nightclubs.

Lined with classic paperbacks and original printing paraphernalia, **L'Edito** (aka Imprimerie Concorde), 2 place Darcy (www.brasserie-imprimerie-dijon.fr; © **03-80-30-69-43**) is an atmospheric place for a glass or two of beer. A young, student crowd flocks to **Le Quentin,** 6 rue de Quentin (© **03-80-30-15-05**) opposite Les Halles market, to knock back beer while listening to DJs spinning a mix of electro, jazz, and funk until the early hours from Monday to Saturday and until 10pm on Sundays. Those who like boisterous Irish pubs should head to **Le Flannery's,** 4 place Sainte Bénigne (℗ **03-80-44-94-53**) and **Le Kilkenny,** 1 rue Auguste-Perdrix (℗ **03-80-30-02-48**).

An older crowd and a calmer ambience reigns at expensive but chic hotel bars such as **Bar de la Cloche** for pre-dinner champagne or a post-dinner whiskey, or **L'Autre Entrée,** 19 rue Berbisey (twinned with Hôtel Philippe Le Bon) for wines by the glass.

The opera season (www.opera-dijon.fr; ℗ **03-80-48-82-82**) in Dijon stretches from the middle of October to June. Operas, dance recitals, and concerts are held in two venues: **Grand Théâtre de Dijon,** place du Théâtre (where you can pop along anytime Tues–Sat from 11am–6pm to buy tickets) and **L'Auditorium,** place Jean Bouhey (that opens just 1 hr. before each performance). Prices range from 8€ to 75€. You can also pick up tickets at FNAC on rue du Bourg.

# Where to Stay

The gastronomic restaurant **Le Pré aux Clercs** now offers bedrooms (see p. 415).

**Hostellerie du Chapeau-Rouge ★★**   Our favorite landmark hotel in central Dijon combines modern conveniences and stylish furnishings with good value as part of the Best Western hotel chain. It has just emerged from an extensive renovation of the reception area and breakfast room in calming green tones, plus the opening of a new basement-level spa with free access for guests to the *hammam,* sauna, and massage showers. Bedrooms vary enormously in style, so guests can choose according to their taste. For those who like ultra-modern interiors, we recommend the recently renovated superior room 121 with its dusky pink and black decor and a large walk-in shower. A more classic superior room with burnt orange fabrics and rich wood furnishings is 129. Because no other hotel restaurant in town serves comparable food, you may want to visit here even if you're not a guest. The Michelin-starred restaurant features innovative fare with French and Asian influences.

5 rue Michelet, Dijon 21024. www.chapeau-rouge.fr. ℗ **03-80-50-88-88.** Fax 03-80-50-88-89. 29 units. 115€–150€ double; 270€ suite. AE, DC, MC, V. Parking 14€. **Amenities:** Restaurant; bar; room service, spa. *In room:* A/C, TV, hair dryer, minibar, free Wi-Fi.

**Hôtel de La Cloche ★**   Legends associated with this site date from the 15th century, but the building evokes a late-19th-century grand hotel, complete with high ceilings and the modernized decor favored by Napoleon III. Part of the Sofitel luxury hotel chain, it's a five-minute walk from the train station and seconds away from Dijon's Arc de Triomphe marking the entrance to the old town center. Overlooking the garden square or the hotel garden, the modern guest rooms have tub/showers. The restaurant overlooks the pretty garden where you can dine in summertime amongst the magnolia trees.

14 place Darcy, Dijon 21000. www.hotel-lacloche.com. ℗ **03-80-30-12-32.** Fax 03-80-30-04-15. 68 units. 200€–240€ double; 320€–800€ suite. AE, DC, MC, V. Parking 30€. **Amenities:** Restaurant; bar; babysitting; exercise room; room service; sauna. *In room:* A/C, TV, hair dryer, minibar, free Wi-Fi.

**Hôtel Wilson** 🎎   Conveniently situated next door to Stéphane Derbord's gastronomic restaurant, this *ancien relais de poste* (coaching inn) dates from the 17th century and has been tastefully restored with exposed old wood ceiling beams and Burgundian wood furniture. Rooms have a worn but comfortable feel with small bathrooms, some with tubs. It's worth noting that rooms overlooking the interior courtyard are quieter.

1 rue de Longvic, Dijon 21000. www.wilson-hotel.com. ✆ **03-80-66-82-50.** Fax 03-80-36-41-54. 27 units. 75€–135€ double. AE, MC, V. Parking 14€. **Amenities:** Bar. *In room:* A/C (in some), TV, hair dryer, free Wi-Fi.

**Le Jacquemart** 🍴  In the center of Old Dijon is one of the town's most affordable hotels. A building from the 1900s was completely restored, yet retains its steep stairwell and high ceilings. It's furnished in a no-nonsense modern style with clean bed linen and small bathrooms. There is no elevator or air-conditioning, but the welcome is genuine. Some of the accommodations are large enough to house three or four guests. For those on a budget that don't mind sharing a shower room and toilet on the landing, the cheapest rooms are good value at 36€. Standard rooms no. 24 and 25 open onto a second-floor terrace. Breakfast is available for 6.50€.

32 rue Verrerie, Dijon 21000. www.hotel-lejacquemart.fr. ✆ **03-80-60-09-60.** 3 units. 36€–68€ double; 68-75€ triple; 82€ quad. AE, MC, V. Parking: 6€. **Amenities:** Breakfast room. *In room:* TV, hair dryer, free Wi-Fi.

# AUXERRE ★★

154km (95 miles) SE of Paris; 148km (92 miles) NW of Dijon

Auxerre was founded by the Gauls and enlarged by the Romans, although there are sadly no Gallo-Roman remains. On a hill overlooking the Yonne River, it's home to many vineyards, famed for their dry white Chablis wine. Joan of Arc spent several days here in 1429. Napoleon met Maréchal Ney here in 1815, on the former emperor's return from Elba. Louis XVIII had sent Ney to stop Napoleon, but Ney embraced him and turned his army against the king. For that, Ney was later shot.

This city is a sleepy, pleasant place with beautifully preserved *colombage* (half-timbered) buildings. Its 40,000 residents will admit that not a lot happens here—and that's how they like it. Nearby, you can awaken your taste buds at the celebrated restaurant La Côte Saint Jacques.

Auxerre.

## Essentials

**GETTING THERE**  Visitors often **drive** here because Auxerre is near A6/E15 (the Autoroute du Soleil) motorway from Paris. There are nine trains per day from

Paris (Gare de Bercy; trip time: 1½ hr approx.), and the fare is 26€ one-way. For train information, visit www.voyages-sncf.com or call ℂ 08-92-33-53-35.

**VISITOR INFORMATION**   The **Office de Tourisme** is at 1–2 quai de la République (www.ot-auxerre.fr; ℂ 03-86-52-06-19).

# Exploring Auxerre

The railway station is at the eastern edge of town, about 1.5km (1 mile) from the historic center. Most of Auxerre is on the western bank of the Yonne. Its heart is between place du Maréchal-Leclerc (near the Hôtel de Ville [city hall]) and the Cathédrale St-Étienne.

**Cathédrale St-Étienne ★★** CATHEDRAL   Pay a visit to the flamboyant Gothic Cathédrale St-Étienne, begun in the 13th century but not completed until the 16th. The front facade is remarkable, with sculptured portals. The stained glass, some of it original, is famous. In the crypt, which is all that remains of the Romanesque church that stood on this site, you can see 11th-century frescoes.

Daily from June to mid-August at 10pm (9:30pm from mid-Aug to Sept) a 70-minute sound-and-light show relates the history of the church. It's presented in English, French, and German, and costs 5€ for adults; 4€ for children 13 and under.

Place St-Étienne. ℂ **03-86-52-23-29.** Free admission to church. Admission 1.90€ to treasury, 3€ to crypt. Cathedral daily 7:30am–6pm (till 5pm All Saints Day–Palm Sunday). Crypt and treasury Palm Sunday–All Saints Day Mon–Sat 9am–6pm, Sun 2–6pm; All Saints Day–Palm Sunday Mon–Sat 10am–5pm

# Where to Eat

**Le Jardin Gourmand ★★** FRENCH   The most sophisticated restaurant in town specializes in *cuisine moderne du marché* (modern market cuisine), employing the freshest ingredients to create artfully presented menus that change, often radically, eight times a year. Contemporary interiors set an upbeat tone in this 1870 house a 10-minute walk from the cathedral with seating for just 17. In summer, flowering shrubs shade the wooden terrace. The chefs are devoted to cultivating fresh salad greens and herbs in their garden, and use them to garnish such platters as pan-fried, locally grown cèpe mushrooms. Other tasty dishes include Bigorre black pig's head pâté, roast pigeon with sloes, and line-caught seabass smoked in beech wood.

56 bd. Vauban. www.lejardingourmand.com. ℂ **03-86-51-53-52.** Reservations required. Main courses 35€–48€; fixed-price menu 55€ lunch, 75€–115€ dinner. MC, V. Wed–Sun noon–1:45pm and 7:30–9:15pm (closed on Sun evenings in winter). Closed 4 weeks throughout the year (consult the website for dates).

# Where to Stay

**Hôtel Le Maxime**   Attractive, high-ceilinged rooms, many with views of the river or the old city, highlight this family-run hotel. Most units retain their original wall and ceiling beams. This 19th-century private mansion was turned into a gracious, old-fashioned inn in the 1950s and has been run by the Leclerc family for the last decade. A thorough renovation has upgraded the accommodations.

You can take breakfast in your room or in the quiet salon, amid Oriental rugs, polished paneling, and a sense of the gentility of an earlier era.

2 quai de la Marine, Auxerre 89000. www.lemaxime.com. ✆ **03-86-52-14-19.** Fax 03-86-52-21-70. 27 units. 92€–130€ double; 144€–236€ suite. AE, DC, MC, V. Parking 8€. **Amenities:** Bar. *In room:* A/C, TV, hair dryer, minibar, free Wi-Fi.

**Le Parc des Maréchaux ★**   A gem that outshines the competition, this three-star hotel was a Napoleon III–style private residence in the 19th century, set in its own 4-hectare (1-acre) park. The most secluded choice in the area, it's on the western outskirts of town, surrounded by century-old trees. The decor in the public areas and the lounge is French Empire; the style of the guest rooms is less consistent—a mixture of contemporary and Empire. Rooms vary from cozy (or cramped depending upon your point of view) to medium-sized. Ask for a room overlooking the park, as avenue-side rooms can be noisy. The only available meal is breakfast, but the staff will serve hot food, on special request, in your room or in one of the salons.

6 av. Foch, Auxerre 89000. www.hotel-parcmarechaux.com. ✆ **03-86-51-43-77.** Fax 03-86-51-31-72. 25 units. 97€–146€ double; 134€–168€ triple or quad. AE, DC, MC, V. **Amenities:** Heated outdoor pool; room service. *In room:* A/C, TV, minibar, free Wi-Fi.

# Where to Stay Nearby

**La Côte Saint Jacques ★★★** FRENCH/BURGUNDIAN   This is one of the top Relais & Châteaux members in France, with a 300-year-old foundation, a clientele that has included Catherine Deneuve and several French presidents, and a well-ingrained sense of comfort and culinary style. Chef Jean Michel Lorain's specialties include beef carpaccio and duck foie gras with cèpe mushrooms, roasted blue lobster, and pigeon filet with Goji berries and white mulberries.

La Côte Saint Jacques also offers 32 opulent rooms that are air-conditioned, contemporary, very comfortable, and decorated with individual color schemes and parquet floors. Ten less expensive, non-air-conditioned rooms lie on an older site. An underground tunnel, fashioned from rocks salvaged from old buildings, connects the two sections. Doubles start at 225€, and suites run from 510€ to 640€.

14 Faubourg de Paris (N6), Joigny 89300. www.cotesaintjacques.com. ✆ **03-86-62-09-70.** Fax 03-86-91-49-70. Reservations required. Main courses 50€–100€; fixed-price lunch (from Wed–Sat) 44€ dinner 145€–215€. AE, DC, MC, V. Tues 7.30–9.45pm, Wed–Sun 12:15–2pm and 7:30–9:45pm. Hotel and restaurant closed Mon and early to late Jan. From Auxerre, head north on A6 (toward Sens) for 27km (17 miles). **Amenities:** Restaurant; spa; fitness room; indoor pool; sauna; kids' playroom; shop. *In room:* TV, minibar, free Wi-Fi.

**Auberge La Lucarne aux Chouettes ★ 🎁**   You may remember Leslie Caron—she was that French gamin who won our hearts by sexily pirouetting with Gene Kelly in *An American in Paris* in 1951 and, later, in 1958, portraying a Parisian courtesan-in-training in *Gigi*. She was more recently seen playing a widow who found passion in *Chocolat* (2000). In this village 46km (29 miles) north of Auxerre, she took some 17th-century buildings and turned them into a small inn. The whole is now under new ownership that has brought La Lucarne up-to-date.

Quai Bretoche, Villeneuve-sur-Yonne 89500. www.lalucarneauxchouettes.fr. ✆ **03-86-87-18-26.** Fax 03-86-87-22-63. 4 units. 55€ double; 99€ triple or duplex. AE, MC, V. **Amenities:** Restaurant. *In room:* TV, hair dryer, Wi-Fi.

# VÉZELAY ★★

217km (135 miles) SE of Paris; 52km (32 miles) S of Auxerre

Vézelay, a living museum of French antiquity, stands frozen in time. For many, the town is the high point of a trip through Burgundy. During the 12th century, it was one of the great pilgrimage sites of the Christian world as it contained the alleged tomb of St. Mary Magdalene, that "beloved and pardoned sinner."

Today the medieval charm of Vézelay is widely known throughout France, and visitors virtually overrun the town in summer. The hordes are especially thick on July 22, the official day of homage to La Madeleine.

## Essentials

**GETTING THERE**   If you're **driving** from Paris, take A6 south to Auxerre, then continue south along N6 to Givry and then D951 to Vézelay. Eight **trains** a day travel from Paris Gare de Bercy to Sermizelles, taking 2½ hours and costing 31€ one-way. For train information, visit www.voyages-sncf.com or call ✆ **08-92-33-53-35.** You'll need to take a short taxi ride from there into town.

**VISITOR INFORMATION**   The **Office de Tourisme** is at 12 rue St-Etienne (www.vezelaytourisme.com; ✆ **03-86-33-23-69;** fax 09-70-62-05-62).

## Exploring the Town

On a hill 108m (354 ft.) above the countryside, Vézelay is known for its ramparts and houses with sculptured doorways, corbeled staircases, and mullioned windows. The town began as an abbey founded by Girart de Roussillon, comte de Bourgogne in 858.

On March 31, 1146, St. Bernard preached the Second Crusade here; in 1190, the town was the rendezvous point for the Third Crusade, drawing such personages as Richard the Lionheart and King Philippe-Auguste of France. Later, St. Louis IX came here several times on pilgrimages.

Park outside the town hall and walk through the medieval streets lined with 15th-, 16th-, and 18th-century houses and flower-filled gardens. If you're in the mood to shop, head for rue St-Etienne and rue St-Pierre. You'll find an assortment of stores selling religious books and statuary, including **La Pierre d'Angle,** place de la Basilique (✆ **03-86-33-29-14). Galerie Lieber,** 14 rue St-Etienne (✆ **03-86-33-33-90),** specializes in handmade jewelry, using semiprecious and precious stones in both heavy and delicate settings of silver and gold, including some African and Asian items. You may also want to pick up a bottle or

Basilique Ste-Madeleine.

two of Vézelay wine at **La Cave Henry de Vézelay,** 4 route de Nanchèvres, St-Père-sous-Vézelay (✆ **03-86-33-29-62**).

**Basilique Ste-Madeleine ★★** CHURCH Built in the 12th century, France's largest and most famous Romanesque church is only 9m (30 ft.) shorter than Notre-Dame de Paris. When you enter the narthex of this UNESCO world heritage site, a vestibule of about 370 sq. m (3,983 sq. ft.), raise your eyes to the doorway depicting Christ giving the apostles the Holy Spirit. From the Romanesque nave, with its traverse arches in white-and-gray stone, you'll see the light Gothic chancel. You can visit the Carolingian crypt, where the tomb of Mary Magdalene formerly rested and which now contains some of her relics. There's a panoramic view from the back terrace.

Place de la Basilique, Vézelay 89450. ✆ **03-86-33-39-50.** Free admission. Daily 7am–8pm.

## Where to Eat

**La Bougainville ★**🍴 BURGUNDIAN Not all of us can afford to dine at L'Espérance (see below), so La Bougainville is a more affordable alternative. This elegantly decorated antique house, complete with fireplace, serves as a backdrop for such regional specialties as *oeufs en meurette* (eggs poached in red wine and served with red-wine sauce) or a platter of oysters. After that, you can plunge into *filet de boeuf bourguignon* (beef cooked in burgundy, here with crème fraîche and escargots). The restaurant is also adept at concocting game dishes, such as venison with chestnuts or a delightful hare stew. Leave room for the homemade desserts.

28 rue St-Etienne. ✆ **03-86-33-27-57.** Reservations required. Main courses 10€–30€; fixed-price menus 22€–29€. MC, V. Thurs–Mon noon–2pm and 7–9pm. Closed mid-Nov to mid-Feb.

**L'Espérance ★★★** MODERN FRENCH No other restaurant in Burgundy is as frequently accessed and gossiped about as this one. The two Michelin-starred restaurant has the feel of an old-fashioned farm and bakery, with Napoleon III decor. Located in a fertile valley, it emanates both Burgundian wholesomeness and Parisian chic. Flagstone floors and big windows overlooking a garden complement the superb cuisine. Marc Méneau runs a smooth kitchen producing classic menu items such as *cromesquis de foie gras* (in the form of a cube that melts in your mouth), potato galette with caviar, turbot en croûte, and roasted and caramelized filet of veal. The overworked staff struggles valiantly with the traffic generated by the place's fame.

On the premises of this Relais & Châteaux property are 34 well-maintained and comfortable guest rooms in three historic buildings. The accommodations epitomize French country living at its best. Doubles cost 150€ to 300€, apartments 350€ to 450€.

Saint-Père-en-Vézelay. www.marc-meneau-esperance.com. ✆ **03-86-33-39-10.** Fax 03-86-33-26-15. Reservations recommended. Main courses 75€–120€; fixed-price lunch 39€-95€, dinner 130€–195€. AE, DC, MC, V. Thurs–Sun noon–2pm; Wed–Mon 7:30–9:30pm. Closed mid-Jan to early Mar.

## Where to Stay

**L'Espérance** (see "Where to Eat," above) also rents luxurious rooms.

**Le Compostelle** 🍴 This pleasant two-star hotel is the best of Vézelay's more affordable inns. It's in the center of town, up the hill leading to the basilica, in a late-19th-century building that was transformed into a hotel in 1991. It's reminiscent of an English country house. Guest rooms are midsize and comfortably furnished, with small, shower-only bathrooms. Breakfast is the only meal served.

Place du Champ de Foire, Vézelay 89450. www.lecompostellevezelay.com. ☎ 03-86-33-28-63. Fax 03-86-33-34-34. 18 units. 49€–64€ double. 76€–86€ triple or quad. AE, MC, V. Closed Dec–early Jan.. **Amenities:** Bar. *In room:* TV, free Wi-Fi.

**Poste et Lion d'Or ★** This local favorite is filled with character and tradition. On the main square, at the bottom of the hill that rises to the basilica, this hotel was built in the 17th century as a postal station. With a terrace, garden, and small restaurant, the Poste et Lion d'Or is first-class lodging with surprisingly reasonable rates. The functional guest rooms are conservatively outfitted—in some cases, in a vaguely Louis XVI style.

Place du Champ-de-Foire, Vézelay 89450. www.laposte-liondor.com. ☎ 03-86-33-21-23. Fax 03-86-32-30-92. 38 units. 82€–122€ double; 149€–164€ suite. AE, DC, MC, V. Parking 6€. Closed Jan–Feb. **Amenities:** Restaurant; bar. *In room:* A/C, TV, free Wi-Fi.

# AVALLON ★

214km (133 miles) SE of Paris; 52km (32 miles) SE of Auxerre; 96km (60 miles) NW of Dijon

Eglise St-Lazare.

This fortified town sits behind ancient ramparts, upon which you can stroll. A medieval atmosphere permeates Avallon, where you'll find many 15th- and 16th-century houses. At the town gate on grande rue Aristide-Briand is a 1460 clock tower. The Romanesque **Collégiale St-Lazare** dates from the 12th century and has fantastic doorways, an artfully lit interior, and impressive woodwork. The church, open daily from 8am to 7pm, is said to have received the head of St. Lazarus in 1000, thus turning it into a pilgrimage site. Today Avallon is a destination mainly for its fabulous food.

## Essentials

**GETTING THERE** If you're **driving,** travel south from Paris along A6 past Auxerre to Avallon. Two direct **trains** arrive daily from Paris Gare de Bercy (trip time: almost 3 hrs; 32€ one-way). Bus service from Dijon takes 2 hours and costs 1.50€ one-way; purchase tickets on the bus. For train information and schedules, visit www.voyages-sncf.com or call ☎ 08-92-33-53-35.

**VISITOR INFORMATION** The **Office de Tourisme** is at 6 rue Bocquillot (www.avallon-tourisme.fr; ☎ 03-86-34-14-19).

## Where to Eat

**Les Capucins** BURGUNDIAN   Warm colors and fresh flowers brighten this restaurant, which is just a 12-minute stroll from the heart of town. It's on the ground floor of a little hotel that rents 19 air-conditioned guest rooms for 40€ to 60€ for doubles. Free Wi-Fi is offered in every room. The Burgundian fare includes eggs poached in a red wine *meurettes* sauce, snails in garlic and parsley butter, and *andouillette* sausage casserole cooked in chablis white wine.

6 av. du Président Doumer, Avallon 89200. www.avallonlescapucins.com. ☎ **03-86-34-06-52.** Fax 03-86-34-58-47. Main courses 10€–24€; fixed-price menu 14€–38€. AE, MC, V. Daily noon–2pm and 7–9:30pm.

## Where to Stay

**Château de Vault-de-Lugny** ★★★   Between Avallon and Vézelay is this 16th-century moat-encircled château, with a fortress tower and peacocks on the grounds. It emphasizes service, with two staff members to every guest. The five-star hotel accommodations are sumptuous, with canopy beds, antique furnishings, and fireplaces. Luxurious bathrooms hold tub/showers. You can order cocktails in the salon and then eat dinner by candlelight. Fresh ingredients are the hallmark of the cuisine here. A special bourguignon meal of typical regional dishes is offered nightly. As well as a spa, there's an indoor pool housed in the ancient vaulted cellars. A cottage in the grounds is perfect for family stays.

11 rue du Chateau, Vault-de-Lugny 89200. www.lugny.fr. ☎ **03-86-34-07-86.** Fax 03-86-34-16-36. 16 units. 270€–420€; 450€–700€ suite & king's bedroom. AE, DC, MC, V. Closed mid-Nov to mid-Apr. Take D957 from Avallon, turn right in Pontaubert (after the church) and follow signs; Vault-de-Lugny is about 3km (1¾ miles) away. **Amenities:** Restaurant; bar; babysitting; indoor pool; spa; room service, free Wi-Fi. *In room:* TV, hair dryer, minibar.

**Moulin des Ruats** ★ 🏠   This enchanting country inn sits on the banks of the Cousin. Constructed as a flour mill in the 17th century, it has been a family hotel since 1924. Some guest rooms have exposed beams and intimate alcoves. Each contains a small bathroom with a shower, and some have tubs as well. Try for a room with a balcony overlooking the river. It's worth noting that there is no air-conditioning in the rooms. The elegant dining room serves prix-fixe menus ranging from healthy to traditional fare, complemented by a fine wine list and a terrace. The restaurant and accommodations are equally atmospheric and impressive.

9 rue des Isles Labaumes, Avallon 89200. www.moulindesruats.com. ☎ **03-86-34-97-00.** Fax 03-86-31-65-47. 25 units. 85€–140€ double, 140€ suite. AE, DC, MC, V. Closed mid-Nov to mid-Feb. Take D427 3km (1¾ miles) west outside town. **Amenities:** Restaurant; bar; free Wi-Fi. *In room:* TV.

# SAULIEU ★

250km (155 miles) SE of Paris; 76km (47 miles) NW of Beaune

Saulieu is interesting, but its food put it on the international map. The town (pop. 3,000) has enjoyed a reputation for cooking since the 17th century. Even Mme. de Sévigné praised it in her letters. So did Rabelais.

The main sight is the 12th-century **Basilique St-Andoche,** place Docteur Roclore (☎ **03-80-64-07-03**), which has some interesting decorated capitals.

Next door, in the **Musée François-Pompon**, (✆ **03-80-64-19-51**), you can see works by François Pompon (d. 1930), the sculptor of animals whose works are featured in Paris's Musée d'Orsay. Pompon's large statue of a bull stands on a plaza off N6 at the entrance to Saulieu. Also in the museum are archaeological remnants from the Gallo-Roman era, sacred medieval art, and old tools illustrating aspects of life in Burgundy several centuries ago. Admission is 4€ for adults; 2.50€ for children 12 to 16 and free for children under 12 (Mon 10am–12:30pm; Wed–Sat 10am–12:30pm 2–5:30pm; Sun 10:30am–noon 2:30–5pm). It's closed in January and February.

## Essentials

**GETTING THERE**    If you're **driving**, head along A6 from Paris or Lyon. The **train** station is northeast of the town center. Passengers coming from Paris sometimes opt to take the TGV from the Gare de Lyon, getting off in Montbard, 48km (30 miles) to the north. There are about six TGV trains a day to Montbard and the journey takes just over 1 hour and costs 53€. From Montbard, a series of **buses** timed to the arrival of the TGV carry passengers on to Saulieu for a one-way fare of 1.50€. For bus information, call Transco (www.mobigo-bourgogne.com/transco-lignes.htm; ✆ **03-80-11-29-29**); for rail information, visit www.voyages-sncf.com or call ✆ **08-92-33-53-35.**

**VISITOR INFORMATION**    The **Office de Tourisme** is at 24 rue d'Argentine (www.saulieu.fr; ✆ **03-80-64-00-21**).

## Where to Stay & Eat

**Château Les Roches ★★**    Twelve kilometers (7½ miles) east of Saulieu, just off D36, stands this imposing country residence in a medieval hilltop village, with panoramic views of the countryside. This magnificent B&B, decorated in exquisite taste, was built by a judge at the turn of the 20th century as an abode for his mistress. The face of that long-ago mistress can be found on the hand-painted ceiling panels in the dining room. The architect borrowed freely from styles in Austria, Switzerland, and Germany. Public rooms are adorned with original wood paneling, high ceilings, and intricate plasterwork. Bedrooms are spacious and furnished with a sumptuous mix of antique and contemporary furnishings, half with showers, half with bathtubs. Home-cooked dinners are offered four nights a week, while picnic lunch baskets and cold-cut dinners are available daily.

Rue de Glanot, Mont Saint-Jean 21320. www.lesroches-burgundy.com. ✆ **03-80-84-32-71.** 6 units. 129€–169€ double. Rates include breakfast. MC, V. **Amenities:** Restaurant (Mon, Thurs, Fri, and Sat) exercise room; room service (breakfast only); wine cellar. *In room:* Free Wi-Fi.

**Le Relais Bernard Loiseau ★★★**    This former stagecoach stop with one of the best-known restaurants in France is an excellent choice. If you want to stay overnight, you'll find guest rooms with everything from Empire to Louis XV decor. You'll sleep on a comfortable mattress, on a bed that's likely to be 200 years old.

The 2003 suicide of its famous chef, Bernard Loiseau (rumored to be despondent at the thought of losing a Michelin star), shocked the culinary world. Loiseau's wife, Dominique, and staff are carrying on admirably under Chef Patrick Bertron, who was a culinary disciple of Loiseau for 20 years. The cooking remains in his style: less traditional, emphasizing maximum taste with no excess fat or sugar. With a cellar that holds more than 15,000 bottles, it's not surprising that all the great burgundies are on the wine list. As well as a fixed-priced weekday lunch menu for 68€, there are fixed-price menus ranging from 120€ to 195€. Children are treated well here with young gourmet meals for kids under 12 years and a playroom filled with games and cuddly toys. The English garden is abundant with old-fashioned roses, hydrangeas, and peonies.

2 rue Argentine, Saulieu 21210. www.bernard-loiseau.com. 32 units. ✆ **03-80-90-53-53.** Fax 03-80-64-08-92. 145€–360€ double; 405€–555€ suite. AE, MC, V. Closed Tues and Wed (except on public holidays); Jan 4 to mid-Feb. **Amenities:** Restaurant; bar; exercise room; indoor and outdoor pools; room service; sauna; spa; kids' playroom; pétanque. *In room:* A/C (in some), TV, hair dryer, minibar, free Wi-Fi.

# AUTUN ★★

293km (182 miles) SE of Paris; 85km (53 miles) SW of Dijon; 48km (30 miles) W of Beaune; 60km (37 miles) SE of Auxerre

Deep in Burgundy, Autun is one of the oldest towns in France. In the days of the Roman Empire, it was called "the other Rome." Some relics still stand, including the remains of the largest theater in Gaul, the Théâtre Romain. It was nearly 150m (492 ft.) in diameter and could hold some 20,000 people. Outside the town, you can see the tower of the 24m-high (79-ft.) Temple de Janus.

Autun is a thriving provincial town of 18,000, but because it's off the beaten track, the hordes go elsewhere. Still, it has its historical associations—Napoleon studied here in 1779 at the military academy (today the Lycée Bonaparte).

## Essentials

**GETTING THERE** If you're **driving,** take A6 south until reaching A38, then turn onto N81 towards Autun. Rail links to Autun are awkward. Six high-speed TGV trains a day from Paris's Gare de Lyon run to Le Creusot-Montceau, 40km (25 miles) south of Autun (54.60€–107€ one-way) taking under 1½ hours. From there, take a 45-minute bus connection to Autun. In Autun, **buses** arrive at a parking lot by the railway station on avenue de la République (1.50€ one-way). For bus information, visit www.buscephale.fr or call ✆ **08-00-07-17-10.** For railway information, visit www.voyages-sncf.com or call ✆ **08-92-33-53-35.**

**VISITOR INFORMATION** The **Office de Tourisme** is at 13 rue Général Demetz (www.autun-tourisme.com; ✆ **03-85-86-80-38;** fax 03-85-86-80-49).

## Seeing the Sights

Autun was an important Roman link on the road from Lyon to Boulogne. A legacy of that period is the 17m-high (56-ft.) **Porte d'Arroux,** once the city's Northern gate, which has two archways now used for cars and smaller ones used for pedestrians. Also exceptional is the **Porte St-André (St. Andrew's Gate),** northwest of the Roman theater. Rising 20m (66 ft.), it has four doorways and is surmounted by a gallery of 10 arcades.

**Cathédrale St-Lazare ★★** CATHEDRAL On the highest point in Autun, the cathedral was built in 1120 to house the relics of St. Lazarus. On the facade,

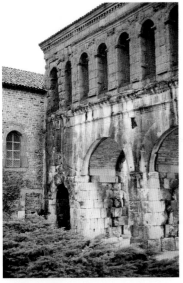

**Porte St-André.**

the tympanum in the central portal depicts the Last Judgment—a triumph of Romanesque sculpture. Inside, a painting by Ingres depicts the martyrdom of St. Symphorien, who was killed in Autun. In the 1850s, Viollet-le-Duc, who restored many monuments in France, had to double the size of some of the columns supporting the roof to avoid a collapse. New capitals matching the Romanesque style of the originals were crafted to top the new columns. The original capitals are on display, more or less at eye level, in the Salle Capitulaire, a flight above street level; especially noteworthy are *La Réveil des Mages* (*The Awakening of the Magi*) and *La Fuite en Égypte* (*The Flight into Egypt*).

Place St-Louis. ✆ **03-85-52-12-37.** Daily 9am–7pm.

**Musée Rolin** ★ MUSEUM This 15th-century mansion was built for a famous lawyer, Nicolas Rolin (b. 1380). An easy walk from the cathedral, the museum displays a collection of Burgundian Romanesque sculpture, as well as paintings and archaeological mementos. From the original Rolin collection are *Nativity,* by the Maître de Moulins, and a statue that's a 15th-century masterpiece, *Our Lady of Autun* (*La Vierge d'Autun,* also known as *La Vierge Bulliot,* after the benefactor who returned the original statue to the cathedral in 1948).

3 rue des Bancs. ✆ **03-85-52-09-76.** Admission 5€ adults, 3€ students and children. Apr–Sept Wed–Mon 9:30am–noon and 1:30–6pm; Oct to mid-Dec and Mar Wed–Mon 10am–noon and 2–5pm (2:30pm reopening on Sun).

## Where to Stay & Eat

**Hôtel les Ursulines** ★ The best hotel in Autun, the three-star Ursulines offers comfortable rooms with views of the countryside and the Morvan mountains. Built in the 1600s as a convent, original features have been preserved in some bedrooms (in particular the Charm rooms) with beamed and mansard ceilings. Most bedrooms are accessible by elevator (with the exception of some rooms on the 2nd floor and in the annex). The hotel is known for its cuisine offering a solid value with fixed-price menus costing from 39€ to 79€.

14 rue de Rivault, Autun 71400. www.hotelursulines.fr. ✆ **03-85-86-58-58.** Fax 03-85-86-23-07. 43 units. 71€–125€ double; 139€–154€ suite. AE, DC, MC, V. Parking 7€. **Amenities:** Restaurant; bar; babysitting. *In room:* A/C (in some), TV, hair dryer, minibar, free Wi-Fi.

# BEAUNE ★★

316km (196 miles) SE of Paris; 39km (24 miles) SW of Dijon

Beaune is the perfect base for exploring the **Côte d'Or** wine region that stretches to the North and South of the city. Burgundy's most influential wine merchants are all based here: Louis Jadot, Joseph Drouhin, and Bouchard Père et Fils, to name but a few. It's one of the best medieval cities in the district, with its girdle of ramparts. Its history spans 2,000 years. Beaune was a Gallic sanctuary, then a Roman town. Until the 14th century, it was the residence of the ducs de Bourgogne. When the last duke, Charles the Bold, died in 1477, Louis XI annexed Beaune.

## Essentials

**GETTING THERE**   If you're **driving,** note that Beaune is a few miles from the junction of four highways—A6, A31and A36. Beaune has good railway connections with Dijon, Lyon, and Paris. From Paris's Gare de Lyon, there are 2 TGV **trains** per day (trip time: just over 2 hr.; 55€–71€ one-way), with many more possibilities via a transfer in Dijon; from Lyon, a dozen or so trains per day (trip time: 1½ hr.; 25€ one-way); and from Dijon, several trains per hour (trip time: under 30 min.; 7.30€ one-way). For train information and schedules, visit www.voyages-sncf.com or call ℂ **08-92-33-53-35.**

### Burgundy by Bike

The best way to see this golden land is by bike. Near the Beaune Rail Station, **Detours in France,** 7 av. du 8-Septembre (www. detours-in-france.com; ℂ **03-80-22-06-03**), rents bikes for 18€ per day.

**VISITOR INFORMATION**   The **Office de Tourisme** is at 6 bd. Perpreuil (www. beaune-tourism.com; ℂ **03-80-26-21-30;** fax 03-80-26-21-39).

**SPECIAL EVENTS**   Beaune comes to life during the weekend preceding the third Sunday in November, when wine buyers and oenophiles from the world over descend on the old town for a 3-day festival and *Ventes des Vins* (wine auction) also called **Les Trois Glorieuses.** The town is packed with wineries offering *dégustations* priced from 20€ to 35€ for "several" glasses each of a different vintage—and with tourists visiting the labyrinth of caves and wine cellars. With all the free spirits (both kinds), visitors crowding the streets can be more than a bit tipsy.

## Exploring the Town

North of the Hôtel-Dieu, the **Collégiale Notre-Dame,** place du Général Leclerc (ℂ **03-80-24-77-95**), is an 1120 Burgundian Romanesque church. Some remarkable 15th-century tapestries illustrating scenes from the life of the Virgin Mary are on display in the sanctuary. You can view them from Easter to mid-November. Admission is 2.50€ for adults, 1.50€ for children 11 to 18; free for children 10 years and under.

The best **shopping** streets are rue de Lorraine, rue d'Alsace, rue Maufoux, and place de la Madeleine. For smaller boutiques, stroll down the pedestrian rue Carnot and rue Monge.

Every Wednesday and Saturday morning, the streets around place de la Halle and place de Fleury are chock-a-block with Burgundy's liveliest market. Arrive early to avoid the tourist crowds and bring bags with you to fill with local produce. The most serious meat and cheese producers have their stalls in the undercover Les Halles market where you'll find stalls specialising in famed Bresse chickens, goats' cheese, or Charolais beef. Outside, the streets nearby are crammed with myriad stalls selling everything from children's toys to fruit and vegetables. Look out for Dijon mustard producers such as Edmond Fallot from Beaune. Other stalls specialize in honey and jams—pick up a *gelée de vignes jaunes* (white-grape jelly) to go with cheese or in sauces.

**Musée de l'Hôtel-Dieu** ★★★ ICON   With its brightly colored patterned roof, one of the town's most visible antique buildings is the 15th-century Hôtel-Dieu. It thrived during the Middle Ages under an order of nuns associated with the famous vineyards of Aloxe-Corton and Meursault. It functioned as a hospital until 1971, and some of the later 18th and 19th-century sections still hold a retirement home. The Musée de l'Hôtel-Dieu displays Flemish-Burgundian art such as Rogier van der Weyden's 1443 polyptych *The Last Judgment* ★★★. In the Salle des Pauvres (Room of the Poor), you'll find painted, broken-barrel, timbered vaulting and mostly authentic furnishings.

Rue de l'Hôtel-Dieu. www.hospices-de-beaune.com. ✆ **03-80-24-45-00.** Admission 6.70€ adults, 2.80€ ages 10–18, free for children 9 and under. Mid-Mar to mid-Nov daily 9am–6:30pm; mid-Nov to mid-Mar daily 9–11:30am and 2–5:30pm.

**Musée des Beaux-Arts** ART MUSEUM   Along with a rich Gallo-Roman archaeological section, this museum has paintings from the 16th to the 19th centuries, including Flemish primitives, and pieces by Beaune-born Félix Ziem, a precursor of the Impressionists. Sculptures from the Middle Ages and the Renaissance are also on display.

6 bd. Perpreuil (Porte Marie de Bourgogne). ✆ **03-80-24-98-70.** Admission (includes Musée du Vin de Bourgogne) 5.50€ adults, 3.50€ students and children 11-18, free for children 10 and under. Daily 11am–1pm and 2–6pm (Dec–Mar closed Tues).

**Musée du Vin de Bourgogne** ★ MUSEUM   Housed in the former mansion of the ducs de Bourgogne, this museum traces the evolution of the region's

Musée de l'Hôtel-Dieu.

# A taste **OF THE CÔTE D'OR**

Beaune is the epicenter of Burgundian winemaking with many of the world's most coveted and expensive wine appellations within an hour's drive. To the North lies the **Côte de Nuits,** famed for its red pinot noir vineyards with mythical appellations such as **La Romanée** and **Richebourg.** To the South lies **Côte de Beaune,** home to the great names of white chardonnay wines such as **Meursault** and **Chassagne-Montrachet.** Unlike Bordeaux, where large estates are usually open to the public for wine-tastings, Burgundy's finest winemakers are notoriously difficult to pin down and often refuse tastings to all but industry professionals.

You may want to start your wine tour in Beaune where many of Burgundy's *négotiants* (wine merchants who process and bottle the produce of smaller wine-makers and then sell under their own name) have their bases. As well as being able to simply turn up with no appointment, you'll often be able to taste a wider variety of appellations than at an individual vineyard. **Patriarche Père et Fils** (www.patriarche.com; ✆ 03-80-24-53-78) offers 1-hour visits to its fabulous 13th-century vaulted tasting cellars where millions of bottles are held along 5km of underground cellars. Tours are aided with interactive video terminals. It's open daily from 9:30-11:30am and 2-5pm, and admission is 13€. **Bouchard Père et Fils,** 15 rue du Château, (www.bouchard-pereetfils.com; ✆ 03-80-24-80-45) has cellars in the 15th-century

Castle of Beaune, a former royal fortress. A guided tour in English and tasting of six wines takes place at 10am from Monday to Saturday. Just opposite the celebrated Hôtel-Dieu, the **Marché aux Vins** (www.marcheauxvins.com; ✆ 03-80-25-08-20) is housed in a former Cordeliers church. With over 100 hectares of vineyards, this wine *négotiant* offers a wide range of appellations to taste. Tastings of 15 wines cost from 10€. It's open daily 9 to 11:30am and 2 to 5:30pm; July through August daily 9:30am to 5:30pm. Its nearby sister property, **Caves du Couvent des Cordeliers,** 6 rue de l'Hôtel-Dieu ✆ 03-80-25-08-20), offers tastings of 5 wines for 8€ including a visit around this 13th-century convent cellars. It's open daily 9 to 11:30am and 2 to 5:30pm.

winemaking. The collection of tools, *objets d'art*, and documents is housed in 15th- and 16th-century rooms. On display in the 14th-century press house is a collection of wine presses.

Rue d'Enfer. ✆ **03-80-22-08-19.** Admission 5.50€ adults, 3.50€ students and children 11-18, free for children 10 and under. Apr–Nov daily 9:30am–6pm; Dec–Mar Wed–Mon 9:30am–5pm.

## Nearby Attractions

Make time to visit the magnificent turreted castle of **Château de Rully** (www.chateau-rully-bourgogne.com; ✆ **03-85-87-20-89**). Originally built in the 12th century as a stronghold for the comte de Ternay, it offers tours in July and August Wednesday through Sunday at 3, 4, and 5pm to visit the castle and temporary art exhibitions at a cost of 4€ to 8€. The castle also produces its own wines under the label **Domaine de la Bressande**: wine tastings are available for group tours of at least 12 people at a cost of 10€ per person.

If you fancy visiting vineyards outside Beaune, head south along D974 to Pommard. **Château de Pommard,** 15 rue Marey Monge (www.chateaudepommard.com; *✆* **03-80-22-12-59**). Built for Messire Vivant de Micault equerry and secretary of Louis XVI in 1726, this castle was bought in 2003 by Maurice Giraud. Visits to the cellars that hold 400,000 bottles and to the castle museum with its collection of antique vintners' tools are available by prior reservation (via their website). Open daily from April to the Vente des Vins (3rd Sun in Nov) from 9:30am to 6:30pm. Next, you can head further along the D974 to Meursault. **Château de Meursault** (www.meursault.com; *✆* **03-80-26-22-75**). This domaine owns over 60 hectares of vineyards covering appellations including Aloxe Corton, Pommard, Puligny-Montrachet, and of course Meursault. You can turn up without prior reservation for a visit to the cellars of this fabulous 19th-century castle followed by a tasting of seven wines in the old castle kitchens for 15€. It is open daily 9:30am to noon and 2:30 to 6pm (no lunchtime closure in summer

months). You may like to stop for a wine-tasting lunch along the way at **La Table d'Olivier Leflaive** (www.maison-olivierleflaive.fr; *✆* **03-80-21-95-27**), 10 place du Monument in Puligny-Montrachet. One of the greats of Burgundy wine, Leflaive has also opened a boutique hotel at the same location and offers cellar visits with his brother Patrick.

For those who'd like to visit independent, family winegrowers but don't know where to start, **Burgundy Discovery** (www.burgundydiscovery.com; *✆* **03-85-49-51-34**) run by English couple David and Lynne Hammond, should be your first port of call. Another well-run, bilingual company that organizes wine tastings at normally inaccessible vineyards is **Tours et Détours**, 4 rue du Chambertin, Gevrey-Chambertin (www.toursetdetours.com; *✆* **03-80-34-16-65**). A good introduction to grape varieties is offered by **Vin Sensation**, 1 rue d'Enfer (www.sensation-vin.com; *✆* **03-80-22-17-57**) in central Beaune with educational wine-tasting sessions of six to nine wines that last 1 to 1½ hours.

## Where to Eat

**Hôtel de la Poste** has two excellent restaurants: the gastronomic **Le Relais** and its more informal, but popular **Le Bistro**. Meanwhile, **Coffee & Deli** at the **Hôtel de Beaune** is the best place for a reasonably priced snack. See "Where to Stay," p. 433.

**Le Jardin des Remparts** ★★ MODERN FRENCH   Just outside the city's medieval wall, this 1930s-era Art Deco *maison bourgeoise* is arguably the finest restaurant in Beaune. Two warmly decorated dining rooms open onto a terrace overlooking the garden. Happily, prices for the well-regarded cuisine are a bit lower than you may expect. Despite having lost its Michelin star (amid much consternation from local fans), the cuisine remains adventurous and creative with dishes such as foie gras (duck liver) pizza, pigs' cheek with Autumn fruits, and wild turbot with softened caramel.

10 rue de l'Hôtel-Dieu. www.le-jardin-des-remparts.com. ℭ **03-80-24-79-41.** Reservations recommended. Main courses 30€–48€; fixed-price lunch menu 28€–45€. fixed-price dinner menus 70€–90€. MC, V. Tues–Sat noon–1:30pm and 7–9pm. Open Mon during July and Aug. Closed mid-Dec to mid-Jan.

**Loiseau des Vignes ★** FRENCH/BURGUNDIAN   The late Bernard Loiseau's mini-empire of restaurants persists under the helm of his charming wife Dominique with two in Paris, his Michelin-starred flagship in Saulieu (see p. 425), and this wine bar in Beaune. The second dining room is lined with wall-to-wall wine fridges for almost 70 burgundy wines that can be served by the glass at the press of a button. Such bold technology moulds seamlessly with the bare stone walls and beamed celings. The wine list is an impressive elogy to Burgundy winemakers with many independent *producteurs* making an appearance, while Christophe Quéant's rich cuisine was rewarded with a Michelin star in 2010. We'd recommend pairing the Gourmet menu with a tasting of five well-paired wines by the glass.

31 rue Maupoux. www.bernard-loiseau.com. ℭ **03-80-24-12-06.** Reservations recommended. Main courses 22€–65€; fixed-price lunch menus 20€–28€; fixed-price lunch menus 59€–75€. AE, DC, MC, V. Tues–Sat noon–2pm and 7–10pm.

**Ma Cuisine ★ 🍴** BURGUNDIAN   Open only 4 days a week, Ma Cuisine enjoys a reputation for well-prepared regional food and an impressively varied wine cellar. The restaurant attracts local residents, many of them wine producers. Fabienne Escoffier produces old-fashioned fare that is delicious enough to ensure that you may re-visit during your trip, while her knowledgeable husband Pierre is on hand to advise on wine choices. Your meal may begin with a platter of thin-sliced cured ham with parsley, or compote of rabbit with fresh tarragon. Main courses include spit-roasted and deboned pigeon or garlicky beef bourguignon. Desserts are 19th-century French brasserie favorites: thin-sliced apple or pear tart, crème brûlée, and almond cake. The setting, a much-renovated 15th-century stable, is appropriately historic.

Passage Ste-Hélène. ℭ **03-80-22-30-22.** Reservations recommended. Main courses 15€–35€; fixed-price menu 26€. MC, V. Mon–Tues and Thurs–Fri noon–1:30pm and 7–9:30pm.

**Relais de Saulx ★** FRENCH   In a 200-year-old stone-trimmed building named after one of the region's ancient and noble families, Relais de Saulx is decorated with heavy timbers and all the accouterments you'd expect from this well-established restaurant. The kitchen prepares traditional Bourguignon cuisine and up-to-date adaptations. Staples are Bresse chicken with morel sauce, scallops with truffle sauce, and roast duck with sauces and garnishes that vary according to the season.

6 rue Louis Véry. ℭ **03-80-22-01-35.** Reservations recommended. Main courses 15€–20€; fixed-price menu 25€–32€. MC, V. Tues and Fri–Sat noon–2pm; Mon–Sat 7–10pm. Closed 1 week in Feb, 2 weeks in Aug, and 1 week in early Dec.

# Where to Eat Nearby

**Maison Lameloise ★★** BURGUNDIAN/FRENCH   This village restaurant was awarded its first Michelin star in 1925. Now one of France's most established Michelin-starred restaurants, Maison Lameloise is a popular stopover on a gourmand's tour through Burgundy. Jacques Lameloise, the grandson of the original owner, leaves most of the cooking in the capable hands of Eric Pras and

Frédéric Lamy. We'd recommend the free-range guinea fowl served in two fashions: roasted breast with a nut crumble and as *confit* (cooked in its own fat). It was less the food that struck us as three Michelin-starred and more the smooth-as-silk service. After a multiple-course meal, you can relax in one of 16 comfortable bedrooms with prices starting at 150€. In 2009, Jacques opened an informal bistro, Pierre et Jean (named after his grandfather and father), in a converted barn complete with stone walls and high-beamed ceilings. There's a well-priced *plat du jour* on weekdays for 19€.

36 place d'Armes, Chagny en Bourgogne 71150. www.lameloise.fr. (℃ **03-85-87-65-65.** Reservations required. Main courses 48€–75€; fixed-price dinner 100€–160€. AE, MC, V. Thurs–Mon noon–1:45pm and 7:30–9:30pm (bistro open Tues–Sun noon–2pm and Tues–Sat 7:30–9:30pm).

## Beaune Nightlife

If you're in the mood for an ale or two, try the English-style **Pickwick's Pub,** 2 rue Notre-Dame (℃ **03-80-22-55-92**). **Le Bout du Monde,** 7 rue du Faubourg Madeleine (www.leboutdumonde.net; ℃ **03-80-24-04-52**), has a beautiful courtyard and offers occasional concerts, theme nights, a wine bar, and tapas.

## Where to Stay

**Hôtel Le Cep ★★**  This former residential mansion in the town center is a great spot for oenophiles, fit for the ducs de Bourgogne. Each antiques-filled guest room is individually decorated and named after a Grand Cru wine of the Côte d'Or vineyards. On the grounds are two of the loveliest arcaded courtyards in Beaune, one from the 16th century, another from the 14th century. A tower housing one of the city's most beautiful stone staircases rises from here. A former wine cellar is the breakfast room. One of Beaune's finest restaurants, Loiseau des Vignes, run by the Bernard Loiseau group, is part of the hotel, featuring a stunning 70 wines by the glass (see "Where to Eat," above).

27 rue Jean-Francois Maufoux, Beaune 21200. www.hotel-cep-beaune.com. (℃ **03-80-22-35-48.** Fax 03-80-22-76-80. 64 units. 174€–214€ double; 254€–334€ suite; 150€ apartment. AE, DC, MC, V. Parking 15€. **Amenities:** Exercise room, restaurant; room service. *In room:* A/C, TV, hair dryer, minibar, free Wi-Fi.

**L'Hostellerie de Bretonnière** ✦  This is the best bargain in town. It's well run, has quiet rooms, and is a 5-minute walk from the center of town. The inn was built as a postal relay station around 1900 and became a hotel in 1950. Management recently enlarged the hotel with a seven-unit garden annex containing only duplex suites complete with kitchenette for an extra 23€, each rustically outfitted in a style that evokes the traditions of rural Burgundy. The accommodations in the rear are the most tranquil, though most visitors prefer those overlooking the garden. Rooms are small but adequate for an overnight, and some have bathtubs. Continental breakfast is available for 9.50€.

43 rue de Faubourg Bretonnière, Beaune 21200. www.hotelbretonniere.com. (℃ **03-80-22-15-77.** Fax 03-80-22-72-54. 32 units. 57€–81€ double; 100€ duplex suite. AE, DC, MC, V. Free parking. **Amenities:** Bar. *In room:* A/C (in some), TV, hair dryer, Wi-Fi (3€ per day).

**L'Hôtel de Beaune ★★**  Marble, mahogany, teak, and Italian stucco abound in this luxurious boutique hotel. Behind the 19th-century stone exterior, it had just eight guest rooms: each is tastefully decorated, with royal-size beds and lustrous black marble bathrooms with Hermès bath products. The hotel maintains an extraordinarily comprehensive wine cellar that, on advance notice, visitors can examine. Wines inside are for sale, either for consumption within the hotel's bar or for takeaway. As well as the pricey hotel restaurant, a wonderful delicatessen serves gourmet breakfasts, sandwiches, and salads from 8am to 10pm daily (10am start on Sun).

3–5 rue Samuel Legay, Beaune 21200. www.lhoteldebeaune.com. ☎ **03-80-25-94-14.** Fax 03-80-25-94-13. 8 units. 270€–370€ double. AE, DC, MC, V. Parking 10€-25€. **Amenities:** Restaurant; bar; babysitting; room service. *In room:* A/C, TV, hair dryer, Internet (10€ per day). Closed mid-Dec to mid-Jan.

## Where to Stay & Eat Nearby

**Hostellerie de Levernois ★★★** FRENCH  Under Jean Croet and his sons, this became one of the most celebrated restaurants of regional France. Now chef Philippe Augé is in charge, the restaurant continues smoothly on its Michelin-starred path. Augé creates seasonally changing grand cuisine in a stone-sided 17th-century *maison bourgeoise* in an idyllic 5-hectare (12-acre) park criss-crossed by the River Bourzaine. The snails in risotto are a pure delight, while the chickens for roasting come from Bresse and are acclaimed as the best in France. The wine list is impressive with over 800 references, many from Burgundy. There's also a stone-vaulted bistro serving an earthier regional cuisine with menus ranging from 29€ to 38€.

The Relais & Châteaux hotel rents 26 beautifully decorated rooms with TV, air-conditioning, and (in most) tub/showers. Rooms are divided between the main building and two annexes: We like the fabulous suites in the main building or rooms in the Pavillon annex with their own garden terrace. Doubles cost 135€ to 265€; the suites go for 215€ to 400€, with free Wi-Fi offered in the rooms.

Rue du Golf, Levernois 21200. www.levernois.com. ☎ **03-80-24-73-58.** Fax 03-80-22-78-00. Reservations required. Main courses 39€–51€; fixed-price dinner 68€–103€. AE, DC, MC, V. Mon–Sat 7–9:30pm; Sun 12:15–1.30pm and 7:15–9pm. Closed late Jan to mid-Mar. Take D970 south of Beaune for 3km (1¾ miles), following signs for lons le saunier.

**La Jasoupe ★★ 👪**  This sumptuous manor house in a quiet village near Beaune is one of those addresses that you'll want to keep to yourself. Kids will love the farm animals and the play area with its trampoline and swings, while the whole family can enjoy the swimming pool. A fitness room is discreetly housed in an annexe at the back of the house. Bed-and-breakfast rooms within the house are furnished to a high standard with period-style furniture and *toile de jouy* fabrics. Scattered around the garden are six gypsy caravans complete with shower-rooms and mini-kitchenettes. These are rented by the week only during summer months. Book early to avoid disappointment.

Rue Jasoupe Bas, Demigny 71150. www.lajasoupe.com. ☎ **06-84-07-58-56.** 5 units; 6 gypsy caravans. 125€–150€ double; from 105€ gypsy caravan. AE, MC, V. **Amenities:** Fitness room. *In room:* A/C (in some), TV, hair dryer, kitchenettes (in caravans only).

# MÂCON

397km (247 miles) SE of Paris; 127km (79 miles) S of Dijon; 87km (54 miles) S of Beaune.

Mâcon is a tale of two towns divided by the River Saône: so close yet so different in character. On the western riverbank lies hard-working Mâcon, the capital of Southern Burgundy and the Saône-et-Loire *département* (district). On the eastern riverbank lies the peaceful backwater Saint-Laurent-sur-Saône in the Ain district of the Rhône-Alpes region. Mâcon is by turns down-at-heel and surprisingly elegant. Wander around its impressive churches or the Lamartine and Ursulines museums. With the splendid exceptions of Restaurant Pierre (see p. 436), the best place for dining is just across the bridge along the Saint-Laurent-sur-Saône riverbank.

## Essentials

**GETTING THERE**  If you're **driving,** take A6 south past Beaune and onto Mâcon. Five high-speed TGV trains a day from Paris's Gare de Lyon run to Mâcon Loche TGV station taking 1½ hours. For railway information, visit www.voyages-sncf.com or call ✆ **08-92-33-53-35.**

**VISITOR INFORMATION**  The **Office de Tourisme** is at 1 place Saint-Pierre (www.macon-tourism.com; ✆ **03-85-86-21-07-07**).

## Seeing the Sights

Mâcon has two churches worth a visit: the Neo-Roman Saint Pierre Church on place St-Pierre and 19th-century Saint Vincent cathédral, designed by Guy de Gisors on Square de la Paix. For information on both churches, call ✆ **03-85-38-00-02**.

**Musée Lamartine** MUSEUM    Housed in an opulent 18th-century mansion, this museum is dedicated to the Mâcon-born, 19th-century poet and politician Alphonse de Lamartine. As well as a fine portrait of Lamartine by Henri Descaisne, there are paintings by his wife Marianne de Lamartine. Lamartine's fluctuating political career is charted through the satirical depictions of newspaper cartoons. There is also a slightly random collection of local landscape paintings, tapestries and ornately carved 19th-century furniture that have been donated by past members of the cultural *Académie de Mâcon* that owns the mansion.

41 rue Sigorgne, Mâcon 71000. ✆ **03-85-38-96-19.** Admission 2.50€ adults, free for ages 26 and under. Tues–Sat 10am–noon and 2–6pm, Sun 2-6pm.

**Musée des Ursulines** ★ MUSEUM    You can chart Maconnais regional history from its Gallo-Roman beginnings at Musée des Ursulines. Of particular interest is a Gallo-Roman potter's oven complete with ancient urns. Other areas of the museum are dedicated to 20th-century naïve artist-cum-sculptor Johé Gormand and to 19th-century landscape paintings by artists including Corot and Monet. A ticket to both this museum and Musée Lamartine (see below) can be bought for 3.40€.

5 rue des Ursulines, Mâcon 71000. ✆ **03-85-39-90-38.** Admission 2.50€ adults, free for ages 26 and under. Tues–Sat 10am–noon and 2–6pm, Sun 2–6pm.

## Where to Eat

Jean-Pierre Delacourt, the former sous-chef at **Restaurant Pierre** (see p. 436) runs **L'Ethym'Sel** (✆ 03-85-39-48-84) on rue Gambetta in central Mâcon where he attracts a loyal local crowd with his fairly priced gastronomic fare. Minutes away on quai Bouchacourt along the Saint-Laurent-sur-Saône riverfront, you'll find two popular French restaurants: **L'Autre Rive** (www.lautrerive.fr; ✆ 03-85-39-01-02) and George Blanc's **Le Saint-Laurent** (www.georgesblanc.com; ✆ 03-85-39-29-19).

**Restaurant Pierre ★★★** FRENCH   This Michelin-starred oasis has just celebrated its 20th anniversary. While chef Christian Gaulin produces deftly executed French fare from the kitchen, his pretty wife Isabelle takes charge in the stone-walled dining room. Christian's twist on classic regional dishes such as *quenelles de brochet* (creamed pike) and Charolais beef tournedos is seen in his choice of imaginatively matched sauces and accompaniments. Leave room for the delicious *mignardises* that follow dessert. Crisp white linen covers the tables that are generously spaced around the dining room. In summertime, there are tables scattered on the pedestrianized street. There's a well-priced lunch menu at 25€.

7–9 rue Dufour. www.restaurant-pierre.com. ✆ **03-85-38-14-23.** Reservations required. Main courses 26€–34€; fixed-price menu 31€–79€. AE, MC, V. Wed–Sun noon–1:45pm; Tues–Sat 7:30–9:45pm. Check website for annual closure dates.

## Where to Stay

**Hôtel du Nord ★**   This two-star riverfront hotel is our favorite choice in Mâcon. It's owned by a Mâconnais couple, Nadine and Daniel, who worked in Parisian hotels before returning six years ago to their hometown. Bedrooms overlooking the river are smaller than those without a view. Superior bedrooms are renovated: some in *toile du jouy* fabrics such as no. 34, some contemporary such as no. 33 with its mock crocodile-skin walls. Breakfast is the only meal served, but there are plenty of nearby restaurants.

313 quai Jean Jaurès, Mâcon 71000. www.hotel-dunord.com. ✆ **03-85-38-08-68.** Fax 03-85-39-01-92. 15 units. 65€–77€ double; 90€ triple. AE, DC, MC, V. **Amenities:** Breakfast room; lift. *In room:* A/C, TV, free Wi-Fi.

## Where to Stay & Eat Nearby

Four generations of Blanc chefs have dominated the restaurant scene around Mâcon. The original Mère Blanc's Bresse chicken in a cream sauce with basmati rice is so legendary that this free-range chicken has become a Blanc trademark, while the current Georges Blanc's menus (designed by Gilles Coudour) have become collector's items. The Blanc restaurant empire now extends from Lyon to its postcard-perfect hub in the village of Vonnas (see below).

**Georges Blanc Parc & Spa ★★★**   130 years of the Blanc family business have led to the creation of this five-star hotel and park that is Disneyesque in its perfection. There are three restaurants to choose from according to your mood and budget: **Georges Blanc** for three Michelin-starred sophistication; **L'Ancienne Auberge** for cozy, French bistro cuisine; and **Côté Sud** for summertime dining overlooking the pool. After a trip to the spa, take time to wander around the garden with its well-stocked orchard and vegetable garden. Very well-heeled guests can arrive by helicopter. Across the square is the more informal and cheaper sister hotel, **La Résidence des Saules Parc & Spa.**

Vonnas 01540. www.georgesblanc.com. ✆ **04-74-50-90-90.** Fax 04-74-50-08-80. 40 units. 180€–320€ double; 480€–800€ suite. AE, DC, MC, V. Parking 10€. **Amenities:** 2 year-round restaurants; 1 summertime restaurant; bar; spa; 3 swimming pools (1 indoor; 2 outdoor); 3 shops; tennis court; helipad; pétanque; babysitting. *In room:* A/C, TV, safe; minibar, free Wi-Fi.

**12**

# THE RHÔNE VALLEY

by Louise Simpson

The mighty River Rhône curves through the gastronomic heart of France. This fiercely independent region fought for its autonomy over many centuries, but the only wars fought here now are culinary. Restaurants with coveted three Michelin stars abound with Maison Pic in Valence, Troisgros in Roanne, and Paul Bocuse in Collonges-au-Mont-d'Or. This land of mountains and rivers is proud of its high-quality local produce: Its chickens from Bresse and chestnuts from Ardèche have even been given their own *appellation d'origine contrôlée* protected legal status.

This is one of France's oldest wine-growing areas with double-dug vines in Côte Rôtie and Hermitage dating back to Roman times when wine-filled amphorae were transported in riverboats down the Rhône. When you've had your fill of hearty Côte du Rhône and light Beaujolais red wines, take time to visit the region's Roman ruins, castles, and canyons.

# LYON ★★★

431km (267 miles) SE of Paris; 311km (193 miles) N of Marseille

France's third largest city is split by the forks of the River Saône and River Rhône. Explore Lyon's historic past atop the Roman ruins on Fourvière hill, in the UNESCO-classified medieval lanes of the old town and in the Baroque splendour of place Bellecour. This undisputed capital of gastronomy consistently knocks Paris off its culinary block, and there's an enthusiasm among chefs and foodies here unseen anywhere else in France. Lyon has also just about completed a landscaped facelift to place Brotteaux and place des Jacobins.

**Things to Do** Meander the cheek-by-jowl medieval streets of Vieux Lyon in search of *traboules*—corridors connecting two streets through a building or courtyard. Learn about the city's Roman past on a visit to **Fourvière hill,** about its silk industry at the **Musée des Tissus et des Arts Décoratifs,** and about its beloved Guignol puppet at the **Musée Gadagne.** Smell the roses and spot rosepink flamingos at France's largest city-based public park, **Parc de la Tête d'Or.**

**Shopping** Glimpse Lyon's illustrious silken past at **L'Atelier de Soierie** in rue Romarin where you can watch silk *carrés* that have been printed here using traditional Lyonnaise techniques since 1890. The wide avenues of the 2nd arrondissement north of place Bellecour are home to designer shops and to one of the oldest shopping arcades in central France, **passage de L'Argue.** To bring home something with history, head for the antique shops concentrated around rue Auguste Comte.

**Restaurants & Dining** Gastronomic capital Lyon is the training ground for many of France's top Michelin-starred chefs. Longtime star Paul Bocuse's

439

Lyon along the Rhône.

**L'Auberge du Pont de Collonges** is the focus of many a foodie's pilgrimage, though up-and-coming chefs such as Mathieu Viannay at **La Mère Brazier** are ready to challenge his culinary crown. Enjoy regional cuisine such as *andouillettes Lyonnaise* (course-grained pork sausages in an onion sauce) and *quenelles de brochet* (creamed pike) at a modest *bouchon*.

**Nightlife and Entertainment**   Grab the weekly guide *Lyon-Poche* at a newsstand for a list of events and venues around town. Drink artisanal beer and listen to live music at **Ninkasi** venues all around the city; dance the night away at **Le Sirius,** a former cargo boat on the Rhône or join the young, kitten-heeled crowd at **First Tendency** in a converted railway station. Opera buffs should head to place de la Comédie, while **Halle Tony Garnier** is the venue for international pop bands.

## Essentials

**GETTING THERE**   If you're arriving from the north by **train,** don't get off at Lyon's first station, Gare de Lyon Part-Dieu; continue to Gare de Perrache, where you can begin sightseeing. The high-speed TGV takes only 2 hours from Paris; the one-way fare is 69€ to 123€. Lyon makes a good stopover en route to the Alps or the Riviera. For information, visit www.voyages-sncf. com or call ✆ **08-92-33-53-35.**

By **plane,** it's a 45-minute flight from Paris to Aéroport Saint-Exupéry (www.lyonaeroports.com; ✆ **08-26-80-08-26**), 25km (16 miles) east of the city. The 30-minute **Rhône Express** tram link from the airport runs every quarter of an hour to central Lyon (100m/328 ft. from TGV train station Lyon Part-Dieu) for 13€. **Taxis** cost about 40€ and take the same amount of time.

If you're **driving** from Paris, head southeast on A6/E15 into Lyon. From Nice, head west on A8 toward Aix-en-Provence, continuing northwest toward Avignon on A7. Bypass the city and continue north along the same route into Lyon. From Grenoble or the French Alps, head northwest on A48 to A43, which will take you northwest into Lyon.

**GETTING AROUND**   A network of Métro lines, trams, and buses branches out to serve the city. A *plan de poche* (pocket map) is available at any office of **TCL** (www.tcl.fr; ✆ **04-26-10-12-12**), which handles all forms of mass transport. Tickets are valid on all forms of public transport, costing 1.60€ for the average ride or else 14€ for a *carnet* of 10 tickets. Most short-time visitors

# Lyon

To Geneva ↑

rue Barrême

pl. de la Croix-Rousse Croix-Rousse

bd. de la Croix-Rousse

r. de Crimée

pont de Lattre de Tassigny

rue Dusquesne

r. des Charteux

rue de la r. du Bon Pasteur

place Colbert

av. du Maréchal Foch

rue de Vendôme

rue de Créqui

r. P. Dupont

r. P. Blanc

r. de la Tourette

rue de Tables Claudiennes

rue Burdeau

r. Malesherbes

quai de Serbie

rue de Sèze

cours du Gén. Giraud

r. Terme

r. des Capucins

Croix-Paquet

place Louis Pradel

pont Morand

quai A. Lasagne

quai de Gén. Sarail

cours F. Roosevelt

quai St - Vincent

r. de la Martinière

r. d'Algérie

place des Terraux

r. du P. Gaillot

r. Jos. Serlin

Foch

rue de Sèze

Saône

quai de Pierre-Scize

rue St-Paul

quai de la Pêcherie

**1**

**2** Hôtel-de-Ville

cours F. Roosevelt

**ST-PAUL**

**3**

pont de la Feuillée

r. du Bât d'Argent

quai J. Moulin

rue Molière

av. du Mar.t de Saxe

rue de Vendôme

**FOURVIERE**

**4**

quai St-Antoine

r. Gentil

passerelle du Collège

cours Lafayette

**5**

rue du Bœuf

rue St-Jean

quai de Bondy

**6**

Cordeliers

rue Grenette

pont Lafayette

**VIEUX LYON**

**7**

funiculaire

r. de la Bombarde

**8**

pont Juin

r. de Brest

r. du Prés. E. Herriot

r. de Carnot

Rhône

rue Rabelais

rue de Bonnel

cours de la Liberté

av. du Maréchal de Saxe

r. P. Corneille

**9**

pl. E. Commette

quai des Célestins

place de la République

pont Wilson

montée St-Barthélémy

**10**

pont Bonaparte

r. E. Zola

quai J. Courmont

V. Augagneur

quai V.-Augagneur

**11**

**ST-JEAN**

passarelle St-Georges

place Bellecour

place Antoine Poncet

r. de la Barre

pont de la Guillotière

rue de Chaponnay

**RIVE-GAUCHE**

funiculaire

pl. des Minimes

**PRESQU'ILE**

r. Villeroy

r. P. Bert

**ST-GEORGES**

quai Fulchiron

quai de Tilsitt

rue Vaubecourt

rue Sala

rue St-Hélène

rue Auguste-Comte

cours Gambetta

r. de Guillotière

To Dijon

rue Franklin

**12**

Ampère

**13**

quai du Docteur Gailleton

quai C. Bernard

rue de Marseille

rue de Condé

**AUGUSTE COMTE**

r. de la Charité

pont de l'Université

**UNIVERSITÉ DE LYON**

rue de l'Université

pont Kitchener

place Carnot

Perrache

cours Verdun

pont Gallieni

rue Chevreul

To Grenoble →

**Bus Station**

To St-Etienne ↘

| | |
|---|---|
| Church | ✝ |
| Information | ⓘ |
| Post Office | ✉ |

0 ____ 1/4 mi
0 ____ 0.25 km

441

may want to purchase a **Ticket Liberté** day pass for 4.90€. For one of the most efficient city taxi services we've ever discovered, call **Taxi Radio de Lyon** (www.taxilyon.com), at ☎ **04-72-10-86-86.**

**VISITOR INFORMATION** The **Office de Tourisme** is on place Bellecour (www.lyon-france.com; ☎ **04-72-77-69-69;** fax 04-78-42-04-32).

**SPECIAL EVENTS** Festivals take place practically every day, especially in summer. Music festivals reign supreme, with the most popular occurring on France's **Fête de la Musique,** which turns the streets of Lyon into performance spaces for local bands around June 21. For 4 days around December 8, the spectacular **Fête des Lumières** lights up Lyon's churches, monuments, and neighborhoods. In June and July, the **Nuits de Fourvière** festival combines music, theater, dance, and cinema in the Gallo-Roman theaters on Fourvière hill and in Parc de Parilly in the suburb of Bron—prices depend on the act and can be purchased by phone at ☎ **04-72-32-00-00** (info at www.nuitsdefourviere.com).

# Exploring the City

The city sprawls over many miles, divided, like Paris, into *arrondissements.* Its heart straddles the Saône, around the east bank's place Bellecour and the west bank's Primatiale St-Jean. Begin your tour of Lyon at **place Bellecour,** one of France's largest and most charming squares. A statue of Louis XIV looks out on the encircling 18th-century buildings.

Urban sociologists are proud of Lyon's efforts to decorate some of its drab facades with *trompe l'oeil* murals. Among the most frequently cited works are the facade of the Musée Tony Garnier, 4 rue des Serpollières, 8e, and the fresco "des Lyonnais célèbres" on rue de la Martinière in the 2e.

## IN VIEUX LYON ★★★

From place Bellecour, walk across pont Bonaparte to the left bank of the Saône River and **Vieux Lyon.** (From elsewhere in the city, you can take bus no. 28 or take the Métro to Vieux Lyon.) Covering about a square mile, Old Lyon contains an amazing collection of medieval and Renaissance buildings, which helped the city attain UNESCO status in 1998. After years of existence as a slum, the area is now fashionable, attracting antiques dealers, artisans, weavers, sculptors, and painters who depict scenes along the **rue du Boeuf,** one of the most interesting streets for exploring.

Your first stop should be the cathedral, **Primatiale St-Jean** (see p. 443). North of the cathedral is the most historically and architecturally evocative neighborhood of Old Lyon, with narrow streets, spiral stairs, hanging gardens, soaring towers, and unusual courtyards whose balconies seem to perch precariously atop medieval pilings or columns.

Lyon is unique for its *traboules,* a series of short covered passageways that connect longer streets running parallel to one another. Scattered throughout Vieux Lyon, they're capped with vaulted masonry ceilings. They often open unexpectedly into flower-ringed courtyards. Ask for a map at the tourist office. The tourism office also offers 2-hour guided *traboule* tours for 10€—call ahead for times.

Try to see the Gothic arcades of the 15th-century **Maison Thomassin,** 2 place du Change, and the 16th-century **Maison du Chamarier,** 37 rue St-Jean, where Mme. de Sévigné lived. You can admire these buildings from the outside, but you are not allowed to enter. The neighborhood also contains **Eglise St-Paul,** 3 place Gerson (*©* **04-78-28-67-93**), consecrated in A.D. 549. Rebuilding began in 1084 after its destruction by the Saracens. Its octagonal lantern tower was completed in the 1100s, and the rest of the premises in the 13th century. You can visit Monday to Saturday noon to 6pm, Sunday 2 to 6pm, and admission is free.

**Musée d'Histoire de Lyon (Musée Gadagne)** ★ MUSEUM This museum is in the Hôtel de Gadagne, an early-16th-century residence that completed a mammoth 10-year restoration in 2009. You'll find interesting Romanesque sculptures on the ground floor. Other exhibits include 18th-century Lyonnais furniture and pottery, antique ceramics from the town of Nevers, a pewter collection, and numerous paintings and engravings of Lyon.

In the same building is the **Musée des Marionnettes du Monde** (same phone and hours), which has three puppets by Laurent Mourguet, creator of Guignol, the best-known French marionette character. The museum also displays marionettes from other parts of France (Amiens, Lille, and Aix-en-Provence) and from around the world.

1 place du Petit-Collège. www.gadagne.musees.lyon.fr. *©* **04-78-42-03-61.** Admission (including Musée de la Marionette) 8€ adults, free for children and students aged 25 and under. Wed–Sun 11am–6:30pm.

**Primatiale St-Jean** ★ CATHEDRAL This cathedral was built between the 12th and the 15th centuries, and its exceptional stained-glass windows date from the same era. Its apse is a masterpiece of Lyonnais Romanesque architecture. A highlight is the Flamboyant Gothic chapel of the Bourbons. On the front portals are medallions depicting the signs of the zodiac, the Creation, and the life of St. John. The cathedral's 16th-century clock is intricate and beautiful. It announces the hour daily at noon, 2, 3, and 4pm in grand style: A rooster crows, and angels herald the event. The treasury is in a wing called **La Manécanterie.** Entrance is free, and hours are Tuesday to Saturday 9.30am to noon and 2 to 6pm (Wednesday from 11am only); every second Sunday 2 to 6pm. The wing of the cathedral that houses the treasury is noted for the beauty and severe dignity of its 12th-century Romanesque facade. Its origins date to the 11th century, when it was established as a music school.

Place St-Jean. *©* **04-78-92-82-29.** Free admission. Daily 8.15am–7pm (Mon–Fri closes at 7.45pm). The cathedral is closed to tourists for mass during the week and on Sun mornings.

## IN FOURVIERE HILL ★

Rising to the west of Vieux Lyon is **Colline de Fourvière** (**Fourvière Hill;** www.fourviere.org). The wooded hill—home to numerous convents, colleges, and hospitals; two Roman theaters; and a superb Gallo-Roman museum—affords a panoramic vista of

Musée des Marionnettes du Monde.

Lyon. You can see the city's many bridges across the two rivers, and the rooftops of the medieval town. In clear weather, you can even view the countryside extending to the snowcapped Alps.

Enthroned on the hill's summit is the 19th-century **Basilique Notre-Dame de Fourvière,** 8 place de Fourvière (© **04-78-25-13-01**), rising fortresslike with four octagonal towers and crenellated walls. Colored mosaics cover its interior, and an ancient chapel adjoins the church. A gilded statue of the Virgin surmounts the belfry. Admission is free; it's open daily 8am to 7pm.

**Jardin du Rosaire** extends along the hillside between the basilica and the Primatiale St-Jean. It's open daily 9am to sunset and promises a scenic walk. You'll see a vast shelter for up to 200 pilgrims. The area can also be reached via a pair of cable-driven **funiculars** that run every 10 minutes from a point immediately adjacent to the Métro station in Vieux Lyon to the top of Fourvière Hill. Priced at 1.60€ each way, they run daily between 6am and 10pm.

**Théâtres Romains,** 6 rue de l'Antiquaille, Montée de Fourvière (© **04-72-32-00-00**), a Roman theater-odeum complex, is in a park south of the basilica. The theater is the most ancient in France, built by order of Augustus from 17 to 15 B.C. and expanded during the reign of Hadrian. The odeum, reserved for musical performances, was once sumptuously decorated; its orchestra floor still contains mosaics of marble and porphyry. The third building was dedicated in A.D. 160 to the goddess Cybele. Only the building's foundations remain. The site is open from 7am until sunset, and entrance is free. Performances are given here in June and July during Les Nuits de Fourvière, when dance recitals, concerts, and plays are staged atop Fourvière Hill (see "Special Events," p. 442).

An altar dedicated to a bull cult and a marble statue of a goddess are on display in the **Musée Gallo-Romain,** 17 rue Cléberg (© **04-72-38-49-30**), near the archaeological site. The museum's collection of Gallo-Roman artifacts is the finest in France outside Paris. The site is open Tuesday through Sunday 10am to

Théâtres Romains.

6pm. Admission is 7€ adults, 4.50€ students, free for ages 17 and under. Entrance is free on Thursday. Guides are available on Thursdays and Sundays at 4:30pm.

## ELSEWHERE AROUND THE CITY

In addition to the sites below, you can visit Lyon's oldest church, the 1107 **Abbaye Romaine de St-Martin-d'Ainay,** 11 rue Bourgelat (© **04-72-40-02-50**), south of place Bellecour, near place Ampère. Admission is free; hours are Monday to Friday 8:30am to noon and 2:30 to 6pm. The rue du Président-Edouard-Herriot extends north from place Bellecour to **place des Terreaux,** dominated by one of the most beautiful of Europe's city halls, the 17th-century **Hôtel de Ville** and by the elaborate **Fontaine Bartholdi** (named after the famous French sculptor of New York's Statue of Liberty).

**L'Institut & Musée Lumière** HISTORIC HOME    Film buffs from all over the world head here. The famous Lumière family, including Antoine (1840–1911), Auguste (1862–1954), and Louis (1864–1948), once lived in Lyon. The brothers were chemists, industrialists, and motion-picture pioneers. In Lyon, they founded a factory for producing photographic plates, paper, and chemicals. They invented the Lumière process of color photography and the Cinématographe, an early motion picture camera, in 1895. They produced films, including *La Sortie de L'Usine Lumière,* released in 1895 and considered the first movie. The complex is dedicated to the memory of the innovators and is a living museum of cinema. Early films are shown, and books, photos, posters, and pre-cinematographic and cinematographic equipment are on display.

25 rue du Premier Film. www.institut-lumiere.org. © **04-78-78-18-95.** Admission 6€ adults, 5€ students and children 7–18, free for children 6 and under. Tues–Sun 10am–6:30pm. Métro: Monplaisir-Lumière.

**Musée de l'Imprimerie de Lyon** MUSEUM    Occupying a 15th-century mansion, this museum is devoted to Lyon's role in the world of printing. Exhibits include a page from a Gutenberg Bible, 17th- to 20th-century presses, 16th- to 19th-century woodcuts, and engravings. This is one of the most important printing museums in Europe, along with those at Mainz and Antwerp. It has a collection of books from "all epochs," including *incunabula,* books printed before Easter 1500.

13 rue de la Poulaillerie. www.imprimerie.lyon.fr. © **04-78-37-65-98.** Admission 5€ adults, 3€ students, free for 26 and under. Wed–Sun 9:30am–noon and 2–6pm.

**Musée des Beaux-Arts** ★★ ART MUSEUM    On the south side of place des Terreaux stands the Palais Saint-Pierre. The former Benedictine abbey was built between 1659 and 1685 in the Italian baroque style. Today it is home to the Musée des Beaux-Arts, which has an outstanding collection of paintings and sculpture. You enter through a courtyard graced with statuary and shade trees, and the ground floor showcases an array of 14th-century paintings. The collection also includes Etruscan, Egyptian, Phoenician, Sumerian, and Persian art. Of special note is Perugino's altarpiece. The top floor holds one of France's richest 19th-century collections, with works by artists from Veronese, Tintoretto, and Rubens to Matisse, Monet, and Picasso. Be sure to see Joseph Chinard's bust of Mme. Récamier, the Lyon beauty who charmed Napoleonic Paris by merely reclining, and the Fantin-Latour masterpiece *La Lecture* (The Reading).

20 place des Terreaux. www.mba-lyon.fr. © **04-72-10-17-40.** Admission 7€ adults, 4€ for students and children. Wed–Thurs and Sat–Mon 10am–6pm; Fri 10:30am–6pm.

**Musée des Tissus et des Arts Décoratifs** ★★★ MUSEUM   In the 1739 Lacroix-Laval mansion by Soufflot (architect of the Panthéon in Paris), the Musée des Arts-Décoratifs contains furniture and objets d'art from the 17th and 18th centuries. The medieval and Renaissance periods are also represented. Look for a five-octave clavecin by Donzelague, the 18th-century creator of musical instruments.

Next door, in the 1730 L'Hôtel de Villeroy, is an even more interesting collection. On view are 2,000 years of priceless fabrics from around the world. Some of the finest fabrics made in Lyon from the 18th century to the present are displayed. The 15th- and 16th-century textiles embroidered with religious motifs are noteworthy, as are the 17th-century Persian carpets. Look for the partridge-motif brocade from Marie Antoinette's bedchamber at Versailles, as well as a 150-color brocaded satin woven for Queen Victoria, which is decorated with birds of paradise and orchids.

34 rue de la Charité. www.musee-des-tissus.com. ℂ **04-78-38-42-00.** Admission 7€ adults, 4.50€ students, free for children under 12. Tues–Sun 10am–noon and 2–5:30pm. Métro: Ampère.

**Amphithéâtre des Trois-Gaules** ★★ RUINS   This ancient amphitheater is one of Lyon's grandest archaeological sites. Constructed in 19 A.D. at the base of the Croix Rousse hill, it was the centerpiece of the **Federal Sanctuary of the Three Gauls**, the administrative and religious complex established in *Lugdunum* (Roman Lyon) to federalise Gaul as an Imperial Province under Emperor Augustus. In the 2nd century, the amphitheatrer was enlarged to hold up to 20,000 spectators: It became the site of gatherings for the 60 Gallic tribes, for gladiatorial combats and later for the Christian persecutions in 177. Classified as a historic monument in 1961, it is now integrated into Lyon's oldest park, the Jardin des Plantes, and is open to visitors.

Rue Lucien Sportisse**.** Admission free.

**Parc de la Tête d'Or** ★★★ ☺ PARK/GARDEN   On the right bank of the Rhône, you can explore the largest city-based public park in France. This 117-hectare (289-acre) park owes its name to the golden head of Christ that, according to legend, is buried in the park. Created in 1856 by the landscape architect Denis Bühler, the park has a magnificent lakeside setting with broad tree-lined avenues, fountains, and rose gardens. Deer wander freely around the grounds, while the **Zoological Park** (open daily 9am to 5pm; ℂ **04-72-82-35-00**) hosts some 1000 animals including rose-pink flamingos, Senegalese dwarf goats, and Indian buffalo with their distinctive sickle-shaped horns. The **Botanical Garden** (greenhouses open daily 9am to 4:30pm; www.jardin-botanique-lyon.com; ℂ **04-72-69-47-60**) features 15,000 plants from around the globe. Five greenhouses host over 6,000 plants with a 21m-high pavilion for luxuriant tropical plants; a Dutch greenhouse for carnivorous plants, a warm orchid greenhouse; a cold horticultural greenhouse for azaleas and cacti; and an aquatic greenhouse containing the splendid *Victoria Cruziana* water lily. Families will be kept busy with pony rides; carousels; swings; pedal cars and pedalos on the lake, as well as a 20-minute train ride around the park.

Entrances on boulevard des Belges, quai Général de Gaulle and avenue Verguin. www.loisirs-parcdelatetedor.com. Admission free. Daily 6am–9pm (until 11pm Apr–Sept).

## OUTSIDE THE CITY

At Rochetaillée-sur-Saône, 11km (6¾ miles) north of Lyon on D433, lies the **Musée Malatre**. This transport museum is in the Château de Rochetaillée, 645 rue du Musée (www.musee-malartre.com; ℂ **04-78-22-18-80**). The château was built in 1131 on even older foundations and rebuilt in the 1700s. The curators are proud of the majestic 15th-century staircase, the Romanesque gateway that's part of the original 12th-century design, and a policy that permits photography, smoking, and any motorcycle-fetish garb you care to wear while admiring the collection of vehicles. The collection includes 100 cars dating to the 1890s, 65 motorcycles from 1903 and after, and 40 bicycles from 1818 and later. Admission to the museum and château is 6€ adults, and free for ages 25 and under. It is open Tuesday through Sunday 9am to 5pm (until 6pm July–Aug). From Lyon, take bus no. 40 or 70.

# Where to Eat

Lyon is the gastronomic capital of France with around 1,000 restaurants to choose from. Nowhere are the winners and losers of coveted Michelin stars more keenly felt than in this metropolitan bastion of cuisine. Competition is so stiff that a number of culinary self-support groups have been set up to hallmark the city's most credible establishments. Look out for restaurants labeled *Toques Blanches Lyonnaises* for gastronomic French and regional cuisine and *Authentique Bouchon Lyonnais* for bistro-style Lyonnais fare.

## VERY EXPENSIVE

**Mère Brazier ★★★ 🖋 FRENCH**   This celebrated Lyon institution is run by the charismatic darling of French food critics, Mathieu Viannay. Since taking over in 2008, Viannay has revisited Mère Brazier classics such as Bresse chicken *demi-deuil* (poached with truffles), as well as introducing his own seasonally changing menu based on precision cooking of the best ingredients. His efforts have been rewarded with Michelin stars: it is now the only two Michelin–starred restaurant in central Lyon. Many features of the original 1920s dining room have been preserved such as its Art Deco windows and tiles. Given its star rating, prices remain surprisingly uninflated.

12 rue Royale. www.lamerebrazier.fr ✆ **04-78-23-17-20.** Reservations recommended. Main courses 47€–55€; fixed-price lunch menus 37€–40€. dinner menus 61€–125€. AE, DC, MC, V. Mon–Fri noon–1:30pm 7:45–9:30pm.

## EXPENSIVE

**Au 14 Février ★★ 🖋 FRENCH**   The latest newcomer to the Michelin-starred club, this restaurant has set the a new gastronomic standard in the heart of the old town. Chef Tsuyoshi Arai brings Japanese nuances to his French cuisine. Menu choices are left to the chef who surprises diners with his trompe-l'oeil dishes such as his sugary interpretation of a Big Mac, complete with meringue buns and red-berry ketchup. We'd recommend opting for the wine pairings menu with wines adapted to each course. Decorated with Raymond Peynet's romantic drawings, the tiny dining room has just six tables so be prepared to book months in advance.

6 rue Mourguet. www.au14fevrier.com. ✆ **04-78-92-91-39.** Reservations required. Fixed-price menu 75€. AE, DC, MC, V. Tues–Sat noon–1:30pm and 7:30–9:30pm.

**Maison Clovis ★★★ 🍴 FRENCH**   A quiet hum of contented local diners pervades this contemporary restaurant in Lyon's 6th arrondissement. Despite winning a Michelin star in 2010, prices remain reasonable at this discreet gastronomic mecca. The finest ingredients are sourced from all corners of France: lobsters from Brittany, free-range pork from the Auvergne, scallops from Normandy, and pigeon from Challans. In a city that prides itself on meat and potato–based dishes, it's refreshing to find so many vegetables. Pan-fried scallops are accompanied by no fewer than three types of turnip. Leave room for a home-made sorbet with surprising flavors such as lemon-basil or mango-jasmine. It's best to book early to avoid disappointment.

19 bd. Brotteaux. www.maisonclovis.com. © **04-72-74-44-61.** Reservations required. Main courses 24€–48€; fixed-price lunch menus 22€–26€; fixed-price dinner menus 59€–70€. AE, DC, MC, V. Tues–Sat noon–1:45pm and 7:30–10pm.

## MODERATE

**Brasserie Georges** FRENCH  Georges is the oldest brasserie in Lyon (founded in 1836) and probably the largest in Europe (with 450 seats). Turn-of-the-20th-century French poet Lamartine still owes the restaurant 40 francs for a meal he consumed 100 years ago. If you thrill to nest where the proud and mighty have already nested, you can ask specifically for a table that is identified with a plaque as having hosted Ernest Hemingway, the Lumière brothers, Edith Piaf, Rodin, Jean-Paul Sartre, or Jules Verne. Specialties include roast beef, snails in garlic butter, heaped platters of choucroute, and grilled meats.

30 cours de Verdun. www.brasseriegeorges.com. © **04-72-56-54-54.** Main courses 15€–25€; fixed-price menus 19.50€–25€. AE, DC, MC, V. Daily 11:30am–11:15pm (until 12:15am Fri–Sat). Closed May 1. Métro: Perrache.

**Café des Fédérations ★ 🍴** FRENCH/LYONNAIS  This is one of the busi-est *bouchons* (see below) in Lyon and sometimes the most amusingly raucous. Catering to the office-worker crowd, it's operated with panache by a team of hardworking employees who would probably perform beautifully in the trenches of a war zone. The fixed-price menus offer a selection of appetizers, main courses, and desserts. Each evokes old-time Lyonnais cuisine at its least pretentious, with such options as a green salad with bacon and croutons; eggs *en meurette* (poached in red wine); pork chops; and *andouillette* (tripe sausage) or other kinds of sau-sages, often served with a creamy potato gratin.

8–10 rue Major-Martin. www.lesfedeslyon.com. © **04-78-28-26-00.** Reservations recommen-ded. Fixed-price lunch 19€, dinner 25€. V. Mon–Sat noon–2pm and 8–9:30pm. Closed 1 week in Jan. Métro: Hôtel-de-Ville.

**M Restaurant ★** FRENCH  Between taking this restaurant over from culi-nary star Mathieu Viannay in 2010 and losing his Michelin star in 2011, chef/owner Julien Gautier has had a rough ride trying to escape Viannay's shadow. Luckily Gautier remains resolute as he continues to extend his repertoire and tantalize palates in his ultramodern dining room with colorful chairs and parquet flooring set off by a candelabrum. Try the pumpkin and chestnut soup with smoked duck breast, followed by pan-fried black sea bream. "It's all subject to change," says a smiling Gautier. "When I do one dish too long, I go crazy."

47 av. Foch. © **04-78-89-55-19.** Reservations required. Main courses 14€–21€; fixed-price menu 18€–34€. AE, DC, MC, V. Mon–Fri noon–2pm and 7:30–10pm. Closed Aug 1–25 and 1 week in Feb.

## INEXPENSIVE

**Les Adrets ★** LYONNAIS  This high-end bistro in the heart of Vieux Lyon has become a Lyonnais institution, combining traditional regional cuisine with impressive value. Try poached eggs with cèpes in cream or creamy pumpkin soup with tiny scallops. Follow them with grilled turbot with a veal *jus*, or duck

# LYON'S best bouchons

A *bouchon* is a Lyon-based bistro serving traditional Lyonnais cuisine. The meat-oriented fare favors classics as sausages, duck pâté, and roast pork. Such is the allure of the *bouchon* appellation that an official association has been set up to protect the 20 or so officially-certified *authentique bouchon lyonnais* from the numerous fakes that parade around the old town. Our favorite *bouchons* include the up-and-coming **Le Musée**, 2 rue des Forces (℡ **04-78-37-71-54**); the long-established **Café des Fédérations** (see above); and **Le Garet**, 7 rue du Garet (℡ **04-78-28-16-94**) famously frequented by Jean Moulin, hero of *La Résistance*.

breast with roasted peaches. At 16€ including wine, the lunch prix fixe is one of Lyon's best deals.

30 rue du Boeuf. ℡ **04-78-38-24-30.** Reservations recommended. Main courses 13€–20€; fixed-price lunch menu with wine 16€; dinner 23€–45€. MC, V. Mon–Fri noon–2:30pm and 7–10:30pm. Métro: Cordelier. Closed Aug.

**Pierre et Martine** 🍴 FRENCH  This family-run restaurant in the 5th arrondissement is one of Lyon's secret addresses. While chef Pierre busies himself in the kitchen, smiling Martine welcomes diners into the cozy dining room with its bare-stone walls and gleaming copper pans. Dishes such as filet of zander with risotto or pan-fried beef with *dauphinois* potatoes are sure to delight. Finish with a hearty dessert such as apple-and-raspberry crumble or crème brûlée *façon grandmère*.

4 rue Ferrachat. www.pierre-et-martine.com. ℡ **04-78-42-49-33.** Reservations recommended. Main courses 12€–15€; fixed-price lunch menus 16€–20€; dinner menus 20€–25€. MC, V. Tues–Sat noon–2pm and 7–9:30pm (Sat 8–10pm).

## Where to Eat Nearby

**Paul Bocuse** ★★★ LYONNAIS  Whether the namesake chef is on-site or not, the standards of this restaurant continue to reach for the skies. Paul Bocuse is one of the world's most famous chefs, and serious Parisian foodies take the TGV from Paris just to dine at this citadel of haute cuisine. He specializes in regional cuisine, though long ago he was the leading exponent of nouvelle cuisine (which he later called "a joke"). Because Bocuse, who is now in his 80s, is gone at least part of the time, other chefs carry on with the mass production (for up to 180 diners) of the signature dishes that the master created. There isn't a lot of room for variation. Tired of the conventional facades of most French restaurants, Bocuse commissioned a local artist to paint the history of French cuisine. The tale begins in the 1700s and proceeds through the years to its "defining moment"—a depiction of Bocuse himself.

You can begin your meal with the famous black-truffle soup and then try one of the most enduring dishes in the Bocuse repertoire: Bresse chicken cooked in a pig's bladder. Other options include roast pigeon in puff pastry with baby cabbage leaves, and red mullet served in a potato casing.

40 quai de la Plage, Pont de Collonges, Collonges-au-Mont-d'Or. www.bocuse.fr. ℡ **04-72-42-90-90.** Reservations required as far in advance as possible. Main courses 52€–64€; fixed-price menu 140€–225€. AE, DC, MC, V. Daily noon–1:30pm and 8–9:30pm. Take N433 9km (5½ miles) north of Lyon.

beaucoup **DE BOCUSE**

A resurgence of interest in chef Paul Bocuse swept across Lyon when Bocuse bought **Le Nord** ★, 18 rue Neuve, (www.nordsudbrasseries.com; ✆ **04-72-10-69-69**), a brasserie where he had worked as a teenager. Its prices (12€–30€ for a main course) signaled that the last of the great chefs had finally decided to go for the mass market. It's one of the most popular places in Lyon for traditional Lyonnais cuisine. A short while later, Bocuse opened a clone of Le Nord, **Le Sud,** 11 place Antonin Poncet (✆ **04-72-77-80-00**), where the culinary venue celebrates all points south (including Provence and, to a lesser degree, French-speaking North Africa) with a Mediterranean-inspired diet that includes tagines and pasta, and a color scheme of vivid blues and yellows. In 1998, he endorsed the opening of **L'Est,** 14 place Jules-Ferry (✆ **04-37-24-25-26**), a large, bustling place offering pan-French and Italian cuisine and a noisy and animated ambience that evokes the *brasseries de gare* of faraway Paris. And finally, the Bocuse empire rounded out the four directions of the compass with the establishment of its final bistro, **L'Ouest,** 1 quai du Commerce (✆ **04-37-64-64-64**). There's a hint of Pacific Rim cuisine here, and its layout is described as "American style," with an open kitchen, wide-open vistas, and a lively theatricality. The latest to open is **Argenson,** 40 allée Pierre de Coubertin (✆ **04-72-73-72-73**), adjacent to the town's biggest soccer stadium, La Stade de Gerland. Each of the five is open for lunch and dinner daily.

## Shopping

The third-largest city in France is a bastion of fashion. The densest concentrations of retail shops lie in the streets leading north of place Bellecour in the 2nd arrondissement (district). The southern end of rue du Président-Edouard-Herriot is home to sought-after international brands with **Louis Vuitton, Hermès, Dior, MaxMara,** and **Furla** for designer clothes and bags, as well as **Mont Blanc** for pens, **Jo Malone** for perfumes, and **Christofle** for tableware. Lyonnais jeweler Jean-Pierre Moreira showcases his exquisite jewelry collection, **Joïa** at no. 104 (www.joia.fr; ✆ **04-72-56-00-69**), while cigar expert Xavier Velasco sells cigars from Havana, Honduras, and the Dominican Republic at **Le Diplomate,** no. 99 (www.lediplomate.fr; ✆ **04-78-42-38-05**).

Around the corner lies our favorite shopping street in Lyon: **rue des Archers**. Here you'll find retro Parisian brand **Antoine et Lili** at no. 4 (www.antoineetlili.com; ✆ **04-78-59-41-40**; also at 2 rue des Fargues) which uses Lyonnais Jacquards for its French-made women's couture; **Vento** at no. 3 (✆ **04-72-41-79-49**) which sells trendy brands such as Dsquared2, Juicy Couture, and Philipp Plein; and **Tartine et Chocolat** on the corner of place des Celestins (www.tartine-et-chocolat.fr; ✆ **04-72-74-16-44**) with elegant outfits for children. Further along, two rival chocolate shops both run by award-winning *chocolatiers* straddle the street: **Bouillet** at no. 14 (www.chocolatier-bouillet.com; ✆ **04-78-42-98-40**; further boutiques at 3 rue d'Austerlitz, 6 bis avenue Général Leclerc and 15 place de la Croix-Rousse) and Bernard Dufoux at no. 15 (www.chocolatsdufoux.com; ✆ **04-72-77-57-95**).

Linking rue du Président-Edouard-Herriot with rue de la République, the historic **passage de L'Argue,** designed by architect Farge in 1827, houses long-established merchants such as Crozet (at no. 50; ✆ **04-72-41-99-92**) for umbrellas, Weiss (at no. 74; ✆ **04-78-37-80-38**) for hats, and Brossard (at no. 65; ✆ **04-78-42-06-05**) for knives and shaving brushes.

South of place Bellcour, antiques dealers concentrate around rue Auguste-Comte. Also consider venturing to the **Cité des Antiquaires,** 117 bd. Stalingrad (www.cite-antiquaires.fr; ✆ **04-72-69-00-00**) in the 6th district, with more than 100 dealers spread over two floors, and merchandise from the 18th century to the 1950s. It's open Thursday, Saturday, and Sunday from 10am to 7pm (Fri by appointment only).

Vieux Lyon has an array of art galleries and one-off boutiques. Made-to-measure chalkboards fashioned in any shape from boats and cars to elephants and wine bottles are on display at **Les Ardoises de Lyon,** 3 rue Soufflot (www.lesardoisesdelyon.com; ✆ **04-78-37-57-89**; open Tues–Sun noon–7:30pm). A new shop, **Natural Soap,** 6 rue de Gadagne (www.naturalsoaplyon.com; ✆ **09-81-37-33-76**) sells artisanal soaps made from fruit and vegetable extracts. For wine, visit **Antic Wine,** one of the best and most amusing wine shops in France, at 18 rue du Boeuf (www.anticwine.com; ✆ **04-78-37-08-96**).

More than 235 shops and boutiques fill the largest shopping center in Lyon, the **Centre Commercial La Part-Dieu,** 17 rue du Dr. Bouchut in the 3rd district (www.centrecommercial-partdieu.com; ✆ **04-72-60-60-62**).

**In Cuisine ★** This shop is dedicated to gourmands. Its shelves are lined with cookbook recipes from around the globe, professional pastry ingredients such as Valrhona *couverture* (coating) chocolate and kitchen accessories from personalised chefs' hats to house-shaped cake molds. At the back of the shop is a cookery school offering courses for French-speaking adults and kids alike. At the front is a small tea shop where you can savor chili-flavored hot chocolate with *financiers* (almond cakes).

1 place Bellecour. www.incuisine.fr. ✆ **04-72-41-18-00.** Cookery courses 30€–70€. AE, MC, V. Tues–Sat 8am–6pm.

**L'Atelier de Soierie ★★** Although Lyon is not the major silk center that it once was, it is home to several silk manufacturers. This workshop in the 1st arrondissement is the perfect place to watch silk *carrés* being printed using traditional Lyonnais techniques, before browsing the scarves and shawls on display in the neighboring boutique.

33 rue Romarin. www.atelierdesoierie.com. ✆ **04-72-07-97-83.** AE, MC, V. Mon-Fri 9:30am–1pm 2–6:30pm; Sat 9am–1pm 2–6pm.

## Lyon Nightlife

Since **Ninkasi** (www.ninkasi.fr) arrived on Lyon's nightlife scene in 1997, this Lyonnais microbrewery chain has gone from strength to strength. You'll find live music, fresh beer, and burgers at each of their nighttime venues around Lyon. Most live concerts are free, although there is sometimes a cover charge for well-known bands playing at the brewery headquarters, **Ninkasi Gerland**. You'll find **Gerland** at 267 rue Marcel Mérieux (✆ **04-72-76-89-00**); **Opéra** at 27 rue de l'Arbre Sec (✆ **04-78-28-37-74**); **Ampère** at 1 rue Henri IV (✆ **04-78-38-14-28**); **Ferrandière** at 22 rue Ferrandière (✆ **04-72-77-91-47**); **Sans Souci** at 26 cours Albert Thomas (✆ **04-78-01-78-12**); and finally **Croix Rousse** at 159 boulevard de la Croix-Rousse (✆ **04-78-28-00-17**), which opened in 2011. Named after the Sumerian goddess of beer, this American-style microbrewery produces 2,500 liters of beer per day, as well as running a *boulangerie* that bakes their own bread and burgers.

A good place to start the evening over a glass or two of wine is **La Cave des Voyageurs** at 7 place Saint-Paul (http://lacavedesvoyageurs.free.fr; ✆ **04-78-28-92-28**) in Vieux Lyon. Around the corner is the Anglophone pub **Smoking Dog,** 16 rue Lainerie (✆ **04-78-28-38-27**), with its bookshelf-lined walls, billiard table, and eight pump beers. It's a popular place to watch live international sports matches. It's open daily from 5pm to 1am (from 2pm on Saturday and Sunday).The best of the former cargo boats parked on the Rhône is **Le Sirius,** Berges du Rhône, 4 quai Augagneur (www.lesirius.com; ✆ **04-78-71-78-71;** Métro: Guillotière). An under-35 crowd packs the ship for dancing to the sounds of Lyon's best DJs on the lower-level floor. There's also an outdoor deck for fair weather. Sometimes big musical acts are booked here, at which time various cover charges are imposed. It's open daily from 4pm to 3am. One of Lyon's largest nightclubs is **First Tendency,** 13/14 place Jules Ferry (www.aperiklub-first.com; ✆ **04-37-24-19-46**) whose house music and chic decor attract a young, kitten-heeled 20s to 30s crowd. Housed in the Brotteaux old railway station, the club has room for 500 people: even so, you should expect a strict door policy.

As you may have expected in a city the size of Lyon, there are a scattering of busy and popular gay bars. A popular spot for men is long-standing **La Ruche,** 22 rue Gentil, 2e (✆ **04-78-37-42-26;** Métro: Cordeliers), which is open daily from 5pm to 3am, while **Le Domaine,** 9 rue du Jardin des Plantes (www.le domainebar.fr; ✆ **04-72-98-85-33**) attracts a young, vibrant lesbian crowd and is open Monday to Saturday 6pm to 3am.

For the theater or opera buff, Lyon's **Théâtre des Célestins,** place des Célestins (www.celestins-lyon.org; ✆ **04-72-77-40-00**), is the premier venue for French-language comedy and drama, and the **Opéra,** place de la Comédie (www.opera-lyon.com; ✆ **08-26-30-53-25**), offers opera, dance, musical concerts and workshops for all ages. **Halle Tony Garnier,** 20 place Antonin Perrin (www.halle-tony-garnier.fr; ✆ **04-72-76-85-85**), originated as a 19th-century food market. The immense 17,000 sq. m (182,986 sq. ft.) space with excellent acoustics is a popular venue for international pop concerts and dance shows. At any newsstand, pick up a copy of the weekly guide *Lyon-Poche,* which lists happenings and venues around town, from bars to classical concerts.

# Where to Stay

## VERY EXPENSIVE

### Cour des Loges ★★★
This landmark, UNESCO-protected hotel in Old Lyon occupies four connected houses dating from the 15th and 16th centuries. Among its lures are a magnificent loggia-ringed courtyard, two restaurants, and a spa with indoor pool. Most of its beautifully furnished rooms and suites face gardens, the square, or the large, sunny lobby. The bedrooms vary in size from bijoux to medium-sized, but all are lavishly decorated. Classic bedrooms often have an open-plan bathroom in the bedroom, while most Superior Rooms have a separate bathroom. The themed suites feature Venetian painted panels or early black-and-white photography; most have separate tub and shower. The immaculate spa uses the Pure Altitude organic product range of its Alpine sister hotel, Les Fermes de Marie. The staff, Lyon's savviest, is courteous and efficient.

# LE 6ème

The 6th is an up-and-coming district. The end of 2012 will see the completion of a long and, at times, controversial plan to put underground parking beneath place Brosset. The upside of this urban project has been the pedestrianization of the square and the area leading down towards the old railway station off place Jules Ferry. Pretty garden beds, stone paving, and children's play areas have given the whole area a new lease of life as witnessed by burgeoning new restaurants and bars nearby.

There are several atmospheric places for an evening drink in the 6th, including the newly-opened **Juliette Café Comptoir**, 41 rue Juliette Récamier (www.cafe juliette.com; ☎ **04-78-52-83-80**), a stylish bar that has been wowing locals with its cocktails. There's also the informal **L'Horloge**, 34 bis boulevard des Brotteaux (www.restaurant-horloge-lyon.com; ☎ **04-37-24-30-15**), which attracts a Lyonnais preppy crowd with its Burgundy wines by the glass served with tapas-style wooden platters of salami and cheese.

2–8 rue du Boeuf, Vieux Lyon 69005. www.courdesloges.com. ☎ **04-72-77-44-44.** Fax 04-72-40-93-61. 61 units. 250€–390€ double; 530€–650€ suite. AE, DC, MC, V. Parking 35€. Métro: St-Jean. **Amenities:** 2 restaurants; bar; spa (with fitness room, indoor pool and sauna); room service. *In room:* A/C, TV, hair dryer, minibar, free Wi-Fi.

**Villa Florentine** ★★★ Conveniently located in Vieux Lyon, this Relais & Châteaux hotel is as stunning as the Cour des Loges (see above). One of the great city hotels along the Rhône, it is a bastion of taste and luxury. The views from the lounges, terraces, and guest rooms are the most panoramic in town. Converted from a 17th-century convent, the building retains many of its original Italianate architectural details. The accommodations are spacious and comfortable, decorated in a style that blends modern Italian design with Renaissance reproductions. A nine-unit annex, just across the street, features rooms and suites that are a bit larger and more modern than those within the hotel's original core.

25 montée Saint Barthélémy, Lyon 69005. www.villaflorentine.com. ☎ **04-72-56-56-56.** Fax 04-72-40-90-56. 28 units. 255€–370€ double; 415€–950€ suite. AE, DC, MC, V. Parking 18€. **Amenities:** Restaurant; bar; babysitting; exercise room; heated outdoor pool; room service; sauna; mini spa. *In room:* A/C, TV, hair dryer, minibar, free Wi-Fi.

## EXPENSIVE

**Le Royal Lyon** ★★★ Overlooking Lyon's place Bellecour, this Haussmanian-style mansion has been a hotel for over a century welcoming numerous famous faces from Sophia Loren to the Beatles. It is also the hotel school of the **Institute Paul Bocuse,** training students in culinary arts and hotel management at the highest level. Fine fabrics by Pierre Frey and Ralph Lauren adorn every corner of the hotel. The dining room overlooks an inviting open-plan kitchen, while the *Salon de Musique* is a scarlet den for tea-drinking or post-dinner *digestifs*. Rooms vary enormously in size and quality. Look out for special web rates for weekend stays.

20 place Bellecour, 69002 Lyon. www.lyonhotel-leroyal.com. ☎ **04-78-37-57-31.** Fax 04-78-37-01-36. 74 units. 145€–390€ double; 235€–500€ suite. AE, DC, MC, V. Parking 19€. **Amenities:** Restaurant; bar; tea room. *In room:* A/C, TV, hair dryer, minibar, free Wi-Fi.

## MODERATE

**Collège Hôtel** The accommodations here, which adopt a tongue-in-cheek theme of a university dorm, are not the spartan affair you might expect; in fact, they are comfortable and include a number of attractive features. Located on the right bank of the Saône within the heart of Vieux Lyon, this three-star hotel offers 39 small but well-furnished bedrooms; some with private terraces or balconies. The minimalist all-white bedrooms might not be to all tastes, but they offer immaculate linens and a choice of modern bathrooms (the best ones are the corner units with hand-held showers, and the top two floors with stunning city views). Street noise is also less of an issue on higher floors. Each floor has a 1960s vintage refrigerator from which "boarders" can help themselves to free nonalcoholic drinks. Best of all is the rooftop garden terrace with a "gym" that humorously reflects the French distaste for exercise. As soon as night falls, the hotel's 130 windows light up as part of a unique light show, enhancing the 1930s facade.

5 place Saint Paul, Lyon 69005. www.college-hotel.com. © **04-72-10-05-05.** Fax 04-78-27-98-84. 39 units. 125€–155€ double. AE, MC, V. Parking 15€. **Amenities:** Bar (with an impressive selection of wines by the glass); library. In room: A/C, TV, free Wi-Fi.

**Hôtel des Célestins ★★** 🎁 On a discreet street midway between place Bellecour and place des Jacobins lies the charming Hôtel des Célestins. This three-star hotel has quietly established itself as one of the best mid-range hotels in Lyon. The secret to their success perhaps lies in the *chez soi* (at home) atmosphere: The old-fashioned breakfast room feels like a private dining room, while the bedrooms contain homey touches such as bookshelves lined with well-worn books. Many of the bedrooms overlook the splendid 18th-century theater on place Célestins. The top-floor bedrooms are the most prized, so book early if you can.

4 rue des Archers, 69002 Lyon. www.hotelcelestins.com. © **04-72-56-08-98.** Fax 04-72-56-08-65. 27 units. 82€–193€ double. 164€–244€ suite. 194€–444€ 2-bedroom apartment. AE, DC, MC, V. **Amenities:** Breakfast room. In room: TV, hair dryer, free Wi-Fi.

**Le Phénix Hotel ★** Overlooking the Saône in Vieux Lyon, this hotel dates in part from the 16th century, when it was a meeting place for theatrical troupes. Today the old structure has been joined with other buildings to create this atmospheric choice with its original Florentine architectural design. Tradition has been respected, but modern touches have been added in all the bedrooms. Rooms are intimate and decorated in warm colors with stylish furnishings; bathrooms have tub/showers. Deluxe rooms have views over the Saône.

7 quai Bondy, 69005 Lyon. www.hotel-phenix-lyon.fr. © **04-78-28-24-24.** Fax 04-78-28-62-86. 36 units. 108€–191€ double. AE, DC, MC, V. Parking 15€. **Amenities:** Bar; room service. In room: TV, hair dryer, minibar, free Wi-Fi.

## INEXPENSIVE

**Hôtel Bayard Bellecour ★** This two-star hotel overlooks one of Lyon's finest squares, place Bellecour. The foundations of this dignified townhouse date from the 16th century. Guest rooms are decorated in romantic French style with creative modern touches. Make sure you ask for one of the renovated rooms: Each room is beautifully outfitted in a style inspired by a period of French history. Most of the compact bathrooms have showers and tubs. There's no elevator and you enter the hotel through a narrow hallway and climb one flight of stairs to the reception area.

23 place Bellecour, Lyon 69002. www.hotelbayard.fr. ☎ **04-78-37-39-64.** Fax 04-72-40-95-51. 22 units. 69€–199€ double. AE, MC, V. Parking 20€ (call ahead). Métro: Bellecour. *In room:* TV, hair dryer, free Wi-Fi.

**Hôtel Saint-Paul** 🖋 "Two-star rating, four-star service" says the Saint-Paul's owner, referring to the French hotel rating system. He's not kidding—along with city knowledge to rival the concierges a few doors down at the Cour des Loges, the people who work here clearly love Lyon and are happy to give you a full, friendly rundown on where to go and what to do, particularly when it comes to food. There's no lift and rooms are plainly furnished; more expensive rooms have tubs. We'd recommend no. 441 with its twins beds and light-infused shower room.

6 rue Lainerie, Lyon 69005. www.hotelsaint-paul.com. ☎ **04-78-28-13-29.** Fax 04-72-00-97-27. 20 units. 75€–82€ double. AE, DC, MC, V. Métro: Hôtel de Ville. *In room:* TV, hair dryer, free Wi-Fi.

# BEAUJOLAIS COUNTRY ★★

The vineyards of Beaujolais start about 40km (25 miles) north of Lyon and finish just South of Mâcon. Though wine lovers tend to include this wine-producing region as part of Greater Burgundy, geographically speaking Beaujolais belongs to the Rhône region. Beaujolais is small—64km (40 miles) long and less than 16km (10 miles) wide—yet it's one of the most famous in France. It's known throughout the world because of the Beaujolais wine craze that began in Paris some 30 years ago. In an average year, this region produces more than 190 million bottles of wine. Some 180 châteaux are scattered throughout this part of France. At many of them, you can sample and buy bottles of Beaujolais.

This region is a colorful and prosperous rural area, with vineyards on hillsides, cottages where the growers live, and historic houses and castles. It has been called the "Land of the Golden Stones," but don't expect architectural monuments.

Unlike Alsace, with its Route du Vin, the Beaujolais country doesn't have a defined route. You can branch off in any direction, stopping at whatever point you desire. Don't be worried about losing your way after meandering off the A6 superhighway. This is one of the easiest parts of eastern France to negotiate, with clear road signs. If you're in doubt, simply follow the signs to the region's capital and commercial center, Villefranche-sur-Saône.

If you're pressed for time, you can tie the highlights together in a one-way drive, beginning at Villefranche-sur-Saône, known as **Villefranche,** which you can reach from A6 between Mâcon and Lyon. (If you're heading north to south, follow the drive in reverse order, beginning in Juliénas, also off A6.)

Start in Villefranche. After an excursion west on D338 to **Bagnols-en-Beaujolais,** return to Villefranche.

**Beaujolais country landscape.**

From here, take the D35 to **St-Julien-sous-Montmelas.** From St-Julien, take D19 to **Salles-Arbuissonnas-en-Beaujolais.** From Salles, take the D20 east back to the A6, then head North on the motorway to **Belleville-sur-Saône.** Then follow D306 North before turning west on the D9 to **Villié-Morgon.** From Villié-Morgon, take D68 to Fleurie and then on to **Juliénas.**

# Villefranche-Sur-Saone: Capital of Beaujolais

Go to the **Office du Tourisme,** 96 rue de la Sous-Préfecture, not far from the marketplace (www.villefranche-beaujolais.fr; ℰ **04-74-07-27-40**), for a booklet on the Beaujolais country. It includes a map and itineraries, and lists the wine-tasting cellars open to the public. It also lists and details some 30 villages.

# Bagnols-En-Beaujolais

To reach Bagnols from Villefranche, head west on D338.

## WHERE TO EAT & STAY

**Château de Bagnols-en-Beaujolais** ★★★    This is lordly living on a grand scale. France's premier château hotel, this one-time Renaissance ruin has been restored by 400 artisans to an exceptionally high standard. This Relais & Châteaux hotel attracts large numbers of oenophiles. Prices are eye-watering, but so are the antiques, paintings, and art (much from the 17th and 18th centuries) that fill the mansion. The individually decorated guest rooms are sumptuous, with antique beds, period velvets, embroidered linen sheets, and down pillows; one unit is named for Mme. de Sévigné, who spent a restless night here in 1673. The bathrooms have tiled floors, brass fittings, and luxurious tubs. La Salle des Gardes, the dining area with cathedral-worthy stonework, serves elegant Beaujolais fare.

Place du Château, Bagnols 69620. www.chateaudebagnols.fr. ℰ **04-74-71-40-00.** Fax 04-74-71-40-49. 21 units. 235€–655€ double; from 335€–990€ suite. AE, DC, MC, V. **Amenities:** Restaurant; lounge; heated outdoor pool; room service. *In room:* TV, hair dryer, Wi-Fi (15€ per day).

# St-Julien-Sous-Montmelas

This charming village is 11km (6¾ miles) northwest of Villefranche (take D35). Claude Bernard, the father of physiology, was born here in 1813. His small stone house—now the **Musée Claude-Bernard** (ℰ **04-74-67-51-44**)—exhibits the scholar's mementos, instruments, and books. Sadly the museum is currently closed for an extensive renovation, but is planned to reopen for summer 2013. A side trip worth taking from St Julien is to **Château de Montmelas** (www.chateau-montmelas.com; ℰ **04-74-67-32-94**). Known locally as the Sleeping Beauty castle, this splendid medieval château is lived in by the Comte Amaury d'Harcourt and his charming wife Delphine. Every Tuesday and Thursday at 2pm during July, tourists can visit the castle (visit the website for details of other opening days during the year). The castle also runs two gîtes. Prices for a weekend are from 400 euros and for a week from 590 euros. From St-Julien, take the D19 west and then the D44 towards the castle.

# Belleville-sur-Saone

For an excellent dining experience, drive east from Salles on D20 back to the A6, then head North on the motorway to Belleville-sur-Saône.

## WHERE TO EAT

**Aux Gourmands de Belleville** ★ MODERN FRENCH  A change of ownership and name (formerly Le Rhône au Rhin) has changed little else. This brightly painted restaurant is a refuge from the more congested regions. Menu items change with the seasons but may include terrine of foie gras, scallops, or farm-raised chicken with morel mushrooms.

10 av. du Port. www.auxgourmandsdebelleville.fr. ℓ **04-74-66-16-23.** Reservations recommended. Fixed-price lunch 15€, dinner 24€–32€. MC, V. Mon-Fri and Sun noon–2pm; Mon-Tues and Thurs–Sun 7–9pm.

## Villié-Morgon

For another wine tour in the Beaujolais country, we suggest driving north from Belleville-sur-Saône on D306 before turning west on the D9 to Villié-Morgon. The village and the surrounding region contain around 250 wine producers. Their product, at its best, is usually judged among the best Beaujolais wines in France.

In the basement of the **Château de Fontcrenne,** immediately adjacent to the Hôtel de Ville, is the **Caveau de Morgon** (www.morgon.fr; ℓ **04-74-04-20-99**). It produces and bottles wine under its own label, **Caveau de Morgon**, using grapes from local independent wine growers. The cellar is open for tours and sales daily 10am to noon and 2 to 6pm in winter, 9:30am to 12pm and 2:30 to 7pm in summer. You'll pay a nominal charge—1€ per glass, 7.50€ per bottle—for wine you consume. Admission is free. Closed first 3 weeks of January.

## Juliénas

Wines are also a reason to travel north on D68 to Juliénas. This village produces a full-bodied, robust wine. Go to the **Cellier de la Vieille Eglise** (ℓ **04-74-04-42-98**), an old church cellar, to sip the wine. A statue of Bacchus with some tipsy, scantily clad girlfriends looks on from what used to be the altar. It's open June to September daily 10am to 12:30pm and 3pm to 7pm; October to May Wednesday to Monday 10am–noon and 3pm–6pm. The local farmers' and wine-growers' cooperative helps support this wine outlet. Admission is free, but expect to pay 6.50€ to 10€ per bottle, depending on the vintage. Closed first 3 weeks of January.

# ROANNE

390km (242 miles) SE of Paris; 87km (54 miles) NW of Lyon

This industrial town on the left bank of the Loire is a popular excursion from Lyon and Vichy because it's home to one of France's greatest three-star restaurants, La Maison Troisgros (see "Where to Eat & Stay," below).

In a neoclassical mansion built at the end of the 18th century, **Musée Joseph Déchelette,** 22 rue Anatole-France (ℓ **04-77-23-68-77**), showcases an exceptional collection of Italian and European earthenware from the 16th though 20th centuries, as well as Gallo-Roman and ancient Egyptian archaeological collections that bear homage to Déchelette, the famous Roannaise archaeologist and benefactor. Hours are Monday & Wednesday to Friday 10am to noon and 2 to 6pm; Saturday 10am to 6pm and Sunday 2pm to 6pm. Admission is 4.60€ for adults, 2.50€ for students, free for ages 25 and under, and free for everyone on Wednesday afternoon.

# Essentials

**GETTING THERE**  **Trains** and some **buses** serve Roanne from nearby cities, notably Lyon, but the train is much more convenient. By train, Roanne lies 3 hours from Paris (with a connection in Le Creusot-Montceau) and 1 hour and 10 minutes from Lyon; for information, visit www.voyages-sncf.com or call ✆ **08-92-33-53-35**. If you're **driving,** follow N7 northwest from Lyon to Roanne. From Paris, follow A6 south to Nemours, then A77 before turning southwest onto N7 at Nevers towards Roanne.

**VISITOR INFORMATION**  The **Office de Tourisme** is at 8 place Maréchal de Lattre-de-Tassigny (www.leroannais.com; ✆ **04-77-71-51-77**).

# Where to Eat & Stay

**La Maison Troisgros ★★★** FRENCH/LYONNAIS  This Relais & Châteaux property is one of the top 10 restaurants in France. It attained that reputation in the 1950s and has since factored into the itineraries of globe-trotting foodies, visiting heads of state, and wealthy people touring the region. Come here with respect for the French *grande bourgeoisie* and the appeal of French culinary finesse. The place is too conservative and devoted to impeccably tailored service for anything radical or provocative.

Decorated in neutral colors and lined with contemporary artwork, the restaurant features superb cuisine at astronomical prices. The current keepers of the three Michelin–starred flame celebrate the bounty of the Lyonnais countryside. Some of the best dishes are sautéed foie gras served with pickled leek, scallops in puff pastry, and three-spiced blackened lamb ribs. To finish the meal, ask for one of the region's best assortments of cheese or perhaps a mint-and-chocolate soufflé. Michel Troisgros also runs the neighboring cafe-deli **Le Central,** selling Troisgros' homemade sweet-and-sour sauces and serving an excellent 23-euro lunchtime menu.

The hotel rents 16 traditionally furnished rooms; a double costs 305€ to 410€, each with free Wi-Fi, while a suite costs 480€ to 600€.

Place de la Gare, Roanne 42300. www.troisgros.com. ✆ **04-77-71-66-97.** Fax 04-77-70-39-77. Reservations required. Main courses 60€–110€; fixed-price menu 95€ lunch, 165€–350€ dinner. AE, DC, MC, V. Thurs–Mon noon–1:30pm and 7:30–9pm. Closed Mon afternoons btw. Oct and Mar, 2 weeks in Feb, and 2 weeks in Aug.

# Where to Eat & Stay Nearby

In the nearby village of **Le Coteau,** you'll find several worthy restaurants. These two are our favorites. To get there, take N7 3km (1¾ miles) southeast from the center of Roanne.

**Auberge Costelloise ★** FRENCH  This is the place to head when you can't afford the dazzling but expensive food at Troisgros. It provides what this region needs: an attractive restaurant with fine cuisine and reasonable prices. The restaurant is adjacent to the banks of the headwaters of the Loire, in a dining room ringed with paintings and wood paneling. Choose one of the fixed-price menus, which change weekly. The well-planned menu includes dishes such as tomato profiteroles with eggplant caviar and curried duck with pumpkin risotto. You can order fine vintages of Burgundian wines by the pitcher.

2 av. de la Libération, Le Coteau 42120. www.auberge-costelloise.fr. ✆ **04-77-68-12-71.** Reservations required. Main courses 14€–32€; fixed-price menus 27€–49€. AE, MC, V. Wed–Sat noon–1:30pm and 7:45–9:30pm; Sun noon–1:30pm. Closed mid-July to mid-Aug.

**Le Grand Couvert** ★★ 🏠 MODERN FRENCH   Surrounded by rolling landscape, this Troisgros *auberge* opened in 2008. Meals are served in a converted barn with huge glass lanterns hanging from the wooden rafters. The earthy French cuisine is astonishingly good. Typical menu items include smoked trout with sorrel and blood sausage with apples. Finish off with toffee cream or shortbread. Accommodations are provided in two beautifully-furnished adjoining *gîtes* and three contemporary eco-friendly *cadoles* (cabins).

Iguerande 71340. www.troisgros.fr. ✆ **03-85-84-07-24.** Fax 03-85-84-17-43. Reservations recommended. Set-price menus 28€–60€. AE, DC, MC, V. Oct–May Mon–Tues and Fri–Sun noon–2pm 7–9:30pm (Jun–Sept also open Thurs).

# PÉROUGES ★★

464km (288 miles) SE of Paris; 35km (22 miles) NE of Lyon

Saved from demolition by a courageous mayor in 1909 and preserved by the government, this thousand-person village of craftspeople has often attracted movie crews: *The Three Musketeers* (1961) and *Monsieur Vincent* (1947) were filmed here. Films had not been made here since the 1970s, since French film production moved primarily to Eastern Europe, but that has changed recently. The town sits on what has been called an "isolated throne," atop a hill northeast of Lyon.

Follow rue du Prince, once the main business street, to place des Tilleuls, at the center of which is the **Arbre de la Liberté (Tree of Liberty),** planted in 1792 to commemorate the Revolution. Nearby, in a 14th-century building, is the **Musée du Vieux-Pérouges,** place de la Halle (✆ **04-74-61-00-88**), displaying such artifacts as hand looms. It's open June to August daily 10am to noon and 2 to 6pm; off season, Saturday and Sunday 10am to noon and 2 to 6pm. Admission is 4€, free ages 10 and under. The price includes access to the museum and, through adjoining doors, to one of the finest houses in the village and a classified historic monument, the **Maison des Princes de Savoie,** with a watchtower (**La Tour de Guet**) and a replica of a 13th-century garden, the **Jardin de Hortulus.** The **Sainte-Marie-Madeleine** church is supremely peaceful.

Wander through town, soaking in the atmosphere of a stone village that's remained virtually unchanged over time.

## Essentials

**GETTING THERE**   It's easiest to **drive** to Pérouges, though the signs for the town, especially at night, are confusing. From Lyon, take A42/E611 northeast and exit near Meximieux.

**VISITOR INFORMATION**   The **Tourist Office (Syndicat d'Initiative,** Cité de Pérouges; www.perouges.org; ✆ **04-74-46-70-84**) lies adjacent to the entrance of this very small village. It's closed in winter.

## Where to Eat & Stay

**Hostellerie du Vieux-Pérouges** ★★ 🏠   This is a treasure in a restored group of 13th-century timbered buildings. Town mayor Thibaut and his family run a museum-caliber inn furnished with cupboards housing pewter plates, iron lanterns hanging from medieval beams, refectory dining tables, and stone fireplaces. The midsize to spacious guest rooms are completely up-to-date with modern amenities, yet they have an old-fashioned atmosphere and style that recall medieval France.

The restaurant's food is exceptional, especially when accompanied by the local sparkling wine, Montagnieu, which has been compared to Asti Spumante. Specialties include Bresse chicken in morel-studded cream sauce, filet of carp stuffed *à l'ancienne* with pike, and *panaché Pérougien* (an omelet stuffed with creamed morels and served with shrimp and crayfish cream sauce). By far the best-selling dessert is a crepe known as a *galette pérougienne à la crème,* made from a century-old recipe. After dinner, ask for a glass of Ypocras, a unique liqueur made from a recipe dating from the Middle Ages. Fixed-price menus range from 38€ to 65€.

Place du Tilleul, Pérouges 01800. www.hostelleriedeperouges.com. ℂ **04-74-61-00-88.** Fax 04-74-34-77-90. 28 units. 128€–246€ double; 159€–318€ triple or quad. AE, MC, V. **Amenities:** Restaurant; bar; room service. *In room:* TV, hair dryer, free Wi-Fi.

# BOURG-EN-BRESSE

425km (264 miles) SE of Paris; 61km (38 miles) NE of Lyon

The ancient capital of Bresse, this farming and business center on the border between Burgundy and the Jura offers fabulous food.

## Essentials

**GETTING THERE**   Bourg-en-Bresse is accessible by **train** from Paris, Lyon, and Dijon. Six TGV (fast) trains arrive from Paris's Gare de Lyon daily (trip time: 2 hr.). From Lyon (40–85 min.), over 20 trains arrive per day. From Dijon (2 hr.), four trains arrive daily. For information, visit www.voyages-sncf.com or call ℂ **08-92-33-53-35.** If **driving** from Lyon, take A42 North, before turning onto A40 for the 40-minute trip; from Dijon (2 hr.), follow A31 to Beaune, then A6 to Mâcon before taking A40 east to Bourg-en-Bresse.

**VISITOR INFORMATION**   The **Office de Tourisme** is at 6 av. Alsace-Lorraine (www.bourgenbressetourisme.fr; ℂ **04-74-22-49-40**).

## Seeing the Sights

If you have time, visit the **Eglise Notre-Dame,** 10 place Clémenceau. Begun in 1505, it contains some finely carved 16th-century stalls. If you'd like to wander around town, check out the 15th-century houses on rue du Palais and rue Gambetta.

**Monastère Royal de Brou ★★** MONASTERY   Art lovers will want to stop here to see its magnificent royal tombs. One of the great artistic treasures of France, this flamboyant Gothic monastery was built in the 16th century for Margaret of Austria, the ill-fated daughter of Emperor Maximilian. Over the ornate Renaissance doorway, the tympanum depicts Margaret and her "handsome duke," Philibert, who died prematurely at the age of 24 after catching a cold on a hunting expedition. The nave and its double aisles are admirable. Look for the ornate rood screen, decorated with basket-handle arching. Ask a guide for a tour of the choir, which is rich in decorative detail; Flemish sculptors and local craftsmen made the 74 choir stalls of oak in just 2 years.

Monastère Royal de Brou.

The tombs are the church's treasure. The Carrara marble statues are of Philibert and Margaret. Another tomb is that of Marguerite de Bourbon, mother of Philibert and grandmother of François I, who died in 1483. See also the stained-glass windows inspired by a Dürer engraving and an alabaster retable (altarpiece) depicting *The Seven Joys of the Madonna.* The monastery occasionally hosts modern art expositions.

63 bd. de Brou. *©* **04-74-22-83-83.** Admission to church, cloisters, and museum 7.50€ adults, free for children 17 and under if accompanied by an adult. July–Sept daily 9am–6pm; Apr–June daily 9am–12:30pm and 2–6pm; Oct–Mar daily 9am–noon and 2–5pm. Closed Jan 1, May 1, Nov 1 and 11, and Christmas.

## Where to Eat

**Au Chalet de Brou ★🍴** TRADITIONAL FRENCH   Moments from the splendid Brou monastery, this unpretentious restaurant serves regional cuisine that won't leave you out of pocket. Specialties include time-worn French dishes such as duck *à l'orange*; frogs' legs in parsley sauce; and at least a half-dozen kinds of Bresse chicken, served with your choice of morel-flavored cream sauce, raspberry vinegar, or chardonnay sauce. Purists may opt for it simply grilled, in order to appreciate the unadorned flavor of the bird in its own drippings. Dessert may be an apple tart presented, according to your choice, hot or cool.

168 bd. de Brou. *©* **04-74-22-26-28.** Reservations recommended. Main courses 11€–28€; fixed-price menu 21€–46€. AE, MC, V. Tues–Wed and Fri–Sat noon–2pm 7–9:30pm; Sun 7–9:30pm.

## Where to Stay

**Hôtel de France ★**   Most of the town's hotels are now run by chains, and this three-star Best Western hotel is the best of the bunch hosting everyone from tourists to film crews (Charlotte Gainsbourg is reported to have been seen here recently). The hotel blends modern and regional styles, and many rooms have baths. In 2011, the hotel was awarded European Ecolabel status, an initiative backed by the European Union which awards environmentally friendly products including hotels and campsites.

19 place Bernard, Bourg-en-Bresse 01000. www.bestwestern-hoteldefrance.com. ✆ **04-74-23-30-24.** Fax 04-74-23-69-90. 44 units. 89€–105€ double. AE, MC, V. Parking 10€. **Amenities:** Bar; restaurant. *In room:* AC, TV, hair dryer, free Wi-Fi.

**Le Griffon d'Or ★ 👤**   A new hotel, Le Griffon d'Or is establishing itself fast as the smartest place to stay in the center of town. This 18th-century former coaching inn has been converted into a stylishly decorated B&B with just sixteen bedrooms and two suites. Guests can enjoy the mini-spa with its Jacuzzi and sauna or play a game of snooker in the billiards room. Breakfast is the only meal served.

10 rue du 4 septembre, Bourg-en-Bresse 01000. www.hotelgriffondor.fr. ✆ **04-74-23-13-24.** Fax 04-74-23-71-61. 18 units. 90€–135€ double. 155€ suite. AE, MC, V. Parking free. **Amenities:** Bar; Jacuzzi; sauna; billiards room. *In room:* TV, hair dryer, minibar, free Wi-Fi.

# VIENNE ★★

489km (303 miles) SE of Paris; 31km (19 miles) S of Lyon

One of ancient Gaul's largest towns, Vienne is home to no fewer than 41 classified historic monuments including a Roman theater, Augustus and Livia temple, and the archaeological Cybèle gardens. Gastronomes know Vienne because it's the home of one of France's leading restaurants, La Pyramide. Even if you can't afford the haute cuisine, you may want to visit.

## Essentials

**GETTING THERE**   **Trains** connect Vienne with the rest of France. Trips require a transfer in Lyon, 20 minutes away. For information, visit www.voyagessncf.com or call ✆ **08-92-33-53-35. Buses** from Lyon arrive a dozen times a day, making many stops and taking about an hour; for information, contact Vienne's Gare Routière (✆ **08-00-86-98-69**), adjacent to the railway station. The one-way bus or train fare from Lyon is about 2€. If you're **driving** from Lyon, take the A7.

**VISITOR INFORMATION**   The **Office de Tourisme** is at cours Brillier (www.vienne-tourisme.com; ✆ **04-74-53-80-30;** fax 04-74-53-80-31).

**SPECIAL EVENTS**   In the first 2 weeks of July, Vienne attracts some of the biggest names in jazz for the annual **Festival du Jazz à Vienne.** Tickets range from 30€ to 40€. You can get tickets and information online (www.jazz avienne.com; ✆ **04-74-78-87-87**).

## Seeing the Sights

Vienne contains many ancient buildings, making it a *ville romaine et médiévale.* Near the center of town on place du Palais is the **Temple d'Auguste et de Livie,** built on the orders of the Roman emperor Claudius and turned into a "temple of reason" during the French Revolution. Another outstanding monument is the **Pyramide du Cirque Romain,** part of the Roman circus. Rising 16m (52 ft.), it rests on a portico with four arches and is sometimes called the tomb of Pilate.

Take rue Clémentine to the **Cathédrale St-Maurice ★★**, place St-Maurice (www.cathedraledevienne.com) which dates from the 12th century and wasn't completed until the 16th. It has three aisles but no transepts. Its west front is built in the

Flamboyant Gothic style, and inside are many fine Romanesque sculptures. The cathedral is open daily 8am to 5pm (until 6pm Apr–Aug); admission is free.

In the south part of town is the **Eglise St-Pierre** ★, place St-Pierre (✆ 04-74-85-20-35). A landmark with origins in the 5th century, it's one of the oldest medieval churches in France. Inside, the **Musée Lapidaire** (✆ 04-74-85-20-35) displays architectural fragments and sculptures from excavations. The museum is open April to October Tuesday to Sunday 9:30am to 1pm and 2 to 6pm; November to March Tuesday to Sunday 1:30 to 5:30pm. Admission is 2.80€ for adults, 2€ for students, and free for children 17 and under. The museum is closed New Year's Day, May 1, November 1, November 11, and Christmas.

A **Roman Theater (Théâtre Romain)** ★, 7 rue du Cirque (✆ 04-74-85-39-23), has been excavated east of town at the foot of Mont Pipet. Theatrical spectacles were once staged here for an audience of thousands. You can visit September and October Tuesday to Sunday 9:30am to 1pm and 2 to 6pm; November to March Tuesday to Friday 9:30am to 12:30pm and 2 to 5pm, Saturday and Sunday 1:30 to 5:30pm; and April to August daily 9:30am to 1pm and 2 to 6pm. Admission is 2.80€.

If you have about an hour for a side trip, in Hauterives, south of Vienne, you'll find one of the world's strangest pieces of architecture. The **Palais Idéal du Facteur Cheval**, or **Palace of the Mailman Cheval** (www.facteurcheval. com; ✆ 04-75-68-81-19), the lifelong work of French postman Ferdinand Cheval, is built of stone and concrete and elaborately decorated, often with clamshells. It's a monumental tribute to one man's whimsical imagination. The work was finished in 1912, when Cheval was 76. Admission is 5.80€ for adults, 4.80€ students, and 4.10€ for children 6 to 16. The palace is open in April to September daily 9:30am to 12:30pm and 1:30 to 6:30pm (until 7pm in July and Aug); November to March daily 9:30am to 12:30pm and 1:30 to 5:30pm 4:30pm.

## Where to Eat

**La Pyramide** ★★★ MODERN FRENCH    This is the area's premier place to stay or dine, and for many, it's the preferred stopover between Paris and the Riviera. The restaurant perpetuates the memory of a superb chef, Fernand Point, who

Detail at the Cathédrale St-Maurice.

died in 1955. Through the continuing efforts of Patrick Henriroux, many of Point's secrets, especially his sauces, have been preserved. Menus change seasonally, but the cuisine is always imaginative. Examples include John Dory cooked in sorrel leaves or scallops with mango and Thai grapefruit sprinkled with Madagascan wild pepper. The cheese platter is wonderful, and desserts are as artfully caloric, and as stylish, as anything else in the Rhône Valley. Henriroux also runs an affordable bistro, Espace PH3, that's open daily for lunch and dinner.

The hotel offers 24 charming, air-conditioned guest rooms, each with minibar, TV, and free Wi-Fi. Doubles go for 200€ to 240€, suites for 390€ to 420€.

14 bd. Fernand Point. www.lapyramide.com. ℂ **04-74-53-01-96.** Fax 04-74-85-69-73. Reservations required. Main courses 40€–95€; fixed-price weekday lunch with wine 61€; fixed-price lunch and dinner menu 115€–172€. AE, DC, MC, V. Thurs–Mon 12–1:30pm and 7:30–9:30pm. Closed mid-Feb to mid-Mar and 1 week in mid-Aug.

**Les Saveurs du Marché ★ ✦** FRENCH   This bustling, high-turnover, and slightly rowdy restaurant is known to many of the hardworking laborers of Vienne, who come here for inexpensive lunchtime meals and for slightly more leisurely and intricate food at night. It's within a 10-minute walk south of the town center. Along one wall is a large paneled bar. Menu items change with the seasons and the availability of raw ingredients but may include a delectable pike soufflé with fresh mussels, and a savory casserole of spicy scallops and crayfish. Expect good value and cheerful informality.

34 cours de Verdun. www.lessaveursdumarche.fr. ℂ **04-74-31-65-65.** Reservations recommended. Main courses 17€–22€. Fixed-price lunch 14€, dinner 19€–31€. DC, MC, V. Mon–Fri noon–1:45pm and 7:30–9:30pm. Closed mid-July to mid-Aug.

## Where to Stay

**La Pyramide** (see above) also offers rooms.

**Le Beau-Rivage**   This four-star hotel originated around 1900 as a simple inn that served food and wine to fishermen who traveled from Lyon to the well-stocked waters of this section of the Rhône. It has evolved into a stylish, nostalgic enclave. The rooms are well furnished; some are larger than you may expect. Most come with a tub/shower.

The Rhône passes by the dining terrace. The traditional cuisine is excellent, if a little overpriced with fixed-price menus from 38€ to 82€. The Côtes du Rhône wines complement the food well.

2 rue du Beau Rivage, Condrieu 69420. www.hotel-beaurivage.com. ℂ **04-74-56-82-82.** Fax 04-74-59-59-36. 30 units. 125€–195€ double; 270€ suite. DC, MC, V. From Vienne, cross the Rhône on D386 and head south 12km (7½ miles); pass through Condrieu and, on the southern outskirts, look for signs on the left. **Amenities:** Bar; restaurant. *In room:* A/C, TV, hair dryer, minibar, free Wi-Fi.

# VALENCE ★

671km (416 miles) SE of Paris; 100km (62 miles) S of Lyon

Standing on the left bank of the Rhône between Lyon and Avignon, Valence is a tidy, business-like town that might easily pass under the radar save for its star attraction: Anne-Sophie Pic, France's only female three-star Michelin chef.

A former Roman colony, it later became the capital of the Duchy of Valentinois, set up by Louis XII in 1493 for Cesare Borgia. Today Valence is a market town and distribution point for Rhône Valley fruit and vegetable producers. It's fitting that François Rabelais, who wrote of gargantuan appetites, spent time here as a student.

The major sight is the **Cathédrale St-Apollinaire,** place des Ormeaux (✆ **04-75-44-90-45**). Built in the Auvergnat-Romanesque style, the cathedral was consecrated by Urban II in 1095 and has been much restored since. The choir contains the tomb of Pope Pius VI, who died a prisoner here in the 18th century. It's open daily from 8am to 7pm.

Adjoining the cathedral is the **Musée Municipal,** 4 place des Ormeaux (www.musee-valence.org; ✆ **04-75-79-20-80**), noted for its nearly 100 red-chalk drawings by Hubert Robert done in the 18th century. The museum is currently closed for renovation works but slated to reopen in early 2013. Call ahead for hours.

Along the RN86 towards Saint-Péray, visitors can climb the ruined 11th-century château atop the white stone **Mont Crussol** (www.chateaudecrussol. com; ✆ **04-75-81-00-51**) to enjoy splendid views, explore protected species in this mountain habitat, and find out about the castle's history at the museum.

## Essentials

**GETTING THERE**   **Trains** run from Lyon, Grenoble, and Marseille. For information, visit www.voyages-sncf.com or call ✆ **08-92-33-53-35**. If you're **driving** from Lyon, take A7 south. From Grenoble, follow E711/A48 North to outside the town of Voreppe, go southwest along E713/A49, and follow N532 into Valence. From Marseille, follow A7 north.

**VISITOR INFORMATION**   The **Office de Tourisme** is at 11 bd. Bancel (www. valencetourisme.com; ✆ **04-75-44-90-40;** fax 04-75-44-90-41).

## Where to Eat & Stay

Valence has no fewer than three Michelin-starred restaurants: the intimate **Flaveurs**, 32 Grande Rue (✆ **04-75-56-08-40**); the well-regarded **La Cachette**,

Mont Crussol.

16 rue des Cévennes (☎ **04-75-55-24-13**) and the incomparable **Maison Pic** (see below). A relaxed place for a glass of wine or Mövenpick ice-cream is **Le Comptoir du Théâtre**, 6 rue du Théâtre (☎ **04-75-84-55-92**).

 **En route to Valence**

If you're travelling to Valence by train, beware the TGV station: a 25-minute taxi ride (costing approximately 30–35 euros) from the city center. If you're arriving from Lyon, the end-to-end journey will be quicker and cheaper if you take a regional TER train instead to the station in Valence city center.

**Maison Pic** ★★★ FRENCH This is the least-known of France's great restaurants, even though it ranks among the top 10. The cooking and the wine list (featuring regional selections such as Hermitage, St-Péray, and Côtes du Rhône) are exceptional. The villa has a courtyard and a contemporary dining room with big tables and ample chairs. Chef Anne-Sophie Pic has been called a fireball in the kitchen, bringing modern (often Asian) touches to classical dishes. Her delightful *amuse-bouches* such as peanut-flavored marshmallow are a talking point. For the main course, a popular choice is the line-caught bar with Aquitaine caviar, the famous dish of her predecessor Jacques Pic. Whatever you choose, you can be sure of the finest ingredients from around the globe such as wild pepper all the way from Madagascar or *Grand Cru* vanilla from Tahiti. Dishes are served by an immaculate army of staff and eaten with her own specially commissioned cutlery.

The on-site brasserie, **Le 7** (☎ **04-75-44-53-86**), serves more affordable regional food without a lot of culinary fuss. Pic also rents 15 individually decorated guest rooms. They cost 290€ to 400€ for a double, 410€ to 890€ for a suite.

285 av. Victor-Hugo. www.pic-valence.com. ☎ **04-75-44-15-32.** Fax 04-75-40-96-03. Reservations required in restaurant. Restaurant: fixed-price menus 90€–210€. MC, V. Tues–Sat noon–1:30pm and 7:30–9:30pm. Brasserie: fixed price menu 30€. Daily 12:30–2:30pm and 8–10pm. Closed Jan.

**Subtil et Thé** 🎁 FRENCH Within minutes of our arrival at this small tea house, every table was taken by locals eagerly awaiting the 13€ lunch. This four-part lunch tends to include a hot dish accompanied by soup, salad, and a *verrine* (savory appetizer served in a glass). Fish and vegetarian options are available. Tempting puddings such as tiramisu and fruit tarts are lined along the counter. The cuisine is decidedly French, despite a Japanese-style decor that emanates from the restaurant's previous incarnation as an Asian restaurant. No one seems to mind the contradiction and a meal is aptly concluded with a Japanese green tea infused with cherry and peony flowers. Subtil et Thé is open all day for breakfast, lunch, and tea (from 3pm when Nutella and jam crepes are served).

2 rue Pelleterie, 26000 Valence. ☎ **04-75-56-75-06.** Fixed-price lunch 13€. AE, MC, V. Mon–Sat 8am–6pm.

# THE ARDÈCHE ★★★

The Ardèche occupies the eastern flank of the Massif Central region, a landscape of jagged, much-eroded granite-and-limestone highlands. Although it defines itself as Le Midi—its southern border lies less than 40km (25 miles) from Avignon and 48km (30 miles) from Nîmes—its culture and landscape are more rooted in the rugged uplands of France's central highlands.

Through its territory flow the streams and rivers that drain the snow and rain of the Massif Central. They include rivers such as the Ligne, Fontolière, Lignon, Tanargue, and, most important, Ardèche. They flow beside, around, and through rocky ravines, feudal ruins, and stone-sided villages perched in high-altitude sites originally chosen for ease of defense in medieval times.

The most famous and visited section of the Ardèche is its southern extremity, with granite-sided ravines 300m (984 ft.) deep, gouged by millions of springtime floodings of the Ardèche River. This area draws thousands of tourists, often with their children, who take driving tours along the highways flanking the ravines.

We recommend that you stop in the southern Ardèche to admire the gorges only briefly. It's better to spend the night in the less touristy northern reaches. The northern Ardèche, in the 45km (28 miles) of hills and valleys separating the hamlets of Vals-les-Bains and Lamastre, is a soft and civilized wilderness, with landscapes devoted to grape growing, shepherding, and hill trekking. For your overnight stop, we'd recommend either Vals-les-Bains or Lamastre.

If you want to kayak in the gorges, go between early April and late November, when the waters are green and sluggish and safer than they are during the winter and spring floods. In Vallon-Pont-d'Arc, you'll find at least three dozen rental agencies for everything from plastic kayaks to horses. One of the best, **Aventure Canoës,** 1 place Allende Neruda, Vallon-Pont-d'Arc 07150 (www. aventure-canoes.fr; ☎ **04-75-37-18-14**), rents canoes and kayaks. A 3-hour *mini-descente* costs around 16€ per person for use of a canoe or kayak. The ride will take you along an 8km (5-mile) route from Vallon-Pont-d'Arc to the downstream hamlet of Châmes. A full-day *grande descente* along the 32km (20-mile) downstream route from Vallon-Pont-d'Arc to Sauze costs around 26€ per person. A 2-day trip by canoe or kayak including camping costs 48€ per person. Prices include transport by minivan back to Vallon-Pont-d'Arc at the end of the ride. Lunch is not included, so bring your own. Picnic fixings are available at dozens of bakeries and delicatessens near each point of origin.

## Vals-Les-Bains

43km (27 miles) W of Montélimar; 138km (86 miles) SW of Lyon

In a depression of the valley of the Volane River, Vals-les-Bains (pop. 3,500) is surrounded by about 150 springs. Discovered in the 17th-century, these springs led to the creation of this *station thermale* (spa town) reputed for the treatment of diabetes, obesity, and nutritional problems. Scientists have never understood why each spring contains a different percentage of minerals: Most contain bicarbonate of soda, some are almost tasteless, and one—La Source Dominique—has such a high percentage of iron and arsenic that it's poisonous. Waters from Dominique are piped away from the town; others are funneled into a Station Thérmale adjacent to the town's casino.

In the park outside the Station Thérmale, a *source intermittante* erupts, Old Faithful style, to a height of around 7.5m (25 ft.) every 6 hours or so. Small crowds gather for eruptions usually at 5:30 and 11:30am, and 5:30 and 11:30pm (1 hr. earlier for all when clocks are changed in the winter).

Other than the scenery, this summertime town's most unusual site is about 23km (14 miles) south, beside the highway to Privas. The 16th-century entrance gate of a ruined feudal château stands here. The views over the confluence of two ravines and the valley are worth the detour.

Vallon Pont d'Arc.

## WHERE TO EAT

**Restaurant Chez Mireille** TRADITIONAL FRENCH   This tiny (26-seat) restaurant occupies a space below vaulted stone ceilings that for centuries sheltered a herd of goats. Known for its earthy warmth, the restaurant serves an ambitious menu of carefully crafted cuisine. Choices range from homemade foie gras and house-smoked salmon to a duck confit in *mille-feuille*. There's a refreshingly strong emphasis on seasonal vegetables.

3 rue Jean-Jaurès. ✆ **04-75-37-49-06.** Reservations recommended in summer. Main courses 12€–18€; fixed-price menus 17.50€–28€. AE, MC, V. Sept–June Thurs–Tues noon–2pm, Thurs–Sat and Mon 7–9pm; July–Aug daily noon–2pm and 7–9:30pm. Closed 1 week in both Feb and Nov.

## WHERE TO STAY

**Grand Hôtel des Bains**   This family-run enterprise is the largest and most authentic hotel in town, with slate floors in the lobby and long, tall hallways. The central wing was built in 1870 in anticipation of a visit from Empress Eugénie. Alas, Eugénie, finding she was comfortable in the nearby resort of Vichy, canceled her visit and died shortly thereafter. Though catering slightly to tour groups, the eco-friendly hotel has a cordial staff and well-maintained, conservatively furnished rooms, most with both tub and shower.

3 montée des Bains, Vals-les-Bains 07600. www.hotel-des-bains.com. ✆ **04-75-37-42-13.** Fax 04-75-37-67-02. 65 units. 79€–112€ double; 146€–162€ suite. AE, DC, MC, V. **Amenities:** Restaurant; bar; 2 outdoor pools; room service. *In room:* TV, hair dryer, free Wi-Fi (in some). Closed Nov–Mar.

**Hôtel Helvie ★**   This three-star hotel is a stylish member of Châteaux & Hôtels Collection. Rooms, many of which look up the valley and onto the beautiful pool, are calm, with pleasant period furnishings. Bathrooms are modern, and most have tub/showers. Closed on Sunday evening and Monday all day, the gastronomic restaurant offers fixed-price menus ranging from 19 to 89 euros.

5 rue Claude Expilly, Vals-les-Bains 07600. www.hotel-helvie.com. ☏ **04-75-94-65-85.** Fax 04-75-37-47-63. 45 units. 69€–135€ double; 125€–160€ suite. AE, MC, V. **Amenities:** Restaurant; bar; pool. *In room:* TV, safe, free Wi-Fi. Closed 2 weeks in Mar.

## Lamastre

42km (26 miles) N of Vals-les-Bains; 30km (19 miles) W of Valence

Many connoisseurs of Ardèche architecture view Lamastre as the most unaltered and evocative village in the district. Its most important site is its church, in Macheville, the upper part of the village. Built of pink Romanesque stone, it encompasses portions that date from the 12th century, and it's a frequent site of weddings. Most visitors use the town as a base for nature walks and hikes through the surrounding hills and valleys. A series of brown-and-white signs marks each trail.

### WHERE TO EAT & STAY

**Château d'Urbilhac ★**  Its history is rich and illustrious, and if you ask them, the congenial owners of this massive stone palace will recite dates, names, and conflicts that date from France's Wars of Religion during the 16th century. For nearly 30 years, this high-altitude château and its 30 hectares (74 acres) of forest has functioned as an upscale hotel with an equally upscale restaurant. Today Mme. Aillaud creates a Provençal-influenced cuisine with many vegetables from their garden; meals are available only to residents and their invited guests, who should make a point to sample at least one meal here. One of the high points is the pool, a 24m-long (79-ft.) watery rectangle that overlooks the valley of the River Doux. Bedrooms are high ceilinged and lavish, furnished with 19th- and early-20th-century antiques. An adjacent house is available for weekly rentals.

Rue de Vernoux, Lamastre 07270. www.chateaudurbilhac.fr. ☏ **04-75-06-42-11.** Fax 04-75-06-52-75. 6 units. 130€–195€ double. Rates include breakfast. Dinner 42€ extra per person. MC, V. From the center of Lamastre, drive 2km (1¼ miles) southeast along the D2 towards Vernoux-en-Vivarais. **Amenities:** Restaurant; bar; outdoor pool; sauna; tennis court. *In room:* Free Wi-Fi. Closed last 2 weeks of both Dec and Mar.

## THE ardèche gorges

The ebbs and flows of the Ardèche, France's fastest-flowing river, have created one of France's most unusual geological areas. The river's final 58km (36 miles), before the waters dump into the Rhône are littered with alluvial deposits, strewn in ravines whose depth can exceed 285m (935 ft.). A **panoramic road (D290)** runs along a rim of these canyons, providing views over an arid landscape of grasses, trees, hardy shrubs, and some of the most distinctive deposits of granite, limestone, and basalt in Europe.

The beautiful driving route, which you can traverse in a few hours even if you stop for sightseeing (follow signs directing you along well-marked footpaths), stretches northwest to southeast between the towns of Vallon-Pont-d'Arc and Pont St-Esprit. The meandering *corniche* roads are a challenge. Beware of other vehicles weaving frighteningly as drivers and passengers admire the scenery and snap photos.

**13**

# THE FRENCH ALPS

by Caroline Sieg

**N**o part of France has more dramatic scenery than the Alps; the western ramparts of the mountains and their foothills are truly majestic. From the Mediterranean to the Rhine, they stretch along the southeastern flank of France. The skiing here is the best in Europe. Some resorts are legendary, such as Chamonix–Mont Blanc, the capital of Alpine skiing, with its 19km (12-mile) Vallée Blanche run. Mont Blanc, at 4,810m (15,777 ft.), is the highest mountain in Western Europe.

Most of this chapter covers the area known as the Savoy (Savoie), taking in the French lake district and the largest Alpine lake, Lac Léman (Lake Geneva).

From January to March, skiers flock to Chamonix–Mont Blanc, Megève, Val d'Isère, and Courchevel 1850; from July to September, spa fans head to Evian-les-Bains. Grenoble, the capital of the French Alps, is the gateway. Grenoble lies 30 minutes by car from the Grenoble–St-Geoirs airport, 40 minutes from the Lyon-Satolas international airport, and 90 minutes from Geneva's Cointrin airport. The city is connected to the Paris-Lyon-Marseille motorway on the west and to the Chambéry-Geneva motorway on the east.

# EVIAN-LES-BAINS ★★★

576km (357 miles) SW of Paris; 42km (26 miles) NE of Geneva

On the château-dotted southern shore of Lac Léman (Lake Geneva), Evian-les-Bains is one of the leading spa resorts in France. Its lakeside promenade, lined with trees and lawns, has been fashionable since the 19th century. Evian's waters became famous in the 18th century, and the first spa buildings were built in 1839. Bottled Evian is considered useful in everything from baby formula to salt-free diets and is seen as a treatment for gout and arthritis.

In the days when Marcel Proust came to enjoy the Belle Epoque grandeur, Evian was the haunt of the very rich. Proust modeled his "Balbec baths" on Evian's. Today the spa, with its promenade and elegant casino, attracts a broader range of guests—it's not just for the rich anymore.

In addition to its **spa buildings,** Evian holds an imposing **Ville des Congrès (Convention Hall)** that has earned the resort the title of "City of Conventions." From late April to September, the **Nautical Center** (✆ **04-50-75-02-69**) on the lake is a popular attraction; it has a 115m (377-ft.) pool with a diving stage, solarium, restaurant, bar, and children's paddling pool.

The major excursion from Evian is a boat trip on Lake Geneva offered by the **Compagnie Générale de Navigation (CGN),** a Swiss outfit whose agent is in Evian. Call the port office directly at ✆ **04-50-70-73-20.** A round-trip ticket from Evian to Lausanne in Switzerland costs 23€, 12€ for children. Contact the company or head for the Office de Tourisme (see "Visitor Information," below) for other prices and hours. If you want to see it all, you can tour both

Haut-Lac and Grand-Lac. The most popular trip is the crossing from Evian to Ouchy-Lausanne, Switzerland (the port for Lausanne), on the north side.

Crescent-shaped **Lake Geneva (Lac Léman)** is the largest lake in central Europe. Covering about 362 sq. km (141 sq. miles), the lake is formed by the Rhône River and is noted for its exceptional blue color.

## Essentials

**Evian-les-Bains.**

**GETTING THERE** The best way to approach Evian-les-Bains by **train** from the French Alps is to the gateway city of Annecy. (Many trains from other parts of France and Switzerland require transfers to the railway junction of Bellegarde.) The one-way fare from Annecy is 15€. For train information and schedules, call ℂ **36-35** or 08-92-35-35-35.

Popular **ferries (CGN)** leave Geneva from quai du Mont-Blanc, at the foot of the rue des Alpes, or from Le Jardin Anglais. From May 28 to September 21, one ferry a day departs Geneva at 9am, arriving in Evian at 11:45am. The return trip leaves Evian at 5:50pm daily and reaches Geneva at 8:45pm. A first-class, one-way ticket costs 49€, a second-class ticket 36€. For ferry information and schedules, visit www.cgn.ch or call ℂ **0848/811-848** or 04-50-70-73-20.

If you're **driving** from Geneva (trip time: 50 min.), take N5 east along the southern rim of the lake. From Paris, take A6 south. Before Mâcon, you'll see signs pointing to the turnoff for Thonon-Evian. From Thonon, N5 leads to Evian. Trip time is about 5½ hours, which can vary depending on traffic.

---

### Driving the Route des Grandes Alpes

Evian can be a starting point for the 741km (459-mile) drive to Nice along the **route des Grandes Alpes ★★★**. One of Europe's great drives, it links Lake Geneva with the Riviera, crossing 35 passes along the way. Leaping from valley to valley, it's open from end to end only in summer (many passes are closed in winter).

You can make the drive in 2 days, but why hurry? The charm of this journey involves stopping at scenic highlights along the way, including Chamonix, Megève, and Val d'Isère. The most

dramatic pass is the **Galibier Pass (Col du Galibier),** at 2,645m (8,676 ft.), which marks the dividing line between the northern and southern parts of the French Alps.

En route to Nice, you'll pass to such towns as St-Veran (1,959m/6,426 ft.), the highest community in Europe; Entrevaux; once a fortress town marking the border between Upper Provence and the Alps; and Touet-sur-Var, a village filled with tall, narrow houses constructed directly against the towering rocky slope.

## The French Alps

Paris

FRANCE
THE FRENCH ALPS

Lausanne

La Cure
N1

Lake Geneva

Moirans-en-Montagne
St-Claude
Nyon
Évian-les-Bains

Thonon-les-Bains
Le Biot
Avoriaz

JURA
St-Genis-Pouilly
Oyonnax
Morzine

Geneva
Annemasse

Nantua
A40
St-Julien-en-Genevois
Bonneville
Flaine
SWITZERLAND

Bellegarde-sur-Valserine
Cruseilles
A410

Cerdon
AIN
Frangy
HAUTE-SAVOIE

Bugey
St-Rambert-en-Bugey
Seyssel
A910
Sallanches
Chamonix–Mont Blanc
A40

Virieu-le-Grand
Alby-sur-Chéran
A41
Talloires
Megève
Mont Blanc
A5

Montalieu-Vercieu
Ruffieux
Annecy
Lac d'Annecy

Belley
Lac du Bourget

Morestel
Yenne
Aix-les-Bains
Albertville

RHÔNE-ALPES
D1504
SAVOIE
Massif des Bauges
Bourg-St-Maurice
ITALY

La Tour-du-Pin
St-Genix-sur-Guiers
Chambéry
Aime
N90

Les Abrets
A43
Montmélian
A43
Chamoux-sur-Gelon
Moûtiers
Tignes
Val d'Isère

Lac d'Aiguebelette
Lac de Paladru

ISÈRE
A48
Voiron
St-Laurent-du-Pont
Goncelin
Courchevel 1850
Vanoise National Park

Rives
Massif de la Chartreuse
A41
St-Jean-de-Maurienne
Lanslebourg

Vinay
A49
St-Ismier
A48
St-Michel-de-Maurienne

Grenoble
Modane

Uriage-les-Bains
Vif
A51
D1091
Alpe-d'Huez
Le Bourg-d'Oisans

0        20 mi
0        20 km

**VISITOR INFORMATION**   The **Office de Tourisme** is on place d'Allinges (www.eviantourism.com; ☏ **04-50-75-04-26;** fax 04-50-75-61-08).

## Taking the Waters at Evian

The clear, cold waters at Evian, legendary for their health and beauty benefits, attract a clientele that possesses both the time and the money to appreciate them.

The most luxurious way to immerse yourself in the resort's hydro-rituals is to check into either of these hotels, both of which maintain private spa facilities open only to well-heeled guests: **Hôtel Royal,** boulevard de Royal, or **Hôtel Ermitage,** avenue du Léman (contact for both www.royalparcevian.com or

*☎* **04-50-26-85-00**). They offer the most expensive packages and are adept at pampering patrons' bodies, souls, and egos.

More reasonably priced are the spa facilities at **Les Thermes Evian,** place de la Libération (*☎* **04-50-75-02-30**). This public spa is adjacent to Débarcadère (the dock), just uphill from the edge of the lake. The hotel spas are more likely to emphasize beauty regimes and stress therapies; the public facility offers a broader range of services, including tanning, massage, and skin and beauty care (but no facilities for overnight guests).

Hôtel Ermitage.

You can indulge yourself with a daylong *thermale*, which provides access to exercise rooms and classes, saunas, steam baths, water from the Evian springs, and two massage sessions. Depending on the program you select, you will spend 60€ to 175€. You can also spend up to 130€ extra per day on additional massage, health, and beauty regimes. The spa is open Monday to Saturday, usually from 9am to 7pm.

## Where to Eat

**Hôtel-Restaurant Le Bourgogne ★** TRADITIONAL FRENCH  Come here for a delectable meal, impeccable service, an attractive setting, and excellent wine. Featured regional wines are Crépy and Rousette. Menu choices in the restaurant are likely to include the house version of foie gras, beef served with morels or a peppercorn sauce, and a poached version of *omble chevalier* (tiny local whitefish) with whiskey sauce.

The inn also offers 30 comfortable rooms with TVs for 75€ to 110€ double.

73 rue Nationale, Evian-les-Bains 74500. www.hotel-evian-bourgogne.com. *☎* **04-50-75-01-05.** Reservations required. Main courses 20€–28€; fixed-price menu 12€–46€. AE, DC, MC, V. Tues–Sun noon–2pm; Tues–Sat 7–10pm. Closed Jan.

## Where to Stay

The **Hôtel-Restaurant Le Bourgogne** (see above) also rents rooms.

**Hôtel de la Verniaz et ses Chalets ★★★**  This glamorous country house stands on a hillside with a view of woods, water (Lac Léman), and the Alps. The antique-filled rooms are in either the main house or one of the separate chalets; the chalets have their own gardens and more privacy but cost a small fortune. Throughout the hotel, you'll find comfortable, even plush accommodations. Main courses in the hotel restaurant run from 25€ to 30€; fixed-price menus, 25€ to 75€.

Avenue D'Abondance, à Neuvecelle Eglise, Evian-les-Bains 74500. www.verniaz.com. *☎* **800/ 735-2478** in the U.S. and Canada, or 04-50-75-04-90. Fax 04-50-70-78-92. 36 units. 110€–295€ double; 269€–370€ suite; 285€–610€ chalet. AE, DC, MC, V. Closed mid-Nov to mid-Feb. **Amenities:** Restaurant; bar; babysitting; outdoor pool; room service; 2 tennis courts. *In room:* TV, hair dryer, minibar, free Wi-Fi.

# ANNECY ★★★

538km (334 miles) SE of Paris; 56km (35 miles) SE of Geneva; 140km (87 miles) E of Lyon

**Lac d'Annecy** is the jewel of the Savoy Alps. The resort of Annecy, which is the region's capital, makes the best base for touring the Haute-Savoie. Once a Gallo-Roman town, the seat of the comtes de Genève, Annecy opens onto one of the best views of lakes and mountains in the French Alps. Since the 1980s, Annecy has become a booming urban center that has managed to preserve its natural setting. In summer, its lakefront promenade is crowded and active.

## Essentials

**GETTING THERE**    If you're **driving,** Annecy is near several highways: From Paris, take A6 southeast to Beaune and connect with A6/N6 south to Mâcon-Nord. Then follow A40 southeast to Seyssel, connecting with N508 going southeast to Annecy. Allow at least 5 hours. From Geneva, follow A40W to St. Julien and take RN201 south toward Annecy. Trip time is 30 minutes.

A car is useful but not essential in the Alps. Annecy has rail links with Paris and Lyon. Nine **trains** arrive daily from Lyon (trip time: 5 hr.), with a one-way fare costing 22€ to 40€. About six trains daily arrive from Paris's Gare de Lyon (trip time: around 5 hr., transfer at Lyon or Bellegarde); the fare is 77€ to 96€ one-way. For information, call ℂ **36-35** or 08-92-35-35-35.

There's also a nearby **airport** (ℂ **04-50-27-30-06**) in the hamlet of Meythet (Aéroport Annecy-Haute-Savoie-Mont-Blanc), with service on Air France from Paris's Orly airport.

**VISITOR INFORMATION**    The **Office de Tourisme** is at 1 rue Jean-Jaurès (www.lac-annecy.com; ℂ **04-50-45-00-33;** fax 04-50-51-87-20).

Gorges du Fier.

Lac d'Annecy.

# Seeing the Sights

Built around the river Thiou, Annecy has been called the Venice of the Alps because of the canals that cut to the old part of town, **Vieil Annecy.** You can explore the arcaded streets where Jean-Jacques Rousseau arrived in 1728.

After seeing Annecy, consider a trek to the **Gorges du Fier** ★★ (www. gorgesdufier.com; ☎ **04-50-46-23-07**), a dramatic river gorge 9.5km (6 miles) to the west. To reach it, take a train or bus from Annecy's rail station to Poisy. From the station, go about 1.5km (1 mile), following the clearly marked signs. This striking gorge is one of the most interesting sights in the French Alps. A gangway takes you to a gully 3 to 10m (9¾–33 ft.) wide, cut through the rock by torrents of water; you'll hear the roar of the river at the bottom. Emerging from this labyrinth, you'll be greeted by a huge expanse of boulders. You can visit the gorge from June 15 to September 10 daily 9:30am to 7:15pm (last trip at 6:25pm), and from March 15 to June 14 and September 11 to October 15 daily 9:30am to 6:15pm (last trip at 5:25pm). The site is closed to the public October 16 to March 14. A hike to its well-signposted depths takes less than an hour and costs 4.90€ for adults, 2.70€ for children 7 to 15; it's free for kids 6 and under.

You can also take a cruise on the ice-blue lake for which the town is famous. Tours of **Lac d'Annecy,** conducted from February to December, last an hour and cost 12€. An English-speaking guide points out the sights. Tours depart between one and six times a day, depending on the season. Inquire at the Office de Tourisme (see above), or call the **Compagnie des Bateaux du Lac d'Annecy** (www.annecy-croisieres.com; ☎ **04-50-51-08-40**).

**Château de Montrottier** CASTLE   Within walking distance of the gorges, in the hamlet of Montrottier, is the 13th- and 14th-century Château de Montrottier. A one-time feudal citadel partially protected by the rugged geology around it, the château's tower offers a panoramic view of Mont Blanc. A small museum features items collected by a local dilettante, showcasing pottery, Asian and African costumes, armor, tapestries, and lace antiques, as well as some bronze bas-reliefs from the 16th century.

Lovagny 74330. www.chateaudemontrottier.com. ☎ **04-50-46-23-02.** Admission 7€ adults, 6.20€ students, 4.50€ children 7–15, free for children 6 and under. Mar 15–May 31 Wed–Mon 2–6pm; June–Aug daily 2–7pm; Sept Wed–Mon 2–6pm; Oct daily 2–6pm.

**Le Palais de l'Ile** PALACE   This is the town's most potent and most frequently photographed visual symbol. Built before the 18th century and connected to the "mainland" of Annecy via a bridge, it resembles a miniature château, surrounded by water, despite its long-term use as a prison (and certainly a very cold one) for local malefactors.

3 passage de l'Ile. ☎ **04-50-33-87-30.** Admission 3.50€ adults, 1.20€ students and persons 12–25, free for children 11 and under. June–Sept daily 10:30am–6pm; Oct–May Wed–Mon 10am–noon and 2–5pm.

**Musée Château d'Annecy** MUSEUM   This forbidding gray-stone monument, whose 12th-century pinnacle is known as the Queen's Tower, dominates the resort. The château contains a museum of regional artifacts that include Alpine furniture, religious art, oil paintings, and modern works. One section is devoted to the geology and marine life of the region's deep, cold lakes.

Place du Château. ☎ **04-50-33-87-30.** Admission 4.80€ adults, 2.50€ ages 12–25, free for children 11 and under. June–Sept daily 10:30am–6pm; Oct–May Wed–Mon 10am–noon and 2–5pm.

The Office de Tourisme (see above) distributes free pamphlets that describe about a dozen easy, family-oriented hiking and biking excursions in the forests around Annecy. More experienced hikers may wish to pick up a free map with a detailed set of challenging walks.

Walks in both categories last 2 to 6 hours. Some begin in the center of Annecy; others require a trip by car or bus from one of several towns in the area—such as Saint-Jorioz or Sevrier, to the west, or Talloires, to the east—to the excursion's origination point. A travel agency in Annecy, **Agence Crolard,** place de la Gare (📞 **04-50-51-74-62**), sells bus tickets to the destinations around Annecy and Lac d'Annecy and Lac Léman. It also arranges excursions by minibus to sites of panoramic interest in July and August (📞 **04-50-45-00-56** for information about these excursions).

# Where to Eat

**La Maison de Marc Veyrat ★★★** MODERN FRENCH    Famous throughout France for owner Marc Veyrat-Durebex's excellent and unusual cuisine, this world-class and horrendously priced restaurant occupies a romanticized version of a Savoyard château at the edge of a lake in the village of Veyrier-du-Lac, 1.5km (1 mile) south of Annecy. Guests dine in a posh room with ceiling frescoes.

The chef has been dubbed *l'enfant terrible* of upscale Alpine cuisine. He offers a unique dining experience, marked by an almost ritualistic etiquette, but the waitstaff advises you on the order in which the meal should be eaten. For example, a "declination of local cheeses," consisting of three large ravioli, each stuffed with a different cheese—a mild cow cheese, a pungent goat cheese, and a very strong blue—is eaten in ascending order of strength. Desserts include a miniature chestnut cake served with essence of truffles.

The *auberge* rents 11 expensive and beautifully furnished rooms. Rates are 260€ to 670€ for a double; a suite costs from 700€ to 880€.

13 vieille rte. des Pensières, Veyrier-du-Lac 74290. www.marcveyrat.fr. 📞 **04-50-60-24-00.** Fax 04-50-60-23-63. Reservations required. Main courses 75€–138€; fixed-price dinner 485€. AE, DC, MC, V. Sat–Sun noon–1:30pm; Wed–Sun 7:30–9pm. Closed Nov to mid-June. From Annecy's lakefront boulevard, follow signs to Veyrier-du-Lac, Chavoires, and Talloires.

**Le Belvédère** FRENCH/SEAFOOD    This is one of the most appealing reasonably priced restaurants in town. On a belvedere above Annecy, about 1.5km (1 mile) west of the town center, it provides views that extend up to 8km (5 miles) over mountains and lakes. Menu items include a salad of Breton lobster with freshwater crayfish and strips of foie gras, a platter containing scallops and red mullet with shellfish-flavored butter sauce, and an unusual pairing of foie gras with a purée of figs and vanilla-flavored bourbon sauce. Dessert may be a selection of tropical-flavored sorbets.

The 10 simple guest rooms are much less opulent than the restaurant. Rooms go for 110€ to 145€ double.

7 chemin du Belvédère, Annecy 7400. www.belvedere-annecy.com. 📞 **04-50-45-04-90.** Reservations recommended. Main courses 16€–40€; fixed-price menus 28€ lunch and 42€–85€ dinner. AE, MC, V. Thurs–Tues 12:15–1:30pm; Mon and Thurs–Sat 7:30–9:30pm. Closed Jan. From downtown Annecy, follow signs leading uphill to Le Semnoz.

## Annecy Nightlife

In the old town, you'll find bars, cafes, pubs, and (in warmer months) street dances, fairs, and even carnivals. A calmer alternative is an evening of theater or dance at the **Théâtre d'Annecy,** 1 rue Jean-Jaurès (www.bonlieu-annecy.com; ✆ **04-50-33-44-00**); tickets cost 15€ to 50€.

If a long day has left you thirsty, try the traditional Irish pub **Le Captain Pub,** 11 rue Pont-Morens (✆ **04-50-45-79-80**), with hearty ales on tap. **Le Vieux Necy,** 3 rue Filaterie (✆ **04-50-45-01-57**), attracts a younger, more boisterous crowd.

The best piano bar in town is **Le Duo,** 104 av. de Genève (✆ **04-50-57-01-46**). It's ideal for quiet conversation. For the most elegant evening on the town, head to the **Casino de l'Impérial,** 33 av. d'Albigny (✆ **04-50-09-30-00**), part of the Belle Epoque–style Impérial Palace hotel on a peninsula jutting into Lac d'Annecy. Entrance to the gaming rooms is free; you must present a passport. The casino is open Sunday to Thursday noon to 2am, and Friday and Saturday noon to 4am.

## Where to Stay

**La Maison de Marc Veyrat** (see "Where to Eat," on p. 477) also rents rooms.

**Hôtel du Nord** 🏆   A government-rated two-star hotel in the center of Annecy, minutes from the train station and Lac d'Annecy, the du Nord is one of the town's better bargains. Guests appreciate the modernity of the soundproof rooms; 20 come with showers only, others with tub and shower. The helpful staff speaks English and can direct you to reasonably priced restaurants nearby. Breakfast is the only meal served.

24 rue Sommeiller, Annecy 74000. www.annecy-hotel-du-nord.com. ✆ **04-50-45-08-78.** Fax 04-50-51-22-04. 30 units. 69€–90€ double. MC, V. *In room:* A/C (in some), TV, dataport.

**Hôtel La Demeure de Chavoire ★★**   One of the most charming accommodations in the area is at Chavoires, about 3km (1¾ miles) east of Annecy. It's intimate and cozy, decorated with well-chosen Savoy antiques. Large doors lead to the gardens overlooking the lake. The guest rooms have names rather than numbers, and each is uniquely decorated with wood beams. Thoughtful service makes this a deserving selection, and it's more tranquil than the hotels in the center of Annecy. The staff will direct you to nearby restaurants.

71 rte. d'Annecy, Veyrier-du-Lac 74290. www.demeuredechavoire.com. ✆ **04-50-60-04-38.** Fax 04-50-60-05-36. 13 units. 126€–195€ double; 225€–275€ suite. AE, DC, MC, V. Parking 10€. From Annecy, follow signs to Chavoires and Talloires. **Amenities:** Bar; tearoom; babysitting; room service; spa. *In room:* TV, hair dryer, minibar, free Wi-Fi.

# TALLOIRES ★★

551km (342 miles) SE of Paris; 32km (20 miles) N of Albertville; 13km (8 miles) S of Annecy

The charming village of Talloires, which dates from 866, is old enough to appear on lists of territories once controlled by Lothar II, great-grandson of Charlemagne. Chalk cliffs surround a bay, and at the lower end a promontory encloses a port. An 18-hole golf course, **Golf Club du Lac d'Annecy** (www.golf-lacannecy.com; ✆ **04-50-60-12-89**), and watersports such as boating, swimming, water-skiing, and fishing make this a favorite vacation spot. Talloires also has one of France's great restaurants, Auberge du Père-Bise, and a Benedictine abbey founded in the 11th century, now the deluxe Hôtel de l'Abbaye.

## Essentials

**GETTING THERE**   From Annecy, you can reach Talloires by **driving** south along N508 for 13km (8 miles). There are about eight daily **buses** from Annecy to Talloires, which take 35 minutes. In Talloires, buses stop in front of the post office. For bus information, call Autocars Frossard in Annecy (✆ **04-50-45-73-90**).

**VISITOR INFORMATION**   The **Office de Tourisme** is on rue André-Theuriet (www.talloires.fr; ✆ **04-50-60-70-64;** fax 04-50-60-76-59).

## Where to Eat

**Auberge du Père-Bise ★★★** FRENCH   Since the 1950s, when it attracted starlets and millionaires, Auberge du Père-Bise has radiated style and charm. A chalet built in 1901, it's one of France's most acclaimed—and expensive—restaurants. In fair weather, you can dine under a vine-covered pergola and enjoy the view of mountains and the lake. The kitchen excels at dishes such as mousse of foie gras, layered potatoes with truffles and foie gras, delicate young lamb, and gratin of crayfish tails.

The inn also offers 34 air-conditioned guest rooms with minibars, TV, and free Wi-Fi. Rates are 240€ to 400€ for a double and 580€ to 680€ for a suite. Reserve at least 2 months in advance, especially in summer.

Rte. du Port, bord du Lac, Talloires 74290. www.perebise.com. ✆ **04-50-60-72-01.** Fax 04-50-60-73-05. Reservations required. Main courses 38€–104€; fixed-price menu 78€–178€. AE, DC, MC, V. Daily noon–2pm and 7–9pm. Closed mid-Nov to mid-Feb.

**La Villa des Fleurs** ✦ TRADITIONAL FRENCH   This *restaurant avec chambres* should be better known, because it's the best place in Talloires for the price. The wonderful meals served here may include *salade landaise* with foie gras, and filet of fera (a Lac d'Annecy fish) with sage sauce. The dining room overlooks the water.

Eight simply furnished rooms with minibars and Victorian-era decor are at the top of a winding staircase—there's no elevator. Doubles cost 98€ to 135€.

779 rte. du Port, Talloires 74290. www.la-villa-talloires.com. ✆ **04-50-60-71-14.** Fax 04-50-60-74-06. Reservations required. Main courses 22€–55€. AE, MC, V. Tues–Sun noon–2pm; Tues–Sat 7–9pm.

## Where to Stay

**Auberge du Père-Bise** and **La Villa des Fleurs** (see above) also rent rooms.

**Hôtel de l'Abbaye ★★**   This 16th-century Benedictine monastery has been a hotel since the French Revolution. It's one of the grand inns of the Alps. With close-up views of the lake, it doesn't equal the cuisine or the luxury of the Auberge du Père-Bise, but it's a lot more affordable. The hotel is rich with beamed ceilings, antique portraits, leather chairs, gardens, and carved balustrades. The great corridors lead to converted guest rooms, of which no two are alike. The furnishings include all the Louis periods, as well as Directoire and Empire. In summer, the restaurant expands onto a shaded lakefront terrace. Overall, this is an extremely pleasant escape from urban life.

Chemin des Moines, Talloires 74290. www.abbaye-talloires.com. ✆ **04-50-60-77-33.** Fax 04-50-60-78-81. 33 units. 150€–320€ double; 345€–620€ suite. AE, DC, MC, V. Closed Nov 17 to mid-Feb. **Amenities:** Restaurant; bar; babysitting; room service; sauna; spa. *In room:* TV, mini-bar, free Wi-Fi.

# GRENOBLE

567km (352 miles) SE of Paris; 55km (34 miles) S of Chambéry; 103km (64 miles) SE of Lyon

The ancient capital of the Dauphine, Grenoble is the commercial, intellectual, and tourist center of the Alps. It's a major stop for travelers, including those driving between the Riviera and Geneva.

A sports capital in winter (it hosted the 1968 Winter Olympic Games) and summer, it attracts many foreign students; its university has the largest summer-session program in Europe. Founded in 1339, the University of Grenoble has a student body of some 50,000. The city (pop. 405,000) is also home to four other universities with a large contingent of English and American students, giving the city a cosmopolitan air.

## Essentials

**GETTING THERE**   An important rail and bus junction, Grenoble is easily accessible from Paris and all the cities in this chapter. About 11 **trains** per day arrive from Paris Gare de Lyon (trip time: 3½ hr.); the one-way fare is 74€ to 97€. Trains arrive almost every hour from Chambéry (trip time: 30 min.; 10€ one-way). For information, call ✆ **36-35** or 08-92-35-35-35.

Until 2004, Grenoble's airport accepted Air France flights from Paris and the rest of Europe. But when Air France transferred all of its inbound flights to nearby Lyon, air traffic to the airport in Grenoble virtually dried up. Flights arrive to Grenoble from London and Bristol (England). **EasyJet** and **British Airways** fly in only September to April, but **Ryanair** also flies in summer. For more information, contact Grenoble's **Aéroport Grenoble-Isère** (✆ **04-76-65-48-48**), 41km (25 miles) northwest of the city center. A shuttle bus meets every flight and takes passengers to and from Grenoble's center; the cost is 4.10€ each way. A taxi (✆ **04-76-65-46-18**) to the town center costs 70€ to 100€.

For information on flying into Lyon, see chapter 14. **Satobus** (✆ **04-72-68-72-17** or 04-76-27-89-29) meets most flights at the Lyon airport and takes passengers to Grenoble. Travel time is an hour; the fare is 20€ each way, 15€ students, and 10€ ages 4 to 12.

If you're **driving,** take A6 from Paris to Lyon and then continue on A48 into Grenoble. Depending on conditions, the drive should take 6 to 7 hours.

**VISITOR INFORMATION**   The **Office de Tourisme** is at 14 rue de la République (www.grenoble-isere-tourisme.com; ✆ **04-76-42-41-41;** fax 04-76-00-18-98). For information about public transportation in Grenoble, call ✆ **04-76-20-66-66.**

## Seeing the Sights

Grenoble lies near the junction of the Isère and Drac rivers. Most of the city is on the south bank of the Isère, though its most impressive monument, the **Fort de la Bastille,** stands on a rocky hilltop on the north bank. A cable car will carry you from the south bank across the river to the top of the fort. The center of Grenoble's historic section is the **Palais de Justice** and **place St-André.** The more modern part of town is southeast, centered on the contemporary **Hôtel de Ville** (town hall) and the nearby **Tour Perret.**

Begin at **place Grenette,** where you can enjoy a drink or an espresso at a cafe. Don't miss the **place aux Herbes** and the **place St-André,** in the very heart of the *centre ville.* Place St-André, dating from the Middle Ages, is the most evocative square in old Grenoble, with the Palais de Justice on one side and the Eglise St-André on the other. The Palace of Justice was built in many stages. The brick church went up in the 13th century. Two great streets for strolling and browsing are rue de la Poste, in the medieval core, and rue J.-J.-Rousseau, a 5-minute walk southwest of the city.

**Grenoble's cable cars.**

Enjoy a ride on the **Téléphérique-Grenoble-Bastille** (www.bastille-grenoble.fr; ℭ **04-76-44-33-65**), cable cars that take you over the banks of the Isère River and its valley. Check the website for the cable car's operating hours, which vary by day and month. A round-trip ticket costs 6.50€ for adults, 5€ for students, and 4€ for ages 5 to 18. It's closed for a period during the month of January (btw. 4 days and 2 weeks). At the belvedere where you land, you'll have a view of the city, the mountains, and the remains of the Fort de la Bastille. Come for the view, not the fort. You can walk up in an hour or so if you're an Olympic athlete; the beginning of the route is signposted to the west of place St-André. We suggest you take the *téléphérique* to the top and then stroll down along the footpath, Montée de Chalmont, that winds to Alpine gardens and past old ruins before reaching a cobblestone walk that leads to the old town.

**Musée Dauphinois ★** MUSEUM    Housed in the 17th-century convent Ste-Marie-d'en-Haut and enhanced by the convent's cloister, gardens, and baroque chapel, this museum lies across the Isère in the Ste-Marie-d'en-Haut section of town. A collection of ethnographic and historical mementos of the Dauphine region is on exhibit, along with folk arts and crafts. This place is a quick course on life in the Alps: No other museum gives such a detailed view of the people. Furnishings, tools, artifacts, and replicas of Alpine settings are on display. Check out the special exhibition on skiing, tracing the development of the sport from its origins to the 21st century's high-tech innovations.

30 rue Maurice-Gignoux. www.musee-dauphinois.fr. ℭ **04-57-58-89-01.** Free admission. June–Sept Wed–Mon 10am–7pm; Oct–May Wed–Mon 10am–6pm. Closed New Year's Day, May 1, and Christmas.

**Musée de Grenoble ★★★** MUSEUM    Founded in 1796, this is one of the country's oldest art museums. It was the first French museum outside of Paris to focus on modern art, a fact appreciated by Picasso, who donated his *Femme Lisant* in 1921. The collection includes Flemish and Italian Renaissance works, but the Impressionist paintings generate the most interest. Note Matisse's *Intérieur aux aubergines* and Léger's *Le Remorqueur.* Ernst, Corot, Klee, Bonnard, Gauguin, Monet—they're all here. On display are a number of older paintings and sculptures, along with artifacts and relics from Greek, Egyptian, and Roman times, including a well-preserved mosaic. The artistic highlight is a sculpted door panel from the 1400s, depicting Jacob and his sons. A collection of 20th-century sculptures occupies the François Mitterrand Esplanade and the Albert Michallon Park surrounding the museum.

5 place de Lavalete. www.museedegrenoble.fr. ℂ **04-76-63-44-44.** Admission 5€ adults, 3€ seniors and students, free for children 17 and under. Free for everyone on 1st Sun of each month. Wed–Mon 10am–6:30pm.

# Where to Eat

**Auberge Napoleon ★★★** FRENCH    No other restaurant in France boasts as intense an association with Napoleon Bonaparte, but that's less important to diners than the fact that the restaurant is the finest in the Grenoble area. In 1815, Napoleon spent the night here at the beginning of a 100-day reign that ended with his defeat by Wellington at the Battle of Waterloo. You'll find enough subtle references to the history of France, from the Revolution to around 1820, to keep a student of French history busy throughout the superb meal. The restaurant seats only 23, in a plush, manicured dining room with upholstered walls and about 20 contemporary floral still lifes by renowned Grenoblois artist Martine Poller. We'd vote the bouillabaisse here as the best in the Alps. Try velvety-smooth crayfish-and-shrimp cream soup or duck foie gras terrine. The chef makes a superb filet of beef in game sauce.

7 rue de Montorge. www.auberge-napoleon.fr. ℂ **04-76-87-53-64.** Reservations recommended. Main courses 22€–36€; fixed-price menu 35€–72€. AE, DC, MC, V. Mon–Sat 7:30–10pm. Closed May 1–15, July 13–14, and Aug 10–25.

**Café de la Table Ronde** FRENCH    This is the second-oldest cafe in France, after the more famous Procope in Paris. Founded in 1739, the cafe has attracted such luminaries as Stendhal and Sarah Bernhardt. It is said to be the spot where Pierre Choderlos de Laclos conceived the plot for his 1784 novel *Les Liaisons Dangereuses.* The menu offers both regional and national cuisine—the ingredients always fresh. We gravitate to *le poisson du jour* (fresh fish of the day), although the *fondue Savoyarde* with charcuterie is a winter delight, as is the Alpine ham. The cafe conducts concerts and poetry readings.

7 place St-André. www.restaurant-tableronde-grenoble.com. ℂ **04-76-44-51-41.** Main courses 10€–23€; fixed-price menus 25€–30€. AE, DC, MC, V. Apr–Oct daily 8am–11pm; off season Mon–Sat 8am–11pm, Sun 1–3pm.

# Grenoble Nightlife

To get things started, walk to **place St-André, place aux Herbes,** or **place de Gordes.** On a good night, these squares overflow with revelers, and the energy level builds in anticipation of an explosion of dancing and partying.

Join fun-loving crowds of students at **Le Couche Tard,** 1 rue Palais (*©* **04-76-44-18-79**), and the **London Pub,** 11 rue Brochene (*©* **04-76-44-41-90**).

**Le Styx,** 6 place Claveyson (*©* **04-76-44-09-99**), is attuned to cutting-edge music from such centers as London and Los Angeles. Expect a mix of hip-hop, R&B, soul, and techno, but be prepared for anything. The dance floor is too small, but it's popular anyway. Young office workers head here after 5pm to sample some of the 70 different cocktails, but beer and pastis are the drinks of choice.

The town's most animated gay disco is **Le Georges V,** 124 cour Berriat (*©* **04-76-84-16-20**), which is open Wednesday from 9pm, Thursday to Sunday from 11:30pm (closing times vary).

## Where to Stay

**Hôtel d'Angleterre Tulip Inn Grenoble**   In the center of town, this hotel features tall windows and wrought-iron balconies, and opens onto a pleasant square with huge chestnut trees. The stylish salons boast wood-grained walls and ceilings and tropical plants. Some guest rooms look out on the Vercors Massif. Most of the small to midsize units are comfortably furnished and come with shower-only bathrooms; some have Jacuzzi tubs. Breakfast is the only meal served.

5 place Victor-Hugo, Grenoble 38000. www.hotel-angleterre-grenoble.com. *©* **04-76-87-37-21.** Fax 04-76-50-94-10. 62 units. 110€–185€ double. AE, DC, MC, V. Free parking. **Amenities:** Room service. *In room:* A/C, TV, hair dryer, minibar, free Wi-Fi.

**Park Hôtel Concorde ★★**   This is the most opulent and prestigious hotel in Grenoble, a government-rated four-star legend that welcomes most of the important politicians and entertainment-industry moguls who visit the region. On the lower four floors of a mid-1960s tower mostly devoted to private condominiums, it's a short drive south of Grenoble's commercial center and close to City Hall. Each guest room is decorated differently, with a blend of dignified (sometimes antique) furniture, state-of-the-art lighting, and modern upholstery.

10 place Paul-Mistral, Grenoble 38027. www.park-hotel-grenoble.fr. *©* **04-76-85-81-23.** Fax 04-76-46-49-88. 50 units. 240€–360€ double; from 450€ suite. AE, DC, MC, V. Parking 16€. Tram: A to Chavant. **Amenities:** Restaurant; bar; babysitting; room service. *In room:* A/C, TV, hair dryer, minibar, free Wi-Fi.

# COURCHEVEL 1850 ★★

633km (392 miles) SE of Paris; 52km (32 miles) SE of Albertville; 97km (60 miles) SE of Chambéry

Courchevel has been called a resort of "high taste, high fashion, and high profile," a chic spot where multimillion-dollar chalets sit on pristine pine-covered slopes. Skiers and geographers know it as part of Les Trois Vallées, sometimes called "the skiing supermarket of France." The resort, with 150km (93 miles) of ski runs in Courchevel and 604km (374 miles) of ski runs in the Trois Vallées around it, employs as many workers in winter as in summer, many of whom do nothing more than manicure and maintain the slopes. Courchevel 1850 has excellent resorts and hotels—with price tags to match—so it draws the super-rich. Travelers on average budgets should avoid it and head for more reasonably priced resorts, especially Chamonix (see "Chamonix–Mont Blanc," later in this chapter).

Skiing at Courchevel 1850.

Courchevel consists of four planned ski towns, each designated by its elevation in meters. They are the less fashionable Courchevel 1300 (Le Prez), Courchevel 1550, Courchevel 1650, and, crowning them all, Courchevel 1850. Courchevel maintains three ski schools with a staff of 700 instructors, a labyrinth of chairlifts, and more than 200 ski runs, which are excellent in the intermediate and advanced categories

Courchevel 1850 is the most attractive ski mecca in the French Alps. It's also the focal point of a chair-hoist network crisscrossing the Les Trois Vallées region. At the center of one of the largest ski areas in the world, Courchevel sits at the base of a soaring amphitheater whose deep snowfalls last longer than those at most other resorts because it faces north. Expect reliable snow conditions, perfectly groomed runs, vertical cliffs, and enough wide runs to appease the intermediate skier. The glacier skiing draws experts from around the world.

**SKI PASSES** A 1-day pass (lift ticket) for Courchevel costs 39€, and a 1-day pass to Les Trois Vallées goes for 47€. A 3-day pass costs 118€ for Courchevel, 165€ for Les Trois Vallées.

## Essentials

**GETTING THERE** If you're **driving** from Paris, take A6 to Lyon, then A42 to Chambéry, and then A430 to Albertville. At Albertville, take N90 to Moutiers and then follow the narrow roads 915 and 75 into Courchevel. Courchevel 1850 is the last stop on a steep Alpine road that dead-ends at the village center. Roads are open year-round, but driving can be treacherous during snowstorms. To go any higher, you'll have to take a cable car from the center of town. Most visitors drive here (you'll need snow tires and chains), but some buses link the city to railway junctions farther down the mountain.

The nearest **train** station is in Moutiers Salins. From Paris's Gare de Lyon, five trains per day leave for Moutiers. The high-speed TGV covers the distance from Paris to Chambéry in about 3 hours. In Chambéry, transfer for Moutiers. From the station in Moutiers, a 1-hour **bus** trip completes the journey to Courchevel. There are five buses per day Monday to Friday and 15 per day on Saturday and Sunday, costing from 10€ to 14€.

The nearest international **airport** is at Geneva. From there, you can catch a bus to Courchevel. There are three buses per day Monday to Friday and eight on Saturday and Sunday. The 4-hour ride costs 70€ one-way. From the airport at Lyon, there are three to five buses a day to Courchevel; the 4-hour trip costs 65€ one-way.

**VISITOR INFORMATION**  The **Office de Tourisme,** at La Croisette in the heart of town (www.courchevel.com; ✆ **04-79-08-00-29;** fax 04-79-08-15-63), provides information on skiing and each of the four Courchevel ski towns.

# Where to Eat

**Chalet des Pierres** FRENCH/SAVOYARD   This is the best of the lunch restaurants scattered across the slopes. Accented with weathered planking and warmed by open hearths, it sits in the middle of the Des Verdons ski slope, a few paces from the path of whizzing skiers. Lunch can be served on a terrace, but most visitors gravitate to the two-story interior, where blazing fireplaces, hunting trophies, and a hip international crowd contribute to the place's charm. Items include air-dried Alpine meat and sausages, the best french fries in Courchevel, pepper steak, and *fondue Savoyarde.* Two appealing dishes are the Beaufort cheese tart and a leg of lamb that's suspended, the traditional way, from a string in the chimney and left to slowly cook in the smoke from the smoldering fire.

Au Jardin Alpin. www.chaletdepierres.com. ✆ **04-79-08-18-61.** Reservations required. Main courses 35€–52€. AE, MC, V. Daily noon–4:30pm. Closed late Apr to mid-July and mid-Aug to early Dec.

**Le Bateau Ivre** ★★★ MODERN FRENCH   This restaurant, one of the greatest in the French Alps, occupies two floors of a hotel in the upper reaches of the resort. The paneled room has parquet floors and big windows that afford a view over the town and its slopes. Enjoyable dishes include *les oeufs cassées* (literally, "broken eggs"), an elegant house specialty accented with roasted crayfish tails and truffles. Also look for frogs' legs in garlic-flavored cream sauce, grilled red snapper with balsamic vinegar and fresh vegetables, polenta with escalopes of foie gras in vinaigrette, and succulent rack of lamb with olives and artichoke hearts.

In the Hôtel Pomme-de-Pin, quartier Les Chenus. ✆ **04-79-00-11-71.** Reservations required. Main courses 35€–110€; fixed-price menu 90€–190€. AE, DC, MC, V. Sat–Sun 12:30–2:15pm; daily 7:30–10pm. Closed Easter to mid-Dec.

**Le Chabichou** ★★★ MODERN FRENCH   This is the second-best restaurant in town (only Le Bateau Ivre, above, is better). Le Chabichou is on the second floor of the hotel of the same name; big windows showcase a view of the slopes. The cuisine includes a number of superlative dishes, such as soup made from "fish from the lake," *magret* of duckling with honey sauce, divine lobster salad, red mullet with vinaigrette sauce, and velvety risotto with giant prawns.

In Le Chabichou hotel, quartier Les Chenus. ✆ **04-79-08-00-55.** Reservations required. Main courses 42€–60€; fixed-price lunch 35€, dinner 70€–160€. AE, DC, MC, V. Daily 12:30–2pm and 7:15–9:30pm. Closed May–June and Sept–Nov.

If you're leaving France and headed toward western Switzerland, specifically Geneva, consider a final R & R stopover at **Jiva Hill Park Hotel ★**, route d'Harée, Crozet 01170 (www.jivahill.com; ℭ **04-50-28-48-48;** fax 04-50-28-48-49). Set on 28 hectares (69 acres) of parkland, it's within France, but only a 10-minute drive from the Geneva airport. This frontier region of the Alpine foothills, where Voltaire was exiled by the French monarchs, seems more closely tuned to Switzerland (especially Geneva) than to the rest of France. Isolated and peaceful, with only 34 rooms, the hotel bills itself as "a boutique resort."

Angular and avant garde, it has interiors by Jean-Philippe Nuel, the famous French hotel designer. Each unit is accented with exposed wood and touches of wrought iron, and manages to be minimalist, stylish, and ultracomfortable at the same time. On the premises is a highly rated deluxe spa, the Carita, decorated like the rest of the hotel, with a spectacular collection of contemporary art and state-of-the-art equipment. Other amenities include a gourmet restaurant, bar, heated indoor pool, two tennis courts, and nearby golf course. Rates, requiring a 3-night minimum stay, range from 320€ to 425€ for a double to 515€ to 615€ for a junior suite.

## Courchevel Nightlife

A chic but seasonal resort, Courchevel offers nightlife that roars into the wee hours in midwinter but melts away with the snow. The area around **La Croisette** (the departure point for most of the lifts) contains lots of restaurants, bars, and clubs that come and go.

**Les Caves de Courchevel,** Porte de Courchevel (ℭ **04-79-08-12-74**), attracts an upscale crowd. A mock Tyrolean facade of weathered wood hides a club evoking a medieval cloister, with stone arches and columns. From December to April, Les Caves is open nightly for drinks from 11pm to 5am. Also appealing is **Piggy's Pub,** rue de la Croisette (ℭ **04-79-08-00-71**), where stiff drinks and recorded music contribute to the sensation that you're far, far away from the French Alps. **Rhumerie Le Kalico,** Au Forum (www.lekalico.com; ℭ **04-79-08-20-28**), is the closest thing in town to a British pub; it's open from December to April only.

## Where to Stay

**Hôtel Bellecôte ★★**   This seven-story chalet, with direct access to the slopes, is known for its collection of unusual antiques. Bored with traditional Alpine motifs, the founder scoured the bazaars of Afghanistan and the Himalayas for objects that lend exotic warmth to the wood-sheathed walls and ceilings. Guest rooms are outfitted with lots of varnished paneling, plush accessories, and carved wooden objects from the Far or Middle East. The hotel has its own ski-rental shop.

Full meals in the elegant dining room include cassoulet of sweetbreads with flap mushrooms, frogs' legs Provençal, and chicken with morels.

Rue de Bellecôte, Courchevel 1850 73120. www.hotels-restaurants-courchevel.com. ℭ **04-79-08-10-19.** Fax 04-79-08-17-16. 54 units. 275€–380€ double; 490€–565€ suite for 2. Rates include half-board. AE, DC, MC, V. Closed mid-Apr to Dec 20. **Amenities:** Restaurant; bar; babysitting; exercise room; Jacuzzi; indoor pool; room service; sauna; free Wi-Fi in lobby. *In room:* TV, hair dryer, minibar.

**Le Chabichou ★★**   This is one of the town's finest hotels, within easy walking distance of many bars and clubs, and boasting a superb restaurant of the same name (see above). Most of the guest rooms in the gingerbread-trimmed chalet are large and well furnished; their daring modern design may not appeal to everyone, however. Beds offer grand Alpine comfort, with quality mattresses and fine linens.

Rue des Chenus, Courchevel 1850 73120. www.chabichou-courchevel.com. ✆ **04-79-08-00-55.** Fax 04-79-08-33-58. 42 units. 470€–830€ double; from 600€ suite for 2. Rates include half-board. AE, DC, MC, V. Parking 30€. Closed May–June and Sept to mid-Dec. **Amenities:** Restaurant; bar; babysitting; exercise room; room service; sauna; spa. *In room:* TV, hair dryer, minibar, free Wi-Fi.

# CHAMONIX–MONT BLANC ★★★

613km (380 miles) SE of Paris; 82km (51 miles) E of Annecy

At an altitude of 1,027m (3,369 ft.), Chamonix is the historic capital of Alpine skiing. This is the resort to choose if you're not a millionaire. Site of the first Winter Olympic Games, in 1924, Chamonix is in a valley almost at the junction of France, Italy, and Switzerland. Skiers the world over know its 20km (12-mile) **Vallée Blanche run,** one of the most rugged, and the longest, in Europe. With exceptional equipment—gondolas, cable cars, and chairlifts—Chamonix is among Europe's major sports resorts, attracting an international crowd with lots of English and Swedish skiers. Thrill seekers also flock here for mountain climbing

**Mont Blanc.**

and hang gliding. An old-fashioned mountain town, Chamonix has a breathtaking backdrop, **Mont Blanc ★★★**, Western Europe's highest mountain, at 4,734m (15,528 ft.).

The 11km (6¾-mile) **Mont Blanc Tunnel** (✆ **04-50-55-39-36**) has made Chamonix a major stop along one of Europe's busiest highways. The tunnel is the easiest way to the mountains to Italy; motorists stop here even if they aren't interested in skiing or mountain climbing. For vehicles originating in France, the round-trip toll for a car and its passengers is 33€ one-way, 41€ round-trip. The return half of the round-trip ticket must be used within 7 days of issue. For information, call ✆ **04-50-55-55-00.**

Chamonix sprawls in a narrow strip along both banks of the Arve River. Its casino, rail, and bus stations, and most restaurants and nightlife are in the town center. Cable cars reach into the mountains from the town's edge. Locals refer to Les Praz, Les Bossons, Les Moussoux, Argentière, and Les Pélerins as satellite villages within greater Chamonix, although, technically, Chamonix refers to only a section around place de l'Eglise.

## Essentials

**GETTING THERE**   Most (but not all) **trains** coming from other parts of France or Switzerland require a transfer in such nearby villages as St-Gervais (in France) or Martigny (in Switzerland). Passengers change trains in either of these villages before continuing on by train to Chamonix. Passengers from Aix-les-Bains, Annecy, Lyon, Chambéry, Paris, and Geneva pass to those villages. There are six daily connections from Paris (trip time: 7 hr.); the one-way fare is 84€ to 102€. From Lyon, there are six relatively complicated rail links per day (trip time: 4 hr.). A one-way fare costs 36€, with transfers at Bellegarde and St-Gervais. For more information and schedules for trains throughout France, call ✆ **36-35** or 08-92-35-35-35.

Year-round, two to six buses a day run from the Geneva airport; the one-way fare is 37€. Buses arrive and depart from a spot adjacent to the railway station. For information, call **Cie S.A.T.** (www.sat-montblanc.com; ✆ **04-50-53-01-15**).

If you're **driving,** you probably won't have to worry about road conditions: Because Chamonix lies on a main road between Italy and the Mont Blanc Tunnel, conditions are excellent year-round. Even after a storm, roads are quickly cleared. From Paris, follow A6 toward Lyon, and then take A40 toward Geneva. Before Geneva, turn south along A40, which runs to Chamonix.

**GETTING AROUND**   Within Chamonix, a local network of small buses (*navettes,* usually painted yellow and blue) make frequent runs from points in town to many of the *téléphériques* (cable cars) and villages up and down the valley. The price of a lift ticket usually includes the fare. Daily ski passes cost 37€ to 47€, depending on the areas you specify. For information, contact **Chambus** (www.chamonix-bus.com; ✆ **04-50-53-05-55**).

**VISITOR INFORMATION**   Chamonix's **Office de Tourisme** is on place du Triangle-de-l'Amitié (www.chamonix.com; ✆ **04-50-53-00-24;** fax 04-50-53-58-90).

# Skiing

With the highest mountain in Western Europe, this is an area for the skilled skier. Regrettably, the five main ski areas are not connected by lifts (you must return to the resort and take a different lift to ski a different area), and lines at the most popular areas are the longest in the Alpine world. Weather and snow conditions create crevasses and avalanches that may close sections for days and even threaten parts of the resort.

Skiing is not actually on Mont Blanc, but on the shoulders and slopes across the valley facing the giant. Vertical drops can be spectacular, with lift-serviced hills rising to as high as 3,150m (10,332 ft.). Glacier skiing begins at 3,740m (12,267 ft.). This is not for beginners or timid intermediate skiers, who should head for Les Houches or Le Tour. World-class skiers come here to face the challenges of the high snows of Brévent, La Flégère, and especially Les Grands Montets, a fierce north-facing wall of snow about 3 city blocks wide.

# Seeing the Area by Cable Car

The belvederes accessible from Chamonix by cable car or mountain railway are famous. For information, contact **Compagnie du Mont-Blanc,** 35 place de la Mer de Glace (℃ **04-50-53-22-75**).

In town, you can board a cable car for the **Aiguille du Midi ★★★** and on to Italy—a harrowing full-day journey. The first stage, a 9-minute run to Plan des Aiguilles at an altitude of 2,263m (7,423 ft.), isn't so alarming. But the second stage, to the Aiguille du Midi station at 3,781m (12,402 ft.), may make your heart leap, especially when the car rises 600m (1,968 ft.) between towers. At the summit, you'll be about 100m (328 ft.) from Mont Blanc's peak. You'll have a commanding view of the aiguilles of Chamonix and Vallée Blanche, the largest glacier in Europe (15km/9¼ miles long and 6km/3¾ miles wide), and of the Jura and the French, Swiss, and Italian Alps.

You leave the tram station along a chasm-spanning narrow bridge leading to the third cable car and the glacial fields beyond. Or you can end your journey at Aiguille du Midi and return to Chamonix; this excursion takes half a day. Generally, the cable cars operate year-round: in summer daily 7am to 5pm, leaving at least every 10 minutes, and in winter daily 8:30am to 3:30pm, leaving every 10 minutes. The first stage, to Plan de L'Aiguille, costs 13€ round-trip. The complete round-trip from Chamonix to Aiguille du Midi goes for 40€.

You can also cross over high mountains and pass jagged needles of rock and ice bathed in dazzling light. The final trip to **Pointe Helbronner,** Italy—at 3,407m (11,175 ft.)—does not require a passport if you want to leave the station and descend on two more cable cars to the village of Courmayeur. From there, you can go to nearby Entrèves to dine at **La Maison de Filippo** (www.lamaison. com; ℃ **01-65-86-97-97**), a "chalet of gluttony." The round-trip from Chamonix to Pointe Helbronner is 60€; the cable car operates from mid-May to mid-October only.

Another cableway takes you up to **Le Brévent ★★★**, at 2,485m (8,151 ft.). From here, you'll have a first-rate view of Mont Blanc and the Aiguilles de Chamonix. The round-trip excursion takes about 1½ hours. Cable cars operate year-round from 8am to 5pm. Summer departures are at least every 15 minutes. A round-trip costs 23€.

Another journey takes you to **Le Montenvers** ★★★ (ℂ **04-50-53-12-54**), at 1,883m (6,176 ft.). Access is not by cable car, but on a **cog railway** known as the **Train Montenvers–Mer de Glace.** It departs from the Gare Montenvers–Mer de Glace, behind Chamonix's Gare SNCF, near the center of town. At the end of the run, you'll have a view of the 6.5km-long (4-mile) *mer de glace* ("sea of ice," or glacier). Immediately east of the glacier, Aiguille du Dru is a rock climb notorious for its difficulty. The trip takes 1½ hours, including a return by rail. Departures are 8am to 6pm in summer, until 4:30pm in the off season; service usually operates year-round. The round-trip fare is 24€.

You can also visit a cave, **La Grotte de Glace,** hollowed out of the *mer de glace*; a cable car connects it with the resort of Montenvers, and the trip takes 3 minutes. The train, cable car, and visit to the cave cost 24€.

## Where to Eat

**Bartavel** ITALIAN   This place is a sporty, informal pizzeria and brasserie. Service is a bit rough, but that's part of its style. Decorated much like a tavern in Italy, this restaurant serves a range of pastas, salads, soups, and rib-sticking platters designed to go well with cold air and high altitudes. Beer and wine flow liberally. Bartavel attracts many outdoor enthusiasts who appreciate its copious portions and reasonable prices.

26 cours du Bartavel. (ℂ **04-50-53-97-19.** Main courses 14€–30€; pasta and pizzas 8.50€–12€. MC, V. Daily 11:30am–11:30pm.

**Le Chaudron** ★ ⚓ TRADITIONAL FRENCH   You'll find fancier places in town, but for good value, honest cooking, and fine mountain ingredients, Le Chaudron is near the top of our list. Chef Stephan Osterberger cooks in front of you, and you're sure to appreciate his specialties, which include house-style sweetbreads, rabbit stew with juniper berries, and fondues. The cellar is filled with well-chosen wines, including Château Mouton-Rothschild and Château Latour.

79 rue des Moulins. (ℂ **04-50-53-40-34.** Reservations recommended. Main courses 15€–35€; fixed-price menu 20€–38€. MC, V. Daily 7–10:30pm. Closed May–June and Oct–Nov.

**Restaurant Albert 1er** ★★★ MODERN FRENCH   This stalwart features a trio of cozily decorated dining rooms, with bay windows opening onto views of Mont Blanc and walls accented by rustic artifacts and antique farm implements. Begin with a broth (*fumet*) of wild mushrooms garnished with ravioli stuffed with foie gras. Main courses include bison steak with green-peppercorn sauce, superb pan-fried scallops with risotto and lobster sauce, and foie gras with truffled chicken rillettes. In summer, dine alfresco in the garden.

In the Hameau Albert 1er hotel, 38 rte. du Bouchet. (ℂ **04-50-53-05-09.** Reservations recommended. Main courses 43€–160€; fixed-price dinner 78€–160€; fixed-price lunch 56€. AE, MC, V. Fri–Mon 12:30–2pm; Thurs–Tues 7:30–9:30pm. Closed mid-May to early June and early Nov to early Dec.

## Chamonix Nightlife

Nightlife in Chamonix runs the gamut from classical to riotous. You'll find the most bars and pubs along rue des Moulins and rue Paccard. Chamonix's most popular disco is **Le Garage,** avenue de l'Aiguille du Midi (www.nightclubgarage.com; (ℂ **06-33-76-86-00**). Open nightly during the height of winter and summer high seasons, but only Thursday to Sunday during rainy months, it's outfitted with a modern format, very artfully "designed" with lots of chrome, steel, and glass. Clientele here could include just about anyone, reflecting the changing hordes of skiers and mountaineers who swarm to Chamonix at regular intervals. Entrance ranges from 5€ to 15€. The **casino,** 12 place H.-B.-de-Saussure (✆ **04-50-53-07-65**), has slot machines and roulette and blackjack tables.

## Where to Stay

**Hôtel Le Faucigny ★★★ ✦**   This place defines contemporary mountain chic. After a massive renovation, the Le Faucigny promptly set itself apart from the rest of the herd. The common areas boast comfortable sofas flanking natural wood benches and tables scattered about. Rooms are soothing muted greys and simple modern furnishings (think IKEA style, but top quality) and more natural wood accents. And then there's the state-of-the-art on site spa decked out on oodles of slate and the decadent terrace with views of the Mont Blanc. Family rooms sleep up to 4 people so you can maximize your budget, but note that in ski and other busy periods there is often a two or three-night minimum stay.

118 place de l'Eglise, Chamonix 74400. www.hotelfaucigny-chamonix.com. ✆ **04-50-53-01-17.** Fax 04-50-53-01-17. 28 units. 100€–180€ double, 130€–240€ family room. AE, MC, V. **Amenities:** Bar; spa. *In room:* TV, free Wi-Fi.

13

THE FRENCH ALPS

Chamonix–Mont Blanc

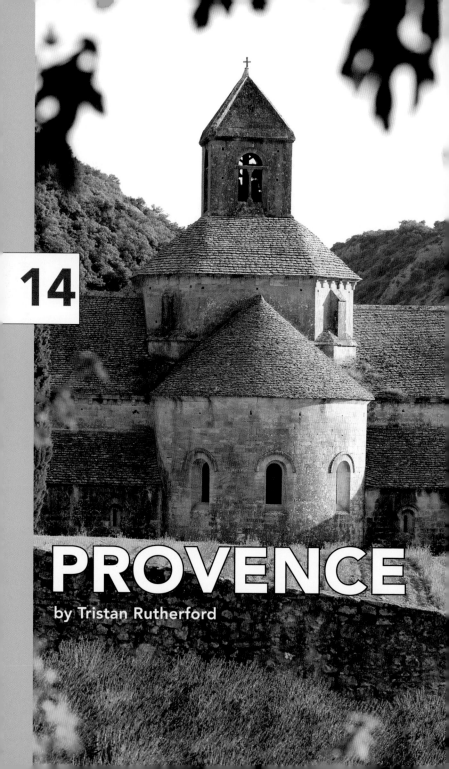

**14**

# PROVENCE
by Tristan Rutherford

T he ancient Greeks left their vines, the Romans their monuments and fortresses, but it was the 19th-century Impressionists who most shaped the romance of Provence today. Cezanne, Gauguin, Chagall, and countless others were drawn to the unique light and vibrant colors brought forth by what van Gogh called "the transparency of the air"—a phenomenon some say is due to the mighty mistral wind that sweeps through the region.

---

Provence, perhaps more than any other part of France, blends past and present in a quiet, almost melancholy way. It has its own language and customs, and some of its festivals go back to medieval times. The region is bounded on the north by the Dauphine River, on the west by the Rhône, on the east by the Alps, and on the south by the Mediterranean. In chapter 17, we focus on the part of Provence known as the Côte d'Azur, or the French Riviera.

For more detailed coverage, see *Frommer's Provence & the Riviera.*

# ORANGE ★

659km (409 miles) S of Paris; 54km (33 miles) NE of Nîmes; 117km (73 miles) NW of Marseille; 31km (19 miles) N of Avignon

Antiquity-rich Orange (pop. 30,600) was not named for citrus fruit, but as a dependency of the Dutch House of Orange-Nassau during the Middle Ages. It is home to two UNESCO world heritage sites: Europe's third-largest triumphal arch and best-preserved Roman theater. Louis XIV, who once considered moving the theater to Versailles, said, "It is the finest wall in my kingdom."

The juice that flows from around Orange today goes into wine. The town is at the heart of the Côtes du Rhône appellation, making it an excellent base for tasting (ask the tourist office for a list of wineries).

## Essentials

**GETTING THERE**    Orange sits on major rail and highway arteries. Trains arrive daily from Avignon (trip time: 20 min.; 5.80€ one-way) and Marseille (trip time: 1 hr. 30 min.; 23€ one-way). From Paris, Orange can be reached in 3¼ hours via the TGV; the fare is 98€. For rail information, visit www.voyages-sncf.com or call ⓒ **36-35**. For bus routes, contact the **Gare Routière,** parking de l'Arc de Triomphe (ⓒ **04-90-34-15-59**). If you're **driving** from Paris, take A6 south to Lyon, then A7 to Orange. The 664km (412-mile) drive takes 6 to 6½ hours.

**VISITOR INFORMATION**    The **Office de Tourisme** is at 5 cours Aristide-Briand (www.otorange.fr; ⓒ **04-90-34-70-88;** fax 04-90-34-99-62).

**SPECIAL EVENTS**    Taking advantage of the dramatic setting and acoustics of the Théâtre Antique, **Les Chorégies d'Orange** features opera and classical music performances for 2 to 3 weeks starting in early July. For information or tickets, contact the office at 18 place Sylvain, adjacent to the theater (www.choregies.asso.fr; ⓒ **04-90-34-24-24;** fax 04-90-11-04-04).

## Exploring the Town

The carefully restored **Théâtre Antique ★★★**, rue Madeleine Roch (www.theatre-antique.com; ⓒ **04-90-51-17-60**), dates from the days of Augustus. Built into the side of a hill, it once held 9,000 spectators in tiered seats. Nearly 105m (344 ft.) long and 38m (125 ft.) high, it's open daily November to February 9:30am to 4:30pm; March and October 9:30am to 5:30pm; April, May, and September 9am to 6pm; and June to August 9am to 7pm. Admission is 8.50€ for adults, 6.50€ for students and children 8-17, and free for children 7 and under. Audioguides are available free of charge.

Théâtre Antique.

Across the street, at the site of a ruined temple, the **Musée d'Art et d'Histoire d'Orange,** place du Théâtre-Antique (ⓒ **04-90-51-17-60**), displays paintings, friezes, and artifacts from local archaeological digs. A ticket to the theater also admits you to the museum. Hours are November to February 9:30am to 4:30pm; March and October 9:30am to 5:30pm; April, May, and September 9am to 6pm; and June to August 9am to 7pm.

The imposing **Arc de Triomphe ★**, avenue de l'Arc-de-Triomphe, comprises a trio of arches held up by Corinthian columns embellished with military and maritime emblems. Also built during the reign of Augustus, it was once part of the original town's fortified walls.

The hilltop park on the **Colline St-Eutrope,** accessible by stairs behind the theater, offers a panoramic view of Orange and the surrounding landscape.

## Where to Eat

**Au Petit Patio** PROVENÇAL   This agreeable little restaurant is excellent value, and gains an ever-increasing stream of fans—particularly during Les Chorégies music festival—each year. The "patio" refers to the small outdoor dining area, which is tucked away rather than on the street like at most other restaurants in town. At the height of summer, you may prefer the colorful, air-conditioned dining room, however. Artfully presented Provençal specialties include eggplant terrine with tomato-basil coulis and veal filet with morels. The service is laid-back and efficient.

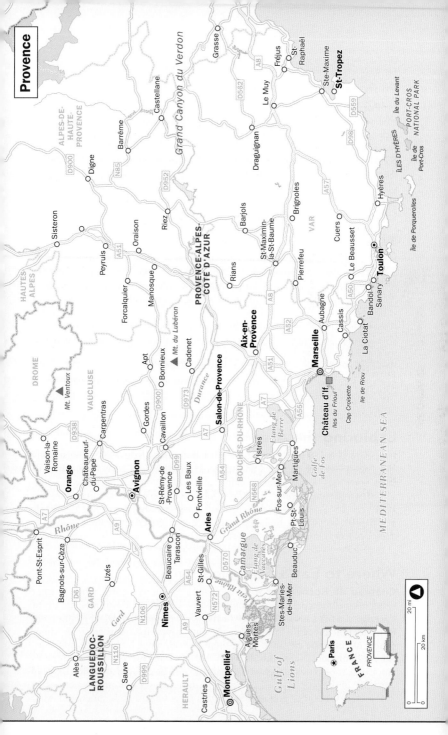

# Provence

495

58 cours Aristide Briand. ☏ **04-90-29-69-27.** Reservations recommended. Main courses 15€–18€; fixed-price lunch 18€, dinner 25€–35€. MC, V. Mon–Sat noon–1:30pm and 7–9:30pm (closed Wed evening year round, Thurs evening Nov–Mar).

**Le Parvis** PROVENÇAL   In a rather austere dining room, classic Provençal cuisine is served based on the freshest ingredients available from land or sea. Try braised sea bass with fennel and asparagus, lamb chops with goat cheese, or, for dessert, olive oil ice cream with wine-marinated figs. The staff is efficient and polite. There is a children's menu, but the hushed atmosphere could be a challenge for families.

55 cours Pourtoules. ☏ **04-90-34-82-00.** Reservations required. Main courses 17€–26€; fixed-price lunch 18€, dinner 28€–48€; children's menu 10€. AE, MC, V. Tues–Sun noon–2:30pm; Tues–Sat 7–11pm. Closed last 3 weeks in Nov.

# Where to Stay

**Hôtel Arène ★ ▮▮**   On a leafy pedestrian street in the center of the historic district, this Best Western's bull's-eye location is a big draw. The complex, freshly renovated in 2011, consists of four antique town houses joined together to offer 35 rooms. "Provençal" rooms are modestly furnished with French-style decor, while those on the Executive Floor are larger, with newer bathrooms. Try to get a room with a balcony opening onto the old square in front; they have more personality. During the summer months, the hotel's outdoor swimming pool makes a welcome respite from the heat.

Place des Langes, Orange 84100. www.hotel-arene.fr. ☏ **04-90-11-40-40.** Fax 04-90-11-40-45. 35 units. 68€–155€ double; 150-210€ junior suite. AE, DC, MC, V. Parking 9€. **Amenities:** 2 restaurants; in-room breakfast; indoor and outdoor pools. *In room:* A/C, TV, hair dryer, minibar, free Wi-Fi.

# Exploring the Area

Just 13km (8 miles) south along the A9 is **Châteauneuf-du-Pape,** a prestigious appellation known for its bold and spicy red wines. Spend a day visiting the village's numerous tasting rooms, winding your way up to the ruins of a castle that served as a summer residence for Pope John XXII. A pleasant option for lunch is Le Verger des Papes, 4 rue du Château (www.vergerdespapes.com; ☏ **04-90-83-50-40**). Steps away from the castle, it serves grilled specialties (monkfish, beef, lamb, or Camargue bull) or pasta on an outdoor terrace with stunning views of the Rhône Valley. The set-price lunch menu is 30€.

# Where to Eat & Stay Nearby

**Château de Rochegude ★★**   A true 12th-century castle—whose former residents include a pope and a dauphin—this Relais & Châteaux member sits at the edge of a hill surrounded by 10 hectares (25 acres) of parkland. Fabrics and furniture influenced by 18th- and 19th-century local traditions create an atmosphere of authentic elegance in the rooms, which range from cozy to spacious. All the bathrooms have tub/showers. The gastronomic restaurant offers an ample selection of regional wines. Meals can also be enjoyed alongside the pool or on one of the property's many tucked-away terraces. Fixed-price lunches cost 26€ to 35€, fixed-price dinners 49€ to 95€; there's also a children's menu available for 20€.

# SHOPPING FOR brocante IN PROVENCE

In France, there's a wide gap between true antiques and old knickknacks, and it's wise to know the difference. For serious purchases, stick to well-established *antiquaires*, found in almost every town and city. If you're looking for more affordable treasures and enjoy flea markets, what you really want is a *brocante*. These are usually held outside on specific days (the markets in Cannes are a good example; see chapter 15). Furniture and objects can also be found in warehouses known as *depot-ventes*.

A village that specializes in *brocante* is **Isle-sur-la-Sorgue,** situated 23km (14 miles) east of Avignon, 11km (6¾ miles) north of Cavaillon, and 42km (26 miles) south of Orange. The **Déballage Brocante** is held on Sundays; the activity starts at 9am and finishes around 6pm. From 8am to 2pm, there's also a Provençal food market. If you're driving, try for a parking space in the Parking Portalet or Parking Allée des Muriers (both free). The *brocante* is concentrated in the southern part of town, where you'll find warehouses filled with dealers and loot—although there are plenty of small stalls dotted throughout the pedestrianized town center too.

Isle-sur-la-Sorgue's Office de Tourisme is at place de la Liberté (www.oti-delasorgue.fr; ℂ **04-90-38-04-78**).

Place du Château, 26790 Rochegude. www.chateauderochegude.com. ℂ **04-75-97-21-10.** Fax 04-75-04-89-87. 25 units. 170€–430€ double; 350€–540€ suite. AE, DC, MC, V. Parking 7€. Closed Sun and Mon Nov 1–Mar 31. Take D976 13km (8 miles) north of Orange, following signs toward Gap and Rochegude. **Amenities:** Restaurant; bar; outdoor pool; room service; tennis court. *In room:* A/C, TV, hair dryer, minibar, free Wi-Fi.

# AVIGNON ★★★

691km (428 miles) S of Paris; 83km (51 miles) NW of Aix-en-Provence; 98km (61 miles) NW of Marseille

In the 14th century, Avignon was the capital of Christendom. What started as a temporary stay by Pope Clement V in 1309, when Rome was deemed too dangerous, became a 67-year golden age. The cultural and architectural legacy left by the six popes who served during this period makes Avignon one of Europe's most beautiful medieval destinations.

Today this walled city of some 95,000 residents is a major stop on the route from Paris to the Mediterranean. In recent years, it has become known as a cultural center, thanks to its annual international performing arts festivals and wealth of experimental theaters and art galleries. To make the most of the many galleries, museums, and the papal complex, plan to spend at least 2 days here.

## Essentials

**GETTING THERE**   Over the summer months, you can **fly** from Paris's Beauvais Airport to **Aéroport Avignon-Caumont** (www.avignon.aeroport.fr; ℂ **04-90-81-51-51**), 8km (5 miles) southeast of Avignon (trip time: 1 hr.). Taxis from the airport to the center cost approximately 25€. Call

**Avignon**

Ile de la Barthelasse

Pont St-Bénézet

Porte du Rocher

quai de la Ligne

Porte de la Ligne

Porte St-Joseph

Musée du Petit Palais

Rocher des Doms

r. St-Joseph

Paris

FRANCE

Avignon

Pont Daladier

Ile Piot

rue Limas

pl. du Palais

Notre-Dame des Doms

r. des Infirmières

Porte Crillon

Palais des Papes

rue Banasterie

rue Ste-Catherine

rue de la Croix

rue Carnot

rue Portail Matheron

r. Louis Pasteur

Rhône

ch. de l'Ile Piot

rue Joseph Vernet

r. Petite Fusterie

rue Racine

Hôtel de Ville

pl. de l'Horloge

place Carnot

pl. du Change

place Pignotte

rue Paul Sain

rue Thiers

Porte St-Dominique

r. Victor Hugo

r. d'Annanelle

Musée Calvet

rue Bouquerie

rue de la République

pl. de la Principale

rue de Roi René

rue Bonneterie

rue Guillaume Puy

J. Vernet

Musée Angladon

r. des Études

r. des Lices

Collection Lambert

r. Henri Fabre

rue des Lices

r. des Teinturiers

Velouterie

bd. Raspail

r. St-Charles

cours J.-Jaurès

rue St-Michel

r. de Portail Magnanen

route de Montfa

Porte Limbert

Porte St-Roch

rue du Rempart St. Louis

av. du 7e Génie

Porte Magnanen

Porte St-Charles

Porte de la République

Gare d'Avignon-Centre

Porte St-Michel

Information

0     1/4 mi
0     0.25 km

*℃* **04-90-82-20-20.** However, it's nearly as quick to hop aboard one of the frequent TGV **trains** from Gare de Lyon: the ride takes 2 hours and 40 minutes and arrives at a modern station 10 minutes from town by shuttle bus. The one-way fare is between 65€ and 90€, depending on the date and time, although it can also be as cheap as 30€ if booked well in advance. Trains arrive frequently from Marseille (trip time: 80 min.; 19.40€ one-way) and Arles (trip time: 20 min.; 7€ one-way), arriving at either the TGV or Avignon's central station. Hourly trains from Aix-en-Provence (trip time: 20 min.; 29€ one-way) shuttle exclusively between the two towns' TGV stations. For rail information, call *℃* **36-35** (www.voyages-sncf.com). The regional **bus** routes go from Avignon to Arles (trip time: 1 hr., 20 min.; 8.50€ one-way) and Aix-en Provence (trip time: 1 hr., 15 min.; 15€ one-way). The bus station at Avignon is the **Gare Routière,** 5 av. Monclar (*℃* **04-90-82-07-35**). If you're **driving** from Paris, take A6 south to Lyon, and then A7 south to Avignon.

Eco-friendly **Baladine** vehicles (Mon–Sat 10am–1pm and 2–6pm; during July and Aug Mon–Sat 10am–8pm) zip around within the city walls for 0.50€ per ride. The **Vélopop** bicycle-sharing scheme (www.velopop.fr, from 1€ per day) allows registered riders to borrow any of the city's 200 bikes for up to 30 minutes at a time for free. To explore the surrounding countryside, **Provence Bike,** 7 av. St-Ruf (www.provence-bike.com; ☎ **04-90-27-92-61**), rents different models for around 9€ to 25€ per day. A deposit of 150€ to 450€, in cash or a credit card imprint, is required. It is possible to reserve a bike online.

**VISITOR INFORMATION**  The **Office de Tourisme** is at 41 cours Jean-Jaurès (www.avignon-tourisme.com; ☎ **04-32-74-32-74;** fax 04-90-82-95-03).

**SPECIAL EVENTS**  The international **Festival d'Avignon,** held for 3 weeks in July, focuses on avant-garde theater, dance, and music. Tickets cost 13€ to 38€. Prices for rooms and meals skyrocket during this period, so make reservations well in advance. Contact the **Bureau du Festival,** Cloître Saint-Louis, 20 rue du Portail Boquier, Avignon 84000 (www.festival-avignon.com; ☎ **04-90-27-66-50**). An alternative and edgier festival, the **Avignon Off,** takes place in July, with theater performances in various improbable venues. For information, contact the **Le Village du OFF,** Ecole Thiers, 1 rue des Ecoles, Avignon 84000 (www.avignonleoff.com; ☎ **04-90-85-13-08**).

# Exploring the Town

Every French child knows the ditty *"Sur le pont d'Avignon, l'on y danse, l'on y danse"* ("On the bridge of Avignon, we dance, we dance"). The bridge in question, **Pont St-Bénézet ★★** (www.palais-des-papes.com; ☎ **04-90-27-51-16**), was constructed between 1177 and 1185. Once spanning the Rhône and connecting Avignon with Villeneuve-lèz-Avignon, it is now a ruin, with only 4 of its original 22 arches remaining (half of it fell into the river in 1669). On the third pillar is the **Chapelle St-Nicolas,** its first story in Romanesque style, the second in Gothic. The remains of the bridge are open November through February daily 9:30am to 5:45pm, first two weeks of March daily 9:30am to 6:30pm, mid-March through June and mid-September through October daily 9am to 7pm, July and first two weeks of September daily 9am to 8pm, and August daily 9am to 9pm. Admission is 4.50€ for adults, 3.50€ for seniors and students, and free for children 7 and under. Entrance to the chapel is included.

**Pont St-Bénézet.**

**Cathédrale Notre-Dame des Doms** CATHEDRAL  Near the Palais des Papes, this majestic 12th-century cathedral contains the elaborate tombs of popes Jean XXII and Benoît XII. Crowning the top is a 19th-century gilded statue of the Virgin. From the cathedral, enter the **Promenade du Rocher-des-Doms** to stroll its garden and enjoy the view across the Rhône to Villeneuve-lez-Avignon.

Place du Palais des Papes. ℂ **04-90-82-12-21.** Free admission. Daily 8am–6pm. Hours may vary according to religious ceremonies.

**La Fondation Anglandon-Dubrujeaud** ★★ ART MUSEUM  The magnificent art collection of Jacques Doucet (1853–1929), the Belle Epoque dandy and designer of Parisian haute couture, is on view here. Doucet and his wife collected the early works of artists including Picasso, Max Jacob, and van Gogh. Wandering through their former home, you'll see rare antiques; 16th-century Buddhas; Louis XVI chairs designed by Jacob; and canvases by Cézanne, Sisley, Degas, and Modigliani.

5 rue Laboureur. www.angladon.com. ℂ **04-90-82-29-03.** Admission 6€ adults, 3€ students and children 13–17, 1.50€ children 7–12, free for children 6 and under. Tues–Sun 1–6pm. Closed Tues in winter, New Year's Day and Christmas.

**Musée Calvet** ★ MUSEUM  Based on the collection of native son Esprit Calvet, who bequeathed a lifetime's worth of acquired art and artifacts to the city upon his death, this is Avignon's premier fine art museum. The 18th-century mansion displays dozens of sculptures and paintings, including works by Vernet, David, Corot, Manet, and Soutine, plus a collection of ancient silverware. Look for a copy of Bosch's *Adoration of the Magi,* plus sculptures by Camille Claudel.

65 rue Joseph-Vernet. www.musee-calvet.org. ℂ **04-90-86-33-84.** Admission 6€ adults, 3€ students, free for children 12 and under. Wed–Mon 10am–1pm and 2–6pm. Closed New Year's Day, May 1, and Christmas.

**Musée du Petit-Palais** ★ ART MUSEUM  This museum, located within Palais des Archevêques (the former Archbishops' Palace), exhibits paintings from the Italian schools of the 13th to 16th centuries, with works from Florence, Venice, Siena, and Lombardy. Salons display 15th-century paintings created in Avignon, and several galleries contain Roman and Gothic sculptures.

Place du Palais des Papes. www.petit-palais.org. ℂ **04-90-86-44-58.** Admission 6€ adults, 3€ students, free for children 12 and under. Wed–Mon 10am–1pm and 2–6pm. Closed New Year's Day, May 1,and Christmas.

**Musée Lapidaire** MUSEUM  A 17th-century Jesuit college chapel houses this impressive collection of Greek, Egyptian, Etruscan, and Gallo-Roman artifacts that grew from the original Calvet collection (see "Musée Calvet," above). Gargoyles, statues, and broken pillars, as well as everyday items such as tools and ornate vases, are on display in the nave and side chambers.

Chapelle des Jésuites, 27 rue de la République. www.musee-lapidaire.org. ℂ **04-90-85-75-38.** Admission 2€ adults, 1€ students 13–18, free for children 12 and under. Tues-Sun 10am–1pm and 2–6pm. Closed New Year's Day, May 1, and Christmas.

**Palais des Papes** ★★★  Dominating Avignon from a hilltop is one of the most famous, or notorious, palaces in the Christian world. Headquarters of a schismatic group of cardinals who came close to destroying the authority of the

**Palais des Papes**

**1er étage (First Floor)**

Tour de Trouillas
Tour des Latrines
Tour des Cuisines
Cuisine Haute
Chapelle St-Martial
Tour St-Jean
Ancien Dressoir
Grand Tinel
Tour de l'Etude
Tour des Anges
Tour de la Garde-Robe
Studium
Chambre à Coucher
Chambre du Cerf
Tour St-Laurent
Chambre de Parement
Revestiaire
Chapelle de Benoit XII
Aile du Conclave
Fenêtre de l'Indulgence
Grande Chapelle de Clément VI
Tour de la Campane
Aile des Familiers
Galerie du Conclave
Chambre des Notaires
Appartement du Trésorier
Ch. du Camérier
Aile des Grands Dignitaires
Tour de la Gâche
Tour d'Angle

**Rez-de-chaussée (Ground Floor)**

Enceinte de Clément VI et d'Urbain V
Verger d'Urbain V
Jardin de Clément VI
Rempart de Benoit XII
Tour du Jardin
Tour de Trouillas
Tour des Latrines
Tour des Cuisines
Jardin de Benoit XII
Chapelle St-Jean
Tour St-Jean
Cuisine Basse
Aile du Consistoire
Tour de l'Etude
Tour des Anges
Tour de la Garde-Robe
Boutellerie
Vestiaire
Chambre du Camérier
Salle de Jésus
Garde-Robe
Pte. de la Peyrolerie
Tour St-Laurent
Chapelle de Benoit XII
Cour du Cloître
Aile du Conclave
Grande Cour
Salle des Herses
Grande Audience
Tour de la Campane
Aile de Familiers
Porte Notre-Dame
Aile des Grands Dignitaires
Tour d'Angle
Salle des Gardes
Petite Audience
Entrée du Palais
Porte des Champeaux
Tour de la Gâche

Palais Vieux    Palais Neuf

Palais des Papes.

popes in Rome, this fortress is the city's most popular monument. Because of its massive size, you may be tempted to opt for a guided tour—but these can be monotonous. The detailed audioguide, included in the price of admission, will likely suffice.

A highlight is the Chapelle St-Jean, known for its frescoes of John the Baptist and John the Evangelist, attributed to the school of Matteo Giovanetti and painted between 1345 and 1348. The **Grand Tinel (Banquet Hall)** is about 41m (134 ft.) long and 9m (30 ft.) wide; the pope's table stood on the south side. The walls of the **Pope's Bedroom,** on the first floor of the Tour des Anges, are painted with foliage, birds, and squirrels. The **Studium (Stag Room)**—the study of Clement VI—was frescoed in 1343 with hunting scenes. The **Grande Audience (Great Receiving Hall)** contains frescoes of the prophets, also attributed to Giovanetti and painted in 1352. If you have time, consider a visit to the Musée du Petit-Palais (see above), at the northern end of the Palace's square.

Place du Palais des Papes. www.palais-des-papes.com. ℭ **04-90-27-50-00.** Admission (including audioguide) 10.50€ adults, 8.50€ seniors and students, free for children 8 and under. Mar 1–14 9am–6:30pm; March 15–June and Sept 16–Oct daily 9am–7pm; July and Sept 1–15 daily 9am–8pm; Aug 9am–9pm; Nov–Feb daily 9:30am–5:45pm; Christmas and New Year's Day 10:30am–5:45pm.

## Shopping

The chain boutique **Souleiado,** 19 rue Joseph-Vernet (ℭ 04-90-86-32-05), sells reproductions of 18th- and 19th-century Provençal fabrics by the meter or made into clothing and linens. There is also a large selection of housewares and gifts.

**Hervé Baume,** 19 rue Petite Fusterie (ℭ 04-90-86-37-66), is the place to buy a Provençal table—or something to put on it. A massive inventory includes French folk art and hand-blown hurricane lamps. **Jaffier-Parsi,** 42 rue des Fourbisseurs (ℭ 04-90-86-08-85), is known for copper saucepans from the Norman town of Villedieu-les-Poêles, which has been making them since the Middle Ages.

A covered market with 40 different merchants is **Les Halles,** place Pie, open Tuesday through Sunday from 6am to 1:30pm. The **flower market** is on place des Carmes on Saturday (8am–1pm), and the **flea market** is in the same place on Sunday (6am–1pm).

## Where to Eat

**Hôtel d'Europe** and **La Mirande** (p. 504 and p. 505) offer excellent dining.

**Christian Etienne** ★★★ PROVENÇAL   The stone house containing this restaurant was built in 1180, around the same time as the Palais des Papes next door. Etienne's fixed-price menus center on featured ingredients such as duck or lobster; the pricier tasting menu relies on his imagination for unique combinations. In summer, look for the vegetable (not vegetarian) menu entirely based on ripe tomatoes, the main course a mousse of lamb, eggplant, tomatoes, and herbs. The a la carte menu includes innovative desserts such as jellied beets with green pepper coulis and lemongrass sorbet. The dining room contains early-16th-century frescoes honoring the marriage of Anne de Bretagne to the French king in 1491.

10 rue de Mons. www.christian-etienne.fr. ⓒ **04-90-86-16-50.** Reservations required. Main courses 30€–50€; fixed-price lunch 31€, dinner 75€–150€. AE, DC, MC, V. Tues–Sat noon–1:15pm and 7:30–9:15pm.

**Hiély-Lucullus** ★★ FRENCH   Before Christian Etienne (see above), this restaurant reigned supreme in Avignon. It's still a worthy competitor, with young brothers Laurent and Gérald Azoulay having taken over to update the restaurant's slightly stuffy reputation. Fresh ingredients are imported daily and cooked to perfection, resulting in dishes such as grilled scallops with black truffles and celery purée, and roast hare. The recipe for *marmite de pecheur au saffron* (fish stew)

Place de l'Orloge in Avignon.

dates back to the restaurant's original 1938 menu. An impressive wine list includes a good selection of Côtes du Rhônes.

5 rue de la République. www.hiely-lucullus.com. ℂ **04-90-86-17-07.** Reservations required. Main courses 28€–35€; fixed-price lunch 19€–125€, dinner 29€–59€. AE, MC, V. Thurs–Tues noon–1:30pm and 7:30–9:30pm. Closed Thurs and Sat lunch.

**La Fourchette** 🖋 PROVENÇAL   An upscale bistro serving innovative cuisine at a moderate price, La Fourchette is open only on weekdays. Its homey decoration (with collected items arranged on the walls) and large bay windows create a pleasant atmosphere. Among the dishes created by the sixth-generation chef: fresh sardines flavored with citrus, haddock-filled ravioli, and beef stew à l'Avignonnaise. It's popular with locals, so reservations are a must.

17 rue Racine. ℂ **04-90-85-20-93.** Main courses 19€; fixed-price menu 33€. MC, V. Mon–Fri 12:15–1:45pm and 7:15–9:45pm. Closed 3 weeks in Aug.

**L'Isle Sonnante** ★ PROVENÇAL   There are only 20 seats in this little gem steps away from the Palais des Papes, though a few tables are added for terrace dining in summer. Chef Boris Chevtchenko transforms market-fresh produce into dishes such as ravioli with foie gras, rabbit with olives, and calamari risotto with saffron. The cuisine is in tune with the cozy, elegant dining area. Save room for the dessert cart, which offers up to 10 delicacies prepared daily. The wine list is dedicated exclusively to Côtes du Rhone.

7 rue Racine. ℂ **04-90-82-56-01.** Reservations essential. Main courses 22€; fixed-price lunch 14.50€, dinner 25€–45€. AE, DC, MC, V. Tues–Sat noon–2pm and 7–9:30pm.

## Avignon Nightlife

**Le Grand Café,** 4 rue des Escaliers-Sainte-Anne (www.legrandcafe-avignon.fr; ℂ **04-90-86-86-77**), is a restaurant-bar-cafe and one of the town's most popular watering holes. Behind the Palais des Papes, it's in an entertainment complex in a former military supply warehouse. The beautiful people frequent **Les Ambassadeurs,** 27 rue Bancasse (www.lesambassadeurs.fr; ℂ **04-90-86-31-55**), an upscale dance club. The **Red Zone DJ bar,** 27 rue Carnot (www.redzonedjbar.com; ℂ **04-90-27-02-44**), offers a different musical theme every night (salsa, electronic, and more). **83 Vernet,** 83 rue Joseph Vernet (www.83vernet.com; ℂ **04-90-85-99-04**), switches from restaurant into dance club mode around 10pm, under the high-ceilinged hallways and stone courtyards of a former 1363 Benedictine convent.

Behind the Hôtel d'Europe, the bar and disco **L'Esclave,** 12 rue du Limas (www.esclavebar.com; ℂ **04-90-85-14-91**), is a focal point of the city's gay community.

## Where to Stay

### VERY EXPENSIVE

**Hôtel d'Europe** ★★★   This deluxe property, in operation since 1799, has welcomed luminaries from Charles Dickens to Jacqueline Kennedy. The entrance is though a shady courtyard dominated by a gurgling fountain, where dining is possible in warmer months. Antiques fill the grand hall and salons, and the guest rooms are handsomely decorated with period furnishings. Two top-floor suites offer private terraces with views of the Palais des Papes. Overall, accommodations are comfortable, with spacious, well-equipped bathrooms. The hotel's Michelin-starred restaurant, La Vieille Fontaine, specializing in traditional French and Provençal cuisine, is one of the best in Avignon.

12 place Crillon, Avignon 84000. www.heurope.com. ℂ **04-90-14-76-76.** Fax 04-90-14-76-71. 44 units. 210€–540€ double; 690€–920€ suite. AE, DC, MC, V. Parking 18€. **Amenities:** Restaurant; bar; babysitting; room service. *In room:* A/C, TV, hair dryer, minibar, free Wi-Fi.

**La Mirande ★★★**   In the heart of Avignon behind the Palais des Papes, this 700-year-old townhouse is one of France's greatest small hotels. In 1987, Achim and Hannelore Stein transformed it into a haven of opulence. On display are 2 centuries of decorative art, ranging from the 1700s *Salon Chinois* to the *Salon Rouge*, with striped red walls. The rooms are breathtaking, with hand-printed wall fabrics, antiques, and huge bathtubs. Number 20 is the most sought after—its lavish premises open onto the garden. The superb restaurant, which offers a chef's table in its medieval cellar on Tuesday and Wednesday evenings (86€ per person), is Michelin-starred.

4 place de l'Amirande, Avignon 84000. www.la-mirande.fr. ℂ **04-90-14-20-20.** Fax 04-90-86-26-85. 20 units. 330€–616€ double; 690€–1,419€ suite. AE, DC, MC, V. Parking 25€. **Amenities:** Restaurant; bar; babysitting; room service. *In room:* A/C, TV, hair dryer, minibar, free Wi-Fi.

## EXPENSIVE

### Hôtel Clarion Cloître St-Louis ★
Steps from Avignon's downtown train station, this hotel is in a former Jesuit school built in the 1580s. Many of the original features remain, including the baroque facade, wraparound arcades, and soaring ceiling vaults. Though the guest rooms are modern and functional—in line with what you would expect from a chain hotel—the dining area made from a glassed-in section of the cloisters is beautifully atmospheric. During the summer, the hotel's rooftop swimming pool—although petite—is a delight.

20 rue du Portail Boquier, Avignon 84000. www.cloitre-saint-louis.com. ℂ **04-90-27-55-55**. Fax 04-90-82-24-01. 80 units. 210€–280€ double; 250€–320€ suite. AE, DC, MC, V. Parking 12€–15€. **Amenities:** Restaurant; bar; outdoor pool; room service. *In room:* A/C, TV, hair dryer, minibar, free Wi-Fi.

## MODERATE

### La Banasterie ★ 🎁
Just a short walk from the papal palace, this charismatic B&Bs is run by Françoise and Jean-Michel, who left Paris to open it and share their passion for all things chocolate. The cozy and elegant bedrooms are beautifully furnished, and some have balconies or terraces. All are named for varieties of chocolate or the Aztec god credited with bringing chocolate to humans as a divine gift. You're offered a decadently rich cup of cocoa before retiring. In the morning, a copious continental breakfast (included in the rate) is left in a basket on your door.

11 rue de la Banasterie, Avignon 84000. www.labanasterie.com. ℂ **06-87-72-96-36.** 5 units. 110€ double; 190€ suite. MC, V. **Amenities:** Breakfast room. *In room:* AC, TV, hair dryer, free Wi-Fi.

### Thames Résidences ★🍴
Just a five-minute stroll from the main train station, these pretty, Provençal-styled apartments (some with kitchenette) make an ideal base. Each one offers satellite television, a Nespresso Pixie expresso machine, DVD players, and free telephone calls abroad. North-facing apartments look out over Avignon's city walls, while apartments at the back have their

own private balconies. Note that Thames Résidences shares its entrance with the Grand Hotel, although the two are separately owned and managed.

36 bd. Saint Roch, Avignon 84000. www.thames-residences.com. © **04-32-70-17-01.** 9 units. 105€–161€ 2-person apartments, 131€–187€ 4-person apartments. MC, V. Free parking. *In room:* A/C, TV, hair dryer, free Wi-Fi.

### INEXPENSIVE

**Hôtel d'Angleterre** This three-story Art Deco structure in the heart of Avignon is the city's best budget hotel, with the advantage of being located inside the city walls and close to the train station. It was built in 1929 in gray stone, emulating the style that local builders imagined was characteristic of English houses. The rooms are on the small side but comfortably furnished; most have compact shower-only bathrooms. Breakfast is the only meal served.

29 bd. Raspail, Avignon 84000. www.hoteldangleterre.fr. © **04-90-86-34-31.** Fax 04-90-86-86-74. 38 units. 70€–100€ double. AE, MC, V. Free parking. *In room:* A/C, TV, free Wi-Fi. Closed mid–Dec to mid–Jan.

**Hôtel le Colbert** On a tiny residential street close to the tourist office, this small hotel is known for its eclectic ambience, great breakfasts, and especially helpful owners. Rooms have modern conveniences and are decorated in vibrant colors with an assortment of avant-garde posters; they have showers only. There is no elevator, but there's a coin laundry just a few steps away. The postage stamp–sized back garden is the perfect place to sit with a coffee and street map—or one of the hotel's iPads, available for rental—and plan your day.

7 rue Agricol Perdiguier, Avignon 84000. www.lecolbert-hotel.com. © **04-90-86-20-20.** Fax 04-90-85-97-00. 14 units. 80€–134€ double. MC, V. Closed Nov–Feb. Parking 18€ in nearby garage. *In room:* A/C, TV, hair dryer, free Wi-Fi.

# Stepping Back in Time in Villeneuve-Lez-Avignon ★

While the popes lived in exile, cardinals built palaces, or *livrées,* just across the Rhône in sleepy Villeneuve-lez-Avignon. Many visitors prefer to stay or dine here—it's quieter and less modernized, while still convenient to Avignon's major attractions. Take bus no. 11, which crosses the larger of the two relatively modern bridges, the **Pont Daladier.**

For information, contact the **Office de Tourisme,** place Charles David (www.tourisme-villeneuvelezavignon.fr; © **04-90-25-61-33;** fax 04-90-25-91-55).

**Église Notre-Dame** CHURCH This church was founded by Cardinal Arnaud de Via in 1333. Other than its architecture, the church's most popular attraction is an antique copy (by an unknown sculptor) of Enguerrand Charonton's *Pietà,* the original of which is in the Louvre.

Place du Chapître. © **04-90-25-61-33.** Free admission. May–Sept daily 10:30am–12:30pm and 2:30–6:30pm; Oct–Apr daily 2–5pm. Closed Jan, Nov 1, Nov 11, Christmas and Dec 26.

**Fort St-André ★** RUINS Crowning the town is Fort St-André, founded in 1360 by Jean-le-Bon to serve as a symbol of might to the pontifical powers across the river. Within its walls, you can visit a formal garden with a rose-trellis colonnade, fountains, and flowers. Also inside is the Abbaye St-André, opened in the 18th century but now privately owned.

Mont Andaon. www.fort-saint-andre.monuments-nationaux.fr. ⓒ **04-90-25-45-35.** Admission 5.50€ adults, 4€ students and ages 19–25, free for European nationals 18–25 and children 18 and under. May 16–Sept 15 10am–1pm and 2–6pm; Apr–May 15 and Sept 16–30 10am–1pm and 2–5:30pm; Oct 1–Mar 31 10am–1pm and 2–5pm.

### La Chartreuse du Val-de-Bénédiction MONASTERY France's largest Carthusian monastery, built in 1352, comprises a church, three cloisters, cells that housed the medieval monks, and a 12th-century graveyard where Pope Innocent VI is entombed. Part of the complex houses the *Centre National d'Ecritures du Spectacle,* a workshop for artists and playwrights who live rent-free for up to a year to pursue their crafts. Art exhibits, concerts, and theater take place throughout the year.

Rue de la République. www.chartreuse.org. ⓒ **04-90-15-24-24.** Admission 7.70€ adults, 5.10€ students and under 25, free for children 18 and under. July-Sept daily 9am-6:30pm; Apr–June daily 9:30am–6:30pm; Oct–Mar Mon–Fri 9:30am–5pm, Sat–Sun 10am–5pm.

### Musée Pierre de Luxembourg (Musée de Villeneuve-lez-Avignon) ★ ART MUSEUM Villeneuve's most important museum occupies a 14th-century home constructed for a local cardinal. Since its designation as a museum in 1996, it's been the richest repository of medieval painting and sculpture in the region. The remarkable *Coronation of the Virgin,* by Enguerrand Charonton, painted in 1453, depicts the denizens of hell supplicating the eternally calm mother of Christ. Equally important is a rare 14th-century ivory statue of the Virgin by an unknown sculptor; it's one of the finest of its type anywhere.

2 rue de la République. ⓒ **04-90-27-49-66.** Admission 3.20€ adults, free for children 18 and under. May–Sept 10:30am-12:30pm and 2:30–6:30pm; Feb–Apr and Oct–Dec 2–5pm. Closed Jan, Nov 1, Nov 11, Christmas and Dec 26.

### Tour Philippe le Bel RUINS Philippe the Fair built this tower in the 13th century, when Villeneuve became a French possession; it was a gateway to the kingdom. If you have the stamina, climb to the top for a view of Avignon and the Rhône Valley.

Rue Montée-de-la-Tour. ⓒ **04-32-70-08-57.** Admission 2.20€ adults, free for children 18 and under. May–Sept Tues–Sun 10:30am–12:30pm and 2:30–6:30pm; Feb–Apr and Oct Tues–Sun 2–5pm. Closed Nov–Jan, May 1, and Nov 1 and 11.

# GORDES ★★★

720km (446 miles) S of Paris; 38km (24 miles) E of Avignon; 77km (48 miles) N of Aix-en-Provence; 92km (57 miles) N of Marseille

Everything about Gordes is rocky—from the low walls flanking the hilltop access road, to the tiered houses clinging to the cliffside, to its *rues caladés* (streets paved with local river stones). From afar, it is a pastiche of beiges, grays, and terra cotta that blushes golden at sunrise and sunset.

The village unwinds downhill from the Château de Gordes, the Renaissance rehabilitation of a 12th-century fortress. The windows in its four machicolated towers still bear grooves from the bows and arrows used to protect Gordes during Gallo-Roman times, when it was a border town.

Today Gordes is more likely to be invaded by easels. Its austere beauty has drawn many artists, including Marc Chagall and Hungarian Victor Vasarely, who spent summers here gathering inspiration for his geometric abstract art.

## Essentials

**GETTING THERE** Gordes is not easily reached via public transportation. The closest train station is Cavaillon, where trains arrive from the Avignon central station (trip time: 35 min.; 6.60€ one-way). Buses leave from the Cavaillon SNCF station and arrive at place du Château in Gordes (trip time: 35 min.; 2€ one-way). For rail information, visit www.voyages-sncf.com or call ✆ **36-35.** For information on bus routes, visit the Vaucluse regional website at www.vaucluse.fr or contact the Gordes tourist office (✆ **04-90-72-02-75**). Another option is to take a 1-day coach tour from either Avignon or Aix-en-Provence.

Gordes.

**Autocars Lieutaud** (www.excursionprovence.com; ✆ 04-90-86-36-75) offers this service in Avignon, as does the tourist office in Aix-en-Provence (www.aixenprovencetourism.com; ✆ 04-42-16-11-61).

By car, Gordes is a 38km (24-mile) drive from Avignon via A7. Take exit 25 for Cavaillon; at the village of Coustellet, follow the signs to Gordes.

**VISITOR INFORMATION** The **Office de Tourisme** is at the place du Château (www.gordes-village.com; ✆ **04-90-72-02-75;** fax 04-90-72-02-26).

## Exploring the Town

**Caves du Palais St. Firmin ★** RUINS  Steep Gordes lacks an abundance of surface area, so early settlers burrowed into the rock itself. Below the Palace of St. Firmin is an underground network of crude rooms and stairways, on seven levels, that over the centuries housed the village's production of olive oil and grain, among other industries. Though the tunnels are adequately lit, children are provided with a small headlamp to give them the feeling of being true explorers.

Rue du Belvédère. www.caves-saint-firmin.com. ✆ **04-90-72-02-75.** Admission 5€ adults, 4€ students. Free audioguide. May–Sept daily 10am–6pm. Oct–Apr by reservation only.

**Château de Gordes** HISTORIC HOME/ART MUSEUM  Housed inside the Château (and the only way to see its interior) is a museum dedicated to the work of contemporary Flemish painter Pol Mara (1920–98), a former resident of

Gordes. The visit begins with a Renaissance-era spiral staircase to the third floor. Over 200 of the artist's works are displayed chronologically as you make your way back downstairs to the *Salle d'Honneur*, dominated by a monumental 16th-century chimney—the largest of its kind in Europe.

Place du Château. ℭ **04-90-72-02-75.** Admission 4€ adults, 3€ children 10–17, free for children 9 and under. Daily 10am–noon and 2–6pm. Closed New Year's Day and Christmas.

**Village des Bories** ★ RUINS    Bories are beehive-shaped dwellings made of intricately stacked stone—and not one ounce of mortar. They date back as far as the Bronze Age and as recently as the 18th century in Provence. An architectural curiosity, their thick walls and cantilevered roofs beg the question: How did they do that? The Village des Bories is the largest extant group of these structures in the region, comprising 30 huts grouped according to function (houses, stables, bakeries, tanneries, and more). Traditional objects and tools are on display, along with an exhibit on the history of dry stone architecture in France and around the world.

1.5km (1 mile) west of Gordes on the D2. ℭ **04-90-72-03-48.** Admission 6€ adults, 4€ children 12–17, free for children 11 and under. Daily 9am to sundown.

## Where to Eat

**L'Artegal** PROVENÇAL    Due to its location on the place du Château, one might mistake this restaurant for a tourist trap. Not so. It serves well-conceived dishes such as sea bass with fresh herbs, duck with honey, and spinach-stuffed lamb, as well as lunchtime salads that are copious and meal-worthy. Dining inside or outside with a view of the castle (busier during the day but tranquil at night). Prices may be higher than what one is used to for this type of restaurant—perhaps understandable when you consider the difficulty of delivering fresh and

Village des Bories.

varied ingredients to such a hard-to-reach location. In season, try the strawberry gazpacho for dessert.

Place du Château, Gordes 84220. ℭ **04-90-72-02-54.** Main courses 16€–22€; fixed-price menu 24€–35€. MC, V. Noon–1:45pm and 7:15–8:45pm. Closed mid-Jan to mid-Mar.

**Un Jour, Charlotte ★** MEDITERRANEAN   Serge and Muriel Alvarez run this eclectic restaurant and photo space. Uncomplicated but refined Mediterranean cuisine here highlights organic ingredients and herbs from their garden. Plates include white truffle ravioli with Parmesan shavings, tapenade-marinated rabbit, and supreme of guinea hen with morel mushrooms and local potatoes. Serge is the photographer—his work decorates the walls, as well as a nearby studio. Because of its laid-back, artsy atmosphere (Muriel is a florist and manages a side wedding flower business, which means beautiful buds are everywhere), the restaurant is popular with in-the-know locals. In good weather, there is outdoor dining under a hundred-year-old plane tree. Reservations are advised.

Hameau Les Imberts, Gordes 84220. www.unjourcharlotte.fr. ℭ **04-90-72-61-98.** Reservations recommended. Main courses 15€–22€; fixed-price menu 27€. MC, V. Daily (dinner only) 7:30–10pm. Closed Jan–Mar.

# Where to Stay

## VERY EXPENSIVE

**Hôtel Les Bories & Spa ★**   During a stay here, you're sure to rub elbows with the pampered and privileged. The hotel is known for its extensive spa; it's not unusual to see blissed-out, bathrobed guests padding back to their rooms after a treatment. There is a large heated indoor whirlpool, as well as an outdoor pool overlooking the Cavaillon plain. The best way to describe the guest rooms is very white—but this is set off nicely by the lavender, orange flowers, and silvery plants of the aromatic garden seen from the windows and private terraces. Enjoy Michelin-starred cuisine in the restaurant or on the terrace at twilight in summer.

Route de l'Abbaye de Sénanque, Gordes 84220. www.hotellesbories.com. ℭ **04-90-72-00-51.** Fax 04-90-72-01-22. 33 units. 300€–450€ double; 550€ or 820€ suite. AE, MC, V. Free parking. **Amenities:** Restaurant; bar; room service; rooms for those w/limited mobility; indoor/outdoor swimming pools; tennis courts; sauna; spa services; steam room. *In room:* A/C, TV, hair dryer, minibar, free Wi-Fi.

## MODERATE

**La Ferme de la Huppe ★ 📑**   Ten minutes down the road from Gordes, within 30 minutes of other famous Luberon villages such as Bonnieux and Roussillon, this former silkworm farm was remodeled into a casually elegant hotel. Its authenticity has been preserved thanks to the use of materials salvaged from old properties in the area. Arranged on different levels, the guest rooms are named after different functions—The Stable, Hay Loft, Wine Cellar, and so on. Though slightly dark, they are very tastefully decorated, with wooden furniture, real quilts, and modern bathrooms. The carefully tended garden and pool are romantically lit at night. Make sure to reserve at the restaurant, which is also open to the public. Expertly prepared dishes such as partridge with chestnut cream, and lamb with thyme and artichoke ravioli mean it's almost always full.

# THE LAST HOME OF albert camus

Author of *The Stranger,* among many other works, Algerian-born Albert Camus (1913–1960) moved to France at the age of 25. A member of the French Resistance, he was first known as a political journalist before being recognized as a philosopher. He was awarded the Nobel Prize for Literature in 1958 "for his important literary production, which with clear-sighted earnestness illuminates the problems of the human conscience in our times."

That same year, drawn by its "solemn and austere landscape despite its bewildering beauty," Camus and his wife moved to Lourmarin. Just 2 years later, Camus was killed in a car accident south of Paris. According to his wishes, he was buried in the village cemetery.

In 1999, former French president Nicolas Sarkozy—with whom Camus would have had little in common philosophically or politically—proposed moving the writer's ashes to the Panthéon in Paris, to rest beside literary giants such as Alexander Dumas, Victor Hugo, and Emile Zola. His descendants politely declined.

R.D. 156, Les Pourquiers, Gordes 84220. www.lafermedelahuppe.com. ☏ **04-90-72-12-25.** Fax 04-90-72-25-39. 10 units. 110€–185€ double. Breakfast (mandatory) 16€ per person. Half-board available. Free parking. DC, MC, V. **Amenities:** Restaurant, outdoor pool. *In room:* A/C, TV, hair dryer, minibar, free Wi-Fi. Closed Nov–mid Mar.

## INEXPENSIVE

**L'Auberge de Carcarille**   Three kilometers (1¾ miles) from the center of Gordes, the heart of this modest hotel is its well-respected restaurant, which draws locals as well as guests. The dry stone main building is hidden at the end of long driveway with manicured trees, housing spacious, attractively decorated rooms that all have private terraces or balconies and access to a large swimming pool. The rates for this property are extremely reasonable, though the management is hoping you'll choose the more expensive half-board option (two meals per day for two people). If you're staying a few days, consider paying full price for a meal in the restaurant, in order to have the flexibility of sampling others in the region. As with La Ferme de La Huppe (see above), the hotel's position is a great base for exploring the Luberon (picnic baskets can be provided on request).

Route d'Apt (D2), Gordes 84220. www.auberge-carcarille.com. ☏ **04-90-72-02-63.** Fax 04-90-72-05-74. 20 units. 75€–102€ double; 115€ suite. Half-board available. MC, V. Free parking. **Amenities:** Restaurant; outdoor pool. *In room:* A/C, TV, hair dryer, free Wi-Fi.

## Exploring the Area

Gordes is part of the Parc Naturel Régional du Luberon, made up of three mountain ranges and their common valley. Author Peter Mayle brought attention to the area with his "A Year in Provence" series extolling the virtues of picturesque villages such as Bonnieux, Lourmarin, and Menerbes, where Mayle restored his first French home. Most of these are within 12km (7½ miles) of each other, making the Luberon well worth an afternoon's drive.

**Abbaye Notre-Dame de Sénanque** ★    One of the prettiest sights in the Luberon—indeed, in all of Provence—is the Abbaye Notre-Dame de Sénanque—particularly when the lavender is in bloom. Five kilometers (3 miles) down the road from Gordes, it was built by Cistercian monks in 1148. Just a handful of monks continue live on the premises today. The structure is noted for its simple architecture and unadorned stone—though standing in a sea of purple, from June to late July, it's dramatic indeed. The abbey is open daily to visitors. A gift shop sells books and items made by the resident monks, as well as lavender honey.

Abbaye Notre-Dame de Sénanque, Gordes 84220. www.senanque.fr. ℂ **04-90-72-17-92.** Admission 7€ adults, 5€ students and 19-25s, 3€ children 6–18, 20€ families; free for children 5 and under. Days and hours vary; call or see website.

# ST-RÉMY-DE-PROVENCE ★

710km (440 miles) S of Paris; 24km (15 miles) NE of Arles; 19km (12 miles) S of Avignon; 10km (6¼ miles) N of Les Baux

Though Nostradamus, the physician and astrologer, was born here in 1503, most associate St-Rémy with Vincent van Gogh, who committed himself to a local asylum in 1889 after cutting off his left ear. *Starry Night* was painted during this period, as were many versions of *Olive Trees* and *Cypresses.*

Come to sleepy St-Rémy not only for its history and sights, but also for an authentic experience of daily Provençal life. The town springs into action on Wednesday mornings, when stalls bursting with the region's bounty, from wild-boar sausages to olives, elegant antiques to local crafts, and bolts of French country fabric, huddle between the sidewalk cafes beneath the plane trees.

## Essentials

**GETTING THERE**    A regional bus, the Cartreize, runs four to nine times daily between Avignon's Gare Routière and St-Rémy's place de la République (trip time: 45 min.; 3.10€ one-way). For bus information, see www.lepilote.com or call ℂ **08-10-00-13-26.** The St-Rémy Tourist Office also provides links to up-to-date bus schedules on their website (see below). If you're driving, head south from Avignon along D571.

**VISITOR INFORMATION**    The **Office de Tourisme** is on place Jean-Jaurès (www.saintremy-de-provence.com; ℂ **04-90-92-05-22;** fax 04-90-92-38-52).

## Seeing the Sights

**Monastère Saint Paul de Mausole** ★ MONASTERY    This former monastery and clinic is where Vincent Van Gogh was confined from 1889 to 1890. It's now a psychiatric hospital for women. You can't see the artist's actual cell, but there is a reconstruction of his room. The Romanesque chapel and cloisters are worth a visit in their own right, as Van Gogh depicted their circular arches and beautifully carved capitals in some of his paintings. The path between the town center and the site (east of the D5 and opposite Glanum, see below) is dotted with reproductions of Van Gogh's paintings from the period he resided here.

Route des Baux-de-Provence. www.cloitresaintpaul-valetudo.com. ℂ **04-90-92-77-00.** Admission 4€ adults, 3€ students, free for children 12 and under. Apr–Oct daily 9:30am–7pm; Nov–Mar daily 10:15am–4:45pm. Closed Nov 1, Nov 11, and Christmas.

Ruines de Glanum.

**Le Site Archéologique de Glanum** ★★ RUINS A Gallo-Roman settlement thrived here during the final days of the Roman Empire. Its monuments include a triumphal arch from the time of Julius Caesar; garlanded with sculptured fruits and flowers, it dates from 20 B.C. and is the oldest in Provence. Another interesting feature is the baths, which, back in the day, had separate chambers for hot, warm, and cold. You can see entire streets and foundations of private residences from the 1st-century town, plus some remains from a Gallo-Greek town of the 2nd century B.C.

Route des Baux-de-Provence. http://glanum.monuments-nationaux.fr. ✆ **04-90-92-23-79.** Admission 7.50€ adults, 4.50€ students, free for European nationals 18-25 and children 18 and under. Apr–Aug daily 9:30am–6:30pm; Sept Tues–Sun 9:30am–6:30pm; Oct–Mar Tues–Sun 10am–5pm. Closed Jan 1, May 1, Nov 1, Nov 11, and Christmas. From St-Rémy, take D5 1.5km (1 mile) south, following signs to Les Antiques.

## Shopping

St-Rémy is a decorator's paradise, with many antiques shops and fabric stores on the narrow streets of the old town and surrounding boulevards. **Broc de Saint Ouen,** route d'Avignon (✆ **04-90-92-28-90**), is a 6,000-sq.-m (64,583-sq.-ft.) space, open every day from 9am to 8pm, selling everything from architectural salvage to furniture, to *tchotchkes*. The town's famous market is held Wednesday mornings.

## Where to Eat

The **Hostellerie du Vallon de Valrugues** (see p. 514) offers excellent dining.

**L'Estagnol** 🎁 MEDITERRANEAN Run by Corinne Meynadier and her husband chef Fabrice, L'Estagnol ("little pond" in the local dialect) sits within the light, bright environs of a former orangery glasshouse. Mediterranean cuisine

513

focuses on top-notch local ingredients like Bouzigues oysters, and regional recipes, such as *cassoulet Languedocien*. The wine list is particularly strong on Corbières AOC offerings from the Languedoc-Roussillon region, where the Meynadiers owned a restaurant for 18 years. During summertime, dining takes place on the pretty garden terrace.

16 bd. Victor Hugo. www.restaurant-lestagnol.com. ℰ **04-90-92-05-95.** Reservations recommended. Main courses 17€–35€; fixed-price lunch 13€, dinner 34€; children's menu 11€. MC, V. May–Sept Tues–Sun noon–2:30pm and 7:15–10pm; Oct–Apr Tues–Sun noon–2:30pm, Fri–Sat 7:15–10pm.

**La Maison Jaune** ★★ FRENCH/PROVENÇAL One of the most enduringly popular restaurants in St-Rémy is in the former residence of an 18th-century merchant. Today, in a pair of dining rooms occupying two floors, you'll appreciate cuisine prepared and served with flair. In warm weather, additional seats extend onto the terrace overlooking the Hôtel de Sade. Menu items include pigeon roasted in wine and honey, braised artichoke hearts with white wine and tomatoes, mussel soup with fennel, and roast rack of lamb served with tapenade of black olives and anchovies.

15 rue Carnot. www.lamaisonjaune.info. ℰ **04-90-92-56-14.** Reservations required. Fixed-price menu 38€–68€. MC, V. Wed–Sun noon–1:30pm; Tues–Sat 7:30–9pm. Closed Nov–Feb.

## St-Remy Nightlife

**Le Cocktail Bar,** in the Hôtel les Ateliers de l'Image, 36 bd. Victor Hugo (ℰ **04-90-92-51-50**), is an unusual destination in this laid-back town. In a former Art Deco movie theater, it is open June to September daily 5pm to 2am.

## Where to Stay

### EXPENSIVE

**Château des Alpilles** ★★★ For luxury and refinement, this former castle is the only hotel in the area that can equal the Vallon de Valrugues (see below). It sits in the center of a magnolia-studded park 2km (1¼ miles) from the center of St-Rémy. Built by the Pichot family in 1827, it counted Chateaubriand among its guests. Françoise Bon converted the mansion in 1980, with the aim of creating a "house for paying friends." The rooms combine antiques, plush upholstery, whimsical accessories such as porcelain panthers flanking one of the mantels, and travertine-trimmed bathtubs. Units in the 19th-century annex—as well as within the little ex-chapel and two-story former washhouse—are equally comfortable.

Route de Rougadou, St-Rémy-de-Provence 13210. www.chateaudesalpilles.com. ℰ **04-90-92-03-33.** Fax 04-90-92-45-17. 22 units. 195€–350€ double; 310€–440€ suite. AE, DC, MC, V. Free parking. Closed early Jan to mid-Mar. **Amenities:** Restaurant; bar; outdoor pool; room service; sauna; 2 tennis courts. *In room:* A/C, TV, hair dryer, minibar, free Wi-Fi.

**Hostellerie du Vallon de Valrugues** ★★★ Surrounded by a park, this hotel has the best accommodations and restaurant in town. Constructed in the 1970s, it resembles an ancient Roman villa. Rooms are tastefully decorated in neoclassical style; many were recently renovated. All have huge, comfortable beds and marble bathrooms. Activities include an outdoor pool, bicycles, and the brand-new spa, La Maison d'Ennea. The restaurant's terrace is as appealing as its cuisine; its Italian-influenced dishes have earned a Michelin star (www. restaurant-marcdepassorio.fr). Fixed-price menus are 59€ to 105€. A less formal bistro is open in the afternoons.

9 Chemin Canto-Cigalo, St-Rémy-de-Provence 13210. www.vallondevalrugues.com. ✆ **04-90-92-04-40.** Fax 04-90-92-44-01. 48 units. 210€–340€ double; 270€–1,200€ suite. AE, MC, V. Free parking. Closed 3 weeks in Jan. **Amenities:** 2 restaurants; bar; babysitting; bikes; exercise room; outdoor pool; ping-pong table; pool table; room service; sauna; spa. *In room:* A/C, TV, hair dryer, minibar, free Wi-Fi.

## MODERATE

**La Maison du Village** ★★ 🏠   This meticulously restored 18th-century town house in the center of St-Rémy appears regularly in French decorating magazines. Welcoming and quietly chic, it comprises five suites with wrought-iron beds and tasteful fabrics, each named after its dominating color: beige, raspberry, violet, and so on. The luxurious bathrooms feature old-fashioned, free-standing bathtubs large enough for a romantic duo. On request, the innkeepers serve organic meals in the family-style dining room or the "secret garden" out back. You can even do your gift shopping on the premises—a corner of the lobby sells France's famous Diptyque brand of perfumes and scented candles (try fig or anise).

10 rue du 8 Mai 1945, St-Rémy-de-Provence 13210. www.lamaisonduvillage.com. ✆ **04-32-60-68-20.** Fax 04-32-60-68-21. 5 units. 170€–210€ suite. MC, V. **Amenities:** Lounge. *In room:* A/C, TV, free Wi-Fi.

## INEXPENSIVE

**L'Amandière**   This simple hotel is one of the best deals in the region. It's probably best suited to drivers, though the center of St.-Rémy is only 10 minutes away on foot. Basic but pleasant rooms come with a bath or shower, balcony or terrace, depending on which you choose. Guests have access to a swimming pool, and there is an exercise trail nearby. There is no restaurant, but breakfast is served in various indoor and outdoor seating areas. A good option if you're just passing through or prefer to spend your travel budget on gourmet restaurants—the hotel's rates are at least a third of what you'd pay at some of the other local favorites.

Av. Théodore Aubanel, Plaisance du Touch, St-Rémy-de-Provence 13210. www.hotel-amandiere. com. ✆ **04-90-92-41-00.** Fax 04-90-92-48-38. 25 units. 65€–75€ double; 85€ triple. AE, MC, V. Free parking. **Amenities:** Outdoor pool; free Wi-Fi in public areas. *In room:* TV, hair dryer.

# ARLES ★★

744km (461 miles) S of Paris; 36km (22 miles) SW of Avignon; 92km (57 miles) NW of Marseille

On the banks of the Rhône River, Arles (pop. 52,000) attracts art lovers, archaeologists, and historians. To the delight of visitors, many of the vistas van Gogh painted so luminously remain. Here the artist was even inspired to paint his own bedroom (*Bedroom in Arles*, 1888).

The Greeks are said to have founded Arles in the 6th century B.C. In the 1st century, Julius Caesar established a Roman colony (controversy continues over whether a bust bearing his likeness recovered from the Rhône as recently as 2008 is authentic). Constantine the Great named Arles the second capital of his empire in A.D. 306, when it was known as "the little Rome of the Gauls." The city was incorporated into France in 1481.

Arles is not as pristinely preserved as, say, Avignon, but it's still very charming, with first-rate museums, excellent restaurants, and summer festivals. Its position on the river means it is a gateway to the Camargue (see chapter 16), giving the town a healthy dose of Spanish influence.

## Essentials

**GETTING THERE**  Trains run almost every hour between Arles and Avignon (trip time: 20 min.; 7€ one-way), Marseille (trip time: 50 min.; 14.30€), and Nîmes (trip time: 30 min.; 8€ one-way). Be sure to take local trains from city center to city center, not the TGV, which, in this case, takes more time. For rail information, go to www.voyages-sncf.com or call ✆ **36-35**. There are **buses** from Aix-en-Provence (trip time: 1 hr., 20 min.; 9.20€ one-way) and other major towns; for information, see www.lepilote.com or call ✆ **08-10-00-13-26**. If **driving,** head south along D570 from Avignon.

For bicycles, head to **Europebike Provence** (www.europbike-provence.net; ✆ **06-38-14-49-50**), which rents bikes from 14€ per day. Pick-up is from several locations around Arles, and they deliver to certain hotels. It is possible to reserve online.

**VISITOR INFORMATION**  The **Office de Tourisme** is on esplanade Charles-de-Gaulle (www.arlestourisme.com; ✆ **04-90-18-41-20;** fax 04-90-18-41-29).

**SPECIAL EVENTS**  **Les Rencontres d'Arles,** held for 3 weeks in July, focuses on international photography, much of contemporary. Tickets range from free to 8€ per exhibition, although passes are also available for 27€ to 35€. The ticket office is located in place de la République for the duration of the festival (www.rencontres-arles.com; ✆ **04-90-96-76-06**).

## Exploring the Town

The **place du Forum,** shaded by plane trees, stands around the old Roman forum. The Terrasse du Café le Soir, immortalized by van Gogh, is now the square's Café van Gogh. You can see two Corinthian columns and fragments from a temple at the corner of the Hôtel Nord-Pinus. Three blocks south is **place de la République,** dominated by a 15m-tall (49-ft.) red granite obelisk.

One of the city's great classical monuments is the Roman **Théâtre Antique ★★**, rue du Cloître (✆ **04-90-49-59-05**). Augustus began the theater in the 1st century; only two Corinthian columns remain. The *Venus of Arles* (now in the Louvre in Paris) was discovered here in 1651. The theater is open May through September

Place du Forum.

**Arles**

daily 9am to 7pm; March, April, and October daily 9am to 6pm; and November through February daily 10am to 5pm. Closed public holidays. Admission is 6.50€ for adults, 5€ for students, and free for children 18 and under. The same ticket admits you to the nearby **Amphitheater (Les Arènes)** ★★, rond-point des Arènes (📞 **04-90-49-59-05**), also built in the 1st century. Sometimes called Le Cirque Romain, it seats almost 25,000. For a good view, climb the three towers that remain from medieval times, when the amphitheater was turned into a fortress. Hours are the same as those for the Théâtre Antique.

**Le Cloître et l'Église St-Trophime** ★ CHURCH    This church is noted for its 12th-century portal, one of the finest achievements of the southern Romanesque style. Frederick Barbarossa was crowned king of Arles here in 1178. In the pediment, Christ is surrounded by the symbols of the Evangelists. The cloister, in Gothic and Romanesque styles, possesses noteworthy medieval carvings: during July's Les Rencontres d'Arles festival, photographs are exhibited here.

East side of place de la République. 📞 **04-90-49-59-05**. Free admission to church; cloister 3.50€ adults, 2.60€ students, free for children 18 and under. Church daily 10am–noon and 2–5pm; cloister May–Sept daily 9am–7pm; Mar, Apr, and Oct daily 9am–6pm; Nov–Feb daily 10am–5pm. Closed New Year's Day, May 1, Nov 1, and Christmas.

## Les Taureaux

Bulls are a big part of Arlesien culture. It's not unusual to see bull steak on local menus, and *saucisson de taureau* (bull sausage) is a local specialty.

The first bullfight, or *corrida*, took place in the amphitheater in 1853. Appropriately, Arles is home to a bull-fighting school. Bulls are run through the streets during major festivals, while spectators behind metal barriers look on. Today *corridas* are held on Easter weekend, during the Festival of Arles in July, and on one weekend in September. The bull is killed only during the Easter *corrida;* expect a few protestors. During the others, the bull is spared. The Easter event begins at 11am, others around 5pm. A seat on the stone benches of the amphitheater costs 18€ to 97€. Tickets are usually available a few hours before-hand at the ticket office on Les Arènes d'Arles (1 rond-point des Arènes). For information or advance tickets, go to www.arenes-arles.com or contact ℂ **08-91-70-03-70**.

**Les Alyscamps ★** RUINS  Perhaps the most memorable sight in Arles, this once–Roman necropolis became a Christian burial ground in the 4th century. Mentioned in Dante's *Inferno*, it has been painted by both van Gogh and Gauguin. Today it is lined with poplars and studded with ancient sarcophagi. Arlesiens escape here to enjoy a respite from the heat.

Av. des Alyscamps. ℂ **04-90-49-59-05.** Admission 3.50€ adults, 2.60€ students, free for children 18 and under. May–Sept daily 9am–7pm; Mar, Apr, and Oct daily 9am–noon and 2–6pm; Nov–Feb daily 10am–noon and 2–5pm. Closed New Year's Day, May 1, Nov 1, and Christmas.

**Musée de l'Arles et de la Provence Antiques ★★** MUSEUM  About 1km (½ mile) south of the town center within a hypermodern setting built in 1995, you'll find one of the world's most famous collections of Roman Christian sarcophagi, plus sculptures, mosaics, and inscriptions from the Augustinian period to the 6th century A.D. Eleven detailed models show ancient monuments of the region as they existed in the past.

Presqu'île du Cirque Romain. www.arles-antique.cg13.fr. ℂ **04-13-31-51-03.** Admission 6€ adults, 4.50€, free for children 17 and under. Wed–Mon 10am–6pm. Closed New Year's Day, May 1, Nov 1, and Christmas.

**Musée Réattu ★** ART MUSEUM  This collection, which belonged to the local painter Jacques Réattu, includes etchings and drawings by Picasso. Other pieces are by Pierre Alechinsky, Raoul Dufy, and Ossip Zadkine. Artworks are exhibited within the former Grand Priory of the Order of Malta, built during the late fifteenth century.

10 rue du Grand-Prieuré. www.museereattu.arles.fr. ℂ **04-90-49-37-58.** Admission 7€ adults, 5€ students, free for children 18 and under. July–Sept Tues–Sun 10am–7pm; Oct–June Tues–Sun 10am–12:30pm and 2–6:30pm. Closed New Year's Day, May 1, Nov 1, and Christmas.

# Where to Eat

**L'Hôtel Particulier** (see p. 520) offers excellent dining.

**L'Atelier de Jean-Luc Rabanel ★★** MODERN MEDITERRANEAN  Not only Michelin-starred, but an advocate of all-organic ingredients too, Jean-Luc

Rabanel is one of Provence's most innovative chefs. Gentle cooking methods, paired with fruits and vegetables from the restaurant's farm in the nearby Camargue, means Southern French flavors remain vibrant. The daily menu (there's no ordering a la carte) may include herb-smoked Camargue bull steak, lamb "maki" with candied ginger or Jerusalem artichokes, crusted and mousse, with green tea milk sorbet. Next door, Bistro A Côté (www.bistro-acote.com; **04-90-47-61-13**) is softer on the wallet. It's open from noon to 2pm and 7:30pm to 9pm daily, and offers a slightly more traditional daily menu (foie gras with Espelette pepper, fresh cod *brandade*) and tapas.

7 rue des Carmes. 🕻 **04-90-91-07-69.** Reservations recommended. Fixed-price lunch 55€–160€, dinner 95€–160€. MC, V. Wed–Sun noon–1:30pm and 8pm–9pm.

**Restaurant Lou Marquès ★★** PROVENÇAL   Lou Marquès, at the Hôtel Jules-César, has an excellent local reputation. Seating is in the formal wood-paneled dining room or on the terrace. The cuisine features creative twists on Provençal specialties. A first course could be crème brûlée of foie gras and celeriac, or chilled Provençal melon soup. As a main course, try Camargue risotto with roasted langoustines and black truffles. Desserts include unique combinations such as pineapple prepared with balsamic vinegar and black olives.

At the Hôtel Jules César, 9 bd. des Lices. 🕻 **04-90-52-52-52.** Reservations recommended. Main courses 26€–68€; fixed-price lunch 21€–28€, dinner 28€–60€. AE, DC, MC, V. Daily noon–1:30pm and 7:30–9:30pm.

## Arles Nightlife

Because of its relatively small population, Arles doesn't offer as many nightlife options as Aix-en-Provence, Avignon, or Marseille. The town's most appealing choice is the bar–cafe–music hall **Le Cargo de Nuit,** 7 av. Sadi Carnot (www.cargodenuit.com; 🕻 **04-90-49-55-99**). Open Wednesday to Saturday, it has live music—salsa, jazz, rock—and then club dancing until 3am. Cover ranges from 8€ to 25€.

---

### 📷 Mistral, Two Ways

Born north of Arles, Frédéric Mistral (1830-1914) dedicated his life to defending and preserving the original Provençal language known as Occitan. A poet who won the Nobel Prize for his epic work *Mirèio* and overall contributions to French literature, Mistral joined with six other Provençal writers in 1854 to found Félibrige, an association for the promotion of Occitan language and literature. He is the author of *Lo Tresor dóu Félibrige,* the most comprehensive dictionary of the Occitan language to this day.

Many think Mistral lent his name to the notorious glacial wind that roars through Provence every year. However, in this case, *mistral* is the Occitan word for "master"—and those who experience the phenomenon regularly say it's a cruel one. Tearing through the Rhône River Valley toward the Mediterranean, the mistral reaches speeds of 100km (62 miles) per hour and can blow up to 100 days per year. Most of these occur in winter, but it is also common in the spring and, in unlucky years, can persist until early summer.

---

# Where to Stay

## VERY EXPENSIVE

**L'Hôtel Particulier ★★★ 🎁** Occupying an 18th-century pavilion, this edifice was the last of the private town houses built in the center of Arles. It may not be as grand as the Jules César, weighing in at just a fraction of the size, but its distinctive elegance has made it a formidable challenger. Behind a monumental gate, you'll encounter ancient yew trees and a courtyard with teak lounges and a limestone-built *bassin* containing a lap pool. Each bedroom is decorated individually in cool, neutral tones with Provençal antiques, elegantly draped fabrics, and designer knickknacks. Gourmet dining is available in the crisp white dining room or outside.

4 rue de la Monnaie, Arles 13200. www.hotel-particulier.com. ✆ **04-90-52-51-40.** Fax 04-90-96-16-70. 14 units. 259€–329€ double; 299€–429€ suite. AE, MC, V. Parking 19€. **Amenities:** Restaurant; outdoor pool; room service; small spa and *hammam. In room:* A/C, TV, minibar, free Wi-Fi.

## EXPENSIVE

**Grand Hôtel Nord-Pinus ★** Depending on your taste, you'll find this legendary hotel either steeped in history and nostalgia—or just plain quirky. On the site of a bakery at the turn of the 20th century, it sits on a tree-lined square in the heart of Arles. The public spaces are crammed with antiques and memorabilia. The guest rooms, up an ornate staircase with wrought-iron balustrades, are glamorous, even theatrical, graced with rich upholsteries and linens. The designer Christian Lecroix recently redecorated the third floor. Many bullfighters, artists, and actors have stayed here; their photographs, as well as a collection of safari photos by Peter Beard, are hung throughout.

Place du Forum, Arles 13200. www.nord-pinus.com. ✆ **04-90-93-44-44.** Fax 04-90-93-34-00. 26 units. 160€–340€ double; 295€–375€ suite; 390€–600€ suite. AE, MC, V. Parking 17€. **Amenities:** Restaurant; bar; room service. *In room:* A/C, TV, hair dryer, free Wi-Fi.

## MODERATE

**Hôtel Calendal ★** Because of everything it offers, the Calendal is a favorite in its price category. On a quiet square near the arena, it provides high-ceilinged accommodations decorated in bright colors. Most rooms have views of the hotel's garden, filled with palms and palmettos. Each unit comes with a compact shower-only bathroom. There is a spa on-site, as well as a boutique selling regional products.

5 rue Porte de Laure, Arles 13200. www.lecalendal.com. ✆ **04-90-96-11-89.** Fax 04-90-96-05-84. 38 units. 119€–169€ double; 129€–169€ triple; 139€–169€ quad. AE, DC, MC, V. Parking 8€. **Amenities:** Summer-only restaurant; bar; cafe; spa. *In room:* A/C, TV, hair dryer, free Wi-Fi.

**Hôtel de l'Amphitheatre** Originally built in the 1600s, this hotel is ideally situated between the Roman amphitheater and the Théâtre Antique (though the entrance is on a tiny side street that can be a little tough to find). Its Old-World atmosphere is enhanced by hand-hewn wood ceiling beams, bright fabrics, soft lighting, reproductions of Provençal furniture, and bedrooms that, in some cases, have views over the terra-cotta roofs of historic Arles. A favorite is the Belvedere Suite, whose windows offer 360-degree views over the town. Only breakfast is served, but many dining options lie within a short walk.

5–7 rue Diderot, Arles 13200. www.hotelamphitheatre.net. ☏ **04-90-96-10-30.** Fax 04-90-93-98-69. 28 units. 56€–116€ double; 126€–156€ suite. AE, MC, V. Parking 6€. **Amenities:** Breakfast room. *In room:* A/C, TV, fridge, hair dryer, free Wi-Fi.

# LES BAUX ★★★

720km (446 miles) S of Paris; 18km (11 miles) NE of Arles; 85km (53 miles) N of Marseille

Les Baux de Provence is the kind of natural/man-made monument often featured in aerial films. Its situation and geology are extraordinary. Cardinal Richelieu called the massive, 245m-high (804-ft.) rock rising from a desolate plain "a nesting place for eagles." A eagle's-eye view of the outcropping would be part moonscape, dotted with archeological ruins and a vast plateau, and part civilization, with boxy stone houses stacked like cards on the rock's east side. The combination is so cinematic that it seems like a living movie set.

*Baux,* or *baou* in Provençal, means "rocky spur." The power-thirsty lords who ruled the settlement took this as their surname in the 11th century, and by the Middle Ages had control of 79 other regional fiefdoms. After they were overthrown, Les Baux was annexed to France with the rest of Provence, but Louis XI ordered the fortress demolished. The settlement experienced a rebirth during the Renaissance, when structures where restored and lavish residences built, only to fall again in 1642 when, wary of rebellion, Louis XIII ordered his armies to destroy it once and for all.

Today the fortress compound is nothing but ruins, but fascinating ones. The surrounding countryside, including Le Val d'Enfer (the Valley of Hell), has its own mysterious allure. The area gives its name to bauxite (aluminium ore), discovered here in 1821 by French geologist Pierre Berthier.

Now the bad news: Because of its dramatic beauty, plus a number of quaint shops and restaurants in the village, Les Baux is virtually overrun with visitors. It's not unlike Mont-St-Michel in this respect.

## Essentials

**GETTING THERE**  Les Baux is best reached by car; there is no rail service. From Arles, take the express highway D570 northeast until you reach the turnoff for a secondary road (D17), which will lead you northeast to Fontvieille. From there, follow the signs east into Les Baux. By **train,** most passengers get off at

**Les Baux ruins.**

Arles, then take a 35-minute local bus (2.10€ one-way). The same line runs in the opposite direction from St-Remy. For bus information, see www.lepilote.com or call ✆ **08-10-00-13-26**. You can also book 1-day coach tours through **Autocars Lieutaud** (www.excursionprovence.com; ✆ **04-90-86-36-75**) in Avignon or the tourist office in Aix-en-Provence (✆ **04-42-16-11-61;** www.aixenprovencetourism.com).

**VISITOR INFORMATION**   The **Office de Tourisme** (www.lesbauxdeprovence.com; ✆ **04-90-54-34-39;** fax 04-90-54-51-15) is at Maison du Roy, near the northern entrance to the old city.

# Exploring the Town

The ghostly ruins cover an area of 7 hectares (17 acres), much larger than the village itself. Consider visiting them early in the morning before the sun gets too strong, then retire to one of the village restaurants during the hottest part of the day. By afternoon, everything may be so overrun with tourists that you'll choose to escape.

The **Château des Baux** and medieval compound are accessed via the 15th-century **Hôtel de la Tour du Brau,** which also houses the **Musée du Château des Baux.** Beneath the high vaulted ceilings of this former bourgeois residence are historical exhibits that will help you to understand the ruins. Models of the fortress explain how the site has evolved architecturally.

Beyond this building are replicas of wooden military equipment that would have been used in the 13th century. Built to scale—that is to say, enormous— are a battering ram, trebuchet (the largest in France), and other catapults capable of firing huge boulders every few minutes. From April to September, these are fired every day at 11am and 1:30, 3:30, and 5:30pm, with an extra show during July and August at 6:30pm.

Other stopping points include the **Chapel of St-Blaise** (inside which a film of aerial views of Provence is shown), a windmill, the skeleton of a hospital built in the 16th century, and a cemetery. The **Tour Sarrazin,** named because it was used to spot Saracen invaders coming from the south, yields a sweeping view.

Admission to the Château, including the museum and access to the ruins, is 8€ for adults, 6€ children 7 to 17 from October to March. The rest of the year, it is 9€ for adults, 7€ children 7 to 17. Open daily in spring from 9am to 7:15pm, summer from 9am to 8:15pm, autumn from 9:30am to 6pm, and winter from 10am to 5pm. For information, go to www.chateau-baux-provence.com or contact ✆ **04-90-54-55-56**.

**Église St-Vincent** CHURCH   This church was constructed in stages between the 12th and 16th centuries. Its oldest nave comprises three troglodyte chapels. To the left of the building is a circular tower known as the *Lanterne des Morts* (Lantern of the Dead), after the old custom of lighting a flame inside whenever a resident of Les Baux died. The modern stained-glass windows were a gift from Prince Rainier III of Monaco when he was the marquis des Baux during the 1980s. Today Prince Albert fills the honorary/ceremonial duties associated with that role—although you're more likely to see Princess Caroline, who has a private home in nearby St-Rémy-de-Provence.

Place St.-Vincent. No phone. Free admission. Daily 9am–5pm (until 7pm June–Aug).

**Fondation Louis Jou** ART MUSEUM   Barcelona-born artist Louis Jou (1882–1968) is considered the most important contemporary artist to come out of Les Baux. A collection of his engravings and seriographs, along with a few small-scale works by Rembrandt, Dürer, and Goya, is carefully preserved in the Renaissance-era Hôtel Jean-de-Brion. Visits are by appointment only.

Hôtel Jean-de-Brion, Grande Rue. www.fondationlouisjou.org. ✆ **04-90-54-34-17.** Admission 3€ adults, 1.50€ children 8-17. Free for children 7 and under. Visits by telephone appointment only.

**Musée des Santons** MUSEUM   Housed in the **Ancien Hôtel de Ville,** this museum is dedicated to the traditional wooden crèche figurines. It exhibits Neapolitan pieces from the 17th and 18th centuries, 19th-century *santons* with papier-mâché faces and glass sulfur eyes made by Carmelite nuns in Avignon, and scenes illustrating the traditions of Provence and Les Baux. A documentary film on the making of the figurines is shown.

Place Louis Jou. ✆ **04-90-54-34-39.** Free admission. Daily 10am–5pm.

**The Yves Brayer Museum** ART MUSEUM   Inside the 16th-century Hôtel de Porcelet, this museum is devoted to the works of figurative painter Yves Brayer (1907–90). An adopted Provençal son, he became famous for his paintings of everyday life between World War I and World War II—landscapes of France, Italy, Morocco, and Spain, and bullfighting scenes. He also created the frescoes inside the **Chapelle des Pénitents Blancs,** on place St.-Vincent just down the street. Brayer is buried in the village cemetery.

Intersection of rue de la Calade and rue de l'Église. www.yvesbrayer.com. ✆ **04-90-54-36-99.** Admission 5€ adults, free children 18 and under. Daily Apr–Sept 10am–12:30pm and 2–6:30pm; Oct–Mar Wed–Mon 10am–12:30pm and 2–5pm. Closed Jan and Feb.

# Where to Eat

**La Cabro d'Or** and **Oustau de Baumanière** (see p. 524) offer outstanding dining.

**La Riboto de Taven** ★★★ PROVENÇAL   Known for its flawless cuisine and market-fresh ingredients, this is one of the great restaurants of the area. When the Novi family opened guest rooms, they decided to stop chasing the favor of picky reviewers and focus completely on pleasing their clientele. It was a good decision, for today you can enjoy award-winning cuisine in an intimate family atmosphere free of food snobs. The heady perfumes of Provence characterize the cuisine, which can include sea bass in olive oil, lamb en croûte with olives, or, in late autumn and winter, medallions of venison served with caramelized root vegetables. The menu changes every day and always features an intelligent and tasteful use of local ingredients and produce.

The hotel is located in and around the 1835 *mas* the family has owned for nearly 2 decades. Accommodations include four rooms within the thick walls of the main farmhouse and two troglodyte suites carved into the grottoes at the far end of the fragrant garden. There is also a swimming pool.

Vallon de la Fontaine, Les Baux de Provence 13520. www.riboto-de-taven.fr. ✆ **04-90-54-34-23.** Fax 04-90-54-38-88. Reservations required. Fixed-price menu 56€. AE, MC, V. Thurs–Tues 7:30–9:30pm. Hotel: 6 units. 180€–200€ double; 230€–300€ suite. **Amenities:** Outdoor pool. *In room:* A/C, TV, hair dryer, minibar, free Wi-Fi. Closed Nov–Feb.

# Where to Stay

**La Riboto de Taven** (see "Where to Eat," on previous page) rents rooms.

## VERY EXPENSIVE

**La Cabro d'Or ★★★**   This is the lesser-known sibling of the nearby Oustau de Baumanière (see below). You'll find some of the most comfortable accommodations in the region here, with a Michelin-starred restaurant. Set in a vast, well-manicured garden, the original building is an 18th-century farmhouse, while the dining room is situated in another building from the same period (meals are also served on the terrace). The massive ceiling beams are works of art in their own right. Guest rooms evoke authentic Provence with art and antiques; some have views over the tranquil countryside. Unlike the Oustau de Baumanière, the annexes in this hotel are not as impressive as the original buildings.

Route d'Arles, Les Baux de Provence 13520. www.lacabrodor.com. ℭ **04-90-54-33-21.** Fax 04-90-54-45-98. 26 units. 165€–390€ double; 293€–600€ suite. AE, DC, MC, V. Free parking. Closed Sun-Mon mid–Oct to Mar. **Amenities:** Restaurant; babysitting; bar; outdoor pool; room service; spa; 2 tennis courts. *In room:* A/C, TV, hair dryer, minibar, free Wi-Fi.

**Oustau de Baumanière ★★★**   Ask a French person to name the top three must-stays in France, and this one is likely to make the list. Raymond Thuillier bought the main building, a remote 14th-century farmhouse, in 1945 and transformed it into a hotel that became a hotspot for the glitterati during the 1950s. Today the Relais & Châteaux member is managed by his grandson, who was born the year the hotel opened. Though not as exclusive now, l'Oustau's dramatic location at the base of the Val d'Enfer—less than 10 minutes from the village of Les Baux on foot—contributes to its lasting magic. Guest rooms are elegantly furnished in 16th and 17th century style and include large sitting areas. If there's no vacancy in the main building, the hotel will assign you to one of the annexes. Request Le Manoir, the most appealing, next to the less-frequented of the hotel's two swimming pools. The faithful return not least for the two-star Michelin restaurant.

Les Baux de Provence 13520. www.oustaudebaumaniere.com. ℭ **04-90-54-33-07.** Fax 04-90-54-40-46. 30 units. 180€–440€ double; 293€–720€ suite. AE, DC, MC, V. Free parking. Closed 1st week of Jan to 1st week of Mar. Hotel closed Tues–Wed Mar and mid-Oct to early Nov. Restaurant closed Tues evening, Wed, and Thurs lunch Mar and mid-Oct to early Nov. **Amenities:** Restaurant; babysitting; 2 outdoor pools; room service; spa; 2 tennis courts. *In room:* A/C, TV, hair dryer, minibar, free Wi-Fi.

## EXPENSIVE

**Auberge de la Benvengudo ★**   In a quiet location about 1.5km (1 mile) south of town, this elegant *auberge* is a 19th-century farmhouse surrounded by sculptured shrubbery and parasol pines. The property has an outdoor pool, tennis court, and terrace heavy with the scent of lavender and thyme. About half the rooms are in the original building, above the gourmet restaurant, and the rest in an attractive stone-sided annex. All are sunny and well maintained. Each has a private terrace or balcony, and some have antique four-poster beds. The hotel can prepare picnic baskets to take along on your sightseeing trips.

Quartier de l'Arcoule, Les Baux de Provence 13520. www.benvengudo.com. ℭ **04-90-54-32-54.** Fax 04-90-54-42-58. 27 units. 130€–210€ double; 220€–405€ suite. AE, MC, V. Free parking. Closed Nov 1–Mar 15. Take RD78f for 1.5km (1 mile) southwest of Les Baux, following signs to

Arles. **Amenities:** Restaurant; babysitting; outdoor pool; room service; tennis court. *In room:* A/C, TV, hair dryer, free Wi-Fi.

# AIX-EN-PROVENCE ★★

760km (471 miles) S of Paris; 84km (52 miles) SE of Avignon; 34km (21 miles) N of Marseille; 185km (115 miles) W of Nice

One of the most surprising things about Aix is its size. Frequently guidebooks and travel programs proclaim it the very heart of Provence, evoking a sleepy town filled with flowers and fountains. Which it is—in certain quarters. But Aix is also a bustling judicial center and university town of nearly 143,000 inhabitants (the Université d'Aix dates from 1413).

Founded in 122 b.c. by Roman general Caius Sextius Calvinus, who named the town Aquae Sextiae, after himself, Aix originated as a military outpost. Its former incarnations include a civilian colony, the seat of an archbishop, and official residence of the medieval counts of Provence.

Paul Cézanne, Aix's most celebrated son, immortalized the countryside in his paintings. Just as he saw it, the Montagne Ste-Victoire looms over the town today, though a string of high-rises now interrupts the landscape.

Time marches on, but there are still plenty of decades-old, family-run shops on the narrow streets of the old town. A lazy summer lunch at one of the bourgeois cafes on the cours Mirabeau is an experience not to be missed.

## Essentials

**GETTING THERE**   **Trains** arrive daily from Marseille (trip time: 1 hr.; 8.70€ one-way), Nice (trip time: 3 hr.; 38€ one-way), and Cannes (trip time: 2 hr., 30 min.; 32.70€ one-way). High-speed TGV trains—from Paris as well as Marseille and Nice—arrive at the modern station near Vitrolles, 18km (11 miles) west of Aix. For rail information, see www.voyages-sncf.com or call ✆ **36-35**. Bus transfers to the center of Aix cost 3.60€ one-way. There are **buses** from Marseille, Avignon, and Nice; for information, see www.lepilote.com or call ✆ **08-10-00-13-26**. If you're **driving** to Aix from Avignon or other points north, take A7 south to A8 and follow the signs into town. From Marseille or other points south, take A51 north.

Eco-friendly **Diabline** vehicles (www.la-diabline.fr; Monday through Saturday 8:30am to 7:30pm) operate three routes, running along cours

---

### ○ Aix Through the Eyes of Cézanne

One of the best experiences in Aix is a walk along the well-marked *route de Cézanne* (D17). From the east end of cours Mirabeau, take rue du Maréchal-Joffre across boulevard Carnot to boulevard des Poilus, which becomes avenue des Ecoles-Militaires and D17. The stretch between Aix and the hamlet of

Le Tholonet is full of twists and turns where Cézanne often set up his easel. The route makes a lovely 5.5km (3½-mile) stroll. Le Tholonet has a cafe or two where you can refresh yourself while waiting for one of the frequent buses back to Aix.

Mirabeau and through most of the Old Town for 0.50€ per ride. To explore the region by bicycle, head for **Aixprit Vélo,** 20 rue Fernand Dol (www.aixprit velo.com; ✆ **04-42-21-24-05**). Here you can rent 10-speed racing bikes or sturdier mountain bikes from 10€ per half-day to 80€ per week. You must leave a credit card deposit of 200€ to 300€, depending on the bike. It is possible to reserve online.

**VISITOR INFORMATION** The **Office de Tourisme** is at Les Allées Provençales, 300 av. Giuseppe Verdi (www.aixenprovencetourism.com; ✆ **04-42-16-11-61;** fax 04-42-16-11-62).

Dining al fresco in Aix-en-Provence.

**SPECIAL EVENTS** The **Festival International d'Art Lyrique & de Musique,** created in 1948 (www.festival-aix.com; ✆ **08-20-92-29-23**), in late July, features music and opera from all over the world.

## Exploring the Town

Aix's main street, **cours Mirabeau ★**, is one of Europe's most beautiful. A double row of plane trees shades it from the Provençal sun and throws dappled daylight onto its rococo fountains. Shops and sidewalk cafes line one side; 17th- and 18th- century sandstone *hôtels particuliers* (mansions) take up the other. The street begins at the 1860 fountain **La Rotonde,** on place du Général-de-Gaulle, and is named for Honoré Gabriel Riqueti, Count of Mirabeau, the revolutionary and statesman. Boulevard Carnot and cours Sextius circle the heart of the old quarter (Vieille Ville), which contains the pedestrian zone.

**Atelier de Cézanne ★★** MUSEUM   Cézanne was the major forerunner of cubism. This studio, surrounded by a wall and restored by American admirers, is where he worked. As the building remained locked up and virtually untouched for decades after Cézanne death in 1906, visitors are offered a unique glimpse into the artist's daily life, "his coat hanging on the wall, his easel with an unfinished picture waiting for a touch of the master's brush," as Thomas R. Parker wrote.

9 av. Paul-Cézanne (outside town). ✆ **04-42-21-06-53.** Admission 5.50€ adults, 2€ students and children 13-25, free for children 12 and under. July–Aug daily 10am–6pm, English tour at 5pm; Apr–June and Sept daily 10am–noon and 2–6pm, English tour at 5pm; Oct–Mar daily 10am–noon and 2–5pm, English tour at 4pm. Closed New Year's Day, Jan 2, Jan 3, May 1, and Christmas, and Sun Dec–Feb.

**Cathédrale St-Sauveur ★** CATHEDRAL   The cathedral of Aix is dedicated to Christ under the title St-Sauveur (Holy Savior or Redeemer) and dates from the 4th and 5th centuries. Its pièce de résistance is a 15th-century Nicolas Froment triptych, *The Burning Bush.* One side depicts the Virgin and Child; the other, Good King René and his second wife, Jeanne de Laval.

Place des Martyrs de la Résistance. www. cathedrale-aixenprovence-monument.fr. (f) **04-42-23-45-65.** Free admission. Daily 8am–noon and 2–6pm. Mass Sun 10:30am and 7pm.

**Musée des Tapisseries** MUSEUM
Three series of tapestries from the 17th and 18th centuries line the gilded walls of this former archbishop's palace. The prelates decorated the palace with *The History of Don Quixote,* by Natoire; *The Russian Games,* by Leprince; and *The Grotesques,* by Monnoyer. The museum also exhibits rare furnishings from the 17th and 18th

Cathédrale St-Sauveur.

centuries, as well as a section dedicated to the history of the city's annual Festival International d'Art Lyrique.

28 place des Martyrs de la Résistance. (☎ **04-42-23-09-91.** Admission 3.20€ adults, free for ages 25 and under. Apr 15–Oct 15 Wed–Mon 10am–6pm; Oct 16–Apr 14 Wed–Mon 1:30–5pm. Closed Jan, May 1, and Dec 25–26.

## Shopping

Opened more than a century ago, **Béchard,** 12 cours Mirabeau (☎ **04-42-26-06-78**), is the most famous bakery in town. They specialize in the famous *Calissons d'Aix,* a candy made from ground almonds, preserved melon, and fruit syrup. **Puyricard**, 7-9 rue Rifle-Rafle (www.puyricard.fr; ☎ **04-42-21-13-26**) creates sensational chocolates filled with candied figs, walnuts or local lavender honey.

Founded in 1934 on a busy boulevard just east of the center of town, **Santons Fouque,** 65 cours Gambetta (www.santons-fouque.com; ☎ **04-42-26-33-38**), stocks close to 2,000 traditional *santons* (crèche figurines).

For a range of truly useful souvenirs, including copper pots and pocket knives by famous French forgers such as Laguiole, try **Quincaillerie Centrale,** 21 rue de Monclar (☎ **04-42-23-33-18**), a hardware/housewares store that's been offering a little bit of everything since 1959.

## Where to Eat

### EXPENSIVE

**Le Clos de la Violette ★★★** MODERN FRENCH    This innovative restaurant is a few steps from La Villa Gallici (see "Where to Stay," below) in an elegant neighborhood that most visitors reach by taxi. The Provençal villa has an octagonal reception area, several serenely decorated dining rooms, and tables outside. Chef Jean-Marc Banzo's Michelin-starred cuisine is both seasonal and creative, highlighting the flavors of Provence. A tempting example is appetizer of grilled eggplant with foie gras and Serrano ham. Roasted filet of lamb may be served with goat cheese gnocchi and spinach shoots. For dessert, look out for tiramisu with lemon, olive oil, and thyme sorbet.

10 av. de la Violette. www.closdelaviolette.fr. (☎ **04-42-23-30-71.** Reservations required. Main courses 45€–55€; fixed-price lunch 50€, and dinner 50€–130€. AE, MC, V. Tues–Sat noon–1:30pm and 7:30–9:30pm. Closed last week of Dec.

### MODERATE

**Brasserie Les Deux Garçons** PROVENÇAL    Few come here for the food alone—though it's not bad, just standard. The draw is the nostalgia and atmosphere of a brasserie founded in 1792 and frequented by the likes of Emile Zola,

---

 **To the Markets We Will Go**

Aix offers the best markets in the region. Place Richelme holds a **fruit-and-vegetable market** every morning from 8:30am to 12:30pm. Come here to buy exquisite products such as olives, lavender, local cheeses, and fresh produce. There's a **flower market** every day, with the same hours, at either place Richelme or place des Prêcheurs (the former on Tues, Thurs, and Sat; the latter on Mon, Wed, Fri, and Sun). The **fish market** is daily in the morning on place Richelme.

Cézanne, Picasso, and Winston Churchill. In winter, the upstairs piano bar is one of the coziest spots in Aix, attracting jazz lovers. In summer, linen-draped tables spill onto the cours Mirabeau. Provençale fare includes *daube de boeuf* (stewed beef marinated in a garlic purée), wild rabbit, soupe de poisson, and fresh fruits and vegetables of the season.

53 cours Mirabeau. www.les2garconsrestaurant.com. ⓒ **04-42-26-00-51.** Main courses 17.50€– 34€; fixed-price menu 25€. AE, MC, V. Daily 7am–2am.

**Le Mille Feuille ★** PROVENÇAL   This small restaurant and tea shop is one of Aix's best-kept secrets. It was opened by two former staff of the l'Oustau de Baumanière in Les Baux. The talented Nicolas Monribot is a pastry chef by training and also a musician, which shows through in his melodious savory dishes such as cream of Jerusalem artichoke soup, roasted lamb with soft polenta, and monkfish with orange-flavored curry. You'll be competing with some serious local fans, particularly at dinnertime, so be sure to reserve in advance. Wine expert Sylvain Sendra offers an unusual collection of local vintages, most of them biodynamic.

8 rue Rifle-Rafle. ⓒ **04-42-96-55-17.** Dinner reservations essential. Main courses 15€; fixed-price lunch 22€–27€, dinner 32€–37€. MC, V. Tues–Sat noon–2pm and Wed–Sat 7:45–10pm. Closed 3 weeks in Aug.

## Aix Nightlife

An establishment that manages to be convenient and hip at the same time lies almost directly across from the city's tourist office. Open daily 8am until at least 2am, **La Rotonde,** 2A place Jeanne d'Arc (www.larotonde-aix.com; ⓒ **04-42-91-61-70**), is a bar, cafe, and rendezvous point for friends and business associates throughout the day and evening. Students meet up at **Le Sextius Bar,** 13 cours Sextius (ⓒ **04-42-26-07-21**), to kick off their evenings.

Under-30s who like thumping electronic beats head for **Le Mistral,** 3 rue Frédéric-Mistral (www.mistralclub.fr; ⓒ **04-42-38-16-49**), where techno and house music pumps long and loud for a cover charge of around 20€ (females enter free on Tues). **Le Divino,** 4039 route de Sisteron (www.divino.fr; ⓒ **04-42-21-28-28**), draws a lively gay/straight crowd for weekend dancing until 6am (cover charge 8€–16€).

For jazz produced by a changing roster of visiting musicians, head for the **Scat Club,** 11 rue de la Verrerie (ⓒ **04-42-23-00-23**), a preferred venue for more mature local patrons.

Last but certainly not least is the **Joïa Glam Club** (www.discotheque-aixenprovence.com; ⓒ **06-80-35-32-94**), chemin de l'Enfant, in the hamlet of Les Milles, 8km (5 miles) south of Aix (follow the signs to Marseille). There is also a shuttle bus from La Rotonde in Aix proper—probably a safer bet anyway. On-site is a restaurant, several bars, an outdoor swimming pool, and indoor/outdoor dance floor. Be forewarned that there are long lines on Fridays (when females get in free) and Saturdays. Entrance usually costs around 16€, unless you're a star or self-confident enough to schmooze the doorman.

## Where to Stay
### VERY EXPENSIVE

**La Villa Gallici ★★★**   This elegant inn, which began life in the 18th century as a private home, is now one of Aix's most stylish hotels. The rooms are chic but homey, thanks to soft furnishings in dozens of different Provençal fabrics. Many have a private terrace or garden, and each one comes with a tub/shower. The villa sits in a large, enclosed garden with a swimming pool. It's a 5-minute walk to the town center.

Av. de la Violette, Aix-en-Provence 13100. www.villagallici.com. ✆ **04-42-23-29-23.** Fax 04-42-96-30-45. 22 units. 230€–690€ double; 430€–945€ suite. AE, DC, MC, V. Free parking. Closed Jan. **Amenities:** Restaurant; bar; babysitting; outdoor pool; room service. *In room:* A/C, TV, hair dryer, minibar, free Wi-Fi.

**28 à Aix** ★★★ 🎁 The owners of this sophisticated *hotel particulier* have created an oasis of charm, tranquillity, style, and comfort, just steps away from the cours Mirabeau. A cozy town house created from a restored 17th-century mansion, it houses only four rooms, each one decorated in a well-executed mix of sumptuous textiles and modern accents. Enjoy pastries and afternoon tea near the fireplace or outside on the intimate garden patio.

28 rue du 4 Septembre, Aix-en-Provence 13100. www.28-a-aix.com. ✆ **04-42-54-82-01.** 4 units. 250€–500€ double. Rates include breakfast. MC, V. Parking 20€. **Amenities:** Breakfast lounge; in-room breakfast. *In room:* A/C, TV, hair dryer, minibar, free Wi-Fi.

## EXPENSIVE

**Hôtel Cézanne** ★★ Colorful and chic, Aix's finest boutique hotel pays homage to Provence and the paintings of Cézanne. Conceived by one of the designers of both Villa Gallici and 28 à Aix (see above), the Cezanne could be considered a younger, hipper cousin, with details such as mother-of-pearl-inlaid walls and elaborate tile in some of the bathrooms. Bedrooms are spacious and filled with light; amenities include rain showers and free cold drinks in the minibar. Breakfast, served until noon, might include smoked salmon and champagne. Modern art is exhibited in the public spaces, which include a bar.

40 av. Victor Hugo, Aix-en-Provence 13100. www.hotelaix.com/cezanne. ✆ **04-42-91-11-11.** Fax 04-42-91-11-10. 55 units. 200€–250€ double; 290€–350€ junior suite; 380€ suite. AE, MC, V. Free parking, by reservation. **Amenities:** Bar; business center. *In room:* A/C, TV, hair dryer, minibar, free Wi-Fi.

## MODERATE

**Hôtel des Augustins** ★ Converted from the 12th-century Grands Augustins Convent, this hotel has retained its ribbed-vault ceilings, stained glass, stone walls, and terra-cotta floors. The reception desk is in a chapel, and paintings and watercolors decorate the public rooms. The convent won a spot in history by sheltering an excommunicated Martin Luther on his return from Rome. Rooms are outfitted in a Provençal country style, with dark-wood furniture and high ceilings. Breakfast is the only meal served.

3 rue de la Masse, Aix-en-Provence 13100. www.hotel-augustins.com. ✆ **04-42-27-28-59.** Fax 04-42-26-74-87. 29 units. 99€–250€ double. AE, DC, MC, V. *In room:* A/C, TV, hair dryer, minibar, free Wi-Fi.

## INEXPENSIVE

**Hôtel du Globe** A good budget option for a city where expensive is the norm. A short walk from the Cathédrale St-Sauveur, this hotel is just on the northwest edge of Aix's old town, and around a ten-minute walk to cours Mirabeau. Rooms are basic but clean; at the press of a button, an automatic shade descends to shield them from sun or unwanted noise. Bathrooms are on the small side. Some rooms have balconies, and a rooftop terrace is open to all. The staff is especially helpful and will do everything to ensure a pleasant stay.

74 cours Sextius, Aix-en-Provence 13100. www.hotelduglobe.com. ✆ **04-42-26-03-58.** Fax 04-42-26-13-68. 46 units. 78€–90€ double; 102€–119€ triple. AE, DC, MC, V. Parking 9.80€. **Amenities:** Breakfast in room. *In room:* A/C, TV, free Wi-Fi.

**Hôtel St. Christophe**   The brasserie attached to this hotel was purchased in 1936 as a garage. It was made into a restaurant and art gallery that featured local artists such as Marcel Arnaud. Arnaud's family now runs the hotel and brasserie; his paintings decorate the premises. Regular rooms are unassuming, with time-worn Art Deco decor, and have tubs rather than showers. Superior rooms, recently renovated, have more contemporary furnishings with fully modern bathrooms. The hotel's location near the Rotonde fountain and the cours Mirabeau is a plus.

2 av. Victor Hugo, Aix-en-Provence 13100. ✆ **04-42-26-01-24.** Fax 04-42-38-53-17. 67 units. 92€–120€ double; 174€ suite. AE, DC, MC, V. **Amenities:** Restaurant. *In room:* A/C, TV, free Wi-Fi.

# MARSEILLE ★★

776km (481 miles) S of Paris; 203km (126 miles) SW of Nice; 32km (20 miles) S of Aix-en-Provence

Marseille, with nearly 1.5 million inhabitants, is the second-largest city in France. It is, in fact, the country's oldest metropolis, founded as a port by the Greeks in the 6th century B.C.

Alexandre Dumas called teeming Marseille "the meeting place of the entire world." It's an industrial city with many faces, both figuratively and literally. A

**View from up above at Basilique Notre-Dame-de-la-Garde.**

view from high up reveals the colorful Vieux Port, with its elegant old buildings, boat-filled harbor, and the Mediterranean beyond—as well as an ocean of concrete comprising business districts and tenement suburbs. The city is sprawling and can be down at heel in parts, but it's also a place of unique sounds, smells, and sights—unlike any others in France.

Marseille is twice the size of Paris, and its age-old problems include a drug industry, unemployment, the Mafia, and racial tension (around a quarter of the population is of North African descent, with significant Armenian, Jewish, and Asian communities too). Nevertheless, there is strong city pride and an eye toward the future, as evidenced by the ongoing **Euroméditerranée** urban regeneration project (www.euromediterranee.fr). Marseille also assumes its proud role as **European Capital of Culture 2013** (www.mp2013.fr), reopening many of its newly renovated museums and completing long-term architectural projects, particularly in the old docklands neighborhood north of the Vieux Port.

## Essentials

**GETTING THERE**   **Marseille Provence Airport** (www.mrsairport.com; ☎ 04-42-14-14-14), 27km (17 miles) northwest of the city center, receives international flights from all over Europe. From the airport, shuttle buses (*navettes*) make the trip to Marseille's St-Charles rail station, near the Vieux-Port, for 8€, 5.60€ for passengers 12-26 and 4€ for children under 12. The shuttle buses run daily every 20 minutes from 5am until midnight; the trip takes 25 minutes. For information, see www.navettemarseilleaeroport.com or call **08-92-70-08-40**.

Marseille has **train** connections from all over Europe, with especially good connections to and from Nice, and on to Italy. The city is the terminus for the TGV bullet train, which departs almost every hour from Paris's Gare de Lyon (trip time: 3 hr., 30 min.; 66€–108€ one-way). For rail information, see www.voyages-sncf.com or call ☎ **36-35**. **Buses** serve the **Gare Routière,** rue Honnorat (www.gareroutieremarseille.fr; ☎ **04-91-08-16-40**), adjacent to the St-Charles railway station. Several buses run daily between Aix-en-Provence and Marseille (trip time: 40 min.; 5€ one-way). If you're **driving** from Paris, follow A6 south to Lyon, and then continue south along A7 to Marseille. The drive takes about 8 hours. From Provence, take A7 south to Marseille.

**GETTING AROUND**   Parking and car safety can be problematic enough that your best bet is to park in a garage and rely on public transportation.

**Métro** lines 1 and 2 both stop at the main train station, Gare St-Charles, place Victor Hugo. Line 1 makes a U-shaped circuit from the suburbs into the city and back again; Line 2 runs north and south in the downtown area. Also with two lines, the tramway services the Canabière and the refurbished Joliette Docks district, as well as continuing out to the suburbs. Individual tickets are 1.50€; they're valid on Métro, tram, and bus lines for up to 60 minutes after purchase. If you plan to take public transport several times during your stay, buy a **pass journée,** valid for one day for 5€ or three days for 10.50€. Maps and transit information are also available at **Espace Info** kiosks, located at strategic points throughout the city, usually in or near Métro stations. Public transit maps are downloadable from the Régie des Transport de Marseille (www.rtm.fr; ☎ **04-91-91-92-10**).

Alternatively, it's also possible to purchase a one-day (22€) or two-day (29€) **City Pass** from the Marseille Tourist Office. This pass covers all

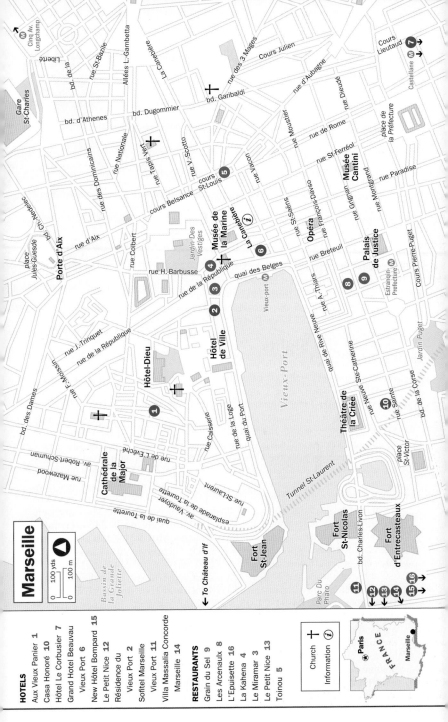

# Marseille

0 100 yds
0 100 m

**HOTELS**

Aux Vieux Panier 1
Casa Honoré 10
Hôtel Le Corbusier 7
Grand Hotel Beauvau
Vieux Port 6
New Hôtel Bompard 15
Le Petit Nice 12
Résidence du
Vieux Port 2
Sofitel Marseille
Vieux Port 11
Villa Massalia Concorde
Marseille 14

**RESTAURANTS**

Grain du Sel 9
Les Arcenaulx 8
L'Epuisette 16
La Kahena 4
Le Miramar 3
Le Petit Nice 13
Toinou 5

✝ Church
ⓘ Information

FRANCE
Paris
Marseille

533

public transport, including the round-trip ferry trip to Château d'If (see below), as well as entrance to 15 of the city's museums and a ride on the *petit-train* (see below) up to the Basilique Notre-Dame de la Garde (see below).

The major arteries divide Marseille into 16 *arrondissements.* As in Paris, the last two digits of a postal code tell you within which *arrondissement* an address is located.

Call ✆ **04-91-02-20-20** for a taxi.

**VISITOR INFORMATION** The **Office de Tourisme** is at 4 la Canebière (www.marseille-tourisme.com; ✆ **08-26-50-05-00;** fax 04-91-13-89-20; Métro: Vieux-Port).

**Daily catch at Vieux-Port.**

## Seeing the Sights

Many travelers never visit the museums, preferring to absorb the life of the city on its busy streets and at its cafes, particularly those along the main street, **La Canebière.** Known as the "Can of Beer" to World War II GIs, it is the heart and soul of Marseille. Lined with hotels, shops, and restaurants, it used to be a very seedy street indeed, saturated with sailors from every nation and people of every nationality. However with the relatively new tramway running along, paired with Marseille's ongoing urban regeneration, it's slowly becoming gentrified.

La Canebière joins the **Vieux-Port ★★**, dominated at its western end by the massive neoclassical forts of St-Jean and St-Nicolas. The harbor is filled with fishing craft and yachts, and ringed by seafood restaurants. For a panoramic view, head to the **Parc du Pharo,** a promontory facing the entrance to the Vieux-Port. From the terrace of the Château du Pharo, built by Napoleon III, you can clearly see the recently redeveloped docklands, now the **Cité de la Méditerranée,** which includes Fort St-Jean and the brand-new **MuCEM** (Museum of European and Mediterranean Civilizations, which will open in 2013), as well as the city's old and new cathedrals.

One of the most efficient, and easiest, ways to see Marseille's centrally located monuments is aboard the fleet of **Le Grand Tour Buses** (www.marseille legrandtour.com; ✆ **04-91-91-05-82;** Métro: Vieux-Port). Each bus is painted white, blue, and yellow, and sports an open-air deck that you'll either appreciate for its unobstructed view or avoid because of its exposure to the searing heat of the midsummer sun. The buses run every month but January; more buses run between March and mid-November (about eight per day, usually 10am to 4:30pm or 5:30pm) than the rest of the year (four per day, usually every other hour 10am–4:30pm). A 1-day pass costs 18€ for adults and 15€ for seniors and students with proper ID; the fare for children ages 4 to 11 is 9€. Two-day passes are available. You can hop off at any of 13 different stops en route and back on to the next bus in the day's sequence, usually arriving between 1 and 2 hours later, depending on the season.

The motorized **Trains Touristiques de Marseille** (www.petit-train-marseille.com; ℭ **04-91-25-24-69**; Métro: Vieux-Port), or *petit-trains*, make circuits around town. Year-round, train no. 1 drives a 75-minute round-trip to Basilique Notre-Dame-de-la-Garde and Basilique St-Victor. From April to mid-November, train no. 2 makes a 65-minute round-trip of old Marseille by way of the cathedral, Vieille Charité, and the Quartier du Panier. Both trains make a 30-minute stop for sightseeing. The trains depart from quai des Belges at the Vieux-Port. The fare for train no. 1 is 7€ for adults and 4€ for children; train no. 2 is 1€ less for both. From mid-June through August, it's also possible to hop aboard the new "By Night" circuit. It runs between 6:40pm and 10:30pm; tickets cost 4€ for adults and 2€ for children.

Boat tours to the **Calanques**, a series of stunning limestone cliffs, fjords, and rocky promontories stretching along the coast for 20km (12 miles) southeast of Marseille, are popular. Many tour operators with different prices and formulas (for example, 3 Calanques in 45 min., or 8 in 2 hr.) can be found on the quai des Belges at the Vieux-Port.

You can also take a 25-minute ferry ride to the **Château d'If,** a national monument built by François I as a fortress to defend Marseille. Alexandre Dumas used it as a setting for the fictional adventures of *The Count of Monte Cristo.* The château is open daily from May 15 to September 20 9:40am to 5:40pm, September 21 through May 14 9am to 5:30pm. It's closed on Mondays between September 15 and March 31.

Entrance to the island is 5.50€ adults, free for children 18 and under (ℭ **04-96-11-03-50;** http://if.monuments-nationaux.fr for information). Boats leave approximately every 45 to 60 minutes, depending on the season; the round-trip transfer is 10€. For information, contact the **Frioul If Express** (www.frioul-if-express.com; ℭ **04-96-11-03-50;** Métro: Vieux-Port).

North of the old port is **Le Panier**, Marseille's original old town, criss-crossed with winding alleys; to its south, the **corniche Président-J.-F.-Kennedy** is a 4km (2½-mile) promenade. You'll pass villas and gardens facing the Mediterranean, before reaching the popular **Plages du Prado.** These spacious, sandy beaches have lifeguards during summer, as well as children's

**Basilique Notre-Dame-de-la-Garde.**

playgrounds, sunloungers and waterside cafes. Serious hikers can continue south of here and on into the Calanques.

**Abbaye St-Victor** ★ RELIGIOUS SITE   This semifortified abbey was built above a crypt from the 5th century, when St. Cassianus founded the church and abbey. You can visit the crypt, which also reflects work done in the 10th and 11th centuries.

3 rue de l'Abbaye. www.saintvictor.net. © **04-96-11-22-60.** Admission to crypt adults 2€, children 1€. Church and crypt open daily 9am–7pm. Head west along quai de Rive-Neuve. Métro: Vieux-Port.

**Basilique Notre-Dame-de-la-Garde** ★ CHURCH   This landmark church crowns a limestone rock overlooking the southern side of the Vieux-Port. It was built in the Romanesque-Byzantine style popular in the 19th century and topped by a 9.7m (32-ft.) gilded statue of the Virgin. Visitors come for the view (best at sunset) from its terrace. Spread out before you are the city, the islands, and the sea.

Rue Fort-du-Sanctuaire. www.notredamedelagarde.com. © **04-91-13-40-80.** Free admission. Daily Apr–Sept 7am–7:15pm, Oct–Mar 7am–6.15pm. Métro: Estrangin-Préfecture. Bus: 60.

**Cathédrale de la Major** CATHEDRAL   One of the largest cathedrals (some 135m/443 ft. long) built in Europe in the 19th century, this massive structure has almost swallowed its 12th-century predecessor, built on the ruins of a temple of Diana. Its striped exterior is in a bastardized Romanesque-Byzantine style with domes and cupolas; the intricate interiors include mosaic floors and red-and-white marble banners.

Place de la Major. © **04-91-90-01-82.** Free admission. Hours vary. Head west of Le Panier district. Métro: Vieux-Port.

**Musée Cantini** ★ ART MUSEUM   The temporary exhibitions in this *hôtel particulier* (private mansion) are often as good as the permanent collection. The latter is dedicated to modern art, specifically fauvism, cubism, surrealism, and abstraction, with masterpieces by Picasso, de Stael, Ernst, and others. The museum was fully renovated in 2012 as part of the city's preparations for European Capital of Culture 2013.

19 rue Grignan. © **04-91-54-77-75.** Admission 3€ adults, 2€ seniors, free for children 18 and under. June–Sept Tues–Sun 11am–6pm; Oct–May Tues–Sun 10am–5pm. Métro: Estrangin/Préfecture.

**Musée d'Archéologie Méditerranéenne** MUSEUM   Antiquities from all periods and civilizations of the Mediterranean basin are represented here, going all the way back to the Iron Age. Rooms are dedicated to the Near East, Cyprus, Greece, Etruria, and Rome. The Egyptian collection is the most extensive outside of Paris.

2 rue de la Charité. ✆ **04-91-14-58-59.** Admission 3€ adults, 2€ seniors, free for children 18 and under. June–Sept Tues–Sun 11am–6pm; Oct–May Tues–Sun 10am–5pm. Closed public holidays. Métro: Joliette. Bus: 35, 49, 55, or 83. Tram: République-Dames.

**Musée Grobet-Labadié** ★ MUSEUM   After the death of music professor Louis Grobet from the Spanish flu, his wealthy wife, Marie Labadié, bequeathed their house and its rare contents to the city in 1919. Here you'll see Louis XV and Louis XVI furniture, as well as an outstanding collection of medieval Burgundian and Provençal sculpture. Other exhibits showcase 17th-century Gobelin tapestries; 15th- to 19th-century German, Italian, French, and Flemish paintings; and 16th- and 17th-century Italian and French faïence.

140 bd. Longchamp. ✆ **04-91-62-21-82.** Admission 3€ adults, 2€ seniors, free for children 18 and under. June–Sept Tues–Sun 11am–6pm; Oct–May Tues–Sun 10am–5pm. Closed public holidays. Métro: Cinq Avenues. Bus: 81. Tram: Longchamp.

## Shopping

Only Paris and Lyon can compete with Marseille for its breadth and diversity of merchandise. Your best bet is a trip to the **Vieux-Port** and its surrounding streets, crowded with stores of all kinds.

On the rue Paradis and rue Saint Ferréol, you'll find many of the same upscale fashion boutiques found in Paris. There is also a Galeries Lafayette, France's largest chain department store. For more bohemian wear, try **cours Julien** and **rue de la Tour** for richly brocaded and beaded items on offer in North African boutiques.

For unique souvenirs, head to **Ateliers Marcel Carbonel,** 49 rue Neuve-Ste-Catherine (www.santonsmarcelcarbonel.com; ✆ **04-91-13-61-36**). This 70-year-old business specializes in *santons,* clay figurines meant for Christmas nativities. In addition to personalities you may already know, the carefully crafted pieces depict Provençal common folk such as bakers, blacksmiths, and milkmaids. More than 600 figurines sell for 10€ and up.

*Navettes,* small cookies that resemble boats, are a Marseillaise specialty. Flavored with secret ingredients that include orange zest and orange flower water, their origin is subject to debate. Some associate them with the legend of *Les Trois Maries*—Mary Magdalene, Mary Salome, and Mary Jacobe—who reportedly came ashore with St.-Lazarus near Marseille to Christianize ancient Provence. Others say they commemorate the 13th-century tradition of parading a statue of the Virgin from the Abbaye St.-Victor through the streets of Marseille. In any case, the cookies were invented in 1791 and are still sold at **Le Four des Navettes,** 136 rue Sainte (www.fourdesnavettes.com; ✆ **04-91-33-32-12**), for around 8.50€ per dozen.

A sampling of the best markets in Marseille: The **Capucins Market** (Mon–Sat 8am–7pm), place des Capucins, has fruit, herbs, fish, and food products; there is one of the region's most authentic fish markets at **quai des Belges** (daily 8am–1pm) on the old port; **allées de Meilhan,** on La Canebière (Tues and Sat 8am–1pm), sells flowers year-round (from the last Sun in Nov–Dec, vendors sell *santons* in the same location daily 8am–7pm). On **cours Julien** near Notre-Dame du Mont, you'll find a market with fruits, vegetables, and other foods (Tues, Thurs, and Sat 8am–1pm); stamps (Sun 8am–1pm); and second-hand goods (3rd Sun of the month 8am–1pm). Also on cours Julien, there are old-book vendors (3rd Sat of the month 8am–1pm) and organic products (Wed 8am–1pm).

## Where to Eat

**Le Petit Nice** (see p. 540) offers exceptional dining.

**Les Arcenaulx ★ 🎁** PROVENÇAL    At the Vieux Port, this restaurant is captivating for three reasons. One, it's housed in a former weapons arsenal built by the navy of Louis XIV. Two, its tables share space with hundreds of books (it's inside what is now a bookstore and publishing house owned by Jeanne Laffitte, who was instrumental in conserving the building itself). Three, run by Laffitte and her sister, Sabine, the restaurant offers excellent cuisine with a Marseillais accent, such as roasted pigeon or duckling with caramelized quince; roasted scallops with hearts of violet artichokes; and assorted *petites légumes farcies* (Provençal vegetables stuffed with minced veal and herbs).

25 cours d'Estienne d'Orves. www.les-arcenaulx.com. 📞 **04-91-59-80-30.** Reservations recommended. Main courses 17€–34€; fixed-price lunch 20€, dinner 59€; children's menu 10€. AE, DC, MC, V. Mon–Sat noon–2pm and 8–11pm. Métro: Vieux-Port.

**L'Epuisette ★★** SEAFOOD/MEDITERRANEAN    This Michelin-starred restaurant is perched on a rocky outcropping in the tiny fishing port of Vallon des Auffes, 2.5km (1½ miles) south of the Vieux Port along the corniche. Serenely decorated in blue and white, the dining room is separated into intimate spaces by long drapes. A large mirror reflects an unobstructed view of the sea and the Château d'If. The menu is changed three times a year, though classics such as *bouillabaisse* and *bourride* are always available. Examples of other dishes: red mullet with sea urchin risotto, lamb shoulder with spices and bacon, and monkfish *osso buco* with young violet artichokes. If you're willing to go a little out of your way, you'll be rewarded with a memorable meal in one of Marseille's most romantic restaurants.

Vallon des Auffes. www.l-epuisette.fr. 📞 **04-91-52-17-82.** Reservations required. Main courses 40€–48€; fixed-price dinner 60€–125€. AE, MC, V. Tues–Sat 12:15–2:30pm and 7:30–9:30pm. Closed Aug.

**Le Grain du Sel ★ 🎁**    MODERN MEDITERRANEAN    Opened in early 2011, this petite restaurant rapidly stole many a local's heart. Chef Pierre Giannetti dishes up contemporary takes on classic Mediterranean cuisine, his years of cooking in Barcelona shining through: look out for Sardinian gnocchi with clams, seared tuna with chickpeas and scallions, or orzo pasta risotto with truffles. The menu changes daily, depending on morning market finds, and there's a carefully considered wine list. The tiny courtyard out back is a cozy spot for dining on a sunny day. Chef Giannetti has plans to begin supplying much of the restaurant's produce directly from his farm in nearby Martigues.

39 rue de la Paix Marcel Paul. 📞 **04-91-54-47-30.** Reservations recommended. Main courses 21€–28€; fixed-price lunch 14€–17€. MC, V. Tues–Sat noon–1:30pm and 8–9:30pm. Closed Aug.

**La Kahena** TUNISIAN    This welcoming spot is one of the busiest and most respected Tunisian restaurants in a city that's loaded with worthy competitors.

Established in 1976 and set close to the Vieux-Port, it takes its name from a 6th-century-B.C. Tunisian princess who was legendary for uniting all the Berber tribes of North Africa. Served in an ornately tiled, lofted dining room, the menu includes roasted vegetable *méchouia* salad; a succulent version of roasted lamb; and 10 varieties of couscous, including versions with lamb, chicken, fish, spicy sausages known as *merguez*, and a "complete" version with a little bit of everything.

2 rue de la République. ℂ **04-91-90-61-93.** Reservations recommended. Main courses 10€–18€. MC, V. Daily noon–2:30pm and 7:30–10:30pm. Métro: Vieux-Port.

**Le Miramar** ★★★ SEAFOOD   After Le Petit Nice (see below), Le Miramar offers the grandest dining in Marseille. Bouillabaisse aficionados flock here to savor a version that will surely be a culinary highlight of your trip. The Miramar's presentation bears no resemblance to the original rough-and-tumble recipe favored by local fishermen, a way of using the least desirable portion of their catch—the bouillabaisse here involves lots of labor and just as much costly seafood. Fresh fish is poached in saffron-infused soup; the final product is served as two separate courses, accompanied by *rouille*, a mayonnaise-like sauce made with garlic, olive oil, and egg yolks, flavored with cayenne and saffron. The setting is a room with frescoes of underwater life and big windows that open onto the Vieux-Port, plus a sidewalk terrace that overlooks Notre-Dame-de-la-Garde. For diners keen to recreate an identical meal at home, Miramar runs bouillabaisse cooking classes (120€, 5-hr. lesson including lunch). Contact the Marseille Tourist Office for further details.

12 quai du Port. www.bouillabaisse.com. ℂ **04-91-91-10-40.** Reservations recommended. Main courses 31€–45€; bouillabaisse from 59€ per person (minimum 2). AE, DC, MC, V. Tues–Sat noon–2pm and 7–10pm. Métro: Vieux-Port.

**Toinou** SEAFOOD   In a massive building that overshadows every other structure nearby, this landmark restaurant serves more shellfish than any other restaurant in Marseille. They even deliver. There's no question where your meal comes from—the fish market is just down the road. Dining rooms are on three floors, served by a waitstaff who are true *Marseillais*, from their accents right down to their attitudes. Don't come here unless you're really fond of shellfish, over 40 species of which can be served raw or cooked. The wine list is extensive, with excellent whites and rosés from nearby Cassis and Bandol.

3 cours St-Louis. www.toinou.com. ℂ **08-11-45-45-45.** Reservations recommended. Shellfish by 6 or the dozen 1.40€–31€; fixed-price platter for 2 people 34€, or 86€ with lobster. DC, MC, V. Daily 11:30am–11:30pm. Métro: Vieux-Port.

# Marseille Nightlife

For an amusing and relatively harmless exposure to the town's saltiness, walk around the **Vieux-Port,** where cafes and restaurants angle their sightlines for the best view of the harbor.

**L'Escale Borély,** avenue Pierre-Mendès-France, is 20 minutes south of the town center (take bus no. 83 or 19). With a dozen bars and cafes, plus restaurants of every possible ethnicity, you'll be spoiled for choice. The animated promenade buzzes at night. There is the potential for conversation with friendly strangers. It's a hint of Santa Monica in Marseille.

Unless the air-conditioning is powerful, Marseille's dance clubs produce a lot of sweat, especially **Le Passe Temps,** 6 rue Fortia (www.lepassetemps.net;

**℃ 06-77-02-22-46;** Métro: Vieux-Port), a small club that accommodates only 80 people. Music aficionados praise the playlist here, and it's open from midnight till dawn. You can also try the nearby **Trolley Bus,** 24 quai de Rive-Neuve (www.letrolley.com; **℃ 04-91-54-30-45;** Métro: Vieux-Port), known for techno, house, hip-hop, jazz, and salsa.

For jazz right on the port, head to **La Caravelle,** 34 quai du Port (www.lacaravelle-marseille.fr; **℃ 04-91-90-36-64;** Métro: Vieux-Port), an aperitif bar and dinner club that serves a different flavor almost every night, including *manouche,* the French gypsy style most associated with Django Reinhardt. **Le Paradox,** 127 rue d'Aubagne (www.leparadox.fr; **℃ 04-91-63-14-65;** Métro: Notre-Dame du Mont/cours Julien), is a restaurant and concert venue featuring a wide variety of indie musicians playing everything from folk to rock, to world music, starting at around 10pm. At least once a month, there is a DJ night, focusing mainly on funk.

More animated is **l'Exit,** 12 quai de Rive-Neuve (**℃ 04-91-54-29-43;** Métro: Vieux-Port), a bar/disco with a terrace that profits from Marseille's sultry nights, and two floors of seething nocturnal energy (happy hour starts at 5pm). The **New Can Can,** 3–7 rue Sénac (www.newcancan.com; **℃ 04-91-48-59-76**), is a lively, sprawling bar-and-disco that identifies itself as a gay venue but draws many straight folks too. On Sunday nights, there are cabaret performances at 2am. Fridays and Saturdays are themed nights with names like "French Kiss" and "Special Blondes" (Madonna, Britney, and Gaga, whether you worship them or just want to dress like them). Open Thursday through Sunday from 11pm until dawn, there is no cover charge except on Friday and Saturday (15€).

# Where to Stay

## VERY EXPENSIVE

**Le Petit Nice ★★★**   This is the most prestigious address in Marseille. It opened in 1917, when the Passédat family joined two villas in a secluded area below a main street paralleling the beach. The spacious Marina Wing across from the main building offers rooms individually decorated in an antique style, opening onto sea views. The rooms in the main house are more modern and avant-garde. Four units are inspired by the cubist movement, with posh geometric appointments and bright colors. The triple Michelin-starred restaurant is beautiful, if pricey, with a view of the Mediterranean and the Calanques. In summer, dinner is served in the garden facing the sea.

Anse-de-Maldormé, corniche Président-J.-F.-Kennedy, Marseille 13007. www.petitnice-passedat.com. **℃ 04-91-59-25-92.** Fax 04-91-59-28-08. 16 units. 150€–685€ double; 535€–1,165€ suite. AE, DC, MC, V. Free parking. **Amenities:** Restaurant; bar; babysitting; free bikes; outdoor pool; room service. *In room:* A/C, TV, hair dryer, minibar, free Wi-Fi.

**Sofitel Marseille Vieux Port ★★★**   This five-star hotel is the highest-rated lodging in the city. Less exclusive than Le Petit Nice, it's a glistening modern palace, towering above the embankments of the old port. Some guest rooms have panoramic views of the Vieux-Port; all are chic, elegant, and fairly generous in size. Buffet breakfast at the hotel's top-floor restaurant, Les Trois Forts, is award-winning—as well as tropical smoothies, smoked salmon and omelettes, look out for delicious sugar-free and gluten-free offerings too. Guests can use the hotel's steam baths, Jacuzzi, and outdoor pool; alternatively staff can provide a local jogging map. The hotel is about a 15-minute walk to the city center.

36 bd. Charles-Livon, Marseille 13007. www.sofitel.com. ✆ **04-91-15-59-00.** Fax 04-91-15-59-50. 134 units. 174€–550€ double; 660€–1,080€ suite. AE, DC, MC, V. Parking 18€. Métro: Vieux-Port. **Amenities:** Restaurant; bar; babysitting; outdoor pool, room service; spa. *In room:* A/C, TV, hair dryer, minibar, free Wi-Fi.

## EXPENSIVE

### Grand Hotel Beauvau Vieux Port ★★  Now completely restored, the Beauvau is the oldest hotel in Marseille, having hosted Frédéric Chopin and George Sand in the 19th century. It is decorated in the various epoch styles of France, including Louis XIII, Napoleon III, and Empire—in line with new hotel chain MGallery's hip and historical branding. The bedrooms are well furnished and comfortable; suites come with terraces. The two-story duplex suite is a good choice for families. There is no restaurant on-site, but many are available nearby. The hotel bar overlooks the port.

4 rue Beauvau, Marseille 13001. www.accorhotels.com. ✆ **04-91-54-91-00.** Fax 04-91-54-15-76. 73 units. 125€–275€ double; 315€–575€ suite. AE, DC, MC, V. **Amenities:** Bar; breakfast room; room service. *In room:* A/C, TV, hair dryer, minibar, free Wi-Fi.

## MODERATE

### Casa Honoré 🛏  Just south of the Vieux Port, this snug bed and breakfast resides within a former print shop. Interior designer Annick Lestrohan, creator of the Honoré brand of homewares, has transformed what was once her family home into a chic, ultra-contemporary "mini-hotel." Floors are polished concrete; much of the furnishings have been created from reclaimed wood. Like a Moroccan riad, all four rooms look out over the courtyard's bougainvillea-trimmed swimming pool. Note that like many B&Bs, Annick and her husband continue to live on the premises.

123 rue Sainte, Marseille 13007. www.casahonore.com. ✆ **04-96-11-01-62.** 4 units. 150€–200€ double. MC, V. **Amenities:** Breakfast room; outdoor pool. *In room:* A/C, TV, free Wi-Fi.

### Hôtel le Corbusier ★  The radical designs of Swiss-born architect Le Corbusier (aka Charles-Edouard Jeanneret, 1887–1965) have long been associated with Marseille. Between 1952 and 1954, he designed La Cité Radieuse, a nine-story building that combines shops and apartments for 1,500 residents. The plans included a hotel, which, beginning in 1959, opened its doors on the building's third and fourth floors.

The current owners, Alban and Dominique Gérardin, are dedicated to the combination of expressionism and functionalism for which Le Corbusier was known: rooms are outfitted with the kind of spartan and functional furniture, lighting fixtures, and accessories of which the architect would have approved. Note that fire damage to the building means both the hotel and its restaurant, Le Ventre de l'Architecte, were temporarily closed down in early 2012. The hotel's location, 2km (1¼ miles) south of Vieux-Port, means you'll have to access most of the city's attractions by public transport or vehicle.

On the 3rd and 4th floors of La Cité Radieuse, 280 bd. Michelet, Marseille 13008. www.hotelle corbusier.com. ✆ **04-91-16-78-00.** Fax 04-91-16-78-28. 21 units. 70€–129€ double; 139€ suite. MC, V. Bus: 21. **Amenities:** Restaurant; bar; exercise room; rooftop jogging track; wading pool for children. *In room:* A/C, TV, fridge, Wi-Fi (4€ per hour).

### New Hôtel Bompard  This tranquil retreat, built after World War II, lies atop a cliff along the corniche, about 3km (1¼ miles) east of the Vieux-Port. Partly

because of its garden, it may remind you of a well-appointed apartment complex. A separate Provençal *mas* houses four large rooms that are more luxurious and atmospheric than those in the main building. Some have canopy beds, and all come with large bathrooms featuring tub/showers. Rooms in the main building are less expensive, more modern, and streamlined, but not terribly romantic.

2 rue des Flots Bleus, Marseille 13007. www.new-hotel.com. ⓒ **04-91-99-22-22.** Fax 04-91-31-02-14. 51 units. 160€–180€ standard double; 180€–220€ Provençal *mas* double. AE, DC, MC, V. Free parking. **Amenities:** Restaurant; bar; outdoor pool. *In room:* A/C, TV, hair dryer, minibar, free Wi-Fi.

### INEXPENSIVE

**Aux Vieux Panier** ◢  Tucked into the heart of Le Panier, Marseille's Old Town, this unique bed and breakfast occupies two floors of a pretty 17th-century townhouse. A different international artist has decorated each one of the hotel's five rooms, from Provençal local Clement Jolin to L.A.-raised Justin Blyth: expect clean lines, quirky accessories and plenty of unique photographs and prints. A rotating roster of exhibitions fills the corridors and common spaces. The panoramic roof terraces takes in cityscapes from Notre-Dame-de-la-Garde to Marseille's brand-new Zaha Hadid-designed skyscraper. A buffet breakfast is served.

13 rue du Panier, Marseille 13002. www.auvieuxpanier.com. ⓒ **04-91-91-23-72.** 5 units. 85€–120€ double. MC, V. **Amenities:** Breakfast room. *In room:* A/C, TV, hair dryer, free Wi-Fi.

# ILES D'HYÈRES ★

39km (24 miles) SE of Toulon; 119km (74 miles) SW of Cannes

Off the Riviera in the Mediterranean, a small group of islands encloses the southern boundary of the Hyères anchorage. During the Renaissance, they were called the Iles d'Or (Golden Islands), named for the glow the rocks give off in sunlight. Nothing today hints at their turbulent past, when they were attacked by pirates and Turkish galleys, or saw Allied landings during World War II.

As you might expect, their location only half an hour from the French coast means the islands are packed with tourists in summer. Thousands of day-trippers arrive, often with children, for a day of sun, sand, and people-watching.

If you have time for only one island, choose the beautiful, lively Ile des Porquerolles. The Ile de Port-Cros is quieter—and perhaps better for an overnight stay in order to take advantage of the great hiking, biking, and snorkeling that would be too rushed for a 6-hour day trip. As for the Ile du Levant, 80% belongs to the French army and is used for missile testing; the majority of the remainder is a nudist colony.

## Essentials

**GETTING TO ILE DE PORQUEROLLES**  Ferries leave from several points along the Côte d'Azur. The most frequent, most convenient, and shortest trip is from the harbor of La Tour Fondue on the peninsula of Giens, a 32km (20-mile) drive east of Toulon. Depending on the season, there are 5 to 19 departures per day. The round-trip fare for the 15-minute crossing is 18€ for adults, 16€ for children 4 to 10. For information, call the **Transports Maritimes et Terrestres du Littoral Varois,** La Tour Fondue, Giens 83400 (www.tlv-tvm.com; ⓒ **04-94-58-21-81**). The next-best option is the ferry from Port Miramar in La Londe-les-Maures, 18km (11 miles) east of Giens, operated by the **Bateliers de la Côte d'Azur** (www.bateliersdelacoted azur.com; ✆ **04-94-05-21-14**). There are three to four daily departures between April and October only (trip time: 30 min.; 23€ adults, 15.50€ children 4–11 round-trip). Another option is **Les Vedettes Ile d'Or & Le Corsaire** (www.vedettesilesdor.fr; ✆ **04-94-71-01-02**). They depart from the *Gare Maritime* in either Le Lavandou (trip time: 40 min.; 34.20€ adults, 26.50€ children 4–12 round-trip) or Cavalaire (trip time: 90 min.; 39.50€ adults, 32€ children 4–12 round-trip).

**GETTING TO ILE DE PORT-CROS**    The most popular ferry route to the island is the 35-minute crossing that departs from Le Lavadou 3 to 7 times daily, depending on the season (27€ adults, 22€ children 4–12 round-trip). For information, contact **Les Vedettes Ile d'Or & Le Corsaire** (www.vedettesilesdor.fr; ✆ **04-94-71-01-02**). The company also runs a ferry once daily from Cavalaire during July and August (trip time: 1 hr.; 31€ adults, 25€ children 4–12 round-trip). The **Transports Maritimes et Terrestres du Littoral Varois** and **Bateliers de la Côte d'Azur** (see above) also service Ile de Port-Cros. Some of the former's services also stop at Ile de Levant en route.

**VISITOR INFORMATION**    Other than temporary, summer-only kiosks without phones that distribute brochures and advice near the ferry docks in Porquerolles and Port-Cros, there are no tourist bureaus on the islands. The offices in Hyères and Toulon try to fill in the gaps. Contact the **Office de Tourisme,** Rotonde du Park Hôtel, av. de Belgique, Hyères (www.hyerestourisme.com; ✆ **04-94-01-84-50**), or the **Office de Tourisme,** 12 place Louis Blanc, Toulon (www.toulontourisme.com; ✆ **04-94-18-53-00**). Information can also be found at www.porquerolles.com.

# Ile de Porquerolles ★

Ile de Porquerolles is the largest and westernmost of the Iles d'Hyères. It has a rugged south coast, but the northern strand, facing the mainland, boasts a handful of pristine white sand beaches. The island is about 8km (5 miles) long and 2km (1¼ miles) wide, and is 4.8km (3 miles) from the mainland. The permanent population is only 400.

The island is said to receive 275 days of sunshine annually. The landscape is one of rocky capes, pine forests twisted by the mistral, sun-drenched vineyards, and pale ocher houses. The **place d'Armes,** former site of the garrison, is home to several quaint cafes—your best bet for lunch if you're just here for a day trip.

The island has a history of raids, attacks, and occupation by everyone from the Dutch and the English to the Turks and the Spaniards. Ten forts, some in ruins, testify to its fierce past. The most ancient is **Fort Ste-Agathe,** built in 1531 by François I. In time, it was a penal colony and a retirement center for soldiers of the colonial wars.

In 1971, the French government purchased a large part of the island and turned it into a national park. Indigenous trees such as fig, mulberry, and olive are protected, as well as plants that attract butterflies.

## WHERE TO EAT & STAY

**Hotel et Residence Les Medes ★**    This hotel is 400m (1,312 ft.) from Courtade Beach and only a short walk from the wharf. Simple guest rooms

**Beach at Ile de Porquerolles.**

and apartments are available; all come with a kitchenette, and some have bunk beds for children. The more desirable units open onto private terraces with a view. Guests gather in the lounge, with its bar, fireplace, and public Internet. Main courses in the simple restaurant include local seafood with Asian accents (fish and scallop ceviche with mango, sesame-peanut crusted prawns) and Moroccan-style tagine. There is a coin laundry nearby, making this hotel a good choice for families.

Rue de la Douane, Porquerolles 83400. www.hotel-les-medes.fr. ☎ **04-94-12-41-24.** Fax 04-94-58-32-49. 48 units. 95€–223€ double; 174€–478€ apartment. MC, V. Closed Nov 8–Dec 26. **Amenities:** Restaurant; bar. *In room:* A/C, TV, free Wi-Fi.

### Mas du Langoustier ★★

In a large park on the island's western tip—secluded from most of the tourists—this tranquil resort hotel is an old *mas* with a view of a lovely pine-ringed bay. Employees greet guests in minivan by the jetty. The rooms, in antique Provençal style, are the most elegantly decorated on the island. Bathrooms are roomy, and most have tub/showers. Should you visit for a meal, the hotel's Michelin-starred restaurant is the islands' only seriously gourmet spot. Dishes such as seared *rougets* (red mullet) with artichoke hearts, or olive-crusted lamb filet are featured; the wine list includes Ile du Porquerolles vintages. The hotel's second restaurant is for guests only (half-board is mandatory). The Langoustier is the only luxury hotel on the islands—a fact reflected by its rates.

Ile de Porquerolles 83400. www.langoustier.com. ☎ **04-94-58-30-09.** Fax 04-94-58-36-02. 50 units. 215€–310€ double; 335€–345€ suite; 320€–330€ apartment. Rates include half-board. MC, V. Closed Oct to late Apr. **Amenities:** 2 restaurants; bar; babysitting; outdoor pool; tennis court. *In room:* A/C, TV, minibar, free Wi-Fi.

# Ile de Port-Cros ★

The most mountainous island of the archipelago, Port-Cros has been France's smallest national park since 1963. It's just 5km (3 miles) long and 2km (1¼ miles) wide. Though the island was devastated by a fire in 1892, today it's blanketed with beautiful beaches, pine forests, and subtropical vegetation (birders flock here to observe nearly 100 different species). A hiker's paradise, it also has a number of well-marked trails. The most popular and scenic is the easy, one-hour *sentier des plantes.* The more adventurous and athletic take the 10km (6¼-mile) *circuit de Port-Man* (and pack their lunch). There is even a 274m (899-ft.) "underwater trail" along the coast where you can snorkel past laminated signs identifying the plants and fish you'll see. See www.portcrosparcnational.fr for information.

## WHERE TO EAT & STAY

**Le Manoir de Hélène**   This is the only bona fide hotel on the Ile de Port-Cros. Originally, it was the grandiose home of the family that owned the island (the hotel is run by their descendants). Today it consists of an 18th-century whitewashed and turreted main building, plus an annex containing most of the guest rooms. Accommodations are basic, but the point is to take advantage of your surroundings—by hiking around the island or lounging by the pool, surrounded by eucalyptus trees. Half-board is mandatory; dinner includes local fish and cheeses.

Ile de Port-Cros 83400. http://hotelmanoirportcros.monsite-orange.fr. ✆ **04-94-05-90-52.** Fax 04-94-05-90-89. 22 units. 170€–210€ double; 200€–370€ suite. MC, V. Closed Oct–Apr. **Amenities:** Restaurant; bar; outdoor pool; room service. *In room:* Hair dryer.

# THE FRENCH RIVIERA

by Tristan Rutherford

**15**

**E**ach resort on the French Riviera, also known as the Côte d'Azur (Azure Coast), offers its own unique flavor and charms. This fabled real estate, ribboning for 200km (125 miles) along the Mediterranean, has long attracted artists and jet set alike with its clear skies, blue waters, and a carefree cafe culture.

A trail of modern artists captivated by the light and setting has left a rich heritage: Matisse at Vence, Cocteau at Villefranche, Léger at Biot, Renoir at Cagnes, and Picasso at Antibes and seemingly everywhere else. The finest collection of artworks is at the Foundation Maeght in St-Paul-de-Vence. New museums dedicated to Jean Cocteau in Menton and Pierre Bonnard near Cannes offer a colorful introduction to the Riviera's art scene.

A century ago, winter and spring were considered high season on the Riviera. In recent decades, July and August have become the most crowded months, and reservations are imperative. The region basks in over 300 days of sun per year, and even December and January are often clement and bright.

The ribbonlike corniche roads stretch across the western Riviera from Nice to Menton. They have been depicted in scores of films, including Cary Grant's *To Catch a Thief* and Robert de Niro's *Ronin*. The Alps literally drop into the Mediterranean here, and roads were carved along the way. The lower road, the 32km (20 miles) long Corniche Inférieure, takes in the resorts of Villefranche, Cap-Ferrat, Beaulieu, Monaco, and Cap-Martin. The 31km (19-mile) Moyenne Corniche (Middle Road) winds in and out of mountain tunnels and takes in the picture-perfect village of Eze. Napoleon built the Grande Corniche—the most panoramic—in 1806. La Turbie is the principal town along the 32km (20-mile) stretch, which reaches more than 480m (1,574 ft.) high at Col d'Eze.

**Note:** For more extensive coverage of this region, check out *Frommer's Provence & the Riviera*.

# ST-TROPEZ ★★

874km (542 miles) S of Paris; 76km (47 miles) SW of Cannes

An air of hedonism runs rampant in this sun-kissed town, but Tropezian style is blissfully understated—not in-your-face. St-Tropez attracts artists, novelists, and the film colony each summer, with a flamboyant parade of humanity trailing behind. In winter it morphs back into a boho fishing village, albeit one studded with modern art galleries and some of the best restaurants along the coast.

The Brigitte Bardot movie *And God Created Woman* put St-Tropez on the tourist map. Yet more decadent tourists, baring almost all on the peninsula's white-sand beaches, followed in her wake. In 1995, Bardot pronounced St-Tropez dead, "squatted by a lot of no-goods, drugheads, and villains." But 1997 saw her return, followed in recent years by celebrity A-listers including Keith Richards, David Beckham, Paris Hilton, Jay-Z, and Beyoncé.

# Essentials

**GETTING THERE**   The nearest rail station is in St-Raphaël, a neighboring coastal resort. **Boats** depart (www.bateauxsaintraphael.com; ✆ **04-94-95-17-46**) from its Vieux Port for St-Tropez (trip time: 50 min.) every 15 minutes in high summer, reducing to twice-daily sailings in winter. The one-way fare is 14€. Year-round, 10 to 15 Varlib **buses** per day leave from the Gare Routière in St-Raphaël (✆ **04-94-44-52-70**; www.varlib.fr) for St-Tropez. The trip takes 1½ to 2 hours, depending on the bus and the traffic, which during midsummer is usually horrendous. A one-way ticket costs 2€. Buses and boats run directly to St-Tropez from Toulon and Hyères. Buses also run from the nearest airport, at Toulon-Hyères, 56km (35 miles) away.

If you **drive,** note that parking in St-Tropez is very difficult, especially in summer. For parking, follow the signs for **Parking des Lices** (✆ **04-94-97-34-46**), beneath place des Lices, or **Parking du Nouveau Port,** on waterfront avenue Charles de Gaulle (✆ **04-94-97-74-99**). To get here from **Cannes,** drive southwest along the coastal highway (RD98), turning east when you see signs pointing to St-Tropez.

**VISITOR INFORMATION**   The **Office de Tourisme** is on quai Jean-Jaurès (www.ot-saint-tropez.com; ✆ **08-92-68-48-28**; fax 04-94-97-82-66).

# A Day at the Beach

The hottest Riviera beaches are at St-Tropez. The best for families are closest to the center, including **Plage de la Bouillabaisse, Plage des Graniers,** and **Plage des Salins.** More daring is the 5km (3-mile) crescent of **Plage de Pampelonne,** about 10km (6¼ miles) from St-Tropez. Here around 35 hedonistic beach clubs dot the sand. For better or worse, the cash-only **La Voile Rouge**—where Champagne was sprayed over diners, who regularly proceeded to dance on the table tops—closed in late 2011. Equally decadent is **Club 55** (www.club55. fr; ✆ **04-94-55-55-55**) a former Bardot hangout, while American-run **Nikki Beach** (www.nikkibeach.com; ✆ **04-94-79-82-04**) is younger and more understated, but nevertheless painfully chic. Gay-friendly **Aqua Club** (www.aqua-club-plage.fr; ✆ **04-94-79-84-35**) and bare-all **Plage de Tahiti** (www. tahiti-beach.com; ✆ **04-94-97-18-02**) are extremely welcoming. More relaxed still are **Tropicana** (✆ **04-94-79-83-96**) and **Plage des Jumeaux** (www. plagedesjumeaux.com; ✆ **04-94-55-21-80**), the latter drawing many families with young kids.

You'll need a car, bike, or scooter to get from town to Plage de Pampelonne. Parking is around 10€ for the day. More than anywhere else on the Riviera, topless bathing is the norm.

# Outdoor Pursuits

**BOATING**   In St-Tropez port, **Octopussy** (www.octopussy.fr; ✆ **04-94-56-53-10**) rents boats 5 to 16m (16–52 ft.) long. Larger ones come with a captain at the helm. Prices begin at 320€ per day.

**DIVING**   Multilingual scuba tuition and equipment hire is available from the **European Diving School** (www.europeandiving.com; ✆ **04-94-79-90-37**), on Plage de Pampelonne. Regular dives, including all equipment, cost 37€.

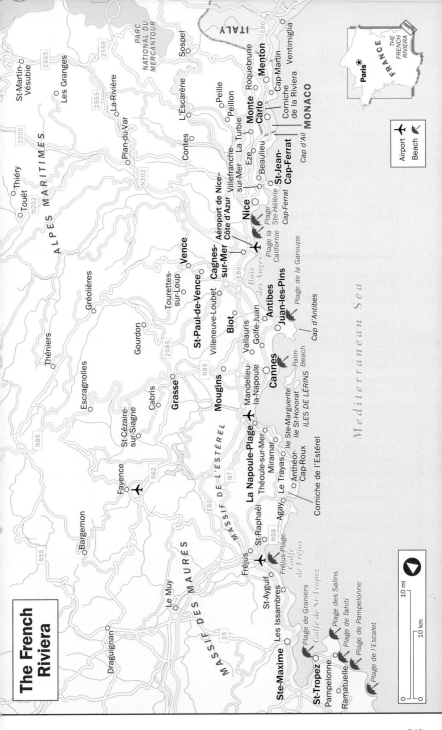

# The French Riviera

# Shopping

St-Tropez is awash with stylish shops. The merchandise is mostly Mediterranean, breezy, and sophisticated. Chic labels include Hermès, Sonia Rykiel, and Dior. The Chanel outlet opened as a pop-up shop inside the old Hotel la Mistralée near place des Lices in 2012, but will move into the Hotel de Paris, St-Tropez's newest hotel, in 2013. There are also scores of one-off designers around the Vieille Ville (old town), on rue Gambetta, and near place des Lices, which also hosts an excellent **outdoor market,** Marché Provençal, with food, clothes, and *brocante* on Tuesday and Saturday mornings. **Galeries Tropéziennes,** 56 rue Gambetta (✆ **04-94-97-02-21**), packs loads of leather, designer clothes, and shoe stores into its showrooms near place des Lices.

# Exploring the City

At the foot of St-Tropez's yacht-filled port lies the bronze **Statue de Suffren,** paying tribute to Vice Admiral Pierre André de Suffren. This St-Tropez native was one of the greatest sailors of 18th-century France and fought in the Franco-American wars against the British in the 1780s.

In the old town, one of the most interesting streets is **rue de la Miséricorde.** It's lined with stone houses that hold boutiques and evokes medieval St-Tropez better than any other in town. At the corner of rue Gambetta is **Chapelle de la Miséricorde,** with a blue, green, and gold tile roof. Towering above town is the **Citadelle,** a fortified castle complete with drawbridges and stunning views across the Bay of St-Tropez. It's open daily from 10am to 6:30pm (until 5:30pm from October to March). Admission is 2.50€; entrance is free for those 8 and under.

**Port Grimaud** ★ makes an interesting outing. From St-Tropez, drive 4km (2¼ miles) west on A98 to route 98, and then 1.5km (1 mile) north to the Port Grimaud exit. If you approach the village at dusk, when it's bathed in Riviera pastels, it looks like a 16th-century hamlet. However, the vision is a mirage: Port Grimaud is the dream of its promoter, architect François Spoerry, who carved it out of marshland and dug canals. Flanking the canals, fingers of land extend from the square to the sea. The homes are Provençal style, many with Italianate window arches. Boat owners can anchor at their doorsteps, and visitors can putter around the 'village' on a rented electric boat. One newspaper called the port "the most magnificent fake since Disneyland."

**Musée de l'Annonciade (Musée St-Tropez)** ★★   Near the harbor, this museum showcases one of the Riviera's finest modern art collections of post-Impressionist masters. Many of the artists, including Paul Signac, painted the port of St-Tropez, a backdrop that lies right outside the building. The collection includes such works as Van Dongen's *Women of the Balustrade* and paintings and sculpture by Bonnard, Matisse, Braque, Dufy, Marquet, Seurat, Derain, and Maillol.

Quai de l'Epi le Port. ✆ **04-94-17-84-10.** Admission 6€ adults, 4€ children 11 and under. July–Oct daily 10am–noon and 2–6pm; Dec–Jun Wed–Mon 10am–noon and 2–6pm.Closed Nov.

# Where to Eat

**Auberge des Maures** ★ PROVENÇAL   One of our favorite restaurants lies close to one end of the all-pedestrian rue Allard. The stone-sided building, highlighted with Provençal murals, has a rollaway roof and garden seating (both

Church ✝

Information ⓘ

**St-Tropez**

*Golfe de St-Tropez*

Tour du Portalet

La Glaye

Tour Vieille

La Ponche

**Paris** ✶

FRANCE

St-Tropez

Citadelle

Môle Jean-Réveille

quai F. Mistral

Château Suffren

Hôtel de Ville

place du Revelin

To Plage des Graniers

quai J.-Jaurès

Eglise

place des Remparts

rue des Remparts

rue du Clocher

place de l'Ormeau

Tour Jarlier

Montée de la Citadelle

*Vieux Port*

ⓘ

rue du Portail Neuf

rue du Petit Bal

av. Paul-Signac

quai de l'Epi

quai Suffren

Statue de Suffren

rue Gambetta

rue de la Miséricorde

Chapelle de la Miséricorde

**Musée de l'Annonciade**

quai G.-Péri

av. du 8 Mai 1945

av. du 11 Nov. 1918

rue Mermoz

rue H.-Seillon

rue Gén.-Allard

rue des Tisserands

rue F.-Sibill

rue G.-Clemenceau

av. du Maréchal-Foch

Montée G.-Ringrave

place Carnot

rue Morbier

rue J.-Quaranta

bd. Vasserot

place des Lices

place de la Croix-de-Fer

bd. Louis-Blanc

place du XVe Corps

av. A.-Grangeon

Théâtre

av. Gén.-Leclerc

rue de la Résistance

To Plages de Tahiti, Pampellone, Moorea, Bora-Bora

To Plage des Salins

rue du Temple

↓ To Plage de Bouillabase

↓ To Chapelle Ste-Anne

0 ___ 100 yds

0 ___ 100 m

experienced during nice weather). The open kitchen affords views of the staff preparing Provençal specialties, including stuffed zucchini blossoms and *gigot d'agneau* (lamb with rosemary confit), and *petits farcis* (stuffed vegetables). The Salinesi family takes pride in using seasonal, all-fresh ingredients.

4 rue du Docteur Boutin. www.aubergedesmaures.fr. ⓒ **04-94-97-01-50.** Reservations recommended. Main courses 42€–60€; fixed-price menu 51€. AE, DC, MC, V. Daily 7:30pm–1am. Closed mid-Nov to Mar.

**Salama** ★ MOROCCAN 🍴 Regulars claim it serves the best couscous on the Cote d'Azur. On a narrow backstreet leading up from St Tropez's main harbor, Salama is a true find without the pretence or prices of other resort restaurants. Dinner is served in an oriental salon or alfresco in a small Moroccan garden. Kick off with bowls of hummus, spicy tomato dip, and roast aubergine puree. Mains include lamb tajine, slow-baked with prunes, dates, and North African spices. Moroccan wine is served along with classic French vintages. Meals may be rounded out by sticky-sweet desserts, and a glass of mint tea.

1 rue des Tisserands. ⓒ **04-94-97-59-62.** Reservations recommended. Main courses 18€–31€. AE, MC, V. Daily 8pm–1am. Closed Nov–Mar.

**Pizzeria Bruno** ITALIAN 🍴 This cozy hole-in-the wall diner has been whipping out peerless pizzas from its wood-fired oven since 1959. Even Bardot was once a regular. A limited menu of grilled meats and steaks also features, as do five top-notch salads including Niçoise and *aux coquilles Saint-Jacques,* the latter brimming with warm scallops, green beans, potato, and onion. While the flavors and prices rank among St-Tropez's best, the stool and banquette seating is far from the most comfortable in town.

2 rue de l'Eglise. ☎ **04-94-97-05-18.** Main courses 11€–18€. AE, MC, V. Daily noon–2pm and 7:30pm–midnight. Closed Oct–Apr.

**Spoon Byblos** ★★ FRENCH/INTERNATIONAL Originally launched in Paris, Spoon's Riviera incarnation draws special inspiration from Catalonian, Andalusian, and Moroccan cuisine. It also offers more than 300 wines from around the world. It's terribly fashionable, as you might expect, given its location in one of the world's hippest hotels. Diners are advised to concentrate on the imaginative cuisine rather than the self-conscious sense of chic. The restaurant opens onto a circular bar made of blue-tinted glass and polished stainless steel. Dig into shrimp and squid consommé with a hint of jasmine and orange, or pan-seared tuna. Local favourites for two people sharing include farm-reared shoulder of lamb with fennel and *socca* pancakes, and whole-roasted lobster with onion confit.

In the Hôtel Byblos, av. Paul Signac. ☎ **04-94-56-68-20.** Reservations required. Main courses 25€–49€; fixed-price menu 86€. AE, DC, MC, V. Daily 8–11pm. Closed Nov to mid-Apr.

## St-Tropez Nightlife

On the lobby level of the Hôtel Byblos, **Les Caves du Roy,** avenue Paul Signac (☎ **04-94-97-16-02**), is the most self-consciously chic nightclub in St-Tropez. Entrance is free, but drink prices are eye-wateringly high. Any riffraff (or paparazzi, for that matter) are kept away from the beautiful people by owner Jean de Colmont. It's open nightly from Easter to late September from 11:30pm until dawn. **Le Papagayo,** in the Résidence du Nouveau-Port, rue Gambetta (☎ **04-94-97-95-95**), is one of the largest nightclubs in town. The decor was inspired by the psychedelic 1960s. Entrance is around 20€ and includes one drink, although those dining at the attached restaurant can routinely sneak in free. Adjacent to Le Papagayo is **Le VIP Room,** in the Résidence du Nouveau-Port (☎ **04-94-97-14-70**), a younger yet similarly chic version of Les Caves du Roy. Paris Hilton and Snoop Dogg have been known to drop by. Cocktails hover around the 20€ mark.

**Le Pigeonnier,** 13 rue de la Ponche (☎ **04-94-97-84-26**), rocks, rolls, and welcomes a mostly gay or lesbian crowd between 20 and 50. Most of the socializing revolves around the long, narrow bar, where patrons from all over Europe chatter. There's also a dance floor. **L'Esquinade,** 2 rue de Four (☎ **04-94-56-26-21**), is the habitual sweaty follow-on club.

Below the Hôtel Sube, **Café de Paris,** sur le Port (☎ **04-94-97-00-56**), is one of the most popular—and most friendly—hangouts in town. It has 1900s-style globe lights, an occasional 19th-century bronze artifact, masses of artificial flowers, and a long zinc bar. **Café Sénéquier,** sur le Port (☎ **04-94-97-00-90**), is historic, venerable, snobbish by day, and off-puttingly stylish by night.

## Where to Stay

### VERY EXPENSIVE

**Hôtel Byblos** ★★★ The builder said he created "an anti-hotel, a place like home." That's true—if your home resembles a palace in Beirut and has salons decorated with Phoenician gold statues from 3000 B.C. On a hill above the harbor, this complex has intimate patios and courtyards. It's filled with antiques and rare objects such as polychrome carved woodwork and marquetry floors. Every room is unique, and all have elegant beds. Unusual features might include a fireplace on a raised hearth or a bed recessed on a dais. The rooms range in size from medium to spacious, often with high ceilings and antiques or reproductions. Some units have such special features as four-posters with furry spreads or sunken whirlpool tubs. Le Hameau, a stylish annex, contains 10 duplex suites built around a small courtyard with an outdoor spa. However, service can be snooty, and the crown of St Tropez's coolest hotel may pass from Byblos to the new Hotel de Paris, when the latter opens for its first full season in 2013.

Av. Paul Signac, St-Tropez 83990. www.byblos.com. ℰ **04-94-56-68-00.** Fax 04-94-56-68-01. 91 units. 395€–950€ double; from 650€ suite. AE, DC, MC, V. Parking 30€. Closed Nov–Mar. **Amenities:** 2 restaurants; 1 bar; nightclub; babysitting; concierge; exercise room; massage; outdoor pool; room service; sauna; spa. *In room:* A/C, TV, hair dryer, minibar, free Wi-Fi.

**Hôtel Sezz ★★ ☺** This designer dream took on the mantle of St-Tropez's hippest hotel with the opening of 35 wow-factor suites in 2010, plus 2 stand-out villas in 2011. Accomplished French hotelier Shahé Kalaidjian has combined practical architecture (curved bedroom ceilings that draw eyes skyward) with smile-inducing additions (secluded outdoor showers with rainforest heads). The resulting atmosphere, no doubt aided by the vast palm-lined pool with huge concrete stepping stones, is laid back, beachy, and communal, although those craving luxurious privacy can doze in their own secret grassy garden that lies to the rear of each unit. Sunrise yoga and open-air massage are the order of the day at the Payot Spa. The restaurant Colette sprouts from inside the glass cube dining room and creeps right around the pool. Dining under the innovative eye of rising star Patrick Cuissard is a delight. Light, summery dishes are prepared with élan: think carpaccio of seabass bathed in coconut milk.

Rte des Salins, St-Tropez 83990. www.hotelsezz-sainttropez.com. ℰ **04-94-55-31-55.** Fax 04-94-55-31-51. 37 units. 400€–850€ double; from 1400€ suite. AE, DC, MC, V. Free parking. Closed mid-Oct to mid-Apr. **Amenities:** 1 restaurant; 1 bar; babysitting; bikes; concierge; exercise room; massage; outdoor pool; room service; sauna; free shuttle to beach; spa. *In room:* A/C, TV, hair dryer, minibar, free Wi-Fi.

## EXPENSIVE

**Pastis Hôtel-St-Tropez ★★ 📱** Two expat Brits, John and Pauline Larkin, have taken a portside Provençal house and transformed it into this chic little hotel. They have decorated it in a sophisticated eclectic style, even featuring their collection of framed album artwork that includes the Sex Pistols and the Rolling Stones. Guests can mingle as they sip an aperitif by the pool in the courtyard. You get the feeling that you're staying in a private home when you lodge here, one discreetly decorated with a fantastic eye for design. Like the guest-only lounge, the rooms are furnished in an inspired mix, and each unit comes with a spacious bathroom as well as (in most of the rooms) a balcony or breakfast terrace. Some accommodations are large enough for extra beds or cots. Indian rugs, Chinese armoires, and beds adorned with Provençal *boutis* spreads enhance the warm, intimate ambience.

61 av. du Général Leclerc, St-Tropez 83990. www.pastis-st-tropez.com. ℰ **04-98-12-56-50.** Fax 04-94-96-99-82. 10 units. 175€–675€ double. AE, MC, V. Free parking. Closed mid-Nov to Dec. **Amenities:** Outdoor pool. *In room:* A/C, TV, minibar, free Wi-Fi.

**Hôtel La Ponche** ★   The same family has run this hotel overlooking the port for more than half a century. The cozy nest has long been a favorite of ours, as it's the most discreet, most charming, and least celebrity-flashy establishment downtown, making Byblos (see above) look nouveau riche and a bit strident in comparison. It's filled with the original airy paintings of Jacques Cordier, who died in 1978. Each floor holds two or three rooms, all of which are well equipped and open onto sea views. Sun-colored walls with subtle lighting lend a homey feeling. The beds are elegantly appointed with linen and quality mattresses, and the mid-size to large bathrooms have tub/showers or a shower only. There's also a convivial attached restaurant with outdoor terrace, specializing in *fruits des mer*.

Port des Pécheurs, St-Tropez 83990. www.laponche.com. ℰ **04-94-97-02-53.** Fax 04-94-97-78-61. 18 units. 240€–550€ double; 290€–750€ suite. AE, MC, V. Parking 25€. Closed Nov to mid-Mar. **Amenities:** Restaurant; bar; babysitting; room service. *In room:* A/C, TV, hair dryer, minibar, free Wi-Fi.

## MODERATE

**Hôtel Les Palmiers**   Accompanied by a verdant garden, this pleasant and practical three-star hotel was created in 1955 with the union of two once-separate houses, the older of which dates from the late 18th century. One of the best things about it is its location directly astride place des Lices in the center of St-Tropez. Bedrooms are simple and compact, and outfitted in Provençal hues of blue, soft orange, and ocher. There's a bar on the premises, but no restaurant.

24–26 bd. Vasserot (place des Lices), St-Tropez 83991. www.hotel-les-palmiers.com. ℰ **04-94-97-01-61.** Fax 04-94-97-10-02. 25 units. 78€–225€ double. AE, MC, V. **Amenities:** Room service. *In room:* A/C, TV, hair dryer, minibar, free Wi-Fi.

**Hôtel Sube**   If you want to be right on the port, in a location that's perfect for yacht- and celebrity-watching, this might be your first choice. It's directly over the hip Café de Paris bar. The two-story lounge has a beamed ceiling and a glass front, allowing a great view of the harbor. The rooms aren't large, but are comfortable and decorated in French provincial style. The more expensive units have scenic views of the port. Each comes with a private bathroom with a shower and tub.

15 quai Suffren, St-Tropez 83990. www.hotelsube.net. ℰ **04-94-97-30-04.** Fax 04-94-54-89-08. 25 units. 90€–290€ double. AE, MC, V. Closed Nov–Mar. **Amenities:** Cafe; bar; free Wi-Fi. *In room:* A/C, TV.

---

 **FRENCH** boules

Second only to charging around St-Tropez's medieval Citadelle, a game of *pétanque*, or French *boules*, is seriously cool for kids. Hop to Le Café (www.lecafe.fr; ℰ **04-94-97-44-69**), one of many alfresco bars in place des Lices, and request a handful of *pétanque boules* to toss around the tree-dappled square. The game was created down the coast and is about as Provençal as it gets. Pick up some tips by watching the locals first. Games begin with a toss of the jack, or *bouchon*. Teams then take turns to throw. Whoever is farthest away keeps trying to get closest to the ball, with any remaining balls tossed in at the end. A point is awarded for each steel ball that's closer to the jack than any balls from the opposing team.

# CANNES ★★★

905km (561 miles) S of Paris; 163km (101 miles) E of Marseille; 26km (16 miles) SW of Nice

When Coco Chanel came here and got a suntan, returning to Paris bronzed, she shocked the milk-white society ladies—who quickly began to copy her. Today the bronzed bodies, clad in nearly nonexistent swimsuits, line the beaches of this chic resort and continue the late fashion designer's example. A block back from the famed promenade de la Croisette are the boutiques, bars, and bistros that make Cannes the Riviera's capital of cool. The opening of a museum dedicated to French painter Pierre Bonnard in the suburb of Le Cannet in 2011 added a cultural string to the resort's sophisticated charms.

## Essentials

**GETTING THERE**  By **train,** Cannes is 15 minutes from Antibes, 35 minutes from Nice, and 50 minutes from Monaco. The TGV from Paris reaches Cannes in an incredibly scenic 5 hours. The one-way fare from Paris is 50€ to 100€. For rail information and schedules, visit www.voyages-sncf.com or call ✆ **36-35. Rapide Côte d'Azur,** place de l'Hôtel de Ville, Cannes (www.rca.tm.fr; ✆ **04-93-85-64-44**), provides bus service to Nice via Antibes and Cagnes-sur-Mer every 20 minutes during the day (trip time: 1½ hr.). The one-way fare is 1€.

Nice **international airport** (www.nice.aeroport.fr; ✆ **08-20-42-33-33**) is a 30-minute drive east. **Buses** pick up passengers at the airport every 30 minutes during the day (hourly at other times) and drop them at the Gare Routière, place de l'Hôtel de Ville (www.rca.tm.fr; ✆ **04-93-85-64-44**). The one-way fare is 15.60€.

By **car** from Marseille, take A51 north to Aix-en-Provence, continuing along A8 east to Cannes. From Nice, follow A8 southwest to Cannes.

**VISITOR INFORMATION**  The **Office de Tourisme** is at 1 bd. de la Croisette (www.cannes.travel; ✆ **04-92-99-84-22;** fax 04-92-99-84-23). There is an additional office by the train station.

**SPECIAL EVENTS**  Cannes is at its most frenzied in mid-May during the **International Film Festival** at the Palais des Festivals, on promenade de la Croisette. It attracts not only film stars (you can touch the cement moulds of their handprints), but also seemingly every photographer in the world. You have a better chance of being named prime minister of France than you do of attending one of the major screenings. (Hotel rooms and tables at restaurants are equally scarce during the festival.) But the people-watching is fabulous. If you find yourself here at the right time, you can join the thousands who line up in front of the Palais des Festivals, where the premieres are held. With paparazzi shouting and gendarmes holding back fans, the guests parade along the red carpet, stopping for a moment to strike a pose. *C'est Cannes!*

You may be able to get tickets for some of the lesser films. For information, see "France Calendar of Events" in chapter 2, or visit **www. festival-cannes.com**.

From international regattas and galas to *concours d'élégance* (an extravagant car show), summertime fireworks, winter ballet, and even a Mimosa Festival (focusing on flowers and local handicrafts) in February, something's always happening at Cannes.

# A Day at the Beach

Beachgoing in Cannes has more to do with exhibitionism than actual swimming. Plage de la Croisette extends between the Vieux Port and the Port Canto. The beaches along this billion-dollar stretch of sand are *payante,* meaning entrance costs 15€ to 30€. You don't need to be a guest of the Martinez or Carlton to use the beaches associated with these high-end hotels (see "Where to Stay"), and there are heaps more buzzing beach clubs dotted around, including sassy 3.14 Beach (✆ **04-93-94-25-43**).

Why should you pay a fee at all? Well, it includes a full day's use of a mattress, a chaise longue (the seafront is more pebbly than sandy), and a parasol, as well as easy access to freshwater showers. There are also outdoor restaurants and bars (some with organic menus, others with burgers and sushi) where no one minds if you appear in your swimsuit. Every beach allows topless bathing, and you're likely to find the same forms of décolletage along the entire strip.

Looking for a free public beach without renting chaises or parasols? Head for **Plage du Midi,** sometimes called Midi Plage, just west of the Vieux Port, or **Plage Gazagnaire,** just east of the Port Canto. Here you'll find families with children and lots of caravan-type vehicles parked nearby.

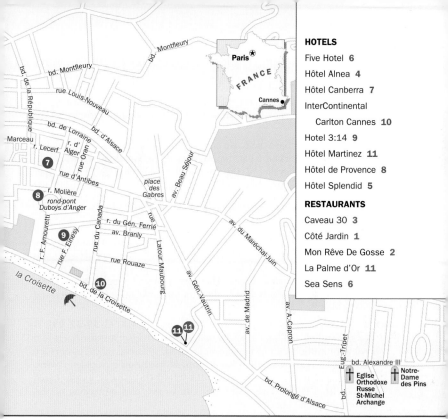

**HOTELS**

Five Hotel **6**

Hôtel Alnea **4**

Hôtel Canberra **7**

InterContinental
Carlton Cannes **10**

Hotel 3:14 **9**

Hôtel Martinez **11**

Hôtel de Provence **8**

Hôtel Splendid **5**

**RESTAURANTS**

Caveau 30 **3**

Côté Jardin **1**

Mon Rêve De Gosse **2**

La Palme d'Or **11**

Sea Sens **6**

# Outdoor Pursuits

**BICYCLING & MOTOR SCOOTERING**   Despite the summertime traffic, the flat landscapes between Cannes and satellite resorts such as La Napoule are well suited for riding a bike or motor scooter. At **Daniel Location,** 7 rue Suffern (www.daniel-location-2roues.com; ☎ **04-93-99-90-30**), *vélos tout terrain* (mountain bikes) cost 12€ a day. Motorized bikes and scooters cost 35€ per day; renters must be at least 16 years old. For larger scooters, you must present a valid driver's license. Another purveyor of bikes is **Mistral Location,** 4 rue Georges Clemenceau (www.mistral-location.com; ☎ **04-93-39-33-60**), which charges 16€ per day.

**BOATING**   Several companies around Cannes's vieux port rent boats of any size, with or without a crew, for a day, a week, or even longer. An outfit known for short-term rentals of small motorcraft is **Elco Marine,** 110 bd. du Midi (www.elcomarine.fr; ☎ **04-93-47-12-62**). For kayak rental and guided tours of the coastline by canoe, try **SeaFirst,** 110 bd. du Midi (www.sea first.fr; ☎ **04-93-65-06-14**).

**GOLF**   Cannes is ringed by 10 golf courses, almost all within a 20-minute drive. The Old Course, route de Golf, Mandelieu (☎ **04-92-97-32-00;**

www.golfoldcourse.com), is a leafy gem dating from 1891. Green fees start at 90€, with big reductions for lunch deals and afternoon tee-offs. The prestigious Royal Mougins Golf Club, 424 av. du Roi, Mougins (www.royalmougins.fr; ✆ **04-92-92-49-69**), also boasts a gourmet restaurant and spa. Green fees start at 175€ including buggy hire, half-price for nine holes.

**TENNIS**   Some resorts have their own courts. The city of Cannes also maintains 16 synthetic courts and 6 clay-topped ones at the **Garden Tennis Club,** 99 av. Maurice Chevalier (✆ **04-93-47-29-33**). You'll pay 12€ to 15€ per hour, depending on the court and the time you want to play, plus 3.50€ per hour for floodlights.

## Shopping

Cannes achieves a blend of resort-style leisure, glamour, and media glitz more successfully than many of its neighbors. You'll see every big-name designer you can think of (Saint-Laurent, Rykiel, and Hermès), plus a legion of one-off designer boutiques and shoe stores. There are also real-people shops; resale shops for star-studded castoffs; flea markets for fun junk; and a fruit, flower, and vegetable market.

**BOOKS**   **Ciné-Folie,** 14 rue des Frères-Pradignac (✆ **04-93-39-22-99**), is devoted entirely to film. Called *La Boutique du Cinema,* it is the finest film bookstore in the south of France; vintage film stills and movie posters are also for sale. **Wally's English Bookshop,** 11 rue Bivouac Napoleon (www.cannesenglishbookshop.com; ✆ **04-93-99-40-08**), stocks locally based classics from Peter Mayle and Carol Drinkwater, plus bestselling novels, travel guides, and maps.

**DESIGNER SHOPS**   Most of the big names in fashion, for both men and women, line **promenade de la Croisette,** also known as **La Croisette,** the main drag running along the sea. Among the most prestigious are **Dior,** 38 La Croisette (✆ **04-92-98-98-00**), and **Hermès,** 17 La Croisette (✆ **04-93-39-08-90**). The stores are in a row, stretching from the Hôtel Carlton almost to the Palais des Festivals, with the best names closest to the **Gray-d'Albion,** 38 rue des Ferbes (✆ **04-92-99-79-79**), which is both a mall and a hotel (how convenient). Near the train station, department store **Galeries Lafayette** has all the labels crammed into one smallish space at 6 rue du Maréchal-Foch (✆ **04-97-06-25-00**).

Young hipsters should try **Bathroom Graffiti,** 52 rue d'Antibes (✆ **04-93-39-02-32**), for sexy luggage, bikinis, and designer homeware. The rue d'Antibes is also brilliant for big brand bargains including Zara and MaxMara, as well as one-off boutiques.

**FLEA MARKETS**   Cannes has two regular flea markets. Casual, dusty, and increasingly filled with castaways from estate sales, **Marché Forville,** just north of the vieux port, is a stucco structure with a roof and a few arches but no walls. From Tuesday to Sunday, it's the fruit, vegetable, and flower market that supplies the dozens of grand restaurants in the area. Monday is *brocante* day, when the market fills with dealers selling everything from Grandmère's dishes to bone-handled carving knives.

## SEEING CANNES FROM A petit train

One of the best ways to get your bearings in Cannes (and to get an idea of the difference between the city's new and old neighborhoods) is to climb aboard the Petit Train touristique de Cannes. The diesel-powered vehicles roll through the streets on rubber tires. They operate every day from 10am to between 7 and 11:30pm, depending on the season. Two itineraries are offered: For views of glittery modern Cannes, board the train at a designated spot in front of either of the town's two casinos for a ride along La Croisette and its side streets. For a ride through the narrow streets of Vieux Cannes (Le Suquet), board the train at a clearly designated site on the seaward side of La Croisette, opposite the Hôtel Majestic. Both tours depart every 30 to 60 minutes. They last around 45 minutes, depending on traffic, and cost 7€ for adults and 3€ for children 9 and younger, depending on the tour. A combination ticket to both tours (good on separate days, if you prefer) costs 10€ for adults and 5€ for children 9 and under. For details, check out www.cannes-petit-train.com or call ✆ **06-22-61-25-76**.

On Saturdays, from 8am to 12:30pm, a somewhat disorganized and busy **Marché aux Fleurs** takes place outdoors along the edges of the allée de la Liberté, across from the Palais des Festivals.

**FOOD**   The **Marché Forville** and the surrounding streets are unsurprisingly the best places to search for picnic supplies. For bottles of Côtes de Provence, try **Cave du Marché,** 5 rue Forville (✆ **04-93-99-60-98**). It also serves up glasses of local rosé and olive crostini on tables outside. **La Compagnie des Saumons,** 12 Marché Forville (✆ **04-93-68-33-20**), brims with caviar, bottles of fish soup, and slabs of smoked salmon. Local cheese shop **La Fromagerie Gourmet,** 8 rue des Halles (✆ **04-93-99-96-41**) is a favorite of celebrated chef Alain Ducasse.

The street with the greatest density of emporiums selling wine, olives, herbs, cheese, bread, and oils is the appealing **rue Meynadier,** which leads east from Marché Forville. Heading farther east still is charming **Cannolive,** 16–20 rue Vénizelos (✆ **04-93-39-08-19**), which was founded in 1880 by ancestors of the current owners, the Raynaud family. It sells Provençal olives and their byproducts—tapenades that connoisseurs refer to as "Provençal caviar." For the ultimate in French cheeses try **La Ferme Savoyarde,** 12 rue Meynadier (✆ **04-93-39-63-68**).

## Seeing the Sights

For many visitors, Cannes might as well consist of only one street, the **promenade de la Croisette**—or just La Croisette—curving along the coast and split by islands of palms and flowers.

A port of call for cruise liners, the grand hotels, apartments, and boutiques that line the seafront are the first things that visitors arriving by ship will see. Many of the bigger hotels, some dating from the 19th century, indulge their guests with exclusive beach clubs on the sand. Above the harbor, the old town of

Cannes sits on Suquet Hill, where you'll see the 14th-century **Tour de Suquet,** which the English dubbed the Lord's Tower.

**Musée de la Castre** ★ MUSEUM   In the Château de la Castre above Cannes' old town, this large museum displays paintings of Cannes from yester-year, plus sculpture and works of decorative art. The ethnography section includes objects from all over the world, including spears from the South Seas and Maya pottery. There's also a gallery devoted to relics of Mediterranean civili-zations, from the Greeks to the Romans, from the Cypriots to the Egyptians. The best part, however, is climbing the 101 steps of the museum's viewing tower: The views across the Riviera are astounding.

Quai de l'Epi le Port. ✆ **04-93-38-55-26.** Admission 3.40€ adults, 2.20€ ages 18–25, free for children under 17. July–Aug daily 10am–7pm; Sept–Mar Tues–Sun 10am–1pm and 2–5pm; Apr–June Tues–Sun 10am–1pm and 2–6pm.

**Musée Bonnard** ★★ ART MUSEUM   The first museum in the world dedi-cated to the impressionist ace Pierre Bonnard opened 3km (1¾ miles) north of Cannes in 2011. Bonnard lived nearby in the later years of his life, capturing the colors of Cannes, Antibes, and St-Tropez on canvas. This sparkling new museum may be petite, but its collection of portraits, sculptures, and sketches is set to grow over the coming years. Interaction helps to bring the current exhibits to life. Visitors may take an audio tour delivered on a state-of-the-art iPod Touch. Mod-ern art enthusiasts may also follow a 90-minute walking tour of the surrounding lanes, which links the very backdrops that Bonnard used in his art.

6 bd. Sidi Carnot, Le Cannet. www.museebonnard.fr. ✆ **04-93-94-06-06.** Admission 6€ adults, 3.50€ ages 12–8, free for children 11 and under. Apr to mid-Oct Tues–Sun 10am–8pm; mid-Oct to Mar Tues–Sun 10am–6pm. Closed Nov.

# Ferrying to the Iles de Lérins ★★

Bobbing in the shimmering Mediterranean across the bay from Cannes, the Lérins Islands are the major excursion from the port. For access to Ile Ste-Mar-guerite, head for the quai Laubeuf on the western side of the port, where ferry-boats operated by **Trans-Côte d'Azur** (www.trans-cote-azur.com; ✆ **04-92-00-42-30**) whiz passengers back and forth year-round at intervals of between every 15 and 75 minutes, depending on the season. For access to Ile St-Honorat, head for the same quay, to the ferryboats operated by **Transports Planaria** (www.cannes-ilesdelerins.com; ✆ **04-92-98-71-38**). Boats depart daily year-round at intervals of between 30 and 90 minutes, depending on the season. Round-trip transport to both islands costs 13€ per adult, 6.50€ for children 5 to 10, and free for children 4 and under.

## ILE STE-MARGUERITE

This island was named after St-Honorat's sister, Ste-Marguerite, who lived here with a group of nuns in the 5th century. Today it's one big botanical garden ringed by crystal clear sea. Cars, cigarettes, and all other pollutants are banned, making it the ultimate escape from the Riviera commotion. From the dock, you can stroll along the island (signs point the way) to Fort Royal, built by Spanish troops from 1635 to 1637 and used as a military barracks and parade ground until World War II. The infamous "Man in the Iron Mask" was allegedly imprisoned here, and you can follow the legend back to his horribly spooky cell.

Boat en route to the Iles des Lerins.

**Musée de la Mer,** Fort Royal (📞 04-93-38-55-26), traces the history of the island, displaying artifacts of Ligurian, Roman, and Arab civilizations, plus the remains discovered by excavations, including paintings, mosaics, and ceramics. The museum is open June to September daily 10am to 5:45pm, and October to May Tuesday to Sunday 10:30am to 1:15pm and 2:15 to 4:45pm (closing at 5:45pm Apr–May). Admission is 3.20€ for adults, free for students and children 17 and under.

### ILE ST-HONORAT ★★

Only 1.6km (1 mile) long, the Ile St-Honorat is much quieter than neighboring Ste-Marguerite. But in historical terms, it's much richer than its island sibling and is the site of a monastery whose origins date from the 5th century. The **Abbaye de St-Honorat** ★, Les Iles de Lérins, Cannes 06400 (www.abbayedelerins.com; 📞 04-92-99-54-00), is a combination of medieval ruins and early-20th-century ecclesiastical buildings, and is home to a community of about 25 Cistercian monks. The monks transform the island's herbs, vines, and honey into a wealth of organic products, including lavender oil and wine. All can be purchased in the monastery shop. There is also an excellent lunch-only seafood restaurant, **La Tonnelle** (www.tonnelle-abbayedelerins.com; 📞 04-92-99-54-08). It's closed from November to mid-December. And no, it's not the monks who cook, but they can organize a wine-tasting or small island tour if arranged in advance.

Most visitors content themselves with a wander through the pine forests on the island's western side, a clamber around the ruined monastery on the island's southern edge, and a sunbath on its seaweed-strewn beaches.

## Where to Eat

### VERY EXPENSIVE

**La Palme d'Or** ★★★ MODERN FRENCH   The ultimate dining experience in Cannes is this double-Michelin-starred restaurant, commanding panoramic sea views from the second floor of the Hotel Martinez. Top chef Christian Sinicropi has presided over the inventive cuisine for more than a decade. He routinely greets diners at their table to best assess their culinary desires before wowing them over six, seven, or eight courses. Although the food is the true star, a celebrity fan base has put this on the see-and-be-seen circuit. Menu items change with the seasons but are likely to include warm foie gras with fondue of rhubarb; or crayfish, clams, and squid marinated in peppered citrus sauce. Intriguing bites on the tasting menus may include olive-flavored marshmallows, beetroot sorbet, and bread made with squid ink. The service is worldly without being stiff.

In the Hôtel Martinez, 73 bd. de la Croisette. www.hotel-martinez.com. © **04-92-98-74-14.** Reservations required. Main courses 48€–85€; fixed-price menu 95€–185€. AE, DC, MC, V. Wed–Sat 12:30–2pm and 8–10pm. Closed Jan–Feb.

## MODERATE

**Le Caveau 30 ★ 🎁** SEAFOOD   Bow-tied staff balancing huge trays of *fruits de mer* on beds of ice sum up this age-old establishment. Le Caveau 30 is a timeless brasserie devoted to excellent service and top-notch but well-priced seafood and harbor-fresh fish. The Belle Epoque is evoked by the decor: hexagonal crystal chandeliers, red banquettes, and heavy white crockery. Dining spreads onto a smart outdoor terrace from Easter to October. Best value is the 25.50€ prix-fixe menu, which pairs homemade red mullet terrine with fish stew and grilled seabream. More expensive à la carte options include with stuffed mussels and crab tartare, and bouillabaisse.

45 av. Félix Fauré. www.lecaveau30.com. © **04-93-39-06-33.** Main courses 17€–38€; fixed-price menu 17€–38€. AE, MC, V. Tue–Sun 7–11:30pm.

**Sea Sens Restaurant 🎁** MODERN FRENCH   Famed restaurateur brothers Jacques and Laurent Pourcel specialize in light, contemporary, Asian-inspired French cuisine. At this sunny rooftop hideaway a block back from La Croisette, they have added an enviable location to their award-winning mix. Market inspired daily dishes may include scallops with sautéed beetroot with a sea broth foam, and Thai-style wagyu beef tartare. Desserts come courtesy of Jérôme de Oliveira, France's young World Pastry Champion, most recently of the Plaza Athénée in Paris. Service is beach club–style: polite but informal staff are dressed in blue and white waiter costumes. The rooftop restaurant also offers one of Cannes' only brunch options. This 55€ blowout breakfast starts with fruits and smoothies, continues with bagels, oysters, and sashimi, the finishes some hours late with a main fish or meat course.

1 rue Notre-Dame. © **04-63-36-05-06.** Reservations recommended. Main courses 26€–42€; fixed-price lunch 19€–60€; fixed-price lunch 60€–80€. AE, MC, V. Mon–Sat noon–2pm and 7.30–11pm; Sun 11am–3pm.

## INEXPENSIVE

**Côté Jardin 🗡** PROVENÇAL   Set near the courthouse (Palais de Justice) in the heart of commercial Cannes, just north of the train station, this restaurant attracts loyal locals because of its unpretentious ambience and its reasonably priced and generous portions. You're offered three different choices as seating options: on the street-level glassed-in veranda, at a table amid the flowering shrubs of the garden terrace, or upstairs within the cozy Provençal dining room.

Classic French menu items include scallops in a basil cream, bavette of beef with shallots, roast Atlantic seabass, and saffron mussels.

12 av. St-Louis. (℡ **04-93-38-60-28.** Reservations required, especially in summer. Fixed-price menus 24€–40€. AE, DC, MC, V. Tues–Sat noon–2pm and 7:30–10pm.

## Cannes Nightlife

Cannes is invariably associated with easygoing permissiveness, filmmaking glitterati, and gambling. If the latter is your thing, Cannes has some world-class casinos loaded with high rollers, voyeurs, and everyone in between. The better established is the **Casino Croisette,** in the Palais des Festivals, Esplanade Lucien Barrière (www.lucienbarriere.com; (℡ **04-92-98-78-50**). A well-respected fixture in town since the 1950s, a collection of noisy slot machines it is most certainly not.

Its main competitor is the newer **Palm Beach Casino,** place F-D-Roosevelt, Pointe de la Croisette (℡ **04-97-06-36-90**), on the southeast edge of La Croisette. Inaugurated in 1933 and rebuilt in 2002, it attracts a younger crowd with a summer-only beachside poker room, a beach club with pool, a restaurant, and a disco that runs until dawn. Both casinos maintain slots that operate daily lunchtime to 5am. Smarter dress is expected for the *les grands jeux* salons (for (blackjack, roulette, craps, poker, and chemin de fer), which open nightly 8pm to 4am. The casino also pulls in daytime visitors with tasty inexpensive lunches and Sunday brunches, both of which come with free gaming chips.

After-dark diversions continue to grow, with a strip of sundowner bars stretching along rue Félix Fauré. Most are chic, some have happy hour cocktails, and several have DJs after dinner. It's best to walk by and take your pick. Nearby is **Chokko,** 15 rue Frères Pradignac (℡ **04-93-39-62-70**), where killer cocktails are served by haughty waiting staff. Dance floor–filling tunes get everyone on their feet after 10pm. Less showy is **Morrison's Irish Pub,** 10 rue Teisseire (℡ **04-92-98-16-17**), which has become the meeting place for visiting yachties and the expat community. There's a live DJ on Thursday, Friday, and Saturday in the attached **Morrison's Lounge** club.

The **Bar l'Amiral,** in the Hôtel Martinez, 73 La Croisette (℡ **04-92-98-73-00**), is where deals go down during the film festival. Directors, producers, stars, press agents, screenwriters, and wannabes crowd in here at festival time. The bow-tied barmen have won several world championship cocktail mixing trophies. Places around the bar come complete with a nametag of the star that once propped it up, Humphrey Bogart among them.

Gay and lesbian bar **Zanzibar,** 85 rue Félix Fauré (℡ **04-93-39-30-75**), is the oldest stop on Cannes's scene. The pace picks up at midnight and throbs until 4am. Cannes's most uplifting option is gay-friendly club **Le Nightlife,** 52 rue Jean-Jaurès (℡ **04-93-39-20-50**). It has been reoutfitted with white walls, a busy bar, occasional fashion shows, and lots of randomly scheduled parties that last until dawn.

## Where to Stay

### VERY EXPENSIVE

**Hôtel Martinez** ★★★   When this Art Deco masterpiece was built in the 1930s, it rivaled any other lodging along the coast in sheer size. Over the years,

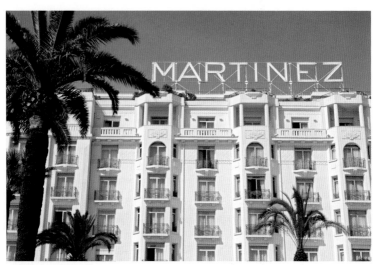

Hôtel Martinez.

however, it fell into disrepair. But in the '80s, the hotel and its restaurants were given a Belle Epoque makeover and returned to their former luster. The suite-laden penthouse floor has become most sought-after in town following a recent restyling. Several more suites look out over the sea from the first floor, including the Suite des Oliviers, a pleasure palace of upholstered silk bedsteads, a sauna, crystal chandeliers, and a 250-sq.-m (2,691-sq.-ft.) terrace with its own Jacuzzi. All units have full marble bathrooms, wood furnishings, and writing desks. The Martinez also possesses ZPlage (a beach club for the glitterati), plus a water-skiing school, a kids' club, a very cool bar for grown-ups, and one of the finest restaurants in the South of France (La Palme d'Or, p. 561). A new seventh-floor spa with products by L. Raphael opened in spring 2012.

73 bd. de la Croisette, Cannes 06406. www.hotel-martinez.com. ℂ **04-92-98-73-00.** Fax 04-93-39-67-82. 412 units. 690€–890€ double; from 3,300€ suite. AE, DC, MC, V. Parking 38€. **Amenities:** 3 summer restaurants, 2 winter restaurants; bar; babysitting; private beach; children's center; concierge; exercise room; outdoor pool; room service; sauna; spa. *In room:* A/C, TV, hair dryer, minibar, free Wi-Fi.

**InterContinental Carlton Cannes ★★★** Here you'll see vehicles of every description dropping off huge amounts of baggage and fashionable guests. The twin gray domes at either end of the facade are often the first things recognized by starlets planning their grand entrances, grand exits, and grand scenes in the hotel's public and private rooms. In 2012, the Carlton celebrated a century of attracting the most prominent members of Europe's *haut monde*. In summer (especially during the film festival), the vast public rooms still fill with all the voyeuristic and exhibitionistic fervor that seems so much a part of the Riviera. Guest rooms are obscenely plush. The entire seventh floor is dedicated to luxurious suites, including the Grace Kelly suite, with multiple bedrooms and a set of personal photos donated by Prince Albert of Monaco in 2010; and the Sir Sean Connery suite, which has a spa room inside one of the Carlton's cupolas and, in a James Bond–esque touch, a private lift.

58 bd. de la Croisette, Cannes 06400. www.intercontinental.com. ✆ **04-93-06-40-06.** Fax 04-93-06-40-25. 343 units. 149€–765€ double; from 699€ suite. AE, DC, MC, V. Parking 38€. **Amenities:** 3 summer restaurants; 1 winter restaurant; 2 bars; health club; room service. *In room:* A/C, TV, hair dryer, minibar, free Wi-Fi.

## EXPENSIVE

**Five Hôtel** ★★   Open since summer 2011, Cannes' hippest hotel offers designer opulence that harks back to the 1920s, when international travel was a high society preserve. Décor is light, luxurious, and laced with art deco. Furnishings are clearly inspired by Louis Vuitton's classic luggage sets. Rooms and suites are arranged like a Wallpaper* photo shoot. Each features hardwood rocking chairs, a Mac Mini computer, Nespresso machine, and Asprey bath products. New for 2012 is the Cinq Mondes spa and Intuitions sweet shop, created by 27-year-old World Pastry Champion Jérôme de Oliveira. The rooftop terrace tops of the Five's inspired design. It features an infinity pool, linen-shaded sun loungers, and a cocktail bar backed up by DJs and frequent live music. The terrace is also the location of the acclaimed Sea Sens restaurant (see p. 562).

1 rue Notre Dame, Cannes 06400. www.five-hotel-cannes.com. ✆ **04-63-36-05-05.** No fax. 45 units. 295€–805€ double; from 595€ suite. AE, DC, MC, V. **Amenities:** Restaurant; bar; concierge; outdoor pool; room service; spa. *In room:* A/C, TV, hair dryer, minibar, free Wi-Fi.

**Hotel 3:14** ★   This is the only hotel in Cannes that was designed following feng shui principles and that serves all-organic cuisine. This incredibly playful establishment also has a Disney-esque design ethic: Each floor is themed around a different continent, although the designs are now starting to date. "Africa" rooms are Lion King meets Arabian nights: red, purple, and gold drapes and cushions with art from the Serengeti. "Asia" occupies the fifth floor, where a zenlike geometry coupled with patchouli and jasmine scents lend a calming edge to each room. The top-floor terrace and spa area hosts yoga, massage, an outdoor pool, and hammam quarters. More painfully hip is the 3.14 Resto-Bar-Club, with an organic kitchen overseen by Italian chef Mario d'Orio. Just 50m (164 ft.) away, on La Croisette, is 3.14's supercool beach club (Paris Hilton was a recent visitor).

5 rue François Einesy, Cannes 06400. www.3-14hotel.com. ✆ **04-92-99-70-00.** Fax 04-92-99-72-12. 96 units. 180€–510€ double; from 865€ suite. AE, DC, MC, V. **Amenities:** Restaurant; bar; babysitting; concierge; outdoor pool; room service; spa. *In room:* A/C, TV, hair dryer, minibar, free Wi-Fi.

## MODERATE

**Hôtel Canberra** ★★   An oasis of calm midway between La Croisette and the rue d'Antibes, its unique location allows guests to lounge and sunbathe around a small swimming pool in calm and privacy. Both public areas and rooms are the epitome of design-led sophistication. Tradition and Privilege rooms (the latter are poolside) have soft, marbled carpets and funky, retro chairs. Terrace Privilege rooms have deck chairs in the sun. Suites boast sofas and period prints from Cannes's elegant past.

20 rue d'Antibes, Cannes 06400. www.hotel-cannes-canberra.com. ✆ **04-97-06-95-00.** Fax 04-92-98-03-47. 35 units. 140€–350€ double; 230€–500€ suite. AE, DC, MC, V. Parking 25€. **Amenities:** 2 summer restaurants; 1 winter restaurant; bar; babysitting; health club; outdoor pool. *In room:* A/C, TV, hair dryer, minibar, free Wi-Fi.

**Hôtel Splendid ★** ⚓  Opened in 1871 and sympathetically renovated over the following decades, this hotel is a favorite of scholars, politicians, actors, and musicians. The portside location is central as they come, but don't expect boutique: the Splendid is fabulously retro and *très* French. The ornate white building with wrought-iron accents looks out onto the sea, the old port, and a park. La Croisette is just a minute's walk south. Rooms are appointed with antique furniture and paintings; about 15 have kitchenettes. Each comes with a good bed and a small but tidy bathroom. The more expensive rooms have sea views.

4–6 rue Félix Fauré, Cannes 06400. www.splendid-hotel-cannes.fr. ℂ **04-97-06-22-22.** Fax 04-93-99-55-02. 62 units. 93€–275€ double. Rates include breakfast. AE, MC, V. **Amenities:** Babysitting; room service. *In room:* A/C, TV, hair dryer, free Wi-Fi.

### INEXPENSIVE

**Hôtel Alnea** 🏨  A class act packed with fun and flavor, but books up weeks in advance. The small but perfectly formed Alnea correctly advertises itself as being 1 minute from the Palais des Festivals, 2 minutes from La Croisette, and 5 minutes from Le Suquet. Stylish rooms are divided into two sizes. Pichtoune rooms are petite, to say the least, but Confort class rooms have enough space to swing a few shopping bags around. Both overflow with art and color.

20 rue Jean de Riouffe, Cannes 06400. www.hotel-alnea.com. ℂ **04-93-68-77-77.** Fax 09-63-49-97-89. 14 units. 60€–98€ double. AE, MC, V. *In room:* A/C, TV, free Wi-Fi.

**Hôtel de Provence** ⚓  Built in the 1930s, this hotel is small and unpretentious—a contrast to the intensely stylish, larger hotels in the immediate area. Most of the rooms have private balconies, and many overlook the shrubs and palms of the hotel's walled garden. Guest rooms are modern and simple, with wooden parquet floors and simply tiled bathrooms. For Cannes, they represent a real bargain. In warm weather, breakfast is served under the flowers of an arbor.

9 rue Molière, Cannes 06400. www.hotel-de-provence.com. ℂ **04-93-38-44-35.** Fax 04-93-39-63-14. 32 units. 105€–195€ double; 155€–275€ suite. AE, MC, V. Parking: 16€. **Amenities:** Bar; room service. *In room:* A/C, TV, hair dryer, minibar, free Wi-Fi.

# MOUGINS

903km (560 miles) S of Paris; 11km (6¾ miles) S of Grasse; 8km (5 miles) N of Cannes

This former fortified town on the crest of a hill provides an alternative for those who want to be near the excitement of Cannes but not in the midst of it. Picasso discovered the tranquil maze of flower-filled streets in the company of his muse, Dora Marr, and photographer, Man Ray, in 1935. In time, Jean Cocteau, Paul Eluard, Fernand Léger, Isadora Duncan, and even Christian Dior called Mougins home.

Mougins now preserves the quiet life in a postcard-perfect manner. Real estate prices are among the highest on the Riviera, and the wealthy residents support a dining scene that punches well above its weight. The Etoile des Mougins food festival held each September is a highbrow gastronomic love-in featuring Michelin-starred chefs from across Provence. The town's artsy legacy has blessed the town with several must-see galleries plus the new Museum of Classical Art, which opened in summer 2011.

**Statue in Mougins.**

# Essentials

**GETTING THERE**   The best way to get to Mougins is to **drive.** From Nice, follow E80/A8 west and then cut north on route 85 into Mougins. From Cannes, head north of the city along N85.

In 2005, the French railway, **SNCF,** reactivated an antique rail line stretching between Grasse (the perfume capital) and Cannes, linking the hamlet of Mouans-Sartoux en route. Mouans-Sartoux lies only 457m (1,499 ft.) from the center of Mougins. Rail service costs 2.90€ one-way from Cannes to Mouans-Sartoux, or 2€ from Grasse to Mouans-Sartoux. There are **trains** every hour. By bus, **Société Tam** (www.cg06.fr; ✆ **08-00-06-01-06**) runs **buses** between Cannes and Grasse. Bus no. 600 stops in Val-de-Mougins, a 10-minute walk from the center of Mougins. One-way fares from either Cannes or Grasse cost 1€. Given the complexities of a bus transfer from Cannes, it's a lot easier just to pay 30€ to 40€ for a **taxi** to haul you and your possessions northward from Cannes.

**VISITOR INFORMATION**   The **Office de Tourisme** is at 15 av. Jean-Charles-Mallet (www.mougins.fr; ✆ **04-93-75-87-67;** fax 04-92-92-04-03).

# Seeing the Sights

**Chapelle Notre-Dame de Vie** RELIGIOUS SITE   The romantic chapel and its tree-dappled grounds, once painted by Churchill, lies 1.5km (1 mile) southeast of Mougins. It was built in the 12th century and reconstructed in 1646. The priory next door is even more famous. It was Picasso's studio and private residence for the last 12 years of his life. It's still a private home occupied intermittently by the Picasso heirs.

Chemin de la Chapelle. Admission free.

**Musée d'Art Classique de Mougins** ★ MUSEUM   In a typically Mougins twist, the town's fascinating new museum shows Egyptian, Greek, and Roman artifacts from across Provence and the Mediterranean, alongside works from the Renaissance and modern day. Classically inspired sculptures, drawings, and canvases from Matisse, Dufy, Cézanne, Henry Moore, and Antony Gormley are thus transposed against pieces from a bygone age. The juxtaposition of an ancient statue of Venus right next to a Venus sculpture by Yves Klein and a *Birth of Venus* print by Andy Warhol gets our vote.

5 rue des Mûriers. www.mouginsmusee.com. ✆ **04-93-75-18-65.** Admission 12€ adults, 5€ children 17 and under. Apr–Oct daily 9:30am–8:30pm; Nov–Mar Tues—Sun 9:30am–7pm.

**Musée de la Photographie André Villers** ★ ART MUSEUM    Mougins is awash with art. A great place to start is this permanent collection of photography by Picasso's friend André Villers. Villers chronicled his friend's Mougins years in black-and-white photos, some scarily prescient, others hilarious (the photo showing Picasso sitting down for breakfast in his trademark Breton shirt pretending he has croissants for fingers will surely raise a smile). Temporary photography exhibitions fill the remaining floors of this traditional village house.

Porte Sarrazine. *(C)* **04-93-75-85-67.** Free admission. Tues–Fri 10am–12:30pm and 2–7pm; Oct Sat–Sun 11am–7pm.

# Where to Eat

**Le Mas Candille** (see below) is noted for its sublime cuisine; you may want to call to reserve a table.

**Le Moulin de Mougins** ★★ FRENCH    Once this address was arguably the most celebrated dining spot on the Riviera when it was the domain of Roger Vergé, now long retired but formerly one of France's top chefs. The current chef Sébastien Chambru does an admirable job filling Vergé's Michelin-starred shoes, without all the hype. Like Vergé, he employs market-fresh ingredients in his "cuisine of the sun," a reference to Provence's sun-drenched countryside. Dishes are earthy yet incredibly upscale, often with modern twists on culinary traditions from both Provence and other regions of the country. Some of the chef's best-known creations include pan-fried foie gras, carpaccio of scallops, and a truly delectable filet of sole stuffed with prawns.

The inn has six rooms and five suites. Each is individually designed, modern, and extremely luxurious. Double rooms cost 150€ to 200€, suites 200€ to 350€.

Notre-Dame de Vie, Mougins 06250. www.moulindemougins.com. *(C)* **04-93-75-78-24.** Fax 04-93-90-18-55. Reservations required. Main courses 38€–80€; fixed-price menu 39€–120€ lunch, 85€–120€ dinner. AE, DC, MC, V. Wed–Sun noon–2pm and 7:30–10pm.

# Where to Stay

**Le Moulin de Mougins** (see "Where to Eat," above) offers rooms and suites.

**Le Mas Candille** ★    This 200-year-old Provençal *mas* (farmhouse) is bathed in five-star luxury. It gained six high-end villa suites in 2009, and its Shiseido spa picked up a best wellness award in 2011. The public rooms contain many 19th-century furnishings, and some open onto the vast gardens that are awash with lavender and olives, and dotted with sculptures. Rooms are individually decorated in different styles, including Japanese, medieval, French colonial, and Provençal. Its restaurant offers prix-fixe lunch and evening menus (each fairly priced, considering the quality on offer), which include dishes such as red mullet and mussels with quince jelly; and scallop tart with cèpes, Jerusalem artichokes, and Tio Pépé cappuccino.

Bd. Clément Rebuffel, Mougins 06250. www.lemascandille.com. *(C)* **04-92-28-43-43.** Fax 04-92-28-43-40. 51 units. 295€–490€ double; from 750€ suite. AE, DC, MC, V. **Amenities:** 2 restaurants; bar; exercise room; 2 outdoor pools; room service; spa. *In room:* A/C, TV, hair dryer, minibar, free Wi-Fi.

**Royal Mougins** ★    Guests rave about this luxurious country resort 1.5km (1 mile) west of outside Mougins for the golf, spa, and food, in that order. The 18-hole course, created in 1993, is broken by streams and waterfalls, and offers preferential rates for guests. The rest of the grounds are an organized chaos of olives, succulents, yuccas, and pine, all interspersed with giant sun-loungers covered in cushions. It's frequented by a wealthy local and European clientele. The indoor/outdoor spa performs microdermabrasion for men and "royal facials" for women. A smart restaurant overlooks the 18th green. It uses fabulously lavish, not to mention expensive, ingredients. Sumptuous suite-only rooms come with a private outdoor sun terrace in Deluxe and Premium categories.

Bd. Clément Rebuffel, Mougins 06250. www.royalmougins.fr. (℃) **04-92-92-49-69.** Fax 04-92-92-49-72. 46 units. 213€–543€ suite. AE, DC, MC, V. **Amenities:** Restaurant; bar; exercise room; room service; spa. *In room:* A/C, TV, hair dryer, minibar, free Wi-Fi.

# GRASSE ★

906km (562 miles) S of Paris; 18km (11 miles) N of Cannes; 9.5km (6 miles) N of Mougins; 23km (14 miles) NW of Antibes

Grasse, a 20-minute drive from Cannes, is the most fragrant town on the Riviera. Surrounded by jasmine and roses, it has been the capital of the perfume industry since the Renaissance. It was once a famous resort, attracting such royals as Queen Victoria and Princess Pauline Borghese, Napoleon's lascivious sister.

Today some three-quarters of the world's essences are produced here from foliage that includes violets, daffodils, wild lavender, and jasmine. It takes 10,000 flowers to produce just over 1 kilogram of jasmine petals. Almost a ton of petals is needed to distill 1 liter of essence. The quaint town, which formed the backdrop for the 2006 movie *Perfume,* has several free perfume museums where visitors can enroll in workshops to create their own scent. The surrounding hills offer a tranquil respite from the coastal bustle, thanks in part to the wonderful selection of country hotels that stud the Provençal countryside.

## Essentials

**GETTING THERE**   **Trains** run to Grasse from Nice, Cannes, and all stations in between. It deposits passengers a 10-minute walk south of town. From here, a walking trail or shuttle bus leads visitors into the center. One-way train tickets cost 4€ from Cannes and 9.20€ from Nice. For train schedules and more information, visit www.voyages-sncf.com or call (℃) **36-35. Buses** pull into town every 30 to 60 minutes daily from Cannes (trip time: 50 min.). The one-way fare is 1€. There are also about 14 buses every day from Nice (trip time: 1 hr). The one-way fare is around 1€. They arrive at the Gare Routière, place Notre Dame des Fleurs ((℃) **04-93-36-37-37**), a 5-minute walk north of the town center. Visitors arriving by **car** take A8, which funnels in traffic from Monaco, Aix-en-Provence, and Marseille.

**VISITOR INFORMATION**   The **Office de Tourisme** is at place du cours Honoré Cresp (www.grasse.fr; (℃) **04-93-36-66-66;** fax 04-93-36-86-36).

## Seeing the Sights

**Musée International de la Parfumerie ★** MUSEUM   This architectural wonder serves as a neat lesson on Grasse's scented history. It runs through the raw materials, trade routes, innovation, and marketing of both perfume's beginnings and its modern-day megabrands.

Display at the Musée International de la Parfumerie.

2 bd. du Jeu de Ballon. www.museesdegrasse.com. ☏ **04-93-36-80-20.** Admission 3€ adults, free for children 18 and under. May–Sept daily 11am–7pm; Oct—Apr Wed–Mon 11am–6pm. Closed Nov.

**Parfumerie Molinard** FACTORY TOUR   This firm is well known in the United States, where its products are sold at Saks, Neiman-Marcus, and Bloomingdale's. In the factory, you can witness the extraction of the essence from the flowers and even make your own scent. You'll also learn all the details of the process of converting flowers into essential oils. You can admire a collection of antique perfume bottle labels and see a rare collection of perfume *flacons* by Baccarat and Lalique. The nearby Parfumerie Fragonard factory, 20 boulevard Fragonard, which emerged fresh from a thorough renovation in 2012, offers a similar experience.

60 bd. Victor Hugo. www.molinard.com. ☏ **04-93-36-01-62.** Free admission. Daily 9.30am-6.30pm (until 7pm July—Aug).

**Villa Musée Fragonard** ★ HISTORIC HOME/ART MUSEUM   The setting is an 18th-century aristocrat's town house with a magnificent garden in back. The collection displayed here includes the paintings of Jean-Honoré Fragonard, who was born in Grasse in 1732; his sister-in-law, Marguerite Gérard; his son, Alexandre; and his grandson, Théophile. Alexandre decorated the grand staircase. Curiously, this is the least-visited museum in town but is surely one of the loveliest.

23 bd. Fragonard. ☏ **04-97-05-58-00.** Free admission. May–Sept daily 11am–7pm; Oct—Apr Wed–Mon 11am–6pm. Closed Nov.

## Where to Eat

For inexpensive dining, you can head for **Hôtel La Bellaudière** (see next page).

**La Bastide St-Antoine (Restaurant Chibois)** ★★★ FRENCH/ PROVENÇAL    La Bastide St-Antoine offers one of the grandest culinary experiences along the Riviera. Jacques Chibois and his restaurant have attracted national attention since 1996. In a 200-year-old Provençal farmhouse surrounded by 2.8 hectares (7 acres) of trees and shrubbery, the restaurant serves a sophisticated array of dishes. Exquisite examples are oysters flavored with yucca leaves, a terrine of foie gras with celery, roasted suckling lamb with a fricassee of fresh vegetables and basil, and roast pigeon risotto with artichokes and truffles. Desserts may include strawberry soup with spice wine or ice cream made with olives and a hint of olive oil. The chef also does wonders with wild duck.

You can stay in the attached five-star accommodation of nine rooms and seven suites, decorated in upscale Provençal style. They have air-conditioning, free Wi-Fi, hair dryers, iPod docks, minibars, and TVs. Outside there's a pool, jogging track, and *boules* court. Doubles cost 250€ to 435€, suites from 480€.

48 av. Henri Dunant. www.jacques-chibois.com. © **04-93-70-94-94.** Fax 04-93-70-94-95. Reservations required. Main courses 50€–79€; fixed-price lunch Mon–Sat 59€–190€, dinner 180€– 190€. AE, DC, MC, V. Daily noon–2pm and 8–9:30pm.

# Where to Stay

**Terre Blanche Hotel and Spa** ★★    Just 20km (12½ miles) east of Grasse, or a 30-minute drive north from Cannes, this golf, spa, and sporting retreat is popular with international guests for good reason. Accommodation takes the form of a series of luxury villas, which are dotted around several acres of landscaped parkland. Each has a private terrace with sun loungers, Provençal furnishing, sumptuous bathrooms with l'Occitane products, plus golf and forest views. Families find the resort particularly attractive, not least because of the vast kids club complete with Lego room. Golf buggy routes and walking path span the resort. The two 18-hole golf courses also feature a performance centre and a David Leadbetter Golf Academy. The courses and grounds are studded with fabulous outdoor sculptures, all of which can be discovered on a bespoke resort audio tour. Calories amassed in the gourmet Faventia restaurant can be burned off in the Terre Blanche spa.

Domaine de Terre Blanche, Grasse, 83440 Tourettes. www.terre-blanche.com. © **94-39-90-00.** Fax 94-39-90-91. 115 units. 380€–675€ double; from 480€ suite. AE, DC, MC, V. **Amenities:** 3 restaurants; 2 bars; babysitting; concierge; exercise room; golf, large indoor pool; room service; spa; sauna; tennis. *In room:* A/C, TV, hair dryer, minibar, free Wi-Fi.

**Hôtel La Bellaudière** 🍴    Part of the respected Logis de France chain, this unpretentious family-run hotel is 3km (1¾ miles) east of the town center in the hills above Grasse. The stone-sided farmhouse was constructed in stages beginning 400 years ago, with most of what you see today built in the 1700s. Guest rooms are simple but dignified and outfitted with Provençal motifs. Many boast views of the sea. A garden terrace is lined with flowering shrubs, and guests are genuinely welcomed by the hosts. Fixed-price meals in the dining room cost 25€ each. Triples and quad rooms also available.

78 av. Pierre Ziller. www.labellaudiere.com. © **04-93-36-02-57.** Fax 04-93-36-40-03. 17 units. 65€–145€ double. AE, DC, MC, V. Free parking. **Amenities:** Restaurant; Internet; room service. *In room:* TV, free Wi-Fi.

# BIOT ★

918km (569 miles) S of Paris; 9.5km (6 miles) E of Cagnes-sur-Mer; 6.5km (4 miles) NW of Antibes

Biot has been famous for its pottery since merchants began to ship earthenware jars to Phoenicia and throughout the Mediterranean. Settled by Gallo-Romans, Biot has a long, war-torn history, but somehow the potters persevered at their ancient craft. Biot is also where Fernand Léger painted until the day he died. A magnificent collection of his work is on display at a museum just outside town.

## Essentials

**GETTING THERE** The **bus** lines no. 7 and no. 10 from Antibes's Gare Routière, place Guynemer (*℃* **04-89-87-72-00**), direct to Biot are way more convenient than the train. Tickets cost 1€. To **drive** to Biot from Nice, take N7 west. From Antibes, follow N7 east.

**VISITOR INFORMATION** The **Office de Tourisme** is at 46 rue St-Sébastien (www.biot-tourisme.com; *℃* **04-93-65-78-00;** fax 04-93-65-78-04).

## Exploring the Town

Exploration of the historic village begins at **place des Arcades**. Here you can see the 16th-century gates and the remains of the town's ramparts. **L' Eglise de Biot,** place des Arcades (*℃* **04-93-65-00-85**), dates from the 15th century. It's the work of Italian immigrants who resettled the town after the Black Death. The church is known for two stunning 15th-century retables (altarpieces): the red-and-gold *Retable du Rosaire,* by Ludovico Bréa, and *Christ aux Plaies,* by Canavesio.

  **Musée d'Histoire Locale et de Céramique Biotoise,** 9 rue St-Sebastien (*℃* **04-93-65-54-54**), has assembled the best works from local artists, potters, ceramists, painters and silver- and goldsmiths. Hours are July to September Wednesday to Sunday 11am to 7pm, October to June Wednesday to Sunday 2 to 6pm (from 10am Thurs and Fri). Admission is 4€, free ages 16 and under.

  In the late 1940s, glassmakers created a bubble-flecked glass known as *verre rustique.* It comes in brilliant colors such as cobalt and emerald, and is displayed in many store windows on the main shopping street, **rue St-Sebastien.** On the same avenue, visitors may rent an electric vehicle with which to tour Biot and the surrounding countryside. Buggy hire costs from 10€ per person per hour (*℃* **06-78-37-94-25**). Nearby is **Galerie Jean-Claude Novaro,** place des Arcades (*℃* **04-93-65-60-23**), run by a master glass blower whose colorful creations beguile and tempt.

  **Musée du Bonzaï** MUSEUM    Privately owned and maintained by members of the Okonek family, this arboretum and showroom contains the largest collection of bonsai in France. Most of the potted trees were crafted from local fig, almond, oak, and even apple trees. Especially noteworthy are bonsai versions of rare tropical cypresses and tropical figs, some as tall as 2m (6½ ft.), loaded with aerial root systems and miniaturized trunks and branches. A 5-minute walk from the Musée National Fernand Léger.

299 Chemin de Val de Pôme, Biot 06410. 3km (1¾ miles) south of Biot. www.museedubonsai-biot.fr. *℃* **04-93-65-63-99.** Admission 4€ adults, 2€ students. Wed–Mon 10am–noon and 2–6pm.

  **Musée National Fernand Léger ★★** MUSEUM    Léger's widow assembled this collection and donated it to the French government after the artist's

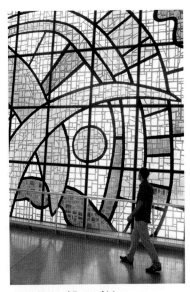

**Musée National Fernand Léger**

death in 1955. This museum is a light-filled rich celebration of paintings, ceramics, tapestries, and sculptures. It opened in 1960, an event that was attended by long-term friends Picasso and Chagall. The collection shows the artist's bright, jazzy pieces, which abound with cranes, acrobats, scaffolding, railroad signals, and buxom nudes. Temporary exhibitions are held on the ground floor and are habitually excellent. The shabby-chic alfresco cafe in the grounds serves cheap *pichets* of wine on mismatched tables, no doubt as the artist would have wanted.

Chemin du Val-de-Pôme (on the eastern edge of town, beside the road to the rail station). www.musee-fernandleger.fr. ℰ **04-92-91-50-20.** Admission 5.50€ adults, 4€ ages 12–18, free 17 and under. May—Oct Wed–Mon 10am–6pm, Nov—Apr Wed–Mon 10am–5pm.

## Where to Eat

**Les Terraillers ★★★** MODERN MEDITERRANEAN   This stone-walled restaurant is .8km (about ½ mile) south of Biot, in a 16th-century studio for the production of clay pots and ceramics. Over the years, it has become a reliable favorite of many a restaurant critic, with its elegant display of modern Provençal cooking. Stunningly presented dishes from head chef Michaël Fulci include line-caught sole with truffle-laden *farcis*, local lamb served with "virtual vegetables" constructed from semolina, and roast scallops atop celery branches and preserved lemon. Justifiably popular.

11 rte. du Chemin-Neuf. www.lesterraillers.com. ℰ **04-93-65-01-59.** Reservations required. Main courses 42€–47€; fixed-price lunch 43€–69€, dinner 69€–110€. AE, MC, V. Dec–Oct Fri–Tues noon–2pm and 7–10pm. Take rte. du Chemin-Neuf, following signs to Antibes.

# GOLFE-JUAN & VALLAURIS

Golfe-Juan: 913km (566 miles) S of Paris, 6.5km (4 miles) E of Cannes; Vallauris: 910km (564 miles) S of Paris, 6.5km (4 miles) E of Cannes

Napoleon and 800 men landed at Golfe-Juan in 1815 to begin his march to Paris and famous Hundred Days in power. Today it's a family resort known for its beaches and a noteworthy restaurant (see "Where to Eat," below).

The 2km-long (1¼-mile) RN135 leads inland from Golfe-Juan to Vallauris. Once simply a stopover along the Riviera, Vallauris's ceramic industry was in terminal decline until it was "discovered" by Picasso just after World War II. The artist's legacy lives on both in snapshots of the master in local galleries and in his awesome *La Paix et La Guerre* fresco.

# Essentials

**GETTING THERE**   You can **drive** to Golfe-Juan or Vallauris on any of the Riviera's coastal highways. Although route numbers are not always indicated, city names are clear once you're on the highway. From Cannes or Antibes, N7 east is the fastest route. From Nice or Biot, take A8/E80 west.

Golfe-Juan's rail station, on avenue de la Gare, is linked to Cannes, Juan-les-Pins, Antibes, and Nice every 30 minutes. A one-way ticket to Cannes costs 1.80€. For railway information, visit www.voyages-sncf.com or call ✆ **36-35.** A flotilla of **buses** operated by Envibus (www.envibus.fr; ✆ **04-89-87-72-00**) makes frequent trips from Cannes; the 20-minute trip costs 1€ each way.

**VISITOR INFORMATION**   There's an **Office de Tourisme** (www.vallauris-golfe-juan.fr) on boulevard des Frères-Roustan, Golfe-Juan (✆ **04-93-63-73-12;** fax 04-93-63-21-07), and another on square du 8-Mai, 1945 Vallauris (✆ **04-93-63-82-58;** fax 04-93-63-13-66).

## A Day at the Beach

Because of its position beside the sea, Golfe-Juan long ago developed into a warm-weather resort. The town's twin strips of beach are **Plage du Soleil** (east of the Vieux Port and the newer Port Camille-Rayon) and **Plage du Midi** (west of those two). Each stretches 1km (½ mile) and charges no entry fee, with the exception of small areas administered by concessions that rent mattresses for between 15€ and 20€ for a day's use. Like everywhere else on the Riviera, Golfe-Juan indulges bathers who choose to remove their bikini tops.

## Seeing the Sights

In Vallauris, Picasso's *l'Homme au Mouton* (*Man and Sheep*) is the outdoor statue at place Paul Isnard in front of which Prince Aly Kahn and screen goddess Rita Hayworth were married. The local council had intended to enclose this statue in a museum, but Picasso insisted that it remain on the square, "where the children could climb over it and the dogs water it unhindered."

**Musée Magnelli, Musée de la Céramique & Musée National Picasso La Guerre et La Paix** ★★ ART MUSEUM   A chapel of rough stone is the focal point of a three-in-one sightseeing highlight. The museum grew from the site of a chapel that Picasso decorated with two paintings: *La Paix* (*Peace*) and *La Guerre* (*War*). The paintings offer contrasting images of love and peace on the one hand, and violence and conflict on the other. In 1970, a house painter illegally gained entrance to the museum and substituted one of his designs after whitewashing a portion of the original. When the aging master inspected the damage, he said, "Not bad at all." In 1996, the site added a permanent exposition devoted to the works of the Florentine-born Alberto Magnelli, a pioneer of abstract art. A third section showcases ceramics, both traditional and innovative, from potters throughout the region.

Place de la Libération. ✆ **04-93-64-71-83.** Admission 3.25€ adults, free for children 15 and under. June–Aug daily 10am–7pm; June 15–30 and Sept 1–15 Wed–Mon 10am–12:15pm and 2–6pm; Sept 16–June 14 Wed–Mon 10am–12:15pm and 2–5pm.

## Shopping

A gallery to seek out is **Galerie Madoura,** rue Georges et Suzanne Ramié (www.madoura.com; ℭ **04-93-64-66-39**), which sells limited editions of Picasso's work. Both the late artist and his friend Chagall sculpted at the studio, and black-and-white portraits of the pair are still tacked to the walls. Picasso took his relationship with this studio-gallery a step further in 1961 by marrying one of the sales staff, Jacqueline Roque.

A host of excellent, not to mention less expensive, ceramic stores line avenue Georges-Clemenceau. **Market days** in Vallauris are Tuesday to Sunday 7am to 12:30pm, at **place Paul Isnard.**

## Where to Eat

**Chez Tétou ★★** SEAFOOD    In its own colorful way, this is one of the Côte d'Azur's most famous restaurants, capitalizing on the beau monde that came here in the 1950s and 1960s, and still pulling in the stars today. Retaining its Provençal earthiness despite its overly high prices, it has thrived in a white-sided beach cottage for more than 70 years. Appetizers are limited to platters of charcuterie, *salade Niçoise,* or several almost-perfect slices of fresh melon. Most diners order the house specialty, bouillabaisse. Also on the limited menu are grilled sea bass with tomatoes Provençal, sole meunière, and several preparations of lobster—the most famous is grilled and served with lemon-butter sauce and fresh parsley.

6 av. des Frères-Roustan, sur la Plage, Golfe-Juan. ℭ **04-93-63-71-16.** Reservations required. Main courses 77€; bouillabaisse 97€–124€. No credit cards. Thurs–Sun noon–2:30pm; Thurs–Tues 8–10:30pm. Closed Nov to early Mar.

# JUAN-LES-PINS ★★

913km (566 miles) S of Paris; 9.5km (6 miles) S of Cannes

This suburb of Antibes is a resort that flourished during the 1920s under American property developer Frank Jay Gould. In the 1930s, Juan-les-Pins drew a chic summer crowd as the Riviera "season" flipped from winter respites to the hedonistic pursuit of summer sun, sea, and sensuality. It has been attracting the young and the young-at-heart from across Europe and the U.S. ever since. F. Scott Fitzgerald decried Juan-les-Pins as a "constant carnival." If only he could see it now . . . .

## Essentials

**GETTING THERE**    Juan-les-Pins is connected by **rail** and bus to most other Mediterranean coastal resorts, including Nice (trip time: 30 min.; 3.60€ one-way). For rail information and schedules, visit www.voyages-sncf.com or call ℭ **36-35**. **Buses** arrive from Nice and its airport at 40-minute intervals throughout the day. A bus leaves for Juan-les-Pins from Antibes at place Guynemer (ℭ **04-89-87-72-00;** www.envibus.fr) daily every 20 minutes and costs 1€ one-way (trip time: 10 min.). To **drive** to Juan-les-Pins from Nice, travel along N7 south; from Cannes, follow the signposted roads.

**VISITOR INFORMATION**    The **Office de Tourisme** is at 51 bd. Charles-Guillaumont (www.antibes-juanlespins.co.uk; ℭ **04-97-23-11-10;** fax 04-97-23-11-09).

**SPECIAL EVENTS** The town offers some of the best nightlife on the Riviera, and the action reaches its height during the annual 10-day **Festival International de Jazz** (www.jazzajuan.com) in mid-July. It attracts jazz, blues, reggae, and world music artists who play nightly on the beachfront Parc de la Pinède. Recent performers have included George Benson, Maceo Parker, and B. B. King. Tickets cost 25€ to 65€ and can be purchased at the Office de Tourisme in both Antibes and Juan-les-Pins, as well as online.

## A Day at the Beach

Part of the reason people flock here is for the town's wealth of sandy beaches, all lapped by a calm bay. Juan-les-Pins also basks in a unique microclimate, making it one of the warmest places on the Riviera to soak up the sun, even in winter. **Plage de Juan-les-Pins** is the most central beach, although quieter stretches of sand wrap around the Cap d'Antibes and include family-friendly **Plage de la Salis** and chic **Plage de la Garoupe.** If you want to stretch out on a sunlounger, go to any of the beach bar concessions that line the bay, where you can rent a mattress for around 12€ to 20€. Topless sunbathing and overt shows of cosmetic surgery are the norm.

## Watersports

If you're interested in scuba diving, try **Easy Dive,** Port Gallice (www.easydive. fr; ☎ **04-93-61-26-07**). A one-tank dive costs 30€ to 55€, including all equipment. **Sea kayaking**, **pedalos, parascending,** and **donuts** are available at virtually every beach in Juan-les-Pins. **Water-skiing** was invented at the Hôtel des Belles-Rives in the 1920s, and it's still a great place to try out the sport. A 10-minute session costs around 30€, 1 hour goes for 110€.

## Where to Eat

**Le Bijou Plage ★ ♪** FRENCH/PROVENÇAL  This upscale brasserie has flourished beside the seafront promenade since 1923. The marine-style decor includes lots of varnished wood and bouquets of flowers. Menu items include excellent bouillabaisse, grilled sardines, risotto with John Dory and truffled butter, steamed mussels with *sauce poulette* (frothy cream sauce with herbs and butter), and a supersize platter of *coquillages et fruits de mer* (shellfish and seafood). This informally elegant establishment spills out onto a private beach with cocktail bar. Toes-in-the-sand outdoor tables are also available. To find the establishment, look out for the grand Moorish villa on the Juan-les-Pins beach road, which was freshly renovated in 2012.

Bd. du Littoral. www.bijouplage.com. ☎ **04-93-61-39-07.** Reservations recommended. Main courses 18.50€–111€; fixed-price menu 24€–48€. AE, DC, MC, V. Daily noon–2:30pm and 7:30–10:30pm.

**Le Perroquet ★** PROVENÇAL  Known as the best restaurant in town for the last decade or so, this restaurant's ambience is carefully synchronized to the resort's casual and carnival-like summer aura. It's across from the Parc de la Pinède and is decorated with depictions of every imaginable form of parrot, the restaurant's namesake. Look for savory fish dishes, at their best when grilled simply with olive oil and basil, and served with lemons. A worthwhile appetizer is the *assortiment Provençale,* which includes tapenade of olives, marinated peppers, grilled sardines, and stuffed vegetables. The set lunch menu changes daily and is especially good value.

Av. Georges-Gallice. www.restaurantleperroquet.fr. ✆ **04-93-61-02-20.** Reservations recommended. Main courses 16€–31€; fixed-price lunch 16€; fixed-price dinner 30€–37€. AE, MC, V. Daily noon–2pm and 7–10:30pm. Closed early Nov to Dec 26.

## Juan-les-Pins Nightlife

Try your luck at the roulette wheel or poker tables at **Eden Casino,** bd. Baudoin, in the heart of Juan-les-Pins (✆ **04-92-93-71-71**). Slot machines are open every day 10am to 4am; gaming tables from 9pm. A photo ID is required, preferably in the form of a passport.

For a faux-tropical-island experience, head to **Le Pam Pam,** 137 bd. Wilson (www.pampam.fr; ✆ **04-93-61-11-05**), a time-honored establishment where guests sip rum and people-watch while reggae beats float around the bar. More modern is **La Réserve,** av. Georges Gallice (✆ **04-93-61-20-06**), where a younger crowd sips pastis and rosé on leopard-print seats under a large plane tree.

If you prefer high-energy partying, you're in the right place. The entire Riviera descends upon Juan-les-Pins's many discos every night in summer, and it's best to follow the crowds to the latest hotspot. **Le Village,** 1 bd. de la Pinède (✆ **04-92-93-90-00**), is one of the more established clubs and boasts an action-packed dance floor with DJs spinning the latest dance sounds. The cover charge is usually 10€, more for themed evenings.

## Where to Stay

### VERY EXPENSIVE

**Hôtel Belles-Rives** ★★★   Once a holiday villa occupied by Zelda and F. Scott Fitzgerald, this luxurious hotel is one of the Riviera's most fabled addresses. It was the scene of many a drunken brawl in the 1920s, a history illustrated in Fitzgerald's semi-autobiographical novel *Tender Is the Night*. It later played host to the illustrious, such as the duke and duchess of Windsor, Josephine Baker, and Edith Piaf. As befits a hotel of this age, rooms come in a variety of shapes and sizes, from small to spacious; each one has a luxurious bathroom filled with L'Occitane beauty products. The lower terraces hold garden dining rooms, a waterside aquatic club with a snack bar and lounge, as well as a jetty. There is also a private beach and a dock.

33 bd. Edouard Baudoin, Juan-les-Pins 06160. www.bellesrives.com. ✆ **04-93-61-02-79.** Fax 04-93-61-43-51. 43 units. 225€–723€ double; 950€–1,615€ suite. AE, DC, MC, V. Parking 25€. Closed Jan–Feb. **Amenities:** 2 summer restaurants; 1 winter restaurant; 2 bars; room service. *In room:* A/C, TV, hair dryer, minibar, free Wi-Fi.

### MODERATE

**Hôtel des Mimosas**   This elegant 1870s-style villa sprawls in a subtropical garden on a hilltop, a 10-minute walk to Juan-les-Pins' sandy public beach. The decor is a mix of high-tech and Italian-style comfort, with antique and modern furniture. Guest rooms come in a variety of shapes and sizes—some are tiny. Try for one of the four rooms with a balcony or one of the nine rooms with a terrace. A pool sits amid huge palm trees. The hotel gets fully booked in summer, so reserve as far in advance as possible.

Rue Pauline, Juan-les-Pins 06160. www.hotelmimosas.com. ℭ **04-93-61-04-16.** Fax 04-92-93-06-46. 34 units. 99€–155€ double. AE, MC, V. Free parking. Closed Oct–Apr. **Amenities:** Bar; outdoor pool; room service; free Wi-Fi. *In room:* A/C, TV, hair dryer, minibar.

### INEXPENSIVE

**Hôtel La Marjolaine** 🐾 A stone's throw from Juan-les-Pins train station and a 3-minute stroll to the beach. Granted, the decor of this century-old villa hasn't changed much since the 1980s, but rooms are clean, homey, and easily the best value in town. Most have exposed ceiling beams, hefty Provençal furniture, and solid wooden beds. The south-facing terrace is ideal for savoring breakfast outdoors on sunny days. A friendly welcome is assured.

15 av. Dr Fabre, Juan-les-Pins 06160. ℭ **04-93-61-06-60.** Fax 04-93-61-02-75. 17 units. 65€–95€ double. AE, MC, V. Free parking. Closed Jan–Feb. **Amenities:** Bar. *In room:* A/C, TV, hair dryer, free Wi-Fi.

# ANTIBES & CAP D'ANTIBES ★★

913km (566 miles) S of Paris; 21km (13 miles) SW of Nice; 11km (6¾ miles) NE of Cannes

On the other side of the Baie des Anges (Bay of Angels) from Nice is the pretty port of Antibes. The town has a quiet charm unique on the Côte d'Azur. Its harbor is filled with fishing boats and pleasure yachts, and its winding streets are packed with promenading locals and well-dressed visitors. A pedestrianized port and several car-free squares make it a family-friendly destination, too. There's also an excellent covered market located near the harbor, open every morning except Mondays.

Spiritually, Antibes is totally divorced from Cap d'Antibes, a peninsula studded with the villas of the super-rich. But the less affluent are welcome to peek at paradise, and a lovely 6km (3¾ miles) coastal path rings the headland, passing picnic and diving spots en route.

Harbor at Antibes.

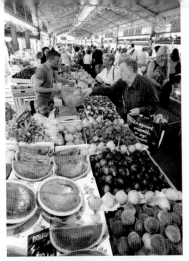

Antibes's bustling market.

## Essentials

**GETTING THERE** **Trains** from Cannes arrive at the rail station, place Pierre-Semard, every 20 minutes (trip time: 15 min.); the one-way fare is 2.70€. Trains from Nice arrive at the rate of 25 per day (trip time: 20 min.); the one-way fare is 4.20€. For rail information, visit www.voyages-sncf.com or call ✆ **36-35**. The **bus** station, La Gare Routière, place Guynemer (✆ **04-89-87-72-00**), receives buses from throughout Provence. Bus fares to Nice, Cannes, Grasse, and Cagnes-sur-Mer cost 1€ one-way.

If you're **driving,** follow E1 east from Cannes and take the turnoff to the south for Antibes, which will lead to the historic core of the old city. From Nice, take E1 west until you come to the turnoff for Antibes. The Cap d'Antibes is clearly visible from most parts of the Riviera. To drive here from Antibes, follow the coastal road, boulevard Leclerc, south—you can't miss it.

**VISITOR INFORMATION** The **Office de Tourisme** is at 11 place du Général-de-Gaulle (www.antibesjuanlespins.com; ✆ **04-97-23-11-11;** fax 04-97-23-11-12).

## Seeing the Sights

**Musée Napoléonien** ☺ MUSEUM   In this stone-sided fort and tower on the Cap d'Antibes, built in stages in the 17th and 18th centuries, you'll find an interesting collection of Napoleonic memorabilia, naval models, and paintings. A toy-soldier collection depicts various uniforms, including one used by Napoleon in the Marengo campaign. A wall painting on wood shows Napoleon disembarking at Golfe-Juan on March 1, 1815, to start his 100 days' march to Paris. In contrast to Canova's Greek-god image of Napoleon, a miniature pendant by Barrault reveals the general as he really looked, with pudgy cheeks and a receding hairline. In the rear rotunda is one of the many hats worn by the emperor. You can climb to the top of the tower for a view of the coast that's worth the admission price alone.

Batterie du Graillon, bd. J.-F.-Kennedy. ✆ **04-93-61-45-32.** Admission 3€ adults; 1.50€ seniors, students, and ages 19–25; free for children 18 and under. Mid-June to mid-Sept Tues–Sat 10am–6pm; mid-Sept to mid-June Tues–Sat 10am–4:30pm.

**Musée Picasso** ★★ ART MUSEUM   On the ramparts above the port is the Château Grimaldi, once the home of princes from the Grimaldi family, who ruled the city from 1385 to 1608. Today it houses a stunning collection of Picasso artworks. The Spanish artist came to town after the war in 1946 and lived and worked in the chateau at the invitation of the municipality. When he departed, he gifted all the work he'd completed to the chateau museum: 23 paintings, 80 ceramics, 44 drawings, 32 lithographs, 11 oils on paper, 2 sculptures, and 5 tapestries. In addition to this collection, a gallery of contemporary art exhibits works

**THE FRENCH RIVIERA**

Antibes & Cap d'Antibes

**Musée Picasso.**

by Léger, Miró, Ernst, and Calder, among others. An expansive outdoor terrace offers views over the Cap d'Antibes, which Picasso aficionados may recognize from his paintings.

Château Grimaldi, place du Mariejol. ⓒ **04-92-90-54-20.** Admission 6€ adults, 3€ students and seniors, free for children 18 and under. Mid-June to mid-Sept Tues–Sun 10am–6pm; mid-Sept to mid-June Tues–Sun 10am–noon and 2–6pm.

## Where to Eat

The Zelda and Scott Fitzgeralds of today head for the **Eden Roc Restaurant** at the Hôtel du Cap–Eden Roc for grand service and grand cuisine. The excellent restaurants at the **Cap d'Antibes Beach Club** (p. 581) are also open to the public.

**Bistro La Rustic** ⬥ FRENCH/PIZZA A family-run restaurant where grandmother mans the kitchen while grandson fields the outdoor tables on buzzing place Nationale. Cuisine, simple as it is, is based around a wood-fired oven. Delicious chargrilled steaks, half-chickens, and breasts of duck are cooked to perfection, the latter on a shovel (which makes it easier to whip it out of the stove at the last minute). Platters of prawns, salads filled with lardons, and melon with ham make up the appetizer menu. One of the author's picks for a great-value traditional feast.

33 place Nationale. ⓒ **04-93-34-10-81.** Main courses 9€–17€; fixed-price menu 13€–18€. MC, V. Daily noon–3pm and 7–11pm.

**La Taverne du Safranier** PROVENÇAL Earthy and irreverent, this brasserie in a century-old building serves a changing roster of Provençal specialties. Zany art is hung up the walls of the car-free square that the restaurant occupies, making this spot a favorite of bohemian locals (who are all actually wealthy in this part of the world). It's also great for kids, as they can run around freely. Menu examples include a platter of *petits farcis* (stuffed vegetables), a mini bouillabaisse for single diners, savory fish soup, and an assortment of grilled fish (including sardines) that's served with just a dash of fresh lemon.

1 place du Safranier. www.taverne-du-safranier.fr. © **04-93-34-80-50.** Reservations recommended. Main courses 18€–28€; fixed-price menu 26€-32€. MC, V. Tues–Sun noon–2pm; Tues–Sat 7–10pm. Closed mid-Nov to mid-Feb.

**Restaurant de Bacon ★★★** SEAFOOD    The Eden Roc restaurant at the Hôtel du Cap is more elegant, but Bacon serves the best seafood around, and has done so for over 6 decades. Surrounded by ultraexpensive residences, this restaurant on a rocky peninsula offers a panoramic coast view. Bouillabaisse aficionados claim that Bacon offers the best in France. In its deluxe version, saltwater crayfish float atop the savory brew; we prefer the simple version, where a waiter adds the finishing touches at your table. If bouillabaisse isn't your favorite, try fish soup with garlic-laden rouille sauce, fish terrine, sea bass, or John Dory, or see what's on offer on the two fixed-price menus.

Bd. de Bacon. www.restaurantdebacon.com. © **04-93-61-50-02.** Reservations required. Main courses 45€–145€; fixed-price lunch 49€–79€, dinner 79€. AE, DC, MC, V. Wed–Sun noon–2pm; Tues–Sun 8–10pm. Closed Nov–Feb.

# Where to Stay

## VERY EXPENSIVE

**Hôtel du Cap–Eden Roc ★★★**    Legendary for the glamour of both its setting and its clientele, this Second Empire hotel, opened in 1870, is surrounded by a maze of manicured gardens. It's like a country estate, with spacious public rooms. Accommodation is among the most sumptuous on the Riviera. Guest rooms recently benefited from a thorough renovation, with sleek modern fittings, iPod docks, and LED screens in every room. Even though the guests snoozing by the pool appear artfully undraped during the day, evenings are upscale, with lots of emphasis on clothing and style. The stunning Restaurant Eden Roc spills out onto a panoramic sea view terrace, and the Bellini Bar is the summertime meeting place of the stars. Casual visitors normally won't even get a look in, but the hotel has become somewhat less elitist.

Bd. J.-F.-Kennedy, Cap d'Antibes 06600. www.edenroc-hotel.fr. © **04-93-61-39-01.** Fax 04-93-67-76-04. 67 units. 350€–1,250€ double; 1,130€–5,800€ suite; 5,200€–12,500€ villa. AE, DC, MC, V. Closed mid-Oct to mid-Apr. Bus: A2. **Amenities:** 2 restaurants; 2 bars; babysitting; exercise room; massage; outdoor pool; room service; spa. *In room:* A/C, TV, hair dryer, free Wi-Fi.

## MODERATE

**Le Bosquet ★** 💼    This fabulous, family-run bed and breakfast midway along the Cap d'Antibes is as far removed from the Riviera bustle as you can get. A leafy, unkempt garden laps up against the pink-hued main villa, which is 2½ centuries old. It's here that the four boutique guest rooms are housed. All are utterly charming: The Chambre Sable has traditional *tomette* floors and antique fittings; the Chambre Galet has a large bathroom and sitting area, and is large enough for a family.

14 chemin des Sables, Cap d'Antibes 06160. www.lebosquet06.com. © **04-93-67-32-29.** 4 units. 100€–200€ double. MC, V. Free parking. Closed mid-Nov to last week Dec. **Amenities:** Bar. *In room:* A/C, TV, hair dryer, fridge, free Wi-Fi.

## INEXPENSIVE

**La Jabotte** ★ 🍴  Only 54m (177 ft.) from the beach, this one-story villa with a trio of bungalows is built around a citrus garden. Yves and Claude are gracious hosts, welcoming you into their cozy environment, where they serve breakfast on the terrace with homemade jams, freshly squeezed orange juice, and "the surprise of the morning." Each day the bar proposes a different aperitif. Bedrooms are small but elegantly decorated, with rich colors, original paintings, and an intriguing hodgepodge of furnishings. Accommodation is frequently themed, ranging from birds to angels. Many of the paintings and ceramics on display are also for sale.

13 av. Max Maurey, Cap d'Antibes 06160. www.jabotte.com. ℭ **04-93-61-45-89.** Fax 04-93-61-07-04. 10 units. 86€–142€ double; 146€–189€ suite. MC, V. Limited free parking. Closed Nov to mid-Feb. **Amenities:** Garden; bar; room service (breakfast only). *In room:* A/C, TV (in some), free Wi-Fi.

# CAGNES-SUR-MER ★

918km (569 miles) S of Paris; 21km (13 miles) NE of Cannes

Cagnes-sur-Mer has two visitor-friendly centers. Perched on a hill overlooking the Riviera, **Haut-de-Cagnes** is one of the most stunning hill villages on the Riviera. At the foot of the hill is an old fishing port and beach resort, **Cros-de-Cagnes,** which lies midway between Nice and Antibes.

For years Haut-de-Cagnes attracted the French literati, such as Simone de Beauvoir. A colony of painters, including Amedeo Modigliani, also settled here. Renoir said the village was "the place where I want to paint until the last day of my life." His museum is the highlight of any visit to the area. The coastal racecourse is one of the most fun-packed in France, with evening races all summer.

## Essentials

**GETTING THERE**  The **train** station, Gare SNCF, lies in Cagnes-Ville (the nondescript commercial part of town) at avenue de la Gare. It serves trains that run along the Mediterranean coast, with arrivals every 30 minutes from both Nice (trip time: 10 min.; 1.80€ one-way) and Cannes (trip time: 25 min.; 4.20€ one-way). For rail information, visit www.voyages-sncf.com or call ℭ **36-35. Buses,** costing 1€ from Nice and Cannes, stop at Cagnes-Ville and at Les Collettes, within walking distance of both Cros-de-Cagnes and the Renoir Museum. For information, contact **Ligne d'Azur** (www.lignesdazur.com; ℭ **08-10-06-10-06**). The climb from Cagnes-Ville to Haut-de-Cagnes is strenuous; a free minibus runs daily about every 15 minutes year-round from place du Général-de-Gaulle in the center of Cagnes-Ville to Haut-de-Cagnes. By **car** from any of the coastal towns, follow the A8 coastal highway, exiting at Cagnes/Sur-Mer/Cros-de-Cagnes.

**VISITOR INFORMATION**  The **Office de Tourisme** is at 6 bd. Maréchal-Juin, Cagnes-Ville (www.cagnes-tourisme.com; ℭ **04-93-20-61-64;** fax 04-93-20-52-63).

**SPECIAL EVENTS**  The verdant gardens of the Renoir Museum are the site, for 2 days in mid-March or early April, of an **Olive Festival (La Fête de l'Olivier).** Highlights include olive oil tasting and gourmet food samples from local restaurants. Entrance is free.

# Exploring the Towns

Cros-de-Cagnes, a part of Cagnes-Sur-Mer, is known for its 4km (2½ miles) of beach, the **Plages de Cros-de-Cagnes.** It's covered with light-gray pebbles smoothed by centuries of wave action.

The orange groves and fields of carnations of the upper village of Haut-de-Cagnes provide a beautiful setting for the narrow flower-filled streets and 17th- and 18th-century homes. Head to the top, where you can enjoy the view from **place du Château** and have lunch or a drink at a pavement cafe.

**Château-Musée Grimaldi (Musée de l'Olivier & Musée d'Art Moderne Méditerranéen)** ★ HISTORIC HOME/MUSEUMS   Château-Musée was a fortress built in 1301 by Rainier Grimaldi I, a lord of Monaco and a French admiral (his portrait is in the museum). In the early 17th century, the castle was converted into a gracious Louis XIII château, which now contains two museums. The Museum of the Olive Tree shows the steps involved in cultivating and processing the olive. The Museum of Mediterranean Modern Art displays works by Kisling, Carzou, Dufy, Cocteau, and Seyssaud, plus temporary exhibits. In one salon is an interesting *trompe l'oeil* fresco, *La Chute de Phaeton*. The tower affords a view of the Côte d'Azur.

7 place Grimaldi, Haut-de-Cagnes. ℂ **04-92-02-47-30.** Admission to both museums 4€ adults, 2€ students, free for children 17 and under. May–Oct Wed–Mon 10am–noon and 2–6pm; Nov–Apr Wed–Mon 10am–noon and 2–5pm.

**Musée Renoir & Les Collettes** ★★ HISTORIC HOME/MUSEUM   After more than a year of renovations, Les Collettes will reopen its doors in July 2013. Its appearance will remain true to the period when the great Impressionist painter Renoir lived here, from 1908 until his death in 1919. However, a new sculpture area as well as an audio-visual room will be added, and the garden paths will be restored to their original layout.

The house was built in 1907 in an orange grove. Explore the drawing room and dining room on your own before going up to the artist's bedroom. In his atelier are his wheelchair, easel, and brushes. The terrace of Mme. Renoir's bedroom faces stunning views over Cap d'Antibes and Haut-de-Cagnes. On a wall hangs a photograph of one of Renoir's sons, Pierre, as he appeared in the 1932 film *Madame Bovary.* Although Renoir is best remembered for his paintings, in Cagnes he began experimenting with sculpture, a form he found easy to manage, given his growing arthritis. The museum has 20 portrait busts and portrait medallions, most of which depict his wife and children. For many, the orange groves, olive plantation, and unkempt gardens that so inspired the artist are a definite highlight.

During the first half of 2013, the Musée Renoir's permanent collection of artworks can be viewed at the Château-Musée Grimaldi.

19 chemin des Collettes. ℂ **04-93-20-61-07.** Admission 4€ adults, 2€ students, free for ages 18 and under. May–Oct Wed–Mon 10am–noon and 2–6pm; Nov–Apr Wed–Mon 10am–noon and 2–5pm.

# Where to Eat

## IN HAUT-DE-CAGNES

**Josy-Jo** ★★ TRADITIONAL FRENCH   Behind a 200-year-old facade covered with vines and flowers, this ever-popular restaurant was the home and studio of Modigliani and Soutine during their hungriest years. Paintings cover the walls, and the Bandecchi family runs everything smoothly. The menu features grilled meats and a variety of fish. You can enjoy brochette of gigot of lamb with kidneys, calves liver, homemade terrine of foie gras of duckling, stuffed Provençal vegetables, and an array of salads. Desserts, including the mousse infused with local Riviera lemons, are all homemade.

2 rue Planastel. www.restaurant-josyjo.com. © **04-93-20-68-76.** Reservations required. Main courses 22€–45€; fixed-price lunch 30€–42€. AE, MC, V. Tues–Sat 12:30–2:30pm and 7:30–10:30pm. Closed mid-Nov to Dec.

## Where to Stay

### IN CAGNES-SUR-MER

**Appart'é** A friendly, well-run spot that makes a fine budget option, this fine little hotel is set back from the beach at Cros-de-Cagnes. Rooms have benefited from a recent overhaul and have modern fittings, from comfy beds to high-powered showers. They range from tiny singles to suites capable of fitting a family of five, the latter with a kitchenette thrown in. All are simply furnished, all have a balcony or terrace, and some have sea views.

3 av. de la Serre, Cagnes-sur-Mer 06800. www.hotel-aeva.fr. © **04-93-73-39-52.** Fax 04-93-08-07-26. 21 units. 80€–120€ double; 120€–205€ suite. MC, V. Free parking. **Amenities:** Bar. In room: TV, minibar, free Wi-Fi.

### IN HAUT-DE-CAGNES

**Le Cagnard** ★ Several 13th-century houses were joined in the 1960s to form this glamorous little hotel. The property reopened in spring 2012 after a sympathetic renovation, which saw the arrival of a small swimming pool in the leafy gardens. Public areas are covered with frescoes, and there's a vine-draped terrace. The rooms and salons are furnished with antiques such as provincial chests, armoires, and Louis XV chairs. Each room has its own style: Some are duplexes, others have terraces and views of the countryside. The luxurious bathrooms are spacious, with tub/showers.

Rue du Pontis-Long, Le Haut-de-Cagnes, Cagnes-sur-Mer 06800. www.le-cagnard.com. © **04-93-20-73-21.** Fax 04-93-22-06-39. 23 units. 240€–380€ double; from 340€ suite. AE, DC, MC, V. Free parking. **Amenities:** Restaurant; bar; babysitting; room service; pool. In room: A/C, TV, hair dryer, minibar, free Wi-Fi.

# ST-PAUL-DE-VENCE ★★

926km (574 miles) S of Paris; 23km (14 miles) E of Grasse; 28km (17 miles) E of Cannes; 31km (19 miles) N of Nice

Of all the hilltop villages of the Riviera, St-Paul-de-Vence is by far the most famous and the most chic. It gained popularity in the 1920s, when artists including Picasso, Chagall, and Matisse frequented the town, trading their paintings for hospitality at the Colombe d'Or hotel. Contemporary art is now the town's principal attraction, and the winding streets are studded with galleries and museums. Circling the town are magnificent old ramparts (allow about 30 min. to walk the full loop) that overlook flowers and olive and orange trees. From the north ramparts, you can look out on Baou de St-Jeannet, a sphinx-shaped rock that was painted into the landscape of Poussin's *Polyphème*.

**St-Paul-de-Vence.**

# Essentials

**GETTING THERE** The nearest **rail** station is in Cagnes-sur-Mer. Some 20 **buses** per day (no. 400) leave from central Nice, dropping passengers off in St-Paul-de-Vence (1€ one-way), then in Vence. For information, contact Ligne d'Azur (www.lignesdazur. com; ℂ 08-10-06-10-06). If you're **driving** from Nice, take the coastal A8 highway west, turn inland at Cagnes-sur-Mer, and follow signs north to St-Paul-de-Vence.

**VISITOR INFORMATION** The **Office de Tourisme** is at 2 rue Grande (www. saint-pauldevence.com; ℂ 04-93-32-86-95; fax 04-93-32-60-27).

## Exploring the Town

*Note:* Driving a car in St-Paul's old town is prohibited, except to drop off luggage at your hotel.

If you phone at least a day (and sometimes a few hours) in advance, the local tourist office can arrange any of ten themed walking tours of the town's historic core or town outskirts. Most tours last for about an hour and are priced at 5€ each; all of them depart from the tourist office. Depending on your interests, tours may highlight the city's history and architecture, the artists who lived here and the works they created, and even the lessons and lore of the French pastime of *pétanque* (also known as *boules*), wherein a practice session with seasoned locals is included as part of the experience.

The pedestrian-only **rue Grande** is the most evocative street, running the length of St-Paul. Most of the stone houses along it are from the 16th and 17th centuries, and many still bear the coats of arms placed there by the original builders. Today most of the houses are antiques shops, arts-and-crafts galleries, and souvenir and gift shops; some are still artists' studios.

The village's chief sight is the **Collégiale de la Conversion de St-Paul ★**, constructed in the 12th and 13th centuries and much altered over the years. The Romanesque choir is the oldest part, containing some remarkable stalls carved in walnut in the 17th century. Look to the left as you enter: You'll see the painting *Ste-Catherine d'Alexandrie,* which has been attributed to Tintoretto. The **Trésor de l'Eglise** is one of the most beautiful in the Alpes-Maritimes, with a spectacular ciborium. Look also for a low relief of the *Martyrdom of St-Clément* on the last altar on the right. It's open daily 9am to 6pm (to 7pm July–Aug). Admission is free.

Near the church is the **Musée d'Histoire de St-Paul,** place de l'Eglise (ℂ **04-93-32-41-13**), a museum in a village house that dates to the 1500s. A collection of rather silly dioramas illustrates the history of the village. It's open from April to September daily 11am to 1pm and 3 to 6pm, and October to March daily from 2 to 5pm. Admission is 3€ adults, 2€ students and children 6 to 18, and free for children 5 and under. The same ticket grants entrance to the

**15**

**THE FRENCH RIVIERA**

St-Paul-de-Vence

Foundation Maeght.

awe-inspiring **Chapelle des Pénitents Blanc** (same hours), just across the street. The artist Folon, who worked on his masterpiece until his death in 2005, decorated the church using modern plaster effects and mosaics. The vast interior is alive with airy frescoes and sunny paintings. It opened to the public in 2008.

**Foundation Maeght** ★★★ ART MUSEUM   This avant-garde building houses one of the most famed modern art museums in Europe. On a hill in pine-studded woods, the Foundation Maeght is like Shangri-La. Nature and the creations of men and women blend harmoniously in this unique achievement of the architect José Luis Sert. Its white concrete arcs give the impression of a giant pagoda.

A stark Calder sculpture rises like a futuristic monster on the lawn. In a courtyard and beyond, the bronze works of Giacometti, marble statues by Miró, and mosaics by Chagall form a surrealistic garden. Artworks are displayed inside, but the museum is at its best in a natural setting of terraces and gardens. It's built on several levels, its many glass walls providing an indoor-outdoor vista. The foundation, a gift "to the people" from Aimé and Marguerite Maeght, also provides a showcase for new talent. On the property are a library, a cinema, a cafeteria, and a magnificent museum store.

623 chemin des Gardettes, outside the town walls. www.fondation-maeght.com. (✆ **04-93-32-81-63**. Admission 14€ adults, 9€ students and ages 10–18, free for children 9 and under. July–Sept daily 10am–7pm; Apr–June daily 10am–6pm; Oct–Mar daily 10am–1pm and 2-6pm.

## Where to Eat

The dining room at the **Hôtel Le St-Paul,** 86 rue Grande (www.lesaintpaul.com; (✆ **04-93-32-65-25**) also features exceptional cuisine based on market-fresh ingredients.

**La Colombe d'Or** ★ PROVENÇAL   For more than a decade, "The Golden Dove" has been St-Paul's most celebrated restaurant—not for cutting-edge cuisine or exotic experiments, but for its remarkable art collection. You can dine amid Mirós, Picassos, Klees, Dufys, Utrillos, and Calders. In fair weather, everyone vies for a seat on the terrace. Begin with smoked salmon or foie gras from Landes if you've recently won at the casino. If not, you can opt for a soup made with fresh seasonal vegetables. The house specials are Bellini champagne cocktails and simple roast chicken, neither of which will break the bank.

The guest rooms (13 doubles, 12 suites) contain French antiques and Provençal accessories. They're in the original 16th-century stone house and in two wings added in the 1950s, one of which stretches into the garden next to the pool. Some units have exposed stone and ceiling beams; all are luxurious, with air-conditioning, minibars, and TVs. Prices are 250€ for a double, 430€ for a suite, including free Wi-Fi.

1 place du Général-de-Gaulle, St-Paul-de-Vence 06570. www.la-colombe-dor.com. ℂ **04-93-32-80-02.** Fax 04-93-32-77-78. Reservations required. Main courses 17€–35€. AE, DC, MC, V. Daily noon–2pm and 7:30–10pm. Closed Nov–Dec and Jan 10–20.

# Where to Stay

**La Colombe d'Or** rents deluxe rooms (above).

## EXPENSIVE

**Le Mas de Pierre ★**    The newest addition to St-Paul's accommodation scene is a vision of Provençal elegance with a dash of boutique charm thrown in. It's located about 2km (1¼ miles) from the village center. Of all the five-star hotels in the area, this spot is the most family friendly and the least stuffy. Eating in jeans and a jacket inside the superb Table de Pierre restaurant, or outside on its poolside terrace, is completely acceptable. The surrounding gardens loop around the pool and are dotted with wooden cabanas, each one with a linen canopy roof that can be pulled shut for a mischievous snooze. The "enchanted garden" contains a collection of orchids in an ancient glasshouse, hidden away next to the hotel's vegetable plot.

2320 route de Serres, St-Paul-de-Vence 06570. www.lemasdepierre.com. ℂ **04-93-59-00-10.** Fax 04-93-59-00-59. 48 units. 205€–600€ double; 295€–1,230€ suite. AE, DC, MC, V. Free parking. **Amenities:** Restaurant, bar; outdoor pool; spa. In room: A/C, TV, hair dryer, free Wi-Fi.

## MODERATE

**Hôtel des Messugues ★ ▐**    Visitors wishing to escape the hordes head to this idyllic retreat set in a flowery park with a sizeable swimming pool. Only a few steps from the Maeght Foundation and overlooking Provençal vineyards, the hotel offers a countrylike environment—although at only 1km (½ mile) from the village center, it's still close to the action. Bedrooms are small to midsize but attractively furnished and most comfortable.

Allée des Lavandes, impasse des Messugues, St-Paul-de-Vence 06570. www.hotel-messugues-saintpaul.com. ℂ **04-93-32-53-32.** Fax 04-93-32-94-15. 15 units. 95€–170€ double. AE, DC, MC, V. Free parking. Closed Nov–Mar. Amenities: Breakfast room; outdoor pool; room service. In room: A/C, TV, hair dryer, free Wi-Fi.

**Hotel Le Hameau ★ ✦**    This romantic Mediterranean villa is on a hilltop on the outskirts of St-Paul-de-Vence, on the road to Colle-sur-Loup. Built as a farmhouse in the 1920s and enlarged and transformed into a hotel in 1967, it contains high-ceilinged rooms with period detail. They range from the tiny Traveler's

Rooms (perfect for a night's pit-stop in the area), to Provençal suites with double sinks in the bathroom and ancient stone floors. View of the surrounding hills and valleys are remarkable. There is also a vineyard and a sunny terrace with fruit trees, flowers, and a pool.

528 rte. de la Colle (D107), St-Paul-de-Vence 06570. www.le-hameau.com. ℂ **04-93-32-80-24.** Fax 04-93-32-55-75. 17 units. 105€–190€ double; 230€–280€ suite. AE, MC, V. Free parking. Closed Nov 15–Feb 15. From the town, take D107 about 1km (½ mile), following the signs south of town toward Colle-sur-Loup. **Amenities:** Bar; outdoor pool; free Wi-Fi. *In room:* A/C, TV, hair dryer.

# VENCE ★

926km (574 miles) S of Paris; 31km (19 miles) N of Cannes; 24km (15 miles) NW of Nice

Travel into the hills northwest of Nice—across country studded with cypresses, olive trees, and pines, where carnations, roses, oleanders, and other flowers grow in profusion—and Vence comes into view. Outside the town, along boulevard Paul-André, olive presses carry on their age-old duties. The main attraction here is the **Vieille Ville (Old Town),** a working town center with a blissful medieval backdrop. Visitors pose for photographs on place du Peyra in front of the **Vieille Fontaine (Old Fountain),** a feature in several films. If you're wearing sturdy shoes, the old town's narrow streets are worth poking around, particularly the cathedral on place Godeau.

Of great interest to art fans is the **Chateau de Villeneuve Fondation Émile Hugues,** 2 place du Frêne (www.museedevence.com; ℂ 04-93-58-15-78), a temporary exhibition space dedicated to modern greats. Recent shows have included artists such as Matisse, Cézanne, Jean-Michel Basquiat, and Cy Twombly. Hours are Tuesday to Sunday 10am to 12:30pm and 2 to 6pm. Admission is 5€, 2.50€ for students and children 16 and under.

Vence's main draw, however, lies just outside the fortified main town. The Chapelle du Rosaire represents one of Matisse's most remarkable achievements.

## Essentials

**GETTING THERE**     Frequent **buses** (no. 94 or 400) originating in Nice take 45 minutes to reach Vence; the one-way fare is 1€. For information, contact Ligne d'Azur (www.lignesdazur.com; ℂ 08-10-06-10-06). The nearest **rail** station is in Cagnes-sur-Mer, about 10km (6¼ miles) southwest from Vence. From there, about 20 buses per day priced at 1€ make the trip to Vence. For train information, visit www.voyages-sncf.com or call

Vieille Fontaine, Vence.

*C* **36-35**. To **drive** to Vence from Nice, take D6007 west to Cagnes-sur-Mer, and then D36 north to Vence.

**VISITOR INFORMATION**   The **Office de Tourisme** is on place Grand-Jardin (www.ville-vence.fr; *C* **04-93-58-06-38**).

## A Matisse Masterpiece

**Chapelle du Rosaire** ★★ RELIGIOUS SITE   It was a beautiful golden autumn along the Côte d'Azur. The great Henri Matisse was 77, and after the turbulence of World War II, he set out to design his masterpiece. Matisse created the Chapelle du Rosaire for the Dominican nuns of Monteils. (Sister Jacques-Marie, a member of the order, had nursed him back to health after a serious illness.) From the front, you might find the structure unremarkable and pass it by—until you spot a 12m (39-ft.) crescent-adorned cross rising from a blue-tile roof.

Matisse wrote: "What I have done in the chapel is to create a religious space . . . in an enclosed area of very reduced proportions and to give it, solely by the play of colors and lines, the dimensions of infinity." The light picks up the subtle coloring in the simply rendered leaf forms and abstract patterns: sapphire blue, aquamarine, and lemon yellow. In black-and-white ceramics, St. Dominic is depicted in only a few bold strokes. The most remarkable design is in the black-and-white-tile Stations of the Cross, with Matisse's self-styled "tormented and passionate" figures. The bishop of Nice came to bless the chapel in the late spring of 1951, when the artist's work was completed. Matisse died 3 years later.

466 av. Henri-Matisse. *C* **04-93-58-03-26.** Admission 3€ adults, 1.50€ children 16 and under; contributions to maintain the chapel are welcome. Mon, Wed, and Sat 2–5:30pm; Tues and Thurs 10–11:30am and 2–5:30pm. Closed mid-Nov to mid-Dec.

## Where to Eat

**Auberge des Seigneurs** and **Le Château du Domaine St-Martin** (see reviews for both in "Where to Stay," below) offer excellent dining.

**La Farigoule** PROVENÇAL   In a century-old house that opens onto a rose garden, this restaurant specializes in Provençal cuisine and is generally regarded as one of the most genial establishments in town. Menu items are traditional but flavorful: They include roast pigeon in a truffle-laden cassoulet, scallop and foie gras risotto, and classic roast lamb with local herbs and potatoes. In the summer, you can dine in the flowering garden.

15 av. Henri-Isnard. www.lafarigoule-vence.fr. *C* **04-93-58-01-27.** Reservations recommended. Main courses 25€–29€; fixed-price menus 29€–45€. MC, V. Wed–Sun noon–2pm and 7:30–10pm. Closed mid-Nov to mid-Dec.

## Where to Stay
### VERY EXPENSIVE

**Le Château du Domaine St-Martin** ★★★   If you're heading into the hill towns above Nice and you seek luxury and refinement, this is the address for you. The château, in a 14-hectare (35-acre) park with terraced gardens, was built in 1936 and has been continuously upgraded ever since. The main building holds the standard units; suites are in the tile-roofed villas. You can walk through the gardens on winding paths lined with tall cypresses, past the chapel ruins and olive trees. The spacious rooms are distinctively decorated, and the large rose-colored bathrooms have tub/showers. The double Michelin-starred restaurant has a view of the coast and serves superb French cuisine under the accomplished command of Yannick Franques, a former protégé of Alain Ducasse. Rates include breakfast.

2490 av. des Templiers B.P. 102, Vence 06140. www.chateau-st-martin.com. © **04-93-58-02-02.** Fax 04-93-24-08-91. 39 units, 6 villas. 360€–585€ double; 465€–1,290€ suite; 900€–3,150€ villa. AE, DC, MC, V. Closed mid-Nov to mid-Feb. From the town center, follow signs toward Coursegoules and Col-de-Vence for 1.5km (1 mile) north. **Amenities:** Restaurant; bar; babysitting; outdoor pool; room service; spa; 2 tennis courts. *In room:* A/C, TV, hair dryer, free Wi-Fi.

## MODERATE

**La Maison du Frêne ★ 🎁**　In the heart of Vence, this Provençal guesthouse, now an elegant retreat, was once a private home in the 18th century. Vence has far more lavish and luxurious retreats, but none with this snug, cozy comfort—much of it revolving around a modern art theme, with pop-art designs and playful touches everywhere. Guest rooms are midsize to spacious. An old ash tree planted in front of the house during the reign of François I and the manse itself have been the subject of countless paintings. The original architecture has been preserved, although all modern comforts have been added. The reception area contains original sculptures and paintings, and it's linked to the country kitchen, where delicious homemade breakfasts are prepared.

1 place du Frêne, Vence 06140. www.lamaisondufrene.com. © **04-93-24-37-83.** 4 units. 165€–190€. MC, V. Parking 13€. **Amenities:** Dinner upon request in winter, lounge library. *In room:* A/C, TV, free Wi-Fi.

## INEXPENSIVE

**Auberge des Seigneurs ★**　This 400-year-old stone hotel gives you a taste of old Provence. Decorative objects and antiques are everywhere. The guest rooms are well maintained, although most of the management's energy is directed at their restaurant. Nevertheless, the Provençal-style rooms are comfortable, with lots of exposed paneling and beams. Two have decorative fireplaces. The small, tiled bathrooms contain showers. The restaurant is in a stone building that used to be the kitchen of the Château de Villeneuve, where François I spent part of his youth. The specialty is grills prepared on an open spit in view of the dining room, which holds a long wooden table and an open fireplace with a row of hanging copper pots and pans.

1 rue de Docteur Biret, Vence 06140. www.auberge-seigneurs.com. © **04-93-58-04-24.** Fax 04-93-24-08-01. 6 units. 85€–95€ double. MC, V. Closed mid-Dec to mid-Jan. **Amenities:** Restaurant; bar; room service. *In room:* Hair dryer, free Wi-Fi.

# NICE ★★★

929km (576 miles) S of Paris; 32km (20 miles) NE of Cannes

Nice is known as the "Queen of the Riviera" and is the largest city on this fabled stretch of coast. It's also one of the most ancient, founded by the Greeks, who called it Nike (Victory). By the 19th century, Russian aristocrats and the British upper class—led by Queen Victoria herself—were flocking here. But these days, it's not as chichi as Cannes or St Tropez. In fact, of all the major French resorts,

Nice is the most down-to-earth, with an emphasis on fine dining and high culture. Indeed, it hosts more museums than any other French city outside of Paris.

It's also the best place to base yourself on the Riviera, especially if you're dependent on public transportation. You can go to San Remo, a glamorous town over the Italian border, for lunch and return to Nice by nightfall. From Nice airport, the second largest in France, you can travel by train or bus along the entire coast to resorts such as Antibes, Juan-les-Pins, and Monaco.

Because of its brilliant sunshine and liberal attitude, Nice has long attracted artists and writers, among them Dumas, Nietzsche, Flaubert, Hugo, Sand, and Stendhal. Henri Matisse, who made his home in Nice, said, "Though the light is intense, it's also soft and tender." The city averages 300 sunny days a year.

Book market at the place du Palais-de-Justice.

## Essentials

**GETTING THERE**  **Trains** arrive at Gare Nice-Ville, avenue Thiers (www.voyages-sncf.com; ☎ **36-35**). From there you can take trains to Cannes for 6.10€, Monaco for 3.40€, and Antibes for 4€, with easy connections to Paris, Marseille, and anywhere else along the Mediterranean coast.

**Buses** to and from Monaco (no. 100), Cannes (no. 200), and all points in between serve the streets immediately around the **Gare Routière,** 5 bd. Jean-Jaurès (www.lignesdazur.com; ☎ **08-10-06-10-06**), the former main bus station, which is currently under renovation.

Transatlantic and intercontinental flights land at **Aéroport Nice–Côte d'Azur** (www.nice.aeroport.fr; ☎ **08-20-42-33-33**). From there, municipal bus nos. 98 and 99 depart at 20-minute intervals for Gare

---

 **A Note on Nice Buses**

If you plan to use the city's buses, consider buying a 1- or 7-day pass, available from tobacco stands and newspaper kiosks throughout the city. The pass allows unlimited transit on any municipal buses that run along the coast, the airport bus, and Nice's tramway. The price is 4€ for a 1-day pass.

For additional information, call Ligne d'Azur (www.lignesdazur.com; ☎ **08-10-06-10-06**). The most useful lines are the no. 15 that runs up to the Matisse and Chagall museums in Cimiez, and lines no. 11 and 52 that run along the Promenade des Anglais.

Routière (see above) and Gare Nice-Ville, respectively; the one-way fare is 4€. A **taxi** from the airport into the city center will cost between 30€ and 40€ each way. Trip time is about 20 minutes.

Ferryboats operated by **Trans-Côte d'Azur** (www.trans-cote-azur. com; ℂ **04-92-00-42-30**), on quai Lunel on Nice's port, link the city with Ile Ste-Marguerite (see "Ferrying to the Iles de Lerins," p. 560) in July and August, and St-Tropez from June to September.

**VISITOR INFORMATION**    Nice maintains three **tourist offices.** The largest and most central of is at 5 promenade des Anglais, near place Masséna (www. nicetourisme.com; ℂ **08-92-70-74-07**). Additional offices are in the arrivals hall of the Aéroport Nice–Côte d'Azur and the railway station on avenue Thiers. Any office can make a hotel reservation (but only for the night of the day you show up), for a modest fee.

**GETTING AROUND**    Most local buses serve the streets around the main bus station, or **Gare Routière,** 10 av. Félix Faure (ℂ **08-92-70-12-06**), which is currently under renovation near place Masséna. Municipal buses charge 1€ for rides within the entire Alpes-Maritime province, even as far as Monaco or Cannes. The same ticket can also be used on Nice's tramway, which connects the Gare Routière with Gare Nice-Ville and northern Nice. Tickets can be purchased at tobacco shops or at electronic kiosks around the city.

Nice is very walkable, and no point of interest downtown is more than a 10-minute walk from place Masséna, including the seafront Promenade, Old Town, and harbor.

A recent addition to the transport scene is **Vélo Bleu** (www.velobleu. org), a bike-sharing scheme with over 175 stations throughout the city. However, registering for the scheme on the electronic stands takes a degree of patience, so register in advance online if possible. A more human place to rent both bikes and scooters is **Holiday Bikes,** 23 rue de Belgique (www. holiday-bikes.com; ℂ **04-93-16-01-62**), by Nice-Ville train station. Open Monday to Saturday 9am to 12.30pm and 2 to 6.30pm, and on Sunday 10am-noon and 4-6pm, it charges from 12€ per day for a bike, or from 30€ per day for a 50cc scooter. A valid driver's license and deposit are required.

One of the most fun ways to quickly gain an overview of Nice involves boarding a **Nice–Le Grand Tour** (www.nicelegrandtour.com; ℂ **04-92-29-17-00**) double-decker bus. Every day of the year, between 9:45am and 6:15pm, one of a flotilla of this company's buses departs from a position adjacent to the Jardins Albert I. The panoramic 90-minute tour takes in the harbor, the museums of Cimiez, the Russian church, and the promenade. Per-person rates for the experience are 20€ for adults, 18€ for students, and 5€ for children 4 to 11. Participants can get off at any of 12 stops en route and opt to reboard any other buses, which follow at roughly 40-minute intervals, after they've explored the neighborhood. Advance reservations aren't necessary, and commentary is piped through to headsets in seven different languages.

Another easy way to see the city is by the small **Train Touristique de Nice** (www.trainstouristiquesdenice.com; ℂ **06-08-55-08-30**), which also departs from the Jardins Albert I. The 45-minute ride passes many of Nice's most-heralded sites, including place Masséna, promenade des Anglais, and quai des Etats-Unis. Departing every 30 minutes, the train operates daily

# Nice

**St-Etienne**

To Gare du Sud →

**Carabacel**

**Vieille Ville**

**Palais des Expositions**

Palais des Congrès et de la Musique Acropolis

Gare Riquier

Gare Maritime

Parc Vigier

Bassin L'Olympia

Musée Naval

Le Château

Marché aux Fleurs

Baie des Anges

Castel Plage

l'Opéra Plage

Galion Plage

Ruhl Plage

Le Lido

Palais Masséna

promenade des Anglais

## ATTRACTIONS

Cathédral Orthodoxe Russe
St-Nicolas à Nice **2**
Musée Massena **13**
Musée des Beaux-Arts **6**
Musée International d'Art
Naïf Anatole-Jakovsky **4**
Palais Lascaris **10**

## HOTELS

Hôtel Gounod **3**
Hôtel Hi **5**
Hôtel Négresco **11**
Palais de la
Méditerranée **12**
Nice Pebbles **9**
Hôtel Pérouse **15**
Hôtel du Petit Palais **8**
Hôtel St-Exupéry **1**
Hôtel Suisse **14**
Hôtel Windsor **7**

FRANCE

★ Paris

Nice

To Cannes,
Airport

Beach
Information
Post Office

0        1/4 mi
0   0.25 km

593

10am to 5pm (until 6pm April–May and Sept, until 7pm June–Aug). The round-trip price is 7€ for adults and 4€ for children 9 and under.

Possibly the coolest way to get around Nice is by Segway, the two-wheeled electronic scooters. Bespoke tours are run by **Mobilboard, 2 rue Halévy** (www.mobilboard.com; ✆ **04-93-80-21-27**). Children 18 and under must be accompanied by an adult. An hour-long tour of Nice costs 25€ per person. Another novel addition to the Nice transport scene is **Auto Bleue** (www.autobleue.org; ✆ **09-77-40-64-06**). The scheme allows visitors to rent an electric Peugeot car from one of 70 vehicle stands around Nice for 50€ per day, inclusive of electricity, parking, and insurance.

**SPECIAL EVENTS**   The **Nice Carnaval** (www.nicecarnaval.com) draws visitors from all over Europe. The "Mardi Gras of the Riviera" runs from mid-February to early March, celebrating the return of spring with 3 weeks of parades, *corsi* (floats), *veglioni* (masked balls), confetti, and battles in which young women toss flowers at the audience.

The **Nice Festival du Jazz** (www.nicejazzfestival.fr) runs for a week in mid-July, when jazz, funk, and reggae artists perform in the Jardins Albert I near the seafront. Recent performers have included Herbie Hancock, Ray Charles, and Toots and the Maytals.

# Exploring the City

In 1822, Nice's orange crop had an awful year. The workers faced a lean time, so the English residents employed them to build the **promenade des Anglais ★★**, today a wide boulevard fronting the bay, split by "islands" of palms and flowers and stretching for about 7km (4¼ miles) all the way to the airport. Along the beach are rows of grand cafes, the Musée Masséna, villas, and the city's most glamorous hotels.

Crossing this boulevard in the tiniest bikinis are some of the world's most attractive bronzed bodies. They're heading for the **beach.** Tough on tender feet, *le plage* is made not of sand, but of pebbles (and not small ones, either).

Rising sharply on a rock at the eastern end of the promenade is **Le Château,** where the ducs de Savoie built their castle, which was torn down in 1706. The hill has since been turned into a wonderful public park complete with a waterfall, cafes, and a giant children's play area. To reach the site and take in the view, board an elevator from the quai des Etats-Unis; the fit can walk up one of five sets of steep steps. The park is open daily from 8am to dusk. At the north end of Le Château is the famous old **graveyard** of Nice, known primarily for lavish monuments that form their own enduring art statement. It's one of the largest in France.

Continuing east from "the Rock" (the site of Le Château), you reach the **Vieux Port,** or harbor**,** where the restaurants are even cheaper and are filled with locals. While lingering over a drink at a sidewalk cafe, you can watch the boats depart for Corsica. The harbor was excavated between 1750 and 1830. Since then, it has gained an outer harbor, protected by two jetties, and is great for a stroll around.

The "authentic" Niçoise live in **Vieille Ville ★**, the old town, beginning at the foot of the Rock and stretching to place Masséna. Sheltered by sienna-tiled roofs, many of the Italianate facades suggest 17th-century Genoese palaces. The old town is a maze of narrow streets, teeming with local life and studded with the least expensive restaurants in Nice. Buy a Niçoise-style onion pizza (*pissaladière*) from a vendor. Many of the buildings are painted a faded Roman gold, and their banners are laundry flapping in the sea breezes.

Cathédrale Orthodoxe Russe St-Nicolas à Nice.

While here, try to visit the **Marché aux Fleurs.** This flower market lies on the **cours Saleya,** the old town's principal walkway, which is filled with alfresco restaurants and cafes. A flamboyant array of carnations, violets, roses, and birds of paradise, the market operates Tuesday to Sunday 8am to 6pm in summer, and 8am until between 2 and 4pm in winter, depending on the vendors' remaining inventory and energy level. On Monday the same space is occupied by a superb antiques market, with vendors carting wares from across France and Italy.

Nice's newly pedestrianized centerpiece is **place Masséna,** with pink buildings in the 17th-century Genoese style and fountains with water jets. Stretching from the main square to the promenade is the **Jardin Albert 1er,** with an open-air terrace and a Triton Fountain. With palms and exotic flowers, it's the most relaxing oasis in town.

**Cathédrale Orthodoxe Russe St-Nicolas à Nice ★** CATHEDRAL Ordered and built by none other than Tsar Nicholas II, this cathedral is the most beautiful religious edifice of the Orthodoxy outside Russia and a perfect expression of Russian religious art abroad. It dates from the Belle Epoque, when some of the Romanovs and entourage turned the Riviera into their stomping ground (everyone from grand dukes to ballerinas walked the promenade). The cathedral is richly ornamented and decorated with icons. You'll spot the building from afar because of its collection of ornate onion-shaped domes. During church services on Sunday morning, the building closes to tourist visits.

Av. Nicolas II (off bd. du Tzaréwitch). www.acor-nice.com. ℂ **04-93-83-94-08.** Admission 3€ adults, 2€ students, free for children 12 and under. May–Sept daily 9am–noon and 2:30–6pm; Oct–Apr daily 9:30am–noon and 2:30–5pm. From the central rail station, head west along av. Thiers to bd. Gambetta, and then go north to av. Nicolas II.

**Musée des Beaux-Arts ★★** ART MUSEUM   This collection is housed in the fabulous former residence of the Ukrainian Princess Kotchubey. It is devoted to the masters of the Second Empire and the Belle Epoque, with an extensive collection of 19th-century French experts. Many of the canvases depict the South of France. The gallery of sculptures includes works by J. B. Carpeaux, Rude, and Rodin. Note the important collection by a dynasty of painters, the Dutch Vanloo family. One of its best-known members, Carle Vanloo, born in Nice in 1705, was Louis XV's premier *peintre.* A fine collection of 19th- and 20th-century art includes works by Ziem, Raffaelli, Boudin, Guillaumin, and Sisley. Armed robbers broke into the museum 5 minutes before closing on a quiet summer Sunday in 2007, stealing a Monet canvas in the process.

33 av. des Baumettes. www.musee-beaux-arts-nice.org. ℂ **04-92-15-28-28.** Free admission. Tues–Sun 10am–6pm. Bus: 3, 8, 9, 10, 12, 22, or 23.

**Musée International d'Art Naïf Anatole-Jakovsky (Museum of Naive Art)** ★ ART MUSEUM   This museum is in the beautifully restored Château Ste-Hélène in the Fabron district. The museum's namesake, for years one of the world's leading art critics, once owned the 600-piece collection of colorful collages, far-out sculptures, and 3-D artworks. Its playful nature and surrounding gardens make it one of the few art galleries in Nice that will appeal to children. Artists from over 25 countries are represented by everything from primitive painting to 20th-century works.

Château St-Hélène, av. de Fabron. ℂ **04-93-71-78-33.** Free admission. Wed–Mon 10am–6pm. Bus: 9, 10, or 23; 10-min. walk.

**Musée Masséna** ★★★ MUSEUM   Reopened after a seemingly endless renovation, this is Nice's key museum. It is surrounded by carefully planted gardens and housed in a Belle Epoque villa with traces of the White House about it. Housed inside is a potted history of the French Riviera. A timeline traces the first Victorian visitors to the roaring 1920s. Costumes from the age, train tickets from London to Nice, and portraits of the holidaying rich bring the past to life. Of additional note are the paintings and objets d'art dedicated from the Masséna family, a noble set of locals who constructed the villa and married themselves off to various European royals.

65 rue de France. ℂ **04-93-91-19-10.** Free admission. Wed–Mon 9am–6pm.

**Palais Lascaris** ☺ PALACE   The baroque Palais Lascaris in the city's historic old town is associated with the Lascaris-Vintimille family, whose recorded history dates back over 7 centuries. Built in the 17th century, it contains elaborately detailed ornaments and suits of armor. An intensive restoration by the city of Nice in 1946 brought back its original beauty, and the palace is now classified as a historic monument. The most elaborate floor, the *étage noble*, retains many of its 18th-century panels and plaster embellishments. A pharmacy, built around 1738 and complete with many of the original accessories, is on the ground floor.

15 rue Droite. www.palais-lascaris-nice.org. ℂ **04-93-62-72-40.** Free admission. Wed–Mon 10am–6pm.

# Nearby Attractions in Cimiez ★★

In the once-aristocratic hilltop quarter of Cimiez, 5km (3 miles) north of Nice, Queen Victoria wintered at the Hôtel Excelsior. Half the English court traveled down from Calais with her on a luxurious private train. Founded by the Romans, who called it Cemenelum, Cimiez was the capital of the Maritime Alps province. Excavations have uncovered the ruins of a Roman town, and you can wander the dig sites, which are shaded with olive trees. The arena was big enough to hold at least 5,000 spectators, who watched contests between gladiators and wild beasts. To reach this suburb and its attractions, take bus no. 15 from place Masséna.

**Monastère de Cimiez (Cimiez Convent)** ★ CONVENT   The convent embraces a church that owns three of the most important works by the locally prominent Bréa brothers, who painted in the late 15th century. In a restored part of the convent where some Franciscan friars still live, the Musée Franciscain is decorated with 17th-century frescoes. Some 350 documents and works of art from the 15th to the 18th centuries are on display. The magnificent gardens are a photographer's dream, and there's rarely a tourist in sight. Panoramic views pan

Musée National Message Biblique Marc Chagall.

over Nice and the Baie des Anges. Artists Matisse and Dufy are buried in the cemetery nearby.

Place du Monastère. ✆ **04-93-81-00-04.** Free admission. Museum Mon–Fri 8:30am–12:30pm and 2:30-6:30pm. Church daily 9am–6pm.

**Musée Matisse** ★★ ART MUSEUM    This museum in a beautiful old Italian villa honors Henri Matisse, one of the 20th century's greatest painters. He came to Nice for the light and made the city his home, living in the Hotel Beau Rivage and on the cours Saleya, and dying in Cimiez in 1954. Seeing his playful nude sketches today, you'll wonder how early critics could have denounced them as "the female animal in all her shame and horror." Most of the pieces in the museum's permanent collection were painted in Nice (you may recognize a few of the backdrops). These include *Nude in an Armchair with a Green Plant* (1937), *Nymph in the Forest* (1935–42), and the famous *Portrait of Madame Matisse* (1905). There's also an assemblage of designs he prepared as practice sketches for Matisse's final masterpiece, his *Chapel at Vence*. Also here are *The Créole Dancer* (1951), *Blue Nude IV* (1952), and around 50 dance-related sketches he did between 1930 and 1931.

In the Villa des Arènes-de-Cimiez, 164 av. des Arènes-de-Cimiez. www.musee-matisse.nice.org. ✆ **04-93-81-08-08.** Free admission. Wed–Mon 10am–6pm.

**Musée National Message Biblique Marc Chagall** ★★ ART MUSEUM In the hills of Cimiez, this handsome museum, surrounded by pools and a garden, is devoted to Marc Chagall's treatment of biblical themes. Born in Russia in 1887, Chagall became a French citizen in 1937 and painted with astonishing light and color until his death in St-Paul-de-Vence in 1985. The artist and his wife donated the works—the most important Chagall collection ever assembled—to France in 1966 and 1972. On display are 450 of his oils, drawings, pastels, lithographs, sculptures, and ceramics; three stained-glass windows; and a tapestry. Chagall decorated a concert room (where recitals are often performed) with brilliantly hued stained-glass windows.

Av. du Dr.-Ménard. www.musee-chagall.fr. ☏ **04-93-53-87-20.** Admission 7.50€ adults, 5.50€ students, free for children 17 and under. May–Oct Wed–Mon 10am–6pm; Nov–Apr Wed–Mon 10am–5pm.

## Outdoor Pursuits

**BEACHES**   Along Nice's seafront, beaches extend uninterrupted for more than 7km (4¼ miles), going from the edge of Vieux-Port (the old port, or harbor) to the international airport. Tucked between the public areas are several rather chic private beaches. Many of these beach bars provide mattresses and parasols for 12€ to 20€. The coolest clubs include Hi Beach (www.hi-beach.net; ☏ **04-97-14-00-83**), which has a sushi bar, weights room, and swing chairs; and Castel Plage (www.castelplage.com; ☏ **04-93-85-22-66**), which is a celebrity hangout in summer. The most family friendly, with its giant pile of outdoor toys, is Opera Plage (☏ **04-93-62-31-52**).

**SCUBA DIVING**   Of the many diving outfits in Nice harbor, **Nice Diving,** 14 quai des Dock (www.nicediving.com; ☏ **04-93-89-42-44**) offers bilingual instruction and *baptêmes* (dives for first-timers) around Nice and Cap Ferrat. A two-tank dive for experienced divers, equipment included, costs around 150€; appropriate diver's certification is required.

## Shopping

Nice's densest concentrations of clothes, shoes, and electronic shops are around **rue Masséna** and **avenue Jean-Médecin.** Both are great for hip French brands. For more high-end couture, the streets around **place Magenta,** including **rue de Verdun, rue Paradis,** and **rue Alphonse Karr** are a credit card's worst nightmare. A shop of note is **Cotelac,** 12 rue Alphonse Karr (☏ **04-93-87-31-59**), which sells chic women's clothing.

Men should try **Façonnable,** 7–9 rue Paradis (☏ **04-93-16-22-35**). This is the original site of a chain with several hundred branches worldwide. The look is youthful and conservatively stylish. Find men's suits, overcoats, sportswear, and jeans in this branch, and an outlet for women's wear (Façonnable Femmes) immediately across the street at 10 rue Paradis (☏ **04-93-88-06-97**).

The winding streets of Nice's old town are the best place to find local crafts, ceramics, gifts, and foodie purchases. If you're thinking of indulging in a Provençale *pique-nique,* **Nicola Alziari,** 14 rue St François de Paule (☏ **04-93-62-94-03**), will provide everything from olives, anchovies, and pistous to aiolis and tapenades. It's one of Nice's oldest purveyors of olive oil, with a house brand that comes in several strengths and flavors. Also for sale are objects crafted from olive wood. For an olive oil tasting session—with chance to buy the goods afterward—check out **Oliviera**, 2 rue Benoit Bunico (☏ **04-93-11-06-45**), run by the amiable Nadim Beyrouti.

The best selection of Provençal fabrics is at **Le Chandelier,** 7 rue de la Boucherie (☏ **04-93-85-85-19**), where you'll see designs by two of the region's best-known producers of cloth, Les Olivades and Valdrôme. For antiquarian books, contemporary art, kitsch, and comicbooks, wander out of the old town to **rue Delille**, just past the MAMAC modern art gallery.

Nice is also known for its **street markets.** In addition to the flower market, **Marché aux Fleurs** (see "Exploring the City," p. 594), the main flea market, **Marché à la Brocante,** also at cours Saleya, takes place Monday 8am to 5pm. Another flea market on the port, **Les Puces de Nice,** place Robilante, is open Tuesday to Saturday 9am to 6pm.

Also in the harbor is **Confiserie Florian,** 14 quai Papacino (ℂ **04-93-55-43-50**). Opened in 1949 by Joseph Fuchs, the grandfather of the present English-speaking owners, their specialty is glazed fruit crystallized in sugar or artfully arranged into chocolates. Look for exotic jams (rose-petal preserves, mandarin marmalade) and the free recipe leaflet, as well as candied violets, verbena leaves, and rosebuds. Back near the opera house, one of the oldest chocolatiers in Nice, **Confiserie Auer,** 7 rue St-François-de-Paule (ℂ **04-93-85-77-98**), was established in 1820. Since then, few of the original decorative accessories have changed. The shop specializes in chocolates, candies, and fruits comfits, the signature Provençal goodies.

# Where to Eat

## VERY EXPENSIVE

**Le Chantecler** ★★★ TRADITIONAL/MODERN FRENCH   This is Nice's most prestigious, most formal, and most commended restaurant. Its walls are decked with panels removed from a château in Pouilly-Fuissé, rich tapestries hang from the ceilings, and bow-tied multilingual waiters anticipate your every move. The menu is revised each week to include the most sophisticated and creative dishes in the city. Dishes may include turbot filet served with purée of broad beans, sun-dried tomatoes, and asparagus; flash-fried sea bass served with baked red onion confit; and a melt-in-your-mouth fantasy of marbled hot chocolate drenched in almond-flavored cream sauce. Michelin-starred dining doesn't come any better value than the lunchtime set menu, which costs 65€ including wine.

In the Hôtel Negresco, 37 promenade des Anglais. ℂ **04-93-16-64-00.** Reservations required. Main courses 48€–80€; fixed-price lunch 55€–130€, dinner 90€–130€. AE, MC, V, DC. Wed–Sun 12:30–1:45pm and 7:30–10pm. Closed Jan.

## EXPENSIVE

**La Merenda** ★★ 🎁 NIÇOISE   Because there's no phone, you have to go by this place twice—once to make a reservation and once to dine—but it's worth the effort. Forsaking his chef's crown at Le Chantecler (see above), Dominique Le Stanc took over this tiny local bistro serving sublime cuisine. Though he was born in Alsace, the chef's heart and soul belong to the Mediterranean, the land of black truffles, wild morels, sea bass, and asparagus. His food is a lullaby of gastronomic unity, with texture, crunch, richness, and balance. Le Stanc never knows what he's going to serve until he goes to the market. Look for specials on a chalkboard. Perhaps you'll find stuffed cabbage, fried zucchini flowers, or oxtail flavored with fresh oranges. Service is discreet and personable.

4 rue Raoul Bosio. No phone. Reservations required. Main courses 14€–29€. No credit cards. Mon–Fri noon–2pm and 7:30–10pm.

## MODERATE

**Flaveur** ★★ 🎁 MODERN FRENCH   This chic little diner was set up by two chef brothers, Gaël et Mickaël Tourteaux, in 2009. After a combined 25 years working in the Riviera's finest kitchens (including the Negresco and the Moulin de Mougins) they wanted to create something with novel tastes, far-out decor, and memorable service, all laced with a good splash of self-belief. As the restaurant's name suggests, the end flavors are sublime; so sublime in fact that Flaveur picked up its inaugural Michelin star in 2011. Cuts of beef are paired with aubergine caviar, steak tartare is blended with panisse chips, and local seafood is placed on a bed of cauliflower and grilled taragon. Servings are as artistically displayed as they are generous. Lunchtime set menus allow for gourmet bites on a budget.

25 rue Gubernatis. www.flaveur.net. (C) **04-93-62-53-95.** Reservations required. Main courses 16€–35€; fixed-price lunch 29€–37€, fixed-price dinner 45€–70€. MC, V. Tues–Fri noon–2pm and 7:30–11pm; Sat 7:30–11pm. Closed early Jan.

**L'Ane Rouge ★★** PROVENÇAL    Facing the old port and occupying an antique building—the owners have carefully retained its ceiling beams and stone walls—this is one of the city's best-known seafood restaurants. In the two modern yet cozy dining rooms, you can enjoy traditional specialties such as bouillabaisse, *bourride* (stew), cannelloni stuffed with spiced filets of seabream, mussels stuffed with bread crumbs and herbs, and sea bream sautéed in local Bandol wine. Service is commendable. Cooking lessons and market tours with head chef Michel Devillers are also available.

7 quai des Deux-Emmanuels. www.anerougenice.com. (C) **04-93-89-49-63.** Reservations recommended. Main courses 24€–48€; fixed-price lunch 23€-35€, fixed-price dinner 35€–68€. AE, DC, MC, V. Fri–Tues noon–2pm and Thurs–Tues 7–10:30pm. Closed early Feb to late March. Bus: 30.

**La Zucca Magica ★ 👔** VEGETARIAN/ITALIAN    The chef at this popular harborside restaurant has been named the best Italian chef in Nice. That this honor should go to a vegetarian restaurant was the most startling part of the news. Chef Marco, who opened his restaurant in 1997 after cooking for many years in Rome, certainly has a fine pedigree—he's a relative of the late Luciano Pavarotti. He serves refined cuisine using recipes from Italy's Piedmont region and updating them with no meat or fish. The red-and-green decor (the colors of Italy) will put you in the mood for the creative cuisine. You'll have to trust Marco, though, because everyone is served the same meal based around a set fixed-price menu, normally comprising five or six courses. You can count on savory cuisine using lots of herbs, Italian cheeses, beans, and pasta.

4 bis quai Papacino. www.lazuccamagica.com. (C) **04-93-56-25-27.** Reservations recommended. Fixed-price lunch 20€, dinner 29€. No credit cards. Tues–Sat 12:30–2pm and 7–9:30pm.

## INEXPENSIVE

**Vinivore ★ 👔** MODERN FRENCH    Since opening in 2011, Vinivore's Asian-Niçoise winebar-restaurant concept has been a huge hit. The establishment's co-owner, 30-year-old Bonaventure Blankstein, is regarded as one of the most knowledgeable young sommeliers in Nice. Patrons can sip from over 500 bottles of wine, which 'Bono' has hand-selected from boutique wineries – many of which are organic – across southern France. Bono's partner, Hong Kong born Chun Wong, mans the industrial-sized gas burner in the open kitchen. Chun's fish, fowl, and fusion dishes were honed at several of the Riviera's finest restaurants, including Le Palme d'Or in Cannes, and blend Provençal freshness with Chinese élan.

10 rue Lascaris. ℂ **04-93-14-68-09.** Reservations recommended. Main courses 11€–18€. MC, V. Tues–Sat noon–3pm and 7–11.30pm.

# Nice Nightlife

Nice has some of the most active nightlife and cultural offerings along the Riviera. Big evenings out usually begin at a cafe or bar; take in a restaurant, opera, or film; and finish in a club. The website http://riviera.angloinfo.com lists all the week's English-language movies in *version originale*.

The major cultural center on the Riviera is the **Opéra de Nice,** 4 rue St-François-de-Paule (www.opera-nice.org; ℂ **04-92-17-40-00**), built in 1885 by Charles Garnier, fabled architect of the Paris Opéra. It presents a full repertoire, with emphasis on serious, often large-scale operas. It's 2012 season included *Il Trovatore*, *Tristan and Isolde*, and *La Boheme*, as well as a *saison symphonique* dominated by the Orchestre Philharmonique de Nice. The opera hall is also the major venue for concerts and recitals. Tickets are available (to concerts, recitals, and full-blown operas) right up until the day of performance. You can show up at the box office (Mon–Thu 9am–5:30pm; Fri until 7.45pm, Sat until 4.30pm) or buy tickets in advance online. Tickets run from 10€ for seats up in the gods, to 80€ for front-and-center seats on opening night.

**Cabaret du Casino Ruhl,** in Casino Ruhl, 1 promenade des Anglais (www.lucienbarriere.com; ℂ **04-97-03-12-22**), is Nice's answer to the more ostentatious glitter of Monte Carlo and Las Vegas. It includes just enough flesh to titillate. The casino contains an area exclusively for slot machines, open daily from 9am to 4am; entrance is free. A more formal gaming room (jacket required, but not a tie) offering blackjack, baccarat, and chemin de fer opens from 3pm. A more chic alternative is the **Casino in the Palais de Mediterranée,** 15 promenade des Anglais (www.casinomediterranee.com; ℂ **04-92-14-68-00**), which offers a similar experience daily from 10am for slot machines, 8pm for gaming tables.

At the hip end of the spectrum is **Smarties,** 10 rue Defly (ℂ **04-93-62-30-75**), a cool cocktail lounge with great DJs. The old town's most happening spot is currently **Villa,** 7 rue Raoul Bosio ℂ **04-93-87-99-45**), whose house aperitif is the wickedly named Putain du Palais: crushed strawberries topped with champagne. More laid back for cocktails, conversation, and understated cool is **Bliss,** 12 rue de l'Abbaye (ℂ **04-93-16-82-38**).

The party spirit is best lapped up in the alfresco bars on the **cours Saleya**. Otherwise, head one block back to **Chez Wayne's,** 15 rue de la Préfecture (ℂ **04-93-13-46-99**), where dancing on the tables to raucous cover bands is the norm. Another adjacent bar with roughly equivalent decor, clientele, and sports priorities is **Le Master Home Bar,** 11 rue de la Prefecture (ℂ **04-95-85-51-64**). **La Bodeguita,** 14 rue Chavin (ℂ **04-93-92-67-24**), serves tapas, wine by the glass, and lots of beer, and re-creates some of the sun-and-salsa motifs of nightlife at its best in the Caribbean and South America.

## GAY NIGHTLIFE

A trend-conscious gay bar in Nice is **Le Klub,** 6 rue Halevy (ℂ **04-93-16-87-26**), near the Casino Ruhl. Entrance costs between 10€ and 20€, and includes one drink. Expect a hard-dancing, high-energy crowd of mostly gay men, many of them under 35, as well as lots of straight people who come for the house tunes and nonstop dancing.

# Where to Stay

## VERY EXPENSIVE

**Hôtel Negresco ★★★**    The Negresco, on the seafront in the heart of Nice, is one of the Riviera's superglamorous hotels. This Victorian wedding-cake hotel is named after its founder, Henry Negresco, and has hosted each era's superstars, from The Beatles to Michael Jackson. The hotel's decorators scoured Europe to gather antiques, tapestries, and art for the ritzy interior and domed central salon. Guestooms benefitted from a modern makeover in 2011, mixing sea views with state-of-the-art wetrooms and contemporary furniture. The entire fifth floor is now dedicated to VVIPs (that's right, "very, very important persons") and has a private luncheon area and bar. Dining is among the best in town, with the Michelin-starred Chantecler and the funky brasserie-style Rotonde, which was also given a thorough makeover in 2011. Despite the changes, the staff still wear 18th-century costumes and are as fawningly polite as ever.

37 promenade des Anglais, Nice 06000. www.hotel-negresco-nice.com. ✆ **04-93-16-64-00.** Fax 04-93-88-35-68. 117 units. 240€–610€ double; from 595€ suite. AE, DC, MC, V. Free parking. **Amenities:** 2 restaurants; bar; babysitting; exercise room; massage; room service. *In room:* A/C, TV, hair dryer, minibar, free Wi-Fi.

**Palais de la Méditerranée ★★★**    This glittering seaside palace on the promenade des Anglais reigned from 1929 to the late 1970s as the chicest hotel in Nice. In its heyday, the hotel's theater stage hosted everyone from Maurice Chevalier to American chanteuse Josephine Baker. But in 1978, it was shuttered up, a sad tale involving the probable murder of heiress Agnès Le Roux, who was a major shareholder in the establishment. In 2004, it reopened with great fanfare. The complete restoration left its Art Deco facade intact, but the interior of this place was gutted. It was turned into a marble palace, with glamorous touches such as plush hallways and a heated outdoor swimming pool on the third floor. Also kept in the renovation were the hotel's monumental chandeliers and stained-glass windows. Bedrooms, midsize to grandly spacious, are outfitted in a tasteful modern decor. Ninety of the bedrooms also open onto sea views. The hotel's casino was also restored to its former glory.

13–15 promenade des Anglais, Nice 06000. http://palais.concorde-hotels.com. ✆ **04-92-14-77-30.** Fax 04-92-14-77-14. 188 units. 195€–625€ double; from 450€ suite. AE, DC, MC, V. **Amenities:** 2 restaurants; bar; babysitting, casino; exercise room; 2 pools (indoor and outdoor); room service; solarium; Turkish bath; watersports equipment/rentals. *In room:* A/C, TV, hair dryer, minibar, free Wi-Fi.

## EXPENSIVE

**Hôtel Hi ★ 🎁**    The Japanese word *hi* describes the black mottling on the back of an ornamental carp, which has traditionally been associated with good luck. An architectural and decorative statement, this hotel occupies a former boarding house that dates to the 1930s. Spearheaded by Matali Crasset, a one-time colleague of Philippe Starck, a team of architects and engineers created one of the most aggressively avant-garde hotels in the south of France. The angular seven-story hotel opened in 2003. Each of the nine high-tech room concepts is different. They range from white-on-white to birch-wood veneer and acid green, to cool violet and gray. The unconventional layouts may include a bathtub tucked behind a screen of potted plants or elevated to a position of theatrical prominence. Electronic gizmos include state-of-the-art iPod docks and power showers. The Hi's highly regarded beach club and spa are hip hangouts in their own right.

3 av. des Fleurs, Nice 06000. www.hi-hotel.net. ✆ **04-97-07-26-26.** Fax 04-97-07-26-27. 38 units. 119€–269€ double; from 440€ suite. AE, DC, MC, V. Parking 24€. Bus: 23. **Amenities:** Organic restaurant; 24-hr. bar and snack bar; rooftop swimming pool; Turkish bath. *In room:* A/C, TV, free Wi-Fi.

**Hôtel La Pérouse ★★** 🎁   Once a prison, La Pérouse has been reconstructed and is now a spectacular and unique Riviera hotel. Set on a cliff, it's built right in the gardens of the ancient château hill, with a secluded swimming pool almost carved out of the rock to the rear. No hotel aside from the adjoining Hotel Suisse affords a better view over both the old city and the Baie des Anges. Inside it resembles an old Provençal home, with low ceilings, white walls, and antique furnishings. The lovely, spacious rooms are beautifully furnished, often with Provençal fabrics. Most have balconies overlooking the bay. The bathrooms are large, clad in Boticino marble, and hold tubs and showers.

11 quai Rauba-Capéu, Nice 06300. www.hotel-la-perouse.com. ✆ **04-93-62-34-63.** Fax 04-93-62-59-41. 65 units. 170€–540€ double; 630€–1,700€ suite. AE, DC, MC, V. Parking 25€. **Amenities:** Restaurant (mid-May to mid-Sept); bar; babysitting; exercise room; Jacuzzi; outdoor pool; room service; sauna. *In room:* A/C, TV, hair dryer, minibar, free Wi-Fi.

## MODERATE

**Hôtel du Petit Palais** 🎁   This whimsical hotel occupies a mansion built around 1890; in the 1970s, it was the home of the actor and writer Sacha Guitry (a name that's instantly recognized in millions of French households). It lies about a 10-minute drive from the city center in the Carabacel district near the Musée Chagall. Many of the Art Deco and Italianate furnishings and Florentine moldings and friezes remain intact. The preferred rooms, and the most expensive, have balconies that afford sea views during the day and sunset views at dusk. Bathrooms are small and tidy, and each has a shower and tub. Breakfast is served in a pretty salon or outdoors in the garden.

17 av. Emile-Bieckert, Nice 06000. www.petitpalaisnice.com. ✆ **04-93-62-19-11.** Fax 04-93-62-53-60. 25 units. 130€–220€ double. AE, DC, MC, V. Parking 10€. **Amenities:** Bar; babysitting; room service. *In room:* A/C, hair dryer, minibar, free Wi-Fi.

**Hôtel Windsor ★**   One of the most arts-conscious hotels on the Riviera is in a *maison bourgeoise* built by disciples of Gustav Eiffel in 1895. It's near the Negresco and the promenade des Anglais. Each unit is a unique decorative statement by a different artist. The heir and scion of the longtime owners, the Redolfi family, commissioned manifestations of his mystical and mythical visions after years of traveling through Asia, Africa, and South America. In the "Ben" room, for example, the Provençal artist of the same name painted verses of his own poetry, in tones of blue, orange, yellow, and green, on a white background. You can take your chances or select a room based on the photos on the hotel website. Most units have a combination tub/shower. The fifth floor holds the health club, steam room, and sauna. The garden contains scores of tropical and exotic plants, a tiny pool, and, to top it off, a parrot who chirps away as happily as the guests.

11 rue Dalpozzo, Nice 06000. www.hotelwindsornice.com. ✆ **04-93-88-59-35.** Fax 04-93-88-94-57. 54 units. 79€–190€ double. AE, DC, MC, V. Parking 15€. **Amenities:** Restaurant; bar;

babysitting; health club; outdoor pool; room service; sauna; smoke-free rooms. *In room:* A/C, TV, hair dryer, minibar.

**Nice Pebbles** ★   We cannot recommend this apartment rental company highly enough. Nice Pebbles manages around 100 high-class properties in the city's premier zones, including the old town and harbor, and along the promenade des Anglais. All of its properties are carefully selected, presumably to minimize any complaints or hassles. Its stock is thus in excellent condition and has first-class amenities (generally iPod docks, high-definition TVs, and designer bathrooms). Sizes vary from one-bedroom properties with large terraces, to large seaview places sleeping 10 or more guests. When booked by the week, prices work out much more competitively than a hotel, especially when traveling with a family. Booking can be made online, although due to high demand, reservations are best made as far in advance as possible.

23 rue Gioffredo, Nice 06000. www.nicepebbles.com. ✆ **04-97-20-27-39.** 100 units. 90€–350€ per apartment per night. MC, V. **Amenities:** Babysitting. *In apartments:* A/C (generally in all), TV, hair dryer, free Wi-Fi.

## INEXPENSIVE

**Hôtel Gounod** ★   A top choice in the city center, this hotel is a 5-minute walk from the sea. It was built around 1910 in a neighborhood where the street names honor composers. Ornate balconies, a domed roof, and an elaborate canopy of wrought iron and glass embellish the Gounod. The attractive lobby and adjoining lounge are festive and stylish, with old prints, copper flowerpots, and antiques. The high-ceilinged guest rooms won't win any luxury hotel awards, but are clean are quiet; most overlook the gardens of private homes. The tiled bathrooms are small but efficiently organized, mainly with shower units. Guests have free unlimited use of the pool and Jacuzzi at the Hôtel Splendid next door.

3 rue Gounod, Nice 06000. www.gounod-nice.com. ✆ **04-93-16-42-00.** Fax 04-93-88-23-84. 45 units. 100€–160€ double; 160€–260€ suite. AE, DC, MC, V. Parking 17€. Closed Nov 20–Dec 20. Bus: 98. **Amenities:** Babysitting; free Internet; Jacuzzi; outdoor pool; room service; spa. *In room:* A/C, TV, hair dryer, minibar.

**Villa Saint-Exupéry** ✐   This former Carmelite monastery has been completely renovated and turned into an award-winning hostel for young and old alike. It won the Best Hostel in France award in 2011. It's busy year-round with seasoned travelers on a budget, artists, musicians, families, hikers, and, of course, students on summer break. The restored and comfort-filled villa offers standard hotel rooms (some with kitchenette), as well as some dormitory accommodations at youth hostel tariffs. Echoing its past life, the former chapel preserved its stained-glass windows. There is also a bar with all drinks at 1€, free Wi-Fi, free luggage storage, free breakfast, and a barbeque area. Guests are also welcome to use a fully equipped kitchen. A new sister hostel offering the same facilities, **Villa Saint Exupéry Beach,** 6 rue Sacha Guitry (✆ **04-93-16-13-45**), opened downtown opposite Galleries Lafayette in 2010.

22 av. Gravier, Nice 06100. www.villahostels.com. ✆ **04-93-84-42-83.** Fax 04-92-09-82-94. 60 units. 27€–40€ per person in a single or twin-bedded room; 16€–30€ per person for dormitory bed. Rates include continental breakfast. MC, V. Free parking. **Amenities:** Bar; cooking facilities; free Wi-Fi. *In room:* Kitchenettes (in some).

# VILLEFRANCHE-SUR-MER ★

935km (580 miles) S of Paris; 6.5km (4 miles) E of Nice

Soaking up the sun in a big blue bay, Villefranche's beauty is legendary. Its medieval old town literally tumbles downhill into the shimmering sea. It's little wonder than countless artists made this beachy getaway their home, or that it's served as the backdrop for countless movies. About 6.5km (4 miles) east of Nice, it's the first town you reach along the Lower Corniche.

## Essentials

**GETTING THERE**   **Trains** arrive from all the Côte d'Azur's coastal resorts from Cannes to Monaco every 30 minutes or so. For rail information and schedules, visit www.voyages-sncf.com or call ⓒ **36-35**. Ligne d'Azur (www.lignes dazur.com; ⓒ **08-10-06-10-06**) maintains a **bus** service at 15-minute intervals aboard line no. 100 from Nice to Monte Carlo via Villefranche. One-way fares costs 1€. Buses deposit their passengers just above the old town, almost directly opposite the tourist information office. Many visitors **drive** via the Basee Corniche (Lower Corniche).

**VISITOR INFORMATION**   The **Office de Tourisme** is on Jardin François-Binon (www.villefranche-sur-mer.com; ⓒ **04-93-01-73-68;** fax 04-93-76-63-65).

## Exploring the Town

Villefranche's long curve of beach, **plage des Marinières,** is the principal attraction to most visitors. From here, **quai Courbet** runs along the sea to the colorful old town. This quay runs past scores of bobbing boats and is lined with waterside restaurants.

Old-town action revolves around **place Amélie Pollonnais.** This delightful square is shaded by palms and spread with the chairs and table of six easygoing restaurants. A Sunday antiques market also takes places here. People from across the Riviera come to root through vintage posters, silverware, 1930s jewelry, and ex-hotel linens.

The painter, writer, filmmaker, and well-respected dilettante Jean Cocteau left a fine memorial to the town's inhabitants. He spent a year (1956–57) painting frescoes on the 14th-century walls of the Romanesque **Chapelle St-Pierre,** quai Courbet (ⓒ **04-93-76-90-70**). He presented it to "the fishermen of Villefranche in homage to the Prince of Apostles, the patron of fishermen." In the apse is a depiction of the miracle of St. Peter walking on the water, not knowing that an angel supports him. Villefranche's busty local women, in their regional costumes, are honored on the left side of the narthex. Admission is 2.50€, free for ages 15 and under. In summer, it is open daily 10am to noon and 3 to 7pm; off-season hours are daily 10am to noon and 2 to 6pm.

A short coastal path leads from the car park below place Amélie Pollonnais to the **16th century citadel.** This castle dominates the bay, and its ramparts can be wandered around at leisure.

## Where to Eat

**La Mère Germaine** FRENCH/SEAFOOD   This historical restaurant is the best of the string of eateries stretching along the quay from the tiny port. Plan to relax over lunch while watching fishermen repair their nets. Mère Germaine opened the place in the 1930s, and these days a descendant, Remy Blouin, handles the cuisine, producing bouillabaisse celebrated across the Riviera. We recommend grilled sea bass with fennel, sole Tante Marie (stuffed with mushroom purée), lobster ravioli with shellfish sauce, and roast cod with chorizo sausage. Perfectly roasted *carré d'agneau* (lamb) is prepared for two.

Quai Courbet. www.meregermaine.com. © **04-93-01-71-39.** Reservations recommended. Main courses 35€–48€; fixed-price menu 42€. AE, MC, V. Daily noon–2:30pm and 7–10:30pm. Closed mid-Nov to Christmas.

## Where to Stay

**Hôtel Welcome ★**   The Welcome was a favorite of author and filmmaker Jean Cocteau and is still the best hotel in town. Every room in this modernized six-story villa has shutters, a balcony, and a view over the bay. Rooms range from midsize to spacious and are comfortably furnished, each with a small bathroom and most with a combination tub/shower. The sidewalk cafe is the focal point of town life. The on-site wine bar has an open fireplace.

3 quai Amiral-Courbet, Villefranche-sur-Mer 06230. www.welcomehotel.com. © **04-93-76-27-62.** Fax 04-93-76-27-66. 35 units. 105€–255€ double; 215€–425€ suite. AE, DC, MC, V. Parking 25€. **Amenities:** Bar; babysitting; room service. *In room:* A/C, TV, hair dryer, minibar, free Wi-Fi.

# 15 ST-JEAN-CAP-FERRAT ★★

939km (582 miles) S of Paris; 9.5km (6 miles) E of Nice

Of all the oases along the Côte d'Azur, no other place has the snob appeal of Cap-Ferrat. It's a 15km (9¼-mile) promontory sprinkled with luxurious villas and outlined by sheltered bays, beaches, and sun-kissed coves. In the charming port of St-Jean, the harbor accommodates yachts, fishing boats, and a dozen low-key restaurants.

## Essentials

**GETTING THERE**   Many visitors drive or take a **taxi** from the rail station at nearby Beaulieu. Buses from the station at Beaulieu depart hourly for Cap-Ferrat; the one-way fare is 1€. There's also an hourly bus, the no. 81, from Nice. For bus information and schedules, contact Ligne d'Azur (www.lignes dazur.com; © **08-10-06-10-06**). By **car** from Nice, take D6098 (the *basse corniche*) east.

**VISITOR INFORMATION**   The **Office de Tourisme** is on 59 av. Denis-Séméria (www.saintjeancapferrat.fr; © **04-93-76-08-90;** fax 04-93-76-16-67).

## Seeing the Sights

One way to enjoy the scenery here is to wander along the public pathway that circles the entire peninsula. It winds past deserted coves and alongside the gardens of countless millionaire dwellings. The most scenic section runs from **plage de Paloma** to **pointe St-Hospice,** where a panoramic view of the Riviera landscape unfolds. You can also wander around the hamlet of **St-Jean,** a colorful fishing village with bars, bistros, and inns.

Villa Ephrussi de Rothschild.

**Villa Ephrussi de Rothschild** ★★ HISTORIC HOME/MUSEUM    Built by
Baronne Ephrussi de Rothschild, this villa is one of the Côte d'Azur's most legendary. Born a Rothschild, the baronne married a Hungarian banker and friend of her
father. She died in 1934, leaving the Italianate building and its gardens to the Institut de France on behalf of the Académie des Beaux-Arts. The museum preserves
the wealth of her collection: 18th-century furniture; Tiepolo ceilings; Savonnerie
carpets; screens and panels from the Far East; tapestries from Gobelin, Aubusson,
and Beauvais; Fragonard drawings; canvases by Boucher; Sèvres porcelain; and
more. It's also amusing to witness the sheer spending power of a young madame
whose hero was Marie Antoinette. The gardens, set in French, Japanese, Spanish,
and Florentine styles, with additional rose and exotic gardens, are a particular
delight. An attractive tea salon overlooks the Bay of Villefranche.

1 av. de Rothschild. www.villa-ephrussi.com. ℂ **04-93-01-33-09.** Admission 12€ adults, 9€ students and children 7–17, free for children 6 and under. July–Aug daily 10am–7pm; Feb 15–June
and Sept–Oct daily 10am–6pm; Nov–Feb 14 Mon–Fri 2–6pm, Sat–Sun 10am–6pm.

## Hitting the Beach

The town's most visible and popular beaches are **plage Passable,** on the northwestern "neck" of the Cap-Ferrat peninsula, close to where it connects to the
French mainland; and **plage de Paloma,** near the peninsula's southernmost tip,
overlooked by the Chapelle St-Hospice. Both are lined with soft pebbles,
although these are easy on sensitive feet. Both have classy beach bars and a restaurant apiece.

## Where to Eat

**Capitaine Cook** ★ PROVENÇAL/SEAFOOD    Next door to the fancy La
Voile d'Or hotel (see "Where to Stay," p. 608), a few blocks uphill from the center

of the village, this restaurant specializes in seafood served in hearty portions. You'll have a panoramic view of the coast from the terrace; inside, the decor is maritime and rugged. Oysters, served simply on the half-shell or in several creative ways with sauces and herbs, are a specialty. Roasted catch of the day is the mainstay, but filet mignon is also popular.

11 av. Jean-Mermoz. (C) **04-93-76-02-66**. Main courses 17€–30€; fixed-price menu 27€–32€. MC, V. Fri–Tues noon–2pm; Thurs–Tues 7:15–10pm. Closed mid-Nov to Dec.

**Le Sloop** FRENCH/PROVENÇAL A justifiably popular bistro specializing in harbor-fresh seafood. Outfitted in blue and white inside and out, it sits at the edge of the port, overlooking the yachts in the harbor. A meal may begin with a carpaccio of sea bass dotted with capers, or perhaps tartare of salmon with aioli and lemon crepes. You could follow with a filet of bream served with red-wine sauce, or a mixed fish fry of three kinds of Mediterranean fish, bound together with olive oil and truffles. Low-key celebrities who holiday nearby have been known to drop in for lunch on the outdoor terrace.

Port Plaisance. www.restaurantsloop.com. (C) **04-93-01-48-63**. Reservations recommended. Main courses 22€–26€; fixed-price menu 30€. AE, DC, MC, V. July-Aug Thurs-Mon noon-2pm and Thurs-Tues 7-10pm; Sep-June Thurs–Tues noon–2pm and 7–10pm. Closed mid-Nov to mid-Dec.

# Where to Stay

## EXPENSIVE

### Grand Hôtel du Cap-Ferrat ★★★
This grande dame hotel, set in vast gardens of semitropical trees and manicured lawns, has reawakened after an extravagant renovation. It has been the retreat of the international elite since 1908 and occupies the same celestial status as La Réserve de Beaulieu (p. 611). Parts of the exterior have open loggias and big arched windows; you can also enjoy the views from the elaborately flowering terrace over the sea. Accommodation is modern and unfussy. A handful of suites benefit from the recent addition of private plunge pools. Another alluring feature is the Cellu M6 spa, which spills outside into curtained cabanas, where massages and other treatments can take place. Le Cap, the hotel's acclaimed gourmet restaurant, is overseen by top chef Didier Aniès. Admission to the pool (the first on the Riviera, and still apparently the largest) and the seaside Club Dauphin beach club incurs a hefty extra charge, even for guests.

71 bd. du Général-de-Gaulle, St-Jean-Cap-Ferrat 06230. www.grand-hotel-cap-ferrat.com. (C) **04-93-76-50-50**. Fax 04-93-76-04-52. 73 units. 265€–990€ double; 580€–4,100€ suite. AE, DC, MC, V. Parking 35€. Closed Jan and Feb. Amenities: 3 restaurants; bar; babysitting; bikes; Olympic-size heated outdoor pool; room service; spa; 2 tennis courts. In room: A/C, TV, hair dryer, minibar, free Wi-Fi.

### La Voile d'Or ★★
Established in 1966, the "Golden Sail" is a tour de force. It provides intimate luxury in a converted 19th-century villa at the edge of the little fishing port and yacht harbor, with a panoramic coast view. It's equal to the Grand Hôtel in every feature except cuisine, which is just a notch lower. The guest rooms, lounges, and restaurant open onto terraces. Accommodations are individually decorated, with hand-painted reproductions, carved gilt headboards, baroque paneled doors, parquet floors, antique clocks, and paintings. The luxurious bathrooms have tub/showers. Guests gather on

the canopied terrace for lunch, and in a stately room with Spanish armchairs and white wrought-iron chandeliers for dinner.

7 av. Jean-Mermoz, St-Jean-Cap-Ferrat 06230. www.lavoiledor.fr. ℂ **04-93-01-13-13.** Fax 04-93-76-11-17. 45 units. 270€–900€ double; 710€–900€ suite. Rates include continental breakfast. AE, MC, V. Parking 25€. Closed mid-Oct to late Apr. **Amenities:** 2 restaurants; bar; babysitting; exercise room; 2 saltwater outdoor pools; room service; sauna; free Wi-Fi. *In room:* A/C, TV, hair dryer, free Internet, minibar.

### MODERATE

**Hôtel Brise Marine**   Built around 1878, this heavenly little villa with front and rear terraces sits on a hillside between St-Jean village and Paloma Plage. A long rose arbor, beds of subtropical flowers, palms, and pines provide an attractive setting. The atmosphere is casual and informal, and the rooms are comfortably but simply furnished. They have small, tiled bathrooms with shower and tub. You can have breakfast in the beamed lounge or under the rose trellis. The little corner bar serves afternoon drinks.

58 av. Jean-Mermoz, St-Jean-Cap-Ferrat 06230. www.hotel-brisemarine.com. ℂ **04-93-76-04-36.** Fax 04-93-76-11-49. 16 units. 148€–188€ double; 178€–218€ triple; 168€–198€ studio. AE, DC, MC, V. Parking 14€. Closed Nov–Jan. **Amenities:** Bar; room service. *In room:* A/C, TV, hair dryer, minibar, free Wi-Fi.

# BEAULIEU-SUR-MER ★★

939km (582 miles) S of Paris; 9.5km (6 miles) E of Nice; 11km (6¾ miles) W of Monte Carlo

Beaulieu-sur-Mer is a Belle Epoque resort cradled between a bustling pleasure harbor and the beach-lined base of Cap Ferrat. Its casino and fine restaurants have attracted *bonnes vivantes* since the days of Riviera tourism began. Like many of the more classic resorts along the Côte d'Azur, it is popular with old-money holidaymakers and the wintering wealthy.

## Essentials

**GETTING THERE**   Most visitors **drive** from Nice on D6098, the coastal highway. **Trains** connect Beaulieu with Nice, Monaco, and the rest of the Côte d'Azur every 30 minutes. For **rail** information, visit www.voyages-sncf.com or call ℂ **36-35**. **Bus** line no. 100 from Nice to Monte Carlo also passes through Beaulieu. One-way fares costs 1€. For bus information and schedules, contact Ligne d'Azur (www.lignesdazur.com; ℂ **08-10-06-10-06**).

**VISITOR INFORMATION**   The **Office de Tourisme** is on place Georges Clémenceau (www.beaulieusurmer.fr; ℂ **04-93-01-02-21**).

## Fun on & off the Beach

Beaulieu has popular public beaches at both ends of town. The beaches aren't as rocky as those in Nice or other nearby resorts, but they're still closer to gravel than to sand. The longer of the two is **Petite Afrique,** just past the yacht harbor. It has a submerged diving platform, a beach bar, and a family-friendly atmosphere. The shorter is **Baie des Fourmis,** which lies beneath the casino at the foot of Cap Ferrat.

The town is home to an important church, the late-19th-century **Église de Sacré-Coeur,** a quasi-Byzantine, quasi-Gothic mishmash at 13 bd. du Maréchal-Leclerc (© **04-93-01-01-46**). It's open daily 8am to 7pm. At the same address (same phone) is the 12th-century Romanesque chapel of Santa Maria de Olivo, used mostly for temporary exhibits of painting, sculpture, and civic memorabilia. Unlike the Eglise de Sacré-Coeur, the chapel is not an active house of worship and is open only for special exhibitions.

As you walk along the seafront promenade, you can see many stately Belle Epoque villas that evoke the days when Beaulieu was the height of fashion. Although you can't go inside, you'll see signs for **Villa Namouna,** which once belonged to Gordon Bennett, the owner of the *New York Herald,* and **Villa Léonine,** former home of the marquess of Salisbury.

Villa Kérylos.

For a memorable 90-minute walk, start north of boulevard Edouard-VII, where a path leads up the Riviera escarpment to **Sentier du Plateau St-Michel.** A belvedere here offers panoramic views from Cap d'Ail to the Estérel. An hour-long alternative is the stroll along **promenade Maurice-Rouvier.** The promenade runs parallel to the water, stretching from Beaulieu to St-Jean. On one side you'll see the most elegant mansions in well-landscaped gardens, including the pink palace of former resident David Niven on place Niven; on the other, views of the Riviera landscape and the peninsular point of St-Hospice.

**Villa Kérylos ★★** MUSEUM   Jutting out into the Mediterranean is this replica of an ancient Greek residence, painstakingly designed and built by the archaeologist Theodore Reinach. A collection of Greek figurines and ceramics fills the cabinets, while an imposing line of larger-than-life statues line several walls. Also interesting is the reconstructed Greek furniture, much of which would be fashionable today. One curious mosaic depicts the slaying of the Minotaur and provides its own labyrinth. Outside, a series of walkways loops around by the sea.

Impasse Gustave Eiffel. www.villa-kerylos.com. © **04-93-01-01-44.** Admission 10€ adults, 7.50€ seniors and children 7–17, free for children 6 and under. Mid-Feb to Oct daily 10am–6pm (until 7pm July–Aug); Nov to mid-Feb Mon–Fri 2–6pm, Sat–Sun 10am–6pm.

## Where to Eat

**The African Queen ★** FRENCH/INTERNATIONAL   Superb food meets a raucous holiday crowd on Beaulieu's bustling port. This ever-popular institution is the meeting point of celebrities, yachties, and the painfully newly rich. The awesome salads are the most popular starters, and it's hard to eat a better bowl of greens on the entire Riviera. The remaining cuisine comes direct from the wood-fired oven: pizzas, fillets of steak, and the African Queen's classy take on the traditional burger.

Port de Plaisance. www.africanqueen.fr. (✆ **04-93-01-10-85**. Reservations recommended. Pizzas 11€–26€; main courses 14€–35€. MC, V. Daily noon–midnight. Closed some holidays.

**La Pignatelle** *❦* FRENCH/PROVENÇAL   Even in this expensive town, you can find an excellent, affordable Provençal bistro. Despite its relatively low prices, La Pignatelle prides itself on the fresh ingredients in its robust cuisine. Specialties include mushroom-stuffed ravioli with truffled cream sauce, succulent *soupe de poissons* from which the kitchen has labored to remove the bones, cassoulet of mussels, fricassee of sea bass with shrimp, and *petite friture du pays,* which incorporates small fish using age-old Provençal traditions.

10 rue de Quincenet. (✆ **04-93-01-03-37.** Reservations recommended. Main courses 9€–27€; fixed-price lunch 22€–32€, dinner 32€. AE, DC, MC, V. Fri-Tues noon–2pm, Thurs–Tues 7–9:30pm. Closed mid-Nov to mid-Dec.

**Les Agaves** ★★ MODERN FRENCH   One of the most stylish restaurants in Beaulieu is in an early-1900s villa across the street from the railway station. It's also one of the most reliable and highly rated, despite its relatively moderate prices. Of note are curry-enhanced scallops with garlic-flavored tomatoes and parsley, lobster salad with mango, ravioli with flap mushrooms, chopped shrimp with Provençal herbs, and several preparations of foie gras. Filet of sea bass with truffles and champagne sauce is delectable. Les Agaves is a hit with visiting restaurant critics, actors, and the Monaco royal family.

4 av. Maréchal Foch. www.lesagaves.com. (✆ **04-93-01-13-12.** Reservations required. Main courses 24€–40€; fixed-price menu 38€. AE, MC, V. Daily 7–10pm. Closed Nov 15–Dec 20.

# Beaulieu Nightlife

Sir Winston Churchill was once a regular at the Art Deco **Grand Casino de Beaulieu,** 4 av. Fernand-Dunan (✆ **04-93-76-48-00**). The house still encourages jackets for men in its fancier areas. It requires that patrons show a passport. The slot machine section, where dress is more casual, is free to enter and doesn't require identification. Of note is the casino's summertime gaming room, where poker and roulette are played under the stars, just across from the Baie des Fourmis beach.

# Where to Stay

## EXPENSIVE

**La Réserve de Beaulieu** ★★★   This pink-and-white *fin de siècle* palace is one of the Cote d'Azur's most famous hotels. Here you can sit, have an (expensive) aperitif, and watch the sunset while a pianist plays Mozart. A number of the lounges open onto a courtyard with bamboo chairs, grass borders, and urns of flowers. Social life revolves around the main drawing room. Like Beaulieu's classic heritage, the clientele is older and more moneyed than in the Riviera's other glamorous hotels. The individually decorated guest rooms range widely in size and design, but all are large; all feature the most subtle of mod cons, such as Bang & Olufsen televisions and stereos, and push-button room service. Most overlook the Mediterranean, while others have a view of the mountains. Some have private balconies. With a name like Restaurant des Rois (*Restaurant of*

*Kings*), it's obvious that the hotel's double Michelin-starred restaurant is very special, too.

5 bd. du Maréchal-Leclerc, Beaulieu-sur-Mer 06310. www.reservebeaulieu.com. ℂ **04-93-01-00-01.** Fax 04-93-01-28-99. 39 units. 240€–1,755€ double; 545€–3,615€ suite. AE, DC, MC, V. Parking 36€. Closed mid-Oct to mid-Dec. **Amenities:** Restaurant; bar; babysitting; exercise room; massage; outdoor pool; room service. *In room:* A/C, TV, hair dryer, minibar, free Wi-Fi.

## INEXPENSIVE

**Hôtel Le Havre Bleu** ⚭ This petite hotel is a great bargain if you don't require a lot of services and amenities. Le Havre Bleu has one of the prettiest facades of any inexpensive hotel in town. In a former Victorian villa, the hotel has arched ornate windows and a front garden dotted with flowering urns. The impeccable guest rooms are comfortable, functional, and tidy, and all feature satellite television. Many have small outdoor terraces. Breakfast can be served alfresco.

29 bd. du Maréchal-Joffre, Beaulieu-sur-Mer 06310. www.lehavrebleu.com. ℂ **04-93-01-01-40.** Fax 04-93-01-29-92. 20 units. 66€–86€ double; 83€–105€ triple. AE, MC, V. Parking 8€. **Amenities:** Babysitting; breakfast room. *In room:* A/C, TV, free Wi-Fi.

**Inter-Hôtel Frisia** Most of the Frisia's rooms, decorated in a modern style, open onto views of the harbor. The sea-view units are the most expensive. All rooms have small bathrooms, with a combination tub/shower. Two spacious suites with kitchenettes are in free-standing villas near the hotel's main building. Public areas include a sunny garden and inviting lounges. English is widely spoken here, and the management makes foreign guests feel especially welcome. Breakfast is the only meal served, but many reasonably priced restaurants are nearby.

2 bd. Eugène-Gauthier, Beaulieu-sur-Mer 06310. www.frisia-beaulieu.com. ℂ **04-93-01-01-04.** Fax 04-93-01-31-92. 35 units. 60€–139€ double; 110€–195€ suite. AE, DC, MC, V. Parking 9€. Closed early Nov–mid-Dec. **Amenities:** Bar; babysitting; room service; free Wi-Fi. *In room:* A/C, TV, hair dryer, minibar.

# EZE & LA TURBIE ★★

942km (584 miles) S of Paris; 11km (6¾ miles) NE of Nice

The hamlets of Eze and La Turbie, 6.5km (4 miles) apart, are picture-perfect hill villages that literally cling to the mountains. Both have fortified medieval cores overlooking the coast, and both were built during the early Middle Ages to stave off raids from Saracen pirates. In Eze's case, it's now tour buses, not coastal raiders, which make daily invasions into town. Its impossibly cute streets contain galleries, boutiques, and artisans' shops. La Turbie is much more authentic and offers a welcome respite from the coast's summertime heat.

Eze is accessible on the Moyenne (Middle) Corniche, La Turbie by way of the Grande (Upper) Corniche. Both are spellbindingly pretty routes. Signs along the coastal road indicate the direction motorists should take to reach either village.

Aside from its pretty lanes, the leading attraction in Eze is the **Jardin d'Eze ★**, avenue du Jardin Exotique (ℂ **04-93-41-10-30**), a showcase of exotic plants in Eze-Village, at the pinnacle of the town's highest hill. Admission is 6€ for adults, 2.50€ for students and ages 12 to 25, and free for children 11 and under. In July and August, it's open daily 9am to 7.30pm; the rest of the

**Trophée des Alps.**

year, it opens daily at 9am and closes between 4.30 and 7pm, depending on the time of sunset.

La Turbie boasts a ruined monument erected by Roman emperor Augustus in 6 B.C., the **Trophée des Alps (Trophy of the Alps) ★**. It's near a rock formation known as La Tête de Chien, at the highest point along the Grand Corniche, 450m (1,476 ft.) above sea level. The Roman Senate ordered the creation of the monument, which many locals call La Trophée d'Auguste, to celebrate the subjugation of the people of the French Alps by the Roman armies.

A short distance from the monument is the interactive **Musée du Trophée d'Auguste,** cours Albert 1er de Monaco, La Turbie (*✆* **04-93-41-20-84**), a mini-museum containing finds from digs nearby, a historical 3D film, and information about the monument's restoration. Both the trophy enclosure and the museum are open Tuesday to Sunday mid-May to mid-September 9:30am to 1pm and 2:30 to 6:30pm, and mid-September to mid-May 10am to 1:30pm and 2:30 to 5pm. Admission to both sites is 5.50€ for adults and free for children 17 and under.

Eze's **Office de Tourisme** is on place du Général-de-Gaulle, Eze-Village (www.eze-riviera.com; *✆* **04-93-41-26-00;** fax 04-93-41-04-80). La Turbie's small **tourist information point** is at 2 place Detras, La Turbie (www.ville-la-turbie.fr; *✆* **04-93-41-21-15**).

## Where to Eat

**Le Troubadour** FRENCH/PROVENÇAL The stone-fronted medieval house that contains this well-known restaurant has, since World War I, housed businesses that have included a bar, a delicatessen, and the local post office. Today, within three dining rooms, each accented with thick ceiling beams, you can order succulent and flavorful dishes that include braised rabbit served with warm hearts of artichoke, foie gras, and carrots; a delightful filet of John Dory with stuffed and deep-fried zucchini blossoms; and other dishes that each manage to showcase some aspect of the Mediterranean diet. You'll find the restaurant close to the village church, in the upper heights of Eze Village.

4 rue du Brec, Eze Village. *✆* **04-93-41-19-03.** Reservations recommended. Main courses 22€– 38€; fixed-price menus 39€–52€. MC, V. Tues–Sat 12:30–2pm and 7:30–9:30pm. Closed mid-Nov to mid-Dec.

## Where to Stay

**Château de la Chèvre d'Or ★★★** This is one of the grandest resort hotels along the eastern Riviera, and a favorite of royalty and A-list celebrities.

The miniature-village retreat was built in the 1920s in neo-Gothic style. The decor of the "Golden Goat" maintains its character while adding modern comfort. Each sumptuously decorated suite is essentially a grand apartment with an expansive view of the coastline. La Chèvre d'Or boasts a variety of restaurants dotted across its outdoor terraces serving classic French and Asian cuisine. The best is its fabulous signature restaurant, which boasts two Michelin stars. Even if you don't eat or spend the night, try to visit for a drink in the lounge, which has a panoramic view.

Rue du Barri, Eze-Village 06360. www.chevredor.com. ✆ **04-92-10-66-66.** Fax 04-93-41-06-72. 37 units. 280€–780€ double; 720€–3,500€ suite. AE, DC, MC, V. Parking 15€. Closed Dec–Feb. **Amenities:** 4 restaurants; bar; babysitting; exercise room; outdoor pool; room service; sauna. *In room:* A/C, TV, hair dryer, minibar, free Wi-Fi.

# MONACO ★★

939km (582 miles) S of Paris; 18km (11 miles) E of Nice

As a tableau on the Rock of Monaco explains, this sunny stretch of coast became the property of the Grimaldi clan in 1297 when one Francesco Grimaldi tricked his way into the fortress protecting the harbor. The dynasty has maintained something resembling independence ever since. In a fit of impatience, the French annexed it in 1793, but the ruling family recovered it in 1814.

Hemmed in by France on three sides and the Mediterranean on the fourth, this feudal anomaly harbours the world's greatest number of both millionaires and billionaires per capita. And as almost everybody knows, the Monégasques do not pay taxes. Nearly all their country's revenue comes from banking, tourism, and gambling. Better still, in an astute feat of cunning, local residents aren't allowed to gamble away their inheritance, so visitors must bring a passport to play on the Principality's famed poker, roulette, and blackjack tables.

Monaco, or, more precisely, its capital of Monte Carlo, has for a century been a symbol of glamour. The 1956 marriage of Prince Rainier III to American actress Grace Kelly enhanced its status. She met the prince when she was in Cannes to promote *To Catch a Thief.* Their daughter Caroline was born in 1957; a son, Albert, in 1958; and a second daughter, Stephanie, in 1965. The Monégasques welcomed the birth of Caroline but went wild for Albert, a male heir. According to a 1918 treaty, Monaco would become an autonomous state under French protection, should the ruling dynasty become extinct. Though not always happy in her role, Princess Grace won the respect and admiration of her people. The Monégasques still mourn her death in a 1982 car accident on the Moyenne Corniche, near La Turbie.

In April 2005, Prince Rainier died after suffering ailing health for many years. Upon his father's death, Prince Albert became the reigning prince. Unlike his father's storybook marriage to Grace Kelly, Albert remained unmarried and heirless, even though he's admitted to having a son out of wedlock. (His illegitimate son cannot ascend to the throne.) Fortunately for the Grimaldi line, Albert married his girlfriend, South African swimmer Charlene Wittstock, in July 2011, who became Her Serene Highness The Princess of Monaco. Despite rumours of a pre-wedding fallout, the couple are idolized in the Principality. Their official portrait (which some commentators claim looks a litttte strained) has pride of place in every bar, hotel, and bakery.

The second-smallest state in Europe (Vatican City is the tiniest), Monaco consists of four parts. The old town, **Monaco-Ville,** on a promontory, "the Rock," 60m (197 ft.) high, is the seat of the royal palace and the government building, as well as the Oceanographic Museum. To the west, **La Condamine** is at the foot of the old town, forming its ritzy harbor and port sector. Up from the port (Monaco is steep) is **Monte Carlo,** once the playground of royalty and still the center for the wintering wealthy, the setting for the casino, and the luxurious hotels. The fourth part, **Fontvieille,** is a neat industrial suburb housing the Monaco Football club.

Monaco used to be slow in summer, but now July and August tend to be so crowded that it's hard to get a room. Dine alfresco, and you'll be passed by a motorcade of Bugattis, Lamborghinis, and Rolls Royces (regular Porches and Mercedes are considered parvenu here). As always, you can lose your shirt at the gaming tables year-round.

## Essentials

**GETTING THERE** Monaco has rail, bus, and highway connections from other coastal cities, especially Nice. There are no border formalities when entering Monaco from mainland France. The 19km (12 miles) **drive** from Nice takes around 30 minutes and runs along the N7 Moyenne Corniche. The pretty D6098 coast road takes a little longer. Ligne d'Azur (www.lignes dazur.com; ✆ 08-10-06-10-06) runs a **bus** service at 15-minute intervals aboard line no. 100 from Nice to Monte Carlo. One-way bus transit from Nice costs 1€. **Trains** arrive every 30 minutes from Cannes, Nice, Menton, and Antibes. For more rail information, visit www.voyages-sncf.com or call ✆ 36-35. Monaco's underground railway station (Gare SNCF) is on place St. Devote. A system of pedestrian tunnels, escalators, and elevators riddle the Principality, and such an underground walkway links the train station to Monte Carlo. If you'd rather take a **taxi** but can't find one at the station, call ✆ 08-20-20-98-98. A recent addition to Monaco is the **Monaco–Le Grand Tour** (www.monacolegrandtour.com; ✆ 97-70-26-36) open-top minibus, which allows visitors to hop-on and hop-off at the Principality's 12 main sights. Day passes cost 17€ for adults; 7€ for children between 4 and 11; free for chilren under 4.

**CAM** (www.cam.mc; ✆ 97-70-22-22) runs buses inside the Principality. Lines nos. 1 and 2 link Monaco-Ville with the Casino area. CAM's solar-powered **shuttle boat** hops between the banks of Monaco's port every 20 minutes. The ride is great for kids and connects the Casino area with foot of Monaco-Ville. All CAM tickets cost 1€.

**VISITOR INFORMATION** The **Direction du Tourisme et des Congrés** office is at 2A bd. des Moulins (www.visitmonaco.com; ✆ 92-16-61-16).

**SPECIAL EVENTS** Two of the most-watched **car-racing events** in Europe are in January (Le Rallye) and May (the Grand Prix). The **Monte-Carlo Masters** ATP tennis tournament (www.monte-carlorolexmasters.com) takes place in April. The **Monte-Carlo International Fireworks Festival** lasts all summer long. The skies above the harbor are lit up several times a week as millions of euros go up in smoke, courtesy of those who can assuredly afford it.

To call Monaco from within France, dial 00 (the access code for all international long-distance calls from France); followed by the **country code, 377;** and then the eight-digit local phone number. (Don't dial the 33 code; that's the country code for France.)

To call Monaco from North America, dial the international access code, 011;

the country code, 377; and then the eight-digit Monaco number.

To call any other country from within Monaco, dial 00 (the international access code), then the applicable country code, and the number. For example, to call Cannes, you would dial 00, 33 (France's country code), 4 (the city code, without the zero), and the eight-digit number.

# Fun on & off the Beach

**BEACHES**  Just outside the border, on French soil, the **Monte-Carlo Beach Club** adjoins the Monte-Carlo Beach Hotel, 22 av. Princesse-Grace (✆ 98-06-54-54). Princess Grace used to come here in flowery swimsuits, and now it's an integral part of Monaco social life. The sand is replenished at regular intervals. The entire establishment was given a chic overhaul in 2009 and now encompasses two mosaic-lined pools, a La Prairie spa, cabanas, a poolside fine dining restaurant called Le Deck, and a low key Mediterranean restaurnat with lunch buffet called La Vigie. New for 2011 was Sea Lounge, an afternoon and late evening club, which features live DJs and *nargile* hubble-bubble pipes. Beach activities include donuts, jet skis, and parachute rides. As the temperature drops in September, the beach closes for the winter. The admission charge of 45€ to 130€, depending on the season, grants you access to the changing rooms, toilets, restaurants, and bar, along with use of a mattress for sunbathing. As usual, topless bathing is common.

More low-key swimming and sunbathing is also available at **Plage du Larvotto,** off avenue Princesse-Grace. Part of this popular man-made strip of sand is public. The other part contains private beach clubs with bars, snacks, and showers, plus a kids club. A jogging track runs behind the beach.

**SPA TREATMENTS**  In 1908, the Société des Bains de Mer launched a seawater (thalassotherapy) spa in Monte Carlo, inaugurated by Prince Albert I. **Les Thermes Marins,** 2 av. de Monte-Carlo (www.thermesmarinsmontecarlo.com; ✆ 98-06-69-00), is now one of the largest spas in Europe and is wellness at its most chic. Spread over four floors is a pool, Turkish *hammam* (steam bath), healthy restaurant, juice bar, tanning booths, fitness center, beauty center, and private treatment rooms. A day pass, giving access to the sauna, steam rooms, fitness facilities, and pools, costs 90€. Therapies include an hour-long Néo-Jeunesse fibro stimulation massage for 130€.

**SWIMMING**  Overlooking the yacht-studded harbor, the **Stade Nautique Rainier-III,** quai Albert-1er, at La Condamine (✆ 93-30-64-83), a pool frequented by the Monégasques, was a gift from Prince Rainier to his subjects. It's open May to October daily 9am to 6pm (until 8pm July–Aug).

# Monaco

To Grande Corniche

To Menton

Paris

FRANCE

Monaco

To Nice

av. des Combattants en Afrique du Nord

Moyen Corniche

av. du Villaine

BEAUSOLEIL

av. de la République

bd. Princesse Charlotte

bd. des Moulins

bd. de Grand-Bretagne

LARVOTTO

Larvotto

Princesse Grace

av. du

Plage de Larvotto

**6**

**7**

*i*

place du Casino

**5**

Casino de Monte Carlo

Gare de Monaco

bd. de Suisse

av. de Costa

MONTE CARLO

place St-Dévote

av. Prés. Kennedy

Moyen Corniche

MONEGHETTI

bd. du Jardin Exotique

Rainier III

bd. de Belgique

rue Grimaldi

Albert 1er

MONACO

Port de Monaco (Port Hercule)

Stade Nautique Rainier-III

quai Antoine 1er

MEDITERRANEAN SEA

LA CONDAMINE

place d'Armes

place du Canton

Palais du Prince

MONACO-VILLE

av. St-Martin

**1**

Jardin Exotique

bd. Charles III

av. du Prince Héréditaire Albert

**2**

**3**

pl. du Palais

Cathédrale

Jardins St-Martin

**4**

Musée Océanographique

Port de Fontvieille

Information *i*

Post Office ✉

av. du 3 Septembre

FONTVIEILLE

Stade Louis II (AS Monaco)

Parc Paysager de Fontvieille

Roseraie Princesse Grace

Collection des Voitures Anciennes
de S.A.S. 1$^e$ Prince de Monaco **2**

Monte-Carlo Casino **5**

Nouveau Musée National de Monaco **1, 6**

Musée Océanographique de Monaco **4**

Musée du Palais du Prince/
Les Grands Appartements du Palais **3**

Sun Casino **7**

0 ——— 1/4 mi
0 ——— 0.25 km

Admission costs 5.10€ per person. Between November and April, it's an ice-skating rink.

**TENNIS & SQUASH**   The **Monte Carlo Country Club,** 155 av. Princesse-Grace, Roquebrune-Cap Martin, France (www.mccc.mc; ☎ **04-93-41-30-15**), has 21 clay and 2 concrete tennis courts. The 43€ fee provides access to a restaurant, health club with Jacuzzi and sauna, putting green, beach, squash courts, and well-maintained tennis courts. Guests of the hotels administered by the Société des Bains de Mer (Hôtel de Paris, Hermitage, Monte Carlo Bay, and Monte Carlo Beach Club) pay half-price. It's open daily 8am to 8 or 9pm, depending on the season.

## Seeing the Sights

### Collection des Voitures Anciennes de S.A.S. le Prince de Monaco ☺

MUSEUM    Prince Rainier III opened a showcase of his private collection of more than 100 vintage autos, including the 1956 Rolls-Royce Silver Cloud that carried the prince and princess on their wedding day. Monaco shopkeepers gave it to the royal couple as a wedding present. Other cool exhibits include a 2009 Mercedes McLaren SLR and a 1986 Lamborghini Countach. The most recent exhibit is a Toyota Lexus with a bulletproof glass roof. It served as the royal wedding car for the marriage of Prince Albert and Charlene Wittstock in 2011.

Les Terrasses de Fontvieille. www.palais.mc. ✆ **92-05-28-56.** Admission 6€ adults, 3€ students and children 8–14, free for children 7 and under. Daily 10am–6pm. Closed Christmas.

### Les Grands Appartements du Palais ★ PALACE

Most summer day-trippers want to see the home of Monaco's royal family, the Palais du Prince, which dominates the principality from the Rock. A tour of the Grands Appartements allows you a glimpse of the Throne Room and some of the art, including works by Bruegel and Holbein, as well as Princess Grace's state portrait. The palace was built in the 13th century, and part dates from the Renaissance. The ideal time to arrive is 11:55am, to watch the 10-minute **Relève de la Garde (Changing of the Guard).**

Place du Palais. www.palais.mc. ✆ **93-25-18-31.** Admission 7€ adults, 3.50€ children 8–14, free for children 7 and under. Daily Apr 10:30am–6pm; May–Sept 9:30am–6:30pm; Oct 10am–5:30pm. Closed Nov–Mar.

### Musée Océanographique de Monaco ★★ ☺ AQUARIUM

Albert I, great-grandfather of the present prince, founded this museum in 1910. You'll see models of the ships aboard which he directed his scientific cruises from 1885 to 1914. Some of the exotic creatures he found on travels were unknown before he captured them. Skeletons of specimens, including a whale that drifted ashore in

Musée Océanographique de Monaco.

1896, are on the main floor. An exhibition devoted to the discovery of the ocean is in the physical-oceanography room on the first floor. Underwater movies are shown in the lecture room. There is also a shark lagoon and over 90 aquariums re-creating tropical reefs, arctic zones, and jellyfish feeding grounds.

Av. St-Martin. www.oceano.mc. (℃ **93-15-36-00.** Admission 13€ adults, 6.50€ children 4–18, free for children 5 and under. Apr–June and Sept daily 9:30am–7pm; July–Aug daily 9:30am–7:30pm; Oct–Mar daily 10am–6pm.

**Nouveau Musée National de Monaco ★★** ART MUSEUMS    The Villa Sauber and the Villa Paloma are two stunning new art spaces set in palatial former homes. Both make up the Nouveau Musée National de Monaco, although they are set on the other side of the city—well, country, actually—from each other. They explore contemporary art themes by way of paintings, sculpture, and installations. The exhibitions that have been carried in so far have been magnificent, such is the pulling power of these state-backed galleries.

Villa Sauber, 17 av. Princess Grace; Villa Paloma, 56 bd. du Jardin Exotique. www.nmnm.mc. (℃ **98-98-16-82.** Admission to both 10€ adults, admission to individual gallery 6€ adults, free entrance for visitors 26 and under. May–Sept daily 10am–7pm. Oct–Apr daily 10am–6pm.

# Where to Eat

## EXPENSIVE

**Restaurant Joël Robuchon ★** MODERN FRENCH    In keeping with its house style, the Hotel Métropole's restaurant offering from superstar chef Joël Robuchon balances elegance with informality. Robuchon is the world's most decorated restaurateur, and the cuisine managed  by his protégé, head chef Christophe Cussac, doesn't disappoint. Half-portions of almost every dish are available for culinary experimentation, including scrambled eggs with black truffles from Alba, and tagine of violet artichoke with chorizo. A variety of set lunch menus allow for further foodie exploration: the slightly more expensive let diners loose on the ten-dish dessert trolley or the cheese counter. Dinner is a more reserved affair, although fine yet unpretentious service and a chef-side dining table make each meal memorable. Thanks to a light redesign, the restaurant remains light, bright and—a rarity in a double Michelin-starred establishment—fun.

In the Hôtel Métropole, 4 av. de la Madone. www.metropole.com. (℃ **93-15-15-10.** Reservations required. Main courses 56€–79€; fixed-price lunch 51€-199€, dinner 199€. AE, MC, V. Daily 12.15–2pm and 7.30–9.30pm.

**Le Café de Paris** TRADITIONAL FRENCH    Its *plats du jour* are well prepared, and its location, the plaza adjacent to the casino and the Hôtel de Paris, allows a front-row view of the comings and goings of the Principality's nerve center. Despite its very public location, this re-creation of old-time Monaco still attracts the stars and a sampling of Monte-Carlo old money. The menu has taken on a classic edge since late 2011 under new head chef Jean-Claude Brugel, who trained alongside several top Riviera chefs including Roger Vergé and Joël Garault. Hors d'ouevre platters include steak tartare, carpaccio of beef, and gambas fricassée. Mains are mostly very classic: sautéed veal escalope, Provençal beef stew and, as a very un-French addition, hamburger.

Place du Casino. (℃ **98-06-76-23.** Reservations recommended. Main courses 12€–45€; fixed-price menu 35€. AE, DC, MC, V. Daily 8am–2am.

## INEXPENSIVE

**Adagio** ★ 🎁 MODERN ITALIAN    This budget contemporary restaurant has been ranked among Monaco's best restaurants since its inception in 2010. Smart wooden tables are set against lightly adorned white walls in a sunlight-filled dining room. Granted, it's a 10-minute hike north of the harbor, but Adagio's bargain set-lunch menu, complete with coffee and a generous slug of wine, has some locals calling it their second home. Simple starters include tuna and fresh fava bean salad, and *ravioli di verdure;* equally uncomplicated mains range from roast beef and green beans to *papillotes* of salmon.

1 rue Biovès. 🕻 **97-98-15-56.** Main courses 14€–20€; fixed-price lunch 15€. AE, MC, V. Mon-Fri noon–2:30pm and 7:30–11pm; Sat 7:30-11pm.

**Stella Polaris** ITALIAN    The Stella won't win any awards for haute cuisine, but for quality Italian cuisine at honest prices, it's hard to beat. And its open dining room, which spills out onto Monaco harbor and the Formula One Grand Prix racetrack, is surely prize-winning in itself. Freshly cooked pizzas, pastas, and grilled meats are served with inexpensive Italian red and white wines.

3 av. President Kennedy. 🕻 **93-30-88-63.** Main courses 9€–17€; pizzas 9€–12€. MC, V. Daily noon–3pm and 7pm–midnight.

# Shopping

If you insist on the likes of Hermès, Gucci, and Lanvin, you'll find them cheek by jowl with the Hôtel de Paris and the casino, lining the streets leading to the Hôtel Hermitage. **Allée Serge-Diaghilev** is just that, an alley, but a very tiny one filled with designer shops.

The prize for Monaco's hippest store goes to **Lull,** 29 rue de Millo (🕻 97-77-54-54), which is awash with labels like Dries Van Noten and Raf Simmons. It has a clothes re-engineering workshop to the rear. Almost next door, **Une Femme à Suivre** (🕻 97-77-10-52) sells French classics from the likes of Tara Jarman and Mariona Gen. For less expensive bags, head to designer outlet **Stock Griffe,** 5 bis av. St-Michel (🕻 93-50-86-06). It slashes prices on Prada, Pucci, Escada, and the like. The place may be small, but not the discounts, some of which add up to an astonishing 90%.

The Galeries du Métropole is packed with high fashion and specialty stores. As well as Dunhill and Gant, try **McMarket** (🕻 97-77-12-12). Serious labels in this fashion emporium include Balenciaga, Christian Louboutin and Jimmy Choo. **FNAC** (🕻 08-25-02-00-20) is recommended for English-language novels, Monaco history books, and the latest electronics from the PSP Vega to the iPad 3. Nearby in the Galerie du Sporting, the **L'Oenothèque,** 2 avenue Princesse Alice (🕻 93-25-82-66) vends rare French vintages and local rosé wines under the watchful eye of a former sommelier.

For real-people shopping, stroll **rue Grimaldi,** the principality's most commercial street, near the fruit, flower, and food market (see below); and **boulevard des Moulins,** closer to the casino, where you'll see glamorous boutiques. There's also a pedestrian thoroughfare with shops less forbiddingly chic than those along boulevard des Moulins: **rue Princesse-Caroline** is loaded with bakeries, flower shops, and the closest thing you'll find to funkiness in Monaco. Also check out the **Formule 1** shop, 15 ruc Grimaldi (🕻 93-15-92-44), where everything from racing helmets to specialty key chains and T-shirts celebrates the roaring, high-octane racing machines.

**MARKETS**   For a look at the heart and soul of the real Monaco, head to place des Armes for the **fruit, flower, and food market,** which starts daily at 7:30am. The indoor and outdoor market has a fountain, cafes, and hand-painted vegetable tiles beneath your feet. The outdoor market packs up at noon, and some dealers at the indoor market stay open until 2pm.

## Monaco Nightlife

**CASINOS & CULTURE**   The **Casino de Monte-Carlo,** place du Casino (www. montecarlocasinos.com; ✆ **98-06-21-21**), is one the most famous in the world. Its creation by architect Charles Garnier (of Paris Opera house fame) in 1863 turned the tables for Monaco, turning a weary port into a world-class destination.

The building encompasses the casino and other areas for different kinds of entertainment, including a theater (Opéra de Monte-Carlo; see below) presenting opera, ballet, and jazz, plus the new Buddha Bar (see "Dancing & Drinking," below).

The casino's marble-floored **Atrium,** containing only slot machines, opens at 2pm Monday to Friday, noon on weekends. Doors for roulette and *trente et quarante* in the rococo **Salon Europe** open at the same time, or at 3pm for private players. Blackjack opens in the hallowed **Salle des Amériques** at 5pm (2pm weekends). The gambling continues until very late (or early), depending on the crowd. The casino classifies its "private rooms" as the more demure, nonelectronic areas without slots. To enter the casino, you must show a passport or other photo ID and be at least 18. After 8pm, the staff will insist that men wear jackets and neckties for entrance to the

Monte-Carlo Casino.

private rooms. Entrance costs 10€ to anywhere past the Atrium; 20€ to the Salons Privés. And entrance to the Les Salons Supers Privés? It's by invitation only (they've got our number).

No dress code or entry fee applies in the **Café de Paris Casino,** place du Casino (📞 **98-06-77-77**), across the square. Video gaming machines open at 10am, with roulette and blackjack tables in operation from 8pm.

The **Opéra de Monte-Carlo** (www.opera.mc; 📞 **98-06-28-28**) is headquartered in the lavish, recently renovated Belle Epoque **Salle Garnier** of the casino. The grand salon hosted the wedding reception of Prince Albert of Monaco and Charlene Wittstock in July 2011. Tickets to the operas and other events scheduled inside range from 20€ to 120€. Tickets to events within the Salle Garnier are available from a kiosk outside the Café de Paris Casino; tickets can be purchased Tuesday to Saturday from 10am to 5:30pm.

The **Grimaldi Forum,** 10 av. Princesse-Grace (www.grimaldiforum. com; 📞 **99-99-20-00**), is Monaco's live entertainment showpiece. It's big hit in 2012 was the musical *Chicago*. It also lines up big-name jazz acts, ballet, and even house music DJs. Regular exhibitions also take place here. Concert and performance tickets cost 20€ to 150€. The **Orchestre Philharmonique de Monte-Carlo** (www.opmc.mc; 📞 **98-06-28-28**) performs concerts and classical recitals in both the Grimaldi Forum and the Salle Garnier.

**DANCING & DRINKING**   Monaco's newest bars are currently its most hopping. **Buddha Bar** (📞 **98-06-19-19**), in the Monte-Carlo Casino complex, is bedecked with chinoiserie, Asian statues, and a raised DJ booth. It attracts a classy crowd from 7pm onward. **Café Llorca,** in the Grimaldi Forum, 10 av. Princesse Grace (📞 **97-97-76-15**), also opened in late 2010. It combines a smart bistro run by top Riviera chef Alain Llora, with an upscale bar overlooking the Mediterranean. In 2011, two brand new gastropubs offered a relaxed alternative to the often showy scene. **Bouchon,** 11 avenue princesse Grace (📞 **97-97-08-80**), is a hip French bistro bar across the street the Grimaldi Forum. Explorers, 36 route de la Piscine (📞 **97-97-70-70**), offers world food, live DJs and beer from Tahiti to Brazil.

For sheer class, the new **Crystal Bar** (📞 **98-06-98-99**), inside the Hôtel Hermitage, pulls out all the stops. Elegant dress, vintage champagne, and the odd feather boa sets the scene. It opens from noon until 1am. Under the same management is timeless **Jimmy'z,** (📞 **98-06-36-36**), open nightly 11pm to 5am, which moved to a new home on place du Casino in 2012. It's a nightly blowout of champagne-laced celebrity culture and rocking music. Drinks are very, very expensive.

# Where to Stay
## VERY EXPENSIVE

**Hôtel de Paris ★★★**   On the resort's main plaza, opposite the casino, this is one of the world's most famous hotels. Elegant fabrics, classic accessories, and one of the finest restaurants in France (Louis XV) combine to make this a favorite of the world's most discerning travelers. The fabulous Art Nouveau lobby is fresh from a sympathetic renovation in 2011 and includes statues and crystal chandeliers. Leading off is Le Bar Americain, a classic wood-paneled watering hole lined with photos of Monaco's greatest patrons, among them Cary Grant and Grace Kelly. The guest rooms come in two principal styles: period and contemporary. Some units are enormous. Bathrooms are awash with marble and elegant brass fittings and are stocked with La Prairie products. Most fabulous of all are the Garnier Suite, which overlooks place du Casino and is the ultimate stage for watching the Formula One Grand Prix; and the Churchill Suite, overlooking the harbor, where the former British Prime Minister's furniture still resides. Additional restaurants include Michelin-starred Le Grill, which has an electronic roof that slides opens to the heavens, and the Côté Jardin, a Mediterranean restaurant spilling onto private gardens.

Place du Casino, Monaco 98007. www.montecarloresort.com. © **98-06-30-00.** Fax 98-06-59-56. 182 units. 435€–1,020€ double; from 740€ suite. AE, DC, MC, V. Valet parking 38€. **Amenities:** 3 restaurants; bar; babysitting; concierge; exercise room; large indoor pool; room service; sauna; Thermes Marins spa offering thalassotherapy. *In room:* A/C, TV, hair dryer, minibar, Wi-Fi (free in lobby, or 20€ per day).

**Hôtel Métropole** ★   The Métropole vies for the title of Monaco's finest hotel, yet is intimate and more boutique than its larger, more intimidating rivals. Its historic lobby off Casino Square is awash with flowers and boasts a Dalí-designed sofa. Public areas are similarly inventive and fresh. Guest rooms are more classic. Thick pile carpets combine with Bulgari bath products and Bang & Olufsen televisions to lend a refined five-star hotel feel. That said, the single Philippe Starck designed suite is eye-poppingly vibrant. Other designers have added their touch to the hotel too, most notably German fashion guru Karl Lagerfeld, who redesigned the chic pool zone in 2012. Métropole guests enjoy VIP access to the Casino de Monté Carlo, the onsite Espa spa, and – for an extra fee – the Rose des Vents beach club.

4 av. de la Madone, Monaco 98007. www.metropole.com. © 93-15-15-35. Fax 93-15-15-34. 113 units. 350€–800€ double; from 1,650€ suite. AE, DC, MC, V. Parking 37€. **Amenities:** 2 restaurants; 2 bars; babysitting; concierge; exercise room; large indoor/outdoor pool; room service; sauna; Espa spa. *In room:* A/C, TV, hair dryer, minibar, free Wi-Fi.

## EXPENSIVE

**Fairmont Monte Carlo** ★   A vision of modern opulence that hugs one of the most valuable pieces of real estate on the Côte d'Azur. The Fairmont is the pinnacle of comfortable luxury: Guests may wear casual dress at dinner yet still expect exemplary service from the multilingual team of staff. The hotel was architecturally daring when built in 1975. Some of its foundations were sunk into the seabed, and some of the Principality's busiest highways (including part of Monaco's F1 Grand Prix track) sweep beneath it. The Fairmont contains Monaco's highest concentration of restaurants, bars, and nightclubs including the Horizon Deck rooftop restaurant (open Mar–Oct) and the Saphir Bar (open 24 hr.); both have heart-stopping panoramic views that stretch all the way over the Italian border. The restaurant, L'Argentin, is a South American steakhouse, with a fabulous wine list and similar views. The guest rooms and suites are furnished in contemporary style with a maritime theme. Many benefit from sea views, terraces, and lashings of fine Italian marble.

15

THE FRENCH RIVIERA

Monaco

12 av. des Spélugues, Monaco 98000. www.fairmont.com/montecarlo. ✆ **93-50-65-00.** Fax 93-30-01-57. 602 units. 279€–879€ double; from 889€ suite. AE, DC, MC, V. Parking 45€. **Amenities:** 2 restaurants; 2 bars; babysitting; concierge; health club; 2 outdoor pools; room service; spa. *In room:* A/C, TV, hair dryer, minibar, Wi-Fi (20€ per day or free if you enroll in the Fairmont President Club at no charge at check-in).

**Monte Carlo Bay Hotel & Resort** ★★★  Occupying a 4-hectare (10-acre) Mediterranean garden, this is a plush garden of Eden in the principality. It's the most child-friendly and business-friendly of all the Monaco hotels. Vast lagoons, pools, exotic gardens, the Cinq Mondes spa, and an indoor pool covered with a monumental glass dome are linked by a network of teak footbridges. A network of five restaurants, bars, and a summer casino round out the complex. Of the beautifully furnished bedrooms, more than three-quarters of them open onto sea views. Rooms are decorated with white-oak furnishings, often sandstone floors, and soft Mediterranean pastels.

40 av. Princesse-Grace, Monaco 98000. www.montecarlobay.com. ✆ **98-06-02-00.** Fax 98-06-00-03. 334 units. 335€–920€ double; from 860€ suite. AE, DC, MC, V. Parking 30€. **Amenities:** 4 restaurants; 2 bars; nightclub; casino; disco; babysitting; concierge; exercise rooms; 3 pools (indoor, outdoor, and children's); spa. *In room:* A/C, TV, hair dryer, minibar, Wi-Fi (free in lobby, or 20€ per day).

### INEXPENSIVE

**Hôtel de France**  Not all Monégasques are rich, as a stroll along workaday rue de la Turbie will convince you. Here you'll find some of the cheapest accommodations and eateries in the high-priced Principality. This 19th-century hotel, 3 minutes from the rail station, has modest furnishings but is well kept and comfortable. It benefitted greatly from thorough renovation, which was completed in 2012. The guest rooms and bathrooms are small, and each unit has a shower.

6 rue de la Turbie, Monaco 98000. www.monte-carlo.mc/france. ✆ **93-30-24-64.** Fax 92-16-13-34. 27 units. 85€–135€ double. MC, V. Parking nearby 7.50€ for 24 hours. **Amenities:** Bar; room service. *In room:* TV, hair dryer, free Wi-Fi.

# ROQUEBRUNE & CAP-MARTIN ★★

Roquebrune: 953km (591 miles) S of Paris, 7km (4½ miles) W of Menton, 58km (36 miles) NE of Cannes, 3km (1¾ miles) E of Monaco. Cap-Martin: 4km (2½ miles) W of Menton, 2.5km (1½ miles) W of Roquebrune.

Roquebrune, along the Grande Corniche, is a charming mountain village with vaulted streets. The views over the Mediterranean rival the village of Eze, and are equally immense. Artists' workshops and boutiques with their pricey merchandise line rue Moncollet.

Down the hill from Roquebrune, Cap-Martin is a pine-covered peninsula, long associated with the rich and famous since the empress Eugénie wintered here in the 19th century. In time, the resort was honored by the presence of Sir Winston Churchill, who came here often in his final years. The long, pebbly plage de la Buse lies underneath Roquebrune-Cap-Martin train station. Its tranquillity is disturbed only by the odd paraglider looping down to the beach from Roquebrune village.

# Essentials

**GETTING THERE**    To **drive** to Roquebrune and Cap-Martin from Nice, follow N7 east for 26km (16 miles). Cap-Martin has **train** and bus connections from the other cities on the coast, including Nice and Menton. For **railway** information and schedules, visit www.voyages-sncf.com or call ℂ **36-35.** To reach Roquebrune, you'll have to take a **taxi** or follow the hiking signs for 30 minutes uphill. For bus information, contact the Gare Routière in Menton (ℂ **04-93-28-43-27**).

**VISITOR INFORMATION**    The **Office de Tourisme** is at 218 av. Aristide-Briand, Roquebrune (www.roquebrune-cap-martin.com; ℂ **04-93-35-62-87;** fax 04-93-28-57-00).

More than any other municipality in the region, Roquebrune and Cap-Martin have at least three guided walking tours of its attractions. The most popular of the three is a 90-minute guided tour of the old town, priced at 6€ for adults and 3€ for students. Tours depart whenever there are enough (at least five) participants to justify it. More esoteric tours, conducted for the most part exclusively in French, are tours of the municipality's wealth of public buildings, one of them a rather humble cabin, Le Cabanon, designed by world-famous architect Le Corbusier. It's conducted every Tuesday and Friday at 9:30am.

# Seeing the Sights

## IN ROQUEBRUNE

Exploring Roquebrune will take about an hour. You can stroll through its colorful streets, which retain their authentic feel. **Château de Roquebrune** (ℂ 04-93-35-07-22) was originally a 10th-century Carolingian castle; the present structure dates in part from the 13th century, although it was jazzed up by its wealthy British owner, Sir William Ingram, nearly a century ago. From the towers, there's a panoramic view along the coast. The interior is open in February to May daily 10am to 12.30pm and 2 to 6pm; June to September daily 10am to 1pm and 2:30 to 7pm; and October to January daily 10am to 12:30pm and 2 to 5pm. Admission is 4.50€ for adults, 3.50€ for seniors, 2.50€ students and children 7 to 11, and free for children 6 and under.

Rue du Château leads to place William-Ingram. Cross this square to rue de la Fontaine and take a left. This leads you to the **Olivier millénaire** (millenary olive tree), one of the oldest in the world—it's at least 1,000 years old.

## IN CAP-MARTIN

Once the exclusive domain of Belgian despot King Leopold II, Cap-Martin is still a fabulously rich spit of land. At its base, you can see the ruins of the **Basilique St-Martin,** a ruined priory constructed by the monks of the Lérins Islands in the 11th century. After pirate raids in later centuries, notably around the 15th century, it was destroyed and abandoned. Privately owned, it is not open to visitors.

You can also take one of the most scenic walks along the Riviera here, lasting about 2 hours. The coastal path, **Sentier Le Corbusier ★**, extends between Pointe du Cap-Martin to the eastern (meaning, the closest) frontier of Monaco. If you have a car, you can park it in the lot at avenue Winston-Churchill and begin your stroll. A sign labeled PROMENADE LE CORBUSIER marks the path. As

**Sentier Le Corbusier.**

you go along, you'll take in a view of Monaco set in a natural amphitheater. In the distance, you'll see Cap-Ferrat and, high above, Roquebrune village. The final stages of the path run past Corbusier's Cabanon log cabin and, almost next door, the Villa E-1027. The latter is a modernist beach home designed in 1924 by the famed Irish architect Eileen Gray. The scenic path ends at Monte-Carlo Beach and takes about 2 hours. Walkers can then take the line no. 100 bus back to their rough starting point. An alternative is to return on foot from either Monte-Carlo Beach or Roquebrune-Cap-Martin train station, following the walking signs back through the Parc des Oliviers, which occupies the central spine of Cap Martin.

# LANGUEDOC-ROUSSILLON

by Mary Anne Evans

anguedoc is a loosely defined area encompassing the cities of Montpellier, Nîmes, Toulouse, and Carcassonne. One of the leading wine-producing areas of the world, it's also fabled for its art treasures.

Both Languedoc and Roussillon are old provinces of France, the first named for the language *(langue)* spoken by its occupants, called Occitan, and the second from the Roman name Ruscino. Languedoc covers the present-day *départements* (departments) of Lozère, Gard, Hérault, and Aude, and Roussillon covers the Pyrénées Orientales, on the border with Spain. To the west, the city of Toulouse is in the Haute-Garonne *département* of the Midi-Pyrénées region.

The coast of Languedoc-Roussillon, from Montpellier to the Spanish frontier, might be called France's "second Riviera" (after the Côte d'Azur). This land of ancient cities has an almost continuous strip of sand stretching west from the Rhône toward the Pyrénées, covered by sun-baking bodies in July and August.

The area around the regional capital of Perpignan is French Catalonia. From the 13th to the 17th centuries, it passed between the kings of Aragón, Majorca, and France. In 1659, it became part of Louis XIV's centralized kingdom. Though officially French today, cultural links with Spain are strong, and the high-speed rail link to Barcelona has brought the two Catalan cities ever closer.

The Camargue is a marshy delta between two arms of the Rhône. South of Arles it's cattle country, where black bulls are bred for the bullfighting arenas of Arles and Nîmes. The cattle are herded by *Gardians* (French cowboys), riding white horses said to have been brought here by the Saracens. The whitewashed houses, plaited-straw roofs, plains, sandbars, and pink flamingos in the marshes make this area different, even exotic.

As for wine, Hérault, Aude, and Garde are some of the largest wine producers in the world. Huge investment has improved the vineyards out of all recognition with many now granted an Appellation d'Origine Contrôlée. It's an area to discover small, boutique producers, unknown labels and the local co-operatives. Also look for Fitou in the Hautes-Corbières district near Narbonne, and Minervois, from west and northwest of Narbonne.

# NÎMES ★★★

721km (447 miles) S of Paris; 43km (27 miles) W of Avignon

Nîmes, the ancient Nemausus, is one of the best places for wandering among Roman relics. The city grew to prominence during the reign of Caesar Augustus (27 B.C.–A.D. 14). It possesses one of the best-preserved Roman amphitheaters in the world and a near-perfect Roman temple. The city is more like Provence than Languedoc, in which it lies. And there's a touch of Pamplona, Spain, in the

PREVIOUS PAGE: **Church of St-Sernin, in Toulouse's Old Town.**

Languedoc-Roussillon

festivals of the *corridas* (bullfights) at the arena. The Spanish influence is even more apparent at night, when its bodegas fill up, often with students drinking sangria and listening to flamenco.

By 1860, the togas of Nîmes's citizenry had long given way to denim, the cloth *de Nîmes*. An Austrian immigrant to Nîmes, Levi Strauss, exported the heavy fabric to California to make into work pants for gold-rush prospectors. The rest, as they say, is history.

## Essentials

**GETTING THERE** The entire town center is now free of vehicular traffic. Nîmes has bus and train services from the rest of France and is near several auto-routes. It lies on the main **rail** line between Marseille and Bordeaux. Regular TGV trains arrive daily from Paris's Gare de Lyon; the one-way fare is from 87€. Train information and schedules are on www.voyages-sncf.com, or call *C* **36-35**. If you're **driving,** take A7 south from Lyon to the town of Orange and connect to A9 into Nîmes.

**VISITOR INFORMATION** The **Office de Tourisme** is at 6 rue Auguste (www.ot-nimes.fr; *C* **04-66-58-38-00;** fax 04-66-58-38-01).

**SPECIAL EVENTS** The 5-day **Féria de Pentecôte** that revolves around the bull (and also includes plenty of drinking and merrymaking), is one of Europe's most popular festivals, attracting almost a million people each year. It takes place over Pentecost, 7 weeks after Easter, around the beginning of June. A second *féria,* **Féria des Vendanges,** celebrating the grape harvest, takes place the third weekend of September.

Every Thursday night during July and August, many of Nîmes's squares burst with music, crowds of pedestrians, and a rich choice of paintings, crafts, used objects, and sculpture during **Les Jeudis de Nîmes** (Nîmes Thursdays).

## Exploring the City

If you want to see all of the city's monuments and museums, consider buying the **Nîmes romaine** combined ticket, sold at the ticket counter of all the local attractions. It provides access for a 3-day period to Maison Carrée, les Arènes de Nîmes, and Tour Magne. The fee is 10€ for adults, 7.70€ for children aged 7 to 17, and free for children 7 and under. For more information, call **Culturespace** (www.arenes-nimes. com; *C* **04-66-21-82-56**).

The pride of Nîmes is the **Maison Carrée ★★★**, place de la Maison Carrée (*C* **04-66-21-82-56**), built during the reign of Caesar Augustus. Consisting of a raised platform with tall Corinthian columns, it's one of Europe's most beautiful, best-preserved Roman

Corinthian column at the Maison Carrée.

**Nîmes**

Church ✝
Information ⓘ

Castellum

rue Rouget de Lisle

rue de Combret

rue de la Tour Magne

① Tour Magne

② Mont Cavalier

rue Ménard

rue Clérisseau

place St-Charles

des Bénédictins

pl. de la Révolution

rue Pasteur

sq. de la Bouquerie

bd. Gambetta

r. du Bât d'Argent ⑦

To Avignon →

rue Nationale

place Gabriel Péri

③ Jardins de la Fontaine

rue Trajan

square Antonin

rue du Gén. Perrier

Cathédrale

rue Séguier

rue

④ Le Temple de Diane

Jardin de la Fontaine

quai de la Fontaine

bd. A. Daudet

Tour de l'Horloge

pl. aux Herbes

ⓘ

pl. du Maréchal Foch

rue Grétry

Carré d'Art ⑤

rue Madeleine

⑥ Musée du Vieux-Nîmes

r. de l'Aspic

r. Dorée

rue des Greffes

⑧ Musée de Préhistoire

sq. de la Couronne

rue Notre-Dame

r. F. Pelloutier

pl. de la Madeleine

rue Emile Jamais

rue de l'Etoile

bd. Victor Hugo

rue de la Fresque

Hôtel de Ville

bd. des Greffes

Admiral Courbet

rue Roussy

rue Monjardin

pl. Jules Guesde

av. Jean Jaurès

av. Florian

rue des Tilleuls

rue Delon-Soubeyron

rue du Bec-de-Lièvre

rue de la Porte de France

rue Jean-Reboul

⑨ Ampithéâtre

bd. de la Libération

Fontaine Pradier

rue Pradier

av. Georges Pompidou

rue Bigot

rue de l'Hôtel-Dieu

pl. des Arènes

esplanade Charles de Gaulle

bd. Feuchères

To Montpellier ↓

rue du Mail

rue de la République

rue de la Cité Foulc

rue Briçonnet

Gare de Nîmes

0 — 1/4 mi
0 — 0.25 km

rue du Cirque-Romain

place Montcalm ⑩

**FRANCE** ★ Paris · Nîmes

Ampithéâtre Romain de Nîmes **9**
Jardins de la Fontaine **3**
Le Temple de Diane **4**
Maison Carrée/Carré d'Art **5**
Mont Cavalier **2**
Musée Archéologique **8**
Musée d'Art Contemporain **5**

Musée des Beaux-Arts **10**
Musée de Préhistoire
 et d'Histoire Naturelle **8**
Musée du Vieux-Nîmes **6**
Porte d'Auguste **7**
Tour Magne **1**

temples. It inspired the builders of La Madeleine in Paris, as well as Thomas Jefferson. It schedules cultural and art exhibits, presented beneath an authentically preserved roof. Admission is 4.50€ for adults or 3.70€ for students and children (free ages 9 and under). Open March and October daily 10am to 6pm; April, May, and September daily 10am to 6:30pm; June daily 10am to 7pm; July and August daily 10am to 8pm; and November through February daily 10am to 1pm and 2 to 4:30pm.

Across the square stands its modern-day twin, the **Carré d'Art ★**, whose understated design by Norman Foster was inspired by (but doesn't overpower) the ancient monument. Inside is the **Musée d'Art Contemporain** (ⓒ **04-66-76-35-70**), containing a permanent collection of art from 1960 to the present

Amphithéâtre Romain de Nîmes

day and temporary exhibitions. It's open Tuesday through Sunday 10am to 6pm. The permanent collection is free; changing exhibitions cost 5€ for adults and are free for anyone aged 25 and under and for everybody on the first Sunday of each month. Note that this building's terrace provides a panorama of most of the ancient monuments and medieval churches of Nîmes.

Scholars call it **Amphithéâtre Romain de Nîmes ★★★**, and locals refer to it as **Les Arènes de Nîmes.** The monument at place des Arènes (www. arenes-nimes.com; ✆ **04-66-21-82-56;**) is a better-preserved twin of the one at Arles, and far more complete than Rome's Colosseum. It's two stories high— each floor has 60 arches—and was built of huge stones painstakingly fitted together without mortar. It once held more than 20,000 spectators who came to see gladiatorial combat and wolf or boar hunts. Today it's used for everything from ballet recitals to bullfights. Admission is 7.90€ for adults and 6€ for students and children from 7 to 17 years, free for child 7 years and under. Open March and October daily 9am to 6pm; April, May, and September daily 9am to 6:30pm; June 9am to 7pm; July to August daily 9am to 8pm; and November through February daily 9:30am to 5pm.

One of the most beautiful gardens in France, **Jardins de la Fontaine ★★**, at the end of quai de la Fontaine, was laid out in the 18th century using the ruins of a Roman shrine as a centerpiece. The garden is open from April to mid-September daily 7:30am to 10pm, and from mid-September to March daily 7:30am to 6:30pm. Within the garden are the ruined **Le Temple de Diane ★** and the remains of some Roman baths. Over the park, within a 10-minute walk north of the town center, is **Mont Cavalier,** a low, rocky hill on top of which rises the sturdy bulk of the **Tour Magne ★** (✆ **04-66-21-82-56**), the city's oldest Roman monument. You can climb it for 2.80€ for adults and 2.40€ for students and children 7 to 17, free for children 7 and under. It's open March and October daily 9:30am to 1pm and 2 to 6pm; April and May daily 9:30am to 6pm; June daily 9am to 7pm; July and August 9am to 8pm; October 9:30am to 1pm and 2 to 6:30pm; and November through February 9:30am to 1pm and 2 to 4:30pm.

Nîmes is home to many museums. The largest and most respected, the **Musée des Beaux-Arts ★,** rue Cité-Foulc (📞 **04-66-67-38-21**), contains French paintings and sculptures from the 17th to the 20th centuries, as well as Flemish, Dutch, and Italian works from the 15th to the 18th centuries. Seek out one of G. B. Moroni's masterpieces, *La Calomnie d'Apelle,* and a well-preserved Gallo-Roman mosaic. The museum is open Tuesday to Sunday 10am to 6pm. Admission is free for the permanent collection. Exhibitions are 5€ for adults and free for those under 25. Free admission the first Sunday of the month.

If time allows, visit the **Musée du Vieux-Nîmes,** place aux Herbes (📞 **04-66-76-73-70**), housed in an Episcopal palace from the 1700s to the north of the Arenas. Its rich collection has antiques, antique porcelain, and workaday objects from the 18th and 19th centuries. Admission is free; hours are Tuesday to Sunday 10am to 6pm.

About 45m (148 ft.) east you'll come to the **Musée d'Histoire Naturelle** (📞 **04-66-76-73-45**) and the **Musée Archéologique ★** (📞 **04-66-76-74-80**), in the same building, at 13 bis bd. l'Amiral-Courbet. Admission is free; hours are Tuesday to Sunday 10am to 6pm. Then walk north along one of the city's busiest thoroughfares, **boulevard de l'Amiral-Courbet,** to the **Porte d'Auguste (Porte d'Arles)**—the remains of a gate built by the Romans during the reign of Augustus.

Outside the city, 23km (14 miles) northeast, the **pont du Gard ★★** spans the Gard River; its huge stones, fitted together without mortar, stand as one of the region's most vivid reminders of the ancient glory. Consisting of three tiers of arches arranged into gracefully symmetrical patterns, it dates from about 19 B.C. Frédéric Mistral, national poet of Provence and Languedoc, recorded a legend that the devil constructed the bridge with the promise that he could claim the soul of the first person to cross it. To visit it, take the highway D6086 from Nîmes to a point 3km (1¾ miles) from the village of Remoulins, where signs are posted.

The pont du Gard visitors' complex offers a range of activities. The interactive museum, **La Grande Expo du Pont du Gard** (www.pontdugard.fr; 📞 **0820 903 330**) shows you the bridge's complex construction, its function throughout the Middle Ages, and its status through the ages as a symbol of the architectural savvy of ancient Rome. You can also wander through the **Mémoires de Garrigue** garden of nature trails, and take the children to the interactive Ludo center. The large site also has a restaurant, cafe, and gift shop. It's open June to September daily 9:30am to 7pm, October and March to May daily 9:30am to 6pm, and November through February daily 9:30am to 5pm. Admission is by car, costing 18€ for up to five people.

During July and August, artificial beaches and small shelters are installed on the right bank of the Gardon near the bridge for **"Rendez-vous à la rivière,"** with lifeguards surveying river swimming.

## Shopping

Head to the center of town and **rue du Général-Perrier, rue des Marchands, rue du Chapître,** and the pedestrian **rue de l'Aspic** and **rue de la Madeleine.** A Monday flea market runs from 8am to around 1pm in boulevard Jean Jaurès in the town center.

To appease your sweet tooth, go to just about any pastry shop in town and ask for the regional almond-based cookies called *croquants villaret* and *caladons.* They're great for a burst of energy or for souvenirs. *Santos,* wood or clay figurines sculpted into characters from Provençal country life, can be found at **Boutique Provençale,** 10 place de la Maison Carré (☎ **04-66-67-81-71**).

# Where to Eat

The dining room at the **Imperator Concorde** (see p. 635) is a good choice.

**Alexandre (Michel Kayser)** ★★★ FRENCH/LANGUEDOCIENNE    The most charming restaurant around is on the outskirts of Nîmes, 9km (5 miles) south of the center. It's the elegantly rustic domain of Michel Kayser, who adheres to classic tradition, with subtle improvements. His wife, Monique, assists him in the ultramodern dining room, which is outfitted in tones of soft red and ocher. Menu items are designed to amuse as well as delight: *île flottante*, a playful update of old-fashioned floating island, with truffles and velouté of cèpe mushrooms; scallops in olive oil with sea urchin and Jerusalem artichokes; and filet of bull from the Camargue in red-wine sauce with Camarguais herbs.

Rte. de l'Aéroport de Garons. www.michelkayser.com. ☎ **04-66-70-08-99.** Reservations recommended. Main courses 44€–66€; fixed-price menus 48€–165€. AE, DC, MC, V. July–Aug Tues–Sat noon–1:30pm and 8–9:30pm; Sept–June Wed–Sun noon–1:30pm, Wed–Sat 8–9:30pm. Closed 2 weeks in Feb–Mar. From town center, take rue de la République southwest to av. Jean-Jaurès; then head south and follow signs to the airport (toward Garons).

**Wine Bar le Cheval Blanc** 🍴 TRADITIONAL FRENCH    This mahogany-paneled place has leather banquettes evocative of an early-1900s California saloon. It's a good place for a quick lunch of salads and platters or a menu of an appetizer, a garnished main course, and two glasses of wine. Typical dishes are *magret* of duckling, top-notch beefsteaks, and fresh (usually grilled) fish. You can also enjoy lunch on the terrace in the courtyard. A restaurateur extraordinaire, Michel Hermet makes his own wine at vineyards that have been associated with his family for generations. More than 300 other varieties of wine are in stock, 15 of which are available by the glass or by the pitcher.

1 place des Arènes. www.winebar-lechevalblanc.com. ☎ **04-66-76-19-59.** Main courses 11€–26€; fixed-price lunch 12.50€, dinner 16€–24€. AE, MC, V. Mon–Sat noon–2pm; Mon–Thurs 7–11pm; Fri–Sat 7pm–midnight.

# Nîmes Nightlife

In the warm weather, the arena hosts many events, including open-air concerts and theater. The Office de Tourisme has a complete listing.

If you like hanging out with the locals, head to the famous neighborhood **Café Le Napoleon,** 46 bd. Victor-Hugo (☎ **04-66-67-20-23**). Popular with the intelligentsia is **Haddock Cafe,** 13 rue de l'Agau (☎ **04-66-67-86-57**), which books occasional rock concerts. **O'Flaherty's,** 26 bd. Amiral-Courbet (☎ **04-66-67-22-63**), apart from British beer, serves up great Irish, country, and bluegrass music on Thursdays.

Modern jazz venue, **Jazzpanazz,** 14 rue Michel Debré (☎ **04-66-84-93-96),** books all kinds of jazz musicians, from improvised electronic groups to Afro-Brazilian. Entrance from 6€ to 10€. Sexy, hip **La Comédie,** 28 rue Jean-Reboul (☎ **04-66-76-13-66**), is hands-down the best for dancing and attracts a pretty crowd of youthful danceaholics. A little less flashy, but great fun, **Lulu Club,** 10 impasse de la Curaterie (www.lulu-club.com; ☎ **04-66-36-28-20**), is the gay and lesbian stronghold in Nîmes. Open Thursday to Saturday, it's a magnet for hip and straight folk as well. A youth-oriented contender is **Le Club Kafé Fash-ion-CKF,** 20 rue de l'Etoile (© **04-66-21-59-22**), open Thursday to Saturday at 11pm, it rocks 'n' rolls to music from L.A. to London.

Streets to explore on virtually any night of the week include **place de la Maison Carrée** and **boulevard Victor-Hugo.**

## Where to Stay

**Best Western Marquis de La Baume** ★ 🏨   The Marquis de la Baume family built this mansion in the 17th century. Grand in style, its best feature is the magnificent open staircase in the interior courtyard. During the hotel conversion, the designers carefully preserved the original architecture, keeping the feel both modern and traditional. Purchased in 2011 by a private family, and completely renovated, the guest rooms are pretty and contemporary, while the tiled bathrooms are right up to date. Nice touches include Nespresso machines. Ask for a room at the back to avoid any noise from the street.

21 rue Nationale, Nîmes 30000. www.hotel-marquis-de-la-baume-nimes.com. © **04-66-76-28-42.** Fax 04-66-76-28-45. 34 units. 140€ double; 170€ junior suite. AE, DC, MC, V. **Amenities:** Bar; room service. *In room:* A/C, TV, hair dryer, minibar, safe, free Wi-Fi.

**Imperator Concorde** ★★   This hotel, part of the Concorde chain, is the largest and finest in town, and is adjacent to Les Jardins de la Fontaine—it's the one with the pale-pink Italianate facade. The original Art Deco building underwent a major renovation in 2005. The artful and cozy good-size rooms have fresh colored fabrics and traditional or French furniture in one or another of the Louis styles. You can dine in the hotel's verdant rear gardens or in the high-ceilinged gourmet dining room, L'Enclos de la Fontaine.

Quai de la Fontaine, 15 rue Gaston Boissier, Nîmes 30900. www.hotel-imperator.com. © **04-66-21-90-30.** Fax 04-66-67-70-25. 60 units. 155€–195€ double; 255€ suite. AE, DC, MC, V. Parking 13€. **Amenities:** Restaurant; bar; babysitting; room service. *In room:* A/C, TV, hair dryer, minibar, safe, free Wi-Fi.

# AIGUES-MORTES ★★

750km (465 miles) SW of Paris; 63km (39 miles) NE of Séte; 40km (25 miles) E of Nîmes; 48km (30 miles) SW of Arles

South of Nîmes, you can explore much of the Camargue by car. The most rewarding place to focus on is Aigues-Mortes, the city of the "dead waters." In the middle of swamps and lagoons, Aigues-Mortes is France's most perfectly preserved walled town. Louis IX and his crusaders once set forth from Aigues-Mortes, which was then a thriving port, the first in France on the Mediterranean. Now 6.5km (4 miles) inland from the sea, it stands on four canals. The **ramparts** ★★, which still enclose the town, were constructed between 1272 and 1300. The **Tour de Constance** ★★ (www.monuments-nationaux.fr; © **04-66-53-61-55**) is a model castle of the Middle Ages. A panoramic view of the marshes unfolds at the top, which you can reach by elevator. Admission is 7.50€ for adults, 4.50€ for ages 18 to 25, and free for children 17 and under. The monument is open May to August daily 10am to 7pm, and September to April daily 10am to 5:30pm.

Aigues-Mortes's main appeal is the medieval feeling that permeates virtually every building, rampart, and cobble-covered street. The city's religious centerpiece is the **Eglise Notre-Dame des Sablons,** rue Jean-Jaurès. Constructed of

The Camargue, where the cowboys of France ride the range, is an alluvial plain inhabited by wild horses, fighting black bulls, roaming Gypsies, pink flamingos, and gluttonous mosquitoes. You can explore the rugged terrain by boat, bike, horse, or jeep.

With the most fragile ecosystem in France, the Camargue has been a nature reserve since 1970. You cannot drive into the protected parts, and some are accessible only to the *Gardians*, the cowboys of the Camargue who guard the wild horses and small black bulls that are reared for the *course Camarguais*, a type of bull-fighting where men in white run through the arena with nothing but a knuckle-duster to protect them. The *Gardians* wear large felt hats, and their ancestors may have been the first American cowboys, who sailed on French ships to the port of New Orleans, where they rode the bayous of Louisiana and east Texas, rounding up cattle—in French, no less.

There's no more evocative sight than the proud snow-white horses running at liberty through the marshlands, with hoofs so tough that they don't need shoes. The breed was brought here by the Arabs long ago, and it is said that their long manes and bushy tails evolved over the centuries to slap those pesky mosquitoes.

Exotic flora and fauna abound where the delta of the Rhône River empties into the Mediterranean. The bird life is the most luxuriant in Europe. The area, which resembles the Florida Everglades, is known for its colonies of pink flamingos *(flamants roses)*. They share living quarters with some 400 other bird species, including ibises, egrets, kingfishers, owls, wild ducks, swans, and ferocious birds of prey. The best place to see flamingo colonies is the area around Ginès, a hamlet on D570, 5km (3 miles) north of Camargue's capital, Stes-Maries-de-la-Mer.

Exploring the Camargue is best undertaken on the back of a Camarguais horse. The steeds can take you into the interior, which you couldn't see otherwise, fording waters to places where the black bulls graze and wild birds nest. You'll find two to three dozen stables (depending on the time of year) along the highway from Arles to Stes-Maries. Virtually all of them charge the same rate, 35€ for 2 hours. The rides are aimed at the neophyte, not the champion equestrian. They're so easy that they're recommended even for those who have never been on a horse before.

wood in 1183, it was rebuilt in stone in 1246 in the ogival style. Its modern stained-glass windows were installed in 1980 as replacements for the badly damaged originals. The church is open May to September daily 8:30am to 6pm, and October to April daily 10am to 5pm.

## Essentials

**GETTING THERE** Five **trains** and four **buses** per day connect Aigues-Mortes and Nîmes. Trip time is about an hour. Train information and schedules are on www.voyages-sncf.com, or call $\textcircled{C}$ **36-35** or 00-33-8-92-35-35-35 from outside France. If you're **driving** to Aigues-Mortes, take D979 south from Gallargues, or A9 from Montpellier or Nîmes.

VISITOR INFORMATION   The **Office de Tourisme** is at place St. Louis (www. ot-aiguesmortes.fr; ⓒ **04-66-53-73-00;** fax 04-66-53-65-94).

# Where to Eat

**Hôtel Les Templiers** (see below) is also a good choice for dining.

**Restaurant Les Arcades** ★★ ☺ CAMARGUAISE   Almost as old as the nearby fortifications, the restaurant is especially charming on sultry days, when the thick masonry keeps the interior cool. The good, reasonably priced food runs from oysters to foie gras salad, from grilled beefsteak from the Camargue to turbot poached in hollandaise sauce. A Camargue Gypsy guitarist sometimes plays flamenco on Saturdays. The owner also rents nine large, comfortable rooms with air-conditioning and TVs. Doubles go for 98€ to 104€.

23 bd. Gambetta, Aigues-Mortes 30220. www.les-arcades.fr. ⓒ **04-66-53-81-13.** Reservations recommended. Main courses 20€–30€; fixed-price lunch 20€, dinner 35€–45€; children's menu 14€. AE, DC, MC, V. Wed and Fri–Sun noon–2pm; Tues–Sun 7:30–10pm; daily July–Aug noon–2pm and 7:30–10pm. Closed 3 weeks in Mar and 2 weeks in Oct.

# Where to Stay

**Restaurant Les Arcades** (see "Where to Eat," above) also rents rooms.

**Hostellerie des Remparts**   Opened about 300 years ago, this weather-worn inn lies at the foot of the Tour de Constance, beside the medieval fortifications. Inexpensive, popular, and often fully booked (especially in summer), it evokes the defensive atmosphere of the Middle Ages, albeit with charm. Narrow stone staircases lead to small, simply furnished rooms. Breakfast is the only meal served.

6 place Anatole-France. www.remparts-aoguesmortes.fr. ⓒ **04-66-53-82-77.** Fax 04-66-53-73-77. 12 units. 50€–180€ double. AE, MC, V. **Amenities:** Restaurant; bar; room service. *In room:* A/C, TV.

**Hôtel Les Templiers** ★   This old inn is a haven of peace and tranquillity. Protected by the medieval ramparts built by St. Louis, king of France, this 18th-century residence has small to medium-size rooms decorated in Provençal style, with just enough odd decorative objects to make you feel at home. You can relax in the courtyard, which is also open for breakfast. The restaurant serves traditional food, and there's a second, less formal bistro.

23 rue de la République. www.hotellestempliers.fr. ⓒ **04-66-53-66-56.** Fax 04-66-53-69-61. 14 units. 125€–190€ double. MC, V. **Amenities:** 2 restaurants; bar; outdoor pool; room service. *In room:* A/C, TV, hair dryer, free Wi-Fi.

# MONTPELLIER ★★

758km (470 miles) SW of Paris; 161km (100 miles) NW of Marseille; 50km (31 miles) SW of Nîmes

The capital of Languedoc-Roussillon, the ancient university city of Montpellier is renowned for its medical school, founded in the 13th century. Nostradamus qualified as a doctor here, and Rabelais studied at the school. Petrarch came to Montpellier in 1317 and stayed for 7 years.

Today Montpellier is a bustling metropolis with a population of 288,000, one of southern France's fastest-growing cities, thanks to an influx of new immigrants and high-tech corporations. There's a good public transport system and cars are banned from the center. With a quarter of the population made up of students, Montpellier is dynamic and lively. The city has a handsome core, with tree-flanked promenades, broad avenues, and historic monuments, and it is minutes from the beach.

## Essentials

**GETTING THERE**   The fastest way to get to Montpellier is to fly from Paris's Orly or Charles de Gaulle airports to Aéroport Montpellier Méditerranée (www.montpellier.aeroport.fr; © **04-67-20-85-00**), 8km (5 miles) southeast of Montpellier (trip time 1 hr. 17 min.). Taxis (© **04-67-20-65-29**) from the airport to the center cost from approximately 40€. The airport shuttle Ligne 120 goes to place Europe and costs 1.50€. Trains arrive regularly daily from Avignon (trip time: from 49 min.; one-way fare is 16€), from Marseille (trip time: 1½ hr.; one-way fare is from 27€), from Toulouse (trip time: 2 hr.; one-way fare is from 38€), and from Perpignan (trip time: 1½ hr.; one-way fare is from 24.70€). Fourteen TGV trains arrive daily from Paris Gare de Lyon, taking less than 3½ hours. The one-way fare is 87€. Train information and schedules are on www.voyages-sncf.com, or call © **36-35** or 00-33-8-92-35-35-35 from outside France.

If you're **driving,** Montpellier lies off A9.

**VISITOR INFORMATION**   The **Office de Tourisme** is at 30 allée Jean de L. de Tassigny (www.ot-montpellier.fr; © **04-67-60-60-60;** fax 04-67-60-60-61).

**SPECIAL EVENTS**   From June 24 to July 7 (approximately), classical and modern dancers leap into town for the **Festival International Montpellier Danse.** Tickets for performances range from free to 35€ and can be purchased through the box office, 18 rue Ste-Ursule (www.montpellierdanse.com; © **08-00-60-07-40** or 04-67-60-83-60). During the last 3 weeks of July, the **Festival de Radio France et de Montpellier** presents orchestral music, jazz, and opera. Tickets run from free to 48€. Information can be found at www.festivalradiofrancemontpellier.com; call © **04-67-61-66-81** or contact **Cité des Congrés Le Corum,** esplanade Charles de Gaulle (© **04-67-61-67-61**).

## Exploring the Town

The expansive **place de la Comédie** is the living room of Montpellier, where you can admire the 18th-century "Fountain of the Three Graces," and watch students hurry to lectures from a cafe terrace. A former military parade ground spreads out from here, where you'll find the **Tourist Office, Musée Fabre,** and **Le Corum** convention and arts venue. Head up **rue de la Loge** to explore the Old Town.

At the top of the Old Town, you'll find the 17th-century **promenade du Peyrou ★★**, a terraced park with views of the Cévennes and the Mediterranean. The broad esplanade sits at the loftiest point in Montpellier. Opposite its entrance at the end of rue Foch is the **Arc de Triomphe,** erected in 1691 to celebrate the victories of Louis XIV. In the center of the promenade is an equestrian statue of the Sun King, and at the end is the **Château d'Eau,** a pavilion with Corinthian columns that is a monument to 18th-century classicism. Water travels here along a 15km-long (9¼-mile) conduit and an aqueduct. Just to the east are the cathedral and botanical gardens.

Place de la Comédie.

**Cathédrale St-Pierre** CATHEDRAL   The town's spiritual centerpiece was founded in 1364. Once associated with a Benedictine monastery, the cathedral suffered badly during the religious wars of the 16th and 17th centuries. After 1795, the medical school occupied the monastery. Today it has a somewhat bleak western front with two towers and a canopied porch.

Place St-Pierre. ℭ **04-67-66-04-12.** Free admission. Mon–Sat 9am–noon and 2:30–7pm; Sun 9am–1pm.

**Jardin des Plantes** PARK/GARDEN   Paul Valéry met André Gide in the Jardin des Plantes, the oldest such garden in France. The botanical garden, filled with exotic plants and a handful of greenhouses, opened in 1593.

163 rue Auguste-Broussonnet (enter from bd. Henri-IV). ℭ **04-67-63-43-22.** Free admission. Jun–Sept Tues–Sun noon–8pm; Oct–May Tues–Sun noon–6pm.

**Musée Fabre ★★★** MUSEUM   One of France's great provincial art galleries occupies the former Hôtel de Massilian, where Molière once played for a season. The collection originated when Napoleon sent Montpellier an exhibition of the Académie Royale in 1803. François Fabre, a Montpellier painter, contributed its most important works in 1825. After Fabre's death, other paintings from his collection were donated to the gallery, including Poussin's *Venus and Adonis*. The impressive collections run from the 15th to the 20th centuries and include an entire wing devoted to abstract expressionist Pierre Soulages. For a glimpse at aristocratic 18th and 19th century living, visit the **Hôtel Cabrières** opposite with its ornate furniture and luxurious textiles. The Poucel brothers (see Le Jardin des Sens, below) run the superb restaurant.

2 rue Montpelliéret. ℭ **04-67-14-83-00.** Admission 6€ adults, 7€ inc. Hôtel Cabrières, 4€ ages 6–26, free for children 6 and under and the 1st Sunday of the month. Tues–Sun 10am–6pm; Hôtel Cabrières Tues–Sun 2-6pm.

# Where to Eat

**La Compagnie des Comptoirs** ★ INTERNATIONAL   Owned by the Poucel brothers (see below) and in a road adjacent to their Le Jardin des Sens, this
restaurant evokes the aesthetic and internationalism of the late-19th-century
French colonies in India, North Africa, or Indochina. There's room inside for
about 130 diners; a big terrace with flowering shrubs and a splashing fountain;
and a mix of Mediterranean and Asian influences in the flavorful cuisine. Try
lobster with spiced tomato chutney and shellfish vinaigrette, followed by Mediterranean lamb with fricassée of girolles and artichokes in thyme jus, and a winning collection of desserts. The lounge bar operates until around 1am.

51 ave. de Nîmes. www.lacompagniedescomptoirs.com. ℭ **04-99-58-39-29.** Reservations
recommended. Main courses 19€ –39€. Fixed-price menus 22€–28€. AE, DC, MC, V. Tues–Fri,
Sun and Mon noon–2:30pm; Tues–Sun 8–11pm (1am for the lounge bar).

**Le Grillardin** FRENCH   The best choice on this charming, tree-shaded
square, Le Grillardin serves succulent grills such as lamb shank, *filet de boeuf*,
and veal steak, accompanied by wok-fried vegetables, green beans, or your own
choice of vegetables. Fish choices such as scallops, monkfish, and sea bass are
equally well prepared. Sit on the heated terrace and chat to the Parisian émigrés
who have discovered this idyllic spot.

2 place de la Chapelle Neuve. www.restaurantlegrillardin.com. ℭ **04-67-66-24-33.** Main
courses 16€–22€; fixed-price lunch (weekdays) 23€, dinner 42€. AE, MC, V. Mon, Thurs, Fri, Sun
noon–2pm and 7–11pm; Sat 7–11pm.

**Le Jardin des Sens** ★★★ FRENCH   This is one of the great restaurants
of southern France. The chefs, twins Laurent and Jacques Pourcel, have taken
Montpellier by storm, and their cuisine could involve almost anything, depending on where their imaginations take them. Start with filet of grilled red mullet
on a mix of herbed potatoes and nuts and roasted foie gras and shaved ham; follow with three cuts of lamb flavored with sesame and lime, accompanied by
potatoes and dried fruit and a sauce using curry, cocoa, and citrus. Finish with
a dessert such as bitter chocolate soufflé with warm ganache and vanilla and
bourbon ice cream.

Le Jardin des Sens also rents 13 guest rooms, plus 2 suites, each designed
in cutting-edge style. They cost 175€ to 285€ for a double and 315€ to 485€ for
a suite.

11 av. St-Lazare. www.jardindessens.com. ℭ **04-99-58-38-38.** Fax 04-99-58-38-39. Reservations
required. Main courses 47€–82€; fixed-price lunch Tues–Fri 49€; fixed-price menus 84€–173€.
AE, MC, V. Tues, Thurs–Sat noon–2pm and 8–10pm, Mon and Wed 8–10pm.

**La Réserve Rimbaud** ★★ FRENCH   The oldest restaurant in Montpellier,
founded in 1835, continues to delight locals and visitors with its gorgeous position on the banks of the Lez. Light and spacious inside, the terrace is the place
for summer dining. Passionate about local ingredients, young chef Charles
Fontès produces dishes ranging from pig's trotters with herb salad to scallops
with beetroot and Granny Smith apples, and roast pigeon with spinach, cabbage,
and pumpkin. Desserts are superb and there are good local wines on offer.

820 ave. Saint-Maur. www.reserve-rimbaud.com. ℭ **04-67-72-52-53.** Reservations recommended. Main courses 32€; fixed-price lunch 25€–32€, menus 60€. AE, MC, V. Tues–Fri and Sun
noon–2pm, Tues–Sat 810pm.

**Les Vignes** ★ PROVENÇAL/LANGUEDOCIENNE   This small restaurant near the Préfecture building serves fine regional cuisine. Walk down the stairs into a spectacular 13th-century arched dining room where you can enjoy the products of the land, including fresh thyme, olives, and other herbs. Bull from the Camargue is served, along with fish caught in the Mediterranean. Specialties include sole and scallops braised with anis, and lamb confit with Provence flavors and aubergine gateau. A selection from Languedoc vineyards accompanies most dishes.

2 rue Bonnier d'Alco. www.lesvignesrestaurant.com. (C) **04-67-60-48-42.** Reservations recommended. Main courses 16€–22€; fixed-price lunch 14€–22€, dinner 28€–75€. AE, MC, V. Mon–Sat noon–1:30pm and 7:45–9:30pm.

## Montpellier Nightlife

After the sun sets, head for **place Jean-Jaurès, rue des Ecoles Laïques, place St-Ravy,** or the more sophisticated area around **rue du Palais de Guilhems,** where you'll find the lounge bar **Les Pampilles** at no. 25 ((C) **06-88-23-59-63**).

   **Rockstore,** 20 rue de Verdun (www.rockstore.fr; (C) **04-67-06-80-00**), draws students with 1950s rock memorabilia and live concerts. This huge venue has several bars while up a flight of stairs its disco pounds out techno and rock. No cover, except on concert nights. For the best jazz and blues in town, check out **JAM,** 100 rue Ferdinand-de-Lesseps (www.lejam.com; (C) **04-67-58-30-30**). In a noisy, smoky, and even gritty space, its regular concerts attract jazz enthusiasts from miles around. Concert tickets average 10€ to 25€.

   If you're after a pint of Guinness, make it to **Fitzpatrick's,** 5 place St-Côme ((C) **04-67-60-58-30**), where fans gather to watch major sporting events. It's noisy, convivial, and has live traditional Irish music on Friday evenings after 10pm. Students gather in crowds at **Cargo,** place St.-Denis ((C) **04-67-92-56-05**) for its Wednesday night student party nights. Otherwise expect blues, funk, soul, and Latin from their DJs. Gays, lesbians, and a club-loving crowd gather at the town's most animated bar and disco, **La Villa Rouge,** route de Palavas (www.la-villarouge.fr; (C) **04-67-06-50-54**), in Lattes, about 5km (3 miles) south of the town center.

## Where to Stay

**Le Jardin des Sens** (p. 640) also rents rooms.

**Hôtel du Palais** ★ 🎣   This hotel in the heart of a neighborhood loaded with antiques dealers is one of the best bargains in town. Built in the late 18th century, Hôtel du Palais is at the top of the Old Town, amid a labyrinth of narrow streets and monumental plazas and parks. Much of the decor dates from around 1983, when the hotel was richly restored using lots of fabrics, big curtains, and faux marble finishes on the walls of the public areas. Subsequent renovations have kept the property up-to-date. The well-maintained guest rooms are relatively large and appealing, with antique reproductions.

3 rue du Palais des-Guilhem. www.hoteldupalais-montpellier.fr. (C) **04-67-60-47-38.** Fax 04-67-60-40-23. 26 units. 77€–92€ double. MC, V. Parking 6.50€. **Amenities:** Room service. In room: A/C, TV, hair dryer, minibar, free Wi-Fi.

**Hôtel Le Guilhem** ★ 🎒   Two 16th-century houses make up this oasis, located on a back street. In its transformation to a hotel, the connected buildings were given all the modern conveniences, including an elevator. Each room is furnished and decorated in individual style, with pretty striped wallpaper and flowery spreads. Although small, the rooms are comfortable. Begin the day with breakfast on the terrace overlooking the garden and the cathedral. The location in the old town makes it an ideal base for sightseeing.

18 rue Jean-Jacques-Rousseau, Montpellier 34000. www.leguilhem.com. ℂ **800/528-1234** or 04-67-52-90-90. Fax 04-67-60-67-67. 35 units. 96€–190€ double. AE, DC, MC, V. Parking 7.50€ in nearby garage. **Amenities:** Room service. *In room:* A/C, TV, hair dryer, minibar, free Wi-Fi.

**La Maison Blanche ★**   Few other hotels in the south of France so successfully emulate the gingerbread and French Creole ambience of old New Orleans. Suites are stylishly furnished in rattan and wicker with plenty of wood paneling, whereas standard guest rooms are outfitted with oak. Bathrooms are midsize to roomy. Parts of the interior, especially the dining room, seem more Louis XIII's France than Louisiana, but overall, the setting in a verdant park (a 10-min. drive northeast of Montpellier's center) is charming and unusual.

1796 av. de la Pompignane. www.hotel-maison-blanche.com. ℂ **04-99-58-20-70.** Fax 04-67-79-53-39. 34 units. 83€–136€ double; 165€–203€ suite. AE, DC, MC, V. Free parking. Take bd. d'Antigone east until you reach the intersection with av. de la Pompignane, and head north until you see the hotel on your right (trip time: 5 min.). **Amenities:** Restaurant; bar; outdoor pool; room service. *In room:* A/C, TV, hair dryer, minibar, free Wi-Fi.

**Pullman Montpellier Antigone ★**   In the heart of Montpellier, this angular, modern, glass-sheathed hotel is the city's top hotel for comfort and first-class amenities. Mainly a business hotel, it does quite a trade with visitors in summer. Renovated in 2011, a particularly appealing feature is the pool, which, along with a bar and breakfast room, occupies most of the top floor. The rooms are chain format but first class. The Antigone is a winning choice, with very efficient staff, and a cozy hideaway bar.

1 rue des Pertuisanes. www.pullmanhotels.com. ℂ **04-67-99-72-72.** Fax 04-67-65-17-50. 88 units. 163€–284€ double. AE, DC, MC, V. Parking 3€–10€. **Amenities:** Restaurant; bar; exercise room; outdoor pool; room service. *In room:* A/C, TV, hair dryer, free Wi-Fi.

# NARBONNE ★

845km (524 miles) SW of Paris; 61km (38 miles) E of Carcassonne; 93km (58 miles) S of Montpellier

Narbonne was the first town outside Italy to be colonized by the Romans. At that time, it was the largest town in Gaul after Lyon, and even today you can see evidence of its former wealth. Some visitors come for the beach, but it also attracts history buffs and others drawn to memories of its glorious past.

Some 50,500 Narbonnais live in this sleepy backwater, and if many of the vineyards have been torn up for holiday homes around here, others are trying to raise the profile of their vineyards. You can visit vineyards in the surrounding area (the tourist office will advise you). If you want to go to the beach, head to the nearby village of **Gruisson** and its adjoining beach, Gruisson-Plage, or to the suburb of **St-Pierre la Mer** and its adjoining beach, Narbonne-Plage. Both are 15km (9¼ miles) south of Narbonne. Buses from the town are frequent, each marked with its destination.

# Essentials

**GETTING THERE** Narbonne has rail, bus, and highway connections with other cities on the Mediterranean coast and with Toulouse. Rail travel is the best to get here, with regular **trains** per day arriving from Perpignan (trip time: 35 min.; one-way from 11€), 13 per day from Toulouse (trip time: 1¼ hr.; one-way fare from 19€), and 42 per day from Montpellier (trip time: 1 hr.; one-way fare is 16€). From Paris, the TGV runs directly to Narbonne (trip time: 4½ hr.; one-way from 73€). Train information and schedules are on www.voyages-sncf.com, or call ✆ **36-35** or 00-33-8-92-35-35-35 from outside France. If you're **driving,** Narbonne is at the junction of A61 and A9, easily accessible from either Toulouse or the Riviera.

**VISITOR INFORMATION** The **Office de Tourisme** is at 31 rue Jean Jaurès (www.narbonne-tourisme.com; ✆ **04-68-65-15-60;** fax 04-68-65-59-12).

## Exploring the Town

Start at the oldest site, the **Horreum,** 7 rue Rouget de Lisle (✆ **04-68-32-45-30**), an underground warren of granaries and grain chutes built by the Romans in the 1st century B.C. It's in the restored medieval quarter, which is now full of attractive shops and restaurants. In the center of town, dominating the main place de l'Hôtel-de-Ville, the huge palace and cathedral complex, built from the 12th to the 14th centuries, reveals vaunting ecclesiastical ambitions. The **Cathédrale St-Just et St-Pasteur ★,** rue Armand Gautier ★★ (✆ **04-68-32-09-52;** free admission; daily 9am–noon and 2–6pm), is just the chancel of the original cathedral plan, but it is still magnificent, decorated with 14th-century statues, stained glass, and Aubusson tapestries. Cloisters join it to the **Palais des Archevêques**

(Archbishop's Palace), which contains several museums, including the **Archaeology Museum ★** and the **Museum of Art and History** (for all, ✆ **04-68-90-30-54**). Additional sights include the **Donjon Gilles-Aycelin,** place de l'Hôtel-de-Ville (✆ **04-68-90-30-65**), a watchtower and prison from the late 13th century, with an observation platform offering a view of the cathedral, the plain, and the Pyrénées; and the **Maison Charles Trenet,** 13 av. Charles Trenet (✆ **04-68-90-30-66**), birthplace of the sentimental songwriter beloved of the French. There are pleasant walks by the canal, which is lined with 18th-century houses and *chais* (wine warehouses).

All Narbonne museums and the Horreum have the same opening hours and prices: Admission to one museum is 6€ (4€ students and

**Cathédrale St-Just et St-Pasteur.**

children aged 10 to 17, children 9 and under free); a pass for all museums, the Donjon Gilles-Aycelin, the Cathedral treasure, and Charles Trenet's birthplace is 9€ (6€ students and children aged 10 to 17, children aged 9 and under free). They're open April to July 14 Wednesday to Monday from 10am to noon and from 2 to 5pm, July 15 to October 31 daily from 10am to 1pm and from 2:30 to 6pm, and November to March Wednesday to Monday from 2 to 5pm.

## Where to Eat

**La Table St-Crescent ★★★** FRENCH/LANGUEDOCIENNE One of the region's best-respected restaurants is just east of town, on the road leading to Perpignan, in a complex of wine-tasting boutiques established by a local syndicate of growers. The restaurant delivers refined, brilliantly realized dishes, with sublime sauces and sophisticated herbs and seasonings. The creative dishes change four times a year based on the availability of seasonal ingredients and the inspiration of the owners. Some of the best main courses include guinea fowl with celery and truffle, and pigeon in pastry with foie gras. There's even Wagyu beef for those who really want to push the boat out.

In the Palais des Vins, 68 av. Général Leclerc, rte. de Perpignan. www.la-table-saint-crescent. com. ⓒ **04-68-41-37-37.** Reservations recommended. Main courses 26€–41€; fixed-price lunch Tues–Fri 25€; fixed-price dinner and Sun lunch 48€–79€. AE, DC, MC, V. Tues–Fri and Sun noon–1:30pm; Tues–Sat 8–9:30pm.

## Where to Stay

**Hôtel du Languedoc** Despite frequent modernizations, the grand stone structure of this Belle Epoque hotel still stands out from the cityscape around it. Beside the canal du Rhône, it's the site of municipal meetings and social events, with high-ceilinged public rooms and a mishmash of decors. The rooms come in a variety of shapes and sizes, many with some of the hotel's original wood furniture and pastel color schemes.

22 bd. Gambetta. www.hoteldulanguedoc.com. ⓒ **04-68-65-14-74.** Fax 04-68-65-81-48. 40 units. 62€–77€ double; 95€ suite. AE, DC, MC, V. Parking 9€. **Amenities:** Bar/Breton-style crêperie; room service. *In room:* TV, hair dryer, free Wi-Fi.

**La Résidence ★** Our favorite hotel in Narbonne is near the Cathédrale St-Just. The 19th-century La Résidence, converted from a stately villa, is comfortable and decorated with antiques. Midsize rooms are spacious, tastefully furnished, and very well maintained. Most of the good-size bathrooms have tub/showers. The hotel has no restaurant but serves breakfast.

6 rue du 1er-Mai. www.hotelresidence.fr. ⓒ **04-68-32-19-41.** Fax 04-68-65-51-82. 26 units. 86€–125€ double. AE, DC, MC, V. Parking 9€. Closed mid-Jan–mid-Feb. **Amenities:** *In room:* A/C, TV, hair dryer, minibar, free Wi-Fi.

# COLLIOURE ★★

929km (576 miles) SW of Paris; 28km (17 miles) SE of Perpignan

A port established by the Greeks in 6000 B.C. and later owned by the kings of Majorca, Collioure is best known as the home of a colony of artists who included Derain, Dufy, Picasso, and Matisse. Attracting art lovers from all over the world, it has some of the charm of a pre-Bardot St-Tropez.

The beach at Collioure.

## Essentials

**GETTING THERE**   Collioure has frequent **train** and **bus** service, especially from Perpignan (trip time: 20 min.). Train information and schedules are on www.voyages-sncf.com, or call ✆ **36-35** or 00-33-8-92-35-35-35 from outside France. Many visitors **drive** along the coastal road (RN114) leading to the Spanish border.

**VISITOR INFORMATION**   The **Office de Tourisme** is on place du 18-Juin (www.collioure.com; ✆ **04-68-82-15-47**; fax 04-68-82-46-29).

## Exploring the Town

The two curving ports sit on either side of the heavy masonry of the 13th-century **Château Royal,** place de 8-Mai-1945 (✆ **04-68-82-06-43**). It's of interest in its own right for its medieval fortifications, but between the months of May and September, it's also the home to a changing series of exhibitions by contemporary artists. Entrance costs the same regardless of whether there's an exhibition: 4€ for adults, 2€ students and children ages 10 to 18, and free for children 9 and under. In July and August, hours are daily 10am to 7pm; rest of the year daily 9am to 5pm.

The **Eglise de Notre-Dame-des-Anges,** rue de l'Eglise (✆ **04-68-82-06-43**), is the town's most famous monument; half lighthouse, half church, it looks austere from the outside, but inside features a floor-to-ceiling altarpiece dripping with gold. The church is open daily from 9am to noon and 2 to 6pm. Also try to visit the **Modern Art Museum,** founded by Jean Peské in the Villa Pams, route de Port-Vendres (✆ **04-68-82-10-19**), home to a collection of works by artists who painted here. It's open mid-June to September 10am to noon and 2 to 6pm. From September to June it has the same hours, but is closed on Tuesdays. Admission is 5€ for adults, 1.50€ for children 12 to 16 and students, and free for children 11 and under. The **Chemin du Fauvisme** lists 20 stops where you can see reproductions of paintings by Matisse, Dérain, and other fauvists beside the actual scene they painted—and the colors that inspired this vibrant but short-lived movement are just as alive in the area today. Pick up a map at the tourist office or **Espace Fauve,** av. Camille Pelletan (✆ **04-68-98-07-16.**)

## Where to Eat

**Restaurant La Balette,** at the Relais des 3 Mas (see below), is the best hotel dining room in town.

**Neptune ★★** FRENCH/CATALAN    This is the best restaurant in Collioure, but much to the credit of its owners and staff, it's easygoing and remarkably unpretentious. You'll find it on the southeastern edge of town in a salmon-toned Provençal *mas* (farmhouse). Main courses change with the seasons but may include bouillabaisse; several versions of lobster; or rack of suckling lamb from the nearby salt marshes in a herb-flavored pastry crust.

9 rte. de Porte-Vendres. www.leneptune-collioure.com. ✆ **04-68-82-02-27.** Reservations recommended. Main courses 22€–54€; fixed-price menus 38€–79€. AE, MC, V. Wed–Mon noon–2pm and 7:30–9pm.

## Where to Stay

**Casa Pairal ★**    This pleasant family-operated hotel is in a 150-year-old house a very short walk from the port and beach. In the guest rooms, charming antiques blend with more modern pieces. The best doubles have *petits salons* plus small balconies. Breakfast is the only meal served, but there are many restaurants nearby. On sunny days, guests can take a dip in the pool, in the shadow of century-old trees.

Impasse des Palmiers. www.hotel-casa-pairal.com. ✆ **04-68-82-05-81.** Fax 04-68-82-52-10. 27 units. 89€–219€ double; 184€–253€ suite. AE, DC, MC, V. Parking 16€. **Amenities:** Outdoor pool; room service. *In room:* A/C, TV, hair dryer, minibar, safe, free Wi-Fi.

**Relais des 3 Mas ★★**    This is the town's premier hotel and the restaurant of choice. In its beautiful rooms, the hotel honors the famous artists who lived at Collioure. The rooms, which have spacious bathrooms with Jacuzzis, open onto water views. Even if you aren't a guest, you may want to have a meal in the Restaurant La Balette and take in its vistas of the harbor. The cooking is inventive—often simple but always refined. Fixed-price menus cost 29€ to 95€.

Rte. de Port-Vendres, Collioure. www.relaisdes3mas.com. ✆ **04-68-82-05-07.** Fax 04-68-82-38-08. 23 units. 100€–300€ double; 190€–465€ suite. AE, MC, V. Free parking. Closed Dec–mid-Feb. **Amenities:** Restaurant; babysitting; outdoor pool; room service; sauna; free Wi-Fi. *In room:* A/C, TV, hair dryer, minibar.

# PERPIGNAN ★★

905km (561 miles) SW of Paris; 369km (229 miles) NW of Marseille; 64km (40 miles) S of Narbonne

Perpignan is a flourishing city. The former capital of the kingdom of Majorca and second city of Catalonia has a new TGV (high-speed train) station, and by 2014 will be only 45 minutes from Barcelona, making it a new Catalan cultural and business hub. Perpignan's new Espace Méditerranée neighborhood around the Théâtre de l'Archipel arts complex was designed by France's favorite architect, Jean Nouvel.

Perpignan.

Southern as it is, Perpignan retains the relaxed pace it is famous for. You'll have time to smell the flowers that grow here in great abundance. It also embodies the late-night culture and love of partying of its Spanish neighbors.

This is one of the sunniest places in France, but during summer afternoons in July and August, it's a cauldron. That's when many locals catch the 9.5km (6-mile) ride to the beach resort of Canet. Bus no. 1 runs from the center of Perpignan every 15 minutes in the summer and costs 4€. A young scene brings energy to Perpignan, especially along the quays of the Basse River, site of impromptu nighttime concerts, beer drinking, and the devouring of tapas, a tradition adopted from nearby Barcelona.

## Essentials

**GETTING THERE**  Ten TGV **trains** per day arrive from Paris from both Austerlitz and Gare de Lyon (trip time: around 5 hr.); others change at Montpellier; the one-way fare starts at 97€. Trains run regularly from Marseille (trip time: from 3 hr. 23 min., depending on the route; from 44.90€ one-way). Train information and schedules are on www.voyages-sncf.com, or call ✆ **36-35** or 00-33-8-92-35-35-35 from outside France. If you're **driving** from the French Riviera, take the A9 west to Perpignan.

**VISITOR INFORMATION**  The **Office Municipal du Tourisme** is in the Palais des Congrès, place Armand-Lanoux (www.perpignantourisme.com; ✆ **04-68-66-30-30;** fax 04-68-66-30-26).

**SPECIAL EVENTS**  Perpignan is the only city in France to celebrate Holy Week in the same way as in Spain: with remarkable processions of penitents dressed in hooded gowns. The **Procession de la Sanch** leaves from Eglise St-Jacques on Good Friday morning and moves through the city center, accompanied by chants and the beating of drums. In the heat of July, **Les Jeudis de Perpignan** (www.perpignantourisme.com; ✆ **04-68-66-30-30**) take over the city with an international cultural festival of street arts.

The first 2 weeks of September, Perpignan is host to the most widely discussed celebration of photojournalism in the industry, **Visa pour l'Image** (www.visapourlimage.com; ✆ **04-68-62-38-00**). Photographs are exhibited in at least 10 sites of historical (usually medieval) interest. Entrance to the shows is free, and an international committee awards prizes.

## Exploring the City

**Place de la République** is at the heart of the pedestrianized city center, whose inviting streets make it a good town for shopping. Catalan is the style indigenous to the area, and its influence is evident in the textiles, pottery, and furniture. A good selection of Catalan-inspired home-decorating items is found at **La Maison Quinta,** 3 rue Grands-des-Fabriques (www.maison-quinta.com; ✆ **04-68-34-41-62**). For one of the best selections of Catalan pieces, including pottery, furniture, carpets, and antiques, visit **Centre Sant-Vicens,** rue Sant-Vicens (www.santvicens.fr; ✆ **04-68-50-02-18**), where about a dozen merchants sell ceramics, pottery, and art. It's 4km (2½ miles) south of the town center; follow signs to Enne and Collioure. All the flavor of Perpignan's colorful street life is found at the outdoor market **Marché Cassanyes,** place Cassanyes, selling fruit, vegetables, preserves, and cheap clothes. It happens daily from 7:30am to 1:30pm.

A 2-hour guided **walking tour** is a good way to see the attractions in the town's historic core. Tours begin at 5pm on Monday and Wednesday in July and August. The rest of the year, they start at 2:30pm on Wednesdays only. They depart from in front of the Palmarium tourist information point on place Arago and cost 5€ per person. Check which are in English. There are also popular themed walks on Sundays. For more details, contact the tourist office (see above).

**Cathédrale St-Jean ★** CATHEDRAL   The cathedral dates from the 14th and 15th centuries and has an admirable nave and interesting 17th-century retables (altarpieces). Leaving through the south door, you'll find on the left a chapel with the *Devost-Christ* (Devout Christ), a magnificent woodcarving depicting Jesus contorted with pain and suffering, with his head, crowned with thorns, drooping on his chest. On Good Friday, the statue is promenaded through the streets of the town center.

Place Gambetta/rue de l'Horloge. ✆ **04-68-51-33-72.** Free admission. Daily 7:30am–6pm. Closes at 5:30pm Dec–Feb.

**Le Castillet ★** MONUMENT/MUSEUM   This crenelated red-brick building is a combination gateway and fortress from the 14th century. You can climb its bulky tower for a view of the town. Also here is the **Musée des Arts et Traditions Populaires Catalans** (also known as La Casa Païral), with exhibitions of Catalan regional artifacts and folkloric items, including typical dress.

Place de Verdun. ✆ **04-68-35-42-05.** Admission 4€ adults, 2€ students, free ages 18 and under. Tues–Sun 10:30am–6pm.

**Musée Rigaud** MUSEUM   Housed in an 18th-century *hôtel particulier,* just off the cafe-lined place Arago, the main collection of Perpignan's art museum is from native son Hyacinthe Rigaud, the official court painter of Versailles who painted four generations of Bourbons. Other artists who visited the area, including Picasso, Dufy, Maillol, and Miro, are represented, along with Catalan ceramics and 210 contemporary artists.

16 rue de l'Ange. (✆ **04-68-35-43-40.** Admission 4€ adults, free ages 25 and under. Tues–Sun 10:30am–6pm.

### Palais des Rois de Majorque (Palace of the Kings of Majorca) ★

CASTLE  At the top of the town, the massive Spanish citadel encloses the now restored former Palace of the Kings of Majorca. Built in the 13th and 14th centuries around a court encircled by arcades, it was the heart of the city. Entering via a huge ramp you come to a park with the castle ahead. From the courtyard you climb to the first floor grand throne room, with its large fireplaces. The square tower with its double gallery gives panoramic views of the Pyrénées. A free guided tour, in French only, departs four times a day if demand warrants it.

Rue des Archers. (✆ **04-68-34-48-29.** Admission 4€ adults, 2€ students and children 12–18, free for children 11 and under. June–Sept daily 10am–6pm; Oct–May daily 9am–5pm.

## Where to Eat

**La Villa Duflot** (see next page) has a good restaurant.

**L'Assiette Catalane** 🍴 CATALAN  Known to virtually every resident of Perpignan, this restaurant resembles something you'd expect across the Pyrénées in Spain. Hand-painted ceramic plates, rugby and flamenco posters, and antique farm implements cover the thick stone walls. Even the long, lively bar is inlaid with Iberian mosaics, and copies of works by Dalí and Picasso seem to watch you as you dine. Tapas features strongly so sample calamaris, ham, anchovies, red peppers, and cheese as small plates. Or try a main dish of *parrillade de poissons*—a mixed fish grill cooked on a hot slab of iron brought directly to your table—and zarzuelas, paella, and tapas. Finish with a portion of the flan *crème Catalane*.

9 rue de la République. (✆ **04-68-34-77-62.** www.assiettecatalane.com. Reservations recommended. Main courses 12€–17.50€; fixed-price lunch 8€–11€, dinner 16€–27€. MC, V. Mon–Sat noon–2pm; Tues–Sat 7:15–10:30pm.

**Le Clos des Lys** ★ 🍴 FRENCH/CATALAN  This well-recommended restaurant, in a stately building that sits apart from its neighbors, has an outdoor terrace overlooking a copse of cypresses and bubbling fountains. There's a selection of fixed price menus, giving you either Catalan or French choices. Dishes are inventive, mixing ingredients and influences. Try salmon done various ways with a tandoori/cocoa sauce followed by a classic beef fillet with herbs and spices and either caramalized onions or Roquefort and nut sauce.

660 chemin de la Fauceille. www.closdeslys.com. (✆ **04-68-56-79-00.** Reservations recommended. Main courses 21€–40€; fixed-price lunch 17.50€–24€, dinner 29€–65€. AE, DC, MC, V. Tues–Sun noon–2pm; Tues and Thurs–Sat 7pm–midnight. Closed 2 weeks in Feb. From the center of Perpignan, drive 2.5km (1½ miles) west, following rte. d'Espagne.

## Perpignan Nightlife

Perpignan's cultural life is centered around the new **Théâtre de l'Archipel**, av. du Général Leclerc (www.theatredelarchipel.org; (✆ **04-68-62-62-00**) which holds multi-cultural events all year round.

Perpignan shows its Spanish and Catalan side at night, getting lively only when other cities go to bed. The streets radiating from **place de la Loge** offer a higher concentration of bars and clubs than any other part of town.

Begin at **Le Habana Bodegita-Club,** 5 rue Grande-des-Fabriques (✆ **04-68-34-11-00**), where salsa and merengue play and sunset-colored cocktails flow. Suds with an Irish accent are the attraction at **Le O'Shannon Bar,** 3 rue de l'Incendie (✆ **04-68-35-12-48**). **Le Cosy Club,** 4 rue du Théâtre (✆ **04-68-66-02-57**), is a piano bar where local jazzers play and a fun-loving crowd congregates over cocktails. It offers the elegance and warmth promised by its name, with a great bar and soothing lighting.

Nightclubs in Perpignan open around 11pm. A good option for dancing is the **Uba-Club,** 5 bd. Mercader (✆ **04-68-34-06-70**), which has a smallish dance floor and, thankfully, some sofas and chairs.

During summer, the beachfront strip at the nearby resort of **Canet-Plage,** 12km (7½ miles) east of Perpignan's historic core, abounds with seasonal bars and dance clubs that come and go with the tourist tides.

## Where to Stay

**La Villa Duflot ★★★**   This is the area's greatest hotel, yet its prices are reasonable for the luxury it offers. Located in a suburb 4km (2½ miles) from Perpignan, the Mediterranean-style dwelling is surrounded by a park of pine, palm, and eucalyptus. You can sunbathe in the gardens surrounding the pool and order drinks from the outside bar. The good-size guest rooms are spacious and soundproof, with stylish Art Deco interiors. The restaurant is reason enough to stay, using market ingredients for dishes such as Iberico ham with white haricot beans, foie gras with almond biscuits and sweet wine, or a platter of fish of the day. It's open daily noon to 2pm and 8 to 11pm, with main courses from 20€ to 28€, a weekday fixed-price lunch menu at 20€–25€, and weekend menu at 29€.

Rond-Point Albert Donnezan, Perpignan 66000. www.villa-duflot.com. ✆ **04-68-56-67-67.** Fax 04-68-56-54-05. 24 units. 150€–190€ double; 210€–275€ suite. AE, DC, MC, V. From central Perpignan, follow signs to Perthus–Le Belou and A9, and travel 3km (1¾ miles) south. Just before you reach A9, you'll see the hotel. **Amenities:** Restaurant; 2 bars; babysitting; outdoor pool; room service. *In room:* A/C, TV, hair dryer, minibar, safe, free Wi-Fi.

**Suitehotel Perpignan ★**   Right next to the Théâtre de l'Archipel and its exciting new district, the Suitehotel has 50 studio apartments. It offers everything an urban nomad could want: spacious suites with bath *and* shower; free Wi-Fi through the "Suitebox," which also offers free calls to French landlines; music; a gym; an ironing room; and a bar and "boutique gourmande," where you can buy luxurious snacks like mini boxes of foie gras or ready-meals for your own microwave. There are free 15-minute massages on Thursdays between 7:30pm and 9:30pm. The contemporary decor, with rooms in soothing slate tones, strikes the right *Elle Decor* note and feels more like a hip bachelor pad than a business hotel.

23 Espace Mediterranée. www.suitehotel.com. ✆ **04-68-92-72-72.** Fax 04-68-64-11-54. 50 units. 81€–140€ suite. Free parking. AE, DC, MC, V. **Amenities:** Bar; gym; self-service meals. *In room:* A/C, TV, hair dryer, minibar, free Wi-Fi.

# CARCASSONNE ★★★

797km (494 miles) SW of Paris; 92km (57 miles) SE of Toulouse; 105km (65 miles) S of Albi

Evoking bold knights, fair damsels, and troubadours, the greatest fortress city of Europe rises against the background of the Pyrénées. Seen from afar, it suggests fairy-tale magic, but in its heyday in the Middle Ages, it wasn't so romantic. Shattering the peace and quiet were battering rams, grapnels, a mobile tower (inspired by the Trojan horse), catapults, flaming arrows, and the mangonel (a type of catapult).

Today the city that once served as a backdrop for the 1991 movie *Robin Hood, Prince of Thieves* is overrun with visitors and tacky gift shops. But the elusive charm of Carcassonne emerges in the evening, when thousands of day-trippers have departed and floodlights bathe the ancient monuments.

## Essentials

**GETTING THERE**   Carcassonne is a major stop for **trains** between Toulouse and destinations south and east. There are 17 trains per day from Toulouse (trip time: 1 hr.; 15€ one-way), 16 per day from Montpellier (trip time: 1½ hr.; from 20€ one-way), and ten per day from Marseille (trip time: from 3 hrs.; from 46€ one-way). Train information and schedules are on www. voyages-sncf.com, or call © **36-35** or 00-33-8-92-35-35-35 from outside France. If you're **driving,** Carcassonne is on A61 south of Toulouse.

**VISITOR INFORMATION**   The **Office de Tourisme** has locations at 28 rue de Verdun (www.carcassonne-tourisme.com); (© **04-68-10-24-30;** fax 04-68-10-24-38) and in the medieval town at Porte Narbonnaise (© **04-68-10-24-36**).

**SPECIAL EVENTS**   The town's nightlife sparkles during its summer festivals. During the **Festival de Carcassonne** (www.festivaldecarcassonne.com), from mid-July to mid-August, concerts, modern and classical dance, operas, and theater fill the city, with big stars such as Duran Duran and Alice Cooper appearing at the **Théâtre Jean Deschamps,** an amphitheater seating 5,000 in La Cité. Tickets run 19€ to 65€. To purchase call © **04-68-11-59-15** or 04-68-77-74-31. On July 14, **Bastille Day,** one of the best fireworks spectacles in France lights up the skies at 10:30pm.

Carcassonne's medieval citadel.

Basilique St-Nazaire.

Over 6 weeks in July and August, the merriment and raucousness of the Middle Ages take over the city during the **Spectacles Medievaux,** in the form of jousts, food fairs, and street festivals. For information, contact the **Office de Tourisme** (see previous page).

## Exploring the Town

Carcassonne consists of two towns: the **Bastide St-Louis** (also known as Ville Basse, or "Lower City"), and the upper town, or medieval **Cité ★★★**, which is among the major attractions in France. The impressive fortifications here consist of the inner and outer walls, a double line of ramparts. The Visigoths built the inner rampart in the 5th century. Clovis, king of the Franks, attacked it unsuccessfully in 506. The Saracens overcame the city in 728, but Pepin the Short (father of Charlemagne) drove them out in 752.

The epic medieval poems *Chansons de Geste* tell the tale of the origin of the town's name. During a siege by Charlemagne, the starving populace of the city was near surrender until a local noblewoman, Dame Carcas, reputedly gathered up the last of their grain, fed it to a sow and tossed the pig over the ramparts. The pig burst, scattering the grain. Dame Carcas then demanded a parley and cried, *"Carcas te sonne!"* (Carcas is calling you!) The Franks, concluding that Carcassonne must have unlimited food supplies, ended their siege.

Carcassonne's walls were further fortified by the vicomtes de Trencavel in the 12th century but were overcome by anti-Cathar crusaders and Simon de Montfort. The city passed to Louis IX who laid out the Ville Basse. But by the mid–17th century, the city had lost its position as a strategic frontier, and the ramparts were left to decay. In the 19th century, builders began to remove the stones for use in new construction. But interest in the Middle Ages revived, and the government ordered Viollet-le-Duc (who restored Notre-Dame in Paris) to repair and, where necessary, rebuild the walls. Reconstruction continued until recently.

In the highest part of the Cité, on rue Cros Mayrevielle, you'll find the **Château Comtal,** place du Château (http://carcassone.monuments-nationaux.fr; ✆ **04-68-11-70-72**), a restored 12th-century fortress that's open April through September daily 9:30am to 6:30pm, October through March daily 9:30am to 5pm. Entrance includes an obligatory 45-minute guided tour, in French and broken English. It's also the only way to climb onto the city's inner ramparts. The cost is 8.50€ for adults, 5.50€ ages 18 to 25, and free age 17 and under. The tour includes access to exhibitions that display the archaeological remnants discovered on-site, plus an explanation of the 19th-century restorations.

Another major monument in the fortifications is the **Basilique St-Nazaire ★**; place de l'Eglise (✆ **04-68-25-27-65**), dating from the 11th to the 14th centuries and containing some beautiful stained-glass windows including two exceptional rose windows. It has other attractions: a soaring Romanesque nave, and a Gothic choir and transept. The 16th-century organ is one of the oldest in southwestern France and there are well-preserved tombs of Bishop Radulphe (1266) and Bishop de Rochefort (14th to 15th centuries). The cathedral is open Monday through Saturday 9 to 11:45am and 1:45 to 6pm, Sunday 9 to 10:45am and 2 to 5pm. It closes slightly earlier in winter. Mass is celebrated on Sunday at 11am. Admission is free.

## Shopping

Carcassonne has two distinct shopping areas. In the Lower City, the major streets for shopping, particularly if you're in the market for clothing, are **rue Clemenceau** and **rue de Verdun.** In the walled medieval city, the streets are chock-full of tiny stores and boutiques; most sell gift items such as antiques and local arts and crafts.

Stores worth visiting, all in the Cité, include **Comptoir des Vins,** 3 rue du Conte Roger (✆ **04-68-26-44-76**), where you'll find a wide selection of regional wines. Some antiques stores of merit are **Faye Henriette,** 4 place du Château (✆ **04-68-47-09-45**), for antique furniture; **Antiquités Safi,** 26 rue Trivalle (✆ **04-68-25-60-51**), for paintings and art objects; and **Maison du Sud,** 13 porte d'Aude (✆ **04-68-47-10-06**), for home decoration.

## Where to Eat

**Brasserie Donjon,** run by Le Donjon et Les Remparts hotel, is recommended, and in Ville-Basse, the moderately priced restaurant at **Trois Couronnes** (see p. 654) serves well-prepared regional cuisine.

**La Barbacane ★** FRENCH   Named after its medieval neighborhood, this celebrated restaurant is in the Hôtel de la Cité. Its soothing looking dining room has green walls and lots of paneling. Menu items are based on seasonal ingredients, with just enough zest. The chef Jerome Ryon has gained a top reputation for a style of cooking mixing seasonal ingredients with skill. Order soft eggs with a lobster and mushroom ragout with passion fruit and mushroom soup, followed by wild braised turbot with potato gnocchi and mushrooms or Bresse pigeon stuffed with crayfish and gratinée potatoes. A star dessert is the warm caramel soufflé, or go for a classic apple tarte with Calvados and apple ice cream.

In the Hôtel de la Cité, place de l'Eglise. www.hoteldelacite.com. ✆ **04-68-71-98-71.** Reservations recommended. Main courses 35€–65€; fixed-price menu 80€–160€. AE, DC, MC, V. Thurs–Mon 7:30–9:30pm. Closed Feb–beginning of Mar.

**Le Jardin en Ville** 🍴 FRENCH   Along with the restaurant, a shop and exhibition space make this new venue a lively meeting place. Eat upstairs in the simple room with bright colored art on the walls, or on the terrace in summer. The menu jogs along nicely with favorites such as crisp fresh salads and pastas followed by lamb chops in thyme and a good fish selection. Vegetables are picked each morning from the garden; meat comes from Carcassone's best butcher. It's a good choice for a fun, casual meal.

5 rue des Framboisiers. www.lejardinenville.fr. ✆ **04-68-47-80-91.** Reservations recommended. Main courses 17€–20€; fixed-price lunch 13€–14.50€. MC, V. Tues–Sat noon–2pm, Thurs–Sat 7pm–9:30pm; July & Aug Tues–Sat lunch and dinner.

**Le Parc Franck Putelat** ★★★ FRENCH   Franck and Céline are making waves in Carcassone at their contemporary designed restaurant, which is the jewel in their particular local crown. In a long room decorated with bold colors, refined, inventive cooking produces dishes ranging from Andalusian gazpacho with Spanish charcuterie and goat cheese to a stunning bouillabaisse as good as you get in Marseilles. Service is charming; the wine list notable. Luxury ingredients like summer truffles appear regularly, and if you can afford it, this is the place to go for the tasting menu at 118€, which varies according to the seasons, the availability of top ingredients, and the chef's personal inspiration.

80 chemin des Anglais. www.restaurantleparcfranckputelat.fr. ✆ **04-68-71-80-80.** Reservations necessary. Fixed-price menus 31€–118€. MC, V. Tues–Sat noon–2pm and 7:30–10pm. Closed Jan and mid-Apr for 2 weeks.

## Carcassone Nightlife

Carcassonne nightlife centers on **rue Omer-Sarraut** in La Bastide and **place Marcou** in La Cité. **La Bulle,** 115 rue Barbacane (✆ 04-68-72-47-70), explodes with techno and rock dance tunes for an under-30 crowd that keeps the place hopping until 5am Wednesday to Sunday. The cover charge begins at 10€ per person. Another enduringly popular disco, 4km (2½ miles) southwest of town, is **Le Black Bottom,** route de Limoux (✆ 04-68-47-37-11), which plays every conceivable kind of dance music Thursday through Sunday beginning at 11pm. Entrance costs 10€ on Saturday only.

## Where to Stay

### IN THE CITÉ

**Hôtel de la Cité** ★★★   Originally a palace for whichever bishop or prelate was in power at the time, this has been the most desirable hotel in town since 1909. It's in the actual walls of the city, adjoining the cathedral. The Orient-Express Hotel group acquired the hotel in the '90s and fluffed it up to the tune of $3 million. You enter through a long Gothic corridor-gallery that leads to the lounge. Many rooms open onto the ramparts and a garden, and feature antiques or reproductions while a few have four-poster beds. The ideal unit is no. 308, which opens onto the most panoramic view of the city. The hotel is renowned for its restaurant, **La Barbacane** (above).

Place Auguste Pierre Pont. www.hoteldelacite.com. ✆ **04-68-71-98-71.** Fax 04-68-71-50-15. 60 units. 185€–510€ double; 315€–1,000€ suite. AE, DC, MC, V. Parking 16€–20€ (garage). **Amenities:** 3 restaurants; bar; babysitting; outdoor pool; room service. *In room:* A/C, TV, hair dryer, i-Pod dock station, minibar, free Wi-Fi.

## AT THE ENTRANCE TO THE CITÉ
**Best Western Le Donjon et Les Remparts ★★ ✦** This little hotel is big on charm and is the best value in the moderate price range. Built in the style of the old Cité, it has a honey-colored stone exterior with iron bars on the windows. The interior is a jewel, with elaborate Louis XIII–style furniture gracing the reception lounges. A newer wing contains additional rooms in medieval architectural style. Their furnishings are more severe, consistent with the medieval look of the nearby ramparts. The hotel also runs the nearby Brasserie Le Donjon. In summer, the garden is the perfect breakfast spot.

2 rue du Comte-Roger. www.hotel-donjon.fr. ✆ **04-68-11-23-00.** Fax 04-68-25-06-60. 61 units. 105€–185€ double; 150€–405€ suite. AE, DC, MC, V. Parking 12€. **Amenities:** Restaurant; bar; room service. *In room:* A/C, TV, hair dryer, minibar, safe, free Wi-Fi.

## IN VILLE BASSE
**Trois Couronnes ★★** This dependable modern hotel makes the most of its Lower City location by offering great views of the Cité and the Aude River from its 44 "panoramic" rooms and one suite, and from the fourth-floor restaurant and bar. A government-rated three-star hotel, "Three Crowns" has good facilities, including an indoor pool. The well maintained rooms are functionally comfortable, with tasteful furnishings. Service is top rate. Good regional cuisine is served in the on-site restaurant.

2 rue des Trois Couronnes. www.hotel-destroiscouronnes.com. ✆ **04-68-25-36-10.** Fax 04-68-25-92-92. 69 units. 95€–150€ double; 210€–250€ suite. AE, DC, MC, V. Parking 6€–9€. **Amenities:** Restaurant; bar; indoor pool; room service. *In room:* A/C, TV, hair dryer, minibar, free Wi-Fi.

# CASTRES ★
728km (451 miles) SW of Paris; 42km (26 miles) S of Albi; 70 km (43.5 miles)

On the bank of the Agout River, Castres is the gateway for trips to the Sidobre, the mountains of Lacaune, and the Black Mountains. Once a Roman military town, it became a religious center after the founding of a Benedictine monastery in the 9th century, then fell under the sway of the comtes d'Albi in the 10th century. During the wars of religion, it was Protestant. The Eglise St-Benoît in French baroque style was started in 1677 on the Benedictine site but never finished. Echoes of Castres as a wool producing town from the 14th century are found in the old tanners' and weavers' houses by the river. Today the town has a population of 43,500.

## Essentials
**GETTING THERE** From Toulouse, there are regular **trains** each day (trip time: around 1 hr. 10 min.; one-way fare is 14€). Train information and schedules are on www.voyages-sncf.com, or call ✆ **36-35** or 00-33-8-92-35-35-35 from outside France. If you're **driving,** Castres is on N126 east of Toulouse and N112 south of Albi.

**VISITOR INFORMATION** The **Office de Tourisme** is at 2 place de la République (www.tourisme-castres.fr; ✆ **05-63-62-63-62;** fax 05-63-62-63-60).

## Exploring the Town
**Jean-Jaurès Museum** Jean-Jaurès, born in Castres, was one of France's most liberal political activists. He supported Dreyfus, founded the newspaper

*L'Humanité*, was leader of the socialist party and campaigned for causes like abolishing the death penalty and colonialism. Though much of the documentation is in French, the large collection of satirical cartoons and lithographs gives a good picture of political life in France in the 1900s.

2 place Pélisson. ℂ **05-63-62-41-83.** Admission 2€ adults. July–Aug daily 10am–noon and 2–6pm; Oct–May 10am–noon and 2–5pm.

**Musée Goya ★**   The museum is in the town hall, an archbishop's palace designed by Mansart in 1669. Some of the spacious public rooms have ceilings supported by a frieze of the archbishop's coats of arms. The largest collection of Spanish art outside the Louvre, the museum houses 16th-century tapestries, some outstanding sculpture and the works of Spanish painters from the 15th to the 20th centuries including works by Velázquez and Murillo. But it is the works of Goya, all donated to the town in 1894 by Pierre Briguiboul, son of the Castres-born artist Marcel Briguiboul, that attract visitors. *Les Caprices* is a study of figures created in 1799 after the illness that left Goya deaf. It fills much of an entire room and consists of symbolic images of demons and monsters, a satire of Spanish society.

In the Jardin de l'Evêché. ℂ **05-63-71-59-30.** Admission 3€ adults, 1.50€ 18 to 26 years, free for children 18 and under. July–Aug daily 10am–6pm; Oct–Mar Tues–Sat 9am–noon and 2–5pm, Sun 10am–noon and 2–5pm.

# Where to Eat

**La Mandragore ★** LANGUEDOCIENNE   On an easily overlooked narrow street, this restaurant, named for a legendary plant with magic powers, occupies a small part of one of the many wings of the medieval château-fort of Castres. The decor is simple, with stone walls and tones of autumn colors. The regional cuisine is served with a smile. Among the best dishes are ravioli stuffed with

Painting by Francisco Pacheco at the Musée Goya.

truffles, snails, and pink garlic, flavored with basil; rack of suckling veal with exotic mushrooms; and *magret* of duckling with natural Canadian maple syrup.

1 rue Malpas. ℰ **05-63-59-51-27.** Reservations recommended. Main courses 12€–18€; fixed-price menu 13€ lunch, 20€–27€ dinner. DC, MC, V. Tues–Sat noon–2pm and 7–9pm. Closed 2 weeks in Sept and 2 weeks in Mar.

**Restaurant Bistrot Saveurs ★★** FRENCH  Englishman Simon Scott worked in the kitchens of the Ritz and Savoy hotels in London before moving to France with his French wife and gaining a Michelin star. His modern, stone-vaulted restaurant attracts both locals and visitors who appreciate his classically based cooking with its distinct modern take. Specialities to order include foie gras two ways: with apples, and with spiced cake, beetroot, and squash chutney; and sea bass cooked *a la plancha* with squash, gnocchi and truffled potatoes. Imaginative desserts and a good cellar are all pluses, as are the good value menus. The staff is charming.

5 rue Sainte-Foy. www.bistrot-saveurs.com. ℰ **05-63-50-11-45.** Reservations recommended. Main courses 37€–40€; fixed-price lunch 16.50€–24€; dinner 28€–65€. MC, V. Mon–Fri noon–2:30pm and 7–10:30pm.

## Where to Stay

**Hôtel Renaissance ★**  Built in the 17th century as a courthouse, this hotel was restored in the '90s. Today you'll see a dignified building with *colombages*-style half-timbering and a mixture of stone blocks and bricks. Some of the larger comfortable rooms have exposed timbers. Some rooms are in the style of Napoleon III, some are 18th-century Asiatic, and others are country-comfortable with safari-themed fabrics.

17 rue Victor-Hugo. www.hotel-renaissance.fr. ℰ **05-63-59-30-42.** Fax 05-63-59-21-38. 20 units. 65€–85€ double; 85€–120€ suite. AE, DC, MC, V. Parking 10€. **Amenities:** Restaurant; bar; room service. *In room:* A/C, TV, hair dryer, minibar, free Wi-Fi.

# ALBI ★★★

697km (432 miles) SW of Paris; 76km (47 miles) NE of Toulouse

The "red city" (for the color of its bricks) of Albi straddles both banks of the Tarn River and is dominated by its 13th-century cathedral, which is at the center of the remarkable brick-built Episcopal city. The whole of this medieval city center was added to UNESCO's World Heritage List in 2010. Toulouse-Lautrec was born in the Hôtel Bosc in Albi; it's still a private home and not open to visitors, but there's a plaque on the wall of the building, on rue Toulouse-Lautrec in the town center. The town's major attraction is the renovated and reopened Toulouse-Lautrec museum with a world-class collection of the artist's work.

## Essentials

**GETTING THERE**  Twenty **trains** per day link Toulouse with Albi (trip time: from 1 hr; the one-way fare is 13€.). Train information and schedules are on www.voyages-sncf.com, or call ℰ **36-35** or 00-33-8-92-35-35-35 from outside France. If you're **driving** from Toulouse, take A68 northeast.

**Cathédrale Ste-Cécile.**

**VISITOR    INFORMATION**  The
**Office de Tourisme** is in the Palais de la Berbie, place Ste-Cécile
(www.albi-tourisme.fr; ✆ **05-63-
49-48-80;** fax 05-63-49-48-98).

## Exploring the Town

### Cathédrale Ste-Cécile ★★

CATHEDRAL  Fortified  with
ramparts and parapets, this 13th-
century cathedral was started by a
local lord-bishop after the religious struggle with the comte de
Toulouse (the crusade against the
Cathars) but took 200 years to
complete. It holds three records:
the largest brick-built cathedral in
the world, the oldest Medieval
depiction of the Last Judgment,
and the largest surface area of
Italian Renaissance frescos in
France. Note the exceptional
16th-century rood screen with a
unique suit of polychromatic statues from the Old and New Testa-
ments. Free classical concerts take place in July and August on Wednesday at
5pm and Sunday at 4pm.

Near place du Vigan, in the medieval center of town. ✆ **05-63-43-23-43.** Cathédrale: Free
admission. Choir 1€, audioguide 3€ adults, free children 11 and under; Treasury 3€ adults, 2€
ages 12–25, free 11 and under. June–Sept daily 9am–6:30pm; Oct–May daily 9am–noon and
2–6:30pm.

**Musée de Lapérouse** MUSEUM    Set on the opposite bank of the Tarn from
the bulk of Albi's medieval core (take the pont Vieux to reach it), this museum
honors the achievements of Albi's native son, Jean-François de Lapérouse, and
tries to penetrate the mystery of his shipwreck off the Salomon Islands in 1788.
Commissioned as an explorer by Louis XVI in the late 1600s, he mapped and
charted the coastlines of Alaska, California, and China, bringing the French up
to speed against England in its rush for colonies outside of Europe.

Square Botany Bay. www.laperouse-france.fr. ✆ **05-63-46-01-87.** Admission 3€ adults, 2€ students and ages 13–25, free for children 12 and under. Mar–June and Sept–Oct Tues–Sun 9am–
noon and 2–6pm; July–Aug Mon–Fri 9am–noon and 2–6pm, Sat–Sun 10am–noon and 2–7pm;
Nov–Feb Tues–Sun 10am–noon and 2–5pm.

**Musée Toulouse-Lautrec** ★★★ MUSEUM  The Palais de la Berbie
(Archbishop's Palace) is a fortified structure dating from the 13th century. This
museum contains the world's most important collection of Toulouse-Lautrec's
paintings, more than 1,000 in all. After ten years of major renovation work and a
temporary closure, the spectacular new museum has been completely rehung. Its

new approach is both chronological and thematic, and includes sections on his family, on the prostitutes he painted, and his portraits of Yvette Gilbert and Jane Avril. The museum also owns paintings by Degas, Bonnard, Matisse, Utrillo, and Rouault, and there's a new gallery on Albi's Episcopal city.

Place Ste-Cécile. www.musee-toulouse-lautrec.com ✆ **05-63-49-48-70.** Admission 8€ adults, 4€ students, free 14 and under. Mid-June–Sep daily 9am–6pm; Apr–May daily 10am–noon and 2–6pm; first three weeks in Jun daily 9am–noon and 2–6pm; Jan Wed–Mon 10am–noon and 2–5pm; Feb-Mar Wed–Mon 10am–noon and 2–5:30pm; Oct Wed–Mon 10am–noon and 2–6pm; Nov–Dec Wed–Mon 10am–noon and 2–5:30pm. Closed Jan 1, May 1, Nov 1, and Dec 25.

# Where to Eat

Both **Hostellerie du Grand St-Antoine** and the **Hôtel Chiffre** are good choices. See "Where to Stay," below.

**Jardin des Quatre Saisons** ★★ MODERN FRENCH    Georges Bermond believes that menus, like life, should change with the seasons, which is how the restaurant got its name. Served in his two simple dining rooms, fine-tuned menu items include beef carpaccio with Parmesan, or crayfish with shitake mushroom, followed by lamb roasted with thyme or a superb *pot-au-feu* of the sea, with three or four species of fish garnished with crayfish-cream sauce.

19 bd. de Strasbourg. www.lejardindesquatresaisons.fr. ✆ **05-63-60-77-76.** Reservations recommended. Fixed-price lunch 14€; menu 27€–38€. AE, DC, MC, V. Tues–Sun noon–2:30pm; Tues–Sat 7:30–10pm.

**Le Lautrec** TRADITIONAL FRENCH    Part of this restaurant's charm derives from its associations with Toulouse-Lautrec—it lies across the street from his birthplace and is decorated with paintings by local artists. Also appealing is the rich patina of its interior brickwork. Skillfully prepared dishes include scallops that come with rose oil and essence of shrimp, and roasted rack of lamb marinated in an infusion of Provençal thyme. Hearty regional dishes—beloved by local diners—are a cassoulet of codfish, savory sweetbreads (an acquired taste for some), and duckling *en confit*.

13–15 rue Toulouse-Lautrec. www.restaurant-le-lautrec.com. ✆ **05-63-54-86-55.** Reservations recommended. Main courses 18€–38€; fixed-price lunch Tues–Sat 16€–18€; fixed-price lunch or dinner 18€–52€. AE, MC, V. Tues–Sun noon–2pm; Tues–Sat 7–9:30pm. Closed 1 week in Jan, 1 week in Aug, and 2 weeks in Nov.

# Where to Stay

**Hostellerie du Grand St-Antoine** ★★    One of the oldest continuously operated hotels in France, the building went from monastery to a medieval hospital, then became an inn in 1734 when the present building was constructed. The same family has owned it for five generations; today the father-son team of Jacques and Jean-François Rieux manages it. Jacques's mother focused on Toulouse-Lautrec when designing the hotel, as her grandfather was a friend of the painter and was given a few of his paintings, sketches, and prints. Several are in the lounge, which opens onto a rear garden. The rooms have been delightfully decorated, with a sophisticated use of color, reproductions, and occasional antiques. Even if you're not staying, visit the dining room. The Rieux culinary tradition is revealed in their traditional yet creative cuisine.

17 rue St-Antoine. www.hotel-saint-antoine-albi.com. © **05-63-54-04-04.** Fax 05-63-47-10-47. 44 units. 110€–168€ double; 165€–228€ suite. AE, DC, MC, V. Parking 7€. **Amenities:** Restaurant; bar; babysitting; room service. *In room:* A/C, TV, hair dryer, minibar, free Wi-Fi.

**Hôtel Chiffre** 🍴   This hotel in the city center was built as an inn for passengers on the mail coaches that hauled letters and people across France. The renovated building retains the original porch that sheltered carriages from the rain and sun. The simple rooms are cozy, with floral-patterned fabric-covered walls; some have views of the inner courtyard. The hotel restaurant's fixed-price menus are popular among locals. The menu, priced at 20€ to 27€ per person, consists of choices that were compiled after Toulouse-Lautrec's death by his friends such as suprême of *sandre* (fish), and duckling roasted with garlic.

50 rue Séré-de-Rivières. www.hotelchiffre.com. © **05-63-48-58-48.** Fax 05-63-38-11-15. 39 units. 96€–136€ double; 250€ suite. AE, MC, V. Parking 9€. **Amenities:** Restaurant; bar; room service; free Wi-Fi. *In room:* A/C, TV, hair dryer.

# CORDES-SUR-CIEL ★★

678km (420 miles) SW of Paris; 25km (16 miles) NW of Albi

This remarkable site is like an eagle's nest on a hilltop, opening onto the Cérou valley. In days gone by, celebrities such as Jean-Paul Sartre and Albert Camus considered this town a favorite hideaway. In low season, the population is just under 1,000, but it swells to 10,000 in midsummer.

Through the centuries, Cordes has been known for its textile, leather, and silk industries. Even today, it's an arts-and-crafts city, and in many of the old houses on the narrow streets, artisans—blacksmiths, enamelers, graphic artists, weavers, engravers, sculptors, and painters—ply their trades. Park outside and then pass under an arch leading to the old town.

Cordes-sur-Ciel.

## Essentials

**GETTING THERE**   If you're **driving,** take A68 northeast from Toulouse to Gaillac, turning north at exit 9 on D922 to Cordes-sur-Ciel. If you're coming by **train,** get off in Cordes-Vindrac and walk, rent a bicycle, or take a taxi the remaining 3km (1¾ miles) west of Cordes. Train information and schedules are on www.voyages-sncf.com, or call © **36-35** or 00-33-8-92-35-35-35 from outside France. For a **minibus,** call Taxi Barrois (© **05-63-56-14-80**). The one-way fare is 5€ per person Monday through Saturday, rising to 8€ after 7pm and on Sunday. There's no regular bus service.

**VISITOR INFORMATION** The **Office de Tourisme** is at 8 place Jeanne Ramel-Cals (www.cordessurciel.fr; ⓒ **05-63-56-00-52;** fax 05-63-56-19-52).

# Exploring the Town

Often called "the city of a hundred Gothic arches," Cordes contains numerous *maisons gothiques* ★★ of pink sandstone. Many of the doors and windows are fashioned of pointed (broken) arches that retain their 13th- and 14th-century grace. Some of the best-preserved ones line **Grande Rue Raymond VII,** also called **rue Droite.**

**Eglise St-Michel** CHURCH The church, the most important historic building in town, dates from the late 13th century and has undergone many alterations. Most of the lateral design of the side chapels probably comes from the cathedral at Albi. Before being shipped here, the organ (dating from 1830) was in Notre-Dame in Paris.

Rue St-Michel. ⓒ **05-63-56-00-25** (tourist office). Free admission. Summer tours daily 10:30am–12:30pm and 3–6:30pm.

**Musée Charles Portal** MUSEUM Small, quirky, and relatively unvisited even by residents of Cordes, this somewhat sleepy museum is near a pass-through (Painted Gate) in the fortifications surrounding the city's medieval center. It's named after Charles Portal (d. 1936), a 1920s-era archivist of the Tarn region and a local historian. In a medieval house whose foundations date from the Gallo-Roman era, it contains artifacts of the textile industry, farming implements, samples of local embroidery, a reconstruction of an old peasant home, and a scattering of medieval pieces.

Porte des Ormeaux. ⓒ **05-63-53-44-41.** Admission 2.50€ adults, 1.50€ students and ages 12–25, free for children 11 and under. July–Aug Wed–Mon 2–6pm; Easter–June and Sept–Oct only Sat–Sun 2–5pm.

# Where to Eat & Stay

**Hostellerie du Parc** 🍴 TRADITIONAL FRENCH This inn originated in the 18th century as a landowner's thick-walled home. Today, in a verdant park, the stone house is a charming *restaurant avec chambres.* It serves generous meals in a garden or paneled dining room. Specialties include homemade foie gras, duckling, *poularde* (chicken) *occitaine,* rabbit with cabbage leaves, and confit of roasted rabbit with pink garlic from the nearby town of Lautrec.

The hotel offers 13 comfortable and well-furnished rooms; a double costs 65€ to 100€ including free Wi-Fi.

Les Cabannes. www.hostellerie-duparc.com. ⓒ **05-63-56-02-59.** Fax 05-63-56-18-03. Reservations recommended. Main courses 14€–32€; fixed-price menu 22€–45€. AE, DC, MC, V. June–Oct daily noon–2pm and 7–9:30pm; off season Fri–Sun noon–2pm, Fri–Sat 7–10pm. Closed 3 weeks in Jan. From the town center, take rte. de St-Antonin (D600) for about 1km (½ mile) west.

**L'Hostellerie du Vieux Cordes** ★★ MODERN FRENCH A warm mellow stone old building, this inn in the center of town has decent sized rooms, simply decorated. Some have the original stone walls and old beams; others are modern. Eat in the pretty restaurant, or in summer on the terrace or patio. Starters run from snails on a bed of ravioli and mushrooms to tart of *andouillette* with pig's trotters; mains might include rack of lamb in truffle crust or poached turbot with cream truffle risotto. It's all good honest fare.

21 rue St-Michel. www.vieuxcordes.fr. ☎ **05-63-53-79-20.** Fax 05-63-56-02-47. 19 units. 58€–132€ double; 128€–168€ suites. Main courses 14€; fixed-price menu 26€–36€. AE, MC, V. Wed–Sat noon–2pm and 7:30–9pm; Sun noon–2pm. Closed Christmas and Jan to mid-Feb.

# TOULOUSE ★★★

705km (437 miles) SW of Paris; 245km (152 miles) SE of Bordeaux; 97km (60 miles) W of Carcassonne

The old capital of the vast Languedoc region, and France's fourth-largest city, Toulouse (known as La Ville Rose) has a cosmopolitan flavor. The major city of the southwest in the Haute-Garonne *département* of the Midi-Pyrénées region and filled with gardens and squares, it's the gateway to the Pyrénées. Most of Toulouse's fine old mansions date from the Renaissance, when this was one of the richest cities in Europe. Today Toulouse is an artistic and cultural hub and a high-tech center, home to two huge aircraft makers—Airbus and Aerospatiale. Also making the city tick is its great number of students: some 89,000 out of a total population of 917,000.

A city with a distinguished past, Toulouse is also a city of the future. The National Center for Space Research has been headquartered here since 1968. The first regularly scheduled airline flights from France took off from the local airport in the 1920s. Today Airbus planes are assembled in a gargantuan hangar in the suburb of Colombiers.

## Essentials

**GETTING THERE**  The Toulouse-Blagnac international **airport** lies in the city's northwestern suburbs, 11km (6¾ miles) from the center; for flight information, go to www.toulouse.aeroport.fr, or call ☎ **00-33-1-70-46-74-74** from abroad or 08-25-38-00-00 in France. **Air France** (www.airfrance.fr; ☎ **09-69-39-02-15**) has about 25 flights a day from Paris and flies to Toulouse from London twice a day in high season.

Five TGV **trains** per day arrive from Paris Montparnasse (trip time: 5½ hr.; from 70€ one-way), 14 trains (TGV and local) from Bordeaux (trip time: 2 hr., 10 min.; from 24€ one-way), and 8 from Marseille (trip time: from 3 hr. 42 min.; from 44€ one-way). Train information and schedules are on www.voyages-sncf.com, or call ☎ **36-35** or 00-33-8-92-35-35-35 from outside France. The **drive** from Paris takes 6 to 7 hours. Take A10 south to Bordeaux, connecting to A62 to Toulouse. The Canal du Midi links many of the region's cities with Toulouse by waterway.

**VISITOR INFORMATION**  The **Office de Tourisme** is in the Donjon du Capitole in the square de Gaulle (www.toulouse-tourisme.com; ☎ **892/180-180** (0.34€/min.; fax 05-61-23-74-97).

## Exploring the City

In addition to the sights listed below, architectural highlights include the Gothic brick **Eglise des Jacobins ★★**, parvis des Jacobins (☎ **05-61-22-21-92**), in Old Toulouse, west of place du Capitole along rue Lakanal. The church and the restored convent, daring in its architecture and its use of palm tree–shaped vaults, form the largest extant monastery complex in France. Open daily 9am to

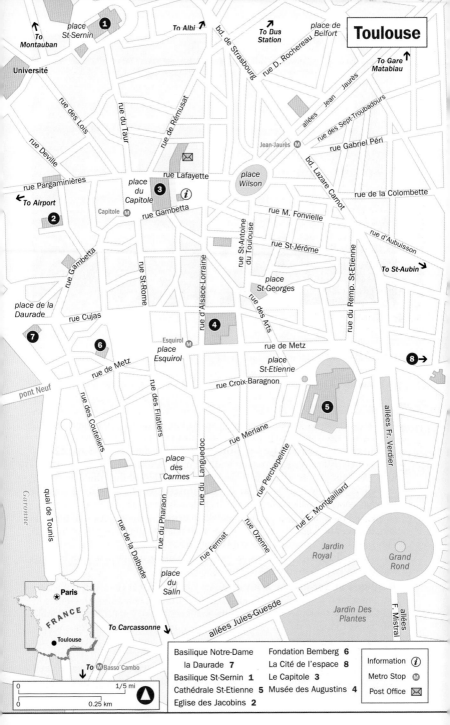

# Toulouse

| | |
|---|---|
| Basilique Notre-Dame la Daurade **7** | Fondation Bemberg **6** |
| Basilique St-Sernin **1** | La Cité de l'espace **8** |
| Cathédrale St-Etienne **5** | Le Capitole **3** |
| Eglise des Jacobins **2** | Musée des Augustins **4** |

| | |
|---|---|
| Information | *i* |
| Metro Stop | Ⓜ |
| Post Office | ✉ |

Le Capitole.

Basilique St-Sernin.

7pm, admission to the complex is free apart from the cloisters which cost 3€, free on first Sunday of the month and for 17 and under.

Small, charming, and dating mostly from the 18th century, **Notre-Dame de la Daurade,** 1 place de la Daurade (*C* **05-61-21-38-32**), gets its name from the gilding that covers its partially baroque exterior. Its prized possession is a statue of the Black Virgin, about 1m (3¼ ft.) tall. The one you'll see today was crafted in 1807 as a replacement for a much older statue burned during the French Revolution. Admission is free, and it is open daily 8:30am to 7pm (6:30pm in winter).

In civic architecture, **Le Capitole ★**, place du Capitole (*C* **05-61-22-34-12**), is an outstanding achievement and one of the most potent symbols of Toulouse. Built in a baroque style in 1753, it houses the **Hôtel de Ville** (City Hall), as well as the **Théâtre National du Capitole** (*C* **05-61-63-13-13**), which presents concerts, ballets, and operas. Its Italian-inspired 18th-century style uses shades of scarlet and gold. Admission, which usually includes a view of the theater, is free. The Capitole complex is open Monday through Saturday 8:30am to 7pm, and from 10am to 9pm on public holidays.

After all that sightseeing, head for **place Wilson,** a showcase 19th-century square (actually an oval) lined with fashionable cafes.

**Basilique St-Sernin ★★★** BASILICA   Consecrated in 1096, this is the largest, finest, and purest Romanesque church in Europe, containing the tombs of the Counts of Toulouse. Entering by the main west door, you can see the double side aisles that give the church five naves, an unusual feature in Romanesque architecture. An upper cloister forms a passageway around the interior. In the crypt (ask for permission to enter) are the relics of 128 saints, plus a thorn said to be from the Crown of Thorns. The old baroque retables (altarpieces) and shrine in the ambulatory have been reset; the relics here are those of the apostles and the first bishops of Toulouse.

13 place St-Sernin. www.basilique-st-sernin-toulouse.fr. 𝒸 **05-61-21-80-45.** Free admission to church; combined admission to the crypt and ambulatory 2€. Church June–Sept Mon–Sat 8:30am–7pm, Sun 8:30am–7:30pm; Oct–May Mon–Sat 8:30am–6pm, Sun 8:30am–7:30pm. Crypt and ambulatory June–Sept Mon–Sat 10am–6pm, Sun 11:30am–6pm; Oct–May Mon–Sat 10am–noon and 2–5:30pm, Sun 2–5:30pm.

**Cathédrale St-Etienne** ★ CATHEDRAL    Because it took so long to build (it was designed and constructed from the 13th–17th c.), this extraordinary cathedral is a fascinating mix of architectural styles. The rectangular bell tower is from the 16th century. A Gothic choir has been added to its unique ogival nave.

Place St-Etienne, at the eastern end of rue de Metz. 𝒸 **05-61-52-03-82.** Free admission. Mon–Sat 8am–7pm; Sun 9am–7pm.

**Fondation Bemberg** ★ MUSEUM    Opened in 1995, this quickly became one of the city's most important museums. Housed in the magnificent Hôtel Assézat (built in 1555), the museum provides an overview of 5 centuries of European art, showcasing world-class paintings from the Renaissance to the late 19th century. The nucleus of the collection represents the lifelong work of German-French collector *extraordinaire* Georges Bemberg, who donated 331 works. The largest bequest was 28 paintings by Pierre Bonnard, including his *Moulin Rouge.* Bemberg also donated works by Pissarro, Matisse *(Vue d'Antibes),* and Monet, plus the fauves. The foundation also owns Canaletto's much-reproduced *Vue de Mestre.* The mansion houses the **Académie des Jeux-Floraux,** which, since 1323, has presented literary awards in the form of wrought-metal flowers to poets.

Place d'Assézat, rue de Metz. www.fondation-bemberg.fr. 𝒸 **05-61-12-06-89.** Admission 6€ adults, 3.50€ students and children 8–18, free for children 7 and under. Tues–Wed and Fri–Sun 10am–12:30pm and 1:30–6pm; Thurs 10am–12:30pm and 1:30–9pm.

**La Cité de l'Espace** ★★ ☺ MUSEUM/PLANETARIUM    Some half a million visitors a year come to this hich-tech attraction to experience what it's like to program the launch of a satellite or how to maneuver one in space. You learn, for example, how easy it is to lose a satellite by putting on a burst of speed at the wrong point during a launch. The IMAX cinema and planetarium take you into space on spectacular journeys while the Gyro-extreme shows you what it's like to be a real astronaut grappling with navigating while your sense of direction is disturbed. In the grounds, you can walk through a replica of Russia's Mir space station. It's a great place for children with special play areas and their own planetarium, the Stellarium. Each year there's a major temporary exhibition on subjects such as extraterrestrials or Mars.

Av. Jean Gonord. www.cite-espace.com. 𝒸 **08-20-37-72-23.** Admission 20€–23€ adults, 17€ ages 5–15, free for children 4 and under. Feb, Mar, and Sept–Dec Tues–Fri 9:30am–5pm, Sat–Sun 9:30am–6pm; Apr–June Mon–Fri 9:30am–5pm, Sat–Sun 9:30am–6pm; July 1–15 9:30am–6pm, mid-July to Aug daily 9:30am–7pm. Closed Jan. Bus: 37 (Sat–Sun only). Follow N126 from the center of town to the E. Peripheral route and take exit 17.

**Musée des Augustins** ★★ MUSEUM    The museum was established here in 1793, shortly after the French Revolution, when revolutionaries closed what was one of the city's most important monasteries and adapted it for public use. In addition to the fabulous paintings, a stroll through this place gives you the chance to view a 14th-century monastery in all its mystical splendor. The original cloisters contain the world's largest and most valuable collection of Romanesque capitals. The sculptures and carvings are magnificent, and there are some fine examples of early Christian sarcophagi. On the upper floors the large, painting collection includes works by Toulouse-Lautrec, Gérard, Delacroix, Ingres, and others. The museum also contains several portraits by Antoine Rivalz, a local artist and major talent.

21 rue de Metz. www.augustins.org. ℂ **05-61-22-21-82.** Admission 3€, free for children 18 and under and first Sun of the month. Wed 10am–9pm; Thurs–Tues 10am–6pm. Closed public holidays.

## Shopping

Head for **rue d'Alsace-Lorraine,** which is rich in clothing and housewares. At the well-stocked shopping mall, the **Centre Commercial St-Georges,** rue du Rempart St-Etienne, you can fill your suitcases with all kinds of glittery loot. For upscale boutiques, head to **rue Croix-Baragnon, rue des Arts,** and **rue St-Antoine du T.** The pearly gates of antiques heaven are on **rue Fermat.** More down-market antiques spread out each Sunday 6am to 1pm during the weekly **flea market** by the Basilique St-Sernin. Also here is a *brocante* sale on the first weekend (Fri–Sun) of each month from 8am to 1pm. There's an organic farmers' market in place du Capitole on Saturday mornings and around Eglise St-Aubin on Sunday mornings.

Violets grow in abundance in meadows near Toulouse. Two shops that sell everything related to violets include **Violettes & Pastels,** 10 rue St-Pantaléon (ℂ **05-61-22-14-22**), and **La Maison de la Violette,** 4 bd. Bonrepos (ℂ **05-61-99-01-30**). Items include violet-scented perfume, and clothing—especially scarves—patterned with the dainty purple flower.

La Maison de la Violette.

## Where to Eat
### EXPENSIVE

**Chez Michel Sarran** ★★★ MODERN FRENCH   At the most stylish restaurant in Toulouse, you can enjoy the cuisine of master chef Michel Sarran. Sarran's wife, Françoise, oversees the main dining room, and the three private rooms, all decorated in a modern, smart style with colorful chairs and art on the walls, in a building in the heart of town near the Novotel Centre. The food brings out the flavors of southern and southwestern France. Start with a warm soup of foie gras and oysters. Move on to a succulent version of poached sea bass served with a creamy polenta lightly flavored with bok choy and caviar sauce; or perhaps a portion of roasted pigeon from the Bigorre region, served in a casserole with thyme and wine-roasted potatoes.

21 bd. Armand Duportal. www.michel-sarran.com. ℂ **05-61-12-32-32.** Reservations recommended. Main courses 40€–70€; fixed-price lunch 49€; menus 98€–150€. AE, DC, MC, V. Mon–Fri noon–1:45pm and 8–9:45pm (closed Wed for lunch). Closed Aug and 1 week around Christmas. Métro: Capitole.

**Les Jardins de l'Opéra ★★★** FRENCH   The entrance to the city's best restaurant is in the 18th-century Florentine courtyard of the Grand Hôtel de l'Opéra (p. 668). The dining area is a series of salons, several of which face a winter garden and the swimming pool. Here you can enjoy classic dishes reinterpreted by a master with a light modern touch. Seemingly simple sounding dishes, such as risotto with white truffle, cassoulet of lobster and foie gras, lamb braised in sweet spices with a couscous of vegetables, and bavette of beef cooked in pepper with an onion and apple comfit are masterly lessons in retaining the flavors and textures of the best ingredients.

In the Grand Hôtel de l'Opéra, 1 place du Capitole. www.lesjardinsdelopera.com. ✆ **05-61-23-07-76.** Reservations required. Main courses 25€–37€; fixed-price lunch 19€, menus 29€–99€. AE, DC, MC, V. Tues–Sat noon–2pm and 8–10pm. Métro: Capitole.

**Metropolitan ★★★** FRENCH   This bright modern restaurant, slightly outside the center, is a showcase for one of Toulouse's most celebrated chefs, Jeremy Morin. Trained at the Hotel Meurice in Paris, Morin offers sublime dishes that are not only creative, but prepared with well-chosen ingredients. Try his carpaccio of veal and caviar with little croquettes of veal and a shellfish and citrus vinaigrette, followed by roasted veal sweetbreads with truffles and Roman hazelnuts, or go for a gutsy tasting pork confit with pig's trotters and black pudding. The predominately orange dining room (not for traditionalists), contains a chic bar, and there's a small terrace draped with vines.

2 place Auguste Albert. www.metropolitan-restaurant.fr. ✆ **05-61-34-63-11.** Main courses 38€–54€; fixed-price lunch 23€–30€, dinner 45€–110€. AE, MC, V. Tues–Fri noon–2pm and Tues–Sat 8–10pm.

## MODERATE

**Le Bibent ★★★** MODERN FRENCH   In June 2011, starred chef Christian Constant took the reins at Le Bibent, a classic brasserie in a historic monument. Closed for two years for renovation, this legendary brasserie is gorgeous with its huge room, high ceiling, frescoed panels, gilding, blond wood floors and banquettes running around the outside. Looking more like a grand palace than a restaurant, it nonetheless swings along with a great buzz. Open seven days a week from 7am to 11:30pm, it's the place for breakfast, Caesar salad for lunch, and foie gras for dinner, as well as all the classic brasserie dishes. Or toy with an oyster; it's all there, right on the place du Capitole in the heart of Toulouse.

5 place du Capitole. www.maisonconstant.com. ✆ **05-61-23-89-03.** No reservations taken. Main courses 17€–26€; fixed-price breakfast 19€. MC, V. Daily 7am–11:30pm. Métro: Esquirol.

**Emile ★** TOULOUSIAN   This special restaurant is in an old-fashioned, red-brick house on one of Toulouse's most beautiful squares. In winter, meals are served upstairs overlooking the square; in summer, seating moves to the street-level dining room and flower-filled terrace. Menu choices include cassoulet Toulousian (cooked in goose fat), *magret* of duckling in traditional style, and a very fresh *parillade* (mixed grill) of fish with a pungently aromatic cold sauce of sweet peppers and olive oil. The wine list is filled with intriguing surprises.

13 place St-Georges. www.restaurant-emile.com. ✆ **05-61-21-05-56.** Reservations recommended. Main courses 20€–32€; fixed-price lunch 20€–55€, dinner 41€–55€. AE, DC, MC, V. Mid-May to Sept Tues–Sat noon–2pm, Mon–Sat 7–10:30pm; Oct to mid-May Tues–Sat noon–2pm and 7:30–10pm. Closed Dec 23–Jan 8. Métro: Capitole or Esquirol.

## INEXPENSIVE

**Le Bon Vivre** ★ SOUTHWESTERN FRENCH    One of downtown Toulouse's most appealing bistros occupies the street level of a historic 18th-century mansion right beside the Hôtel de Ville (Town Hall). Established in 2004, it provides cost-conscious dining. Menu items feature contemporary twists on time-tested French specialties, popular with locals who appreciate good value. The best examples include an unusual version of spaghetti sautéed with duck confit, and a version of cassoulet (the specialty of France's southwest) made with both duck and pork.

15 bis place Wilson. www.lebonvivre.com. ✆ **05-61-23-07-17.** Reservations recommended. Main courses 15€–36€; fixed-price menus 25.50€–39€. AE, DC, MC, V. Mon–Fri 11:30am–2:30pm and Sat–Sun 8am–11:30am and 11:30am–3pm; Sun–Tues 6:45–11:30pm; Wed–Sat 6:45pm–12:30am. Métro: Esquirol.

**Le Colombier** ★ TOULOUSIAN    Try this bastion of regional cookery, going strong since 1873. Alain Lacoste arguably serves the best cassoulet in Toulouse. His duck foie gras comes with figs and, of all things, gingerbread. Nearly all locals order the cassoulet; it's slow-cooked to perfection. The restaurant itself is a simple stone-and-brick dining room with paintings decorating the walls. Cut all this fat with the acidity of strawberry soup with lime sorbet. Or opt for the apple "croustade."

14 rue Bayard. www.restaurant-lecolombier.com. ✆ **05-61-62-40-05.** Reservations recommended. Main courses 19€–26€; fixed-price menus 18€–49€. MC, V. Tues–Fri noon–2pm and Mon–Sat 7:15–10pm. Métro: Jeanne d'Arc.

# Toulouse Nightlife

Toulouse's theater, dance, and opera are often on a par with those found in Paris. To stay on top of the arts scene, pick up a copy of the free monthly magazine produced by the municipality, *A Toulouse* from the Office de Tourisme.

## PERFORMING ARTS

The city's most notable theaters are **Théâtre du Capitole,** place du Capitole (www.theatre-du-capitole.fr; ✆ **05-61-63-13-13**), which specializes in operas, operettas, and works from the classical French repertoire; and **Halle aux Grains,** place Dupuy (✆ **05-61-63-13-13**). The home of the Orchestre du Capitole, Halle aux Grains is the venue for mostly classical concerts. **Théâtre Garonne,** 1 av. du Château d'Eau (www.theatregaronne.com; ✆ **05-62-48-56-56**), stages everything from works by Molière to current dramas. Another important venue is the **Zenith de Toulouse,** 11 av. Raymond-Badiou (✆ **05-62-74-49-49**), which has a large stage and seating capacity. It schedules rock concerts, variety acts, and musical comedies from other European cities. A smaller competitor, with a roughly equivalent mix of music, theater, and entertainment, is **Théâtre de la Cité,** 1 rue Pierre Baudis (www.tnt-cite.com; ✆ **05-34-45-05-05**).

## BARS & CLUBS

The liveliest squares to wander after dark are **place du Capitole, place St-Georges, place St-Pierre,** and **place Wilson.**

For bars and pubs, **La Tantina de Bourgos,** 27 rue de la Garonette (✆ **05-61-55-59-29**), has a Latin flair that's popular with students; and the rowdier **Chez Tonton,** 16 place St-Pierre (✆ **05-61-21-89-54**), has an *après-match* atmosphere, complete with the winning teams boozing it up. The busiest English-style pub in town, **Le Frog & Le Roast Beef,** 14 rue de l'Industrie (�C **05-61-99-28-57**), is woodsy and Celtic looking, and often very crowded with the city's English-speaking community. **La Pelouse Interdite,** 72 av. des Etats-Unis (℃ **05-61-47-30-40**), offers a charming restaurant and bar behind a simple, discreetly marked green door. The venue incorporates a garden, a restaurant, a bar, and lots of charm. **The I-Bar,** 3 rue Gabrielle-Peri (www. i-bar.fr; ℃ **05-61-62-08-07**), with restaurant, bar, and club lounge, is the smart place for tapas and cocktails before dancing to the music spun by energetic DJs.

**L'Ubu Club,** 16 rue Saint Rome (℃ **05-61-23-26-75**), right in the heart of town, is a series of cellars with a restaurant and a discotheque that starts the evening as a piano bar and notches up the beat later.

The oldest and most deeply entrenched gay bar in Toulouse is **Shanghai Express,** 12 rue de la Pomme (℃ **05-61-23-37-80**), a man's dance domain playing the latest in techno. Entrance is free, and it's open every night. **Le Beaucoup,** 9 place du Pont-Neuf (℃ **05-61-12-39-29**) opens Wednesday to Sunday at 10am, which makes this gay restaurant and bar popular for brunch. Music takes over in the evenings.

# Where to Stay

## EXPENSIVE

### Grand Hôtel de l'Opéra ★★★
This is the most elegant oasis in Toulouse, and the owners have won several awards for transforming a 17th-century convent into a sophisticated hotel. The public rooms contain early-19th-century antiques and Napoleonic-inspired tented canopies over the bars. Some of the spacious and stylish guest rooms have curving balconies overlooking formal squares, and all have high ceilings and modern amenities. The beds are elegant with tasteful fabrics and soft pillows. The hotel restaurant, Les Jardins de l'Opéra (p. 666), is the town's most prestigious, with the hotel's 1930's brasserie catering for traditionalists after dishes like huge seafood platters or lamb from the sweet-smelling pastures of the Pyrénées.

1 place du Capitole. www.grand-hotel-opera.com. ℃ **05-61-21-82-66.** Fax 05-61-23-41-04. 50 units. 220€–390€ double; 490€ suite. AE, DC, MC, V. Parking 17€. Métro: Capitole. **Amenities:** Restaurants; brasserie; bar; room service; sauna, Turkish hammam. *In room:* A/C, TV, hair dryer, minibar, free Wi-Fi.

## MODERATE

### Les Bains-Douches ★★
Small and intimate, Toulouse's best boutique hotel is the latest word in modernity. It is so sleek, it's almost self-consciously so, and its cocktail lounge has become a chic rendezvous spot. All the bedrooms are tasteful and stylish, the beds comfortable with fine linens, and the bathrooms reflect a designer's touch. A terrace opens up during the summer months.

4 and 4 bis rue du Point Guilheméry. www.hotel-bainsdouches.com. ℃ **05-62-72-52-52.** Fax 05-34-42-09-98. 22 units. 140€–210€ double; 280€–330€ suite. AE, MC, V. Parking 12€. **Amenities:** Breakfast room; room service. *In room:* A/C, TV, hair dryer, minibar, free Wi-Fi.

### Hôtel des Beaux-Arts ★
Just by the banks of the Garonne river in the center of town, this 18th-century building makes a charming hotel. Individually decorated guest rooms are smart with bold-colored fabrics and some overlook the riverside.

Ask for Number 432 for a small terrace and the best view. The restaurant looks like a Parisian brasserie and offers good traditional and regional cooking.

1 place du Pont-Neuf. www.hoteldesbeauxarts.com. (2) **05-34-45-40-60.** Fax 05-34-45-42-43. 19 units. 135€–195€ double; 215–255€ family room for 2 adults and up to 2 children. AE, MC, V. Parking nearby 18€. Métro: Esquirol. **Amenities:** Restaurant; bar. *In room:* A/C, TV, hair dryer, minibar, safe, free Wi-Fi.

## INEXPENSIVE

**Hotel de France ★**    In the heart of Toulouse, this hotel in a restored historic monument from 1890 stands near the landmark squares Wilson and Capitole. Restaurants, cafes, cinemas, markets, and shops lie just a few feet from the hotel's doorstep. The midsize bedrooms combine charm, convenience, and comfort, and each is tastefully decorated, with a travertine-tiled bathroom. Ask for one with a balcony. The facade may suggest the halcyon days of Belle Epoque, but the interior is modern and sophisticated.

5 rue Austerlitz. www.hotel-france-toulouse.com. (2) **05-61-21-88-24.** Fax 05-61-21-99-77. 63 units. 69€ double; 99€ quad. AE, MC, V. **Amenities:** Breakfast room; room service. *In room:* A/C, TV, free Wi-Fi.

# THE BASQUE COUNTRY

by Jane Anson

A land rich in folklore, the Basque Country extends to the Spanish border in southwest France. The Basque capital, Bayonne, and the resorts, Biarritz and St-Jean-de-Luz, are on the coast, while Pau and Lourdes are the gateway to the Pyrénées.

The vast Pyrénean region is a land of glaciers, summits, thermal baths, subterranean grottoes and caverns, winter-sports centers, and trout-filled mountain streams. **Pau** is a good base for excursions to the western Pyrénées.

# PAU ★★★

768km (476 miles) SW of Paris; 196km (122 miles) SW of Toulouse

High above the banks of the Gave de Pau River, Pau is the most cosmopolitan city in the western Pyrénées and the capital of the Pyrénées-Atlantiques *département* (ministate). It was once the capital of the Béarn region, the land of the kings of Navarre, the most famous and beloved of whom was Henri IV, who was born in Pau. The British discovered Pau in the early 19th century, launching such practices as fox hunting, a custom that lingers. Even if you're just passing through, follow boulevard des Pyrénées, an esplanade erected on Napoleon's orders, for a famous panoramic view.

## Essentials

**GETTING THERE**   **Pau-Uzein airport** is 12km (7½ miles) north of town; call ✆ 05-59-33-33-00 for flight information. There are good **train** connections from Biarritz (three direct per day, taking 1 hr. 40 min. and the same again via Bayonne); the one-way fare is 19€. For train information, call ✆ **36-35. Driving** to Pau is relatively easy because of the new A65 motoway, which opened in December 2010 and has dramatically speeded up access times from the north. From Paris, take A10 south to Bordeaux, the N230 ringroad around Bordeaux, the A62 Autoroute des Deux Mers, until joining the new A65 motorway, at Langon just south of Bordeaux, which runs all the way to Pau. Alternatively, from Toulouse, the smaller N117 runs to Pau.

**VISITOR INFORMATION**   The **Office de Tourisme** is on place Royale (www.tourismepau.com; ✆ **05-59-27-27-08;** fax 05-59-27-03-21).

**SPECIAL EVENTS**   In late May and early June, there's the **Grand Prix de Pau** (www.grandprixdepau.com; ✆ **01-42-59-73-40**), when race cars compete for speed records in what may remind you of a small-scale replica of the Grand Prix in Monaco.

## Exploring the City

The city center is 30m (98 ft.) up from the river and the railway station, and if you arrive by train, you'll have the pleasure of ascending in its historic **Funicular** from

PREVIOUS PAGE: **Cathedral and Basque houses in Bayonne, with people dressed for the July festival.**

The Basque Country

near the station to Place Royale. Restored in 2010 and more than a century old, it runs Monday to Saturday from 6:45am to 9:40pm and on Sundays from 1:30 to 8:50pm, and is free. Place Royale is in the center of the 2km-long (1¼-mile) **boulevard des Pyrénées,** a popular promenade since the 19th century for its views over palm-landscaped slopes to the distant mountains. At the eastern end is Parc Beaumont, where the **Palais Beaumont** (www.pau-congres.com; ✆ **05-59-11-20-00**), built as a casino and winter garden, now hosts concerts, theater performances, and exhibitions; and at the western end is the **Château de Pau ★,** 2 rue du Château (www.musee-chateau-pau.fr; ✆ **05-59-82-38-00**), dating from the 12th century and steeped in the Renaissance spirit of the bold Marguerite de Navarre, who wrote the bawdy novel *Heptaméron* at age 60. Inside are many souvenirs, including a crib made of a single tortoiseshell for Henri de

Navarre, who was born here, and a splendid array of Flemish and Gobelin tapestries. The great rectangular tower, **Tour de Gaston Phoebus,** is from the 14th century. The château is open for visits mid-June to mid-September daily 9:30am to 12:30pm and 1:30 to 6:45pm (last admission 5.45pm), and mid-September to mid-June daily 9:30 to 11:45am and 2 to 5pm. Guided tours (conducted in French and English) depart at 15-minute intervals during open hours. Admission is 6€ for adults, 4.50€ for students 18 to 25, and free for ages 17 and under.

The **Musée des Beaux-Arts** ★, 1 rue Mathieu-Lalanne (✆ **05-59-27-33-02**), displays a collection of European paintings, including Spanish, Flemish, Dutch, English, and French masters such as El Greco, Zur-

View in Pau.

barán, Degas, and Boudin. It's open Wednesday to Monday 10am to noon and 2 to 6pm. Admission is 4€ adults, 3.50€ students, and free for children 18 and under. Pau is also famous for its **Haras National** (National Stud), created by Napoléon, which is well worth a visit if you are equine minded. It's situated south of the Gave de Pau at 1 rue du Maréchal Leclerc (www.haras-nationaux. fr; ✆ **05-59-35-06-52**). Guided visits Monday to Friday are at 10am, 2pm, and 4pm in July and August; 2pm and 4pm in May, June, September, and October; and 2pm only November to April. Admission is 5€ for adults, 3€ for children 7 to 18, and free for ages 6 and under.

A little further out of town, heading towards the foothills of the Pyrénées, the **Zoo d'Asson** is an excellent place for children, with over 500 species of animals, kept in large, open spaces and carefully-maintained enclosures. Of particular interest is the kangaroo sanctuary, one of the biggest in Europe. In total, the zoo covers 5 hectares (12 acres), and is entered at 6 Chemin du Brouquet 64800 Asson (www.zoo-asson.org; ✆ **05-59-71-03-34**). It's open daily April to September 9am to 7pm, and the rest of year from 9am to 6pm. Admission is 11€ adults, 7€ children.

## Where to Eat

**Au Fin Gourmet** ★★ 🍴 BASQUE   This restaurant, in the Joantho gardens near the bottom of the funicular, is maintained by the sons of the retired founder, Clément Ithurriague. The postmodern, circular dining room opens onto a terrace for warm-weather dining. The cuisine is based on regional ingredients. Some of the best menu items include grilled scallops with fennel, preceded by an appetizer of foie gras with mushrooms. Rack of lamb with fresh herbs from the Pyrénées is an always-reliable choice.

24 av. Gaston-Lacoste. www.restaurant-aufingourmet.com. ✆ **05-59-27-47-71.** Reservations recommended. Main courses 22€–25€; fixed-price lunch 28€–76€, dinner 38€–74€. AE, DC, MC, V. Tues–Sun noon–2pm; Tues–Sat 7:30–9:30pm.

**Au Grain du Raisin** ★ FRENCH/WINE BAR    This cozy wine bar is tucked away into a side street in the historic center of Pau. You'll find live music most weekend evenings and regular art exhibitions, and there is a small choice of grazing plates to accompany your wine. These are mainly focused around charcuterie and cheese, but sometimes specials wander further afield—and larger meals can be organized on request. You'll find a warm and friendly welcome and an expectedly brilliant choice of wines from little-known southwest France regions, including Madiran, Jurançon, and Gaillac.

11 rue Sully, Quartier du Chateau. ✆ **05--59-82-98-44.** Tasting plates 15€ MC, V. Mon–Sat 6pm-1.30am.

**Chez Ruffet** ★★ BEARNAISE    The most famous restaurant in the region is on the southern outskirts of Pau, within an old-fashioned stone-built house with a slate roof and a bell tower. Many guests opt for the 64€ five-course menu, but guests in a group of four or more can opt for a 45€ menu where everyone eats the same thing. The choices change weekly, but examples of dishes served here include sea scallops that are first smoked, then grilled, and served with chicken-stuffed ravioli and a sweet pepper–and–mango sauce; braised sweetbreads with a butter-flavored cream sauce and vanilla-flavored brioches; and line-caught sea bass glazed with miso.

3 av. Charles Touzet, Jurançon. www.restaurant-chez-ruffet-64.com. ✆ **05-59-06-25-13.** Reservations required. Main courses 34€–42€; fixed-price lunch (Tues–Fri) 30€, dinner 45€, 64€ and 80€. AE, DC, MC, V. Tues–Sat noon–1.30pm and 7:30–9.30pm.

# Shopping

Pau's shopping streets don't quite live up to its surrounding scenery and its cultural attractions, but it does offer authentic regional specialties such as chocolates, sweet jams, and Basque antiques. The pedestrian **rue Serviez** and **rue des Cordeliers** harbor an array of boutiques and shops that carry these items, as do **rue Louis-Barthou** and **rue du Maréchal-Foch,** which are all around the central **place Georges Clemenceau.**

Pau is home to some of the best antiques shops in the region, such as **Antiquites Delan,** 4 rue Gassion (www.delanpatrick.com; ✆ **05-59-27-45-62**).

One of the best-known shops in Pau is **La Féerie Gourmande,** 48 rue du Maréchal Joffre (✆ **05-59-27-69-51**). The owner, M. Francis Miot, has been voted best jam and candy maker in France several times. If you're interested in seeing where his confections are made, head for the suburbs of Pau, about 1.5km (1 mile) southeast of the center, to the residential hamlet of Uzos. Here you'll find **Musée de la Confiture** (www.francis-miot.com; ✆ **05-59-35-05-56**), where exhibits display the history of jams from medieval times to the present, as well as offering numerous workshops and tastings detailing his techniques. It's open Monday to Saturday 10am to noon and 2 to 6pm; admission is 4.60€ adults and 3€ ages 3 to 12; closed in December. It has a special price of 3€ adults, 2€ ages 3 to 12 during Jul-Aug,

# Pau Nightlife

Nightlife in Pau has always centered on **Le Triangle,** an area in the town center that's flanked by the rue Emile Garet, rue Lespy, and rue Castetnau, although in recent years, it's been augmented with a few new bars along **boulevard des Pyrénées** near place Clemenceau.

Within the borders of Le Triangle, **Le Garage Bar,** at 47 rue Emile Garet (www.legaragebar.com; © **05-59-83-75-17**), has been going strong since 1993. Set within an old auto repair shop, it retains many of its original industrial-looking fixtures, plus a collection of antique traffic lights, road signs, and mopeds hanging from chains in the ceiling. It's open Monday to Friday noon to 1:30am, Saturday and Sunday 3pm to 1:30am.

The new live music venue **Show Case Time,** 8–10 rue d'Arribes (www. showcasetime.fr; © **05-59-06-94-62**), has a full program ranging from rocka-billy through salsa to jazz, blues, and indie. Entrance is usually free except on Fridays and Saturdays, when prices range from 5€ to 15€, depending on the band. Art is exposed on the walls of the lounge bar. It's open Tuesday to Saturday from 6pm to 2am.

## Where to Stay

**Best Western Hôtel Continental**   In a classic Haussmannian building with a rotunda (ask for a "rotunda" room to experience a room with no corners), the centrally located Continental is decorated with antiques and paintings. Many of the rooms are spacious. About 60 have midsize bathrooms with tub/showers; the rest have showers. Redecoration is being done room by room, and some look distinctly old-fashioned, so bear this in mind when booking.

2 rue du Maréchal-Foch, Pau 64000. www.hotel-continental-pau.com. © **05-59-27-69-31.** Fax 05-59-27-99-84. 75 units. 72€–100€ double. AE, DC, MC, V. Free parking. **Amenities:** Restaurant; room service. In room: TV, hair dryer, minibar, free Wi-Fi.

**Villa Navarre**   Very close to the center of Pau, this charming hotel is located in the middle of large gardens, and has a luxury feel. The spacious rooms are divided between the main Villa building and the Pavillon, converted from former stables, and there is also a pool and spa onsite. Views over the Pyrenees from all suites, and 12 of the largest bedrooms, while the rest have still-impressive views over the park, and are slightly less expensive. Another plus here is the restaurant, which has an extensive wine list.

59 avenue Trespoey, Pau 64000. www.villanavarre.fr. © **05-59-14-65-65.** Fax 05-59-14-65-64. 30 units. 189€–229€ double; 329€ suite. AE, DC, MC, V. **Amenities:** Bar; restaurant, swimming pool, spa. In room: A/C, TV, minibar, free Wi-Fi.

# BAYONNE ★★

770km (477 miles) SW of Paris; 184km (114 miles) SW of Bordeaux

Bayonne is the leading port and pleasure-yacht basin of the Côte Basque, divided by the Nive and Adour rivers. A cathedral city and the capital of the Pays Basque, it's characterized by narrow streets, quays, and ramparts. Enlivening the scene are bull-fights, *pelote* (jai alai), and street dancing at annual fiestas. You may want to buy some of Bayonne's famous chocolate at one of the arcaded shops along rue du Port-Neuf, and then enjoy coffee at a cafe along place de la Liberté, the hub of town.

## Essentials

**GETTING THERE**   Four TGV **trains** per day link Bayonne and Paris (trip time: 5 hr., 10 min.; 85€ one-way). Nine trains per day arrive from Bordeaux (trip time: 1 hr., 50 min.; 28€ one-way). For train information and schedules, call © **36-35.**

**Pont de Bayonne.**

There's a **bus** service from Biarritz, 15 minutes away. Bus no. 1 departs from Biarritz at 12-minute intervals throughout the daylight hours, depositing passengers on place de la Mairie in Bayonne; the one-way fare is 1€, and tickets can be bought on the bus. There's also bus service between Bayonne and outlying towns and villages not serviced by train. For bus information in Bayonne, call ℂ **05-59-59-04-61.**

Bayonne is near the end of the N117 roadway, easily accessible by **car** from Toulouse and other cities in the south of France. From Paris, take A10 south to Bordeaux, and then the N10 and A63 down the Atlantic coast towards Bayonne.

**VISITOR INFORMATION**    The **Office de Tourisme** is on place des Basques (www.bayonne-tourisme.com; ℂ **08-20-42-64-64;** fax 05-59-59-37-55).

**SPECIAL EVENTS**    During the 4-day **Fête de Bayonne,** the last week in July, a frenzy of outdoor concerts and dancing fills the streets. The celebration is intense. For **free concerts** on fair-weather Thursday evenings in July and August, head to the gazebo on place de Gaulle, where styles range from jazz to traditional Basque. Contact the Office de Tourisme (see above) for more information.

## Exploring the Town

**Vieux Bayonne,** the old town, is inside the ramparts, on the left bank of the Nive. The early-13th-century **Cathédrale Ste-Marie** (www.cathedrale-de-bayonne.fr.st; ℂ **05-59-59-17-82**) dominates this part of town on rue d'Espagne and rue des Gouverneurs. The spiny 19th-century steeples are the best-known landmarks in Bayonne. The cathedral is worth half an hour of your time and is a good retreat on a hot day. It was begun in 1258 when Bayonne was under English rule; it fell to the French in 1451. That explains the cathedral's ornamentation, mixing such elements as the English coat of arms (three lions) with the fleur-de-lis of France. Don't miss the gorgeous 14th-century cloisters. They're like a secret garden from the Middle Ages. The cathedral is open Monday through Saturday 7:30am to 12:30pm and 3 to 7pm, Sunday 7:30am to noon and 3:30 to 8pm.

**Atelier de Chocolat de Bayonne Andrieu** FACTORY TOUR    Bayonne's chocolate tradition began with the Jewish community that fled here from the Spanish Inquisition. Come to this industrial-looking neighborhood near the railway station for an insight into history and ingredients for one of the world's most sought-after confections, followed of course by a tasting.

7 allée de Gibéléou, Zone Artisanale Sainte-Croix. www.atelierduchocolat.fr. 🕾 **05-59-55-70-23.** Entrance 5.60€ adults, 2.80€ children 4–12. July–Aug Mon–Sat 9:30am–6:30pm; Sept–June Mon–Sat 9:30am–12:30pm and 2–6pm.

**Musée Basque ★★** MUSEUM    Bayonne's major museum showcases the traditions, architecture, and decorative arts (including textiles and furniture) of the Basques in a state-of-the-art format that's more advanced and sophisticated than any equivalent museum in the Basque-speaking world.

37 quai des Corsaires. www.musee-basque.com. 🕾 **05-59-59-08-98.** Admission 5.50€ adults, free for children and under 26s; free for all first Sun of each month. July–Aug Wed 10am–9:30pm, Thurs–Tues 10am–6:30pm; Sept–June Tues–Sun 10am–6pm.

**Plaine d'Ansot et Musée d'Histoire Naturelle ★★ ☺** MUSEUM    Just outside the city, this natural history "eco-museum" reopened its doors—on its new site, in a conservation area—after 60 years of closure. The only museum of its kind in France, located within a protected area of outstanding natural beauty, it offers, besides exhibits of local flora and fauna, walking and bike paths, as well as nature trails and bird watching stations. At the entrance, the Maison Barthe has information on activities, as well as temporary exhibits, and a traditional Natural History museum forms a separate building. The rest of the sights are laid out around the lakes, open spaces, and rivers of the 220-acre park itself.

Plaine d'Ansot, 64100 Bayonne. www.ansot.bayonne.fr. 🕾 **05-59-42-22-61.** Free admission. Maison Barthe mid-Apr to mid-Oct Tues to Sun 10.30am to 6pm, rest of year 1:30 to 5pm, Museum Tues–Sun 10:30am–6pm (Thurs during term time for school groups only), rest of park 9:30am to 7pm. Closed May 1, 1 week Christmas, 1 week Jan, 1 week Fête de Bayonne.

# Shopping

Most of Bayonne's specialty shops and boutiques lie inside the ramparts of the old town, Grand Bayonne. The pedestrian streets of **rue Port Neuf** (aptly nicknamed the "street of chocolate shops"), **rue Victor-Hugo,** and **rue de la Salie** are major shopping destinations. For antiques, walk along the **rue des Faures** and the edges of **place Montaut,** behind the cathedral. Most of the modern shops and French chain stores are on **rue Thiers** and **quai de la Nive,** outside the old town. Visit **Maison Jean Vier** shop, carrefour Cinq Cantons (www.jean-vier.com; 🕾 **05-59-59-16-18**), to get your Basque bathroom, kitchen, and bed linens. **Cazenave,** 19 rue Port Neuf (www.chocolats-bayonne-cazenave.fr; 🕾 **05-59-59-03-16**), specializes in *chocolats de Bayonne,* which include rich, dark, strong chocolate nougats; stop in the tearoom here for warm chocolate mousse.

The accessories of one Basque tradition have become something of a fine art. In olden days, the *makhila* was used as a walking stick, a cudgel, or—when equipped with a hidden blade—a knife. Today carved *makhilas* are sold as collectors' items and souvenirs. For safety's sake, they almost never come with a blade.

One of the best outlets in town is **Makhilas-Leoncini,** 37 rue Vieille Boucherie (℃ **05-59-59-18-20**). Another famous product of the Basque country is *jambon de Bayonne,* its cured hams, which taste best shaved into paper-thin slices and consumed with one of the region's heady red wines. An establishment that prepares and sells these hams is **Saloir et Séchoire à Jambon Pierre Ibaialde,** 41 rue des Cordeliers (www.pierre-ibaialde.com; ℃ **05-59-25-65-30**), where the hams are sold either whole or in thin slices. Also available is an impressive roster of sausages, pâtés, and terrines.

## Where to Eat

**Auberge du Cheval Blanc ★★** BASQUE    The finest restaurant in Bayonne occupies a half-timbered Basque-style house built in 1715 in the heart of the historic center. Menu items vary with the season but may include slices of foie gras with caramelized endive and pine nuts, ravioli stuffed with wild boar and flavored with local red wine and confit of baby onions, and corn blinis with flap mushrooms. Dorado may be simmered in garlic and served with *crépinette de marmitako* (diced tuna with red and green peppers, bound in a pig's stomach). One of the best desserts is a Grand Marnier soufflé.

68 rue Bourgneuf. www.cheval-blanc-bayonne.com. ℃ **05-59-59-01-33.** Reservations recommended. Main courses 18€–35€; fixed-price menu 25€–82€. AE, MC, V. Tues–Fri and Sun noon–1:30pm; Tues–Sat 7:45–9:30pm. Closed Feb.

**La Cidrerie TTiPia ★ 🍴** BASQUE    This restaurant has become famous throughout Bayonne for its resuscitation of the cider-making traditions of the Basque country. Owned and managed by an amiable Basque nationalist known simply as Isabelle, it serves two brands of (mildly alcoholic) cider and a very limited array of old-fashioned Basque food. This is configured into a "one choice fits all" set-price menu whose four courses include omelets with morels, grilled steaks, and a slab of local goat's cheese with walnuts. This place gets boisterous and gregarious, with sports fans sometimes singing over their cups after important matches.

27 rue des Cordeliers. http://ttipia.364.fr. ℃ **05-59-46-13-31.** Set-price menu 29€. MC, V. Tues–Sun noon–2pm; Mon–Sat 8–11pm; Fri–Sat 8pm-12am.

## Bayonne Nightlife

Nightlife centers on the neighborhood known as Petit Bayonne, the town's historic core. **Rue des Tonneliers, rue Pannecau,** and **rue des Cordeliers** are the liveliest areas after dark. Le Caveau des Augustin, 7 rue des Augustins, is a good choice for live music and jam sessions, and its vaulted stone cellars allow excellent acoustics (www.lecaveaudesaugustins.com; ℃ **05-59-25-69-76**). Good choice of tapas and wine also. For an equally interesting taste of local color, with slightly more traditional music, head to **Le Cabaret La Luna Negra,** also on rue des Augustins (www.lunanegra.fr; ℃ **05-59-25-78-05**). The 6€-to-10€ cover charge includes cabaret, jazz, or blues performances and popular French songs.

## Where to Stay

**Best Western Grand Hôtel ★**    The best chain hotel in town was originally built in 1835 on the ruins of a medieval Carmelite convent. Rooms were recently refurbished in a comfortable, contemporary style with quality beds. Each midsize bathroom has a tub and shower. There is an English club–style bar, and breakfast is served in a pleasant vaulted courtyard covered by a glass roof.

21 rue Thiers. www.bw-legrandhotel.com. © **800/528-1234** in the U.S. and Canada, or 05-59-59-62-00. Fax 05-59-59-62-01. 54 units. 140€–170€ double. AE, DC, MC, V. Parking 13€. **Amenities:** Restaurant (breakfast only); bar; room service. *In room:* A/C, TV, hair dryer, minibar, free Wi-Fi.

**La Villa Bayonne** ★★   If you can manage to get a room here, you'll enjoy a dreamy setting and the owners' personal touch. On a hill overlooking the River Nive, 900m (½ mile) from the town center, this lovely 1905 villa, surrounded by an Italianate garden, offers a peaceful stay. The rooms, either ground floor or in the eaves, are exquisitely decorated in mauve, gray, and gold, and the reception rooms make it feel like your own splendid home.

12 Chemin de Jacquette. www.bayonne-hotel-lavilla.com. © **05-59-03-01-20.** 10 units. 90€–150€ double. AE, MC, V. Free parking. *In room:* A/C, TV, free Wi-Fi.

# BIARRITZ ★★★

779km (483 miles) SW of Paris; 193km (120 miles) SW of Bordeaux

One of the most famous seaside resorts in the world, Biarritz was once a fishing village. Empress Eugénie and her husband, Napoleon III, put it on the map and started a constant stream of royal visitors. In the 1930s, the Prince of Wales (before and after his brief reign as Edward VIII) and Wallis Simpson did much to make Biarritz more fashionable as they headed south with these instructions: "Chill the champagne, pack the pearls, and tune up the Bugatti." Although those legendary days are long gone, the resort is still fashionable and has become the surfing capital of France, with plenty of surf shops, snack bars, and even some reasonably-priced hotels.

## Essentials

**GETTING THERE**   More than twenty **trains** arrive daily from Bayonne (trip time: 10 min.), which has rail links with Paris and other cities in the south of France. The one-way fare is 2.60€. The rail station is 3km (1¾ miles) south of the town center, in La Négresse. For information, call © **36-35.** Bus no. 2 carries passengers from the station to the center of Biarritz; the one-way fare is 1€. You can also take a cab for around 15€ to 20€. If you're **driving,** Biarritz is at the end of the N117 roadway, the major thoroughfare for the Basque country. From Paris, take A10 south to Vierzon, and then N20 south to Limoges. Continue on N21 south to Tarbes, and then head west on N117.

**VISITOR INFORMATION**   The **Office de Tourisme** is on square d'Ixelles (www.biarritz.fr; © **05-59-22-37-00;** fax 05-59-24-14-19).

**SPECIAL EVENTS**   If you're in town in mid-September, check out the modern dance and ballet performances during the 9-day festival **Le Temps d'Aimer** (www.letempsdaimer.com). Tickets cost 102€ for admission to six performances, with reduced rates for children, students, and families. For reservations and ticket sales for the festival, contact the tourist office above. At the end of September, the **Festival Biarritz Amérique Latine** (www.festivaldebiarritz.com) is the most important Latin American film festival in the world. It's much more laid-back than Cannes—you'll find yourself rubbing shoulders or even salsaing with top Latin directors in the casino complex, where most events are held. Entry to the whole week's films is 55€, and single-film entry is 6€.

Biarritz is the surfing capital of France, and each year dozens of competitions are held through the summer months. One of the most recent, started in mid-July 2011, is the 5-day **Roxy Jam,** an event known as the **Women's International Festival of Long Board Surfing.** It's centered on the waves offshore from La Plage de la Côte Basque. For more information, contact the tourist office. Biarritz also has 10 golf courses within a short drive of the town. A good practice setting is the **Center d'Entraînement d'Ilbarritz-Bidart,** avenue du Chateau, Bidart 64210 (www.golfilbarritz.com; ✆ **05-59-43-81-30**); you can play 9 holes for 23€ to 36€. The **Biarritz Cup** is a nationwide competition attended by mostly French golfers in the third week in July at the Golf du Phare, avenue Edith-Cavell (www.biarritz-cup.com; ✆ **05-59-03-71-80**). Information on both festivals is available from the tourist office.

## A Day at the Beach

Along the seafront facing the Casino is the **Grande Plage.** During the Belle Epoque, this was where Victorian ladies promenaded under parasols and wide-brimmed veiled hats. Today's bathers are more likely to be in wetsuits or surfy combos.

**Promenade du Bord de Mer,** along the coast within the city limits, is still a major attraction. The paths are often carved into cliffs, and sections have been designed as rock gardens with flowers, turning the area into a public park. From here, you can head north to **Pointe St-Martin,** where you'll find more gardens and a staircase (look for the sign DESCENTE DE L'OCEAN) leading you to allée Winston-Churchill, a paved path going along **Plage Miramar.**

**La Perspective de la Côte des Basques,** a walk that goes up to another plateau, leads to one of the wildest beaches in France: **Plage de la Côte des Basques,** with breakers crashing at the base of the cliffs. This is where serious surfers head.

If you like your beaches calmer, the safest beach is the small, horseshoe-shaped **Plage du Port-Vieux,** along the path from plateau de l'Atalaye. Its tranquil waters, protected by rocks, make it a favorite with families.

## Exploring the Town

**Eglise St-Martin,** rue St-Martin (✆ **05-59-23-05-19**), is one of the few vestiges of the port's early boom days. In the 12th century, Biarritz grew prosperous as a whaling center. The mammals' departure from the Bay of Biscay marked a decline in the port's fortunes. The church dates from the 1100s and was restored in 1541 with a flamboyant Gothic chancel. It's in the town center between two of Biarritz's major arteries, rue d'Espagne and avenue de Gramont, and is open daily 8am to 7pm. Admission is free.

Biarritz's turning point came with the arrival of Queen Hortense, who spent lazy summers here with her two daughters. One of them, Eugénie, married Napoleon III in 1853 and prevailed on him to visit Biarritz the next year. The emperor fell under its spell and ordered the construction of the **Hôtel du Palais** (p. 683). The hotel remains the town's most enduring landmarks. When Biarritz's star started to wane in the 1950s, the municipality showed a great deal of foresight in buying the hotel and the equally monumental casino, the essence of Biarritz's fading glamour. In a commanding spot on Grande Plage, the hotel is worth a visit even if you're not a guest. You can view the palatial trappings of its public rooms.

Across from the Hôtel du Palais, the **Eglise Orthodoxe Russe,** 8 av. de l'Impératrice (✆ **05-59-24-16-74**), was built in 1892 so that wintering Russian aristocrats could worship when they weren't enjoying champagne, caviar, and Basque prostitutes. It's noted for its gilded dome, the interior of which is the color of a blue sky on a sunny day. It can be visited only on weekends: Saturday 3 to 6pm and Sunday 4 to 7pm. After you pass the Hôtel du Palais, the walkway widens into **quai de la Grande Plage,** Biarritz's principal promenade. This walkway continues to the opposite end of the resort, where a final belvedere opens onto the southernmost stretch of beach. This whole walk takes about 3 hours. At the southern edge of Grande Plage, steps will take you to **place Ste-Eugénie,** Biarritz's most gracious old square. Right below place Ste-Eugénie is the colorful **Port des Pêcheurs** (fishers' port). Crowded with fishing boats, it has old wooden houses and shacks backed up against a cliff, along with small harborfront restaurants and cafes.

The rocky **plateau de l'Atalaye** forms one side of the Port des Pêcheurs. Carved on orders of Napoleon III, a tunnel leads from the plateau to an esplanade. Here a footbridge stretches over the sea to a rocky islet that takes its name, **Rocher de la Vierge (Rock of the Virgin),** from the statue crowning it. Alexandre-Gustave Eiffel (designer of the tower) directed construction of the footbridge. The walk out onto the edge of the rock, with crashing surf on both sides, is the most dramatic in Biarritz. You can see all the way to the mountains of the Spanish Basque country, far to the south.

Here you can visit the **Musée de la Mer,** 14 plateau de l'Atalaye (www. museedelamer.com; ✆ **05-59-22-33-34**), which houses 24 aquariums of fish native to the bay, and has been recently given a facelift, and doubled its aquarium space from 3,500-square meters to 7,000-square meters. The seals steal the show at their daily 10:30am and 5pm feedings. The museum also houses sharks that are fed on Tuesday and Friday at 11am and Wednesday and Sunday at 4:30pm. Admission is 13€ adults, 9.50€ students and children 4 to 16, and free for children 3 and under. It's open in July and August daily 9:30am to midnight, April to June and September-October daily 9:30am to 8pm, and November to March 9:30am-7pm.

## Shopping

The major boutiques, with all the big designer names from Paris, are on **place Clemenceau** in the heart of Biarritz. From this square, fan out to **rue Gambetta, rue Mazagran, avenue Victor-Hugo, avenue Edouard-VII, avenue du Maréchal-Foch,** and **avenue de Verdun.** Look for the exceptional Biarritz chocolates and confections, and textiles from the Basque country.

The finest chocolatiers are **Pariès,** 1 place Bellevue (www.paries.fr; ✆ **05-59-22-07-52**), where you can choose from seven kinds of *tourons* (nougats), ranging from raspberry to coffee; and **Henriet,** place Clemenceau (www. chocolaterie-henriet.com; ✆ **05-59-24-24-15**), where the house specialty is *rochers de Biarritz* (morsels of candied orange peel and roasted almonds covered in dark chocolate). At the other end of the gastronomic spectrum, try **Mille et**

**Un Fromages,** 8 rue Victor Hugo (www.milleetunfromages.com; ✆ **05-59-24-67-88**), specializing in, as the name suggests, French cheeses, as well as a host of hearty wines to accompany them.

Virtually every souvenir shop and department store in the region sells **espadrilles,** the canvas-topped, rope-bottomed slippers which originate from the Pyrénées. A simple off-the-shelf model begins at around 15€, and made-to-order versions (special sizes and colors) rarely top 70€.

## Where to Eat

The restaurant at **Château de Brindos** (see "Where to Eat & Stay Nearby," p. 683) also serves excellent Franco-Basque cuisine.

**Clos Basque** ★★ BASQUE/FRENCH The best regional specialties are showcased here in this Basque kitchen known for its savory offerings from both the land and sea nearby. The creative cuisine varies with the season, the availability of ingredients, and the chef's inspiration on any given day. One of the best fish dishes is a local Atlantic whitefish known as maigre. Their codfish platter with chorizo and artichokes reflects inspiration from neighboring Spain.

12 rue Louis Barthou. ✆ **05-59-24-24-96.** Reservations recommended as far in advance in summer as possible. Main courses 15€ each; fixed-price menu 25€. MC, V. Tues–Sun noon–1:30pm and Tues–Sat 8–9:30pm. Closed 1 week June, 1 week Oct, 3 weeks Feb.

**Negresse & Co.** ★ 🍴 BASQUE/FRENCH This restaurant takes its name from a 19th-century slave who escaped from an American plantation by hiding in the bottom of a French ship returning home. She established an inn in Biarritz, which was used by Napoleon's army en route to Spain. Inside, the decor is somber and dignified, opening onto a summer terrace. At lunch, typical brasserie food is served. At dinner, the menu is more gastronomic. Menus change every month for the relatively young and fashionable crowd that flocks here.

44 rue Luis Mariano. www.negresseco.com. ✆ **05-59-41-28-51.** Reservations required. Lunch main courses 15€–18€; dinner main courses 20€; fixed-price lunch 13€, dinner 35€. AE, DC, MC, V. Mon–Fri noon–2:30pm and Tues–Sat 7–9:30pm.

## Biarritz Nightlife

Start the night with a stroll around **Port des Pêcheurs,** an ideal spot for people-watching, with its sport fishermen, restaurants, and fascinating crowds.

Fortunes have been made and lost at **Le Casino Municipal,** 1 av. Edouard-VII (✆ **05-59-22-77-77**), where you can easily catch gambling fever. The less formal section, containing only slot machines, is open daily 10am to 3am (until 4am Sat). Entrance is free, no ID is required, and there's no dress code. The more elegant section (for *les jeux de table,* or table games) is open Sunday to Thursday 8pm to 3am, Friday and Saturday 8pm to 4am. This section requires a passport or photo ID. "Correct" dress for this section means no shorts or sloppy attire—jackets for men aren't required.

The hippest nightclub in town is **Le Copa,** 24 av. Edouard-VII (✆ **05-59-22-29-43**), which plays Latin (particularly Cuban) salsa, and virtually every other kind of dance music. **Ibiza,** 1 rue Poste (✆ **05-59-22-33-10**), concentrates on salsa, rock, and pop music; is right by the main beach; and has good views over the ocean. Equally appealing is **Disco Le Caveau,** 4 rue Gambetta (✆ **05-59-24-16-17**), where a well-dressed and attractive crowd of gay and straight people mingle. **Le Carré Coast,** 21 av. Edouard VII (www.lecarrecoast. com; © **05-59-24-64-64**), is open nightly between 7:30pm and 4am June and September, but closed Sunday to Wednesday the rest of the year. It combines a view of the sea, an outdoor terrace, a minimalist decor with lots of burnished steel, and a dance floor. Entrance is free, but a whiskey with soda begins at around 10€.

## Where to Stay

**Hôtel Atalaye** ◆  For economy with a bit of style, head to this simple govern-ment-rated two-star lodging. In the heart of town on a tranquil spot overlooking the ocean, this early-20th-century hotel gets rather sleepy in winter. Rooms are well maintained and traditionally furnished; most of the small, tiled bathrooms have showers. Breakfast is provided anytime you request it. The location is right off place Ste-Eugénie near the beaches, lighthouse, and casino.

6 rue des Goelands, Plateau de L'Atalaye, Biarritz 64200. www.hotelatalaye.com. © **05-59-24-06-76.** Fax 05-59-22-33-51. 24 units. 47€–92€ double; 67€–119€ triple. MC, V. Closed mid-Nov to mid-Dec (and last week of Jan). *In room:* A/C, TV.

**Hôtel du Palais** ★★★ ☺  There is no finer hotel along the Basque coast than this one. The Hôtel du Palais has been the grand playground for the inter-national elite for over a century and has truly come into vogue again after opening its Spa Impérial in 2006. Of course, the hotel has elaborately furnished suites, but even the double rooms have period furniture and silk draperies, plus spacious private bathrooms. Try to get a room facing west, to enjoy the sunsets over the Basque coast.

1 av. de l'Impératrice, Biarritz 64200. www.hotel-du-palais.com. © **800/223-6800** in the U.S. and Canada, or 05-59-41-64-00. Fax 05-59-41-67-99. 153 units. 325€–650€ double; 750€–1,900€ suite. AE, DC, MC, V. **Amenities:** 3 restaurants; bar; children's program and playground; exer-cise room; indoor pool and outdoor seawater pool; room service; sauna; spa. *In room:* A/C, TV, hair dryer, minibar, free Wi-Fi.

**Hotel de Silhouette** ★★  By all means enjoy the spas and thalassotherapy centers at the main Biarritz hotels, but for a more intimate hotel experience, try this understated but luxurious place, in the city's Les Halles district. Located in a 17th century building once owned by Louis XV's finance minister, Etienne de Silhouette, a full restoration has turned it into a glamorous hotel. Spacious rooms have good-quality beds, each one individually designed in a range of warm colors. The hotel has a lovely terrace for eating breakfast outside, a large garden, and a good restaurant offering seafood and regional specialties.

30 rue Gambetta, Quartier des Halles. www.hotel-silhouette-biarritz.com. © **05-59-24-93-82.** 20 units. 119€–340€ double. AE, DC, MC, V. Parking 15€ **Amenities:** Restaurant; bar room ser-vice. *In room:* A/C, TV, hair dryer, minibar, MP3 player, free Wi-Fi.

## Where to Eat & Stay Nearby

**Château de Brindos** ★★ 🎒  This is one of the most architecturally and cul-turally unusual homes in the southwest of France, with a history entrenched in the Jazz Age. Built by an American heiress in 1920, it occupies 11 hectares (27 acres) of inland park and garden. With a facade inspired by the architecture of Spain, and an interior loaded with architectural remnants such as fireplaces and staircases from the Gothic age, this is the most romantic stopover on the Côte

Basque. All rooms have a balcony or a terrace. The nearby village of Anglet is a good spot for surfing.

1 allée du Château, Anglet 64600. www.chateaudebrindos.com. ☏ **05-59-23-89-80.** Fax 05-59-23-89-81. 29 units. 220€–335€ double; 250€–600€ suite. AE, DC, MC, V. From town center, follow aeroport signs; after the 2nd roundabout *(rond-point),* follow signs to château; it's about 2.5km (1½ miles) north of Biarritz. Closed last 2 weeks of Feb. **Amenities:** Restaurant; bar; exercise room; heated outdoor pool; room service; sauna. *In room:* A/C, TV, hair dryer, minibar, free Wi-Fi.

# ST-JEAN-DE-LUZ ★★

791km (490 miles) SW of Paris; 15km (9¼ miles) S of Biarritz

This tuna-fishing port and beach resort is ideal for a seaside vacation. St-Jean-de-Luz lies at the mouth of the Nivelle, opening onto the Bay of Biscay, with the Pyrénées in the background. Tourists have been flocking here since the 1920s, when H. G. Wells, Aldous Huxley, and friends "discovered" the town.

## Essentials

**GETTING THERE**    25 **trains** per day arrive from Biarritz (trip time: 11 min.; from 3.10€ one-way), and seven trains per day arrive from Paris (trip time: 5 hr 40 min.; from 62€ one-way). For train information and schedules, call ☏ **36-35. Buses** pulling into town from other parts of the Basque country arrive at the Gare Routière (☏ **05-59-26-06-99**), in front of the railway station. St-Jean-de-Luz is a short **drive** from Biarritz along N10 south.

**VISITOR INFORMATION**    The **Office de Tourisme** is on 20 bd. Victor Hugo (www.saint-jean-de-luz.com; ☏ **05-59-26-03-16;** fax 05-59-26-21-47).

**SPECIAL EVENTS**    In July and August on Wednesday after 10:30pm and Sunday after 10:30pm, people pile into place Louis-XIV to take part in **Toro de Fuego,** a celebration of the bull. Revelers take to the streets to dance and watch fireworks. The highlight of the festivities is a snorting papier-mâché bull carried around place Louis-XIV. During the second half of June, the city celebrates the **Festival of St-Jean** *(Fêtes Patronales de la Saint Jean)* with concerts and a series of food kiosks along the harborfront. For 4 days during the first half of October, a small film festival, **Festival International des Jeunes Réalisateurs** (www.jeunes-realisaeurs.com; ☏ **05-59-51-65-30**), showcases the work of filmmakers from southwestern France. For information about festivals, contact the Office de Tourisme (see above).

## Fun on & off the Beach

The major draw here is the gracefully curving stretch of the white-sand **La Grande Plage St-Jean-de-Luz;** it's one of the best beaches in France and, consequently, very crowded in July and August. The beach lies in a half-moon-shaped bay between the ocean and the source of the Nivelle River. St-Jean-de-Luz is also a **working port,** where garishly painted fishing boats jut right up to the shopping streets. Eating seafood recently plucked from the sea is one of the reasons to visit, especially when Basque chefs transform the big catch into intriguing platters. This port's many narrow streets flanked by old houses are great for strolling. For one of the best views, climb up to the top of the **Colline**

**Grand Plage St-Jean-de-Luz.**

de Saint-Barbe, a large hill at one end of the waterfront. It has a walking path and lovely views over the city.

## Exploring the Town

In the town's principal church, the 13th-century **Eglise St-Jean-Baptiste ★★**, at the corner of rue Gambetta and rue Garat (*©* **05-59-26-08-81**), Louis XIV and the Spanish Infanta, Marie-Thérèse, were married in 1660. The interior is among the handsomest of all Basque churches. Surmounting the altar is a statue-studded gilded *retable* (altarpiece). The interior is open to visitors Monday to Saturday 9am to noon and 2 to 6pm, and Sunday 3 to 6:30pm.

Two houses are associated with the couple. **La Maison Louis XIV,** place Louis XIV (*©* **05-59-26-01-56**), was the scene of the royal wedding night. Built of chiseled gray stone between 1644 and 1648 beside the port, it is richly furnished with antiques and mementos. It's open daily for guided tours in July and August at 10:30am and 12:30, 2:30, and 6:30pm; and from April to June and September to October at 3, 4, and 5pm. Entrance is 5.30€. **La Maison de l'Infante,** 1 rue de l'Infante (*©* **05-59-26-36-82**), is where the Infanta lived at the time of her marriage. It was designed and built by wealthy weapons merchant Johannot de Haraneder. Its pink façade, made from bricks and local stones, evokes an Italian palazzo. Inside is a "grand" reception room with a 17th-century fireplace and ceiling beams richly adorned and painted. It is open from June to October 15, and October 25 to November 11, Tuesday to Saturday from 11am to 12:30pm and 2:30 to 6:30pm, and Sunday and Monday from 2:30 to 6:30pm. Entrance is 2.50€.

## Where to Eat

You may also like to check out Le Rosewood at the **Grand Hôtel Loreamar** (see p. 686).

**Auberge Kaïku ★** BASQUE/FRENCH   On a narrow street off place Louis-XIV, Auberge Kaïku is the best restaurant in town outside the hotels. The structure, with hand-hewn beams and chiseled masonry, dates from 1540 and is said to be the oldest in town. Examples of the cuisine are roast suckling Pyrénéan lamb, John Dory with fresh mint, filet of beef with essence of truffles, and duckling in honey.

17 rue de la République. *©* **05-59-26-13-20.** Reservations recommended. Main courses 20€–25€; fixed-price lunch 25€, dinner 32€. MC, V. July–Aug daily 12:15–2pm and 7:30–10pm; Sept–June Thurs–Mon 12:15–2pm and 7–10pm.

**Chez Kako** BASQUE   "Kako who?" you might ask. He's Jean-Claude Ascery (which translates from the Basque as "fox"), whose childhood nickname, Kako, is known to virtually every longtime resident of St-Jean-de-Luz. You'll find his rustic, artfully old-fashioned bodega within Les Halles, point of sale for the town's freshest meats and produce. Come here for beefsteaks prepared for two diners at a time, tapas, fresh fish—especially hake—and slices of aromatic goat cheese from local farmsteads. There's a full list of French and Spanish wines, but many diners here prefer bottles of the moderately alcoholic local cider instead.

18 rue du Maréchal Harispe at the place des Halles. www.restaurant-kako-saintjeandeluz.com. ✆ **05-59-85-10-70.** Reservations recommended. Main courses 15€–20€; set-price menu 43€. AE, MC, V. Tues–Sat noon–2:30pm and 7:30–10pm (till 11pm Fri–Sat). Open Mon in summer.

**Chez Pablo** ✔ BASQUE   Housed in a traditional red-and-white Basque building, this relaxed restaurant offers fantastic value. Expect plentiful servings of regional specialties, from fish soup and Basque omelette, to freshly-caught local river fish And the Gateau Basque is pretty hard to beat. Wine list concentrates on Rioja and the Navarre.

5 rue Mlle Etcheto ✆ **05-59-26-37-81.** Reservations recommended. Main courses from 9€; fixed-price menu 13€–20€ MC, V. Mon–Tues noon–2pm; Thurs–Sun noon–2pm, 7.30–10pm.

# Shopping

You'll find the best shopping along pedestrian **rue Gambetta** and around the Eglise St-Jean-de-Luz. There you can find anything from clothes and leather handbags to books and chocolates, to dishes and linens.

You can also ramble around the port, sip pastis in a harborfront cafe, and debate the virtues of the beret. Then scout out **Maison Adam,** 49 rue Gambetta (www.macarons-adam.com; ✆ **05-59-26-03-54**), which has sold almond-based confections from this boutique since 1660. For quality tablecloths, throws, bedding and other gorgeous linen, the traditional **Mendiburutegia Tissus**, 3 rue Renau-d'Elissagaray (✆ **05-59-26-02-63**), is hard to beat.

# St-Jean-De-Luz Nightlife

You can start by taking a walk along the promenade to watch the sunset. Around place Louis XIV, you'll find a hotbed of activity at the cafes and bars. A fun spot in the center of town is Pub du Corsaire, 16 rue de la République (✆ **05-59-26-10-74**), for unpretentious merrymaking.

# Where to Stay

**Grand Hôtel Loreamar** ★★★   This Belle Epoque beauty has been brought back to its original splendor. Spruce chintzes and impressionist paintings in the rooms and vintage trunks in the corridors evoke a more elegant age—one where you could nip down to the English-style bar and have a jazz-era cocktail perfectly mixed, just like today. The restaurant has a superb open kitchen where you can watch the chefs put finishing touches to the Basque-influenced cuisine. And then there's the spa, with direct access to the beach: an aesthetic delight with candlelight and watery ripples, and an utterly gorgeous sea-water swimming pool.

43 bd. Thiers. www.luzgrandhotel.fr. ✆ **05-59-26-35-36.** Fax 05-59-51-99-84. 55 units. 170€–320€ double; 590€–620€ suite. AE, DC, MC, V. Parking 20€. **Amenities:** Restaurant; bar; indoor pool; room service; spa. *In room:* A/C, TV, hair dryer, minibar, free Wi-Fi.

**Auberge Basque** ★★   Clean lines abound here, both outside and in, echoing traditional Basque architecture but bringing it squarely into the 21st century.

A home in Espellete.

Surrounded by a large park, and facing La Rhune mountain, this is a wonderfully calm and elegant hotel, with a good restaurant offering a modern-take on traditional local food. Every detail has been well thought out—there are glass chandeliers and bedroom furniture by Flamant, wine glasses by Jean-Pierre Lagneau, tea from Bentheman & Barton, geothermal heating throughout the hotel, and large flatscreen TVs in the bedrooms. It's located 7km outside St-Jean-de-Luz, but is well worth the five-minute drive.

D307 vieille route de St-Jean-de-Luz, 64310 Helbarron—Saint-Pee. www.aubergebasque.com. ✆ **05-59-51-70-00.** Fax 05-59-51-70-17. 12 units. 96€–250€ double; 250€–260€ 2 suite. AE, MC, V. Parking: free. **Amenities:** Restaurant; bar; spa. *In room:* A/C, TV, hair dryer, minibar, free Wi-Fi.

**Le Parc Victoria ★★** 🎁  The most secluded and tranquil hotel at the resort is a white 19th-century villa, saved from destruction and lovingly restored. The chandelier-lit salon of the main building, decorated in Napoleon III fashion, sets the tone. Guest rooms include antiques, tasteful but comfortable Art Deco furnishings, and marble-clad bathrooms. The restaurant's cuisine and wines are first class.

5 rue Cepé. www.parcvictoria.com. ✆ **05-59-26-78-78.** Fax 05-59-26-78-08. 20 units. 175€–340€ double; 290€–455€ suite. AE, DC, MC, V. Free parking. Closed mid-Nov to mid-Mar. **Amenities:** 2 restaurants; bar; babysitting; outdoor pool. *In room:* A/C, TV, hair dryer, minibar, free Wi-Fi.

## exploring **BASQUE VILLAGES**

The entire Basque region is dotted with atmospheric, beautifully-preserved villages. From Saint-Jean-de-Luz, the most easily reached is **Guéthary**, 3km (1.9 miles) away either on the main N10 road to Biarritz, or along the pretty coastal backroads. A traditional fishing village which has become something of a gourmet center and artistic refuge, the old town is laid out around the lovely church and fishing port, and a walk takes you along the headland, past some dramatic coves. Heading the other way from Saint-Jean-de-Luz, along the D932 up into the hills of the Pyrénées, both **Saint-Jean-Pied-de-Port** and **Espelette** are unmissable. They epitomize the traditional Basque village—classic half-timbered houses in red, white and green, shops offering local cheeses and hams, Irouléguy wines, and other specialities, all with the mountains rising dramatically behind. Espelette is known for its tiny red peppers, often seen strung outside the houses around the main square like cheerful garlands, while Saint-Jean-Pied-de-Port has a 17th century citadelle and is located along banks of the pretty river Nive.

**18**

# BORDEAUX & THE ATLANTIC COAST

by Jane Anson

From La Rochelle to the Bordeaux wine district, the southwest of France is often just a quick stopover for visitors driving from Paris to Spain. However, this area is well worth a more in-depth visit for its Atlantic beaches, medieval and Renaissance ruins, Romanesque and Gothic churches, vineyards, and delightful inns serving splendid regional cuisine.

This intriguing region merits a detour inland to sample cognac in Cognac and to visit nearby art cities such as Poitiers and Angoulême. If you can manage it, allow a week here—enough time to sample the wine, savor the cuisine, and see some of the sights.

# POITIERS ★★

333km (206 miles) SW of Paris; 177km (110 miles) SE of Nantes

Poitiers stands on a hill overlooking the Clain and Boivre rivers—a strategic location that tempted many conquerors. Everybody has passed through here—from Joan of Arc to Richard the Lion-Hearted. Charles Martel chased out the Muslims in A.D. 732 and altered the course of European civilization. Poitiers was the chief city of Eleanor of Aquitaine, who had her marriage to pious Louis VII annulled so she could wed England's Henry II.

For those interested in history, this is one of the most fascinating towns in France. The Battle of Poitiers was fought on September 19, 1356, between the armies of Edward the Black Prince and King John of France. It was one of the three great English victories in the Hundred Years' War, distinguished by the use of the longbow in the skilled hands of English archers.

After decades of slumber, the town came alive with the opening of **Futuroscope,** a cinema theme park in 1987, which now gets upward of 3 million visitors per year. The thriving student population (25,000 of Poitiers's 92,000 residents are students) adds vitality as well.

## Essentials

**GETTING THERE** Frequent **rail** service is available from Paris, Bordeaux, and La Rochelle. Around 15 high-speed TGV trains arrive daily from Paris's Gare Montparnasse (trip time: 90 min.; 55€ one-way). Another 14 TGVs arrive daily from Bordeaux (trip time: 1¾ hr; 38€ one-way), and 12 regular trains arrive from La Rochelle (trip time: 1¾ hr.; 23€ one-way). For train information, visit www.voyages-sncf.com or call ℂ **36-35. Bus** service from Poitiers is so badly scheduled that it's virtually nonexistent. If you're **driving,** Poitiers is located on the A10 highway; from Paris, follow A10 south through the cities of Orléans and Tours, and on to Poitiers.

**VISITOR INFORMATION** The **Office de Tourisme** is at 45 place Charles de Gaulle (www.ot-poitiers.fr; ℂ **05-49-41-21-24**).

PREVIOUS PAGE: **La Rochelle.**

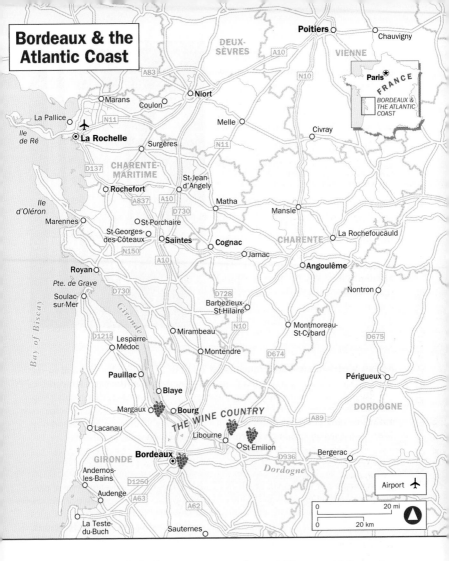

# Bordeaux & the Atlantic Coast

**SPECIAL EVENTS**    The liveliest time to visit is from mid-June to mid-September during **Poitiers l'Eté,** a festival of free live jazz, theater, opera, rock, and fireworks. Free concerts and theater pieces, both in and out of the streets, take place at various parks and churches around the city. Check with the tourist office for schedules.

## Exploring the City

**Baptistère St-Jean** ★ RELIGIOUS SITE    From the cathedral, you can walk to the most ancient Christian monument in France. It was built as a baptistery in the early 4th century on Roman foundations and extended in the 7th century. It contains frescoes from the 11th to the 13th centuries and a collection of funerary sculpture.

Rue Jean-Jaurès. (℡ **05 49 41 21 24.** Admission 2€ adults, 1€ children 11 and under. July–Aug daily 10:30am–12:30pm and 3–6pm; Sept and Apr–Jun Wed–Mon 10:30am–12:30pm and 3–6pm; Oct–Mar Wed–Mon 2:30–4:30pm.

**Cathédrale St-Pierre** ★ CATHEDRAL In the eastern sector of Poitiers is the twin-towered Cathédrale St-Pierre, begun in 1162 by Henry II of England and Eleanor of Aquitaine on the ruins of a Roman basilica. The architecturally undistinguished cathedral was completed much later. The interior, 89m (292 ft.) long, contains some admirable 12th- and 13th-century stained glass.

Place de la Cathédrale. (℡ **05-49-41-23-76.** Free admission. Daily 8:30am–7:30pm (until 6pm in winter).

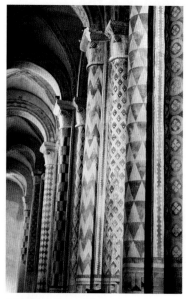

Eglise Notre-Dame-la-Grande.

**Eglise Notre-Dame-la-Grande** ★★ CHURCH This church, built in the Romanesque-Byzantine style and richly decorated, is from the late 11th century. See in particular its western front, dating from the mid–12th century. Surrounded by an open-air market, the facade, carved like an ivory casket, is characterized by pine cone–shaped towers. It was thoroughly cleaned and restored in 1996. Carvings on the doorway represent biblical scenes.

Place Charles de Gaulle. (℡ **05-49-41-22-56.** Free admission. Mon–Sat 9am–7pm; Sun noon–7pm.

**Futuroscope** ★★ ☺ AMUSEMENT PARK This multimedia amusement park in a suburb of Poitiers is a wonderland of technology that lets you experience sounds, images, and sensations with the world's most advanced film-projection techniques and largest screens. The architecture is extraordinary—take a peek at the **Kinémax**, a 400-seat cinema shaped like a rock crystal covered with mirrors, or the **Cité du Numérique** (Digital City), a giant glass triangle with a huge white globe sitting in the middle. There are no less than six IMAX theatres here, projecting viewers into the heart of the action; as well as attractions that use "increased reality" 3D technology, motion simulators, and sophisticated lighting effects. Attractions let you rocket deep into space, dive under the ocean, or fly up in the air for a virtual sky tour. New rides include a roller coaster following the wild adventures of a futuristic pizza delivery man, and an IMAX Arthur and the Dance with the Robots ride. In July and August every night until 10pm, *les nocturnes* are staged with illuminated fountains, lights, and recorded music.

The park's success is such that it has its own TGV train station with direct connections to Bordeaux, Paris, and other major cities, as well as a selection of hotels and restaurants (detailed on the website) so that you can stay overnight.

Jaunay-Clan. www.futuroscope.com. ✆ **05-49-49-30-80.** Admission 37€ adults, 34€ over 60, 28€ children 5–16, free for children 4 and under. Daily 10am–dusk. Bus: Vitalis line 1 and E direct from Poitiers Centre train station. Driving: From Poitiers, take D910 or A10 autoroute about 12km (7½ miles) north. Closed Jan to mid-Feb.

**Musée Ste-Croix** MUSEUM    On the site of the old abbey of Ste-Croix, this museum has a fine arts section devoted mainly to painting—especially 16th- and 17th-century Flemish art and 19th-century salon painting. Works by Bonnard, Sisley, and Moreau are on display, as well as an impressive collection of sculptures, including Maillol, Rodin, and seven statues by Camille Claudel. A separate archaeological section documents the history of Poitou, from prehistoric times through the Gallo-Roman era and the Renaissance, to the end of the 19th century.

3 rue Jean-Jaurès. www.musees-poitiers.org. ✆ **05-49-41-07-53.** Admission 4€ adults (2€ Sundays) free for ages 17 and under. June–Sept Tues 10am–noon and 1:15–8pm, Wed–Fri 10am–noon and 1:15–6pm, Sat–Sun 10am–noon and 2–6pm; Oct–May Tues 10am–5pm, Wed–Fri 10am–noon and 1:15–5pm, Sat–Sun 2–6pm.

# Where to Eat

**Alain Boutin** ★ FRENCH/SEAFOOD    Chef Boutin has awakened the sleepy taste buds of the town with his market-fresh cuisine combined with his culinary imagination. A regional influence enhances his clever dishes, especially when he uses produce of the area, as he does most effectively. You might begin with a shellfish soup flavored with saffron with a rouille sauce, followed by filet of zander or veal kidneys with a piquant sauce and zucchini flan. Located near the Jardins de Blossac, the restaurant has one large dining room, plus another smaller one seating only 15.

65 rue Carnot. www.alainboutin.com. ✆ **05-49-88-25-53.** Reservations required. Main courses 16€–30€; fixed-price menus 25€–36€. MC, V. Tues–Fri noon–1:30pm; Mon–Sat 7:30–9:30pm. Closed 1st week of Sept and 1st week of Jan.

**Poitevin** 🐟 FRENCH    Shoppers and office workers descend on this restaurant en masse at lunchtime, but evening meals are less rushed. There are six cozy dining rooms: One contains an 18th-century fireplace transported here from a demolished building nearby; another abounds with butterflies (on the carpets, curtains, and napery, and mounted in frames). Menu items may include *mouclade Charentaise* (mussels in white wine–and–cream sauce); scallops with sauterne sabayon; and an unusual stewpot containing filets of eel and sole, served with lemon sauce. For dessert, try a semisoft slice of oozing chocolate cake.

76 rue Carnot. ✆ **05-49-88-35-04.** http://le-poitevin.fr. Reservations recommended. Main courses 16€–40€; fixed-price menu 24€–36€. AE, DC, MC, V. Mon–Sat noon–2pm, 7–10pm. Sun noon–2pm. Closed 2 weeks at Easter, 3 weeks in late July and Aug, and 2 weeks at Christmas.

**La Tartignole** ★ 🐟 MODERN EUROPEAN    One of the rising culinary stars in Poitiers, this is a great destination for foodies. Located near the pont de Rochereuil, the cozy dining room manages to be low-key but chic, and the food is a careful blend of traditional French seasonal food, with some interesting touches from elsewhere in Europe. A typical menu might offer organic Scottish smoked salmon (smoked on the premises), and duck breast poached in chestnuts.

2 rue des Quatres Roues. ✆ **09-81-37-79-04.** Reservations recommended. set-price lunches and dinners 19€–37€. AE, MC, V. Tues–Sun noon–2pm and 7pm–11pm. Closed weekend lunches.

## Where to Stay

**Hôtel de l'Europe ★ 📷** Composed of several buildings, one of which dates from the 19th century, these comfortable lodgings offer a combination of both modern and *fin-de-siècle* style. The breakfast room features curlicue moldings and a grand fireplace, while most of the rooms are modern and sleek. Sixty rooms were fully renovated in 2009, some with a vaguely colonial or Asian theme; the older ones in the main building are smaller (and cheaper) and accessible only by staircase.

39 rue Carnot, Poitiers 86000. www.hotel-europe-poitiers.com. ✆ **05-49-88-12-00.** Fax 05-49-88-97-30. 88 units. 65€–99€ double. AE, MC, V. Parking 6€. **Amenities:** Room service. *In room:* TV, hair dryer, minibar (in some), free Wi-Fi. Closed btw. Christmas and New Year's Day.

**Hôtel du Plat d'Etain 🖋** One of the best bargains in Poitiers, this renovated hotel is on a narrow alley close to the landmark place du Maréchal-Leclerc. The much-renovated, much-simplified building dates from 1895. It's named after the medieval inn, the "Pewter Plate," that stood on the site. (That inn became infamous for unwittingly housing Ravaillac, the deranged zealot who fatally stabbed King Henri IV in 1610.) Rooms are compact and simply but comfortably furnished, in warm shades of gold, beige, and red.

7–9 rue du Plat-d'Etain, Poitiers 86000. www.poitiers-leplatdetain.com. ✆ **05-49-41-04-80.** Fax 05-49-52-25-84. 20 units. 51€–67€ double. AE, MC, V. Parking 5€. *In room:* TV, minibar, free Wi-Fi. Closed last 2 weeks in Dec.

**Le Grand Hotel** It's the most imposing Art Deco monument in town, with an exterior that is pure 1920s and bedrooms that have maintained the same style in spirit. With four stories and a location in the heart of the city's commercial core, it often hosts French actors and entertainers, thanks to a good reputation for solid quality and its proximity to the Théâtre National. There is an expansive terrace where breakfasts are served on clement summer mornings, overlooking a quiet inner courtyard. While there's no on-site restaurant, there are plenty nearby. Bedrooms, depending on what floor you're on, may have a modernized 1920s-inspired decor and monochromatic color schemes. All rooms have been recently upgraded to include air-conditioning throughout the hotel and new beds throughout, and the main entrance area is just about done with its own upgrade.

28 rue Carnot, Poitiers 86000. www.grandhotelpoitiers.fr. ✆ **05-49-60-90-60.** Fax 05-49-62-81-89. 47 units. 92€–96€ double; 120€ suite. AE, DC, MC, V. Parking 6€. **Amenities:** Bar; room service. *In room:* TV, hair dryer, minibar, free Wi-Fi.

# LA ROCHELLE ★★★

467km (290 miles) SW of Paris; 145km (90 miles) SE of Nantes; 183km (113 miles) N of Bordeaux; 142km (88 miles) NW of Angoulême

La Rochelle is a historic port and ancient sailors' city, formerly the stronghold of the Huguenots. It was founded as a fishing village in the 10th century on a rocky platform in the center of a marshland. Eleanor of Aquitaine gave La Rochelle a charter in 1199, freeing it from feudal dues. After becoming an independent city-state, the port capitalized on the wars between France and England. It was the departure point for the founders of Montreal. From the 14th to the 16th century, La Rochelle was one of France's great maritime cities. It became the principal

La Rochelle.

port between France and the colony of Canada, but France's loss of Canada ruined its Atlantic trade.

As a hotbed of Protestant factions, it armed privateers to prey on Catholic vessels but was eventually besieged by Catholic troops, led by Cardinal Richelieu (with his Musketeers) and Jean Guiton. When Richelieu blockaded the port, La Rochelle bravely resisted. It took 15 months to starve the city into submission, during which time 25,000 citizens perished from hunger. On October 30, 1628, Richelieu entered the city and found only 5,000 survivors.

Today La Rochelle, a city of 77,000, is the cultural and administrative center of the Charente-Maritime *département* (administrative region). Its famous city lights have earned it the title "City of Light." While many of La Rochelle's sights are old, the city is riddled with high-rise condos and home to the largest pleasure-boat basin in Europe. In summer, the city is overrun with visitors.

## Essentials

**GETTING THERE** The La Rochelle–Ile-de-Ré **airport** (www.larochelle. aeroport.fr; © 05-46-42-86-70) is on the coast, 4km (2½ miles) north of the city. Take bus no. 7 or 47 to reach it; for information and schedules, visit www.rtcr.fr or call © 05-46-34-84-58. Six to eight **trains** from Bordeaux and Nantes arrive daily (trip time: 2 hr.; 28€–30€ one-way). There are a few direct TGVs from Paris's Gare Montparnasse, although most require a transfer at Nantes (trip time: 3 hr.); the one-way fare is 66€ to 83€. For train information, visit www.voyages-sncf.com or call © 36-35. **Buses** leave from place de Verdun (© 05-46-00-95-15 for information). If you're **driving** to La Rochelle, follow A10 south from Poitiers to exit 33 toward La Rochelle/Niort/St-Maixent, and then take N11 west to the coast and La Rochelle.

**VISITOR INFORMATION** The **Office de Tourisme** is on quai Georges Simenon, Le Gabut (www.larochelle-tourisme.com; © 05-46-41-14-68).

**SPECIAL EVENTS** The busiest month is July; the **Festival International du Film de La Rochelle** rolls in at the beginning of the month. It attracts a huge following of fans, press, actors, directors, and, of course, paparazzi. Screenings are held around town; a pass for 10 screenings costs 45€. For information, contact the festival office, at 10 quai Georges Simenon (www. festival-larochelle.org; ☎ **05-46-52-28-96** or 01-48-06-16-66). For a week in mid-July, **Les Francofolies,** a festival of French-speaking music, features big names as well as not-so-famous groups, many of them international pop musicians. The town is overrun with groupies and fans, and a party atmosphere prevails. Tickets range from 20€ to 35€. Call ☎ **05-46-28-28-28** for details (www.francofolies.fr). The Office de Tourisme can also provide details on both festivals.

La Rochelle is also the site of the biggest showcase of boats and yachts in Europe, **Le Grand Pavois–Salon Nautique.** It's a 5-day extravaganza in mid-September. The action is based in and around La Rochelle's Port de Plaisance (better known as the Bassin des Yachts, or Yacht Basin). Sellers and buyers of boats and marine hardware, as well as weekend sailors from everywhere, usually attend. For information about dates and venues, check www.grand-pavois.com or call ☎ **05-46-44-46-39**.

# Exploring the City

There are two sides to La Rochelle: the old and unspoiled town inside the Vauban defenses, and the modern and industrial suburbs. Its **fortifications** have a circuit of 5.5km (3½ miles), with a total of seven gates.

The town, with its arch-covered streets, is great for strolling. The port is a fishing harbor and one of Europe's major sailing centers. Try to schedule a visit in time to attend a fish auction. The best streets for strolling, each with a 17th-century arcade, are **rue du Palais, la rue du Temple, rue Chaudrier,** and **rue des Merciers,** with its ancient wooden houses (seek out the ones at nos. 3, 5, 8, and 17).

**Aquarium de La Rochelle ★** AQUARIUM   La Rochelle's blockbuster crowd pleaser, this is one of the biggest aquariums in Europe. It rises from a portside position near the Port des Minimes, north of the old city. Inside are guided walkways stretching over two floors of massive and bubbling seawater tanks loaded with approximately 10,000 species of flora and fauna from the oceans of the world, living in what look like natural habitats. A new exhibit looks at the ecosystem of the Atlantic coastline. It's hard to miss this place; there are signs for it all over town.

Bassin des Grands Yachts, quai Louis Prunier, Le Vieux Port. www.aquarium-larochelle.com. ☎ **05-46-34-00-00.** 15€ adults, 11€ students and children 3–17, free for children 2 and under. English-language audio guide 3.50€. July–Aug daily 9am–11pm; Apr–June and Sept daily 9am–8pm; Oct–Mar daily 10am–8pm.

**Hôtel de Ville (City Hall) ★** GOVERNMENT BUILDING   The town's 14th-century showcase is built in Flamboyant Gothic style with battlements. Inside you can admire the Henry II staircase with canopies and the marble desk of the heroic Jean Guiton. You must visit as part of a guided tour (in French only); advance reservations are not necessary.

Place de la Mairie, in the city center. ☎ **05-46-51-51-51.** Admission 4€ adults, 1.50€ students and children 4–18, free for children 3 and under. Guided tours July–Aug daily 3 and 4pm; June and Sept daily 3pm; Oct–May Sat–Sun 3pm (and some holidays at 3 and 4pm).

**Musée des Beaux-Arts** ★ ART MUSEUM   The museum is in an Episcopal palace built in the mid–18th century. The art spans the 15th to the 20th centuries, with works by Gustave Doré, Brossard de Beaulieu, Corot, and Fromentin. Twentieth-century pieces include works by Maillol and Léger.

28 rue Gargoulleau. www.ville-larochelle.fr. ℂ **05-46-41-64-65.** Admission 4€ adults, free for children 17 and under. Oct–Mar Mon and Wed–Fri 9:30am–12:30pm and 1:30–5:30pm, Sat–Sun 2:30–6pm; Apr–Sept Mon and Wed–Sat 10:30am–12:30pm and 2–6pm, Sun 2–6pm.

**Muséum d'Histoire Naturelle** MUSEUM   Set within an enormous (2,500 sq. m/26,910 sq. ft.) once-private mansion in the heart of town, and reopened in 2007 after a 13-year closing, this museum stockpiles everything of interest, ethnographically and anthropologically speaking. Stuffed animals, African masks, maps of prehistoric migrational patterns, and everything brought back by La Rochelle's 17th-century traders from around the world are on display. A botanical garden gives an insight into the plants these traders also brought back home with them.

28 rue Albert 1er. www.museum-larochelle.fr. ℂ **05-46-41-18-25.** Admission 4€, free for 17 and under. Oct–mid-May Tues–Fri 9am–6pm, Sat–Sun 2–6pm; mid-May to Sept Tues–Fri 10am–7pm, Sat–Sun 2–7pm.

**Musée du Nouveau-Monde** ★ MUSEUM   In an 18th-century town house rich with architectural details, this is one of the most intriguing museums in La Rochelle. It's rich with evidence of the city's prominent role in the colonization of Canada. The displays trace the port's 300-year history with the New World. Exhibits start with LaSalle's discovery of the Mississippi Delta in 1682 and end with the settling of the Louisiana territory. Other exhibits depict French settlements in the West Indies, including Guadeloupe and Martinique. The vast cane sugar and tobacco cultivations they ran there are explored—as is the slavery that accompanied them.

**Money-Saving Museum Pass**

You can buy a **combination ticket** good for entrance to the Musée des Beaux-Arts, Musée Orbigny-Bernon, Muséum d'Histoire Naturelle, and Musée du Nouveau-Monde. Available at any of the museums and the tourist office, it costs 12€, a big savings.

In the Hôtel Fleuriau, 10 rue Fleuriau. ℂ **05-46-41-46-50.** Admission 4€ adults, free for children 17 and under. Oct–Mar Mon and Wed–Fri 9:30am–12:30pm and 1:30–5:30pm, Sat–Sun 2:30–6pm; Apr–Sept Mon and Wed–Sat 10am–12:30pm and 2–6pm, Sun 2–6pm.

**Musée Maritime** MUSEUM   This museum is composed of eight permanently docked boats, two of which can be visited: a meteorological frigate and an antique *chalutier de peche* (fishing trawler). Exhibits evoke the grand days of La Rochelle as a maritime power and its commerce with the New World.

Quai Sénac de Meilhan. www.museemaritimelarochelle.fr. ℂ **05-46-28-03-00.** Admission 8€ adults, 5.50€ for students and children 4–16, free for children 3 and under. Apr–June and Sept daily 10am–6:30pm; July–Aug daily 10am–7pm.

**Tour de la Chaîne** HISTORIC SITE   During the 1300s, this tower was built as an anchor piece for the large forged-iron chain that stretched across the harbor, closing it against hostile warships. The exhibits focus on the history of the first migration to Canada.

Quai du Gabut. www.monuments-nationaux.fr. ℂ **05-46-34-11-81.** Admission, see box below. Oct–Mar daily 10am–1pm and 2:15–5:30pm; Apr–Sept 10am–6:30pm

**Tour de la Lanterne** ★ HISTORIC SITE   Built between 1445 and 1476, this was once a lighthouse but was used mainly as a jail as late as the 19th century. A low rampart connects the cylindrical tower to the Tour de la Chaîne. During the Wars of Religion, 13 priests were tossed from its summit. You climb 162 steps to the top hold; in clear weather, the panoramic view extends all the way to Ile d'Oléron. On the way up, you can still see graffiti scrawled by former prisoners.

Opposite Tour St-Nicolas, quai du Gabut. ✆ 05-46-41-56-04. Admission, see box above. Oct–Mar daily 10am–1pm and 2–5:30pm; Apr–Sept 10am–6:30pm.

**Tour St-Nicolas** ★ HISTORIC SITE   The oldest tower in La Rochelle, Tour St-Nicolas was built between 1371 and 1382. It originally guarded the town against surprise attacks. From its second floor, you can enjoy a view of the town and harbor; from the top, you can see only the old town and Ile d'Oléron.

Quai du Gabut. ✆ 05-46-41-74-13. Admission, see above. Oct–Mar daily 10am–1pm and 2–5:30pm; Apr–Sept 10am–6:30pm.

Tour St-Nicolas.

## Where to Eat

**Bar/Bistro André** 🔱 SEAFOOD   Seafood is an expensive item anywhere in France, but you can't come to this port town without sampling some. Traditional menu items include savory versions of fish soup; an unusual version of *cabillaud fumé* (home-smoked codfish) served with garlic-flavored cream sauce; curried mussels (*mouclade*); and a saltwater fish not very common in other parts of France, filet of *maîgre*, served with chive-flavored cream sauce.

5 rue St-Jean du Pérot/place de la Chaîne. www.barandre.com. ✆ 05-46-41-28-24. Reservations recommended. Main courses 19€–32€. Fixed-price menus 18€–45€. AE, DC, MC, V. Daily noon–2:30pm and 7–10:30pm.

**Chez Lulu** FRENCH/INTERNATIONAL   Located a 3-minute walk from La Rochelle's Old Port, this unpretentious and fun restaurant is owned by

Betty Rechaux, who quit her job as a financial auditor in Paris to return to her hometown to open this place. She named it after her recently deceased grandmother, Lulu. Inside you'll sit on armchairs or sofas and may dine to the tune of a live pianist, who sometimes plays in the evenings. The best menu items include foie gras with figs and fig granita; medallions of lamb with pear, eggplant, and almond chutney; squid with a squid-ink risotto; and duck magret with black olive butter.

19 ter place du Maréchal Foch. www.chezlulu.net. ⓒ 05-46-50-69-03. Main courses 17€; fixed-price menu 18€ lunch, 28€–38€ (dinner). MC, V. Mon–Sat noon–2pm and 7–10pm.

**Le Bistrot Baroque** ⓥ FRENCH This simple and elegant restaurant elevates classic French bistro fare. Husband and wife team Ludovic and Elodie Boutet are in charge here, working with chef Francois Lepoul (who spent some time in Vietnam, which has clearly influenced parts of the menu). Food ranges from Vietnamese-inspired *nem* prawn rolls, to more traditional terrine of local fish and *parmentier de canard* served with green salad.

21 rue des Dames. www.restaurant-le-baroque.com. ⓒ 05-46-43-40-05. Reservations recommended. Main courses 9€–15€; fixed-price menu 14€–25€. AE, DC, MC, V. Thurs–Tue noon–2pm and 7:30–10pm. Wed 7:30–10pm.

**Richard et Christopher Coutanceau** ★★★ MODERN FRENCH This is not only the city's most glamorous and prestigious restaurant, but also one of the finest along the coast. Delectable cuisine is served in an airy dining room with big bay windows overlooking the adjacent beach and sea. Clearly an artist, Richard Coutanceau, the owner and genius chef, prepares "modernized" cuisine. For an appetizer, roasted frogs' legs come with crisp vegetables and bitter almond foam. The signature fish dish is line-caught sea bass cooked within its own crusty skin and served with chard and lardons. Among the meat dishes, you can sample boned pigeon bourguignon with vegetable minestrone, or medallions of venison with beets and stuffed dates in a cacao-flavored sauce.

Plage de la Concurrence. www.coutanceaularochelle.com. ⓒ 05-46-41-48-19. Reservations required. Main courses 42€–62€; fixed-price menus 55€–115€. AE, DC, MC, V. Mon–Sat noon–1:30pm and 7:30–9:30pm.

# La Rochelle Nightlife

From July to September, head for **quai Duperré, cours des Dames,** and **cours des Templiers.** Once the sun starts to set, this becomes one big pedestrian zone peppered with street performers. It's a fun, almost magical area that sets the tone for the rest of the night.

# Where to Stay

**La Monnaie Art & Spa** ★★ Located in the historic center of La Rochelle close to the marina, the hotel is housed within a 17th-century building, but has been successfully restored to show perfectly-detailed contemporary styling. Modern art exhibits, from sculptures to photography, are placed around the hotel, in both public spaces and bedrooms. A spa with Jacuzzi and sauna can be reserved in advance, and there is an excellent bar open daily from 3pm.

3 rue de la Monnaie, La Rochelle 17000. www.hotelmonnaie.com. ⓒ 800/337-4685 in the U.S. 05-46-50-65-65. 36 units. 159€–204€ double; 259€–319€ suite. AE, DC, MC, V. Parking 15€–20€,

reserve in advance. **Amenities:** Room service. *In room:* A/C, TV, hair dryer, minibar. Free Wi-Fi in lobby of hotel, ADSL in bedrooms.

**Les Brises ★ 🌊** This nautically decorated seaside hotel opposite the Port des Minimes, 1.5km (1 mile) north of the old city, offers a view of the sea and of a soaring 19th-century column dedicated to the Virgin. You can enjoy the view from the front balconies of the six-story building as well as the parasol-shaded patio. The immaculate rooms have cherrywood furniture and comfortable beds.

1 chemin de la Digue de Richelieu, La Rochelle 17000. www.hotellesbrises.cabanova.fr. **𝄐 05-46-43-89-37.** Fax 05-46-43-27-97. 48 units. 80€–130€ double; 160€–210€ family room for 4. AE, DC, MC, V. Free parking. **Amenities:** Room service. *In room:* TV, hair dryer, free Wi-Fi.

## 🎁 sailing THE PORTS OF LA ROCHELLE

La Rochelle has always earned its living from the sea and from the ships that make its harbor their home. Four distinct harbors have grown up over the centuries, each a world unto itself, rich with local nuance and lore. They include the historic **Vieux-Port,** the **Port de Plaisance** (a modern yacht marina), the **Port de Pêche** (the fishing port), and the **Port de Commerce,** which is mostly used by large container ships.

The best way to appreciate them is to take a boat tour. Visit the tourist office (see "Essentials," earlier in this chapter), which acts as a clearinghouse for the outfitters (Croisières Inter-Iles, Navipromer, Ré Croisières). Tours combine a look at the modern facilities with a waterside view of the historic ramparts—which, despite their girth and height, did not protect the city's 17th-century Protestants from starvation and eventual annihilation.

The company with the most frequent departures is the **Croisières Inter-Iles** (www.inter-iles.com; 𝄐 **08-25-13-55-00**). Every day from April to October, there are about a half-dozen cruises into each of the six ports. In winter, they're offered less frequently, usually only on school vacations. Tours last 70 to 180 minutes each, are conducted in French, and average 20€.

Another excellent waterborne outing—but only during the warmer months—involves taking a ferry from the Vieux-Port of La Rochelle to **Ile de Ré.** The island, 26km (16 miles) off the coast of La Rochelle and ringed with 69km (43 miles) of sandy beaches, holds nature preserves crisscrossed with biking and hiking paths, and a number of excellent restaurant in the island's main town, St-Martin-de-Ré. Croisières Inter-Iles (see above) serves the island. If you want to get here during July or August, and if you don't have a car, we recommend taking the ferry for a round-trip fare of 22€. It's worth spending a few days on the island if you have time, joining the many Parisians who escape here during the summer months.

You can also drive your car across the bridge that connects the Ile de Ré to the French mainland. It's accessible from a point 3km (1¾ miles) south of La Rochelle. The toll is 17€ in summer, 9€ in winter. The local bus company, **Les Mouettes** (www.lesmouettes-transports.com; 𝄐 **08-11-36-17-17**), offers 14 round-trips per day year-round (line 3), and charges 4.40€ one-way or 7.40€ round-trip from La Rochelle to several stops along the island.

**La Residence de France ★**   This is a charming hotel in a 16th-century building, close to the cathedral and the place du Verdun. A laid-back atmosphere pervades the grounds, which have a pretty garden with a heated outdoor pool. Inside, a piano bar offers entertainment most evenings, and a large fire ensures this hotel works year-round. Breakfast is free for those under 17. There are a few larger suites (for additional cost) that are able to house up to six people. Next door, a large residence offers cheaper rooms and apartments with small kitchens.

43 rue du Minange, La Rochelle 17000. www.hotel-larochelle.com. ⓒ **05-46-28-06-00.** Fax 05-46-28-06-03. 16 units. 130€–230€ double; 150€–290€ suite. AE, DC, MC, V. 10€ Parking. **Amenities:** Bar; room service. *In room:* TV, hair dryer, free Wi-Fi.

# COGNAC

478km (296 miles) SW of Paris; 37km (23 miles) NW of Angoulême; 113km (70 miles) SE of La Rochelle

The world enjoys 163 million bottles a year of the nectar known as cognac, which Victor Hugo called "the drink of the gods." It's worth a detour to visit one of the château warehouses of the bottlers. Martell, Hennessy, and Otard welcome visits from the public, as well as other worthy *maisons de négoce;* visits usually include free tastings.

## Essentials

**GETTING THERE**   Five **trains** per day arrive from Angoulême (trip time: 40 min., ticket price 9.60€ one-way), and six trains pull in from Saintes (trip time: 20 min., ticket price 5.40€ one-way). For train information and schedules, visit www.voyages-sncf.com or call ⓒ **36-35.** There is limited **bus** service from Angoulême; the trip takes 50 minutes and costs 4.50€; visit www.vtpc.fr or call ⓒ **05-45-95-95-99** for schedules. If you're **driving** to Cognac, the best route from Saintes (which lies along the major route A10) is N141 east.

**VISITOR INFORMATION**   The **Office de Tourisme** is at 16 rue du 14-Juillet (www.tourism-cognac.com; ⓒ **05-45-82-10-71**).

**SPECIAL EVENTS**   Cognac grapes are among the last picked in France. Harvest time usually begins in mid-October.

Cognac is home to several annual festivals, the best of which is **Cognac Blues Passions,** a jazz festival featuring performers from throughout France and the world, including stars like B. B. King, Liz McComb, and Taj Majal that takes place over 5 days in July. Most events cost between 30€ and 40€, although a *passeport* granting access to all the concerts in the venue sells for 130€. For information, check www.bluespassions.com or call ⓒ **05-45-36-11-81.**

More closely tuned to French-speaking audiences is the annual **Coup de Chauffe/Festival du Théâtre de la Rue,** where for a 3-day period in September, street performers present social or political satires in the open air without any admission charges. Although a working knowledge of French is useful, many of the presentations are more "performance art" than traditional drama and can be appreciated for their visuals. For information, visit www.avantscene.com or call ⓒ **05-45-82-32-78.**

# Exploring the Town

Many visitors don't realize that this unassuming town of some 20,000 people is more than just a drink. Though the air is perfumed with the sweet scent from the distilleries, business goes on as usual in the cobbled streets, some of which still sport a few half-timbered houses from the Renaissance.

Cognac at Hennessy.

If you'd like to visit a distillery, go to its main office during regular business hours and request a tour, or visit the tourist office for assistance. On a tour, you'll see some brandies that have aged for as long as 50 or even 100 years. You can have a free taste and then purchase a bottle or two. As far as we're concerned, **Otard** offers the most informative and insightful tours, partly because of the sheer majesty of its headquarters, in the late-medieval **Château de Cognac,** 127 bd. Denfert-Rochereau (www.otard.com; ℂ **05-45-36-88-86**). The tour is half historical overview of the castle, half a technical explanation of cognac production. Parts of the château are appropriately baronial (King François I was born here), and enormous other sections hold tens of thousands of bottles of cognac. Tours last about 1 hour and cost 9€ for adults, 4€ for students 12 to 18, and are free for children 11 and under. From April to October, tours depart at frequent intervals daily. During November to March, you need to contact them in advance to arrange the tour. Call the tourist office or the company several days in advance for exact schedules. The château lies within a 10-minute walk from the town center, near the Hôtel de Ville (city hall).

Other distilleries that conduct tours are **Hennessy,** 1 quai Hennessy (www.hennessy.com; ℂ **05-45-35-72-68;** closed Jan–Feb, Mar–Apr, Oct–Dec Mon–Fri, May–Sept, open daily, 9€); **Camus,** 21 rue de Cagouillet (www.camus.fr; ℂ **05-45-32-70-14;** closed Oct–May, Jun–Sept Mon 2–6pm, Tues–Sat 10–12:30pm, 2–6pm, 7€, master sommelier class where you blend your own cognac, 160€); and **Martell,** place Edouard-Martell (www.martell.com; ℂ **05-45-36-33-33;** by appointment only Nov–Mar, Apr–Oct Mon–Fri 10am–5pm, Sat-Sun noon–5pm, 7.50€ up to 30€ for tasting older cognacs). **Rémy Martin** maintains a battered but authentic-looking wine storehouse in the countryside, at Domaine de Merpins, and a glossier, more media-hip information center and sales outlet in the heart of Cognac. Known as the **Maison Rémy Martin,** it's at 20 rue de la Société Vinicole (www.visitesremymartin.com; ℂ **05-45-35-76-66**) and offers a variety of tours of the estate, the cellars, a combination of the two, or various themed tastings. Priced from 15€, the most elaborate costs 75€ and punctuates its insights into the world of Rémy Martin with frequent dégustations of esoteric cognacs and lots of bite-sized canapés to accompany them. Exclusive visits and Afficonado Journeys are also available, at more elaborate prices. For all tours, call in advance for reservations.

If you're short on time, a good retail outlet is **La Cognathèque,** 8 place Jean-Monnet (www.cognatheque.com; ℂ **05-45-82-43-31**), which prides itself on having the widest selection from all the region's distilleries, large and small (some 400 different cognacs), though you'll pay for the convenience of having everything under one roof.

No one ever accused the cognac industry of not knowing how to promote its products in its hometown. The **Musée des Arts de Cognac** lies in the town center, at place de la Salle Verte (www.musees-cognac.fr; ℂ **05-45-36-21-10**). Within, you'll find exhibits showcasing everything associated with the cognac trade, from cultivation of grapes to bottle and barrel making, to insights into global marketing and sales. A few rooms have been tastefully renovated over the last year. Entrance costs 4.80€ for adults, 3.50€ for students. Admission is free for anyone 17 and under. It's open as follows: July to August Tuesday to Sunday 10am to 6:30pm; May, June, and September Tuesday to Friday 11am to 6pm, and Saturday and Sunday 1 to 6pm; October to April Tuesday to Sunday 2 to 5:30 pm.

Within a 15-minute walk lies the **Musée d'Art et l'Histoire de Cognac,** 48 bd. Denfert-Rochereau (ℂ **05-45-32-07-25**), which has exhibits on popular arts and traditions, archaeological exhibits, and a fine art collection of paintings, sculpture, decorative arts, and furniture. Accessible with the same ticket that's valid for access to the above-noted Musée des Arts de Cognac (and vice versa), it's open as follows: July to August Wednesday to Monday 10am to 6:30pm; May, June, and September Monday, Wednesday, Thursday, and Friday 11am to 1pm and 2 to 6pm, and Saturday and Sunday from 1pm to 6pm; October to April Wednesday to 2 to 5:30pm.

Cognac has two beautiful parks: the **Parc François-1er** and the **Jardin Public** (accessible from the Musée d'Art et l'Histoire de Cognac**).** The Romanesque-Gothic **Eglise St-Léger,** rue de Monseigneur LaCroix (ℂ **05-45-82-05-71**), is from the 12th century, and its bell tower is from the 15th. Admission is free; it's open daily 8am to 7pm.

## Where to Eat

The restaurant at **Domaine du Breuil** (see "Where to Stay," below) serves worthwhile meals.

**Hostellerie Les Pigeons Blancs** ★★ MODERN FRENCH   This restaurant, run by the Tachet family, has two elegant dining rooms with exposed ceiling beams and limestone fireplaces. Menu offerings depend on the availability of ingredients but may include warm oysters and shrimp in Chardonnay-flavored sauce, sautéed foie gras with cabbage and bacon, and filet of veal with morel sauce. The chef uses cognac vapors to steam many of his raw ingredients, including excellent line-caught sea bass with spices. Come with an appetite—there is no ordering a la carte here, though you are welcome to mix and match on the various two- and three-course fixed-price menus.

110 rue Jules-Brisson. www.pigeons-blancs.com. (ℂ **05-45-82-16-36.** Reservations recommended. Fixed-price menu 24€ lunch, 34€–59€ (dinner). AE, MC, V. Tues–Sun noon–2pm; Mon–Sat 7–9pm.

## Where to Stay

**Domaine du Breuil** ★★   This tranquil 19th-century manor house, studded with magnificent windows, is in a 7.2-hectare (18-acre) landscaped park 2 minutes from the center of Cognac. Rooms are simple but well furnished and well maintained. Cognac aficionados and those in town to do business with the factories head here for the hospitality, the well-appointed rooms, and the excellent cuisine from the southwest of France. The food is reason enough to visit, and, naturally, you'll finish your meal with a cognac in the bar to aid digestion.

104 rue Robert-Daugas, Cognac 16100. www.hotel-domaine-du-breuil.com. © **05-45-35-32-06.** Fax 05-45-35-14-15. 24 units. 69€–162€ double. 230€-261€ suites. AE, MC, V. Free parking. Closed Dec 20–Jan 5. **Amenities:** Restaurant; bar; outdoor pool. *In room:* TV, hair dryer, minibar (in some), free Wi-Fi.

**Hotel Heritage** ★  A 17th century building (with sections dating from the 19th century), the Hotel Heritage is recently renovated and restored to provide warm and luxurious rooms in central Cognac for a very reasonable price. A small restaurant (with outside courtyard) and bar complete the easy atmosphere. And you can't beat the personal connection the owner Jean-Francois Jolivet has with the building—his great-great-grandfather worked as a butler in the building when it was a private house.

25 rue d'Angoulement, Cognac 16100. www.hheritage.com. © **05-45-82-01-26.** Fax 05-45-82-20-33. 19 units. 65€–70€ double. AE, MC, V. 10€ parking. **Amenities:** Restaurant; bar. *In room:* TV, free Wi-Fi.

# ANGOULÊME ★★

443km (275 miles) SW of Paris; 116km (72 miles) NE of Bordeaux

The old town of Angoulême hugs a hilltop between the Charente and Aguienne rivers. You can visit it on the same day you visit Cognac. The town has been a center for the French paper industry since the 17th century, a tradition that carries on today in the five remaining paper mills. These days, Angoulême (pop. 43,000) is probably best known for something that gets printed on that paper: comics. Authors, artists, and fans come from all over the world to attend the **Festival International de la Bande Dessinée,** one of the largest comic book/graphic novel gatherings on earth. Hard-bound comics, or *bandes dessinées*, are not only considered an art form in France (*"le 9eme art"*), but also are big business: They account for a big chunk of the French book market. These comics are not just for children—they cover everything from political humor to adventure stories, to personal memoirs and documentary reporting. The festival takes over the town for 3 days in January, when the latest books are presented, prizes are awarded, and contracts are signed. There are also lots of expositions and events for casual visitors. For more information, contact the festival (www.bdangouleme.com; © **05-45-97-86-50**) or the tourist office (see below). If you miss the festival, you can still explore this graphic world at the **Cité Internationale de la Bande Dessinée et de l'Image (CNBDI);** see "Exploring the Town," on p. 705.

## Essentials

**GETTING THERE**  There are about two TGV **trains** per hour (trip time: 55 min.) and a handful of regular trains (trip time: 1½ hr.) every day from Bordeaux; the one-way fare is 25€. There is also frequent train service from Saintes (trip time: 1 hr.) and Poitiers (trip time: 45 min.). From Paris's Montparnasse Station, some 15 TGV trains make the trip daily (trip time: 2 hr., 40 min.); the one-way fare is 63€-85€. For train information and schedules, visit www.voyages-sncf.com or call © **36-35. Véolia** (www.vtpc.fr;

Comics on display at Cité Internationale de la Bande Dessinée et de l'Image

✆ **05-45-95-95-99**) runs eight **buses** per day between Cognac and Angoulême. The trip takes 1 hour and costs 4.50€ each way. If you're **driving** from Bordeaux, take N10 northeast to Angoulême.

**VISITOR INFORMATION**  The **Office de Tourisme** is at place des Halles (www. angouleme-tourisme.com; ✆ **05-45-95-16-84**).

## Exploring the Town

The hub of the town is **place de l'Hôtel-de-Ville.** The town hall was erected from 1858 to 1866 on the site of the palace of the ducs d'Angoulême, where Marguerite de Navarre, sister of François I, was born. All that remains of the palace are the 15th-century Tour de Valois and 13th-century Tour de Lusignan.

**Cathédrale St-Pierre ★**, 4 place St-Pierre, was built in the 11th and 12th centuries and restored in the 19th. Flanked by towers, its facade boasts 75 statues, each in a separate niche, representing the Last Judgment. This is one of France's most startling examples of Romanesque-Byzantine style. The 19th-century architect Abadie (designer of Sacré-Coeur in Paris) tore down the north tower and then rebuilt it with the original materials in the same style. In the interior, you can wander under a four-domed ceiling. It's open Monday to Saturday 9am to 7pm, Sunday 10am to 6:30pm.

As mentioned above, Angoulême is the European capital of comic book and graphic novel art. In addition to the festival, the city is now home of the **Cité Internationale de la Bande Dessinée et de l'Image,** 121 rue de Bordeaux (www.citebd.org; ✆ **05-45-38-65-65**), which has an exhibition space, a library and research center, and two screening rooms; it hosts seminars and lectures with famous authors, some of whom come to do residencies. It's open in July and August Tuesday to Friday 10am to 7pm, and Saturday and Sunday 2 to 7pm; and September to June Tuesday to Friday 10am to 6pm, and Saturday and Sunday 2 to 6pm. Entrance costs 6.50€ for adults, 4€ for students under 26, free for children 17 and under.

To get out into the city itself, you can walk along the panoramic **promenade des Remparts** ★, a path that flanks the site of the long-gone fortifications that once surrounded the historic core of Angoulême. The most appealing section of the 3km (1¾-mile) walkway is the 1km (½-mile) section that connects the cathedral with Les Halles (the covered market). Views from here stretch over the hills that flank the River Charente almost 75m (246 ft.) below. A more contemporary walk is also available—the **Circuit des Murs Peints** (Grafitti Walk). Famous graphic artists such as Florence Cestac and Marc-Antoine Mathieu have created over 20 piees of grafitti art at various public spots around the city, and a walking circuit has been organized by the tourist office to allow visitors to enjoy them (map available).

## Where to Eat

**La Cité** FRENCH   Set at the northern edge of Angoulême's medieval core, this small and intimate restaurant is pleasantly outfitted in tones of terra cotta and pale green. An enduring house specialty is seafood brochette, where crayfish, scallops, and mussels are spit-roasted and served with a creamy garlic sauce. Most of the menu is devoted to fish, but there are a handful of meat dishes on the menu.

28 rue St-Roch. ✆ **05-45-92-42-69.** Reservations recommended. Main courses 14€–25€; fixed-price menus 15€–30€. AE, MC, V. Tues–Sat noon–2pm and 7–10pm. Closed Aug.

**La Ruelle** ★★ FRENCH   This first-class restaurant, in the oldest part of town, is Angoulême's best. Count on classic French recipes with a modern twist. The menu changes frequently, but some examples of its delights are filet of Limousin beef served with a pine-needle bouillon and chocolate "surprise" served with orange and nougatine, and flambéed in Grand Marnier. The space was originally part of a pair of houses separated by a narrow alleyway (*une ruelle*). Vestiges of the 17th-century structure are visible in the dining room's stonemasonry and painted ceiling beams.

6 rue Trois-Notre-Dame. www.restaurant-laruelle.com. ✆ **05-45-95-15-19.** Reservations recommended. Main courses 29€–38€; fixed-price menu 38€–60€. DC, MC, V. Tues–Sat noon–2pm and 7:30–10pm. Closed 1st week of Jan and 2 weeks at the end of Jul and beginning of Aug.

## Where to Stay

**Hotel du Palais**   Hotel choices are limited in Angoulême, but this well-located hotel has individually-designed rooms and a cheerful feel. The building itself is a former convent dating from the 18th century, and is well located near the Palais de Justice. Recently renovated, the rooms vary quite widely in size, but are comfortable and well decorated. It also serves generous breakfasts.

4 place Francis Louvel, Angoulême 16000. www.hotel-angouleme.fr. ✆ 05-45-92-54-11, fax **05-45-92-01-83.** 41 units. 60€–160€ double. AE, MC, V. Parking 7€. **Amenities:** Bar. *In room:* TV, free Wi-Fi.

## Where to Eat & Stay Nearby

**Hostellerie du Maine Brun** ★★   Originally a flour mill, this property is the premier place to stay and dine in this area. It's surrounded by 32 hectares (79 acres) of lowlands (including a garden, a creek, and open fields), about half of which are devoted to the production of cognac. These are the most luxurious accommodations around, larger than the lodgings at many competitors; each has a terrace. Rooms are individually decorated with 18th- and 19th-century French furniture. The restaurant serves splendid fare. Specialties include terrine of foie gras with cognac, and Porée charentaise, a combination of fish in a creamy Pineau wine sauce. Fixed-price menus range from 30€ to 40€.

RN 141, La Vigerie, Asnières-sur-Nouère 16290. www.hotel-maine-brun.com. (℃) **05-45-90-83-00.** Fax 05-45-96-91-14. 18 units. 120€–130€ double; 170€ suite. AE, DC, MC, V. Hotel and restaurant closed mid-Oct to mid-Apr. Take RN 141 7km (4¼ miles) west of Angoulême and turn right at Vigerie. **Amenities:** Restaurant; bar; outdoor pool; room service; free Wi-Fi. *In room:* TV, hair dryer, minibar.

# BORDEAUX ★★★

578km (358 miles) SW of Paris; 549km (340 miles) W of Lyon

Elegant Bordeaux, capital of Aquitaine, is the hub for the legendary wine-growing region that includes *appellations* like St-Emilion and Médoc. You can visit many of the most famous vineyards and sample their wares. Wines aside, the city of Bordeaux is a treasure in itself. Its wide quays, which curve graciously around the Garonne River, have been given a new, car-free life and are now filled with public gardens, fountains, and playgrounds for both children and adults. Splendid plazas, like the esplanade des Quinconces and place de la Bourse, give way to narrow cobbled streets, 14th-century churches, 18th- and 19th-century mansions, and an exquisite urban landscape that has been hailed as one of the aesthetic triumphs of western France.

**Things to Do**    Let the neoclassical masks of Bacchus and Mercury on **place de la Bourse** lead you to **Quartier Saint Pierre**'s stately old merchants' houses. Or cross tree-lined **esplanade des Quinconces**, with its statues of Montaigne and Montesquieu, to antiques shops and markets in the **Chartrons** district. Back in the historic center, the **Musée des Beaux Arts** displays the works of Titian, Delacroix, and Veronese. Standing 112m (374 ft.) tall, **Basilique St-Martin** provides sweeping panoramas over the city and the Garonne River, whose silvery waters link Bordeaux with the Atlantic.

**Nightlife & Entertainment**    Sensible by day, Bordeaux rocks by night. Bars and bistros line the Garonne's **quays,** leading well-dressed crews to the chic clubs on **quai de Paludate,** while students guzzle cheap wine in grungy bars around **place de la Victoire.** For something more sophisticated, the **Grand Théâtre** is a sumptuous neoclassical venue used for top-notch opera, dance, and theater. The **Bassins à Flots** district at the far end of the quayside is slowly being renovated and offers increasing numbers of bars and restaurants. In the trendy **Bastide** district, just across the pont de Pierre (stone bridge), lights from Bordeaux's rows of mansions twinkle seductively.

**Restaurants & Dining**    Sandwiched between the Atlantic Ocean and fertile land, Bordeaux gets the best of both worlds. Tantalize your taste buds with melt-in-your-mouth Arcachon oysters, tender Pauillac lamb, Aquitaine beef, Périgord truffles, prunes from Agen, and St-Emilion macaroons. The elegant **quays** are freckled with contemporary eateries, or take your pick along **rue St-Rémi** and **place du Parlement,** where French, Chinese, and Italian restaurants fight for space. For a Michelin-starred treat, **Le Chapon Fin** has been serving gourmet French cuisine since 1825.

**Relaxation**   Nothing loosens muscles like Bacchus's old finest, and around Bordeaux, you're spoiled for choice. Escape the city to the verdant vineyards encircling **St-Emilion,** where gently trellised vines have grown since the 12th century and the village's postcard-perfect cobbles conceal an eerie troglodyte church. When the rolling hills beckon again, the great vineyards of **Médoc** (think châteaux Margaux, Lafite Rothschild, Latour, and Mouton Rothschild) produce some of the world's finest wines.

## Essentials

**GETTING THERE**   The local **airport,** Bordeaux–Mérignac (www.bordeaux. aeroport.fr; ✆ **05-56-34-50-50** for flight information), is served by flights from European and North African cities like London, Madrid, Stockholm, and Casablanca, as well as many French destinations. It's 15km (9¼ miles) west of Bordeaux in Mérignac. Paris is an hour's flight away. A **shuttle bus** (Jet'Bus) connects the airport with the train station, departing every 45 minutes (trip time: 45 min.) and costing 7€ one-way for adults, 6€ for 25 and under. Children under 5 ride free. A taxi (✆ **05-56-96-00-34**) between the airport and the train station costs about 45€.

The railway station, Gare St-Jean, is on the west bank of the river, within a 30-minute walk (or 5-min. taxi ride) of the center of the old town. Some 15 to 25 **trains** from Paris's Gare Montparnasse (trip time: 3 hr. by TGV) arrive each day. The one-way fare is 73€-89€. For train information and schedules, visit www.voyages-sncf.com or call ✆ **36-35**.

Bordeaux is easy to reach by **car.** From Paris, follow A10 south through Orléans, Tours, and Poitiers into Bordeaux (trip time: about 5 hr.). Be aware that the streets of Bordeaux are fraught with hazards: narrow 18th-century alleys, traffic jams, and simply too many cars and people. Easily available parking within the city's historic core is scarce. Whenever possible, head for

Streets in Bordeaux leading to its bell tower.

one of the blue-and-white P signs that indicate public garages, mainly located underground.

**GETTING AROUND**    Three lines of a new modern tram system—labeled A, B, and C—have made traveling around Bordeaux easier than at any time in its history. Service is daily from 5am to 1am, with individual tickets (Tickarte) costing 1.40€, transfers included during a 1-hour period. There are also several passes: 1 day Tickarte costs 4.10€, 5.20€ for 5 trips, 11€ for 10 trips, or 11€ for 1 week.

Once aboard, you must validate your Tickarte, which is sold in *tabacs* and other outlets. The combined bus-and-tram system (www.infotbc.com; ☏ **05-56-57-88-88**) serves both inner Bordeaux and its suburbs, with maps available at the train station. The most central information office is at 9 place Gambetta, open Monday to Friday 7am to 7pm and Saturday 9am to 6pm.

**VISITOR INFORMATION**     The **Office de Tourisme** is at 12 cours du 30-Juillet (www.bordeaux-tourisme.com; ✆ **05-56-00-66-00**), with a branch office in the Gare St-Jean (✆ **05-56-91-64-70**).

# Exploring Bordeaux

Wine exporters welcome guests to sample wines and learn about the industry. In "The Wine Country," later in this chapter, we suggest a tour of the region. Plan your trip with maps, guides, and advice about local wines, available free from the **Maison du Vin (House of Wine),** 1 cours du 30-Juillet (www.vins-bordeaux. fr; ✆ **05-56-00-22-88**), opposite the tourist office (which also has a snazzy wine bar for some preliminary tasting, and offers two-hour introductory tasting classes every day from July to September for 25€, tickets from tourist office or Maison du Vin). To make the rounds of the vineyards, consider alternative forms of transport: bus, bicycle, or even walking.

**STROLLS THROUGH TOWN**     The prettiest and most historic neighborhood in Old Bordeaux is the "Golden Triangle," defined by cours Clemenceau, cours de l'Intendance, and les allées de Tourny. Since the new tram came to town, many of the streets are blissfully free of cars. You can traipse around the old town on your own, because it's fairly compact, or take advantage of the 2-hour **walking tour** the tourist office (see above) arranges daily at 10am Monday, Tuesday, Thursday, Friday, and Sunday. Conducted in both French and English, tours take in all the most important sites and begin at the tourist office. Cost is 8.50€ for adults, 7.50€ for students, 6€ for children 13 to 17, and free for children 12 and under. Reserve in advance and call to confirm. There are also a variety of other tours on offer through the tourist office— from a 2-hour bus tour (Sat and Wed at 10am) to an inline-skating excursion on car-free Sundays (the 1st Sun of each month at 2:30pm).

   If you go it alone, your tour of Old Bordeaux can begin in the heart of this old city at **place de la Comédie,** which was once the site of a Roman temple. On this square, one of France's great theaters, **Grand Théâtre ★★**, place de la Comédie (www.opera-bordeaux.com; ✆ **05-56-00-85-95**), the city's cultural symbol, was built between 1773 and 1780 as testimony to the burgeoning prosperity of Bordeaux's emerging bourgeoisie. This is one of the last remaining 18th-century theaters in the world, rivaling those of Naples, Stockholm, and Milan. A colonnade of 12 columns graces its facade. Surmounted on these are statues of goddesses and the Muses. If you'd like to visit the richly decorated interior, there are guided tours on Wednesdays and Saturdays at 2pm, 4pm, and 5.30pm. They cost 3€, and you can reserve ahead in person, by phone, or via Internet.

Detail in Bordeaux's "Golden Triangle"

From here, you can walk north to **esplanade des Quinconces.** It was laid out between 1818 and 1828, and covers nearly 12 hectares (30 acres). From here, you can stroll down the river and enjoy the gardens and fountains of the new promenade along the **quays** to the splendid **place de la Bourse ★**, which opens directly onto the Garonne. It was laid out between 1728 and 1755; the fountain of the Three Graces is at its center. Flanking the square are the Custom House and the Stock Exchange. On warm days, Bordelais (particularly the youngest ones) come here to splash through the huge 1-inch deep water feature, known as the **Miroir d'Eau** (Water Mirror) that lies between the square and the river.

**CHURCHES** The largest and most ostentatious church in Bordeaux is the **Cathédrale St-André ★★**, place Pey-Berland (✆ **05-56-52-68-10**), near the southern perimeter of the old town. The sculptures on the 13th-century Porte Royale (Royal Door) are admirable; see also the 14th-century sculptures on the North Door. Separate from the rest of the church is the 47m (154-ft.) **Tour Pey-Berland** (✆ **05-56-81-26-25**), a belfry begun in the 15th century. Foundations date from 900 years ago. The church is open July to September daily 10 to 12:30am and 2:30 to 6pm. Off season, hours are Tuesday to Sunday 10am to noon and daily 2 to 6pm. The tower is open daily June to September 10am to 1:15pm and 2 to 6pm, October to May Tuesday to Sunday 10am to 12:30pm and 2 to 5:30pm. Tower admission is 5€ for adults and 3.50€ for those 25 and under. Free organ recitals are held in July and August on Tuesdays at 6:30pm.

Foremost among the "secondary" churches is the **Basilique St-Michel ★**, place St-Michel/Canteloup (✆ **05-56-94-30-50**). The church itself was constructed in stages from the 14th to the 16th centuries. More impressive is its bell tower, the **Fleche St-Michel ★**, across the street. This tower, erected in 1472, is the second-tallest stone tower in France (after the cathedral at Strasbourg), rising 112m (367 ft.). The basilica's hours vary, but it is usually open 10am to 6pm. The tower is open for visits June to September only, Tuesday to Friday 10am to 1pm and 2 to 7pm, and Saturday and Sunday 2 to 7pm, for 3.50€. You climb 228 steps to the top, where you have sweeping views over the port and the Garonne. During July and August, every Friday from 5 to 7pm, the bells in the tower are rung as part of a free carillon concert that can be heard throughout the neighborhood.

Another historic church is **Basilique St-Seurin,** place des Martyrs de la Résistance (✆ **05-56-93-89-28**). Its most ancient sections, such as its crypt, date from the 5th century. See the porch left over from an earlier church; it has some capitals from the Romanesque era. In summer, hours are Tuesday to Sunday 8:30 to 6:30pm; off-season hours are Tuesday to Sunday 8:30am to 7:30pm. On Sunday, the basilica may shut down at 1pm.

**Abbatiale Ste-Croix,** place Pierre-Renaudel (✆ **05-56-94-30-50**), gained attention in musical circles when its organ, a marvel built by a monk, Dom Bedos, was restored to its original working order in 1996. In July and August, free organ concerts are presented Wednesday at 6:30pm; otherwise, the church is generally open daily 10am to 6pm.

**MUSEUMS** Admission to the permanent collections of all of Bordeaux's municipal museums (including the three below) is free. For an overview of the

## Buying Wine in Bordeaux

If you've come to Bordeaux to buy wine, try to choose one that carries personal significance because you've visited the vineyard, or consult the experts at the wine shops. We recommend **La Vinothèque,** 8 cours du 30-Juillet (www.la-vinotheque.com; © **05-56-52-32-05**), and **Badie,** 62 allées de Tourny (© **05-56-52-23-72**). Some of the best red

bordeaux wines come from small houses such as **Château Penin,** Genissac, 30km (20 miles) east of Bordeaux (© **05-57-24-46-98**); **Château Bel Air,** Naujan-et-Postiac, 40km (25 miles) east of Bordeaux (© **05-57-84-55-08**); and **Château les Bouzigues,** Saintes Gemmes, 76km (47 miles) south of Bordeaux (© **05-56-61-80-77**).

history and ethnography of the region, visit the **Musée d'Aquitaine ★**, 20 cours Pasteur (www.bordeaux.fr; © **05-56-01-51-00**), which has a good collection of Gallo-Roman sculptures and artifacts, as well as displays and model ships detailing the maritime history of Bordeaux, and its growth as a trading centre during the 17th and 18th centuries. The museum is open Tuesday to Sunday 11am to 6pm.

The **Musée des Beaux-Arts ★★**, 20 cours d'Albret, Jardin du Palais-Rohan (www.bordeaux.fr; © **05-56-10-20-56**), has an outstanding collection from the 16th to the 20th centuries. Works by Perugina, Titian, Rubens, Veronese, Delacroix, and Marquet are on display. The museum is open Wednesday to Monday 11am to 6pm.

Housed in a stunning mansion built in 1779, the **Musée des Arts Décoratifs ★**, 39 rue Bouffard, (© **05-56-10-14-00;** www.bordeaux.fr), has a significant collection of sculptures, paintings, furniture, ceramics, and other art objects dating primarily from the 18th and 19th centuries. Of particular interest are several "period rooms" set up to approximate the world of the rich aristocracy in the 18th century, and a new exhibition detailing 20th century design. This museum is open Wednesday to Monday 2 to 6pm. For modern art, head to the **Musée des Arts Contemporain** (CAPC), 7 rue Ferrere (www.capc-bordeaux.fr; © **05-56-00-81-50**). Just set back from the riverfront, and housed in a vast former sugar warehouse, it hosts some of the most exciting contemporary art displays in southwest France. Open Tues-Sun 11am-6pm (late night til 8pm on Wednesdays).

**BOAT RIDES** The **pont de Pierre,** with 17 arches, stretches 478m (1,568 ft.) across the Garonne and is one of the most beautiful bridges in France. Built on orders of Napoleon I, the bridge proved so difficult to build that it wasn't finished until 1822, after he died. The bridge can be crossed on foot for a view of the quays and the port. For an even better view, we suggest a **tour of the port,** which lasts about 90 minutes and goes up the river and all around the harbor. The tours run from April to October and usually depart from the quai des Chartrons, in the center of town. The cost is 15€ for adults and 12€ for children 10€ and under. For exact times and a description of other cruises, call the tourist office (see "Essentials," above) or **Bateaux "Ville de Bordeaux,"** quai des Chartrons (www.bateaubordeaux.com; © **05-56-52-88-88**). Ask about the occasional floating concerts at night.

# Shopping

If you want antiques, head to **rue Bouffard, rue des Remparts,** and **rue Notre-Dame,** where you'll find an indoor market known as **Village Notre-Dame** (www.antiquitesbordeaux.com; ✆ **05-56-52-66-13**), housing about 30 antiques stands. Another destination is the neighborhood around **Eglise St-Michel,** particularly the passage St-Michel, a narrow alleyway a few steps from the church.

For clothes shopping, go to the couture quarter around **place des Grands Hommes,** as well as **cours Georges-Clemenceau** and **cours de l'Intendance,** with its many upscale and classic emporiums. For the greatest concentration of shops, head to the **rue Ste-Catherine,** the longest pedestrian street in France. It has at least 100 boutiques, from the most luxurious to the cheapest. The **allées de Tourny** are also rife with goodies, including **Cadiot-Badie,** 26 allées de Tourny (www.cadiot-badie.com; ✆ **05-56-44-24-22**), a must for serious chocoholics. Established in 1826, their chocolates are considered the best in Bordeaux.

# Where to Eat

## EXPENSIVE

**La Tupina** ★★ 🍴 SOUTHWESTERN FRENCH   One of Bordeaux's most talented chefs runs this cozy spot with a summer terrace near quai de la Monnaie. It's been called "a tribute to country kitchens and the grandmothers who cooked in them." Jean-Pierre Xiradakis's specialty is duck, so your meal may include *tournedos de canard,* and the kitchen often uses duck giblets, skin, and livers in salads. Other specialties are roasted shoulder of lamb *en confit* with garlic and white beans, and lamprey eel à la Bordelaise.

6 rue Porte de la Monnaie. www.latupina.com. ✆ **05-56-91-56-37.** Reservations recommended. Main courses 14€–55€; fixed-price lunch 18€–35€, dinner 60€. AE, DC, MC, V. Daily noon–2pm and 7–11pm.

**Le Chapon-Fin** ★★★ MODERN FRENCH   Dating from 1825, this prestigious restaurant features an unusual decor that critics have referred to as "organic rococo." Crafted from distressed rocks into an Art Nouveau–style grotto, it soars almost 7.5m (25 ft.) to a skylight that floods the interior with light. The restaurant features artful renditions of classics like fresh duck foie gras with chutney and tamarind, Pauillac lamb grilled with peppers and mushrooms, and seared scallops served with cardamom-scented pineapple pulp. The restaurant is in one of the city's upscale neighborhoods, between place Gambetta and the Marché aux Grands Hommes.

5 rue Montesquieu. www.chapon-fin.com. ✆ **05-56-79-10-10.** Reservations required. Main courses 34€–44€; fixed-price menus 38€–90€. AE, DC, MC, V. Tues–Sat noon–1:30pm and 7:30–9:30pm.

## MODERATE

**Fernand** ★★ FRENCH   You'll get a good dose of traditional bistro atmosphere at this seriously southwestern restaurant, located on the waterfront next to the place de la Bourse. Depending on the season, you'll find an excellent selection of the region's greatest hits: Pauillac lamb, lamprey, game, and a homemade foie gras. The chef specializes in fresh fish, oysters, and other shellfish straight from the day's market. Steaks come from the Blonde d'Aquitaine, a local race of prize-winning beef.

7 quai de la Douane. www.fernand-bordeaux.com. ☎ **05-56-81-23-40.** Reservations recommended. Main courses 20€–34€; fixed-price menus 16€–21 lunch, 34€–48€ dinner. AE, MC, V. Daily noon–11pm.

**Le Mably** ★ 🖊 FRENCH   In the heart of 18th-century Bordeaux, surrounded by art galleries and shops, this restaurant attracts gastronomes, hipsters, politicians, journalists, and locals who enjoy the elegant atmosphere of a 19th-century *brasserie de luxe.* The duck-intensive menu lists salad of duck necks stuffed with pistachios, confit of duckling, *magret* of duckling, and, of course, duck liver. Recommended nonduck items are veal kidneys with fresh coriander, blanquettes of veal, *boeuf bourguignon,* and several kinds of fresh fish. Pay special attention to the comprehensive wine list, rich in esoteric burgundies. There's additional seating on an outdoor terrace during warmer weather.

12 rue Mably. ☎ **05-56-44-30-10.** Reservations recommended. Main courses 15€–28€; fixed-price menu 23€–33€. AE, MC, V. Tues–Sat noon–2:30pm and 7:30–11pm. Closed 3 weeks in Aug.

## INEXPENSIVE

**La Boîte à Huîtres** FRENCH   Inexpensive, quick, friendly, and excellent quality—this is pretty much a perfect spot for lunch if you are craving some oysters, fresh from the Atlantic coast of France. You can have them either on their own with a squeeze of lemon, or vinegar and shallots, or accompanied by the traditional chitterling sausage. A cold glass of local white wine will finish it off perfectly.

35 cours du Chapeau Rouge. ☎ **05-56-81-64-97.** Main courses 10€–20€. MC, V. Tues–Mon lunch noon–2pm, 7–10.30pm.

**L'O de l'Hâ** ★ 🏛 FRENCH/INTERNATIONAL   This name is a play on both the French for "the great beyond" and the name of the cobbled street outside, which commemorates a long-gone medieval prison. Antique masonry, roughly textured plaster, and polished concrete decorate both fashionable dining rooms. Menu items are innovative and intriguing. Examples include butternut squash risotto with foie gras, and veal filet with parsnip purée and heritage vegetables. On Friday and Saturday, a DJ spins disco from 8 until around 11pm.

5 rue du Hâ. www.odelha.fr. ☎ **05-56-81-42-21.** Main courses 18€–27€; fixed-price menus 14€–29€. MC, V. Tues–Fri noon–2pm; Tues–Thurs 8–10pm; Fri–Sat 8–11pm. Tram: A to Musée d'Aquitaine.

# Bordeaux Nightlife

Pick up a copy of *Clubs et Concerts* at the Office de Tourisme or *Bordeaux Plus* at a newsstand; both detail the goings-on in and around town.

Animated street life rules the inner core of Bordeaux by night. Head to **place de la Victoire, place St-Pierre, place du Parlement, place Camille Jullian,** and **place Gambetta;** the latter swarms with students. Night owls in Bordeaux gravitate toward quai du Paludate, where restaurants, bars, and discos remain open until the wee hours.

The hottest drinking spot in Bordeaux is **Le Calle Ocho,** rue des Piliers de Tutelle (☎ **05-56-48-08-68**), a red-and-black enclave of Cuban music, photographs, and posters, all of it richly lubricated with your choice of mojitos and some of the best-looking and most uninhibited people in town. It's open nightly from 6pm till dawn.

If you are feeling trendy and glamorous, try **La Casa Latina,** 59 quai Chartrons (✆ **05-57-87-15-80**), where merengue, salsa, and bachata might make you think that you've landed in the Dominican Republic or Brazil. For a more laid-back night on the town, **Café Populaire** (✆ **05-56-94-39-06**), or Café Pop, as it's known to locals, is a fun place to have a drink and mix with the natives. Filled with relics from the 1950s, it has music to keep you busy into the wee hours.

The leading gay bar, **BHV (Bar de l'Hôtel de Ville),** 4 rue de l'Hôtel de Ville (✆ **05-56-44-05-08**), is in the heart of town, across from the town hall, and is open Tuesday to Sunday 6pm to 2am. Drag shows take place from October to June on Sunday at 10:30pm.

A good choice for dancing is **La Plage,** 40 quai de Paludate (✆ **05-56-49-02-46**), with its 1970s decor and just as classic 25- to 45-year-old crowd. **La Dame de Shanghai,** quai A. Lalande (✆ **05-57-10-20-50**), a restaurant-bar-club in a moored boat in the Bassins a Flot, is another good bet for a late night.

## Where to Stay

### EXPENSIVE

#### Grand Hotel de Bordeaux & Spa ★★★
Located opposite the Opéra National de Bordeaux, Grand Hotel de Bordeaux has been restored to its former glory, bringing five-star luxury to the historic center. Rooms still evoke the 19th century, with their reproduction period furniture. Black lacquer wrought-iron lamps and pleated silk shades add more elegance. Rooms have all the modern amenities, including flatscreen TVs and Bose radio systems. Enjoy market-fresh seafood in the Michelin-starred dining room of Le Pressoir d'Argent, the hotel's acclaimed restaurant. A large spa with swimming pool is located across the top three floors of the hotel.

2–5 place de la Comédie, Bordeaux 33000. www.ghbordeaux.com. ✆ **05-57-30-44-44.** 310€–450€ double; 485€–2000 suite. AE, DC, MC, V Parking 35€. **Amenities:** Restaurant; bar; room service; spa. *In room:* A/C, TV, hair dryer, minibar, free Wi-Fi.

#### Seeko'O Hotel ★★
This daringly modern hotel makes a statement on the 18th-century quays of the Garonne. Its jagged glistening white exterior evokes a block of ice. It's got enough electronic gadgetry to launch itself into space—well, almost. The location of this surreal hotel is near the quai des Chartrons, a once-seedy neighborhood that is now about as happening as it gets in Bordeaux. Bedrooms have been likened to a space-age bachelor pad, with some circular beds and color schemes of black and white with red splashes like a woman would "slash on" her lipstick. Most of the bedrooms are in essence junior suites, and bathtubs are designed for two.

54 quai de Bacalan, Bordeaux 33300. www.seekoo-hotel.com. ✆ **05-56-39-07-07.** 45 units. 190€–234€ junior suite; 398€ panoramic suite. AE, MC, V. Parking 10€. **Amenities:** Bar; room service; sauna, Turkish baths. *In room:* A/C, TV, hair dryer, minibar, free Wi-Fi.

### MODERATE

#### Hôtel Tour Intendance ★★
This former mansion has been transformed into a cozy hotel that successfully blends modern comfort with the building's 18th-century charm. Rooms are light filled and airy, with lots of exposed stone walls and blonde wood. Antique wood beams support the ceiling in the breakfast room; terra-cotta tiles cover the floor. Located on a quiet side street off the cours de l'Intendance, the hotel provides easy access to the historic center.

14–16 rue de la Vielle Tour, Bordeaux 33000. www.hotel-tour-indendance.com. ☎ **05-56-44-56-56.** Fax 05-56-44-54-54. 34 units. 115€–165€ double. AE, DC, MC, V. Parking 12€ overnight; during the day hourly rate 2.50€. *In room:* A/C, TV, hair dryer, free Wi-Fi.

**L'Avant Scene ★**    Located on trendy rue Borie, you are within a few minutes' walk of both the quays and the bistros and galleries of Chartrons. The hotel itself is intimate and well-designed, housed in a traditional stone building in this former wine merchant's district (a museum to the history of wine in the area is a few doors down). Bedrooms are sleek and modern, with luxurious touches such as Philippe Starck furniture and Bose stereos.

36 rue Borie, Bordeaux 33300. http://lavantscene.fr. ☎ **05-57-29-25-39.** Fax 05-57-29-25-40. 9 units. 110€–175€ double; 195€ suite. AE, DC, MC, V. Parking 15€. **Amenities:** Restaurant; bar; room service. *In room:* A/C, TV, hair dryer, minibar, free Wi-Fi.

### INEXPENSIVE

**Hôtel Continental ★ ⚲**    To get a certain class, charm, and elegance in Bordeaux at this price is a rarity. In the center of the "Golden Triangle," on a semipedestrian mall dotted with boutiques, this 18th-century town house wins new fans every year. You'll get a warm welcome and a fine dose of Bordelaise hospitality. Rooms, although a bit small (especially the singles), are warmly decorated and furnished, each with a compact bathroom; a few have tiny balconies. Breakfast is included in the price of the room.

10 rue Montesquieu, Bordeaux 33000. www.hotel-le-continental.com. ☎ **05-56-52-66-00.** Fax 05-56-52-77-97. 51 units. 96€–135€ double; 190€–210€ suite. AE, DC, MC, V. Parking 1.50–2.50€. *In room:* A/C (in some), TV, hair dryer (in some), free Wi-Fi.

**Hôtel de France ★ ⚲**    A mere 2-minute walk to the Grand Théâtre, this family-run hotel is about as central as it gets—and a whole lot cheaper than 90 percent of the lodging in the neighborhood. The friendly owners keep their rooms clean and simple, with white walls and modern bedsteads; the quiet side street ensures peace and tranquillity at night.

7 rue Franklin, Bordeaux 33000. www.hotel-france-bordeaux.fr. ☎ **05-56-48-24-11.** 20 units. 72€ double. AE, MC, V. *In room:* TV, free Wi-Fi.

# THE WINE COUNTRY

The major Bordeaux wine districts are Graves, Médoc, Sauternes, Entre-deux-Mers, Libourne, Blaye, and Bourg. North of the city of Bordeaux, the Garonne River joins the Dordogne to form the Gironde, a broad estuary. Some 117,000 hectares (298,990 acres) of vines produce over 150 million gallons of wine a year, some of which are among the greatest reds in the world. (The white wines are less well known, although worth exploring.)

Many of the famous vineyards welcome visitors, but most don't have a permanent staff to accommodate sightseers. Don't just show up—call first or check with local tourist offices about appropriate times to visit. A typical tour includes information about the winemaking process and a tour of the cellars. Most châteaux have historical artifacts on display. Tours end with a tasting, in which visitors 18 and older may participate.

Before heading out one of the many Wine Roads, or Routes des Vins, make sure you get a detailed map from the Bordeaux tourist office (see "Essentials" under the "Bordeaux" section, earlier in this chapter), because trails aren't always well marked.

# Libourne

This is a sizable market town with a high-speed railway connection. At the junction of the Dordogne and Isle rivers, Libourne is roughly the center of the St-Emilion, Pomerol, and Fronsac wine districts. The center of town is in the form of a *bastide,* which was cutting-edge urban planning in the Middle Ages. This gridlike setup was perfect for both commerce and defense, and centered on a large town square lined with arcades. In Libourne, this square still contains some houses from the 16th century, including the lovely **Hôtel-de-Ville** (Town Hall). There is an open-air market on the square every Tuesday, Friday, and Saturday morning, one of the nicest in the region. You can also explore the remains of 13th-century ramparts. In the town center is the **Office de Tourisme,** 45 allée Robert Boulin (✆ **05-57-51-15-04**), where you can get details on visiting the vineyards.

## WHERE TO EAT

**Chez Servais** ★★ 🍴 FRENCH   The setting for our favorite restaurant in Libourne is an antique (probably 19th-c.) house whose sculpted facade occupies a prominent position in the town center. In the dining rooms—one small and intimate, the other more convivial—a hardworking, professional staff serves items from a menu that changes at least every 6 weeks. Our favorite dishes include sautéed foie gras with white grapes, scallops with salsify chips, and *magret* of duck with red seasonal berries.

14 place Decazes. ✆ **05-57-51-83-97.** Reservations recommended. Fixed-price menu 19€ lunch, 27€–39€ dinner. AE, MC, V. Tues–Sun 12:30–2pm; Tues–Sat 7:45–9:30pm. Closed 1 week in May and last 2 weeks in Aug.

# Médoc ★

The Médoc, an undulating plain covered with vineyards, is one of the most-visited wine regions in southwestern France. The city of Bordeaux and the Pointe de Grave, at the mouth of the Gironde Estuary, mark its borders. Throughout the region are many châteaux producing grapes; only a handful of these, however, are of true star quality. The most-visited château is that of Mouton-Rothschild, said to be second only to Lourdes among attractions in southwestern France. Be advised that you cannot buy wine directly at most of the chateaux below.

## EXPLORING THE AREA

**Château Lynch Bages** HISTORIC HOME   This chateau boasts excellent visitor facilities. Tours include a tasting of the estate, classified as one of the region's best in 1855. There's also a cluster of shops and eateries in the village of Bages directly behind the chateau. Here you'll find a traditional butcher's and patisserie, alongside a wine boutique, a wine school, a children's play area, and several artisanal workshops.

Craste des Jardins, Pauillac 33250. www.lynchbages.com. ✆ **05-56-73-24-00.** Daily tours by appointment 9.30am–1pm, 2–6.30pm. 8€ per person, including tasting. Tours in English on request.

**Château Margaux** HISTORIC HOME   Known as the Versailles of the Médoc, this Empire-style château was built in the 19th century near the village of Margaux. The estate covers more than 263 hectares (650 acres), of which 80 hectares (198 acres) produce Château Margaux and Pavillon Rouge du Château Margaux; almost 12 hectares (30 acres) are devoted to producing Pavillon Blanc du Château Margaux. To see the vat rooms and wine cellars, make an appointment by e-mail, letter, or phone.

On D2, Margaux 33460. www.chateau-margaux.com. ℭ **05-57-88-83-83.** Vat rooms and wine cellars by appointment only, Mon–Fri. Closed Aug. Free admission. Tours in English on request.

**Chateau Pichon Longueville** HISTORIC HOME    One of the most visitor-friendly classified chateaux in Bordeaux, the tour takes you through the subterranean cellars, created by architect Alain Triaud in 2010, and into the visitor center for tasting of their main wine, and second wine Les Tourelles de Longueville. Bring your camera—the stone turrets and reflective pool are the stuff of chateaux dreams.

Pauillac 33250. www.pichonlongueville.com. ℭ **05-56-73-17-17.** 10€ with tasting. Daily 9am–12:30pm, 2-6:30pm. by appointment only. Tours in English on request.

## WHERE TO EAT & STAY

**Cordeillan-Bages** ★★    In a region obsessed with fine wine and fine food, this emerges as the most consistently celebrated restaurant and hotel. The setting is a 18th-century mansion surrounded by vineyards. While most come for the restaurant, many also spend the night after indulging in wine with dinner. A la carte main courses go for 46€ to 70€; there's a 60€ fixed-price menu at lunch. Menu items may include a velouté of cockles and razor clams with seaweed and salmon roe, cod with French caviar and white beans, or rabbit with caramelized apples and wild mushrooms. For dessert, indulge in a cooked pear filed with liquid chocolate, or a sinful combination of caramel, peanuts, licorice, and yogurt sherbet. The spacious guest rooms are decorated with formal curtains, upholstered walls, a scattering of antiques, and an airy minimalism. About half are contemporary, with monochromatic color schemes; the rest are in traditional country house style.

Rte. D2, Pauillac 33250. www.cordeillanbages. com. ℭ **05-56-59-24-24.** Fax 05-56-59-01-89. 28 units. 199€–292€ double; 392€ junior suite; 517€ 2-bedroom apt for 4. AE, DC, MC, V. Closed Dec 15–Feb 14. **Amenities:** Restaurant; bar; exercise room; outdoor pool; room service; sauna. *In room:* TV, hair dryer, free Wi-Fi.

# St-Emilion ★★

Surrounded by vineyards, St-Emilion is on a limestone plateau overlooking the valley of the Dordogne; a maze of wine cellars has been dug beneath the town. The town, constructed mostly of golden stone and dating from the Middle Ages, is also known for its *macarons*, a light-as-air cookie made with almonds and egg whites.

St-Emilion.

St-Emilion maintains the ancient tradition of La Jurade, a society dedicated to maintaining the highest standard for the local wine and promoting and honoring it around the world. During the Jurade wine festival in September, members of this society wear silk hats and scarlet robes edged with ermine. **Note:** The town is jammed during the Jurade, and hotel prices tend to rise during the festival.

## ESSENTIALS

**GETTING THERE**   St-Emilion lies 35km (22 miles) northeast of Bordeaux, between Libourne, 8km (5 miles) away, and Castillon-la-Bataille, 11km (6¼ miles) away. **Trains** from Bordeaux make the 45-minute trip to St-Emilion 8 to 10 times per day; the one-way fare is 8.20€. Trains from other parts of France usually require transfers in either Bordeaux or Libourne, a 10-minute train ride from St-Emilion. For train information in St-Emilion, visit www.voyages-sncf.com or call ✆ **36-35**.

**VISITOR INFORMATION**   The **Office de Tourisme** is on place des Créneaux (www.saint-emilion-tourisme.com; ✆ **05-57-55-28-28**).

## EXPLORING THE TOWN

At the heart of St-Emilion is the medieval **place du Marché,** also called **place de l'Eglise Monolithe,** between two hills. St-Emilion abounds with unusual monuments, some of them dug, for defensive reasons, into the limestone bedrock that adds such verve to the vineyards.

Foremost among the monuments is the **Eglise Monolithe ★**, place de l'Eglise Monolithe (✆ **05-57-55-28-28**), the largest underground church in Europe, carved by Benedictine monks during the 9th to 12th centuries. Three 14th-century bay windows mark its facade. A 14th-century sculpted portal depicts the Last Judgment and Resurrection of the Dead. The church is 11m (36 ft.) high, 20m (66 ft.) wide, and 38m (125 ft.) long. It can be visited only as part of an organized tour. The daily tours last 45 minutes, and English-language tours are regularly scheduled between April and October. Each tour includes a visit to the church, its **catacombs,** the 13th-century Chapelle de la Trinité, and its underground grotto—a site known as the Hermitage—where St-Emilion sequestered himself during the latter part of his life. The entire complex was kept alive during the heyday of its use by underground springs, which were surrounded in the 1500s by ornate balustrades (the monks charged admission). The tour, which lasts 45 minutes, costs 7€ for adults, 4.50€ for students, and is free for children 11 and under. Another excellent way to get an overview of the history of St-Emilion is at **Chateau Villemaurine**, ✆ **05-57-74-47-30**, which is walking distance from the tourist office, and offers a sound-and-light show in its extensive underground limestone cellars, retelling the story of area since the 8th century.

You can visit two additional monuments without an organized tour. The first is the **bell tower** (*clocher*) of the Eglise Monolithe (see above). It rises on place des Créneaux, near place de l'Eglise Monolithe. Built between the 1100s and the 1400s, it's the second-highest tower in the La Gironde region and, for years after its construction, was the only aboveground landmark that indicated the position of the underground church. You can climb the bell tower and take in the panoramic view daily between 9am and 6pm for a 1.25€ fee. To do this, go to the tourist office, where someone will give you a key to the tower door in exchange for an ID card. (When you return the key, you'll get your ID back.)

You may want to visit the **Château du Roi** (📞 **05-57-24-72-09**), founded by Henry III of the Plantagenet line during the 13th century. Don't expect a full-fledged castle. The tall *donjon,* or keep, was the first section built, and the construction that followed was either demolished or never completed. Until 1608, this building functioned as the town hall. From its summit, you can see as far away as the Dordogne. You can climb the tower (the procedure is the same as for visiting the bell tower) during daylight hours from April to October for 1.25€.

## WHERE TO EAT & STAY

**Hôtel Palais Cardinal ★**   Though parts of the building date from the 13th century, when it was a cardinal's mansion, today this gracious inn is loaded with modern comforts. Carefully tended by the same family for five generations, rooms in these pleasant lodgings are swathed in warm colors and period prints, in keeping with the building's history. Comfort ranges from smaller rooms with views of the cobbled streets to larger, "luxury" rooms with views of the vineyards and marble bathrooms. All guests have equal access to the pool and the private garden, as well as to the dining room, which serves elegant regional classics (fixed-price menus are 28€–48€, with half-board rates available for hotel guests). The restaurant offers wine from the adjacent Clos de Sarpe, the hotel's very own vineyard.

Place du 11 Novembre 1918, St-Emilion 33330. www.palais-cardinal.com. 📞 **05-57-24-72-39.** Fax 05-57-74-47-54. 27 units. 88€–162€ double; 176€–216€ suite. AE, DC, MC, V. Free parking. Closed Dec–Mar. **Amenities:** Restaurant; outdoor pool. *In room:* TV, hair dryer, free Internet.

**Comptoir St Genes ★**   A 15-minute drive from Saint Emilion, in the vineyards of Castillon Cotes de Bordeaux, this relaxed and low-key restaurant is worth a detour. It serves classic French bistro cuisine and only wines from the surrounding area. The service is friendly and the food excellent.

5 Croix, Saint Emilion 33350. www.comptoirdegenes.com. 📞 **05-57-47-90-03.** Fax 05-57-47-99-47. Menus 15€-21€.

# THE DORDOGNE & THE LOT

by Jane Anson

**19**

overs of foie gras, truffles, and exceptional landscapes have always sought out the Dordogne and Périgord regions of France. Our first stop, Périgueux, was the capital of the old province of Périgord. After admiring Cro-Magnon artwork in prehistoric caves and taking in the beauty of the Dordogne Valley, we explore the lofty heights of Rocamadour and then visit Cahors, the ancient capital of Quercy.

Though the larger towns are inviting, the countryside is the main attraction here. Exquisite villages are, in some cases, literally carved into the limestone cliffs framing the Dordogne River. Medieval fortresses peer down from craggy bluffs. As evidenced by the stunning cave paintings they left behind, humans have been taken with this splendid natural setting since prehistoric times. Now it's your turn to take a few days to explore.

# PÉRIGUEUX ★

485km (301 miles) SW of Paris; 85km (53 miles) SE of Angoulême; 113km (70 miles) NE of Bordeaux; 101km (63 miles) SW of Limoges

Capital of the old province of Périgord, Périgueux stands on the Isle River. In addition to its food products (foie gras and truffles reign supreme here), the town is known for its medieval and Renaissance architecture and its Gallo-Roman ruins. The city is divided into three sections: Le Puy St-Front (the medieval town), on the slope of the hill; the Cité (the old Roman town); and, to the west, the modern town.

Though Périgueux (pop. 29,600) is very pretty, it is basically a sleepy provincial town. Its attractions probably won't hold your interest for more than a day, but you'll likely pass through on your way to the Dordogne Valley and the cave paintings at Les Eyzies.

## Essentials

**GETTING THERE**  At least a dozen **trains** per day arrive from Paris from either Montparnasse or Gare d'Austerlitz (trip time: 4–5 hr.; 68€–85€ one-way), 11 direct trains from Bordeaux (trip time: 1½ hr.; 21€ one-way), and 1 or 2 direct trains per hour from Limoges (trip time: 1 hr.; 16€ one-way). For train information, visit www.voyages-sncf.com or call ☎ **36-35.** If you're **driving** from Paris, take A10 south to Orléans and then A20 south to Vierzon, where you'll pick up the A89 to Périgueux.

**VISITOR INFORMATION**  The **Office du Tourisme** is at 26 place Francheville (www.tourisme-perigueux.fr; ☎ **05-53-53-10-63**).

You may want to rent a bike and explore the countryside; a map is available at the tourist office. Rent from MBK 15 cours Fenelon (☎ **05-53-53-44-62**) from 6€ per half-day. The Vinci car parks also offer free bike hire to their customers.

PREVIOUS PAGE: **Rocamadour.**

The Dordogne
& the Lot

Juillac
Objat
Hautefort
Ayen
D901
CORRÈZE
Donzenac
Vézère

Paris ★
THE DORDOGNE
& THE LOT

FRANCE

Périgueux

A89
Thenon
A89
Terrasson-
Lavilledieu
Brive-la-
Gaillarde

St-Pierre-
de-Chignac
D6809
Larche

FORÊT BARADE

DORDOGNE
Montignac
D62
A20
Cressensac

Vergt
D706 ■ Lascaux II
D704
D60
D38
Beaulieu-sur-
Dordogne

St-Léon-
sur-Vézère
St-Genies
Salignac-Eyvigues

D710
Martel

Les Eyzies-de-Tayac
Souillac
LOT

D703
Sarlat-
la-Canéda
D47
D703
Vallée de
la Dordogne

Trémolat
St-Cyprien
Beynac-
et-Cazenac
Lacave

Le Buisson-
de-Cadouin
Payrac

Vallée de la Dordogne
Domme
Rocamadour

D25
Belvès
D704
Gourdon

Beaumont-
du-Périgord

Monpozier
D2
A20

D104
D673

D673
Puy-l'Evêque
D820

Fumel
Lot

N21
Cahors
Limogne-
en-Quercy

D911
Villeneuve-
sur-Lot
Tournon-
d'Agenais
D656

Penne-
d'Agenais
D653
Montcuq

0          10 mi
0          10 km

## Exploring the Town & Environs

Give yourself the time to amble through the **Puy St-Front,** Périgueux's well-preserved medieval quarter, rich with ancient houses, cobbled alleyways, and Renaissance facades. It's hard to miss the imposing **Tour Mataguerre,** a 15th-century tower that is all that's left of the city's fortifications. Follow the winding streets up to the **Cathedral St-Front** (see below) and the **place de Coderc,** once a literal pigsty, and later the administrative center of the medieval town. Today there is an outdoor market here on Wednesdays and Saturdays from 8am to 1pm that snakes down to place de la Cautre and the Hôtel de Ville.

Périgueux is a treasure trove of Gallo-Roman antiquities. The most visible is the **Tour de Vésone,** a partially ruined site that stands 26m (85 ft.) tall, just southwest of town beyond the railway station. Here you'll see the remains of a Roman temple dedicated to the goddess Vesuna, but you can't enter the site. The remains of a large 1st-century Gallo-Roman villa were discovered next to the temple, and in 2003, a sleek new museum was opened, **Vesunna–Site-Musée Gallo-Romain** (see below).

Nearby is the **Jardin des Arènes,** a public garden that holds a few remains of an amphitheater that held as many as 22,000 spectators back in the 2nd century. Near the arena are the ruins of the **Château Barrière,** rue Turenne, built in the 11th or 12th century on Roman foundations.

Gastronomy reigns supreme in Périgueux, especially when it comes to smooth, melt-in-your-mouth foie gras. Stores that sell this delicacy abound. One of the best is **La Maison Léon,** 9 place de la Clautre (www.maisonleon.fr; ✆ **05-53-53-29-96**). If you want an adventure, head for a goose farm that makes its own foie gras, such as **A la Ferme de Puy Gauthier,** about 15 minutes south of town in Marsaneix (✆ **05-53-08-87-07;** http://puygauthier24.pagesperso-orange.fr). To get there, take the D2 and follow signs to Brive.

Périgueux.

Truffles are another local specialty, and fans of this extremely expensive and delectable fungus come from far and wide, especially during the **Truffle Festival** (Fête de la Truffe), which takes place in mid-December. Truffle markets are held during the winter months in place St-Louis in Périgueux, and in a few local villages, most notably in Saint-Genies and Brantome. In July and August, although not the season for truffles, there is a singing competition in honor of the local **delicacy in Périgueux itself.**

**Cathédrale St-Front ★** CATHEDRAL   This 12th-century cathedral is one of the rare Byzantine-style churches to be found in France. Left in ruins after the Wars of Religion, it was restored with more than a few 19th-century flourishes by Paul Abadie, who, thus inspired, went on to design the Sacre-Coeur in Paris. With its five white domes and colonnaded turrets, St-Front evokes Constantinople. The cathedral's bell tower is one of the only authentic vestiges of the original church. The interior is built on the plan of a Greek cross, unusual for a French cathedral. The recently restored cloisters, which date from the 9th century, can be visited for a fee of 1.50€.

Place de la Clautre. www.amiscathedralesaintfront.fr. ✆ **05-53-53-23-62.** Free admission. Daily 8am–7pm (closes at 6pm in winter).

**Eglise St-Etienne-de-la-Cité** CHURCH   Périgueux's other remarkable church—this one in the Cité area—was a cathedral until 1669, when it lost its

Display at Musée d'Art et d'Archéologie du Périgord.

position to St-Front. The church was built in the 12th century but has been much damaged since. It contains a 12th-century bishop's tomb and a carved 17th-century wooden reredos depicting the Assumption of the Madonna.

10 av. Cavaignac. ✆ **05-53-06-48-10.** Free admission. Daily 8am–6pm.

**Musée d'Art et d'Archéologie du Périgord** ★ MUSEUM   Built on the site of an Augustinian monastery, this museum has an exceptional collection of prehistoric relics (one of the largest in France), as well as sculptures and medieval and Renaissance treasures. Many of the artifacts were recovered from digs in the Périgord region, which is rich in prehistoric remains.

22 cours Tourny. ✆ **05-53-06-40-70.** http://musee-perigord.museum.com. Admission 4€ adults, 2€ students, free for children 17 and under. Apr–Sept Mon and Wed–Fri 10:30am–5:30pm, Sat–Sun 1–6pm; Oct–Mar Mon and Wed–Fri 10am–5pm, Sat–Sun 1–6pm.

**Vesunna—Site-Musée Gallo-Romain** ★ MUSEUM   One of the most talked-about museums in central France is housed in a mostly glass shell that was designed by the renowned architect Jean Nouvel. A short walk from the center of Périgueux, it's positioned directly above excavations, which revealed an extensive, albeit ruined, ancient Roman villa, replete with mosaics and many of the workaday artifacts of everyday life in the ancient Roman provinces. Visitors will be intrigued by the juxtaposition of the hypermodern shell and the ancient artifacts within. Recent improvements include several interactive displays, including a 3D movie.

Rue du 26e Régiment d'Infanterie. www.vesunna.fr. ✆ **05-53-53-00-92.** Admission 6€ adults, 4€ students and children ages 6–25, free for children 5 and under. Oct–Mar Tues–Fri 9:30am–12:30pm and 1:30–5pm, Sat–Sun 10am–12:30pm and 2:30–6pm; Apr–June and Sept Tues–Fri 9:30am–5:30pm, Sat–Sun 10am–12:30pm and 2:30–6pm; July–Aug daily 10am–7pm. Closed 1st and 2nd week of Jan.

# BIKING AND CANOEING DOWN THE
## Dordogne

The Dordogne's rivers meander through countryside that's among the most verdant and historic in France. This area is underpopulated but dotted with monuments, châteaux, 12th-century villages, and charming churches.

As you bike around, the rural character of the area unfolds before you. No château, hotel, or inn treats you disdainfully if you show up on two rather than four wheels. (*Au contraire*, the staff will probably offer advice on suitable bike routes.) If you're ever in doubt about where your handlebars should lead you, know that you'll rarely go wrong if your route parallels the riverbanks of the Lot, the Vézère, the Dordogne, or any of their tributaries. Architects and builders since the 11th century have added greatly to the visual allure of their watersides.

The SNCF makes it easy to transport a bike on the nation's railways. However, if you don't want to bring your own wheels on the train, there are plenty of rental shops throughout the region. (We recommend rentals in this chapter's sections on Périgueux and Les Eyzies-de-Tayac.)

Exploring the rivers by canoe is another option. Every summer, a flotilla of bathing-suited visitors can be seen paddling down the Dordogne; the Lot and the Vézère get less traffic and are also beautiful. The rivers tend to be shallow and lazy, perfect for a family outing.

**Le Comité Départemental du Tourism,** 25 rue du Président Wilson, Périgueux 24000 (www.dordogne-perigord-tourisme.fr; ℂ 05-53-35-50-24), provides information about all the towns in the *département* and will help you organize biking, hiking, kayaking, and canoeing trips. Two of the best outdoors outfitters are **Canoë Loisir,** Vitrac, 24200 (www.canoes-loisirs.com; ℂ 05-53-31-22-92), and **Adventure Plein Air,** St-Léon sur Vézère, 24290 (www.canoevezere.com; ℂ 05-53-50-67-71).

## Where to Eat

**Château des Reynats ★★** MODERN FRENCH   This slate-roofed 19th-century manor has a yellow and soft-red Empire dining room in which you can enjoy the finest *cuisine du marché* in the entire region. Someone on the staff may relay stories of the role the château played during France's disastrous exit from its former department of Algeria, when it functioned as a kind of refugee center for French citizens booted off their estates. Menu items are likely to include salmon with caviar, foie gras with mango tartare, and a well-prepared version of scallops with velvety chestnuts.

The château also rents 45 beautiful rooms. Thirteen of the rooms lie in the château, the other 37 in l'Orangerie, a guesthouse of comfort but less grand, of course, than the château. Rooms in the château range from 132€ to 213€ in a double, 243€ to 279€ in a suite, whereas doubles in the guesthouse go for 103€ to 115€.

5 av. des Reynats, Chancelade 24650. www.chateau-hotel-perigord.com. ℂ **05-53-03-53-59.** Fax 05-53-03-44-84. Reservations recommended. Main courses 33€–20€; fixed-price menu 28€ lunch, 44€–89€ dinner. MC, V. Tues–Fri 12:30–1:30pm; Mon–Sat 7:30–9pm. Closed (restaurant) first 3 weeks of Jan.

**Le Clos Saint Front** ★ MODERN FRENCH   Regional specialities are the watchword here—that means duck, foie gras, pork, and local fish, all cooked with precision and imagination. It has a lovely garden for summer months, but this is a year-round destination.

5-7 rue de la Vertu, Périgueux 24000. www.leclossaintfront.com. ✆ **05-53-46-78-58.** Fax 05-53-46-78-20. Reservations recommended. Main courses 20€; fixed-price menu 26€ lunch, 40€–62€ dinner. MC, V. Lunch Tues–Sun noon–1:45pm; Dinner Tues–Sat 7–9:45pm.

## Périgueux Nightlife

If the weather is clement, begin your evening with a stroll in the streets and alleyways surrounding **place St-Silain, place St-Louis,** and **place du Marché.** One of the town's best wine bars is **Le Cercle,** 18 cours Montaigne (www.hotel restaurantlunivers.fr; ✆ **05-53-53-34-79**).

For the high-energy crowd, the leading disco is **La Reg,** 16 rue Chancelier de l'Hôpital (✆ **05-53-53-10-55**). It's open Wednesday to Saturday nights from midnight till dawn.

## Where to Stay

The **Château des Reynats** (see "Where to Eat," p. 725) also has rooms.

**Hôtel Bristol**   This modern hotel, the best in the town center, is centrally located and offers recently renovated comfortable rooms, often with sleek styling. It's your best bet in a town with a limited, lackluster selection. Bathrooms are a bit small but come with a combination tub/shower. Breakfast is the only meal served, but it's only a 5-minute walk to the town's best restaurants and major points of interest.

37–39 rue Antoine Gadaud, Périgueux 24000. www.bristolfrance.com. ✆ **05-53-08-75-90.** Fax 05-53-07-00-49. 29 units. 69€–82€ double. AE, MC, V. Free parking. Closed btw. Christmas and New Year's Day. **Amenities:** Room service. *In room:* A/C, TV, hair dryer, minibar, free Wi-Fi.

# LASCAUX (MONTIGNAC) ★★

496km (308 miles) SW of Paris; 47km (29 miles) SE of Périgueux

The **Caves at Lascaux,** 2km (1¼ miles) from the Vézère River town of Montignac in the Dordogne region, contain the most beautiful and most famous cave paintings in the world. Unfortunately, you can't view the actual paintings (the caves have been closed to the public to prevent deterioration), but a precise replica gives you a clear picture of the remarkable works.

Four boys looking for a dog discovered the caves in 1940. They opened to the public in 1948, quickly becoming one of France's major attractions and drawing 125,000 visitors annually. However, the hordes of tourists caused atmospheric changes in the caves, endangering the paintings. Scientists went to work to halt the destructive fungus plaguing the paintings, known as "the green sickness," and a detailed facsimile was constructed nearby for visitors. The town of Montignac itself is worth a stop, for its well-preserved medieval streets and houses.

## Essentials

**GETTING THERE**   By far, the easiest way to reach Montignac is to **drive** northeast from Les Eyzies on D65 for 19km (12 miles).

**Rail** service is to the neighboring hamlet of Condat-Le-Lardin, 9.5km (6 miles) northeast. From there, taxis (*②* **05-53-51-80-46**) take visitors to Montignac for 20€. If no taxis are waiting, a railway station employee will call one for you. For train information, visit www.voyages-sncf.com or call *②* **36-35**.

**VISITOR INFORMATION** The **Office de Tourisme** in Montignac is on place Bertrand-de-Born (www.tourisme-vezere.com; *②* **05-53-51-82-60**).

## Exploring the Caves & Other Attractions

Public visits to the original Lascaux caves ceased in 1963. Permission to visit for research purposes is given only to qualified archaeologists, so unless you've got an advanced degree and good connections, you will have to make do with the facsimile. That said, Lascaux II is nothing to sniff at. Years of painstaking artistic and scientific labor went into re-creating the cave, including the use of prehistoric painting techniques and natural colorants. While some of the magic is lost, what you see is virtually identical to the real thing. For more virtual reality, you can visit the original cave online at an extensive site set up by the French government: www.lascaux.culture.fr.

**Lascaux II** ★★ HISTORIC SITE   A short walk downhill from the real cave is an impressive reproduction of the original, duplicated and molded in concrete to look and feel like the original stone. The 39m-long (128-ft.) tunnel faithfully reproduces the section of the cave harboring 90 percent of the famous paintings, so you will get a good idea of what the "Sistine Chapel of Prehistory" looks like. You'll see majestic bulls, wild boars, stags, horses, and deer, the originals of which

Lascaux cave paintings.

were painted by Cro-Magnon peoples 15,000 to 20,000 years ago. No one has yet figured out exactly what purpose these paintings served, but the artistry of these prehistoric painters is startling. Try to show up as close to opening time as possible—the number of visitors per day is limited to 2,000, and tickets usually sell out by 2pm. During the winter, you can buy tickets directly at Lascaux II (remember, it's closed Mon in off season), but from April to October, you must purchase them from a kiosk adjacent to the Montignac tourist office, place Bertran-de-Born. You will be given a specific time for your guided visit; be sure to ask for a tour in English, if needed.

2km (1¼ miles) from Montignac, off D706. www.semitour.com. ✆ **05-53-51-95-03.** Admission 9.50€ adults, 6€ children 6–12, free for children 5 and under. July–Aug daily 9am–7pm; Oct to mid-Nov daily 10am–12:30pm and 2–6pm; mid-Feb to Mar Tues–Sun 10am–12:30pm and 2–5:30pm; Apr–June and Sept daily 9am–6pm. Closed mid-Nov to mid-Feb.

**Le Thot** ☺ ZOO/MUSEUM   This attraction includes a zoo with live animals that approximate those depicted on the walls of Lascaux, like Przewalski horses and European bison. Projection rooms show short films on the discovery of cave art at Lascaux, and exhibits explore prehistoric painting techniques and Cro-Magnon life in the Dordogne. After your visit to Le Thot, walk out on the terrace for a view of the Vézère Valley and the Lascaux hills.

Thonac, 7km (4¼ miles) southwest of Montignac along D706 (follow the signs for Les Eyzies). www.semitour.com. ✆ **05-53-50-70-44.** Admission 7€ adults, 4.50€ children 6–12, free for children 5 and under. July–Aug daily 10am–7pm; Oct to mid-Nov daily 10am–12:30pm and 2–6pm; mid-Feb to Mar and mid-Nov to Dec Tues–Sun 10am–12:30pm and 2–5:30pm; Apr–June and Sept daily 10am–6pm. Closed Jan. Single tickets for visits of both Lascaux and Thot available. 13€ adults, 8.50€ children 6-12.

**Site Préhistorique de Regourdou** ☺ MUSEUM   About 450m (1,476 ft.) uphill from Lascaux, a minor road branches off and runs through a forest until it reaches this site, discovered in 1954 by Roger Constant when he conducted an archeological dig in front of his house. Found at the site was a sepulcher with a skeleton of a Neanderthal man and a bear and several other bear skeletons nearby, possibly evidence of a prehistoric bear cult. The house has been made into an archaeological museum; nearby, six semiwild bears roam around a naturalized habitat that's barricaded against humans. Depending on the time of year, you may be required to take a guided tour (available in English and French, at no extra cost).

✆ **05-53-51-81-23.** www.regourdou.fr. Admission 5€ adults, 3€ children 6–12, free for children 5 and under. July–Aug daily 10am–7pm; Sept–Nov and Feb–June daily 11am–6pm. Closed Dec to mid-Feb.

**Préhisto Parc** ☺ MUSEUM   Around 15km from Montignac and 5km from Les Eyzies, but well worth the detour, this is a highly child-friendly overview of how Neanderthal and Cro-Magnon man lived. The exhibits are set out around a wooded walkway through a five-hectare park, with recreations of scenes from daily life, such as a Wooly Mammoth hunt, and a family making tools and cooking around an open fire. Workshops during school holidays and the summer months teach skills such as fire-making, flint-cutting, and spear-throwing. **La Madeleine**, a riverside cave village just a few minutes drive away, also makes an excellent visit.

La Faure Reignac, Tursac 24020. www.prehistoparc.fr. ℂ **05-53-50-73-19.** Admission 6.80€ adults, 3.20€ children 6–12, free for children 5 and under. July–Aug daily 9:30am–7.30pm; Sept–Nov and Feb–June daily 10am–6pm. Closed mid Nov to mid-Feb.

## Where to Eat & Stay

**Aux Berges de la Vézère** ★ MODERN FRENCH/ITALIAN This is a wonderful restaurant, right on the banks of the river, with views over the medieval streets and houses of the village on the far banks of the Vézère. The main food is bistro-style French, with a good range of freshly-caught river fish, and classics such as *filet mignon de porc*. Their Italian pizza menu may seem odd, but it is expertly done, with quality touches such as 36-month aged Parmesan and 24-month aged Prosciutto ham. Books for children add to the relaxed feeling—and in a town where restaurants can be tourist traps in the summer, this is a great choice.

Place Tourny, Montignac 24290. ℂ **05-53-50-56-31.** DC, MC, V. Main courses 9.90€–15€. Menus 20€. July–Aug daily noon–2:30pm, 9–11pm. Rest of year Tues–Sun noon–2pm, 7:30–10:30pm

**Hostellerie la Roseraie** ★ 🦯 In the heart of the medieval village, this little charmer is both affordable and cozy. It was converted from a comfortable home built for one of the town merchants in the 19th century on the banks of the Vézère. The midsize bedrooms have individual character and well-kept bathrooms with either a tub or shower. Adding to the charm is a rose garden in back. There is a pleasant terrace to enjoy in the summer months, and the restaurant is one of the better choices in town, serving traditional French cuisine; fixed-price menus cost from 28€ to 49€.

11 place d'Armes, Montignac 24290. www.laroseraie-hotel.com. ℂ **05-53-50-53-92.** Fax 05-53-51-02-23. 14 units. 85€–185€ double; 200€–280€ family apartment. AE, DC, MC, V. Parking 8€. **Amenities:** Restaurant; bar; outdoor pool. *In room:* TV, hair dryer, Wi-Fi (in most; 3€ per 2 hr.). Closed Nov–Easter.

# LES EYZIES-DE-TAYAC ★★★

533km (330 miles) SW of Paris; 45km (28 miles) SE of Périgueux

When prehistoric skeletons were unearthed here in 1868, the market town of Les Eyzies-de-Tayac (known as Les Eyzies) suddenly became an archaeologist's dream. This area in the Dordogne Valley was found to be one of the richest in the world in ancient sites and deposits. Some of the caves contain primitive drawings made 30,000 years ago. The most beautiful and most famous are at Lascaux (see above), but many caves around Les Eyzies are open to the public.

## Essentials

**GETTING THERE** Local **trains** run from Le Buisson, 19km (12 miles) away. The several daily trains from Périgueux are more direct. For information, visit www.voyages-sncf.com or call ℂ **36-35.** To **drive** from Périgueux, start along D710 southeast to Le Bugue, and then follow the signs to Les Eyzies-de-Tayac.

**VISITOR INFORMATION** The **Office de Tourisme** (www.tourisme-vezere.com; ℂ **05-53-06-97-05**) is open year-round at 19 rue de la Préhistoire (place de la Mairie).

## Exploring the Area

Many of the caves in this area limit the number of daily visitors they admit; you can call ahead for reservations up to a year in advance. We recommend that you do so, especially if you plan to visit in the summer.

If you want to pedal around the countryside, you can rent bicycles at the tourist office. Prices begin at 10€ per half-day, 15€ per full day. A 20€ deposit is required; no credit cards are accepted.

Whether you're biking or driving, the loveliest villages in the **Dordogne Valley ★★★** include Sarlat-la-Canéda, 17km (11 miles) southeast of Les Eyzies, and La Roque-Gageac, 14 km (8¾ miles) south of Sarlat. Smaller villages, including Beynac-et-Cazenac, Castelnaud, Domme, and Montfort, lie beside the road that meanders through the Dordogne Valley. Throughout the region, routes are country roads marked only with signs leading to the above-mentioned destinations.

Make a special effort to stand in the shadow of the foreboding **Château de Beynac ★★**, Beynac-et-Cazenac (✆ **05-53-29-50-40**), a remarkably intact 12th-century fortress that peers out over the Dordogne Valley from a rocky crag. The fortress played an important role in the 100 Years' War and at one point was seized by Richard the Lion-Hearted. The Grosso family, who live on-site, have been renovating the monument for almost 40 years, and they've done a amazing job; the castle has served as a backdrop in several movies, including Luc Besson's *Jean d'Arc*. The view alone is worth the hike up the hill; fans of knights in shining armor will surely appreciate the visit. It's open April through September daily 10am to 6:30pm, and October to March daily 11am to sundown. Free 1-hour guided tours (in French) begin once or twice an hour. Admission, with or without the tour, costs 7.50€, 4.30€ ages 12 to 16, and 3.20€ ages 5 to 11. There's a worthy restaurant in the nearby **Hôtel du Chateau** (✆ **05-53-29-19-20**), located on the river at the base of the chateau.

**Grotte de Font-de-Gaume.**

**Grotte de Font-de-Gaume ★★**
HISTORIC SITE This is the last cave with multicolored prehistoric paintings that is still open to the public (although there are rumors that this too will be closed within a few years, so move fast). Only 180 visitors are allowed per day, so be sure to reserve well in advance, particularly in the summer. You will be on a 45-minute guided tour (tours are limited to 12 persons, and make sure to request one in English when you reserve) through a rather narrow cave (claustrophobes beware). Discovered in 1901, the paintings and etchings in the cave date from the Magdalenian period (17,000– 9,000 B.C.). While the paintings are not as spectacular as those at Lascaux, here you are seeing the real thing, including depictions of bison,

Musée National de la Préhistoire.

mammoths, horses, and other animals. The knowledgeable guides will point out how prehistoric artists used the shape of the caves walls to make their paintings more lifelike. They may also show some eerie prehistoric hand prints.

On D47, 1.5km (1 mile) outside Les Eyzies. ℂ **05-53-06-86-00.** http://eyzies.monuments-nationaux.fr/en. Admission 7€ adults, 4.50€ 18–25, free for ages 17 and under. May 15–Sept 15 Sun–Fri 9:30am–5:30pm; Sept 16–May 14 Sun–Fri 9:30am–12:30pm and 2–5:30pm.

### Grotte des Combarelles ★ HISTORIC SITE  Discovered at the turn of the 20th century, this wide cave on the southeast edge of town has over 400 etchings of animals, including musk oxen, horses, bison, and aurochs (prehistoric oxen). Think of it as a gallery of Magdalenian art. Advance reservations are vital—only 60 visitors per day are admitted.

On D47, 17km (11 miles) north of Bergerac. ℂ **05-53-06-86-00.** http://eyzies.monuments-nationaux.fr/en. Admission 7€ adults, 4.50€ 18–25, free for ages 17 and under. May 15–Sept 15 Sun–Fri 9:30am–5:30pm; Sept 16–May 14 Sun–Fri 9:30am–12:30pm and 2–5:30pm.

### Grotte du Grand-Roc ★ NATURAL ATTRACTION  The artistic marvels here are all created by nature, not man; this cave is a geological wonder of crystals, stalagmites, and stalactites. The cave is about 1.5km (1 mile) northwest of Les Eyzies on the left bank of the Vézère (signs point the way on D47). There are no limits to visitors at this venue.

48 av. Préhistoire, Les Eyzies 24620. www.semitour.com. ℂ **05-53-06-92-70.** Admission 7.€ adults, 4.50€ children 6–12, free for children 5 and under. July–Aug daily 10am–7pm; Sept to mid-Nov and Easter–June Sun–Fri 10am–12:30pm and 2–6pm; mid-Nov to Dec and Feb–Mar Mon–Thurs 10am–12:30pm and 2–5:30pm. Closed Jan. Ensure you have a sweater, as it gets chilly underground.

### Musée National de la Préhistoire ★★ MUSEUM  In the shadow of the limestone cliff that hovers above the village, this museum had a major overhaul and is now set in a modern limestone building next to a fortress-castle from the 16th century. One of the largest collections of prehistoric artifacts in Europe ("only" 18,000 of its 5 million objects are on display), this museum traces 400,000 years of human history, from the origins to the end of the Ice Age (around 10,000 B.C.). Highlights include an exquisite **15,000-year-old etching of a bison ★**

carved on a bone, showing its head licking its flank; a **40,000-year-old skeleton** of a newborn; **Neanderthal jewelry;** and **stone tools** dating back 150,000 years. Also on display are the first replicas of the first-known human footprints, dating from around 3.6 million years ago.

1 rue du Musée, Les Eyzies 24640. www.musee-prehistoire-eyzies.fr. © **05-53-06-45-45.** Admission 5€ adults, 3.50€ 18–25, free for children 17 and under. July–Aug daily 9:30am–6:30pm; June and Sept Wed–Mon 9:30am–6pm; Oct–May Wed–Mon 9:30am–12:30pm and 2–5:30pm.

## Where to Eat & Stay

**Hôtel Le Centenaire ★★**   This charm-filled oasis is even better known for its cuisine than for its accommodations. The good-size, comfortable rooms are conservatively modern, with period touches like reproduction antiques and small canopies over the beds. The verdant grounds include a shady terrace and an outdoor pool. Even if you're not a hotel guest, consider a visit to the restaurant, where fixed-price menus cost 35€ to 70€. Specialties include sautéed foie gras with homemade spice bread, sautéed scallops with truffle risotto, and veal fricassee with wild mushrooms.

Rocher de la Penne, Les Eyzies-Tayac-Sireuil 24620. www.hotelducentenaire.fr. © **05-53-06-68-68.** Fax 05-53-06-92-41. 24 units. 120€–195€ double; 195€–215€ suite. AE, MC, V. Closed Jan to mid-Feb. **Amenities:** Restaurant; bar; exercise room; heated outdoor pool; room service; sauna. *In room:* TV, hair dryer, minibar, free Wi-Fi.

### The Scoop on Cave Tickets

To prevent deterioration of the art, a limited number of visitors are allowed into the caves of **Les Eyzies-de-Tayac** each day (specifically Font-de-Gaume and Combarelles). Tickets are available up to 3 months in advance, and we advise you to reserve that far ahead, if possible.

**Hôtel Le Moulin de la Beune ★ 🛈**   This is the best bet for the frugal traveler—a transformed 17th-century mill (complete with working waterwheel) just off the main street. The simple but cozy rooms are nicely decorated with homey touches. A small stream runs through the property, so if you open the window, you'll be lulled to sleep by the sound of splashing water. Ivy covers the outside of the hotel and the restaurant, Au Vieux Moulin, which serves elegant regional classics with set menus starting at 31€. In good weather, you can dine on a shaded terrace or just laze in a lounge chair next to the babbling brook.

2 rue du Moulin Bas, Les Eyzies-de-Tayac 24620. http://moulindelabeune.com. © **05-53-06-94-33.** Fax 05-53-06-98-06. 20 units. 64€–79€ double. MC, V. Closed Nov–Apr. **Amenities:** Restaurant. *In room:* A/C, hair dryer.

**Hôtel Les Glycines ★ 🛈**   We'd stay here just for the flower garden. Housed in a building that dates from 1862, this establishment offers regional cuisine, comfortable accommodations, and drinks on a veranda with a grape arbor. Rooms are done up in relaxing shades of beige, combining regional charm with designer style. Some rooms look out over the ample grounds, which include a pool and lots of the aforementioned flowers. Restaurant specialties include new twists on foie gras, cèpes, and truffles. Fixed-price menus range from 28€ (lunchtime only) to 95€. Many ingredients come from the hotel's impressive kitchen garden.

Rte. de Périgueux (D47), Les Eyzies-Tayac-Sireuil 24620. www.les-glycines-dordogne.com. ✆ **05-53-06-97-07.** Fax 05-53-06-92-19. 23 units. 95€–165€ double; 195€–235€ junior suite. AE, DC, MC, V. Closed Nov–Apr. **Amenities:** Restaurant; bar; babysitting; outdoor pool; room service. *In room:* A/C, TV, hair dryer, free Wi-Fi.

# SARLAT-LA-CANÉDA ★★

9.5km (6 miles) E of Les Eyzies-de-Tayac; 530km (329 miles) SW of Paris; 60km (37 miles) NW of Cahors

The capital of Périgord Noir (Black Périgord), Sarlat is possibly the best-preserved medieval town in southwestern France, almost a living museum. Its inner core is filled with so many ancient buildings that it's like stepping back into another age as you wander past stone structures of ocher color along cobblestone streets.

Sarlat grew up around a Benedictine abbey back in the 9th century and was awarded a city charter in 1299. The zenith of its fame came in the 14th century, when it was known as a bustling center of artisans, painters, and students. Old Sarlat, called **Vieille Ville ★★★**, the main reason to visit, is split by the 19th-century main street, **rue de la République,** which defines the commercial heart of town and is lined with shops and restaurants.

With more medieval buildings than in any town in France, Sarlat is often a movie backdrop. Robert Hossein's *Les Misérables* was shot here in 1982, as was Danny Huston's *Becoming Colette,* in 1991. Watch out in summer, though—traffic can snarl on the approach to the town, so try to plan your arrival for as early in the morning as possible.

## Essentials

**GETTING THERE**   There are good direct train connections from Bordeaux (trip time: 2½ hr, 25€), about seven trains per day. Trains from Paris go to Souillac, about 30km (19 miles) by bus from Sarlat; buses run fairly frequently (trip time: 40 min.); visit www.ter-sncf.com/Regions/Aquitaine/fr for schedules. For train information and schedules, visit www.voyages-sncf.com or call ✆ **36-35.** The terminus in Sarlat lies 1km (½ mile) south of the old town. You can walk it in 15 minutes or else take a taxi.

Motorists **drive** the A10 autoroute from Paris, going by way of Poitiers, Angoulême, and Périgueux to reach Sarlat. Or you can take the A89 from Bordeaux. Sarlat lies 180km (112 miles) east of Bordeaux.

**VISITOR INFORMATION**   The Office de Tourisme, 3 rue Tourny (www.sarlat-tourisme.com; ✆ **05-53-31-45-45**), sells maps of the area and offers English-language tours from May to October.

**SPECIAL EVENTS**   In the summer, the streets of Sarlat are bustling with people, many of whom come to attend the **Féstival des Jeux de Théâtre de Sarlat** (www.festival-theatre-sarlat.com; ✆ **05-53-31-10-83**), a theater festival that runs from mid-July to the first week of August. During the month of August and into the first week of September, Sarlat also hosts the **Féstival de Musique du Périgord Noir** (www.festivalduperigordnoir.fr; ✆ **05-53-51-61-61**). The November film festival, **Le Féstival de Film de Sarlat** (www.ville-sarlat.fr/festival; ✆ **05-53-29-18-13**), is the biggest such event in France after Cannes and Deauville.

# Exploring the Town

Start your tour of Old Sarlat at **place du Peyrou ★**, and allow at least 2 hours to wander around. Opening onto place du Peyrou is the **Cathédral de Saint-Sacerdos,** which enjoyed its greatest prestige when it was an Episcopal seat between 1317 and 1790. The cathedral has a Romanesque bell tower, but most of the structure dates from the 16th and 17th centuries. Much of the interior is in the late Gothic style. The structure stands to the right of the tourist office (see above). Leave by the south doorway.

Behind the cathedral is **Lanterne des Morts,** or "Lantern to the Dead" **★★**, which was reputedly built in the 1100s to honor St. Bernard's pilgrimage to Sarlat, and is a fine example of early medieval sepulchral architecture.

Also opening on place du Peyrou, **Maison de la Boétie ★** stands opposite the cathedral. You can admire its facade, as it's the most charming Renaissance house in Sarlat. Dating from 1525, the house has mullioned windows and a painted gable. It was once inhabited by the town's most famous son, Etienne de la Boétie, who was born about the time the house was completed. A criminal magistrate, he had a lifelong friendship with Montaigne, who was at La Boétie's bedside when he died in 1563. That death inspired Montaigne's famous essay "Friendship."

The second square to visit is **place du Marché aux Oies ★**, known for its bronze statue of three geese by Lalanne. For centuries, this market sold live fowl, and the statue commemorates that long-ago role. The most stunning Renaissance facade on this square belongs to the Hotel Chassaing.

One of Sarlat's most colorful medieval streets is **rue des Consuls ★★**, whose greatest buildings include **Hôtel Plamon,** its Gothic windows making it look like a church. Beyond the doorway of Plamon is a series of five arcades on

**Rue Montaigne.**

## A Side Trip to Gorodka

After a few days exploring the prehistoric and medieval riches of the Dordogne, a trip to **Gorodka-Za village of modern art** ★ (www.gorodka.com; ✆ **05-53-31-02-00**), 4km (2 miles) from Sarlat in La Canéda, is a refreshing change. The brainchild of artist Pierre Shasmoukine, you might find exhibits by various artists-in-residence; live theater shows; or sculptures and multimedia exhibits, either dotted around a forest with three separate walkways or within 8 art galleries displaying over 400 works. It's a particularly interesting place at night, as many of the works of art start glowing and moving when you least expect them to. The site seems to be constantly threatened by local opposition, but it remains for now one of the most unusual and inspiring sites in the region. Gorodka can be visited daily (July–Aug 10am–midnight, Sept–June 2–6pm). Free admission (although certain exhibits have entrance fees).

the ground floor opening onto a covered market. A trio of Gothic bay windows on the second floor have been restored to their original appearance.

If you follow **Jardin des Enfeus** (behind the cathedral), you reach **rue Montaigne** ★ where the great 16th-century philosopher was born and once lived. The buildings along this street are extremely photogenic.

Feel free to roam the back streets of Sarlat. You can allow yourself to get lost, as you'll invariably wind up back at **place de la Liberté,** in the center of town, and the 18th-century Hôtel de Ville, or City Hall.

Sarlat is celebrated by French gastronomes for its foie gras and truffle market, **Le Marché aux Truffles et au Gras,** held at the bottom of rue Fénelon every Saturday from 9am to noon December to February. Sarlat is also known for its wines, and the best selection is found at **Julien de Savignac,** place Pasteur (✆ **05-53-31-29-20**).

## Where to Eat

**Auberge de Mirandol** ★ FRENCH    A 15th century building makes a fine setting for this popular restaurant. The menu offers the full range of southwestern classics—foie gras, duck breast, coq au vin, walnut bread, and plentiful truffles when they are in season. Three separate dining rooms allow a large number of diners to be seated, but even so, it's best to book ahead in the summer.

7, rue Consuls, Sarlat 24200. www.restaurant-auberge-mirandol-sarlat.fr. ✆ **05-53-29-53-89.** Reservations recommended in the restaurant. Main courses 15€–25€; set menus 15€–29€; DC, MC, V. noon–2pm, 7:30–10pm.

**Le Quatre Saisons** FRENCH    Only in a town as rich in medieval monuments as Sarlat could a well-recommended restaurant be tucked into a 14th-century stone tower. You'll climb an exterior stairway to reach the dining room, which is outfitted in a minimalist contemporary style in tones of gray and soft orange. A separate corkscrew-style staircase leads upstairs to a terrace with additional tables and a view over town. Menu items might include foie gras with caramelized apples, lamb with an herb-cream sauce, and a moist chocolate cake served with licorice-flavored ice cream.

2 côte de Toulouse. www.4saisons-sarlat-perigord.com. ☏ **05-53-29-48-59.** Reservations recommended. Set-price menus 25€–49€. AE, DC, MC, V. Sept–June Thurs–Mon 12:15–1:30pm and 7:15–9:30pm; July–Aug daily 12:15–1:30pm and 7:15–9:30pm. Closed 1 week in Jan and 1 week in Mar.

## Where to Stay

The most sumptuous way to live in and around Sarlat is at the **Château de Puymartin,** which rents two of the most elegant guest rooms in the entire area. Surrounded by antiques, you get to live like a count (or countess) of medieval times, but with all the modern comforts. The cost of a double is 120€ to 150€ per night.

D47, Marquay 24200. www.chateau-de-puymartin.com. ☏ **05-53-59-29-97.** The château is open for visits also, at 7€ for adults and 5€ for children 6–12. Apr–Oct.

**Les Chambres du Glacier ★ 🍴**   Well located on the pedestrianized place de la Liberté, this *chambres d'hotes* is housed in an 18th century building and is full of character. There are well-sized bedrooms with slightly old-fashioned private bathrooms. A brasserie (and ice cream parlor, hence the name) is on the ground floor, making plans easy with children in the evenings.

9 place de la Liberte, Sarlat 24200. www.hotel-recollets-sarlat.com. ☏ **05-53-29-99-99.** 4 units. 70€ double; 90€ family room. MC, V. *In room:* A/C, TV, free Wi-Fi.

**La Maison des Peyrat ★ 🛏**   Up a hill and away from the crowds that flock to Sarlat in summer, this is the most tranquil retreat in walking distance, lying only 1.6km (1 mile) from the center. The oldest section of this one-story stone structure dates from 1343, when it was a hospital for victims of the Black Death. Those unhappy memories are long gone now. In 1843, a local baron turned it into a hunting lodge. Today it's a small hotel and preserves much of its original character, with simply furnished bedrooms in pastel and rattan furnishings. Exposed beams and original artwork add to its character. On a terrace shaded by a massive chestnut tree, breakfast and dinner are served (for hotel guests only; dinner is 23€).

Le Lac de la Plane, Sarlat 24200. http://maisondespeyrat.com. ☏ **05-53-59-00-32.** 10 units. 56€–103€ double. MC, V. Closed Nov 15–Apr 1. **Amenities:** Restaurant for hotel guests (dinner served Mon–Tues and Thurs–Sat); outdoor pool; free Wi-Fi. *In room:* TV, hair dryer.

# ROCAMADOUR ★★★

541km (335 miles) SW of Paris; 66km (41 miles) SE of Sarlat-la-Canéda; 55km (34 miles) S of Brive; 63km (39 miles) NE of Cahors

Rocamadour reached the zenith of its fame and prosperity in the 13th century, when it was one of the most famous pilgrimage sites in Christendom. Countless miracles were said to have taken place there, thanks to the sacred aura of the Chapel of Notre-Dame and, specifically, the statue of the Black Madonna. Pilgrims still come here (in significantly smaller numbers), but most visitors are secular tourists who come to admire this spectacular village that seems to be carved into sheer rock. It's definitely worth a detour, even if it's out of your way. The setting is one of the most unusual in Europe: Towers, churches, and oratories rise in stages up the side of a cliff on the slope of the usually dry gorge of Alzou.

Only around 600 people live in the village year-round, but in the summer that numbers skyrockets during the day, when crowds of tourists arrive. For obvious logistical reasons, vehicles are prohibited in the town and there is a lot of stair

**Rocamadour.**

climbing to do. The faint of heart or the mobility-impaired can take an elevator from the village at the base of the cliff up to the religious sanctuary, and from the religious sanctuary to the castle (see below). It's a short walk from the parking lot to the village.

## Essentials

**GETTING THERE**    The best way to reach Rocamadour is by **car.** From Bordeaux, travel east along A89 autoroute to Brive-la-Gaillarde, then take the A20 to exit 54 toward Gramat. Then continue on D840 and take the D673 south to Rocamadour.

Rocamadour and neighboring Padirac share a **train** station, **Gare de Rocamadour-Padirac,** that isn't really convenient to either—it's 4km (2½ miles) east of Rocamadour on N140. Trains arrive about five or six times a day from Brive in the north and Capdenac in the south; for transport from the station, your only option is to call a **taxi** (phone numbers posted at the station). For train information and schedules, visit www.voyages-sncf.com or call ✆ **36-35**. There is no **bus** service.

**VISITOR INFORMATION**    The town maintains two separate **tourist offices,** one in the village Hôtel de Ville, rue Roland-le-Preux (✆ **05-65-33-62-59**), and another well-signposted branch office in l'Hospitalet, a small village in the heights that you will pass through on your way to Rocamadour (www.rocamadour.com; ✆ **05-65-33-22-00**).

## Exploring the Town

The **site ★★★** of this gravity-defying village rises abruptly across the landscape. Its single street, lined with souvenir shops, runs along the side of a steep hill. It's best seen when approached from the road coming in from the tiny village of L'Hospitalet. Once in Rocamadour, you will want to get from the lower town (Basse Ville) to the town's **Cité Réligieuse,** a cluster of chapels and churches halfway up the cliff. The main way of getting from bottom to top is a narrow street/staircase that loops and twists its way upward. Called the "Chemin de la Croix," or the Stations of Christ, it was the route medieval penitents used to make their way to the sacred chapel—the most penitent did it on their knees.

For the unrepentant, and others who are loath to negotiate the town's steep inclines, the town maintains two elevators. One goes from Basse Ville to Cité Réligieuse, midway up the rocky heights of Rocamadour. The ride costs 2€ one-way, 3€ round-trip. The other goes from Cité Réligieuse to the panoramic medieval ramparts near the hill's summit; it costs 2.50€ one-way, 4€ round-trip. A tourist train also trundles up and down at regular intervals from April to September, for 2.50€ one-way, 3.50€ round-trip.

For a superb **view,** head toward the **Château de Rocamadour,** which perches on a rock spur high above the town center. You can reach it by way of Chemin de la Croix or take the elevator. It was built in the 14th century and restored by the local bishops in the 19th century. Its interior is off-limits, except for guests of the church officials who live and work here. You can, however, walk along its panoramic **ramparts ★★,** which open at 8am daily year-round. Closing times vary, usually just before sunset and no later than 9pm in the summer. Admission to the ramparts costs 2€. **Note:** You must buy your entrance ticket at a machine; be sure to have exact change, or you will have made the trip up for nothing.

**Cité Réligieuse ★★★** RELIGIOUS SITE   This cluster of chapels and churches is the town's religious centerpiece, visited by both casual tourists and devoted pilgrims. Site of many conversions, with mystical connotations that date to the Middle Ages, it's accessible from the town on the **Grand Escalier,** a stairway of 216 steps. Climbing the weathered steps will lead you to the **parvis des Eglises,** place St-Amadour, with seven chapels. Free tours are conducted by volunteers; schedules change frequently, according to holidays and church schedules. Two to five 1-hour tours take place each day (depending on the season); times are prominently posted at the entrance.

The three most important churches are detailed below.

**Basilique St-Sauveur** RELIGIOUS SITE   Set against the cliff, this small basilica was built in the Romanesque-Gothic style from the 11th to the 13th centuries. It's decorated with paintings and inscriptions recalling visits of celebrated persons, including Philippe the Handsome.

**Chapelle Notre-Dame ★★** RELIGIOUS SITE   This is the "chapelle miraculeuse," the holy of holies, where St. Amadour is said to have carved out an oratory in the rock (who exactly St. Amadour was, however, is subject of debate). After caving in during the 15th century, it was rebuilt in Flamboyant Gothic style, and it underwent various alterations in the 19th century, when it was restored. It shelters the venerated **Black Madonna,** a small sculpture carved out of wood that dates from the 12th century, depicting the Virgin seated with a small Jesus on her knee. Hanging from the roof is a 9th-century **bell** that was rung when a miracle occurred. Outside, above the door leading to the chapel, is an iron sword stuck in the rock that is said to be **Durandal,** the sword of Roland, the legendary 8th-century knight.

**Chapelle St-Michel** ★ RELIGIOUS SITE   Sheltered by an overhanging rock on the outside of this Romanesque chapel are two impressive **12th-century frescoes** representing the Annunciation and the Visitation. There are more frescoes inside, though many are damaged.

Free admission; donations appreciated. Suggested donation for tour 6€ adults, 3.50€ children 8–18. Daily 9am–11pm.

## Where to Eat & Stay

**Grand Hôtel Beau-Site** ★   With its entrance evoking a medieval hall, this is one of the finest inns in the village. The stone walls were built in the 15th century by an Order of Malta commander, Jehan de Valon (1440–1516). Today the rear terrace provides a view of the Val d'Alzou. The reception area has heavy beams and a cavernous fireplace. Rooms (23 of which are in the air-conditioned main building, the rest in a less desirable annex) are comfortable and conservatively decorated; many have beautiful views, and some have spa bathtubs.

The restaurant serves regional cuisine prepared by the Menot family, who have owned the place for generations. Specialties include truffle pie, and duck magret with fig sauce. Dessert may be a slice of caramelized apple tart or Poire Belle Hélène (poached pears in chocolate sauce). Fixed-price menus cost 19€ at lunch and 26€ to 58€ at dinner.

Cité Médiévale, Rocamadour 46500. www.bw-beausite.com. © **800/528-1234** in the U.S. and Canada, or 05-65-33-63-08. Fax 05-65-33-65-23. 38 units. 99€–145€ double. AE, DC, MC, V. Free parking. Closed mid-Nov to mid-Feb. **Amenities:** Restaurants; bar; free Internet; outdoor pool. *In room:* A/C, TV, hair dryer, free Wi-Fi.

**Hôtel-Restaurant Le Belvedere** ★   This is a good option offering very reasonable value, and well located with views over the streets of Rocamadour, particularly beautiful with the illuminations at night. There is a contemporary-styled restaurant, with fixed-price menus from 18€ to 34€. On summer evenings, ask for a table on the terrace.

L'Hospitalet, Rocamadour 46500. www.hotel-le-belvedere.fr. © **05-65-33-63-25.** Fax 05-65-33-69-25. 17 units. 55€–76€ double. AE, DC, MC, V. Free parking. Closed Feb-Mar on Tues and Wed. **Amenities:** Restaurants; bar; outdoor pool. *In room:* A/C, TV, hair dryer, free Wi-Fi.

## Where to Eat & Stay Nearby

**Château de La Treyne** ★★   For a treat away from the tourist bustle, try this Relais & Châteaux property 20 minutes away, in Lacave. Built in the 14th and 17th centuries, this superb chateau sits on the edge of a particularly tranquil bend of the Dordogne River. Blessed with lush grounds and a classic French garden, the property is surrounded by 120 hectares (296 acres) of forest for hiking and truffle hunting. The spacious rooms feature Pierre Frey fabrics, antiques, and exposed beams; the more luxurious ones feel like private apartments from another era. The restaurant has been awarded a Michelin star for chef Andrieux's delectable creations, like langoustine risotto, foie gras in a spice crust, wild mushroom ravioli, and grilled Quercy lamb. If you've gone this far, you may as well indulge in an orange-rhubarb semolina roll with lemon-infused ice cream. Set menus are 48€ at lunch and 96€ to 138€ at dinner.

Lacave 46200. http://chateaudelatreyne.com. ☎ **05-65-27-60-60.** Fax 05-65-27-60-70. 16 units. 200€–440€ double; 600€–900€ suite. AE, DC, MC, V. Closed mid-Nov to Christmas and Jan to mid-Mar. Take the D32 and D247 from Rocamadour to Lacave. **Amenities:** Restaurant; bar, outdoor pool. *In room:* A/C, TV, hair dryer, minibar, free Wi-Fi.

**Domaine de La Rhue ★ 🏠**   This property's charming owners, Christine and Eric Jooris, gutted a 19th-century stable and turned it into a series of spacious and light-filled rooms, each simply but elegantly decorated in superb taste. Some have terraces, some have minibars, and all are equipped with compact bathrooms, mainly with shower units. On the lower level is an inviting reception and breakfast room with a welcoming fireplace. Eric is a pilot and can takes guests for a 45-minute hot-air balloon ride over the canyon of Rocamadour.

Rocamadour 46500. www.domainedelarhue.com. ☎ **05-65-33-71-50.** Fax 05-65-33-72-48. 14 units. 95€–130€ double. Studio La Forge 750€ per week. MC, V. Closed Nov–Easter. Follow D673, then N140 signposted rhue for a total of 5km (3 miles) from town. **Amenities:** Outdoor pool; free Wi-Fi. *In room:* A/C (in some), hair dryer, minibar (in some), kitchenette (in some).

# CAHORS ★

541km (335 miles) SW of Paris; 217km (135 miles) SE of Bordeaux; 89km (55 miles) N of Toulouse

The ancient capital of Quercy, Cahors was a thriving university city in the Middle Ages, and many antiquities from its illustrious past remain. Today Cahors is best known for the red wine that's made principally from the Malbec grapes grown in vineyards around this old city. Firm but not harsh, Cahors is one of the most deeply colored fine French wines.

Since the mid-1990s, the city of Cahors has funded the redesign and replanting of at least 21 municipal gardens, most of them laid out in medieval patterns, using historically appropriate plants. The most spectacular of these gardens lie immediately adjacent to Town Hall. Overall, they function as a magnet for horticultural societies throughout France.

## Essentials

**GETTING THERE**   To **drive** to Cahors from Toulouse, follow the A62 autoroute north to the junction with A20 and continue on A20 north into Cahors.

   **Trains** serve Cahors from Toulouse, Brive, and Montauban. For train information and schedules, visit www.voyages-sncf.com or call ☎ **36-35.** There's infrequent **bus** service from some of the outlying villages, several of which are of historical interest, but it's vastly easier to drive.

**VISITOR INFORMATION**   The **Office de Tourisme** is on place François-Mitterrand (www.tourisme-cahors.com; ☎ **05-65-53-20-65;** fax 05-65-53-20-74).

**SPECIAL EVENTS**   The **Festival du Blues** turns this town upside down for a week in mid-July, when blues groups, including some from the United States, descend. Most of the performances are free outdoor affairs along boulevard Gambetta. Main concerts are usually at the open-air **Théâtre des Verdures,** a courtyard in the heart of the medieval city. Ticket prices vary, but range from 25€ to 45€. For exact dates and information, contact the Office de Tourisme (see above) or visit the site of **Cahors Blues**

Festival (www.cahorsbluesfestival.com). You can buy tickets on the website or at any FNAC bookstore (www.fnac.fr). Every other year in April and May (next one 2013), La Diagonale des Arts reunites contemporary artists for exhibitions around the city. Info can be found at http://ladiagonaledesarts.org.

## Exploring the Area

The town is on a rocky peninsula almost entirely surrounded by a loop of the Lot River. It grew near a sacred spring that still supplies the city with water. At the source of the spring, the **Fontaine des Chartreux** stands by the side of **pont Valentré ★★** (also called pont du Diable), a bridge with a trio of towers. It's a magnificent example of medieval defensive design erected between 1308 and 1380 and restored in the 19th century. The pont, the first medieval fortified bridge in France, is the most eye-catching site in Cahors, with crenelated parapets, battlements, and pointed arches.

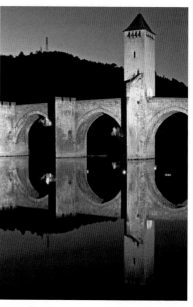

Pont Valentré.

Dominating the old town, the **Cathédrale St-Etienne ★**, 30 rue de la Chanterie (✆ **05-65-35-27-80**), was begun in 1119 and reconstructed between 1285 and 1500. It was the first cathedral in the country to have cupolas, giving it a Romanesque-Byzantine look. One remarkable feature is its sculptured Romanesque north portal, carved around 1135 in the Languedoc style. It's open daily from 9am to 7pm; in winter the cathedral is closed Sunday mornings. Adjoining the cathedral are the remains of a Gothic cloister from the late 15th century. The admission-free cloister is open during the same hours as the cathedral. The **Musée de Cahors Henri-Martin,** 792 rue Emile Zola (www.mairie-cahors.fr/musee), is also worth a few hours browsing with its extensive range of 18th and 19th century art, although several of the display rooms have temporary exhibits only, as some restoration work is underway. Admission is 3€ adult and free for those under 18, and it's open Wed-Sat 11am-6pm, Sun 2-6pm.

## Where to Eat

Le Balandre, the restaurant at **Hôtel Terminus** (see p. 742), serves well-recommended cuisine.

**Le Rendez-Vous ★** FRENCH  One of the most appealing restaurants in Cahors's historic core occupies the stone-walled, ocher-colored premises of a 13th-century private house. It turns out an array of well-prepared and reasonably priced dishes that guarantee an animated crowd. Menu items change with the season but may include fried foie gras with spice bread; a tart layered with anchovies and confit of onions; and superb farm-raised veal.

49 rue Clément Marot. ⓒ **05-65-22-65-10.** Reservations recommended. Main courses 14€; fixed-price lunch 16€, dinner 22€. MC, V. Tues–Sat noon–2pm and 7:30–9:30pm.

**L'O à la Bouche** ★ 🍴 MODERN FRENCH   One of Cahors's best brasseries recently moved to a restored mansion from the turn of the 20th century in the center of town. Meals at this popular spot involve full fixed-price menus, each with a choice of at least four food items per category (that is, a minimum of four starters, four main courses, and four desserts). Menu items might include fresh trout from the Pyrénées served with leeks in vinaigrette, and Quercy lamb flavored with walnuts and Espelette peppers, all created by renowned chef Jean-Francois Dive. The wine list includes an excellent sampling of Cahors vintages.

56 allée Fénelon. ⓒ **05-65-35-65-69.** Reservations recommended. Fixed-price menu 26€-50€. MC, V. Tues–Sat noon–1:30pm and 7–9:30pm.

## Where to Stay

**Hôtel de France**   Hotel choices are limited in Cahors, but these 1970s-era lodgings, positioned midway between pont Valentré and the train station, provide some of the best rooms in the town center. They're well furnished and modern, if not particularly chic. Each unit comes with an average-size bathroom, most with a shower unit. Breakfast is the only meal served, but there are plenty of restaurants nearby.

252 av. Jean-Jaurès, Cahors 46000. www.hoteldefrance-cahors.fr. ⓒ **05-65-35-16-76.** Fax 05-65-22-01-08. 39 units. 69€ double. AE, DC, MC, V. Parking 1.50€. *In room:* A/C, TV, hair dryer, minibar, free Wi-Fi.

**Hôtel Terminus** ★   On the avenue leading from the railway station into the heart of town, this hotel oozes turn-of-the-20th-century character with its original stone construction. Rooms are conservative yet tasteful, with floral prints, fresh flowers, and firm beds. On the premises is Le Balandre, the town's best restaurant, which specializes in regional dishes from the surrounding Périgord-Quercy district. Fixed-price menus are 18€ to 31€ at lunch and 36€ to 75€ at dinner. Even if you don't opt for a meal in its quaint dining room or on the outdoor terrace, you may want to stop into the 1920s-style bar for a drink.

5 av. Charles de Freycinet, Cahors 46000. www.balandre.com. ⓒ **05-65-53-32-00.** Fax 05-65-53-32-26. 21 units. 77€-100€ double; 130€-160€ suite. AE, DC, MC, V. Parking free in courtyard, 7€ in garage. Closed last 2 weeks in Nov. **Amenities:** Restaurant; bar; room service; free Wi-Fi. *In room:* TV, hair dryer, minibar.

# SIDE TRIP TO LIMOGES ★

396km (246 miles) S of Paris; 311km (193 miles) N of Toulouse; 93km (58 miles) NE of Périgueux

Limoges, the ancient capital of Limousin in west-central France, is world famous for its exquisite porcelain and enamel works. Enamel production is a medieval industry revived in the 19th century and still going strong. In fact, Limoges is the economic capital of western France. Occupying the Vienne's right bank, the town has historically consisted of two parts: La Cité (aka Vieux Limoges), with its narrow streets and old *maisons* on the lower slope, and La Ville Haute (aka "Le Château"), at the summit.

## Essentials

**GETTING THERE**   Limoges has good **train** service from most regional cities, with direct trains from Toulouse, Poitiers, and Paris. Ten trains depart daily from Paris's Gare d'Austerlitz for Limoges (trip time: 3 hr.; 56€ one-way). There are 12 trains a day from Périgueux (trip time: 1 hr.; 16€ one-way). For complete train information, visit www.voyages-sncf.fr or call ℂ **36-35** or 08-92-35-35-35 (calls cost 0.34€/min.). **Bus** transit in and out of the small towns and villages nearby can be arranged through the **Régie des Transports de la Haute-Vienne,** place des Charentes (ℂ **05-55-10-31-10;** www.rdthv.com). If you're **driving** from Périgueux, take N21 north for the 1½-hour trip. If driving from Cahors, take A20 north for the 2-hour trip.

**VISITOR INFORMATION**   The **Office de Tourisme** is at 12 bd. de Fleurus (www.tourismelimoges.com; ℂ **05-55-34-46-87;** fax 05-55-34-19-12).

## Exploring the Town

If you'd like to see an enameler at work or an operating porcelain factory, ask at the tourist office (see above) for a list of workshops, or go directly to the famous **Pavillon de la Porcelaine** (see p. 745).

Thanks to the rich deposits of kaolin (known locally as "white gold") found near Limoges in the 18th century, more than 30 manufacturers of porcelain have set up operations through the years. Many maintain factory outlets, sometimes offering good-quality seconds at reduced prices. In the center of town, you'll find **Raynaud,** 14 ancienne rte. d'Aixe (www.raynaud.fr; ℂ **05-55-01-77-65**), and **Porcelaines Philippe Deshoulières-Lafarge,** 77 bis rue Armand Dutreix

Shopping in Limoges.

(www.deshoulieres.com; ☎ **05-55-50-33-43**). Largest of all, with the best publicity operation, is **Bernardaud,** 27 av. Albert-Thomas (www.bernardaud.fr; ☎ **05-55-10-55-91**), where a small-scale museum offers regularly changing exhibitions, and a tearoom adjoins the showroom. Guided visits are available through the summer months, with a chance to get hands-on with the process of making pottery (June–Sept, 9:45–11:15am, 1:30–4pm, Oct–May by appointment). Adults 4.50€, free for children 12 and under.

**Cathédrale St-Etienne** CATHEDRAL   The cathedral was begun in 1273 and took years to complete. The choir was finished in 1327, but work continued in the nave until almost 1890. The cathedral is the only one in the old province of Limousin built entirely in the Gothic style. The main entrance is through Porte St-Jean, which has carved wooden doors from the 16th century (constructed at the peak of the Flamboyant Gothic style). Inside, the nave appears so harmonious it's hard to imagine that its construction took 6 centuries. The rood screen is of particular interest, built in 1533 in the ornate style of the Italian Renaissance. The cathedral also contains some bishops' tombs from the 14th to the 16th centuries.

Place de l'Evêché. ☎ **05-55-34-46-87.** Free admission. Mon–Sat 2:30–5pm, Sun 2:30–6pm.

**Eglise St-Michel-des-Lions** CHURCH   Two stone lions guard the entrance to this church. Constructed between the 14th and 16th centuries, it features a typically Limousin bell tower surmounted by a strange copper globe and splendid vaulting supported by slender pillars. Despite its name, the church is the center of the cult of St-Martial, a Limoges hometown bishop who died in the 3rd century. The church is the home of what's reputed to be his skull, stored in an elaborately enameled reliquary. Les Ostensions is a religious pilgrimage, established in 994, that occurs every 7 years from February to November. The skull, La Châsse de St-Martial—which some believers credit with healing powers—is removed from storage and exhibited as part of religious processions that attract as many as 100,000 devout adherents. The next such procession is scheduled for 2016.

Place St-Michel. ☎ **05-55-34-46-87.** Free admission. Mon–Sat 8am–6pm; Sun 8–11:45am and 4–6pm.

**Musée des Beaux-Arts de Limoges** MUSEUM   This former municipal museum has been renovated, with double its space and a new museography to live up to its new title as a museum of fine arts. The main part of the museum is housed in the 18th-century archbishops' palace, now joined by luminous modern galleries for temporary exhibitions. It is surrounded by the Jardins de l'Evêché, which offer a view of the Vienne and the 13th-century pont St-Etienne. The collections are divided into four parts: an outstanding collection of Limoges enamels from the 12th century to the present day; an Egyptian collection of 2,000 pieces; archeology, sculptures, and stained glass from now-defunct abbeys; and fine art, including works by Auguste Renoir, who was born in Limoges.

1 place de l'Evêché. www.museebal.fr. ☎ **05-55-45-98-10.** Free admission to permanent collections; temporary exhibitions 5€ adults, 3€ age 18 and under. Apr–Sept Wed–Mon 10am–6pm; Oct–Mar Mon and Wed–Sat 10am–noon and 2–5pm, Sun 2–5pm.

**Musée National de la Porcelaine Adrien-Dubouché** MUSEUM   This museum has the largest public collection of Limoges porcelain. Its 12,000 pieces illustrate the history of glassmaking and ceramics (porcelain, earthenware, stoneware, and terra cotta) throughout the ages. In France, its porcelain collection is second in quantity only to that of Sèvres. From summer 2012, the 3-million-euro renovation project will be completed, with a new modern building alongside the 19th-century traditional space, tripling the previous area of exhibition rooms. A restaurant and cafe are also planned, as well as an expanded boutique.

8 bis place Winston-Churchill. www.musee-adriendubouche.fr. ☎ **05-55-33-08-50.** Admission 4.50€ adults, 3€ ages 6–18. Wed–Mon 10am–12:25pm and 2–5:40pm (hours correct during the renovation work, when just boutique open).

Limoges porcelain.

**Pavillon de la Porcelaine–Musée Haviland** FACTORY TOUR Haviland has been exporting its porcelain to the United States and other countries since 1842, when a group of American entrepreneurs immigrated to France from Boston to found the first American-owned company ever established in Europe. Over the years, it has used the designs of artists such as Gauguin and Dalí. In the museum, you can see masterpieces as well as original pieces created for the U.S. White House. A video screening can tell you more about the manufacturing process, and a large shop also sells the porcelain.

40 av. John-Kennedy. www.haviland-limoges.com. ☎ **05-55-30-21-86.** Free admission. Mid-Mar to June daily 10am–1pm and 2–6:30pm; July–Aug daily 10am–6:30pm; Sept to mid-Mar Mon–Sat 10am–1pm and 2–6:30pm.

**Parc Victor Thuillat** PARK Besides porcelain, Limoges is one of the greenest cities in France, with numerous open spaces, and attractive walks along the river Vienne. Victor Thuillat is one of the largest and most attractive parks, with a large collection of centuries-old sequoia and cypress trees. A *boules* court and childrens' play area make this a pleasant place to while away a few hours.

Avenue Emile Labussiere. ☎ **05-55-45-62-67.** Free admission. Open dawn til dusk daily.

## Where to Eat

**La Table du Couvent** FRENCH This recently opened bistro in the former Carmes convent is part of the excellent cookery school Les Paroles de Chef. The man in charge here is Pascal Robert, and besides the excellent bistro, you will find an epicerie selling freshly-made pasta and other goodies, and plenty of kitchen accessories. Menus change weekly depending on seasonal produce, but expect fresh local ingredients put together with imagination and a delicate touch.

20 place d'Aine. www.latableducouvent.com. $\textcircled{C}$ **05-55-32-30-66.** Reservations recommended. Main courses 15€–32€; set-price menus 19€–24€ (weekday lunch), 32€ and 38€ (dinner). AE, MC, V. Tues–Thurs noon–2pm, 7:30–10:30pm, Fri noon–2pm.

## Where to Stay

**Art Hotel Tendance**    Finding small, non-chain hotels in Limoges is not easy, but this simple hotel has undergone a full renovation in recent years, with a real effort to introduce individual design and charm. Each room is differently themed, with good-sized beds, if small bathrooms in most cases. You're not getting any luxuries here, but it is clean and friendly.

37 rue Armand Barbes. www.arthoteltendance.com. $\textcircled{C}$ **05-55-77-31-72.** fax: 05-55-10-25-53. 76 units. 71€–90€ double. DC, MC, V. **Amenities:** Bar; breakfast room. *In room:* A/C, TV, hair dryer, free Wi-Fi.

**Best Western Hotel Richelieu ★**    Not far from the town center, this hotel in a 1930s building was recently renovated with an attractive contemporary decor using quality fabrics. Extras like free Wi-Fi, tea- and coffeemakers, slippers, and an exercise room make it a good value.

40 av. Baudin. www.hotel-richelieu.com. $\textcircled{C}$ **05-55-34-22-82.** Fax 05-55-34-35-36. 43 units. 88€–118€ double. AE, DC, MC, V. **Amenities:** Bar; breakfast room; exercise room. *In room:* A/C, TV, hair dryer, minibar (in some), free Wi-Fi.

**19**

THE DORDOGNE & THE LOT | Side Trip to Limoges

# PLANNING YOUR TRIP TO FRANCE

by Lily Heise

O f almost any destination in the world, flying into France is one of the most effortless undertakings in global travel. There are no shots to get, no particular safety precautions, and more and more French people now speak English. With your passport, airline ticket, and enough money, you just go. Of course, before you lift off the ground in your native country, you can do some advance preparation. In the pages that follow, you'll find everything you need to know about the practicalities of planning your trip: finding the best airfare, deciding when to go, getting around the country, and more.

# GETTING THERE

## AIRPORTS

The two Paris airports—Orly (airport code: ORY) and Charles de Gaulle (airport code: CDG)—are about even in terms of convenience to the city's center, though taxi rides from Orly may take less time than those from de Gaulle. Orly, the older of the two, is 13km (8 miles) south of the center; Charles de Gaulle is 22km (14 miles) northeast. Air France serves Charles de Gaulle (Terminal 2C) from North America. U.S. carriers land at both airports. Flight status and other useful information for both airports can be found online (www.aeroportsdeparis. fr). Beauvais airport (www.aeroportbeauvais.com) is located 70km (40 miles) north of Paris and is served by European continental budget airlines such as Ryanair or WizzAir. There is a frequent bus service to and from Paris Porte Maillot bus depot (Métro: Porte Maillot). This takes 1 to 1½ hours and costs 15€ one-way. To return to Beauvais, you must be at the bus depot 3 hours and 15 minutes before your flight departure.

Most airlines charge their lowest fares between November 1 and March 13. Shoulder season (Oct and mid-Mar to mid-June) is a bit more expensive, though we think it's the ideal time to visit France.

## GETTING THERE FROM THE U.K. & CONTINENTAL EUROPE

### By Train

Paris is one of Europe's busiest rail junctions, with trains arriving at and departing from its many stations every few minutes. If you're in Europe, you may want to go to Paris by train. The cost is relatively low—especially compared to renting a car.

Rail passes as well as individual rail tickets are available at most travel agencies or at any office of **Rail Europe** (www.raileurope.com; ✆ **888/382-7245** in the U.S.;) or **Eurostar** (www.eurostar.com; ✆ **800/EUROSTAR** [387-6782] in the U.S.).

PREVIOUS PAGE: **Musée d'Orsay in Paris.**

## By Bus

Bus travel to Paris is available from London, as well as from many cities on the Continent. In the early 1990s, the French government established incentives for long-haul buses not to drive into the center of Paris. The arrival and departure point for Europe's largest operator, **Eurolines France,** 28 av. du Général-de-Gaulle, 93541 Bagnolet (www.eurolines.fr; ✆ **08-92-89-90-91**), is a 35-minute Métro ride from central Paris, at the terminus of line no. 3 (Métro: Gallieni), in the eastern suburb of Bagnolet. Despite this inconvenience, many people prefer bus travel, and it is the often the most economical means of travel.

Long-haul buses are equipped with toilets, and they stop at mealtimes for rest and refreshment.

Because Eurolines does not have a U.S. sales agent, most people buy their ticket in Europe or online. Any European travel agent can arrange the sale. If you're traveling to Paris from London, contact **Eurolines (U.K.) Ltd.,** 52 Grosvenor Gardens, Victoria, London SW1 0AU (www.nationalexpress.com; ✆ **0871/781-81-81;** for information or credit card sales).

## By Car

The major highways into Paris are A1 from the north (Great Britain and Benelux); A13 from Rouen, Normandy, and northwest France; A10 from Bordeaux, the Pyrénées, the southwest, and Spain; A6 from Lyon, the French Alps, the Riviera, and Italy; and A4 from Metz, Nancy, and Strasbourg in the east.

## By Ferry from England

Ferries and hydrofoils operate day and night, with the exception of last-minute cancellations during storms. Many crossings are timed to coincide with the arrival and departure of trains (especially those btw. London and Paris). Trains let you off a short walk from the piers. Most ferries carry cars, trucks, and freight, but some hydrofoils take passengers only. The major routes include at least 12 trips a day between Dover or Folkestone and Calais or Boulogne.

Hovercraft and hydrofoils make the trip from Dover to Calais, the shortest distance across the Channel, in just 40 minutes during good weather. The ferries may take several hours, depending on the weather and tides. If you're bringing a car, it's important to make reservations—space below decks is usually crowded. Timetables can vary depending on weather conditions and many other factors.

There are various operators of ferries across the channel depending on your destination. **P&O Ferries** (www.poferries.com; ✆ **0871/664-5645** in the U.K.) operates car and passenger ferries between Dover, England, and Calais, France (over 20 sailings a day; 90 min. each way). **Brittany Ferries** (www.brittanyferries. com; ✆ **0825/828-828**) operates ferry service from Portsmouth, Pooles and Plymouth, England, to Cherbourg, Caen, or St-Malo, France (one or two departures a day; 3–4 hr., each way). **L D Lines** (www.ldlines.co.uk; ✆ **0844/576-8836** in the U.K.) operates night crossings between Portsmouth and Le Havre, France (one departure nightly 8 hr. each way).

# GETTING AROUND

## BY PLANE

France has few domestic competitors. **Air France** (www.airfrance.com; ✆ **800/237-2747**) is the primary carrier, serving about eight cities in France and eight others in Europe. Air travel time from Paris to almost anywhere in France is about an hour. Low cost airline **easyJet** has started to offer some routes between Paris and Brest, Toulouse, and Nice (www.easyjet.com).

## BY CAR

The most charming châteaux and country hotels always seem to lie away from the main cities and train stations. Renting a car is often the best way to travel around France, especially if you plan to explore it in depth.

But Europe's rail networks are so well developed and inexpensive that we recommend you rent a car only for exploring areas little serviced by rail, such as Brittany, rural Burgundy, and the Dordogne. Or take trains between cities and rent a car on the days when you want to explore independently.

Driving time in Europe is largely a matter of conjecture, urgency, and how much sightseeing you do along the way. Driving time from Paris to Geneva is 5½ hours minimum. It's 2½ hours from Paris to Rouen, 3½ hours to Nantes, and 4 hours to Lyon. The driving time from Marseille to Paris (771km/478 miles) is a matter of national pride, and tall tales abound about how rapidly the French can do it. Flooring it, you may conceivably get there in 7 hours, but we always make a 2-day journey of it.

**RENTALS**    To rent a car, you'll need to present a passport, a driver's license, and a credit card. You also have to meet the company's minimum-age requirement. (For the least expensive cars, this is 21 at Hertz, 23 at Avis, and 25 at Budget. More expensive cars may require that you be at least 25.) It usually isn't obligatory within France, but certain companies have asked for the presentation of an International Driver's License, even though this is becoming increasingly superfluous in Western Europe.

*Note:* The best deal is usually a weekly rental with unlimited mileage. All car-rental bills in France are subject to a 19.6% government tax. Though the rental company won't usually mind if you drive your car into, say, Germany, Switzerland, Italy, or Spain, it's often forbidden to transport your car by ferry, including across the Channel to England.

In France, **collision damage waiver (CDW)** is usually factored into the overall rate quoted, but you should always verify this, of course, before taking a car on the road. At most companies, the CDW provision won't protect you against theft, so if this is the case, ask about purchasing extra theft protection.

Automatic transmission is a luxury in Europe, so if you want it, you must specifically request it and you'll pay dearly.

**Budget** (www.budget.com; ✆ 800/472-3325) has about 30 locations in Paris and at Orly (✆ 01-49-75-56-05) and Charles de Gaulle (✆ 01-48-62-70-22). For rentals of more than 7 days, you can usually pick up a car in one French city and drop it off in another, but there are extra charges. Drop-offs in cities within an easy drive of the French border (including Geneva and Frankfurt) incur no extra charge; you can arrange drop-offs in other non-French cities for a reasonable surcharge.

**Hertz** (www.hertz.com; ✆ 800/654-3001 in the U.S. and Canada) maintains about 15 locations in Paris, including offices at the city's airports. The main office is at 27 place St-Ferdinand, 17e (✆ 01-45-74-97-39; Métro: Argentine). Be sure to ask about promotional discounts. **Avis** (www.avis.com; ✆ 800/331-1084 in the U.S. and Canada) has offices at both

Paris airports and an inner-city headquarters at 5 rue Bixio, 7e (✆ **01-44-18-10-50**; Métro: Ecole Militaire), near the Eiffel Tower.

**National** (www.nationalcar.com; ✆ **800/CAR-RENT** [227-7368] in the U.S. and Canada) is represented in Paris by Europcar; one office is at 78 rue du Rocher, 8e (✆ **01-45-22-77-91**; Métro: St. Philippe du Roule). It has offices at both Paris airports and at about a dozen other locations. For the lowest rates, reserve in advance from North America.

Two U.S.-based agencies that don't have Paris offices but act as booking agents for Paris-based agencies are **Kemwel Drive Europe** (www.kemwel.com; ✆ **877/820-0668**) and **Auto Europe** (www.autoeurope.com; ✆ **888/223-5555**). They can make bookings in the United States only, so call before your trip.

The city of Paris has started a shared car service called **Autolib** (www.autolib.fr). In order to be able to use this service you must have a valid E.U. driver's license; therefore it is not applicable for most overseas travelers to France.

**GASOLINE**    Known in France as *essence,* gas is expensive for those accustomed to North American prices. All but the least expensive cars usually require an octane rating that the French classify as *essence super,* the most expensive variety. Depending on your car, you'll need either leaded (*avec plomb*) or unleaded (*sans plomb*).

Beware the mixture of gasoline and oil, called *mélange* or *gasoil,* sold in some rural communities; this mixture is for very old two-cycle engines.

**Note:** Sometimes you can drive for miles in rural France without encountering a gas station; don't let your tank get dangerously low.

**DRIVING RULES**    Everyone in the car, in both the front and the back seats, must wear seat belts. Children 11 and under must ride in the back seat. Drivers are supposed to yield to the car on their right, except where signs indicate otherwise, as at traffic circles.

If you violate the speed limit, expect a big fine. Limits are about 130kmph (81 mph) on expressways, about 100kmph (62 mph) on major national highways, and 90kmph (56 mph) on country roads. In towns, don't exceed 60kmph (37 mph).

**Note:** It's illegal to use a cellphone while you're driving in France; you will be ticketed if you're stopped.

**MAPS**    For France as a whole, most motorists opt for **Michelin map 989** (www.viamichelin.com). For regions, Michelin publishes a series of **yellow maps** that are quite good. Big travel-book stores in North America carry these maps, and they're commonly available in France (at lower prices). In this age of congested traffic, one useful feature of the Michelin map is its designations of alternative *routes de dégagement,* which let you skirt big cities and avoid traffic-clogged highways.

**BREAKDOWNS/ASSISTANCE**    A breakdown is called *une panne* in France. Call the police at ✆ **17** anywhere in France to be put in touch with the nearest garage. Most local garages offer towing. If the breakdown occurs on an expressway, find the nearest roadside emergency phone box, pick up the phone, and put a call through. You'll be connected to the nearest breakdown service facility.

## BY TRAIN

The world's fastest trains link some 50 French cities, allowing you to get from Paris to just about anywhere else in the country in hours. With 39,000km (24,180 miles) of track and about 3,000 stations, SNCF (French National Railroads) is fabled for its on-time performance. You can travel in first or second class by day and in couchette by night. Many trains have light dining facilities.

**INFORMATION**   If you plan to travel a lot on European railroads, get the latest copy of the *Thomas Cook Timetable of European Passenger Railroads*. This 500-plus-page book documents all of Europe's main passenger rail services with detail and accuracy. It's available online at www.thomascookpublishing.com.

**In the United States:** For more information and to purchase rail passes before you leave, contact **Rail Europe** (www.raileurope.com; ℭ **877/272-RAIL** [272-7245]).

**In Canada:** Call Rail Europe at ℭ **800/361-RAIL** [361-7245].

**In London:** SNCF has offices at Rail Europe, 179 Piccadilly, London W1V 0BA (ℭ **0870/584-8848**).

**In Paris:** For information or reservations, go online (www.voyages-sncf.com). You can also go to any local travel agency. If you have a chip credit card and know your PIN, you can use your card to buy your ticket at the easy to use *billetteries* (ticket machine, often with an English menu option) in every train station.

**FRANCE RAIL PASSES**   Working cooperatively with SNCF, Air Inter Europe, and Avis, **Rail Europe** (www.railfrance.com) offers three flexible rail passes to North Americans that can reduce travel costs considerably.

The **France Railpass** provides unlimited rail transport in France for any 3 days within 1 month, at $297 in first class and $240 in second. You can purchase up to 6 more days for an extra $45 per person per day. Children 4 to 11 travel for half-price.

The **France Rail 'n' Drive Pass,** available only in North America, combines good value on both rail travel and Avis car rentals. It is best used by arriving at a major rail depot and then striking out to explore the countryside by car. It includes the France Railpass (see above) and use of a rental car. A 2-day rail pass (first class) and 2 days' use of the cheapest rental car (with unlimited mileage) is $326 to $424 per person. The best deal if you're traveling in France with a friend—or even three or four friends—is the **France Saverpass,** granting 3 days of unlimited travel in a 1-month period. The cost is $297 per person first class or $240 second class. There's also a **France Youthpass** for travelers 25 or under, granting 3 days of unlimited train travel within a month. The cost is $209 in first class or $177 in second class. For those over 60, the **France Senior Pass** offers all the same features as the France Railpass, but with a savings. You get 3 days of unlimited train travel in 1 month for $259, with additional rail days costing $38 each. Travel days may be used consecutively or nonconsecutively.

A **France Rail Day Pass** allows you to take day trips from Paris to such cities as Lyon, Reims, Dijon, or Nantes. The cost is $161 in first class or $114 in second class. The pass grants you 1 day of unlimited travel in a 1-month period on the national rail network.

**EURAILPASS** The **Eurailpass** permits unlimited first-class rail travel in any country in western Europe except the British Isles (good in Ireland). Passes are available for purchase online (www.eurail.com) and at various offices/agents around the world. Travel agents and railway agents in such cities as New York, Montreal, and Los Angeles sell Eurailpasses. You can purchase them at the North American offices of CIT Travel Service, the French National Railroads, the German Federal Railroads, and the Swiss Federal Railways. It is strongly recommended that you purchase passes before you leave home, as not all passes are available in Europe; also, passes purchased in Europe will cost about 20% more. Numerous options are available for travel in France.

The **Eurail Global Pass** allows you unlimited travel in 20 Eurail-affiliated countries. You can travel on any of the days within the validity period, which is available for 15 days, 21 days, 1 month, 2 months, 3 months, and some other possibilities as well. Prices for first-class adult travel are $767 for 15 days, $990 for 21 days, $1,219 for 1 month, $1,722 for 2 months, and $2,122 for 3 months. Children 4 to 11 pay half fare; those 3 and under travel for free.

A **Eurail Global Pass Saver,** also valid for first-class travel in 20 countries, offers a special deal for two or more people traveling together. This pass costs $652 for 15 days, $842 for 21 days, $1,036 for 1 month, $1,464 for 2 months, and $1,805 for 3 months.

A **Eurail Global Youth Pass** for those 12 to 25 allows second-class travel in 18 countries. This pass costs $500 for 15 days, $645 for 21 days, $793 for 1 month, $1,119 for 2 months, and $1,380 for 3 months.

The **Eurail Select Pass** offers unlimited travel on the national rail networks of any three, four, or five bordering countries out of the 22 Eurail nations linked by train or ship. Two or more passengers can travel together for big discounts, getting 5, 6, 8, 10, or 15 days of rail travel within any 2-month period on the national rail networks of any three, four, or five adjoining Eurail countries linked by train or ship. A sample fare: For 5 days in 2 months, you pay $484 for three countries. **Eurail Select Pass Youth,** for travelers under 26, allows second-class travel within the same guidelines as Eurail Selectpass, with fees starting at $316. **Eurail Select Pass Saver** offers discounts for one or more people traveling together in first-class travel within the same guidelines as Eurail Selectpass, with fees starting at $411.

# TOURS

In a country as diverse and popular as France, there are numerous options.

## Adventure & Wellness Trips

**BALLOONING** **Buddy Bombard's Private Europe,** 605 Belvedere Rd., Suite 15, West Palm Beach, FL 33405 (www.buddybombard.com; © **800/862-8537** or 561/837-6610; fax 561/837-6623) maintains about three dozen hot-air balloons, some in Burgundy. The 5-day tours, costing $9,834 per person (double occupancy), incorporate food and wine tasting and all meals, lodging in Relais & Châteaux hotels, sightseeing, rail transfers to and from Paris, and a daily balloon ride over vineyards and fields.

**BARGE CRUISES**   Before the advent of the railways, many crops, building supplies, raw materials, and finished products were barged through France on a series of rivers, canals, and estuaries. Many of these waterways retain their old-fashioned locks and pumps, allowing shallow-draft barges easy access through the idyllic countryside.

**French Country Waterways, Ltd.,** 24 Bay Rd. # 1, Duxbury, MA 02332 (www.fcwl.com; ✆ **800/222-1236** or 781/934-2454), leads 1-week tours through Burgundy, the Loire Valley, Alsace-Lorraine, and Champagne. For double occupancy, the price ranges from $5,095 to $6,695.

**Go Barging** (www.gobarging.com; ✆ **800/394-8630**) operates Great Island Voyages, featuring river cruise ships. Fares range from $2,790 to $4,790 per person (double occupancy) for a 6-night cruise, including room, breakfast, and dinner. Bicycles are carried on board for sightseeing trips. This company also offers cruises in the Loire Valley and the south of France.

**BICYCLING TOURS**   Some of the best cycling tours of France are offered by **VBT (Deluxe Bicycle Vacations),** 614 Monkton Rd., Bristol, VT 05443 (www. vbt.com; ✆ **800/245-3868**), which offers trips in five of the most scenic parts of France. Rides range from Burgundy wine tours to more challenging tours through Provence. Prices start at $2,545 per person, with airfare packages also available.

**Classic Adventures,** P.O. Box 143, Hamlin, NY 14464 (www.classic adventures.com; ✆ **800/777-8090**), sponsors 6- to 7-day June and September tours of the Loire Valley and Burgundy. Accommodations are upscale, and tours are van supported and escorted. Tours, including room, breakfast, and dinner, begin at $2,789 per person.

**Cycling for Softies** (www.cycling-for-softies.co.uk) is ideal for easygoing travelers with little cycling experience. Tours cover most of France, from Champagne and Alsace-Lorraine to Cognac and Provence. Prices vary according to type of tour (both self-guided and small groups are available); buffet breakfasts and gourmet dinners are included.

# Cooking Schools

The famous/infamous Georges-Auguste Escoffier (1846–1935) taught the Edwardians how to eat. Today the Hôtel Ritz maintains the **Ecole Ritz Escoffier,** 15 place Vendôme, Paris 75001 (www.ritzescoffier.com; ✆ **01-43-16-30-50**), with culinary, cocktail, and pastry workshops, as well as lessons for kids. These cost 75€ to 170€ each. Professional-level courses, taught in French and English, start at 1,100€, with a Master's in French Gastronomy costing 27,800€.

**Le Cordon Bleu,** 8 rue Léon-Delhomme, 75015 Paris (www.cordonbleu. edu; ✆ **01-53-68-22-50**), was established in 1895 and is the most famous French cooking school—where Julia Child learned to perfect her *pâté brisée* and *mousse au chocolat.* The best-known courses last 10 weeks and cost 8,500€, after which you are awarded a certificate. Many enthusiasts prefer a less intense immersion and opt for a 4-day workshop or a 1- to 2-hour demonstration class. Enrollment in either is online; costs start at 45€ for a demonstration and at 880€ for a 4-day workshop. Classes are in English.

**At Home with Patricia Wells** (www.patriciawells.com) is a Paris- and Provence-based cooking school taught by Patricia Wells, cookbook author and famed former restaurant critic for the *International Herald Tribune*. The extremely popular 5-day classes are limited to 12 students and cost $5,000 (accommodation not included).

**Les Petits Farcis** (www.petitsfarcis.com), run by Cordon Bleu-trained Canadian chef Rosa Jackson, offers tours of the Nice's colorful produce market, followed by daylong gourmet cooking sessions. Prices begin at 195€ per person and include a four-course lunch with wine.

## Language Classes

The **Alliance Française,** 101 bd. Raspail, Paris 75006 (www.alliancefr.org; ☎ **01-42-84-90-00**), a nonprofit organization with a network of 1,100 establishments in 138 countries, offers French-language courses to some 350,000 students. The school in Paris is open all year; month-long courses range from 360€ to 848€, depending on the number of hours per day. Request information and an application at least 1 month before your departure. In North America, the largest branch is the **Alliance Française,** 53 W. Jackson Blvd., Ste. 1225, Chicago, IL 60604 (☎ **312/431-1880;** www.afusa.org).

Just outside of Nice, the **Institut de Francais,** 23 av. Général-Leclerc, Villefranche-sur-mer 06230 (www.institutdefrancais.com; ☎ **04-93-01-88-44**), offers month-long French immersion courses. Each day includes 8½ hours of lessons, plus breakfast and lunch taken together with professors. Prices range from 2,700€ to 3,300€.

A clearinghouse for information on French-language schools is **Lingua Service Worldwide,** 14½ Long Ridge Rd., West Redding, CT 06896 (www.linguaserviceworldwide.com; ☎ **800/394-LEARN** [5327]). Its programs are available in many cities throughout France. They cost $147 to $5,800 per week, depending on the city, the school, and the accommodations.

## Music Tours

One outfit that coordinates hotel stays in France with major musical events is **Dailey-Thorp Travel,** P.O. Box 670, Big Horn, WY 82833 (www.daileythorp.com; ☎ **800/998-4677;** fax 307/674-7474). Sojourns last from 3 to 9 days and, in many cases, tie in with performances in other parts of Europe (often London, Berlin, or Milan). Expect accommodations in deluxe hotels, such as Paris's Hôtel du Louvre or the Hôtel Scribe, or onboard small luxury cruise ships.

# [FastFACTS] FRANCE

**Area Codes** All French telephone numbers consist of 10 digits, the first two of which are like an area code. If you're calling anywhere in France from within France, just dial all 10 digits. If you're calling from the United States, drop the initial 0 (zero). See "Telephones" later in this section for further information.

**Business Hours** Business hours in France are erratic. Most banks are open Monday through Friday from 9:30am to 4:30pm. Many, particularly in small towns, take a lunch break. Hours are usually posted on the door. Most museums close 1 day a week (often

Tues), and they're generally closed on national holidays. Usual hours are from 9:30am to 5pm. Refer to the individual listings. Generally, offices are open Monday through Friday from 9am to 5pm, but always call first. In Paris or other big French cities, stores are open from 9, 9:30, or (often) 10am to 6 or 7pm, without a break for lunch. Some shops, delis, cafes, and newsstands open at 8am and close at 8 or 9pm. In some small stores, the lunch break can last 2 hours, beginning at 1pm. This is more common in the south than in the north.

**Car Rental**   See "Getting There: By Car," earlier in this chapter.

**Cellphones**   See "Mobile Phones," later in this section.

**Crime**   See "Safety," later in this section.

**Customs**   **What you can bring into France:** Citizens of E.U. countries can bring in any amount of goods, as long as the goods are intended for their personal use and not for resale. Non-E.U. citizens are entitled to 200 cigarettes, 100 small cigars, 50 cigars, or 250g of tobacco duty-free. You can also bring in 2 liters of wine or beer and 1 liter of spirits (more than 22% alcohol). In addition, you can bring in 50g (1.76oz) of perfume.

**What you can take out of France:**

**Australian Citizens**   A helpful brochure is available from the Australian Customs and Border Protection Service: *Know Before You Go,* online under "Information for Travelers." For more information, call the **Australian Customs Service** (www.customs.gov.au; ℭ **1300/363-263,** or 612/6275-6666 if you're abroad). The duty-free allowance in Australia is A$900, or, for those 17 or younger, A$450. If you're returning with valuables you already own, you should file the "Goods Imported in Passenger Baggage" form.

**Canadian Citizens**   For a clear summary of Canadian rules, ask for the booklet *I Declare,* issued by the **Canada Border Services Agency** (www.cbsa-asfc.gc.ca under "Going on Vacation?," ℭ **800/461-9999** in Canada, or 204/983-3500 from abroad). Canada allows its citizens a C$750 exemption, and you're allowed to mail gifts to Canada from abroad valued at less than C$60 a day, provided they're unsolicited and don't contain alcohol or tobacco (write on the package "Unsolicited gift, under C$60 value"). All valuables, including serial numbers of valuables you already own, should be declared on the Y-38 form before departure from Canada.

**New Zealand Citizens**   The answers to most questions regarding customs can be found on the website of the **New Zealand Customs Service** (www.customs.govt.nz; ℭ **0800/4-CUSTOMS** [0800/428-786], or 649/300-5399 from outside New Zealand).The duty-free allowance for New Zealand is NZ$700. Fill out a certificate of export listing the valuables you are taking out of the country so that you can bring them back without paying duty.

**U.K. Citizens**   When returning to the U.K. from an E.U. country such as France, you can bring in an unlimited amount of most goods. There is no limit on what you can bring back from an E.U. country, as long as the items are for personal use (this includes gifts) and you have already paid the duty and tax. However, if you bring in more than these levels, you may be asked to prove that the goods are for your own use. For information, contact **HM Revenue Customs** (www.hmrc.gov.uk; ℭ **0845/010-9000**).

**U.S. Citizens**   For specifics on what you can bring back and the corresponding fees, download the invaluable free pamphlet *Know Before You Go,* online at **www.cbp.gov**. Or contact the **U.S. Customs & Border Protection (CBP)** (ℭ **877/CBP-5511** [227-5511], or 703/526-4200 for international calls). Returning U.S. citizens who have been away for 48 hours or more are allowed to bring back, once every 30 days, $800 worth of merchandise duty-free. You're charged a flat rate of duty on the next $1,000 worth of purchases, and any dollar amount beyond that is subject to duty at whatever rates apply. On mailed gifts, the duty-free limit is $200. To avoid having to pay duty on foreign-made personal items you owned before your trip, bring along a bill of sale, insurance policy, jeweler's appraisal, or receipt of purchase, or register items before you leave. You cannot bring fresh foodstuffs into the U.S.

**Disabled Travelers**    Facilities for travelers in France, and nearly all modern hotels, provide accessible rooms. Older hotels (unless they've been renovated) may not provide elevators, special toilet facilities, or wheelchair ramps. The TGVs (high-speed trains) are wheelchair accessible; older trains have compartments for wheelchair boarding. If you visit the Paris tourist office's website (www.parisinfo.com) and click on "Paris Pratique," you'll find links to a number of guides and websites dedicated to travelers with disabilities. With the exception of Line 14 and several other stations, most Paris Métro lines do not have disabled access and are not always equipped with either escalators or elevators. Buses are a much better option for disabled visitors, as many lines are now equipped with lowering floors and space for wheelchairs. RER lines and some SNCF services are wheelchair-accessible (look at www.infomobi.com for a useful disabled-access version of the Paris Métro map or call ✆ **08-10-64-64-64**).

**Doctors**    Doctors are listed in the *Pages Jaunes* (French equivalent of the Yellow Pages; www.pagesjaunes.fr) under "Médecins: Médecine générale." If you're using the website, you can search for a doctor by typing the town in the "Où" box. The minimum fee for a consultation is about 23€—for this rate, look for a doctor who is described as "conventionée secteur 1." The higher the "secteur," the higher the fee. **SOS Médecins** (✆ **36-24** or 01-47-07-77-77) makes house calls, which cost 70€ before 7pm and from 110€ after 7pm or on holidays (prices quoted are for people without French social security). See also "Emergencies" and "Health" later in this section.

**Drinking Laws**    Supermarkets, grocery stores, and cafes sell alcoholic beverages. The legal drinking age is 18, but persons under that age can be served alcohol in a bar or restaurant if accompanied by a parent or legal guardian. The law regarding drunk driving is tough. A motorist is considered "legally intoxicated" if their blood-alcohol limit exceeds .05%. If it is under .08% (the limit in the U.K., Ireland, and some U.S. states) the driver faces a fine of 135€. Over .08%, and it could cost 4,500€ or up to two years in jail. If you cause an accident while driving drunk, the fine could be increased to 30,000€, and if you cause serious injury or death, you face 10 years in jail and a fine of up to 150,000€.

**Driving Rules**    The French drive on the right. At junctions where there are no signposts indicating the right of way, cars coming from the right have priority. Many roundabouts now give priority to those on the roundabout. If this is not indicated, priority is for those coming from the right.

**Drugstores**    You'll spot French *pharmacies* by looking for the green neon cross above the door. If your local pharmacy is closed, there should be a sign on the door indicating the nearest one open. You can also have the front-desk staff at your hotel contact the nearest Commissariat de Police; an agent there will have the address of a nearby pharmacy open 24 hours a day. *Parapharmacies* sell medical products and toiletries, but they don't dispense prescriptions. In Paris, one of the most central all-nighters is the **Pharmacie des Champs-Elysées** (84 av. des Champs-Elysées; Métro: George V; ✆ **01-45-62-02-41**). See also "Emergencies" and "Health" later in this section.

**Electricity** Electricity in France runs on 220 volts AC (60 cycles). Adapters or transformers are needed to fit sockets, which you can buy in branches of Darty, FNAC, or BHV. Many hotels have two-pin (in some cases, three-pin) sockets for electric razors.

**Embassies & Consulates** If you have a passport, immigration, legal, or other problem, contact your consulate. Call before you go—they often keep odd hours and observe both French and home-country holidays.

The Embassy of **Australia** is at 4 rue Jean-Rey, 15e (www.france.embassy.gov.au; ✆ **01-40-59-33-00;** Métro: Bir Hakeim), open Monday to Friday 9am to noon and 2 to 4pm.

The Embassy of **Canada** is at 35 av. Montaigne, 8e (www.amb-canada.fr; ✆ **01-44-43-29-00;** Métro: Franklin-D-Roosevelt or Alma-Marceau), open Monday to Friday 9am to noon and 2 to 5pm.

The Embassy of **Ireland** is at 4 rue Rude, 16e (✆ **01-44-17-67-00;** www.embassyof ireland.fr; Métro: Etoile), open Monday to Friday 9:30am to noon.

The embassy of **New Zealand** is at 7ter rue Léonard-de-Vinci, 16e (www.nzembassy. com; ✆ **01-45-01-43-43;** Métro: Victor Hugo), open Monday to Thursday 9am to 1pm and 2 to 5:30pm, Friday 9am to 1pm and 2 to 4pm (reduced hours in July and August).

The Embassy of the **United Kingdom** is at 35 rue du Faubourg St-Honoré, 8e (✆ **01-44-51-31-00;** http://ukinfrance.fco.gov.uk; Métro: Concorde or Madeleine), open Monday to Friday 9:30am to 1pm and 2:30 to 6pm.

The Embassy of the **United States,** 2 av. Gabriel, 8e (http://france.usembassy.gov; ✆ **01-43-12-22-22;** Métro: Concorde), is open Monday to Friday 9am to 6pm.

**Emergencies** In an emergency while at a hotel, contact the front desk. Most staffs are trained in dealing with a crisis and will do whatever is necessary. If the emergency involves something like a stolen wallet, go to the police station in person. Otherwise, call ✆ **112** from a mobile phone, or call the fire brigade *(Sapeurs-Pompiers)* at ✆ **18;** they are trained to deal with all kinds of medical emergencies, not just fires. For an ambulance, call ✆ **15.** For the police, call ✆ **17.**

**Etiquette & Customs** Parisians like pleasantries and take manners seriously: Say "Bonjour, Madame/Monsieur" when entering an establishment and "Au revoir" when you depart. Always say "Pardon" when you accidentally bump into someone. With strangers, people who are older than you and professional contacts use *vous* rather than *tu* (*vous* is the polite form of the pronoun *you*).

**Family Travel** To locate accommodations, restaurants, and attractions that are particularly kid-friendly, look for the "Kids" icon throughout this guide.

**Health** For travel abroad, Non-E.U. nationals should consider buying medical travel insurance. For U.S. citizens, Medicare and Medicaid do not provide coverage for medical costs incurred abroad, so check what medical services your health insurance covers before leaving home. U.K. nationals will need a **European Health Insurance Card (EHIC)** to receive free or reduced-cost medical care during a visit to a European Economic Area (EEA) country or Switzerland (go to www.ehic.org.uk for further information).

If you suffer from a chronic illness, consult your doctor before your departure. Pack prescription medications in your carry-on luggage and carry them in their original containers, with pharmacy labels—otherwise, they won't make it through airport security. Carry the generic name of prescription medicines, in case a local pharmacist is unfamiliar with the brand name.

For further tips on travel and health concerns, and a list of local English-speaking doctors, contact the **International Association for Medical Assistance to Travelers (IAMAT;** www.iamat.org; ✆ **716/754-4883** in the U.S., or **416/652-0137** in Canada). You can also find listings of reliable medical clinics overseas at the **International Society of Travel Medicine** (www.istm.org). See also "Doctors," "Drugstores," "Emergencies," and "Hospitals."

**Holidays**  Major holidays are New Year's Day (Jan 1), Easter Sunday and Monday (late Mar/Apr), May Day (May 1), VE Day (May 8), Ascension Thursday (40 days after Easter), Pentecost/Whit Sunday and Whit Monday (seventh Sun and Mon after Easter), Bastille Day (July 14), Assumption Day (Aug 15), All Saints Day (Nov 1), Armistice Day (Nov 11), and Christmas Day (Dec 25). For more information on holidays, see "France Calendar of Events," p. 49.

**Hospitals**  Dial ℭ **15** for medical emergencies. In Paris, the **American Hospital,** 63 bd. Victor-Hugo, in the suburb of Neuilly-sur-Seine (www.american-hospital.org; ℭ **01-46-41-25-25**; Métro: Pont-de-Levallois or Pont-de-Neuilly; bus no. 82), operates a 24-hour emergency service. The bilingual staff accepts Blue Cross and other American insurance plans. Hospitals in other major cities include **Hôpital de Rouen,** 1 rue de Germont (www.chu-rouen.fr; ℭ **02-32-88-89-90**), in Rouen; **Hôpital Bretonneau,** 2 bd. Tonnellé (www.chu-tours.fr; ℭ **02-47-47-47-47**), in Tours; **Hôpital Civil de Strasbourg,** 1 place de l'Hôpital (www.chru-strasbourg.fr; ℭ **03-88-11-67-68**), in Strasbourg; **Hôpital Edouard Herriot,** 5 place Arsonval (www.chu-lyon.fr, ℭ **08-20-08-20-69**), in Lyon; **Hôpital d'Avignon,** 305 rue Raoul Follereau (www.ch-avignon.fr; ℭ **04-32-75-33-33**), in Avignon; **Hôpital St-Roch,** 5 rue Pierre Dévoluy (www.chu-nice.fr; ℭ **04-92-03-33-33**), in Nice; and **CHU de Rangueil,** av. du Prof. Jean-Poulhes (www.chu-toulouse.fr; ℭ **05-61-32-25-33**), in Toulouse.

**Hot Lines**  S.O.S. Help is a hotline for English-speaking callers in crisis at ℭ **01-46-21-46-46** (www.soshelpline.org). Open 3 to 11pm daily.

**Internet & Wi-Fi**  In French cities, many hotels and cafes have Internet access, and Wi-Fi (pronounced *wee-fee*) is becoming increasingly common in cafes and public spaces. There are also hundreds of cybercafes all over France. To find cybercafes, check **www.cybercaptive.com** and **www.cybercafe.com**. A reasonably priced option in Paris is **Luxembourg Micro,** 81 bd. Saint-Michel, 5e (www.luxembourg-micro.com; ℭ **01-46-33-27-98;** Métro: Luxembourg). It's open daily from 9am to 10pm.

**Language**  English is increasingly understood in France, especially among younger people who have studied it in school. People are more likely to understand English in centers such as Paris and the Riviera than in the more remote provinces. Service personnel in hotels tend to speak English, at least at the front desk. For handy French words and phrases, as well as food and menu terms, refer to chapter 21, "Useful Terms & Phrases." A good phrasebook is *Frommer's French PhraseFinder & Dictionary.*

**Legal Aid**  In an emergency, especially if you get into trouble with the law, your country's embassy or consulate will provide legal advice. See "Embassies & Consulates" above.

**LGBT Travelers**  France is one of the world's most tolerant countries toward gays and lesbians. "Gay Paree" boasts a large gay population, with many clubs, restaurants, organizations, and services. Lesbian or bisexual women can pick up a copy of *Lesbia* or *La Dix-ième Muse* (www.ladixiememuse.com). These publications and others are available at Paris's largest, best-stocked gay bookstore, **Les Mots à la Bouche,** 6 rue Ste-Croix-de-la-Bretonnerie, 4e (www.motsbouche.com; ℭ **01-42-78-88-30;** Métro: Hôtel-de-Ville), which carries publications in both French and English. In addition, both www.paris-gay.com and www.gayvox.com have updated listings about the gay and lesbian scene and events.

**Lost & Found**  To speed the process of replacing your personal documents if they're lost or stolen, make a photocopy of the first few pages of your passport and write down your credit card numbers. Leave this information with someone at home (to be called in an emergency) and your traveling companion. If your credit card is stolen, you can call **American Express** (call collect U.S. ℭ **336-393-1111**), **MasterCard** (ℭ **08-00-90-13-87;** www.mastercard.com), or **Visa** (ℭ **08-00-90-13-87;** www.visaeurope.com). In Paris, all lost objects—except those found in train stations or on trains—are taken to the **Bureau des Objets Trouvés** (36 rue des Morillons, 15e ℭ **08-21-00-25-25;** www.prefecture-police-paris.interieur.gouv.fr). It's better to visit in person than to call, but be warned that there are huge delays in processing claims. It's open from Monday to Thursday 8:30am to 5pm and Friday 8:30am to 4:30pm. Objects lost on the Métro are held by the station agents before being sent on to the Bureau des Objets Trouvés. If you lose something on a train or in a train station, go to the Lost Property office of the SNCF station in question.

Mail    Most post offices in France are open Monday to Friday from 8am to 5pm (in Paris some are open until 8 pm) and every Saturday from 8am to noon. A 24-hour post office is located in Paris at 52 rue du Louvre 1e (ℭ **01-40-28-20-00).** Allow 5 to 8 days to send or receive mail from home. Stamps are also sold in *tabacs* (tobacconists). Tariffs depend on the weight and size of the letter or package, but more information can be found at www.laposte.fr.

Medical Requirements    Unless you are arriving from an area of the world known to be suffering from an epidemic, especially cholera or yellow fever, inoculations or vaccinations are not required for entry in France.

Mobile Phones    The three letters that define much of the world's wireless capabilities are **GSM** (Global System for Mobile Communications), a big, seamless network that makes for easy cross-border mobile phone use throughout Europe and dozens of other countries worldwide. You can use your mobile phone in France, provided it is GSM and triband or quad-band; just confirm this with your operator before you leave.

Using your phone abroad can be expensive, and you usually have to pay to receive calls, so it's a good idea to get it "unlocked" before you leave. This means you can buy a SIM card from one of the three main French providers: **Bouygues Télécom** (www.bouyguestelecom.fr), **Orange** (www.orange.fr), or **SFR** (www.sfr.fr). A SIM card with 5€ call credit costs about 10€. Alternatively, if your phone isn't unlocked, you can buy a cheap mobile phone. To top-up your phone credit, buy a Mobicarte from *tabacs,* supermarkets, and mobile phone outlets. Prices range from 5€ to 100€. It is also possible to buy a foreign SIM card prior to your departure. Various mobile phone services for travelers are available such as Ekit (www.ekit.com) and Telestial (www.telestial.com). Travelers with smart phones can make cheaper phone calls within Wi-Fi and 3G networks using apps like nextgencel.com.

Money & Costs    Frommer's lists exact prices in the local currency. The currency conversions quoted below were correct at press time. However, rates fluctuate, so before departing, consult a currency exchange website such as www.oanda.com/convert/classic to check up-to-the-minute rates.

## THE VALUE OF THE EURO VS. OTHER POPULAR CURRENCIES

| Euro (€) | US$ | C$ | UK£ | A$ | NZ$ |
|---|---|---|---|---|---|
| 1 | 1.32 | 1.31 | 0.83 | 1.23 | 1.58 |

For decades, Paris was known as one of the most expensive cities on earth. It still is a pricey destination, but London has not only caught up with Paris, it has surpassed it. Paris is not as expensive as Tokyo or Oslo, but it's increasingly difficult to find even an average hotel for less than 150€.

It's always advisable to bring money in a variety of forms on a vacation: a mix of cash, credit cards, and traveler's checks. You should also exchange enough petty cash to cover airport incidentals, tipping, and transportation to your hotel before you leave home, or withdraw money upon arrival at an airport ATM. In many international destinations, ATMs offer the best exchange rates. Avoid exchanging money at commercial exchange bureaus and hotels, which often have the highest transaction fees. ATMs are widely available in Paris, but if you're venturing into rural France, it's always good to have cash in your pocket.

Not just Paris, but all of France is a very expensive destination. To compensate, you can often find top-value food and lodging. Part of the cost is the value-added tax (VAT in English, TVA in French), which adds between 6% and 33% to everything. Rental cars (and fuel) are expensive, and flying within France costs more than within the U.S. Train travel is relatively inexpensive, especially with a rail pass or by booking three months in advance. Prices in Paris and on the Riviera are higher than in the provinces. Three of the most visited areas—Brittany, Normandy, and the Loire Valley—have reasonably priced hotels and restaurants offering superb food at moderate prices.

Visa (known as Carte Bleue in French) is the most common credit card in France, but most international credit cards are widely used. In an attempt to reduce credit card fraud, French credit cards are issued with an embedded chip and a PIN to authorize transactions. Non-French cards (which don't have a chip) do work, but they print a slip that requires a signature. This does mean, however, that they cannot be used in automated machines, such as those in Métro stations. There are still shops, restaurants, and bars, often family run, that don't accept credit or debit cards, so it's always good to both check in advance and have cash on you. The minimum amount you have to spend to use a credit or debit card is slowly decreasing, but in some shops and bars—again, often smaller businesses—it can be as high as 15€.

You can buy traveler's checks at most banks, and they are widely accepted in France, although, frankly, merchants prefer cash. Because of difficulties with credit cards (see above) or ATMs that can reject your card for no apparent reason, travelers are once again buying traveler's checks for security in case something goes wrong with their plastic. They are offered in denominations of $20, $50, $100, $500, and sometimes $1,000. Generally, you'll pay a service charge ranging from 1% to 4%. The most popular traveler's checks are offered by **American Express, Visa,** and **MasterCard.** You can change traveler's checks at most post offices. If you carry traveler's checks, keep a record of their serial numbers separate from your checks, in the event that they are stolen or lost—you'll get your refund faster.

For help with currency conversions, tip calculations, and more, download **Multicultural Travelers**.

## Newspapers & Magazines
Only 20% of French people read a national paper. The most famous is the serious, center-left **Le Monde,** which is strong on both politics and economic issues. **Le Figaro** is more conservative and tends to favor lifestyle features over controversial issues. **Libération,** founded in the late 1960s by Jean-Paul Sartre and Simone de Beauvoir, has good news and arts coverage and is considered more left-wing.

English-language newspaper *International Herald-Tribune,* based in Paris and published Monday to Saturday, is distributed all over France and sold at newspaper kiosks and in the lobbies of first-class hotels. Copies of *Time* and *Newsweek* are also widely sold. A

Fast Facts: France

PLANNING YOUR TRIP TO FRANCE

far larger selection of U.K. magazines and newspapers is available. London newspapers arrive in Paris an hour or so after publication. WHSmith (248 rue de Rivoli 75001 Paris. www.whsmith.fr; © **01-44-77-88-99**), the largest English language bookstore in Paris, carries a wide selection of English-language press.

Passports    Citizens of the U.K., New Zealand, Australia, Canada, and the United States need a valid passport to enter France. The passport is valid for a stay of 90 days. To prevent international child abduction, E.U. governments have initiated procedures at entry and exit points. These often (but not always) include requiring documentary evidence of relationship and permission for the child's travel from the parent or legal guardian not present. Having such documentation on hand, even if not required, facilitates entries and exits. All children must have their own passports.

Allow plenty of time before your trip to apply for a passport; processing normally takes several weeks but can take longer during busy periods (especially spring). Keep in mind that if you need a passport in a hurry, you'll pay a higher processing fee.

**For Residents of Australia:** You can pick up an application from your local post office or any branch of Passports Australia. Visit the government website at www.passports.gov. au for more details.

**For Residents of Canada:** Passport applications are available at Passport Canada agencies throughout Canada. Forms and further information can be found at www.ppt. gc.ca).

**For Residents of Ireland:** You can apply for a passport using the Passport Express service at most post offices. Further information can be found at www.foreignaffairs. gov.ie.

**For Residents of New Zealand:** You can pick up a passport application at any New Zealand Passports Office or download it from their website, www.passports.govt.nz.

**For Residents of the United Kingdom:** To pick up an application for a passport, visit your nearest passport office or major post office, or download the forms from the website www.ips.gov.uk.

**For Residents of the United States:** Whether you're applying in person or by mail, you can download passport applications from the U.S. State Department website at http:// travel.state.gov.

Police    In an emergency, call © **17** or **112** from a mobile or land line phone anywhere in France.

Safety    The most common menace, especially in large cities—particularly Paris—is the plague of pickpockets. Take precautions and be vigilant at all times: Don't take more money with you than necessary, keep your passport in a concealed pouch or leave it at your hotel, and ensure that your bag is firmly closed at all times. In cafes, bars, and restaurants, it's best not to leave your bag under the table, on the back of your chair, or an empty chair beside you. Keep it between your legs or on your lap, to avoid it being stolen. Never leave valuables in a car, and never travel with your car unlocked.

Much of the country, particularly central France, the northeast, Normandy, and Brittany, remains relatively safe, although no place in the world is crime-free. Those intending to visit the south of France, especially the Riviera, should exercise caution; robberies and muggings are more likely to occur here than in other parts of the country. It's best to check your baggage into a hotel and then go sightseeing instead of leaving it unguarded in the trunk of a car, which can easily be broken into. Marseille is among the most dangerous French cities.

In general, Paris is a safe city and it is safe to use the Métro late at night, though it is always best to not drawn attention to the fact you are foreign by speaking loudly in English. Certain Métro stations (and the areas around them) are best avoided at night: Châtelet-Les Halles, Gare du Nord, Barbès-Rochechouart, and Strasbourg–St-Denis. Violent incidents and robberies have been known on the RER, particularly RER B, so it is best to find alternative transport to and from the airport (such as buses or taxis) late at night or early in the morning. Also, around the major sites, it is quite common to be approached by a young Roma girl and asked if you speak English or approaching you with a ring "checking" to see if you have dropped it by accident and then soliciting money for finding it. It's best to avoid these situations, and any incident that might occur, by shaking your head and walking away.

The government of France maintains a national antiterrorism plan; in times of heightened security concerns, the government mobilizes police and armed forces and installs them at airports, train and Métro stations, and high-profile locations such as schools, embassies, and government installations.

Most nonwhite travelers won't experience any problems. Although there is a significant level of discrimination against West and North African immigrants, there has been almost no harassment of African-American tourists to Paris or France itself. **S.O.S. Racisme** (51 av. de Flandre, 19e (www.sos-racisme.org, ℰ **01-40-35-36-55**) offers legal advice to victims of prejudice and will even intervene to help with the police.

Female travelers should not expect any more hassle than in other major cities, and the same precautions apply. Avoid walking alone at night and never get into an unmarked taxi. If you are approached in the street or on public transportation, it's best to avoid entering into conversation and walk away.

Senior Travel   Many discounts are available to seniors—men and women over 60. Although they often seem to apply to residents of E.U. countries, it pays to announce at the ticket window of a museum or monument that you are 60 years old or more. You may not receive a discount, but it doesn't hurt to ask. "Senior," incidentally, is pronounced *seenyore* in France. Senior citizens do not get a discount for traveling on public transport in Paris, but there are senior discounts on national trains. Check out www.voyages-sncf.com for further information. Frommers.com offers more information and resources on travel for seniors.

Smoking   Smoking is now banned in all public places in France, including cafes, restaurants, bars, and nightclubs, but it is permitted on outdoor and semi-enclosed terraces.

Student Travel   Student discounts are less common in France than other countries, but simply because young people under 26 are usually offered reduced rates. Some discounts apply only to residents of E.U. countries, but it's worth carrying ID to prove your age and announcing it when buying tickets. Look out for the **Ticket Jeune** when using the Métro in Paris. It can be used on a Saturday, Sunday, or bank holiday, and provides unlimited travel in zones 1 to 3 for 3.50€ (see "Public Transport" above). SNCF also offer discounts for under-26-year-olds traveling on national trains (www.voyages-sncf.com).

Taxes   As a member of the European Union, France routinely imposes a value-added tax (VAT in English; TVA in French) on most goods. The standard VAT is 19.6%, and prices that include it are often marked TTC (*toutes taxes comprises*, "all taxes included"). If you're not an E.U. resident, you can get a VAT refund if you're spending less than 6 months in France, you purchase goods worth at least 175€ at a single shop on the same day, the goods fit into your luggage, and the shop offers vente en détaxe (duty-free sales or tax-free shopping). Give them your passport and ask for a *bordereau de vente à l'exportation* (export sales invoice). This is then signed by the retailer and yourself. When you leave the country, you need to get all three pages of this invoice validated by France's customs officials. They'll keep one sheet, and you must post the pink one back to the shop. Once the shop receives its stamped copy, it will send you a *virement* (fund transfer) using the payment method you requested. It may take several months.

**Telephones**   Public phones can still be found in France. They all require a phone card (known as *télécarte*), which can be purchased at post offices, tabacs, supermarkets, SNCF ticket windows, Métro stations, and anywhere you see a blue sticker reading *"Télécarte en vente ici"* ("Phone card for sale here"). They usually cost 7.50€ for 50 calling units and 15€ for 120 units.

The country code for France is 33. To make a local or long-distance call within France, dial the 10-digit number of the person or place you're calling. Mobile numbers begin with 06 or 07. Numbers beginning with 0-800, 0-804, 0-805, and 0-809 are free in France; other numbers beginning with 8 are not. Most four-digit numbers starting with 10, 30, and 31 are free of charge.

For operator assistance and French directory inquiries, dial 📞 **12.**

**Time**   France is on Central European Time, which is 1 hour ahead of Greenwich Mean Time. French daylight saving time lasts from the last Sunday in March to the last Sunday in October, when clocks are set 1 hour ahead of the standard time. France uses the 24-hour clock (so 13h is 1pm, 14h15 is 2:15pm, and so on).

**Tipping**   By law, all bills in **cafes, bars, and restaurants** say *service compris,* which means the service charge is included. However, it is customary to leave 1€ or 2€, depending on the quality of the service, in more upscale restaurants leave 5€-10€. **Taxi drivers** usually expect a 5% to 10% tip, or for the fare to be rounded up to the next euro. The French give their **hairdressers** a tip of about 15%, and if you go to the theater, you're expected to tip the **usher** about 2€.

**Toilets**   If you're in dire need, duck into a cafe or brasserie to use the lavatory. It's customary to make a small purchase if you do so. Some toilets require a *jeton* coin to access them, which you need to obtain from a waiter. Paris is full of gray-colored automatic street toilets, which are free to use and are washed and disinfected after each use. France still has some hole-in-the-ground squat toilets, so be warned.

**VAT**   See "Taxes," earlier in this section.

**Visas**   E.U. nationals don't need a visa to enter France. Nor do U.S., Canadian, Australian, New Zealand, or South African citizens for trips of up to 3 months. Nationals of other countries should make inquiries at the nearest French embassy or consulate before they travel to France. If Non-E.U. citizens wish to stay for longer than 3 months, they must apply to a French embassy or consulate for a long-term visa.

**Visitor Information**   Before you go, your best source of information is the **French Government Tourist Office** (www.franceguide.com), which can be reached at the following addresses:

- **United States:** 825 Third Ave., 29th Floor, New York, NY 10022 (📞 **1-212-838-7800;** fax 212/838-7855); 205 N. Michigan Ave., Chicago, IL 60601 (📞 **312/327-0290**); or 9454 Wilshire Blvd., Ste. 715, Beverly Hills, CA 90212 (📞 **310/271-6665** )

- **Canada:** 1800 av. McGill College, Ste. 490, Montreal, QC H3A 2W9 (📞 **514/288-2026;** fax 514/845-4868)

- **United Kingdom:** Lincoln House, 300 High Holborn, London WC1V 7JH (☏ **09068/244-123** [60p per min.]; fax 020/7061 6646 )

- **Australia:** 25 Bligh St., Sydney, NSW 2000 (☏ **02/9231-5244;** fax 02/9221-8682)

Water   Drinking water is generally safe. If you ask for water in a restaurant, it'll be served bottled (for which you'll pay), unless you specifically request *une carafe d'eau* or *l'eau de robinet* (tap water). Your waiter may ask if you'd like your water *avec gas* (carbonated) or *sans gas* (without bubbles).

Wi-Fi   See "Internet & Wi-Fi," earlier in this section.

Women Travelers   See "Safety," earlier in this section.

# USEFUL TERMS & PHRASES

## GLOSSARY OF FRENCH-LANGUAGE TERMS

It's often amazing how a word or two of halting French will change your hosts' dispositions in their home country. At the very least, try to learn a few numbers, basic greetings, and—above all—the life raft, *"Parlez-vous anglais?"* As it turns out, many French do speak passable English and will use it liberally if you demonstrate the basic courtesy of greeting them in their language. Go on, try our glossary out, and don't be bashful. *Bonne chance!*

### BASICS

| English | French | Pronunciation |
|---|---|---|
| Yes/No | Oui/Non | **wee/nohn** |
| Okay | D'accord | **dah-*core*** |
| Please | S'il vous plaît | **seel voo *play*** |
| Thank you | Merci | **mair-*see*** |
| You're welcome | De rien | **duh ree-*ehn*** |
| Hello (during daylight hours) | Bonjour | **bohn-*jhoor*** |
| Good evening | Bonsoir | **bohn-*swahr*** |
| Goodbye | Au revoir | **o ruh-*vwahr*** |

| English | French | Pronunciation |
|---------|--------|---------------|
| What's your name? | Comment vous appellez-vous? | **ko-mahn voo za-pell-ay-voo?** |
| My name is . . . | Je m'appelle . . . | **jhuh ma-pell . . .** |
| Happy to meet you | Enchanté(e) | **ohn-shahn-tay** |
| Miss | Mademoiselle | **mad-mwa-zel** |
| Mr. | Monsieur | **muh-syuh** |
| Mrs. | Madame | **ma-dam** |
| How are you? | Comment allez-vous? | **kuh-mahn tahl-ay-voo?** |
| Fine, thank you, and you? | Très bien, merci, et vous? | **tray bee-ehn, mare-ci, ay voo?** |
| Very well, thank you | Très bien, merci | **tray bee-ehn, mair-see** |
| So-so | Comme ci, comme ça | **kum-see, kum-sah** |
| I'm sorry/excuse me | Pardon | **pahr-dohn** |
| I'm so very sorry | Désolé(e) | **day-zoh-lay** |
| That's all right | Il n'y a pas de quoi | **eel nee ah pah duh kwah** |

## GETTING AROUND/STREET SMARTS

| English | French | Pronunciation |
|---------|--------|---------------|
| Do you speak English? | Parlez-vous anglais? | **par-lay-voo ahn-glay?** |
| I don't speak French | Je ne parle pas français | **jhuh ne parl pah frahn-say** |
| I don't understand | Je ne comprends pas | **jhuh ne kohm-prahn pas** |
| Could you speak more loudly/more slowly? | Pouvez-vous parler un peu plus fort/plus lentement? | **poo-vay-voo par-lay un puh ploo for/ploo lan-te-ment?** |
| Could you repeat that? | Répetez, s'il vous plaît? | **ray-pay-tay, seel voo play** |
| What is it? | Qu'est-ce que c'est? | **kess kuh say?** |
| What time is it? | Qu'elle heure est-il? | **kel uhr eh-teel?** |
| What? | Quoi? | **kwah?** |
| How? or What did you say? | Comment? | **ko-mahn?** |
| When? | Quand? | **kahn?** |
| Where is . . . ? | Où est . . . ? | **ooh eh . . . ?** |
| Who? | Qui? | **kee?** |
| Why? | Pourquoi? | **poor-kwah?** |
| Here/there | ici/là | **ee-see/lah** |
| Left/right | à gauche/à droite | **a goash/a drwaht** |
| Straight ahead | tout droit | **too drwah** |

| English | French | Pronunciation |
|---------|--------|---------------|
| I'm American/Canadian/British | Je suis américain(e)/canadien(e)/anglais(e) | **jhe sweez a-may-ree-kehn/can-ah-dee-en/ahn-glay (glaise)** |
| Fill the tank (of a car), please | Le plein, s'il vous plaît | **luh plan, seel voo play** |
| I'm going to . . . | Je vais à . . . | **jhe vay ah . . .** |
| I want to get off at . . . | Je voudrais descendre à . . . | **jhe voo-dray day-son-drah ah** |
| I'm sick | Je suis malade | **jhuh swee mal-ahd** |
| airport | l'aéroport | **lair-o-por** |
| bank | la banque | **lah bahnk** |
| bridge | pont | **pohn** |
| bus station | la gare routière | **lah gar roo-tee-air** |
| bus stop | l'arrêt de bus | **lah-ray duh boohss** |
| by means of a bicycle | en vélo/par bicyclette | **ahn vay-low/par bee-see-clet** |
| by means of a car | en voiture | **ahn vwa-toor** |
| cashier | la caisse | **lah kess** |
| cathedral | cathédral | **ka-tay-dral** |
| church | église | **ay-gleez** |
| dead end | une impasse | **ewn am-pass** |
| driver's license | permis de conduire | **per-mee duh con-dweer** |
| elevator | l'ascenseur | **lah-sahn-seuhr** |
| stairs | l'escalier | **les-kal-yay** |
| entrance (to a building or a city) | une porte | **ewn port** |
| exit (from a building or a freeway) | une sortie | **ewn sor-tee** |
| fortified castle or palace | château | **sha-tow** |
| garden | jardin | **jhar-dehn** |
| gasoline | du pétrol/de l'essence | **duh pay-trol/de lay-sahns** |
| highway to . . . | la route pour | **la root por** |
| hospital | l'hôpital | **low-pee-tahl** |
| museum | le musée | **luh mew-zay** |
| no entry | sens interdit | **sehns ahn-ter-dee** |
| no smoking | défense de fumer | **day-fahns de fu-may** |
| on foot | à pied | **ah pee-ay** |

| English | French | Pronunciation |
|---|---|---|
| 1-day pass | ticket journalier | **tee-kay jhoor-nall-ee-ay** |
| one-way ticket | aller simple | **ah-lay sam-pluh** |
| police | la police | **lah po-lees** |
| rented car | voiture de location | **vwa-toor de low-ka-see-on** |
| round-trip ticket | aller-retour | **ah-lay-re-toor** |
| slow down | ralentir | **rah-lahn-teer** |
| store | le magasin | **luh ma-ga-zehn** |
| street | rue | **roo** |
| subway | le Métro | **le may-tro** |
| telephone | le téléphone | **luh tay-lay-phone** |
| ticket | un billet | **uh bee-yay** |
| ticket office | vente de billets | **vahnt duh bee-yay** |
| toilets | les toilettes/les WC | **lay twa-lets/lay vay-say** |

## NECESSITIES

| English | French | Pronunciation |
|---|---|---|
| I'd like . . . | Je voudrais . . . | **jhe voo-dray . . .** |
| a room | une chambre | **ewn shahm-bruh** |
| the key | la clé (la clef) | **la clay** |
| I'd like to buy . . . | Je voudrais acheter . . . | **jhe voo-dray ahsh-tay . . .** |
| aspirin | des aspirines/des aspros | **deyz ahs-peer-eens/deyz ahs-prohs** |
| condoms | des préservatifs | **day pray-ser-va-teefs** |
| dictionary | un dictionnaire | **uh deek-see-oh-nare** |
| dress | une robe | **ewn robe** |
| envelopes | des envelopes | **days ahn-veh-lope** |
| gift (for someone) | un cadeau | **uh kah-doe** |
| handbag | un sac | **uh sahk** |
| hat | un chapeau | **uh shah-poh** |
| magazine | une revue | **ewn reh-vu** |
| map of the city | un plan de ville | **unh plahn de veel** |
| matches | des allumettes | **dayz a-loo-met** |
| necktie | une cravate | **eun cra-vaht** |
| newspaper | un journal | **uh jhoor-nahl** |
| phone card | une carte téléphonique | **ewncart tay-lay-fone-eek** |

| English | French | Pronunciation |
|---|---|---|
| postcard | une carte postale | **ewn carte pos-*tahl*** |
| road map | une carte routière | **ewn cart roo-tee-*air*** |
| shirt | une chemise | **ewn che-*meez*** |
| shoes | des chaussures | **day show-*suhr*** |
| skirt | une jupe | **ewn jhoop** |
| soap | du savon | **dew sah-*vohn*** |
| socks | des chaussettes | **day show-*set*** |
| stamp | un timbre | **uh *tam*-bruh** |
| trousers | un pantalon | **uh pan-tah-*lohn*** |
| writing paper | du papier à lettres | **dew pap-pee-ay a *let*-ruh** |
| How much does it cost? | C'est combien? / Ça coûte combien? | **say comb-bee-*ehn*?/ sah coot comb-bee-*ehn*?** |
| That's expensive | C'est cher/chère | **say share** |
| That's inexpensive | C'est raisonnable/C'est bon marché | **say ray-son-*ahb*-bluh/ say bohn mar-*shay*** |
| Do you take credit cards? | Est-ce que vous acceptez les cartes de credit? | **es-kuh voo zaksep-*tay* lay kart duh creh-*dee*?** |

## NUMBERS & ORDINALS

| English | French | Pronunciation |
|---|---|---|
| zero | zéro | **zare-*oh*** |
| one | un | **uh** |
| two | deux | **duh** |
| three | trois | **twah** |
| four | quatre | ***kaht*-ruh** |
| five | cinq | **sank** |
| six | six | **seess** |
| seven | sept | **set** |
| eight | huit | **wheat** |
| nine | neuf | **nuf** |
| ten | dix | **deess** |
| eleven | onze | **ohnz** |
| twelve | douze | **dooz** |
| thirteen | treize | **trehz** |
| fourteen | quatorze | **kah-*torz*** |
| fifteen | quinze | **kanz** |

| English | French | Pronunciation |
|---|---|---|
| sixteen | seize | **sez** |
| seventeen | dix-sept | **deez-set** |
| eighteen | dix-huit | **deez-wheat** |
| nineteen | dix-neuf | **deez-nuf** |
| twenty | vingt | **vehn** |
| twenty-one | vingt-et-un | **vehnt-ay-uh** |
| twenty-two | vingt-deux | **vehnt-duh** |
| thirty | trente | **trahnt** |
| forty | quarante | **ka-rahnt** |
| fifty | cinquante | **sang-kahnt** |
| sixty | soixante | **swa-sahnt** |
| sixty-one | soixante-et-un | **swa-sahnt-et-uh** |
| seventy | soixante-dix | **swa-sahnt-deess** |
| seventy-one | soixante-et-onze | **swa-sahnt-et-ohnze** |
| eighty | quatre-vingts | **kaht-ruh-vehn** |
| eighty-one | quatre-vingt-un | **kaht-ruh-vehn-uh** |
| ninety | quatre-vingt-dix | **kaht-ruh-venh-deess** |
| ninety-one | quatre-vingt-onze | **kaht-ruh-venh-ohnze** |
| one hundred | cent | **sahn** |
| one thousand | mille | **meel** |
| one hundred thousand | cent mille | **sahn meel** |
| first | premier | **preh-mee-ay** |
| second | deuxième | **duhz-zee-em** |
| third | troisième | **twa-zee-em** |
| tenth | dixième | **dees-ee-em** |
| twentieth | vingtième | **vehnt-ee-em** |
| thirtieth | trentième | **trahnt-ee-em** |
| one-hundredth | centième | **sant-ee-em** |

## THE CALENDAR

| English | French | Pronunciation |
|---|---|---|
| Sunday | dimanche | **dee-mahnsh** |
| Monday | lundi | **luhn-dee** |
| Tuesday | mardi | **mahr-dee** |
| Wednesday | mercredi | **mair-kruh-dee** |

| English | French | Pronunciation |
|---------|--------|---------------|
| Thursday | jeudi | *jheu*-dee |
| Friday | vendredi | *vawn*-druh-dee |
| Saturday | samedi | *sahm*-dee |
| yesterday | hier | ee-*air* |
| today | aujourd'hui | o-jhord-*dwee* |
| this morning/this afternoon | ce matin/cet après-midi | suh ma-*tan*/set ah-preh-mee-*dee* |
| tonight | ce soir | suh *swahr* |
| tomorrow | demain | de-*man* |

## BASIC MENU TERMS

**Note:** When ordering, simply preface the French-language name with the phrase *"Je voudrais"* (jhe voo-dray), which means "I would like . . ."

| English | French | Pronunciation |
|---------|--------|---------------|
| beef stew | du pot au feu | dew poht o *fhe* |
| chicken | du poulet | dew poo-lay |
| chicken, stewed with mushrooms and wine | du coq au vin | dew cock o vhin |
| frogs' legs | des cuisses de grenouilles | day cweess duh gre-*noo*-yuh |
| ham | du jambon | dew jham-bohn |
| lamb | de l'agneau | duh lahn-*nyo* |
| rabbit | du lapin | dew lah-pan |
| steak | du bifteck | dew beef-*tek* |
| eggplant | de l'aubergine | duh loh-ber-*jheen* |
| green beans | des haricots verts | day ahr-ee-coh *vaire* |
| green peas | des petits pois | day puh-tee *pwah* |
| lemon/lime | du citron/du citron vert | dew cee-*tron*/dew cee-tron *vaire* |
| orange | une orange | ewn o-*rahnj* |
| potatoes | des pommes de terre | day puhm duh *tehr* |
| french fried potatoes | des pommes frites | day puhm *freet* |
| strawberries | des fraises | day *frez* |
| beer | de la bière | duh lah bee-*aire* |
| milk | du lait | dew *lay* |

| English | French | Pronunciation |
|---------|--------|---------------|
| water | de l'eau | **duh lo** |
| red wine | du vin rouge | **dew vhin *rooj*** |
| white wine | du vin blanc | **dew vhin *blahn*** |
| coffee | un café | **uh ka-*fay*** |
| tea | du thé | **dew *tay*** |

# Index

776